FROMMER'S

GREECE ON $30 A DAY

Including Istanbul & Turkey's Aegean Coast

by John Levy
and Kyle McCarthy

1988–89 Edition

Published by Prentice Hall Press
A Division of Simon & Schuster Inc.
Gulf + Western Building
One Gulf + Western Plaza
New York, NY 10023

ISBN 0-13-365123-1

Manufactured in the United States of America

CONTENTS

MAPS

ACKNOWLEDGMENTS

As our third edition goes to press we see a better, more thorough and practical guidebook, and for this we have our readers to thank. Without your diligent search for the best food and housing, your patience with our vagueness and very (!) occasional inaccuracies, and your thoughtful and informative letters, we would never have completed such a far-reaching revision.

Love and appreciation to our co-writers, researchers and indefatigable travel companions: Keith McCarthy and Ron Bozman. Your stamina, enthusiasm, and hard work enabled us to review and explore anew two of our favorite countries.

A heartfelt *efkaristoh* to Lisa Antonaki Greenberg and George Selimis of E.O.T. in Athens, to Fran Pappas at the N.T.O.G. in New York, to Thanos, Maria, and Iannis, and to the many Greek friends who made our work such a pleasure. *Teşekkür ederim* to Kamil Muren and Oktay Ataman of the Turkish Tourism and Information Office in New York, and to the warm hospitable people of Turkey.

Thanks to Olympic Airways and Lufthansa for their cooperation with this edition, and our final credits above the title: to our publisher, Paul Pasmantier, and editor-in-spirit, Marilyn Wood, for giving us a third chance.

J.L. and K.M.

INFLATION ALERT: Any book bold enough to quote prices had better say something about inflation. And a book about Greece and Turkey had better say something loud and strong about inflation. A radical devaluation of the drachma or Turkish lira against the dollar or pound has softened the impact of an inflation rate that traditionally exceeds any currency realignment. As both countries enter the economic mainstream, prices are bound to rise to the level of most other European countries. Expect inflation rates between 20% and 25% in Greece and Turkey. The prices in this volume have a built-in inflation figure, and to avoid confusion, are quoted in dollars as well ($1 = 130 drachmas; $1 = 800 TL). Before setting off, check your local bank for current exchange rates. Compare these to the exchange rates we found in mid-1985 and you'll see how fast things change.

A DISCLAIMER: Although every effort was made to ensure the accuracy of the prices and travel information appearing in this book, it should be kept in mind that prices do fluctuate in the course of time, and that information does change under the impact of the varied and volatile factors that affect the travel industry. Readers should also note that the establishments described under Readers' Selections or Suggestions have not in many cases been inspected by the authors and that the opinions expressed there are those of the individual reader(s) only. They do not in any way represent the opinions of the publisher or authors of this guide.

THE SOUL OF A CIVILIZATION

1. About This Book
2. Suggested Itineraries
3. The $35-A-Day Travel Club—
How to Save Money on All Your Travels

LIKE SOME PRIMORDIAL MEMORY, we all respond to the most basic elements in Greece. Of course there are symbols such as the Acropolis in Athens and the ruins, scattered on the mountaintops in every village and town, but it's the sun, the deep blue of the Aegean, and the blinding white of cube-shaped houses that stir the imagination. Why else would we respond this way, with such a strong, sensual feeling, if these more basic elements of Greek life weren't so pure? When friends return from Greece they always come back looking so healthy and alive, revived from the spiritual and physical pleasure of just being there. Even now, after researching and writing, traipsing up and down harborfronts, exhaustively looking at hotel after hotel, the most basic memories remain: sitting under a tree in a mountain village on Crete, eating a plate of freshly made yogurt and honey; standing on a hill on a North Aegean island, watching the silvery green leaves of a million olive trees shimmering in the breeze; the shock of jumping into the cool, clear water from a rocky ledge on Hydra's north coast. These are the images that travelers paint of their journey to Greece.

Aside from the elemental urge that attracts people to Greece, visitors come with their own ideas of what to see and do. Many come on ships, enjoying the luxury that is unique to sailing on a fully outfitted cruise vessel. For them, relaxing on deck with an occasional stopover at one of Greece's more popular ports is heavenly. Others arrive by combination train and ferry, armed with EurailPass, backpack, and a keen instinct for hunting down the best beach and the wildest party. The greatest number of travelers bring suitcases, cameras—don't forget the guidebook—and a desire to touch a little bit of Greek magic wherever it is found: archeological sites, bouzouki clubs, tavernas, open-air markets, museums, and beaches. It's for these people that our guide is written.

AND TURKEY TOO: Including Turkey in a book about Greece raised a few eyebrows in both countries, but seems to connect with the movement of a growing number of tourists. Though the two countries seem destined to be eternal enemies, their common features and extreme contrasts make for interesting travel. Turkey offers, on the whole, better preserved and more "accessible" archeological ruins, though the ancient cities and palaces in Greece are of greater historical importance. Greece has the islands; Turkey has Istanbul and a splendid coast. Whether it's one country or the other, the game of competition is inevitable. We really don't care which country claims what, and neither should you. Enjoy Greece and Turkey for what they are: two of the most fascinating countries in the world.

The best news for our readers is the continued strength of the dollar against both the drachma and the Turkish lira, making both countries among the better values in Europe.

As for Turkey, that country's growth and increasing sophistication as a tourist destination is the main news for Asia-bound travelers. Since our last visit, Istanbul has begun a major clean-up program (with the help of a fleet of New York City sanitation vehicles), many more international hotels and resorts have sprung up along the Aegean coast, and historic monuments and museums have undergone restoration and preservation. The new economic policies of the government and the influx of foreign investment have buoyed the economy. Italian-style fashions, Mercedes-Benz luxury cars, and Saudi caftans vie with kebab and sweet shops on the streets of every city.

1. About This Book

$30 A DAY—WHAT IT MEANS: We've tried hard in this book to keep costs down for the budget traveler. Those readers familiar with the $$$-a-Day guidebook series know that that means spending (per person) about $30 a day for food and lodging—about $15 a day for your hotel room (usually in a C- or D-class hotel or first-class pension, rarely with private toilet/bath/shower facilities) and about $15 a day for three meals (dining in the Greek style: usually a big meal at midday, a snack about 6 p.m., and a light supper later in the evening). You won't live like a jet-setter on this sum, but you can live quite comfortably if you follow our recommendations. Needless to say, however, if you insist on doing things American style, it will cost you more.

For new readers, you should note that that's all the $30-a-day is meant to cover—meals and lodging—*not* transportation, admission to museums or historic sites, souvenirs for your friends back home, a night out to check out the local after-dark activities, and so on. However, we have listed the best budget choices for transportation, sightseeing, shopping, nightlife, and excursions so that in these categories too you'll get the most for your drachmas.

WE NEED YOUR HELP: In both countries, we've tried to find the best values, the most interesting and unusual destinations, and at the same time to throw in some of our point of view. But things change. Quality or service at some of our recommendations may go out the window, prices may rise unexpectedly, or a brand-new place may open up just down the road that is far superior to what we have listed here. We trust that you'll help us, and our future readers, by sending your suggestions, comments, tips, and—yes, even criticisms—to us: John Levy and Kyle McCarthy, c/o Frommer Books, Gulf + Western Building, One Gulf + Western Plaza, New York, NY 10023.

2. Suggested Itineraries

The idea of including suggested itineraries is more a method of recommending certain destinations in a reasonable, logical order than an offering of finely tuned travel schedules. In fact, we'd encourage departing from these plans to tailor your journey to your own interests, needs, and desires. (Although

Turkish travel spots are included in three of the four proposed itineraries, you'll find additional suggestions in the introductory chapter on Turkey.)

Greek Highlights

This trip is designed for those who want to visit Greece's most spectacular sites and islands but have only two weeks in which to travel. The main points to see, after visiting the Acropolis, Archeological Museum, Museum of Cycladic and Ancient Greek Art, and Plaka in **Athens** and the Temple of Poseidon at **Sounion** are **Ancient Corinth**, the theater at **Epidaurus** (especially during the summer when they offer a full schedule of classical Greek plays), the extensive excavations at **Mycenae**, the elegant museum and site at **Olympia**, and Greece's premier destination, **Delphi**. This first portion can be done in about a week, especially if you take a tour; we particularly like Viking's three- and five-day bus Classical Tours for their efficiency. The second week should be spent island hopping, bouncing from one island to another within one of the country's island groups. It's preferable to limit your travels to one particular group to ease potential transportation problems, since the ferry system is designed, roughly, to service individual island groups.

The two most varied and easily accessible island groups are the **Cyclades** and the **Sporades**. Within the Cyclades first-time travelers might consider visiting **Mykonos** (and by all means, **Delos**), **Paros**, and **Santorini**. The best of the Sporades include **Skiathos**, **Skopelos**, and **Skyros**. The Cyclades offer an excellent combination of archeological sites, fine beaches, a sophisticated resort and shopping scene, and classic island architecture. The somewhat less developed Sporades are less crowded and less expensive. They also have sensational beaches and offer travelers the chance to sample a more traditional Greek lifestyle (especially on Skyros).

An Introduction to Greece and Turkey

This trip is for people who have a minimum of a month and want to see the very best of both countries (remember that in the case of Turkey the scope of this book is limited to Istanbul and the Aegean coast; there are certainly other fascinating destinations in the central part of the country that we'd encourage you to visit). The itinerary begins and ends in **Athens**. After exploring the capital, continue to **Mykonos**, with a visit to **Delos**. Travel to **Santorini**, where you can tour the Minoan excavation at Akrotiri. Then it's on to **Crete** (by air or ferry), visiting Iraklion, the Archeological Museum, and Knossos. If you have extra travel time consider several side trips, including the mountain village of **Spili**, **Matala**'s caves and beaches, the Minoan excavation at **Phaistos**, **Chania's** Venetian harbor city, or the dramatic hike through the **Samaria Gorge**. From Crete continue to **Rhodes**, where you'll see the medieval city and the picturesque Acropolis and beach cove at **Lindos**.

There are two nearby crossings to **Turkey**. The first is from Rhodes itself to **Marmaris**, Turkey's yachting center (where you can take a side trip south to **Fethiye**, among the best and least developed beaches in the Aegean); the second approach is to travel north (by hydrofoil, plane or ferry) to the island of **Kos**, where you can tour the Asclepion, and cross over by ferry to **Bodrum**, the Mykonos of Turkey. Travel north to **Kuşadasi**, the base for a tour of **Ephesus** in nearby Selçuk. Continue north to **Istanbul** with a stop in **Bergama** to hike ancient Pergamum and an overnight in **Izmir**, **Ayvalik**, or **Bursa**.

Istanbul requires a minimum of three days to see Topkapi Palace, the Blue Mosque, Hagia Sophia, and Suleymaniye; shop in the Grand Bazaar; boat up the Bosporus; and sample the city's fine restaurants. Either fly, train, or bus to **Thessaloniki** (in Northern Greece) to view the fantastic Archeological Museum and nearby excavations at Philippi and Vergina. Take a bus down the coast to Volos, the jumping-off point to **Skiathos**, the jewel of the Sporades. Return by hydrofoil or ferry to Volos (where you can take another side trip to the verdant, mansion-lined **Mount Pelion** region) and travel west to Kalambaka, the gateway to the medieval monasteries atop **Meteora**'s peaks and pinnacles.

From Kalambaka take the train or bus to Patras and continue to **Olympia** (if you have a car don't miss the Apollo Temple at Vassae). Visit the Peloponnesian highlights, including **Nafplion**, **Mycenae**, **Epidaurus**, **Corinth**, and **Delphi** (a bit to the north). After communing with the Oracle at Delphi return to Athens.

Before going home consider a vacation within a vacation at one of our favorite resting spots on the nearby island of **Hydra** (you can take the Flying Dolphin hydrofoil for extra speed). In case you haven't seen enough, don't miss the Temple of Afaia on nearby **Aegina**. Return to Athens and pat yourself on the back for completing what is truly an epic journey.

Greek and Turkish Art and Archeology

These destinations offer a stripped-down version of the previous itinerary, concentrating on archeological excavations, museums, and medieval cities. This trip will take between three weeks and a month.

Athens (Acropolis, Archeology Museum, Museum of Cycladic
    and Ancient Greek Art, Sounion, and Aegina)
Mykonos (Delos)
Santorini (Akrotiri)
Iraklion (Knossos and Archeology Museum)
Rhodes (Lindos)
Kos (Asclepion)
Samos (Tunnel and crossing to Turkey)
Kuşadası (Ephesus with optional trips to Aphrodisias, Pamukkale, Priene,
    Didyma, and Miletos)
Bergama (Pergamum)
Istanbul (Topkapi Palace, Blue Mosque, Hagia Sophia, Grand Bazaar,
    Ibrahim Pasha Palace, Suleymaniye, Rustam Pasha, Kariye Camii,
    Museum of Ancient Orient, and Carpet Museum)
Thessaloniki (Archeology Museum, walking tour of churches, Philippi,
    Vergina)
Meteora
Olympia (optional trip to Vessae if traveling by car)
Mycenae
Epidaurus
Ancient Corinth
Delphi
Athens

Beach and Island Hopping

This is how Kyle and I imagine our visits to Greece and Turkey will be, but somehow we just never have enough time to wander, relax in one place, and slip into the Greek and Turkish pace of life. This is not to say that you shouldn't try it if you have the time. Instead of an itinerary we've listed some of our favorite beaches and party spots.

Beaches: Not in any order, we'd recommend the many beaches on **Mykonos**, the beaches outside of Naoussa on **Paros**, Milopotas beach on **Ios**, Matala on **Crete**, the sandy strips on the island of **Kos**, Emborio on **Chios**, several beaches on **Skiathos**, the island of **Antipaxos**, Myrtos beach on **Kefalonia**, and lastly—perhaps the best of all—the undeveloped beaches at **Fethiye** in Turkey. There are many other smaller beaches in more remote locations, but those mentioned above are all of sufficient quality to warrant a special visit if you're longing for a place in the sun.

Island Hopping: If you want to escape the hordes of summer tourists we'd recommend traveling off the well-trod tracks to places we call "on the frontiers of tourism." In these out-of-the-way locations you're bound to find that empty beach you've dreamed about or that perfect Greek fishing village that seems to have disappeared. Other than the Cyclades (try the **Western Cyclades**) and Sporades (**northern Skopelos, Alonissos,** and **Skyros**) we particularly enjoy visiting the **Dodecanese** and the **Ionian** islands. Not only can one journey to **Rhodes** and **Kos**, but the Dodecanese also include such gems as **Simi** and **Patmos**. The Ionians offer **Corfu**, but more intrepid island-hoppers make stops on **Paxos, Antipaxos,** and **Kefalonia**.

3. The $35-A-Day Travel Club—How to Save Money on All Your Travels

In this book we'll be looking at how to get your money's worth in Greece, Istanbul, and Turkey's Aegean Coast, but there is a "device" for saving money and determining value on *all* your trips. It's the popular, international $35-A-Day Travel Club, now in its 26th successful year of operation. The Club was formed at the urging of numerous readers of the $$$-A-Day and Dollarwise Guides, who felt that such an organization could provide continuing travel information and a sense of community to value-minded travelers in all parts of the world. And so it does!

In keeping with the budget concept, the annual membership fee is low and is immediately exceeded by the value of your benefits. Upon receipt of $18 (U.S. residents), or $20 U.S. by check drawn on a U.S. bank or via international postal money order in U.S. funds (Canadian, Mexican, and other foreign residents) to cover one year's membership, we will send all new members the following items.

(1) Any *two* of the following books
Please designate in your letter which two you wish to receive:

Frommer's $-A-Day Guides
   Europe on $30 a Day
   Australia on $25 a Day
   Eastern Europe on $25 a Day
   England on $40 a Day
   Greece (including Istanbul and Turkey's Aegean Coast) on $30 a Day
   Hawaii on $50 a Day
   India on $25 a Day
   Ireland on $30 a Day
   Israel on $30 & $35 a Day
   Mexico (plus Belize and Guatemala) on $20 a Day
   New York on $50 a Day
   New Zealand on $40 a Day
   Scandinavia on $50 a Day
   Scotland and Wales on $40 a Day
   South America on $30 a Day
   Spain and Morocco (plus the Canary Is.) on $40 a Day

Turkey on $25 a Day
Washington, D.C. (including Historic Virginia) on $40 a Day

Frommer's Dollarwise Guides
Dollarwise Guide to Austria and Hungary
Dollarwise Guide to Belgium, Holland, & Luxembourg
Dollarwise Guide to Bermuda and The Bahamas
Dollarwise Guide to Canada
Dollarwise Guide to the Caribbean
Dollarwise Guide to Egypt
Dollarwise Guide to England and Scotland
Dollarwise Guide to France
Dollarwise Guide to Germany
Dollarwise Guide to Italy
Dollarwise Guide to Japan and Hong Kong
Dollarwise Guide to Portugal, Madeira, and the Azores
Dollarwise Guide to the South Pacific
Dollarwise Guide to Switzerland and Liechtenstein
Dollarwise Guide to Alaska
Dollarwise Guide to California and Las Vegas
Dollarwise Guide to Florida
Dollarwise Guide to the Mid-Atlantic States
Dollarwise Guide to New England
Dollarwise Guide to New York State
Dollarwise Guide to the Northwest
Dollarwise Guide to Skiing USA—East
Dollarwise Guide to Skiing USA—West
Dollarwise Guide to the Southeast and New Orleans
Dollarwise Guide to the Southwest
Dollarwise Guide to Texas
(Dollarwise Guides discuss accommodations and facilities in all price ranges, with emphasis on the medium-priced.)

Frommer's Touring Guides
Egypt
Florence
London
Paris
Venice
(These new, color illustrated guides include walking tours, cultural and historic sites, and other vital travel information.)

Arthur Frommer's New World of Travel
(From America's #1 travel expert, a sourcebook with the hottest news and latest trends that's guaranteed to change the way you travel—and save you hundreds of dollars. Jam-packed with alternative new modes of travel that will lead you to vacations that cater to the mind, the spirit, and a sense of thrift.)

A Shopper's Guide to Best Buys in England, Scotland, and Wales
(Describes in detail hundreds of places to shop—department stores, factory outlets, street markets, and craft centers—for great quality British bargains.)

A Shopper's Guide to the Caribbean
(Two experienced Caribbean hands guide you through this shopper's paradise,

offering witty insights and helpful tips on the wares and emporia of more than 25 islands.)

Beat the High Cost of Travel
(This practical guide details how to save money on absolutely all travel items—accommodations, transportation, dining, sightseeing, shopping, taxes, and more. Includes special budget information for seniors, students, singles, and families.)

Bed & Breakfast—North America
(This guide contains a directory of over 150 organizations that offer bed & breakfast referrals and reservations throughout North America. The scenic attractions, and major schools and universities near the homes of each are also listed.)

Dollarwise Guide to Cruises
(This complete guide covers all the basics of cruising—ports of call, costs, fly-cruise package bargains, cabin selection booking, embarkation and debarkation and describes in detail over 60 or so ships cruising the waters of Alaska, the Caribbean, Mexico, Hawaii, Panama, Canada, and the United States.)

Dollarwise Guide to Skiing Europe
(Describes top ski resorts in Austria, France, Italy, and Switzerland. Illustrated with maps of each resort area plus full-color trail maps.)

Fast 'n' Easy Phrase Book
(French, German, Spanish, and Italian—all in one convenient, easy-to-use phrase guide.)

Guide to Honeymoon Destinations
(A special guide for that most romantic trip of your life, with full details on planning and choosing the destination that will be just right in the U.S. [California, New England, Hawaii, Florida, New York, South Carolina, etc.], Canada, Mexico, and the Caribbean.)

Marilyn Wood's Wonderful Weekends
(This very selective guide covers the best mini-vacation destinations within a 175-mile radius of New York City. It describes special country inns and other accommodations, restaurants, picnic spots, sights, and activities—all the information needed for a two- or three-day stay.)

Motorist's Phrase Book
(A practical phrase book in French, German, and Spanish designed specifically for the English-speaking motorist touring abroad.)

Swap and Go—Home Exchanging Made Easy
(Two veteran home exchangers explain in detail all the money-saving benefits of a home exchange, and then describe precisely how to do it. Also includes information on home rentals and many tips on low-cost travel.)

The Candy Apple: New York for Kids
(A spirited guide to the wonders of the Big Apple by a savvy New York grandmother with a kid's-eye view to fun. Indispensable for visitors and residents alike.)

Travel Diary and Record Book
(A 96-page diary for personal travel notes plus a section for such vital data as passport and traveler's check numbers, itinerary, postcard list, special people and places to visit, and a reference section with temperature and conversion charts, and world maps with distance zones.)

Where to Stay USA
(By the Council on International Educational Exchange, this extraordinary guide is the first to list accommodations in all 50 states that cost anywhere from $3 to $30 per night.)

(2) A one-year subscription to *The Wonderful World of Budget Travel*

This quarterly eight-page tabloid newspaper keeps you up to date on fast-breaking developments in low-cost travel in all parts of the world bringing you the latest money-saving information—the kind of information you'd have to pay $25 a year to obtain elsewhere. This consumer-conscious publication also features columns of special interest to readers: **Hospitality Exchange** (members all over the world who are willing to provide hospitality to other members as they pass through their home cities); **Share-a-Trip** (offers and requests from members for travel companions who can share costs and help avoid the burdensome single supplement); and **Readers Ask . . . Readers Reply** (travel questions from members to which other members reply with authentic firsthand information).

(3) A copy of *Arthur Frommer's Guide to New York*

This is a pocket-size guide to hotels, restaurants, nightspots, and sightseeing attractions in all price ranges throughout the New York area.

(4) Your personal membership card

Membership entitles you to purchase through the Club all Arthur Frommer publications for a third to a half off their regular retail prices during the term of your membership.

So why not join this hardy band of international budgeteers and participate in its exchange of travel information and hospitality? Simply send your name and address, together with your annual membership fee of $18 (U.S. residents) or $20 U.S. (Canadian, Mexican, and other foreign residents), by check drawn on a U.S. bank or via international postal money order in U.S. funds to: $35-A-Day Travel Club, Inc., Frommer Books, Gulf + Western Building, One Gulf + Western Plaza, New York, NY 10023. And please remember to specify which *two* of the books in section (1) above you wish to receive in your initial package of members' benefits. Or, if you prefer, use the last page of this book, simply checking off the two books you select and enclosing $18 or $20 in U.S. currency.

Once you are a member, there is no obligation to buy additional books. No books will be mailed to you without your specific order.

Chapter I

A BRIEF HISTORY OF GREECE

1. The Earliest Settlers
2. Minoan Civilization
3. Mycenaean Civilization
4. Classical Civilization
5. The Hellenistic Era
6. Greece Under the Roman Empire
7. The Byzantine Era
8. Tourkokratia
9. Modern History

THESE FEW INTRODUCTORY PAGES should orient those who wish to journey to the many ancient cities and sites in Greece and Turkey. By no means exhaustive, this section is an overview to supplement the facts, speculative tidbits, and mythological tales found in the regional sections later in this book.

Greece's ancient history is that of three civilizations: Minoan, Mycenaean, and Classical. The years 2000 to 1500 B.C. were dominated by the Minoan culture which flourished on Crete and, some speculate, in the coastal colony of Akrotiri, Santorini. The Mycenaean civilization, which lasted from about 1600 to 600 B.C. (including 400 years of what is referred to as the Dark Ages), was centered in the Peloponnese. The Classical Era, so-called because the arts, culture, and democracy of the Greeks reached their peak at this time, spans the years from 600 to 321 B.C., the death of Alexander the Great.

1. The Earliest Settlers

Pottery dating from as early as 6000 B.C. has been found in mainland villages, indicative not only of agricultural settlements but also a primitive Neolithic culture. Cultivation of wheat and barley and the presence of fishermen in the coastal villages suggest that these first settlers came by sea from the Middle East. About 2600 B.C., a new wave of immigrants from Asia brought copper to Greece. Archeologists have found traces of another race at Phaistos, on Crete, from about 2300 B.C.; several sites abandoned about 2000 B.C. suggest that northern invaders overran Greek settlements about this time. After this transitional period, Minoan culture became predominant during the middle Bronze Age (2000–1570 B.C.).

A READY REFERENCE FOR ANCIENT GREEK HISTORY

Period	Approx. dates	Key events and people
Minoan	3000 to 1400 B.C.	Knossos (Crete); King Minos; the Minotaur; Theseus
Mycenaean	1400 to 1150 B.C.	Agamemnon; Jason and the Argonauts; Achilles; Troy
Dark Age	1200 to 1100 B.C.	
Aristocratic Age	800 to 600 B.C.	Athens unites with towns of Attica; Draco proclaims severe laws; Solon reforms constitution; Homer composes the *Iliad* and the *Odyssey*
Persian Wars	520 to 430 B.C.	Themistocles fortifies Piraeus; Greeks win at Marathon and Salamis; Aeschylus wins Athens Drama festival
Classical Age	480 to 430 B.C.	Parthenon built; Pericles in power; Aeschylus, Sophocles, and Euripides at work
Peloponnesian War	430 to 400 B.C.	Naval battle of Syracuse; Erechtheum on Acropolis completed; Aristophanes writes comedies: Pericles dies; Socrates drinks hemlock; Sparta triumphs
Macedonian Age	360 to 300 B.C.	Alexander the Great conquers; Aristotle founds school
Roman	200 B.C. to A.D. 300	Rome sacks Corinth
Byzantine	A.D. 300 to 1200	Constantine builds Constantinople; Crusaders build forts, sack Constantinople

2. The Minoan Civilization

Sir Arthur Evans shocked contemporary scholars when he began excavating a Cretan hillside south of Iraklion and uncovered the remains of an enormous palace. The reconstruction of this extremely complex architectural wonder enables visitors to easily imagine how legend could transform a sacrificial bull, once penned inside its mazelike corridors, into the diabolical Minotaur in his labyrinth.

In architecture, physical works, commerce, and the arts, the Minoans achieved a rare degree of sophistication. They were gifted artisans, producing beautiful frescoes for the Cretan palaces and, many think, for homes in their colony at Akrotiri. (The best-preserved of these frescoes are on display in the archeological museums of Iraklion and Athens.) By the 16th century B.C. the Minoans had founded colonies at Miletos, Asia Minor, and on Kalymnos, Rhodes, and Kythera. Goods from as far away as Egypt and Syria have been excavated at Minoan sites and the eggshell-thin, multicolored "kamares" ware they produc civilization. Professor Marinatos, who headed the excavation of Minoan Akrotiri (see Chapter VIII), and other archeologists postulate that the severe volcanic eruption of Santorini about 1500 B.C. caused a tidal wave that wiped out Knossos and Crete's north shore; their theory is very popular with Atlantis buffs. Other scholars conclude from "Linear B" tablets, written in the script later used at Mycenae, that invaders from the north destroyed this society. It was about this time that a new race was prospering in the Peloponnese, in the towns of Pilos, Tiryns, and Mycenae.

3. Mycenaean Civilization

As early as 2600 B.C. Asian tribes, later called Pelasgians, were settling in the Peloponnese. Their pottery and sculpture, found in Asia Minor, Egypt, the Cyclades, and on Crete, indicates that the Minoans had direct contact with their eventual successors. It took Heinrich Schliemann's hard work and imagination to forge the link. In 1870, in a quest to prove the veracity of Homer's *Iliad*, Schliemann began excavating at Hissarlik, Turkey. After six years of exploring the multilevel ruins of ancient Troy, he continued to the east coast of the Peloponnese, searching for evidence of Homer's Greek heroes. The royal shaft graves he uncovered at Mycenae, filled with gold masks, jewelry, and pottery, convinced him, albeit wrongly, that he'd found King Agamemnon's tomb. Nevertheless, these early shaft graves, which clearly show Minoan influence, indicated that here was a culture that had supplanted the Minoan in its artistic, cultural, and social dominance of Greece.

These peoples, centered in Mycenae (see Chapter VI), achieved new heights in architecture and bronze work. By the 14th century shaft graves had evolved into *tholos* tombs, beehive-shaped burial vaults cut into the mountainside, a significant engineering feat for that time. Nestor's Palace at Pilos displays another Mycenaean invention. Unlike Minoan palaces, it was built around a *megaron*, a reception hall with a central hearth and columned portico at one end, the forerunner of the classic Greek temple. "Linear B" tablets found at Pilos (deciphered in 1953 by Michael Ventris) tell us that their syllabic script also was an early form of ancient Greek. Then, a more militaristic mood prevailed in the Mycenaean centers. Cyclopean wall fortifications (so-called because only huge monsters could stack the tremendous boulders seen today) began appearing about 1300 B.C., the same time that smaller villages were falling to outside invaders. Decadence accompanied the declining civilization. Once used only commercially, Mycenaean trading ships ran pirate raids against other Mediterranean sailors. Archeologists think it was the Dorians (from the Balkans) who eventually destroyed this civilization. Although the Dorians were Greek-speaking, they were barbarians, and Greek history plummeted into the Dark Ages.

The only archeological evidence from the period 1100–750 B.C. comes from the Kerameikos Cemetery in Athens. Old-fashioned cist graves, not seen for a millennium, and new iron jewelry pieces indicate that culture retrogressed. Scholars think that bronzeworking may have lapsed because trade restrictions made it difficult to obtain the component tin. However, many associate the use of iron for metalwork with Anatolian and Middle Eastern tribes and believe that these peoples were related to the Dorians. Historians think that the Trojan Wars, which Homer chronicled in his *Iliad* nearly 500 years later, occurred during this period.

Art historians call this the protogeometric period because the pottery found from Athens was decorated with concentric circles or painted geometric forms. Many examples are on display at the National Archeological Museum in Athens. Trade with the more sophisticated cultures of Africa, Spain, and Italy seems to have resumed after 900 B.C. Highly skilled geometric period vases have been excavated in Phoenicia and Egypt, indicating that a new, broader range of trading partners helped pull Greece from the Dark Ages.

4. Classical Civilization

The Classical period in ancient history, from about 600–321 B.C., is considered Greece's Golden Age. In three centuries the Greeks left an unrivaled cultural legacy. Some examples: the democratic government of Solon and Pericles; the natural science of Pythagoras and Hippocrates; literature from Homer, Herodotus, and Thucydides; drama from Sophocles, Euripides, and Aristophanes; the philosophy of Socrates and Plato; the art of Phidias and of Praxiteles and the work of countless others. Several factors contributed to this cultural flowering.

THE GROWTH OF THE CITY-STATE: The mountainous, inhospitable Greek terrain made the city-state a very practical social unit. By 800 B.C. barbaric tribes who'd overrun Greece during the Dark Ages were settling down into agricultural communities. The economy had decentralized; inhabited settlements clustered into fertile valleys, isolated from their neighbors by mountain barriers. Homes were built upon any plateau (*acropolis*) that could be easily safeguarded from invaders. As trade increased, agriculture became more specialized. The city-state of Athens, for example, planted its farmland with vineyards and olive groves, not only for their export value but because of the crops' suitability to the arid terrain. The once fertile inland was being eroded by over-foresting (to build ships) and over-grazing. In the 4th century Plato wrote of the region: "What now remains, just as on small islands, compared with what used to be, is like the body of a sick man, with all the rich and fertile earth fallen away. . . ." The lack of arable land to satisfy an increasing population forced the city-states to found colonies abroad. Greece was now entering what archeologists call the Archaic Age. About 750 B.C. the colony of Cumae (north of Naples) was founded by Greeks from Kymi, Chalkis, and Eretria on Evia. Soon after, Syracuse (Sicily), Messalia (Marseilles), and Byzantion (Istanbul) were settled by Greeks. By 600 B.C., there were 1,500 overseas colonies linked to mainland Greece by language, custom, and religion. All others in the ancient world were considered *barbaroi.*

The largest growing city-states were Corinth and Megara on the Peloponnese, Aegina and Athens in Attica, and the islands of Rhodes and Samos. The responsibility of maintaining their colonies forced these city-states to expand commercially and industrially. Metal tools and weapons, pottery and textiles were heavily traded, so much so that even small neighboring city-states became rivals. The ability to amass wealth by the lower class pursuits of trade, commerce, and craftsmanship began to equalize society. The army, once the exclusive province of the landed gentry, now recruited "hoplites," soldiers who could pay for their own armor. Usurers began to prey on small farmers who were hard hit by the growing specialization in food for trade. Social upheaval in every class generated changes in government.

THE FIRST DEMOCRACY: At the dawn of the Classical period some city-states attempted democratic governments, where assemblies ruled, and some established oligarchies, where aristocratic council members ruled. All governments had similar precepts: a magistracy (which evolved from the old tribal kings) led by a religious, military, or judicial figure; a council or senate made up of elder advisors, often the aristocracy; and an assembly of the people, who could act on the council's recommendations.

In 594 B.C. Solon established a code of laws and a democratic framework for Athens. He cancelled farmers' debts and attempted to restore an egalitarian social order. Solon established public works programs, festivals, and athletic events. Later, under Pericles, civil servants would collect salaries so that none were prevented from participating in the democratic process. Taxes came from voteless foreign residents, customs, and allied city-state "protection" revenues. The rich in Athens were always "super-taxed" by financing the equipping of a trireme or the staging of a play or chorus rehearsal as their tax burden.

The next government reform in Athens came from the tyrant Kleisthenes, who acceded to the revolutionary demands of Athens's aristocratic council (*Areopagus*), which had allied itself with the Peloponnesian League against him. Now citizenship depended on being a member of a *demos,* or civil parish; there were 168 in the *polis* of Athens. These were divided into groups of ten and then mixed so that a geographic and ethnic blend of tribal members would be achieved. A Supreme Court of nine representatives from the council was voted on annually and the people's assembly was increased to 500 members. A president was elected by the assembly on a rotational basis from among tribal leaders.

Athenian leaders dispensed with their critics through the process of *ostrakismos,* whereby each winter the assembly would be asked to vote on whether there was anyone worthy of expulsion. Affirmative answers would lead to a spring vote, in which members wrote the undesired person's name on a discarded pottery fragment (*ostrakos*). The top scorer (6,000 votes was the minimum) would be banished for ten years, but without loss of property or status.

Aristotle summed up democracy this way: "You can't have a state of ten citizens. But when you have 100,000, it is no longer a *polis.* [It should be small enough for] the citizens to know each other's characters. Where this is not the case, both elections and decisions at law are bound to suffer." The Greeks were very proud of their political democracy; in fact, it was a defense of their political system in the Ionian colonies that led Greece into its first great challenge, the Persian Wars.

THE PERSIAN WARS: The mighty Persian Empire had long kept a watchful eye on Greece, targeting her as a potential conquest. Emperor Cyrus consolidated the Greek colonies in Asia Minor under Persian rule in 546 B.C., but not until 499 B.C. did the Ionian cities, now under Darius, openly revolt. Aristagoras, the tyrant of Miletos, went first to Sparta, then to Athens to plead for their help against Darius. The following year, 20 ships from Athens and five from Eretria sailed for Ephesus. After four years of battle the Persians prevailed, but Darius was determined to punish Athens for her aid. In 492 B.C. his first naval expedition was shipwrecked off Mount Athos, but he soon sent another, this time to the Bay of Marathon. The Athenian general Miltiades, his troops, and their Plataean allies camped at Marathon (see Chapter III, "Exploring Attica") to await requested Spartan reinforcements. The messenger Pheidippides ran 240 kilometers to Sparta in less than two days, but found the willing Spartans unable to march before the lunar holiday. Miltiades was forced to attack and boldly defeated the enemy by concentrating on the vulnerable Persian wings. Darius' troops fled back to their ships and sailed immediately for Cape Sounion, hoping to find an unguarded Athens. Miltiades' men rushed back by land to defend their city. The following day the Spartan reinforcements arrived, so delighted at the Athenians' victory that they marched north to Marathon to see the Persian dead for themselves. By the way, it was Pheidippides' 26.2-mile run to Athens to announce victory that gave us our modern-day "marathon."

The Persians did not take well to their defeat at Marathon. Under Darius' son, Xerxes, two pontoon bridges were constructed across the Hellespont and a canal was dug through what is now Chalkidiki to prevent the possibility of another storm delaying Persian revenge. In May of 480 B.C. Xerxes set off with about 180,000 troops, including exotic Indian, Ethiopian, Egyptian, and Phoenician infantry and Arabs on camelback. Countless tales are told of collapsed bridges, Persian stupidity, and needless naval losses. The Greeks had their naval defense at Cape Artemision (north of Evia) and a land defense at the Thermopylae Pass. After several days of intense battle at sea, the Greeks were chased south to Salamis. The Spartan general Leonidas and 7,000 men were guarding the Thermopylae Pass, a natural land barrier (see Chapter IX) preventing the Persians from reaching southern Greece. After three days of fighting, the traitor Ephialtes led the Persians over another mountain pass and Leonidas' troops were surrounded. Aware of the hopeless situation, Leonidas chose to remain behind with his 300 Spartans and Boetian soldiers to guard the others' retreat. Herodotus has immortalized their bravery in battle; all fought till none were left. Their epitaph, still seen by the side of the national highway paved through Thermopylae Pass, reads: "Passerby, tell them in Sparta that here in obedience to their laws we lie."

The Greek navy managed an astonishing victory after this crushing land defeat. At Salamis the Athenian leader Themistocles heeded the Delphic Oracle's prophecy that "wooden walls" would save their city by manning all of Athens' warships. Themistocles then sent a Greek slave in traitor's guise to encourage Xerxes to attack immediately. Because of his clever timing, the Persians were lured into a narrow bay where the much smaller Greek navy easily defeated them. Xerxes and the Persian navy withdrew to the Hellespont. In the spring, the Persian General Mardonios recaptured Attica, inflicting heavy damage. The Spartan leader Pausanius rallied his troops to battle the Persians at Plataea; their unshakable determination and bravery brought them victory. Soon after, the enemy was run out of its base in Thebes (which, years later, would still be mistrusted for siding with the Persians) and the remaining Persian fleet was burned off Cape Mykale. The time had come to organize a united defense for all the Greek city-states.

Athens took the lead in 478 B.C. by founding the Delian League, the

NATO of its day. Two hundred city-states in the Aegean and Thrace and on the coast of Asia Minor contributed ships or funds to remain under Athens's protection. Of course, their support also consolidated Athens's power. In fact, after 449 B.C. Athens was using Delian League funds (transferred from Delos to Athens for "safekeeping") to support public works projects at home. By treaties with league members, Athens improved her trade position, imposed democratic constitutions on members, and transferred their judicial claims to her jurisdiction. Now that military strength was deemed the first priority, the brilliant general Pericles was elected to lead. Under his tenure, governmental reform gave back much of the citizens' power to the politically held council.

ATHENS UNDER PERICLES: During the fifteen consecutive terms that Pericles was re-elected (461–429 B.C.), Athens blossomed socially and culturally. Pericles established payment for all government servants, creating a more widespread democracy. Magistrates had to be elected and government operations were centralized in the *tholos,* next to the council in the Agora. All business was screened by the council before it went to the people's assembly, but at 40 openhouse meetings each year any citizen could bring an injustice up before the assembly.

Because there were 250 council members and the position could only be held twice, nonconsecutively, in a lifetime, many Athenians were involved with the political process. Wealthy landowners and the military had traditionally controlled local politics; now a new breed of orators (demagogues) rose to represent the naval and civilian working class. Slaves were still common but many were skilled, had the right to vote, and kept their own businesses, paying their owners a royalty on earnings. Actually, many contemporary Greeks felt the Athenians were too lenient with their slaves.

Pericles himself came from an aristocratic background but was a staunch supporter of democratic government. Even though his enemies called him a dictator, his unquestioned rule over Athens was fairly maintained in regular elections. Contemporary writers describe him as an intelligent, skillful orator and a brilliant military strategist. Lesser politicians conceded that he was uncorrupted by his almost total power over the city, yet they used his highly publicized affair with a "barbaric" girl against him in his declining years.

In 447 B.C. funds from the Delian League coffers were used to begin work on the Parthenon. Pericles justified their use to detractors: after all, as long as Athens protected her allies in wartime, none of them should care what she did with League funds. The Parthenon was part of a public works program established to reduce the unemployment caused by Pericles' Thirty Years' Truce (445 B.C.) with Sparta. In 437 B.C. the Propylaea and a new, covered *Odeion* were added to the Acropolis. Pericles also commissioned the Temples of Poseidon at Cape Sounion, of Nemesis at Rhamnous, of Hephaestus overlooking the Agora, and the Hall of Mysteries at Eleusis (see Chapter IV, "Exploring Attica"). Plutarch writes in his *Lives* that Pericles was an avid enthusiast of the arts. It was no coincidence that his politically astute social programs also served to promote his personal interest in the performing and visual arts. In 460 B.C. Pericles commissioned his friend Pheidias to sculpt a huge chryselephantine (gold and ivory) statue of Zeus for the sanctuary at Olympia. (Art historians believe that it was from this superb sculpture that the custom began of representing Christ with a beard.) Pheidias was already known to Athenians by his Athena Promachus, a huge bronze statue of the goddess constructed on the Acropolis to celebrate victory over the Persians. When the architects Iktinos and Kallicrates began designing the Parthenon, Pheidias was put in charge of all its sculptural ornamentation.

During Pericles' time the theater flourished. The first dramatic diversion from the solemnity of religious rituals came in 520 B.C., when Thespis introduced a *hypokrites,* or play actor, reciting narratives. In 477 B.C. in his play *The Persians,* Aesychylus added a second actor and additional dialogue to create a more complex plot. The young playwright Sophocles, who won the Athens playwriting competition in 468 B.C., introduced a third actor and painted scenery to this form. Best known for his *Antigone* and *Oedipus the King,* Sophocles actually wrote over 100 popular plays. They were presented in the usual way: four at a time, usually three tragedies and one farce of about an hour each in length. *Medea, The Trojan Women,* and *The Bacchae* are three of the 19 plays which have survived from the many tragedies of Euripides. He was born in 480 B.C. to a very poor family, and lived and wrote in a cave on Salamis. Although he won dramatic competitions at a young age, his realistic, politically conscious drama was not well understood in his day.

In contrast, the sarcastic and witty social commentaries of Aristophanes were very popular. His 12 comedies, including *The Knights* and *The Wasps,* satirized politicians, modern music, and other themes. In *The Clouds* (423 B.C.) he mocked the great philosopher Socrates who ran "a logic factory for the extra-clever. They teach you (if you pay enough) to win your arguments, whether you're right or wrong." Some historians believe the success of his play led fellow Athenians to condemn Socrates to death by drinking hemlock, in 399 B.C.

Athens's unique Golden Age under Pericles was short-lived. In 430 B.C. the first of two devastating plagues struck Athens, killing nearly a third of her population. Many felt that the gods were indicating their displeasure with Pericles, whose aggressive attempts at land expansion were frowned upon by the other super city-state, Sparta. At a time when Athens was at her weakest, her unbridled urge for conquest led to the first major intra-Greek conflict, the Peloponnesian War.

THE PELOPONNESIAN WAR: Sparta was the mainstay of the Peloponnesian League, a military alliance that was a truly powerful force. Pericles' initial forays outside of Attica had angered Sparta and her allies, but not until Athens began meddling in Corinth's affairs in the Ionian Sea (431 B.C.) was war openly declared. Pericles directed Athens's offense at sea and was usually victorious. Spartan land raids into Attica were ineffective; Athens defended herself by remaining safely behind her fortifications and the "Long Walls," which connected the city to Piraeus and Phaleron. The war was devastating to both sides: in the captured colonies, men were killed and their wives and children sold off into slavery. After Pericles died in 429 B.C., a disorganized Athenian leadership chose a bolder offense. Political greed motivated most of their forays, and the resultant anger of many Delian League allies only accelerated Athens's downfall. After inconclusive fighting, in 421 B.C. a truce was declared, which was to last only three years.

Athens then turned a covetous eye on the prosperous colony of Sicily. The huge fleet and thousands of troops sent failed to capture the island; the Sicilian expedition marked the second phase of the wars. Thucydides blamed Athenian arrogance for its humiliating defeat; only a few sailors escaped after the last great battle at Syracuse harbor in 413 B.C. Alcibiades, who some called the lover of Socrates and some the nephew of Pericles, first betrayed Athens in the Sicilian fiasco by turning to Sparta, then betrayed Sparta by joining the Athenian fleet off Samos for the last phase (412–404 B.C.) of the war. By this time, Sparta had traded in her Ionian colonies for Persian support. After years of battling in the Ionian and the Aegean, Athens's fleet was defeated. Xenophon writes that her Long Walls were immediately torn down "to the music of flute-girls and with great enthusiasm" the victors required surrender of all but 12 ships. Perhaps the greatest tragedy of this outcome was that Athens, fit to rule and at her prime culturally, was denied the only chance she'd ever have to unite all of Greece under her aegis.

SPARTA: Webster's *New World Dictionary* defines "spartan" as "warlike, hardy, disciplined," adjectives that the ancient world would surely have used to describe the inhabitants of Sparta (see Chapter V). In the 7th century B.C., under the leadership of the legendary Lykourgos, the Spartans decided to make their city-state a model of disciplined life and martial training.

According to Plutarch, a committee of elders judged babies at birth and left weaklings on the slopes of Mount Taygetos to die. Hardier infants were bathed in wine (this was thought to bring out the "fits" in sickly ones) and raised to be unafraid of the dark, tolerant of all foods, and uncomplaining. At the age of seven, the state took all boys for athletic training and basic education. They were underfed to encourage stealing and were punished not for stealing but for being caught at it. Violent team games and long, solo Outward Bound-like wilderness missions developed endurance. Women lived at home but received rigorous physical training to ensure that they would bear strong children. At 20, young men attempted to win election to a *syssition*, a cultural/military unit where they lived out their adulthood. Wives could only meet their husbands secretly at night, but were often lent by sterile men to others so they could bear children.

The government of Sparta was run by two kings who kept a check on each other. There was no political unrest among the citizenry because Spartiates (land-owning, full-blooded descendants of Spartan parents) lived without class distinctions and left all necessary work to their *helots* (state-owned slaves). Thucydides described their city as "formed of villages in the old Greek manner," indicating that in architecture as in the arts, the strict Spartan lifestyle discouraged artistic expression. Nevertheless, history has proven that the Spartans were extremely patriotic, brave, and proud of their city's achievements, and their political stability was the envy of many of their contemporaries.

THE DECLINE OF THE CITY-STATES: Twenty-seven years of warfare was financially devastating for every city-state involved. There was rampant inflation, widespread unemployment, and constant food shortages. There was no work for the slaves, the poor sought jobs as mercenary soldiers, and the rich sustained the farmers with living subsidies. In 399 B.C. war broke out again. This time the Persians were asking Sparta to support them against the Asian Greek colonies. Within four years, an unlikely alliance comprised of the Boeotian League (a confederation of city-states) the city-state of Thebes, several Peloponnesian League members who had been betrayed by Sparta, and a new ally, Athens, was formed to battle Sparta and Persia. The Persian king Artaxerxes became concerned with rebel forces fighting in the Persian colonies of Egypt and Cyprus. Fearful of a protracted and costly war on Greek soil, Artaxerxes demanded that Sparta make peace with the other Greek city-states.

From 378 to 371 B.C. Thebes (see Chapter X), under the leadership of the brilliant King Epaminondas, was the major power on the Greek mainland. After the Theban victory at the Battle of Leuctra, in which the powerful Spartans were totally crushed, Epaminondas led his troops on a conquest of the Peloponnese, liberating Messenia and founding the model city of Megalopolis (see Chapter VI). Athens was so fearful of the Thebans that she sided with Sparta, and despite repeated assaults, Sparta itself never fell. The fighting came to a climax at Mantinea in 362 B.C. Here a Boeotian army from Thebes and its Peloponnesian allies fought Sparta, Athens, and their Peloponnesian allies. It is said that when Epaminondas fell in battle, it so disheartened the winning Boeotians that all lost interest in fighting, retreated to their own sides, and gave up claims of victory. In less than a generation, the Greek city-states, now in hopeless disarray, would be united under Philip of Macedon.

PHILIP OF MACEDON: After the Battle of Leuctra, Athens regained stability under the leadership of the lawyer and orator Demosthenes. Both she and her old enemy, Thebes, began aggressive intervention into the "barbarous" regions of Thessaly and Macedonia. Young Prince Philip was taken hostage during one Theban raid but assumed the Macedonian throne after his return in 359 B.C. Philip began his conquest of Greece by making forays into Chalkidiki and Thessaly, but was careful to retain the friendship of Thebes and Athens. Demosthenes urged Athenians to be aware of the threat of this seemingly equitable ruler; despite his proclaimed admiration for Athenian culture, Philip was sure to attack. Demosthenes swayed the citizenry and raised money to strengthen the Athenian fleet so they could protect the Straits of Dardanelle. The Persians joined Athens, Thebes, and other Greek cities to put up a united front against Philip. Nevertheless, Philip and his son, Alexander, defeated the combined Greek forces at the Battle of Chaironeia (338 B.C.). Philip dealt sternly with Thebes, an ally which had double-crossed him, but leniently with his favored Athens, after ousting Demosthenes.

Philip's life was cut short; scholars blame his ex-wife's jealousy of his new marriage for his public assassination. Only through the accomplishments of his son, Alexander, can we imagine what Philip might have achieved had he lived to rule a unified Greece.

ALEXANDER THE GREAT: The intellectual climate in Greece was consonant with Alexander's ideals. Two great thinkers were very influential in the 4th century. Plato, a free-thinking tutor hired to teach the son of a Sicilian tyrant, was so outspoken that his boss sent him to the slave market. Luckily, Plato was bought by a Greek and freed to found a school (348 B.C.) in a local Athenian park, under a statue of Akademos. His philosophy was based on truth as a way of life; nothing disgusted him more than imitation in art or life. His *Republic* mocked democratic politics and his *Laws* condemned religion. Plato wrote the definitive treatise on Socrates' ideas, but never formalized his own in writing. Nevertheless, the Academy he started continued to draw the top Greek minds until A.D. 529, when Emperor Justinian put an end to all pagan institutions.

The scholar Aristotle was born in Chalkidiki, but went to Athens as a young man to join its respected academic community. Philip brought him to Macedonia to tutor young Alexander, who surely benefitted from his vast knowledge of the natural world, logic, and rhetoric. When he left Alexander's court in 335 B.C., Aristotle founded a school in Athens in a park near the Temple of the Apollo Lykeios. His Lyceum offered courses in rhetoric, logic, ethics, politics, and biology, and his research was financed by Alexander. Although Aristotle was greatly admired, he was forced to flee Athens after Alexander's death because of the ill will towards anyone with Macedonian ties. Without the influence of these far-thinking men it would be hard to understand Alexander's breadth of interest and his commitment to unifying all the known races of the world in one kingdom.

So many legends surround the life and death of Alexander the Great that our whole book could be devoted to him. It is said of the young man that every time he heard of his father's military victories, he complained that Philip would leave him nothing to conquer. Plutarch recounts the story of the wild steed, Boukephalas, an unmanageable horse that Philip and his elder trainers rejected. When Alexander succeeded in mounting him, Philip reportedly said, "My son, look for a kingdom big enough for yourself. Macedonia is too small. . . ." The stallion spent the rest of his life with Alexander, who named an Indian town "Boukephalas" in memory of him. Alexander served as a general in the Battle of Chaironeia and learned many effective military maneuvers from Philip. After Philip's mysterious death, Alexander took over the Macedonian throne and Philip's position as general of the League of Corinth.

In 334 B.C. Alexander began his conquest of Persia, ostensibly motivated to avenge past invasions of Greece (though many say it was to replenish Macedonian coffers). Alexander brought his 35,000 troops to Troy, where he made sacrifices to Athena in imitation of his hero Achilles. (Alexander reportedly carried a copy of the *Iliad* with him throughout his Asian campaign.) In the first two years he captured Miletos, Tyre, Phoenicia, Palestine, and Egypt after difficult fighting, personal injuries, and great hardship for his troops. Darius fled eastward and Alexander took captive the Persian king's mother, wife, and daughters. He spent the winter of 332–331 B.C. in Egypt and founded the city of Alexandria, the first and greatest of the sixteen Alexandrias he would found along his route of conquest. Later that year he routed Darius at Gaugamela, but refused Darius' attempt at a settlement. Instead Alexander continued east to Babylon, Sousa, and Persepolis, where he burned down the old palace of Xerxes in revenge for the slaughter at Thermopylae. Darius was now left with minimal troops from his former empire. He had great trouble controlling them and was killed at Ekbatana by an allied leader, Bessos, who hoped to impress Alexander by his deed. When Alexander found out, he gave Darius a royal funeral and had Bessos, the murderous Satrap of Baktria, executed. Alexander continued east until all opposition had been crushed in the rugged, inhospitable eastern mountains, and in 327 B.C. he decided to invade India.

About this time Alexander began emulating Persian ways, including having his many new Persian advisors prostrate themselves on the ground before him. His Greek troops, who would only bow down before the gods, were offended by his behavior and refused to cooperate. Most were anxious to return to their homeland and felt that they'd accomplished all they set out to do; few shared his curiosity to visit the legendary India. Alexander dealt with any signs of discontent harshly, but his troops continued to follow him because of their personal loyalty and respect. Within the year, Alexander and his army crossed the River Indus (now Pakistan), but the seasonal monsoon vanquished his troops' morale. They refused to continue across the Hyphasis River, and after fruitless pleading (including shutting himself in his tent and refusing food) Alexander agreed to turn back. He split his remaining troops into three groups: one took a direct route back to Persia; a fleet under his senior commander, Nearchos, followed the south coast of Asia to the Persian Gulf; and the remaining division marched along the coast in support of the fleet. It took nearly a year of arduous trekking, hunger, thirst, and natural disasters before Alexander arrived back at Sousa. There he celebrated by marrying Darius' daughter and presiding at a ceremony where 10,000 of his men married Asian women. He retired thousands of Macedonian soldiers and tried to replace them with Persian recruits, which angered many troops who felt betrayed after their loyalty to him.

Alexander was planning to conquer Arabia when he fell ill (some say from malaria, others poisoning, alcoholism, or venereal disease). He died in Babylon in June of 323 B.C. This brilliant military tactician and charismatic ruler contributed much knowledge to the natural sciences from his great venture and exposed the known world to Greek culture. Unfortunately no one else was capable of governing his unwieldy empire. When it disintegrated into manageable parts, all grew under the influence of Hellenistic civilization.

5. The Hellenistic Era

The years from Alexander's death (323 B.C.) to the crowning of Octavian as the first Roman emperor (31 B.C.) are remarkable for the dominance of Greek culture in a world where the Greeks had little political control. A common form of the Greek language, *koine*, spread throughout the Mediterranean; the New Testament was later written in it. Individual city-states and colonies were absorbed by and influenced large kingdoms. The increase in worldwide trade and travel integrated Greeks with other races. Although slavery increased and racial strife was not uncommon, the mixture of new cultures and traditions would evolve, by the Roman era, into a very cosmopolitan and sophisticated whole.

After Alexander's death Greece itself united into the Hellenic League, intent on winning its freedom from the Macedonian leader Antipatros. After its unsuccessful attack on his troops at Lamia, Antipatros sent the Macedonian navy to the Dardanelles, where they soundly defeated the Athenian navy. Athens surrendered. Antipatros disenfranchised any citizen without the requisite minimum of property, abolished democracy, and offered land to anyone who would resettle in Thrace. His policies so weakened the city that Athens never regained her former status. For twenty years the rest of Alexander's empire was at war. Antipatros' son, Kassandros, ruled Macedonia and installed Demetrios to rule over Athens. Alexander's former bodyguard, Ptolemy, headed the Hellenistic Empire from Alexandria, Egypt. He worked to sustain Alexander's ideals, and even smuggled Alexander's corpse into Alexandria so that a tomb could be built for him. Ptolemy's empire flourished until 31 B.C., when Cleopatra and Mark Anthony were defeated. The leader of Alexander's footguards, Seleukos, consolidated his Asian holdings along the lines of the old Persian Empire and established his capital at Antiochos (named after his son) in Syria. The Seleucid Empire was the most visible remnant of Alexander's former glory, but it, too, slowly dwindled in strength since no effort was made to unite its diverse people.

6. Greece Under the Roman Empire

Greece and Carthage allied themselves against the Romans for the first Macedonian War in 215 B.C. Troops under King Philip V resisted the Romans through another war, but in 205 B.C. Greece fell. Not until the Romans defeated the combined forces of the Achaean League (146 B.C.) was Greece made a province, subjected to Roman laws, and forced to pay tribute. The Romans were ruthless in putting down the rebellion of the poorer classes, while rewarding some property holders with positions as local magistrates. In 146 B.C. Corinth was leveled; in 86 B.C. Athenians were massacred by Sulla to quash an uprising. Roman civil wars fought on Greek soil (such as Julius Caesar's battle at Pharsalus and Augustus' at Actium) also caused much damage to Greece and its economy.

After the second century A.D., when little of value was left in Greece, the Romans became more lenient with their subjects. They began building public works in Greece, restored some cities, and brought Greeks into local government. Hadrian revived old religious festivals and founded a new Panhellenic League. The Romans enthusiastically adopted the Hellenistic culture and its artisans. In the arts, this was a period of "antiquarianism"; artists reproduced early masterpieces, old dramas were restaged, classical philosophies and old dialects were revived. The writer Plutarch (46–120) stirred Roman interest by praising Greek heroes, ethics, religion, and philosophy in his series of biographies, *The Lives.* In the mid-second century Pausanius wrote a scholarly account of Greece's archeological history which helped sustain Roman interest in Greek culture and, of course, contributed to educating the Western world about its past.

7. The Byzantine Era

In Greece the third century was marked by barbaric invasions; Goth and Heruli tribes from Europe caused great destruction. Although the declining Empire couldn't afford to repair the damage, Emperor Claudius II guaranteed the Greeks' physical safety. Christianity, starting when St. Paul built his first church in Corinth, had grown into a powerful force within the Roman Empire. At the end of the third century, Diocletian divided Greece into several dioceses, each governed by *dekeprotoi* (ten men) and paying land taxes to Constantinople, the Christian Empire's capital. Greek art and goods were shipped to the Asian city, increasing trade and bolstering local Greek communities. In 394 Emperor Theodosius I abolished the Olympic Games and all "pagan" rituals, but many Greeks continued to follow their old beliefs.

Under the Isaurian Dynasty (eighth century) the country was divided into *themes;* many of these counties prospered as the wealth of the Byzantines grew. The *themes* became feudal principalities after the fall of Constantinople to the Crusaders in 1204. New Latin conquerors and old Byzantine rulers, notably the Venetians, French, Aragonese, Sicilians, and Catalans fought over and traded principalities. The Frank, Geoffroy de Villehardouin, administered the principality of Morea, one of the most prosperous of its day. The Byzantine rulers, the Palaeologi, retook Morea in 1262, renamed it the Peloponnese, and founded their capital at Mystra (see Chapter V). From 1204 to 1797 Venice held many Greek duchies, endowing them with an architectural legacy still admired today. The Ionian Islands, Methoni, Koroni, Argos, Monemvassia, and Nafplion on the Peloponnese, Crete, Evia, Naxos, and other islands still bear evidence of their Venetian heritage. Overall the ecclesiastical rule of the Byzantine Era provided a period of self-confidence and growth for Greece, which rose from a state of neglect at the end of the Roman period to the nationalistic spirit and strength it would need to defend itself against its next conqueror.

8. Tourkokratia

This Greek word for the period of history under the rule of the Ottoman Empire (1453–1821) is said today in hushed, pensive tones, reminding the modern visitor of the tensions it caused between Greece and Turkey. Much of the Greek mainland had already been taken when Constantinople (now Istanbul) fell to Sultan Mohammad II in 1453. Although some individual islands resisted annexation to the Empire for years, many Greek cities found Ottoman rule preferable to that of the Franks or Venetians. In theory, the Greek Orthodox religion was tolerated so long as it permitted political loyalty to the Ottomans; under Suleiman the Magnificent the Greeks enjoyed freedom of trade and language. Strong Ottoman forces protected the mainland from attack by its former feudal overlords and extended a small amount of autonomy to local governments.

For the Greeks, of course, life without freedom was intolerable. They were obligated to pay a per capita tax for the "privilege" of living under Ottoman rule, real estate and commerce were taxed, and, worst of all, about 20% of the male children were sent to Istanbul for training as *janizaries,* servants to the sultan. This system was abolished in the 1600s, but until then, some Greeks actually took advantage of this educational opportunity to rise within the ranks of Turkish government. (When the revolution came, the "Turkish" Greeks did not forget their homeland.) In the 18th century Catherine the Great, Empress of Russia, encouraged rebellion amongst her Orthodox brethren. The first uprising, centered in the Peloponnese in 1770, was forcibly put down with no Russian intervention. When Catherine tried to stir up trouble in 1786 most of the Greeks ignored her, but in Epirus there was an unsuccessful revolt against the local Sultan, Ali Pasha.

The next few decades were inspirational: the oppressed Greeks witnessed the French Revolution, the American Revolution, the fall of Napoleon, and other nationalist rebellions. Ali Pasha had eroded Ottoman rule in the north by annexing all of the neighboring territories. In response, the aristocratic and intellectual classes contemplated revolt, while Greeks in Europe sought support for their cause. When Ali Pasha decided to split from the Empire in 1820, it provided a perfect opportunity for the Greeks to demand their freedom. The War of Independence (1821–1829) eventually won liberation for the Greeks, but the fledgling nation's fragmented forces, conflicting allegiances, and disparate goals laid a rough road for the new government.

During the two years between the decisive Battle of Navarino (which granted Greece independence under the Treaty of London) and Russia's war on Turkey (settled by the Treaty of Adrianople), Greece had extended its boundaries north and south of the originally negotiated borders. Alexandros Mavrokordatos and Dimitrios Ypsilantis, who consolidated this expansion, played an important part in foreign policy. Kapodistrias, a noted leader in foreign affairs, took office as president on January 18, 1828. During his presidency, the European powers tried to install a king, Prince Leopold of Saxe-Coburg. The wealthy Greeks thought Kapodistrias' democratic reforms were excessive, while liberals felt he was autocratic and too willing to accept a king. Kapodistrias' was assassinated by an aristocratic dissident in Nafplion in 1831, leaving the government in chaos. An ineffective government coalition, including Kapodistrias' brother and Theodoros Kolokotronis, was created. While awaiting a policy decision, the European powers took action to support the weakened democracy by sending in French troops to keep order. Under their auspices, the hastily convened Conference of London finally proclaimed Greece an independent kingdom.

9. Modern History

The establishment of a monarchy is one hallmark of Greece's modern history; territorial disputes is another. At the Conference of London, Greece was granted the Peloponnese, the mainland north to the Arta-Volos line, and some of the Aegean Islands (but not Crete or Samos), all to be guarded by Britain, France, and Russia. Greece's first monarch, Prince Otto (Othon) of Bavaria, arrived in February 1833. Two issues caused resentment among the country's former war heroes: Greece had yet to expand to its previous boundaries, and all positions in Othon's government were held by Bavarians. On September 14, 1843, Greek wartime leaders and rebel forces stormed the royal palace, demanding the removal of foreign rulers and a new constitution. Othon complied and a National Assembly including representatives from the still unliberated areas of Macedonia, Thessaly, and Epirus drafted a new constitution. For the next twenty years Orthon ruled over the *Vouli* (Lower House) and the *Yerousia* (Senate). When the Crimean War began, England and France sided with Turkey against Russia, but Othon supported Russia against Greece's old enemy. In 1854 Greek troops unsuccessfully tried to take back Epirus and Thessaly but were expelled from Smyrna (Izmir) and Istanbul by the Turks. For the next three years, English and French troops remained in Greece to enforce its neutrality.

Although Othon was still popular, the people began to resent the king's autocratic rule. In 1862 minor mutinies led to a full-scale revolt in Athens, leading to Othon's fall. While the Europeans quickly searched for a new king, Britain voted to cede the Ionian Islands to Greece. On October 30, 1863, young Prince William of Denmark accepted the Greek throne under the name of George I.

THE REIGN OF KING GEORGE I: In the fifty years of George's reign (1863–1913), Greece flourished, independent of the European powers. Thessaly, Macedonia, Epirus, and most of the Aegean islands were reunited. Kharilaos Trikoupis and Eleutherios Venizelos distinguished themselves during this period. Today, their statues dot the plazas of nearly every Greek town. This new breed of politician, modern-day democrats, reduced the king's authority and reinforced the popular will with a new, liberal constitution.

Trikoupis was the prime minister from the 1880s until his death in 1896. His tenure, in a period of prosperity, tranquillity, and great capital improvement, was hampered by his militant rival, Theodoros Diliyiannis, who assumed the post after Trikoupis' death. That year, a major uprising in Crete gave Diliyiannis the excuse he needed to send an armed navy to annex the island, but he was halted by the arrival of European troops. The Greeks demanded a fight; on April 17, 1897, Turkey declared war. Turkey won easily and a peace treaty was signed; the Europeans decided to install Prince George of England as the island's High Commissioner under the sultan's *suzerainty*. Venizelos actively opposed this compromise and set up Alexandros Zaimis in a provisional Cretan government in 1905. Because of his effective leadership, the European powers withdrew their troops in mid-1908.

THE BALKAN WARS: In Turkey the liberal Young Turks movement demanded a constitutional government from Sultan Abdul Hamid I and finally deposed him in 1909. Their powerful presence in Thessalonica caused the Bulgars, Serbs, and Greeks to unite in the Military League, led by Venizelos. Venizelos came to Athens, where he quickly assumed power, became prime minister, revised the Greek constitution, and remade the Military League into the Balkan League. In 1912 Turkey declared war on Bulgaria and Serbia. The protectorate of Crete was allowed to join the Balkan League. The league fought successfully and won back Epirus, Macedonia, Samos, and Crete. As so often happened in Greek politics, an unexpected event shook the country's fragile order: the military hero Constantine had to assume the throne when King George I was assassinated.

The Treaty of London abolished the Turkish Empire and returned occupied lands to the Balkan League. Disputes over their disposition led to the Second Balkan War, in which Serbia and Greece were allied against Bulgaria. The Truce of Bucharest (August 10, 1913) left Bulgaria a small part of Macedonia and access to the Aegean and created Albania from part of Epirus. However, the Turks and Italians refused to leave their occupied positions on the Aegean and Dodecanese islands. World War I put an end to this shell game.

WORLD WAR I: The war provoked an international crisis over the interpretation of the Greco-Serbian alliance. King Constantine openly favored neutrality in case of a Serbian invasion (many felt he really sided with brother-in-law Emperor Wilhelm II of Germany). However, Prime Minister Venizelos sided with the entente, voted to support Serbia, and pledged Greek troops to their cause if the Turks decided to join the war against them. Venizelos was dismissed. Constantine maintained Greece's neutrality until June 1917, when the Allies demanded Greek participation. Constantine left the country in protest and Venizelos returned as prime minister. Military successes in Macedonia and the Ukraine strengthened Venizelos' bargaining position with the Allied powers.

In 1919 the Allies encouraged the Greeks to retake Smyrna (now Izmir). The Greco-Turkish War that ensued was disastrous for the Greeks. In 1923 the League of Nations insisted on the resettlement of Muslim and Orthodox citizens; half a million Turks emigrated to Greece. Because of the Turkish fiasco, King Constantine was relieved of his throne, but his successor, young George II, reigned for only a year after him. The revolutionary activity of Nikolaos Plastiras ushered in a constitutional government amid the confusion of internal problems and border disputes.

On March 25, 1924, Admiral Pavlos Koundouriotis was proclaimed first president of the new Republic of Greece. The republic lasted only eleven turbulent years. Venizelos, as leader of the Liberal Party, reappeared several times in an effort to take control. Panayiotis Tsaldaris headed for the royalist Popular Party, which stepped in after one of Venizelos' failed coups and restored the monarchy of George II in 1935.

The first general election showed the people divided between a Liberal/Republican coalition and a Right wing/Popular Party coalition. On August 4, 1936, King George II permitted a military takeover to protect the country from a Communist coup; the Fourth of August Government of General Metaxas assured strong leadership just as Greece was about to face the next crisis: World War II.

WORLD WAR II: After the outbreak of war, the British guaranteed protection to the neutral Greeks and defended the country against Italy's invasion through Albania in 1940. The following year Bulgaria and Yugoslavia were overrun by the Germans, who then overpowered the British and occupied Greece until 1944.

During the war a heroic resistance movement against the Germans grew throughout the country. Communist-organized forces (the EAM-ELAS) and democratic rebel forces (the EDES) fought the Germans as well as each other. After Italy's surrender in the fall of '43, through the summer of '44, the Communist EAM-ELAS consolidated their power and formed a provisional government in the north. Liberal Greeks, with British help, attempted to unite the guerrilla forces, but at the end of 1944, civil war broke out in Athens. (This period and the personal devastation it caused are the subject of a film called *Eleni,* based on the powerful novel by Greek-born *New York Times* writer Nicholas Gage.) The psychological damage caused by the five years of civil war left a greater mark on Greek politics than any conflict since the Peloponnesian Wars. The Communists were finally defeated and after a few years of disorganized government rule, an election ratified the monarchy of George II. In less than a year he died, and in 1947 his brother Paul became king. A renewed Communist guerrilla movement was proving too strong for the British forces. Under the aegis of the Truman Doctrine, the U.S. sent massive amounts of aid and finally quelled the insurgents in the north. On October 16, 1949, after great losses, family feuds, and much bitterness, the Communists laid down their arms. Unstable coalition governments, supported by U.S. aid, came and went until the military leader Papagos, backed by his Greek Rally party, was elected prime minister in 1952. During these tumultuous years, the Dodecanese Islands were returned to Greece (1948) and Greece joined the Council of Europe (1949) and NATO (1951).

POSTWAR GREECE: 1952 was an important year for Greece: women were given the right to vote and Konstantinos Caramanlis, public works minister under Papagos, was elected prime minister. During his tenure the issue of Cyprus's sovereignty was resolved with Turkey by signing the Zurich Accord of 1959, which granted Cyprus independence.

Caramanlis and his ERE party remained in power until 1963, when the Centre Union party led by Georgios Papandreou forced his resignation. King Paul, after his death in 1964, was succeeded by his son, Constantine. On July 15, 1965, King Constantine II dismissed Georgios Papandreou, accusing him of aiding his son (Andreas, head of the left wing ASPIDA group) to infiltrate the army. Two years of erratic leadership followed; in 1967, a military coup installed Konstantinos Kollias as prime minister. Both Georgios and Andreas Papandreou were arrested, along with Communists, authors, academics, and others opposed to the current regime. At year's end, when his radio appeal failed to overturn the military *junta*, King Constantine II and his family fled to Rome. The dictatorial triumvirate of generals Zoitakis, Patakos, and Papadopoulos held firm control of the country. After many prisoners were released in a political amnesty, Andreas Papandreou organized an opposition party from Europe. The Council of Europe resolved on January 31, 1968 that the Greek government would be expelled if parliamentary procedures weren't restored within the year. A new constitution was approved by 92% of the voters later that year, reaffirming the traditional constitutional monarchy.

Nevertheless, the military *junta* continued their complete hold over Greek politics. Regular purges led to the exile or imprisonment of all opponents, and reports of torture were common. On June 1, 1973, Prime Minister Papadopoulos announced the abolition of the monarchy. He made himself president, promised the restoration of civil liberties, and scheduled a parliamentary election for the following year. In November 1973 General Ioannidis, chief of the military police, mounted another coup to oppose the president's overly liberal concessions. In July 1974 Constantine Caramanlis was brought back from Paris and sworn in as prime minister. A public referendum abolished the monarchy, and within a year a constitution was drafted for the new republic. Under it, the republic was divided into 52 *nomoi*, each headed by a *nomarch* or governor. The president was to be elected by Parliament to serve a five-year term; the head of the government, the prime minister, would be appointed by the president. Parliament elected the new president, Constantine Tsatsos. Caramanlis remained popular and was re-elected premier in 1977 and president in 1980. In 1981 Greece, previously an associate member, became a full-fledged member of the EEC (Common Market). On October 18th of that year, Andreas Papandreou, a Harvard-educated economist and once-imprisoned son of the former premier, now head of the Panhellenic Socialist (PASOK) Party, was elected prime minister. In March 1985 he shocked President Caramanlis (who expected renomination) and the world by nominating Supreme Court Judge Christos Sartzetakis for the presidential post. In June an overwhelming number of Greece's 10 million citizens voted PASOK the majority party. Whatever the outcome, tourists can be sure that Greeks everywhere will be hotly debating their favorite topic—politics. Brush up on your knowledge of current events with the English-language paper the *Athens News* or the monthly magazine *The Athenian*. Both will provide enough insight to enable you to keep up with the conversation raging around you. We can guarantee that ferryboat captains, waiters, and your Greek friends will continue to criticize and exercise their democratic freedoms as they have tried on and off for the last 3500 years.

Chapter II

GETTING TO GREECE

IN THE OLD DAYS, getting to Greece meant arriving by ship. Whether starting out from the docks in New York or taking the ferry from Italy, travel by sea was the dominant mode of transportation. Now, of course, nearly everyone flies. Although ferries from Italy are nearly always full, airports greet the greatest number of incoming visitors. Flying is fast, and considering the multitude of price breaks, promotions, and charters available, traveling by air can be a real bargain. Open up any Sunday travel section in the newspaper and you're bound to see "Special Flyaway," "Escape with Us," and "Charters by the Pound" (English).

The selection of available deals is staggering and confusing; each airline has different rules and regulations governing the terms of its promotion and most fares change according to season. Decide where and when you want to go, and then call up a travel agent who understands the ins and outs of discount fares. If you don't understand the "fine print," your "bargain" flight could turn out to be something less than inexpensive. Obviously, the prices listed below are subject to change . . . which they will.

BY AIR: Olympic Airways is the national carrier of Greece and has daily nonstop flights from New York to Athens, as well as frequent flights from Montréal and Toronto to Athens. Olympic is the only airline that flies within Greece, so you can buy a through ticket that includes your ultimate destination (for an extra charge). During the high season, a round-trip ticket costs $888 (tickets must be purchased at least 14 days prior to departure). Olympic also offers lower fares in the off-season ($699). Olympic Airways' main office is in New York at 647 Fifth Ave. (tel. 212/838-3600 or toll free 800/223-1226). Most other major scheduled carriers, including TWA, Pan Am, Lufthansa, and KLM fly to Athens as well; many have fares that are comparable to those offered by Olympic. Lufthansa also flies to Thessaloniki and Heraklion (Crete).

Charter Flights to Greece

Each year different companies offer charter flights to Athens. The prices change even more than those of the regular airlines, and there are very different rules for booking seats. Generally, you must book a seat a month or so in advance to get on a flight in June, July, or August, and the prices depend on how many days you intend to stay, what day of the week you're leaving, and at what time of year. **Homeric Tours** (tel. 212/753-1100 or toll free 800/223-5570) is one of the established and more reliable charter companies. In 1987 they charged $449 to $549 for flights departing in the low season and $659 during July, August, and September. Homeric normally offers flights leaving three times a week from New York in the high season and once a week during the rest of the year. The company also offers low-priced tours, car rental, and hotel packages.

Their prices at the Athens deluxe-category Caravel are particularly attractive. **Tourlite International** (tel. 212/599-2727 or toll free 800/272-7600) charged $499 to $650 for their flights to Athens.

Warning: We're the first ones to play down the political implications of including both Greece and Turkey in this guidebook because, the truth is, they're two of our favorite countries and are very complementary tourist destinations. However, governments competing for the same tourist dollars sometimes don't think so. Since 1985 a long-ignored airline regulation regarding charter flights has been enforced by Greece. Charter flights are legally restricted to providing transportation at discount fares between two countries only. Tickets are not supposed to be used to facilitate travel to a third country; i.e., those flying by charter between New York and Athens are not supposed to visit Turkey during their holiday. After interviewing several Greek and Turkish travel agents, we've found that this ruling has only been enforced against tourists flying directly by charter to a Greek island such as Kos or Rhodes (where travel to Turkey is just a brief ferryboat ride away). Since American charter companies only fly direct to Athens, few Americans have been confronted with having to pay the difference between a one-way charter and one-way economy-fare ticket for their return flight. Turkish travel officials have talked about the possibility of issuing visas that could be removed from your passport (the only proof of your overnight stay in a "third" country), a technique that Israel has employed with Mideast-bound tourists for years. Until official policy has been established, WE STRONGLY URGE ALL READERS POSSESSING CHARTER AIR TICKETS TO CONSULT WITH THEIR TRAVEL AGENCY OR CHARTER AIRLINE BEFORE DEPARTURE REGARDING THEIR POLICY ON TRAVEL TO A THIRD COUNTRY.

Flights to Europe

Many people want to visit other parts of Europe before coming to Greece. For them it makes sense to fly to another capital, such as London, Paris, or Rome, and arrive in Greece by train, bus, or ferry. For many a year Icelandic, now called **Icelandair** (tel. 800/223-5500), has shuttled North Americans by the planeload to Europe at low prices. As of the time of writing they charged $599 (off-season) and $809 (high season) for a round-trip ticket from New York to Athens via Icelandair's Luxembourg Gateway (depending on times of departure). The extra bonus for flying on Icelandair is that there are no restrictions on stays within Europe for up to one year and (this may appeal to somebody out there) you're entitled to a stopover in either Iceland or Luxembourg. Icelandair normally has daily flights to Europe from New York and Chicago, with additional departures from Baltimore/Washington, Boston, and Orlando, Florida.

This year it's possible to fly to Europe on cheapie airlines like **Virgin Atlantic** (tel. 212/242-1330 or toll free 800/862-8621) for prices well below other airlines. Virgin Atlantic flies daily from New York and five times a week from Miami to London for about $520 round trip on their Late Saver fare ($600 from Miami). Standby fares are about 10% less. Most charter fares to Europe range from $400 to $800 round trip. One-way tickets, though less restrictive, are generally more expensive than round-trip fares. Again, these fares change with the wind. Check your newspaper or travel agent for details.

Travel Agents

Few travel agents keep up on the best values for every country; it's impossible to track all of the changes. However, Ms. Rina Annousis, a multilingual Greek who works in New York, specializes in travel to Greece and makes it her business to know. She runs an agency called **The Travel Business** (tel. 212/279-3700) and can book air and land reservations for your entire trip.

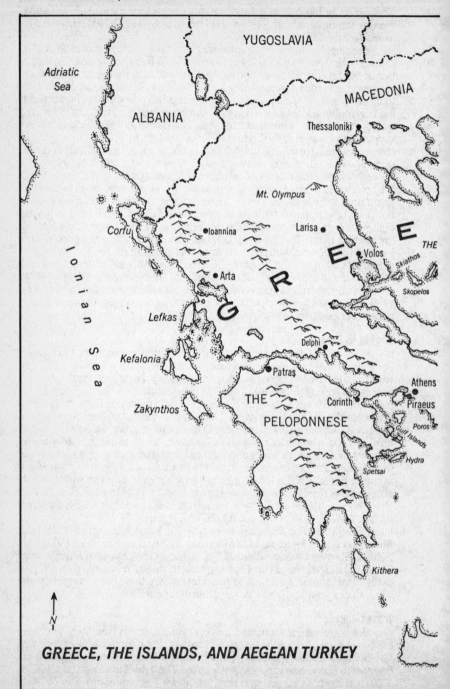

GREECE, THE ISLANDS, AND AEGEAN TURKEY

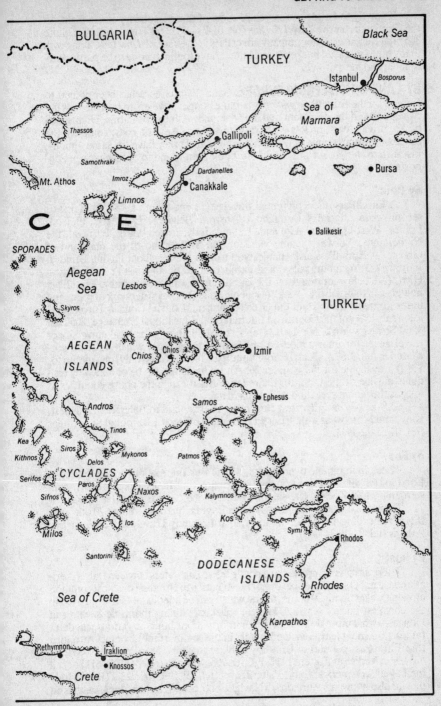

BULGARIA

TURKEY

Black Sea

Istanbul

Bosporus

Sea of Marmara

Thassos

Samothraki

Mt. Athos

Imroz

Dardanelles

Canakkale

Gallipoli

Bursa

Limnos

C E

Balikesir

SPORADES

Aegean Sea

Skyros

Lesbos

TURKEY

AEGEAN

ISLANDS

Chios

Chios

Izmir

Andros

Samos

Ephesus

Tinos

Kea

Siros

Mykonos

Patmos

Kithnos

Delos

Serifos

CYCLADES

Paros

Naxos

Kalymnos

Sifnos

Ios

Kos

Milos

Symi

Rhodos

Santorini

DODECANESE

ISLANDS

Rhodes

Sea of Crete

Karpathos

Rethymnon

Iraklion

Knossos

Crete

If you fly to London in search of some of those legendary cheap flights to the Continent, try the **Travel Arcade** (tel. 01-734-5873) at Triumph House, Suite 305, 189 Regent St. The company advertises in the back of *Time Out,* along with many other so-called bucket shops, but we have found this one to be particularly reliable and inexpensive.

BY LAND OR SEA FROM EUROPE: Since 1978 Greece has been joined to Europe on the EurailPass system, enabling budget travelers to ride the rails between parts of the continent and Thessaloniki, Athens, or Patras. High-speed buses, private cars, or low-cost cruises from the Adriatic coast complete the range of transport options. Those coming from Turkey have the same options; just turn to the Turkey portion of our book for a roundup of magic-carpet opportunities.

By Train

A **EurailPass** offers unlimited travel (e.g., one month for $440) in first or second class on trains throughout Austria, Belgium, Denmark, Finland, France, West Germany, Holland, Ireland, Italy, Luxembourg, Portugal, the Netherlands, Norway, Spain, Sweden, and Switzerland to the mainland of Greece. A EurailPass also enables you to ride the ferryboat linking Brindisi, Italy, to Corfu, Igoumenitsa, and Patras on the Ionian coast. The Naviatica/HML (see below for details) is the Eurail correspondent company. EurailPass holders can then use the O.S.E. (Hellenic State Railways) network of trains and buses for travel throughout the Greek mainland. Contact Council Travel Service, a subsidary of the Council on International Educational Exchange, 205 East 42nd St., New York, NY 10017 (tel. 212/661-1450) or your local university or travel agent for information on obtaining a EurailPass, which must be purchased in the U.S. A special Eurail Youthpass (second class only; one month for $310) is available for those under 26. An InterrailPass can be obtained by residents outside of the U.S., for unlimited travel through the above countries as long as the purchaser is under 26 years of age.

O.S.E.'s *Venezia Express* runs from Thessaloniki to Belgrade, Budapest, Kiev, and Moscow as well. Contact their main office at 1 Karoulou St., Athens (tel. 01/52-22-491).

By Bus

Those indomitable overlanders, **Magic Bus International,** have offices in London (tel. 499-37-75), throughout Germany (in Munich call 59-18-24), Amsterdam (tel. 26-44-34), Thessaloniki (tel. 263-566), and Athens (tel. 01/323-74-71). Their twice-weekly London–Athens Express bus costs about $70 one way. If you're heading north, check fares also at **Economy Travel,** 18 Venizelou St., Athens (tel. 01/36-34-045).

By Boat

There are several cruise ships plying the scenic waters between Italy's Adriatic coast and Greece's Ionian coast. From Patras to Brindisi (the most common crossing) takes about 20 hours, a time which can be adequately survived even in the cheapest bucket seats. A lounge, snackbar, dining room, deck with sun lounges—what more do you need? For information about the various schedules (at least one boat leaves each port daily in the summertime), contact **Adriatica** (the EurailPass people) in Brindisi, Italy, at Stazione Maritima (tel. 0831/23-825) or in Venice at Zattere 1411, P.O.B. 705, Venezia (tel. 041/781-611) or call their agent in America, Extra Value Travel (tel. toll free 800/223-2712). In Italy they're also known as Adriatica di Navigazione, S.p.A. **Ionian Star Lines** has an office in Ancona, Italy, at Cagidemetrio S.R.L., Piazza Roma 21 (tel. 53-696). **Minoan Lines** also has an office in Ancona; their car ferries make the run to Iraklion and Chania, Crete, as well. In Ancona they're at O. Paroletti and Co., 4 Via XXIX Settembre (tel. 071/201-933).

In 1987 the average fare in tourist class was $95 for adults; many companies offer 20% to 25% off for those with student identification cards.

Information about leaving Greece via ferry can be found in Chapter VI, "The Peloponnese" (see Patras). For information about sailings to Turkey from the various Greek Aegean islands, check the individual island listings in Chapter IX, "The Dodecanese" (see Rhodes or Kos), and Chapter XV, "The Northeast Aegean Islands" (see Samos, Chios, Lesbos).

Bon voyage! Or as the Greeks would say, *kalo taxidi!*

Chapter III

THE ABC'S OF GREECE

THIS CHAPTER is an easy, alphabetized way to organize a lot of basic information that will help you plan your trip to Greece. More specific information about various aspects of travel is included in "Athens ABCs" in Chapter IV.

AIR TRANSPORT: Olympic Airways is the exclusive domestic carrier in Greece. During the high season they are so overburdened by tourists that service and efficiency sometimes suffer, but, overall, their frequent flights and reasonable fares make them indispensable to the island hopper. To obtain a copy of Olympic's Summer Timetable, contact their offices at 647 Fifth Ave., New York, NY 10022 (tel. toll free 800/223-1226) or in Athens at 6 Othonos St., Syntagma Square (tel. 01/92-92-444). The 1987 sample air fares to the islands are listed below; all fares are one way from Athens:

Chios	4570 drs ($35.10)	Mytilini (Lesbos)	5290 drs ($40.70)
Iraklion (Crete)	6630 drs ($51)	Rhodes	8400 drs ($64.60)
Kerkyra (Corfu)	7680 drs ($59.10)	Skiathos	5020 drs ($38.60)
Kos	6400 drs ($49.20)	Thira (Santorini)	5960 drs ($45.90)
Mykonos	5020 drs ($38.60)	Paros	5610 drs ($43.10)

ARCHEOLOGICAL SITES: Ever since the amazing discovery of King Philip of Macedonia's tomb at Vergina (he was Alexander the Great's father) in the late 1970's, there has been a rekindled interest in Greek archeology. The spectacular museum show, "The Search for Alexander," traveled to America and around the world. New excavations and older digs, such as those at Delos, that have been going on for more than 100 years are attracting the greatest interest in decades. Kyle and I have spent a great deal of time over the years visiting sites, near and far, throughout Greece. Our intention was to provide sufficient background and description for those ancient-rock hounds to decide which sites are for now and which will be seen on a return visit. A complete description of the sites goes far beyond the scope and ability of this book and its authors. We recommend using one of the fine books written by such qualified Greek archeologists as Manolis Andronicos, Spiros Marinatos, or J. A. Papapostolou (all published by Ekdotike Athenon).

ART CENTERS: There are four art centers in Greece (Delphi, Hydra, Mykonos, and Rhodes) where "well-known" artists and "recipients of special awards" are given an opportunity to live virtually rent free in an artistic community for up to three weeks each year. Interested artists should apply to the Rector of the School of Fine Arts, 42 Patission St., Athens (tel. 01/36-16-930).

BATHROOMS: John wasn't very interested in this section but I think it's important. Let's start with Greek toilets. For the most part, they're clean and they work, even in unlikely places such as public parks and museums. Carry tissues with you because you can't always count on finding a supply outside the hotels. What should you do with that soiled tissue? Pay attention to the signs you see everywhere, and don't try to flush it down the toilet. Put it in the bin like they ask; if one is not provided, carry it out with you. Even if there's no sign, don't put any paper products in the toilets. Believe me, it's easier to find a trash bin than to explain in Greek that the toilet has just flooded. (All this fuss is because of the peculiarly narrow pipes of the Greek sewage system.)

The Greek shower is the next topic. A bath is a bath, and many of the older hotels have large, soak-in-able tubs. If you're trying to wash your hair, you'll have to tackle the European shower. Typically it's a small nozzle connected to a coiled metal tube that will lash out at you and soak the towels when you first turn it on. Once you've mastered steering it with one hand, you'll have to figure out how to open the shampoo, lather, and rinse with the other (if there's enough water pressure to make all this possible). You'll soon be grateful for the small pensions that charge extra if you take a shower. What you'll spend your vacation wondering about is what happened to shower curtains. (We'd be delighted to discuss with any readers our scheme to market plastic shower curtains with taverna menus printed on them. You thought Onassis was rich? This could be bigger than shipping!)

BOATS AND SCHEDULES: The only thing to say is that there are a lot of them, they're unreliable, subject to weather and personal calamities, fun, and a great way to meet people. Of course they're a necessity, and the best way to plan your island itinerary is to get a National Tourist Organization of Greece (E.O.T.) map, which indicates, by dotted lines, most of the routes between islands. (Within each island group, there are many local ferries that connect the smaller islands) E.O.T. always publishes a weekly schedule of departures from Piraeus (the major port) and Rafina (a nearby Attica port which services the Cyclades more quickly and cheaper than Piraeus). Within each chapter on an island group, we've tried to indicate the frequency and variety of sailings and have suggested that you talk to the local Tourist Office or travel agents for schedule information. Here's a list of sample ferryboat fares (all tourist class), and remember—just because the next guy told you he took that ferry last week doesn't mean it will be there this week!

1987 One-Way Tourist-Class Fares from Piraeus to:

Crete (Iraklion)	2320 drs ($17.80)
Rhodes	2790 drs ($21.50)
Mykonos	1430 drs ($11)
Samos	2140 drs ($16.50)
Ios	1820 drs ($14)
Naxos	1460 drs ($11.20)
Patmos	2020 drs ($15.50)
Monemvassia	1420 drs ($10.90)
Santorini (Thira)	1820 drs ($14)
Lesbos (Mytilini)	2140 drs ($16.50)
Kos	2520 drs ($19.40)
Igoumenitsa to Corfu (Kerkyra)	380 drs ($2.90)
Patras to Kefalonia	1000 drs ($7.70)
Volos to Skiathos	1270 drs ($9.80)

(From Piraeus, the embarkation tax is a few drachmas for all classes.) Fares will be about 10% less in the low season; make sure to double-check with the local Port Authority to confirm schedules.

Hydrofoils are a new luxury on the Greek sea-scene, and they can save you a great deal of time and seasickness. They currently service the Sporades and the Saronic Gulf Islands and some Peloponnese coastal cities (see those chapters for more information).

CLIMATE: Greece has a generally mild climate (notwithstanding the phenomenal heat wave of 1987): cool winters (which hover around 55° to 60°F in Athens and the south and 45° to 50°F in Thessaloniki and the north) and *meltemi* breeze-cooled summers (about 85° to 95°F throughout the country). E.O.T. claims that Greece has 3,000 hours of sunshine each year! The best seasons to visit are late April to June (spring) and mid-September to November (fall); the sun is less intensely blinding, the wildflowers are out, and the tourists are gone.

CUISINE: Kyle will eat anything and wasn't too concerned about your introduction to Greek cuisine, so I, gustatory dilettante, will attempt this section. Greece is definitely a three-meals-a-day kind of country. Here the emphasis is on a big midday lunch (about 2 p.m.), followed by a siesta, a revival coffee or snack at 6 p.m., and then a light dinner about 10 or 11 p.m. If you can work yourself into this schedule (easy to do when the sun doesn't set until 9:30 or 10 p.m.), you'll see and enjoy the best of Greek dining.

Most of us are familiar with *souvlaki, moussaka,* Greek salads, and *baklava* pastry, but in Greece there's a wide variety of other foods (usually prepared with the same vegetables, meats, fish, and olive oil) that will keep you trying something new every day for weeks.

Breakfast: Our pet peeve is the usually outrageous price imposed on you for inclusive "brekfest complet": an awful serving of dried-out bread or packaged toast, Nescafé, and an airline packet of butter and marmalade. Your best bet is to go out to a local *kafeneion* for a fresh-brewed Greek coffee and fresh bread, yogurt, or cheese pie.

Lunch: Lots of options here, from retsina and fish to *tost,* those uniquely Greek sandwich shops where your combination of fast eats is pressed onto a roll or hero with a waffle iron and served.

Dinner: This is the time to let loose, sample everything, drink some wine, and stroll it off. There's a list of sample menu items in Appendix II. Don't worry about pronouncing them: most tavernas welcome you right into the kitchen to sniff, peek, and point out what you want. The only rule of thumb about Greek restaurants is that if it's got tablecloths instead of plastic sheets, it's going to cost you more.

CURRENCY: The unit of currency in Greece is the **drachma (dr),** a coin or bill in use for thousands of years (money buffs should visit Athens's Numismatic Museum). As of this writing there are about 130 drachmas (drs) to U.S. $1; therefore each drachma is worth less than a penny.

Note: Although the drachma has recently been devalued against the dollar by about 15%, you'll find that the country's 25% inflation rate keep values somewhat comparable to those we've listed. However, in the last two years inflation and currency fluctuations with the dollar and the drachma have made things very confusing for the average tourist.

CUSTOMS: Up to a total of 10 kilograms (about 22 pounds) of food, 1 liter of alcohol or 2 liters of wine, and any gift articles up to a value of $85 may be imported to Greece duty free. Tourists can also bring in 200 cigarettes, 50 cigars, and two packs of playing cards. Automobiles can be imported for the tourist's personal use for up to four months (a permit is issued upon arrival at one of the land borders). There is no restriction on the amount of foreign currency that can be brought into Greece. The export of antiquities is forbidden by law. *Note:* Check with your travel agent or local government office, as regulations change frequently.

DOCUMENTS: U.S., Canadian, and British citizens can enter Greece without a visa and remain for up to a three-month period. Three-month visas are issued showing the date and port of entry upon arrival. For a resident permit allowing up to six months in the country, apply to the local Aliens Bureau (tel. 77-05-771 or 36-28-301 in Athens) or contact your embassy.

EMBASSIES AND CONSULATES: See this same heading in the ABCs of Athens in Chapter IV.

EMPLOYMENT: A high unemployment rate has made it more difficult to remain in Greece for reasons of employment. To inquire about obtaining a work permit, contact the local Tourist Police, Aliens Bureau, or your embassy.

FESTIVALS AND EVENTS: The following is only a sampling of the hundreds of special events—folkloric, religious, festive, cultural—that take place throughout the year all over Greece. For a complete list, contact the Greek National Tourist Organization.

January: Feast of St. Basil—a general celebration with traditional New Year's cake and national costumes (1st).

Epiphany—the "Blessing of the Waters" ceremony throughout Greece. The most spectacular spot to visit is Piraeus (6th).

February: In mid-February it's carnival time throughout Greece. Patras has one of the largest and most gala parades.

March: Greek National Holiday, honoring the War of Independence with military parades throughout the country (25th).

April: Sound-and-light performances in Athens and Rhodes (through October).

Anniversaries dedicated to St. Spyridon, patron saint of Corfu (mid-month).

Good Friday, Holy Saturday, and Easter Sunday in the Greek Orthodox church, a public holiday weekend and the most important religious holiday in the Greek calendar (movable).

May: Labor Day and Flower Festival, a public holiday (1st).

The anniversary of the union of the Ionian Islands with Greece, celebrated mostly on Corfu (21st). Sound-and-light performances begin in Corfu and run through mid-September.

Navy Week Festival celebrated throughout Greece. In Volos there's a re-enactment of the sailing of the Argonauts' expedition; on Hydra it's a celebration of Admiral Miaouli (end of month).

June: Wine Festivals at Daphni (11 kilometers from Athens), Rhodes, and other locations—wine-tasting, tavernas, dancing.

The Athens Festival of international music, drama, and dance begins at the Herod Atticos Theater on the Acropolis.

July: Wine Festival at Alexandroupolis (midmonth).

Epidaurus Festival—performances of ancient Greek drama in open-air theater (through August).

Northern Greece National Theater performances of ancient Greek drama in the open-air theaters at Philippi and on the island of Thassos.

"Dionysia" Wine Festival on island of Naxos (midmonth).

August: Ancient Greek dramas performed in the open-air theater at Diou, near Mount Olympus (midmonth), and at the ancient theater at Dodona.

Art exhibition on Skyros island (first week of month).

Holiday honoring the Virgin Mary, celebrated on the island of Tinos (15th).

Hippokrateia Festival, featuring ancient drama, musical performances, and a re-enactment of the Hippocratic Oath, on the island of Kos.

September: Thessaloniki International Trade Fair.

Film Festival and Festival of Popular Song, Thessaloniki.

October: Demetrius Festival—music, opera, ballet—in Thessaloniki.

National Anniversary (28th).

November: St. Andrew's Day, celebrating the patron saint of Patras (30th).

GETTING AROUND: Despite the language barrier most of us face, getting around Greece is relatively simple, efficient, cheap, and pleasant.

Airplanes make it possible to fly between island groups (such as Crete to Santorini or Rhodes to Mykonos) or hop between them via Athens. However, the deluge of tourists in the high season makes this more of an ordeal than it should be: bumped passengers, delayed flights, and incorrectly written tickets are common frustrations. We can only suggest you make Olympic Airways reservations *as far in advance as possible* and stick to them. Domestic flights cancelled (or changed) within 24 hours of departure cost a 30% penalty; within 12 hours, 50% of your ticket price will be demanded.

Most readers will sample the **ferryboats,** either the large ocean liner-like ships leaving from Piraeus and major ports or the smaller, inter-island boats. For both, check the local E.O.T. office or travel agents to determine the current schedule and arrive at least 15 minutes before departure to purchase tickets from the dockside agents. *Note:* those taking ferries crossing to Turkey will need to submit their passport and payment one day in advance of departure.

Public buses will take you to far-off beaches on the islands or to the corners of the Peloponnese, northern Greece, or even Athens. Kiosk news vendors are a good source of *local bus* information; have exact change ready when you hop on. *Long-distance buses* usually leave from a convenient central station, but check with the E.O.T. for current schedules as their posted schedules are often only in Greek and/or totally inaccurate. After you've clarified your destination (make sure you know the correct pronunciation—our friend heading to Mycenae was sent to Messenia by a misunderstanding), try to sit near the driver so he can tell you where to get off. Fares are usually paid to the ticket collector on board after you depart.

DISTANCE BETWEEN GREECE'S MAJOR CITIES (AND SIGHTS)
Distance in Kilometers

	Athens	Corinth	Igoumenitsa	Livadia	Nafplion	Patras	Thessaloniki	Trikala	Volos
Athens		83	475	118	147	213	508	328	316
Corinth	83		396	153	61	134	535	357	344
Igoumenitsa	475	396		425	446	276	443	239	359
Livadia (Delphi)	118	153	425		217	168	396	210	208
Nafplion	147	61	446	217		184	600	421	408
Patras	213	134	276	168	184		489	302	298
Thessaloniki	508	535	443	396	600	489		214	215
Trikala (Meteora)	328	357	239	210	421	302	214		120
Volos	316	344	359	208	408	298	215	120	

Mopeds are probably the most common form of private tourist transportation. They're a fun, practical, and cheap (about $10 to $20 per day) way to sightsee in the islands. Before renting one make sure you feel comfortable about riding along steep, sand- or gravel-strewn roads where cars know no speed limit. Since no tourist ever accepts a helmet from the few vendors who offer them, make sure you choose a slower, easier-to-balance *moped*, rather than a small 25cc or 50cc *motorcycle*. Organize your possessions so that luggage straps are secure. And, last but not least, take a close look at your moped before driving off. Check especially for faulty brakes. Since many tourists have accidents and fail to report them to the rental shops, their successors end up with bent frames which make steering and balancing the bikes difficult and unpredictable.

Rental cars are widely available, but expensive by U.S. standards (about $45 per day plus $3 per gallon of gas). Nevertheless, a car is ideal for sightseeing in the hinterlands; try to pick up other tourists to carpool and share expenses. Drive extremely cautiously and make sure you've purchased the maximum insurance plan available. For most companies, drivers are required to show a valid drivers' license, be at least 21 years of age for some cars (24 years for other models), and leave a cash deposit if they don't have a major credit card for payment.

Buses too slow or inconvenient? Moped too wild? Car too expensive? You may qualify for our least favorite mode of transportation, the **taxi**. *In Athens* they're impossible to find—they're either already carrying a local who's not going in your direction (group rides are sanctioned because of a taxi shortage; each passenger pays the difference between the final meter reading and the reading when they entered) or, if empty, refuse to pick you up when they realize you're a tourist (it's usually because they have so many problems with them!). *On the islands,* they're no better. Typical taxi tricks: (1) Some taxi drivers will pick up a group of tourists and insist (illegally) that every passenger pay the full metered fare. (2) Some taxi meters include a decimal point for the obsolete *lepta* (1/100th of a drachma), and drivers don't complain when unwitting tourists pay 1200 drs instead of 120 drs for their ride. (3) Late at night, taxis at airports, train and bus stations refuse to use their meters and demand a flat rate, usually 30% to 50% higher than normal. (4) Taxis at airports often overcharge tourists for the nominal fees imposed on each piece of luggage (15 drs in 1987), on trips to the airport (30 drs), or on rides after midnight (40 drs). (5) Drivers often adjust their meter so that it counts at twice the speed, even though your destination is not outside the city limits where this practice is authorized. Check the small window to the right of the drachma display on the face of the meter; it should read "1" in town and "2" only if you're leaving the city limits. (6) Another trick is when the driver tells you the hotel you want to go to is fully booked and he knows another with a room. Drivers get commissions from some hotels. Now that you've been warned, let us say that New York cabbies may be worse, that taxi rides are usually cheap anyway, and that there are some wonderful Greek drivers filled with good-natured advice, news, and gossip. Try to determine from a local what the approximate fare will be before entering a taxi so that you'll have some basis for judgment—*we want to warn you, not make you totally paranoid.*

HOTELS: If you've traveled with a Frommer "$30-A-Day" guidebook before, you know we believe that first-class budget travel comes from spending less than $15 a day on your hotel room and less than $15 a day for three meals. Then you can spend those extra dollars on luxuries you want. If two or three are traveling together, you'll be able to economize by sharing a room. Conversely, singles may be spending more on a per-day basis.

A general note about Greek hotels is in order. Until recently, all Greek lodgings were rated by the government as Deluxe, Class A, B, C, D, and E hotels or first-, second-, and third-class pensions. Rooms-to-let in private homes, or guesthouses, though regulated, were not rated. The government ensured equal standards for equal accommodations, enforced strict guidelines as to the prices these facilities could charge, and made sure those prices were posted for the traveler.

Now, however, the price structure has been discontinued and the rating system seems to us to be an anachronistic shorthand for explaining expensive "foreign-style" or better bargain "Greek-style" accommodations. We have concentrated on reviewing the C- and D-class hotels and first-class pensions (which generally run $15 to 35 for a double, often with continental breakfast, in the summertime) but have thrown in a classy, modern A- or B-class hotel (with all the amenities of an American hotel) when we felt you'd treat yourself like royalty for only a lord's ransom.

We rank cleanliness and character as top priority, with size of the room and private bathroom as lesser concern. In almost all the Greek accommodations we've found, you pay more for a toilet/shower/bath inside your room and much less for a sink in the room and a toilet/shower/bathroom directly across the hall. (Better to save your drachmas for a linen tablecloth, an extra ouzo, or another plane fare to a far-off island.)

Those traveling during the high season (mid-June to mid-September) to any of the popular island resorts should make reservations as far in advance as possible. You can write directly to any of the hotels we recommend, or write the **Hellenic Chamber of Hotels**, 24 Stadiou St., Athens, Greece (tel. 32-36-962; cable address; XENEPEL; telex-214269 XEPE GR). They will expedite your reservation and can suggest alternative accommodations in a similar category if your first choice is not available. If you're traveling without reservations, the Tourist Office or travel agents in each town may help you find a hotel or private room upon arrival.

Because most hotels were built over the last decade to keep up with the boom in tourism, the majority of new hotels are nondescript C-class ones, cut from the Holiday Inn "no surprises" mold. The C-class hotels in larger cities tend to be larger facilities with elevators, private bathrooms, air conditioning (for an extra fee), telephones, and a TV lounge or bar.

We always list these facilities, but our personal preference runs to the converted mansions, private villas, restored older hotels, or the small, newer ones with a very European or Greek feel. Here, usually for less money, you'll find a fresco or an ornate ceiling, a winding staircase or wrought-iron balcony, French doors or marble floors. In the smaller lodgings you'll be more likely to have more contact with your hosts, because often this family team (the Greeks employ their relatives first in everything!) can mean a friendly, helpful, and honest source of advice on local restaurants, shops, and sights. On most of the Greek islands, families rent out rooms in their homes to visitors. There's no better way to appreciate a country than by staying with a native. And over the eye-opener Greek coffee each morning, you'll learn a great deal about the Greek people and their culture.

Note: We welcome any comments you have about our recommendations or about the hotels and wonderful discoveries you've made. Only through this dialogue can we keep up with your needs and preferences.

ISLANDS: "The isles of Greece, the isles of Greece!/Where burning Sappho loved and sang . . . /Eternal summer gilds them yet." Lord Byron was one of the first, and best known, island hoppers. The Greeks say that when God was done creating the world, he took the leftover stones in his hand and threw them

away—this is Greece. There are over 3,000 islands, about half of them uninhabited, but only about 500 have electricity and other amenities of modern life. No
tour to Greece is complete without sampling some of them.

LANGUAGE: In Greece, naturally, the national language is Greek. And in
Greece almost everyone appreciates the effort when you attempt to speak to
them in their own language. In fact, because so many visitors already know the
basic pronunciation of many Greek letters from their fraternity or sorority days,
the Greeks have come to expect it. Don't be shy—start with the basic expressions listed in Appendix I and then let the Greek people you meet teach you the
more subtle expressions in their language.

Note: Try to memorize the basic sounds associated with the letters of the
Greek alphabet. It will help a lot when you're lost if you can sound out the
names of bus stops, restaurants, villages, etc., from the many signs around you.

METRIC MEASURES: Greece uses the European (soon to be American) system of measurements and weights. The following should help you get around:

1 kilometer = 0.62 (⅝) miles	50°F = 10°C
1 kilogram = 2.2 lbs.	77°F = 25°C
1 liter = 1.06 quarts	98°F = 37°C

RECOMMENDED READING: Greece has produced or inspired some of the
greatest literary works ever created. The following list is a sampling of books
that we've enjoyed during our travels and that would make worthy companions
on any journey through Hellas.

Over the years more people have become Grecophiles after reading Mary
Renault's books than from just about anything else—including traveling to
Greece. Ms. Renault, who died in 1983, wrote more than a dozen books, mostly
historical novels, that breathe life into the ancient Greek past. Among her best-
known books are *The King Must Die, The Mask of Apollo,* and *The Persian
Boy.*

If you haven't already done so in school, there's nothing like reading Homer's *The Odyssey* and *The Iliad,* the blind poet's mythological/historical epics.
The translations by Robert Fitzgerald capture more of the original spirit than
Edith Hamilton's more widely read Penguin edition. Speaking of Edith Hamilton, her *Mythology* is a good reference book and makes for lively reading.

Henry Miller's *The Colossus of Maroussi* and the novels and travel books
by Lawrence Durrell (try *The Alexandria Quartet, Prospero's Cell,* and
Durrell's guide, *The Greek Islands*) are fine works by modern writers. *The
Magus,* which takes place on Spetsai, is one of John Fowles's best, and is a perfect book to read while lying on the beach.

No list of suggested books about Greece would be complete without including the country's national writer, Nikos Kazantzakis. *Zorba the Greek* and
A Modern Sequel to the Odyssey (which is 33,333 lines long) capture the essence
of the Greek soul. The poems of C. P. Cavafy (translated by Rae Davin) are
to verse what Kazantzakis is to prose; he is Greece's most important modern
poet.

Finally, one of our favorite books on Greece is about the Greek alphabet.
Actually it uses the ancient Greek alphabet to describe some of the more remarkable aspects of ancient Greek life, all the while winding you around the
authors' etymological finger. The name of this fascinating volume is *From*

Alpha to Omega (The Life and Times of the Greek Alphabet), by Alexander and Nicholas Humez.

SEASICKNESS: This is an unpleasant subject that's not often discussed, but one that's very much a part of island hopping, particularly in May and August when seas can be rough. Consult with your doctor. He may prescribe *Transdermscop*, a new medication on an adhesive tape that you press behind your ear: *voila!* no motion sickness for up to three days. If you're reading this while bobbing around on a ferry boat, don't stay inside (unless there's a threat of being washed overboard!). Get fresh air, try to focus on the horizon (the only unmoving thing around), and breathe deeply. If you haven't gotten sick yet, eat dry soda crackers and don't drink fluids (even Greek sailors do it). A doctor friend from Harvard recommends taking a Dramamine the *night before* a cruise. Without going into a long explanation, this technique works and doesn't make you drowsy.

TELEPHONES: See this same heading in the ABCs of Athens in Chapter IV.

TIME: Both Greece and Turkey are ahead of North American time zones by seven hours (EST), eight hours (CST), nine hours (MST), or ten hours (PST). In Greece the European system of a 24-hour clock is used, so that noon = 1200, 4 p.m. = 1600, and 11 p.m. = 2300, etc.

TIPPING AND TAXES: A 10% to 15% service charge is included in most restaurant bills and is reflected in the two columns of prices next to menu items. It's customary to leave an additional 5% to 10% for the waiter or busboy; often, on small bills, change up to the nearest 100 drs is left. This rule applies to taxi fares as well. Although Greeks do not usually tip taxi drivers, it's expected of tourists. Small tips to chambermaids and porters (100 to 300 drs) are always appreciated. Greek taxes are already included in hotel and restaurant bills.

TOURIST INFORMATION: The **Greek National Tourist Organization (E.O.T.** in Greek, or **G.N.T.O.** in English abbreviation) is one of the most helpful, informative tourist services around, although they are usually located only in the most popular tourist centers. Unfortunately, in 1985 the helpful, friendly, and reassuring **Tourist Police,** which guided tourists for years in lesser known towns and islands, was consolidated with the regular Police Force. Since then, many local communities have opened their own tourist offices offering many helpful services.

For information before your departure, write or visit the G.N.T.O. at the following North American addresses:

Olympic Towers
645 Fifth Ave., 5th floor
New York, NY 10022
(tel. 212/421-5777)

National Bank of Greece Bldg.
168 North Michigan Ave., 4th floor
Chicago, IL 60601
(tel. 312/782-1084)

611 West 6th St., Suite 1998
Los Angeles, CA 90017

(tel. 213/626-6696)

1233 De la Montagne
Montréal, Québec H3G 1Z2, Canada
(tel. 514/871-1535)

68 Scollard St.
Unit E
Toronto, Ontario M5P 1G2, Canada
(tel. 416/968-2220)

YACHTING: Is there anything more romantic or glamorous than chartering a yacht to sail the Greek islands? Information and a listing of yacht brokers can be obtained from your nearest G.N.T.O. office. For information on special rules and regulations governing yachting and chartering these boats in Greece, contact the **Greek Yacht Brokers and Consultants Association,** 36 Alkyonis St., P. Phaliron, Athens (tel. 98-16-582). Our budget suggestion for sampling the high life: contact **Viking Yacht Cruises and Tours,** Filellinon St., Athens (tel. 01/32-29-383), to find out about their low-cost cruises through the Cyclades, Ionian Islands, or the Dodecanese Islands and Turkish Aegean coast.

Chapter IV

ATHENS AND ATTICA

ATHENS IS a city unique among the great capitals of Western Europe.
To see the golden marble columns of the Parthenon crowning the rocky slope of the Acropolis is an awesome experience that has brought travelers to the capital of the ancient world for over 2,000 years. Yet Athens's renown for its role as the birthplace of democracy as well as its store of antiquity's finest art and architecture represent just two aspects of this fascinating city. Side by side with the reminders of the great Classical Age, today's visitors find intriguing evidence of Athens's Byzantine heritage in its tiny old churches, bustling Eastern-style markets, and, more mundanely, in the pungent coffee made Turkish-style and served in coffeehouses throughout the city. Put all this in the midst of a sprawling, fast-growing city of 3½ million people and you'll have some idea of the vibrancy and excitement that is contemporary Athens. While other cities are fast asleep in the early morning and late night hours, Athens is at its liveliest.

The shops and markets, particularly those at Monastiraki and the fruit and vegetable stalls around Omonia Square, open early in the morning, well before 7 a.m. Traffic is heavy at that hour; taxis weave in and out of the paths of tethered trolley buses and the sound of car horns signal the start of another day. The cafés quickly fill with bleary-eyed Athenians grabbing a quick coffee before work. At one o'clock businesses shut their shutters for siesta, an officially sanctioned rest time at the height of the midday heat. The whole city heads home for lunch (the biggest meal of the day) and an hour or two of sleep before returning to work. Businesses reopen around 6 p.m., many staying open until 8 in the evening. Crowds pour into Athens's tavernas, restaurants, and bars beginning at 10 or 11 p.m. when the city gets its second wind, lasting well past midnight. Sometime around 2 a.m. Athenians wander home to begin anew after only a few hours of shut-eye.

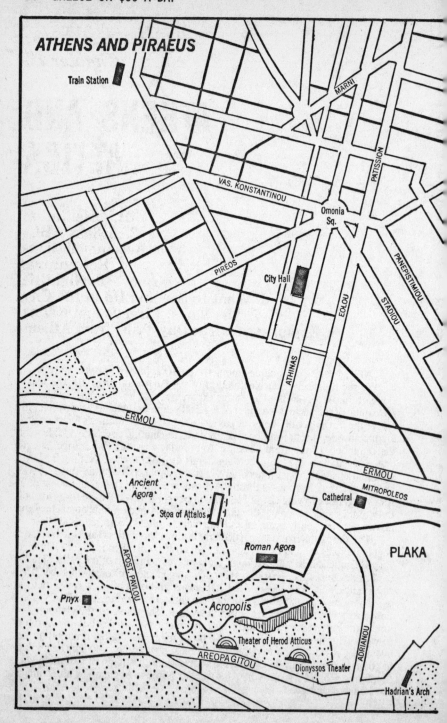

ATHENS AND PIRAEUS

Train Station

MARNI

PATISSION

VAS. KONSTANTINOU

Omonia Sq.

PIREOS

City Hall

EOLOU

PANEPISTIMIOU

STADIOU

ATHINAS

ERMOU

ERMOU

MITROPOLEOS

Ancient Agora

Cathedral

Stoa of Attalos

Roman Agora

PLAKA

APOST. PAVLOU

Pnyx

Acropolis

ADRIANOU

Theater of Herod Atticus

AREOPAGITOU

Dionyssos Theater

Hadrian's Arch

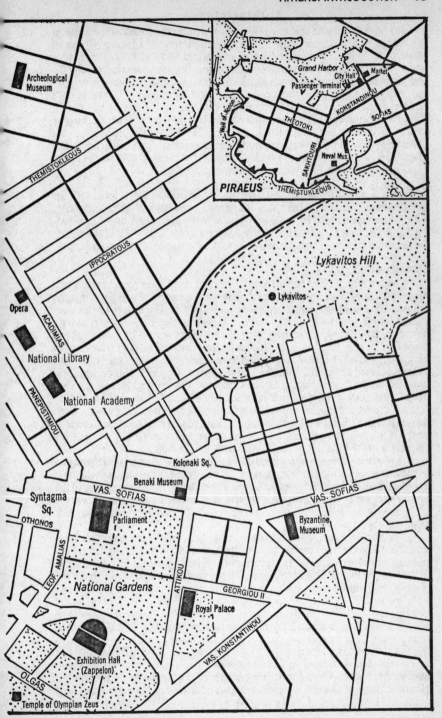

Archeological Museum

THEMISTOKLEOUS

IPPOCRATOUS

Opera

ACADIMIAS

National Library

PANEPISTIMIOU

National Academy

Lykavitos Hill

Lykavitos

Kolonaki Sq.

Benaki Museum

VAS. SOFIAS

VAS. SOFIAS

Syntagma Sq.

OTHONOS

Parliament

LEOF. AMALIAS

Byzantine Museum

ATTIKOU

National Gardens

GEORGIOU II

Royal Palace

VAS. KONSTANTINOU

Exhibition Hall (Zappeion)

OLGAS

Temple of Olympian Zeus

PIRAEUS

Grand Harbor

City Hall

Market

Passenger Terminal

Wall of Konon

THEOTOKI

KONSTANDINOU

SOFIAS

SAKHTOURI

Naval Mus.

THEMIS.TUKLEOUS

1. Orientation

It's hard to imagine that only 150 years ago, after the ouster of the Turks in the War of Independence, Athens was little more than an obscure outpost of fewer than 10,000 inhabitants. Period engravings show shabby, single-story wood homes flanking the Acropolis and Agora. Beyond them the barren hills and plains of the Attica peninsula spread far into the distance. Today metropolitan Athens incorporates the center city, with Syntagma ("Constitution") Square as its hub, and the surrounding suburbs of Kifissia to the north, Kaisariani to the east, Piraeus (it was gobbled up by Athens years ago) to the west, and Vouliagmeni to the south. Athens's 3½ million people live within a 150-square-mile area that's rapidly bumping up against the city's final limits, the mountains and sea. The city is such a magnet that roughly 40% of the entire population of Greece lives within the Athenian borders!

ATHENS'S LANDMARKS AND NEIGHBORHOODS: Let's take a closer look. Most of the sites and services of interest to tourists are in the center city, within a triangle defined by Syntagma Square to the east, the Acropolis (including Koukaki) to the south, and Omonia Square to the north. All of the sights, except when otherwise noted, are within walking distance of Syntagma Square.

Syntagma Square

Draw a straight line between the Acropolis and Lykavitos, Athens's two major hills, and with a geometrician's delight the midpoint will be Syntagma Square, the tourist, government, and business center. The history of this busy square is tied closely with that of modern Greece and centers on the country's first monarch, Otto I. Otto chose the palace site in present-day Syntagma because of its central location. Less obvious is why democracy-loving Greeks had a king at all, and why a Greek king should have the unlikely name Otto (of course, some would argue that the "auto" is still the king of Greece). This decision was imposed on the new nation by its allies, Britain, France, and Russia, who believed that only a nonpartisan outsider could steer a safe course around Greece's turbulent parties and regional factions. That's how the German-born son of Bavaria's King Ludwig became the king of Greece (he also introduced beer to Greece). The palace's neoclassical design and creamy yellow façade is a testament to the taste of Greece's 19th-century German king.

A plan for Athens was designed during Otto's 30-year reign with Syntagma as the city center. King Otto's royal palace is now home to the Greek Parliament and the Tomb of the Unknown Soldier. It stands high on the eastern side of the square and overlooks Syntagma's central landscaped island. These days the main draw is the delightfully theatrical changing of the guard by white-skirted, pompom-shoed *evzones*.

The northern perimeter of Syntagma has two of Athens's luxury class hotels: the King George, replete with white-gloved doormen, an opulently appointed lobby, and a chic rooftop restaurant; and the slightly fading grand dame of Athens hotels, the Grand Bretagne. The western quarter of Syntagma is the place to see and be seen: a succession of overpriced outdoor cafés overflows with exhausted tourists, pickpockets, and blasé Athenians. Cocky young Greeks on the trail of gorgeous foreign girls wear tight-fitting blue jeans and strut in front of the café set. Busy waiters with nerves of steel defy all notions of sanity and gravity by carrying trays of drinks across the street—also known as the speedway—to tables on the park side of the square. Behind these streetside cafés is the always-buzzing American Express office, one of Athens's most popular meeting spots. On the northwest corner of the square is the even-busier National Bank of Greece, where currency and travelers' tales are exchanged throughout the day and evening. Many of Athens's public buses stop on this side of Syntagma, momentarily obscuring the view of café society. Syntagma's southern side is home to a half-dozen airlines, including Olympic. Across the street is a taxi-dispatching station, where even the hardest-boiled Athenian can become unnerved by his inability to find an empty cab.

Kolonaki

Kolonaki, the chic shopping district at the base of **Lykavitos Hill**, is a ten-minute walk northwest of Syntagma. Though it has lost some of its glamour to the nouveau suburbs in far-off places like Kifissia and Glyfada, Kolonaki remains Athens's best in-town address. Lykavitos (or Lycabettus) Hill offers the best view imaginable (when the smog clears) of the entire metropolitan area. There's a funicular railway running up and down the hill, though walking is encouraged.

Plaka

The Plaka, located just a few blocks to the southwest of Syntagma and extending to the base of the **Acropolis**, was settled in the 19th and early 20th centuries by wealthy merchants. They built luxurious multi-story wood and marble mansions with finely crafted interiors. Tavernas and *ouzerie* sprang up, followed by middle-class housing, and, by the 1950s, nightclubs. From the 1950s on the Plaka became less a real neighborhood—arguably Athens's finest—and more a tourist magnet. Visitors were drawn in droves to bouzouki clubs where wildly amplified strummers, sad-eyed singers, and sweat-soaked Greeks gracefully slid through their dances. During this invasion a lot of plates were broken and so was elegant old Plaka. By the late 1960s most of the mansions, shabby and forgotten, were transformed into flophouses and dives. The Plaka was run-down, noisy, and avoided by Athenians—other than the exploitive few who knew that a steady flow of tourists meant a steady flow of drachmas. It hit rock-bottom a few years ago when the government shut down over 100 guesthouses and restaurants. The Plaka, once Athens's most architecturally distinguished neighborhood, has recovered from its long series of shocks, due primarily to the efforts of Melina Mercouri. Like Fanueil Hall in Boston or the South Street Seaport in New York, the Plaka was singled out by the government for renovation and development. A few relics of the bad old times remain, but the Plaka has undergone an amazing facelift that is transforming it, once again, into Athens's premier showplace.

Koukaki

Koukaki is one of Athens's best-kept secrets, a quiet middle-class neighborhood that's hidden behind the southern flank of the Acropolis. The streets are a mix of early 20th-century and modern town houses, the restaurants are little frequented by tourists, and there's nary a souvenir shop to be found. Buses and trolleys run frequently from Koukaki's main streets, making stops at the Temple of Olympian Zeus, Syntagma Square, Omonia Square, the National Archeological Museum, and Fokinos Negri. **Syngrou,** the wide boulevard leading toward Piraeus, Glyfada, and the two airports, is only a block or two away from Koukaki's main street; you'll also find most of the rental-car agencies, the public bus to Piraeus, and Olympic Airways' in-town terminal—where the airport bus arrives and departs—along Syngrou.

Omonia Square

If you look at a map of Athens, you'll come to the conclusion that all roads lead to Omonia (pronounced like the pungent cleaning fluid). Two parallel streets connect Omonia with Syntagma: **Panepistimiou**, along which is the university, the National Library, and the Academia; and **Stadiou**, with Platia Kolokotroni and the main O.T.E. office. **Eolou** and **Athinas Streets** complete the triangle from Omonia to the northern base of the Agora and Acropolis; running due south from Omonia, both streets intersect Ermou Street at **Monastiraki**, Athens's largest outdoor market. There are a great many hotels, office buildings, markets, and modes of transportation—including the subway to Piraeus—available in the Omonia Square area. The square was for many years the commercial and tourist center of Athens; however, many businesses have moved out of the precinct and the hotels have gone precipitously downhill. Today it strongly resembles Times Square; don't stay in Omonia unless you have to. It may not be the most attractive part of town, but it certainly is an interesting place. The vigor of the early-morning markets is Athens at its best. The huge department stores, with lower-priced goods than the tourist shops, are deluged with Athenians looking for bargains. The bus stop on the square and the *Poste Restante* line at the main post office are among the best places in the city to meet fellow travelers. The ladies, and men who like to dress like them, wander the back streets at all hours of the day and night looking for a hand to hold.

The Suburbs

Like everywhere else in the world, the suburbs are not the most interesting part of Athens (no matter how much people may dislike New York, for example, have you ever heard of anyone going there to visit Great Neck?), though like everywhere else in the world, people keep flocking to them. About the ritziest suburb of all is **Kifissia**, to the north of downtown Athens. The houses are big and modern, and a stroll down one of Kifissia's nicer streets would remind you very much of an American neighborhood. The only reason for a tourist to go there is for restaurants (there are some good ones) and the discos (also good). To the north is pine-covered **Drossia**, a suburb which has the distinction of always being 10° cooler than Athens and serving the best *peynirli* in Greece. **Glyfada** is to the south of Athens, and most people associate it with the airport, a controversial U.S. military base, and the residential area for diplomats. The people and shops are cosmopolitan and chic. **Vouliagmeni** is, like Glyfada, on the coast; people go there for the beach. One of Greater Athens's best hotels, the Astir Palace, is located in Vouliagmeni.

GETTING TO SYNTAGMA: If Athens is your first introduction to Greece, you may be surprised at what a big city it appears to be. As a transportation center, it's laid out somewhat like Los Angeles; all terminals are outside the heart of the city. Whether you've come by plane, boat, train, or bus, you'll probably need to get back to Syntagma Square to reorient yourself to the Big City.

From the Airport

To reach downtown Athens from Hellinikon International Airport, you have four alternatives that vary in cost and speed: taxi, Olympic Airways bus, the yellow bus, or the public bus. **Taxis** are easy to hail at both the East (international) and West (Olympic international and domestic) terminals. From the airport to Syntagma Square should cost 400 to 500 drs ($3 to $4), quite a bargain if you consider cab fares in most Western countries. Watch the meter when you leave the airport; drivers must keep it on the single-fare counter and there should be a "1" in the small window next to the meter's drachma display window. If there's a "2" in this window, it means that your meter is running at twice the rate (acceptable for drivers who have out-of-town or midnight-to-4 a.m. passengers). Be bold—question this immediately, as if you're an old hand at the game. (It's an old trick and it happened to Kyle, only by then she was accustomed enough to the rates that she could see that something was wrong.) Back to your fare! Watch the meter, add 50 drs airport charge, plus 15 drs for every piece of luggage over 22 pounds, and with the base fare of 115 drs you should arrive at the sum you're being asked to pay. Don't forget to add a small tip. Most Greeks just round off the meter (for example, a 123-dr fare will get 130 drs; a 281-dr fare will get 300), but we'd recommend trying to figure in a 10% to 15% tip on most rides (maybe a little more from the airport). With no traffic the trip from the airport should take 20 to 30 minutes, but during rush hour it could take 1 to 1½ hours.

The **Olympic Airways bus** leaves every half-hour from outside Olympic's domestic or international terminal and takes Olympic passengers to the airlines' office at 96 Sygrou Ave. (a 15-minute walk from Syntagma Square, and there are nearby buses and trolleys that will take you to many other parts of the city). Buses run regularly between 6:30 a.m. and 10:30 p.m.; the fare is 125 drs ($1). If you're arriving or departing from the International Airport (that is, taking an airline other than Olympic) there's a **yellow bus** that leaves from 1 Amalias St. at Syntagma Square. This bus, marked "Airport" in English, runs every 15 minutes after 6 a.m.; its fare is 100 drs (80¢). If you're really broke, **public bus** 133, which plies the coastal route, stops at Posidonios Street outside the airport grounds. For 40 drs (30¢) it too will bring you to Syntagma Square (exact fare required!).

From the Port

The most fun method to reach Athens if you're arriving at the port of **Piraeus** is to ride the yellow-and-red cars of the **Metro**. This old-fashioned subway is the fastest way to cut through the traffic congestion, but only takes you to certain stops within the city. The two closest stops to Syntagma are "Monastiraki" (an area about 20 minutes' walk west, where the flea market is held) and Omonia Square, another major transportation and tourist hub in the city. Tickets cost 40 drs (30¢) to any stop on the line, and should be purchased at the BART-like dispensers in the station (although there's always someone manning a booth). The Metro runs every fifteen minutes between 5 a.m. and 12:10 a.m.

There's also **bus** service to Piraeus from the green bus depot at Filellinon Street, just off Syntagma Square. Bus no. 40 leaves every fifteen minutes between 5 a.m. and 1 a.m., and hourly between 1 a.m. and 5 a.m. If you're returning to Athens from Piraeus, the Metro is much more conveniently located. If you want to take a bus you'll have to walk four blocks from the harbor to catch one; inquire at the news kiosks for the nearest stop.

If you've landed at the port of **Rafina**, up the hill from the ferryboat pier you'll see a sloping bus stop with several buses in line. Inquire about the one to Athens; it runs often and will return you within the hour to the Green Park Terminal at Vass. Alexandras and Patission Street (about 25 minutes by trolley from Syntagma Square). From the terminal, there are buses to Rafina every half-hour.

From the Railroad Station

If you're arriving from northern Europe or the north of Greece, your train will pull into the main station, **Stathmos Larissis,** at Karaiskaki Square (near Omonia Square.) Trains coming from the Peloponnese arrive and depart from the ornate old station next door. The beaux-arts Peloponnesus station has smoked-glass panes, crystal and gilt chandeliers, and a marvelously carved wooden ticket booth with graceful wrought-iron dividers (a treat for the train buff). *Note:* The Larissis station has a National Bank of Greece booth (open 8:30 a.m. to 2 p.m.), a post office, O.T.E., and a police station. Snacks are cheaper and better at the Peloponnesus station than anywhere around; for real meals, see our "Restaurants" section.

Taxis are available at all hours from the parking area outside the stations and should cost less than 200 drs ($1.54) to Syntagma Square. Trolley no. 1 (in front, and to the right of Larissis) goes to Syntagma Square and Koukaki, passing through Omonia Square. Trolley no. 5 is an alternate route to Syntagma Square. The fare is 40 drs (30¢).

From the Bus Station

There are two principal bus stations for the O.S.E. and K.T.E.L. bus lines that cover routes throughout the country. The terminal at 100 Kifissou St. handles buses to Patras, the Peloponnese, the Ionian Islands, and all points south. Public bus 51 will take you from this terminal to Vilara and Menandrou Streets, near Omonia Square, and from here you can catch a bus or trolley to Syntagma. At 260 Liossion St. you'll find the terminal for buses northbound to Delphi, Thebes, Evia, and Meteora. Bus no. 29 will bring you back to Athens Avenue, the street running by the National Gardens, just a block from Syntagma Square. If you're returning from a day trip to one of the public bus terminals (the Kanningos terminal for buses to suburbs like Psychico, Drossia, and Kifissia; the Vass. Olgas terminal for the south-coast beaches of Voula, Varkiza, or Vouliagmeni; or the Thissiou terminal for other local lines), inquire there as to the best Athens bus or trolley to return you to your destination. O.S.E. buses, which are under the control of the Hellenic State Railways, use the Stathmos Larissis railroad station as their terminal.

GETTING AROUND THE CITY: Once you've arrived in the city, how do you get to your next destination? Taxis are so inexpensive—usually less than the 130 drs ($1) minimum—that we recommend you take them everywhere, especially if you're traveling in a pair. Unfortunately, they're not easy to find and you'll probably have to resort to one of the many alternatives.

Taxis

We could write volumes about trying to get a cab in Athens, but it wouldn't help during rush hour. Be warned, however, that, as is the case in most major cities, you will run into ruthless and dishonest drivers. There are several taxi stands throughout Greater Athens, and cabs can be hailed on any of the city's streets. (Hovering around near a popular hotel will usually increase your chances.) Taxis are also required to pick up as many additional passengers as possible going in the same direction, so don't give up if the rooftop light is turned off. Keep waving and one might stop and pick you up! Then check the meter to see that it's registering properly; if you're traveling with a Greek passenger who gets out sooner than you, you'll never know what they paid, so don't be surprised when you get asked to pay the entire fare on the meter.

Trolleys and Buses

Trolleys and local buses are the most convenient way to get around the city, but they're usually so crowded that you can't sightsee out the windows. Head straight to the back for the best view. Trolleys nos. 1 and 5 go everywhere the tourist needs: to Syntagma, the Archeological Museum, Omonia Square, the train station, and the Koukaki region behind the Acropolis. At every stop (signposted with a yellow triangle) there are notices listing the trolley numbers and their final destinations (once you've conquered this formula, you can figure them out on your own). Always check with others waiting at the stop or with your hotel reception desk, as route numbers change frequently.

Note: Many trolley lines stop running at 11 p.m., others at midnight. Athens buses often coincide with the trolley routes or partially overlap them and then take off on their own. For the truly dedicated, a map can be obtained from the E.A.S. office at 166 Leof. Ionias St. in Cato Patissia or by calling 22-35-901. Fares on both are 40 drs (30¢), exact change only, and totally free before 8 a.m. (you lucky early birds!).

The Subway (Metro)

A subway in Athens? Ugh! Actually, they're clean, quiet, fun to ride, and an efficient means of transport. The Metro (as the Greeks call it) works best for those staying in hotels in the Omonia Square region because that's one of the main stops. Other stops include Piraeus (there's a stop at Nea Faliron, which is good for diners heading to Mikrolimano, and one at Alipedou Street, the end of the line at the pier for island-bound ferries); Victorias Square, near the railroad stations; Monastiraki, for sightseeing in the Plaka or Agora or shopping in the flea market and Kifissia (a prosperous outer suburb). Tickets should be purchased before boarding at the dispensing machines; fares are 40 drs (30¢) one way and 80 drs (60¢) round trip. If you don't have exact change, or have questions, there's a manned ticket booth near the entrance toll. The Metro operates every fifteen minutes between 5:30 a.m. and 12:10 a.m.

LEAVING THE CITY: If you're exiting by plane, boat, train, or bus, you'll be able to reverse the above directions and find your way to the appropriate terminal. Check the Athens ABCs for information on purchasing tickets. For those who have rented cars for some mainland sightseeing excursions, the roundabout of Omonia Square is the axis for the many major roads leaving the city.

Make sure when you leave the garage that your car has a black-and-white checkered sticker in the upper right-hand side of the windshield, indicating that you're a foreign driver. This will exempt you from certain traffic restrictions imposed on Greek drivers.

If you're going to Glyfada or Cape Sounion, take Leof. Syngrou Avenue (Amalias Street leads directly into this from Syntagma Square) and follow the signs. Either this route or Vouliagmenis Street (behind the Arch of Hadrian) leads to the airport and Vouliagmeni. The fastest route to Piraeus is to take Pireos Street from Omonia Square. For the Peloponnese (signs indicate Korinthos or Patras), take Ag. Konstantinou from Omonia Square and then bear left on Achilleos Street. Patission Street (a.k.a. 28 Oktovriou Street, which runs in front of the Archeological Museum) is the main road leading north to Evia, Volos, and Thessalonica.

Storing Luggage

Many hotels (and surprisingly, even more hostels) will store your excess luggage for you while you cavort in the islands or wherever. Some will accept it for free; others charge 50 to 75 drs (38¢ to 58¢) per day per piece. One of the best ways to ensure its safety is to feel comfortable with the hotel's management or reputation; if this is in doubt, dial 171 and ask for other recommendations. Otherwise, making a return reservation for a hotel room and leaving a deposit (even if you have to call ahead and change the date) is the most effective way, we found.

In Piraeus there are several travel agents along Akti Miaouli (the main waterside road) who will hold your bags while you plan an itinerary—effective for the day, but not recommended for long periods. Call 32-36-851 for more information. Both railroad stations have luggage-storage facilities, open 6 a.m. to 11 p.m.; the fee is 60¢ per item per day.

Airport Hotels

We can't think of anything worse than sleeping next to an airport, but, of course, those of you who have to catch 5 a.m. planes back home are relieved at the prospect of an airport hotel. We found two that are moderately priced, clean, and pleasant, and assure guests of finding cabs at any hour for the five-minute ride down the highway. The B-class **Albatross**, at 77 Vass. Georgiou B St. (tel. 98-24-981) in Kalamaki, has a parking garage and restaurant and 80 rooms overlooking the you-know-what (unless the noise from the highway bothers you, ask for a front, beach-facing room). High-season doubles with private facilities and air conditioning start at 6870 drs ($52.90) per night. The **Hellinikon** is a 52-room C-class hotel at 76 Vass. Georgiou B St. (tel. 98-17-227). As at the Albatross, the Hellinikon is air-conditioned and has access to a miniature golf course. Doubles with bath run 5250 drs ($40.40) in the high season.

2. Athens ABCs

AIRPORTS: There are two airports in the Glyfada section of Greater Athens, both parts of the **Hellinikon International Airport.** The **East Terminal** handles international flights of all scheduled and charter airlines other than Olympic. For general and flight information, call 96-99-466. The **West** (or Olympic) **Terminal** handles only Olympic Airways flights, both domestic and international. For information, call 98-92-111. There is a shuttle service between the two airports every hour between 8:30 a.m. and 8:30 p.m. See "Getting to Syntagma" for information on airport buses and other transport. By the way, there are no luggage storage facilities at the airport.

AIRPLANE TICKETS: Most international carriers have offices in Athens where you can make reservations or confirm flights. Within Greece, **Olympic Airways** is the sole carrier. For information on schedules and fares, visit their Syntagma Square office at 6 Othonos St. or call 92-92-555 (96-16-161 for reservations). *Note:* Olympic's Airport Bus departs every half hour from their main office at 96 Sygrou, starting at 6:30 a.m. and until 10 p.m.

AMERICAN EXPRESS: The main office is on Syntagma Square (tel. 32-44-975). If you're going to be receiving mail there, the mailing address is: 2 Ermou St., 102 25 Athens, Syntagma Square, Greece. American Express will cash and sell traveler's checks, make travel arrangements or book tours, and accept mail for cardholders; others pay 125 drs ($1) per letter. Office hours are 8:30 a.m. to 5:30 p.m. Monday to Friday, to 1:30 p.m. on Saturday. Emergency check cashing, card replacement, and check replacement service hours are 8:30 a.m. to 2 p.m., except Friday and Saturday when closing hours are 1:30 and 12:30 p.m. respectively. Don't forget your passport.

BANKS: The **National Bank of Greece** on Syntagma Square is open Monday through Friday from 8 a.m. to 9 p.m., on Saturday from 9 a.m. to 8 p.m., and on Sunday and holidays from 9 a.m. to 4 p.m. (This branch has the added bonus of having an E.O.T. office inside.) Official banking hours throughout Greece are 8 a.m. to 2 p.m. Monday to Thursday and 8 a.m. to 1:30 p.m. on Friday. There are several branches of the National Bank of Greece, Ionian Popular Bank, and Commercial Bank, as well as many American and European banks, located on Stadiou and Panepistimiou (Venizelou) Streets.

BOOKSTORES: The biggest of the foreign-language bookstores in Athens is **Eleftheroudakis,** at 4 Nikis St. (tel. 32-29-388), just behind Syntagma Square. Their collection is enormous (especially good on guidebooks!). Also good are **Pandelides,** at 11 Amerikis St. (tel. 36-23-673), and the **American Bookstore,** up the street at no. 23. Another personal favorite (with a much more eclectic, student bent) is **Compendium,** at 28 Nikis St. (tel. 32-26-931). At Compendium they'll even buy used books in return for store credit, a good way to lighten that load if you've been on the road for a while. For a look at the best guides and art- and photography-filled books about Greece published by **Ekdotike** (tel. 36-08-911) go to the retail store at 11 Omirou St. (the third right off Stadiou Street as you're walking away from Syntagma Square). For stationery supplies head straight to the best: **A. Pallis** at the corner of Voulis and Ermou (tel. 32-42-115), near Syntagma.

BUSINESS HOURS: To conserve energy, reduce unemployment, or suit the laid-back lifestyle of the Greek people, work weeks have been set at alternating full-day/half-day hours. The typical six-day week for most vendors and service businesses is Monday, Wednesday, and Saturday from 8:30 a.m. to 1:30 p.m. (or 9 a.m. to 2 p.m.), then Tuesday, Thursday, and Friday from 8:30 a.m. to 1:30 p.m. plus the afternoon hours of 5 to 8 p.m. Grocery and food-related stores are open a half-hour later. Many businesses catering to tourists, especially in the islands, have expanded their hours to 8 a.m. to 10 p.m. daily because they are only open half the year, from April to October. Some government offices work only the morning shift six days; other businesses change their hours in wintertime. We suggest that you call ahead to double-check the hours of any business you're dealing with.

BUS TERMINALS: There are two major bus terminals in Athens for long-distance (or provincial) buses. From **100 Kifissou St.** (telephone information at 51-29-293) buses depart for Patras, Olympia, Mycenae, Sparta, other Peloponnese destinations, Tripolis, Igoumenitsa and the Ionian Islands, Kastoria, Florina, Kavala, and other destinations in the north of Greece. From the terminal at **260 Liossion St.** (telephone information at 83-17-096) buses leave for Amfissa, Delphi, Chalkis and Evia, Ossios Loukas, Volos, and other northeastern destinations. If you're unsure of which station to contact, call 171 for tourist information or 142 for station information. **O.S.E. (the Hellenic State Railways)** also has bus service to the north of Greece (from the Larissis station) and to the Peloponnese (from the Peloponnesus station). Information and advance tickets can be purchased at 6 Sina St. (tel. 36-24-402), 1 Karolou St. (tel. 52-22-491), or, for international destinations only, 17 Filellinon St. (tel. 32-36-747). For bus service to the closer towns of Rafina, Sounion, Porto Rafti, and Attic coast destinations, use the **Green Park Terminal** at the junction of Patission Street and Alexandras Avenue. (E.O.T. publishes a complete schedule of long-distance bus routes and schedules.)

CAMERA EQUIPMENT AND REPAIR: Cameras, accessories, and film are all more expensive in Greece than in the United States, so bring along a good supply. The light is very harsh and bright so you might want to consider using filters over your lenses (at least an ultraviolet or skylight filter) and bringing slow-speed film for daylight photography (some ASA-25 or ASA-64 film). Don't forget to keep film (particularly if it's exposed) out of direct sunlight, and carry it with you on flights so that it can be hand-inspected at Security (checked-in baggage is X-rayed in the larger Greek airports). Any of the vendors near Syntagma Square can do minor repairs or recommend a technician for more extensive work if necessary.

CAMPING: Freelance camping (just dropping your tent down where fancy suits) is forbidden throughout Greece. E.O.T. publishes a listing of all the licensed campgrounds throughout the mainland and islands. We found that in places where there were no licensed campgrounds nearby, free camping was condoned. (Make sure to clean up after yourselves!)

CAR RENTALS: Renting a car in Greece is an extremely expensive proposition, but one that makes sightseeing much easier and more pleasurable. All the major rental companies are represented: **Hertz** (tel. 92-20-102), **Avis** (tel. 32-24-951), **Budget** through its licensees (tel. 92-19-555), and the larger Greek firms such as **Hellascars** (tel. 92-35-353) and **Interrent** (tel. 92-33-452). We had excellent service from Hertz everywhere we went (they have several offices throughout the mainland and the islands) and could book cars in advance. However, both the larger and smaller Greek companies tend to have lower rates. **Viking Tours** (tel. 32-29-383), at 3 Filellinon, can also arrange car rentals at discount rates.

Daily rates are $45 plus 38¢ per kilometer or from $436 per week with unlimited mileage. Remember that gas (*venzina,* sold by the liter) costs about $2.50 per gallon.

Check the brochures that adorn every hotel lobby to determine the best price and model for your needs. The smallest cars (like the Fiat 127 or the Suzuki SS 40) cost least, but usually only have two seats, and are standard shift. The best intermediate for coping with Greek terrain seems to be the four-seater Fiat 128 (the Opel Kadett is another option in this size). Whichever you choose, make sure to take out an additional insurance policy. Driving in Greece can be very adventurous; it has the highest accident rate in Europe.

DRIVING: An International Driver's License (available from all AAA offices in the U.S. with the provision of a valid state driver's license and $10) is recommended, but all American, European, and Australian licenses will be accepted for one year after arrival. An organization called ELPA can extend your license or provide maps and information; call 104 for emergency road service or 174 for tourist information.

DRUGSTORES: Every pharmacy has a list posted on its door indicating where the nearest all-night pharmacy is located; call 107 for a list of 24-hour pharmacies. There are several drugstores around Syntagma Square that have personnel who speak English.

EMBASSIES AND CONSULATES: The **American Embassy** is at 91 Vass. Sophias Ave. (tel. 72-12-951 or 72-18-400; telex 21-5548). Hours for their visa section are 8 a.m. to 12:30 p.m., Monday through Friday. The **Canadian Em-**

bassy is located at 4 I. Gennadiou St. (tel. 72-39-511). Their visa section is open 8 a.m. to noon, Monday through Friday. The **Embassy of Great Britain** is at 1 Ploutarchou St. (tel. 72-36-211). Visa section hours at 8 a.m. to 1 p.m., Monday through Friday. There are also British consular offices in Iraklion, Corfu, Patras, Rhodes, Samos, and Thessalonika. The **Australian Consulate** is at 15 Messoghion St. (tel. 77-57-650); visas are available from 8 a.m. to 2:30 p.m. daily; until 5 p.m. Tuesday and Thursday.

EMERGENCY: The general emergency line for tourists is 171. Dial 100 for emergency police service, 166 for ambulance and first aid, and 199 for the fire department. U.S. citizens can call 72-12-951 for emergency medical assistance.

FERRYBOAT TICKETS: Ferryboat tickets for boats leaving from Piraeus (to most of the Greek islands) or from Rafina (to the Cyclades islands) are usually purchased a half-hour before departure at the ferryboat pier. Each slip will be well marked with banners indicating the boat's destination; even with the summertime crowds, between 7:30 and 9:30 a.m., you can hardly get lost. If you want to purchase your tickets in advance, contact the many travel agencies on Nikis Street. For schedule information in Athens, call 171 (tel. 45-11-311 in Piraeus; tel. 0294/2330 in Rafina).

HOSPITALS: There are several throughout Greater Athens. In an emergency, dial 171 or 166 for information on the nearest one. Citizens of E.E.C. countries will not have to pay for services; other citizens are expected to pay at the time of treatment. Blue Cross/Blue Shield is recognized in Greece, and is the best insurance you have for receiving prompt and proper attention. Check with your insurance agent to make sure that your policy is up to date and applicable.

HYDROFOIL TICKETS: Ceres Flying Hydroways operates regularly scheduled hydrofoils between Piraeus, the Peloponnese, and the Saronic Gulf islands. Tickets can be purchased at the pier, Zea Marina, or at 8 Themistoklis in Piraeus. For information on hydrofoil schedules, call 45-27-107.

INFORMATION: Dial 171 for 24-hour tourist information in the English language. For information about traveling throughout Greece, contact the E.O.T. offices (see Chapter III, "Tourist Information"). When you've decided on your travel plans and need assistance or advice, contact our friends at **Viking Tours,** a travel agency at 3 Filellinon St., just off Syntagma Square (tel. 32-29-383). Dimitri Cocconi and his staff have assisted Frommer readers for years.

LAUNDRY AND DRY CLEANING: The **National Dry Cleaners and Laundry Service** is at 17 Apollonos St. (tel. 32-32-226), next to the Hermes Hotel. A gracious Australian gentleman runs the shop; laundry is done for 425 drs ($3.30) per kilo within 24 hours. Average dry cleaning prices: 625 drs ($4.75) for a dress or 750 drs ($5.75) for a suit. There's a **self-service laundry** in the Plaka, at the corner of Afroditi and 10 Herefontos Sts. Washing machines cost 200 drs ($1.55), and dryers 50 dr (39¢) for ten minutes. Hours are 8 a.m. to 6 p.m. daily.

LIBRARY: The best library for those interested in reading more about modern Greek civilization and culture is the **Hellenic American Union** at 22 Massalias St. (tel. 36-29-886). The seventh-floor Clary Thompson Reading Room is open

Monday to Thursday from 9 a.m. to 1 p.m. and 5 p.m. to 8 p.m.; Friday from 9 a.m. to 4 p.m.

MAPS: We're both map bugs completely—put one in our hands and we feel like we've lived in a place all our lives. The best one we found for Athens (available at all kiosks for 500 drs, or about $3.80), is called *Athinai, Pireefs, Attiki,* published by F. Lappas (tel. 82-35-961). The Athens map given out free by E.O.T. is also quite good and is available at the E.O.T. branches throughout the city.

MONEY CHANGING: In Greece only banks, post offices, and authorized bank representatives (perhaps the general store or travel agent in a small island village) are legally able to change money at government-posted rates of exchange. Often the large hotels will change traveler's checks for guests, but at lower rates than bank rates to compensate them for the service. Because bank holidays and strikes occur rather erratically, we recommend that you always have some extra drachmas on hand.

NEWSPAPERS AND PERIODICALS: The *Athens News* is the daily newspaper published locally in English, available at kiosks everywhere for 60 dr (47¢). Each evening about 6 p.m. that day's edition of the *International Herald Tribune* will hit the newsstands 110 drs (85¢). (It's usually easier to find in the vicinity of Syntagma Square or in one of the big hotels.) *Athenian Magazine* is a monthly periodical published in Athens that's crammed full of information, restaurant reviews, cultural and recreational listings, and articles of interest to English-speaking tourists. It's really a must if you're going to be in Athens more than two days. The *Athenian* is available at most news kiosks, priced at 200 drs ($1.50).

O.T.E.: This is the Overseas Telephone Exchange, an office where long-distance and local calls can be booked through an operator or dialed directly. Collect calls can be made to the U.S. but require up to an hour's wait, as do credit card calls. Self-pay phone calls can be put through immediately with the country's newly installed automatic dialing system. The main office is at 15 Stadiou St. (two blocks from Syntagma Square) and it's open 7 a.m. to midnight. The O.T.E. office at 85 Patission St. (near Victoria Square) is open 24 hours. There are other smaller O.T.E. exchanges in other parts of Athens. They generally have more limited hours of operation.

POLICE: In case of **emergency**, dial 100 on any phone, 24 hours. All questions concerning tourist needs should be addressed to the **Tourist Information Bureau**, tel. 171, 24 hours.

   For **lost and found** information, call the Traffic Police (tel. 52-30-111).

   For **lost passports**, contact the Alien Police (tel. 36-28-301).

   Any theft should be immediately reported to the police, especially if your possessions are covered by a baggage insurance policy which may require a police report for reimbursement. When Kyle was ripped off by a taxi driver (who had his meter set on the "2" or double-speed rating), she was told to write a letter with all the pertinent information to the police, and *voilà!* two months later we received a letter back from them saying that the driver would be appropriately fined for his misdeed.

POST OFFICE: The central post office (or G.P.O.) is a half block from Omonia Square at 100 Eolou St., open Monday to Friday from 7:30 a.m. to 8 p.m. *Poste Restante,* that gift to all voyagers who will be incommunicado for a while, can be directed either to Omonia Square (where anything marked "G.P.O." will go) or to Syntagma Square, a post office at Mitropoleos Street, which is also open until 8 p.m. (Bring your passport when picking up Poste Restante mail.) The post office for sending parcels (surface mail is painfully slow) is at 4 Stadiou St. Leave any internationally bound parcels unwrapped until they've been inspected there.

RAILROAD INFORMATION: The slow but pleasant and efficient railroad system in Greece is under the care of the **Hellenic State Railways,** or **O.S.E.** They maintain both stations in Athens as well as the bus network that's based at the Strathmos Larissis station (for northern Greece) or the Peloponnesus station (for southern Greece). EurailPass holders are entitled to use the O.S.E. train network free of charge, but may find that an occasional **K.T.E.L.** bus (the other nationwide system) is worth the drachmas for its more direct or convenient service. For most intra-Greece trains, tickets can be purchased a half hour before departure from the ticket windows at the train station (open 6 a.m. to 11 p.m.). For international journeys or for information, contact any of the O.S.E. offices, located at 6 Sina St. (off Akadimias Street, near Omonia Square), at Kardoul, near Omonia Square, and at 17 Filellinon, where tickets can be purchased for all international bus and rail trips. All offices are open from 8:30 a.m. to 6 p.m. Monday through Saturday. Information on Peloponnese trains can be had by calling 51-31-601.

RELIGIOUS SERVICES: For Roman Catholic services, contact the **St. Denis Church,** 24 Venizelou (tel. 36-23-603). For interdenominational English-language services, contact the **St. Andrew's Protestant International Church,** 66 Sina St. (tel. 681-8336). For Anglican services, contact **St. Paul's Church,** 29 Filellinon St. (tel. 72-14-906). Athens's only synagogue is the **Beth Shalom Synagogue,** 5 Melidoni St. (tel. 32-52-823).

SHOE REPAIR: Break that heel trying to scale the Acropolis? There's a shoe-repair shop on Filellinon Street, just off the corner of Syntagma Square, next to a fast-food restaurant.

SUBWAYS: The Metro is Athens's subway train network, a small one which services riders between the northern suburb of Kifissia and the port of Piraeus. For more information, see "Getting Around," above.

TAXIS: This lengthy subject is discussed above in our "Getting Around" section. The bottom line: They're great, if you can get 'em.

TELEGRAMS: These can be sent through the O.T.E. offices (see "O.T.E.," above).

TELEPHONES: Pay phones in Athens are a rare treat; if you can find one, it's usually in such a noisy place that you can't hear the other party. In any case, deposit your 5-dr coin first (we know it says "2 dr"; forget it!) and listen for the irregular beeping sound. That's your dial tone. If you get a regular beeping sound the line is busy. If you've found a full-length phone booth, the silver-and-blue ones are for local calls and the silver-and-orange ones are for long-distance (outside of Athens) calls. If you can't find a phone booth, there's often a pay phone attached to the side of news kiosks. If there's nowhere to deposit your coin, just hand the money to the kiosk salesperson. (*Tip:* Kyle's favorite pay phone is in the back of the Everyday Restaurant just off Syntagma Square.)

Long-distance calls and international calls should be made from the O.T.E. offices; see the listing "O.T.E.," above.

Note: All long-distance calls must be prefaced by the appropriate area code. The area code always begins with a zero ("0"), and is in the form 0752/27-776; the number in front of the slash ("0752") is the area code. Since most travelers will only phone ahead to make hotel reservations, throughout this guide we've included the area codes as part of the phone numbers of all accommodations listings, except in Athens. To call Athens from outside the city, use the area code 01. The dialing code for the United States is 001, and then the area code and local number. The larger O.T.E. exchanges usually have a fairly recent and complete collection of international phone books.

TOURIST INFORMATION: Information or emergency assistance can be obtained 24 hours a day by dialing 171 in Greater Athens. However, there's such a wealth of brochures, maps, listings, and advice at the **National Tourist Office of Greece (E.O.T.** in Greek) that you should make it your first stop. The central tourist offices are in the National Bank of Greece office at Syntagma Square (tel. 32-22-545), at 2 Karageorgitis Servias St., and at the General Bank on Syntagma Square at 1 Ermou St. Office hours are Monday to Friday from 8 a.m. to 9 p.m., on Saturday, Sunday, and holidays to 8 p.m. Even if no one is manning the desk, there's usually a wide variety of pamphlets and information listings available. (*Tip:* If you're planning on going to the islands, try to pick up the appropriate brochure here so you don't need to buy a map when you get there.)

TOURS AND TRAVEL AGENTS: Dimitri Cocconi and the staff of **Viking Tours** have assisted Frommer readers for years by providing friendly advice, reliable information, and excellent budget tours of archeological sites on the Greek mainland and the Peloponnese, and Cyclades yacht cruises. Viking is also offering cruises to the Ionian, Sporades, and Dodecanese (with stops in Turkey) island cruises. Viking is located at 3 Filellinon St., about a half block from Syntagma Square. Their hours Monday through Friday, are usually 8:30 a.m. to 3:30 p.m., 8:30 a.m. to 8 p.m. during the summer, and 9 a.m. to 1 p.m. on Saturday. Call 32-29-383 or 32-24-262 for information. Another excellent tour operator is **CHAT Tours,** located at 4 Stadiou St. (tel. 32-23-137 or 32-22-886), which offers 30 different tours on land and sea. (We applaud the nifty litter pails they've installed at most of the major tourist sights.)

Key Tours and G.O. Tours are two companies offering a one-day Athens sightseeing tour. **Key Tours** (tel. 32-32-520), at 2 Ermou, and **G.O. Tours** (tel. 32-25-951), both charge about 5000 drs. ($38.50) for a tour including all ancient and modern points of interest. Viking Tours can help you book either of these programs, often at a discount; they also book yacht and cruise ship tours.

Travel agents who deal in discount, charter, or student-fare flights include **Vital Student Travel Services**, 1 Filellinon St. (tel. 32-47-433), and **Kadmos Travel**, 30 Nikis St. (tel. 32-33-618). There are several "bucket shops," agencies that deal in discount, cash-only, air and boat tickets in the vicinity of Syntagma

Square, along Filellinon, Voulis, and Nikis Streets. Watch local newspapers or the bulletin board at the Magic Bus office, 20 Filellinon St. (tel. 32-37-471), for notices offering discount return flight tickets. Their hours are 9 a.m. to 5 p.m. weekdays and 9 a.m. to 2 p.m. Saturday.

3. Accommodations

It seems no matter how much attention is devoted to hotels in Athens, at the height of the tourist season (sometime between July 1 and August 31) someone, somewhere will be stuck without a room. Athens is not only the starting point for so many travels; it's a fantastic city filled with some of the finest archeological sites in the country. Everyone feels compelled to spend at least a few days in the capital. We strongly recommend that you write ahead to one of the lodgings that interests you for reservations.

Unfortunately, Athens today is a large, crowded, noisy, and badly polluted city; many tourists have complained that it's impossible to find a room quiet enough to get a good night's sleep. There is a solution to that problem: for years, Omonia Square was considered the heart of the city, and since tourists flocked there, most of the newer and better hotels were built in that vicinity. Now, however, Syntagma Square is considered the political and tourist center of the city, and many new lodgings have sprung up in a neighborhood called Koukaki, an older residential section behind the Acropolis. It is quiet and very convenient. The best news of all is that the Plaka, once the center of lower-than-low-cost hostels and hippie hangouts that were closed down by the police, has been resurrected in a historic preservation drive. As this lively and colorful district is restored, more and more of the closed pensions are reopening under new and caring management.

So, with so many choices elsewhere, we're citing fewer of the Omonia Square-area hotels, which are in the noisiest and most crowded streets of the city. We're including many suggestions sent in by readers of the previous edition, and we welcome your comments on some of our finds.

KOUKAKI: There are two high-end accommodations in this neighborhood worthy of mention for the splurge urge in some of our readers. The **Hotel Acropolis View** (tel. 92-17-303) is set at 10 Webster, at the corner of Rovertou Galli Street, near Phillipapou Hill. It's a lovely hotel in the truly "classic" setting for Athens —a quiet, winding street—with rooms and a rooftop bar that overlook the Acropolis. In the summertime the rooftop bar becomes an elegant barbecue with a perfect sunset view. The Acropolis View's 32 rooms are small, but filled with the most modern amenities, including air conditioning, phone, and private bathroom. In the high season, double-room rates including breakfast and taxes are 7020 drs ($54); singles run 5355 drs ($42).

The **Hotel Hera** (tel. 92-36-682) is an attractive addition to the Athens scene. Located at 9 Falirou St., off Makrigianni Street (within minutes of the Plaka), the Hera's large, arcaded picture windows and slate-tiled rooftop bar both overlook the Acropolis in the distance. The spacious lobby is two-tiered to create a coffeeshop/breakfast lounge that has a view of the Hera's back garden. The compact rooms are simply furnished and have phones, air conditioning, piped-in music, and private facilities. High-season doubles in this 49-room inn rent for 6625 drs ($51), including continental breakfast.

Most hotels in the Koukaki area are in fact pensions or restored homes. Many draw a student crowd, but all are suitable for families or older travelers who feel young at heart. The **Marble House Pension** is the best of these more intimate inns. Its façade has been decorated in sheaths of creamy marble, and the two plaster columns that flank its main door give it a regal air. Iannis and Thanos treat all their guests like royalty. The Marble House (tel. 92-34-058) is located at 35A Zinni St., two blocks up the street from the Olympic Airways office on Sygrou. For being so close to a major thoroughfare its back-facing rooms are remarkably quiet, the perfect place to grab a bed if you have an early flight to catch (and they'll store your luggage for free). The rooms facing the cul-de-sac have balconies and large shuttered doors that allow a flood of light to enter the simply decorated space. Those that face the other direction are not as bright, but they're functional and clean. The 20 rooms vary in price: singles cost 2330 drs ($18); doubles run 2760 drs ($21); triples go for 3560 drs ($27). The recently renovated snackbar and reception area is a popular hub for guests trading tales of their recent travels. Even before its renovations, the Marble House was one of our favorites. Good has gotten better.

Tony's Pension (tel. 92-30-561) is a tastefully modern update of the wildly popular hostel he's been running for over a decade; he's even added a slightly lower-priced wing for overflow during the peak season. It's at 26 Zaharitsa St., a few blocks in from Dion. Aeropagitou Street. From time to time Tony's given the pension a new look; now the freshly painted and wallpapered rooms sparkle. Solar heating panels provide 24-hour hot water in some rooms. Some rooms have a telephone. Doubles are 3445 drs ($26.50) and singles run 2860 drs ($22). Students and singles dominate the ever-lively scene at Tony's, and have spread the word so that it's usually impossible to get a room after 10 a.m. In that case, good-natured Tony will contact his pension peers and try to accommodate the overflow crowds.

Margarita's Apartments (tel. 98-29-664), at 43 Karatassou, is just down the block from Tony's but it's miles away in ambience. Margarita and Fondas Elossitis run this artists' hostel on a weekly and month-to-month basis, housing dancers, musicians, and models from abroad who relish the high ceilings and antique furnishings as a glamorous home away from home. Some of the 11 uniquely furnished rooms have baths, some share a private bathroom with one other room. A double with bath is 8125 drs ($62.50) per week.

Another pension near Margarita's that has an artistic bent: the **Art Gallery Pension,** at 5 Erechthiou St. (tel. 923-8376). Bright orange awnings open out over the balconies adjoining the rooms. Polished hardwood floors and natural oak furniture add a warm, homey feeling to a house whose old parlor has luxurious molding, French doors, and traditional architectural detail. Manager and architect Yannis Assimacopoulos told us that this 40-year-old family house had been home to a number of artists who left behind a legacy of paintings that are now displayed everywhere (hence the name). Singles are 2815 drs ($21.60), doubles are 3750 drs ($29).

Clare's House at 24 Sorvolou (tel. 92-22-288) is a popular choice among students. Its 23 double rooms are modern and clean; there is a communal kitchen upstairs, laundry facilities, and a large rooftop area for sunbathing. A double with breakfast runs 4000 drs ($31), with private bath 5000 drs ($38.50).

THE PLAKA: The Plaka, bounded by Ermou and Filellinon Streets and the slopes of the Acropolis and Agora, once housed the elite of Athens. Great private mansions, villas, and luxury hotels lined the narrow, twisting, stone-paved lanes of a European-style neighborhood. About 20 years ago, as Athens became plagued with big-city ills, many of the old families moved out; their homes became rooming houses and run-down residences. The Plaka's charm attracted great numbers of tourists; nightclubs, bouzouki joints, fast-food parlors, and souvenir shops opened up in the crowded lanes, creating such a furor that soon

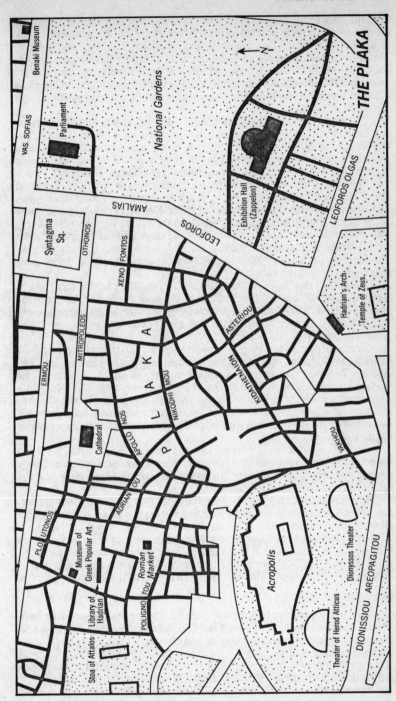

THE PLAKA

N

Benaki Museum

VAS. SOFIAS

Parliament

National Gardens

Exhibition Hall
(Zappeion)

LEOFOROS OLGAS

AMALIAS

LEOFOROS

OTHONOS

Syntagma
Sq.

XENO FONTOS

Hadrian's Arch.

Temple of Zeus.

ERMOU

MITROPOLEOS

ASTERIOU

KIDATHENAION

VAKHOU

P   L   A   K   A

APOLLO NOS

NIKODHI MOU

ADRIAN OU

Cathedral

PLO UTONOS

Museum of
Greek Popular Art

Roman
TOU Market

POLIGNO

Library of
Hadrian

Stoa of Attalos

Acropolis

Theater of Herod Atticus

Dionyssos Theater

DIONISSIOU   AREOPAGITOU

even the local residents couldn't sleep. The once low-budget accommodations soon housed only those who couldn't afford anywhere else to go; standards sank so low that in 1982 the police came in and closed down almost every lodging. The Greek government committed large sums to restore this classic neighborhood, and the hotels and hostels that are now open have worked hard to get relicensed. The Plaka has once again become a terrific place to stay, in the midst of all the action, and yet in the late hours a quiet untrafficked area in which to get a good night's sleep.

The small, charming **Hotel Nefeli** (tel. 32-28-044), at 16A Iperidou St. (now Ag. Hatzimihali), is a perfect example. Its 18 rooms are spotless, if small. The marble-floored hallways are lined with botanical prints in soft pastel shades painted by Greek artists. A continental breakfast is served in their comfortable lounge. Bed-and-breakfast doubles are 5000 drs ($38) in the summer.

Our next hotel comes from a suggestion offered to us by readers Betty and Stuart Hunter from Tucson, Arizona, whom we met in the Viking Tours office. The Hunters loved the **Hotel Hermes** (tel. 32-35-514), at 19 Apollonos, with one of the more modern and imposing façades in the Plaka. The Hermes has very plain rooms, all with showers, and 36 of the 45 have air conditioning. Doubles are 7250 ($56) with breakfast, plus a 650 ($5) additional air-conditioning charge. The Hermes has always had a large following, even though its prices have caught up with its fancy facade.

Another C-class hotel, with rather plain rooms but a pleasant roof garden, is the **Adonis** (tel. 32-49-737), at 3 Koudrou, at Voulis Street. Ask for one of the large-balconied rooms facing the Acropolis; though there isn't a terrific view, each is roomy enough to sunbathe. Bed-and-breakfast rates for two at the Adonis begin at 5522 drs ($42.50).

Are you planning a lengthy stay in Athens? The **Hotel Ava,** at 9–11 Lissikratous St. (a half block from Hadrian's Arch), may be just the thing. The Ava has 20 rooms that are well-equipped, comfortable utility apartments for those who like to keep up a bit of the home life during their visit. It's both a residence for many Athenians and a hotel for visiting guests, so write ahead to Mr. Fissendjidis or call 32-37-478 for reservations. Efficiency apartments for two run 4000 drs ($31); rooms with air conditioning cost 650 drs ($5) extra per night.

Also in a quiet section of the Plaka is the **Adams Hotel** (tel. 32-25-381), at the corner of Herefontos and Thalou Streets. Mrs. Katsimpras maintains 15 tidy rooms, with private baths, phones, and balconies. Bathless doubles are 3250 drs ($25); with bath doubles are 3750 ($29).

In the same price range is the **Imperial Hotel** (tel. 32-27-617), whose manager, Nicholas Klisouris, delighted John by insisting that he see for himself that all the lights, plumbing, phones, and keys actually worked (they do). The Imperial is at 46 Mitropoleos, which grants its corner rooms an extremely close-up view of the Athens cathedral, with the Acropolis in the background. John says to ask for Room 47—it's got a huge balcony with table and chairs and Arthur Frommer once slept here. The Imperial's rates are 3500 drs ($27) for two.

Budget Bets in the Plaka

Are you wondering by now about those enticing small hotels that have been resurrected from the old villas and mansions of this area? They're all included in this section, because they're less expensive than the newer C-class places. Since many of you may want an elevator and a private toilet, we listed accommodations with those facilities first. The more daring reader will appreciate the other assets these intimate pensions have to offer.

Our first choice is the B-class pension **Hotel Acropolis House**, located at 6–8

Kodrou (tel. 32-22-344), at the corner of Voulis Street and opposite the Adonis. (Once you've found your hotel, you'll begin to understand the Plaka's convoluted layout!) Panos and members of the Choudalakis family are the friendly and helpful hosts who've restored this 150-year-old villa. The original classic architectural details, the molding, and a decorative frieze combine with lace curtains and traditional two-tone painted walls to re-create an era. Spiral wooden stairs lead up to the now-famous Room 107, a spacious double whose large balcony has a splendid Acropolis view. The Choudalakis have added a "newer" wing (it's 30 years old) that's not as special, but it's clean and the toilets (there's one to a room, but across the hall) are fully tiled and modern; Rooms 401 and 402 were the best choices in this wing. Bathless doubles are 3800 drs ($29), 4200 drs ($32) with bath, in any wing of the hotel. Breakfast—an additional 450 drs ($3.50) is served in a small dining room opposite the old parlor, which now doubles as a TV lounge.

John's Place (tel. 32-29-719), at 5 Patrou St., near the Hotel Hermes between Apolonos and Mitropoleos, is one of the closed-down, now reopened hostels in the area, and still draws mostly a student crowd. There are parquet wooden floors and beautiful dark-wood doors (with their ornate wrought-iron trim) that open onto each floor and a cheerful, dormitory atmosphere. Singles are 1600 drs ($12) and doubles are 2125 drs ($16).

The **Dioskouros Guest House** (tel. 32-48-165), off Amalias Street at 6 Pittakou St., is another old home with a dramatic, winding staircase. Many rooms overlook a tree-filled courtyard, which enhances the quiet. Private double rooms run 2250 drs ($17) per night with shared bath.

AROUND SYNTAGMA SQUARE: There are very few budget hotels close to Syntagma Square because it's the most convenient choice location. The old world-class hotels like the Grande Bretagne and the King George (doubles about $200) are fun to walk into for a look, but you wouldn't want to blow your whole holiday budget in one night. The **Hotel Diomia** (tel. 32-38-034) is one of Athens's rarest finds—a moderate-priced hotel around Syntagma Square. At 5 Diomia St., just four blocks south of the square off the corner of Ermou, it's so quiet that contemplating the Acropolis from your personal balcony is a relaxing experience. Rooms are simply decorated but spacious, modern, and air-conditioned. The Diomia's friendly staff mans a small restaurant and popular sidestreet snackbar. At this full-service hotel, high season doubles rent for 5800 drs ($45); reservations are recommended.

The **Hotel Phoebus** (tel. 32-20-142), at 12 Peta St., is a much simpler choice, but still a good value. To reach it, walk down Filellinon and turn right just before it merges with Amalias Street. The Phoebus is on a quiet, narrow lane behind St. Paul's Church. This attractive building is well maintained by Drina and Marcos, a resourceful couple who have made the Phoebus into a fine hotel. Its 23 neat rooms have French doors opening out onto balconies. There is an elevator, and on the ground floor a very comfortable dining and sitting room, complete with fireplace, stereo, and library where visitors swap paperbacks. Bed-and-breakfast singles are 3325 drs ($26), doubles 4300 drs ($33).

Our last Syntagma choice is **George's Student House**, at 46 Nikis (tel. 32-26-474). The second-floor dorms, with their 20-foot-high ceilings and ornate, painted molding and plasterwork, are the best value. Dorm beds cost 500 drs ($3.85) each, including use of hot showers. George's also provides free luggage storage, quite a plus for those interested in island hopping. (By the way, George's glorious villa was built by Hadgi Nikolas, a war hero in the 1821 battle for liberation against the Turks.) You must check in early in the day if you hope to get a room in this popular hostel. The additional good news at George's is that there is a basement laundry room, with coin machines at 350 drs ($2.75) per load, a welcome treat for road dirty travelers. George and his friendly staff close the house in January and February.

READER'S HOTEL SUGGESTION: "We recently completed our second trip to Greece and returned, once again, to the **Hotel Cleo** at 3 Patrou, near Syntagma Square. We found it to be in a perfect location, near the Plaka, the Acropolis and other sights, as well as to airport transportation and other amenities. It is very reasonably priced with a double room and bath running about 2500 drs ($19.20); the rooms are large and comfortable" (David A. Lehmann, New York, N.Y.).

AROUND THE ARCHEOLOGICAL MUSEUM: There are two fine hotels situated near the Archeological Museum, the right place to stay for readers who've come to Athens precisely to spend time with this extraordinary collection of ancient art. The **Hotel Exarchion** (tel. 36-01-256), at 55 Themistokleous St., on Exarchion Square, has 49 comfortable rooms with private bath, most with balcony. There is an elevator and a large rooftop where you can eat or drink while you watch students debate in the square below. Exarchia Square, which is really a triangle, has restaurants on all three sides and tables and chairs in the middle. It's a ten-minute walk to the Archeological Museum. The summer rates are 2400 drs ($18.50) for a single and 2900 drs ($22) for a double room.

The **Museum Hotel** (tel. 36-05-611), at 16 Bouboulinas St., is so close behind the Archeological Museum that all of its balconies overlook the museum's tree-filled park. The Museum Hotel is clean and bright, and there's a phone and bathroom in every one of its 60 rooms—a worthwhile home a little farther away from the madding crowd. Doubles between mid-March and October run 3560 drs ($27) per night with breakfast. Flight fans will appreciate the large jet engine showroom next door to the hotel!

The **Hotel Orion** (tel. 36-27-362) is set on a green hillside above Strefi Park, about 15 minutes' walk from the museum. The mailing address is Kostas Tastes, c/o Hotel Orion, 105 Emm. Benaki, at Anexartisias, but if you approach the Orion from this direction you'll have to scale that green hillside (quite a hike!). A double without bath rents for 2400 drs ($18.50) including breakfast. Call the Orion to double-check the route your cab driver should take up the back road.

KOLONAKI: Kolonaki Square is one of the most sophisticated, elegant, expensive, and chicest neighborhoods in Athens, a slope of Lykavitos Hill that's filled with fine boutiques, the poshest restaurants, "in" cafés, and beautiful people. There is one hotel in this area, the **Athenian Inn** (tel. 72-38-097), at 22 Haritos St., and it's one of those hideaway places that people who travel a lot love to know about. The international clientele prize its quiet location, inexpensive accommodations, and friendly, informative staff. (A quote from the guest book: "At last the ideal Athens hotel, good and modest in scale but perfect in service and goodwill. Hurrah. Lawrence Durrell.") Double rooms, many of which have balconies looking out to Lykavitos Hill, are 5760 drs ($44) or 6740 drs ($52), according to season, including breakfast in the cozy lounge (decorated with a fireplace, piano, and two Mexican sombreros).

AROUND OMONIA SQUARE: Don't be discouraged if you have trouble finding some of these hotels: they're set mainly on the small, back streets that radiate from the busy Omonia traffic circle. Generally, they're much less noisy at night.

There's a gem of a hotel at 9 Vilara St., the **Hotel Athinea** (tel. 52-43-884), easily distinguished by its cream marble façade and the multicolored flags flying over its front door. The cream marble lobby is elegant, quiet, and intimate, in a low-key style complemented by the muted colors of the decor. Plaster casts of classical sculptures and friezes decorate the hallways; sparkling-clean rooms have modern, all-tiled bathrooms. Doubles at the Athinea are 4840 drs ($37), singles are 3180 drs ($24.50), and both rates include breakfast. The Athinea is truly a find for any neighborhood in Athens. It fills up early, so if you plan on staying here you should make reservations.

The **Keramikos** (tel. 52-47-631), at 30 Keramikou St., is an older hotel on a quiet, tree-lined street. There's a pleasant roof garden, many of the terraces have good views, and the spacious guest rooms (with private baths) cost only 4147 drs ($32), including breakfast. (Kyle was wondering why so many of the guests had red hair; it turns out that the Keramikos hosts many Irish tour groups.)

The **Hotel Omega** (tel. 32-12-421), 15 Athinas at Aristogitonos, overlooks the vast vacant lots that serve in the working hours as a (noisy) marketplace for fruits and meat—lots of atmosphere. The Omega's rooms are clean, large, replete with black-and-white photos of Grecian sights. Back-facing, high-floor rooms command a fine view of the Acropolis. For those who've always wanted to experience the bustle of a major food market while relaxing in bed, doubles with bath are 3840 drs ($29.50).

There are freshly painted, pale pink wrought-iron balconies at the old **Hotel Carolina** (tel. 32-20-837), at 55 Kolokotroni St., between Omonia and Syntagma Squares. Clean comfortable doubles (with bath) overlooking the narrow lanes of shops run from 3560 drs ($27.50) to 3775 drs ($29), according to season.

The **Hotel Alkistis** (tel. 32-19-811), at 18 Platia Theatrou, is set on a quiet lane near Omonia Square. The 08, 09, 10 series of rooms overlook the Acropolis; the 01 to 06 rooms have terraces facing the street. All doubles with private bathrooms run 5000 drs ($38.50), with breakfast. The Alkistis has a large, clean roof with seating for sunbathers to enjoy a great view of the Acropolis. Let's urge the management to start serving drinks up there as well.

There are clean, simple rooms at the **Hotel Amaryllis** (tel. 52-38-738), located at 45 Veranzerou St., a few blocks from the traffic circle. This hotel is favored by many English tour groups who like its budget prices: 3015 drs ($23) for a single, 4350 drs ($33.50) for a double. It's an old, fairly clean abode that's rather charmless. Nevertheless, the management is helpful and informative, and Veranzerous is a safe street.

A low-budget alternative for the student crowd is the **Hotel Tempi** (tel. 32-13-175), at 29 Eolou St. This 26-room hotel, across from placid St. Irene Square, is a well managed, freshly painted D-class lodging that's clean and friendly but a bit worn. The homey touches include a café bar, laundry room with ironing facilities, free luggage storage, and a lending library. The Tempi is conveniently located just ten blocks from Syntagma. At 2190 drs ($17) for a bathless double, it's a good deal.

Another popular lodging alternative with past readers of this guide is the **Attalos Hotel** (tel. 32-12-801), at 29 Athinas St. The venerable Attalos is a large, multistory building with comfortable rooms, an accommodating staff and a rooftop view of you know what. In addition, they offer free luggage storage. Double rooms with bath and breakfast run 5090 drs ($39.10).

READERS' HOTEL SUGGESTIONS: "We arrived in Athens during the peak season without making arrangements for our accommodation. We happened upon the **Pan Hotel** (tel. 32-37-816), at 11 Mitropoleos St., just off Syntagma Square. There we found a perfectly comfortable and clean room for 2870 drs ($22.10) and the staff was absolutely wonderful"

(D. Strike and P. Scontlebury, London, England). . . . "When last in Athens I stayed in a very recommendable hotel, the **Ermeion** (tel. 32-12-753), at 66 Ermou St., right in the center of Athens—a short walking distance from Syntagma Square and Monesteraki. The hotel, run by friendly proprietors, was clean, convenient and very reasonable at 2300 drs ($18)" (Helen Bayerian, Los Angeles, Calif.).

NEAR THE RAILROAD STATION: Readers who will be dashing in and out of Athens quickly may find a hotel near the railroad station particularly convenient. If you're going to stay for more than two nights, though, there are much better areas to sleep in. Since this book went to press several new establishments have opened, particularly in the A and B classes. Those listed below are C-class inns.

The **Hotel Nana** (tel. 88-42-211), at 29 Metaxa St. at Deligianni Street, is directly across from the Larissis station and is probably the best, if not the cheapest, hotel in the area. Built in 1982, the Nana's 50 rooms have all the B-class amenities, including air conditioning. The decor could only be described as modern: the use of stucco swirls, bamboo siding, and Formica is rather startling. Doubles at the Nana cost 4375 drs ($33.70) plus 330 drs ($2.50) per breakfast.

The 37-room **Hotel Sofos** (tel. 82-26-402) is at 18–20 Hormovitou St., right around the corner from the busy Liossion Street. It's a mite older than the Nana and a little more modest, though the lobby boasts a half-quarry's worth of veined gray marble tiles. Doubles at the Sofos are 3775 drs ($29), with private facilities.

At 45 Liossion and Ipirou Streets, about five minutes from the train station, is the high-rise, 83-room **Hotel Balasca** (tel. 88-35-211). The Balasca is dimly lit and somewhat dull, but if you're stuck for a place, shell out the 4000 drs ($31) for an air-conditioned double.

Budget Bets Around the Railroad Station

When we visited the budget hotels near the station we heard that the government was threatening to close many of them that refused to update their aging facilities. Those listed below were still open when we visited last summer; by the time you visit they may be closed.

The **Hotel Astra** (tel. 82-13-772) is an old villa whose pleasant, flowering garden slopes down to meet the square in front of the Larissis station. The hosts at this friendly lodging at 46 Deligianni St. (off Psiloriti St.) speak halting English, but they'll try to welcome everyone. Old-fashioned, spacious rooms and use of the large, clean, common bathrooms cost 1000 drs ($7.70) for a single or 1750 drs ($13.50) for a double; low-season rates are 20% less.

It's hard to miss the pink neon **Hotel Rea** sign on the roof of this baby-blue art-deco wonder. The old, worn Rea (tel. 82-13-760), at 31 Metaxa St., has ornate, wrought-iron balconies, tooled doorknobs, and an elevator that long ago forgot how to stop flush with the floor. If offbeat kitsch is your thing, the Rea has small, balconied doubles for 1800 drs ($14), with bathroom down the hall.

A three-story, pale-blue house with white trim at the corner of Peniou Street (at no. 52) is within sight of the Larissis station, to the left. It has been transformed into the **Diethnes Hostel** (tel. 88-32-878), a clean, well-managed dorm-style place where prices range from 625 drs ($4.80) to put your sleeping bag on the roof to 2000 drs ($15.40) for a single bed in a private room. The manager, Mr. Nalbantis, is filled with tips on student discounts, cheap restaurants, bargain air fares, and behind-the-scenes Athens. Definitely a good place for EurailPass holders who've just arrived.

YOUTH HOSTELS: There are several **Greek Youth Hostel Federation**

(G.Y.H.F.) lodgings throughout Greece. For a complete listing, contact the E.O.T. For more information, contact the **Greek Youth Hostels Association,** 4 Dragatsaniou St., Athens (tel. 32-34-107 or 32-37-590).

Rooms are available at the **YWCA (XEN** in Greek), at 11 Amerikis (tel. 36-24-291). The **YMCA (XAN)** (tel. 36-26-970) has closed its accommodations in recent years but is renovating new quarters at 6 Akadimias St.

We've noted hostels that we ourselves have inspected in the sections above, according to geographic region; here's a listing of others that have come to our attention recently. All offer beds in dorm-style accommodations for about 625 drs ($5.20) to 875 drs ($6.75) per night, and most have some cooking facilities, a laundry area, luggage storage, and information service.

Athens Connection, Patission at 20 Ioulianou St. (tel. 82-13-940), behind the Archeological Museum.

Joy's Hostel, 74 Acharnon at 38 Ferron (tel. 82-31-012), near the Victoria Square Metro stop.

Paradise Hostel, 20 Mezonos, at Akominatou Street (tel. 52-20-084), near the Larissis railroad station.

SPLURGE ACCOMMODATION: The **Athens Hilton** (tel. 72-81-453), at 46 Vasilissis Sophis Ave. (near the American Embassy), is something of an institution in the capital. Not only is it the home to many an international businessperson or diplomat, but for years it has been a place to meet for a swim and a drink or to dine in one of the hotel's many restaurants. Because it is the Hilton flagship in Greece it is only appropriate that everything in this newly renovated complex be made of polished marble. The lobby and other public spaces glisten; when we visited (after completion of the renovation), everything seemed brand new. Room rates for two are $126 per night; however, Hilton often runs promotional sales so check with your travel agent before booking. Last year they offered a $96 weekend rate for two, making this a very affordable splurge. For those on business, there is a full floor of executive rooms and suites, a separate business center, and a higher level of service.

4. Restaurants

Food is not only the key to someone's heart, it's also often the key to a successful and pleasurable vacation. Because of the wide variety of international, Greek, formal, and casual dining establishments, Athens is the perfect place to begin your education in the ways of Greek cuisine. There is enough variety so that you can mix in a dose of Greek with burgers and spaghetti until you reach the point where you're craving moussaka and taramosalata at every meal!

A QUICK OVERVIEW: This section is divided into geographic regions of the city, making it easy to find an eatery when you're hungry right nearby. If you want to plan a night on the town, turn directly to the "Splurge" section, which recommends fine restaurants of several cuisines, regardless of their locale. If you're hankering after a particular taste, here's a quick index to recommended restaurants by specialties:

Tavernas

The most expensive (good too) is Kostoyiannis (Splurge). The best casual Greek place is Xinos (Plaka), open evenings (closed weekends). The best of the fancier Greek places is Fatsios, open for lunch and dinner. Excellent, moderately priced food and a young and lively crowd can be found at Socrates Prison (Koukaki).

Continental Cuisine

The most expensive is L'Abreuvoir (Splurge), for gourmet French fare with a touch of Greek. The best of the less formal, moderately priced continental/Greek restaurants is Herodion (Koukaki), open for dinner only. The best European old-world ambience with an exquisite light-snacks menu is found at De Profundis Tea Room (Plaka).

Vegetarian

The best vegetarian restaurant in Athens is the Eden, noted in the Plaka section. It's open from 5 p.m. to 12 a.m. at 3 Flessa St. Near Syntagma, at the corner of Amerikis and Elef. Venizelou, is the Si Snack Bar, a very good health-food restaurant.

Ouzeris

These casual bars are a superb Greek invention, a place to nurse an ouzo (strong, anise-flavored liquor) and munch on varied hors d'oeuvres (or mezzedes). Usually a variety of wine or beer is served also, but the food is mostly limited to finger food. The most elegant Athens ouzeri is Salamandre (Kolonaki); Remezzo (Kolonaki) is another bar known for its lively crowd.

Dessert and Coffee

For a midday break, midafternoon lift, or late-night treat, try Zonar's (Syntagma), a typical ice cream and confection parlor. The most mind-boggling display of sweets is undoubtedly at Select (Fokinos Negri). For low-profile sweetaholics, the murals and brass 1930s decor of the Brazilian (Syntagma) is the most comfortable.

KOUKAKI: A local favorite for budget travelers residing near the Acropolis, perched on sloping Agelikara Street off Propileon, is the picturesque **Herodion** (tel. 92-35-291). You must climb up steps to reach the large outdoor patio (so drenched in bougainvillea that you might easily miss it from the street) that's been erected on the roof of this 50-year-old house. Inside is an intimate, glowing dining room decorated with prints and paintings of musicians and dancers. There's a piano (for guests with talent, please) and large ceramic jugs filled with retsina. The soft lighting and tablecloths give the Herodion a pleasing, formal air. Herman, the charming Belgian owner, speaks several languages and is delighted to explain the day's specialties: perhaps a Greek lamb stew or pork chops baked with cheese and peppers; veal with cinnamon or grilled fresh swordfish. Hors d'oeuvres are a specialty of the Herodion (and an excellent way to sample a variety of Greek foods); their combination platter of hors d'oeuvres includes seven kinds and makes a great meal for four people. Entrees run about 750 drs ($5.80). Herodion (also spelled "Irodio" on some signs) is open 8 p.m. to 2 a.m. daily; closed Tuesday.

One lively taverna that's certainly been discovered—it's always packed with students and families—is **Socrates Prison** (tel. 92-23-434), at 20 Mitseon, a half block in from Dion. Aeropagitou Street. The meat dishes are tender and well prepared, their salads are fresh and full, portions are large, retsina is tasty, and you dine at long, family-style tables. We dare any reader to walk out of Socrates without having met at least half a dozen other diners. It's open at 7:30 p.m. nightly; dinners for two with wine start at 1060 drs ($8).

The best setting in Koukaki, replete with a rooftop view of the Acropolis at sunset, is at **Taverna Strofi**, a longtime favorite, at 25 Rovertou Galli, at the corner of Propileon Street (tel. 92-14-130). Strofi has two dining levels and a pleasant rooftop summer dining area; typical Greek fare is well presented and served. Their excellent lamb and veal entrees average 900 drs ($7). Strofi is open daily (except Sunday) for dinner only, and credit cards are accepted.

Koukaki's best pizza is found at **Castle Pizzeria** (tel. 92-16-474), at 10 Lepta St., on the east side of Sygrou. Castle (the Greeks all say "Kastul") will deliver to local hotels at no extra charge. Their large pizza is the size of a small American pizza.

For Koukaki residents with late-night munchies, the nearest souvlaki, fast-food, and pizza place is located around the Drakou Square, between Propileon and Falirou Streets. Sweet tooths will find many local bakeries, but nothing as

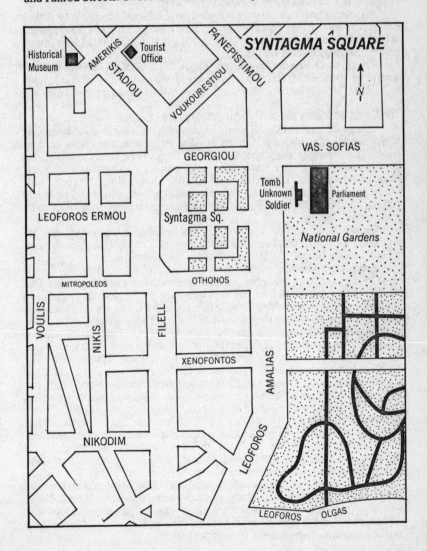

shockingly rich and ornate as the variety carried by **Kosmidis Pâtisserie,** at 24 Drakou St. It's open daily from 8 a.m. to 10:00 p.m. for take-out treats.

SYNTAGMA SQUARE: Most travelers find themselves collapsing into a café chair or grabbing a fast-food snack when it comes to eating at Syntagma Square. Try to put aside a lunch hour for **Kentrikon** (tel. 32-32-482), a large taverna behind the Historical Museum at 3 Kolokotroni. The Kentrikon is a spacious, air-conditioned, modern, clean taverna with cloth-covered tables and a bar. Service is prompt and polite, a great combination when you're waiting for a delectable lamb ragoût with spinach, chicken with okra, or their special macaroni. Don't be afraid to walk into their kitchen and peek into the pots; it's the Greek way. Expect to pay 600 to 800 drs ($4.60 to $6) per person.

A more expensive 1150 drs ($9), good, and different lunch can be had at **Corfu** (tel. 36-13-011), next door to the King's Palace Hotel at 6 Kriezotou. What's different here are the regional specialties from the Ionian Isles (many piquant tomato sauces!); try them.

The menu at **Taverna Lengos** (tel. 32-31-127) at 22 Nikis includes seafood specialties and continental entrees. A meal with wine will run 1500 drs ($11.50) to 2000 drs ($15.40) for two. Their small, quiet patio is a pleasant midday haven.

The Cafés and Snackbars of Syntagma Square

One block from Syntagma, at 1B Voukourestiou, is the bustling **Brazilian,** a 1930s-style coffeehouse filled with working Athenians, newspaper-reading travelers, or shoppers deep in conversation. There are no tables or chairs, yet it's a popular spot to stand and drink a quick espresso, grab a pastry, contemplate a sandwich, loaf of bread, or piece of cake. There's always lots of in-and-out traffic at the Brazilian. Snacks are reasonably priced; coffees and espressos still run 100 drs (77¢) to 150 drs ($1.16). The Brazilian is open from 7 a.m. to 10 p.m., closed Sunday.

On the corner two doors down from the Brazilian is **Every Day,** the new "in" place for Athenians. Here you can sit down, and though the menu is more varied than the Brazilian, it doesn't have that early bird charm.

Zonar (tel. 32-30-336) is the quintessential *zacharoplasteion*, the Greek term for a pastry shop, coffee bar, candy store, and bakery rolled into one. The Syntagma Square branch (can you miss that huge awning and the bright sidewalk tables filled with travelers gorging themselves on ice-cream sundaes?) is at 9 Panepistimou St. It's not cheap, but it's worthwhile for a splurge.

American-style snacking can be done at the **American Restaurant,** a bright, Formica-and-vinyl coffeeshop at Apollonos St. The breakfast special is eggs, toast, coffee, and jam for 375 drs ($2.90), but anytime between 8 a.m. and 11:30 p.m. there are people enjoying the air conditioning and comfy booths. It's closed Sunday. The management has studied American taste and offers the homesick and lonely a chiliburger, orange juice, sodas with ice, a "Constitution" burger with fries, or a bowl of chili with beans.

A special place that's best to go to with a Greek friend, a knowledge of the language, or moxie and a phrasebook is the sophisticated ouzeri **Salamandre.** It's located on sloping Matzarou Street, off Solonos about two blocks behind the university. Salamandre is open from 12:30 p.m. to 5 p.m., 7 p.m. to 2 a.m. daily except during the summer, when it's 11 a.m. to 6 p.m. weekdays only. It offers an especially good collection of wine from all over Greece (wines from Limnos, Crete, and Santorini are particularly good). We sampled *ladotiri* (a fried cheese with olive oil), *manidaria* (baked mushrooms with garlic), *spensofai* (sausage and peppers), and what Kyle recorded as *chtapovi* (a squid dish). Everything was delicious and cost about $2.50 to $6 per portion.

THE PLAKA: The Plaka's been Athens's "Restaurant Row" for decades. In every corner of its narrow streets you'll find a lively taverna, fast-food snack stand, or plugged-in bouzouki joint. There's one classic that's worth making reservations for (but get them after 9 p.m.) and that's **Taverna Xinos.** It's tucked in back of a narrow pebble-paved lane leading off Angelou Geronta Street, off Iperidou Street, opposite the K.K.E. building. Dionysian folk-art murals grace the walls; the informal atmosphere draws guests in aloha shirts or suits and ties (former President Karamanlis is a frequent customer!). Xinos is highly recommended by Greeks, who consider it one of the finest restaurants in Athens. When not playing, the charming gentlemen in the band sit back and watch the clientele. The food is superb: excellent lemony stuffed grape leaves, a tasty moussaka with fresh ground spices, lamb fricassee in an egg-lemon and dill sauce, and a veal stew with tomatoes and potatoes in rich olive oil. You can't go wrong with any entrée at Xinos. An unforgettable meal with wine will cost 2000 drs ($15.40) to 3000 drs ($23) for two. Call 32-21-065 for reservations; if you don't have them you may wait an hour, but do! Walk around the Plaka until your turn comes.

There's a lot of atmosphere at **Tsekoura's,** at 3 Tripodon Street, on the corner of Epiharmou (tel. 32-33-710). Two trees grow inside the white-washed dining room, right up through the floor (one of the trees, a Greek psychia, appears to be making headway toward taking over the taverna—eat fast). Fanis and Despina Tsehouras wrote to us correctly pointing out that the tree is a "sikia" (fig), not a "psychia"; however, we prefer the more poetic transliteration. Dear reader/eater, judge for yourself. Tsekoura's, with its charming ambience and excellent location, represents good-value dining with dinner for two running 1000 drs ($7.70) to 1500 drs ($11.50).

Ornate wrought-iron tables and chairs fill the rooftop terrace, which surrounds a traditional sitting room (now converted to a dining area that looks like an ice-cream parlor). Robust young tourists munch on fruit salad in yogurt, fluffy vegetable pie *bourrekis,* and tasty spinach-based vegeburgers in yogurt sauce. Timos, an engaging host who lived in Boston for nine years, is a vegetarian sympathetic to the vegetarian tourists who arrive in a country where lamb is roasting on spits at every corner. He opened **Eden** in a renovated villa at 3 Flessa St. (tel. 32-48-858). Prices are inexpensive at Eden with a tasty meal running 600 drs ($4.60) to 900 drs ($7). Hours are 12 noon to midnight daily.

Greeks and tourists alike dine on traditional taverna fare at **To Fagadiko** (tel. 32-53-728), on Adrianou St. in the middle of the Plaka. This neighborhood restaurant, with its spacious, airy fan-cooled dining room, serves a vegetarian plate featuring seasonal produce in a slightly tangy sauce, a flavorful macaroni with octopus, and a fine Greek salad. Two can eat well for 1200 drs ($9.20).

Timos told us about a natural-foods market selling herbs and vitamins called **Propolis,** at 3 Fidou St., near Omonia Square, that is excellent and inexpensive.

T. Stamatopoulos' taverna is **Palia Plakotiki,** one of the oldest in the Plaka, at 26 Lisiou (tel. 32-28-722). Eating typical taverna fare in such a beautiful garden with vines tumbling down its trellised walls is a refreshing change on a hot summer's night. The Palia is a bit more expensive than some of the others— about 2000 drs ($15.40) for two—but it also features Greek music.

The Cafés and Snackbars of the Plaka

The **De Profundis Tea Room** (tel. 72-14-959), at 1 Hatzimichali, is one of the best examples of the new surge in renovation. This entry in the Plaka's highly competitive eatery market takes a new tack in dining: furniture has been culled from old cafés throughout Greece; classical music plays softly: natural juices, herbal teas, imported coffees, and a liquor bar combine to make De Profundis satisfactory to everyone. The atmosphere is quiet and very English at midday and soft-spoken, elegant Athenian at night. Bread with homemade jams, pastries, or spinach-and-cheese pies can be ordered. De Profundis is open from noon until 1 a.m., daily; even if you don't eat there, peek through its lace curtains to see what an attractive French-speaking Greek couple can do with an old mansion.

Our favorite breakfast place in Athens is **To Tristrato**, a small 1920s style tearoom at the corner of Asteriou and Dedalou at the top of the hill. Run by a large and lovely woman who loves to meet people, this milk shop has it all: fresh fruits and yogurt, eggs and bacon, fresh squeezed lemonade, croissants—you name it. To Tristrato is open daily during the high season from 10 a.m. to midnight. The sum of 575 drs ($4.40) will provide you with a terrific meal in a gorgeous setting. And you can sit inside or out.

Paragoti, at 11 Apollonos St., is like Little Italy; you sit at small marble-top tables in the back of a grocery store or on the sidewalk. No one here speaks English, but the menu features "Roll lixurious and Breatoast." You get the picture. Better value than their continental breakfast is just a cup of Greek coffee, a pastry or cheese pie, cornflakes, or delicious yogurt. Two can eat well for 600 drs ($4.60).

KOLONAKI:
The majority of cafés and restaurants in Kolonaki are places to be seen, not to eat in. **Kioupi** (pronounced "Q-pee") is down below street level with a pine-paneled entrance at 3 Filkis Estaria on Kolonaki Square, and it's one of the rare exceptions. This neighborhood taverna is known for its tasty food. Writes Steven Werthimer of New York City: "Kioupi is plain looking but has a large selection of well-prepared taverna fare and excellent moussaka!"

Remezzo, at 6 Haritos near Kolonaki Square, is the same style as the more obvious "in crowd" outdoor cafés on the square, but it's intimate, chic, quiet, and dimly lit. Remezzo is more for bar chatter than for dining, but if you find hungry company and you don't want to go far, the food (primarily French fare) is fine. (If you've sampled the Remezzo on Mykonos, Hydra, or Corfu, you'll have an idea of what to expect from the mother one—which, by the way, is closed in the summer!) Reservations are recommended (tel. 36-27-426).

FOKINOS NEGRI:
This is a long, broad avenue broken up by a traffic island filled with trees and benches, planters randomly cemented into the street to reduce the speed of traffic, and an atmosphere all its own. Fokinos Negri, reached by trolley 3 or 12 (they pass in front of the university or Archeological Museum), is the youth capital of Athens—sort of a Malibu, East Village, or Valley Girls heaven. At night, it's the place to go for a good look at the country's future leaders and a really good time.

If you walk three blocks up from the trolley and turn right, you'll reach **Mr. Goody's,** the most popular hamburger joint, although it looks like any other fast-food emporium. This is the place to mix with Athenian youth. The really cool order the "Double Burger Special" at 300 drs ($2.30), a big burger with an egg on top and potato salad on the side. Then try **Vivoli's,** at 31 Fokinos Negri, up the block, for Italian-style ices and ice cream.

Select, at the corner of E. Anizolou Street, is the café for grownups (over 20) along Fokinos Negri. (If you can't spot any grownups, look for the white neon, scalloped marquee that makes this café look like a wedding cake.) Inside you'll find what may be the largest selection of Greek and European pastries and cakes in the country, if not the world. It's just fun to walk in and drool; 500

drs ($3.85) will buy you coffee and a pastry. Sit there and admire the cigarette man, wending his way through aisles of Fila and Lacoste with a tray of smokes suspended from his neck, moving with the panache of a true Copa girl!

Taverna I Thraka is one of the few restaurants on Fokinos Negri, and it's a pleasant place from which to watch the action. Service is attentive; sample the baked lamb leg for two, a homemade cheese pie that resembles a fried cheese dumpling stuffed with eggplant, or their tasty shrimp salad with diced peppers, pickles, and tomatoes. A couple can savor a delicious meal in a calm, tastefully quiet ambience for about 2500 drs ($19.20).

OMONIA SQUARE: As you approach Omonia Square along Panepistimiou, at

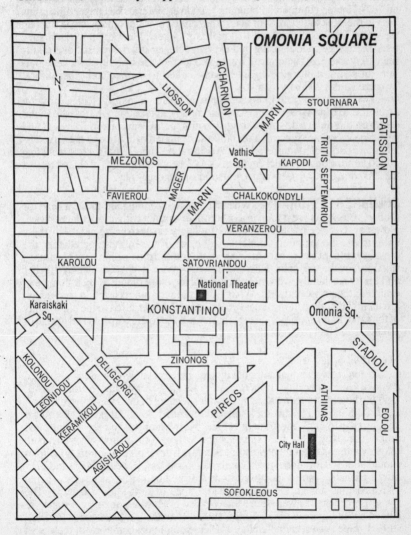

no. 46 on the right you'll find the simple wood façade of the **Ideal Restaurant**. The Ideal (tel. 36-14-604) has high-quality Greek food and a variety of continental dishes. It's an Athenian classic, one that's displayed the day's specialties (wrapped in plastic wrap with a price flag imbedded in them) in the front window for years. Even the "I refuse to taste Greek food" crowd will like the Ideal and its waiters (dressed in jackets and ties). Since 1922 the Ideal has served happy customers in the all-wood dining room. For about 1000 drs ($7.70) per head you can try it too.

Another taverna worthy of mention that's not exactly in Omonia Square is **Sigalas**. Taverna Sigalas is located at Monastiraki Square, opposite the delightful flea market (and just a one-stop Metro ride away from Omonia Square, which is why it got into this section). Spiros opened his wildly popular eatery in an 1879 vintage commercial building. The lively interior has huge, old retsina kegs in the back and dozens of black-and-white photos of Greek movie stars on the walls. Between 8 a.m. and 10 p.m. there's Greek Muzak; from 10 p.m. to 2 a.m. there's frenzied dancing and experimental *sirtaki* movement overtaking the eating space. At all hours, Greeks and tourists are wolfing down large portions of stews, moussaka, gigante beans, baked tomatoes, and other dishes. Two can eat for 2000 drs ($15.40).

Two blocks up from Omonia Square at 6 Satovriandou, off 28 Oktovriou St., is the **Ariston Greek Grill**. A bright canopy shades the outdoor café tables set up on this quiet side street. Inside the grill, in full view of a whirling spit and barbecue racks, are several other tables surrounded by murals of the Greek islands and national monuments. The Ariston serves a full meal for two including grilled lamb, a quarter chicken, Greek salad, beer, and carafes of chilled retsina for 2000 drs ($15.40), between 9 a.m. and 1 a.m. every day.

SPLURGE RESTAURANTS: When it comes to spending $15 to $25 a head for dinner, you expect great food in a beautiful restaurant with immaculate service. However, Greek cuisine doesn't lend itself very easily to being judged by these criteria: the food is often simple though made of the freshest ingredients; the most beautiful places to eat are those where you can dine within view of nature's splendor, by the sea, in the hills; and the best service is that provided by the chef and his or her family, who make you feel like you're dining in their home and sampling their special dishes. What unites the restaurants listed in this section are their higher than "low-budget" cost, general consensus as to the high quality of the food, and a special ambience that allows you to dress up and feel formal or go casual and feel pampered.

The Greek Splurge

If you're in search of authenticity try a taverna known for its widely varied menu of Greek specialties from *tsadziki* to *kataifi*, **Kostoyiannis** (tel. 82-12-496). One of the oldest tavernas in the area, it's located behind the Polytechnic off Leof. Alexandras Avenue on a small street called Zaimi, at no. 37. If you get lost, just say to any pedestrian or cabbie "Kostoyiannis," and they'll smile and point the way. In the summertime reservations are recommended. (Kostoyiannis is open nightly except Sunday, from 8 p.m. to 2 a.m.). Couples should allot $60 for dinner; light eaters can spend less. Readers Diana and Timothy Bianchi, both doctors from Brookline, Massachusetts, write: "Kostoyiannis has an impressively wide range of dishes for a taverna. The swordfish brochettes were excellent. We had at least ten appetizers which included stuffed mussels, fried brains, stuffed tomatoes, cooked beans (tourlu), stuffed grape leaves, cannelloni . . ." Please don't take home any of their new, personalized dishware as a souvenir! The brand-new extension should keep waiting time to a minimum.

You've heard there's no judging a book by its cover, so don't be horrified by the name attached to one of the expense-account crowd's favorite lunch hangouts: **Fatsios.** Fatsios is at 5 Efroniou, in the Pangrati section of town, about a block south of the Hilton Hotel. Between noon and 5 p.m. (make reservations if you'd like to dine between 2 and 4 p.m. at 72-17-421) you can enjoy an excellent Greek meal at a lively, ritzy taverna where attractive murals and a frescoed ceiling are the decor. Their meals may set you back from $12 to $18, but will not make you "fatsio." (By the way, the charming Mr. Fatsios is usually in attendance.)

Myrtia, located up the hill behind the Olympic Stadium at 35 Markou Moussourou St. (tel. 70-12-276), is the most famous of the fixed-menu tavernas in Athens, and one that provides an unforgettable (though expensive, up to $25 per person) gastronomic bacchanalia that's as much a part of the Greek experience as your first sight of the Parthenon. The atmosphere is meant to transport you to a wonderfully Greek world of villages, goatherds, rocky coastlines, and lively dancing; landscape paintings, shiny brass lamps, worn ceramic pottery, the thatched straw matting of so many taverna roofs—all contribute. A trio of strolling musicians tops it off. They weave in and out of the waiters who are burdened with large trays of *mezedes* (appetizer dishes), jugs of wine, then selected roast chicken or lamb (the best!) entrées, and then more wine, more vegetables, fruits, sweets, more wine. Anyone who can still walk out needs to hail a cab back to Syntagma (about $5), but we guarantee that your evening will not be easily forgotten. Myrtia is open from 8:30 p.m. to 2 a.m., Monday through Saturday. Dinner is served in the garden from Mid-May to October. Call ahead for reservations.

O Anthropos (tel. 72-27-914) is our favorite fish taverna in Athens. No, it's not a fancy place catering to the ultra-chic, nor does it have the tourist appeal of Piraeus's Microlimano, but if what you want is a simply prepared fish or seafood entrée in a homey, garden atmosphere, O Anthropos is the place to go. This unassuming presence doesn't mean that it is a secret—which is to say, call for reservations; Athenians in the know come here often. Also we heard that the chef was Aristotle Onassis' cook for many years, adding some panache to this intimate eatery. O Anthropos is located at 13 Archelaou, near the intersection of Vass. Konstantinou and Vass. Georgiou. Two should expect to spend $35.

The International Splurge

For a romantic, candlelit evening under a mulberry tree canopy, there's no better choice than **L'Abreuvoir**, in the Kolonaki district at 51 Xenokratous (tel. 72-29-061). L'Abreuvoir (which means "watering hole") has a comfortable, welcoming ambience that's suited to a dress-up evening or a gourmand's casual night out. It's frequented by wealthy Athenians, tawny-haired shipping magnates' wives and resident expatriates longing for a European feast. Most of L'Abreuvoir's specialties are French, and all are excellently prepared and artistically presented. From the light spinach soufflé-like tart or smoked trout to the steak au poivre, entrecôtes Provençales (a filet cooked in a marvelous garlic, mushroom, and parsley sauce) to the strawberry pie or chocolate mousse, it's all a delight. L'Abreuvoir has all the attributes of a perfect splurge evening: an elegant setting, wonderful food, and superb service. For such gourmet fare and first-class treatment, the prices are reasonable. A complete dinner for two (it's open for lunch and dinner daily) will cost $25 to $30 per person. Reservations recommended.

Splurges by the Sea

Athenians love to get away from the heat and *nefos* (smog) of their city for an evening at the seashore. Whether it's a meal at Microlimano (the charming port of Piraeus) or under the screaming whines of overhead jetcraft in the suburb of Glyfada, Greeks are always ready to sit outside, sip retsina, and stare out to the sea.

If a tourist asks "Where's the best seafood restaurant in Athens?" he or she will always be told "Microlimano." There are so many seaside tavernas lining the picturesque, broad, rounded cove that no one can agree on which one is best (it's like asking a New Yorker to name the best restaurant in Chinatown). Cheek to cheek are the canopy-shaded vinyl chairs of Capt. John's, Three Brothers, Semiramis, and a myriad of others. The menus and prices are similar: that is, the charge for fish by the kilo is similar. Whether or not the waiter weighing your portion of fish does it honestly is what differs in most cases. Many Greeks won't go to Microlimano anymore. Though still charmed by the setting, they're fed up with being overcharged—or worse, badly treated by waiters who realize that because they speak the language they cannot be cheated.

The majority of restaurants are kept alive by group-bound tourists who don't distinguish between quality and prices. Here are two that seem to be better than most: **Zephyros** (tel. 41-75-152), at 48 Koumoundourou, and the most celebrated one, **Kanaris** (tel. 41-22-533), which has maintained its reputation for excellent seafood since 1922. Bring $25 to $40 per person with you and then follow these steps: First, try to grab a seat in one of the above-mentioned restaurants or in one that you've chosen after price-shopping the posted menus. The best tables are by the waterside, where you'll have a closeup view of the yachts and cruisers bobbing up and down in the marina. Order some tangy retsina, a bottle of Domestica (one of the cheapest but, to our palates, best of the local white wines), or a Heineken. When you've established territorial control over your table, saunter back into the kitchen and ask a waiter to show you the day's catch in the large silver freezers. (The Greeks' favorite, and most expensive, is *barbounia*, red mullet, but we feel any of the lesser priced fish which are freshly caught and grilled are just as tasty.) Make sure he weighs your portion and explains how much it will cost before you leave the kitchen. After you've gotten an eyeful of the seafood hors d'oeuvres, you'll probably need one to tide you over until your grilled *(skara)* or fried *(tiganiti)* fish arrives. A Greek, or peasant's, salad *(choriatiki)* or a plateful of cool, crisp cucumbers and tomatoes rounds out the feast. After supper, stroll along the harbor to the Royal Yacht Club at its tip and admire just how regal these sailing ships can be.

From Microlimano, a five-minute walk to the Metro station at Nea Faliron will bring you back to Omonia Square for 20 drs (16¢). Otherwise, you can opt for a taxi, about 650 drs ($4.80) back to Syntagma Square.

Another seaside splurge? How about brunch at the luxury-class, super-chic, swank resort in Vouliagmeni, the **Astir Palace Hotel and Bungalows**. Public bus no. 118 will bring you south to this white-on-white high-rise community. Over an enormous, elaborate presentation of the best in Western and Greek morning foods you can sit and stare out over the swimming pool to the sea. Call 89-60-211 for information and reservations.

5. Nightlife

No one can match Athenians when it comes to enjoying the night. Their midafternoon siestas (from 2 to 5 p.m., a time when you could be napping too) enable these carousers-at-heart to keep dining and drinking and dancing till 4 or 5 a.m. (while still reporting to work at 7:30 or 8 a.m.) almost every night of the week. If there's an evening when things taper off, it might be Sunday; during the summertime though, when so many Greeks are on holiday, you probably won't be able to judge what night it is because the crowds will always look like Saturday night prime. Put on your dancing shoes and enjoy: dining, dancing, and listening at Athens's many bouzouki clubs, international nightclubs, discos, or boîtes . . . romantic night-time vistas from mountaintop restaurants and bars . . . gambling at an elegant world-class resort . . . cultural events and performances by international and Greek artists at the Athens Festival, Lykavitos Hill Festival, Sound-and-Light Show, Dora Stratou Folk Dance Theatre . . . movies, taverna-hopping, people-watching, holding hands, chasing girls, and more. . . .

BOUZOUKI CLUBS: If Anthony Quinn or Melina Mercouri are what brought you to Greece, you cannot avoid the lure of the bouzouki clubs, those noisy nightspots where free-flowing wine, an amplified band, and willing guests join hands to dance up a storm. Plate-smashing, the accepted method of showing appreciation, has been outlawed but persists in some clubs; check with the management *before* you join in because you'll be charged by the plate! (If you really get into it, they're sold before the show begins, by the dozen.) Then go to it.

The bouzouki "sound" (or *rebetika*, as the Greeks know it) actually began in the 1920s in the back streets of Piraeus. The port of Athens was filled with *rebetes*, down-and-out prostitutes, druggies, and a new wave of impoverished immigrants. These immigrants from Asia Minor brought with them a Turkish musical heritage and began playing soulful folk music on their acoustic bouzoukis (a mandolin-like instrument) in the smoky dives on the harbor.

Manos Hatjidakis, composer of the film score for *Never on Sunday,* has been quoted on the subject of rebetika: "[I was] dazed by the grandeur and depth of the melodic phrases. . . . I believed suddenly that the song I was listening to was my own—utterly my own story. . . ."

A style of music developed much in the same way the blues did in America, and by the 1950s these tunes caught the fancy of well-to-do Greeks, who empathized with their lyrics of lost love, unemployment, death, family squabbles, sunken ships, and other crises. Popular musicians added a rhythm section, amplification, and often piano accompaniment to create the lively, spirited sound we now associate with Greek films and modern bouzouki clubs. Whereas once in *Zorba the Greek* Anthony Quinn was carried away and danced a *zeibekiko* (or intensely personal expression of feeling) to Mikis Theodorakis' haunting music, tourists now leap up en masse to join hands in the *syrtaki,* one of the simpler folk dances taught by light-footed waiters. So the next time you see a Greek transported in dance or caught up in the frenzy of throwing dinner plates, look for the tears behind the smiles and the laughter.

The Plaka has always been the center of the tourist-oriented bouzouki clubs, an area where a few key streets are just wall-to-wall sound and the clubs have only pink or blue neon signs to differentiate them. Many of the tavernas with musicians or elaborate floor shows serve a high-priced meal beforehand to get you in the mood; count on spending $25 a head at such places as **Taverna Kalokerinou** (tel. 32-32-054), at 10 Kekropos St. Music usually begins at about 9 p.m., heavy singing and dancing after 10:30 p.m., but call ahead to make sure.

The intersection of Lissiou and Mnisikleos Streets, about two blocks from the Tower of the Winds, is bouzouki heaven. **Mostrou**, at 22 Mniskleos St. (tel. 32-25-558), is one of the biggest and most touristy, but their slick, fully costumed and choreographed floor show pleases many. Across the street is **Palia Taverna Kritikou**, at no. 24 (tel. 32-22-809), just before you reach the steps scaling the Acropolis. This is a simpler taverna, one of the oldest in Plaka, and for less money you can enjoy singers, an orchestra, and, as the night wears on, some lively dancing by a mixed Greek/tourist audience. **Taverna Sissifos**, at no. 31 (tel. 32-46-042), is known for its good food as well as music.

The **Palia Athena**, 4 Flessa (tel. 32-38-175), and **Diogenes**, at 255 Sygrou Ave. (tel. 94-24-267), are two of the more expensive and ritzier Greek bouzouki clubs. Watch yourself here; a drink can cost as much as $20 and a bottle of whiskey up to $120. Iannis Paraos, a Greek superstar on the order of Frank Sinatra, appeared at Diogenes last year; the Greeks who go there expect to pay well for the quality entertainment they'll get.

Note: Those who are serious about bouzouki-ing should consult with their hotel receptionist or the current issue of the *Athenian* to find out which clubs are featuring the best performers. Then purchase a copy of *Greek Dances* by Ted Petrides (Lycabbetus Press; 750 drs [$5.77], available at many bookstores), which has a lively, informative introduction to dance forms in prose, accompanied by explicit foot diagrams so that even a clutz can learn the syrtaki.

READERS' NIGHTCLUB SUGGESTION: "On both our first and second visits we spent a delightful evening at **O Fantis**, a bouzouki club that is definitely not a tourist trap; we were the only non-Greeks there. The night will run about $15–$25 a head, but the music goes well on into the night with everyone up on the floor. Make a reservation. O Fantis is on 12 Lissiou St. (tel. 32-24-249)" (Barbara, Charlie, and Michael Eigner, Spotswood, N.J.).

DISCOS: Those of you who aren't very comfortable with the idea of doing as the locals do may prefer to go out and old-fashioned disco dance. Some of the better spots this year . . .

The number one club by all accounts is **Aftokinesis** (tel. 68-43-855), located in the wealthy suburb of Kifissia at 7 Kifissias Avenue between Flocas and Maroussi. Sophisticated neon lighting and exciting decor, a good selection of the latest in American and European dance music, and a crowd that takes "aftokinesis" (self-movement) seriously make this the place. During the winter Aftokinesis moves indoors but manages to retain its lead.

Close on its heels is **Divina**, a more intimate, cozy place serving dinner before the fun begins. Divina (tel. 80-15-884) is in Kifissia's Shopping Land mall, where you can cool off by window-shopping between numbers.

Some of the hottest clubs are in the Kolonaki area. **Disco 14** (tel. 72-45-938) was the hot new club when we visited. Just up the block is **Disco Place**, a predominantly gay club with the best disc jockey in Kolonaki. The **Make-Up Club** (tel. 36-42-160), on Panepistimiou, is another contender for the throne. The other area that is saturated with discos is Koukaki, on Syngrou Avenue not far from Olympic's in-town terminal. The two best that we found were **Video Disco** (tel. 25-25-391), at 255 Syngrou, and **Barbarella** (tel. 64-25-601), right next door. The Video features mostly new wave (American and British), while Barbarella cooks with Eurodisco and occasional flourishes of American Top Ten. In the ritzy area of Kiffisia there is another good club called **Amnesia** (tel. 68-23-326), at 45 Kiffisias Ave. (closed Tuesday). On the way to the airport is **Ergostasio** (tel. 97-12-852), at 268 Vouliagmenis Ave., which features the latest hits from Europe and Greece.

At all the above clubs, entrance is free but drinks run $5 to $10 each for the first drink, then less for each following drink. Most open up around 9 p.m. but don't get hot until after midnight, although the 2 a.m. government-imposed curfew cuts short your boogying time. Dress casually but well: the Greek men wear jackets and sometimes ties; the women wear light cocktail dresses, diaphanous Greek creations, or the latest in European glitter and Spandex.

BOÎTES: If disco isn't your thing, you don't have to go music-less into the night.

Something that's become very popular with young Athenians in search of their own musical identity is the *boîte*, or small club, where new or old music is performed live in front of an attentive, drinking, and smoking audience.

This year's popular clubs include **Apanemia**, in the Plaka at 4 Tholou (tel. 32-48-580), which offers one show at 9 p.m. or 10 p.m. nightly and two shows on Saturday. **Medusa** is near the Acropolis, at 2 Makri and Dion. Areopagitou Avenue. The performer Marinos manages this hall; call 92-18-272 for show information. Dionysis Savopoulos and his band play regularly at **Skorpios**, one of the oldest of the clubs, at 15 Kydathineon, in the Plaka (tel. 32-25-064). **Zygos**, on the same block at no. 22 (tel. 32-25-595), also features many well-known performers.

The musical offerings vary from night to night, from unknown and experimental to traditional rebetika performers or major pop stars. Admission price is about 800 drs ($6.15) and often includes the first drink.

Recently boîtes known as "Public Bars" have sprung up. These are bars that feature disc jockeys (starting around 10 p.m.) standing behind the bar and spinning sounds until 2 a.m. or 3 a.m. nightly. One of the best is in Exarchion Square: **Padis** (tel. 36-32-564), at 5 Exarchia St. The music here is mostly reggae and American FM, and it's good enough to keep things hopping at this very busy bar. One of the bartenders, Christos Ridopoulos, is especially kind and in perfect English will discuss anything with you from politics to where the nearest café is. Another hot spot is in the **Plaka**, on Adrianou, between Kydathineon and Nikodimou. It's on the second floor of a building halfway between these streets. You'll hear the party from the street. A double row of painted arrows point the way up, and when you push open the double doors you'll be hit by the crowd, the music, and the Kamaki kamikazes standing around waiting for the beautiful foreign girls to arrive. This place is always packed and always jumps! It's also expensive, as is Padis: a beer runs you twice what it normally would. Still, that's only about 300 drs ($2.30) for entry into Athens's fastest-moving hangout. This place is owned and run by three brothers who look almost identical. One operates the door, one the music, and one the bar!

DINING WITH A VIEW: We must make mention of the Dionyssos Restaurants, at least the two that have monopolized the best panoramic views in the entire city. What you're going for is the unforgettable view; better food at better prices you can get elsewhere. Raised up on the side of Philopappou Hill with a magnificent view of the Acropolis is **Dionyssos** (tel. 92-31-936), on Dion. Aeropagitou Avenue at the entrance to the Sound-and-Light Show. The decor is modern and not very interesting, the international menu is high priced (although there's an undistinguished coffeeshop on the lower level), but nothing can detract from the view of the Parthenon, especially after 9:30 p.m. when it's façade is mottled by the dramatic lighting of the Sound-and-Light display. Dionyssos is open daily for lunch or dinner.

The Dionyssos atop Mount Likavitos (open March 1) can be reached by the funicular which begins at the head of Ploutarchou Street above Kolonaki Square (just getting to the ticket booth is a climb!). The funicular deposits you at the top of Athens's highest peak, just perfect for an overview of the glittering city, especially at sunset. This **Dionyssos** (tel. 92-33-182) also features an international menu, but is more moderately overpriced; it's open for lunch and dinner.

Budget Tip: About halfway up (or at the halfway point if you're walking down) is the **Lykavitos Hill ouzeri**, a popular bar meant for the leisurely consumption of ouzo or wine with a wide variety of inexpensive and tasty hors d'oeuvres. The view from here, over the city to Piraeus and the distant Saronic

Gulf, is best at sundown, and for less than 1200 drs ($9.25) per person you can sit out nightfall and dream what dreamers dream.

THE CASINO MONT PARNIS: This year, Greece's two casinos have become three (after the resurrection of the Achilleon on Corfu) and include the Astir Grand Palace on Rhodes and a nightclub, restaurant, and casino complex at the resort on top of Mount Parnis (about 35 kilometers out of town). If you're driving (we wouldn't want to imagine the cab fare to get here!) you can shave off the last eight kilometers by taking the Parnis cable car directly to the hotel's front door. The casino is open from 8 p.m. to 2 a.m. nightly except Wednesday. For information, call 32-29-412; for reservations, 24-69-111.

THE ATHENS FESTIVAL: Since 1955 the Athens Festival, held in one of the world's most beautiful ancient theaters, the Herod Atticus Odeon (built in 161 and reconstructed after World War II) has entertained international audiences with theater, ballet, and musical performances by acclaimed traditional and modern artists. Martha Graham and Maurice Béjart's companies have performed in a revival of the Dionysia performances begun by Peisistratus, tyrant of Athens during the sixth century B.C. In addition, the Bolshoi and Kirov ballets from the USSR, the London Philharmonic, and the Deutsche Staatsoper Berlin, among many other international cultural luminaries, have appeared here, along with the celebrated National Theater of Greece, which produces classic Greek drama in the modern Greek language. Performances are also held in the open air theater on Lykavitos Hill.

Performances are held frequently (almost daily; some very popular shows are carried over a few extra days) and are sold out often far in advance. Contact the E.O.T. for the current schedule or call 32-22-545 for information. Tickets go on sale two weeks prior to the performance at the Festival Box Office, 4 Stadiou St. at Voukourestiou (the pedestrian shopping mall near Syntagma Square), open daily. Call 32-23-111, ext. 240, or 32-21-459 for Festival information. Tickets for the Epidaurus Theater Festival (see Chapter VI, "The Peloponnese") can also be purchased here. Athens Festival tickets cost from 500 drs ($3.80) to 2500 drs ($19.20); remaining seats can be purchased from the Herod Atticus Odeon box office between 6:30 p.m. and 9 p.m. on the day of the performance. Each June jazz comes to Athens via the **Praxis Jazz Festival.** From traditional to avant-garde, the Praxis Festival covers it all and tickets are inexpensive, about $4 each. Check with the E.O.T. *Athenian* magazine for concert information.

LYKAVITOS HILL FESTIVAL: A lesser known, but equally delightful, open-air festival is held each summer at the theater on top of Lykavitos Hill. The funicular running from the top of Ploutarchou Street will sweep you up to the panoramically situated modern bowl, where contemporary dance, music, and theatrical performances are given every few evenings, after 9:30 p.m. Past performers include the Japanese Theater Company Nakane, the pop group Tangerine Dream, Memphis Slim, the Indian Padma Subramaniyan Dancers, and many notable Greek composers. For schedule and ticket information, contact the E.O.T. at 32-22-545.

SOUND-AND-LIGHT (SON ET LUMIÈRE) AT THE ACROPOLIS: Sound-and-light shows can be one of the most effective ways to bring an architectural monument to life. From the top of Philopappou Hill (grab the seats farthest away from the P.A. system) you can let yourself imagine the flawless grandeur that was. The silhouettes of the Parthenon, the Erectheum, and particularly the Acropolis walls are enhanced by the ever-changing light. For those who are disappointed by their daytime view when scaffolding and the effects of pollution on the temples are so obvious, a distant examination of the glowing gem perched above a twinkling Athens skyline may be the cure. If you insist on listening to the melodramatic delivery, have a few glasses of retsina before the show. It's a skimpy review of the Acropolis's history; the program (200 drs, or $1.54) will enable you to read it later on.

Performances are given from April 1 to October 31, daily, in English at 9 p.m. (in French on Thursday, Saturday, and Sunday at 10 p.m., and in German on Tuesday and Friday at 10 p.m.). Bring a sweater and a camera (if you have high-speed film) and wear your good walking shoes. The cost is 500 drs ($3.85) for adults, 250 drs ($2) for students. The entrance is on Dion. Areopagitou, opposite the Acropolis, where you'll have a brief climb up Philopappou Hill.

If this gets you in the mood for live entertainment, attend the Dora Stratou Folk Dance Show (a two-minute walk farther on), timed to go on after the English-language performances, nightly.

DORA STRATOU FOLK DANCERS: The Dora Stratou Theater, a short walk on Philopappou Hill from the Sound-and-Light Show, is one of the few opportunities you'll have to see Greek folk dances presented the way they're performed in villages (as opposed to, say, the contrived bouzouki dances in the ultra-touristy tavernas). Since her company's first performance in 1953, Dora Stratou has achieved the status of grande dame of all Greek traditional dances, and a night's concert will feature up to six different styles. Typically, a program will include dances from Macedonia, the Peloponnese, and several island groups. The choreography is accompanied by a *zygia,* an orchestra of five musicians (clarinet, drums, violin, santouri, and lute). Each dance is performed in costumes from the appropriate region, and in between dances (while the dancers change outfits) the zygia plays folk music. Actually, the charm of the evening is that you can see traditional Greek dances and costumes and hear music all in one place. If you're not an aficionado, you might find many of the dances repetitive, but under a starlit night sky, the theater itself, with comfortable lawn chairs in an idyllic Greek setting, make this a much-recommended evening.

Shows are presented daily at 10:15 p.m. with additional "matinees" at 8:15 p.m. on Wednesday and Sunday (tel. 92-14-650). Tickets range from 500 drs ($3.85) to 800 drs ($6). The theater is small, so all of the seats are good. A final note: All seats are reserved and your ticket will indicate a specific row and seat number; however, none of the rows of seats are labeled in the theater itself. The ushers will grab you, seat you at your supposed chair, and unabashedly stick out their hands for a tip. Try walking in and finding a seat that suits you, or moving to a closer view once the majority of the audience is in. If you're corralled, a tip of 10 or 20 drs is appropriate.

MOVIES: One of the cheapest forms of entertainment in Greece is the open-air cinema, sort of a drive-in without the cars. For 250 drs ($1.93) to 400 drs ($3.08) you can grab a bridge chair out in a fenced-off lot, make yourself comfortable, and settle in for a series of commercial announcements, shorts, trailers, and mini-films about subjects you never thought people made movies about. Then the feature begins.

In Athens there are several cinemas that show primarily "foreign" films— English-language, French, and German fare. In the center of town there's the **Aigli**, in the Zappeion (tel. 32-38-950), and the **Vox**, at 46 Panepistimiou (tel. 36-25-842), for the newest Greek films. Try the **Kolossion Cinema**, 25 Velvendous (tel. 86-41-650), in Platia Kipseli for new wave and classic European films; the **Elena Cinema**, 47 Antifilou, in Illisia (tel. 77-89-120), for new American films and alternate "theme week" festivals; the **Cinema Thission**, 7 Ap. Pavlou (tel. 34-70-980), for revivals of American and European comedies and classics. In the summertime most of the indoor theaters close down (only a few have air conditioning), and al fresco cinema becomes the only way to go.

EVENING STROLLS: Perhaps the very best entertainment of all is the Greek people themselves: watch the glee and exuberance with which Athenians soak up the night air, promenade along the seafront, overtake a sidewalk café table, devour a taverna feast. We'll point you in the right direction and then let serendipity guide you; stop when you're in the mood.

The Plaka

The narrow, winding streets, cobblestoned footpaths, and uneven stone steps of the Plaka never fail to delight the first-time visitor. From Syntagma Square, walk to the corner of Othonos and Filellinon Streets (Olympic Airways is on Othonos) and head away from the square along Othonos Street (this is where Othonos and Mitropoleos become one). The first left will be Nikis Street; turn here to the first right, which is Apollonos Street, and follow Apollonos through the small streets till you reach the wider, brighter Adrianou (it's the block after the Hermes Hotel). You can make a left and take the second street, Nikodimou, for some fine old buildings, or continue along Adrianou to the fifth left, which is Kydathineon; here you'll find several late-night boutiques, tavernas, strolling musicians, and tourists. If you make a right turn on Adrianou at the intersection of Apollonos Street, and then make the first left, you'll reach Mniskleos Street. In two blocks it joins Lissiou Street, where you'll find the outdoor and indoor bouzouki clubs, cafés crowded with drinking Greeks and dancing tourists, and some late-night action for the adult crowd.

Youth on Parade

For a closeup look at the teen crowd in Athens, there's no better place than Fokinos Negri, a long, broad avenue of cafés quite a way up from the Archeological Museum. Trolley no. 3 or 12 stops in front of the university (on Panepistimiou) and along 28 Oktovriou St. Ask the trolley driver to point you in the right direction when he's gotten to the last stop. Young and old alike will delight in the scene here (see the "Restaurants" section, above, for more information).

Chic Watching and a Sky-High View

For a closeup look at the chic crowd in Athens, stroll up to Kolonaki. From Syntagma Square, walk up past the Grande Bretagne and King George hotels, across Panepistimou Street to the street now called Vass. Sofias. At the fifth intersection, on the left, is the Benaki Museum. Make a left turn up the sloped Koubari Street and you'll soon walk right into Kolonaki Square. Try Bokolas or Neo Lykovrysi, two jam-packed cafés that overlook the little planted green. All the streets emanating from the square offer elegant boutique window-shopping, if you can tear yourself away from the cafés.

Even better, make your first stop (hopefully around sundown) the top of Lykavitos Hill. If you walk through Kolonaki Square and take Patri. Ioakim Street on the right, in three blocks you'll reach the uphill Ploutarchou Street. At the head of this, where stairs also ascend, is the funicular which speeds you to the top (though underground!) for 100 drs (80¢), until midnight daily.

At the top of Lykavitos is the whitewashed (rather undistinguished, if you want to see the interior) Chapel of St. George. When you're up there with the thousands of other tourists, pay-per-view telescopes, outdoor café, and theater, you'll be astonished to realize that all this action is nestled 1,000 feet atop "that barren-looking hill with the little white blob on it" that you've been seeing throughout your stay. Nevertheless, the view is quite spectacular from here. If you decide to stay a while, check out the "Dining with a View" section for a review of the restaurants. If you've had your fill and vertigo is setting in, by all means funicular your way back down to Kolonaki Square, where the chic scene will peak between midnight and 1:30 a.m.

The Seaside

The Metro from Omonia Square will whisk you down to Piraeus. Those seeking entertainment of a strictly adult nature should exit at the last stop and then walk left along the harbor until you reach the docks for the steamers to Crete and the Cyclades. Opposite these piers is Leof. Merarchias Street. Make a left, and along the first narrow intersection (Filonos Street) and the second (Notara) you'll find a lot of neon—and a lot of company.

The more romantically inclined should exit at the Neo. Faliron stop, from where they can walk ten minutes to Microlimano. This picturesque harbor, filled with busy tavernas, Greeks and their families, yachts and fishing boats, is covered in the "Seafood Restaurants" section.

FOR ADULTS ONLY: After-hours company can be found in several areas of Athens: near Omonia Square, try Sokratous, Sofokleou, and Menandrou Streets; near the Plaka, try Androutsou and Byzantiou Streets off Sygrou Avenue (behind the Olympic Airways terminal); and try the bars by the large hotels on Ag. Konstantinou (near Omonia) or Ermou and Karageorgi Streets (near Syntagma).

The police have asked us to warn readers about the scam that's most often reported to them by tourists. This is how it goes: A young woman will approach a gentleman either inside or outside one of the bars, bouzouki clubs, nightclubs, or cafés frequented by tourists and will ask to be bought a drink. It's almost always "champagne" (usually just a carbonated beverage or super-cheap local brew) that she'll consume while the gentleman nurses his own drink. When the bill comes, it runs from $50 to $150 a bottle for the "champagne." The bartender gets his money, the girl gets her cut, the gentleman storms out furious and is too embarrassed, too drunk, or too enraged to get a receipt, so when he calls the police to report it, they have no proof and can investigate no further. *Caveat Emptor!*

6. What to See and Do in the City

You've recuperated from your flight (your voyage, your train trip, your auto exodus) and now what? Even those who've sworn off sightseeing forever cannot leave the capital without a firsthand experience of the Acropolis, still one of the great Wonders of the World. Athens also boasts several excellent museums of art, history, religious icons, folk craft, even money and war, but none touches the splendor of the National Archeological Museum, which houses priceless remains of the Greece that was. If you've got only *one day* in Athens, it better not be a Monday when the National Archeological Museum is closed, because a visit there after your communion with the Acropolis will be all you'll be able to absorb that day. *Two-day* visitors can see the other archeological sites, stroll through the Plaka, take in another museum (we recommend the Museum of Cycladic and Ancient Greek Art). *Three-day* stopovers will enable you to see things more leisurely: stop in cafés for a spree of people-watching between the more mundane sights, sample different kinds of Greek foods and wines, shop for trinkets in the flea market or plastic worry beads and Parthenon ashtrays in Omonia Square.

Most visitors, especially first-timers, have had enough of Athens after three days. The smog, the heat, the noise of traffic, the rude shock of modern development that's blanketed one of the world's legendary cities in a shroud of concrete and dust becomes too oppressive to bear. Aim straight for the heart, though, the luminous and ancient Acropolis, and all of the city's unfortunate development magically recedes into the background. The magnificent achievements of the fifth century B.C., concentrated on a 512-foot-tall limestone mound of relatively small physical dimensions (some 126,000 square feet), still manage to dominate this revved-up metropolis. No matter how far the elastic bounds of Athens press, the Acropolis remains the storehouse of the city's soul. And for good reason. In contrast to contemporary Athens, the Athens of Pericles was a historical epiphany: the origin and implementation of political democracy, the outpouring of revolutionary forms of drama, poetry, and philosophy, and the creation of extraordinary works of art and architecture set off an explosion that within 150 years would shake the world as far away as China. A visit to the Acropolis, the Herod Atticus Theater, and the nearby Agora will jolt you with their power and nobility. Within this concentration of buildings, spanning a mere 200 years, Athens produced the cornerstones of Western civilization: the philosophers Plato and Aristotle; the dramatists Sophocles, Euripides, Aeschylus, and Aristophanes; the historians Thucydides and Xenophon; and the orators Isocrates and Demosthenes. The Acropolis, both physically and spiritually, is certainly among the most astonishing sites of the world.

THE ACROPOLIS: The Acropolis ("High Place") of Athens was considered a sacred spot even in Neolithic times; archeological evidence has suggested that mystical cult worship was practiced on this ledge as long as 5,000 years ago. Under the present-day Erectheum stood the "Ancient Temple" dedicated to Poseidon, god of the spring which bubbled up life-giving water to previous generations of Acropolis inhabitants, and to Athena, goddess of the sustaining olive tree.

Over the centuries the early inhabitants were forced down the slopes of the Sacred Rock, while more and more holy places were built on its summit. This land-use battle would continue until the fifth century B.C.

By the time of the Mycenaean kings the Acropolis had become a fortified citadel. During the sixth-century B.C. rule of the tyrant Peisistratus, other temples and sacred buildings were constructed. In 480 B.C. the Persians invaded Athens and burned the city and the Acropolis structures. After the Greek naval victory at Salamis and land battle at Plataia, the returning Athenians swore that rather than restore the destroyed temples, they would leave them as a reminder of the barbarian invaders. What archeologists uncovered in the excavations between 1885 and 1891 were the "Persian Deposit," the pits filled with sculptural and architectural fragments that had been carefully buried over 2,200 years before. The magnificent architecture that can be seen today dates from the Periclean, or Golden, Age of Athens (fifth century B.C.), when the wealthy, newly democratic, and invigorated city-state decided to rebuild the Acropolis in even greater splendor.

There are four major monuments whose impressive ruins convey the grace, style, and technical achievement of the Golden Age. The **Propylaia,** a grand entryway that led worshippers from the temporal world into the spiritual atmosphere of the sanctuary, was begun in 437 B.C. Pericles commissioned Mnesikles, a renowned Athenian architect, to design the new *propylon* (temple entry) because he'd sent Iktinos (the architect of the Parthenon) out to Eleusis to work on a temple to Demeter. Mnesikles designed a graceful structure that would introduce newcomers to one of the Acropolis's revolutionary design concepts: the mixture of the Doric and Ionic principles. The Propylaia has an outer and inner façade of six Doric columns, which created five entryways on both sides of the building. To support the massive roof, internal support columns in the lighter, more graceful Ionic style were installed.

To the right of the Propylaia and below the final staircase to the Acropolis plateau visitors can look up to the **Temple of Athena Nike.** This trim, elegant white marble monument was built over the site of an altar dedicated to the goddess of Victory for the Panathenaic Festival almost 150 years before. Pericles commissioned the architect Kallicrates to build a new temple at a time when Athens was about to embark on the Peloponnesian War. In 425 B.C. an additional protective parapet decorated with a sculptural frieze expressing the Athenians' hope for final victory was added to the temple. Fragments of this frieze can now be seen in the Acropolis Museum (at the site). One in particular, the lovely fifth century B.C. *Nike Unlacing Her Sandals,* depicts such graceful movement that someone should consider using her for sneaker ads!

Climb slowly up the last stairs and stone pathway that brings you to the foot of the Parthenon. Was it the ancient praying Athenians or the modern preying visitors who've worn these stones so smooth?

Let's talk about the **Erectheum** first, leaving the best for last. From Mycenaean times on there'd been a temple here honoring Poseidon and Athena that has come to be known as the "Ancient Temple." Pericles had ordered a new temple built to replace the one burned by the Persians, one grand enough to hold the wooden statue of Athena that the fleeing Athenians rescued when Themistocles warned them to abandon their city before the onslaught of Xerxes. The icon was of Athena Polias (the Provider or Patron), and it was of great spiritual importance to Pericles and his ideals for the Athenian state. Unfortunately, work on the temple was halted by the Peloponnesian War and by Pericles' sudden death in a plague that swept through Athens. In 421 B.C. a radical new design concept was created to solve the many constraints faced by the unknown architect: the temple would be on several levels which would provide enough space to enshrine the many icons and altars necessary to satisfy all the cult worship carried out there, and at the same time could solve the problems of the uneven, rocky surface. Many scholars now believe that the sophistication of the Erectheum could only be the work of Mnesikles. It is designed in three basic parts: the main temple, the north extension, and the famous Porch of the Maidens **(Karyatides).** The main temple is divided to accommodate both deities, the east half dedicated to Athena Polias and the west to Poseidon Erectheus. The covered porch, used in many rituals, has graceful, hefty stone *kore* (called Karyatides) to support its entablature. The original five maidens have parted ways: one sailed with Lord Elgin back to London and is now in the British Museum, while her four sisters have been removed from the destructive air pollution to the Acropolis Museum, where they are enveloped in a protective casing of nitrogen gas. The fat and frumpy cement copies that were thrown up in their place don't even deserve a second glance.

The **Parthenon** is suffering most sorely from the effects of Athens's *nefos,* the cloud of sulfur dioxide that combines with rain and dew to create an acid rain which dissolves the marble first into plaster and then into dust. At last, the Greek government, with the assistance of UNESCO, has committed restoration funds and the talents of an international advisory committee of architects and scientists to try to preserve what's left. In fact, efforts are now underway to literally rebuild the structure from fragments that surround the site.

The Parthenon can only be spoken of in superlatives. It's the largest Doric temple ever completed in Greece, and it's the only one made entirely of marble, which was shipped from Mount Pentelicus, more than 16 kilometers north of the Acropolis. Most of it was built in only nine years (447-438 B.C.) thanks to the labor and funds of hundreds of thousands of Athenians and their allies. It's been estimated that the Parthenon cost over $150 million to build!

Pericles commissioned architects Iktinos and Kallicrates to design a temple that would give Athenians "eternal honor." The sculptor Phidias insisted that it be wide and tall enough to house his planned 12-meter-tall statue of Athena Parthenos (the Virgin), to be made of gold and ivory. Their design followed much of the floor plan of the temple the Persians had destroyed on that site, but was expanded to include eight Doric columns on its shorter sides and 17 on the longer (thereby meeting the classical requisite that the long sides must be twice as long plus one column more to add grace). Every stone in the structure was trapezoidal in shape and cut to fit its own unique position. Iron support beams, where needed, were sheathed in flexible lead to allow for expansion and prevent corrosion. Phidias is always credited as the master of the Parthenon for the huge amount of sculptural work he did ornamenting the facade. Another first was his insistence on carving all 92 metopes that circled the building. Those on the eastern side depict Athena's fight against the Giants (the Gigantomachy); many fragments of this exciting work can be seen in the Acropolis Museum. The western side (Amazonomachy) depicted Theseus leading a band of Athenians in battle against the Amazons. The south side showed Theseus joined with King Peirithoos and the Lapiths against the Centaurs (Centauromachy); the north side portrayed a number of Attic heroes from the Trojan Wars.

The famous frieze of the Parthenon (the bulk of the "Elgin Marbles" that Cultural Minister Mercouri is so anxious to get back) depicted the Panathenaic Procession, the annual event that drew hundreds of thousands of worshippers to the Acropolis, wending their way up the hillside, bearing gifts, children, and the aged in hand. The individualism and expressiveness of these Athenians is an incredible feat; even the worn and pollution-eroded frieze left in place on the western side of the Parthenon evokes a feeling for the beauty that must have been. As Manolis Korres, chief archeologist for the restoration project, put it: "We are obliged to accept that the perfect lines and surfaces have been lost forever and that the monument has a new character—that of a ruin."

This ruin, the whole of the Acropolis, is one that was turned into a Christian church by the Byzantine Emperor Theodosius II; that had its wall crenellated and a tower constructed in the Propylaia by the Franks; that became a mosque in the 15th century for Turkish conquerors, who kept a harem in the Erectheum; that had the Propylaia, then filled with gunpowder, struck by lightning and virtually destroyed; and that was turned into a powder hold which was hit by a Venetian bombardment in 1687. This explosion caused a fire that raged for two days; 28 columns fell, most of the interior *cella* collapsed, and much of the frieze of Phidias was destroyed. The Turks then returned and had the nerve to mask this disfigurement with the trappings of a mosque, replete with minaret. Since the day the Turks left in 1834, excavation and restoration has been taking place. At the turn of the century Thomas Bruce, seventh Earl of Elgin and ambassador to the sultan, obtained permission to diagram, analyze, and finally take away the carved stones and masonry which remained at the Acropolis. Whether you believe this was the best thing for the infamous "Elgin Marbles" or a gross injustice to Greece, they remain now in the possession of the British Museum, which wrangled them away from the lord at a fraction of what they cost him, after his fortunes at home had failed. The Parthenon survived as a barrack's for British troops during World War II, but was jolted more than an inch off its base by an earthquake in 1981. The restoration team cites the now-rusting and expanding iron support rods that turn-of-the-century restorers mistakenly put into the precious marble as cause for the total destabilization of the monuments. Part of their task will be to locate these rods with X rays and then replace them with an expensive titanium alloy (a light but sturdy metal used in aircraft). We look forward to 1991, the projected end date for completion of restoration, and perhaps the day when the Acropolis will be secure at last.

The Acropolis Museum

Housed in a discreet white building just below the Parthenon, this small collection of finds from the Acropolis contains some superb sculpture, including the Gigantomachy pediment from the Ancient Temple to Athena that stood before the Erectheum. There are a few extraordinary classical-era sculptures attributed to Phidias, which do justice to the reputation that has come to us through the centuries. The large collection of *kore* (statues of the young women in attendance to Athena) are particularly beautiful. In their strong faces, bright eyes and robust figures we can trace the lineage of so many of the Greek faces we see today. The coloration still preserved on their pure marble surface also makes vivid how horrified we might be if we got up to the Acropolis and saw it and its statuary painted in Alexander Calder colors!

Other Monuments on the Acropolis

A major thoroughfare, Dion. Aeropagitou, parallels the south side of the Acropolis rock. At its east end are the rocky remains of the fifth century B.C. **Theater of Dionysos,** the birthplace of drama and the place where 13,000 eager Athenians came to watch works by Aeschylus, Euripides, Sophocles, and Aristophanes. Next to it was the site of the **Asclepion,** built when Socrates brought that cult worship to Athens. The long, arcaded **Stoa of Eumenes,** built by the king of Pergamon in the second century B.C., runs west to the **Herod Atticus Odeon.** Herod was a great patron of the arts and used his enormous wealth to create many monuments in Athens. This 5,000-seat theater was built between A.D. 161 and 174 for his wife, Regilla. The theater impressed audiences of the day with its mosaic floor, white marble seats, and huge cedar roof. Today the partially restored theater continues to impress audiences at the Athens Festival with its beauty of proportion and style. Both sites are open 9 a.m. to 2:45 p.m. daily, 9 a.m. to 1:45 p.m. on Sunday. Admission is 250 drs ($2).

Hours and Admission

The Acropolis and its monuments can be seen daily between 7:30 a.m. and 6:45 p.m., 8 a.m. to 5:45 p.m. on Sunday. Admission is 625 drs ($4.80); students pay half price. The Acropolis Museum is open noon to 6 p.m. on Tuesday, the same hours as the site on all other days. Check with the E.O.T. for shortened hours during the winter months or call the museum (tel. 32-10-219), as these vary according to weather. *The Acropolis* by Manolis Andronicos (Ekdotike Press) is one of the best guides to the site and includes illustrations that attempt to re-create the Acropolis as it once was.

THE AGORA: The huge open-air excavation site called the Agora covers the plain just north of the Acropolis. From Monastiraki, the flea market area, you can enter the scene of American archeological work that in the past 50 years has turned up an enormous amount of artifacts and information about life in the Hellenistic period. The Agora or Roman Forum was the center of political and social life (a huge fire that roared through Athens's present-day market in 1884 helped to reveal these enormously important ruins). If you walk down Adrianou Street you'll see eight elegant Corinthian columns that line the side of

Hadrian's Library, currently being excavated. At the head of Areos Street, on the right, is the Agora, and across from the entrance, on Epaminondou Street, an intriguing, white octagonal structure called the Horologion (Clock) of Andronikos Kyrrhestes, known as the **Tower of the Winds**. Dating from the first century B.C., this tower contained a hydraulic clock and probably a planetarium; each of its sides is decorated with a frieze depicting the wind that would blow from that specific direction. The angles of each face of the tower suggest it could also have been used as a sundial.

At the entrance to the Agora is an excellent site map made of tiles. (Once you enter the grounds, don't be surprised if the roar of a Metro train zooming by disturbs your reverie.) At the entrance are three huge statues, two Tritons and one Giant who once held up the propylon (entry porch) of the **Gymnasium**. Bearing right to the spectacular Thission, you'll pass a bold, headless sculpture of the Emperor Hadrian (A.D. 117-138), which is the perfect height for someone 5'7" or taller to insert his head and have a quick photo taken!

The **Thission (Theseion)** is also known as the Temple of Hephaestus and Athena or the **Hephaisteion** because of its location on Ag. Kolonos Hill, site of the ancient iron and metal works over which these patrons presided. Built between 449 and 444 B.C., the Thission is the best preserved temple in all of Greece (because of its conversion to a Christian church dedicated to St. George). The Thission was the work of the architectural genius who created the Temple of Poseidon at Cape Sounion and the Temple of Nemesis near Marathon. You can still appreciate the friezes under the portico on the east and west sides.

The huge, orange-roofed temple across the open Agora from the Thission is the **Stoa of Attalos**, now the **Agora Museum**. Constructed of marble, the stoa has 134 columns arranged in double rows of Doric, Ionic, and Aeolic capitals to form two stories. It's thought to have been a shopping bazaar in the Hellenistic era.

The Agora Museum that's been created in the renovation is quite interesting; the range of scientific inventions, tools, games, and machinery makes this the Smithsonian of the ancient world. Of particular interest to us are a display of Neolithic to first-century B.C. pottery, pottery-making tools, and bronze-casting and ceramic molds. A display of antique wine jugs and tools designed by the Archaia Clauss Vineyards (did you visit them in Patras?) colorfully depicts the history of wine making and the jugs used to contain the wine. A second- or third-century B.C. *kleroterion* is a slotted marble rock which held name plates for choosing chairmen of the Twelve Tribes, and worked with balls that dropped and kept score. The *klepsydra* was a six-minute water clock used to limit the speeches given in court. A double-layer wine cooler, from the eighth century B.C., was stored in cold water. There's also a collection of Roman theatrical masks and charming toys and a pretty ivory statuette of the Apollo Lykeios, a replica of a work by Praxiteles.

The Agora Archeological Site and Museum is open Monday to Saturday from 8 a.m. to 7 p.m., on Sunday from 8 a.m. to 5 p.m. The admission fee is 400 drs ($3.85) for adults, half price for students. The Agora Museum is *closed on Tuesday*.

The hardy can wander up the few paving stones that remain of the Panathenaic Way, which leads directly up the hill to the Acropolis, for more sightseeing. This is the shortest route to the Parthenon.

THE OLYMPIUM: At the foot of busy Leof. Amalias Street, just before it reaches the even busier Sygrou Avenue, you'll find two lonely monuments to antiquity: the Temple of the Olympian Zeus and Hadrian's Arch.

The **Temple of the Olympian Zeus** (Naos Olympiou Dios), begun under Peisistratus in 515 B.C., is the largest temple to the Father of the Gods ever built in Greece. Work was discontinued on it after the fall of Peisistratus' tyranny, but commenced again under the Syrian king, Antiochus IV Epiphanes. A Roman architect, Cossutius, was brought in to complete the temple according to the original plans, but added a new Corinthian flair of his own. When Antiochus died, work was halted once more. Finally, in Hadrian's reign (about A.D. 131) the 104 Corinthian columns were raised to the god. Fifteen tall columns and the base of the colossal structure still stand; one column, as if to demonstrate its grandeur close up, lies in fluted segments among the wildflowers.

The squat archway overlooking the site, **Hadrian's Arch** (Pili Adrianou), was built to honor the emperor during his reign, perhaps in congratulations for the completion of Zeus' temple. The arch symbolically separates Hellenic Athens (Theseus' city) from Roman Athens (Hadrian's city).

The Temple of the Olympian Zeus is enclosed; to visit it more closely, go between 9 a.m. and 3 p.m. daily; 9:30 a.m. to 2:30 p.m. on Sunday and holidays. The admission fee is 250 drs ($1.90). Hadrian's Arch is always open for exploration.

THE NATIONAL ARCHEOLOGICAL MUSEUM: This is one of the most exciting collections of antiquity in the world. If not for its checkered history, this treasure trove of Greek finds might indeed be the world's best. Unfortunately, during the centuries of foreign domination many other countries had their chance to pick and choose among the antiquities they wanted in their own palaces and museums. The Louvre may have the *Winged Victory of Samothrace* and the *Venus de Milo,* the British Museum may have the Elgin Marbles, the Arsenal of Venice may be guarded by a Lion of Delos, and the Metropolitan Museum may have the most complete collection of Greek ceramics, but in Athens there remain works of art of such caliber that we will label them "Must Sees."

It wasn't until 1881 that the Greek government settled on building a central museum to house the scattered collections of archeological societies, scholars, and wealthy patrons. Years of cataloguing, organizing, and displaying were interrupted by World War II, when every artwork in the building was removed and buried underground. After 1945, aid received through the Marshall Plan and other funds enabled the Greeks to dig out their collection and renovate their museum, yet not until 1964 was there a unified plan for the exhibition space. As other countries move rapidly into contemporary design schemes and high-technology preservation techniques, the National Archeological Museum looks more and more behind the times. Nevertheless, its collection is an unparalleled legacy that we all should be proud to share in, and to miss a face-to-face confrontation with some of these masterworks is to miss one of traveling's rare privileges.

Must Sees

Room 4—The Mycenaean Room includes gold jewelry, artifacts, and masks from the chamber tombs discovered by Schliemann. The famous "Mask of Agamemnon" brings to life Homer's words from the *Iliad:* "He was the King of Men . . . distinguished amongst many and outstanding amongst heroes. . . ."

Room 6—The Cycladic Room contains marble figurines (mostly of women) from the third millennium B.C.

Rooms 7–11—The Archaic Sculpture rooms hold a collection of huge *kouros* statues, which once filled the great temples.

Room 15—The Poseidon Room houses bronze sculptures and the 6½-foot-tall bronze of the sea god himself, poised gracefully, (once) trident in hand, arms and legs outspread, sensuous curls weaving through his hair and beard. The hand of this masterpiece was discovered off Evia (near Artemision) in 1926; two years later divers found the rest of the body and said it was Poseidon's wrath that caused the Roman ship that had stolen it to be sunk in Greek waters.

Room 40—The New Bronzes Room contains the handsome *Marathon Boy,* a bronze Hermes from the school of Praxiteles, found in 1926 off the coast of Marathon. His eyes are limestone with pupils of glass; his nipples were inlaid with copper.

Room 48—The Fresco or *"Thera" Gallery,* at the top of the stairs, displays the reconstructed frescoes found at Akrotiri, a Minoan city on the island of Santorini (Thera).

Rooms 49 to 56—The Vase Galleries contain an incredible range of sophisticated and folk ceramics from throughout the Greek world.

Hours and Admission

The National Archeological Museum (tel. 82-17-717) is located at 1 Tossitsa, recessed off 28 Oktovriou St. It's a ten-minute walk from Omonia Square, or a no. 1 or no. 3 trolley ride from Syntagma Square. The museum is open daily from 8 a.m. to 7 p.m., Sunday until 6 p.m.; *closed on Monday.* Admission is 500 drs ($3.85) for adults, half price for students. Three or four guides are available at the entry daily, and they charge 3000 drs ($23) for a one-hour tour for one to ten people.

MUSEUM OF CYCLADIC AND ANCIENT GREEK ART: In 1986 the Nicholas P. Goulandris Foundation gave Athens a new museum filled with the earliest sculpture, pottery, and bronzes from the Cycladic, Minoan, and Mycenaean civilizations (3000 B.C.–A.D. 300). This collection of 230 objects, distinguished by the early Cycladic pieces, is one of the most impressive in the world. Goulandris' superbly displayed marble figurines, their physical attributes so simply defined, are wonderfully exhibited and informatively labelled. Their new white marble home is as simply elegant as the work it contains.

The Museum of Cycladic and Ancient Greek Art is located above the National Gardens at 4 Neophytou Douka St., off Vass. Sophias Street. It's open daily from 10 a.m. to 4 p.m., Saturday till 3 p.m. (call 72-28-321 for summer hours), and *closed Tuesday and Sunday.* Admission is 150 drs ($1.20). To leave Athens without seeing it would be to miss a rare glimpse at a prehistoric art that speaks eloquently of Western man's beginnings.

THE BENAKI MUSEUM: The private collection and life's work of Anthony Benaki from Cairo, this eclectic display of Hellenic, Byzantine, and post-Byzantine jewelry is delightful to some and totally unappreciated by others. Mr. Benaki's library contained some valuable illustrated manuscripts, which are displayed; we liked the Coptic fabrics from Egypt and the Chinese ceramics on the first floor. In the basement there's an interesting collection of Greek folk art, embroidery, and costumes, which appeals to many visitors interested in traditional handicrafts. The Benaki (tel. 36-11-617) is on Vass. Sophias and Koumbari Streets. It's open from 8:30 a.m. to 2 p.m. daily; closed Tuesday. Admission is 200 drs ($1.50) for adults, 60 drs (46¢) for students.

ATHENS'S SPECIAL COLLECTIONS: The **National Gallery of Art** (tel. 72-11-010), at Vass. Sophias (#46) and Vass. Konstantinou Streets, opened in 1976 with a commitment to display modern work by Greek and European artists. On the first floor you'll find four El Grecos among the Renaissance through impressionistic paintings of other Greek artists. Last year the National Gallery included "The New American Theatre," a performance of one-act plays, as part of their revolving exhibition schedule. The National Gallery is open from 9 a.m. to 3:30 p.m. Tuesday to Saturday, 10 a.m. to 3 p.m. on Sunday; closed Monday. Admission is 200 drs ($1.50).

The **Byzantine Museum** (tel. 72-11-027), at 22 Vass. Sophias, is housed in an 1840 mansion built by an eccentric French aristocrat, the Duchesse de Plaisance. Beyond the open-air court is an interesting reproduction of a Byzantine "domed-cross-in-square" Orthodox church from the 12th or 13th century. The well-labeled architectural details and sculptural fragments provide an excellent introduction to Byzantine architecture, one of Greece's best represented art forms. To the right of the entry is a reconstruction of an early Christian basilica with sculptures (from the fifth to seventh centuries A.D.) brought from many parts of Greece and reassembled here. After walking clockwise through chronologically progressing displays, you'll arrive at a late 17th- to 19th-century chapel lit by an exquisite carved wood chandelier. The floor above has a fine collection of religious icons, frescoes, jewel-encrusted vestments, and other ecclesiastical memorabilia. The museum is open from 9 a.m. to 3 p.m. weekdays, 8:30 a.m. to 2 p.m. Sunday (closed Tuesday). Admission is 250 drs ($1.90), students half-price.

The **Museum of Greek Folk Art and Kyriazopoulos Collection of Folk Ceramics** is housed in the mid-18th-century Tzesdaraki Mosque, constructed by the Turks in Monastiraki Square. It can be admired when you're visiting the flea market. The museum is open daily from 10 a.m. to 2 p.m.; closed Monday.

The **Museum of National History** (tel. 32-37-617) is housed in the old Greek Parliament building on Stadiou Street. In its collection of Greek and Athenian historical items are portraits of war heroes from the 1821 War of Independence (for those who've often wondered who all the squares and main boulevards are named after). One small but charming aspect of this museum is the collection of 12 watercolors by P. Zographos that General Makyrgiannis commissioned, and then personally supervised, which depict famous battles from the War of Independence. The National History Museum is open Tuesday to Friday from 9 a.m. to 2 p.m., on Saturday and Sunday to 1 p.m.; closed Monday. (There's a very pleasant shaded café next door, Maccheroncino, where you can splurge on home-made ice creams, real cappuccino, elaborate pastries, and fresh fruit à la Roma.)

The **Numismatic Museum** (tel. 82-17-769) is a collection of Greek, Roman, Byzantine, medieval, and modern coins, lead seals, weights, and engraved stones that's housed in the first-floor corner wing of the National Archeological Museum. See that listing for hours and fees. The museum is slated to move to new quarters in Schliemann's house on Panepistimiou Street, near Syntagma Square.

The **Beth Shalom Synagogue and Jewish Museum** is a living testament to the tenacity of a people and the perseverance of their faith. Prior to the Holocaust there were 77,000 Jews living in Greece. After the war there were fewer than 11,000, 3,000 of whom lived in Athens. A fascinating account of one man's survival in the deathcamps is told in *Athens to Auschwitz* (Lycabetus Press). Remarkably, a synagogue, called Beth Shalom, was built in Athens during 1939 which, after extensive renovation and rebuilding in the 1970s, is again an active place of worship. The milk-white marble façade in modern style is reason enough to make a visit, but also notice the copper bema (pulpit) in similar period design. Across the street, above the synagogue offices, is a reconstruction of the interior of an older synagogue. To get to the synagogue walk along Ermou from Syntagma and turn left to 8 Melindori (tel. 32-52-773). The synagogue is open daily from 9 a.m. to 1 p.m. with services on Monday and Thursday morning at 8 a.m., Friday evening, and Saturday morning.

One of the best discoveries we made during our last visit to Athens was the **Jewish Museum** (tel. 32-31-577), located across the Columns of Zeus at 36 Amalias. This small, though expanding, collection, presents a fascinating story of the region's once flourishing Jewish culture. Few, if any, museums in Greece present objects with more care and understanding than does this dedicated staff. Along with changing exhibitions, the museum publishes a newsletter of great interest. Though much of the community disappeared during the Second World War, the motivation of the Jewish Museum is to celebrate the spirit and proud history of Jews in both Turkey and Greece, rather than create a memorial for those who died in the Holocaust. When we first visited we thought we'd stick our heads in for a few minutes; instead we stayed for about two hours. In case you're not convinced, read the following note:

READER'S SIGHTSEEING SUGGESTION: "I think this is actually the most interesting museum I visited in all of Greece, not so much for its collection, but for the enthusiasm of its young conservators. They not only gave us a private tour of the exhibits, but also a 1½-hour discourse on the history of religion—Christianity, Judaism, and Islam—in Southeast Europe and Asia Minor. And I'm not even Jewish!" (Ms. Gale Rutan, Pittsburgh, Pa.). [*Author's Note:* The museum is open daily from 9 a.m. to 1 p.m.; closed Saturday. We'd suggest you call in advance to make sure that they're actually open as the museum has a very small full-time staff. Their Museum shop sells interesting artifacts.]

ATHENS'S "LITTLE" SIGHTS: One of the delights of the modern city is the number of sights, events, and plain, ordinary happenings that make the tourist stop to watch with delight.

The **Panathenaic Stadium**, behind the National Gardens at Vass. Konstantinou, is a re-creation in solid white marble of the original stadium at Olympia, now over 2,000 years old. This 60,000-seat theater was opened for the 1896 Olympic Games, the first held since antiquity, and is still in use today. Pause and soak up the immense accomplishment the event must have been in 1896, and then imagine men in togas doing the same thing!

The neoclassic **Parliament Building**, located at the head of Syntagma Square, is guarded by two stiff-faced young men *(evzones)* in traditional garb. You can watch the Changing of the Guard ceremony at 6 p.m. daily in front of the Tomb of the Unknown Soldier. Go early and buy chick-peas (50 drs, or 49¢) from any of the many vendors to feed the hordes of pigeons who know supper's coming. Then stick around for the formal marionette march as the guards' pompommed red leather shoes clomp in unison across the marble square.

The **National Garden** is one of the most civilized places in Athens: several square blocks without traffic, noise, or heat. It is also the cat capital of Greece, with hundreds of meandering stray cats all looking for love and food. It's open sunrise to sunset, and the many entrances include Amalias Street at Syntagma Square, Amalias at Hadrian's Arch, and Vass. Konstantinou opposite the Panathenaic Stadium. Joggers will find the city's freshest air within its confines, with several routes of packed gravel paving weaving in and out of the exotic plantings. (Joggers beware: The park entrances are marble-paved and a run over them can lead to shin splints!) Food kiosks, birds, haggard tourists, and smiling Greeks abound.

The **Zapion** is a large neoclassical building used primarily for exhibitions and international conferences. It's usually closed to the public, but if you're strolling through the National Gardens, take a minute to peek in and admire the fine entranceway and interior columns.

Another side of Athens rarely seen is expressed vividly in **Anafiotika**, a small quarter of island-style whitewashed homes built high up on the Acropolis Hill by immigrants from Anafi. This volcanic Cyclades isle sent many workers to Athens in the 19th century, and the low-slung stucco homes built around large courtyards filled with caged birds reflect the traditional Cycladic architecture of that time.

Next to the Monument of Lysikratous at Epimandou and Byronos Streets in the Plaka is a perfect example of a **mid-city excavation** in progress. The Athens law requiring that all contractors with building permits submit to an archeological review of the planned site before construction begins has indefinitely postponed more projects than you can imagine. This sixth- to tenth-century B.C. site spans the Classical, Roman, and Byzantine eras; pottery shards, jewelry, and coins have already been found. Renovation on this square began in 1982, when the site was discovered.

We found in the Plaka a gallery that's really an artists' collective, and a very special place. It's the **Gallery Kreonidis** (tel. 32-47-146), at 7 Iperidou (corner Nikis Street). It's a guild of about a dozen artists, each working in a different medium. There are textile, ceramic, woven sculpture, mineral, and papier-mâché artists, who create very beautiful modern and "folk art" type of pieces. In addition the collective puts on puppet theater each night during the tourist season. The performances are for children, but all ages will be charmed and amused by the antics of these wonderful puppets. The work these artists create is for sale; you can browse through their shop and talk to the artists themselves while you look. Try and make this a part of your itinerary while you're in Athens.

SHOPPING: The best values in Athens are items that are uniquely Greek, be they locally produced clothing or folk arts or internationally designed merchandise that's been manufactured in Greece. What's cheaper than what you get back home? Shoes, furs, and bathing suits. What's uniquely Greek? Hand-knit woolen sweaters, flokati rugs, cotton embroideries from the islands, and some museum-reproduction ceramics. What are the best souvenirs? Copper trinkets from the flea market, *komboloi* (worry beads), sponges, and the things you find in the small towns, villages, or islands you'll visit.

Shopping Around Syntagma Square

Just off Syntagma Square is elegant little **Voukourestiou Street**, which has become a high-fashion international shopping mall. Along the stone-paved street you'll find such acclaimed designers as Ungaro, Yves St. Laurent, Pierre Cardin, and Ted Lapidus. Unfortunately these items are all imported and cost just as much, if not more, than the same things in the international boutiques of New York, Los Angeles, Chicago, or Boston. Better menswear (if you need to dress up for something) can be found along Akadimias Street, near Amerikis and Pindarou Streets. Again, the most fashionable garments will probably be of Italian or French design and thus very expensive.

Surprisingly enough, designer shoes by such names as Charles Jourdan, Bally, and Valentino cost about half of what they do in New York! Why? Because although they're not labeled as such, many of these shoes are actually manufactured in Greece, where the labor is cheaper. At the corner of Voukourestion and Valaoritou there is an excellent tobacconist.

Between Syntagma and Omonia Squares you'll find many shops along

Stadiou and Panepistimiou Streets (the latter is more expensive). For Greek couture design, try the shop of Nikos and Takis on Panepistimiou. For the finest in modern jewelry, try Lalaounis and Zolatas, nearby. Both feature unique art pieces in gold and precious stones; Zolatas has the license to reproduce all the museum pieces and does superb reproductions of the best antiquities.

Some of the best fur shops are around Syntagma Square, but it's the less-than-the-best that will carry good-value, well-styled coats in the less precious furs. Furs from the Kastoria region are a good value in Greece not because the animals are raised there, but because European designers bring in skins and patterns to the Kastoria workshops where the cheaper labor can produce expertly tailored coats. The ones that are not re-exported are therefore cheaper to buy here.

High-end shoppers can also take a stroll along Kolonaki Square.

Shopping Around Kolonaki Square

What makes shopping here so much fun is that all the stores are concentrated in six square blocks. The boundaries running north-south are Solonos and Anagnostopolou; east-west, Omirou and Iraklitou. Inside this area you'll find Laura Ashley (28 Irodotou), Fiorucci (9 Haritsos), Free Kid (a beautiful clothing store for kids, at 19 Anagnostopolou), Parolas (a great Italian store just down the block at number 11), Lacoste (Iraklitou and Solonos), and a whole spate of gorgeous designer-wear shops on Iraklitou: Lapis, Costa Anghelopoulos, and Negativo. The above shops are between Skoufa and Solonos Streets. For ladies' leather goods there is a chain of stores called Again (18 Omirou) that have nice pieces. And there is Dervis (16 Amerikis St.), which has the motto: "Quality women's fashion—for the chic." These shops are not budget finds: most have high-end prices that reflect the beauty and craftsmanship of the products. Which brings us to the National Welfare Organization shops, one of which is at 24A Voukourestiou. These are shops run by the government to keep the native handicrafts alive and thriving. If it's real Greek crafts you're looking for, this is the place. Each of the four N.W.O. shops have jewelry, carpets, tapestries, ceramics, and more at reasonable prices. We applaud this laudable project and urge you to check it out for yourself.

Shopping Around Omonia Square

Omonia Square is definitely the workers' part of town, and the big, efficient department stores and budget boutiques reflect the market. There are three main department-like stores: Lambroupouli is at Eolou and Lykougos Streets, Athenee is down Stadiou Street at no. 33, and Minion, the largest and most varied, is at no. 103 Septemvriou St. (the avenue running parallel to 28 Oktovriou St.).

Omonia Square has a number of small fruit-and-nut stores, a whole-wheat macrobiotic bakery, at Stadiou and Eolou Street next to the G.P.O., and a lot of souvenir stands in narrow arcades off Stadiou Street and in the underground Metro stop. Souvenirs are also sold at streetside kiosks and by mobile vendors.

The Flea Markets

Monastiraki (or Yousouroum, as the locals call it) is a daily market area radiating from a picturesque old square below the Plaka. If you're walking, the easiest way to go is to walk down Pandrossou Street. The Metro will take you right there; when you exit you'll find Pandrossou Street on the right and Ifestou Street on the left, both main arteries for shoppers and impassable knickknack displays when the Sunday flea market is held. Try to get there on a Sunday (hours are from 8 a.m. to 2 p.m.), when the park behind the Thission is filled with young and old alike walking their canaries, watching them kiss and sing and feeding them like lovers. Compared to this show, the flea market is tame! It's a great place for campers: plates, kitchen utensils, jars, flashlights, gas burners, Greek cotton underwear (the Greek sizes are *very* narrow), watches, new and used music cassettes and records, Chinese alarm clocks, punk clothes and Sears coveralls, leather goods, wispy cotton Isadora Duncan dresses, *komboloi*. Dig deeper.

Hephaistos, at 12 Ifestou and an arcade at no. 24, is filled with old and new copper and brass (remember—you can't *cook* in copper pots that are unlined, but you can serve in them).

At 89 Pandrossou St. is the leather shop of **Stavros Melissinos**, resident bard to the flea market, acclaimed poet, celebrity, and shoemaker to the stars. For $10 to $15 you can walk away in a pair of sandals that may be similar to those (reputedly) ordered by Jacqueline Onassis, the Beatles, or Rudolf Nureyev (who knows from good shoes).

You may find some bulk-knit homespun wool sweaters here or in the Plaka, at one of the pricier tourist-only shops. If you're off to the islands soon, you can probably find better designed and more finely knitted ones; if you're off to Crete or Delphi and north, you can find equally folksy ones at better prices.

The **Piraeus Flea Market** is a worthwhile Sunday excursion (open 8 a.m. to noon), when the enclosed, older market heads outdoors. It's located off Ippodamius Street near the terminus of the Metro and specializes in old ship bric-a-brac, lamps, hand-embroidery, and whatever else gets washed ashore.

Both flea market areas function as regular shopping malls during the work-week; most keep 8 a.m. to 2 p.m. and 5:30 to 8 p.m. hours Monday to Friday (depending on the season, Saturday is a half or full day).

Bargaining

Kyle hates it but John loves it, and when we go shopping, John does all the talking. The First Rule of Bargaining is "Take yourself seriously." Really believe that you're only going to pay a certain amount and be prepared to walk away if the vendor doesn't meet your price (in fact, walking away anyway seems to reduce the price a lot!) Carry small bills as evidence of your limited budget, always use cash, and talk fast and firm. Remember, too, that someone else has the exact same merchandise, and that you can always come back the next day to buy it because no one will remember the scene you created.

Handcrafts

The **National Organization of Greek Handicrafts**, at 9 Mitropoleos St. (tel. 32-21-017), is a trade office which displays examples of handcraft work done by member companies. Only their carpets are for sale retail. The Tourist Office and the **Hellenic Artisan Trades Cooperative** (tel. 32-33-458) endorse the following shops:

Lyceum Club of Greek Women, 17 Democritou St. (tel. 36-37-698), for ceramics, jewelry, embroidery and woven fabrics.

Greek Women's Institution, 3 Kolokotroni St., next to Kentrikon Restaurant (tel. 36-24-038), where embroidery from the islands, replicas of Benaki Museum embroideries, and very fine work can be found.

The **XEN (YWCA)**, 11 Amerikis St. (tel. 36-24-291), has a small collection of embroideries for sale.

National Welfare Organization (Ethniki Pronia) has four shops that carry the woven, ceramic, copperware, and jewelry work of local Greek craftsmen. The shops are located throughout the Athens area and are uniformly high-quality. Their store in the Plaka is at 6 Ipatias (tel. 32-40-017) and features an amazing stock of tapestries and small goods guaranteed to delight. They also have a shop in the Hilton and at 135 Elefteriou Venizelou.

The **Museum of Cycladic and Ancient Greek Art**, at 4 Neophytou St., the **Benaki Museum**, at 1 Koumbari St. (corner of Vass. Sophias), and the **National Archeological Museum**, at 1 Totsitsa St. (28 Oktovriou St.), all sell reproductions of items in their collections. The Benaki also sells other items such as scarves, needlepoint kits, linens whose designs are inspired by traditional Greek motifs; the National Archeological Museum also sells castings of items exhibited in other Greek museums and copies of paintings and murals.

7. The Ports: Piraeus and Rafina

Piraeus (Pireefs) has been the port of Athens since antiquity; although the Greek maritime industry isn't what it once was, the thousands of tourists who board ferries bound for the Aegean islands each day contribute to maintaining Piraeus's position as number one port in the Mediterranean. As a city it has the conveniences and amenities of Athens without any of the charm; as a port it has the seamier sides of a sailors' lair but all the color and life of an active harbor. In Greece the chances are that if it moves by water, you'll find it at Piraeus.

In direct contrast to the commercialized shipping industry in Piraeus is the casual car ferry that runs from Rafina to the Cyclades. This sleepy, charming fishing port is about 45 minutes by bus north of Athens; it's a refreshing drive and an instant change of pace once you reach the harborside. Everything seems much more manageable in Rafina, and for those heading off to Tinos, Mykonos, Siros, Paros, or Naxos, we recommend saving time and money by sailing from this calmer port.

PIRAEUS: The port of Athens is one of the most seen, least appealing places on the Greece itinerary. If you're trying to visit the Cyclades (you can also go from Rafina), Saronic Gulf, Dodecanese, Northeast Aegean islands, or Crete, you'll have to pass through. Nighttime visitors should confine their wanderings to the port if they're waiting for a ferryboat or to Microlimano's expensive but scenic harborside tavernas.

Useful Information

Dial 171 for tourist information, 24 hours. The closest **E.O.T.** office is in Athens at Syntagma Square.

Ferry tickets can be purchased one hour before departure; for booking first-class cabins or advance sale tickets, see one of the harborside travel agents (around Karasklaki Square by the domestic ferries and along Akti Miaouli opposite the Crete ferries). Most open at 6 a.m. and will hold your baggage for the day, if requested. **E.O.T.** publishes a list of weekly sailings, but the **Port Authority** (tel. 41-72-657) can also provide you with schedule information.

If you need a travel agency to make reservations or to recommend a particular service, try **Explorations Unlimited** (tel. 41-16-395) at 2 Kapodistriou and 36 Akti Posidonos St. Michalis (Mike) Hadgiantoniou and his English-speaking staff are very helpful, particularly with making ferry and hydrofoil arrangements as well as hotel bookings.

Getting to **Piraeus** is very easy from any of Athens's centers. From Omonia Square take the Metro to the last stop (40 drs or 30¢), which will leave you one block from the domestic port. Trolley no. 20 from Navarinou Street near the terminus goes to Microlimano. From Syntagma Square take the Green Depot bus no. 40 from the corner of Filellinon Street, which will leave you one block from the international port, about a ten-minute walk along the water from the domestic port. A taxi will cost about 650 drs ($5) from **Syntagma** Square.

There are several banks in Piraeus but the **National Bank of Greece** and **Commercial Bank** branches inside the Customs House (at the international port) are open daily from 9 a.m. to 3 p.m.; the National Bank's office on Ethniki Anastasious Street is also open from 6 p.m. to 8 p.m. Some of the post offices in the area also change money during extended hours. . . . There's a post office branch inside the Metro station, open till 4 p.m. daily. The main branch is at Ethn. Antistaseos and Dimitriou Streets . . . The **O.T.E.** is a block away from the post office, off Filinos Street. There is another branch in front of the International Port Terminal, open from 7:30 a.m. to 10 p.m.

On midsummer eves, open-air theatrical performances are given at the **Kastella Theater**, a few blocks inland from Microlimano. In the wintertime the theater goes indoors to the Dimotiki (Public) Theater, on the green at Leof. Vass. Konstantinou Street (where you can also catch the bus to Syntagma) . . . The **Piraeus Archeological Museum** (tel. 45-21-598) is at 31 Trikoupi, near the Zea Marina (closed Tuesday), the **Maritime Museum** (tel. 45-16-822) is at Akti Themistokleous and Freatida Streets, near the Flying Dolphins pier at Zea Marina (closed Sunday and Monday).

The *Aegina Dolphin* leaves from the domestic pier. Schedules are posted and tickets are sold for the same day's voyage either at the domestic pier or at 8 Themistokleous, Zea Marina.

Accommodations

If you absolutely have to stay here, try the **Ideal Hotel** (tel. 45-11-727), at 142 Notara St., two blocks in from the waterfront opposite the Crete ferries. The Ideal is a clean, pleasant C-class hotel that accepts American Express and will allow you to charge meals at the Happy Eater Restaurant (across the street) to your room, which may just rescue someone fresh off the boat and clean out of cash. Their 29 rooms all have private bathrooms, air conditioning, and telephones; doubles are 3870 drs ($29.80) in the high season.

A more budget-conscious choice is the **Hotel Faros** (tel. 45-26-318), next door at no. 140. The Faros's 23 rooms—2060 drs ($15.90) for a double and 1610 drs ($12.40) for a single—have private baths and are clean but spartan. This small hotel has a bar, elevator, and TV lounge and will store luggage free as per Mr. Faros. Try to get a back room; it'll be quieter.

An older, but reasonably maintained, choice is the **Electra Hotel**, at 12 Navarinou (tel. 41-77-057), a pleasant street a block from the Metro terminus and just behind the domestic port. The 19 bathless rooms have some semblance of traditional charm and cost 2120 drs ($16.30) for two.

Dining

Rio-Antirio is an inexpensive taverna with good salad, souvlaki, pasta, and chicken. You can peek around their display case till you're sure you understand what you're eating. Rio-Antirio is located at 14 Menarchias, up the block opposite the Crete ferries.

At 8 Menarchias, just before the cinema, is **Posidonion,** a moderately priced taverna for seafood and probably the best dining alternative in the area. Posidonion is large and comfortable and has tables outside on the bustling street.

If you're over near the Customs House or international pier, try **Dennis Dan** at 73 Akti Miaouli. This cheap bright fast-food emporium is open daily from 8 a.m. to 7 p.m., on Saturday from 8 a.m. to 2 p.m., and offers a range of sandwiches, drinks, a dartboard for company, a clean toilet upstairs, and a working pay phone.

Boat-bound travelers should get to Piraeus early enough to walk into the **market** area behind Akti Posidonios and the Aegina Dolphins. There are a lot of outdoor fruit vendors, dried fruit-and-nut shops, bakeries, and knickknack traders. Microlimano is a high-end dining region treated in the "Athens Restaurants" section of this chapter.

RAFINA: One way to beat the high cost of ferries is to start your trip to the Cyclades from Rafina. Buses leave Athens from the Areos Park, 29 Mavromateon St., at 6:30 a.m. daily and continue every half hour till 5:30 p.m., crossing the 27 kilometers to this Aegean port through small cities and grape fields. Once there, you'll find that boats run from 7:45 a.m. daily (twice a day in summer) to Andros, Siros, Tinos, and Mykonos (call 0294/25-200 for specific sailing times); five times weekly to Siros, Paros, and Naxos (daily in summer), and once a week to Amorgos, at a savings of 20% to 40% over the fares from Piraeus (tel. 0294/22-700). The **Anne L. Ferry** (tel. 0294/23-561) runs daily service to Karystos, Evia, and Andros.

You'll notice many small beaches near Rafina. Villas and condos dot the coastline and big resort hotels for Athenian weekenders crowd **Golden Beach,** the stretch south from Nea Makri. A large Greek-American naval base gets the prime beachfront here, leaving tourists with an incredibly diverse selection of junk-food parlors and cheap motels along the coastal highway until the charming **Marathon Beach.** Though Rafina doesn't have a palatable beach of its own, the small harbor and sea breezes compensate by making it a refreshing change from the *nefos* of the Greater Athens region. Life centers around the large Central Platia, whose elevated position gives it an air of small-town dignity quite different from the dockside hustle that goes on at sea level below.

Accommodations

Spending a night in Rafina is a pleasant alternative to an early-morning schlep to steamy Piraeus. Because many budget tour groups use Rafina as their base for day trips, the hotel scene is made up mostly of a few huge C-class places. The **Hotel Avra**, to the right of the port (tel. 0294/22-781) is by far the most pleasant. Its doubles go for 3850 drs ($30), breakfast included. (They say they'll waive their half-board requirement for independent travelers.)

We couldn't agree on whether the port-view **Hotel Akti** (tel. 0294/24-776) at 14 Vithnyias, open April through October, was any better than the **Hotel Corali,** on the Platia (tel. 0294/22-477), open all year. The Corali is a little cheaper at 2650 drs ($20) for a double room; both charge 250 drs ($2) extra for a shower. If you want to get clean (or do some laundry or pamper yourself) before you hit Mykonos, better stick with the Hotel Avra.

The nicest lodging is the immaculate **Kokkino Limenaki Campgrounds** (tel. 0294/26-601). This means "red port" in Greek, and the multitiered site sits above a beautiful red-cliff cove with a pebble beach. It's only one kilometer from the ferry, and at 440 drs ($3.10) per sleeping bag, with hot showers and a laundry room, it's probably worthwhile to check in just for a swim if you have a long wait for the ferry. One block away is the public bus stop for Marathon (17 kilometers north).

Dining

There are two general areas to grab a bite in Rafina, either up around the Central Platia or down by the car ferry pier. Colorful awning-shaded cafés, banks, and other tourist essentials surround the spacious square. Of the cafés, **Vesuvio's** is the best bet here for reasonably priced pizza, spaghetti, or a nightcap.

On the east end of town (a two-minute walk) a road slopes down to sea level, bearing the weight of cars that will soon be loaded onto ships bound for the Cyclades. Interspersed with the ferryboat ticket agencies are several seafood tavernas. At lunchtime or supper watch out for the gregarious restaurateurs who'll try to rope you in for an expensive (though certainly scenic) fish fry. Try **To Express** (tel. 0294/23-556 in case you need to call and find out how to tell it apart from the others), which is neatly tucked in next to a BP gas pump. An excellent calamari and fried filet meal cost us about 675 drs ($5.20) to 950 drs ($7.30) each. These tavernas are great fun when the ships are pulling in—you're far enough away to eat peacefully, yet close enough to enjoy.

8. Exploring Attica: Day Trips from Athens

It's sometimes hard to take the midsummer heat in Athens (in the summer of 1987 temperatures actually exceeded 120°F!), and those of you waiting for a train or a plane or a friend may be interested in spending the day in another environment. Our first recommendation for getting away is to head south to the beaches; all along the Apollo Coast between Piraeus and Cape Sounion are resorts, beaches, tavernas, nightlife, and a relaxing change of pace. Your day could begin at the beautiful-to-behold Temple of Poseidon at Sounion and stretch into an afternoon of beach sampling, an easy thing to do by public bus.

A cool, forested retreat that's very popular with Athenians is the Kesariani Monastery, located on the verdant slopes of Mount Imitos within a half hour of the urban center. Archeology buffs will enjoy an opportunity to head west to Daphni (where the Wine Festival will have to console those who find the monastery closed) and then onto Elefsina, site of the quite fascinating Eleusinian Mysteries of antiquity. Archeologists have uncovered an incredible variety of remains in a spot thought holy to many over the centuries, but fit only for heavy industry today. The east coast of the Attic peninsula features the Plain of Marathon, site of the famous battle against the Persians. The museum and tombs uncovered there, combined with a lighthearted dip in the nearby bay, make a very interesting mini-journey. North of Marathon is the welcoming Temple of Nemesis (goddess of vengeance), while south of Marathon is the welcoming Temple of Artemis (goddess of fertility, chastity, and all animals) at Brauron.

Several tour operators offer one-day excursions to Epidaurus (see Chapter VI, "The Peloponnese"), Delphi (see Chapter X), and to the Saronic Gulf Islands of Aegina, Hydra, and Poros (covered in Chapter V). We think these sights deserve more than one day of your time, but if you're pressed, contact our friends at **Viking Tours,** 3 Filellinon St. (tel. 32-29-383 or 32-24-262), for more information about the budget-wise packages they have available.

SOUNION: Our first-choice day trip would begin with a visit to the incredible **Temple of Poseidon** at Cape Sounion. The temple's 15 sun-bleached columns stand out starkly against the Mediterranean sky, their power enhanced by the hilltop placement in view of the sea. Their bold Doric design (no entasis, or bulging effect at the midriff, and only 16 flutings instead of 20) comes from the same master hand that designed the Thission temple in the Agora. Scholars believe this fifth-century B.C. temple was built over the remains of an earlier Poseidon and Athena Temple as part of Pericles' master plan.

Very little remains of the propylon (entryway) or the stoa (covered arcade) that protected worshippers from the blazing sun. Yet the strong columns (one of which supposedly is engraved with Lord Byron's initials; we haven't found them, but if you do please write to us) and the solid base which you can still walk on (one of the few temples in Greece that can be entered) convey an immediate sense of the respect felt by the architect and the worshippers for the god Poseidon. From his height only can you look straight out to the sea; the fortress walls that once surrounded it defended this strategic highpoint over the Saronic Gulf and the shipping lanes to Evia. Northeast of Poseidon's sanctuary was the Temple of Athena Sounias, though little remains today.

The archeological site is open from 9 a.m. to sunset daily (10 a.m. on Sunday). Admission is 300 drs ($2.30) for adults. K.T.E.L. (tel. 82-13-203) buses for Sounion leave from 14 Mavromateon St. at Areos Park, costing 425 drs ($3), every hour between 6 a.m. and 5:30 p.m.

We recommend coming first thing in the morning so that you can have some time alone with this unforgettable monument. After your first visit, walk down the hill to the tempting **Hotel Aegaeon** (tel. 0292/39-200). On its beach, notice the hollowed-out storage niches in the encircling cliffs, where the Athenians drydocked their triremes. You can picnic, lunch at one of the tavernas, or have the full lunch—2000 drs ($16) for lobster and fish—or à la carte menu at the Aegaeon's café. Make sure to wander into the lobby to admire the barnacle-crusted amphorae and gemstones found in the seas below the temple.

You can rent a pedalboat for about 650 drs ($5) an hour—a bargain!—or take a sailing lesson and admire Poseidon's sanctuary from the lowly point of view most mortals once had.

Don't leave without first returning to the Temple of Poseidon to admire it in the waning light of sunset. Looking west over the blue Aegean, your view restricted by the majestic white columns, nearly 2,500 years old, is an experience every traveler should have.

THE APOLLO COAST: The 65 kilometers of coastline curling around the Saronic Gulf between Athens and Cape Sounion is known fondly by travel agents as the Apollo Coast. In actuality, the first 20 kilometers are just an indistinguishable outgrowth of Athens. The first city south of Piraeus is Glyfada, home of the Olympic (West) and international (East) airports.

Glyfada is a well-to-do, but hardly quiet, suburb. The streets are lined with cafés, restaurants, and chic sportswear shops. There are many expatriates and members of the military and diplomatic corps who make Glyfada their home, and the style and taste of the area reflect this "foreign" presence. The one bizarre and noisy aspect of life in this suburb is that jets from the nearby Olympic airport seem to hover over the avenues on their way in or out of Greece.

Other than the occasional rattle of windows, life in Glyfada is lots of fun. It's a great place to visit for those of you who may be homesick. The main drag, Leof. Georgiou Street, is lined with cafés and restaurants, but for serious eating go around the corner from the Bank of Greece to Konstantinopolos Street. There are several eateries, sophisticated pizza parlors, steak restaurants, and bars. Greek-style fast-food.

READER'S RESTAURANT SELECTION: "On our last night in Greece we stayed in Glyfada for its proximity to the airport and found the most memorable feast of our vacation. Mahmoud Kaoosh is the host and owner of **Yildizlar,** on the second floor at 1 Konstantinopoleos St. What a treat for the senses! Arabic music filled the air and the exotic decor made us feel as if we had been transported to the Middle East. The food was an explosion of taste experiences and we were dumbstruck with culinary ecstasy. The cost for the two of us was $28 including wine" (Barbara Wells, Great Barrington, Mass.)

If you're after a beach, head south to **Varkiza,** at the 27-kilometer point. The nice public beach will be packed on summer weekends but at other times it makes a good day trip. When you're there, you can walk or bus the two kilometers to **Vari,** a small town due north of Varkiza known for its grilled lamb.

Around the small platia are several barbecues, and the **Stani Grill House** (tel. 89-70-005) on Poziari Street is one of the best. Their private label retsina and lamb on a spit are delicious and well worth the splurge at 1300 drs ($10) each. For those of you who are missing the Greek Easter feast, this is a way to experience every Greek's favorite meal.

The **beaches** improve in direct proportion to their distance from Athens. As you continue to Cape Sounion, you can stop at Lagonissi or at the small beach opposite the Eden Beach Hotel. Depending on the crowds and the season, seaside hotels may claim rights to the sand in front of their cafés and will extract 300 drs to 500 drs ($2.30 to $4) from you for placing your towel there. Several blue public buses leave from Vass. Olgas Avenue near the Zappion.

MOUNT IMITOS AND THE KESARIANI MONASTERY: A refreshing half-day trip for tourists weary of the Big City is to the **Kesariani Monastery**, just seven kilometers east in a cool, bird-infested forest at the foot of Imitos. The healing spring waters pouring forth from the marble goat's head at the monastery's entrance have distinguished this as a holy site for centuries. Kesariani, dedicated to the Presentation of the Virgin, was built over the ruins of a fifth-century Christian church, which in turn probably covered an ancient Greek temple.

The small church is constructed in the form of a Greek cross, with four marble columns supporting the dome. The lovely frescoes date from the 16th century, with the exception of those in the narthex, signed "Iannis Hypatos, 1689." On the west side of the paved, flower-filled courtyard are the old kitchen and refectory, which now houses some sculptural fragments. To the south, the old monks' cells and a bathhouse are being restored, exploration at your own risk is permitted.

The Kesariani Monastery (tel. 72-36-619) is open daily from 9 a.m. to 3 p.m., till 2 p.m. Sunday, and Bus no. 224 leaves from Venizelou and Vass. Sophias every 20 minutes to the monastery; the fare is 50 drs (40¢).

Mount Imitos offers beautiful prospects over Athens, Attica, and the Saronic Gulf (try to come up here on a smogless day). At every scenic parking spot you'll find men playing backgammon, couples holding hands, and old people strolling. After sunset Imitos becomes Athens's favorite Lover's Lane. The road winds around these forested slopes for nearly 18 kilometers, and the choice of sun, shade, cool breezes, and picnic spots is unlimited.

In antiquity, Imitos is believed to have been crowned with a statue of Zeus Hymettios, and ancient caves (including a sixth-century B.C. altar) have been found near the summit. More recently the mountain was cherished by Athenians for the Hymettos honey produced by bees which fed off the mountain's fragrant flowers and herbs. Most of the bees have migrated now, though a few apiaries still exist for heather-fed bees.

MONASTERY OF DAFNI: The recently restored 11th-century monastery, one of the finest examples of Byzantine mosaics, architecture, and design in all of Greece, is situated off the main Athens-Corinth highway about ten kilometers from Athens. **Dafni Monastery** (tel. 58-11-558) is open every day from 9 a.m. to 3 p.m., Sunday from 9:30 a.m. to 2:30 p.m. Admission is 250 drs ($2). From mid-July to mid-September an annual Wine Festival is held on the grounds; for 525 drs ($4) you can sample many different kinds of wine. Check with the E.O.T. for Festival hours; public bus 873 leaves regularly from Eleftherias Square in Athens.

ELEUSIS (ELEFSINA): Disappointment befalls all those who enter the unattractive, industrial city of Elefsina, for nowhere are there signs of the mystical and heavenly spirits that governed here for centuries. The archeological site of Eleusis, topped by a forested acropolis with a small church and clocktower, is astonishingly large and picturesque despite the power plants and tract housing that crowd its perimeter. At first sight it's just a cave in the hillside with an amazing disarray of Greek marble slabs, red brick Roman walls, medieval hewnstone ramparts, pits, and wells—all vestiges of the many civilizations which built over their predecessors in trying to establish this as a sacred place for their own religion.

The most fascinating aspect of the remains are those pertaining to the **Eleusinian Mysteries** that were performed here nearly 3,000 years ago. These mysteries were begun by Eumolpus to honor Demeter, goddess of the harvest, whose daughter Persephone had exited from the Underworld at this site. Scholars believe that these mysterious ceremonies (never revealed by any of the participants) were part purification, fasting, ritual, and drama. It is thought that priestesses promised happiness, resurrection after death, or immortality to the initiated. Homer wrote in the *Odyssey:* "[the initiated go to] the Elysian Plain and the world's end . . . where life is easiest for men. No snow is there, nor yet great storm, nor any rain . . ." Herodotus tells us: "Every year the Athenians celebrate a festival in honor of the Mother and the Maid, and anyone who wishes, from Athens or elsewhere, may be initiated in the mysteries . . ." To find the Mysteries' traces among all the generations of rubble, follow us:

After entering the site, on the right behind the labeled Temple of Artemis is the **Eschara**, a Roman-era pit where sacrificial victims were burned. To the left of the huge, sculpted marble medallion of Antonius Pius (its builder) is the **Greater Propylaea**, from the second century A.D., modeled after the Propylaea of Athens's Acropolis. Built on top of a fifth-century B.C. version, this entrance to the Sacred Way had balustrades to curb the flow of devotees to the Sanctuary behind it. To the left of the Greater Propylaea can be seen one of two **triumphal arches** dedicated to the Great Goddesses and to the Emperor Hadrian. This arch inspired the Arc de Triomphe, which caps the Champs-Élysées (Elysian Fields) in Paris.

Nearby, the pit (**Callichoros Well**) marks the area where the Eleusinian women danced and chanted in praise of Demeter. Turning back, up the marble-paved Sacred Way is the **Plutonium**, the sacred cave where Persephone disappeared with Hades (Pluto, to the Romans) to the Underworld and from which she emerged six months of the year to make the earth bloom. Climbing up beyond this will bring you to roofed-over areas where walls of several eras have yet to be fully excavated. On the right, the small carved stone steps are thought to have led to a terrace altar to worship the goddesses. Behind the church is the **Telesterion**, a large square with rows of seats carved in the stone embankment, at right. This was thought to be the Hall of Initiation (designed by Iktinos, of Parthenon fame), where devotees would gather to receive their mysterious rites.

The site and archeological museum are open from 8:45 a.m. to 3 p.m. daily, from 9:30 a.m. to 2:30 p.m. on Sunday, closed Tuesday. Admission is 250 drs ($2). Public bus no. 853, 862, and 864 leave Eleftherios Square regularly for the one-hour trip to Elefsina, located just off the old Athens-Corinth coastal route.

MARATHON: The bravery of the Athenian troops who fought against and successfully defeated the invading Persian hordes at Marathon in 490 B.C. has been heralded since that time as one of history's greatest testimonies to the spirit of freedom and democracy. An archeological museum, the Tomb of the Plataeans, and the Tomb of the Athenians are all that mark the spot of that battle, but the realization that this scrub-brush, rocky plain and the clear blue bay beyond it were the site of such a momentous event transforms this day trip into an elevating experience. No one tells the story better than Herodotus, the second-century Roman who recorded events of the Hellenic world in *The Histories:*

"The part of Attica nearest Eretria [site of the last Persian victory] and also the best ground for cavalry to maneuvre in—was at Marathon. To Marathon, therefore, Hippias directed the invading army, and the Athenians, as soon as the news arrived, hurried to meet it. The Athenian troops were commanded by ten generals, of whom the tenth was Miltiades. . . .

"Before they left the city the Athenian generals sent off a message to Sparta. The messenger was an Athenian named Pheidippides, a trained runner still in the practice of his profession. . . . The Spartans, though moved by the appeal, said they could not take the field until the moon was full. So they waited for the full moon, and meanwhile Hippias, the son of Pisistratus, guided the Persians to Marathon. . . .

"The previous night Hippias had dreamed that he was sleeping with his mother, and he supposed that the dream meant that he would return to Athens, recover his power, and die peacefully at home in old age. . . . On the following day, he led the fleet to anchorage at Marathon and got the troops into position when they had disembarked. While he was busy with this he was seized by an unusually violent fit [and] coughed one [of his teeth] right out of his mouth. It fell somewhere in the sand . . . nowhere to be seen. Hippias turned to his companions and said with a deep sigh, 'This land is not ours; we shall never be able to conquer it. The only part I ever had in it my tooth possesses. . . .'

"The Athenian troops were drawn up on a piece of ground sacred to Heracles, when they were joined by the Plataeans, who came to support them with every available man. Amongst the Athenian commanders opinion was divided. Miltiades turned to the polemarch, or War Archon.

"'It is now in your hands, Callimachus, either to enslave Athens, or to make her free. . . . Never in the course of our long history have we Athenians been in such peril as now. If we refuse to fight I have little doubt that the result will be the rise in Athens of bitter political dissension: our purpose will be shaken, and we shall submit to Persia. But if we fight before the rot can show itself in any of us, then if God gives us fair play, we can not only fight but win. . . . Vote on my side, and our country will be free—yes, and the Mistress of Greece. . . .'

"Miltiades would not fight until the day came when he had supreme command. When it did come, the Athenian army moved into position. The right wing was commanded by Callimachus, then followed the tribes, and finally, on the left wing, was the contingent from Plataea. The struggle at Marathon was long drawn out. In the center, held by the Persians themselves and the Sacae, the advance was with the foreigners who were so far successful as to break the Greek line and pursue the fugitives inland from the sea; but the Athenians on one wing and the Plataeans on the other were both victorious. Having gotten the upper hand, they left the defeated Persians to make their escape and then, drawing the two wings together into a single unit, they turned their attention to the Persians who had broken through in the center. Here again they were triumphant, chasing the routed enemy, and cutting them down as they ran right to the edge of the sea. Then, plunging into the water, they laid hold of the ships, calling for fire. . . . In the Battle of Marathon some 6,400 Persians were killed; the losses of the Athenians were 192. . . .

"After waiting for the full moon, 2,000 Spartans set off for Athens. They were so anxious not to be late that they were in Attica on the third day after leaving Sparta. They had, of course, missed the battle; but such was their passion to see the Persians, that they went to Marathon to have a look at the bodies. That done, they complimented the Athenians on their good work, and returned home. . . ." [excerpted from the Penguin Classics edition].

The Archeological Museum

Marathon's archeological museum is next to the recently restored Tomb of the Plataeans, two kilometers west of the highway turnoff marked "Marathon." The museum is well worth a visit. It's very well organized (labels are in English) and features Neolithic to Byzantine-era finds from throughout the Marathon region. The small courtyard, filled with bitter orange and kumquat trees, has a large Ionic capital thought to be the top of a huge pedestal which supported a trophy honoring the victorious soldiers at Marathon. Archeologists think this column is similar in purpose to that of the Naxian Sphynx at Delphi.

Tumulus of the Plataeans

Near the base of Agrieliki Hill, the command post for the Athenian troops and their allies, a large grave site (tumulus) was discovered. The tumulus has been rebuilt so that you can enter and see the opened graves of the Plataean warriors. Herodotus tells us that Plataea contributed 1,000 troops to fight alongside the Athenians at Marathon. They've been laid to rest about 200 meters from the archeological museum.

Tomb of the Athenians

Located across the highway and about three kilometers south of the archeological museum turnoff is the Tomb of the Athenians at Marathon, where the cremated remains of the 192 Athenian soldiers who died defending Hellas from the Persians are buried. The site is marked with a simple stele (dating from 510 B.C.) carved with the likeness of Aristion, a *strategoi* who led the Athenians. The Tomb of Miltiades has been found near the site of the present-day museum.

Useful Information

The archeological museum (tel. 0294/931-1477), the Tomb of the Plataeans, and the Tomb of the Athenians are open to view from 8 a.m. to 5:30 p.m. There is no fee to enter any of the sites except at the Tomb of the Athenians, where the charge is 250 drs ($2).

Orange buses to Marathon leave from 29 Mavromateon at Areos Park; contact tourist information (tel. 171) for schedules.

The nearby town of **Marathon Beach** has the closest accommodations, restaurants, and a pleasant (can get very crowded) beach. The 24-room **Hotel Marathon** (tel. 0294/55-222) is in a quiet, eucalyptus-lined roadway about two kilometers from the archeological museum turnoff. It's a good idea to check before taking one of their large (usually clean), cheerful doubles with terraces and private facilities, which run 5000 drs ($38.50) in the summertime; a comfortable restaurant serves three meals here as well. **Camping Marathon** is at the "Marathon Beach" turnoff, half a kilometer from the beach. **Camping Rhamnous** is three kilometers from the port, but along the beach. Marathon Beach has several food markets, touristy tavernas, and a cinema.

The Athens Open International Marathon

Held every October since 1972, this race commemorates the run of Pheidippides to announce the Athenian victory over the Persians at the Battle of Marathon (490 B.C.). The race begins outside the village of Marathon and continues along Pheidippides' course for exactly 42.195 kms (26.2 miles) to the Panathenaic Stadium built for the first modern Olympic Games (1896) in Athens. There is no qualifying time to enter the race. Applicants should contact **Mondial Tours**, 6 Ermou St., in Athens (tel. 32-30-731) or **Marathon Tours** (tel. 1-800-343-5088 in Cambridge, Mass.) in the United States for information.

THE TEMPLE OF NEMESIS: A possible excursion from Marathon is to the Temple of Nemesis (goddess of vengeance) at the nearby Acropolis of Rhamnous. From this temple, which sits atop the fortress, comes the worst possible revenge: it is only accessible by taxi—3000 drs ($23.10)—or car from Marathon Beach, and for all your effort you are rewarded with knee-high ruins and sky-high frustration. Very little is left of the once-graceful work of the unknown architect who designed the Temple of Poseidon at Sounion and the Thission in the Agora. And worse still, the beautiful wildflowers that blanket the site are painful; Rhamnous means "place of spiny buckthorn." Nemesis wasn't kidding.

But the Greeks have had the last laugh. The impressive three-tiered base of her temple is scarred with Greek graffiti, particularly feet pointing in opposing directions. As for the ironic touch of constructing a much smaller Temple of Themis (the goddess of eternal justice, who was also Zeus' lawyer) behind that of Nemesis—well, relative to the size, its ruins are more impressive. The beautiful promontory was once lined with white marble towers guarding the Euripos Channel. It's now a scrub-brush slope, blocked off with fencing, but still offers a beautiful view of Marathon Bay and, beyond, the island of Evia. The Temple of Nemesis site is open daily from 9 a.m. to 3 p.m., 9:30 a.m. to 2:30 p.m. on Sunday and holidays, at no fee. Cars should follow road signs to the ferry at Aghia Marina, then bear left up the road toward the hills.

THE TEMPLE OF ARTEMIS AT BRAURON: In the small, once-waterside village of Vravona (also called Brauron) there stands a Temple of Artemis that's a fabulous surprise. Not well known or frequented, this lovely site is dedicated to the goddess of fertility (who was also the patroness of unmarried girls and chastity). Apollo's twin sister Artemis was the protective mistress of all beasts; her role as goddess of the hunt was often chronicled in mythology.

Scholars believe the temple was constructed in the Middle Helladic era (2000 to 1600 B.C.) to appease Artemis' anger over the killing of a bear. The bear was her favorite animal, and after the sanctuary was built, it was decreed that in the spring all the young girls from neighboring towns should dress like bears to serve Artemis. Every five years the Brauronia Festival was held, and girls between the ages of five and ten years would come in yellow chitons and dance like bears in the sanctuary grounds. Many young women remained to grow up there, creating what might be called the first "feminist cell." King Agamemnon's daughter Iphigenia remained at Brauron when she returned from Tauris with Orestes to become an Artemis priestess. While Artemis was venerated in gratitude for motherhood and good health, Iphigenia was brought votive offerings when a baby or mother died in childbirth. Brauron became a sanctuary for many Greek women fleeing a world about which Euripides could claim, "A woman should be good for everything at home, but abroad good for nothing" (*Meleager*, trans. M. H. Morgan).

The best preserved part of the site is the stoa, a colonnaded way once called the Parthenon (of the Virgin), perhaps because the young devotees of Artemis lived there during festivals. These ruins date primarily from the fifth century B.C. and were constructed over much earlier shrines at this site. The proportions of the temple are more square; the squat Doric columns end abruptly on the limestone terrace and appear more primitive than the graceful supports of the more famous Doric temples, such as Sounion or the Parthenon. Yet their placement, set back in a broad, marshy plain overlooking the Aegean in the distance (a distance, by the way, which was much shorter before it became silted up), is very powerful and appropriate to a sanctuary where men would have to let women be themselves.

The archeological museum of Vravona is a kilometer away from the site, up a road that winds through vineyards and grazing fields. Inside are fourth-century B.C. votive reliefs and friezes from the sanctuary, geometric-era ceramics from early tombs, and other finds from a prehistoric settlement discovered on a hill above the temple. The most interesting displays are those which illuminate the activities of temple inhabitants; there are terracotta plaques carved in relief which depict Artemis in her many incarnations, gold jewelry and ornamental objects found in the silty deposit from the sacred spring, and charming ceramic *arktos,* statuettes of the young girls who came to perform and worship here.

The museum and the archeological site are open from 9 a.m. to 3 p.m. on weekdays, 9:30 a.m. to 2:30 p.m. on Sunday and holidays; both are closed Tuesday. The 250 drs ($2) admission covers both places. Vravona can be reached by public bus from Athens (it's 35 kilometers southeast) or Rafina (15 kilometers south).

Chapter V

THE SARONIC GULF ISLANDS

1. Aegina
2. Poros
3. Hydra
4. Spetsai

THE BODY OF WATER separating Attica from the Peloponnesian coast hosts the island chain closest to Athens, the Saronic Gulf islands of Aegina, Poros, Hydra, and Spetsai. Each has its unique charm. Above Aegina's pine-covered hills stands the graceful Temple of Afaia, one of Greece's best preserved Doric structures. Below the temple are groves of pistachios and coves for swimming. Poros is an island for dancing, wandering the town's terraced back streets, and visiting Lemonodasos, a giant lemon grove adjoining a fine sandy beach. Visiting Hydra is a sublime experience; the entire island has been declared a national monument because of its wealth of elegant stone mansions, monasteries, and natural beauty. Spetsai offers wonderful architectural sights, long walks through pine forests, and lovely beaches.

The Saronic Gulf islands are preferred by Athenians as weekend destinations. From Friday to Sunday during the summer these islands take on a carnival atmosphere with festivals, parades, and a giant influx of visitors from around the world. During midweek the ports and beaches return to relative calm, the only time when restaurants and hotels have vacancies and the best time to see the sights. All of these islands can be treated as day trips from Athens or can be visited on a three-isle day cruise. Either way, they're all perfect getaway destinations for those who've been beaten down by the rigors of sightseeing in Athens.

GETTING AROUND: One of the joys of touring the Saronic Gulf is that, with little exception, you can go to any island from any other island at almost any time of day. Boats and hydrofoils run constantly. Rarely will you have to wait any longer than an hour or two for a boat to take you to your desired destination.

This efficient state of affairs is bolstered by the operation of the so-called **Flying Dolphins**, a fleet of yellow-and-blue Russian-built ships that fly on the surface of the water at more than twice the speed of a normal ferry. These sports cars of the sea travel with the speed of a destroyer, skimming blithely over ocean swells. The cabin is laid out like the interior of an airplane, with bucket seats and fore-and-aft sections.

Generally a hydrofoil takes half the time of a regular ferry and costs 35% more for a ticket. For example, a normal ferry to Aegina takes 90 minutes and costs 475 drs ($3.65), while a hydrofoil travels the same distance in 40 minutes and costs 650 drs ($5).

Most hydrofoils depart from Zea Marina in Piraeus; the ferries and most Aegina-bound hydrofoils leave from the main Piraeus docks. The ferries and hydrofoils begin operating at 6 a.m. and continue service until the late evening. Hydrofoils stop at Aegina, Poros, Hydra, Spetsai, Kyrapassi, Hermione, Leonidion, Porto Heli, Monemvassia, and in the high season, at Tyros, Tolo, Neapolis, Nafphlion, and Kythira. Generally, the Flying Dolphins follow an interisland route, making local stops, but there are express runs as well. Flying Dolphin tickets can be booked in Piraeus (tel. 45-27-107) at the Ceres Hydrofoil Joint Service office at 8 Akti Themistokleus, along the waterfront. Check carefully for schedules and departure port.

The other interesting way to see the Saronic Gulf islands is on a three-isle day cruise aboard the *Saronic Star*. These cruises, which can be booked through **Viking Tours**, at 3 Filellinon (tel. 32-29-383), make stops on Aegina (to see the Temple of Afaia), Poros, and Hydra. Lunch is served on board and the cruise line provides transportation to and from the ship from Athens. Cost of the one-day cruise is 5625 drs ($43.30). It's a wonderful introduction to island-hopping and the forgotten luxury of traveling by cruise ship.

1. Aegina

Aegina is the largest of the Saronic Gulf islands and the closest to Piraeus, making it a convenient and pleasurable day-long introduction to the Greek islands. The island is so close to Athens that many treat it as an extension of the capital (in fact Aegina *was* the capital in the early years of the modern Greek nation), commuting on the Flying Dolphins as if taking the train to work. An even-larger group of Athenians visit Aegina on weekends (when it's most crowded).

Despite the pressures of tourism and development, Aegina manages to maintain its own identity. The countryside supports the usual Greek staples (olives, figs, and almonds), but in between are strange-looking pistachio trees. Farmers set up temporary booths along the road to peddle these exotic nuts.

Most people come to Aegina to visit the Temple of Afaia, one of the best preserved sanctuaries in Greece, on a par with the Temple of Poseidon at Sounion. If you take binoculars, you can see the Parthenon and the Temple of Poseidon; the ancients built the three temples in an equilateral triangle and in sight of each other so they could communicate by fire.

Aegina is convenient enough to visit as a day trip from Athens, though we'd recommend beginning your tour of the Saronic Gulf islands with a stop at Aegina and continuing on to Poros, Hydra, Spetsai, and the Peloponnese peninsula.

ORIENTATION: Both the ferry and the Flying Dolphin dock at **Aegina town** on the northeast coast, where the G-shaped breakwater creates calm waters for mooring the many yachts that visit. The port is a comfortable village with big, crowded family beaches north and south of the harbor. The harbor is a busy part of town: merchants sell fresh fruit and vegetables brought over from the mainland, signs on the bobbing fishing boats advertise prices for the day's catch, farmers from the cooperative shovel pistachios into paper bags 625 drs ($4.80) for 500 grams—to sell them to groups of wide-eyed German tourists, and bicyclists roam up and down the waterfront road.

Buses leave from the port to all parts of the island. It only takes a short ride for the village to recede and the island's farms and rugged hills to appear. The leafy pistachio trees grow so close to the winding gravel road that buses occasionally pull off a branch or two. Aegina's erratically sculpted coastline is a terror to sailors and a delight to swimmers, with rocky coves on nearly every inch of the perimeter. **Perdika**, on the southwest side, is the favored beach. Set on a pine-covered crest above Aegina's dramatic shoreline is the noble Temple of Afaia. Athens and the Parthenon are visible somewhere off in the hazy distance. The bus travels as far as the east coast honky-tonk beach town of Ag. Marina, where groups of German and English tourists annually lay siege.

USEFUL INFORMATION: The **Police** (tel. 22-391) maintain an office right off the port on a small street behind the bus station, open 8:30 a.m. to 2 p.m. and 5 to 7 p.m. The **National Bank of Greece** (open 8 a.m. to 2 p.m. Monday through Friday), a bakery, cafés, markets, hotels, and nearly anything you'll need are on the long waterfront street. The **post office** (open 8 a.m. to 8 p.m. Monday through Friday; 9 a.m. to 1:30 p.m. Saturday and Sunday) and **bus station** are off to the left and around the corner as you disembark from the ferry. The Port Authority **information booth** is on the port near the pistachio cooperative booth. The **O.T.E.** (the **area code** for Aegina is 0297) is five blocks from the port on Aeakou Street. The island **hospital** (tel. 22-209) is on the northeast edge of town and can handle most medical emergencies, as does the in-town Center of Health Clinic (tel. 22-902).

The **bus** to the Temple of Afaia and Ag. Marina runs every half hour during the summer. If you feel so inclined, **taxis** are available next to the bus depot. **Bicycle**-rental stands are located on the other side of the paralia, near the southern beach. Watch out—some of the shops have been known to charge tourists outrageous prices for a barely functioning two-wheeler! The price should be around 625 drs ($4.80) a day.

Anne Yannoulis' *Aegina* (Lycabettus Press) is an excellent and useful guide. **Pipinistours** (tel. 24-456) is extremely helpful and also serves as the Ceres Hydrofoil agent.

AROUND THE ISLAND: The **town of Aegina** has a good feeling about it. Wander down the back streets of the port and you'll get a hint of yesteryear on the island, especially when one of the horse-drawn carts passes by (carriages are rented for 1250 drs ($9.60) per half hour). On our last visit, we enjoyed visiting the recently restored Markelos Tower, a squat 15th-century structure in the middle of town. Just past the north side beach is the Hill of Kolona, where a sole Doric column stands above the remains of ancient Aegina. The museum in town (open 8 a.m. to 4 p.m. daily, closed Tuesday) contains objects dating from prehistoric times and includes a good collection of fifth-century B.C. sculpture.

If you plan to spend the night, Aegina town is as good a place as any to find a hotel. The C-class **Hotel Brown** (tel. 0297/22-271), on the south side of the harbor, has an elegant neoclassical façade and equally distinguished common spaces and garden. Most of the hotel's 25 rooms have private baths; doubles with breakfast run 5225 drs ($40.40) with bath, 4000 drs ($30.80) without.

A cheaper alternative is the **guesthouse of E. Pavlou** (tel. 0297/22-795), near the Brown and just behind the church overlooking the paralia. Simple, clean rooms are 3670 drs ($28.20) with bath, 3190 drs ($24.50) without. Mr. and Mrs. Pavlou have additional rooms nearby at similar rates.

Of the many cafés and tavernas we like **Afaia** (to the left of the pier), **Mondraki, Vostitsanos, Taverna Baroutis, Stratigou** (two kilometers south in Faros), and the **Retro Bar** (next to the post office). Try the **Inoi disco** in Faros or

Disco Elpianno in Aegina for lively nightspots. Bar-hoppers will enjoy the **Taverna Belle Epoque** for a nightcap.

The road winds through hilly terrain up to the graceful **Temple of Afaia.** The sanctuary we see now is the third structure built on the site and dates from 490 B.C. It was dedicated to Afaia, a Creto-Mycenaean god whose cult later merged with that of Athena. When the temple was originally excavated archeologists found numerous statues and friezes in high relief, all done in Archaic style. Only a few statues remain on Aegina (in the museum); the others were removed to Athens and Munich. The temple is one of the finest examples of Archaic architecture in the Hellenic world, its 6 by 12 inward-sloping Doric columns all in an excellent state of preservation. The site is open from 10 a.m. to 5 p.m. Monday through Saturday, on Sunday from 8 a.m. to 1 p.m. and 2:30 to 5 p.m. Admission is 300 drs ($2.30) for adults, 150 drs ($1.15) for students.

Either a long walk down the donkey path or a short bus ride will lead you to the unappealing village of **Ag. Marina,** a group tourist resort that has defaced what was otherwise a perfectly lovely stretch of sandy beach. If you decide to overnight in Ag. Marina, we recommend the somewhat pricey **Hotel Apollo** (tel. 0297/32-271). This resort inn is set away from the throng and courts a more sophisticated clientele. Double rooms run 7500 drs ($57.70), bed and breakfast, 10,000 drs ($76.90) for half board. Far preferable is the beach community at **Perdika** (try Dimitri's El Greco Taverna), where boats ply the water to Moni Island, an ideal camping spot.

For those who want to leave the group scene behind, head over to the nearby island of **Agistri.** Small boats make the 20-minute commute every couple of hours (or whenever the boat is filled with passengers). Though the services are pretty basic you'll still find tavernas, rooms for rent, and Skala Liminaria, one of the few nudist beaches on the Saronic Gulf.

2. Poros

Poros means "passage," and the name could not be more appropriate. The island is actually made up of two islands, Speria and Kalavria, linked by a narrow isthmus, and the two are separated from the mainland of the Peloponnese by a narrow body of water. **Kalavria** contains 95% of the land mass of the island, but it is **Spheria,** with the town of Poros, that attracts most of the populace and has a small naval base. An armada of water ferries links Poros with the mainland city of Galatas, almost a stone's throw away.

Kalavria (the island's ancient name) is a rustic, thickly wooded haven which in ancient times was a refuge for political outcasts and sailors. The greatest of all Athenian orators, Demosthenes, fled to Poros in 338 B.C. after Athens was defeated in the battle of Chaeronia against the forces of Philip of Macedon. Demosthenes led a stirring call to arms to awaken a lethargic Athens against the powerful Macedonian army. When Philip made peace with the defeated city-state, Demosthenes went to the Temple of Poseidon on Kalavria to commit suicide (his grave is near the site). Today there is little to see at the site of the temple; most of the marble was hauled away centuries ago to build other structures, pirates raided it, and the rest was leveled by earthquakes. Kalavria's rocky coastline has many natural harbors and beaches. Wealthy Athenians have built luxurious villas, nestled in the dense pine forests of this secluded part of the island.

THE TOWN OF POROS: There are two ways to get to Poros. Most people arrive by ferry or hydrofoil, landing at the port in Poros town. Some cross over from the Peloponnese (a 370-meter journey, costing 15 drs) after visiting Epidauros. The **waterfront** is a blur of activity; boats of all sizes load and unload their human cargo, the cafés are full, music pours out from the bars and clubs, and hundreds of Greek weekenders and foreign tourists parade up and down the paralia.

Poros is best appreciated at night and away from the harbor. Climb up to the residential quarter where cube-shaped houses rest on ever-higher terraces. Henry Miller visited the island years ago, but his description is still apt: "To sail slowly through the streets of Poros is to recapture the joy of passing through the neck of the womb. It is a joy too deep almost to be remembered."

Hotels are not Poros's strong suit, but the **Seven Brothers** (tel. 0298/23-412) has 16 clean, pleasant rooms. A double with bath is 4700 drs ($36.20). The taverna downstairs may be somewhat noisy, so ask for rooms in the back. Far preferable to the hotels, however, are private rooms in the town above the paralia. The rooms of **Maria Christofa** (tel. 0298/22-058) can be found next to the clock tower at the highest point above the harbor. Many of her six rooms have breathtaking views of the town and the harbor. The 2500 drs ($19.20) for a double without bath is the bargain of the island. Contact the **Tantours** office (tel. 22-112), on the harbor, for other choices; they also offer excursions to the Peloponnese and the other Saronic Gulf islands.

Our two favorite dining spots are to the right of the port. The outdoor **Lucas Restaurant** is run by a Greek dancer and his English wife, Susie. Their food is good and cheap. The Lucas is located about 500 meters from the center of town on the paralia. Closer in is the **Caravella Restaurant,** specializing in fish entrées. Though more expensive than the Lucas, dinner for two should run a reasonable 1300 drs ($10). The **Three Brothers** is another local favorite, a small place with a large kitchen, one block off the port.

Dionysos is one of the island's better eateries and is found on the left side of the port, about 400 meters from the center. If you continue for another 600 meters you'll come to the only gas station on the island. Just beyond this landmark is a fine, super low-budget souvlaki-and-grilled chicken joint, **Ovelix.** If you're in the mood, you can also launder your clothes or buy secondhand English books at nearby **Suzi's Laundrette** and **Anita's Books.** And you thought nothing was happening on sleepy Poros.

Poros is a dancer's island. You're sure to find a club where people will be doing the steps to a fast-paced *hasapiko* (a regional dance designed for weight loss), getting crazier as the night wears on. As for discos, the best is **Scirocco,** about one kilometer from the center of town.

The **Police** are on the port three blocks down to the right of the dock (tel. 22-462) and are open daily to help tourists. The **National Bank of Greece** is on the far right of the port, as is the post office. The **O.T.E.** (the **area code** is 0298) is on the paralia.

AROUND THE ISLAND AND BEYOND: Unfortunately the two most often suggested excursions on the larger part of the island are pretty much a bust. The Temple of Poseidon is rubble on a picturesque plateau, while the Monastery of Zoodochos Pighi is just another monastery. (By the way, the Lycabettus Press guide, *Poros,* by Niki Stavrolakes is an excellent publication dealing with the entire area.)

Instead of touring Kalavria, head over to the mainland. If you visit **Galatas** in the middle of June you might be lucky enough to witness the Flower Festival. Parades, floats, marching bands, and floral arrays are the stuff of the Flower Festival. (Did you know that Greece exports flowers to Holland?) A bus from Galatas runs eight kilometers to the village of **Troizena,** thought to be the birthplace of Theseus (certainly the birthplace of Theseus' son, Hippolytos) and site of the ancient Temple of Asklepios. There is a lovely walk, along the Devil's

Gorge (so named because of a face that looks like you-know-who on one of the walls), leading to the site. Again there isn't much to see, but it's a pleasant stroll through fields of carnations and will be of interest to those who enjoyed Mary Renault's *The King Must Die*.

Far more sensual is **Lemonodasos**, a 25,000-tree lemon grove that was planted after Greece's War of Independence. This is one excursion that's hard to resist: a walk through a citrus grove whose fragrant flowers and fruit will send your nose into ecstasy. Suddenly like an oasis, a taverna comes into view that dispenses freshly squeezed lemonade and such intensely strong retsina that it made an entire Australian rowing team tipsy. On the far side of Lemonodasos is a sandy beach (called Aliki). And you wondered why you ever came to Poros.

Warning: As the authors of this book we like to think that we make most of the mistakes so that you don't. On our way to Poros from Aegina, John rushed to disembark when the ferry first pulled into port. However, instead of landing at Poros we ended up on the Peloponnesian coast at Methana. It's a sedate, middle-class Greek thermal resort where you'll see more women playing bridge in the cafés than naked girls on the beach or wild men doing handkerchief dances. You've been warned.

3. Hydra

Even among such a glittering array of jewels as the Greek islands, Hydra stands out as a jewel among gems. Nature's scenic elegance has been matched by man's handiwork; grand domestic architecture wrought a century ago by Italian architects is well preserved and a nationally recognized monument. Best of all, Hydra has banned all motorized vehicles. Pedestrians peacefully strolling the port's back lanes encounter only donkeys and, occasionally, the island's lone garbage truck. Nary a moped to be found . . .

The slate-gray town of Hydra rises up a natural amphitheater from the port; to appreciate its peacefulness, just take a short (but challenging) walk up-hill. Follow the worn cobblestones up to the stone wall, which surrounds a white-washed monastery and local cemetery. At this distance, the sounds of the town and land wash over you in a flood of fresh sensations. The tinkle of goat bells and the chatter of children float up from below, joining the singsong chant of a monk above you. The Hydriots have created a uniquely human environment, where natural sounds dominate. It's an overwhelming delight, not to be missed.

The most important migration to Hydra took place in the 1600s, when Orthodox Albanians, on the run after the fall of Mistras to the Turks, took refuge on the island. Over the years these mountain people became excellent sailors, hired by other nations to run blockades and fight in foreign wars. The island amassed tremendous wealth and avoided the burden of taxation by the Turks in exchange for training the Ottoman navy. When the winds of revolution swept over the nearby islands, Hydriots were a little reluctant to join forces, not wanting to upset a favorable relation with the occupying Turks. As it turned out, Hydra joined in the War of Independence and won several stunning victories (Admiral Miaoulis was a Hydriot). Today the major migration is composed of glitzy Athenian and international jet setters who weekend on this special island. In this century, Hydra's main business after tourism must be training real estate agents, because prices for houses on the island are astronomical.

If you plan to stay overnight on any of the Saronic Gulf islands you'll be hard pressed to find a nicer place than Hydra. Visit in midweek when the weekend crowd is busy at work and the island is a virtual paradise. If you can, arrange your travels to arrive on Hydra toward the end of June for the special **Miaoulia Festival**. This celebration commemorates the Hydriot commander's victory over the superior Ottoman navy by recreating the battle, complete with the burning of a fireship, exploding cannons, and fireworks.

ORIENTATION: The boat, whether ferry or hydrofoil, docks on the left side of the port and main town. The **Police** (tel. 52-205) are at 9 Votsi St., two blocks up from the waterfront. They maintain a list of rooms for rent and can advise you about hotels and pensions. The **National Bank of Greece** and the **Commercial Bank** both have offices on the harbor, open 8 a.m. to 2 p.m., with extended evening hours in the summer. The **post office** is just off the paralia at Tombazi Street and is open Monday through Friday from 8 a.m. to 2:30 p.m. Across the street from the Police is the **O.T.E.** (the **area code** for Hydra is 0298), which is open from 7:30 a.m. to 11 p.m. Monday through Friday, on Saturday and Sunday from 8:30 a.m. to 1:30 p.m. Information regarding the **boats** is available from the Port Authority, next to the ferry dock, or by looking on the big yellow signboard at the point of departure. *Hydra* (Lycabettus Press), by Catherine Vanderpool, is a fine companion guide, particularly for its detailed descriptions of the mansions and island architecture. There is a **newstand** on the paralia that sells English language periodicals and a small selection of books. At the far end of the port is the new **Hydra Museum,** housing a fine collection of island historical documents and artifacts.

We're always reticent to recommend a particular shop, but one that we found to our tastes was **Loulaki** (tel. 52-292), at 22 Miaouli, a combination gallery and boutique that carries many objets d'art in the local shade of Hydra blue. You'll understand when you visit!

ACCOMMODATIONS: Once again we found a hotel that deserves exceptional mention: the **Hotel Miranda Hydra** (tel. 0298/52-230), located several blocks off the harbor up Miaouli Street. Set in an 18th-century sea captain's house, the Miranda is decorated with Oriental rugs, tattered wooden chests, marble tables, and period naval engravings. The 16 renovated rooms are extremely spacious; some have lovely painted ceilings and antique wooden furniture. Hosts Iannis, Miranda, and Phoebe are as gracious a staff as one can imagine, transforming their home into a veritable Greek shangri-la. Double rooms rent for 7700 drs ($59.20) a night including breakfast, and it's an absolutely worthwhile splurge. You're advised to make a reservation because, as you might imagine, such an establishment is much in demand.

Just across from the Miranda and having the same ownership is the newly redone **Hotel Leto** (tel. 0298/52-280), a simple C-class affair with rates averaging 4500 drs ($34.60) for a double room.

A short walk from the Leto and Miranda is the recently restored Hydriot mansion, **Orloff** (tel. 0298/52-564). Though these 10 rooms aren't quite up to the standard of the Miranda, they are richly atmospheric and among the best the island has to offer. Rooms range in price from 5000 to 7500 drs ($38.50 to $57.70), depending on size, location, and facilities (with or without bath).

Another Hydriot mansion open to visitors is the **Hotel Hydra** (tel. 0298/52-102), a two-story gray stone hotel on the western cliffs above the port. The building was purchased from the National Tourist Office by Dimitri Davis and has been beautifully restored. The rooms are carpeted, with balconies overlooking the town and harbor. Eight of the 12 rooms have private baths. The double with bath is 5750 drs ($44.20), 5250 drs ($40.40) without, including breakfast. Call for reservations, particularly if you want to come on a weekend.

In the same neighborhood but on a lower level is **Savvas Rooms to Let** (tel. 0298/52-259), run by Marina Kehagioglou. The rooms are eclectically furnished, and the two clean bathrooms are in a garden-filled courtyard. Climbing up the steep wooden stairs with the narrow pipe handrail may remind some of their sailing days. There's no doubt that you're in Marina's own home. Rooms range from 960 drs ($7.40) for a double to 1200 drs ($9.25) for a room for three.

The **Amaryllis Hotel** (tel. 0298/52-249) is a C-class inn built in traditional Hydriot style. Two of the Amaryllis's ten rooms come with private facilities and the location is most convenient, one block behind the paralia. Doubles cost 4500 drs ($34.60) with bath, 4000 drs ($30.80) without.

On the quiet, western side of the harbor lies the **Pension Douglas** (tel. 0298/ 52-597), presided over by Douglas Wilson, a charming, philosophical Englishman, whose loving hand has made this seven-room inn a most pleasant place. All rooms open to the harbor, with world-class views. Douglas keeps a clean house and even irons the sheets. A double is 2225 drs ($17.30); a single, 1250 drs ($9.60), all without bath.

The **Pension Agelika** (tel. 0298/53-202) is on Miaouli Street, two blocks above the Miranda. Its 18 rooms are plain, simple, and clean. All have private baths and overlook a quiet courtyard. Prices range from 3560 drs ($27.40) for a double to 2310 drs ($17.80) for a single.

RESTAURANTS: As usual, the waterfront taverns are to be avoided for anything but coffee or a quick snack. Head into town for a better deal.

Our own favorite is **Taverna The Garden** (tel. 0298/52-329), several blocks up the hill from the waterfront Pan Travel. Behind whitewashed garden walls lies Hydra's finest grill. The meat is superb and swordfish souvlaki divine; don't pass up the *exohiko* (lamb wrapped in phyllo leaves). A meal for two should run about 1875 drs ($14.40).

For a European-style café, try **Loulaki** (named for the indigo dye used in its blue-and-white decor), located opposite the Amaryllis Hotel. Its cool patio, facing the hills, is a respite from the hot sun. Host Enrique Llorca offers fine pastries, a continental breakfast, and good French and Italian coffees (a treat for those fleeing Nescafé).

Taverna Douskos, on Rafaelias Street, is one of the oldest on Hydra, and an unusually serene garden café. An excellent bakery is behind the harborside Pan Travel Agency (where hydrofoil tickets are sold). Nearby is **The Three Brothers,** a garden taverna that serves such delicacies as a special tiropita, bourekakia, and a tasty lamb with lemon sauce. Dinner for two should run 1750 drs ($13.50).

Many of the best restaurants are in Kaminia, to the west of the town. Of particular mention are **To Kamini,** on the harbor, and **Georges and Anna,** a family-run fish taverna one block from the harbor.

READER'S RESTAURANT SELECTION: "I've just returned from Hydra and want to recommend a charming taverna called **Captain George**, built, owned, and run by an American, Peter, and his Greek wife, who does the cooking. I spent many an enjoyable evening there and already miss his grilled whole fish, the best I've had anywhere" (Eleanor S. Cook, Santa Monica, Calif.)

WHAT TO SEE AND DO: Hydra is a small island, but there's enough to do to keep busy for several days. A brief **walking tour** of the town is a good introduction to the island's architectural splendor. Beginning at the port, the Tsamados mansion is now the School of the Merchant Marine, the oldest in Greece. Next door is the site of Hydra's island museum, soon to be completed. If you carefully ascend the worn stairs, you'll find the **fortress** and cannons that once protected the harbor.

Walk west, along the waterfront, to the **Clock Tower** and the monastery of the Assumption of the Virgin Mary. Today the monastery houses the island's administrative offices, but enter the courtyard and you'll feel the serenity of an isolated mountain retreat.

Continue down the paralia, where up the hill to the right is the most impressive of all the **Hydriot mansions**, built by the Tombazis family. This four-story slate villa is now an annex of the School of Fine Arts of Athens. Each year students from the school and artists from around the world stay at the Tombazis mansion to study and pursue art. At the far western edge of the port is a three-story stone mansion owned by the Economou-Miriklis family. Around the other side of the port, above the rocks, is the gigantic mansion of George Koundouriotis, the largest on Hydra. The closest swimming area is immediately below the mansion, where you can just dive off the rocks into the deep-blue sea.

Leave the town, and a pleasant hike will bring you to the wonderful **beaches** along the western coast; some have fish tavernas and showers. To the east of the town is Miramare beach, dominated by the hotel of the same name and a water sports center.

If you feel like stretching your legs consider ascending the trail that leads from Miaouli Street to the **monastery** of Prophet Elijah and the **convent** of Ag. Efpraxia. Both communities are active, and from the top you'll have a fabulous view of the town and beyond. Walk farther south beyond these compounds to the convent of Ag. Taxiarchi, and you will have reached the south coast of the island. The trails are rewarding, but rugged, so wear good shoes. *Warning:* Women in shorts will not be allowed in some of the monasteries.

On our last visit we took a wonderful stroll to the coastal town of Vlichos. A nice way to get to this lovely spot (there is a taverna/bar in the town as well as a small beach for swimming) is to walk up to the top of Hydra town and take the upper trail west past a small monastery and graveyard. The trail continues through hilly farmland and winds down to remote Vlichos. It's a good idea to ask passersby for directions or you might end up on the other side of the island!

Inquire at the Port Authority about caïques that offer **around-the-island cruises**; many have full- and half-day trips that stop at the more remote beaches.

Hydra has several **discos**, all of them low key. Of these we enjoyed visiting Cavos and Heaven, both on the western side of town up on the hill. As for **bars**, the Pirate on the paralia near the Clock Tower is perhaps the best magnet for Hydra's celebrants.

4. Spetsai

Spetsai, the farthest island from Athens in the Saronic group, was once (after Hydra) the "in" weekend destination for tourist-weary Athenians. However, the tourists have caught up with them, and tour groups from England now inundate the island. There are still many reasons to visit the island (its museum, pine forests, and wonderful beaches), but the quiet peace of yesteryear has been tainted by the proliferation of mopeds and cars. Still, Spetsai's horse-drawn carriage can take you away from it all and into the quiet of the old port or the forests.

ORIENTATION: Spetsai is oval shaped; the ferry and hydrofoil dock at the Dapia, which is a 20-minute walk to *paleo limani*, or old harbor. The northeast corner of Spetsai is the most developed region of the island. The lush interior is covered with Aleppo pines and fragrant spices. Of Spetsai's beaches, Paraskevi and Anarghiri, on the south coast, are the best; neither is sandy, but the scruffy foliage and casual feeling (there's no sense of being at an international resort) make for pleasant swimming and sunning. To the east of the island is Spetsopoula, the domain of the Niarchos family.

DAPIA AND THE OLD HARBOR: Most people stay in Dapia and from there take walks and day trips. The local **Police** (tel. 73-100) are 150 meters up from the harbor and can be reasonably helpful. **Banks** (open from 8 a.m. to 2 p.m., Monday through Friday), the **post office,** and **O.T.E.** (the **area code** for Spetsai is 0298) are all within 100 meters of the waterfront. **Takis Spetse Tours** (tel. 72-215), on the road between Dapia and the old harbor, knows every room on the island (try to avoid the group "villas"; they're usually the least attractive accommodations) and can help you with travel arrangements and tours. Australian Mary Bichard is particularly helpful and knows the island exceedingly well.

Perhaps Dapia's only interesting sight is the **museum,** housed in the family home of Hatziyannis Mexis, an island celebrity. Walking through this small collection you'll see the usual unspectacular artifacts, archeological relics, and recent folk objects. The treat here is paying homage to the island's great lady, the indomitable **Bouboulina.** All that's left are a bunch of bones in an aging casket, but when she was better fleshed, Bouboulina was a terror on the open seas. Born in prison of Hydriot parents, Bouboulina was rumored to be half-pirate, half-revolutionary, serving the cause against the Turks during the War of Independence. With her powerful fleet, she sealed off the harbor at Nafplion to defeat the Turks. Legends contend that this less-than-slim warrior forced men to submit at gunpoint. To what, you ask? Bouboulina did have many children, one of whom eloped with a young man whose parents objected, leading to Bouboulina's assassination—but that's another story.

The clumps of instant villas and private rooms, mostly at the service of English tour companies, are changing the face of Spetsai. Finding a good quality, inexpensive, room is difficult. If you wish to book a room, expect to pay from 1500 drs ($11.50) to 3000 drs ($23.10) per night. Takis Tours can help book a room.

As for hotels, we found a topsy-turvy relationship between price and quality: the cheaper inns offer better facilities than the more established and expensive lodgings. The following guide lists our favorites in terms of offering the best value.

The 12-room **Pension Alexandris** (tel. 0298/73-073) is a spiffy clean inn with balconies overlooking the horse-cart stand and the harbor. Pleasant modern rooms with private bath are 2500 drs ($19.20) for two.

The D-class **Hotel Klimis** (tel. 0298/73-777) is a remodeled pension, also on the waterfront but about 50 meters from the square. Its 18 rooms all have baths and balconies. The style is austere, but the facilities are very clean. A double runs 3320 drs ($25.60).

The two C-class waterfront hotels, the **Roumani** (tel. 0298/72-344) and the **Soleil** (tel. 0298/72-488), are similarly constructed and equipped inns. All rooms have a balcony and private bath; the front facing rooms command a view of the harbor. Doubles cost 4150 drs ($31.90) at the Roumani and 5100 drs ($39.30) at the Soleil. Each hotel has a shaded café, where breakfast and afternoon snacks are served. The new **Ship Side Bar** in the Soleil is one of the nicest on the island. For a nonalcoholic beverage at either café, try the lemonade (called a fresh lemon): a half-filled glass with straight lemon juice and ice along with another glass of water and sugar served on the side—heaven!

Restaurants

Consistent with an island that is known for good living, Spetsai has its share of fine restaurants. Our favorite island eatery has three names: **Siora's, Giorgio's,** or **Exedra.** Whatever you end up calling it, this excellent seafood taverna overlooks the old harbor, where yachts pull in and out from all corners of Europe. The specialty here is fish *spetsiota,* a tasty fish-and-tomato casserole;

order a salad and a bottle of wine and the total bill for two will run 1800 drs ($13.90) to 2200 drs ($16.90).

If you're in the mood, there's a pizza parlor just down the street from Siora's. Above the bar/bistro is the thoroughly cozy and intimate **Amoni Restaurant,** with lovely views of the paleo limani, a wide variety of food, and a new bar, the Cabouni, overlooking the harbor.

Back in Dapia is the **Bakery,** just before the Tourist Police. They serve an island specialty called *amigdalato;* as Andrew Thomas describes it in his guide, *Spetsai* (Lycabettus Press), "a small cone-shaped almond cake covered in icing sugar and flavoured with rosewater." We also like the **Verandah,** opposite the little church on the way to the police station.

The **Bakery Restaurant,** one block up from the harbor on the way to the police station and above one of Spetsai's more popular pâtisseries, is a tourist's dream: a good Greek taverna where the food is prepared with very little oil and served hot. This is one cook who understands foreign palates. The Bakery is open for dinner only.

Beyond the police station is a Dapian favorite, **Lazaro's Taverna,** where good food mixes with a normally lively local crowd. **Saropolla** and **Patralis** are also local favorites, to the west of town.

Nightlife

There's lots of it on Spetsai, with bars, discos, and bouzouki dancing from Dapia to the old harbor and even at a few far-flung beaches. Beginning with bars, in Dapia there's **Socrates,** which at this point is an English-Greek (or vice-versa) pub. Groups from the Mother Country inhabit this bar exclusively. The **Rendezvous Bar** at the town beach is also popular with visiting English. We had a good time at the **Mourayo Piano Bar,** at the Old Harbor, where Manolis, one of a steady stream of Greek singers, croons romantic songs to an appreciative audience. Ag. Marina, beyond the old harbor, has **Aloni and Pitioussa** restaurants (with some entertainment), also frequented by foreign guests, especially the yachting crowd. For discos, there's **Figaro,** on the old harbor, and **Fever,** with an all-white interior and John Travolta (isn't this 1988 already?) lighting. Bouzouki dancing goes on all night at **George's.**

AROUND THE ISLAND: The way one used to get around the island, other than by bus or foot, was by horse-drawn carriage. Spetsai has finally succumbed to the motorized demons from Detroit. Mopeds can now be rented on the waterfront.

Speaking of horses, there are at least two kinds of carriage drivers. The first is polite, drives slowly, and is usually talkative and hospitable. The second, and the kind we seek, doesn't say a word but is a terror on wheels; with this driver, just sit back and let the inertia that presses hard against your chest eviscerate your cowering little body. All of the excitement takes place one block from the harbor behind the Remetzo Café, also known as Spetsai's most dangerous intersection. Here one can enjoy the sight of buggies tearing out from between the lone alleyway and Katerine's Boutique. Thrill rides, or the more sedate version, cost between 200 drs ($1.55) and 250 drs ($1.95) from Dapia to the old harbor.

Beaches on Spetsai are a composite of sand and shingle. The best, **Paraskevi** and **Anaghiri,** are on the opposite coast from Dapia and can be reached by excursion boat, bus (in the case of Anaghiri), or buggy. Paraskevi is bordered by pine trees and is favored for its setting, while Anaghiri is a longer, more spacious beach on a perfect C-shaped cove.

Speaking of these two beaches, set in between them is a large white house near Bourani. This little-known location is the setting for John Fowles's novel

The Magus. Fowles taught on Spetsai at Anargyrios and Korgialenios College (the Eton of Greece) during the early 1950s; he returned later to write this famous work.

Another interesting site is the **Bekiris Cave,** down below the right side of Anaghiri beach. Follow the three steps down and crouch through the opening and there you'll find a grotto hideaway. For those who are in search of a nudist beach, try climbing up on the red rocks on Paraskevi. Remember, you didn't hear it from us! **Kosta beach**, on the mainland, is a popular day trip. There are tavernas at both Anaghiri and Kosta, but plan on taking a picnic to Paraskevi.

Chapter VI

THE PELOPONNESE

1. Corinth
2. Nafplion (Nauplion)
3. Epidaurus
4. Mycenae
5. Argos
6. Tripolis
7. Megalopolis
8. Andritsena and Vassae (Bassae)
9. Sparta
10. Mistra (Mystra)
11. Monemvassia
12. Kythira
13. Pilos
14. Methoni and Koroni
15. Githio (Gythion)
16. Areopolis
17. Kalamata (Calamata)
18. Olympia
19. Pirgos (Pyrgos)
20. Kyllini
21. Patras

THOUGH FAMOUS CHIEFLY for its unforgettable artifacts from Greece's classical era, the Peloponnese today has some of the most exquisite beaches and mountainous terrain Greece has to offer. This peninsula, separated from the mainland by the Corinth Canal, is the ideal place to start your love affair with the glory that is Greece. The archeological sites at Corinth, Mycenae, and Olympia, are some of the most expressive ruins of ancient times, leaving visitors with a tangible feeling of life as it must have been over 3,500 years ago. Though there are ruins to be seen everywhere in Greece, the most extensive, best preserved, and most important seem to be in a line between Athens and Olympia (Athens, Corinth, Mycenae, Tiryns, Epidaurus, Nafplion, Olympia).

There are five convenient points of entry to the Peloponnese: from Athens a bus will take you into Corinth, from Italy you can ferry to Patras, boats to/from Crete and Piraeus leave/arrive at Gythion and Monemvassia, and several port towns in the Argolid are serviced by ferry. There are daily flights to Kalamata (southwest) from Athens.

Once you arrive in the Peloponnese, the path of least resistance to maximum sightseeing is your own car combined with foot power; however, all the major areas of interest are serviced regularly by public bus. Even though those tough-to-get-to gems, like the Mani, have poor service, this is offset by the fact that most of these towns can be seen in a day or less using another Peloponnese town as a home base. (The larger towns also have train service between them, which can be combined with buses for the most efficient touring.) *Note:* Pick up the printed bus and train schedules from E.O.T. before you leave Athens so you can plan ahead.

If you visited the places that we liked best it would take you about a week by car. The thought of that much driving may not appeal to you greatly; neither might the patience you will need at some of the bus stops. If the comfort and security of a tour are more your thing, **Viking Tours** (tel. 32-29-383), located at 3 Filellinon St. in Athens, books other companies' tours (principally the excellent Chat Tours), often at a discount if done a day or so before departure. Viking has a four-day tour of the Peloponnese and Delphi; the best of the classical sites for $300 (first-class hotels), including a professional guide. (Viking offers discounts to senior citizens, professors and students, and military personnel.) Their four-day tour goes from Delphi to Anti-Rion, where you ferry over to the Peloponnese at Rion; then to Patras, Olympia, Tripolis, Mycenae, Nafplion, Epidaurus, Corinth, and back to Athens.

Whether it's tours or yours, the first stop in the Peloponnese should be . . .

THE ARGOLID (NORTHEAST PELOPONNESE)

The Argolid is that part of the northeast Peloponnese consisting of Corinth, Nafplion, Mycenae, and Argos, an area which is a pilgrimage for lovers of the classics. In addition to the magnificent ruins all around you there is a timeless quality that infuses the air, a feeling that it must have been exactly like this all those many centuries ago when this was indeed the cradle of human civilization. Surrounded by mountains on the west and north and by the sea on the east and south, the Argolid is a combination of yesterday and today and eternity, blending the relics of the past with the ongoing beauty of its bays and slopes and plains.

Archeological evidence now dates the first inhabitants of the Argolid back to 3000 B.C. Some 1,500 years later, around 1450 B.C., it was the heart of the Greek Empire. The Mycenaean component of this society was the dominant one; every aspect of Greek life was influenced by the Mycenaeans, especially so in the Argolid.

Although this region never became a united state (factions were always at war with each other), it has always been considered a single geographical unit, with the plain of Argos as its center. Around the 12th century B.C. Dorians established themselves at Argos, which became their official capital until the Romans subjugated the Peloponnese. At the beginning of the 13th century A.D. the Franks occupied the Argolid region, which in turn was occupied by the Venetians. In the revolution of 1821 the Argolid was the major battleground, and after the cessation of hostilities Nafplion became the capital of all Greece, to be replaced by Athens in 1834.

History was made again when a German archeologist, Heinrich Schliemann, discovered a tomb in 1882 in Mycenae. His discoveries of gold masks and other antiquities alerted the world to this region once more. If you only have time to sample the Peloponnese, head here first.

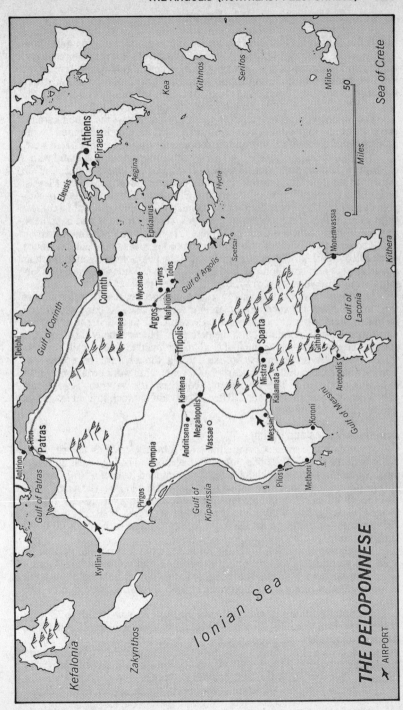

THE PELOPONNESE

✈ AIRPORT

1. Corinth

MODERN CORINTH (CORINTHOS): Corinth, approximately 55 miles from Athens, is the gateway to the Peloponnese. As a city it's not very interesting; in its present form it has existed only since 1928, when an earthquake leveled the town for a second time. Even then the ruins of "New Corinth" were no match for those of ancient Corinth, and today Corinth is still primarily a stop on the way to the magnificent ruins that are seven kilometers out of town.

From Athens, an excellent seven-lane highway follows the winding southern coast of the mainland along the Saronic Gulf, here badly polluted by the industries and commercial shipyards that dominate the view from Piraeus west.

You can break up the 3½-hour drive with a morning stop at **Dafni** with a monastery that is an excellent example of Byzantine art (check with E.O.T. in Athens to see if the monastery is open). Ten kilometers farther west is Eleusis, or Elefsina ("arrival"), site of the ancient Eleusinian Mysteries. Here participants underwent rites commemorating Demeter's gift of corn (and its cultivation) to man. When they "arrived," initiates were given hope and happiness, thus giving Paris the name Champs-Élysées for one of its idyllic boulevards.

The next 60 kilometers offer some sumptuous vistas of the gulf and much truck-filled superhighway. As we approached the Peloponnese, the rolling hills and fruit trees reminded John of southern California. When you reach the Corinth toll, look down as you cross the bridge to admire the canal.

In ancient times Corinth was a wealthy precinct because of its location as the "middle man" between the Ionian and Aegean seas. As early as A.D. 62 Nero saw the wisdom of building a **canal** across Corinth to save ships from the dangerous 185-mile detour around the peninsula. He personally christened the start of the canal by digging the first clod of earth with a gold shovel! A workforce of 6,000 Jewish prisoners continued to dig, though it was never finished. The canal-to-be languished for nearly 2,000 years, until work began on it again in 1881. Completed in 1893 by a French company, the waterway is gorgeous: only 30 yards wide, its sides are 270 feet of smooth, flat rock straight up and its entire length is about four miles.

Accommodations and Dining

If you decide to stay in Corinth, there are some choices. Our favorite hotel is the **Bellevue** (tel. 0741/22-088), at 41 Damaskinou. The high ceilings, pastel paint job, and "wood-look" linoleum floors reminded Kyle of a New England college dorm. The owners have tried hard to give the old Bellevue a new look, and though it's certainly not modern, their efforts have given the city a good-value C-class pension with some charm, but it's often booked by groups. The doubles with bath go for 2400 drs ($18.50), those without for 2000 drs ($15.40).

The **Ephira Hotel** (tel. 0741/22-434) is three blocks from the park at 52 Vass. Konstantinou. From here it's a five-minute walk to the harbor. This C-class, 45-room hotel is on the main drag, so it does tend to be noisy, though the modern, efficient rooms are a good value at 3530 drs ($27.20) for a double with bath.

Saving the best value for last, we have the **Hotel Apollon** (tel. 0741/22-587), at 18 Pirinis. Run by Paul Spiropolis, this is a clean 18-room hotel. The first floor has been remodeled with wood paneling and all-tile bathrooms, so if you need a quick bed, try for this. Many rooms have a small terrace, and all of them are noisy! Singles begin at 2320 drs ($17.80) and doubles at 3360 drs ($25.80); if you stay more than three days you can get a reduced price.

All the above hotels serve breakfast (except the Bellevue). For meals you should go either to the **Diethnes Restaurant,** in the main platia, or **Taverna Anaxagoras,** an excellent and inexpensive place to eat; it's along the water, near the center of town.

Useful Information

Buses from new to old Corinth (Acrocorinth) leave from Ermou and Kolianou Streets, behind the park. They run every hour between 7 a.m. and 8 p.m. and return on the half hour. It's a pleasant 15- to 25-minute ride and the fare is 75 drs (60¢). The buses that run to Nafplion and Athens leave every hour from the corner of Konstantinou and Aratou Streets. . . .

There's a **railway station** for those who ride the rails. . . . If you walk away from the harbor on Vass. Konstantinou, there are two **banks.** . . . The **area code** is 0741. . . .

If you have to kill some time or if you're just in the mood (John always is) you can catch a Greek **movie** at the two theaters on Damaskinou, one near the Ephira Hotel, the other near the Bellevue Hotel.

ANCIENT CORINTH: On a plateau at the base of the Acrocorinth mountain stands the remains of the ancient city of Corinth, all that's left of what once was the most powerful precinct in all of Greece. It occupied the land bridge between the mainland and the Peloponnese, a position it took full advantage of early on in its history by charging exorbitant tolls to those who would cross the isthmus in order to trade. To defend herself Corinth became a great maritime power, able to dominate both the Corinth and Saronic gulfs because of her ability to move ships overland to the sea almost immediately.

Corinth reached its zenith in the fifth century B.C. In 44 B.C. Caesar stepped in to turn it into a Roman colony. Archeologists started to dig in 1896 and have yet to stop (the most recent excavations are across the street from the site where the Asklepion has been found); the remains they've found are those of Roman times. Under Roman rule the name of Corinth became synonymous with luxury and pleasure to excess, an image it shared with Spartan women, said to be the most pampered and glamorous of all. A legend has it that the local harlots wore sandals that left the impression "Follow Me" in the fine sand. One of the Roman ruins found so far is the Peirene Fountain, an enclosed-courtyard type of area with a central "pool" that looks about the size of an Olympic pool, now overgrown with flowers. Arched entryways flanked by pieces of columns complete the sight.

One of the very few remains from the Greek period, and the most outstanding, is the **Temple of Apollo,** built in the sixth century B.C., one of the oldest in Greece. It stands on a bluff overlooking the ancient marketplace, with 7 of the original 17 columns still standing. Next door is the **museum,** filled with sculpture, friezes, and other relics found during the digs there. Be sure to glance at the fine display, next to the museum, of the evolution of Greek columnar architecture, culminating in the highly decorative Corinthian style. With its Roman mosaic floors the museum is the perfect place to come in out of the sun during the summer; you can picnic in the inner courtyard. Admission is 375 drs ($2.90), half price for students. The site is open Monday through Saturday from 8 a.m. to 7 p.m. (8:45 a.m. to 3 p.m. during the off-season), on Sunday from 8 a.m. to 5:45 p.m.

At the top of the Acrocorinth, overlooking the site, is the **Fort of Acrocorinth,** a huge fortress with foundations dating from ancient times. The rest was built and rebuilt by various other groups, including the Byzantines, Franks, and Turks. The uppermost part was originally the Temple of Aphrodite, where 1,000 sacred courtesans "initiated" visitors in the art of love. It is said that merchants from around the world would arrive with fabulous gifts and rare treasures for the girls, who were supposedly masters at their trade (all in the service of the goddess, of course).

If you've brought a picnic, you can wander over to your favorite areas to discover your own secret pleasures. If you haven't there's the **Taverna Acrocorinth**. It features a great view, cool drinks, and souvenirs. Lunch will run about 800 drs ($6.10) per person. You can stop at an ancient fountain at the first bend of the unpaved road, where modern plumbing provides you with cool running water.

To get to the Acropolis, you can hire a taxi for 150 drs ($1.10) per person, each direction. They operate on a shuttle system and usually wait until the cab is full. Otherwise you can hike up to the site, a one- to two-hour trip up an unpaved road. The reward for this sacrifice is the many gorgeous vistas you'll see at every bend in the road.

The **Ekdotike Guide** is very informative and makes a nice souvenir.

Accommodations and Dining

Our number one place to stay *and* dine is the **Taverna Dafni** (tel. 0741/31-225), run by Anastosias Dafni. It's opposite the BP station (the sign was broken when we last visited) on the main road to the ancient site, about 500 meters before the entrance. There are several such taverns on this road, but this one, with its "room" sign and multilingual stenciled tablecloths, caught our fancy. The seven rooms are clean and spacious, with small balconies and a view of the valley. Mr. Dafni prides himself as being something of a "specialista" in local cuisine, and the samples that we tried were delicious. The taverna features spit-roasted lamb, yogurt, fresh fruit, pastries, and retsina. A single room here will run you 2880 drs ($22.10); a double is the same price!

Some people use Athens as their base camp for the Peloponnese, but we think we've found a place much nicer and easier in terms of access to all the little towns; and that's . . .

2. Nafplion (Nauplion)

Nafplion (Nauplion) is a city of Venetian fortresses with an ancient harbor, engaging restaurants and cafés, and an almost idyllic serenity. Flower gardens are scattered throughout the area. If the resonance of the city's church bells don't wake you in the morning, then the street cries, moans, chirps, and whistles will do the trick.

We were in Nafplion the week before the Greek Easter and were treated to a preview of the choral dirge that is traditionally performed on the holiday. The entire city appeared to be in a state of preparation. As we walked the narrow streets, we'd peek into windows and see locals practicing their dances.

Nafplion is so inviting that you might consider taking a breather from the usual "If this is Tuesday it must be Sparta" program that most travelers adhere to. By bus or car, Nafplion is the ideal spot to stay for visits to Corinth, Argos, Mycenae, Epidaurus, and the rest of the Argolid.

In antiquity Nafplion was a great naval power; in the third century B.C. fortifications were built on a sheer rise from the sea straight up on the southern side of town. One fort, the Palamidi, still towers over the town. The town itself is situated right on the Gulf of Acropolis, 90 miles from Athens.

USEFUL INFORMATION: There are no trains to Nafplion, so you'll have to get off in nearby Argos; it's about a five-hour proposition from Athens, and half that from Corinth. You can rent a car in Nafplion from **Staikos** (tel. 27-950) for about $40 per day. The **bus station** is at Nikitara Square. Buses for Argos leave every half hour, those to Athens almost every hour, the bus to Mycenae at 10 a.m., noon, and 2 p.m., and those to other towns three or four times a day. The **O.T.E.** office is open daily from 6 a.m. to 11 p.m. and is across the street from the bus station (the **area code** is 0752). At the bus station in Nafplion you can buy a copy of the best **map** of the area we found. It has a bright orange cover and is called "Peloponnisos" (published by F. Lappas, the same man who did our favorite map of Athens!). The map is in English, French, and German and has street plans for six of the most important towns in the Peloponnese. It costs 500 drs ($3.85) and is well worth it.

We very much liked the shop owned by George Agathos and Sigrid Ebeling, called **Camara,** located at 3 Spiliadou, near the paralia. This fascinating emporium sells contemporary silver jewelry (made by Sigrid) and a wide assortment of antiques, rugs, and other Greek objets d'art.

ACCOMMODATIONS: The **Hotel Dioscouri** (tel. 0752/28-550), at the corner of Zygomala and Byronos, has C-class prices with an A-class view! You'll find this very popular place by walking up the same steps as to the Hotel Leto (see below) and turning right. One more block down and you'll find the Dioscouri. Its 51 rooms are standard, but it's those views from the front and side rooms that make it worthwhile. A double with bath goes for 5250 drs ($40.40), a single for 4000 drs ($30.75). Breakfast is included in the price.

If you don't need a private bathroom or an elevator, there's one pension with such charm and personality that it alone is a good reason to stay in Nafplion. Just off the harbor in a lovely old villa, the **Hotel Otto** (tel. 0752/27-585), named after the first king of the Greek Republic, is a block from the water at 2 Farmakopoulon. A picturesque little garden adjoins the hotel proper, with lemon, orange, and tangerine trees as well as a circular display of violets and roses. The Otto was a private home with a grand spiral staircase and an ornate painted ceiling that in 1962 became a D-class hotel. It charges 2125 drs ($16.35) for a single and 2500 drs ($19.25) for a double. For 250 drs ($1.92) you can savor breakfast in the scent-filled garden, where you can commune with a cage full of parakeets while tiny clay faces stare down at you from the parapets.

Three blocks from the harbor is the **Hotel and Pension Epidaurus** (tel. 0752/27-541), at the corner of Bikakis and Lambropoulos. The hotel has ten bright rooms with small terraces overlooking the street, the pension offers similar accommodations (18 rooms), with baths across the hall, for about 20% less. Highlighting the classic detailing of this old house is a spiral staircase winding up to gray eight-foot double doors framed in fresh sky-blue enamel paint. The rooms are clean and a double without bath is 2250 drs ($17.30); with private facilities, 2500 drs ($19.25).

Next in order of preference is the aforementioned **Leto Hotel** (tel. 0752/28-093), at 28 Zygomala. Paul Rekoumis and his two brothers own both the Leto and Otto hotels, and while the Leto is not as classic as the Otto, its charm is in its location. Follow Farmakopoulon past the Otto to the end of the street and walk up the three flights of stairs. On both sides you'll see the back streets of Nafplion, and they're wonderful. The rooms in the front have the best view; otherwise they're rather nondescript. Breakfast is served on a veranda that has a view of this city's graceful harbor, mountains, and roof tiles. A single without breakfast goes for 3065 drs ($23.55), a double for 3315 drs ($25.50), and a double with bath for about $2.50 more. Breakfast is about 250 drs ($1.92).

Off Platia Syntagma (Constitution Square) is the **Hotel Athena** (tel. 0752/27-695), with simple accommodations near a lovely square which serves as a playground for children and has two outdoor cafés. Singles are 2375 drs ($18.30) and doubles run 3125 drs ($24).

The last of our in-town recommendations is the pricey **Hotel Agamemnon** (tel. 0752/28-021), located on the waterfront to the right of the paralia at 3 Akti Miaouli. Mr. Katsaitis, your host, runs a 40-room establishment (34 doubles and 6 singles) with a large, pretty lobby covered in vines where you can sit and watch the harbor through huge picture windows. Half board is compulsory here, and though it may be lots of drachmas, the large doubles have gorgeous marble terraces which hang over the port. Singles are 4860 drs ($37.40) and doubles run 7645 drs ($58.80).

Finally, a note to campers: Campgrounds are to be found about two kilometers out of Nafplion on the road to Argos. These should be passed by; you'd do better to find accommodations near the harbor or Syntagma Square.

Splurge Accommodations

One of the most luxurious lodgings on the entire Peloponnese is the neoclassical-style **Hotel Amalia** (tel. 0752/24-401). This sprawling complex includes large, comfortable guest quarters, airy garden public spaces, and one of the most inviting swimming pools you'll ever find. The Amalia is located about four kilometers from the center of Nafplion, so a five-minute taxi ride is part of the package. If you don't mind the relative isolation, we couldn't imagine a more relaxing base. Doubles run 10,620 drs ($81.70), singles 7500 drs ($57.70), including breakfast.

DINING AND NIGHTLIFE: On the right-hand side of the harbor, looking out across the gentle waters of the Gulf of Argolis to the island of **Bourdzi**, are several popular cafés where both locals and tourists can sit or swing (yes, big swinging love-seats!) and admire the views. Walk past the Olympia and the Rendez-Vous to the last café, the **Aktaion**, which offers both the ambience of an older, classic café in a quiet setting and a wonderful homemade dessert called *galactaboureka*. Don't miss this special treat. From this vantage point you can see a medieval castle that stands on Bourdzi, the Pasqualigo, seemingly lit to kindle romance.

Be careful of the restaurants on Syntagma Square; most are tourist traps. However, we found one that we liked quite a lot. For at least 50 years the **Taverna Ellas,** on Syntagma Square, has served traditional Greek fare to locals. Though we've visited Nafplion many times it's only on our last trip that we discovered this choice outdoor eatery. Of their many good menu items the stuffed grape leaves were particularly flavorful and well prepared. Also recommended are their many vegetable entrées and an especially well-constructed moussaka. The price for two should be about 1000 drs ($7.70), making it an excellent value.

If you want to escape the more touristy restaurants, head for two ouzeries along the paralia beyond the fortifications (continue past the Hotel Agamemnon). The first waterside eatery is **Banieres** (tel. 28-125), where ouzo and a tasty selection of *mezes* (Greek appetizers) await. A meal of ouzo, *saganaki* (fried cheese), octopus, and salad will run about 500 drs ($3.80). During the high season Banieres is open for lunch and dinner daily. Next door is the **Omolos,** which is very similar in style and price to Banieres.

Another food option in Nafplion, and one that's romantic, is to make your own picnic and eat up at the Palamidi Fort or down by the harbor. Try the supermarket (**Babyfoods**) at 13 Amalias St. (one block from the Amymoni Hotel). It's stocked with a full deli-type selection, including canned fish, biscuits, and a wire rack filled with local specialties. The **Dolce Pâtisserie** across the street will round out your feast with its breadth of European and Greek sweets and homemade ice cream. On summer nights, this is the right place to be (open til 10 p.m.).

If you have a car (or are willing to shell out the drachmas for a taxi) there is a great taverna about five kilometers from Nafplion called **Lakis.** This moderately priced taverna is always jammed with Greeks, who appreciate the fine food that the kitchen turns out. To get there, drive about 10 minutes on the road to Nea Kios. Lakis is on the right.

If you want to sample an interesting segment of Greek nightlife a visit to a *boite* (a small music club) will certainly edify. One such establishment, frequented mostly by young Nafplian men, is **Sirena,** just off the paralia. A small electrified band plays a contemporary form of *rebetika,* a sort of Greek soul music. Dancing is spontaneous but taken seriously. The few women who attend are mostly guests of the Kamakis (young Greek studs) and are encouraged to join the festivities. It's best to go after 11 p.m., when the energy begins to build. Drinks are expensive, at 500 drs ($3.90), but for the same price you get a wonderful show.

WHAT TO SEE AND DO: Although its geographical proximity to Mycenae, Argos, Epidaurus, and Corinth is enough to recommend it as a base for sightseeing, Nafplion is interesting itself. Two blocks from the waterfront is **Syntagma Square**, the perfect small-town square with two cafés, a movie theater, a bookstore with some titles in English, a bank, and the Hotel Athena. On the west side of the square is the **archeological museum** (tel. 22-331), a three-story Venetian barrack with a small symbol of Saint Mark, the guardian of Venice, gracing the façade. Here the visitor finds a good collection of early and late Hellenic pottery, as well as finds from several Mycenaean sites. Top billing, however, goes to a remarkably well-preserved 15th-century B.C. Mycenaean suit of armor. Up front that probably doesn't sound too exciting as far as great treasures go, but see it and you'll understand—it's special. The museum is open 8:45 a.m. to 3 p.m. weekdays, 9:30 a.m. to 2:30 p.m. on weekends and holidays; closed Tuesdays. Admission is 200 drs ($1.54) for adults, half price for students.

The **Public Square** (Kolokotronis Square and Matsikas Street) has a park containing a children's playground, an outdoor taverna, some cafés, a fountain, and fast food! It's somewhat of a local hangout—a lot of life, a lot of color. The prices are better here in the shops and cafés than at other squares.

A light brick Byzantine-style building with a red-tiled dome dominates the west corner of Syntagma Square. This **Turkish mosque**, dating from the 19th century, was once the palace of the Turkish governor. It's used today for music recitals and other local events.

Mentioned earlier as a possible site for an outdoor picnic, the **Palamidi Fort**, perched on a crag over 700 feet high, is worth looking up to. To get to it, you can walk the 857 steps, or take a car, taxi, or bus up the mile and a half. The fort was built by the Venetians in the early 18th century, and its beauty is blinding. You'll enjoy the expansive view of the Argolid; we found the shade of the ramparts an inviting spot for a picnic lunch. Admission is 375 drs ($2.90) for adults, half-price for students. It's open 10 a.m. to 7 p.m. weekdays and closes at 3 p.m. on Sunday.

Staying in Tolos

If your only idea of a holiday in Greece means living every moment within sight of the beach, consider staying at the beach resort of Tolos, just 11 kilometers south of Nafplion. Several hotels line the shore road that overlooks a small beach and the clear waters of the Gulf of Argos. Chic small boutiques line both sides of the main street leading to the beach. On the beach you'll find the **Hotel Artemis** (tel. 59-458), which has a good restaurant. There are 19 rooms, many overlooking the water. A double goes for 3440 drs ($26.50). Another favorite was the **Hotel Tolo** (tel. 59-248), where Dimitris Skalidis makes all his guests feel special. The Tolo is located at 15 Leof. Bouboulinas, quite close to the beach. A clean and modern double room with bath and breakfast can be had for 4850 drs ($37.30). Buses going from Nafplion to Tolos and back leave every hour from their respective stations from 7 a.m. to 7 p.m. daily. It's a twenty-minute ride. Whether you stay in Nafplion or Tolos your first day trip should be to . . .

3. Epidaurus

Today the name of Epidaurus (pronounced E-pi-DAV-ros) is associated with the celebrated amphitheater, where summer productions of the Greek classics are held annually. To the ancient Greeks, though, Epidaurus was home to the most renowned Asclepion in the Hellenic world.

The **Asclepion**, or sanctuary to the god of healing, Asclepios, was built over a seventh-century B.C. shrine to Apollo Maleatas. Historians believe that Asclepios was a Thessalian king blessed with a talent for healing who eventually became deified for his abilities. Eventually the myth developed that he was in fact a son of Apollo who was trained in the healing arts by the wise centaur Chyron. Even the Oracle of Delphi, when prompted, assured his questioners that Asclepios had come from the town of Epidaurus and that a sanctuary there to him would be most important. By the fifth century B.C. the sanctuary, located near the villages of Ligourion and Palea (Old) Epidavros, drew the infirm from all parts of Greece. Within a century the Asclepion reached its peak. Most of the buildings whose remains can be seen date from this period. Belief in cult practices was diminishing, so the priests were training physicians, called *Asklepiadae,* who could treat patients in a more organized manner. Worshippers would come for a miracle cure, but stay for a longer period to rest, exercise, go to the theater, take mineral baths, and diet—then depart (probably healthier).

Stelae displayed in the museum record the 70 miracles of Asclepios and recipes for medicines and various treatments. By the fourth century A.D. foreign invaders and Christians laid waste to what was left of this sanctuary, but Asclepios' importance lives on Socrates' last words: "I owe a cock to Asclepios; do not forget, but pay it" (from *Dialogues of Plato,* "Phaedo").

THE ARCHEOLOGICAL MUSEUM AND SITE: The **museum** at Epidaurus is more than you could want. Tall Corinthian columns grace a façade trimmed with fragments of ancient sculptural frieze. Inside, bright galleries are lined with statuary and sculpture found at the Asclepion sanctuary. Most of the male figures are Asclepios; the female, Hygeia (they're mostly casts from originals in the National Museum of Athens). Plans and watercolors, coupled with reconstructed façades and pediments, give a vivid picture of the scope of the sanctuary. The *tholos* (called La Rotonde by the French archeologists) was an especially noteworthy construction, by Polycleitus the Younger, because of its shape, patterned floor, and interior maze design. Notice too the beautiful carved lilies and acanthus flowers that bloomed from the coffered ceilings.

The archeological site, which is still undergoing excavation, can be reached by a path behind the museum. The many stones in disarray represent the remains of the **Propyleon**, an Ionic-columned entryway; the **Abaton**, or Dormitory of Incubation, where patients slept so that Asclepios could come to cure them in their dreams; and a **Temple of Artemis**, Asclepios' aunt. Nearby was the two-story **Katagogion**, a full-amenities, 160-room guesthouse! The Stadium to the west was the site of the Pan-hellenic Games, held every four years. The huge Temple of Asclepios (380–375 B.C.) was designed by architect Theodotos, and once held a gold-and-ivory statue of the god, seated with his snakes and a dog by his side, that has never been recovered. The most impressive ruin, diagonally across the far end of the site, is the **Tholos**, whose concentric walls can still be discerned.

The archeological museum and site are open daily from 8 a.m. to 7 p.m., on Sunday from 8 a.m. to 6 p.m. The museum is closed on Tuesday. Admission is 375 drs ($2.90) for adults, half-price for students.

THE THEATER OF EPIDAURUS: "I never knew the meaning of peace until I arrived at Epidaurus," wrote Henry Miller. Only in 1900 did archeologists (who began working at the site in 1881) uncover the magnificent amphitheater that's come to symbolize the majesty of ancient Epidaurus. The theater, which is just east of the Asclepion, carved into the side of Mount Kynortion, once seated 14,000 healthy and recuperating spectators. Polycleitus the Younger is credited with designing this architectural masterpiece. Praise goes to the scenic landscaping, excellent acoustics, the orchestra (more than 20 meters in diameter), and well-arranged seating; even the poorest spectators enjoyed good sightlines and fine sound. The theater's excellent state of preservation when found enabled the Greek government to begin presenting the modern *epidauria* (drama festivals) there in 1954. Classic works by Euripides, Sophocles, Aristophanes, Aeschylus, and others are presented in the Greek language, and staged with an eye to their original production. Ignore the large speakers behind the orchestra, which are covered in styrofoam painted to look like rocks! The performances still make for an unforgettable evening of drama in an unforgettable setting.

Tickets to the same night's 9 p.m. performance can be purchased at the box office after 5 p.m. (usually sold out by 8 p.m.). Tickets range from 1000 drs ($7.70) to 2500 drs ($19.20), students 500 drs ($3.80), and can be purchased in advance in Athens at the Athens Festival Box Office, 4 Stadiou St., in the arcade (tel. 01/32-21-459 for information). Performances are given Saturday and Sunday nights between the end of June and mid-September; check with E.O.T. for the summer's schedule. The programs sold at the performance and at the box office beforehand have a translation of the entire play in English and cost 300 drs ($2.30).

USEFUL INFORMATION: The public **bus** goes from Athens twice daily to the site of Epidaurus for 910 drs ($7) each way; there are also several tour operators offering round-trip weekend excursions that include theater tickets and same-day, round-trip transport. There are three public buses daily between the site and the lovely port town of Nafplion, where you'll find a wide range of accommodations. (Palea Epidavros is about 18 kilometers away and has several hotels, but is just not as interesting as Nafplion.) There's an extra late-night bus on Saturday and Sunday returning to Nafplion or Palea Epidavros, at a fare of 400 drs ($3.10).

The tourist pavilion at the site is also the **Epidaurus Xenia Hotel** (tel. 0753/22-005). The 24 Xenia bungalows of hewn stone are neatly tucked in behind the pines and olives so as not to intrude on the classical setting. Double rooms with the Xenia's compulsory half-board plan are 7000 drs ($53.80) with private bath, 6000 drs ($46.10) with shared facilities. Book early.

4. Mycenae

Some of you may remember the name Mycenae (Mikines, pronounced Mi-KEY-nez) from high school, when you were forced to read Homer, or from art history texts depicting the gold masks unearthed there. A famous play was written about its king, Agamemnon, and his unhappy home life. Today Mycenae is a one-street town known for its truly magnificent, world-class archeological site. There are three buses daily from Nafplion to Mycenae, a pleasant one-hour ride that costs 300 drs ($2.30).

ANCIENT MYCENAE: In 1841 excavations were begun, but it wasn't until 33 years later that the German archeologist Heinrich Schliemann took an interest in Mycenae. He unearthed tombs, pieces of palaces and aqueducts, and other relics that were mentioned by Homer, thus establishing that Homer's writing was based on fact. The most famous of his finds is the **Acropolis.** The **Lions Gate,** on the newer, western wall, dates from 1250 B.C. and was the first discovery made by Schliemann when he began in 1876. The gate, once closed by two wooden and bronze doors, is capped by an 18-ton lintel supporting the famous lions, their front paws perched on pedestals. These cats announced to the world that within these walls was the mighty kingdom of Atreus.

As you pass through the Lions Gate, look to your right and you'll find the **Royal Cemetery**, the burial ground of 16-century B.C. Mycenaean kings. These six "shaft" graves (so named because the kings were buried standing up) held many of the most important ancient Greek artifacts. Some of these exquisite gold and silver artifacts—including the famous gold face mask that Schliemann thought was Agamemnon's—can be seen today in the National Archeological Museum in Athens. If you've brought a flashlight or lighter, walk to the top and straight into an ancient cistern.

At the top of the Acropolis are the few remnants of the **Grand Palace**, which archeologists have learned included a throne room, a great court (it's foundations still remain), and the megaron, the offical reception hall, whose frescoed walls can be reconstructed by the imaginative visitor from the fragments on display in the National Archeological Museum in Athens. Athens notwithstanding, there's plenty to see and savor here.

The Acropolis is three kilometers away from the Corinth–Argos road and is open 8 a.m. to 7:30 p.m. daily, Sunday until 6 p.m. Admission is 375 drs ($2.90) for adults, half-price for students.

Keep your ticket from the main site and take it and yourself over to the **Treasury of Atreus,** known also as the Tomb of Agamemnon. It's a huge, magnificent empty cone of gargantuan proportions with extraordinary acoustical characteristics and the coolest spot to be found during the hot Mycenaean summer, so you might consider it before you have lunch somewhere else. The *dromos* (corridor) approach to the tomb is nearly 100 feet long, and the interior of the *tholos* (a beehive-shaped tomb) was once entirely decorated in bronze. The cavity at the right is believed to have been used to store excess skeletons, as the main chamber was filled steadily over generations. Several tholos have been excavated in the vicinity of the Mycenae mound, and because of their scale and grandeur, names of the principal members of the House of Atreus (Agamemnon) have been assigned them. All the great funerary objects discovered here come from the circular grave mounds mentioned above.

As of this writing, the new museum is still under construction. When it finally opens it is planned that it will contain most of the Mycenaean treasures now housed in the National Archeological Museum in Athens.

ACCOMMODATIONS AND DINING: The **Hotel La Petit Planète** (tel. 0751/66-240), run by Dimitrios Dassis, is a bright, sunny, and spacious hotel directly on the road to the ancient site. Many groups stop here and lunch at midday under the hotel's covered veranda. If you're lucky enough to get a room here, you'll have a wonderful view from either the front or back rooms. The Planète is only open from March to October, and in the summer months you have to have a written reservation at least one month in advance. This C-class hotel is very clean and has a bar/restaurant. The price of a single is 3580 drs ($27.50), a double checks in at 5170 drs ($39.75).

La Belle Hélène (tel. 0751/66-225) is also run by Mr. Dassis and has a welcome sign reading "Heinrich Schliemann's Haus, Erbaut 1862." Even if your're not German or an archeology student (take a look at their guest book, dating from 1878, for the list of luminaries), you'll be interested in this charming inn. Take the plank-wood stairs up to Room 3, where the Herr himself slept; its windows open out onto a view of one of his greatest accomplishments. At 2500 drs ($19.25) for a double, including breakfast, this is a find.

The **Hotel Agamemnon** (tel. 0751/66-222), at 3 Ch. Tsounta St., may be a bargain at 3750 drs ($28.85) for a double in this very heavily touristed area. The hotel's modern, grand façade hides eight mediocre rooms and a sunny dining room seating 600! All rooms have bath and shower, and breakfast is 375 drs ($2.90).

For you campers, there are two possibilities: **Camping Atreus**, the first campground as you enter the city (tel. 0751/66-221), which is 310 drs ($2.40) per person; and **Camping Mycenae** (tel. 0751/66-247), opposite the Belle Hélène. This campground has ten sites for pitching tents and 20 for bus groups for about the same sum.

There are several places to eat, all surprisingly similar: **Achilleys**, the **Menelaos**, the **Electra** café, **Omphos Homer**, and the **Iphigenia Restaurant**. Omphos Homer is about one kilometer from the site on the main road, and also has rooms to let, as do the Electra and Iphigenia. the Iphigenia is at the turnoff to the site, has youth-hostel rooms to let, and serves pretty decent food.

5. Argos

Thirteen kilometers from Mycenae is Argos, home of the (surprise!) Argonauts, who actually sailed from Volos. According to legend, Argos is the oldest town of the Argolid, dating from prehistoric times. Around the end of the sixth century B.C. the name Argos became synonymous with fine pottery and sculpture, particularly metal and bronze work, at which Hageladas and Polycleitos excelled to such an extent that their names were known throughout the Hellenic world and still survive today.

As you arrive in Argos you'll notice the hills of **Larissa** and **Aspida**. On top of Larissa (the higher hill), watching over the strategic plains of the Argolid, sits a Venetian fortress on the site of an original acropolis, later joined by Byzantine and Turkish fortifications. It remains in such good condition that its use in the 1821 War of Independence turned the tide for the Greeks (who held the Peloponnese against the Turkish onslaught). The low-to-the-ground white houses of the modern town are on the same site as the ancient city. Today the town has about 16,000 inhabitants, a lively public market, and a yearly fair that takes place on October 1. Argos is a half-hour bus ride from Nafplion. There are buses every half-hour from 6 a.m. to 7 p.m. daily.

WHAT TO SEE: At the southeast foot of Larissa Hill lies the fourth-century B.C. **Amphitheater of Argos**. Even larger (though now less impressive) than the one at Epidaurus, this theater has 81 tiers cut from rock and was designed to seat 20,000. It was remodeled twice, the second time (in the early fourth century B.C.) in order to turn the orchestra into a water tank where nautical combat would be performed! To make it watertight, the floor was paved with blue-and-white marble. Commanding the top row of this wondrous structure is a fat yucca. Excavations continue at the site on the lower levels. You can drive or walk through (off the road to Tripolis) from 9 a.m. to 6 p.m. weekdays, 10 a.m. to 3 p.m. on Sunday.

Next to the theater are the ruins of the **Roman baths**. Actually they're below the amphitheater, but the first thing you see, near the theater, is a large hall with a crypt containing three sarcophagi. This room, thought to be the reception room, is connected to the dressing room by means of a vestibule, which in turn is connected to the *frigidarium* (the cold-water room). Here there are three pools, dating from the second century A.D. The tall red-brick structure to the left (in front of the theater) is what remains of the **aqueduct** that serviced the city of Argos and fed the baths and swimming pool.

Near the main square in the city center is the **archeological museum**, which has the most interesting finds made by the French School at Athens. As you enter the garden in the front of the museum, turn left and you'll come to a covered arcade that houses a fine collection of Roman mosaics from a large private home (probably fifth century). The second floor of this museum houses some wonderful sculpture. Our favorite was a three-foot-tall image of Pyonaysis and a goat, taken from the theater in Argos. Museum hours are the same as for the amphitheater.

If you decide to stay in Argos, there are two small D-class hotels in town (Argos isn't so wonderful that you'll want to go first class): the **Hermes** (tel. 0751/27-510), at 10 Vass. Konstantinou, and the **Theoxenia** (tel. 0751/27-370), up the street at 31 Tsokri; doubles run about 2300 drs ($15.40).

TIRYNS: Twelve kilometers from Argos by a road with mountains on one side and sea on the other are the ruins of the Mycenaean acropolis of Tiryns, with its walls of cyclopean masonry, so called because the ancients believed Cyclops himself built them to protect the king of Tiryns, Proteus. Tiryns was fortified at least two generations before Mycenae; the fortification dates back to the 13th century B.C. and is a great treat for the modern visitor. The upper level, or palace site, is surrounded by those huge, handmade walls (trolleys are used by archeologists working at the lower level to move much smaller stones from the site). The entrance to the palace is chariot width, identical to the one at Mycenae, but these ruins are in better shape and thus more impressive. Excavation is still in progress at the lower level to try to uncover the foundations of several dwellings, among them the Lower Castles, which were rebuilt after a 13th-century B.C. earthquake and survived well into the Mycenaean age. These ruins are open from 9 a.m. to 7 p.m. weekdays, 10 a.m. to 5 p.m. on Sunday. Admission is 375 drs ($2.90) for adults, half price for students.

CENTRAL PELOPONNESE (ARCADIA)

The central Peloponnese, an immensely mountainous region of great beauty, is as it must have been thousands of years ago. Its inhabitants were thought by Herodotus in his *Histories* to be the oldest residents of the Peloponnese. The original Arcadians consisted of several different tribes, who united for the first time when they fought in the Trojan War. Arcadian independence began on September 23, 1821, with the capture of Tripolis, today the capital of the Central Peloponnese. Tripolis itself was then leveled six short years later, and rebuilt completely in 1827.

Several small towns circle Tripolis: Nestani is north of the capital, as is Mantinea, and both have interesting ruins and monasteries. Farther north is Levidion, with its Temple to Artemis Hymnia. To the southwest is Vytina, a famous winter resort for Greeks. Megalopolis lies 34 miles from Tripolis, surrounded by mountains and remnants of its rich past. Nearby is the Temple of Apollo at Vassae (which you will see spelled as "Bassae"). This temple is so extraordinary that we urge you to see it; even if the thought of another ruin makes you wince, let the magic of this Doric masterpiece fill your senses.

All the towns are served well by public transport, but travel is slow. Drivers making an arc through the northern Peloponnese can cut across and see these sites between Nafplion and Olympia. The landscape changes steadily, from the low, dry hills of the Argolid to the often snow-capped peaks of the Taigetos and Parnon mountains that surround Sparta.

6. Tripolis

Today's Tripolis is the communications hub for the Peloponnese. Primarily an industrial center, it still has the markets that historically have always been the source of income for the fertile farms of the outlying towns. There's not a lot to see in Tripolis, but you may find yourself stuck there after the two-hour bus ride from Argos; all the hotels we mention are between the two bus stations.

The **Galaxy Hotel** (tel. 071/22-5195) is at the central square, Georgiou Square. It's an 80-room, C-class establishment run by Mr. Marinakos with spacious clean rooms, piped-in Muzak, and small balconies overlooking the Aghios Vassilious Church. These make the Galaxy a better bet than you'd think if you judged it by its small, spare lobby. Singles are 2235 drs ($17.20); doubles, 3275 drs ($25.20). Even the singles have double beds, and all rooms have baths.

In the B-class category, the **Arcadia Hotel** (tel. 071/22-55-51), right on Kolokotroni Square, offers a great marble-floored dining hall with columns and clean, bright rooms at 3910 drs ($30.10) for a double and 2510 drs ($19.30) for a single. All the rooms have baths, and there's a bar/restaurant also.

There are many pleasant tavernas (all moderately priced) overlooking Georgiou Square, a potentially nice respite in an otherwise unremarkable, busy town. If only they'd turn on the fountains! There is the **Galaxy Café** in Central Square, which is terrific for coffee and Greek pastries. Scout around for cafés; there are plenty from which to choose.

You can reach Tripolis by bus from Nafplion (about 1½ hours) or Argos. There are several trains a day. There's a pleasing variety of color in the country-side between Argos and Tripolis, making the drive a very nice alternative.

7. Megalopolis

Megalopolis today is a large, modern town that stands near the ruins of the ancient town of the same name, about 35 kilometers north of Tripolis. About eight kilometers out of town you descend into a valley by a series of hairpin turns that reward you with a fine view of the entire plain. The fourth-century B.C. ruins of Megalopolis are in such a picturesque setting that they're well worth the minor detour if you're en route from Tripolis, Sparta, or Calamata to Olympia.

An optimistic Epaminondas (famed for his leadership of Thebes) founded Megalopolis ("large city") as a planned Utopian community during the years 371–368 B.C. Hoping to create cities (including Messene and Mantinaea) to contain the aggressive Spartans, he convinced 40 smaller cities to unite into one huge capital. Villagers from all parts of Arcadia emigrated to Megalopolis. Unfortunately, dissension among the relocated inhabitants and the city's forced entry into a coalition against Sparta brought about a very swift decline. Though the town was rebuilt several times, by the time it was visited by Pausanias in the second century A.D. it lay in ruins.

THE ARCHEOLOGICAL SITE: The **amphitheater** of Megalopolis was the largest in all of Greece, seating nearly 20,000. There was a water channel that encircled the stage to allow for enhanced acoustics, so the actors' voices could be heard in the last row! These same rows are now filled with swinging evergreens, which make the bleachers a great spot for a picnic lunch.

Behind the stage, to the north of the site, are the column remains of the **Thersilion,** a congress hall which seated 6,000 and had standing room for an additional 10,000. It was built to ensure that the Arcadian Confederacy had a meeting place, and if you've ever been involved with "government by committee," you can understand why Megalopolis wasn't around for long. The uniformed guard (Mr. Ilias Diavolichin) opens the site when he arrives in the morning (8 a.m.? 9 a.m.?) and closes it at 3:30 p.m.; in the interim he enthusiastically greets all visitors with the facts and figures he knows about Megalopolis, and he does so in almost every language! There's no fee to see the site, and we found out the hard way that he becomes offended if you offer him a tip for his help.

FOOD AND LODGING: If you want to stay over in Megalopolis there are two hotels, both located two blocks off the main square, where you turn off to go to the theater. The **Pan Hotel** (tel. 0791/22-270) charges 3125 drs ($24) for a double, as does the **Achillion Hotel** (tel. 0791/23-276). There is a great produce market every Friday on the street in front of the Achillion Hotel. On the Andritsena road to Karitena is what one archeologist told us was *his* favorite part of excavating this site, the **Karvouniara Taverna.** He claims that they serve the finest grilled baby goat and lamb anywhere in all of Greece. Back in town we enjoyed a simple grill, **Meraklis,** across from the Pan Hotel. Also, **Taverna Karthvelia** serves find Greek food at low prices.

KARITENA: On the road from Megalopolis to Andritsena there is a fork on the right that leads to Karitena; take it. Karitena is a picture-perfect medieval town perched on the slopes of adjoining hills. From the town there's a wonderful view of the Alfios River as it winds through the Likeo Valley below. The bus to Andritsena stops in Karitena, turns around and goes back downhill. If you've been riding too long, deboard at the fork, where there's an ouzeri, and wait the 15 minutes for the bus to return, continuing on to Andritsena.

8. Andritsena and Vassae (Bassae)

ANDRITSENA: This is a lovely mountain village with hillside homes, foliage, and an old church, all of which make it a worthy stop on the way to Vassae (Ba-SEH). The best thing is the air; in the deep summer it's crisp and light, in winter invigorating. If you've ever been to India, summer here will remind you of the imperial retreats to which the British escaped during the summer months, only less luxurious.

If you want to stop in Andritsena for the night (and bus riders may have to), there are two places we can recommend: the Pan and the Xenia Hotel and Restaurant. The **Hotel Pan** (tel. 0626/22-213) is at the north end of town. It has only six rooms: a double is 2000 drs ($15.40) and all the rooms are small and neat. They have a small marble staircase that is lined with voracious plants. The best café in town, which doubles as the bus station, is across the street.

The **Xenia Hotel and Restaurant** (tel. 0626/22-219), at the south end of town, is a somewhat bigger (40 rooms) C-class hotel that is also more expensive: doubles without bath cost 3620 drs ($27.90); with bath 4500 drs ($34.60). The rooms are clean and spacious; they also have a great view of the mountains. The manager is willing to bargain over the rates, so go to it. There is a weird collection of needlepoint, including Greek, European, and Walt Disney pieces!

The main square has a taverna that is good and a hotel opposite that's not. There's a bank up the block, at 340 Apollonos.

VASSAE (BASSAE): Located 14 miles outside of Andritsena, at the end of a winding, mountainous, and dusty road, is Vassae. From this road you have a fine view of the village and the Alpheus Valley; but not until the top can you see one of mankind's greatest works of art, the **Temple of Vassae.**

The temple is set on a rocky plateau nestled in the highlands (and oaks) of Arcadia. Like Delphi, the setting itself is inspiring, commanding a broad view of the surrounding hills and ravines. Respectful of its natural setting, the temple stands alone, aware of its own grace and majesty. Because of its isolated location the temple is not a popular stop for tourists, but those who go will be well rewarded. You'll have to have a car or take a taxi to see it, as there's no public transportation. The taxi from Andritsena costs a steep 1500 drs ($11.50) per person, but it's worth it. The driver will wait up to one hour and then whisk you through the clouds back to town. This isolation served the Phygalians well, who hid in the hills around Vassae during their retreat from the Spartan army. They erected the temple to thank their god for saving them from a plague that descended during the Peloponnesian War.

The Vassae temple was built by the famed architect Iktinos, the same man who brought you the Parthenon in Athens. Unlike the Parthenon, however, the Vassae temple is made of limestone, hewn from the huge deposits in the area. Vassae is a much-studied structure because it encompasses the three great Greek architectural traditions: Doric, Ionic, and Corinthian. As you approach the temple from the main path look carefully at the columns facing you at the front. Then you'll understand how Iktinos was able to integrate these three differing styles into one cohesive whole.

Although the temple is often shrouded in scaffolding, it remains one of the best preserved temples in Greece. Unfortunately, you will have to go to London to see the exquisite frieze that once adorned Vassae, for, like its more renowned Athenian cousin, the sculptures are on display at the British Museum.

From Andritsena, point yourself toward the city that was so famed for the valor and strength of its inhabitants that it never thought it necessary to build protective walls around its perimeters. Only one town fits that description: Sparta. If you're busing it this means backtracking to Tripolis, a 2½-hour ride from Andritsena. You can get to Sparta in half a day, but once you get there you'll probably have to spend the night because you will have missed all the connecting buses to anywhere!

9. Sparta

Ancient Sparta was a mélange of five communities within four villages built on six hills under one set of laws. This curious experiment was launched in the ninth century B.C., when a race of Dorians invaded the Laconian plain and subsequently settled there to mix with the locals. These four villages were brought together by a man who is both a historical *and* a legendary figure, the legislator Lykourgos, who set down the laws and principles of this new state, Sparta. He felt that three classes of inhabitants, two kings, and one senate were needed to ensure stability. The constitution he drafted was so strong this new state remained intact for centuries.

After the Persian war Sparta became increasingly jealous of Athens's influence. This led to the bloodbath known as the Peloponnesian War, which lasted nearly 30 years. Sparta emerged the victor, but her dominance in Hellenic affairs was diminished by the toll the fighting had taken. This decline continued, and today Sparta is little more than a stop on the way to Mystra. The town is devoid of charm or character, and even the ruins disappoint—understandably, since from the sixth century B.C. on austerity was Sparta's modus operandi, and this applied to architecture and the arts as well as to daily life. So ended an experiment in urban development that left its mark on history.

ACCOMMODATIONS: If you plan to stay in Sparta, there are several hotels to choose from. Our favorite was the **Hotel Maniatis** (tel. 0731/22-665), at the corner of Paleologou and Dion. Dafnou. The Maniatis is popular with groups as it has 80 clean, air-conditioned rooms, all with private bath. It also has a large, comfortable TV lounge and restaurant. Its moderate prices—4440 drs ($34.15) for a double with breakfast—also help to make it a popular C-class spot for singles too.

In the same league is the **Hotel Apollon** (tel. 0731/22-491), at Thermopylon and Frederikis Streets. This clean and modern hotel boasts small bright rooms that overlook the surrounding hills. The pale-blue hallway is lit by big picture windows, and potted ivy snakes up the marble staircase. With all the amenities of a deluxe hotel (private bathrooms, elevator, air conditioning, etc.), plus the friendliness of the Katranis family, the Apollon is a warm and comfortable place to rest a while. Single rooms start at 2875 drs ($22.10) and doubles at 3750 drs ($28.50).

If you've come to Sparta primarily to see Mystra, then you might consider staying at the **Hotel Sparti** (tel. 0731/21-343), at 46 Aghissilaou, about three blocks from the bus station on a side street. The Sparti is, well, Spartan: the rooms are clean and spare and the manager is polite and reserved. Doubles are inexpensive—2000 drs ($15.40)—and best of all, it's half a block from the bus stop for Mystra.

Last is the **Hotel Cecil** (tel. 0731/24-980), at 1 Stadiou. Mr. Tzanetakis is your host, and he presides over a 13-room, D-class establishment that is close by the central square in town. Due to this proximity it does tend to be noisy, but the prices are so inexpensive that you may find it worthwhile: singles are 1000 drs ($7.70); doubles, 1850 drs ($14.20). Baths and showers are on each floor.

DINING: Near the Hotel Cecil are three inexpensive and good tavernas. The **Richia Grill**, opposite the Cecil, features souvlaki, grilled lamb, draft Löwenbräu, and fries. Two people can gorge themselves for 1300 drs ($10) by ordering the half kilo of grilled lamb with french fries and salad. Around the corner is the **National Taverna**, which is also good. The **Golden Key** (nearby) features cheap American food if you're feeling homesick, and the **Leski** (by city hall) is great for dessert and coffee afterward, as is the **Entelvais Café,** with its exotic variety of pastries and drinks.

WHAT TO SEE: Just 1½ blocks east of the central square, on Lykourgo Street, is the **Museum of Sparta**. It houses a small, somewhat eclectic collection of statues, friezes, mosaics, and pottery ranging from the sixth century B.C. to the second century A.D., all from Spartan excavation sites. There are also some fine bronze sculptures and clay pieces. This museum is for the classics buff, the hardy Spartaphile, or those with a half hour to kill in town. There's also a fragrant, charming garden in the front laden with shaded benches for contemplation of the statuary that surrounds you. The hours here are 8:30 a.m. to 2:30 p.m. Monday through Saturday, 9 a.m. to 2 p.m. on Sunday. Admission is 350 drs ($2.70).

At the north end of the city (about a ten-minute walk from the Hotel

Apollon) is the site of **Ancient Sparta**. To visit this site, leave town by the Tripolis road until you reach Leonidas Street; turn left, and about 300 yards farther down the road you'll see the "tomb" of Leonidas. Up a dusty road and through a grove of olive trees you'll find five column bases, some old stones, the echo of a theater, and a very nice vista of the city. Beyond are the ruins of two Byzantine churches and a Roman portico. Little remains of such a great power except legend.

10. Mistra (Mystra)

Mistra, the Byzantine ghost town that lies 4½ kilometers west of Sparta in the foothills of Mount Taygetos, is populated today by birds, wildflowers, and rabbits.

If you visit Mistra in spring you'll see the wildflower population running wild on the hills and in the cracks of the ruins. An equally colorful variety of birds and insects have also made Mistra their home. If you hike up the worn stairs and criss-cross the paths of this solitary spot, hearing the donkeys' bells and studying the abstract shapes of the ruined buildings as you ascend, you can then rest in the shade of a tree (older than most countries) that is guaranteed to transport you to a world, ascetic and removed, where you can coexist with the spirits of those monks who inhabited this place 500 years ago.

The spirit of old Mistra is reflected in her beautiful churches, which include **Peribleptos,** with its wall paintings; the **Evangelistria,** which boasts sculptured decor; the **Monastery of Pantanassa** and its frescoes; and **St. Demetrios Church,** in the lower city, whose architecture, paintings, and mosaics are expert examples of Byzantine art. At the summit is **St. George's Church**, which is in the best condition and whose assorted emblems testify to the influence the Franks had here.

GETTING THERE: Drivers will leave Sparta by the Eurotas road, heading toward the Taygetos mountains through groves of orange, almond, and olive trees. The bus stop for Mistra is at the corner of Agisilaou and Leof. Lykourgou. There is a schedule posted on the back of the stainless-steel support on the corner. Buses depart about every 1½ hours, and are 100 drs (77¢). The last bus leaves around 5 p.m., as the site closes at 7 p.m. The town of Mistra itself, one to two kilometers below the ancient city, exists (like many others) solely to service the vast hordes of tourists that pass through. If you're feeling particularly hardy you may want to walk from town to the entrance of old Mistra; if you've come by bus from Sparta (if you're lucky it'll drop you off at the Xenia Restaurant) you will certainly hoof it up the hill. In any case, try to get there during the morning before the noonday sun discourages your most valiant efforts to explore.

Admission to Mistra is 375 drs ($2.90), half-price for students. Hours are 9 a.m. to 7 p.m. weekdays, 10 a.m. to 4 p.m. on Sunday. You should wear suitable clothing (no shorts or halter tops, etc.).

USEFUL INFORMATION: There is one hotel in Mistra and one campground. The hotel is the **Byzantion** (tel. 0731/93-309), a B-class hotel with 22 plain and unexceptional rooms; singles go for 2500 drs ($19.25), doubles for 3750 drs ($28.85). It's closed during the winter, when you're better off staying in Sparta for the night.

If you get hungry you might try the medium-priced **Byzantium** (across from the hotel), which features meat dishes, pasta dishes, and, best of all, cold drinks. Under the maple tree in the main square is a snackbar/cafeteria with very inexpensive prices, where you can privately negotiate for a room, though it's not legal. Just below the site and in a gorgeous setting is Marmara, one of the better cafés in the area.

The **campground** can be found halfway between Sparta and Mistra, behind a gas station that is easily sighted.

We hope you take the time to see Mistra. It isn't only the vestiges of the Byzantine age that make Mistra a must, this is an oasis from modern life, and as such, is very special.

SOUTHERN PELOPONNESE

11. Monemvassia

We could say that the port city of Monemvassia (95 kilometers southeast from Sparta) is in the Top Ten of the most beautiful and unspoiled spots on the Aegean coast. But go three kilometers out of town over a narrow stone causeway to the "Gibraltar of Greece," and you'll find the real Monemvassia, which has earned this exalted standing among visitors in-the-know. It's a 13th-century Byzantine village, more complete than Mistra architecturally, yet more overrun by flowers too. Tucked away on the south face of a hill, shadowed by an imposing fort, is Paradise.

Zeus in his wisdom knew that if he spared Monemvassia from classical ruins or sandy beaches, it would be spared hordes of tourists. When you enter the vaulted gates to this walled community, you'll be delighted by the unspoiled charm and tender beauty of the quiet village. A few cafés and a couple of souvenir shops pepper the main path, but they're nestled in the grottoes of the original Byzantine dwellings. On top of the hillside is the 13th-century **Aghia Sophia,** similar in style to the Byzantine church at Dafni. The crystal-clear, inviting Aegean below you can be gotten to by the paths that corkscrew down the hill.

ACCOMMODATIONS: One of the greatest assets of this mesmerizing, remote paradise is the **Hotel Malvasia** (tel. 0732/61-435), which occupies the restored mansion in the old castle and has 15 handcrafted suites complete with living rooms decorated in woven flokotis, kitchenettes, and solid-marble bathrooms. This is the life-work of Iannis Ilias, its proud and talented owner; we can only direct you to find him as follows: walk to the square in front of the white-and-blue church, then proceed down the footpath through anemones, daisies, and honeysuckle to the nearest geranium bush. If you spot gray hair peeking out from behind the few café tables outside no. 58, then you've found him. The perfect apartments blend in so naturally with the natural setting that Frank Lloyd Wright would have been impressed. It could be a marvelous vacation resort, a romantic port, or an idyllic retreat for the weary traveler who wants something more. Try to get here before it becomes Paradise Lost! The rates are 6250 drs ($48.10) for a double; family suites range from 7000 drs ($53.80) to 11000 drs ($86.50).

For those we have failed to convince, there are other lodgings on the mainland, just a 15-minute walk over the causeway from the medieval city on the headland. In order of preference we'll start with the **Aktaion Hotel** (tel. 0732/61-234), located on the waterfront in Monemvassia village and housed in the second floor of a popular restaurant. Many of the 18 rooms have balconies, which offer the view of a yacht basin and the headland rock; at 2905 drs ($22.30), for a double without shower, the Aktaion is the best value on the mainland. Breakfast is only 300 drs ($2.20).

There is the **Akroyali** (tel. 0732/61-202), on the main street at 17 Spartis, half a block below the post office and two blocks up from the Aktaion. This E-class hotel has eight clean and modern rooms (with toilets in the hall) that at

2700 drs ($20.80) for a double makes this a comfortable place in which to sack out.

The **Minoa** (tel. 0732/61-209) is just down the block, situated a stone's throw from the harbor. It has 15 charming rooms (with inlaid floors of many colors) and balconies that review all that passes by Monemvassia's outcrop. It also adjoins a pâtisserie and café. This C-class hotel has doubles with bath at 3820 drs ($29.40).

The **Monemvassia** (tel. 0732/61-381) is one kilometer out of Monemvassia village heading north. It has a restaurant that makes it a scenic spot for lunch (good, moderately priced local fish specials) or a choice hotel for those who seek quiet isolation. The large sky-blue rooms, with their sunflower bathrooms, echo the nearby Aegean waters, and the gray-green brush of the headland is conspicious from every terrace. Doubles with bath cost the same as the Minoa.

DINING: There are three good places on the mainland to eat; two are across from one another on the right and left sides of the causeway, and the other is opposite the police bureau on 28 Oktobriou Street. Across from one another are the **Castello** and **Dionysus**; our favorite, though, was the **Kyprous** (tel. 61-383), opposite the police station. It's the last restaurant on the harbor, down where the boats dock (on the second floor of the white building with the green canopy). The Kyprous is moderately priced, and the two specialties are calamari and a daily fish platter.

USEFUL INFORMATION: The **bus terminal** to use in Athens is at 100 Kifissou Ave. (tel. 51-24-913); take one of seven daily buses to Sparta (six hours), then change for the bus to Monemvassia, or take the morning bus that goes directly to Monemvassia; it takes eight hours. . . . The **car-ferry** to Kythira from Piraeus makes calls at Monemvassia two or three times weekly; phone from Piraeus (tel. 45-11-311). . . . At the Zea Marina in Piraeus (tel. 45-27-107) you can get a **hydrofoil** to whisk you across. It runs three times weekly (it's called the Flying Dolphin), and costs 3070 drs ($23.60), but it saves you almost three hours in travel time. . . . The **area code** is 0732.

If you follow the blue arrows in town marked "Portello" to the small bathing area off the rocky coast, you'll find a free outdoor shower to rinse off everything but the memory of Monemvassia.

12. Kythira

As you approach the harbor, you're dazzled by the contrast between shore, sky, and sea: this is the island of Kythira, resting off the southernmost cape of the Peloponnese.

It is now believed that the Minoans had a trading post here as early as 2000 B.C., and over the centuries the island followed closely the development of the peninsula, with the Achaeans, Dorians, and Argives all in their turn taking over and settling in before being displaced by someone else. During the Peloponnesian War it was held by Athens and used as a base from which the Athenians could raid the Laconian Plain. They located themselves at the ancient capital (Kythira), which occupied the southern hill of the island, on top of which was a fortified acropolis.

Today the capital city is **Chora**, an ingratiating village with cobbled lanes and crooked streets that faces south toward the Cretan Sea and has, like Mistra, many Byzantine churches. Chora's neighbor to the south is the active port of **Kapsali**, which contains the relics of the ancient Venetian port perched 900 feet overhead on a hill. It is from this port that you get the boats going to and from Piraeus, Crete, and Gythion. Check here for times and dates of departures and arrivals. Just east of the port is the town of **Vroulaia**, with a small beach, some tavernas, and a few rooms to rent.

Kythira is, for all its beauty, home to many villa-owning Greeks. There isn't any real reason for tourists to visit, other than its intrinsic beauty; you'll probably want to skip by and continue on to the western Peloponnese. If you want to stay, there's the B-class **Kytheria** (tel. 0733/33-321), as well as rooms to let in the many private homes that dot the island. Other than that, the Greek Islands Club books villas and rooms from their office in London.

If you're an islandaholic there's **Antikythira**, a smaller island just off the coast that's quite the place for explorers. Art buffs may enjoy scuba-diving off its coast, where in 1900 divers found a wrecked ship full of sculptures in marble and bronze and fragments of superb relief work. In 1802 nearly 20 crates filled with the Parthenon's sculptural frieze (on their way to London under the aegis of the notorious Lord Elgin) "fell" off their freighter and into the deep seas (the Kythira Triangle?) off Kythira.

13. Pilos

Pilos is a small port on the southwestern tip of the Peloponnese, more remarkable for its role in modern history than for ancient sites that might attract the typical tourist. Named Navarino by the Venetians because its Byzantine castle (Paleokastro) reminded them of one of Avars (Avarinon), it was under Venetian dominance until 1715. Navarino, as its celebrated shipping lane is now known, was the site of a major naval battle which inadvertently won Greece her independence! Because of the unique mooring capability of its natural breakwater, the tiny island of Sphacteria was chosen by Ibrahim Pasha in 1825 as the site from which to carry out his invasion and conquest of the entire region. Two years later, at the allied convention, Britain, France, and Russia decided to support the Greek insurgents against the destructive excesses of Ibrahim's forces. They sent a fleet to intimidate him into accepting their proposed treaty with Greece. This allied squadron was fired on at once, and retaliated; their victory was so complete that 60 Turkish warships and 6,000 troops were lost in the battle.

Today in Pilos the central platia (square) is under the sway of five overpowering maple trees. Fishing boats and the occasional yacht bob up and down in the marina, while farther out in the Gulf of Kiparissia a tanker sits idle. Pilos is a very nice town to dine in (on the harbor) while watching the sunset over the Aegean. It's that kind of leisurely tourist stop. Those who need overnight accommodations can stroll down Main Street. Up ahead is the Neokastro, built by the Turks in 1573 and so named to distinguish it from the Paleokastro, from which Pilos took its nickname.

Across from the entrance to the fort, built out onto a rocky cliff at one end of town, is the Hotel Castle. Today the castle *(kastro)* is the property of the city, which in turn leases it out to experienced innkeepers who maintain it. There's an archeological museum at the site, two blocks off the platia on Thilillinon Street. The museum has memorials from the War of Independence. Museum hours are 8 a.m. to 7 p.m. weekdays, 10 a.m. to 4:30 p.m. on Sunday.

The banks are located on the square, as is the bus station. You can rent a car from the Hotel Nestor (tel. 22-226) or a boat at the Bay of Navarino (tel. 22-783).

ACCOMMODATIONS AND DINING: Our number one place to stay opens in April and closes at the end of October: **Karalis Beach Hotel** (tel. 0723/23-021), on Pylos Messinias (walk down to the waterfront and hang a left), has spacious rooms with afternoon breezes that blow in from the harbor. A double with shower runs 5000 drs ($38.50); a triple, 20% more. Breakfast is available for 560 drs ($4.30).

The **Navarinon Hotel** (tel. 0723/22-291) is the best value in town. At this small pension the narrow reception area is glutted with fishing poles, and there is a busy and terrific taverna next door. The sloped wooden stairs to this house lead to 13 tidy rooms that keep watch over the harbor. A double goes for 2400 drs ($18.50).

The **Hotel Galaxy** (tel. 0723/22-780), on the central square (off Marine Street), is a 34-room C-class establishment with a café in front that's the hot spot in town. Doubles go for 3250 drs ($25), and feature large tulip-tile bathrooms, nice rooms, breakfast, and an elevator for your off days. Next door to the Galaxy is the **Trion Navarchon** (tel. 0723/22-206), an aging D-class hotel.

Next to the police station on the Marina is **To Deithnes,** an eatery that has fresh flowers on the tables and an excellent wine list. The restaurant is moderately priced, and the food is satisfying. There's a terrific bakery at 2 Pissistratou, called the **Agilos Karabatsos Bakery**; just walk up the stairs on the south side of the platia to their balcony and sample their wares. You won't be disappointed; try their fresh-made spanokopita.

READERS' HOTEL SUGGESTION: "We decided to stay in Pilos one night and found the new **Hotel Miramare** (tel. 0723/22-226). The hotel is in the B category. Our room had a view of the sea, television, and a private shower, all for 5600 drs ($43.30). We loved Pilos and would recommend the Miramare for those who are willing to spend a little more for B-class luxury" (Twopence and Jamie Lustberg, Scotland).

WHAT TO SEE: In town is the **Neokastro**, the Venetian fortress built in 1573 and open daily. It was undergoing renovation when we were there, but should be open when you arrive.

More interesting is **Nestor's Palace** (the Palace of Pilos), a 30-minute drive heading northeast from Pilos. To get there, take Kalamatas Street, which rises at the north end of the harbor, and follow the signs to Kiparissia. In about two kilometers the road forks at a large cafeteria; to the right is Kalamata, to the left is the coast road. Go left, and after ten kilometers of very pleasant touring through several small villages and lemon groves you'll arrive in Korifas (Romanou), where the unmarked right fork will lead you (after another ten kilometers) right to the site.

The excavations which unearthed the largest palace yet discovered in Greece were begun by the University of Cincinnati in 1939. Archeologists estimate that Nestor, the wealthy king of Pilos, founded this capital in 1300 B.C. After the fall of Troy (to which his fleet had greatly contributed) Nestor returned to settle in Pilos. His fabulous palace has been reconstructed in prints drawn by Piet de Jong (reproduced in the local guidebook); the palace itself fell prey to fire in a Dorian attack around 190 B.C. The site is hard to appreciate, despite what was obviously painstaking effort in excavating and displaying it under a weatherproof hangar; perhaps because the stones and column bases that remain are sealed off from the sky, our imaginations couldn't lift these ruins above knee level. Nonetheless, standing on the hilltop site and surveying the yet-undeveloped natural beauty of the Peloponnese as a whole and the Gulf of Kiparissia (over which Nestor reigned) left us spellbound. The site is open 9 a.m. to 6 p.m. weekdays, 10 a.m. to 4:30 p.m. on Sunday. Admission is 300 drs ($2.30) for adults, half price for students.

The **archeological museum** is located three kilometers beyond the site, in Chora. Pay close attention to the many seemingly conflicting signs that lead there. Museum hours are the same as those at the site, but it's closed Tuesday. There's a comprehensive and good collection of many artifacts uncovered at the palace site as well as examples of Mycenaean art.

14. Methoni and Koroni

METHONI: Methoni is an out-of-the-way treasure, far from the well-known tourist stomping grounds. You're far more likely to run into wealthy Greeks yachting around Methoni's glistening harbor than German tour groups just in for a weekend romp. Like Koroni, Methoni is a medieval town, but it's much less claustrophobic than its neighbor. The Venetians fought long and hard to capture Methoni, and when they eventually succeeded they were less than entirely delighted—the entire town was devastated. Starting with a fresh canvas, these Renaissance men constructed a superb fortress and lighthouse, both of which stand today as a testament to their skill and taste. The site of the castle has a marvelous moat and a series of well-preserved walls that are beautifully engineered; the wall extends out into the harbor, culminating in the medieval lighthouse that is known in these parts as "one of the eyes of Venice." Site hours are 9 a.m. to 3 p.m. weekdays, 10 a.m. to 4:30 p.m. on Sunday.

Useful Information

Methoni is a very comfortable seaside resort town, which has both a modern and timeless feel to it because of the harbor. The bus station is in the center of town: you can't miss it. From Pilos, it's a short and sweet half-hour ride.

If you decide to stay, we have some places for you to try, but there's one that is a definite favorite: the **Hotel Iliodysion** (tel. 0723/31-225). This 12-room hotel is really a veiled family home set back one block from the beach, with a view of both fort and port, an old-fashioned Mark Twain-type whitewashed exterior, and Mr. Paraskevopoulos, the owner, to welcome you. Who can resist? His home is your home for 2020 drs ($15.60), double.

The **Methoni Beach Hotel** (tel. 0723/31-455) is a splurge selection right next to the fort, overlooking a sandy beach. It has an excellent restaurant (with a veranda over the beach), and the 13 rooms run 10,000 drs ($76.90) for a half board double; all rooms have private bath and half board is compulsory.

There are many room-to-let signs all over town, offering the least expensive accommodation. For breakfast or lunch try the **Café Ioniu**, the **Porto Logo**, or **George's Cafeteria**; all are very good, inexpensive, and are practically next door to each other.

From Methoni to Koroni

Traveling directly between the west and east coastal towns can be a jarring experience—the roads are unpaved for more than half the journey. Those who undertake the trip, however, will be amply rewarded by some of the sights. If you're busing it then you'll have to go from Methoni to Pylos to Kalamata to Koroni, a full day of buses to go 16 kilometers! Try to negotiate a shared taxi or thumb your way there. It's faster and easier. About 16 kilometers from Koloni, not long out of Methoni, is the tiny and thoroughly entrancing beach town of **Finikoundas**. This remote coastal village generally attracts the younger crowd who are willing to put up with the modest hardship of getting there to discover something akin to the "soul of Greece." Rooms-to-let are in abundance, and the town square makes a comfortable eating area, with food available. Along the road as you head out of town you'll see cypress trees, vineyards, and rows of tomatoes and vegetables growing under Long Island–style plastic canopies. And before you know it you'll be in . . .

KORONI: This small medieval coastal town is set on the hilly western side of the Messenian Gulf near a 13th-century Venetian fortress: in short, another Greek port-and-fort town. Its compact three- and four-story buildings have wrought-iron "lace" balconies, and the stairways and streets are all narrow and worn. The entire town is built amphitheatrically—spread out at the highest hill, then angled down to the harbor below. Koroni has had thousands of years of foreign armies marching in and out, obliterating what came before them and then leaving their own brand on the town. It is a classic example of this kind of hand-me-down town.

Today's Koroni has a small protected harbor that makes for a pleasant visit, but not much else. There are many rooms-to-let above the various tavernas and restaurants on the waterfront. The E-class **Diana** (tel. 0725/22-312) is both hotel and taverna, and Mr. Sipsas runs a clean, simple eight-room place that has doubles for only 1900 drs ($14.60). The **Taverna Flisvos** (tel. 0725/22-238) is another eight-roomer on the waterfront. It's clean and has doubles with bath for 2500 drs ($19.20); during the off-season you can readily bargain the manager down. The **Panorama** (tel. 0752/22-224), only open during the summer, is situated at the top of this steeply sloped town. In the section on Methoni you may recall that the lighthouse there was referred to by villagers and guidebooks alike as "one of the eyes of Venice"; Koroni is the second eye, directly across the "nose" of the Likodimos region.

From Kalamata to Koroni you'll tour the east coast of the western Peloponnese, a wild, superlative beach along the Gulf of Messenia. Koroni and Methoni are the two principal ports for this region; they are the "two eyes" because of their respective Venetian fortresses (or lighthouses).

If you want to avoid the summer crowds, stop at **Petalidi**, a small white-washed seaside town just 26 kilometers from Koroni. Several "rooms-to-let" signs dot the narrow streets leading in and out of the town's center, and a lush village green surrounds café tables shaded by the old church. Behind the church is a small sandy beach, and about two kilometers north is Eros Beach Camping, featuring bungalows on a pebbly beach. However, there are sure signs of development that portend a McDonald's future for this fruit- and palm-tree-shaded road.

THE MANI

15. Githio (Gythion)

Githio is a small port city on the Gulf of Laconia known in antiquity as the port of Sparta, just 45 kilometers to the north. Called Kranai in ancient days, Githio is also notable as the first refuge of those two lovers, Paris and Helen; they eloped here from her home in Sparta and set off by ship to Troy. We approached Githio along a winding, scenic road that led through the Taygetos range, whose verdant landscaping includes nausea-inducing hairpin turns in the road. Githio is the capital city of the Mani, the isolated southern fringe of the Peloponnese named after Maina Castle, built by William de Villehardouin in the 13th century. He was the same gentleman who gave us the castles at Monemvassia and Mystras.

Though it's the capital of this region, Githio is noteworthy only as a driving point between Sparta and Monemvassia or Areopolis. The tall old houses along the seafront, many of which offer rooms to let, overlook a lighthouse on the tiny island of Marathonissi, now connected by a roadway to the mainland. Several faded tavernas and tourist-worn shops line the seafront until it reaches the triangular Mavromikali Square. Here some of the cafés play host to aging, lounging hippie tourists and retired Greek seamen. The C- and D-class lodgings are only for those who have to await the twice-weekly ferries to Kythira or Crete.

If you are in Githio know that you're in the octopus capital of Greece. Most seaside cafés will include this tasty denizen of the Gulf on their menus. By all means, try it!

USEFUL INFORMATION: **Mavromikali Square** is the heart of Githio; here are the cafés, the bus stop (in front of the Café Ouzeri), and several places to stay. As you face the square from the water, walk up the first street on your left (there's a market on the corner). On Zannimbei Gritolaki Street you'll see a large church on the right. Here, in the first square, is a very good, large cafeteria with a self-service market. Continue up the hill and you'll see **"rooms to let"** signs. Rooms should average 1000 drs ($7.70) to 1800 drs ($13.80), and you should be able to tell from the street how homey and clean these rooms are.

The police station is near the harbor on King George Street (tel. 22-271). There's a bakery nearby that has fresh egg bagels for 50 drs apiece. The **Transmed Shipping Agency**, at 5 King George St., is where you get plane tickets to Athens from Kalamata or ferries to Kythira, Crete, Piraeus, etc. You might also try the **Theo. Rozakis Agency** (tel. 22-455); their departure schedules are posted daily on the front door. The **area code** is 0733.

ACCOMMODATIONS: There are several C-class hotels where you can await transportation out of Githio. But first we want to recommend a rooms-to-let right over the pharmacy near the harbor, run by **Mrs. Kondovannis** (tel. 0733/22-518). This lovely young woman welcomes you into her spotless home, where ivy grows along the doorframes and molding. Her five spacious rooms upstairs offer simple accommodations with a common bath and kitchen for only 1500 drs ($11.50) a night.

On the harbor is the **Hotel Aktaion** (tel. 0733/22-294), run by a rotund and charming host whose name is Vassiliki Minakakis. The hotel is on Thodoros Street, and you can tell it right away by its tall red door and red "sphinx" planters on either side. The lobby has red and black vinyl furniture, 25-foot ceilings, and pink-and-white walls; all this is yours at 1975 drs ($15.20) for a double. None of the rooms has a shower or bath—it's all communal.

The **Hotel Pantheon** (tel. 0733/22-284) is also on the waterfront and has a distinctly 1960s look. Many of the rooms have balconies jutting over the boardwalk: this is the place to be if you want to be in the center of things. Prices range from 4300 drs ($33.10) for a single to 4700 drs ($36.15) for a double, including breakfast. All the rooms have private bath/shower.

The **Hotel Milton** (tel. 0733/22-914) is about two kilometers out of Githio on the road to Areopolis. The hotel is perched on a slope facing Githio's downtown, and you can see the lighthouse from the front balconies. The rooms are small and clean, and the hotel is supremely comfortable, more so than those in Githio. Rooms start at 3125 drs ($24) for a single, 4125 drs ($31.75) for a double, and all rooms have showers.

The bus from Githio to Sparta takes an hour and a half, if you want to go to Kalamata or points east. Our next stop is Areopolis, just a half-hour bus ride away.

By the way, Githio is where the film crew of Paul Mazursky's movie *Tempest* stayed while they were filming off the coast on a small island meant to duplicate Shakespeare's vision of medieval Corfu. Location manager Carl Zucker recommends the weather-worn ouzeri on the square where "soft, slouchy chairs are a great place to relax. The view of the sea, the caiques bouncing out in the waves, just sharing an ouzo with the locals was the perfect way to end a long day on the set. . . ."

16. Areopolis

The first village of the "inner Mani" is Areopolis, known in the old days as Tsimova. The enclosed courtyards and small cobbled lanes and housing give the impression that Areopolis was probably at one time a heavily fortressed place in which to live. This impression is bolstered by a visit to the **Kapetanakos Tower** (tel. 0733/51-233), a "traditional settlement" opened by the Greek government, which has a program to restore indigenous regional housing such as this for use as hotels. This tower, surrounded by a beautiful garden, was built around 1820 and was reconstructed as part of the government's program in 1979 by the architect Babassis. The Tower today has seven rooms with 17 beds in various configurations—some duplexes, some singles, etc. The walls are over three feet thick (you urbanites will appreciate this) and the furnishings are all traditional, employing old Mani motifs throughout. The Tower is open all year; a single goes for 4600 drs ($35.40), with shower, while a double is 5300 drs ($40.80). Bathless rooms run 10% less. Kapetanakos is reason enough for spending the night in Areopolis.

USEFUL INFORMATION: You'll find the **bus station** in the main square, as well as the **tourist office** and the **police station**. You won't find any banks in town, however, so have cash with you.

ACCOMMODATIONS AND DINING: There's a four-year-old coastal resort about five kilometers north of Areopolis on the Gulf of Messiniakos named after a queen from Homer's time: it's the **Hotel Itilo** (tel. 0733/51-300), a very pleasant base for relaxing in style or sightseeing in the picturesque Mani. Situated just outside the charming village of Neo Itilo (a fork in the road on the way to or from Areopolis), this modern wood-sided 21-room hotel is right on a pebble beach. If you are going by bus, you can ask the driver to let you off at the fork in the road for Neo Itilo. The pale-blue rooms have natural-wood furnishings and are decorated with color photographs of other Greek landscapes, none of which competes with the view from your balcony. On the hill above you is Itilo, a typical Mani village of rough stone, tile-roof houses, and narrow paths. There's a café in front of the hotel, or you can have breakfast in for 330 drs ($2.50). A single will set you back 3375 drs ($26); a double, 5000 drs ($38.50).

Good taverna fare is found at many places, but we came up with a honey: the **Taverna Tsimova** (tel. 51-219), at Platia Areopolis. Georgiou Lamprinakou is the manager, and he'll make sure you get a filling, terrific meal for 850 drs ($6.50). The menu features such house specialties as fried eggplant or fried purkins, snapper, and lamb's head. By the way, you'll recognize Mr. Lamprinakou immediately; he looks like Walter Matthau. Another fine choice is **Georgios Taverna**, on the main platia.

If you're looking for a less expensive place to sleep and eat, you might try the **Hotel Mani** (tel. 0733/51-269), right on the main street as you pull into town. The Mani is new, has 16 clean rooms, and offers doubles for 1600 drs ($12.30) without bath, 1800 drs ($13.85) with. Hopefully you'll be flush enough so that you can stay at either Kapetanakos Tower or the Itilo, as they'll make your visit here more worthwhile.

WHAT TO SEE: Seven kilometers south of Areopolis are the famous **Caves of Pirgos Dirou**. They're part of an underground river, and the 5,000 meters that have been exposed reveal fascinating, multicolored stalagmite and stalactite formations. There's a half-hour guided tour by boat you should take; in the summertime you may have to wait for a smaller launch. For those not too interested in caves there's a small but nice bathing beach nearby, as well as some good tavernas. You'll have to telephone (0733/52-222) for the hours and current price, all of which depend on the time of the year. Nearby is the **Taverna Diron,** popular with tourists and locals alike.

For you museum mavens there's the popular **Historical Museum of Mani** (tel. 74-414), located at Koutifari (Thalames). This museum is housed in a Mani dwelling restored by a local Maniot, Mr. Nikon Dimangelo. The small collection of artifacts (unlabeled), lithographs, and costumes is sure to interest those who have become Mani-acs. The loom on display is the actual one used to make the multicolored weavings that you'll see in all the area's shops and hotels. The museum is open from 9 a.m. to 7 p.m. weekdays, April through October. The admission price is 250 drs ($1.90)—no student discount.

17. Kalamata (Calamata)

When we first visited Kalamata it was a large, heavily commercial city choked with smart boutiques, block housing, discothèques, and an old, gorgeous stucco-with-tile train station close to the other travel-related services. A local brochure touted Kalamata as "Europe's southernmost city," and continued with "Kalamata is distinguished for its very climate, because it lies on the 37th parallel, that is the same latitude with Los Angeles and Miami. Besides, its streets are full of palm and banana trees." Kalamata is also famous throughout Greece for having the finest olive oil.

All of that has changed: Kalamata was devastated by that most Greek of disasters, an earthquake. In 1986 the town was completely flattened leaving its most dedicated inhabitants (over two thirds left for other towns) to resettle in tents. Even so, the airport is open, a rental car agency operates and one hotel, on the outskirts of the town, is still open for business. Also, the business of the region, agriculture, is back in full force.

There are some interesting day trips you can take to caves and castles in the area. One travel agent was recommended to us; he's **John Trigilidas** (tel. 26-293), at 4 Policharous St., and he offers day trips through the Mani to the Pirgos Dirou caves, trips to Pilos and Methoni, and others.

USEFUL INFORMATION: The following information is bound to change as the town is being rebuilt, but know that there are still some tourist facilities in operation. The **area code** is 0721.

If you want to rent a car, **Maniatis** (tel. 27-634) is your man. He's located at 1 Iatropoulou St., and cars go for 2250 drs ($17.30) a day plus 30 drs (23¢) a kilometer, plus 20% tax, plus insurance.

ACCOMMODATIONS: As of our last visit the only hotel in full operation was the B-class **Filoxenia** (tel. 0721/23-166), located on the Navarinou Paralia. Before planning on staying here, it's best to call ahead for reservations. Otherwise, head for another town in the area for lodging.

As for **dining,** the harbor has several temporary stands where you'll find souvlaki, pastries, retsina, etc. Fig-ophiles beware! Kyle searched everywhere and found that those plump Kalanet figs found in the U.S. are exported from, but not sold in, this region.

Ten kilometers west of Kalamata is the undistinguished town of Messini, whose name still conjures images of the classic town of Messina, located about 22 kilometers north of this whistle-stop. **Archaea Messina** (Messina) is where you should stop; to get there take a right at the Pirelli station in town, about half a kilometer past the **Hotel Messini** (tel. 0722/23-002), located on the main street opposite the BP station. The hotel, by the way, is a clean and comfortable place run by a gracious family. This C-class hostelry has doubles for about 3125 drs ($24), and everything about it is cheerful and sunny! The village of Mavramati stands beside the ruins of Messina. Make sure you see the "double-gate," a massive entrance in massive walls, perfectly preserved.

The region today is defined as the entire Messenian peninsula and part of the Mani. Its encompasses Kalamata, Messini, Pilos, and Triphylia. And Pilos is our next stop.

WESTERN PELOPONNESE

There are three peninsulas on the southern tip of the Peloponnese; the middle one is the region referred to as the Mani. The history of the Mani is inextricably bound up with agriculture and breeding. But because of the heavy immigration that defined the region, feuds over the use of land were constant and ongoing, to the point where the inhabitants were known as "pirates on the sea and robbers on land." They migrated to the most western peninsula, building homes in the village of Pirgos that were virtual mini-fortresses. Today Pirgos is the modern capital of this area.

18. Olympia

Today's modern Olympia is a half-mile tourist strip, overflowing with high-priced cafés, shops, and hotels. The prices everywhere in town are high, but if you slip off the main drag, either one block up or down, you'll find the air is just as fine and the hotels and tavernas tend to be less expensive and better.

Olympia is at its best in the early spring before the tourist hordes descend. Two gigantic trees smack in the middle of town provide the focal point for everyone's daily activities, as well as shading the two most popular cafés in town.

Most of the town's **banks,** as well as the **bus** station, are on the main street. The **train** station is off Kondyli Street, on the north end of town. If you're planning to visit the sites and have no car, you can either hoof it, take the bus, or call a **taxi** (tel. 22-580) to pick you up. It's an easy 15-minute walk to the site and museum. Just walk right through town and keep following the road.

USEFUL INFORMATION: There is no Tourist Police or E.O.T. in Olympia; however the regular **police** (tel. 22-100) handle all emergencies. For medical attention call the **hospital** at 22-222. The **O.T.E.,** on the far side of the main drag (toward the ancient site), is open Monday through Friday only; check their hours when you arrive (the **area code** is 0624).

ACCOMMODATIONS: Our favorite place is the **Hotel Leonideon** (tel. 0624/22-550), one block off the main street, up from the post office at the far end of town. Mr. and Mrs. Teoharis are your hosts, and they will show you impeccably clean and serviceable (nothing fancy) rooms, seven in all, with singles at 2065 drs ($15.85), doubles at 2425 drs ($18.65), and breakfast at 265 drs ($2). The outdoor café here is shaded by deep-purple grapes that cover a pipe canopy.

Though it is not as well maintained as one would wish in such a recently built hotel, we still like the **Hotel Hercules** (tel. 0624/22-532), just two blocks from the center of town, behind the bus station. The Hercules is tastefully furnished, and the manager, Spiros Karachalios, goes out of his way to ensure you as pleasant a stay as possible. A double with bath (and balcony) runs 3465 drs ($26.65). The C-class **Hotel Phedias** (tel. 0624/22-667) is down the block from the Hercules, whose charming owner is George Bournas. The Phedias has the nicest bathrooms in Olympia: the showers are also half-tubs! All the rooms have a balcony, and a double goes for 3325 drs ($25.55); singles are 2500 drs ($19.25). We found a **youth hostel** that is near the bus depot; it's about 30 meters down the street, with a big sign outside. The hostel closes at 11 p.m. each night; it's 500 drs ($3.85) per bed and a hot shower.

There are two pensions we liked. The **Pension Achilleys** (tel. 0624/22-562), on Stefanopoul Street, has seven clean, large rooms above a market. The keeper often tends the store downstairs. A double is 2600 drs ($20), and there's a shower down the hall. The other is the **Pension Posidon** (tel. 0624/22-567), located one block off the main street. The Posidon is not as nice as the Achilleys, but its ten rooms are adequate, and they have singles for 1875 drs ($14.40) and doubles for 2250 drs ($17.30).

Foremost of the "group hotels" is the **Apollon Hotel** (tel. 0624/22-522), on the corner of Main and Duomo Streets. Though this once-fine hotel is showing its age it still is an acceptable place to stay, with some nice amenities to boot. Contemporary decor and a rooftop swimming pool(!) is yours for 3875 drs ($29.80) in a single, 5875 drs ($45.20) in a double, which, in contrast to some of the other pricey competitors, is a good deal.

DINING: We have a new favorite in Olympia. Run by a Greek named Pete and his German wife, **Pete's Den** (tel. 22-066) reflects a sensational melding of these two culture's cooking styles. The *saganaki,* for example, is served sizzlingly hot and, at the table, doused with cognac and set ablaze. Zucchini pie, Greek sausages, and various salads are served on an appetizer plate that will easily satisfy two. Follow that with lamb oreganato or shish kebab and a carafe of homemade retsina. (We were especially delighted when a basket full of garlic bread appeared instead of the standard issue white bread). Pete's Den is open daily for lunch and dinner and is set one block off the main street, near the Olympia Café. Dinner for two runs about 2200 drs ($16.90).

A soothing, cool drink at the outdoor café of the **Altis Restaurant** complex on the main street makes a delightful rest stop after a long day of rock and museum trekking.

Around the corner from the Olympic Café is the **Taverna Pritannio,** a very good, simple-fare tavern where 950 drs ($7.30) buys a filling and satisfying meal.

About two kilometers out of town is the **Taverna Klimateria,** where we had a very tasty dinner (complete) for 1300 drs ($10).

Dessert lovers should walk up from the Artemis Hotel to a bakery that is scrumptious: the **Dimitri Bakery,** on Tsoreka Street. It's also open late for those of you (like Kyle) who are given to late-night chocaholic attacks. Again, you'll see a lot of places while you're getting acquainted with the town, and one of them is sure to lure you in. If you're feeling feisty you can go dancing at (what else?) **Zorba's,** just off Main Street.

READERS' RESTAURANT SELECTION: "We took the wrong train, ended up in Olympia and found the wonderful **Manos Restaurant** on the main street. Manos features grilled lamb chops, souvlaki, french fries better than in the U.S., and rice better than the Chinese prepare. You can have a beautiful meal for only 1400 drs ($10.80)" (David and June Tung, Raleigh, N.C.).

WHAT TO SEE: If all the hoopla and commerciality of the Olympics today tends to turn you off, a visit to the original site of the games is a moving and sobering way to reacquaint yourself with the origins of this greatest of all athletic events.

The ancient site was in a section of Pissa, which the Eliads from the north invaded and settled. They renamed the new state Elis and built a sanctuary to Zeus which they named Olympia, after the mountain in Thessaly. In 776 B.C. the first Olympic Games were held, in which the contestants were mortal heroes versus gods! Realizing (we suppose) the folly of this approach, by 576 B.C. the games had been restructured as a footrace held every four years for five days, during the summer full moon. At this time messengers would travel to announce the sacred truce, and athletes from all over Greece would stop fighting and compete instead. The regular Olympic events, spanning as they did all these thousands of years, are thought by historians to be the reason the Greek Empire lasted as long and gloriously as it did. To honor the compassion and wisdom of Zeus, not to mention his physical strength, young men would go into training at this religious sanctuary to compete for the honors a laurel-leaf crown would bestow.

The original Olympic event, a run down the length of the Stadium (142.25 meters), was soon expanded to include multilap races, the pentathlon (running, wrestling, discus, jumping, and javelin), boxing, chariot races, and contests of strength. To preserve the integrity of the athletes, strict rules were imposed and stiff fines were levied against offenders. Anybody who bore arms at the sanctuary during the period of this sacred truce was fined, and bronze casts of Zeus were made and displayed from the earnings of these fines. Marble bases from these casts still exist and are dotted throughout the site. By the time Nero took control of the games, by adding such events as guitar playing (events he always won) many years later, there were only 200 or so of these *zanos* (bronze casts) in the entire sanctuary. Women were not allowed to watch the competitions, primarily because the participants were nude. To pacify possible resentment, women had their own Olympics, the *Heraia* (in honor of Zeus' wife).

As Greek civilization declined so did the allure of the laurel, and subsequently corruption and vice plagued the sanctuary at Olympia. In A.D. 393 the Emperor Theodosius banned the games by decree; 30 years later his son ordered all the temples at the sanctuary destroyed.

One of the most moving stories having to do with the games is that concerning a Frenchman by the name of the Baron de Couberton. The baron worked for many years to revive the games as a possible first step toward world peace. In 1896 the first modern Olympiad was held in Athens, followed by another in 1900 in Paris, then again four years later in St. Louis. Except for the First and Second World Wars (oh, for a sacred truce!) the games have continued ever since. By the time of his death in 1938 the baron had seen a large part of his dream come true; he was buried in Paris, and his wife took his heart and buried it in Olympia underneath the monument that stands outside the stadium today in honor of one man and his dream.

In 1936, to revive interest in the flagging morale of the "new" games, the tradition began of bearing a flame from the original sanctuary at Olympia to the site of the new Olympiad. The five entwined circles (that reminded you of Ballantine beer when you were a kid) symbolize the unity of the five continents which participate. Today the flame is lit by focusing the sun's rays through a magnifying glass located at the Temple of Hera (in the ruins of which the beautiful Hermes of Praxiteles was discovered). Having been lit, the torch is then conveyed by a "priestess" through the arched Krypte entrance to the stadium then to the field, where the first runner in the relay to the site starts the journey the whole world watches. (We have fun picking olive branches and making "Olympic" wreaths after our modest marathon jog.) You can also see tour groups compete against one another on a busy day. The site is open from 7:30 a.m. to 7 p.m. daily, 8 a.m. to 6 p.m. on Sunday.

If you want to appreciate this site to the utmost, go to the **archeological**

museum; you'll see signs for it at the site entrance and on the road. Admission is 375 drs ($2.90), half-price for students. Superb pediments from the Temple of Zeus have been reconstructed and displayed in a room of the same spacial dimensions as its original setting. These pediments are remarkable for the attention to detail in the bodies and the fluid facial expressions. After seeing this, you develop a respect for the word "monumental," and it drives home the religious aspect of the original games. The other great treasure here is the statue of Hermes by Praxiteles; notice how the archeologists have reconstructed the legs from the knees down, with only the right foot to work from. Don't forget to check out the statues on the east and west sides of the Temple of Zeus—they're glorious. Finds from continuing excavations at the site are often moved to the museum; the most interesting dig is at the Tomb or Monument of Pelops.

The hours here are 7:30 a.m. to 7 p.m. weekdays (Tuesday noon to 6 p.m.) and 8 a.m. to 6 p.m. on Sunday. The museum is very strict about allowing flash pictures to be taken, which you can only do with a permit purchased for an additional 375 drs ($2.90).

We don't know how persuasive we've been, but this is really a one-of-a-kind museum, and under no circumstances should you miss it.

The **Museum of Olympic Games** is in town, about three blocks north of the bus station. The hours are 8 a.m. to 3:30 p.m. daily, 9 a.m. to 4:30 p.m. Sundays. It costs 125 drs ($1). If you've had your fill of museums and you want to browse there are several good shops. We found two jewelry shops with beautiful pieces whose owners were willing to bargain: **Nicholas** (tel. 22-472), at 17 Praxiteles St., and **Anastasios** (tel. 22-423), farther down the same street. Next to Anastasios is a small shop run by Niki Karargiri, whose husband is the cook and proprietor of the Britannia Restaurant, on Duoma St. She carries mainly clothing and is a good dress-maker. At the other end of town is a fine bookshop, the **Galerie Orphée** (tel. 0624/22-107). The Galerie carries newspapers and magazines from around the world! They also display and sell contemporary Greek art in their adjacent gallery space. Their hours are 8 a.m. to 11 p.m. daily.

WEST TO KYLLINI: Leaving behind the breathless splendor of Olympia you head back to Pirgos and take the main road that leads you to Lechena (Lehena). Past Lechena you turn off onto the road to Kyllini. Just outside of Kyllini, you will see tall eucalyptus groves on either side of the road; this is where the famous **Kyllini Spa** is located, a must on your itinerary. The spa is actually a group of spas and lodgings, hydropathic installations (the spas are famed for treating respiratory ailments), and a public beach. If you've ever sat in hot mineral springs you probably don't need any urging; those of you who haven't should. It is one of life's great pleasures. And a day or two on the beach is the perfect antidote to those "Oh-no-not-another-ruin" blues.

19. Pirgos (Pyrgos)

Pirgos is a transportation center where many find themselves changing trains or buses on the way to Olympia or Athens or anyplace other than Pirgos. From here you head north to Patras for the ferry to Kephalonia or Italy, south to Kiparissia, or east to Tripolis in order to connect with Sparta or Nafplion or . . . we'll spare you the rest. If you want to head to Olympia, **Achtypis Tours** (tel. 26-301) offers excursions there and to other regions.

USEFUL INFORMATION: Local **buses** leave from Ipsilandou Street; the buses going to Athens, Olympia, and Patras leave from Manolopoulou Street. The **train station** is also on Ipsilandou Street, at the foot of the street. . . . It will be fairly easy to find wherever it is you want to go; Pirgos is the capital of the region around it, Elis, and as such is marked well for visitors, Greek and foreign alike. The **area code** is 0621.

ACCOMMODATIONS: If you plan to stay in Pirgos for the night, there are some places we can recommend to ensure you'll have a nice time. Our first choice is the **Ilida Hotel** (tel. 0621/28-046), at the corner of Patron and Deligianni Streets, no. 50. Its 35 rooms all have private baths, there are plants everywhere you look, and the lobby is a döppelganger of the TWA lounge at JFK airport in New York City! Doubles are 2360 drs ($18.10).

The **Hotel Marily** (tel. 0621/28-133) is up the street at the corner of Themistokleous and Deliyanni (you can't miss the bow tie over the door). Cushy chairs, which Kyle calls "chipper decor," and the pervasive scent of rose-water define this 30-room dwelling, which charges 3090 drs ($23.70) for a double with private bath. The **Olympos** (tel. 0621/23-650), on Karkavitsa Street, is clean and neat, and has singles for 2060 drs ($15.90) with doubles going for around 2590 drs ($19.90).

Most hotels have restaurants in them, and just by walking around you'll find lots of options when it's time to munch.

20. Kyllini

Seventy-eight kilometers south of Patras, at the western tip of the Peloponnese, is Kyllini. If you drive there you'll pass through groves of enormous eucalyptus (and mosquitos), then come to a not so wonderful stretch of sandy beach which has been developed by E.O.T.

If you've timed it so you only have a little time to kill, you can walk the side streets (there's a mouthwatering bakery up from the post office) and hang out at one of the half-dozen cafés in the terminal. The café next to the ticket booth is so big you can sit in the shade and never have to purchase anything as you savor the sight of strollers.

In Kyllini proper you'll find a port with a skinny stretch of dirty beach on either side of the busy ferry terminal. Ferries leave daily for Zakinthos and Kefalonia; you should confirm departure times by dialing 92-294. Each trip takes about one and a half hours.

If you happen to miss the last boat, the **Hotel Ionian** (tel. 0623/92-318) is next door to the port and has doubles for 3250 drs ($25) without bath, 3750 drs ($28.80) with.

A better value (though very noisy) and a more campy setting is the 30-room **Hotel Glarentza** (tel. 0623/92-397), on Kyllini's main road. We fondly remember when the sign outside read only "GLAR," but we're proud to report that it's been fixed; doubles with private bath run 3750 drs ($28.80).

At **Loutra Kyllini** there's a campground with two-person bungalows for 1500 drs ($11.50) a night. Tent sites go for 300 drs ($2.30), and if you have 60 drs (45¢) you can park and star gaze.

A little farther back in the gardens is the C-class **Xenia Hotel** (tel. 0623/96-270), where a half-board double with bath runs 7720 drs ($59.40). There's also volleyball, basketball, and tennis. To unwind, you can lower yourself into a spring-water thermal bath (250 drs), famous since antiquity for its curative powers.

If an international resort appeals more directly to your idea of a Greek holiday, or if the Xenia is booked up, the brand-new and costly **Robinson Clubhouse Kyllini Beach Hotel** (tel. 0623/95-205) is open on the coast at Kastron, about two kilometers from the Xenia. We like the sound of this letter from London:

READERS' HOTEL SELECTION: "We strongly recommend the **Chryssi Avgi Hotel** (tel. 0623/ 95-224), in Kastro near Kyllini, run by Christos Lapidas and his French wife, Catherine. At some 3500 drs ($26.90) one finds the place oozes with charm and the standard of everything is noticeably above the average C accommodation. Kastro itself is a pretty little village, about 10 kilometers from Kyllini port and ideal for those whose ferry dictates a night near the port. There is also a fantastically wide and long sandy beach about three kilometers south of the village" (Peter Bennett and family, London, England).

What can we add? The bus stop is on the main street. You should count on having cash, as Kyllini has no bank or American Express offices! It does have a disco though, open from 8 p.m. to 1 a.m. and located at the Xenia Hotel, overlooking the Ionian Sea. The whole region also has a huge number of mosquitos; bring your repellent for a good night's rest. After you've danced and romanced the night away, in the morning you can ferry out to Zakynthos or Kefalonia, or bus north to . . .

21. Patras

The city of Patras stands just below the site of the ancient city where, according to legend, St. Andrew preached Christianity and was crucified for his efforts, later being buried here. Patras is the capital of the region called Achaea, which occupies the northwest part of the Peloponnese. This area is very mountainous, yet ruins indicate that it has been settled since the Paleolithic Age.

Patras today is the third-largest port in Greece and the hub of the business world in the Peloponnese. It got its name from Patreus, its founder, the leader of the Achaeans who drove out the Ionians. The ancient acropolis was capped with a Byzantine castle that still dominates the city, the center of which is laid out with spacious squares flanked by neoclassical-style buildings. The heart of the city is Georgiou tou Protou Square, where the above-mentioned neoclassical styling is apparent everywhere, as are the arches found most every place in the city.

These arches are the first sight many travelers see of Greece, for Patras is where thousands of Europeans disembark from **ferries**, arriving from Brindisi or Ancona, Italy (free on your EurailPass). There are also ferries to Corfu, Igoumenitsa, and Kefalonia, which (as you might have guessed) means that Patras is always crowded with visitors. There's plenty to see for everybody, including the biggest cathedral in all of Greece, **St. Andrew's** (though not a great beauty). Following the trend in Greece, there is the **Patras Festival** in July and August featuring concerts, art shows, and the usual hoopla.

There are vineyards set in the hills surrounding the city that are intoxicatingly fun when you take the tours; once a year during February or March (depending on the year) the annual **Carnival,** featuring a chariot parade, takes top-priority over other gala events. And, needless to say, Patras has its quota of Byzantine and Turkish and Frankish architecture-and-ruins if you still haven't had enough.

John immediately found two movie theaters near the port, the **Cine Elite,** and the **Inteal Theater,** while Kyle headed up Maizonos Street to the **archeological museum** (tel. 061/27-50-70) with its fragments of sculpture and mosaic (you must apply for entrance at the museum; there are no longer regular visiting hours).

If you want to continue the "old-city" route, just get to Haghios Nicolaos Street (which is always packed) and stay on it until you reach the **kastro;** you can't miss it. You'll see an outer enclosure wall; to the east is the main gate, part of a tower built by the Turks. Rather than describe the castle we'll let you discover it for yourself. After the castle you might want to wander along Haghious Georgiou Street toward the best kept ruin around, the **Odeon**, built during the

Roman period and razed in the third century A.D. Not only has the stage wall been restored, but it's still used for concerts and theater performances.

USEFUL INFORMATION: The **American Express** office is inside the **National Bank of Greece**, which is next to the tourist police station (tel. 220-902; open 24 hours) on Othonos and Amalias Streets (no. 46). American Express hours are 8 a.m. to 2 p.m. weekdays only. The bank's hours are 8 a.m. to 2 p.m. weekdays (Saturday until 1 p.m.), 10 a.m. to 1 p.m. on Sunday, and (hooray!) from 5:30 to 8:30 p.m. every day. The **E.O.T.** office in Patras (tel. 420-305) is on Iroon Polytechniu; walk along the water away from town to the New Port and you'll find it. It has the largest collection of free brochures in the entire country. Definitely try to stock up here before you get to Athens, where the variety of free maps and schedules, etc., is often cleaned out. The office is open from 8 a.m. to 10 p.m. daily. The **area code** for Patras is 061.

If it's excursions to the Ionian Isles you want, call **Ionian Cruise Lines** (tel. 336-130) or the **K. Tsimara Tour Office** (tel. 277-783); they're down the street from the bank. If it's ferries to Italy you have in mind, there are 15 boats a day to Brindisi and Ancona; Brindisi is serviced by the Libra, Frak, Hellenic, and Attica lines, and Ancona by the Kargeorgiou, Minoa, and Ionia lines. The **Hellenic-Mediterranean Lines** transport EurailPass holders free; their office is by the pier. There are excursion outings to seaside spots in the direction of Athens, in the direction of Pirgos, and trips along the northern coastline. Usually, boats to Italy arrive in the afternoon.

As for getting around the Greek mainland, there are many alternatives; you can hire a car at one of several agencies or avail yourself of the public transportation. There are two **bus companies: K.T.E.L.** (tel. 273-997), which services Athens, Pirgos, Kalamata, and Salonica; and **O.S.E.**, which is run by the Hellenic State Railways, the train people (tel. 293-694). They're located across the street from the police station. Both K.T.E.L. and O.S.E. go south along the west coast of the Peloponnese. The bus to Athens costs 1415 drs ($10.85) and takes about three hours; the train takes longer (about 4½ hours) but only costs 680 drs ($5.25) and you can use your EurailPass. The **train station** (tel. 277-870) is also across from the police station and services Athens, Pirgos, and Kiparissia. If you want to book a flight or just confirm an existing one, the **Olympic Airlines** office (tel. 222-901) is at 16 Ag. Andreou St. (in the Hotel Astir), at the corner of Aratou Street. The local **P.T.T.** is at Ag. Nichalaou and Riga Fereou. A **camera repair** place is at 65 Ag. Andreou on the second floor (Fotis Kotsakis).

ACCOMMODATIONS: Hotels in Patras fall into two distinct groups: "American style," which are fancier and have private baths with each room, and "Greek style," which have more personality but with common baths on each floor. Starting with American style, we found the **Hotel Adonis** (tel. 061/224-213), at Zaimi and Kasali Streets, to be a nice, quiet, C-class place charging 4000 drs ($30.75) for a double with bath and breakfast (piped-in classical Muzak free). The **Adonis** is also close to the bus depot and the ferry ticket offices.

If you prefer to "go native" when traveling, then the Greek-style hotels are more your style. The **Hotel Mitropolis** (tel. 061/277-535), at Platia Trion Symmachon, is close to the harbor and a nicely kept D-class hotel in the old-world style, which means sheer white curtains and fresh flowers in all the rooms, embroidered pillows in the lounge, etc. Its 22 rooms go for 2500 drs ($19.25) for a double. Although inexpensive, the difference in noise at the older hotels around Patras's main square makes this a bad bargain for light sleepers.

Next is the **Hotel Delphi** (tel. 061/273-050), up Ag. Andreou at no. 63. This is a larger, 45-room D-class place; a double is about 2165 drs ($16.65) and the host, Georgiou Vazouras, welcomes you in English.

The **Hotel Splendid** (tel. 061/276-521) is on the same block (Ag. Andreou has many hotels) at no. 28, and this 21-room D class has an ancient wire-cage elevator, vast rooms that are not very sunny (but clean), and doubles for 3875 drs ($29.80).

There's an **IYHE Hostel** (tel. 061/427-278) at 62 Iroun Politechniou, about 800 meters from the Patras ship terminal along the coast road; the cost is 425 drs ($3.25) a bed for the night. The hostel offers hot showers and laundry facilities.

For those who like to camp, there are several campgrounds outside of Patras, the closest about four kilometers away. It's called **Avia Patron Camping** (tel. 061/424-133) and it can hold 800 people, 250 cars, and 50 trailers! Call for current rates, as they fluctuate seasonally. It should run about 300 drs ($2.30) a person, a bit more for tents.

DINING: As many hotels as there are in Patras, restaurants outnumber them. Most of these places are tourist traps, and we only hope that you can spot them by their telltale tailoring. There are two that we tried that were quite good, one taverna and one fast-food emporium that included a taverna grill, a cafeteria, and a restaurant (the Olympian). This place was called **Better Value Fast Foods,** and it's behind the police building on Ag. Andreou. There's much to choose from, so we'll leave you on your own. The taverna, **Bieneza** (tel. 221-209), at 18 Kolokotroni (opposite the square), has a typical taverna menu—fish and noodles, salads—and the place is clean, really good, and cheap! We give this one a double thumbs-up.

Our favorite dining room in Patras is the **Tricoyia Brothers Restaurant** (tel. 279-421), on the paralia, just off Clock Square. Among the many dishes that we tried, we particularly liked the beef with zucchini, carrots, and potatoes as well as lamb with vegetables in a smooth lemon sauce. Tricoyia is open daily for lunch and dinner. The cost for two people should run about 1600 drs ($12.30).

Before we leave Patras we thought we'd alert you tennis mavens to the existence of a tennis club, the "64 Club," at Koukouli Patron (tel. 277-776), in case you packed a racquet for the ride.

RION AND ANTIRION: Rion's claim to fame is the fact that it's the port city (8 kilometers north of Patras) that connects the Peloponnese to the mainland at Antirion.

The curious and museum-happy crowd will want to head over to the pier where the ruins of **Morea Castle** (built in 1499 by the Sultan Bajazit) are; the let's-get-on-with-it crowd will make a beeline to the souvlaki trucks and the small-and-sometimes-expensive markets.

The 15-minute **ferry** ride across this mile-wide divide will cost your car 375 drs ($2.90); tickets are sold on board. **Bus** riders crossing to and from the Peloponnese will find themselves changing buses before the ferry and paying the 55 drs (45¢) fare, the same as their noncar companions. You will be greeted by the fortress ruins of **Roumelia** when you reach the other side, built by the Turks to fortify the strait. In ancient times a temple to Poseidon stood at both ports, checking out all those who sailed through the Gulf of Corinth.

Chapter VII

CRETE

1. Iraklion
2. From Iraklion to Aghios Nikolaos
3. Aghios Nikolaos and the Northeast
4. The South: Ierapetra to Aghia Galini
5. Rethymnon
6. Chania and the Southwest Coast

THE NATURAL RESOURCES and artistic richness of Crete have made her coveted by every Aegean and Mediterranean culture in history, and today's traveler will find her just as desirable.

Nature lovers make the pilgrimage around the perimeters and through the mountainous heartland of Crete, which for variety of scenic beauty is unparalleled in Greece. The island is the longest link in a geological chain stretching from the mountainous Peloponnese through Kythira, to verdant Rhodes, and beyond to Asia Minor; her terrain reflects these different landscapes, particularly on the east and west coasts. Crete's developed north coast is defined by a national highway linking several harbors on the azure-blue Aegean. Once-great centers of the ancient maritime powers have become overdeveloped beach resorts and picturesque fishing ports. The untamed rugged south coast curls lazily along the Libyan Sea, facing the tropical coast of Africa across the navy Mediterranean. Crete's wealth comes from the south's thriving year-round agribusiness—tomato hothouses line the roads curved above huge canyons and rocky gorges; date palms and vineyards are interspersed with placid, sandy beach coves and dense banana plantations.

The culture that many consider the mother of all Greek civilization originated on Crete. The variety of archeological treasures from the Minoan civilizations will delight even visitors bored with "old stones." The great palaces at Knossos, Malia, and Phaistos are only the first leg of an historical odyssey that leads to Hellenic, Byzantine, and Venetian sites throughout the island.

Whether you're interested in a motor-coach tour of historical sites or an overland expedition to unexplored beaches, Crete has it all.

A BRIEF HISTORY: Crete is known to have been inhabited since the seventh millennium B.C., but it was not until about 2600 B.C., when immigrants from Asia Minor and Africa arrived with bronze tools and implements, that we see the beginnings of the first distinct civilization.

This civilization was dubbed "Minoan," after the island's legendary King Minos, by the preeminent archeologist Sir Arthur Evans, and its history is divided into four periods based on the palace ruins found in Crete. The

Prepalatial period was 2600–1900 B.C.; the Protopalatial, 1900–1700 B.C.; the Neopalatial, 1700–1400 B.C.; and the Postpalatial, 1400–1150 B.C. The great civilization at Mycenae achieved ascendancy over Crete during the Postpalatial era, though the Minoan culture survived for many generations until its conquest in the eighth century B.C. by Dorian invaders from the mainland. The sophisticated social and political systems (and the superb artistic quality achieved by the Minoans) mark this as the first Greek civilization.

The most exciting archeological finds on Crete date from the Protopalatial period, when large palaces were founded at Knossos, Phaistos, and Malia. Here kings, who were also religious leaders, ruled over a society of nobles, craftsmen, farmers, and their slaves. Trade began with Asia Minor and Africa, where Minoan ceramic and bronze artifacts have been found; at home, sophisticated civil projects produced roadways, bridges, aqueducts, and an excellent drainage system that can be seen at Knossos. In the archeological museum (perhaps the finest in all Greece) there's a collection of faïence plaques carved and painted in the shapes of two- and three-story local houses that indicates the high level of sophistication the Minoan builders achieved.

About 1700 B.C. a disaster befell the Minoans (either an earthquake or a massive invasion), and the palaces were destroyed. Over their rubble rose the magnificent palaces now seen at Knossos, Phaistos, and Malia. This marked the beginning of the Neopalatial period, where for 300 years the Minoans produced the beautiful frescoes and pottery we so admire today. Smaller palaces and villas, such as those at Zakros, Ag. Triadha, and Amnissos (the ancient port where a villa with glorious lily frescoes was found), cropped up on the island.

Around 1500 B.C. another disaster, perhaps a conquest by the Achaeans (who then resettled the island), destroyed the Minoan civilization. Such complete destruction is thought by some to have been the result of a huge tidal wave caused by the volcanic eruption of Santorini (just 60 miles north), which occurred during the same period. The eminent archeologist Professor Marinatos surmised this after his excavation at Amnissos revealed layers of volcanic ash; his later work at Akrotiri (on Santorini) proved that this Minoan-like civilization was destroyed by the eruption as well.

The story of Theseus and the Minotaur is one of the best-known Greek myths, and archeologists claim that the story was the Greeks' attempt to explain the strange Minoan culture. According to legend, the Minotaur was a hideous creature with a man's head and a bull's body, the gross offspring of an illicit affair between Queen Pasiphae (Minos' wife) and a beautiful white bull sent by Poseidon to help Minos in battle. When Minos appeared ungrateful for the gift, Poseidon decided to get even. The court architect, magician, and jack-of-all-trades, Daedalus, made it possible for Pasiphae to consummate the passion instilled in her by the angry Poseidon, and she bore the Minotaur. King Minos was horrified. He commissioned Daedalus to build a huge maze, the Labyrinth, through which the Minotaur could wander forever without being seen. Then, from Athens, he exacted the horrible tribute of sending seven young men and seven young maidens each year into the Labyrinth as Minotaur food. Theseus, the Athenian hero, volunteered to join the group when he learned of their plight. With help from Minos' daughter, Ariadne, Theseus slew the beast. Daedalus and his son, Icarus, were imprisoned in the Labyrinth because of their part in these escapades, and it was while trying to fly from here on feathered wings attached with wax that Icarus flew too close to the sun and fell to his death. Meanwhile Theseus and Ariadne fled to Naxos, where their love ended in sorrow and bitterness.

Just a cursory glance at the icons and ceramic artifacts in the archeological museum confirms that the bull was a very important Minoan symbol. Mysterious cult practices, including dance, music, and blood sacrifices, were carried out in every palace and at outdoor shrines. Real bulls, the icons of the double-headed ax (used when sacrificing the bulls), and abstract pairs of horns all probably served in cult rituals as symbols of the Earth Mother's other part, the fertile male that renewed life and provided for continuing harvests. The supreme Cretan deity was the nature goddess (or Earth Mother).

The uniquely Minoan architectural achievements displayed at Knossos may explain the legend of the Labyrinth. Such a complex of three- and five-story buildings, with large rooms centered around courtyards (on many different levels), supported by bright red wooden columns and perfectly spaced stairs, could only be the work of a genius such as Daedalus. If you try to follow a site plan of the remains at Knossos today you'll be convinced of the very same thing.

The Postpalatial period (1400–1150 B.C.), after the disaster, marks the decline of Minoan culture, though scholars agree that many of the achievements of this early civilization were absorbed by the Mycenaeans. By 1000 B.C. the Dorians had invaded Crete, establishing a new aristocratic government while assuming many Minoan legal precepts as the foundation for their new Spartan state on the mainland.

Following this invasion a militaristic mood predominated in Crete. Cities that had flourished while united under Minos became rivals. Successful trading continued with Asia Minor and Africa, introducing Oriental styles to an island mostly isolated from mainland Greece. After several thwarted attempts, the Romans finally took over Crete in A.D. 67 and chose Gortyn as their capital. For 800 years under Roman rule Crete was a prosperous colony, which saw the arrival of Christianity in the fifth century.

In A.D. 826 the Saracens invaded, destroying Gortyn and Iraklion and inhabiting the newly fortified port of Candia (present-day Chania). Nikephoros Phokas retook Crete from marauding pirates in 961, and from Byzantine hands it was purchased by Venice.

Candia was now the artistic and political center of an island settled by Greek and Venetian nobility, all of whom acquiesced to its customs, language, and spirit. Scholars speak of the Cretan Renaissance during the 16th and 17th centuries when local poetry, architecture, and painting flowered. Iraklion's loggia, Rethymnon's fountain, and Chania's stately homes all date from this period. The only extant works from the Cretan School of Painting, which produced several artists (including Theotokopoulous, known to the world as El Greco), are displayed in the Aghia Katerina Church, a Venetian monument in Iraklion.

The Venetians had architect Michele Sammicheli refortify the ramparts of Iraklion's fortress, and it withstood the Turkish onslaught for 21 years. In 1669 the last free port, Candia, fell, and little was heard from Crete until its liberation in 1898. In 1912 the island joined the Greek nation, but even today you hear people say, "Cretans first, Greeks second."

ORIENTATION: Crete is such a varied and exciting island that we suggest allotting the same amount of time and interest you'd give to the Peloponnese or northern Greece. A fully satisfying tour can be made by the excellent **public bus** system, and travelers should allow a minimum of one week to explore. Three- or five-day visitors can see many of Crete's sites, but should consider renting a **car**. Jeeps are particularly popular (and fun) on this island because they expose you to the ever-changing scents and breezes, while allowing free travel on unpaved roads to the more remote areas.

Visitors coming to Crete by **plane** can fly into the Iraklion or Chania airport, although we recommend the Iraklion airport because of its proximity to the capital city of Iraklion, where most of the tourist services are located.

Ferries service Crete at least once a day from Piraeus all year round, though it should be noted that Cretans consider their tourist season as extending only from April 1 through October 31 on the north coast, when many accommodations and restaurants close. The south coast advertises itself as a year-round resort because of its mild climate, but here, too, many accommodations are seasonal. We recommend that visitors planning an extended winter holiday on Crete contact a local travel agent.

1. Iraklion

If you've got only a day or two to devote to Crete, they *must* be spent in its largest city and principal port, Iraklion. This rather unattractive, busy city is graced with a cosmopolitan air and such superb artistic and cultural treasures that it's a vital stopover for any visitor to Greece. A visit to the nearby Palace of Knossos, cradle of Greek civilization, and to Iraklion's world-class archeological museum, is an absolute must.

IRAKLION'S ABC'S: Here's a brief survey of the facts of daily life in Iraklion.

Airlines

Iraklion Airport is serviced by direct charter flights from all over Europe. Otherwise, **Olympic Airways** handles all flights from within Greece; their office is at Eleftherias (Liberty) Square (tel. 225-171). There are several flights daily from Athens to Iraklion, five times daily from Athens to Chania, and 11 times weekly between Iraklion and Rhodes, three times a week to Mykonos and Santorini, and two times a week to Thessalonika.

Airport

Iraklion Airport is 15 minutes outside the city. Buses leave one hour before flight time from the Olympic Airways Office and cost 150 drs ($1.15). Taxis cost approximately 350 drs ($2.69). Olympic also has bus service to and from **Chania Airport** (tel. 63-264), formerly a military airstrip in Aerodromia, to meet flights; these buses cost 350 drs ($2.69). There is a Tourist Information desk at the Iraklion Airport and also a board to make free phone calls for different tourist information.

American Express

The American Express agent for Crete is the **Creta Travel Bureau**, 20 Epimenidou St., Iraklion (tel. 227-002). They're open 9 a.m. to 1 p.m. Monday to Friday for emergency traveler's check services, and handle mail during these hours.

Area Code

When calling from outside the various towns, use area code 081 for Iraklion, 0821 for Chania, 0831 for Rethymnon, and 0842 for Ierapetra. Many smaller districts which have their own district codes are also noted in the text.

Banks

There is a **Bank of Greece** and an **Ionian Bank** on 25 Avgousto Street open the standard 8 a.m. to 2 p.m. banking hours. The **National Bank of Greece**, at

35, 25 Avgousto St., is open Monday to Friday at the same hours. Many of the larger hotels throughout Crete will cash traveler's checks at odd hours for a nominal fee.

Bus Terminals
The bus stations for the east of Crete and Malia are opposite the ferry quay, under the red canopy. Buses to Rethymnon and Chania depart from Venizelou Street opposite the Xenia Hotel. Buses to Matala, Phaestos, and Ag. Galini leave from the terminal at Kalokairinou and Makariou Streets. There is frequent bus service to all parts of the island, and a complete schedule is available from the National Tourist Office of Greece (E.O.T.).

Car Rental
Hertz (tel. 081/225-371 in Iraklion) has 17 offices throughout the island and offers the convenience of reserving your car in advance worldwide, as well as providing an excellent roadmap and guidebook written especially for Crete. **Avis** (tel. 081/282-963) and **Hellascars** (tel. 081/235-796) also have Iraklion offices, as well as the flexibility of having additional offices on the island.

Some of the cheapest rental deals can be made by-the-week with companies such as **Caravel** (tel. 081/242-669) and **Inter Rent** (tel. 081/225-291). It's often difficult to book a car from any of the small companies during the high season; phoning ahead for reservations is recommended.

Camera Shop
Repairs, supplies, and one-day processing are available down the street from the Petra Hotel on Dikeosinas Street.

Doctors
Refer to your hotel reception, or the local E.O.T. office (tel. 081/228-203).

Ferryboats
Several ferryboats depart daily from Piraeus for Iraklion, Chania, or Ag. Nikolaos. The most convenient steamers leave at 6:30 or 7 p.m., and arrive at Iraklion or Chania the following morning after the 12-hour ride. The steamers which service Ag. Nikolaos directly are most often local boats, which make stops throughout the Cyclades islands, then at Ag. Nikolaos and Sitia, then continue onto Kassos, Karpathos, and the other Dodecanese islands. (These could be construed as the poor man's version of a three-day cruise!) For more information on schedules, contact Tourist Information in Athens (tel. 171) or the Piraeus Port Authorities (tel. 45-11-311).

Excursion boats ply the popular Iraklion-to-Santorini route four days weekly. Tickets are available from local travel agents for 1200 drs ($9.25).

Festivals
The island whose most famous native son is Nikos Kazantzakis' fiercely individualistic Zorba the Greek is certain to celebrate many unique holidays. Before departure from Athens you can get information on national holidays such as **Naval Week**, celebrated mid-July at the port of Souda near Chania; **Greek Easter;** the **Wine Festival**, held in August in Rethymnon; the government-sponsored **arts festivals**, such as the Heraklion Festival inaugurated in the capital last summer. Don't forget to check with local N.T.O.G. (E.O.T.) or police offices for information on Sitia's **Sultana Raisin Festival;** Kritsa's **Folk Festival,**

where a mock wedding is performed; Elos' **Chestnut Festival**; or Ag. Galini's **Sheep Shearing Festival**.

Guidebook

There's an excellent archeological guide by J. A. Papapostolou, former director of the archeological museum, called *Crete*, available widely for 800 drs ($6.15).

Hospital

Venizelio Hospital (tel. 235-921) is on Knossos Road, Iraklion. For general first aid info, call 222-222.

Information

The **National Tourist Office of Greece (E.O.T.)**, 1 Xanthoudidou St., off Eleftherias Square in Iraklion (tel. 081/228-203), is open Monday through Friday from 7:30 a.m. to 2:30 p.m., with a very helpful and knowledgeable staff. There is also a telephone board of services at the Iraklion Airport.

Laundry

Lavomatique, 25 Merabelou St., near the archeological museum in Iraklion, is a self-service laundry, open 7 a.m. to 9:30 p.m. daily. Wash costs 375 drs ($2.88); dry, 200 drs ($1.54). Bring your own soap!

There's a **dry cleaners** on Dikeosinis Street (formerly Konstantinou Street) providing one-day service.

Luggage

Left Luggage, at 48 25 Augousto Street, is perfectly located (across the street from the Bank of Greece) and the ideal solution for excessive or cumbersome luggage. Each piece is 125 drs (96¢) a day; this includes insurance on your stuff (about $3 a bag). It's open from 6:30 a.m. through midnight and provides man-on-duty security every day.

Markets

There's a daily meat and produce market at the head of 25 Avgousto Street in Iraklion. It runs along Odos 1866, a few blocks up from the Morosini (Lion) Fountain. You should visit the market early in the morning; it's wild and wonderful!

Post Office

The main post office is on Gianari Street, off Vascolianis Square, in Iraklion. It's open Monday through Friday from 8 a.m. to 8 p.m.

Religious Services

Ag. Iannis Vaptistis (John the Baptist) Church at P. Antoniou Street in Iraklion has Catholic services twice daily. Call E.O.T. for the times.

Shopping

There are several shops carrying a wide variety of Greek souvenirs around Eleftherias (Liberty) Square, along Dikeosinis Street, and parallel to it, along Daedelou Street, a pleasant pedestrian mall.

Taxis

They cruise the city of Iraklion and can be booked by dialing 235-859 or 236-257. There is also a taxi stand across the street from the museum. The taxi problems of Athens also abound in Iraklion. Drivers tell you hotels you ask for are booked and insist they take you elsewhere. Stand up to the drivers or insist on getting out of the cabs. At the airport you will find posted long-distance prices to different parts of Crete. For example—3300 drs ($25.40) to Rethymnon, 3420 drs ($26.30) to Ag. Galini. It might be worth it if you belong to a group of three or four. Inside Iraklion there is a minimum charge of 150 drs ($1.15).

Telephone Office

The O.T.E. is over and down one street from the back of El Greco Park in Iraklion. It is open 24 hours a day but for collect or operator-assisted calls, it closes at 8 p.m.

Tourist Police

The Tourist Police (tel. 081/283-190) are located on Dikeosinis Street near Platias Eleftherias, and are open from 7 a.m. to 11 p.m. daily, all year. They speak English and are very helpful.

Travel Agent

The most helpful travel office in Iraklion is **Polytravel**, on 25 Avgousto (tel. 282-476), run by John Polychronides, who also manages the Poseidon Hotel (tel. 081/235-584). If Crete seems too large to get a handle on, go straight to John.

ACCOMMODATIONS: Many of the C-class hotels originally built to handle Iraklion's tourist boom now find themselves in the middle of a noisy, crowded city. Some of the best of the newer lodgings are located outside the city center, but we've also included many of the older pensions, whose remnants of European charm make up for their area's big-city drawbacks.

By the New Port

Just 1½ kilometers from the old city is a cluster of C-class hotels perched on the cliffs above the new port. It's a short walk from the Piraeus ferry, but a long way away from the heat and congestion of downtown Iraklion.

The outstanding choice here is the **Hotel Poseidon** (tel. 081/285-859 or 222-545), at 46 Possidonos Povos (at the end of the street), because of the hospitality, warmth, and helpfulness of its staff. The owner, John Polychronides, has a sophisticated, well-traveled background and keeps up-to-date on tourists' needs. He and his staff are very knowledgeable about historic sites and the ever-changing resorts on Crete. All the Poseidon's rooms (spotless, with plenty of hot water) have balconies overlooking the port or face west with a view of the Stroumboulis Mountains (which ensures a welcome breeze in Crete's hot summer). Doubles are 5600 drs ($43.07), including a full breakfast (with fresh bread!) served in a lounge filled with embroidery and local handicrafts.

By the Old Port

Overlooking the old Venetian harbor are several C-class hotels that are exceedingly similar in style, but well located and relatively quiet. The first choice for value here is the **Kris Hotel** (tel. 081/223-211), at 2 Epimendou. The 12 doubles in this converted apartment building are 3600 drs ($27.69).

Around the corner at 1 Ariadnis is the **Ilaira** (tel. 081/227-103), with 20 modern, whipped-stucco-walled rooms at 4690 drs ($36.07) per double (including continental breakfast).

The recent **Marin Hotel** (tel. 081/220-737) is another choice on the block, at 10 D. Bofor. Several of its 48 rooms have large balconies overlooking the harbor, and there's a nice roof garden as well. Doubles are 6700 drs ($51.54).

Downtown

Iraklion's downtown might be construed by amateur archeologists as just a neighborhood surrounding its fantastic museum, but we think the nonstop nightlife, centered around the Morosini (Lion) Fountain and the Venetian Church of San Marco, marks this as the heart of the city.

You'll find several good-value hotels if you walk straight past the Morosini Fountain behind El Greco Park. The 25-room **Mirabello** (tel. 081/285-052), at 20 Theotokopolu, occupies an attractive old building, and all its balconies overlook the park and the neighborhood's quiet residential streets. Doubles without bath are 3750 drs ($28.84); with bath, 3900 drs ($30).

Nearby is the **Hotel Lena** (tel. 081/223-280), at 10 Lahana, well run by the Mangonas family. The Lena has 18 somber, bathless rooms that are bargain priced. Doubles are 1875 drs ($14.42) and dorm beds are available for 1000 drs ($7.69).

The **Atlas Guest House** (tel. 081/288-989), at 6 Kandanoleion, is just a block from the café-lined Lion Fountain Square, and if the nightlife doesn't bother you, it's a lovely old home with a roof garden and spacious private rooms with private bathrooms right on the roof. Manolis Neakakis runs a friendly place, and makes the kitchen available to his guests. Some rooms have private baths and some don't, but all doubles are 1900 drs ($14.61), plus 250 drs ($1.92) per shower.

Another nice place is the **Pension Vergina** (tel. 081/242-739), at 32 Chortatson St., near the historical museum. The rooms are clean and spacious and doubles go for 2500 drs ($19.25) a night, and there's a lovely garden with banana trees. "A nice place where somebody can rest" is how the manager suggested we review the Vergina; we couldn't agree more.

Near the Museum

The archeological museum of Eleftherias (Liberty) Square is mostly surrounded by luxury and A-class hotels, but there are two budget accommodations in this elegant quarter. **Mrs. Toupoyannis** has rooms to let above her garden town house at 2 Malikout, right behind the Atlantis Hotel. Mrs. Toupoyannis travels frequently, but you can call 081/226-112, or just knock on the gate that encloses their geranium bushes and swing set. A room will run you 1800 drs ($13.84).

If no one's home, up the street and one block over is the newly built **Eurocreta Pension** (tel. 081/226-700), at 38 Ariadnes. The seven clean, simple doubles are 1900 drs ($14.62), including shower. The pension's owner, Paulos, also runs the rent-a-car company downstairs, and is very helpful; he says guests of his pension will get a discount on car or scooter rentals. Across the street is the Pension Ilias (tel. 226-348), with similar rates and services, if the Eurocreta is full.

Best for the Budget

Iraklion is very erratic in its offerings of lodging, and the low end is no exception. There's a **GYH Youth Hostel** (tel. 081/286-281) at 24 Handakos, a few blocks behind the Fountain Square. About 100 beds are available at 500 drs ($3.85), but the militaristic, overregulated atmosphere lessens its appeal.

If you can't stand the regimen, the **Hotel Chania** (tel. 081/284-282), at 19 Kidonias, is crying out for you to join host George Thiakakis in his wildly festooned courtyard. Country stickers, sport decals, and flag murals turn this 25-bed free-flowing hostel into an *Animal House* college dorm. The one double is negotiable at 1380 drs ($10.62) to 1750 drs ($13.46) per night; in the triples and quads, beds are 575 drs ($4.42) each. The showers are free (a bonus for the impoverished).

The **Rhea Pension** (tel. 081/223-638), at the corner of Kalimeraki and Handakos Streets, has 16 spare, clean rooms that go for only 1875 drs ($14.42) each.

There is a pleasant campground five kilometers west of the city, **Camping Iraklion** (tel. 283-164) is near the beach and has a market, restaurant, bar, laundry facility, and swimming pool!

DINING: Iraklion boasts some excellent restaurants. Their special dishes are attributed to the variety of fresh produce (grown year round in the south) and the Cretan's special flair for cooking. Crete is also known for its subtle wines—the rich, dry Minos Cava white and the Cava Lato reds.

Daedelou Street, a pedestrian mall running between Liberty and Fountain squares, is lined with restaurants that are great for the cuisine and people-watching. The **Minos Taverna**, at no. 10 (tel. 081/281-263), is an excellent choice, our favorite in fact, and is favored by locals for its special Cretan veal with onions and it's exotic lamb-baked-in-yogurt dishes. Harris runs the show here and makes sure that the service is prompt and attentive. Also excellent is the squid, which is uniquely prepared and is simply sensational! Dinner for two runs about 1300 drs ($10). It's also open for lunch. The Minos's prices are similar to Maxim's, it's open for lunch and dinner, and is one of the few eateries in Iraklion open year round. Here, you must sample the house wines. The **Klimateria** (tel. 081/284-708), next door, is also good. At any of these tavernas, ask for a Cretan specialty from among the goodies brewing in the kitchen (take a look for yourself) then allow enough time to linger over your Minos Cava and check out the city life of Iraklion all around you.

Maxim's (tel. 287-239), facing well-kept El Greco Park, is where John claims there are "the most flavorful stuffed tomatoes in Greece." Maxim's will please the most fastidious traveler, from the taverna gourmand to the inhibited eater. All dishes are simply prepared using the freshest local ingredients, and so vary according to season. The sophisticated vegetable dishes are always excellent, but if chef George has meat or fish specialties on the day's menu, order them—you won't be disappointed. Two can eat for approximately 1600 drs ($12.30).

Just down the hill from the Hotel Poseidon above the new port is the **Taverna Faros** (tel. 243-233), an inexpensive choice for a good Greek supper. The seaman's ambience of razor clams, conch shells, and fishnet drapes confirm that the seafood here is very good. Highlighting the decor is the stuffed kri-kri (Crete's unique brand of curly-horned goat) mounted on the wall. After you've seen them depicted on Minoan seals from 3,000 years ago, or if you've tried to find one while hiking through the Samaria Gorge, you'll be thrilled to see one in person (almost).

Also near the Poseidon, two blocks farther down on Ikarou, is **Taverna Stavros**. The place looks, tastes, and feels like your mom's kitchen, and Stavros plays a mean bouzouki when the mood hits him! Two can chow down for less than 1000 drs ($7.69).

CAFÉS AND DISCOS: If you're still sampling Cretan wines or need some coffee, stroll over to the Lion Fountain and grab the nearest empty chair. This is where the action is. You'll find the best ice cream in town at the **Galaxy Hotel** on

Democratias Avenue. A more intimate café is the **Pub La Palma**, at 14 Idomeneos, where you can have a drink on the comfortable patio. Opposite the old Venetian port, at the foot of 25 Avgousto, is **Ta Psaria** (tel. 220-494), "The Fish," a pleasant outdoor café cooled by the sea breeze that swirls around the fortress. Fish can be had elsewhere at steeper prices; and it's a very nice spot to while away the cocktail hour.

When you're ready to boogie try **Disco Piper** (tel. 226-626), directly behind the Astoria Hotel on the central square off Platias Eleftherias. It opens at 9:30 p.m., and the entrance fee is 500 drs ($3.85), which includes a free drink. Just past the bend in the road on Ikarou Street is **Disco Life** (tel. 280-656), the other hot club in town. Things start popping around here at 10:30 p.m., and admission is 700 drs ($5.38).

WHAT TO SEE AND DO: Iraklion has a number of major historic sites from throughout Crete's colorful past. The Minoan Palace at Knossos is just five kilometers south of the heart of the city and within walking distance of the ferry are several fascinating Venetian and Byzantine remains.

A Walking Tour

Ferries from Piraeus arrive daily between 7 a.m. and 8 a.m., a perfect time to explore the still-quiet city. From the new harbor, turn right and continue along the waterfront to the old **Venetian Arsenal**, an arcaded storage area awaiting development. New historic preservation laws have been effected in Iraklion to ensure the restoration and reuse, rather than the destruction, of its historic architectural monuments.

At the tip of the old port is the **"Koules,"** a wonderfully preserved 14th-century fortress, rebuilt between 1523 and 1540. A Lion of St. Mark proudly guards the doorway. Each morning the **old harbor** comes alive, with brisk trading in red mullet, "chopis (a local fish)" and swordfish brought in by the fishing boats. If you continue along the waterfront (Makariou Street) you'll soon see the West bus station, and behind it, the small **historical museum** which houses a private collection of Cretan folk art, Venetian and Turkish antiquities, and memorabilia of Crete's celebrated son, author Nikos Kazantzakis. The museum is supposed to be open from 9 a.m. to 1 p.m. and 4 p.m. to 8 p.m. daily, but you'd better call first to check (tel. 741-689).

If you turn left opposite the old port, at 25 Avgousto St., you'll be on Iraklion's travel agent/ticket office/rental-car row. Behind the first small square on your left is the **Ag. Titus Church**, built in the 16th century and dedicated to Titos, who first brought Christianity to Crete (at the city of Gortyn). Just past the Knossos Hotel is the lovely **Venetian Loggia**, and farther up, the **Church of San Marco** (from 1303, converted into a mosque by the Turks and now used as an exhibition hall). Across the street is the **Lion (or Morosini) Fountain**, built by the Venetian general Francesco Morosini and dedicated in 1628. The lion support, thought to have come from another 14th century fountain, dominates **Platia Venizelou**, named for Eleftherios Venizelou, a Cretan revolutionary and later premier of Greece. The popular square is now more commonly called the Lion (or Fountain) Square. Stop at one of the many cafés for a breakfast of Crete's flavorful bread with local jams or honey. To avoid problems, be sure to ask the prices in advance if a set menu is not offered. As you revive, you can watch the pace of the city quicken.

A few blocks down Katekhaki Street is the **Ag. Minas Cathedral**. On the right side of the transept are four icons credited to Michael Damaskinos, a master of the Cretan School (and perhaps teacher of El Greco). At the nearby **Haghia Ekaterini Church** is a collection of icons by members of this same school. Other Venetian monuments such as the **Porta Khanion** (near the bus station for Phaestos), the **Bembo Fountain** on Kornarou Square, and the **Martinengo Ramparts**, along the Venetian enclosure wall at the southern tip of the city, are recommended for those with an abundance of time.

Guided Tours

Many of Iraklion's visitors arrive on cruise ships in the morning and depart the same evening, so tourist services are geared to catch these hit-and-run sightseers. One of the biggest tour operators is the **Creta Travel Bureau** (tel. 081/22-70-02), on 25th Avgousto at no. 27. Other offices in Aghios Nikolaos and Rethymnon (the maps printed on their brochures are used by E.O.T.) ensures the company a large audience for its varied (and thorough) day trips.

To get the most from a visit to Iraklion's two greatest sites, the archeological museum and the Palace of Knossos, we recommend purchasing the excellent guidebook *Crete* (in the Greece Museums and Monuments series), by J.A. Papapostolou for 1000 drs ($7.69), especially if you'd like to go on your own. Otherwise, a guided tour of what remains of the fascinating Minoan culture is strongly recommended. Half-day guided bus tours to Knossos and the museum are offered daily by several travel agents, either as separate sites—at 2000 drs ($15.38) and 1600 drs ($12.30) respectively—or as a combined tour for 3400 drs ($26.15).

The Archeological Museum

The Archeological Museum of Heraklion [*sic*], on Xanthoudidou Street opposite the E.O.T., merits at least two hours of close examination by anyone interested in the Minoan civilization. The labeled ground-floor exhibits are grouped chronologically in 73 galleries. The archeological museum includes Neolithic, Hellenic, and Roman finds from throughout Crete, but is unique in the world for its comprehensive Minoan collection. Superb examples abound of terracotta icons and ceramic ware, decorated in typically Minoan black swirls and spirals. There are marble, bronze, ivory, and stone figurines worshipping, fighting with bulls, dancing, making music, and performing acrobatic feats. Precious faïence plaques depict styles of housing, clothing, sports, and worship. Several pieces of exquisite gold jewelry are displayed. There are drawings, sculptures, reliefs, and seals representing every aspect of the bull in secular and religious terms. The spirit of the Minoans, their love for natural and physical beauty, their delight in depicting the wonders of the world around them, are to be seen everywhere in this exquisite collection.

Upstairs on the first floor is the marvelous collection of frescoes from the Palaces of Knossos (copies have been installed at the site), Malia, and Phaistos, and the smaller villas of Amnissos and Aghia Triadha. Erect, lean young men with long curls; buxom, topless maidens; graceful lilies and dolphins; bulls and ornate, multicolored decorative patterns bring the Minoan culture back to life.

The museum is open on Tuesday to Saturday from 8 a.m. to 7 p.m., on Sunday and holidays from 8 a.m. to 6 p.m. Closed Monday. Admission is 500 drs ($3.85) for adults, 300 drs ($2.30) for students; a photography permit is 170 drs ($1.30).

Knossos

The archeological site at Knossos, five kilometers south of Iraklion, contains the **Central Palace**, which dominated Minoan civilization from 2000 to 1400 B.C. The remarkable excavation of ruins by archeologist Sir Arthur Evans includes an elaborate re-creation of large parts of the original palace (considered overrestored by some standards). Yet it's still fun and fascinating to explore. Knossos is the archetypal "pop" archeological site, but it's an absolute must for any visitor to Crete.

The Englishman Evans began his work in 1900 (after some 1878 finds by a local scholar) and, as his dig progressed, steadily bought up the land behind the growing port of Iraklion. He found that a town had existed before Minos built his palace, so he conjectured that the king (and spiritual leader of the Minoans) may have been a wealthy landowner. The huge complex (almost 20,000 square meters) is thought to have had 1,400 rooms, on many levels; it's known that the east wing of the palace had five stories and the west had three.

Evans used lots of cement and a color code to evoke images of the original structure. The round red columns were painted wood, used in building because their tensility made them earthquake resistant. Column bases and the lower portion of walls were covered in marble or alabaster, in contrast to the stuccoed top half, decorated with lively, multicolored frescoes. Wood was used in the brick walls and for door and window frames; the panes were alabaster. Remember that the fabulous frescoes have been removed from the site and can be found at the Heraklion archeological museum.

Eighteen storerooms were uncovered containing 150 pithoi (large urns) holding liquids (perhaps olive oil) used to light lamps. Evans believed that the palace was finally destroyed by a fire which roared through its wooden structure, fueled by lamps overturned in an earthquake. The little that remains of the palace is still a marvel.

Most of the lower flights of the original, expertly crafted stairs are still used, and near the queen's Megaron is what's considered to be the first flush toilet! Horizontal and vertical clay pipes (proof of the Minoans' expert sewage system) can still be seen. In the Administrative Wing of the palace, a wooden throne, thought to have been Minos', has been re-created from a void fused in some volcanic ruins by a casting process. Outside the palace buildings are the paved stones of Europe's oldest road and the collapsed steps of Europe's first theater.

Evans also found the remains of what may have been an area (outside the palace grounds) for the celebrated bull dances, part of the mysterious religious cult surrounding this animal.

If the colorful restoration of Knossos is too much for your historical sensibilities, at the knee-high ruins of Malia and Phaestos you can imagine what the palaces must have looked like all by yourself.

The Palace of Knossos archeological site is open Monday through Saturday from 8 a.m. to 7 p.m. and on Sunday from 8 a.m. to 6 p.m. Admission is 500 drs ($3.85) for adults and 300 drs ($2.30) for students. Try to come before 9:30 a.m. or after 11:30 a.m. (when the half-day tours that emanate from the cruise ships have departed) so you'll have space to explore.

Bus 2 runs to Knossos every 20 minutes from outside El Greco Park. It can also be picked up at Eleftherias (Liberty) Square. The fare is 75 drs (58¢).

DAY TRIPS FROM IRAKLION: The region south of Iraklion is Crete's equivalent of the Napa Valley in California or the Bordeaux region in France. Low, rolling hills and gently shaded valleys are resplendent with groves of trellised grapes cultivated for many of Crete's fine wines and powerful *raki*.

Archanes

If you want to experience the full sensuality of this area, drive or take one of the frequent buses to Archanes (15 kilometers south of Iraklion), get out, and then walk to some of the nearby vineyards. You'll be saturated with the fragrance of the air and the exquisite vistas. Stop by a vineyard during August or September (depending on the weather) and you can watch the harvest. Each year a number of visitors hire themselves out as day laborers during the harvest period. Most vineyards pay about 1500 drs ($11.50) a day, and it really is tough, back-breaking work. But there's nothing like jumping in and taking part in a tradition that dates back thousands of years. If you decide to pick grapes, don't be surprised if they pay the Greeks almost twice as much. They tend to be far more experienced and productive than most tourists.

A delightful stop in Pano (upper) Archanes is the shaded ouzeri, **Miriofito**, located at the base of the hill on which the village is built. Miriofito serves local drinks and light food, and you can watch the goings-on from under the cool of the trees.

This region has a long history of wine growing, and this fact is no more apparent than at **Vathipetro**, five kilometers south (you must walk), where excavations in progress have unearthed a Minoan palace (circa 1600 B.C.) with facilities for pressing grapes. Olive presses and kilns for firing pottery have also been found. Nearby, archeologists have uncovered what they believe are the remnants of an early, important center of worship. Traces of blood have led researchers to the conclusion that sacrifices (animal and human) took place near the palace.

Southeast of Archanes is the town of **Thrapsanu**, where local craftsmen still make the huge ceramic urns (*pithoi*) that have been made since Minoan times. **Paradosiaki Keramiki** (tel. 0891/41-374), one kilometer outside Thrapsanu, is an ideal place to watch the age-old method of pottery making. The potter's small shop has some tantalizing bargains, like glazed espresso cups at 250 drs ($1.92) for a set, and makes a worthwhile visit just to see the men mixing clay, fashioning pottery, and applying the simple decorations.

Spili

Spili is a very special place. This gorgeous hillside village is the perfect antidote to the suburban and Dionysian revelries of north- and south-coast beach resorts. Imagine a town of grapevines and roses, where streets lined with old stone houses built on a hillside are wide enough only for donkeys . . . geranium-filled courtyards with bunches of drying herbs left for goats to nibble on . . . freshly made yogurt covered with nuts, which grow behind every home . . . 19 lions' heads pouring out mountain spring water into a fountain above the platia . . . and only one hotel in town, charming and inexpensive.

Spili is the quintessential Cretan village, a community of farmers and their families, little touched by the tourist parade that crosses their main street to reach Aghia Galini. It's the kind of village you came to Greece to see, and the only way to appreciate its beauty is by abandoning the main street and striking out on its narrow stone paths. You'll find whitewashed terraces covered with grape-filled trellises, fragrant flowers, palms, and cherry trees. To get there take the bus from Rethymnon to Ag. Galini and tell the driver to let you off at Spili.

If you come for lunch, there are seven cafés within 100 meters of the Lion Fountain. Walk down the main street to visit the **Green Hotel** (tel. 0832/22-225), and you may just decide to spend the night. John dubbed it "the Green House," and besides the plants that have overtaken its light natural-wood interior, every one of the 15 rooms has a tiled balcony (filled with potted geraniums) overlooking flower-covered houses on the main street or the valley below. George Maravelakis, its owner, claims to speak a "Greek salad" of English, French, and German, but he just couldn't understand our praise for his "green thumb"! Stay and you'll have the opportunity to try his yogurt (drenched in home-grown honey and nuts) for breakfast. At 2300 drs ($17.69) for a double, you may decide to stay for the rest of your life! George's brother, Iannis, runs **Gianni's Restaurant**, nearby, and it's heartily recommended too.

Rest assured that Spili also exists in the real world. There are two gas stations, two banks, a post office, dry cleaner, and a bakery along the main street. The Rethymnon bus stops at the platia.

Gortis

Gortis is one of Crete's most important archeological sites because of the excellent ruins from several eras found there, among them the remains of the three-aisled **Basilica of Ag. Titus**, dedicated in the sixth century A.D. to Titos (he was a pupil of Saint Paul who founded the first Christian community on Crete at this site in A.D. 65). It's considered Crete's finest Christian monument. The basilica is at the foot of the ancient acropolis of Gortyn, which served as the capital of Crete during the Roman Period. Surrounding the basilica are the remains of a second-century **Roman Odeon**. Across the highway, enter the olive grove past the Metropolis road to see the remains of a second-century **Praetorium** (the governor's house), a **Nymphaion**, which the Byzantines converted into a fountain, and the **Temple of the Egyptian Gods**, dedicated to Isis and Sarapis; there's even a temple to the Pythian Apollo. Farther back are remains of a small amphitheater.

The earliest settlement dates from post-Mycenaean times (tenth century B.C.), and almost every succeeding generation has used materials from the existing temples to construct edifices of their own. The best example of this is the **Code of Gortis**, written in an ancient Doric language, that designated the rights and property of man. It's carved in stone blocks that make up part of the much-later Odeon. You'll see the stone tablets in the reconstructed facade behind the theater.

Phaistos

If you've come to see the fascinating ruins of Crete's second-largest Minoan palace, we hope you've purchased the excellent guidebook, *Crete*, by J. A. Papapostolou. (Anyone with an interest in exploring the traces of the Minoan civilization left on the island will appreciate the wonderful drawings reconstructing the original cities, as well as excellent maps of every Minoan site.) The **Palace of Phaistos** is every bit as grand as that at Knossos, but because it hasn't been restored in the Evans color-by-number fullness, a good guide or well-illustrated guidebook is essential for full appreciation. Excavations were begun at Phaistos in the same period that Evans was working at Knossos, but it wasn't until 1950 that Professor Levi completed a systematic examination of the site.

As you walk down the stairs to the site, you'll be in the middle of the court from the older palace (ca. 2000 B.C.). On your right, the grand stairs mark the entrance to the newer palace built on the earthquake-shattered remains of the older one, about 1750 B.C., a grand Minoan palace dominating the Messary plain, where civilization flourished until 1450 B.C.

To the 20th-century traveler the highlight of the palace is the **royal apartments**, found under protective plastic canopies on the north side of the site. In the first apartment, the remains of four columns make it easy to envision the arched roof they supported over the perimeter of the room, and the well of light created in the courtyard. The benches and flooring which have survived in places at the west end of the room are still sheathed in alabaster slabs, mortared with red plaster. A perfect staircase between the royal suites led up to the palace's second story.

The site is open from 8 a.m. to 7 p.m. Monday to Saturday, from 8 a.m. to 6 p.m. on Sunday and holidays. The admission fee is 300 drs ($2.30) for adults, 250 drs ($1.92) for students. Phaistos can be reached by public bus from

Iraklion, or via several daily connections with buses from Rethymnon, Matala, and Aghia Galini. Those with a serious archeological interest may obtain permission to consult with on-site scholars of the Italian Archeological School from the director of antiquities at the museum in Iraklion.

Three kilometers from the Palace at Phaistos is the **Villa of Ag. Triadha**, a small Minoan palace dating from 1700 B.C. It's believed to have been the summer home of the king who resided at Phaistos, and makes a refreshing side trip at midday because of the cool breezes blowing off the Libyan Sea, just ten kilometers south. The archeological museum at Iraklion contains two carved vases, incredible sculpture with reliefs depicting boxers and harvesters, as well as some beautiful frescoes, that were found at this site.

2. From Iraklion to Aghios Nikolaos

The tourist developments along Crete's north coast emanate in both directions from Iraklion. The satellite cities of **Arina** and **Themis Beach** are full-service resorts housing budget tour groups who've jumped on charters in Brussels or Frankfurt for a "Week at the Beach" package that's cheaper than staying at home.

Hersonissos is the first major autonomous town, though the hundreds of white prefab Mediterranean-style hotels, boutiques, and scooter-rental outfits must have been cloned from the model issued at the Bureau of Greek Hotel Standards. For kilometers along the island side of the road, big, small, elegant, and ugly homes sprout "villas to let" signs. Two kilometers out past the main street is **Caravan Camping**, where you can share the narrow sand-and-pebble beach with thousands of others. Believe us, you don't want to visit Hersonissos.

Continuing east, you'll reach **Stalis**, a much smaller development of the same ilk. Here, the **Pension Marina**, just a short walk to the beach, is a cheap place to stay (though in the off-season you should move on to the truly picturesque Ag. Nikolaos for the night).

MALIA: On the way, stop to see the Palace of Malia, an interesting Minoan site just outside this uninteresting, unappealing beach resort. Buses run from Iraklion every 30 minutes, costing 325 drs ($2.50); they turn off the main highway to leave you at the foot of the public beach.

If you feel compelled to stay in Malia, there are several cheaper accommodations along the Hersonissos model. The **Grammatikakis Pension** (tel. 0897/31-366), with rooms right on the beach, is an affordable resort choice at 3450 drs ($26.53) for a double, including breakfast. Its 52 older, clean bungalows are built around a lawn and garden sunning area, and the lobby is filled with racks of suntan lotion, trashy novels, and faded postcards. Write ahead though, as it's often fully booked.

Just 50 meters east is the **Pension Agapi** (tel. 0897/31-264), where 2500 drs ($19.23) includes breakfast for two and the company of sunburned Germans listening to American rock music, tapping their Dr. Scholl's on the barstools around the seaside café.

Certainly as clean, with "cottage cheese" stuccoed walls and newly tiled private bathrooms, are the better value rooms, 200 drs ($15.38), above the **Sirtaki Taverna** and **Cafée Zodiac**, on the main street. If you insist on a private phone and elevator, the **Drossia Hotel** (tel. 0897/31-408) offers less intimate accommodations at 2600 drs ($20) for a double, including breakfast.

The Palace of Malia

Just three kilometers outside Malia are the ruins of a Minoan palace. What's a very pleasant 20-minute walk along the beach could turn into a 35-

minute bus trip, when you wait half an hour for the Ag. Nikolaos–bound bus and then hop aboard for a five-minute ride. The archeological site (tel. 0897/31-597) is open daily from 8:45 a.m. to 3 p.m., on Sunday and holidays from 9:30 a.m. to 2:30 p.m. Admission is 250 drs ($1.92), and "proper" attire is required.

Greek archeologist Joseph Chatzedakis first conducted excavations here in 1915 and found the ruins of what was probably the Minoan city of Miletos. The simple remains of Crete's third Minoan palace (from ca. 1700 B.C.) give the visitor a good impression of what the Palace at Knossos might have looked like before Evans's extraordinary restoration. There the comparison ends. Archeologists think the lack of frescoes and simple style of the Malia palace indicate that it was a provincial outpost—a suburban palace, so to speak.

The quiet site is surrounded by mountains and cooled by a sea breeze. Because it's on one level and can be seen from above, the grandeur of the original palace is very apparent. Rough rectangular bricks are stacked four to five feet high and mortared with a reddish clay. Large areas of flagstone paving are still visible. In the back, covered-over section, where the French Archeological School has continued to dig, you can see subterranean walls with remnants of plaster trim. Some column bases have been revealed, and doors, steps, walls, and a half-exposed vase (frozen in time) are visible.

LASSITHI PLAIN: A visit to the mountainous inland region of the Lassithi Plain can be made as a day trip from Iraklion or as a diversion from the north coast highway on the way to Ag. Nikolaos. Tour guides have earmarked **Psychro** as the best vantage point for clear views over the Lassithi Plain, a sight to see in midmorning when the thousands of white sailcloth windmills are spinning wildly, pumping water to irrigate the lush wheat fields. It is breathtakingly gorgeous.

Nearby is the **Dictaion Cave**, where Rhea secretly gave birth to Zeus. (She was attempting to save him from the fate of his brothers and sisters who were eaten at birth by their father, Kronos.) Legends say that Zeus was suckled by the goat Amalthea in the cave; archeologists have uncovered many icons and votive symbols confirming this as an important worship area during the Minoan era. (Actually, one of the most exciting excavations taking place in all of Greece is at the Grotto of Ideon Andron, south of Rethymnon, the cave where Zeus was raised.) The Dictaion Cave can be visited via donkey or well-shod feet. If you join a tour or go by public bus, you'll exit the north coast highway just before Malia and head south through the fertile Mochas area, past the villages of Potamie and Kera.

A more dramatic mountain road, practical only for tourists with wheels, leads from the mountain town of **Neapolis**. This small city, on a plateau west of the Dicti range, offers its own view of windmills. The left side of the road is covered by the tall stone towers of now-idle, traditional windmills, while the right or valley side of the drive is filled with bright aluminum ones with spinning cloth-covered blades. It seems most of Crete's 30 million olive trees are clinging to the hillsides here, vigorously nurtured by the continuous flow of water.

Just after Neapolis, a left turn off the highway at Kastelli will bring you along the more scenic, original road to Ag. Nikolaos. You can go left at the coast up to **Plaka**, a charming fishing village whose two tavernas overlook the tip of Spinalonga Island. From the dock, skillful negotiation can provide you with a private boat trip to the island.

Bearing right will bring you to the once equally appealing, though now very developed, port at **Elounda**. We recommend that you approach Ag. Nikolaos, the obviously established jewel of this sparkling coastline, via the new highway so that your first impression will be of its idyllic pond, rather than the resort hotel strip that's been developed from its north end up toward Elounda. As you approach Ag. Nikolaos you pass by Istron Bay, a very beautiful stretch of beach. It's being developed now; if you're driving, by all means turn off and check out the bay. There are two hotels, a market, and a taverna.

3. Aghios Nikolaos and the Northeast

The sleepy little port town of Aghios Nikolaos (St. Nicholas) was a well-kept secret for many years. English tourists in small numbers would return season after season to decompress from the hectic pace of everyday life. Even the BBC came to Ag. Nikolaos, to produce one of its acclaimed TV series. About ten years ago hotels started sprouting up like weeds, and now the local publicity hawkers dub it the "St- Tropez of Crete." Nevertheless, it's hard to spoil one of Crete's most ideal vacation spots. Last summer we met an English girl, Sarah, and asked her how long she'd been in Ag. Nikolaos. She replied, dreamily, "Oh, about three years now. . . . I guess I forgot to leave."

Unfortunately, when the summer season cranks up and tourists pour in (after all, most tourists aren't dummies; they know a good spot when they see one) the town can go haywire. Discos, loud tavernas, overcrowding, and moped madness make Ag. Nikolaos an oppressive environment. This is a place to visit in spring and fall if you don't want to be disappointed, when the port is at its best. (You might want to make this a lunch stop if you're only on Crete during the summer.) There is an excellent Tourist Office (tel. 0841/22-357) that can make Ag. Nikolaos sparkle for you. It's open from 7:30 a.m. to 9 p.m. during the week, and 8 a.m. to 3:30 p.m. on Sunday.

LAYOUT: The town is built on a couple of low hills and centered around a small pond—all of the maps and locals refer to it as a lake. In either case it's wet, and one of the best places to while away the hours at a café and watch the little fishing caiques pull in. The town is divided into two parts: the older, quieter, and more picturesque village and the glitzier livelier beach. (The best local **beach** is at Armiros, three kilometers south of town. The locals complain that the water's cold, but that just keeps it less crowded for the hardy.) The local **post office** is on 28 Octovriou St. and the telephone exchange is nearby. The **Tourist Police** (tel. 0841/22-251), are open Monday through Friday and they're located up from the lake on Paleologoli St. The Ag. Nikolaos **General Hospital** (tel. 0841/22-369) is on Lasithiou Street. All town **banks** keep the standard Greek 8 a.m. to 2 p.m. weekday hours. The **area code** is 0841.

ACCOMMODATIONS: Both the village and the beach areas of Ag. Nikolaos have fine accommodations. The trick is finding one that's retained some of the magic that made this such a popular tourist destination in the first place. Another difficulty is that most hotels are often fully booked by groups throughout the season.

In the Village

The number one selections in the village are the Hotel Odysseas and the Pension Milos. The **Hotel Odysseas** (tel. 0841/23-934) is where many longtime English visitors to Ag. Nikolaos now choose to stay. Like many other places in town, the hotel is recently built, but it has a "homely" feel (as the English like to say) and is often filled with guests who are up for a good part of the day and night. Expect to pay 3200 drs ($24.61) for double during the busy summer season. That is, if they have a room at all. Recently they have hosted several tour groups who completely buy out the hotel.

The **Pension Milos** (tel. 0841/23-783) at 24 Sarolidi St., is a spotless sister-run pension that has fine views of the sea. Maria and Georgia live on the first two floors of the villa, and a stay in one of the rooms above theirs will make you feel as if you're visiting a Greek family. High-season double rooms with private facilities go for 2625 drs ($20.19).

The **Pension Istron** (tel. 0841/23-763), on Sarolidi Street near the Milos, is another attractive choice managed by Mrs. Tuttu Dachi and her family. There are nine bathless rooms enlivened by fresh-cut flowers and crisp new paint. Shuttered French doors open up to refreshing sea breezes. The Dachis charge 1850 drs ($14.23) in the low season for a double room and 2200 drs ($16.92) in the high season.

By the Beach

If you want to be in closer proximity to a swimming beach and nightlife, try the **Hotel Linda** or the **Pension Perla**. Sandwiched in between the much larger and more expensive hotels Coral, Hermes, and Rea, you'll find more personality at these smaller lodgings. The **Linda** (tel. 0841/22-130) is newer and a little costlier than the Perla—2500 drs ($19.23) vs. 2300 drs ($17.69) for a double— but both are clean and attractive. The decor of the Hotel Linda's 16 rooms is what one guest called "Hessian Greek moderne" but the bougainvillea-covered, trellised canopy over the breakfast patio is just lovely. The Perla (tel. 0841/23-379) is at 4 Salaminos, across the street from the Linda. The eight spartan rooms are bathless but the common showers are spotless and have abundant hot water.

The **Hotel Athina** (tel. 0841/28-225), at 32 Prigipos Armostou Georgiou, is a good-value B-class hotel above the harbor, in a quieter, more residential neighborhood. The Athina's lobby is warmly decorated with colorful locally woven fabrics, and its 20 rooms are spacious and light. High-season singles are 1700 drs ($13.07); doubles, 2650 drs ($20.38); triples, 3225 drs ($24.80).

The High and Low Ends

Most of our readers wouldn't be interested in the A and B luxury-class resorts that line the coast above Ag. Nikolaos village; those who are should book accommodations through a travel agent before departure. Nevertheless, there are several hotels offering high-priced rooms that are somewhat plusher than those mentioned above. On the village side of the harbor is the **Hotel Panorama** (tel. 0841/28-890), built cleverly on a rise at 5 Kondourou St. As its name implies, the Panorama offers excellent views of the seagoing traffic from its lobby and sunny, enclosed dining balcony. There is elevator service to every floor, and all 29 rooms have private balconies, bathrooms, and fabric-covered furnishings. The Spanish-style lobby has tiled floors, brass chandeliers, and lots of fresh flowers. Doubles at the Panorama are 4100 drs ($31.53).

The **Hotel Victoria** (tel. 0841/22-266), on Akti Koyntourou, is a fancier C-class choice by the beach. This clean, modern hotel is only 100 meters or so from the best beach in Ag. Nikolaos, and all 20 rooms are decorated with locally made handicrafts and artwork. Doubles with private facilities run 4850 drs ($37.30) nightly.

Ag. Nikolaos's cheapest beds can be found at the **Youth Hostel** (tel. 0841/22-823), at 5 Stratiou Koraka. The facility has 70 beds and is surprisingly well maintained; each will cost 425 drs ($3.27). Common showers and an inexpensive restaurant are this hostel's more positive attributes.

DINING: Ag. Nikolaos is endowed with especially good restaurants. **Taverna the Pines** has an odd name but deliciously roasted chicken and lamb. Located opposite the Creta Travel Bureau on the pond, its wooden façade is partially hidden from view by a tall pine tree which shades the front tables. The dark-wood interior decor gives the Pines a formal yet romantic feeling. Dinner for two at what's considered one of Ag. Nikolaos's finest eateries should cost 1800 drs ($13.85) to 2300 drs ($17.69), including a bottle of local wine.

The **Trata Restaurant**, situated opposite the Hotel Delta by the city's southern beachfront, is the local favorite for its excellent preparation of typical Greek specialties, such as stuffed tomatoes or moussaka. Chicken Trata is also a good choice. Best of all, it's got local prices, where two can eat well for 1400 drs ($10.77).

As you might imagine, a port whose biggest industry is fishing should boast some excellent fish restaurants. The problem here is that Ag. Nikolaos has been so overbuilt for tourists that many vessels of its fishing fleet have been diverted to day-cruise use. Still, there are two local favorites for good value in really fresh fish. As might be expected, **Hari's Restaurant**, at the east end of the ferryboat harbor, a little out of the main crush, has the better food and wine list at lower prices. For those who want the Riviera ambience of the busy beach-coast promenade, try **Zefiros**. Even though you'll pay more here, at least you'll be getting a great meal.

The prime location for dining in terms of pedestrian traffic should be the bridge connecting both the harbor and beach halves of town. The one restaurant here, the **Café Agtaion**, has remained owned and operated by the local Cretans for the benefit of the locals, and has good, simple Greek fare at low-budget prices. Their octopus is a specialty (500 drs or $3.85), and try their *raki* as an after-dinner drink.

For a totally different Greek experience, try the **Ikaros Taverna**, next door to the Hotel Coral. This lively and inviting open-air taverna spills out onto the harborside. Young tourists and local mates crowd the big tables to enjoy Greek music, fresh air, song and dance, and mediocre food. Chef Nikos Kokolakis knows best how to whip up a good time. The patrons have been known to provide their own entertainment, dancing to a selection of popular tunes. If no one else gets up, Nikos and his dancing waiters will. If you've been practicing Dora Stratou's routines after seeing her troupe in Athens, this may be your big chance to step out. Dinner for two runs about 2000 drs ($15.38), which is steep for the food but a bargain for the liberating atmosphere.

If you've worked off some calories at the Ikaros, there's one local dessert specialty that shouldn't be missed in Ag. Nikolaos. **Limnis Taverna**, on the lakefront in the heart of town, can't be missed because of the large sign in its window proclaiming "BBC-TV group, headed by Ian Hendry filming 'The Lotus Eaters', ate 90% of their meals here." We all know what to think about such a recommendation; therefore eat elsewhere and arrive after 9 p.m. Then order their famous dessert, yogurt served with walnuts and honey, at 375 drs ($2.88). We overheard one traveler exclaim: "Why, I've counted 32 nuts!"

WHAT TO SEE AND DO: There are many man-made wonders to admire in the naturally beautiful and scenic port. Just two kilometers from the village is a little-known Byzantine church with fine frescoes. The small collection of finds from Myrtos, Mochlas, and Krista are at Ag. Nikolaos's archeological museums (tel. 22-462); it's open Wednesday to Monday 9 a.m. to 3 p.m. Closed Tuesday. At night Ag. Nikolaos sizzles. All the discos, bars, and café's inhabit the main strip on the port. Akti Koundourou Street. Want to boogie? Try **Bora Bora** or, two doors down, the **Lipstick Disco**. Maybe something more upscale? The **Candia Café** and the **Zodiac Bar** are your kind of place: chic, young, and hot. Just check out the strip with a leisurely stroll and stop to smell the roses.

EXCURSIONS UP AND DOWN THE COAST: Both **Grips Tours** (tel. 28-988) and **Creta Tours** (tel. 28-496) offer motor-coach tours around Crete originating in Ag. Nikolaos and local boat excursions. Our favorite was the full-day fishing trip which stopped at a taverna in Elounda, where the day's catch was fried up for lunch. **Spinalonga Island** is one of the most popular destinations from Ag. Nikolaos, and boat tours cost about 1600 drs ($12.30), though small boats can be hired for much less from the ports at Elounda or Plaka for short visits. Check with Deirdre at the **Massaros Travel Agency** (tel. 0841/22-267), at 29 Koundourou St., open 7 days a week. They've got all the info on various trips, and even list villas to rent. Spinalonga was a peninsula until the Venetians built a powerful fortress over the ruins of the ancient city of Olonte. The Venetians restored their bastion in 1526 and reinforced it by cutting a canal through the peninsula. This insular fortress was one of the last three on Crete (along with the fortresses at Grambousse and Souda Bay), providing the Venetians with an impregnable stronghold against the Turks for 50 years, until 1715. In modern times (until 1958) Spinalonga was the site of a leper colony, earning it the poignant nickname "the Island of Pain and Tears."

Elounda

Just ten kilometers north of Ag. Nikolaos, along a resort-encrusted road, is the once-sleepy port of Elounda, now awakening to the tinkle of tourist drachmas. Your first sight of it will be the land bridge that stretches out to meet the island of Spinalonga, forming a natural lagoon. Straddling this spit of land is a solitary, graceful Venetian fortress in ruins.

Elounda is the perfect example of a "picturesque fishing village nestled in a sheltered cove" that's been discovered by beach-resort packagers. Fortunately, though, the severe water shortage in the area has slowed the ravages of overdevelopment.

Flanking both sides of the road into the port are restaurants and gift shops with rooms to let above them. There are several C-class hotels in the village, which will give you a chance to enjoy the pretty sandy beaches without an all-inclusive package. The **Hotel Kalypso** (tel. 0841/41-316), at the north end of the harbor next to the Ag. Constantinos Church, has 20 nicely decorated, well-maintained doubles at 3425 drs ($26.34) above an expensive tavern of the same name.

The best bet here, and one reason to come to Elounda, is the excellent architecture of the new **Hotel Sophia** (tel. 0841/41-482), on the main street. Its 26 spacious rooms are all different, with private entrances off a courtyard, and stacked on many levels like the Palace at Knossos. Many are two-room suites with kitchenettes, at 3700 drs ($28.46)—a good deal if you want to stay a while—and spacious comfortable doubles are 3200 drs ($24.61) nightly.

Elounda is better appreciated as a fun and scenic day trip from Ag. Nikolaos. Its pretty harbor can provide respite from the midsummer crowds.

Kritsa

The hill town of Kritsa is located ten kilometers south of the main north-coast highway, and provides a welcome glimpse of the way life used to be (and rarely is) in this well-touristed part of Crete. The traditional weavings seen throughout the island provide much of the village's income, and the small handicraft shops on the main street offer many good buys. The town is known for its almond juice drink, Soumada, drunk cold in summer and hot in winter.

Just before you arrive in town is the celebrated 14th-century Byzantine Church of Panagia Kera. Within this small community church are the extensive, well-preserved remains of religious frescoes. The style of the renderings is much more primitive than those found on the mainland at Dafni or Ossios Loukas.

Decorative elements (from nature), sombre colors, and the brooding expressions of saints, villagers, kings, and icons are all worthy of close examination. Panagia Kera (open 8:30 a.m. to 6 p.m. Monday through Saturday, 9 a.m. to 2 p.m. on Sunday; fee: 250 drs or $1.92), is a wonderful place to experience the religious devotion once expressed in this isolated village and confirms the town's past as one of the most important centers of Byzantine art during the Venetian period. There are also beautiful frescoes at the Ag. Georgios Kavousiotis Church.

Gournia

The superbly restored remains of the village of Gournia (22 kilometers east of Ag. Nikolaos) are unique on Crete because this is the only Minoan town dating from the "Minoan **I**" period, a distinction earned by the almost total destruction of the first Minoan civilization by an earthquake in 1450 B.C. From the road the rough stone walls and even plan of Gournia's "streets" could be mistaken for a well-organized olive grove, minus the trees. If you climb up the easily distinguished, 3,500-year-old main street to the top of the mound, once site of a modest palace, you'll enjoy a wonderful view of the back alleys, houses, Agora, and Bay of Istron. There's no fee to enter the archeological site of Gournia, which is open till sunset (the knowledgeable guard speaks English and German). Public bus service from Ag. Nikolaos will cost you about 325 drs ($2.50). We're delighted to report that there are no postcard stands (no stands at all, in fact). If you walk a few hundred meters up the main roadway there's an excellent vantage point for photos, which includes a full view of this remarkable site and the bay beyond. Hours at the free site are 8:45 a.m. to 3 p.m. Wednesday to Monday, 9:30 a.m. to 2:30 p.m. Sunday and holidays. Closed Tuesday.

East to Sitia

The bus to Sitia follows the highway, the only road extending to the eastern tip of Crete at Vai. At each bend in the road you will be witness to the most exquisite vistas of mountain and sea on the whole island. **Kavoussion** is a bouquet of a village, literally dripping with pink and white oleanders and bright yellow honeysuckle. The scent of pressed olives wafts through the air, mingling with the sweet flowers in sensual confusion.

As the road climbs, cascades of yellow tumble down the hillside, where olive trees grow at an alarming 45° angle. Donkeys burdened with herbs and grape leaves are led by old farmers in their traditional baggy black pants, and you often see Crete's unique kris-kris, a curly-horned goat, tagging along.

Almost ten kilometers before you reach Sitia is a turnoff for the "**Minoan House of Chamaizi**," a site for avid Minoaphiles. A 1,000-meter walk along the stone road leading down from the highway will take you to the ruins of this old home, safely settled among olive groves. In the nearby hamlet of **Hamesion** you can see local finds at the Cretan Home Museum.

Sitia

Sitia was a Venetian stronghold until the Turkish pirate Barbarossa lay siege to the fort in the late 16th century. Today wreckages of two sunken ferryboats sit off Sitia's beachline, casualties not of the cannons of some hot-tempered Turk, but of Sitia's new invaders, sun-seeking tourists.

Strangely, though, Sitia is really nothing more than a way station between Ag. Nikolaos and the palm-lined beach at Vai. Its unspectacular (and often dirty) three-kilometer-long beach doesn't merit Sitia's almost cult-like status among budget travelers. To its credit, Sitia does have a fantastic and inexpensive restaurant and a couple of lively pensions.

First, the restaurant: **Yura's** is located one block up from the taxi stand at 4 Dimokritou St. The food here (Cretan) is probably the best you'll find. Consistent with the hunting decor (notice the rifle and kri-kri horns on the walls), Yura's serves very fresh meat. Not only that, but the fava beans are just crisp enough, the pasta firm, and all the sauces delicious. The restaurant has an outdoor section across the street, but in the hot summer months the indoor tends to be cooler. If Yura's is closed, you might try **Russo's** or **Zorba's** on La Strada, all nearby on the harbor.

As for pensions, the **Arhontiko Hotel**, at 16 Kondulakis (tel. 0843/28-172), is a real charmer. Its ten spacious and clean rooms are in a 1900 wooden house, with ever-so-slightly sloped wooden floors, surrounded by lemon trees. Apostolis Kamalis and Brigitte Hurdalek are very hospitable and even provide a common kitchen for their guests, at 2150 drs ($16.53) for two.

Victoria's Pension (tel. 0843/28-080) is on the left side of the road to Ierapetra, about 200 meters from the center of town. The pension has two gorgeous gardens and houses its guests (most of whom are young nomads) in small and simply furnished bungalow-style rooms. Victoria's also has a kitchen, and most guests stay for a while. Doubles are 2100 drs ($16.15).

The **Youth Hostel** (tel. 0843/22-693), up the hill from the bus stop, at 4 Therissou St., is a great stop for budget tourists. Lakis, the owner, and Sue, his ever-so-helpful manager, will do everything to make your stay in Sitia pleasant. Beds are 450 drs ($3.46) per night.

The **Hotel Elena** (tel. 0843/22-681) is the best C-class selection, at 3000 drs ($23.07), including breakfast, for a spacious double room with private bath.

People come to Sitia to connect with boats leaving for the Dodecanese and the Cyclades. You can get **ferries** going to Kassos, Karpathos, Diafan, Chalki, or Rhodes. There is also a route that goes to Ag. Nikolaos, Santorini, Ios, Naxos, Paros, and Piraeus. (Both are extensions of lines that leave Ag. Nikolaos.) Nightly activity centers on card games at the Youth Hostel or the two **discos** of note: Zorba's (poor Kazantzakis) and La Nuit.

Vai

A highly touted destination 27 kilometers northeast of Sitia, Vai is a land of palm trees. Cretans and Europeans take this palm-lined, sand-beach inlet very seriously, and those of you who've enjoyed Florida or California beaches will be amused by the ecstatic Germans and Italians who pose for photos under the seaside palm fronds. This is very out of the way for a beach excursion, but the large parking lot, cafeteria, and (best of all) private showers (for 60 drs, 50¢) ensure its popularity year round. An excerpt from the posted regulations follows:

"The aesthetic forest Vai is a unique habitat consisting of the endemic species *Phoenix Theophrastii*. . . . It constitutes the northernmost boundary of the expansion of this species and consequently poses as a natural monument of international interest. . . . Its maintenance is deemed imperative. . . . At a parallel basis this habitat should be studied from all angles. . . . No camping and sleeping in the open air. . . . The safekeeping of forest is carried out by special officials of the forestry department and aims at the preservation of this natural national heritage, giving at the same time to the visitor the opportunity of recreation in a spellbinding natural environment. For this end your cooperation with the game wardens for the success of the common objective, it being the protection of this unique habitat with which nature has endowed our country, is deemed indispensable. . . ."

The far end of the parking lot is an unofficially designated camping spot, and the hardy who scale the hill beyond the tourist restaurant will descend to an out-of-sight cove sanctioned for nude sunbathing. If you really want to test the farthest-out beaches, continue straight for two kilometers, past the right turnoff for Vai.

Itanos

At the northeastern tip of the island is the ancient city of Manos, uncovered by French archeologists. The remains of the eastern acropolis indicate that this picturesque promontory was inhabited from the Geometric through Hellenic periods. On the taller, western acropolis the remains date from the third century. Never ones to miss a good site, the Byzantines occupied the land between the acropolises, and remains of stone houses can still be seen. Of utmost interest to the modern visitor are two isolated sandy coves easily viewed from the height of either acropolis, which provide superb swimming and sunbathing without the Vai crowds.

Zakros

Some of the most magnificent Minoan artifacts have been unearthed at Kato Zakros, located 37 kilometers from Sitia, on Crete's far east end, south from the exotic beach at Vai. Zakros is the fourth **Minoan palace**, and archeologists have determined that its location was of major strategic and commercial import for the Minoan empire. The palace gave the Minoans a base for trading and keeping tabs on the other major powers of antiquity: Syria, Egypt, and the whole of Asia Minor.

Excavation began in the early 1960s and continues, with the major discovery of remarkably carved stone vases excavated from the only unplundered Minoan tomb on Crete. These vessels are one of the highlights of the archeological museum in Iraklion (Gallery 8), and spark the imagination with their brilliant design and craftsmanship. The site, like the other Minoan palaces, was built about 1600 B.C. on top of the remains of an earlier palace. Unfortunately the palace at Zakros is not as well preserved as those at Knossos and Phaestos, but is certainly worth a visit for those fascinated by Minoan culture and history.

The town of Zakros (eight kilometers from the site) has the C-class **Hotel Zakros** (tel. 0843/28-479) and rooms to rent. There is a beach at Kato Zakros, so if the heat of ancient stone gets to you, cool off in the sea.

4. The South: Ierapetra to Ag. Galini

To Cretans, Ierapetra is the star of the south coast, the next willing victim of tourist inundation (because of its sandy beaches and clean waters). Fortunately for Crete it is already the wealthiest city (in terms of per-capita income) because of its thriving agriculture industry. From here tomatoes, eggplants, cucumbers, herbs, and raisins are exported to other parts of Greece and northern Europe. The hothouses seen on both sides of the road as you approach from Sitia keep those ripe tomatoes coming for Greek salads in Athens all year round. Unfortunately for the too-numerous hoteliers, the plants and offices that service this vital cash crop have made Ierapetra a rather ugly, bustling seaside city. Nonetheless, Crete's south coast along the Libyan Sea boasts the clearest waters and warmest climate in Europe, and the national highways system has made Ierapetra its gateway city.

IERAPETRA: For those who need activity and want to sightsee along Crete's beautiful south coast, Ierapetra's long harbor, pleasant if overpriced cafés, and urban activities make an acceptable base, though the smaller, picturesque port of Ag. Galini may be more to your liking. Consult the new **E.O.T.** office (tel. 0842/28-658) in Ierapetra.

Where to Stay

If you decide to make Ierapetra your base, try to get a furnished flat with kitchenette, at 2300 drs ($17.69) for a double, from Mr. Agiannotakis at the **Kafeteria Ierapetra** (tel. 0842/22-846), on the harbor. Avoid his Hotel Coral. There are several rooms to let on Ionanidou Street, which runs parallel to the water (a block in). Here, try the **Gorgona Pension**, or the rooms at no. 44, where **Theo** (tel. 0842/23-394) has seven clean rooms without bath; doubles are 1850 drs ($14.23). The cheery **Hotel Kyrva** (tel. 0842/22-594), one kilometer from town at 27 Em. Lambraki, is the best value, though not the least expensive C-class hotel, at 2900 drs ($22.30) for a double room.

What to Do

If you're only interested in the beach, backtrack east for 27 kilometers to **Makrigialos**, a small fishing village with a long, public beach. Staying in one of the few spartan rooms to let above the main street will give you solo time on the beach before the day-trippers arrive.

From Ierapetra's harbor, three 60-passenger cruise boats depart at 9 a.m. daily April through October for an excursion to the tiny uninhabited **Chrissi (Donkey) Island** (2000 drs or $15.38 round trip). Its sand beaches are considered among the finest (and certainly the least exploited) in Crete. There's only one taverna, so bring a picnic, or adequate supplies if you plan to rough-camp in this nearly African isle.

An easier (and less expensive) excursion is to the less frequented beach at **Ag. Fotia**, 15 kilometers east of town. The K.T.E.L. buses to Sitia, leaving from the central square, will drop you there. Between Ag. Fotia and Makrigialos you can climb down to a beach just past the Coriva Village Resort in **Ferma** (or at **Galini Beach** near Koutsouras).

Within Ierapetra town there's a small **archeological museum** (open Monday through Saturday, 9 a.m. to 3 p.m.). For one of the most pleasant evening activities, try a **sunset stroll**. We recommend starting at the central part of the harbor down from Eletheria Square. Turning right, you'll pass an old, official-looking iron building. A stroll past the drydocked fishing boats and worn hulls in the midst of repair will lead into taverna row, where you can judge the local action. At the west end of the harbor is a Venetian fortress, a broad square framed by an old clock tower, and the Damilaki Church. When you're ready to eat, try the **Konaki Minotauro** or **Kalamnia Tavernas**, both overlooking the harbor. Remember, you haven't eaten in Ierapetra until you've tried their tomatoes!

And most important, if you're doing anything other than passing through, pay a visit to the **Ierapetra Express Tourist Office** (tel. 28-123 or 22-411), the building with Creta Tours and Hertz signs opposite the National Bank, at 24 Eleftherias. The enthusiastic Chrisoula speaks several languages and is overwhelmingly helpful, as is everyone at their office. Ierapetra Express is open from 8:30 a.m. to 1 p.m. and 5:30 p.m. to 8 p.m.

MYRTOS: Myrtos appears from the road like one of the many "hothouse" vegetable towns on Crete's attractive south coast. Walk into town and you'll see lovely gardens in small private homes, grapevines creeping up rickety trellises, and old women dressed in peasant black, sweeping dirt off the sidewalk. If you continue walking you'll come to Myrtos' sandy, long, and often trash-strewn beach. Camping on the beach is forbidden, but you'd never know it if you visited the much cleaner western side of the beach. Here you can see lots of European hippies in loose, gauzy traveling costumes, watching the ebb tide.

Remember, the hipped-out beach of today is the chic and expensive resort of tomorrow!

If this strange combination appeals to you (make no mistake, Myrtos is a nice place), try staying at the **Hotel Myrtos** (tel. 0842/51-226), at 1800 drs ($7.69) for two. There are also rooms to rent above the supermarket, one block from the Cosmos Tavern, and near Myrtos's church.

Cosmos Restaurant is a popular hangout, especially if you want to eat a tomato omelet and listen to old blues tapes at 8:30 a.m.! Myrtos boasts three beachfront cafés and the taverna **Akti**, where the sign proclaims "For the littoral." One comment overheard at a café discussion about the locals' reaction to the vanguard of the tourist invasion: "They're not too friendly, but you've got to make a new culture."

ARVI: After overcoming the initial shock of Crete's sprawling north coast developments, the truly committed beach seeker inevitably opens up the map in search of less inhabited shorelines. If the information grapevine is any measure of consensus, then the tiny village of Arvi is this year's favorite.

Like other points on the island, Arvi's natural surroundings reflect Crete's close proximity to Africa and Asia Minor. Its long, thin beach is within 100 meters of banana plantations and melon groves; there's also a spectacular gorge facing Arvi, 15 to 20 minutes' hiking distance from the town. The path (delightfully void of signs, guard rails, or tourists) leads through tilled fields of bananas, cucumbers, and grapes. You'll probably run across farmers schlepping goods from town, laborers working on the water pipes, goats, and a stray dog or two. The path parallels a small stream; at the mouth of the gorge you have to wade in knee-deep water. The sinewy curves of the rock there were formed by thousands of years of rushing water.

Arvi also has a 300-year-old monastery, **Ag. Antonini**, that is a moderate walk from town. From its hillside perch you have a good view of Arvi's unusual layout.

Most people come to Arvi for the beach, and unfortunately it isn't the paradise that one might imagine. In fact locals prefer the wider beach two kilometers west of the town. We did too. The town beach is certainly adequate, but with the number of tourists who take refuge here in the summer months, it tends to crowd up.

As for hotels, there is a pension, the **Hotel Gorgona** (tel. 0895/71-211), charging 2500 drs ($19.23) for two, and a C-class hotel, the **Hotel Ariadni** (tel. 0895/31-200), where doubles run 1600 drs ($12.30). The pension is spotless, small, and a bit homey, while the Ariadni (situated right on the shore) is a tad bit beach-worn. The Ariadni offers a 25% discount to students, which tends to make it a great congregating place for everyone. There are also numerous rooms to let, and about four or five hotels under construction.

If Arvi isn't to your taste and you don't mind an even bumpier road, a visit to the quiet fishing port of **Tsoutsouros** is worthwhile. It has a wide beach, some of the best fishing (and fish, in its two tavernas) on Crete, and lower priced rooms to rent.

One day, unfortunately, an English tour company will reach this unspoiled hamlet, and today's charm will be tomorrow's postcard heaven.

MATALA: One of Crete's southernmost beach communities, Matala is known for the cave dwellings (carved by Christian refugees) in the cliffs that encircle its beach. Cretan resistance forces hid in them centuries later, during World War II, and young foreigners inhabited them during the 1960s and 1970s. These so-called hippie caves were ostensibly "cleaned out" for health reasons by the Greek government, but arriving in Matala today one can see the real reason for their expulsion: Matala boasts one of the best fine-pebble beaches on Crete, and the natural cove, formed by a horseshoe of sandstone cliffs, has perfectly clear warm water. Busloads of very young vacationers pour in every day, dropping more drachmas on the souvenir and handcraft boutiques than most former cave-dwellers spent in a month. Young travelers still arrive on their own (the public bus from Iraklion runs twice daily; fare: 560 drs, or $4.31), sunbathing nude by day on the hillside terraces formed by the cliff caves and sleeping by night in the nearby campground or pensions.

The most telling testament to Matala's glorious past is the graffiti on the concrete beachfront bulkhead: "Today is Life. Tomorrow *never come*. I live for *today*. Welcome to Matala. George."

Beach aficionados should make sure to climb the hill behind the pensions to **Red Beach**, where some of Matala's visitors sun in blissful seclusion. If you climb over the tourists gaping at the once-inhabited caves (on the opposite side of the cove, but now fenced off to the public), you'll get to **Komo Beach**, another three-kilometer-long stretch of sand. The less hardy can drive (or walk) back through town and take the first unpaved road on the left.

The hotel situation is tenuous, teetering between the clean, newer private facilities where doubles run 3200 drs ($24.61) and the very basic small pensions on the back street where doubles run from about 2500 drs ($19.23) depending on the season, the renter's mood, the facilities, etc. The best choice is the **Nikos Pension** (tel. 0892/42-375) which is a few streets off the beach on an unnamed street. Expect to pay 2800 drs ($21.54) for a double room. At Matala Bay is the **Hotel Matala Bay** (!) (tel. 0892/42-300), where 3500 drs ($26.92) gets you a quiet, clean double just off the beach and close to a handful of good tavernas.

Of the several restaurants on the beach, **George's**, tucked up in the south flank of the cove, has the best prices 500 drs ($3.85) to 800 drs ($6.15) per entrée. For cheap meals minus the view, try **Toast Bar Crete**, featuring J. J. Cale tunes in the parking lot, or **Rio Souvlaki** (playing Dylan songs), four parking spots away. Also good is the restaurant in the **Zativia Hotel** (tel. 0892/42-112).

Note: A word of caution is worth repeating here about the restaurants. Most don't have menus, and owners volunteered upon inquiry that they would charge whatever they felt clients were willing to pay: so ask before you eat!

AG. GALINI: The locals tell of a Byzantine emperor who centuries ago set sail in quest of the Holy Grail. After months of difficult travel he met with a great storm at sea and took refuge in a quiet cove at the Bay of Messara. He prayed fervently for the storm to end, and when it did he built a small church on the nearest shore, dedicating it to Aghia Galini, "Saint Peace."

A small, overbuilt beach community has sprung up at this peaceful spot. The narrow streets, packed with shops and cafés, provide a lively, informal resort atmosphere.

Layout

The steep hill overlooking the mile-long stretch of pebble-and-sand beach is tiered with hotels (which fill up in July and August). From the plusher C-class hotels, like the **Athena** (tel. 0832/91-331), charging 3600 drs ($27.69) for a double, to the older, slightly cheaper **Astoria** and **Christof** (on the topmost tier), there is a terrific view of placid Libyan Sea. We recommend choosing a smaller hotel or rented room closer to the port; there you still have a view, but you're a little closer to the activity (it's also less legwork walking up the switchback road after a few glasses of wine at night!). Below the lowest level are the busy tavernas at **Fountain Square**. This is the main **bus stop** (buses leave once daily at 8:30 a.m. to Iraklion, five times daily to Rethymnon, three times daily to Plakias). By the fountain are the post office and National Bank.

Accommodations and Dining

On the lowest tier is the **Hotel Soulia** (tel. 0832/91-272), whose 22 clean rooms offer harbor views. Doubles are 2500 drs ($19.23) with bath. One tier above the harbor are the **hotels Candia** (tel. 91-203), **Dedalos** (tel. 91-214), and **Selena** (tel. 91-273), where doubles run about 4000 drs ($30.76) with private bath. All are clean and have balconies with views. The Selena is our first choice.

The nautical-style design of the **Ariston Pension** (tel. 0832/91-285) drew us to it. Helen Mougarakis runs a tidy ship, with six spic'n'span doubles with bath for 2400 drs ($18.46).

A budget alternative would be the **Acropol** (tel. 91-234) on the same tier, where doubles without bath are 1400 drs ($10.77) but showers are 200 drs ($1.54) extra. Another choice at this price is the **Livili** (tel. 0832/91-362), above the restaurant of that name on the main street.

Camping Ag. Galini (tel. 0832/91-386) is situated in an olive grove by the sea, just three kilometers south of town. It's on a beach, has 45 spaces, and a restaurant and market.

In the cluttered pedestrian main street, one good choice for good-value, tasty Greek dishes is the **Libykon Pelagos** (Greek for "Libyan Sea"). They serve a great Greek salad for 275 drs ($2.11). The nearby **Mapona Snack Bar** boasts "Our Happy Hour lasts all day," and **Scirocco Bar** offers windsurfing lessons. The **Creta Sun**, at the port, is the café spot for Greek coffee and pastry while you pore over the news from an *International Herald Tribune* (purchased at the foreign-language bookshop next to Christo's Pizza).

What to Do

If you're starting to feel that Ag. Galini is well set up for tourists, you've gotten the point. It's a popular base for budget charter groups that come from England for a week in the sun, and because of this it's very well organized to assist independent travelers who want to explore Crete's south coast from an inexpensive and comfortable resort.

The knowledgeable **Candia Tours Office** (tel. 91-278; office in Iraklion, 285-576) offers trips to all of Crete's outstanding sights. Hours are 8 a.m. to 1 p.m. and 5:30 p.m. to 10 p.m. Day trips include a visit to Samaria Gorge for a hike at 3000 drs ($23.07), several cruises to nearby Libyan Sea beaches, a tour to the Minoan palace at Phaestos, ruins at Gortis, and the lovely beach at Matala for 2200 drs ($16.92). In fact, many visitors pass up Ag. Galini's clean pebble beach, hop on the frequent local bus, and head for the exceptionally scenic Matala or the quieter, less developed fishermen's beach at Plakias.

5. Rethymnon

The port of Rethymnon, dominated by the impressive **Venetian Fortezza** of 1574 on a peninsula at its eastern end, has retained more of a medieval flavor than the port of Iraklion, and is on a bigger scale than the more intimate port of Chania. Rethymnon played a historic role as capital of the province under the Turks and Venetians, and it carried on an active trade with the Orient.

Located 79 kilometers west of Iraklion on the north coast, Rethymnon can be visited as a day trip (buses run several times daily) or used as a vacation base for the beach-smitten. The main bus station, on Moatsou Street, is only a ten-minute walk south of the public beach at Venizolou. There is a very helpful new Tourist Office, located along the harbor on Venizelou Street, next to the beach that is run by the Prefecture of Rethymnon. Hours are 9 a.m. to 6:30 p.m. weekdays; they close at 2 p.m. on weekends.

ACCOMMODATIONS: If you've come to spend the night by the sea, turn right from the bus station and walk along the sand-and-pebble beach where you can inspect the many rooms to let across the road. The **Lefteris Pension** (tel. 0831/23-803), at 26 Plastira St., and the **Kastro Hotel** (tel. 0831/24-973), down the street, are the best bets at the port. Since the beach isn't as good as those near Vai or along the south coast, we'd spend our hotel money at an older lodging within the narrow twisting streets behind the Venetian port. There, many of the buildings crowd the street with their overhanging wooden Turkish balconies.

Turning back to the fortress behind the marina, walk along Arkadiou Street, which runs parallel to the many tavernas and cafés with run-down, grungy rooms above. At 39 Verde Kallergi, near the Spot Café on the harbor, is the one exception to this—the eight double kitchenette apartments (some with balconies and terraces) running from 2750 drs ($21.15) to 3640 drs ($28) per night, **Venetia Apartments** (tel. 0831/25-092). Up the block is the aging **Hotel Minoa** (tel. 0831/22-508), at 58 Arkadiou, whose mild green interior and 25 rooms are spotlessly maintained by a very hospitable family. Comfortable twin-bedded rooms with bath are 2500 drs ($19.23), triples are 2900 drs ($22.30). Up the block is the attractive **Hotel Leo** (tel. 0831/26-197), where doubles are 2500 drs ($19.23); some have a private bath; it's got a cozy bar for hanging out.

Nearby at Arkadiou and 3 Blastou is the totally captivating **Zania Hotel** (tel. 0831/28-169), run by Miss Foni Psaronalou. In excellent French, she'll describe the history of this 150-year-old house, now converted into three spacious doubles at 2050 drs ($15.76) and two triples at 3100 drs ($23.85). The prices are high for sharing a huge old bathroom with others, but the Zania's specialness should sway some readers.

In the center of town, at 45 Topasi St., are 68 beds, at 375 drs ($2.88) per, crammed into the **Greek Youth Hostel** (tel. 0831/22-848). At 303 Arkadiou St. is **Mikonos Rooms-To-Let** (tel. 0831/29-129), which vary from a double without bath at 2000 drs ($15.38) to a great double with kitchenette and private bath at 2500 drs ($19.23). These have balconies overlooking the quieter end of the harbor, and though the simple all-white furnishings may seem a little antiseptic, it's really very pleasant for a longer stay. New and nice too is the **Pension Lane** (no phone yet), near Marouli Street.

DINING: At the foot of Arkadiou Street is everyone's favorite restaurant, **Famagusta**, with bargain prices and a lovely view of the sea. Two can eat various local specialties prepared in the Cretan style, for 2400 drs ($18.46). Another popular choice is **Tassos**, right on the harbor opposite the fishing boats. The various appetizers, including a piquant taramosalata at 160 drs ($1.23), a satisfying accompaniment to a carafe of local wine.

WHAT TO SEE: Sightseers should start from the sheltered end of the harbor and turn left past the well-recommended **Poseidon Restaurant**. A four-minute walk up Paleogolou will bring you to the lovely 17th-century **Rimondi Fountain**, also called "Megali Vrissi." A block away on the left is the **Neratzes Mosque** and its minaret, one of the many signs of Turkish occupation which give Rethymnon so much color. There's also a fine (now empty) mosque near the Great Gate to the Fortezza. On Arkadiou Street is the early 17th-century **Venetian Loggia**, once used as a clearinghouse by local merchants, which has become the region's **archeological museum**, open 9 a.m. to 1 p.m. and 6 p.m. to 8 p.m. Tuesday through Sunday. Closed Monday. Admission is 100 drs (77¢).

During the last half of July, go straight past the Neratzes Minaret to the flower-filled, well-groomed public park, where the annual **Wine Festival** is held. If you can't go far after sampling the many delicious Cretan wines, take a room at the good-value **Park Hotel** (tel. 0831/29-658), across the street, where 18 rooms overlook the bacchanalia below.

Day Trips from Rethymnon

Two excursions that are possible from Rethymnon include a visit to Crete's famous **Monastery of Arcadi**, a 16th-century Venetian work with a lovely church within. Its Renaissance-style door and elaborate columns and arches were not badly damaged in the Turkish siege of 1866. In this famous incident, the Abbott Gabriel chose to ignite the monastery's store of powder kegs, killing 800 refugees and attacking soldiers, rather than surrender to the Turks.

Another excursion is to the nearly perfect mountain village of **Spili** (treated elsewhere in this chapter), which is 30 kilometers south of the national highway. On the way you'll pass by the old church on the square in the village of **Armeni**, a pretty town filled with outspread fan cacti and dripping with bougainvillea.

For the truly adventurous, a full-day trip, camping expedition, or hitchhiking foray should be made to the coast due south of Rethymnon. Head for Plakias and include stops at the Preveli Monastery and Frangokastello along the way.

The **Preveli Monastery** has long been a stronghold of Greek nationalism, a base for resistance against hostile armies. Its remarkable location, high up on the rocks overlooking the blue Libyan Sea, is both remote and strategic. For the monks who live here, it's a sanctuary of calm and beauty. For the Greek Resistance it was a base for counterattack against both the Turks and, during World War II, the Germans. A plaque from World War II commemorates the British, Australian, and New Zealand forces who took part in the Battle of Crete against German submarines.

The monastery was built in 1836 and contains several panels painted in the 1600s. A carved crest above the medieval marble fountain bears a Crusader cross. The monastery maintains a small museum that exhibits priests' vestments, religious symbols, and ornaments.

The monastery is open from 8 a.m. to 1 p.m. and 5 p.m. to 7 p.m. daily. The sign at the gate says: "No shorts." Dress accordingly.

Below the monastery, by the roadside, is a photogenic abandoned village that evokes eerie images of yesteryear. And for those with time on their hands and in search of an uncrowded beach, you can hike down the hill (along a wide dirt path) to a secluded cove under the promontory.

A dominating presence over a wide, gray sandy stretch of coastline, the 14th-century Venetian **Fortress of Frangokastello** will impress even the most blasé tourists. The fort is totally intact, with flowers growing inside and outside its massive walls. The worn sign of Saint Mark (the Lion of Venice) is still visible over the southern portal.

However, the most vital part of Frangokastello is its haunting legend, the story of Fata Morgana. During the War of Independence in 1821 a small battalion of Greek soldiers was hopelessly outnumbered by fierce Turkish forces who moved in and massacred the Greeks. Since that time local inhabitants swear that when the sea is calm (at the end of May or September) and it's late at night, a ghostly image of the gallant battalion appears, hovering above the ocean. The visitation of the restless souls of the soldiers reminds the locals of the terrible day when Frangokastello was the scene of this region's most ghastly event. (There is a coterie of young Greeks and foreigners who return annually to camp out at Frangokastello's primitive pensions and await Fata Morgana.)

PLAKIAS: Plakias is a tiny southern coastal fishing town, whose attractive beach and year-round warm water have only recently been discovered by tourists. It's an ideal place for those who enjoy hiking and climbing over rocks. On the far-left side of the beach is a series of caves, and on either side of the cove are more isolated beaches. Be warned that it is developing at a rapid rate, especially with the completion of the new road.

As you enter the town, on your right is a cherry 45-bed **Youth Hostel** (no telephone yet) that is inexpensive—only 375 drs ($2.88) per bed. The hostel has a good library of American, British, and Greek novels, and is managed by a virile young Greek. Farther on is the main beach that comes to a point where there are several cafés; the **Café Sofia** plays the best music (they probably borrow tapes from the hostel) and has low prices, thus accounting for its popularity. If you walk around the point, you'll find two more tavernas: **Christo Leftari**, with a wide variety of fish and the best view of the cove, and an unnamed eatery that is even cheaper overlooking the rocks in the sea.

There are bargain rooms to rent anywhere between 800 drs ($6.15) and 1100 drs ($8.46) for two, depending on the season. Try **Iosif Thrimeas** (tel. 0832/31-297), at the harbor, or **Markos Stefanakis** (he worked at the U.S. Embassy in Athens for over 25 years), whose rooms are located a bit behind the point. The lively and chic (for Plakias) C-class **Hotel Lamon** (tel. 0832/31-279) has 27 rooms, at 3100 drs ($23.84) for two, including breakfast. A second, less costly choice is the 16-room **Hotel Livykon** (tel. 0832/31-216). The rooms are clean if spartan and not a bad deal at 1900 drs ($14.61) for a double if you take breakfast at the bakery next door. Money can be changed at the hotels.

Getting to Plakias can be a chore. Buses run three times a day (twice on Sunday) from Rethymnon to Plakias. The roadway from Rethymnon (37 kilometers north) stops just a few kilometers' walk outside of town and the scenic bus route passes through the rugged Kotsifou Gorge.

6. Chania and the Southwest Coast

The city of Chania bears the stamp of its Renaissance-era Venetian occupants more than any other city on Crete. Narrow streets with 600-year-old slender wood and stone houses still grace the old city, and thick stone walls fortify the small, secluded harbor. A solitary lighthouse stands watch at the port point.

Surrounding this historic center is a modern vibrant city. Like Iraklion, there are large areas of little interest to tourists, sections filled with busy markets with trucks carting produce in and out amid the endless buzzing of motorbikes and compact cars.

The comparison with Iraklion is a popular sport on Crete, where boosters of each city claim their own to be the island's "Number One." Although the capital was moved from Chania to Iraklion, and the latter is more economically developed, Chania wins hands-down for sheer architectural elegance. This intra-island competition goes back perhaps as far as the second century B.C., when ancient Chania (called Kydonia in those days) battled against its less powerful adversaries at Knossos. Chania was occupied by the Venetians (who built the walls, harbor, and nearby residential area) during the 14th and 16th centuries, then, for over 200 years, the Turks. The Germans moved into Crete during World War II and damaged or flattened much of the old city.

The major sights, aside from the harbor itself, include the old Venetian-era **Municipal Markets** and garden, as well as two museums, one chronicling the city's deep connection with the sea, the other displaying archeological finds from the area. To find the market, walk up Halidon Street from the port and turn left at Skridlof Tsouderon. In a few blocks you'll be at the crucifix-shaped market where you can see the center of Chania's past and present commercial activity. If you continue from the market on Dimocratias Street, you'll come to the lushly planted **Municipal Garden**, dating from 1870. The delightful **Naval Museum of Crete** (open 10 a.m. to 2 p.m. Tuesday through Sunday, from 5 p.m. to 7 p.m. Tuesday, Thursday and Saturday; closed Monday; admission is 100 drs or 76¢) is almost directly on the bulkhead of the harbor. The **archeological museum** (open daily from 8 a.m. to 7 p.m. Monday through Saturday, Sunday 8 a.m. to 6 p.m.) is on Halidon Street, one block from the harbor, so you can peek in on your way to the market. Admission is 250 drs ($1.92).

USEFUL INFORMATION: There's a branch of the **National Tourist Office of Greece (E.O.T.)** in the white mosque at the harbor, at 6 Akti Tombazi (tel. 0821/ 26-426). It's open daily from 8 a.m. to 2:30 p.m., closed Sunday. **Ferry tickets** for the nightly Piraeus boats departing from Souda (15 minutes from the market by bus) are sold by several travel agents for 3618 drs ($27.83). . . . **Olympic Airways** offers bus service one hour before departure time to Chania Airport for 250 drs ($1.92). . . . The **post office**, open 8 a.m. to 7 p.m. weekdays, is behind the Agora on Tzanakaki Street. . . . There's a **laundry** on Tzanakaki Street opposite the post office, as well as one on Kanevarou Street opposite the taxi stand. . . . The local **Chania Hospital** is off Venizelou Street. **Spa Tours** (tel. 0821/21-327), at 10 Mihelidaki St., can take care of all your tour and travel needs. . . . The **area code** is 0821.

ACCOMMODATIONS: One of Chania's most appreciated features is its wonderful offering of hotels, many of which are converted 14th-century Venetian homes and boarding houses. At the top of our list is a special splurge—the **Hotel Contessa** (tel. 0821/23-966). The six rooms, in an exquisite Venetian home with antiques decorating the lobby, run 6900 drs ($53.07) for a double, including breakfast, and it's absolutely worth it for the treat of basking in such old-world elegance. The Contessa is located on the west side of the Old Port at 15 Theofanous St.

If the Contessa sounds inviting but you're running low on drachmas, try one of the three **pensions**, housed in 600- to 700-year-old homes next to the Naval Museum on Angelou Street. The one closest to the harbor is the **Meltemi**, and is followed by **Theresa** and **Stella**. The Theresa is by far the nicest. The manager, Vassilis Baskakis, keeps the place perfect. Doubles go for about 3100 drs ($23.85) for two, including shower. A stay in any of these homes is enjoyable for the portside atmosphere, winding creaky stairs, and high, decorative ceilings. Other, plusher choices are the **El Greco Hotel** (tel. 0821/22-411), also in an old house with wooden floors and flokati rugs, charging from 4200 drs ($32.30) for two, and the C-class, boringly modern (but very clean) **Hotel Lucia** (tel. 0821/ 21-821), charging 4800 drs ($36.92) for two, breakfast included.

The other budget choice on the harbor is the **Hotel Manos** (tel. 0821/29-493). When you see it you might laugh at its collapsing exterior walls, but the interior has been renovated quite recently and still retains touches of its old charm. The Manos charges 3600 drs ($27.69) for doubles with a bath and 3600 drs ($26.15) for doubles without.

On the other side of the harbor is the 12-room **Ariadne**, which has a great view over the east side of the port. The rooms are clean, have very high ceilings, and best of all, go for 2900 drs ($22.30) a night for two.

Pension Kipos (tel. 0821/58-618), located at 23 Tzanakaki St., is clean, friendly, and has a jazz bar on the premises. All this and heaven too for just 2650 drs ($20.38).

DINING AND NIGHTLIFE: Known for its Cretan specialties is the **Vouli Restaurant**, on Gianari Street. The veal dishes, at 550 drs ($4.23) per portion, are a special treat. For the spicy, locally prepared seafood dishes favored by Chaniots, try **Fragio's**. It's at the head of Nea Hora Street and can be spotted by the constant deliveries of octopus, fish, and prawns that cross its threshold. The owner, Michael Ruftakis, also owns and rents rooms at De Minos Pension nearby and is very helpful. Two can have a delicious meal for 1200 drs ($9.23). **Dionyssos** was also highly recommended, but we found the prices comparatively high for Chania's taverna market. Nonetheless its attractive harborside location and flavorful food warrant a mention. Another choice for continental cooking is the **Oleander** (behind the Hotel Lucia), which is run by a young German chef.

For after-dinner entertainment, try **Fagotto**, at 16 Angelou. From 7 p.m. to 2 a.m. The manager, Mr. Kouviades, makes sure a continuous mix of old jazz and blues is played, often by live bands. Fagotto's offbeat crowd includes Greeks rarely seen at the harborside cafés frequented by tourists. For the price of a drink, you can get a behind-the-scenes look at Chania's notable arts and literary crowd. The sign on the door says this is not a place for beer drinkers. If you're now feeling left out, head for the harbor (the hub of the hip). When you get to Halidon Street ask where Odos Skridlof is and look to the right for an Amstel Beer sign—this place has great souvlaki and the cheapest beer around: 100 drs (80¢) for a giant stein!

SHOPPING TIP: For the discerning, there's a fine selection of old and antique Cretan blankets and kilims at 5 Angelou (near the Naval Museum). **Kostas Liapakis** claims that his embroideries and weavings are about 100 years old and made from old, local dowry fabrics. The rich red background and decorative geometric patterns in the fabrics are quite stunning, and you might be seduced into spending around $200 for a three- by five-foot souvenir.

EXCURSIONS FROM CHANIA: The most popular excursion from Chania is a hike through Europe's largest canyon to Crete's south coast.

THE SAMARIA GORGE: The Samaria Gorge (often referred to as the "Grand Canyon of Greece") connects the small inland mountain hamlet of Omalos to the southern coast beach town of Ag. Roumeli. A 17-kilometer footpath leads through the narrow canyon and is the only passage in or out of the area.

The rigorous hike takes about four to five hours. You don't have to be in mountaineer condition, but you should feel comfortable with the idea of walking (albeit downhill) for 17 kilometers. We met hikers of all ages throughout the day; all were healthy and had stamina. Wear light hiking boots or sneakers and bring food for a picnic and a towel and swimsuit for the postdescent dip.

The trail begins at a well-marked entrance at **Omalos**, at the *kosokolon* (or "wooden steps"). The path drops steeply for the first three kilometers, with lots of switchbacks and loose stones. Good views of the gorge are within one kilometer, so if you decide that the full trek isn't your style you can still witness the 600-meter drop to the bottom of the canyon. A multitude of wildflowers line the path, giving the impression of a predetermined design. The trail continues to drop (it's downhill the entire way) until it levels at the deserted town of **Samaria**, seven kilometers into the Gorge. The inhabitants of Samaria were forced to leave in 1962 after the gorge was declared a national park. They were relocated quite conveniently at the end of the trail (ten kilometers away), where they now own and service the lucrative tourist concession. As at many points along the trail, this stop has an abundant supply of fresh mountain water.

The second segment of the journey is the real payoff. The trail finally hits the river bottom, then meanders through the rocky bed. The deep gorge becomes narrower; the water-eroded striations and patterns on the rocks and walls are exquisite. The river-cut trail passes through a chasm for about four kilometers; then, in the more scenic part of the canyon, fast-running, turquoise-hued water suddenly emerges, enticing more than a few to a quick swim, which unfortunately is strictly forbidden. At the end of the official park boundaries the gorge is only nine feet wide (and at its most dramatic). The canyon widens after that, and after four kilometers leads to the great black pebble beach at Ag. Roumeli. Cold drinks, restaurants (our favorite was the Taverna Tara; try their tasty dolmades!) and the inviting water of the Libyan Sea make the end of this journey particularly pleasurable.

Although there are many conveniently packaged tours for visiting the Samaria Gorge, they all tend to arrive at the same time, clogging up the trail and forcing hikers to stay more or less in line instead of just experiencing the canyon. A better, and less costly bet, is to sleep in Chania and take the early-morning (5:45 a.m.) public bus to Omalos. This will get you into the gorge well before the crowds descend.

The gorge is open from April 1 to October 30, and the Parks Department lists many restrictions (including no camping and no singing).

Aghia Roumeli

If you enjoy the beach at Ag. Roumeli, you might consider staying overnight. There are **rooms-to-let** at the Livikon, Tara, Stratos, and Kri-Kri guest houses, and there's an even better beach at St. Pauls (a one-hour walk east). Simple, bathless, beach-shack rooms rent for 900 drs ($6.90) for two, including a hot shower.

The only way out of Ag. Roumeli, short of hiking in reverse, is the **ferry to Chora Sfakion**. Boats run five times a day in the summer between 1 and 5 p.m., and cost 625 drs ($4.80). The ferry makes a brief stop at Loutro, a beautiful, secluded cove with rooms, beach, a place to eat, and almost no tourists—what else do you need? As always, check the schedule. Regular ferry service is also available to Paleochora once a day during the summer, twice weekly during the spring and fall, costing 875 drs ($6.73).

THE SOUTHWEST COAST: The Prefecture of Chania is the least developed part of Crete, due to its poor infrastructure. The snow-capped inland mountain ranges, fertile valleys, and startling palisades that tumble into the navy-blue Mediterranean make it impossible to link the isolated beaches and villages to the national highway system. To reach most of the west's idyllic beaches takes time, patience, and a boat or Jeep.

Chora Sfakion (Sfakia)

Chora Sfakion (Sfakia) is one of the most popular new south coast beaches because it's been linked by a paved road to the yogurt capital, Vrisses. Such a privileged position unfortunately subjects the tiny village to the mad crush of exhausted tourists who arrive between 3 and 7 p.m. each evening after having hiked the 13 miles through the Samaria Gorge. The caïque shuttle service offered by the Sofia Co. connects the lovely (but invaded) beach at Ag. Roumeli (the exit from the gorge) with Sfakia five times daily in summer. The fare is 600 drs ($4.62).

It's easy to become enchanted with the gray pebble beach lying idly below the tour-bus parking lot. Most days (other than in July and August) it's just a great place to get away from it all. In 1941 courageous citizens from this tiny port evacuated Australian and New Zealand troops after the famous Battle of Crete. The spirited Sfakiots have changed little—now the traditionally clothed men sitting in the *kafeneions* have a regular parade of shutterbugs in hiking shorts to watch, though few even lift their eyes from their glasses of ouzo.

There's a pricey **Xenia Hotel** (tel. 0825/91-202) tucked away innocuously behind geraniums, but any of the locals' **rooms-to-let** run only 1400 drs ($10.77) to 2100 drs ($16.15) for a double, many including private baths. They're above the few tavernas and up on the hillside along the road out of town, where you'll also have the benefit of superb views looking out over the Libyan Sea.

Tourist services include a **police station** at 25 Martiou Square (the town bus parking lot), a **National Bank of Greece** (represented in the souvenir shop with the Kodak sign), and a **bakery** and **market** on the tiny lane behind the main port street. Sfakia also has two **taxis** (what for?) and regular bus connections to Chania.

For the Explorer

If things get too busy for you, jump on one of the Sofia's twice-daily runs to Loutro 350 drs $2.69), an even sleepier port just west along the coast. There are rooms to let here, as well as unsanctioned camping in the many nooks and crannies of this lovely coast. The horribly inconvenient Sougia is another choice if you're heading west, with rooms to let. Remember: The harder the work, the greater the reward.

Skipping past Ag. Roumeli (covered in the Samaria Gorge portion of this chapter) we get to **Paleochora**, connected to Aghia Roumeli daily during the summer by Sofia boats, at a fare of 840 drs ($6.46). Because it's also connected by a picturesque and dizzying winding road from the north, the quiet fishing village of Paleochora has been only minimally developed. There are two small D-class hotels, the **Paleochora** (tel. 0823/41-225) and the **Livikon** (tel. 0823/41-250), plus there are several rooms-to-let near the broad sandy beach. Local boats can be hired for the half-day visit to ancient Lissos, where you can still see mosaics in the ruined temples. Paleochora has regular bus connections to Chania, 77 kilometers to the northeast.

Backtracking inland and then cutting over due west (you deserted-beach seekers had better get a good map) we come to the **Monastery of Chrisoskalitisas**, in the southwestern corner of the island. Here too there are a few rooms to let, but where you're going there is *nothing*. Yes, absolutely nothing! You've come all the way to Chrisoskalitisas to walk through the shallow waters to **Elafonisi Island**, a deserted, pure-sand nirvana where Cretans say "the sun sets like on no other place on earth." Now that you've arrived we hope you don't find 30,000 other Frommer readers on beach towels!

The lazy man's way to explore the west coast is along the national highway. In quick succession from Chania you'll pass through the modern beach resorts at Platanias, Malame, and Kolimbari. Just north is Crete's oldest monastery, **Gonia**, at Odigitrias. Heading west through another 20 kilometers of gorgeous scenery is **Kastelion** (also called Kisamos), from which you catch infrequent ferries to Gythion and the Peloponnese. There are rooms to let, and the inexpensive **Morfefs Hotel** (tel. 22-475), with its ten bathless rooms costing from 2200 drs ($16.92) a night.

Beach seekers should continue south to **Platanos**, where a passable but adventurous road veers up to **Fallasarna**, a beach so isolated that nude swimming is condoned. Returning to Platanos and continuing south you'll find another remote beach enclave in the tiny **Sfinarion**, where rooms are available.

If this section doesn't prompt correspondence from all of you, we'll know our trekking has been in vain.

Chapter VIII

THE CYCLADES

STILL REVOLVING AROUND Delos, Greece's spiritual center in classical times, the Cyclades ("Circle") today are a blend of ancient and modern. From the abstract white marble sculpture of a harpist carved nearly 4,000 years ago to the billowing sails of a windmill, snow-white village churches, brilliant blue sky, and a hammy pelican or two, the Cyclades are the quintessential Aegean islands. When people dream of a Greek island, they're imagining the Cyclades.

Mykonos is known the world over for its extraordinary beaches, postcard-perfect villagescapes, and wild nightlife. It's miraculous that with all of the island's development so much of its original beauty and appeal survives. **Delos** is a short commute from Mykonos. The entire island is a vast archeological treasure; the French have been excavating the site for 100 years and they're still going. **Siros** is the capital of the Cyclades, and its wealth is evidenced by the lavish neoclassical mansions that grace its gently sloping hills. Another star in this chain of islands is **Paros**, a destination with all of the attractions of Mykonos, including the nightlife, and several villages to choose from. **Naxos** is directly across from Paros. It's the largest of the Cyclades, and its mountains and steeply terraced villages make it one of the best islands for hiking and camping. **Ios** is a party island, a popular hangout for British and European students since the 1960s, with one of the best beaches in the country. **Santorini** is a volcanic paradise complete with black-sand beaches, astonishing excavations, and donkeys that transport visitors up the switchback trail to the picturesque town of **Fira**. **Oia**, a recently restored village on the northern tip of Santorini, offers a breathtaking view of the rest of the island and adjacent moaning volcanos. Each year Greeks in the tens of thousands descend on **Tinos** to visit the Church of the Panagia Evangelistria in hopes of receiving a cure or blessing. It's hard to miss

Andros, the second-largest island in the chain, but few tourists visit this pine-covered island. Even more overlooked are the western islands, **Serifos**, **Sifnos**, and **Milos**, ideal destinations for those who cherish a solitary beach and rural village life.

There are few island chains easier to get to than the Cyclades: ferries leave everyday from both Piraeus and Rafina, excursion boats and hydrofoils operate between nearly all islands, and Olympic Airways has service, often several flights a day, to Mykonos, Paros, Santorini, and Milos. You can usually knock off an hour or so on sailing time—and about 20% of the ticket price—if you take a ferry from Rafina instead of Piraeus.

A luxurious and convenient way of seeing the best of the Cyclades is with Viking Tours' seven-day yacht cruise. Their yachts ply the Aegean waters, calling at Sounion and the Temple of Poseidon, Kythnos, Serifos, Ios, Santorini, Paros, Naxos, Delos, Mykonos, and Tinos. We found it great fun, relaxing, informative, delicious, and a wonderful way to make new friends. You don't have to worry about hotel reservations, ferry connections, or life in general, and the gourmet three-star meals are among the best in all of Greece. It's an excellent introduction to Greece's most famous islands at a price far below what comparable companies offer: sleeping accommodations, breakfast and lunch, transfers, and an extremely capable English-speaking guide (they really know the islands!) run $745 for one week in a four-berth cabin, $945 in a two-berth cabin. **Viking Tours** of Greece has an office in Connecticut (tel. 800/341-3030) and in Athens (tel. 32-29-383).

1. Mykonos

Nearly everyone planning a trip to Greece dreams of visiting Mykonos, an island of universal appeal. Its special blend of simple and sophisticated pleasures attracts a wide range of visitors. Whether you've come to look or be looked at, the Mykonos scene is a delightful introduction to the latest trends in fashion, music, and lifestyles.

First-time visitors will be pleased to know that even after years of popularity, the island's unique gifts remain unspoiled. The five bold-white windmills that have greeted rock stars and prime ministers still dominate the harbor from their perch on Kato Myli Hill. The island's unofficial host, Petros the Pelican, continues to pose for new arrivals. By now it's become apparent that this pale pink bird prefers to save his showiest antics for bikini-clad nymphettes on arriving sleek Italian yachts.

A TYPICAL DAY: The Mykonos scene changes venue according to the time of day. In early morning, only eager new arrivals are out. At the port of Chora, burly old fishermen scrub their caïques and don captain's hats for the day ahead (of shuttling skimpily clad girls and boys to far-off beaches).

By 11 a.m. the harborside cafés begin to fill. Under bright Metaxa umbrellas, bleary-eyed souls trying to recuperate from the night before nurse double-espressos. Behind the news kiosk at Antonia's Bakery, a fresh-scrubbed coed in a diaphanous caftan shares her first taste of *tiropitta* with a suntanned, brawny guy in a Dartmouth sweatshirt.

On the south side of town past the windmills, queues form for the beach-bound buses. A mélange of vacationers sporting suntans-in-progress wait patiently for a ride to their favorite beach. The largest numbers board the bus for Plati Yialos; from this beach the crowd divides again. Gays and liberated sun worshippers hop the small wooden shuttle boats bound for the world-famous Paradise and Super Paradise beaches.

Back in Chora, the labyrinth of narrow, whitewashed lanes designed to foil pirate raiders does little to thwart determined shoppers. The luxury cruise ship that has just moored at the pier lets loose a swarm of day-trippers, who cart away everything from "I Lost It on Mykonos" T-shirts to high-priced gold jewelry from LaLaounis.

In the afternoon, tranquility prevails. Even the enormous consumer demand doesn't prevent most Mykoniot shop owners from closing their stores during the long, sleepy siesta. The lazy dogs around Taxi Square follow suit, finding shady places to nap, and for a few hours all of Mykonos resembles a calm Mexican village.

At dusk the scene comes back to life. Sunbathers return to town, and galleries fill up with window-shoppers and connoisseurs. The crisp sea breezes and fading rosy sunlight provide the perfect ambience for aimless wandering through Chora's back-street maze. Groups of French-speaking Japanese admire Greek and Italian sweaters, while an older couple buys painted stones for their grandchildren.

Just before sunset, lovers flock to the romantic waterside bars of Little Venice, an old quarter where balconied homes overhang the Aegean.

Mykonos is liveliest at night, when the variety of crowds and diversions will satisfy even the most sophisticated traveler. Restaurants of many cuisines, clubs, and bars featuring every style of music and discos catering to the latest international dance crazes throw open their doors until 2 a.m., when the revelers return home and the cycle begins again.

ORIENTATION: Chora, the port town, owes its special character to the whitewashed, cube-shaped houses, trimmed in every shade of blue, lining its narrow cobblestone streets. The twisting passages and alleyways of the village invariably bewilder visitors; however, on Mykonos serendipity rewards those who are lost.

If you arrive by ferryboat, you'll dock at the modern, northern section of Mykonos's small **harbor**. Most tourist services are located around the southern half of the port, to your right as you exit the boat. (If you arrive by Olympic, their airport bus will drop you off next to the pier.) Past the small, sandy town beach on your right, you'll find **Manto Mavrogenous Square**. "Mavro" or "Taxi Square" is the town's taxi stand (tel. 22-400). Continuing along the crescent-shaped harbor you'll see cafés and souvenir stands on your left and small fishing boats, beach shuttle caïques, and Delos excursion boats on the right. Ferryboat ticket agents and tour operators' offices are in the central section. Foreign newspapers and maps (the Mykonos-Delos map published by Stamatis Bozinakis is particularly good at 80 drs—62¢) can be purchased at nearby kiosks.

What Mykoniots call **Main Street** (officially called **Matoyianni Street**) can be found in the tangle that runs perpendicular to the harbor at Taxi Square. Like so many other streets in town, Matoyianni is jammed with chic bars, boutiques, cafés, and bakeries; if you pass Pierro's Bar, you'll know you're on the right road. The blue arrows labeled "Plati Yialos" that run along Main Street lead to the beach bus station on Chora's south side.

For a quick tour of town, walk to the south end of Main Street, turn right on Enoplan Dinameon (at Vengera's Bar), and turn right again at Mitropoleos Georgouli. *Voilà!* You've made a big circle through the back streets and have returned safely to the southwestern end of the port, having seen the charming quarter known as **Little Venice**. On your left are the O.T.E. and the Folk Art Museum. A quick left turn around the tip of the harbor will bring you to Paraportiani, the island's quintessential Cycladic church. Overheard at the scene: "Looks like a giant kourambiedes" (those delicious shortbread puffs coated in powdered sugar). To visit the windmills, walk around Paraportiani bearing west (right, as you walk away from the port). This lane, **Ag. Anargion**, is one of Mykonos's best shopping areas for artwork and handcrafts. After a three-minute walk you'll see Spiro's Taverna at the base of **Kato Myli Hill**, where the renowned windmills are a short stairway climb away.

GETTING AROUND: One of Chora's greatest assets is the government decree which declared Mykonos an architectural landmark and prohibited all motorized traffic from Chora's back streets. There's only one way to get around the town—walking. As for the rest of the island, frequent and comfortable public transportation is by far the best value.

By Bus

Mykonos has one of the best organized and most useful bus systems in the Greek islands; the buses run frequently and cost 80 drs (62¢) to 150 drs ($1.15) one way. There are two bus stations in Chora: the **Leto Hotel bus station**, by the pier, has buses leaving for Ag. Stephanos beach, northwest-coast hotels, the inland village of Ano Mera, and the far east-coast beaches at Elia and Kalafatis; the airport bus stops at the far side of the Hotel Leto, across from Olympic Airways. Schedules are posted, though subject to change. Ask your driver when buses return if you're planning a trip far from Chora.

The **"Beach" bus station** is on the south side of town, about a ten-minute walk from the harbor. Follow those helpful blue arrows on Main Street and you won't get lost. These southbound buses go to Ornos/Aghios Yiannis and Plati Yialos/Psarou beaches. To get to the island's best sandy stretches (called Paradise and Super Paradise), take the Plati Yialos bus. From the pier, shuttle caïques run continuously. (In the high season, day trips by caïque often leave from Chora's port.) Although there are posted departure times for the beach buses, they often leave as soon as they're full. If you miss the last bus, you can always walk or call a taxi. Beware: cab rides cost about five times the one-way bus fare.

By Moped, Car, and Taxi

Since public transportation to the principal tourist sites is excellent, it's not necessary to spend your drachmas on any motorized transport. However, for those who haven't tried them, **mopeds** can be a fun way to get around. Mopeds and motorcycles (too dangerous for the novice) are available at shops near the southside bus station. Expect to pay 1800 drs ($13.85) to 3000 drs ($23.07) daily, depending on size. Explorers should gather in groups of four to rent Jeeps, available from travel agents for 6250 drs ($48.07) per day, including full insurance.

Getting a **taxi** in Chora is easy; either walk to Mavro Square or telephone 22-400. If you're outside of Chora and call a taxi, you'll be charged from Chora to your pickup point, plus the fare to your destination. Before calling, try to find a taxi returning empty to Chora from the village you're in, or flag one down along the road. The driver will be happy to make a few extra drachmas—be sure to settle on a price before you take off. *Another budget tip:* Many of the posh out-of-town hotels have private shuttle service back to Chora. A friendly request to the concierge may get you a free ride.

USEFUL INFORMATION: There is no official E.O.T. office on Mykonos. Since the Tourist Police next to O.T.E. has been closed, visitors should turn to nearby travel agents for information. The **Mykonos Accommodation Center** (tel. 23-160) is a good place to start.

The area code for Mykonos is 0289.

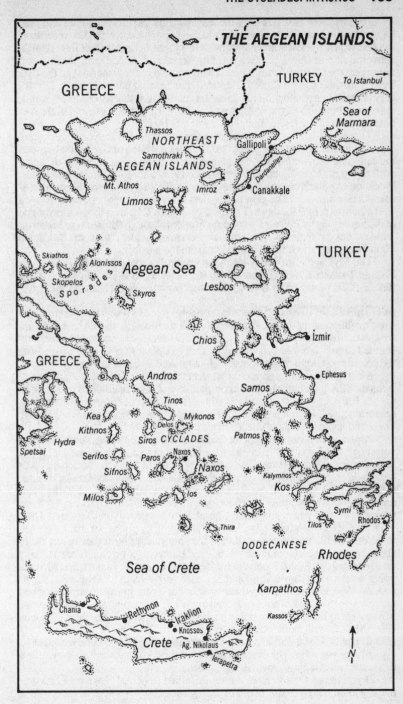

THE AEGEAN ISLANDS

GREECE

TURKEY

To Istanbul

Sea of Marmara

Thassos

NORTHEAST

Gallipoli

Samothraki

AEGEAN ISLANDS

Dardanelles

Mt. Athos

Imroz

Canakkale

Limnos

TURKEY

Skiathos

Alonissos

Aegean Sea

Skopelos

Sporades

Skyros

Lesbos

Chios

İzmir

GREECE

Andros

Ephesus

Tinos

Samos

Kea

Mykonos

Kithnos

Delos

Patmos

Hydra

Siros CYCLADES

Spetsai

Serifos

Paros

Naxos

Sifnos

Naxos

Kalymnos

Milos

Ios

Kos

Thira

Symi

Tilos

Rhodos

DODECANESE

Rhodes

Sea of Crete

Karpathos

Chania

Rethynon

Iraklion

Kassos

Knossos

Crete

Ag. Nikolaus

Ierapetra

N

For **ferryboat** tickets, check the travel agents' current schedules and then be sure to purchase your ticket from whichever portside travel office represents the line which is most convenient; most ferryboat tickets are not interchangeable on different ships. . . . **Sea and Sky Travel** (tel. 22-853), on Taxi Square, represents the Chryssi Ammos Lines, whose luxurious boats service all the Cyclades from their base in Rafina. They also change money at good rates. . . . It's very difficult to get a seat on the 25-seater mini-planes that fly out of Mykonos; make your first stop **Olympic Airways** (tel. 22-490), on the north end of the harbor, open 8 a.m. to 7:30 p.m. daily.

The convenient banks on the harbor make it very easy for you to get spending money. The **Commercial Bank** and the **National Bank of Greece** are between the cafés and souvenir shops, on the harbor; both open 8 a.m. to 2 p.m. and 6 p.m. to 8 p.m. Monday through Friday, and 9:30 a.m. to 1 p.m. on weekends. Weekend traveler's check–cashing service is offered by the Hotel Leto at less-than-bank rates. . . . The **post office**, next door to Olympic Airways, is open 7:30 a.m. to 8 p.m. Monday to Friday. . . . The **O.T.E.** is on the southwest end of the harbor, open 7:30 a.m. to 10 p.m. Monday through Saturday, to 3 p.m. on Sunday, during summer. . . . For a **dry cleaner/laundry,** walk straight down Main Street; it's about four "blocks" in from the harbor.

The **Mykonos Clinic** handles minor medical complaints (tel. 22-274). Dr. George Tsolakis is well recommended (tel. 23-208), as is Dr. Michael Nikolos (tel. 23-026), whose office is down the street from the Hotel Matogianni.

ACCOMMODATIONS: Mykonos is probably Greece's best-known island, and what qualifies as the low season here (April to June 15, and October) would look overcrowded at most other islands. The many visitors who've been enchanted in past years return annually, while neophytes arrive daily, increasing the pressure on hotel rooms that are often booked a year in advance.

Most of the hotels and rooms listed below will accept reservations one to three months in advance *only* if accompanied by a deposit equal to one-third of the fee for your total stay; and this only after their past customers have been accommodated. If at all possible, visit in the low season, when prices are slightly lower and you have a good chance of finding a bed.

For those determined to be in the hottest spot at the hottest time, we have one suggestion—make a reservation early and plan your trip around it. If you don't get any response from these hotels, try an outfit that's the best thing that's happened to Mykonos in years: the **Mykonos Accommodations Center (M.A.C.).** M.A.C. has offices at 3 Filellinon St. in Athens (tel. 32-20-000) and upstairs at 46 Matoyianni (Main) St. (tel. 0289/23-160) on Mykonos; both are geared to finding you a villa, resort, hotel, or private room on the island. Their multilingual and helpful staff will correspond, talk by phone, or meet with you to determine the best accommodation for your budget (and they're not stuffy about booking cheap rooms in local houses, though of course there aren't many on Mykonos). Mykonos is one of Greece's most expensive islands, and M.A.C. offers a very wide range of C- and D-class hotels—from 3500 drs ($26.92) to 6000 drs ($46.15)—and some private rooms. For ensuring you an affordable bed they charge 15% of the rental or a 1250 drs ($9.61) minimum fee, which may be worthwhile to those who can only visit in the peak season. From their Mykonos base, M.A.C. will book rooms at other islands for a minimum of 3000 drs ($23.07) or 15% of the total rental. Owner Michel Le Goff says he has plans to expand the operation. The center is pricey but they do come through for you and can spare you disappointment and heartache.

If you haven't made reservations or talked to M.A.C., we really recommend you do not go to this island in the high season.

If you're reading this in the low season while sunbathing on a ferry speeding toward the island, don't despair. You may find a room in one of the in-town hotels (discussed below), which are all within minutes of the port. If anyone offers you a private room as you disembark, grab it and be grateful if it's affordable and nice (you can always move the next day). Be prepared to accept lodging in another community outside of Chora.

Camping

The official campground on Mykonos is at Paradise Beach. **Paradise Camping** (tel. 0289/22-129 or 22-025) charges 375 drs ($2.88) per person plus 125 drs (96¢) per tent, which includes the use of all facilities. It seems ironic that Mykonos, with its reputation for wealth and glamor, should accord to campers one of the loveliest spots on the island. How could a night in any hotel or villa compare to sleeping under the stars at the edge of Paradise?

In the Town of Chora

Closest to the pier are two of Mykonos's oldest and best-value hotels. The **Hotel Delos** (tel. 0289/22-312 or 22-517) occupies the top floors of what was originally a seafarer's house, whose ground floor has been renovated to accommodate Olympic Airways. The Delos has 14 spacious rooms, with large wood-framed windows overlooking the harbor. You'll have to navigate the sloping wooden floors to the large, clean bathrooms down the hall. In the high season doubles are 2520 drs ($19.38) and singles run 2100 drs ($16.15). The harborside **Hotel Apollo** (tel. 0289/22-223) has a carefully maintained 19th-century façade that blends in with the neighboring commercial establishments in the central section of the port. The Apollo's 12 simply furnished, bathless rooms are slightly higher priced than those at the Delos, and it has eight additional rooms with private facilities at 3480 drs ($26.76) a double.

Just two narrow lanes in from the harbor as you walk down Main (Matogianni) Street is the **Hotel Manto** (tel. 0289/22-330), a small whitewashed lodging on a quiet side street. The 15-room Manto has clean, simple doubles with bath for 5200 drs ($40). Nearby is the older, more homey Delphines, under the same management. The blue-shuttered **Hotel Delphines** (tel. 0289/22-292) is one block behind the taxi stand at Mavrogenous Square. Small, bathless doubles are 5000 drs ($38.46). Singles are 2450 drs ($18.84) a night, not a bad deal in this crowded port (on Mykonos, a single person is often charged for a double room).

Another 50 meters down Main Street you'll find the **Hotel Matogianni** (tel. 0289/22-217) and its older twin, the **Hotel Carbonis** (tel. 0289/22-475), which occupies the upstairs floors. The Matogianni has 22 modernized doubles with baths and private phones, an unnecessary convenience that shouldn't seduce you into avoiding the O.T.E., where metered long-distance calls are much cheaper. (From midday on, the crowded telephone exchange is also a great spot to meet people.) Although the Matogianni's on swinging Main Street, the rooms overlooking their pretty garden are quiet. With breakfast, doubles are 5100 drs ($39.23) a night. The Carbonis, upstairs, has nine "rooms comfortable with running waters," an advertising line that means some rooms have private baths and some don't. If you share a bathroom you can shave 325 drs off the 3750 drs ($28.84) tariff.

At 32 Kalogera (the first right off Main Street past the Matogianni) is the delightful **Hotel Philippi** (tel. 0289/22-294 or 22-295), where 13 homey rooms fetch 3640 drs ($28) per double, with or without bath. Flower-print wallpaper or ruffled bedspreads create the cozy decor unique to each room. The Philippi's owner, Angelique Kontiza, also tends a lush flowering garden that backs onto her son's restaurant. Many evenings these flowers grace the tables of Philippi's, an elegant eatery widely proclaimed as Mykonos's best.

Farther up Kalogera Street is the **Hotel Zorzis** (tel. 0289/22-167), run by Iannis and his friendly family. All of the Zorzis's ten double rooms have private baths and run about 4000 drs ($30.76) in the high season. Just opposite, at 24 Kalogera, is the quaint C-class **Marios Hotel** (tel. 0289/22-704), distinguished by its dark wood-beamed ceilings. The Marios has spotless doubles with modern facilities at 4200 drs ($32.30) a night. Around the corner at 18 Kalogera is the ten-room **Maria Hotel** (tel. 0289/22-317), whose sunny, bathless doubles are 4200 drs ($32.30) also.

The **Hotel Matina** (tel. 0289/22-387), at 3 Fournakion St., is ideally situated inside a large garden. Doubles go for 5625 drs ($43.30).

Rooms-to-Let: The two best areas to find rooms are along Main Street, between the Hotel Matogianni and Kalogera Street, and along Kalogera Street between Ag. Saranta and Ag. Gerasimou Streets. **Maria Chidaki** keeps very tidy and comfortable rooms in the old, green-shuttered white building opposite Paraportiani Church. In the low season Maria will save a room for you if you call ahead (tel. 0289/22-309), but even if you haven't, it's worthwhile to ask. At 2250 drs ($17.30) for a double without bath, her family-style rooms are a good value for such a scenic location.

This year we found an inexpensive and special place to stay. Next door to the Hotel Carbonaki on Fournakia Street is a Rooms-to-Let sign in the window. We investigated and met **Despina Dantou**, who rents rooms in her home for 2500 drs ($19.20). It's like staying with your aunt minus the family squabbling! The place is clean and centrally located (but quiet). A find.

If you're not carrying a lot of luggage and are eager to see the town, follow the blue arrows from the port, which direct you to "Plati Yialos." There are several tour operators' villas near the southside bus stop, and the odd rooms that remain empty are rented out by the group's booking agent, who's usually on the premises.

B-Class Splurges: Built in the middle of a gorgeous garden in the heart of town is the **Hotel Kouneni** (tel. 0289/22-301), 20 "apartments" with private showers and baths, an outdoor terrace where breakfast is served, and a very nice bar where you can unwind after a hard day at the beach. The price tag for all this luxury is 8000 drs ($61.50) and well worth it!

Around the Island

There are hotels clustered around many popular beaches on the island, but most people prefer to stay in town and "commute" to the exquisite beaches of Paradise and Super Paradise. For those who need to curl their toes in the sand before breakfast, a few selections follow.

At Megali Ammos: For any beach lover, a bungalow at the **Mykonos Beach Hotel** (tel. 0289/22-572), on Megali Ammos, is well worth the price of 8590 drs ($66.07), including breakfast for two. Megali Ammos beach, a pleasant ten-minute walk south of Chora, gets very crowded by midday, so you'll probably want to try another of the island's fine beaches in the afternoon.

At Ornos Beach: Just two kilometers farther south is the new **Club Mykonos Hotel** (formerly the Paralos Beach Hotel) (no telephone). Two stories of spacious bungalow-style rooms are contained within the long sleek lines of this modern hotel. Double rooms overlooking the water cost 6625 drs ($50.96), including breakfast, shower and transportation to and from the airport! This beach on calm Ornos Bay is particularly recommended to families, who will appreciate its watersports facilities, tavernas, and shallow waters. The **Hotel Asteri** (tel. 0289/22-715) is near the beach, and a double goes for only 4200 drs ($32.30).

At Plati Yialos: Fifteen minutes by bus or 30 minutes on foot south of Chora is the sandy, crescent-shaped beach of Plati Yialos, better known as the caïque stop for shuttles running to Paradise and Super Paradise beaches. Right on the beach is the **Hotel Platy Gyalos** (tel. 0289/22-343), little more than 11 bathless, simple rooms above a popular restaurant. Doubles are 4650 drs ($35.77) and almost impossible to book. Next door is the newer **Hotel Petinos** (tel. 0289/22-127), whose arcaded façade shades large balconies. Private-facility rooms are also 6830 drs ($52.54), including breakfast. The Petinos management also has private rooms to let at Plati Yialos, where the rates are about 1000 drs less, and some villa apartments near the southside bus station in Chora.

Along the bus route from Chora are other C-class choices, the Cycladic-style **Hotel Magas** (tel. 0289/22-577) and a cluster of hotels sharing one owner and names that start with K—the Korali, Kohyli, Kyma, and Kalypso. The attractive Magas, with balconied doubles overlooking the hot scrubby fields, is a good value at 3950 drs ($30.38). All are within walking distance of the beach by day and the bustling town by night, though buses run every 15 minutes till 10 p.m., and then hourly until midnight. The "K" hotels—three B-class and one C—range in price from 4500 drs ($34.61) to 6000 drs ($46.15), including breakfast. All are new, sparkling clean, and have superb sea views. Call 0289/22-929 for reservations.

At Aghios Stephanos: About four kilometers north of Chora is the popular resort of Aghios Stephanos. Several hotels, pensions, tavernas, and a disco are within reach of a pleasant, though crowded, sandy beach. Near the coast, the best C-class choices are the **Hotel Artemis** (tel. 0289/22-345) and the **Hotel Panorama** (tel. 0289/22-337). The Artemis is slightly cheaper, at 5000 drs ($38.46), and closer to the beach. The small **Hotel Mina** (tel. 0289/23-024) is more "in town," but offers rooms with and without private bath from 3250 drs ($25) to 4000 drs ($30.76).

RESTAURANTS: Mykonos is famed for its restaurants, and the fashionable ones change as rapidly as the value of the drachma. Nevertheless there are several favorites that have stood the test of time.

Light Snacks

For breakfast or snacks, there are two wonderful bakeries just off the harbor. (The harbor itself is lined with expensive cafés, where an early-morning or late-night coffee is the best value.) The **Fournos Bakery** in the tiny lane behind the gold store can be identified by the contented backpackers sitting on the ground outside eating cheese pies. It's run by a grumpy, talented baker. She offers a variety of "kookis," "caik," and "tutti fruitti pies" as well as yummy cheese, spinach, and zucchini pies for 100 drs (77¢). The other bakery, **Andreas**, is behind Mavrogenous Square on Zouganelis Street. Antonia also has a wide variety of bread and pastry snacks. In the square is **Alexis Snack Bar**, open at all hours, which serves good, cheap burgers, souvlaki, and other snacks. For a noon brunch, don't miss the peach-and-yogurt shakes, whole wheat bread, and fresh jams at **Vengera's**—at night, one of the island's best bars.

On Kalogera Street near the Hotel Philippi is the more refined **Hibiscus**

Croissanterie, offering a large variety of you-know-what plus fluffy quiche Lorraine and other authentic delights created by its French owner, Anna. The Hibiscus is open 8 a.m. to 3 p.m. and 6 p.m. to 9 p.m. and is worth a visit if only to admire its spotless, all-white tiled modern kitchen. Next door is a popular and cheap spaghetteria/pizzeria, which is popular during lunchtime.

Tavernas

Nikos Taverna, behind the O.T.E., is one of the few good places in Chora that's open for lunch. Nikos has a varied, inexpensive taverna menu and a very friendly staff and features "spiritual drinks" for those who need a lift. We enjoyed a simple, filling lunch of moussaka and salad for 900 drs ($6.92) each.

Spiro's Taverna is an open-air, casual waterside restaurant long known for its large, moderately priced selection of seafood. The view is lovely, the food, while not inspired, is tasty. Prices run 1000 drs ($7.69) to 1300 drs ($10) for each dinner. Don't miss their shrimp specialties.

Klimateria, run by Maria Stylianou, is another good and reasonably priced choice near Taxi Square. The area is quieter, so if you're looking for a respite from the Mykonos chaos, Klimateria is definitely worth a try.

Antonini's is on Taxi Square, next to the Alexis Snack Bar. This moderately priced taverna serves typical Greek peasant fare; a satisfying dinner for two runs 1500 drs ($11.54).

Near the Lito Cinema is **Eva's Garden**, a popular place for the romantically inclined due to its great garden, terrific cooking, and excellent service. Dinner here runs about 2500 drs ($19.20) for two.

Splurge Restaurants

Having surveyed all manner of elegant eateries to make a splurge recommendation, we've come up with two that fit our criteria of more formal dining, attentive service, interesting menus with Greek specialties, and great food (not necessarily in that order). **Philippi** (tel. 22-294), long a favorite with locals and tourists, is set in an enchanting olive tree garden. Woven fabrics cover the tables and banquettes, which are spaced to provide intimate, romantic dining by candlelight. When you step down into the garden off the busy Main Street, you'll enter a quiet European world where elegant dining prevails. The continental menu includes rabbit dishes, curry, and many elaborately prepared traditional Greek dishes. Dinner for two, including a good choice from their sizable wine list, will run 3500 drs ($26.92) to 5000 drs ($38.46).

Superb food is the attraction of the **Edem Restaurant** (tel. 22-855), a casual garden filled with tables just off Kalogera Street. Edem has a wider range of continental and Greek specialties on its menu (their meat dishes are famous), though prices are about the same as at Philippi. The real treat here, though, is Petros the Pelican, for years the island's mascot, who greets visitors with a great flapping of his huge, soft pink wings. Most evenings Petros dines at Edem, and regales guests with his impatient hopping on a wicker dining chair by the entrance.

We would be remiss if we didn't mention the town's most lavish restaurant, **Katrine's**. Its dark, intimate interior is filled with the rich and near-rich, enjoying excellent seafood. Unless you're prepared to pay Paris prices, join the cognoscenti at Edem or Philippi, where equally fine food is served.

Note: In July and August you'll probably have to make reservations at both Philippi and Edem, but wait until 9:30 p.m. or 10 p.m. to begin supper. It's the Greek way and everything's much livelier at this hour.

BEACHES: Despite what many regard as vast overdevelopment in comparison with Mykonos's virgin years, the island's gorgeous sandy beaches and fresh, clear water remain unspoiled by tourist hordes. The erratically shaped coastline offers several secluded stone-and-sand beaches; we'll review the better-known ones accessible by foot, bus, moped, or caïque.

Note: Mykonos has learned to accommodate every type of tourist—family, single, gay, straight, backpacker, and jet-setter. Each beach draws its own crowd with their own unwritten rules for wardrobe and conduct.

Nearest to Town

Megali Ammos is a pleasant family beach about ten minutes south of the Theoxenia Hotel. This is strictly a family beach, with some topless activity at off-hours on the fringes. Megali Ammos is too accessible to the cruise-ship day-trippers to even be considered by those in search of peace and quiet.

From the southside bus station behind the Theoxenia you can catch a ride or walk the three kilometers south to **Ornos Beach**, on calm and shallow Ornos Bay. Ornos is preferred by families and bathtub bathers who relish its still, tepid clean water. If Ornos becomes too crowded, due west of it on a small peninsula facing the sacred island of Delos is the placid stretch at **Ag. Yiannis**. Bus service from Chora was recently begun to accommodate the hotels that have sprung up nearby, but Ag. Yiannis remains relatively secluded. It's a casual family beach with some watersports and tavernas. The restaurants fill up at sunset, when romantics come for the splendid view.

If you hop on the alternative southbound bus, you have a choice of several other beaches. From the waterfront bus stop you'll find **Psarou Beach** on your right, a popular family beach with diving, waterskiing, and windsurfing facilities. To the left is busy **Plati Yialos**, lined with multicolored striped umbrellas, bright windsurfers, and a mixed bag of sun worshippers. Topless ladies are not unheard of here.

Many visitors stepping off the ferry grab the nearest bus to the popular **Ag. Stephanos**, three kilometers north of Chora. Unfortunately, this mediocre beach, crowded with guests from nearby hotels, isn't really worth the trip. Most watersports facilities are available.

Getting There: All of these beaches are within a half hour's walk from Chora, but we wouldn't recommend attempting it in the midday heat of July and August. Transport from the southside bus station is frequent. **Buses** to Ornos and Ag. Yiannis run five or six times daily for 75 drs (58¢). Buses to Plati Yialos and Psarou begin at 8 a.m. and run every 15 minutes till 10 p.m., then hourly until midnight, for 60 drs (46¢). Schedules for both are posted on the small snack shop at the near side of the square. Buses to Ag. Stephanos leave from the Leto Hotel near the ferryboat pier and run hourly between 8 a.m. and midnight.

Around the Island

From the Plati Yialos pier you can catch caïques to other beaches. One of Mykonos's unforgettable sights has to be the fat old fishermen with twinkling eyes calling out "Paradise and Super Paradise" as if heaven was only a boatride away. Between 9:15 a.m. and 6:30 p.m. their brightly colored caïques shuttle eager tourists back and forth to the pristine, fine sand beaches of Paradise, Super Paradise, and Elia, for fares of 150 drs ($1.15), 175 drs ($1.35), and 190 drs ($1.46), respectively.

As you'd expect, **Paradise** is crowded with blissful souls, mostly bared, who treasure its pure gold sand and crystal-clear water. This was the original nude beach, and today it's still where the action is, in addition to having an excellent taverna. **Super Paradise** is not quite as attainable, and so less crowded. The beach is predominantly gay and bare, and has several good tavernas playing nonstop pop music. Both beaches have eating spots tucked back up on the scrubby, rocky slopes, thereby preserving their idyllic quality. Both are predominantly topless or nude, though clothed sunbathing is condoned. Some watersports are available as well.

Paradise and Super Paradise are also accessible by road with private transport, though the road to Super, in particular, is of dubious quality. Paradise can be reached in a 30-minute hike from Plati Yialos. This walk is highly recommended to the lover of anonymous beaches, who will find many semi-private niches along the way. **Paranga** is a tiny cove which is popular with nudists and is usually not crowded at all.

Caïques from Plati Yialos take about 45 minutes to get to **Elia Beach**, so it's much less crowded than Paradise or Super. Throughout the day some wealthy guests from the hilltop Hotel Ano Mera are shuttled down to Elia for a brush with the sand. It's a clean, pale sand beach, one of Mykonos's largest, with two good tavernas for nourishment. If Elia becomes too busy, head west to **Agrari**, another quiet south-coast beach. Agrari is sheltered by lush foliage, so all types of apparel and nonapparel are accepted. It seems that only a peaceful few are willing to walk the 15 minutes from Elia to this lovely cove. If you've come this far, stay for a lunch of homemade taverna fare at the beach's only eatery.

An amusing sight along this coast is the local shepherds washing their goats and sheep. From atop the cliffs, they toss the burly animals into the pure Aegean below. Every time the matted creatures clamber back onto the slippery rocks, they are mercilessly shoved in again for another rinse.

Around the Cape of Kalafati is another long, sheltered stretch. Guests of the B-class Aphrodite Hotel have appropriated this beach, keeping it clothed and family oriented. From the Hotel Leto in Chora, buses run four times a day to **Kalafatis**. Guests of the Hotel Aphrodite have a regularly scheduled shuttle van for in-town excursions.

WHAT TO SEE: On Mykonos, a "what to see" section should be called "what to do when it rains." For those who are determined, there are a few nonhedonistic pursuits of interest. First and foremost, of course, is a day trip to the sacred island of **Delos**, a marvelous island/museum with vast archeological ruins of great beauty and interest. This island is completely amazing. Organized guided and nonguided excursions leave daily for the 40-minute ride to the island, and cost 1200 drs ($9.23) round trip for transportation alone or 2600 drs ($20) for the (not necessary) guided tour. Boats depart the harbor at 9 a.m. and return at 12:30 p.m., ample time for most visitors. Delos is such an important site that it's treated separately in this chapter.

For those going to Delos, a visit to the archeological museum may be of interest. The **Mykonos Archeological Museum** has a lot of ceramic pieces and some interesting sixth-century B.C. Cycladic finds. It's open 9 a.m. to 3 p.m. daily, 10 a.m. to 2 p.m. on Sunday; closed Tuesday. Admission is 150 drs ($1.15).

The lovely **Paraportiani Church** on the southwest side of the port is considered by architects around the world to be a superb example of the Cycladic style. The sloping, whitewashed stucco exterior reminded John of the sensual adobe churches of Taos, New Mexico. Hidden within its organically shaped walls are four small chapels, each oriented toward a point on the compass. It's not uncommon to see artists of all ages sketching, painting, or maneuvering to photograph this Cycladic landmark. Don't leave until you've walked completely around this amazing building to see it from every angle.

Next to the church on the square is the **Folk Museum**, a fun collection of local handcrafts, furniture, silver figurines, and ship memorabilia. Outstanding in this large collection are some petrified bread samples, baked in braided shapes with red Easter eggs, and the wax life-size sailor who stands beside the huge model of a warship from 1821. The Folk Museum is open from 5:30 p.m. to 8:30 p.m. daily and 6:30 p.m. to 8:30 p.m. on Sunday.

If you haven't climbed up to **Kato Myli** you'll be wondering why we said there were five windmills, when only three tall whitewashed ones are visible from a distance. If you go up to explore, wait until early afternoon, when the windmill closest to the stairs is open for viewing.

NIGHTLIFE: Mykonos really sparkles at night, so whatever your budget, plan on dressing up for the evening and walking the streets to admire everyone else admiring you.

Bars

For early drinks, the **Lotus** on Main Street has replaced Vengera's as "the" popular place. At sunset the intimate **Kastro**, behind the Paraportiani Church, and the **Caprice Bar**, down the block, are perfect for chillier evenings, when the rosy reflection on the calm Aegean can be admired from their picture windows. The **Sundown Café**, a few minutes' walk farther down this seaside lane, is wonderful on warm days, when the sea spray splashing on the edge of Little Venice enhances the dramatic sunset views. For a quiet, civilized drink, try the **Montparnasse**, also along this lane, a cozy bar whose wood-paneled interior is complemented by classical music. **Skarpa** is a favorite of resident Mykoniots. You'll find it just down the street from the Sundown Café.

Longtime "king of the scene" in Mykonos is **Pierro's**, an elegant old bar that's seen so many fads and celebs come and go it's a wonder it's still around. (Last year it was a gay bar). Pierro's, on Main Street just a mob scene away from the harbor, is a must-see for everyone. You may have to go into Mantos Bar next door to buy a beer, because you can't squeeze through the flesh out front, but then you're set for the best people-watching and pickup action on the island—some would say, in all of Greece. Pierro's is in full swing after 11 p.m.

Are you looking for the Party Bar of the Century? Hang a right at Pierro's, proceed about 50 feet and when you see an Irish harp stenciled on the window you'll have reached the **Stavros Irish Bar**. This was the wildest place on the island: English girls dancing on the bar miming Madonna, outside a table of Italian models, there on assignment and living it up, and inside all hell breaking loose, with girls digging boys digging girls. The music is great and everybody is there to have fun and party hearty.

Greek Clubs

By all means, don't stop after dinner. If you're ready for some authentic Greek dancing, try **Thalami**, a small underground club in back of the O.T.E. There's no cover charge, and you can push your way through the beaded curtains to see fine dancing by local men and visiting professionals. Another club worth a visit is **Baboula's**, which draws a very different crowd with a jingling and jangling belly dancer; remember to bring plenty of coins to throw on the floor in appreciation. The **Mykonos Club** is a bouzouki nightclub that is frequented by locals and tourists in search of the road to rebetika (Greek blues).

International Clubs and Discos

For many years the chicest and most popular discos were Remezzo and Nine Muses. **Remezzo** has been rehabilitated and has returned to public favor, but faces tough competition from Mykonos's Number One, **City Disco**. City is an elegantly spare, white-on-white club with excellent lighting, the latest international dance tunes, and a superior sound system. City draws a mixed crowd: gay and straight, black and white. Even if you're not a dancer, drop in to watch the action, which doesn't begin till after midnight. Every night during the summer they put on a drag show, featuring such favorites as Marilyn Monroe, Tina Turner, Maria Callas, Dolly Parton, and others—you won't believe it! City Disco is located on Paraportiani Square. Other after 1 a.m. discos include **T.K.'s** and the **Yacht Club**. For '60s music, especially the Stones (a fav of the DJ), try the **Anchor Club**.

Farther down Matoyianni, after you leave the densely packed square outside Pierro's, you'll come to another type of crowd—all punk, chic, and new wave tough. It's the action behind the unmarked doors of **Kookoo's Nest**, which you'll recognize by the red and green globes on either side of the door.

Movies

The **Lito** and **Artemis** are the town's two cinemas. Each has two shows per night, beginning at 9 and 11 p.m. Unfortunately, no *Zorba the Greek* here; only kung-fu cheapies and B-movies make it to Mykonos. We are told that the August schedule is a bit more uplifting. If you're so inclined, admission to cinema al fresca is 325 drs ($2.50).

GETTING THERE: Mykonos is the most accessible of all the Greek islands. From Piraeus, the **Nomikos Lines** have departures at least once daily, usually at 8 a.m., and a second ship is added in summer leaving in the afternoon. Schedules should be confirmed in Athens at 171, the Tourist Information number, or at 45-11-311. A tourist class ticket runs under 2000 drs ($15.38). There are also daily ferryboat departures from Rafina on the **Chryssi Ammos Lines**, and schedules can be checked at 0294/23-300. Mykonos is also connected by ferry to the islands of Tinos, Siros, Paros, Naxos, Santorini, and Andros, usually daily.

Olympic Airways flies from Athens to Mykonos seven to ten times daily, though reservations must be made in advance. Mykonos is also connected by air to Iraklion, Crete, Rhodes, and Santorini daily. Schedule information can be obtained at Olympic in Athens (tel. 92-92-555) or at their Mykonos office, open 8 a.m. to 7:30 p.m. daily (tel. 22-490).

2. Delos

The tiny island where Apollo and Artemis were born was considered by the Greeks to be the holiest of sanctuaries, the sacred center around which the Cyclades circled. The entire island of Delos is now an archeological museum that's one of the best sites in Greece. Excursion boats from Mykonos sail daily for a half-day visit to Delos.

IN HISTORY: The Homeric Hymns tell us how Zeus, fearing the reprisals of his jealous wife, Hera, abandoned his pregnant mistress, Leto. This helpless mortal was forced to wander the Mediterranean, rejected by lands too fearful to grant her refuge. Zeus begged his brother Poseidon to help her. Poseidon raised up a submerged island and anchored it on a diamond column; Delos was where Leto could give birth. Soon after Leto's arrival, Artemis was born on Mount Kynthos. The next day Artemis, the new goddess of the hunt, helped deliver her twin brother, Apollo. A golden palm tree in the center of Delos's Sacred Lake marked the site of Apollo's birthplace.

Delos was one of the most important religious centers in antiquity, on a par with Delphi and Olympia. Pilgrims from throughout the ancient world visited

Delos bearing fabulous offerings. The sacred island was taken over by a jealous Athens in the fifth century B.C., at which time its rich treasury was moved to the city-state for "safekeeping." As a display of power, Athens insisted on a purification of the island and banned all births and deaths on its shores. The pregnant and the dying had to be moved to nearby Rhenia. Though Delos's wealth and influence were greatly diminished under the Athenians, she regained her independence after the Egyptians took over the region.

From the late fourth to the second century B.C. Delos prospered as a commercial trading port and newly revered religious center. This wealthiest of islands drew merchants from all over Africa and Asia Minor; Delos was soon recognized as a vital commercial port. Roman merchants, backed by an emerging trading empire, eventually seized it from the Greeks and developed it as an alternative free port to Rhodes. The extensive ruins from this prosperous era include docks, warehouses, villas, sanctuaries, and ornate maritime clubs.

In the following centuries the island was pillaged by Greeks and Romans in turn, finally succumbing to the ravagement of pirates in A.D. 69, who carried off whatever hadn't already been carted away to Athens or Rome.

THE ARCHEOLOGICAL SITE: The three hours on Delos allotted by excursion boats should allow even avid archeology buffs enough time to explore the principal sites. To the left of the new pier where you'll dock is the partially filled-in **Sacred Harbor**, where pilgrims and traders from throughout the ancient world used to land. At the ticket kiosk—the site is open daily from 8:30 a.m. to 2:30 p.m. for a fee of 250 drs ($1.92)—site plans and picture guides are for sale, and even the cheapest is adequate enough to serve as your guide. Our favorite, with an excellent text, good pictures, and a fold-out map in the back, was *Delos: Monuments and Museum*, by P. Zaphiropoulou (Kreve Edition), that cost 500 drs ($3.80).

Proceed up past the **Agora,** where festivals were celebrated by the freedmen and traders on the island. Bear right up the hill to explore the south side of the site dominated by **Mount Kynthos**, which the hardy may want to ascend for its fine views over the sanctuary. Along the way, a maze of ruined **warehouses** will be on your right. Be sure to see the various **houses**, or "Maison," once inhabited by wealthy Athenians, where some exquisite mosaics have been found. Most of the mosaics on Delos were designed and installed by artists brought in from Syria.

The large roofed **House of Masks** contains a superb colored mosaic of Dionysos on a panther (Delos's best known treasure) in the room at right and some geometric patterned borders in the central room, where the tiles of five elaborate masks depicting a range of theatrical expression have been taken up for reconstruction. The bright color of these Syrian works, now over 2,000 years old, is astounding.

From the summit of Mount Kynthos there's a spectacular view of the entire site of Delos, as well as the nearby islet of Ekati, the Delian burial ground of Rhenia, and beyond them, Siros. Coming down, you'll cross the **Sacred Way** and the **Egyptian Temple of Isis** and other foreign gods.

If you head back down toward the lush palm groves (the filled-in **Sacred Lake**, where it's thought Leto gave birth to Apollo) you'll soon come across the famous **Delian Lion Walk**. These six skinny guardians, left from the original 16 (one of which guards the Arsenal in Venice), are from the second half of the seventh century B.C. and face east to the Lake. Continuing along this path you'll see the large **Poseidoniasts of Beirut** building, a sort of merchant's club for Mideastern traders. Beyond, several rooms of elegant houses line the stone-paved route. Fragments of painted stucco on the brick walls and some ornate mosaics are sure proof that trading at this port was lucrative for many. Don't forget to look at the bases and their fragments; some bear writing that looks as if it were carved yesterday!

Since 1873, when the French School began their excavations, work has continued each summer at Delos.

ACCOMMODATIONS: Those with a scholarly or professional interest may apply for one of the four spartan double rooms, costing 1400 drs ($10.77) a night, at the **Xenia Hostel** (tel. 0289/22-259), located behind the Tourist Pavilion.

3. Siros

Siros (Syros), whose main port, Ermoupolis, serves as capital of the Cyclades island group, is an inevitable stop for almost all boats plying the Aegean. A stopover on Siros may interest those tourists looking for an island where tourists don't go.

Since antiquity the island's central position has made it a prosperous trading and shipping port. Excavations at Chalandriani have revealed the existence of an early Cycladic civilization from the third millennium B.C. The northern tip of the island is said to have been the home of the philosopher Pherecydas. His best pupil, Pythagoras, was a brilliant mathematician who went to Samos to build an engineering marvel, the Evpalinos Tunnel, which brought water underground for over a mile. After the Greek Liberation of 1821, the North Aegean islanders who'd been driven out by the Turks sought refuge on Siros. Throughout the 19th century Siros flourished as a maritime center, becoming the most important port in Greece.

Unlike most of the Cycladic islanders, the affluent Sirians do not rely on tourism as the mainstay of their economy. Besides the huge shipping industry, textiles and inland greenhouses are Siros's sources of revenue. Most visitors would swear the economy turns on *loukoumi,* the locally produced Turkish delight that looks like Jell-O cubes in powdered sugar, and tastes like . . . well, you'll have to try it yourself. Greeks of all ages adore it, so wildly enterprising vendors run onto every ship that docks at the harbor for a ten-minute sell-a-thon. To Greeks, a visit to Siros without a refill of loukoumi is like spending a weekend in Hershey, Pennsylvania, without buying a chocolate bar. Siros's loukoumi is so superior, in fact, that the most holy Orthodox Church of the Evengelistria on Tinos offers it rather than the Tinos-produced brand to pilgrims. *Halvadopittes,* a locally made nougat sold in tissue-covered pancake slabs, is also extremely popular. (Both make inexpensive, easy-to-carry, and very memorable gifts.)

AROUND THE ISLAND: Ferryboats dock at **Ermoupolis,** which served as the island's major port in ancient times. Today Ermoupolis is still a busy harbor, enlarged by a huge modern breakwater which provides anchorage for many tankers and container cargo ships. Loading cranes line the outer rim of the port. Opposite the ferry pier is a small, uninhabited island hosting a tall lighthouse. Still lovely in their fading glory are the large neoclassic mansions overlooking the water, vestiges of Siros's prosperous past. The city appears to be spread over three hills, with the lowest level of pastel-colored boxy housing butting up against the bulkhead at water's edge. The hill to the east above the new town is topped with the blue-domed Orthodox Church of the Resurrection. This area, known as **Vrontado,** was built up after the Greek immigration of 1821. While the outer harbor has been sullied by today's commercial shipping industry, the narrow streets, large marble-paved squares, and dignified mansions of Vrontado Hill lend a certain old-world charm to the bustling inner city.

The northwest hill (to the left, looking from the water) is the town of **Ano Siros**, a Christian medieval town built by the Venetians in the 13th century. Ano Siros originally spread across the summit of both hills, where its inhabitants were protected from pirate raids. Several Roman Catholic churches still stand, the most important of which is the **Church of San Giorgio**. The large buff-colored square building on the hilltop is the medieval **Monastery of the Capuchins**. Remnants of castle walls, stone archways, and narrow lanes will delight visitors. Ano Siros can be visited by climbing up the old stairs from Ermoupolis or by local bus.

Around the teardrop-shaped island there are quiet **beaches** at Megalos Gialos, Possidonia, and Finikas (or Phoenix), which are great for those bored with seeing other tourists but probably unsatisfactory for true connoisseurs. Most bathing is off the rocky bluffs that jut from the tree-lined shore into the many bays and inlets on the south and west coasts.

ERMOUPOLIS: The main port is the handiest for short-term visitors, who will find several travel agents selling ferryboat tickets and renting mopeds from shops along the waterfront. **Bus** connections can be made to other parts of the island; check the bus station, one block inland from the pier, for information and schedules. The **local police** (tel. 22-630) and **Port Police** (tel. 22-690) are located on the harbor, near the monumental neoclassic Teloneion and other government buildings. Here too is the **National Bank of Greece**, open Monday to Friday from 8 a.m. to 2 p.m.

Venizelou Street will lead you from the pier to the main square of Ermoupolis, **Platia Miaouli**. There are several inexpensive tavernas and ouzeris around this active hub. For evening entertainment, return to Platia Miaouli, where the gregarious Sirians will be crowding the cafés, arguing about politics over a milky ouzo. For cool breezes, stroll along the waterfront, which looks much more appealing in the soft light of the moon. Ermoupolis also offers the usual diversions: you can go to one of the two cinemas, or dance at **Margarita's Disco**.

Accommodations

The bright-white **Hotel Hermes** (tel. 0281/28-011) is a fancy, B-class establishment that's open year round. Spacious doubles overlooking the harbor start at 3600 drs ($27.69) without private bath, or 4300 drs ($33.07) with. The 28-room Mediterranean-style **Hotel Europe** (tel. 0281/28-771, Telex. 29-3133) is just a block behind the harbor. Most rooms face a lovely Rhodian-style inlaid pebble court filled with plants. The hotel has a lounge/bar and serves both continental and English-style breakfasts for 400 drs ($3.07). Doubles with private bath are 4000 drs ($30.76). Less expensive accommodations with shared bath are available at the **Cycladikon** (tel. 0281/22-280) on Miaouli Square, at the **Aktaeon** (tel. 0281/22-675), and at the old **Hotel Ellas** (tel. 0281/22-519), about half a block in from the port.

GETTING THERE: There's really no problem getting to Siros—in fact it's hard to avoid if you're headed elsewhere. Direct ferries run daily from Piraeus and Rafina. "Where to Go" is the fun decision to be made.

Siros is connected twice daily by ferryboat to Tinos and Mykonos, daily to Paros, Ios, Santorini, and Naxos, three times a week to Ikaria and Samos, and once a week to Astipalea, Kos, and Rhodes on the F/B *Nirefs*. The F/B *Kimolos* has the most esoteric routing, offering once-weekly sailings (usually Wednesday or Thursday) to Kimilos, Milos, Sifnos, Serifos, and Kifnos or Sikinos, Folegandros, and Anafi.

All schedules should be checked with a local travel agent; **Syros Travel** (tel. 23-338), on the harbor, handles most of the ferryboat lines.

4. Paros

Paros is a seductive island; as if inhabited by Sirens, every golden beach or patch of honeysuckle, every whitewashed alley or dusty donkey trail beckons, enticing you to further exploration. On Paros, visitors who plan a two-day stay often spend a month.

Paroikia is the island's major port and it's as delightful as the rest of the island. Unlike the port cities of most Aegean islands, the harborside is not the town's main attraction; Paroikia is most alluring in the narrow, stone-paved back streets of the Agora section, where the enveloping and often disorienting whitewashed walls block off all connection with the sea. Even more captivating is the north-coast port of Naoussa. Seemingly a sleepy fishing village, Naoussa hosts gourmet restaurants and stylish hotels, making it one of the Cyclades' most understated resorts.

For many years, Paros was known by only a small coterie of European travelers in search of a quiet island retreat. Several bought villas and settled here. Now the island draws many of the short-term visitors that Mykonos can no longer accommodate. Though thousands arrive each summer, the island has succeeded in maintaining a delicate balance between the customs of traditional Greek village life and the demands of a modern international resort community.

Success has its price, however. Since the airport was completed in 1982, Paros has been able to receive charter-plane loads of group tours. As in the past, Paros's friends and residents will undoubtedly protect their lovely, very "Greek" island from becoming merely another group resort. To our readers we say, "Go now!"

ORIENTATION: Visitors to Paros have a choice of two ports to stay in: **Paroikia**, where the ferry docks, and the smaller, northern haven of **Naoussa.** If you've come to Paros to party, meet people, or luxuriate over a glass of Lagari wine, then Paroikia's the spot for you. Paroikia is the island's capital, a sophisticated resort with a diverse selection of restaurants and discos, comfortable hotels and excellent shops. You can easily explore the island's sights by moped or by joining one of the many excursions offered by local travel agents. Pleasant beaches are within a half hour's walk to the south. (The beaches in town are crowded but acceptable.)

Naoussa is the island's other major port, but it feels like a remote fishing village. If you're coming from Piraeus, the large steamers cannot dock here. However, island-hoppers should note that several smaller boats make excursions from the other Cyclades. We found the lights and sights of bustling Paroikia great fun, but the glowing moonlight and rustle of sailcloth made Naoussa more romantic. Naoussa offers a small selection of good restaurants and shops, most tucked under the trees in the town's main square. Within 40 minutes' walk of the Naoussa Square are the island's most exquisite **beaches**, nestled in the nooks and crannies of the jagged northern coastline. Many of the better hotels are scattered across the rolling hills and narrow, unpaved coastal paths leading to these beach coves. Because of this decentralization, Naoussa appears less developed than it actually is.

GETTING AROUND: A stroller's pace is appropriate for this serene isle; there are many scenic attractions within an hour's walk of both Paroikia and Naoussa. **Bicycles** are another popular alternative for exploring the island, with rolling hills providing just the right amount of workout for weekend bicyclists. Paros has some difficult-to-navigate pebble-and-dirt roads, so don't forget to check your tire pressure if you rent a bike. One-speed bicycles can be rented from stands around Mavrogenous Square for 350 drs ($2.69) per day.

The only **public bus** that provides frequent service is the shuttle between Paroikia and Naoussa (fare: 80 drs, or 61¢. The other public buses from Paroikia run only three or four times a day in two general directions: south to Aliki and southeast to the beaches at Piso Livadhi and Chrissi Akti. Unfortunately, their infrequent service (schedules are posted by the bus station) makes catching a returning late-afternoon bus exceedingly difficult. Most people resort to a brisk walk for the return trip.

An easy and adventuresome alternative is to rent a **moped.** There are several moped dealers along the harbor (between the windmill and the yacht marina to the north) just waiting to accommodate you. It's a seller's market on Paros in the summertime, and most of the rental shops stand firm on their prices. Mopeds, as we've said before, can be dangerous, so check them out carefully before deciding on a rental. Depending on size they will cost 1250 drs ($9.61) to 2000 drs ($15.38). Another alternative is a Jeep or dune buggy. After comparing vehicle quality, the best bets were **Rent-A-Car Acropolis** (tel. 21-830), run by the good-natured Boyztzis Brothers and **Budget Rent-a-Car,** along the harborfront. Groups of three or four might enjoy renting one of the Acropolis's wildly painted dune buggies at 6250 drs ($48.07) per day or a Suzuki Jeep, which costs 6000 drs ($46.15) per day. Rates include third-party insurance. Full insurance, which we recommend, is 750 drs ($5.76) more per day. Acropolis requires that renters have a driver's license for at least one year prior to rental.

Paros Travel (tel. 21-582) is one of many offices that offer round-the-island day trips. It has daily departures at 10 a.m., and tours cost from 1200 drs ($9.23) to 2000 drs ($15.38).

Taxis can be booked (tel. 21-500) or hailed at the windmill taxi stand. If you're coming off the ferry with lots of luggage and a hotel reservation in Naoussa, it's worth the 800 drs ($6.15) to take a taxi directly there.

USEFUL INFORMATION: The **area code** for Paros is 0284. **Ferry** tickets can be purchased from many travel agencies around Mavrogenous Square; schedules are posted on big blackboards outside their offices. Day excursions to Mykonos and Sifnos for about 2000 drs ($15.38) can be found at many of the agencies. **Olympic Airways** tickets can be purchased at the harborside multiservice Travel Office, where a local ticket agent (tel. 21-900) sells all their inter-Greece routes. A company called **Interisland Touring Services** (tel. 21-353) can help you find hotels, villas, and furnished apartments. The **Tourist Information Bureau** is actually inside the windmill on the harbor. It's open from 9 a.m. to 10 p.m. daily, and the staff speaks English and French and has a bulletin board covered with bus and ferry schedules, island information, and maps. There is also a message board to help you locate friends and lovers.

If you're staying a while, pick up the fact-filled guidebook *Paros,* by Jeffrey Carson and James Clark.

There are two banks on Mavrogenous Square, but the **National Bank of Greece** (open 8 a.m. to 2 p.m. and 5:30 p.m. to 8 p.m. Monday to Friday, on Saturday from 9 a.m. to 1 p.m. in the high season) has an ultramodern office with a glass back wall that allows sunlight to filter through. It deserves kudos for its sensitive design. . . . The **post office** is near the Ekatonotapyliani Church, open 7:30 a.m. to 2 p.m. Monday to Friday, with extended hours in July and August. . . . The **O.T.E.** is at the head of the southbound coastal road near the windmill. The long hours (7:30 a.m. to 10 p.m. Monday through Friday) help to offset crowding by the midday throng. If the front door is closed, go around to the back. Wind direction determines which door is left open!

The **Cyclades Laundry/Dry Cleaning** (tel. 22-341) is opposite the Ekatontapyliani Church. . . . Campers should stock up at the **Emborion Supermarket** and **Aristo Bakery** on Agora (Market) Street before leaving town; the prices are better and there's more variety than at the campground markets.

The **Paros Clinic**, down the road from Ekatontapyliani, can be reached at 21-235 or 22-477. **Medical emergencies** should be handled through the Town Police (tel. 21-2221).

PAROIKIA: We'd recommend that you stay in Paroikia if you have only a day or two on the island. If you're going to stay longer, try Paroikia for the first few days and then move on to Naoussa. Each port has its singular appeal, as different from each other as are the separate islands; Paroikia has the shopping and the nightlife, while Naoussa is quieter and more rural.

Layout

Ferryboats land at Paroikia, site of the ancient capital and the largest village on Paros. In front of the pier is Paroikia's best-known landmark, a squat, whitewashed **windmill**. If you turn left and follow the bay, you'll hit the bus station (schedules are posted on their kiosk) and a very handy luggage storage—hours are 8 a.m. to 8 p.m. Each piece of luggage costs 75 drs (58¢) a half day, or 150 drs ($1.15) for an overnight or 24-hour period. With the windmill as a handle, imagine Paroikia's four main streets spreading out like the delicate frame of an open rice-paper fan. To your right, the road curves out of sight and follows the rock and sand coastline around the O.T.E. to the old kastro.

Directly in front of the windmill (facing inland) is **Manto Mavrogenous Square.** Ms. Mavrogenous, whose surly-faced bust is in the middle of this garden setting, has been commemorated on Paros and on Mykonos's (her birthplace) for her heroism during the War of Independence. In the 1820s Mavrogenous successfully quelled a band of Algerian pirates, then led her resistance fighters against Ottoman soldiers in Evia, Thessaly, and Turkey. After Liberation Ms. Mavrogenous settled in the now-Greek capital of Nafplion, but she was forced to leave after her affair with the prominent politician Dimitrios Ypsilantis was discovered. Eventually Mavrogenous settled on Paros where she died, impoverished and forgotten, in 1848.

On the left side of the square are travel agents, ferryboat ticket vendors, round-the-island excursion operators, and an I.T.S. Office, which helps with accommodations.

The lane which runs straight back through the square, between the two banks, leads to the enticing and picturesque **Agora** (Market) section. The Agora is concentrated in a relatively small area of town, but its layout is so convoluted that Theseus himself couldn't find his way around. At dusk the soft light and dimming shadows make it even harder to discern where the whitewashed, Cycladic-style streets begin and end. This confusion only makes the Agora that much more mysterious and romantic. The cavelike storefronts of the Agora host a large variety of painting and ceramics galleries and handcrafts boutiques. In this sector, the lost art of outlining the paving stones in white has been resurrected. Where cement patches have been used to replace broken paving, a local *trompe l'oeil* artist has painted in the outlines to imitate individual stones.

Returning to the harbor, you can't help but notice the graceful lines of the bright white **Ag. Nikolaos Church,** on its own tiny traffic island. This street leads past the public gardens to the unique church called **Ekatontapylian.** This "Church of 100 Doors" is considered the most superb example of Byzantine architecture in the Cyclades. Many of Paroikia's hotels lie in the hidden alleyways that snake between Mavrogenous Square and the Ekatonotapyliani Church.

To the extreme left of the windmill is the waterside road, which runs northwest, past the bus station, the yacht marina, and a slew of new hotels. Continuing north, you'll come upon **Camping Koula** (tel. 22-081), about 800 meters from the ferryboat pier. The site is on Livadhi Beach and it's the first choice campground in the vicinity of Paroikia.

Accommodations

The port of Paroikia has three basic hotel zones: the Agora, the harbor, and the beach. Because of Paros's immense popularity most hotels now require reservations for July and August, and these should be made at least one month in advance. All written requests must be accompanied by a deposit equal to one night's rent. Once you arrive in Greece, a follow-up phone call is highly recommended for those who haven't received a written confirmation.

In the Agora: The Agora is the heart of Paroikia, its pulse beating 24 hours a day. If you roll out of bed early you can catch the Greek vendors receiving donkey-loads of fruits and vegetables. A ravishing smell emanates from the bakery, where fresh-baked loaves have been set out to cool. Throughout the day and evening the Agora takes on its tourist persona, bustling with mercantile activity. Then, after midnight, when only a few remain in the late-night bars, strains of Eartha Kitt or Keith Jarrett drift through the still, whitewashed back alleys.

This is the most intriguing neighborhood in which to stay. In fact, our favorite hotel in Paroikia is on the main street of the Agora, Market Street. The eight-room **Hotel Dina** (tel. 0284/21-325) is a small lodging that would be indistinguishable from its pure-white neighbors if not for the discreet sign mounted outside. When you enter the long, narrow hallway the first thing you'll see are attractive plantings; then, you'll probably find the friendly proprietor, Dina Patelis, relaxing over a Greek coffee in the back garden. The Hotel Dina is spotless; all her simply furnished rooms and bathrooms sparkle. High-season doubles are 2596 drs ($19.96), without bath; rooms with private baths rent for 3000 drs ($23.07).

Other accommodations are available on the outskirts of the Agora in the quiet back streets of Paroikia, where the tourist presence is not so pervasive. The back-street maze can be navigated by walking up Ekatontapyliani Street and making a right down the lane opposite the church. Follow signs that begin here for the **hotels Galinos** and **Louiza** (tel. 0284/21-480 or 22-122). These two hotels, opposite each other on a lane so narrow that you could almost join hands with a friendly neighbor, have merged under the management of Michael Damias. The Galinos and Louiza combined have 47 comfortable rooms with private baths. Singles are available for 3500 drs ($26.92); doubles are 4125 drs ($31.73). When we visited, the hotels were filled with a group of watercolor artists from Oregon who'd come to Paros for ten days of painting. The Agora is certainly the right place to begin.

Down the lane across from the Louiza are two other budget hotels, the **Hotel Acropoli** (tel. 0284/21-521), and across from it, the **Hotel Margarita** (tel. 0284/21-563). The 12-room Acropoli is a little worn but its simple rooms with common bathrooms are clean. Doubles cost 4200 drs ($32.30) in the high season. The Margarita is a newer hotel and all its spacious rooms have private baths. Its rates are the same as the Galinos-Louiza.

Definitely the most cozy and attractive lodging is the **Pension Vanguelistra** (tel. 0284/21-482), on this same lane. You can't miss its flower-covered veranda, which brightens the whole street. Iorgos and Voula Maounis and their outgoing, English-speaking kids make every guest feel welcome. Four spotless, balconied rooms with shared bath are 2600 drs ($20) in the summertime. The Vanguelistra also has two doubles, each with private bath, for 2800 drs ($21.53).

Another gracious family renting rooms in the area is headed by **Mrs. Zambia Mavro** (tel. 0284/21-628). Her large, single-story home is in front of a vineyard off the road leading to the Galinos-Louiza. Mrs. Mavro speaks very little English, but the buzzing, salon-style hair dryers operating in her living room betray her main occupation! Even after coiffing hair all day, Mrs. Mavro manages to keep six neat rooms, which rent for 1650 drs ($12.69) in the low season, 2100 drs ($16.15) in the high.

READER'S HOTEL SUGGESTION: "I want to tell you about the greatest hotel experience I had in Greece. The **Hotel Niko** is located above the Lobster Restaurant, about a block off the Agora. All the rooms have terraces overlooking fields, private toilet and bath, plenty of towels and soap (!)—all for 2250 drs ($17.30) a double. The family who ran it couldn't have been more loving or caring. . . . I stayed on Paros four nights instead of one, I was so comfortable there" (Sara Sherman, Santa Monica, Calif.).

At the Harbor: The harborside nearest the windmill is a convenient and lively place to spend your evenings, and at sunset the views are magnificent. The best value here is the oddly named **Hotel The Kontes** (tel. 0284/21-246), an older inn with a broad arched doorway that faces toward Mavrogenous Square. The second-floor balconied rooms have great views of the windmill and the sea; the first-floor rooms, with shuttered French doors, open out onto a large, pleasant sundeck. The Kontes is a well-maintained, stylish building where cleanliness more than makes up for a little peeling paint. Doubles with bath range from 2450 drs ($18.85) to 2750 drs ($21.15), depending on location and view.

The **Hotel Georgy** (whose sign, "GEORGE V," looks like a take-off on Paris's most elegant first-class establishment) is nearby on Mavrogenous Square. The Georgy (tel. 0284/21-353) features a lively snackbar out front. This 38-room hotel is run by the Kontostavlos family, who take pride in providing good service to their guests. Their recently constructed hotel has large rooms with private, all-tiled bathrooms. You have a choice of views over a richly planted inner courtyard or out toward lively Mavrogenous Square. Doubles are 4820 drs ($37.07); continental breakfast in their café is 325 drs ($2.50) extra per person.

Just north of the windmill, on the street behind the Ag. Nikolaos Church traffic island, are two smaller, cheaper hotels. The **Hotel Kypraios** (tel. 0284/21-383) is five neat, simple, bathless rooms whose balconies shade the car-rental shop below. Anne, a warm and helpful hostess, charges only 2100 drs ($16.15) for two, including hot showers. A night's stay at the Kypraios may get you a discount at her husband's car-rental company downstairs. A few doors down from the Kypraios, above the River of Silver Jewelers, are similar accommodations at the **Hotel Parko** (tel. 0284/22-213), where the hostess, Mary, keeps six clean, bathless doubles that are 2800 drs ($21.54) a night, plus 225 drs ($1.73) extra for each hot-water shower.

At the Beach: The strip of hotels that line Livadhi Beach (about a ten-minute walk north of the windmill) have three common features: bland, C-class decor, proximity to the crowded town beach, and Aegean sea views. We'll review a few of them briefly, in order of their proximity to the ferryboat pier.

Closest to the pier is the **Hotel Polo** (tel. 0284/22-173), affiliated with the

Polo's Tours office (next to the windmill). It's located one street in from the beach, behind the Taverna Skouna. The recently constructed Polo has spacious rooms with private baths. All have balconies complete with tables and chairs (for your cocktail hour), but the harbor view is partially restricted. Bed-and-breakfast for two is 5875 drs ($45.19).

The 19-room **Hotel Stella** (tel. 0284/21-502) and the 12-room **Hotel Paros** (tel. 0284/21-319) have spartan rooms at the same prices as the Polo. The rooms with Aegean views are worthwhile; otherwise stay at the Polo. The **Hotel Dilion** (tel. 0284/21-479), one block behind the Hotel Paros, is another budget alternative to the Polo. Doubles are 5250 drs ($40.38) with private baths.

Farther along the beach are a few more expensive C-class hotels. The best bet is the **Hotel Asterias** (tel. 0284/21-797), an attractive Cycladic-style, white stucco hotel with 36 rooms and a front-facing, flowering garden. Spacious doubles with wooden shuttered doors opening onto balconies are 5625 drs ($43.26), including breakfast.

I.T.S. also rents fully furnished apartments in the area, complete with kitchens. They are a bit isolated but one can walk to town in 20 minutes or take a caïque across the bay. Prices run about 5800 drs ($44.61) for a one-bedroom apartment to 7000 drs ($53.85) for a two-bedroom unit, which sleeps four. Extra beds can be added for about 625 drs ($4.80). Rooms without kitchens run about 3625 drs ($27.88) for a double.

Restaurants

One factor that has greatly influenced Parian life is the number of foreigners who've taken up residence on the island. Their presence is immediately apparent to those who survey the quality restaurants.

Casual Fare: As much a must-see site as a great place to eat is **Nick's Hamburgers** (tel. 22-106), also known as "The Greatest Burgers on Earth." This lively snackbar, on the seaside road to the kastro, features an active message board ("attractive young man seeks companion") and popular lending library. Ask Nick Kossoudjis if you can read "The Nick Hamburger Story," or how a terribly nice fellow from Dayton, Ohio, happened to start a hamburger haven in far-off Paros. Nick uses hand-shaped buns, fresh meat, and island-grown vegetables in his delicious, cooked-to-order burgers, served piping hot! His specialties include the Nikburger at 170 drs ($1.31) and the huge Big Nik, a two-fisted sandwich of juicy ground beef, lettuce, and tomato, topped by Nick's own special sauce, at 320 drs ($2.46). Don't forget the fries! Nick's hours are unique—it's best just to pop by and see if he's open.

For coffee and pastry we liked **Pâtisserie Haniotis**. This reasonably priced café, open 8 a.m. to midnight daily, has wrought-iron tables overlooking lively Mavrogenous Square.

Tavernas: The **Dionysos Taverna** (tel. 22-318) has most of its seating outdoors in a pretty garden filled with bright red geraniums. Inside, a sensual fresco depicts mortals frolicking around Dionysos, who reclines, grape cluster in hand, on a chaise engraved "It is wise never to neglect the Gods." The Dionysos serves a large variety of good Greek wines, including the Parian favorites: Lagari, a strong red wine, and Kavarnis, a dry white, both at about 350 drs ($2.69) a bottle. A satisfying dinner for two, of the popular grilled pork chops or beef casserole, will cost 1500 drs ($11.54) to 3000 drs ($23.07), including wine.

In the Agora you'll come across many places to eat and drink. The **Levantis Tea Room,** on the main Market Street, is one of the nicest. A quick peek inside will lure you to a table: the interior is like a tearoom, and all the furnishings are gorgeous. The menu betrays the fact that it's also a restaurant, featuring coq-au-vin (680 drs [$5.23]), a very fine filet of chicken with mustard sauce (812 drs [$6.25]), various fresh fish dishes and homemade pies, felafel, and cakes (the lemon pie is worth dying for!). There is a large wine cellar stocked with local favorites, such as Kavernis, La Gari, and Crevellier. These run from 500 drs ($3.85) to 750 drs ($5.77) a bottle. The Levantis is open only from 7:30 p.m. to 11 p.m., so make sure you leave enough time at the end of the day to visit, even if it's only for an iced coffee and sweet.

Farther down Market street is the **Balcony Creperie;** it's on the second floor at the juncture in the road. The delicious fruit crêpes are a light answer to hot-weather appetites. And the outdoor seating is perfect.

Katerina's Restaurant, just off Market street, is another good place to dine.

Formal Dining: In the Agora, we loved **To Tamarisko** (tel. 22-170), a lovely trellised garden dripping with grapes and bright purple morning glories. Chefs Alfons and Karin are an attractive German couple who've perfected a sophisticated blend of continental and Greek cuisine. Try their tender veal filet, broiled on a skewer and served with rice, or their lamb in lemon sauce. A delicious dinner for two, including a bottle of Lagari, should be 1680 drs ($12.92) to 2500 drs ($19.23). To Tamarisko is open for dinner only; closed Monday. To find it, walk down the Market street from the square, make a left at the pharmacy, and then a right through the first whitewashed archway. It's behind all the greenery, on the right.

Bars and Late-Night Clubs: Just behind the windmill is Paroikia's second best-known landmark, the **Port Café.** This basic, spacious ouzeri, lit by bare incandescent bulbs, is filled day and night with tourists waiting for the ferry, bus, taxi, or just waiting. The Port Café serves the cheapest ouzo and grilled octopus on the island, as well as salads, sandwiches, and omelets; for about 125 drs (96¢) a setup, you can pass the time kibbitzing with a wide variety of fellow travelers.

The **Saloon D'Or** (tel. 22-176), on the Paralia, is also popular for its cheap drinks, and on good nights gets the liveliest 25- to 35-year-old crowd around.

If partying's not your thing, Paroikia offers several elegant alternatives. The **Ballos Music Bar,** a few doors away from the O.T.E. on the Paralia, is a tastefully decorated bar whose stone interior is braced with dark wooden beams. Mellow jazz and classical music accompany the slightly more expensive drinks (about $2.50 each).

Nearby is the picture-perfect **Apollo Café,** a restored home appointed in Cycladic chic. Dark-wood booths set in whitewashed stone walls form the entrance to the café's garden. Candlelight sets the tone inside the high-ceilinged house. Benches and stools are topped with bright woven cotton cushions. The old low tables are lightly varnished natural wood. Ice-cream desserts, snacks, drinks, and coffees are served to the soothing sounds of classical Western and Greek music. Romantics should head straight for the outside booths, where we whiled away hours one night in our own private world.

Farther down the street is **Psarades,** a Greek music and dance club from about 7:30 p.m. to 11 p.m. and the hottest disco in town from 11 p.m. on to 2 a.m. In fact, the Paralia on this side of town is where almost all the discos and bars are, so a nice waterfront stroll will yield up the night's secrets to you.

Dancing: There are so many discothèques tucked in the back lanes of the

Agora and the Paralia that it would be futile to recommend one over another. Nonetheless we fell into **Disco Magic** (tel. 21-129) one night and were amused by the bowl-size fuschia-colored drinks that were numbing the crowd for 250 drs ($1.92) each. Even if you don't try a "Magic Special," there's no cover charge, and the crowded dance floor and bevy of "No Problem" T-shirts should make all feel at home, as will George and Mikalis, the two managers.

What to Do

Paroikia features excellent **shopping**, particularly in the Agora. The wide range of galleries, handcrafts boutiques, clothing shops, and food markets make Paros one of the best spots in all of Greece for memorable souvenir and folk-art shopping. Just off Market street, almost at its end, you'll find the **Aegean School of Fine Arts**, founded 17 years ago by an American artist, the late Brett Taylor, a highly regarded painter who passed away in 1983. Mr. Taylor left behind an enduring arts institution where artists come to study each summer. Just below it is an excellent gallery of sculpture and ceramics representing some of the finest work of island craftsmen. The **Yria Ceramic Studio**, in the middle of the Agora, features ceramics, weavings, and lovely handmade plates. John loved the large serving platters with an abstract octopus pattern that were 3900 drs ($30). There may be no bargains to be had in the Agora, but then we find it always worthwhile to buy an object that we truly love, regardless of an outsider's appraisal of its "value." Another unique shop in the Agora is **The Teapot**, an herbalist's shop filled with teas, spices, natural foods, dyes, and folk art. It is directly across from the Levantis Tea Room. The assorted packaged herbs and potpourri of local Greek wildflowers make inexpensive and easy-to-carry gifts.

The site that draws thousands of pilgrims annually to Paros is its famous church, the **Panagia Ekatontapylian**. Located just off the private boat harbor, it's a large, graceful example of Byzantine church architecture. The name is thought to mean "100 Doors," but those who try will count only 99. There's a legend that if the 100th door is found then Constantinople (the holiest Greek Orthodox city, known to most of the world as Istanbul) will be returned to the Greek nation. The Ekatontapylian was constructed in the sixth century and rebuilt in the tenth century. Of special note is the ornately carved iconostasis of luminescent Parian marble. The swing doors that lead to the altar are carved wood painted to resemble marble. The marble floors and columns add lightness and grace to the stone walls. At one time the ceiling and walls were covered with frescoes, and remnants can still be seen. Behind the main basilica on the right is the Baptistry, now restored and occupied by several doves. The best time to visit Ekatontapylian is on August 15, the Feast of the Assumption, when great festivities are held at the site. The church is open for viewing daily from 8 a.m. to 1 p.m. and 5 p.m. to 8 p.m.

Behind the Baptistry of the Ekatontapylian is the **Paros Archeological Museum** (open 8 a.m. to 2 p.m. Monday through Saturday, to 1 p.m. on Sunday; closed Tuesday). The museum contains a small collection of finds from the sixth to the third centuries B.C., but will be of interest only to Parian scholars. In the room to the right of the entrance is a fragment of the *Parian Chronicle* (no. 26), an important tablet from which many events in ancient Greek history were dated, including the birth of Homer (the larger portion of the *Parian Chronicle* was taken to Oxford University in England for study and display). The museum also contains a third-century plaque inscribed with a biography of Archilochos, a famed seventh-century B.C. lyric poet and one of Paros's most famous native sons. His poetry reflects a thoroughly 20th-century mentality: "What, breaks me, young friend, is tasteless desire, dead iambics, boring dinners. . . ." Admission to the Paros Archeological Museum is 150 drs ($1.15).

Another neighborhood of great interest to those who delight in the architectural wonder of the Agora is the **kastro,** about a ten-minute walk south of the windmill on the seaside road. The remains of the 13th-century Venetian fortifications are all the more interesting because of the marble fragments from the ancient Temples of Demeter and Apollo that were incorporated into the kastro walls. Traditional Cycladic housing clings to the old Venetian tower and ramparts in a fascinating melange of architectural styles that spans nearly 3,000 years.

NAOUSSA: Naoussa is perched up on Paros's north coast, in the middle of two fat peninsulas lined with rocky coves and sandy beaches. Fortunately, recent tourist development has focused on the beach areas, and this has kept Naoussa village relatively unspoiled. The gnarled, whitewashed back lanes of the port are even more confusing than Paroikia's Agora because of their small size and lack of commercial activity. This enclave of Greek villagers and the active port nearby (where fishermen still fish) give Naoussa its charm.

Orientation and Services

If you're coming the 11 kilometers north from Paroikia, you'll know you're approaching Naoussa by the hotels and restaurants which line the paved roadway. After crossing a street-level bridge, Archilochos Street and Naoussa's main square will be on the right. The square, shaded by tall eucalyptus trees, marks the bus station and the taxi stand. The **Town Police** (tel. 51-202) are behind the dry goods store off the square, and the **O.T.E.** is on Archilochos Street. About 200 meters farther up Archilochos Street, on the left past the right-hand church, is the **post office** (open 8 a.m. to 3 p.m. Monday through Saturday). Tucked in a cool storefront, almost buried beneath ferry schedule signs, is the Nissiotissa Tourist Office, known locally as **Gavalas Travel** (tel. 51-480). Cathy and Kostas Gavalas, both knowledgeable Naoussans, will help you find a hotel, room to let, or villa. Gavalas can also arrange ferryboat and plane tickets, rental cars, and island excursions. Nearby is **Simitzi Tours** (tel. 51-113), where Katerina will help you in any way possible to enjoy your stay on Paros.

If you continue across the square to an arched entryway, you'll be at the medieval gates of the old city. Within are the fascinating back alleys of Naoussa; they are best explored in midafternoon, when the inhabitants retire inside for siesta. Walking softly along the cobblestone paths and peeking into the geranium-filled gardens provides an undisturbed view of timeless Greek life.

Beyond the National Bank is the busy harbor at **St. Demetrios Bay.** It's most active at sunrise and late afternoon, when the fishermen are setting out or returning home with the day's catch. From the portside cafés you can watch the nets being spread out on the dock, then carefully folded for the next day's outing. The blue, green, orange, and yellow caïques are scrubbed, rinsed, and fixed to their moorings. Across the way, the small whitewashed **Ag. Nikolaos Church,** dedicated to the patron saint of sailors, stands out strikingly in a sea of primary colors. A legacy of the 15th-century Venetian occupation of this tiny port is the old stonework of the breakwater on the eastern side. Divers will find ruined ramparts submerged throughout this part of the harbor.

The **area code** is 0284.

Accommodations

There are fewer hotels and rooms to let in Naoussa than in Paroikia, so in July and August advance reservations are even more strongly recommended. If you haven't made reservations and are in Naoussa unable to find a hotel room, try **Gavalas Travel** (tel. 0284/51-480) on the Square. Opposite the Gavalas office is the **Hotel Aliprantis** (tel. 0284/51-571), directly on Naoussa's main square. The attractive C-class hotel has 15 rooms, all with tiled bathrooms. Ask for a front-facing room with a balcony overlooking the aged eucalyptus on the square; doubles are 4860 drs ($37.38) in the summer and 4210 drs ($32.38) from April to early June, and October. Next to Simitzi Tours is **Linardos Rooms-to-Rent** (tel. 0284/51-261), where 1875 drs ($14.42) gets you a clean, nice room in the heart of town.

To reach the **Minoa Hotel** (tel. 0284/51-309 or 51-551), also in "downtown" Naoussa, walk up Archilochos Street to the post office, then turn sharply back to the left. The modern, whitewashed Minoa sits up on a low hill overlooking the back alleys of the village. Natural finished wood tables and chairs from the hotel's popular (but expensive) restaurant fill the cobblestone square in front. All 26 rooms have private baths and carved-wood verandas, though there's not much of a view. High-season doubles are 4850 drs ($37.30); continental breakfast in the Minoa's restaurant is optional at 300 drs ($2.30) per person. The Minoa claims to be booked up by March, but you can try it.

In the quiet back streets surrounding the Hotel Minoa—and in the whole area behind the Sacriotia Monument—you'll find a scattering of whitewashed abodes sporting "Rooms-Chambres-Zimmer" signs.

There are several excellent hotels and bungalows within a 15-minute walk of the square. Our first choice among these would be the **Hotel Naoussa** (tel. 0284/51-207), a bungalow complex run by the Maroulidis family. The Naoussa is open from April to October, though its spacious bungalows overlooking the St. Demetrios Bay are booked early for July and August. A double room costs 3875 drs ($29.80) in the high season and includes private bath, a kitchenette with stocked fridge, sink and utensils, and a large patio which leads onto a back garden. The Naoussa bungalows can also be booked through an Athens office—Iracleous, 46 Kallithea St. (tel. 95-97-631).

On a hillside above the road leading back to Paroikia is the modern, well-run **Hotel Mary** (tel. 0284/51-201). Nikos Karpodinis and his family maintain 16 tastefully decorated, spotless rooms. Double rooms, most with balconies, cost 5750 drs ($44.23) for bed-and-breakfast.

Just down the dry, scrub-brush slope from the Hotel Mary are the **Piperi Bungalows** (tel. 0284/51-295), owned by a dashing Scotsman, Jimmy Clarke-Ames. This David Niven look-alike keeps eight small bungalows; private apartments with baths, kitchenettes, and individual solar-panel hot-water heaters. Each has polished stone floors and raw-wood furniture; local folk art (woven cotton cushions and linens) and blooming flowers give a personal feel. Mr. Clarke-Ames, a charming host, responded to our question of how long he'd lived on Paros with "About eight years, ten years, what?" A bungalow for two or three is 3625 drs ($27.88) until June 1, and then 3950 drs ($30.38) until September 9.

A very nice beachside hotel is the **Kalypso** (tel. 0284/51-488). Located east of Naoussa village, at Agii Anargiri Beach, the attractive Kalypso is built around a cobblestone courtyard, though many of the outer, balconied rooms overlook the sea. Spacious double rooms include private baths and telephones and cost 4750 drs ($36.53) a night. The upper-floor rooms are reached via an ornately carved wooden mezzanine, which overlooks the Kalypso's bar. Again, your only hope here is to book ahead.

Tucked in among the splashier places in this newly constructed resort area is the budget-watchers' **Hotel Cavos** (tel. 0284/51-367, or 89-58-255 in Athens). The immaculately maintained Cavos has 19 double rooms, many with a view of the bay. High-season doubles are 5725 drs ($44.03). There are a number of similar newly built apartments and studios in this area. Most run about 5000 drs ($38.46) a double.

We found a magnificent "splurge" hotel overlooking Kolimbithres Beach: the **Atlantis Hotel** (tel. 0284/51-340), located literally on the left shoulder of the beach. The Atlantis has been exquisitely designed so that each of its 20 rooms has a balcony overlooking the ocean. All rooms have their own phones from which you can dial internationally, a radio, and all the amenities. There is a pool that also overlooks the ocean and around which the hotel sponsors a weekly barbecue for its guests, and a heavily planted outdoor terrace (there are three tiers of balconies and terraces here!), where you can sunbathe during breakfast; it is connected to an indoor bar/lounge, where you can unwind while watching the sunset. The tab for all this? 6625 drs ($50.96) for two, including breakfast. The public bus to the beach stops at the foot of the hotel. You should make reservations here at least three months in advance; we say go for it.

Dining

The number of foreign residents and the sophisticated tourist clientele encourage a more varied, gourmet restaurant scene than one might expect in this seemingly sleepy fishing village. Naoussa's main square has some of the best-value casual eating establishments in the area. Beneath the Hotel Aliprantis are the village's **bread bakery and pâtisserie.** Delicious snacks of cheese pies, biscuits, espresso, and pastries can be consumed under the cooling eucalyptus in the shaded outdoor café, often for less than 150 drs ($1.15).

We usually find that the most scenic restaurants provide the least appetizing food at the highest prices. In Naoussa, there's a welcome exception—the **Restaurant Limanaki.** It's really a taverna at the harborside, where you can watch the fishermen mend their nets and unload the day's catch. Limanaki serves standard taverna fare, but the quality is higher than most; a well-cooked meal for two with local wine will cost 2000 drs ($15.38). Best of all, you can pass the time just watching real life carry on in front of you. What else could you have possibly come to Greece for?

Near the Limanaki on the harbor is **Stratia,** the local ouzeri. One of Naoussa's greatest assets is that there are still enough local Greek citizens in town to support an authentic ouzeri. Old, wind-burnt fishermen sit for hours nursing their milky ouzos (this clear firewater turns white when you add water) and their mini-portions of grilled octopus and olives. If you haven't had time in your busy schedule for an afternoon or evening at an ouzeri, then this is the right time and place. There's nothing more relaxing than sitting outside to drink an ouzo.

On the opposite end of the spectrum for early-evening or late-night drinks or coffee is **Maimou,** an intimate, chic, whitewashed café. Just around the corner from the post office you'll see a sign saying "Creperie"; this is the incredibly beautiful and delicious **Kavarnis Bar.** The Kavarnis's interior reminds you of another time, of Paris in the twenties, or an American private clubhouse from the forties. The menu here is crêpes, ranging from 250 drs ($1.92) to 650 drs ($5) in price and stuffed with everything from fruit to meat to ice cream! Try the famous Cognac Crêpe. The restaurant also serves cocktails (elaborate and about 550 drs [$4.25]) and opens at 8 p.m.

On Mantosmayrogenous Street you'll find the best pastry shop in town, **Delicieux,** just around the corner from **Heavenly Ice Cream,** which lives up to its name. Heavenly Ice Cream is around the corner from the Avra Tours office.

To get to these back streets take the left hand road at the bus stop and follow the white arrow sign with black lettering that says "Telephone office"; after two blocks you're there.

Formal Dining: Taverna Christo's (tel. 51-442), which opens at 7 p.m. nightly, opposite the post office, is known for its eclectic menu of continental and Euro-Greek cuisine. Dinner is served in a beautiful garden filled with red and pink geraniums. The trellised roof is dripping with grape clusters, and their dark purple color in late August is unforgettable. Any of Christo's veal, lamb, or steak dishes costs from 2500 drs ($19.23) to 3000 drs ($23.07) per person including a bottle of Lagari and a fresh-fruit dessert.

Nightlife

If holding hands while strolling under the stars doesn't fill up your evening, you can take in an outdoor "B" picture at the **Makis Cinema**. Nightly shows are usually at 10 p.m. and midnight. If you had something a little more active in mind, try the **Paracato Disco** or the **Banana Moor**. Both are a ten-minute walk up the hill on the main street of Naoussa and they are right next door to each other—double trouble!

Local and Intra-Island Transportation

Naoussa's sudden growth in popularity has meant no expansion of transportation connections to other Paros villages and Cyclades islands.

Buses run from Paroikia to Naoussa approximately every hour between 8 a.m. and 10 p.m. From the bus stop in Naoussa's main square buses run to Paroikia every hour on the half hour until 10:30 p.m. The fare for the 15-minute trip is 95 drs (73¢). Bus service to other island villages is on poorly paved or narrow dirt roads, and is infrequent.

Because there are so many excellent beaches within 20 kilometers of Naoussa village, a **moped** is an expedient way to sample them at your own pace. There are several moped dealers on the square; prices are comparable to those in Paroikia and bargaining is unlikely in the peak-demand summer season. **Alipranti Rent-A-Car** (tel. 51-119), at the foot of the bridge leading into town, were very friendly and accommodating. Their rates (insurance included) for mopeds are 1250 drs ($9.61), motorcycles are 1750 drs ($13.46), and cars go for 5000 drs ($38.46) a day.

Nissiotissa Rent-A-Car rents Renault Jeeps for about 5200 drs ($40) daily in the high season. If you team up with a few others a rental car can be fun and an economical way to sightsee, and the entire island can be covered in one day.

Taxis are an expensive alternative for beach hopping and cannot easily be found outside the village, but for getting to and from Paroikia they're often worth the 800 drs ($6.15) tariff. Luggage costs about 40 drs (30¢) per bag extra.

Daily **excursion boats** leave from the Naoussa harbor for Mykonos and Delos. The two-hour journey can be taken one way for 1025 drs ($7.88); the full-day, round-trip excursion costs 2000 drs ($15.38). Also in summer, daily excursions can be made to Naxos; round-trip fares are 1500 drs ($11.53), though one-way tickets are sold for half price. Local caïques make day trips to the beach of Santa Maria, about six kilometers away around the eastern peninsula, for 600 drs ($4.61) round trip. There's also caïque servece to Kolimbithres Beach (on the west peninsula) for 160 drs ($1.23) each way. Check the boards in front of the many travel agencies for other tours.

AROUND THE ISLAND: Paros is reputed to have some of the best beaches in the Aegean; the island's scenic beauty and archeological sites are additional lures. In fact, Paros's many attractions are sure to keep even the most restless sightseer happy for days.

West Coast Beaches

South from Paroikia, along the west coast, which faces the island of Antiparos, are several fine beaches. Just three kilometers from the port is **Ag. Irini**. This secluded sandy beach cove is visible from the elevated main road just before the turnoff for Petaloudhes (Valley of the Butterflies). At Ag. Irini you'll find a taverna, the Ag. Eirini Campgrounds, and a handful of palm trees. Another ten minutes south by moped is the turnoff for **Pounda**, a popular sandy beach that gets crowded in July and August. Pounda is located at the narrowest stretch of the Aegean between Paros and Antiparos—you can sit in a café and examine Antiparos's main port. South of Pounda the paved roadway disappears and dust, dirt, and gravel begin.

About 20 kilometers south of Paroikia is **Aliki**, a charming, unspoiled fishing village. The residents of Aliki rely more on their harbor than on their tiny village. Tucked around a large clean sandy beach cove are the few new, prefab buildings, yet many hand-built caïques are moored in the small natural harbor.

If you're as charmed as we were by this friendly port and have brought your own bicycle or moped from Paroikia, you might consider staying. (Buses do run three or four times a day from Paroikia, but they're unreliable at best, nonexistent at worst.) The first choice would be the **Hotel Algiliki** (tel. 0284/21-285), a 13-room, C-class place at the far end of the town's pier. Nikoletta Sikalia is one of the friendly proprietors; during our stay there were more staff than guests. Doubles with private bath are 3125 drs ($24.03) in the summer and singles are 2000 drs ($15.38). All the balconies have beautiful views of the busy port and the quiet beach. Besides cleanliness, modern facilities, and warm hosts, the Agiliki has another asset: it's above the **Aliki Restaurant**, the village's seafood taverna and café/pâtisserie all-in-one.

Aliki's other hotel is the **Aphroditi** (tel. 0284/21-986). The Aphroditi, opened in 1980, is managed by the friendly Aliprantis family. Their 20 modern spacious rooms with balconies are spotless and simply furnished; doubles with bath are 4600 drs ($35.38) in the summer and 3650 drs ($28.07) in June and September. The **general store** (where you park your vehicle, because you have to walk through most of the town) has rooms to let, and **free camping** is tolerated on the broad, smooth pebble beach just south of the port.

North Coast Beaches

The north coast beaches, hugging the two peninsulas that jut into St. Demetrios Bay around the village of Naoussa, are the best on the island. To the west of Naoussa, about ten minutes by moped, is the picturesque **Kolimbithres Beach**. Small sandy coves are punctuated by giant, smooth rocks, which must be scaled or swum around to reach the next cove or the open sea. Reminiscent of the weird rocks that jut forth into the air above Meteora are the smaller boulders which spring out of the Aegean at Kolimbithres. This lunar seascape is well worth a visit even for those who can't stand sparkling azure water and golden sand. Nearby is **Camping Naoussa** (tel. 0284/51-595) (not quite as sparkling as the water), where sites cost 375 drs ($2.88) per person per night.

North of Kolimbithres, by the Ag. Ioannis Church, is **Monastery Beach**, the north coast's nudist beach. In this secluded cove clothed and unclothed bathers enjoy the calm waters. West of Naoussa the beaches are often more populated because of the new hotels that have been built along the roads of this peninsula. **Agii Anagiri** is a good example; it's a well-maintained beach but the hotels that border it provide daily crowds.

About four kilometers north of Naoussa on an unpaved road is the popular **Lageri Beach**. Before you reach Lageri, the road forks to the right. Bearing right will bring you to **Santa Maria Beach**, perhaps the most beautiful one on the island because of its purity and seclusion. At Santa Maria there are coves so secluded that free camping is possible. Shallow sand dunes (very rare in Greece) line the broad banks of fine sand that curve around the irregular coastline. Although Santa Maria is only about 20 minutes from Naoussa by moped, most tourists don't make it that far. Those who do will be richly rewarded. Southeast of Naoussa, and connected by public bus, is the beach town of **Ampelas.** Several rooms to rent are now available at this small beach, and there are some good inexpensive tavernas.

You can inquire at Scopas Tours in Paroikia and at the Gavalas Travel Office in Naoussa about **windsurfing** lessons and equipment rental. In both ports the rate is 680 drs ($5.23) hourly or 2300 drs ($17.69) daily.

East Coast Beaches

The east coast beaches, equidistant from Paroikia or Naoussa, can be reached by private transport or public bus. Buses leave three or four times daily from either village.

The east coast roadway runs about half a kilometer inland from the sea, so a window check from a moving bus can't give you a status report on crowd conditions at the beach. Choose wisely; once you've disembarked, it's several kilometers to the next beach. (The local beachbum grapevine in either port town will provide the latest update.)

The beautiful beach at **Ormos Molos**, on a small peninsula near the village of Marpissa, is the closest, therefore the most crowded. **Piso Livadhi**, about ten kilometers from either Paroikia or Naoussa, is a small sandy beach cove surrounded by hotels and pizza parlors; the village feels crowded even when there's no one in sight. The shallow harbor makes an unappealing swimming hole in full view of the overtouristed town. The next cove south, **Logares**, has started to feel Piso Livadhi's crowds, though as yet there are no sanctioned hotels on the beach.

There is a universal consensus on the best beach-for-beach's sake, although only those looking for almost total seclusion will want to stay overnight there. **Chryssi Akti**, the "Golden Beach" on Paros's east coast, is 25 kilometers south of Naoussa over partially paved roads. It's well worth a dusting to get there. The community is one kilometer off the paved main road (turn left just before the Golden Beach Restaurant). You'll see Taverna Zina on the left and a parking lot at the end for beach commuters. At the parking lot, the **Gold Beach Hotel** (tel. 0284/41-366) has 37 C-class rooms with views over the two-kilometer stretch of fine golden sand. Doubles run 2600 drs ($20). Several new hotels are in the works. However unwelcome these signs of development might be, they'll ensure that Chryssi Akti is rid of the hundreds of campers who crashed there and littered it for several summers. If you're planning to stay a while, bring some good books.

What to See

If your time is limited, rent a moped or car pool for a one-day, around-the-island tour. For single travelers, it might be more economical to book one of the bus tours offered by several local travel agents for 2000 drs ($15.38).

A day of sightseeing around the island of Paros should begin in Paroikia, include Petaloudhes and a visit to a beach such as Kolimbithres on the way north, then a stop in Naoussa for a seafood lunch at the picturesque harbor. From Naoussa, the tour continues south to one of the finest east coast beaches, such as Ormos Molos. On the return trip across the heartland of Paros to Paroikia, stops should be made at Lefkes, the medieval capital, and at the marble quarries of Marathi.

Petaloudhes, the Valley of the Butterflies, is a lush oasis of pear, plum, fig, and pomegranate trees just six kilometers from Paroikia. Taking the beach road out of town, continue for about four kilometers until the left-hand turnoff for the Monastery of Christo Dassous, a nunnery since 1805. (The nunnery has always been closed to men, but often seems to be closed to everyone.) Regardless, its continual renovation over the years has left little of architectural interest. From Christo Dassous, take the dirt road on the right for about a kilometer downhill to the home of Kostas Gravalris, the contented owner of this special property. The Greeks call this place "Psychopiana"—the place to lighten the heart and mind—and we couldn't have put it better. Kostas opens his home from 8 a.m. to 8 p.m. daily, closing it for siesta from 1 p.m. to 4 p.m. He recommends coming in the early morning or evening, when the butterflies leave the ivy leaves they cling to and fly around. The butterflies, genus *Panaxia quadripunctaria poda,* look like black-and-white-striped arrowhead flowers when they relax in the shade. Once aroused, they take off. Please don't be aggressive and throw things at them—they are nervous creatures. When they fly, you can see their bright-red undersides. As at Petaloudhes in Rhodes, the butterflies are born and die here. They emerge in June and live until September when they disappear (they're most numerous from July 15 to August 15). The unique combination on this arid island of a freshwater spring, dense foliage, flowering trees, and cool shade is what has lured the butterflies here for at least 300 years (since the Gravalris family has had this property). They run a small snackbar at the site; the butterfly keeper's fee is 100 drs (76¢).

The road south from Petaloudhes to Aliki is partially paved, but it's not worthwhile trying to make a full-circle tour of the island through that southernmost point. The "roads" that curve up the Chryssi Akti Beach on the east are not fit for bus, moped, or bicycle. We think most readers will prefer to double back up to Paroikia and continue north from there, up to Naoussa. Archeology buffs can make a stop at the **Sanctuary of Aphrodite,** though very little remains from antiquity. James A. Clark writes of this excursion: "It's on the way to Naoussa, on the second and higher of the two hills, about 2 kms. from Paroikia, to the left of the Naoussa road. Head for the farmhouse halfway up the hill, and from there to the grotto below the summit. There is a fig tree, a little spring, and a fantastic view." *Paros,* the guidebook written by Mr. Clark and Jeffrey Carson, is highly recommended for its rich historical details, local anecdotes, and many wonderful walking tours.

After a lunch break and tour of Naoussa village, follow the east coast road south from Naoussa to Marpissa. Here the road forks right (or west), to Paroikia. The uphill, inland road to Paroikia is a pleasant change from the hot and dusty coastal route. After winding through ancient olive groves and well-tended farmland, it begins to ascend steep hills. When the road levels out, you've come to the perimeter of **Lefkes.** This classic hill town was constructed in the shape of an amphitheater. The tiers of whitewashed houses with red-tiled roofs surround a central town square. It's said that Lefkes, medieval capital of Paros, was built in the hills to protect inhabitants from the pirates who raided the coastal towns. If the pirates ever reached Lefkes, its sharply angled, narrow streets and confusing levels would have thwarted them. Even today, trying to reach the famed Aghia Triadha Church, whose carved marble towers are easily visible from a distance, is a feat. Once you arrive at Lefkes, leave your vehicle behind and descend the slippery smooth cobblestone paths to the inner core of the village. The small main square will not be apparent until you come to the end of one of the narrow lanes which leads into it.

Parian marble, prized for its translucency and soft, granular texture, was used by ancient sculptors for their best works, including the *Hermes* by Praxiteles and the *Venus de Milo*. The **marble quarries at Marathi** are the last stop on the return trip to Paroikia; to reach them, take the winding mountain roads about five kilometers west of Lefkes, where the tiny farming community of Marathi lives on a plateau. From the road, walk up to the left beyond the few farmhouses toward the deserted buildings that once belonged to a French mining company. When mining became too expensive they abandoned the site, leaving behind two deep shafts in the marble mountain behind their old compound. The French mining firm brought out enough marble from this site in 1844 to construct Napoleon's tomb. If not for the prohibitive cost, modern-day sculptors could still work with this incomparable material.

The last part of the route to Paroikia joins the Naoussa road. Just before town, on your left, is the **Ekatontapylian Church.** After visiting here, continue around the port and follow the coast road past the windmill. You can finish your tour with a stroll through the kastro; afterwards descend to the seashore for a drink at one of the many pleasant cafés.

Antiparos

A visit to Antiparos is popular with today's tourists who want to get away from all the crowds in Paroikia. This 11-kilometer-long island, just anti, or "opposite," the west coast of Paros, was once connected to it by a natural causeway. For centuries its huge cave drew distinguished tourists who otherwise had little reason to go to Paros. The Marquis de Nointel, King Otto of Greece, and even Lord Byron visited the cave and carved their names in the many stalagmites and stalactites.

Tourists who arrive on the excursion caïques from Paroikia no longer descend the 90 meters into the cave by rope—a safer cement staircase has been built. Nonetheless, an hour spent in the dark, echo-filled cave trying to deduce some of the inscriptions is a lot more adventuresome than sitting on a beach (and makes for good storytelling long afterward).

Excursion caïques leave the port of Paroikia regularly beginning at 8 a.m. for the 45-minute ride to Antiparos. Round-trip excursions including a visit to the caves (about a two-hour walk from the village of Antiparos) cost 1400 drs ($10.77). When you dock, you'll have to climb the hill of St. John to the Church of St. John of the Cave. From here you'll have an excellent view south to Folegandros (farthest west), Sikinos, and Ios, with a bit of Paros to your left. There are also local shuttle boats ferrying the channel between Pounda and Antiparos continuously from 9 a.m. The fare is 100 drs (76¢).

Besides several pensions and rooms-to-let, there are now three hotels on Antiparos, the C-class **Chryssi Akti** (tel. 0284/61-227), the D-class **Anargyros** (tel. 0284/61-204), and the **Mantalena** (tel. 0284/61-206). There's also a **campground** (tel. 0284/61-221) with full facilities about a ten-minute walk north from the port. The official campground is on an excellent beach, but free camping is condoned on all the beaches at the north tip of the island. Another popular beach, small but well protected, is at Apantima opposite Aliki on Paros's west coast.

GETTING THERE: Paros is just six hours by ferryboat or 55 minutes by airplane from Athens, making it one of the closest of the Cycladic isles. The major port, Paroikia, is serviced at least once daily from Piraeus. The Nomikos Lines, the

Naxos Maritime Company, and other steamer lines depart Piraeus between 7 a.m. and 9 a.m.; schedules should be confirmed with Tourist Information in Athens (tel. 171) or by dialing 45-11-311. The Chryssi Ammos Lines has daily departures from Rafina via Siros to Paros. The trip from Rafina can take an hour less than from Piraeus if the weather is good, and the fare from Rafina is about 20% cheaper. Their ferryboat schedule can be checked at 0294/23-300. Paroikia is linked to the other Cyclades via daily ferry service to Naxos, Ios, and Thira (Santorini). The F/B *Aigaion* has overnight service to Ikaria and Samos, three times a week. From Samos you can arrange a next-day excursion to Ephesus, Turkey. The F/B *Kimolos* runs once a week to Sifnos. Cruise excursions (one-way tickets are sold, though not legally) leave daily from Paroikia or Naoussa to Mykonos.

Olympic has four daily scheduled flights to Paros. For schedule information and reservations, call Olympic Airways (tel. 92-92-555 in Athens, or 21-900 or 22-015 in Paroikia).

5. Naxos

According to Herodotus, the following report was sent by a roving emissary to King Darius, at the ancient Persian court: "In spite of [Naxos's] small size it is a fine and fertile place. . . . I suggest you attack it." The world and ways of man have changed little since those heady days of the Persian Empire.

ORIENTATION: You can attack Naxos in two ways. The best means of exploring, for those who relish verdant valleys, craggy peaks, and isolated mountain villages, is to hike along the island's trails and backcountry roads. If you're an inveterate cafe hopper, museum hound, or shopper, center your activities around the port and the lovely walled Venetian kastro that overlooks the harbor and sea.

Boats arrive at the harbor on the northern end of Naxos in the main town, called **Naxos,** or **Chora.** Along the harbor are two of the town's most notable landmarks. South of the pier, built on a tiny islet nestled in the harbor, is the whitewashed **Myrtidiotissa Church.** On the north side of the port, to the left as you disembark, is the unfinished yet perfect **Temple of Apollo.** The temple is built on another islet and is connected to the mainland by a narrow causeway. Rising from this rocky site is the Portara (which means "Great Door"), a gargantuan post-and-lintel opening made of tan-colored Naxian marble. This ancient portal, practically all that's left of the temple, is Naxos's best known monument, a grand doorway that has welcomed visitors to the island for over 2,500 years.

If you set off in an easterly direction you'll visit Grotta, Bourgo, and Fountana, the oldest quarters in Naxos town. **Grotta** abuts the northern coast of Chora. This section has just undergone a major transformation, from a sleepy neighborhood to a resort hosting a fresh crop of oceanfront villas and hotels. **Bourgo** and **Fountana** are picturesque districts filled with two- and three-story homes covered in gardenias and bougainvillea. These two areas surround the island's most captivating structure, the 13th-century Venetian **kastro.** Isolated from the town below by an imposing wall, the kastro is a magnificent medieval town-within-a-town.

The southern half of Chora, leading down to the beachfront resort of Ag. Georgios, is where you'll find most of the town's hotels, restaurants, and tourist services. The most direct way to reach Chora's south side is to walk down the Paralia, the café- and souvenir-lined lane that overlooks Naxos' harbor.

GETTING AROUND: Walking Naxos' trails and back roads brings you face to face with the island's hospitable inhabitants. Exchanging a "mera" (shortened form of "good-day") with a passing farmer, listening to the metallic clanging of a goat's bell, or breathing the lemon-scented air from a nearby grove are what visiting Greece is all about. Naxos is ideal for this kind of travel, because the most interesting parts of the island are no more than a half day walk from Chora. Most of all, the scenery within this relatively small area is remarkably varied; a three-hour walk will take you from bamboo groves to the cool air atop Mount Zas, 3,000 feet above the Aegean and the highest point in the Cyclades.

If you plan to walk around the interior section of the island, particularly in the Tragea region, conserve your energy by taking a short **bus trip** from Chora to Chalki, Filoti, or Apeiranthos. There's regular service in the afternoon back to Chora from these points. Buses leave from the northern end of the waterfront, only a short distance from the taxi stand. There is frequent service to Chalki, Filoti, and the beach at Ag. Anna. Fares run from 80 drs (62¢) to 120 drs (92¢). Most other destinations have buses running only two or three times a day. One of the most popular day trips is a visit to Apollon 325 drs ($2.50), on the northern end of the island. However, the bus travels this route only four times a day, and a one-way journey takes two hours and 15 minutes. Competition for seats on the Apollon-bound bus is fierce, so your best bet is to get on the bus as early as possible. It's a long ride, especially if you have to stand the entire way.

Although it's possible to tour the island by bus, you may find its inefficiency more than you can bear, particularly if you intend to visit fairly remote spots. A **moped** or **motorcycle** is an ideal way of getting around. **Jason's Bikes**, near the Lalos Café on the north side of the harbor, has an excellent selection of high-quality rentals. Go to one of the cheaper places near Jason's to establish the going price (about 1500 drs to 2000 drs—$11.54 to $15.38—per day), then try to negotiate with Jason, a Liverpool-born motorcyclist. Remember to check that your bike is in good running order before taking it. Naxos has some major mountains to cross, requiring a strong motor and good brakes.

Those traveling in a group of three or four, or with a few drachmas to burn, might consider exploring the island by **Jeep**. An aptly named outfit called **The Jeep** (tel. 23-395) rents Suzukis and Mini Mokes for 7000 drs ($53.85) per day. Make sure that you get full insurance without a deductible. The Jeep is located near the ferry dock on the north side.

If you're on Naxos for only one day and you want to see everything, consider hiring a **taxi**. Naxos is filled with cabs, and you can hire one for a half-day-around-the-island tour for 4500 drs ($34.60), a little bit less than a full-day rental car. Make sure you bargain with the cabbie and set a price or you may overpay by 2000 drs ($15.38). Each taxi can hold up to four people.

USEFUL INFORMATION: There is no G.N.T.O. office on Naxos, but the **town police** in Chora (tel. 22-100) have a list of hotels and private rooms and will make reservations for you. The station is located two blocks behind the Pantanassa Church, approximately 200 meters from the dock. The **National Bank of Greece** (open 8 a.m. to 2 p.m. Monday through Friday) is on the lower end of the waterfront strip. Opposite the bank, behind the Hotel Coronis, is the **O.T.E.** (summer hours are 7:30 a.m. to 10 p.m. Monday through Thursday, until 5 p.m. on Friday). The telephone **area code** for Naxos is 0285. The **post office** is open from 7:30 a.m. to 3 p.m. during the summer months. There is a **medical clinic** on Naxos (tel. 22-346), but for serious problems contact the police.

Naxos International Tours (tel. 0285/22-095) is run by the owner of the Hotel Coronis, Vassilis Vallindras, who knows the island as well as anyone. The agency offers excursions to the inland villages and Apollon, ferry tickets, and air reservations for Olympic Airways. Another good office is the **Tourist Informa-**

tion Center (tel. 0285/24-525). The staff is knowledgeable and Despina Kitini can take care of all of your needs.

If you plan on staying on the island for a while, or just want to learn more about it, read John Freely's short, colorful account simply called *Naxos* (Lycabettus Press). The book has an excellent description of walking tours as well as a kinky passage about a delightful fellow called Nikos of the Seven League Boots. Also make sure you try two of Naxos's specialties: *kefalotieri,* a superb sharp cheese, and *citron,* a sweet liqueur made from oranges and lemons.

ACCOMMODATIONS: Naxos has experienced an upswing in tourism within the last few years. Unlike most of the other Cycladic islands, Naxos was little dependent on the travel business; the island's economy was self-sufficient. With recent declines in the local economy and skyrocketing land values, tourism has become the island's salvation. Although the face of the island will ultimately change, the immediate benefit is that there is usually a surplus of hotels and private rooms.

In the Town of Chora

The best value in town is the newly constructed **Hotel Grotta** (tel. 0285/22-215), overlooking the bay of Grotta and a ten-minute walk northeast of the ferry dock. The host, Mr. Lianos, is gracious to a fault, and he runs a sparkling inn. The Grotta's 20 spotless rooms have polished marble floors, large balconies, and private facilities. Doubles run 4200 drs ($32.30), and if you call ahead the owner will pick you up at the ferry. Even if you go just to look at a room, you'll have a hard time leaving without accepting Mr. Lianos' offer of a shot glass of *citron,* the island's potent lemon liqueur—it tastes exactly like lemon ouzo!

Closer into Chora, across from Panagia Chrisopolitissa, is the tiny E-class **Hotel Anna** (tel. 0285/22-475). Each of the hotel's six homey rooms has a private bath and a unique character, the result of hostess Anna Glezos' loving hand. Doubles go for 2130 drs ($16.38); singles are about 375 drs ($2.88) less.

The **Hotel Panorama** (tel. 0285/22-330) is located in a very pretty stone-and-stucco building one block east of the kastro's large Venetian tower. This is a perfect choice for those who want to stay in Chora's most atmospheric neighborhood, below the kastro amid whitewashed homes and twisting lanes. The cost for two for one of its 16 C-class rooms is 2875 drs ($22.11).

Right around the corner from the Panorama is the equally attractive **Hotel Apollon** (tel. 0285/22-468). Like many of the nearby homes the hotel has a lovely flower garden in front of its irregular rough stone façade. The Apollon has 19 rooms, some with private bath, for 2600 drs ($20); those without private facilities run 400 drs ($3.10) less.

The **Hotel Coronis** (tel. 0285/22-626) has 32 clean rooms, all with showers. The price is right at 3200 drs ($24.61), including breakfast, but unless you have a reservation it will be difficult to procure a room during the high season. The building itself is drably modern, but the Coronis's portside location is a definite advantage for those who want to be "in the heart of the heart" of the island.

Nearby is the aging but still elegant **Hermes Hotel** (tel. 0285/22-220). All 24 rooms have private baths, but the tariff is steep during the summer: doubles go for 4450 drs ($34.23), without breakfast. Actually the Hermes isn't an old hotel —it was built in the early 1960s—but its style is strictly old-world palazzo.

The splashiest C-class domicile in town is the super-slick **Hotel Aegeon** (tel. 0285/22-852), opposite the O.T.E. Large smoked-glass doors lead to the Aegeon's cool, marble-floored lobby. Everything about the place says 1980s Greco modern. As you might imagine, the Aegeon is a group-oriented inn.

Give it a shot in case they have a cancellation. Doubles run 3500 drs ($26.92), including breakfast.

Near Chora

In between town and Ag. Georgios is the popular **Hotel Ariadne** (tel. 0285/ 22-452). Singled out by the *New York Times* as one of the best of the island hostelries, the charm of the Ariadne is due to its hostess, Despina Kitini. There are 24 rooms, some with private bath; the price for a double including breakfast is 5000 drs ($38.46). Despina also operates the **Tourist Information Center** (tel. 0285/23-328), where she has a currency exchange, boat schedules, and a phone service open from 7:30 a.m. to midnight. You can also leave luggage there for a small charge.

From the Ariadne all the way down to the end of the sandy Ag. Georgios is an endless strip of hotels, bungalows, private rooms, discos, bars, movie theaters, and restaurants. There are so many C-class look-alike hotels and rooms that an image of any one place is an impossibility; they all blur together. Among the best in this C-class pack are the **Hotel Glaros** (tel. 0285/23-131), the **Hotel Kymata** (tel. 0285/22-438), and the lower-priced bungalows at the **Galini** (tel. 0285/22-114). Prices for two are 2500 drs ($19.23) at the Glaros and Galini, and 3500 drs ($26.90) at the Kymata. New hotels, legal and not, are being built every day, so if you can't find a room at one of the suggested places, be assured that there'll be a spanking-new inn to welcome you.

RESTAURANTS AND NIGHTLIFE: Although Naxos isn't the wildest island in the Cyclades, there are enough excellent eateries and nightspots to satisfy gourmands and night owls alike. The most popular restaurant in town, and for once justifiably so, is **Nikos** (tel. 23-153), located above the Commercial Bank on the harborfront. The recently expanded dining room is so enormous that it resembles a suburban country-club banquet hall. Don't be put off though, because the real star at Nikos is the food. Try the *exohiko,* fresh lamb and vegetables cooked with fragrant spices and wrapped in crispy pastry leaves *(filo),* or the barbecued fish—the red snapper and swordfish are perfect—lightly topped with oil and locally grown lemon. Don't overlook Nikos's delightful ice-cream desserts; they're deliciously cool and sweet. Dinner for two will cost about 2700 drs ($20.76), but ice cream can be had for 460 drs ($3.53) per helping. (One hot evening we observed a table of 20 inebriated Swedes pouring their desserts on top of each other in a kind of group ice-cream sponge bath.)

The best situated portside taverna in Chora is the **Meltemi**, named after the infamous northwesterly wind that knocked Theseus out to sea. The Meltemi is best appreciated at sunset when the last of the day's boats slips into the harbor. It serves a wide variety of Naxian specialties at moderate prices. Next door is **Florins** (tel. 23-475), a very civilized bar in an old Naxian mansion and garden. An evening drink at Florins is a perfect way to conclude a day-long stroll through the kastro and the town's back streets. Below Florins in the same house is **Veggera** (tel. 23-567), a steak house-cum-piano bar that is very good, chic, and worthwhile. Both places open around 9 p.m.

The two best tavernas in Chora are both located in the labyrinthine Bourgo, below the kastro, and both are run by fellows named **Vasilis**. The food is tasty and inexpensive, and you'll likely find more locals than tourists. Neither place offers refined dining. Actually both tavernas have a reputation for high-spirited, often boisterous, crowds. Both places are, of course, around the corner from each other off Ag. Nikodemos Street.

There are many snackbars and fast-food joints at Ag. Georgios, but our favorite nighttime hangout is an all-in-one bar, taverna, café, and disco called

Asteria. It's right on the beach, and the decor can only be described as Greek-Polynesian: lots of bamboo, hanging lights, and little grass-covered umbrellas. There's just enough kitsch to make it perfect for outdoor dining and night-long drinking. Taverna food is served after 10 p.m., and there's almost always a live band. Music ranges from jazz to punk (the house band used to be a Greek new wave combo called the Drachmas), with some bouzouki thrown in for local color. The **Onikos Bar** is an ouzeri near Florins, where you can sit and sip comfortably for hours.

The most popular and loudest bars in town are the **Glaros** and **In** (tel. 22-872). Both places are filled with European and American students, and the pickup action is intense. Also on the singles scene is the **Cafe Bizarre** (tel. 24-490), near the post office in Chora.

BEACHES: Some of Naxos's best beaches are near the main town. **Ag. Georgios** is a ten-minute walk from Chora and is considered the town beach. Prior to the tourist explosion, this was *the* beach of Naxos. Now it's lined with hotels and restaurants, and the beach itself is jammed with tourists. Dirt bikers use the beach at night as a racing strip, further diminishing this already-beaten shoreline. These days, most people head south via foot, bus, or caïque for the clean sandy beaches at **Ag. Prokopios** and **Ag. Anna.** Ag. Prokopios is a developed stretch that hosts a few hotels and tavernas. The beach is great, and you'll still find people in the village serving barbecued octopus, homemade dolmades, and other Greek snacks right outside of their houses.

For the true connoisseur the best beach on the island is south of Ag. Anna, known by Naxians as **Plaka beach.** To get there, take the 160 drs ($1.23) caïque from the harbor in Chora, and instead of walking north (toward Ag. Prokopios), head south. There you'll find a five-kilometer stretch of almost completely uninhabited shoreline. It's ideal for nude sunbathing.

The large protected bay at **Pyrgaki** and **Agiassos,** about 20 kilometers south of Chora, is considered the best swimming area on Naxos. There's no local transportation, so you'll have to take a moped or private car.

WHAT TO SEE: Naxos is renowned for its scenic treasures. The Tragea region and Apollonas have been so celebrated throughout time that only the Olympian gods could have created such a wondrous landscape. However, the island's two most fascinating sights are located right in Chora.

In the Town of Chora

Chora's most exquisite monument is the Venetian **kastro,** a medieval citadel that overlooks, and is quite separate from, the town below. The kastro's once-secure walls are crumbling in spots, but even their modest deterioration lends a sense of aged grandeur. Behind these ramparts is a maze of rising and falling streets. Narrow alleyways dead-end and whitewashed steps, long ago attached to shops and homes, now lead only to the sky.

Artists, writers, craftsmen, as well as the descendants of the kastro's original Venetian occupants, live in majestic Renaissance-era mansions—many still bear the crest of the family that built them. As if retreating from the world below, the kastro's residents rarely seem to leave their homes, preferring the seclusion and security of life behind closed doors.

Each street holds its own secrets. Walk through the kastro and perhaps you'll eye an old woman weaving rugs (look in at 617 Sanudo St.), a painter or jeweler huddled over his work, or maybe you'll steal a view inside one of the magnificent homes that grace the streets. At night, when the paths and alleyways are illuminated by flickering lamps, there's a palpable feeling of stepping back in time. For a moment you can imagine the fear that night engendered: the threat of enigmatic shadows, deserted streets, and the unknown that was beyond the city's broad ramparts.

The kastro was built on what was probably the ancient Mycenaean acropolis. In the 13th century Marco Sanudo, a nephew of a Venetian doge, made Naxos the capital of the Duchy of the Archipelago—Venice's claim to the Aegean islands. The kastro was established as the seat of power and from there St. Mark's Republic ruled the islands for over 300 years.

Wandering through the dizzying array of streets will invariably bring you past the kastro's major buildings, all built during the Venetian and Turkish occupations. One of the most interesting is the so-called French School, founded in 1627 for both Catholics and Orthodox Greeks. Among the school's distinguished students was the Cretan writer Nikos Kazantzakis, who studied there in 1896. Nikos's studies were cut short when his father pried him out of the school, fearing that his son was being indoctrinated by "papist dogs" (so much for secular cooperation).

The school is no more, having been converted into the island's **archeological museum** (open 9 a.m. to 1 p.m. and 4 p.m. to 6 p.m. Monday through Saturday, 9 a.m. to 3 p.m. on Sunday; closed Tuesday. Note that these hours are not totally dependable.). The museum is a treasury of early Cycladic pottery, sculpture, and religious knickknacks. A short walk around the corner will bring you to the 13th-century Catholic church, and farther on, to the main tower of Sanudo's original fortress/palace.

The **Temple of Apollo** is Chora's second grand attraction. Archeologists assume that the temple is dedicated to Apollo only from a scant reference in the Delian Hymns—if you visit the temple and it's a very clear day, Delos will be visible far to the north. For hundreds of years it was thought that the temple was dedicated to Dionysus, the island's patron diety. Naxians claimed that the temple was built on the site where Dionysus found the abandoned princess Ariadne. The shrine was to commemorate the god's gallantry and to immortalize the island's most romantic tale.

Ariadne, eldest daughter of the legendary Cretan king Minos, fell in love with the Athenian hero Theseus when he arrived at Knossos to slay the Minotaur (the monstrous half-man, half-bull that lived in the labyrinth). Counseled by Daedalus, the labyrinth's architect, Ariadne secretly brought Theseus a ball of thread so he could find his way out of the maze. After killing the beast, Theseus used the string to retrace his route through the maze and escape. Theseus fled with Ariadne and sailed toward Athens.

This is where the story gets murky. One account suggests that Theseus put Ariadne on shore at Naxos to recover from seasickness when a huge wind came up and blew his ship far out to sea. Theseus returned to Naxos only to find that poor Ariadne had died. Not a pretty story! By far the more romantic, and obviously preferable, version of Ariadne's fate is that Ariadne, left by Theseus on a rocky islet next to the Naxian shore, was rescued by Dionysus, the most orgiastically spirited god in the Pantheon.

Dionysus had been kidnapped by pirates who didn't fully appreciate the true nature, or identity, of their captive. Never one to miss an opportunity for fun, the wine god called upon his viney legion to attack the ship's masts and sails. He magically transformed the oars into slithery serpents, and as if that didn't unnerve his abductors, Dionysus turned himself into a snarling lion. The pirates jumped into the sea and Dionysus calmly sailed into port to save Ariadne. The princess and the deity fell deeply in love and he built a huge palace on the rocky site where he found her. After Ariadne's death, Dionysus placed her bejeweled crown in the sky, forming a shimmering constellation dedicated to love.

Construction of the temple commenced under the reign of Lygdamis, a sixth-century ruler who overthrew the aristocratic regime. In this period the Naxians dedicated the Sphinx that was placed on top of a magnificent column at Delphi. Archeologists and historians believe that construction was halted on the Temple of Apollo when the Naxian army was defeated by a force from Samos. Pieces of marble, thought to be from the temple, have been found at sites all over the island. Apparently the sanctuary was far more complete than the few relics that remain would indicate.

Around the Island

Although many tourists travel the distance to **Apollonas** (especially to stay overnight), it's a wearing journey if you're traveling by bus or moped. Expect to wind up and down curving country roads for at least 2½ hours each way. A more civilized idea is to visit the inland villages of Chalki, Filoti, and especially Apirathos.

The busy road leading from Chora to Chalki bisects well-cultivated farmland shrouded by bamboo windbreaks. Horn-tooting taxis and buses speed out of town, often narrowly missing an overloaded donkey and its master.

It seems that on Naxos, if any two people pass on the road, even traveling by car, they invariably yell at each other. Perhaps that's how slow-walking farmers avoid getting flattened. Many tourists don't know how to respond to such sociality, but we've always enjoyed yelling back. It takes courage, but it's truly invigorating. If you're walking and you scream at a passing car, the driver will often stop and offer you a ride—strange but effective.

The Tragea: The road continues past **Kato Sangri**, a small village distinguished by an abandoned Venetian mansion that stands high on a barren hill. From Kato Sangri to Chalki, marking the beginnings of the Tragea region, the landscape takes on a surreal quality. Mesa Potamia (no joke!), a series of dangerous-looking spiked peaks, lie to the north, and huge, flat stones shaped like cut tiles line the valley floor. The landscape looks decidedly Martian in the glow of the pink late-afternoon light. The blazing summer sun drives up temperatures to extremes, so the approach to **Chalki** comes as a relief (particularly for those traveling by foot or moped). The outskirts of town are resplendent with sweet-smelling lemon and shady olive trees, highlighted by the chanting cicadas hidden in flowering oleanders.

Chalki was the region's commercial center and features two 18th-century Venetian *pirgos* (a cross between a stately mansion or castle and a fortified outpost). Turn right at Panagia Prothonis, a lovely church that's almost always closed, and walk along the ancient cobblestone road. The first pirgos is to your right, a white marble crest advertising the year it was built, 1742. Make sure to climb the worn marble steps. There's a picture-perfect view of the Filoti, one of the largest inland villages, which sweeps down the mountainside like an overturned can of whitewash. Chalki's other pirgos is on the far end of town (toward Filoti), behind a grove of olive trees.

As you head off to Filoti, near the hamlet of **Keramio** there's a sight that cries out, "Hold on, this is it! This is the real Greece!" To the southwest, atop an anonymous peak, sits a lone whitewashed church, small and round in form, perfect in relation to man, mountain, and sky.

Filoti has classically Cycladic cube-shaped homes with pastel shutters and red tiled roofs. The town rises steeply from the platia along the road to the silver-domed church, with its primitive-style figures adorning a three-pronged steeple. To reach the Panagia, walk up the wide stairs near the bus stop and veer left. If you climb a few steps beyond the church and turn right, you'll tour the upper town and dead-end at a pirgos dated 1718. It's still used as a primitive home. Double back a few yards to the grand fig tree, and there will be a small set of stairs leading down to the main road. Filoti has two tavernas and a few private rooms to rent.

If there was a beauty contest among the inland towns of Naxos, **Apirathos** would win hands down. This richly endowed hill town overlooks perfectly stepped vineyards and deep green valleys. The houses, dating from the 18th and 19th centuries, combine Venetian and Cycladic styles. If the homes strike you as ornate, it's because Apirathos was once home to Naxos's wealthiest class, emery mine owners. Most of the mines have closed and many of the houses are deserted, but the town maintains a regal air. There's a small museum near the central platia containing early Cycladic marble idols and some very old and primitive folk ceramics. Take the narrow path leading from the "highway" and ask the man who runs the unnamed taverna a few doors down across from the museum for the key. He doesn't have it, but he knows the witty and informative curator, who will usher you in.

The road from Apirathos to Apollonas is curvy in the extreme (extremely curvaceous?). **Koronos** and **Skado** are both gorgeous mountain villages and are the only towns of note along the way. The road is lined on both sides with honeysuckle-scented yellow wildflowers (readers who know what species they are should write us immediately!). They grow so thickly that they brush passing cars like chamois towels at a car wash. Locals often stop to pick them, sometimes by rolling down a car window and cutting a few stems to decorate the dining table.

Apollonas: A motor-coach view of the Tragea can be had throughout the course of a visit to Apollonas. A day trip to this north-coast port, 54 kilometers from Naxos town, is a popular excursion because it gives you ample introduction to the scenic wonders of the island's interior on the way to an interesting archeological site. Many of the small mountain villages along the route have their own points of interest, principally from the Venetian period, but the island's historical highlight is at Apollonas. Here, in an abandoned marble quarry about a 15-minute walk above town, lies a 30-foot-tall statue that was never completed. Archeologists date it to the seventh century B.C. and presume that this **kouros**, or young man sculpted in a rigid frontal pose, was intended for the huge Temple of Apollo which stood at this tip of the island. The kouros lies lifeless in the chiseled marble rock face from which he was hewn. The long crack across his nose may be the reason why he was left here, but with his eroded strong torso and flexed feet he looks like Frankenstein awaiting the breath of life.

The petite fishing port of Apollonas has a sandy cove and a larger pebble cove ideal for swimming and bathing, which are, however, in full view of the modest town. The friendly villagers offer rooms to let, many with private baths, for about 1700 drs ($13.07). The Matzoulou family runs the clean **Pension Aigaion**, on the road into town. Its seven rooms have harbor views, and a double runs 1450 drs ($11.15). The **Hotel Kouros** (tel. 0285/81-203) is a new, undistinguished C-class hotel on the pebble beach at the far end of town. Doubles currently go for 2150 drs ($16.54). Thanks to its owner's persistence, camping has been prohibited on this pleasant beach since 1979—greatly reducing the number of overnight visitors to Apollonas.

With so many day-trippers the port has a profusion of restaurants, including the **Koronis**, at the end of the pier, the **Apollonas Taverna**, and **John's** snackbar. At the café named simply **Restaurant**, on the corner along the harbor, they serve two Naxian specialties: locally brewed citron and a hard sharp cheese called *Kefalotiri*. Overnight visitors can walk up behind the church to the outdoor **Meltemi Grill,** with views over the point of a nearby marble stone beach. After a filling souvlaki, you can hit the dance floor at **Faros Disco,** underneath the Koronis taverna.

On the Road Back to Chora: Strangely, the unfinished kouros outside Apollonas isn't the island's only one. Eight kilometers outside of Chora is Naxos's other unfinished kouros. Known as the **Felerios kouros,** this statue is much smaller but more distinctly carved than the work at Apollonas. It sleeps in an old woman's garden.

There's a curious power to these unformed monsters, as if one day they might awaken to roam the island. Children sense it. They take great pleasure in climbing and jumping on these giants, doing their bit to keep the demons down.

GETTING THERE: Naxos is in the middle of the heavily trafficked Cycladic ferry system, so you'll have no problems making connections. There are daily boats to Piraeus, as well as to Santorini, Ios, Paros, and Mykonos. In addition, the *Naoussa Express* runs a one-day round-trip excursion to Paros. You can connect to Rafina every day except Thursday.

Boats stop at Amorgos twice weekly, and for those wishing to visit Crete, there's a weekly ferry to Ag. Nikolaos. The Crete-bound boat continues after Ag. Nikolaos, calling at Kassos, Karpathos, and Rhodes; don't forget the legend of Ariadne: watch out for choppy seas.

6. Ios

Ios is an island with a reputation. Since the 1960s, hundreds of thousands have made a pilgrimage here. Sun and sea, music and dancing, cheap carefree living and the revelers, who participate in this modern-day Dionysian carnival, make Ios the celebrated Island of Youth, an electric, plugged-in rock in the Aegean.

Obviously Ios isn't for everyone. The disillusioned compare it to a summer camp for English and European teenagers, or perhaps a perpetual college mixer. More adventurous travelers liken Ios to Kathmandu for cowards, a baby-step from the security of home. Others find little attraction in the vast amount of exposed flesh sprawled out over Ios's beaches. And for those in search of a quaint or quiet traditional village—well, Ios isn't the place. Fortunately there's a self-selection process, so that nearly everyone who goes knows what to expect; and for that, Ios delivers.

ORIENTATION: Like many of the Cyclades Ios is a totally barren, rocky island that suffers from a lack of fresh water. Today, the only foliage is in the center of the island and in the extreme north, although Homer once wrote that he'd like to be buried here, one of the most verdant of isles.

All boats dock at **Gialos,** the port city of Ios. To the left of the pier as you alight from the ferry is a beach that tends to collect debris from the harbor, but is certainly acceptable, especially if you're stuck in the heat waiting for a ferry. Gialos itself has little to offer other than the dock, a large number of travel agents, a bank, and some high-priced C-class hotels. All the action is up the hill in **Chora,** where you'll probably want to stay. On the other side of Chora is highly regarded **Milopotas Beach,** far and away the most popular beach on the island. A bus connects these three spots so frequently that you'll never have to wait for more than 15 to 25 minutes for one to come along.

Many short-term visitors confine themselves to Gialos, Chora, and Milopotas, but longer-term tourists quickly discover that Ios has beaches on almost every cove, indentation, or stretch of coastline. Each beach has its own character, and if you're there long enough you're certain to find one that's a perfect fit. The biggest problem is transportation. Other than Milopotas, most other beaches must be reached by foot or caïque.

GETTING AROUND: Most people who visit Ios shuttle back and forth exclusively between the port, Chora, and Milopotas beach. There is excellent bus service to these destinations—cheap, at 75 drs (58¢) from Gialos to Chora, and frequent (approximately every half hour from 8 a.m. to 11 p.m.). You can walk to these same points, but it can be very hot, especially from Chora down to the beach (about a 30-minute walk). If you plan to walk after dark, bring a flashlight as the path is poorly lit. The island's only other road crosses from the port to Ag. Theodoti on the east coast. There is infrequent bus service to Ag. Theodoti, and it runs only during the summer months. Travel agents also offer a red bus which conveys visitors round trip to Ag. Theodoti for 720 drs ($5.54). Check with them for details. Again, walking is an alternative, although it's about two hours away by foot. There is only one regularly scheduled boat trip, going to Maganari beach, on the southern end of the island, at 750 drs ($5.77).

USEFUL INFORMATION: There is no E.O.T. office on Ios, but the regular **police** (tel. 91-303) have a complete list of private rooms and hotels, as well as official prices for all accommodations. The friendly force is acutely aware of pricing violations, and they encourage tourists who have been overcharged to report the problem. The office is conveniently located directly across from Chora's only bus stop. Hours are 8 a.m. to 2 p.m. Monday through Friday, with extended hours, 6 p.m. to 8 p.m. on Monday and Thursday. The **area code** for Ios is 0286.

The **O.T.E.** and **post office** is located on the south side (on your right as you disembark) of the port, in the village. If you want to make collect calls, be aware that you can only book them through **O.T.E.** (up in Chora) from 7:30 a.m. to 8 p.m. Monday through Friday. The post office is open from 7:30 a.m. to 2 p.m., Monday through Friday.

There are three banks on Ios, one at the port and two up in Chora. The **National Bank of Greece**, located on the south side of Gialos, is open Monday through Friday from 8 a.m. to 2 p.m. The two banks up in the village are also open from 8 a.m. to 2 p.m. Monday through Friday. Bring a book; lines are often very long, especially at the banks in Chora, and don't forget to bring your passport. Try to avoid changing money on Monday morning; it's a complete zoo.

The most knowledgeable and helpful travel agents on Ios are at **Acteon Travel** (tel. 91-207), located on the port platia. They usually stay open until 10:30 p.m., and will assist you in finding a room and booking tickets. They also operate offices in Chora and Milopotas Beach. Also good, and just up from the Acteon, is **Kritikakis Tours.** They're open from 9 a.m. to 9 p.m. and are the agents for Olympic Airways.

There is a **tailor** (that is, if your clothes are not deliberately ripped), Michael Lambares, up in Chora near the large blue-domed church, who also provides **dry cleaning and laundry service.**

ACCOMMODATIONS: Ios is a mob scene in the summer: visitors outnumber islanders 10 to 1. Literally, there are days when the Port Police will not allow ferry passengers to disembark on the island. Most of the upscale C-class hotels are booked for groups by travel agencies, and the best and cheapest private rooms are gobbled up by visitors who arrive as early as May or June to stay for the entire summer. The hotel scene isn't totally hopeless, for on Ios, as on most of the islands during the high season (here, a particularly apt term), you can always go to the police or local travel agency to inquire about a private room. The other alternative is, of course, to make reservations; it may violate the free spirit of life on Ios but at least you'll know that you have a room.

At the Port

The two best conventional hotels are the 56-room **Hotel Mare-Monte** (tel. 0286/91-564), where double rooms with balconies run 4375 drs ($33.65) for bed-and-breakfast, and the equally attractive **Hotel Flisvos** (tel. 0286/91-315). The Flisvos is on the south side of the port and its 14 modern and spacious rooms run 4375 drs ($33.65) for two, including breakfast.

If you want a cheaper room, try the C-class **Hotel Corali** (tel. 0286/91-272), on the beach, where doubles with a view rent for 5625 drs ($43.27), including breakfast. The friendly **Hotel Elena** (tel. 0286/91-276) is an E-class inn, located near the beach behind the Mare-Monte. Its 22 rooms, all bathless, are like old-fashioned beach bungalows centered around a café and courtyard. Double rooms are a very modest 1900 drs ($14.62). Mr. and Mrs. Galiatsou offer conti-nental breakfast for 325 drs ($2.50), and options of bacon, eggs, yogurt, and cakes for slightly higher prices.

Another inexpensive alternative is the **Club Leto** (tel. 0286/91-279), a clus-ter of bungalows on the north side of the port. The Leto's 50 rooms are spartan-ly decorated but clean. All rooms have showers: those with hot water are 3430 drs ($26.38) for two; without hot water, 3000 drs ($23.07). Students are granted a 10% discount.

Next to camping Ios is **Villa Koula,** a bouganvillea-infested home with 8 rooms (private baths), balconies, and friendly managers (Maria and Iannis), who charge 2500 drs ($19.23) a night. This is a very nice place to stay near the harbor.

The **Hotel Parthenon** (tel. 0286/91-275) has 15 rooms; at 3500 drs ($26.92) for a double it's a bargain compared to its C-class cousins. The Parthenon is past the post office on the hill opposite the town; you can watch all the dockside ac-tion from your balcony without having to struggle to sleep through the noise.

Maria Halari (tel. 0286/91-382) offers eight very clean, spacious rooms, conveniently located on the south side of the port. Mrs. Halari charges 1875 drs ($14.42) for two.

The port has one official camping spot—though people are known to camp all over the port when rooms are occupied—**Camping Ios** (tel. 0286/91-329). It's near the beach and fully equipped. Andreas Apostolakis, the manager, loves to exchange "real life" views and charges 525 drs ($4) a night for his wonderful space by the water.

In Chora

Up in the village (which locals call "the jungle") you can choose between the hotels Phillipou and Aphroditi. The **Hotel Phillipou** (tel. 0286/91-290) has 22 clean rooms, all with showers, running 3400 drs ($26.15) for a double. It's above a platia of the same name, a popular and noisy meeting place for late-night café and bar sitters. Not for those with sensitive ears. The **Hotel Aphroditi** (tel. 0286/ 91-546) is in the town but a little off to the side. It has 12 modern, clean rooms, and its all marble floors lend a touch of elegance. Rooms for two are 3750 drs ($28.85), including breakfast.

The town has an extensive offering of private rooms. Visit the police office for a current list and official prices.

At Milopotas Beach

Milopotas Beach is an increasingly popular place to stay, with new hotels going up at an amazing rate. At the top of the donkey path above the beach is the 14-room **Hotel Acropolis** (tel. 0286/91-303). All rooms have showers and most have balconies with great views of the beach below. Doubles are a reasonable 1900 drs ($14.62). At the base of the path, right down on the beach where New Age capitalists give haircuts and massages, are two rooms-to-rent establishments built above tavernas. Both establishments have perfectly comfortable rooms, though neither is luxurious. The first is above the taverna **Orakou** (tel. 0286/91-243), where all nine rooms come with private shower. Doubles go for 2150 drs ($16.54). The taverna below is a popular place for beachside snacking. Next door is the 22-room **Delfini Hotel** (tel. 0286/91-341), where rooms with bath and balcony run 3450 drs ($26.54).

The slick but comfortable **Hotel Milopotas** (tel. 0286/91-301) has 22 rooms for 3200 drs ($24.62) a double, including breakfast. The rooms are clean and the garden well cared for, but groups usually grab all the rooms. Before schlepping your heavy luggage across the long beach, check in advance that the Milopotas has a vacant room.

Perhaps the most popular place on the island for rock-bottom accommodations is the campground **Stars** (tel. 0286/91-302). This place is decked out with all the facilities any camper could possibly need: a restaurant, snackbar, and small market, all inexpensive! It's also situated close to the beach, and the price is right, 375 drs ($2.88) per night.

RESTAURANTS: Food is cheaper on Ios than on many other islands. Restaurateurs are forced to keep prices low because so many visitors buy their food at grocery stores and bakeries.

The taverna in Chora that cooks authentic country cuisine is the **Nest,** an eight-table place that's almost exclusively frequented by Ios's slightly dazed locals. The Nest serves a hearty and tasty bean soup that nearly everyone eats for lunch, with a salad and a beer. Begin by walking up the main street toward the base of the stairs, and then ask directions. Lunch here will run you only 500 drs ($3.80). You might like to try the **Pithari Restaurant,** farther up on the same street. It has an excellent house shrimp casserole and a very tasty veal roast. Two can eat a full meal here for under 1300 drs ($10).

The best food on the island is found on the very highest point in Chora, opposite the windmills. Alternatively called **The Windmill** or **The Mill,** this taverna serves classic Greek food at its best. The salad is made with *risithra* cheese, a delicious alternative to your average feta. The goat meat is flavorful and tender. Even the taramosalata, which seems to be a fairly standard item, is especially tasty and fresh. Our overall favorite at the Windmill is the stuffed eggplant, though others swear by the pork souvlaki surrounded by rich, ripe tomatoes.

Two good breakfast and snack restaurants, though not wholly Greek in inspiration, are the **Romantica Pâtisserie** and the **Déjà Vu Café.** At the Pâtisserie's outdoor tables, inexpensive coffee, sweets, breakfast goodies, and juice are served. The Romantica—and it is, sort of—is opposite a heavenly aromatic bakery and two blocks over from the main street. The Déjà Vu Café is on the other side of the bus street, away from the main concentration of cafés, clubs, and restaurants. Its specialty is omelets, ranging in price from 250 drs ($1.92) to 400 drs ($3.07).

NIGHTLIFE: Imagine a giant all-night street party of intoxicated teenage nomads—this is nighttime on Ios. Chora is the epicenter.

The most blissful way to begin the evening is to climb up to Dimitri Alexiadis' **Ios Club**, a short hop down from the bus stop, for drinks, sunset panorama, and classical music. This open-air sunset theater is popular with people of all ages, possibly because it's the most mellow place in Chora. Prices are on the high side for exotic drinks—500 drs ($3.85) to 750 drs ($5.77). Admission is 100 drs (77¢—applied to your bar tab), but if you're uncontrollably cheap you can always sit on the rock just outside the entrance to the club and enjoy the sunset and music. The classical concert begins at 7 p.m. and continues until 9:30 p.m. The music changes much later, when the club becomes home to disco's dancing fools.

Clubs and discos there are aplenty. A casual stroll up Chora's twisting lanes and main street will take you past at least ten good danceterias. You don't have to poke your head in to hear what kind of music they play—it'll be obvious. The clubs change names and musical styles even more frequently than on Mykonos, but here are the favorites as of summer of 1987. On the main street, below the stairs, is **Disco 69**, where there are cheap drinks and up-to-date tunes. Nearby is the dark and moody **Kalimera Jazz Club**, where the music is played soft and low. For a round of pool, snacks, and drinks, head to the slightly subterranean **Players Club**. Farther on, at the main square, is a concentration of clubs where the amplified music clashes, creating a cacophony of rock 'n roll. **Jon's Electric**, the **Ios Café Bar**, **Iliatroneion**, **My Way**, and **New Look** are all the most crowded night spots.

BEACHES: The nighttime party is in Chora's back streets. The daytime party is on **Milopotas Beach**, one of Greece's longest sandy beaches. The water is clean, and notwithstanding the usual mob scene, it's a fabulous place to spread out a towel or mat to bake under the strong Aegean sun. Perhaps 90% of those visiting Ios go no farther than Milopotas, yet the whole island is ringed with beaches. **Maganari**, on the extreme south coast, has a sandy beach, rooms to rent, and a taverna. A 1½-hour walk northeast from Maganari is the lonely **Three Churches beach**, a haunt of those looking for undisturbed, private bathing. On the east coast are **Psathi** and **Aghia Theodoti**, both with beaches, food, and camping.

Of some historical interest are the swimming cove and caves at **Plakatos**, which archeologists incorrectly claimed to be Homer's tomb. (You'll have to hire a boat to visit the caves.) What's interesting about Homer and Ios is that the poet described it as a green and thickly wooded island, the most beautiful in the Aegean, and an ideal place for him to die. Whether he died on the island is open to dispute, but as for Ios being covered with trees . . .

GETTING THERE: There are daily boats from Piraeus; for specific departure times call the Port Authority in Piraeus (tel. 45-11-311) or the Athens Tourist Information line (tel. 171). Ios is well connected to the surrounding Cycladic islands with daily service to Naxos, Paros, and Santorini; sailing five times a week to Mykonos and Syros; four times a week to Milos and Sifnos; and two times a week to Folegandros, Sikinos, and Anafi.

7. Santorini

Santorini (called Thira by the Greeks) is unique among the arid, white-washed, rocky Cyclades for its dramatic volcanic landscape. Visitors arriving by sea at the old west coast port are stunned by the sheer black cliffs which stretch around a fantastic cauldron-shaped bay, the Caldera. Deep red soil and long streaks of white pumice stripe the cliffs, which are white-capped 250 meters above sea level by the capital city of Fira. Besides the breathtaking first impression, Santorini's black sand beaches, good cheap wine, and folktales linking it to the legendary Atlantis lure American tourists in droves.

HISTORY: The geology of Santorini separates it visually and historically from the other Cyclades isles. Unlike Mykonos or Paros, which delight tourists with their present life, Santorini's fascinating past has intrigued scholars and visitors for years. In ancient times this volcanic island was called Strongyle, or "round," a reference to the almost perfect semicircle that remained after this volcano's eruption and subsequent collapse. The fishermen living in traditional villages on nearby Thirasia inhabit mountain tops of Strongyle which remained above water. In fact a land bridge is submerged between the two islands. To the southwest, the tiny Aspronisi is another peak in the Strongyle ring.

The two islets in the center of the Caldera bay are the original lava cones. The smaller, Palea Kameni ("burnt one"), emerged after an eruption in 197 B.C. and grew, shrank, and grew to its present size over 700 turbulent years. In 1707 a mild earthquake caused the larger, Nea Kameni, to rise. It's been an active volcano ever since, last erupting in 1950. Brave souls can take boat tours to both islands, bathe in the hot springs created off their coasts, and peer down into the sizzling inferno within.

The volcanic eruption of 1500 B.C. that caused the collapse of Strongyle was so forceful that archeologists think it caused tidal waves which totally flattened Crete and touched the shores of Africa. The fascinating city of Akrotiri, uncovered on Santorini by Professor Marinatos in 1967, was apparently an ally or member of the Minoan kingdom that flourished on Crete until 1500 B.C., and may have been the legendary Atlantis. The ruins of Akrotiri, well preserved under lava and volcanic ash, have been immensely important in understanding Minoan culture. The exciting excavations continue today in the "Pompeii of the Aegean," and should not be missed by even the one-day visitor.

In time, the no-longer-round Strongyle was renamed Kalisti, "the beautiful one." In the tenth century B.C. it was renamed Thira, after a Dorian ruler from Sparta who invaded the island and settled seven villages. Ancient Thira can be viewed today. The ruins of the Dorian hilltop capital also reflect the later presence of Roman and Byzantine conquerors. The Venetian crusaders occupied Santorini (European sailors named it after its patron, Saint Irene) from the 13th to the 16th centuries. In the village of Emborion you can see several hillside homes built within the only Venetian fortress walls that remain.

In 1956 an earthquake that registered 7.8 on the Richter Scale destroyed about two-thirds of the housing on the island. Because it struck early in the morning when most of Santorini's residents were working in the fields or on their boats, only 40 people were killed. Many homeless islanders, unable to secure government loans to rebuild, fled to other Greek ports, the U.S., and Australia to begin new lives. Now Santorini's 6,500 inhabitants subsist principally on tourism and the thriving wine industry. Vines hooped in coils over low supports (to protect grapes from the extreme heat and *meltemi* winds) grow everywhere in the rich, volcanic soil.

ORIENTATION: Before your ferry has even docked, it's evident that the volcanic blast that split Strongyle nearly 4,000 years ago has left its mark on all aspects of modern life. In recent years this spectacular and bizarre natural landscape has been marred by the extraction of pumice from the cliffs, to use in the manufacture of high quality cement. For centuries, to the tourists' delight, mules were used to make the steep ascent from the port to Fira. The hardy beasts are now augmented by a Doppelmayer cable car which makes the lava rock cliff look like an Austrian ski resort, and adds 800 tourists per hour to the capital city. They each pay 375 drs ($2.88) for the ride up.

Your first stop will be the hilltop, shopping-mad capital of **Fira,** the central bus station for around-the-island and beach bus connections. A ten-minute walk along the cliff north from Fira (left as you exit the mules or cable car) will lead you to **Firostephani,** where the hotels are a better value and the view back to Fira breathtaking. If you've come for more than two days (or in the height of the season) consider a room in one of the smaller villages. The pace is a little less tourist oriented and nearby local beaches are less congested.

Because no rivers or lakes appeared on this volcanic island after its eruption, Santorini's development has depended on water supplied by the few springs discovered at **Kamari Beach.** Kamari's black sand beaches and natural water supply guaranteed it would be the first resort to be fully developed by charter-tour packages. Off-season, Kamari Beach is one of the island's highlights, but during July and August it's a place you'll want to stay away from. Instead, try the nearby black sand **Perissa Beach,** where there are hotels, pensions, and rooms to let that won't be group booked.

GETTING AROUND: Santorini is one of the few Cycladic islands with acceptable bus service. The square in Fira serves as the island's **central bus station.** A large blackboard notes the ever-changing departure times to all the major tourist centers. The young man or woman wielding a chalk eraser in the vicinity of the bus stop will probably speak some English and can provide information on return departures. Fares average 80 drs (62¢) to 300 drs ($2.31). If you're unfortunate enough to miss the last bus (most routes are serviced till 10 or 11 p.m.) you'll be at the mercy of Fira's rapacious taxi drivers. All taxis must be booked by phone and base their rates from Fira. A cab ride from Oia to Fira can cost 1600 drs ($12.31); from Kamari Beach, 900 drs ($6.92).

Santorini's young crowd seems to prefer transportation on two wheels; **mopeds** far outnumber rental cars. It's not uncommon to see young men in varsity sweatshirts leaning on their mopeds outside the post office or snack shops, waiting to offer some fair damsel a ride. Visiting Europeans prefer rental cars and make hitchhiking an occasional transport option.

FIRA: Most first-time tourists stay in Fira, where the majority of services are located, even if only for a day or two. We call it "shopping mad" because its boutique-lined lanes are filled with the hundreds who arrive daily on cruise ships. They pause briefly to admire the scenery and then gallop up on mules to buy gold, furs, and ceramics that are no better value here than almost anywhere else in Greece.

Layout

Fira is a confusing maze of narrow lanes off three basic main streets. After your ascent from the port, the mule or cable car will leave you at **Nomikos Street,** which becomes **Ag. Mina.** This pedestrian street runs along the cliff wall and offers beautiful views of the Caldera. Scenic dining spots, discos, and boutiques line Ag. Mina. If you walk the other way (north) on Nomikos Street, you'll reach **Firostephani.**

Fira's second street, **Ypapantis,** (a/k/a "Gold Street"), is crammed full of jewelers, clothes boutiques, souvenir stands, and restaurants. The small lane, **Erithrou Stavrou,** runs parallel to part of it. In this central core you'll find the archeological museum (tel. 22-217), which is open 8:30 a.m. to 12:30 p.m., and 4 p.m. to 6 p.m. daily (closed Monday). Admission is 200 drs ($1.54). There is also an international bookshop on the near end. The **O.T.E.** (Santorini's area code is 0286), **post office** (open 7:30 a.m. to 2 p.m. Monday to Friday), and **National Bank** (open 8 a.m. to 2 p.m.) are at the far end, practically next to each other. Many travel agents also change money during their working hours (for most, from 8 a.m. to 9:30 p.m.). The few drachmas you lose changing money here could spare you a 45-minute wait in a bank whose crowds remind us of a Friday lunchtime at a downtown branch of Citibank.

The third street through Fira is **25 Martiou**, which is open to cars and leads north to Oia. In the center of things here is **Platia Theotokopoulou**, the not-square main square from which the buses start. On both sides of the street are travel agents, tour operators, ticket salesmen, tourist information offices—you get the picture. Santorini's tourist flood is well catered to by a torrent of travel services that is unsurpassed in a place this size.

Tourist Services

There is no official government tourist office but we found the **Kamari Tours** office (tel. 31-390), on the square, particularly helpful. If you're stuck for a room or a moped, they'll do what they can. Kamari Tours offers day trips to most of the island's sites. A full-day Akrotiri, Monastery, Beach, and Winery tour is 1620 drs ($12.50); boat tours to the volcano on Nea Kameni and Thirasia Island are 2500 drs ($19.20), and student discounts are available. The smaller **Damigos Tours** (tel. 22-383), across the street, was the first established in Fira and also offers excellent guided tours, at slightly lower rates. Our readers have enjoyed these island tours. **X-Ray Kilo** (!) **Travel Services** (tel. 22-624) is the American Express representative on Santorini. They're in the main square.

Most of the travel offices can provide rental cars from local companies or you can contact **Budget Rent A Car** (tel. 22-900). Their office is on the principal roadway to the village, a block below the square. A 4-Seat Citroen Pony will run you 4120 drs ($31.69) a day, with unlimited mileage. Nearby is the **Olympic Airways** office. **Moped** dealers are ubiquitous and offer single-person mopeds for 1500 drs ($11.54) to 1900 drs ($14.62) per day, depending on the season and duration of rental. There is limited medical treatment on the island; Fira's small **hospital** is on 25 Martiou Street (tel. 22-237).

Accommodations

First, a word of warning regarding housing on the island. Santorini is extremely densely populated in July and August, and travelers without sleeping bags should make a reservation, accompanied by a deposit, at least two months in advance of arrival. Otherwise, head straight from the ferry and catch the bus into Fira's bus stop square and ask one of the travel agents to help you find a room. If anyone offers you one along the way, take a long look before you turn it down. You can always move the next day if you find something better.

In Fira: The **Loucas Hotel** (tel. 0286/22-480) has a terrace bar perched on the cliffs and overlooks the volcano. It's famous as much for its food as its accommodations. Right in the shopping stream is the C-class **Theoxenia** (tel. 0286/22-740), where doubles with private bath are 7150 drs ($55). The top-most of its 13 rooms have views and there's a pleasant large terrace. A better bet in the modern, colorless hotel category is the **Hotel Tataki** (tel. 0286/22-389), whose 11 rooms with private showers are only 5100 drs ($39.23) in the high season.

The newly built **Hotel Asimina** is run by Mendrinos Tours (tel. 0286/22-989). The hotel, located next door to the archeological museum, has ten equally pleasant double rooms for 4900 drs ($37.69) per night.

Off 25 Martiou Street across from Olympic Airways is the **Santorini Hotel** (tel. 0286/22-593), whose entrance is hidden in the back. All 24 rooms have private facilities and the hotel is a bit worn. Doubles are 5250 drs ($40.38). On the same street, back toward the bus stop, is the **Hotel Antonia** (tel. 0286/22-879), whose 14 rooms are 5220 drs ($40.15) for two; however, you must book rooms through Atlantis Travel Agents, on the square. A plus at the Antonia is the presence of many flowering plants from a well-tended garden, which gives the hotel a homey feeling.

The new **Pelican Hotel** (tel. 0286/23-113), run by Manolis Roussos, is a plush addition to the C-class accommodation scene in Fira. Its 13 rooms come with refrigerators, and included in the tariff is a fresh orange juice breakfast. The price is a stiff 8700 drs ($66.92) for a double.

Having described some of the better hotel choices, we can say that the best places to stay on Santorini are always privately run. Since most young visitors (Santorini's tourists are mostly young) seek out the opportunity to live in a real Greek home, "rooms to let" has become such a big business that families just build impersonal multiroom additions to their charming and homey residences. Nonetheless, many have modern private facilities and hotel amenities at a better price than the hotels.

Rooms can be found everywhere, so we'll only mention the **Tasias' home** (tel. 0286/22-915), where seven sky-blue, sparkling rooms are available at 1600 drs ($12.30) for a double. You must have someone who speaks Greek call up so that their cute daughter, Dimitra, can come fetch you and lead you through the maze of streets to get there.

Between April and mid-June and in September and October, doubles can be had from 1000 drs ($7.69) to 1300 drs ($10), while in July and August the prices soar to 1600 drs ($12.31) to 2500 drs ($19.23).

There's also a 50-bed **youth hostel** (tel. 0286/22-577) about 200 meters from the bus stop. Beds are 425 drs ($3.27), including shower, and the hostel offers ferry tickets at a discount to their guests. Another, more recent, hostel is **Kamares Youth Hostel,** up the hill near the cable car. Beds, including showers, are the same price.

Outside Fira: There are accommodations to suit everyone's needs and budget in the vicinity of Fira, where rooms get gobbled up early for July and August. You may not want to live there, but most visitors will want to visit the capital city for an infusion of society. Sleeping in a nearby village may be the solution.

Just a ten-minute walk north along 25 Martiou Street is the community called **Firostephani,** which, to our minds, offers the loveliest view of the Caldera and the active volcano at Nea Kameni. The **Hotel Galini** (tel. 0286/22-336) stands out here for its imaginative, tiered architecture. This style assures that all 15 rooms with private bath have a fabulous view and the privacy of separate entrances off a common veranda. Doubles run 5400 drs ($41.53), without breakfast, but owner George Roussos, whose patience is sometimes sorely tried during the busy season, has a reasonably priced taverna across the pathway.

Hotel Kafieris (tel. 0286/22-189) has ten comfortable rooms with the same view at 5100 drs ($39.23) for a double with private bath. Argiri's Cafieris has three pension-style rooms to let as well, at 4800 drs ($36.92) for a double. These can be very economical for families or long-term visitors, but make sure to get a room facing east. There are other rooms to let, including Anna Kafieri's "**The Nice View,**" along the cliff walls. Budget watchers attracted to this area may prefer the homey atmosphere of the ten-room **Hotel Thira** (tel. 0286/22-863), where doubles with bath are 4300 drs ($33.07). The hotel, whose ten rooms look west over the fields to the sea, at 25 Martiou, is marked by the small windmill atop its roof garden. Two pensions run by the ubiquitous Mendrinos Brothers, the **Faros** and the **Panoramic View** (tel. 0286/22-034 for both) offer clean double rooms with private bath for only 3000 drs ($23.07), a real bargain here.

For those who shun the singles pubs, discos, and jewelers of main-street Fira, there are several rooms to let and some hotels in the attractive, white-washed village of **Kartaradoes,** two kilometers south. Here several of the village women offer rooms attached to their homes at 1500 drs ($11.53) to 2000 drs ($15.38) per double to help offset the cost of water, which is brought every-where on the island by tanker trucks from the springs at Kamari. We stayed with **Maria Roussou** (tel. 0286/22-047), who delighted Kyle by insisting on rehanging all our laundry using clothespins and her special touch. Her large white home is a block below the helpful **Meltemi Travel Office** (tel. 0286/22-890), where Gisella Nomikos will help find you a room or solve other problems.

A few minutes up the road to Fira is the whitewashed **Hotel Cyclades** (tel. 0286/22-948), run by Fanouris Sigalas. The Cyclades looks like your rich Greek aunt's private villa. Its 15 double rooms are 4050 drs ($31.15). Closer to Fira still are the simple accommodations at the **Hotel Palladion** (tel. 0286/22-583), where doubles range from 3800 drs ($23.07) to 4200 drs ($32.30), depending on the season. The treat here is breakfast in the marvelously decorated ground floor, which is cluttered with lace, flowers, and embroidery in traditional—and rarely seen—Santorinian fashion.

Unfortunately, Kartaradoes has only a few unremarkable tavernas. A pleasant exception is the **Glaros Taverna,** where Tom Nichas serves up spaghet-ti, shish kebab, etc. with elan and gusto. For the island's only good bread you'll have to go to the bakery in nearby **Messaria.** This little village, crowded with the hotels Apollon, Messaria, Andreas, Margariti, and Artemidoris, is at the busy crossroads connecting the Fira road to almost every site and beach on the island. When the moped smoke clears you'll see several pleasant tavernas on the main square.

Note: There are literally beds and food available in every corner of this overtouristed island, so if you're hankering after something different, hop on the local bus and explore. Then, please write and let us know what you've dis-covered.

Restaurants

For breakfast, there are several fast-food shops in town and a good bakery (next to the Enigma Disco), which in summer features a tasty raisin bread.

Few of the "better" (for ambience, more than cuisine) restaurants are open for lunch, but **Camille Stefani** (tel. 22-265), considered the island's best, is a lovely exception. The simple, elegant peach-colored interior has a cool, roman-tic ambience well suited to the sophisticated Greek-continental menu. Special-ties include shrimp Stefani, in a tomato and cheese casserole, and a wide variety of hors d'oeuvres. The good house wines are aged, and there's a fine selection of Santorini's celebrated local wines (the white Nykteri is a good choice). You may prefer to save this one for an evening splurge—meals run 1500 drs ($11.54) to 2500 drs ($19.23) per person. Camille Stefani has outdoor dining on a pleasant veranda; reservations are recommended in summer.

The excellent **Galaxy Restaurant** (tel. 22-717), on 25 Martiou, is open for dinner and packed nightly. Jim Chalaris grows all his own vegetables and makes delicious eggplant, tomato, and zucchini dishes. The Galaxy's cavelike interior is decorated with pottery, weavings, and a mural of the island which reminds you that you're actually in Greece. (Sometimes, when diners at the long tables nearby start singing their nations' anthems, it's hard to remember where you are). Pizzas run about 800 drs ($6.15), and a full meal for two will be about 2000 drs ($15.38).

For authentic taverna fare try **Nicholas** (not to be confused with *Nicola's,* near the port), on E. Stavrou in the heart of town. Their fava, a dip made from lentil-type beans, is an island specialty that's prepared very well here. Meals for two run 1000 drs ($7.69) to 1300 drs ($10), and the untrendy decor can be a relief.

Highly recommended is **Zorba's** (tel. 23-070), overlooking the harbor, for their fish and native dishes.

Nightlife

The social scene is one of Fira's most important lures, and if we have to choose, this year's disco would be the **Enigma** (tel. 22-466), near the square. The very popular, preppy **Town Club** (tel. 22-283), next to Nicholas, is a comfortable spot to drink and meet available American companions. You might also try **Casablanca**.

Those who are visiting in August can enjoy classical music at the new **Santorini Festival.** International singers and musicians will perform at Fira's open-air amphitheater over a two-week period. (See Kamari, below, for details of the Santoroni Wine Festival.)

When all is said and done, Fira's unique attribute is her remarkable natural beauty. From the few tavernas below Ag. Mina on the cliff we'd recommend **Franco's Bar** (tel. 22-881), open noon to 1 a.m. for snacks, pastries, coffees, and drinks. The view over the Caldera from this extraordinary setting is unbelievably beautiful, particularly at the magic sunset hour. You can unwind to classical music or flip through a volume from an excellent browsing library of art and photography books. Franco's is expensive, but totally recommended because the charming Italian host has combined his native flair for food with a wonderful aesthetic sensibility to create a delightful, elegant and totally Cycliadic café.

EMPORION: The large southern city of Emporion is at the turnoff for Perissa Beach. It's second in size to Fira and has some unusual houses built inside the ruins of a large Venetian fortress. A popular group excursion is to the local taverna **Stavros** (tel. 81-293) where a plugged-in bouzouki band sends tourists into a dancing frenzy. As John says, the louder the music, the worse the food, but it's still a wild night if you're up for it, and in fact the food here is fine.

KAMARI: Kamari Beach is Santorini's most popular destination because its beautiful eight-kilometer-long black sand beach was long ago discovered and exploited by tour operators. Seven planeloads of Europeans land directly at Santorini's airport each week for a packaged vacation at this unique resort. For those of you able to visit Kamari in the spring or fall, it is possible to find a room at prices comparable to those in Fira or the less attractive Perissa Beach.

There is little to do but dance, dine, drink, or soak up the sun at Kamari Beach. If you want to get out and see the island, local buses will take you to Fira where you can change for transport to other villages. A hike up to Ancient Thira is a wonderful excursion that begins here. The local **Kamari Tours** office (tel. 31-390 or 31-455) runs excursions to all of Santorini's sites, in addition to booking most of Kamari's rooms as well as cruises to other islands. They will also exchange money if you can't get into Fira to the only National Bank branch.

The **Santorini Wine Festival,** hosted by Kamari Tours (tel. 0286/31-390) is held nightly in Exo Gonia. For 1250 drs ($9.62) you get a round-trip bus leaving Kamari/Fira/Karterados/Messaria around 8 p.m., returning at 12:30 a.m. In between is an evening of Greek music, dancing, and drinking (free wine all night).

For an additional 1225 drs ($9.42) you can also order from 2 to 3 different Greek menus. It's a fun way to spend an evening if you're four or more.

Accommodations

Some of the island's plushest accommodations are here as well. The 55-room **Kamari Beach Hotel** (tel. 0286/31-216) has the best beachfront location. All the Kamari's spacious, balconied rooms take advantage of the view over the Aegean and the lovely pool down below. The luxury resort life has its price, but before June 30, doubles with breakfast are 5670 drs ($43.60). From July until the hotel's closing on September 30 the price is 6750 drs ($51.90). If this sounds tantalizing, more information can be obtained through their Athens office (tel. 91-69-06). If you really want to splurge for your even tan, the seven plush **Kallisti Villas** (tel. 0286/31-242) offer fully equipped one- or two-bedroom homes on the beach for 8500 drs ($65.40) double or 9000 drs ($69.20) for four people per night.

Coming back to earth, off-season travelers have a chance at rooms at the **Villa Astro** (tel. 0286/31-366). Group-tour operators also monopolize the less expensive rooms with private baths at the **Dionysos** (tel. 0286/31-310) or **Matina Hotels** (tel. 0286/31-491), which are 4200 drs ($32.30) double.

You should bargain for the rooms-to-let, including some above **Andreas' Restaurant** (considered Kamari's finest). Rooms run about 2600 drs ($20) per double, with shower in the hall.

The **Akis Pension** (tel. 0286/31-670) is just 300 yards from the beach. It has 14 rooms, all with private bath, and a cafeteria/café downstairs that's very good. A double goes for 3400 drs ($26.15).

There are many pensions in Kamari. Consult the free guide (available everywhere) "This Summer In Santorini" for listings.

Dining and Nightlife

The nearby **Gamba's** or **Irini's Restaurants** are local favorites and more reasonably priced than the equally good **Christos**, by the bus stop. The average supper costs 1000 drs ($7.69) per person. For good values in fish, try the swordfish at **George's**, and loukamides addicts will savor the sweet fried puffs at **Café Argiris**.

Pinpointing the favorite bar/disco for next year's readers is always tricky, but we'd suggest the **Sail Inn** (tel. 31-165) or the **Yellow Donkey** (tel. 30-314) where each night certain hours are set aside for disco, rock, or Greek music.

When you can't stand the Club Med ambience any longer, grab a bus for Fira, at 85 drs (65¢). They leave nearly every hour between 7 a.m. and 10 p.m. For spontaneous types, a taxi can be ordered (tel. 22-492), but the ten-minute ride will cost about 700 drs ($5.38).

PERISSA: Perissa Beach has a lot going for it as an alternative to staying in Fira. Here are three reasons why:

First, and most important, the wide, long beach is composed of fine black pebbles, which glitter like sapphires in the sunlight. Second, it's easy to get to— only 15 minutes away from Fira and buses run every half hour until about 11 p.m. in the summer at a cost of 85 drs (65¢). Third, once you get there you'll find many places to eat only a pebble's throw away from the beach. And if you decide to stay, you have a choice of camping, a youth hostel, private rooms, or a hotel. With all this going for Perissa, you might imagine that it gets crowded in the summer. You're right, but the crowds are predominantly day visitors from other parts of the island. If you choose to stay, you'll enjoy the early morning in relative peace and tranquillity.

Accommodations

Perissa Camping has sites from 325 drs ($2.50)—a tent is 185 drs ($1.42) extra—and it's located right behind the beach. It's also the nude sunbathing center of Perissa and has hot showers, a mini-market, and a very active canteen with great music. The **youth hostel** (no telephone yet; call Tourist Kiosk Restaurant) has 78 beds for 400 drs ($3.07) each. The hostel can be found on Perissa's main road opposite the Florida Disco. The **Hotel Christina** (tel. 0286/81-362), one of Perissa's first licensed establishments, has eight clean and comfortable rooms, all with private bath. High-season doubles are 3750 drs ($28.85).

Perissa is still a fledgling resort and most of the newer hotels provide very simple accommodations in a similar price range. The **Hotels Marianna** and **Santa Irini** are the best of the newer hotels, but if they're fully booked there are many other comparable lodgings nearby. Doubles at most of these hotels will run 3500 drs ($26.92) with bath.

Dining

Perissa's best restaurant has the unimaginative name **Tourist Kiosk Restaurant** (tel. 29-205). The building is equally dull and is located at the far end of the beach. Fortunately their food is quite good. The fish is caught very near the beach and grilled fresh to order; red mullet is 800 drs ($6.15) per person. The Kiosk also offers good vegetable dishes. Their shaded café is a blessed haven from the midday sun. The beachside Tourist Kiosk provides diners with free showers and dressing rooms. What more do you need? Another Perissa favorite is the popular snackbar **Pizzeria Galaxy #3**, for light meals. Campers and picnickers will find two grocery stores near the beach.

Note: Information on money changing is available from the locally run **Perissa Tours** (behind the church) or the helpful **Kamari Tours** (on the main street, 500 meters from the beach).

OIA: Ascending from the new port of Armeni—375 drs ($2.88) by donkey, 700 drs ($5.38) by taxi—the village of Oia (pronounced ee-ah) appears as a thin white icing of traditional Cycladic homes atop the dark black and red cliffs that rise from the Caldera. From this northernmost tip of the island you can admire the mist-shrouded, volcanic rock islands that break the gently rippling surface of the Aegean.

Oia's Cycladic architecture merits its distinction as the most beautiful village on Santorini. Like many ports of the island, Oia was nearly leveled by the earthquake of 1956. Its current architectural integrity is due to local efforts to rebuild the damaged village in the indigenous style. New housing was constructed to resemble the traditional vaulted-roof homes that existed before the earthquake of 1956. Some of the most beautiful villas here survived the tremors, but were abandoned by residents who never returned. The National Tourist Organization of Greece has been refurbishing these villas to rent them out as part of their Traditional Settlement Program; information and bookings are available from **Paradosiakos Ikismos Oias**, Oia, Santorini (tel. 0286/71-234). The restored villas accommodate from two to seven people; rates begin at 3750 drs ($28.85) a night. Inhabitants are proud of their picturesque village and not eager to encourage tourism, at least not by the budget crowds. Living in Oia is very costly, but this village is certainly worth a visit for those who can't afford a prolonged stay.

Day Trips

A sunset excursion into this elite town of shipping magnates is the most publicized way to visit. In Fira, hordes climb onto Kamari Tours' buses at midday for some sightseeing and transport to Oia 900 drs ($6.92). What you're paying for primarily is the transportation back if you're not sleeping in Oia. Public buses stop running to Fira at 8 p.m. A taxi back costs from 750 drs ($5.77) to 1100 drs ($8.46); it must be ordered by phone (tel. 22-292) or by CB radio at the Hotel Anemones (tel. 71-220). You may be lucky enough to find a taxi in town, which will make the return trip to Fira for a mere 750 drs ($5.77). So if you don't have wheels, and you don't want to join a group tour, try to round up a few other people to taxi-share for your evening in Oia. Hitchhiking is very difficult because the fuel shortage keeps the few locals off the roads and most tourists rent mopeds.

Budget watchers can take buses one way from Fira (five times daily, last one at 7 p.m.) for 110 drs (85¢). Allow yourself enough time to wander through the village's main street.

Dining

To turn this excursion into a splurge evening, phone ahead to reserve one of the sunset view tables at the **Kyklos Restaurant** (tel. 71-235), the only one built on the cliffs facing west. There's no official menu, but owner M. Darzentos provided us with a full meal, including a carafe of the house Nykteri wine, for 1300 drs ($10). The **Finikia Restaurant** (tel. 71-373) is a good choice. Marinos Markozanes makes sure you get your fill, and for 1000 drs ($7.69) each you'll be well satisfied.

A budget alternative, if you can survive till 9 p.m. without eating, is to continue north up Oia's only street to Lontza Castle, where the view is equally exquisite. Coming back on your left is the charming, inexpensive **Lontza Ouzeri**, where terrace tables have beautiful views east to Fira's twinkling lights. The **Neptune Restaurant** is another budget choice nearby, where dinners for two will cost 800 drs ($6.15) to 1200 drs ($9.23).

Oia's other recommended restaurants include the popular **Petros Taverna**, next to the big church, and the small, cheaper **Milos**, where fresh fish is the best value. The **Panorama**, on the road behind the church, is run by Spyros Kikkalis, who winters in Washington, D.C. The Panorama is a favorite for souvlaki and pizza. A full pie costs 650 drs ($5).

Accommodations

If you get addicted to the views, you'll save time and money by finding a room. The **Hotel Fregada** (tel. 0286/71-221) is one of Oia's most expensive—5850 drs ($45) for a double with bath, including breakfast. A much better value in accommodations is the ten-room **Hotel Anemones** (tel. 0286/71-220), which charges 3950 drs ($30.38) for a double room.

The charming traditional rooms of the **Hotel Lauta** (tel. 71-204), on the cliff side of Oia's only street, are 3360 drs ($25.85) double, and the Caldera view is priceless. There are a few rooms to let as well, but prices run 400 drs ($3.07) to 600 drs ($4.61) above double-room rates in Fira.

For residents, the helpful tour office of **Manolis Karvounis** can book tickets on local day trips (for about 200 drs more than Fira prices), rent cars, or help with accommodations. **Karvounis Tours Ltd.** (tel. 71-209) understands both ends of the tourist spectrum well. They run the pleasant, unofficial **Youth Hostel**, one kilometer south of town, where 46 beds are 625 drs ($4.80) each, a night. They also rent two spectacular villas on the cliffs. Four can enjoy the luxury of the Perivolas for 12,000 drs ($92.30) a night in the high season, all services included.

From the hilltop Oia, the nearest sand beach is **Baxedes**, partially accessible by bus from the town square. A one-kilometer walk over the black sand will bring you to a relatively isolated, undeveloped bathing area. Oia also boasts a marine museum, open 11 a.m. to noon and 4 p.m. to 5 p.m. daily.

WHAT TO SEE AROUND THE ISLAND: A visit to Santorini would not be complete without a stop at the archeological site of Akrotiri. The impact of this startling 1960s find has been compared to the discovery of King Tut's tomb in the 1920s. Those without an archeological background should take advantage of the many excellent local tours and see the site with a knowledgeable guide. The standard around-the-island day tour will also include a visit to the Monastery of Prophitis Elias, reviewed below. A personal favorite was a self-guided tour of Ancient Thira, the Dorian acropolis that can best be visited from Kamari Beach.

Akrotiri

The Minoan satellite city of Akrotiri is an outstanding monument to that culture and to the efforts of the archeologist who discovered it far below layers of volcanic ash. Since the early 1930s Minoan expert Dr. S. Marinatos had devoted his life to the search for Akrotiri. He hoped to find a city buried by the great earthquake and volcanic eruptions of antiquity, which radically altered Santorini. The tidal waves caused by the 16th-century B.C. earthquake were thought to have traveled to Crete, Egypt, and Israel, causing massive destruction. Dr. Marinatos found samples of volcanic ash (perhaps from Santorini) in the ancient Minoan harbor near Knossos, providing the first evidence that the quake that felled Crete and its Minoan palaces and cities was caused by the geological upheaval on Santorini. From that point on, he decided to explore Santorini for evidence that might prove his theory.

Dr. Marinatos returned to areas where pottery shards had been found in earlier decades. Following reports from local farmers that certain areas of earth collapsed under heavy weight, he found this ancient city of Akrotiri in 1966. Excavation began in 1967 and archeologists believe that it may take another 100 years to complete their delicate, tedious work.

The findings from Akrotiri have provided the world with some of the most beautiful Minoan stone artifacts and the most impressive frescos of the prehistoric world. The high artistic quality of the finds suggests that Akrotiri was a city of wealthy merchants and ship captains. Yet the fairly equal distribution of artistic work leads researchers to believe that there was a relatively equal distribution of wealth.

As you enter the covered site you'll be standing on the main street. Most of the remains on either side were stores or warehouses for Akrotiri commercial trade. In one room 400 clay pots were found, all stacked according to size. Another held large urns with traces of olive oil, fava, onion, garlic, and fish inside. Continuing down the street, you'll come to a "square" in the shape of a triangle, and in front of you is the West House. This multi-storied home is also called the Captain's House because of the richly decorated fresco of Minoan and Libyan sea battles unearthed on the second floor.

In 1977 Dr. Marinatos tragically fell from a ramp above the excavated site and broke his neck. He is buried in the ruins of a tile potter's shop where a wreath and flowers mark his grave.

Continuing along the main street, you'll see many more houses where remarkably preserved frescoes were discovered. Unfortunately, all of the best works from Akrotiri were carted away to Athens and are on view at the National Archeological Museum. A new archeological museum is being built in Fira, however, and it is hoped that eventually the frescoes will be housed there. Among the highlights are frescoes depicting the nude fisherboy (thought to be the first surviving representation of a male nude), a free-spirited decorative work representing Spring, a lovely illustration of three young women, an image of two men boxing, and an animal scene of northern Africa. Even without the frescoes, the site itself and the work that continues are so exciting that a visit to Akrotiri is a must for anyone touring Santorini.

The excavation continues, and if you visit during the summer you may have an opportunity to watch as visiting professors from around Greece systematically uncover the rich remains from this important site.

Akrotiri can be reached by public bus or private bus tours. Cost of admission is 425 drs ($3.27) for adults, 250 drs ($1.92) for students. Hours are 8:30 a.m. to 2:45 p.m. Monday to Saturday, and 9 a.m. to 2 p.m. on Sunday. Summers are very hot under the tin roofs at midday and the place gets very crowded. It would be a good idea to arrive first thing in the morning, if possible.

Monastery of Prophitis Elias

The Monastery of the Prophet Elijah, built by two monks from Pyrgos in 1711, is well worth a morning away from the beach. Part of the chapel and the monastery museum were added when King Otto, impressed by the monastery's work, asked the Greek government for funds to enlarge it. From this period come the many small rooms, clustered in a maze around the chapel, which now house fascinating exhibits of local culture. The monastery has always been cherished by the people of Santorini for its role during the Turkish Occupation (1453–1821). The few monks who inhabited it opened a "secret school" where they taught the island's children the Greek language and traditions outlawed by the Turks. In the museum, a model secret school has been created in a monk's cell. By the 1800s its instruction and care for the needy earned Profitis Elias the support of wealthy benefactors. Many of the monastery's fine religious items and valuable gifts were sold off to raise funds for the War of Independence, but the remaining sets of porcelain, silver, and ecclesiastical items are displayed.

The old hostelry and dining quarters of the enlarged monastery were converted into a Museum of Thiran Culture by the three monks who remained when the monastery's fortunes dwindled. They still offer a glass of *Tsikouthia* (Santorinian firewater) and a candy to all who come to visit—but, please, don't take their picture! The folksy museum is in contrast to the classic chapel, which contains a portrait of Elias from 1500 done in the Cretan style. It's on the far right of the altar; you can notice the similarities to the later work of El Greco, the best known exponent of this school.

The cultural museum's workshops include displays of tools, grains, candle-making supplies, and other implements of local cottage industries. The carpentry and blacksmith shop, boasting a 1960s bandsaw, intrigued John, while Kyle liked the petrified, braided wheat bread. We both loved the wax model peasant grinding fava beans, and the ouzo distillery (in the room below the postcard stand), which looks like a Prohibition-era contraption.

Everything in the monastery is well labeled and can be enjoyed by the solo visitor, but several companies offer this as part of a half-day tour. Striped cotton coveralls are provided for those who arrive in shorts. The monastery is open daily (except Sunday) from 8 a.m. to 1 p.m. and 2:30 p.m. to 6 p.m. A warning —the monastery was temporarily closed when we were there. Check whether it's open before you plan your excursion.

Ancient Thira (Archaia Fira)

The acropolis of the island's ancient capital, Thira, was inhabited by Dorian colonists from the ninth century B.C. Its impressive remains are situated on the hill towering 1,200 feet above Kamari Beach, and the highlight of any excursion here is the remarkable views of the ancient port at Kamari and the long black sand streak of Perissa. Make sure you also check out the springs in the cliff. Most of the buildings on the acropolis date from the Ptolemaic period (300–145 B.C.).

After entering the site, follow the path on the left. Carved in the rocks at a small shrine are the eagle symbol of Zeus, the lion of Apollo (you can sit on his throne and put your foot in his imprints) to the left, the dolphin of Poseidon, and a portrait of a Dorian admiral. Just south is the open Agora, and behind it the hewn stone ruins of the Governor's Palace. On the southern tip is a terrace thought to be the center of religious practices; stone tablets found here told of naked young boys who would frolic in homage to Dionysos. From this point you have a fantastic serial view of Santorini's most popular beaches and a clear sense of how valuable this acropolis was to the defense of the ancient capital. Behind this point there's a partially shaded, smooth stone Sanctuary of the Egyptian Gods, ideal for picnicking. Nearby is an underground sanctuary, whose Doric columns still support a stone canopy for an alternative shaded picnic spot.

Getting to Ancient Thira demands some forethought. Travel agents offer half-day excursions by mule up the stone path, perfect for those of you who loved this transport from the port to the new Fira (cost: 2000 drs, or $15.38). It's possible to arrange a round-trip taxi tour from Fira, which costs 3500 drs ($26.92), including waiting time. Skillful negotiation may convince the driver to allow more than two passengers in the taxi for this price.

For those looking for an exciting relief from the beach blues, start out about 8:30 a.m. from Kamari Beach and hike up to the acropolis. The 45-minute walk is uphill, but the beautiful views (which you must stop and admire) provide regular relief. Wear good shoes, bring water, and by all means a picnic, even if it's only bread from a local bakery and café frappé left over from the night before. You'll be so relieved when you arrive that you may just want to sit and enjoy the views. After you've caught your breath, hike onto the site itself and you'll be delighted by the unstructured remains of a once-proud civilization.

Ancient Thira is open 9 a.m. to 3 p.m. daily, to 1 p.m. on Sunday and holidays.

GETTING THERE: In the high season Santorini is serviced at least twice daily from Piraeus by the Kykladiki, Santorini, and other maritime companies. Scheduled **ferries** which call at Siros, Paros, Naxos, Folegandros, Sikinos, and Anafi take 12 hours, but express boats stopping only at Paros, Naxos, and Ios can do the trip in 10. Schedules should be confirmed with Tourist Information in Athens (tel. 171, or at 45-11-311). Once-weekly ferry service from the Dodecanese calls first at Rhodes, Karpathos, Kassos, and Crete. From Crete, there are two daily excursion boats leaving Iraklion which offer one-way transport for 1182 drs ($9.10). (Beware of this open-sea route in stormy weather—six hours of nausea may make the airfare seem cheap.) Ferries via Mykonos run four times weekly.

Piraeus ferries dock at the port Athinios, a 700 drs ($5.38) taxi or a 120 drs (92¢) bus ride from Fira. The exposed port at Skala (below Fira) is too unsafe for the larger steamships; often the small ferries that do dock there have to shuttle passengers in to shore on small caïques. If you dock at Skala you can choose between a tough 45-minute hike uphill around 250 pushy mules; a 425 drs ($3.27) mule ride, including luggage (negotiate in low season); or the 425 drs ($3.27) cable-car ride to reach Fira town. We'd recommend donkey up and cable car down.

Olympic flies direct from Athens to the international airport at Monolithos daily. (The only international flights are charters from Europe.) In the high season there are flights from Iraklion Airport, in Crete, and Rhodes three times a week, and from Mykonos six times a week. Olympic Airways provides a bus to and from the airport to meet flights which returns to their office in Fira; the fare is 150 drs ($1.15). For schedule information and reservations, check their Fira office (tel. 22-493), open daily, or call 92-92-555 in Athens.

8. Tinos

Many visitors find Tinos the least commercial of all the Cyclades and enjoy a visit for exactly that reason. Tinos has some beautiful beaches, an attractive port town, traditional hill villages where little English is spoken, and a green landscape dotted with dovecotes from the Venetian period. Tinos is the most heavily visited island in Greece, but more than 90% of the tourists are Greeks themselves.

CHURCH OF THE EVANGELISTRIA: Tinos is celebrated throughout Greece for its Church of the Evangelistria, which draws thousands of pilgrims annually. Because of its church Tinos is the second "holy island," after Patmos. On August 15 (Feast of the Assumption) and on March 25 (Feast of the Annunciation) the Orthodox, the handicapped, infirm, and sick make the pilgrimage to kiss the holy icon of the Madonna, hang their tin votive representations on the picture, and await a miracle cure. The spiritual and national life of the Tinians has been centered around Panagia Evangelistria ("Our Lady of Good Tidings") since 1823. In 1822 Pelagia, a nun from the Kechrovouniou Nunnery, had a dream that an icon was buried on a nearby farm. Pelagia summoned her neighbors to help excavate, and they soon found the foundation of a Byzantine church. There, on January 30, 1823, a workman found a gold figure of the Madonna, an icon thought to have been sent by the Virgin Mary to cure the faithful of Tinos. Work began immediately on the elegant, traditional-style Greek Orthodox church that can be seen today.

From the ferry port, take the street on the left (where the Tinos Tours office is), Leof. Megalocharis. The walled-in church is just a few minutes' walk away. You'll pass several shops selling candles (up to six feet long!), incense, medallions, books, and silver and gold votive offerings. These votive plaques represent arms, eyes, legs, knees, boats, cars, or whatever else anyone needs to have cured (for a fee these plaques can be custom made).

The church, built on two levels, is of Parian and Tinian marble—notice the prized green-veined marble from Tinos. The bottom level has small chapels and a baptismal font filled with gold and silver offerings. This level is always crowded with Greek children dressed in white. Around the Rhodian-style pebble-paved courtyard are galleries housing other icons, religious artifacts, and the painting and sculpture of some of the famous Greek artists from this island.

Continue up the grand marble stairs (now carpeted in red to protect them from further erosion) to the main chapel. To the left of the central isle is the Sacred Icon of the Madonna, so covered in gold and diamonds that it's hard to discern. The priests conduct services regularly, and during one it's impossible to explore because of the women queued up to kiss the icon, with others kissing the floor, the frescoes, and the small shrines around the altar. Old men scurry about removing just-lit candles to make way for new ones. Outside the main chapel are a few galleries of ecclesiastical art; you can return at the end of the service to admire the wealth of offerings hanging from the chandeliers and censers throughout the church.

The posted hours for the galleries are 8:30 a.m. to 12:30 p.m. and 4 p.m. to 6 p.m. Monday through Saturday, and 9:30 a.m. to 11 a.m. and 3 p.m. to 4:30 p.m. on Sunday, but the posted hours are not always adhered to. Some galleries are closed on Wednesday. And don't forget proper attire (long pants for men, long skirts for women) is required to enter.

ORIENTATION: If you've seen enough tourists to last you a lifetime on other Greek islands, you might find Tinos's pleasant port a refreshing change. Hotels, shops, and restaurants are accustomed to serving only Greek vacationers. Although few locals speak English, their enthusiasm and hospitality overcome any language barrier. The street running north from the harbor by the Panagia Tinos ticket office leads to the Church of the Evangelistria. On the corner of the main street and Lazarou Sochou Street are the **post office** and the **O.T.E.** Next door is a shop renting **mopeds** (at 1300 drs, or $10 a day) and **bicycles** (at 600 drs or $4.62, a day). Another good place for mopeds is Moto Mike (tel. 23-304). The **bus station** and **taxi stand** are at the harbor; you can check at the helpful reception desk of the Posidonios Hotel for schedules and rates. Opposite the waterfront are ferry ticket agents and several banks which keep, well, bank hours (8 a.m. to 2 p.m.) Mr. Zanes has a small **laundry** behind the Lido Hotel. If the icon of the Madonna won't help, there's a **first-aid center** (tel. 22-210). The **area code** is 0283.

ACCOMMODATIONS: The attractive port of Tinos has many C-class hotels which are clean, simply decorated, and well located, with fine views, all similarly priced. You'll have no problems finding a room if you avoid the Panagia festivities in March and August; however, the hotels often become crowded in July, when most Greeks vacation.

We'll mention the harborside hotels in order of preference. First and foremost is the **Hotel Tinion** (tel. 0283/22-261), at 1 Alavanou Street, on the right-hand side of the harbor. Immediately striking is its old-world air—lace curtains, marble floors, and hand-polished wood. Its rooms have 14-foot ceilings, a huge terrace, phones, and old tilework floors. Some rooms have private baths, and the shared baths are old European half-tubs. A double will run you 4300 drs ($33), and the memory of your visit comes free.

East on the waterfront is the 112-year-old **Avra** (tel. 0283/22-242), whose 16 high-ceilinged rooms are built around a plant-filled tiled courtyard. The Avra's spacious doubles with private bath are 2250 drs ($17.30). The **Posidonios** (tel. 0283/22-245) has 39 rooms which rent for 2770 drs ($21.30); the top floor has the best harbor views. The 38-room **Delfinia** (tel. 0283/22-289) is an equally good alternative. This contemporary hotel is built above two lively portside cafés, whose activities spill into the Delfinia's lobby. A double room goes for 3540 drs ($27.23), with breakfast an additional 375 drs ($2.88).

To the left (south) of the ferryboat pier is the 20-room **Hotel Lito** (tel. 0283/22-791). Modern double rooms equipped with telephone/radio are 3566 drs ($27.43). Next door is the **Hotel Aigli** (tel. 0283/22-240), with 15 rooms. Ask for a double with a private bath at 3125 drs ($24.03); the bathless doubles are overpriced at 3000 drs ($23.07).

Tinos's best-value hotel is on the pretty Platia Ierarachon (about two blocks up, behind the Hotel Posidonios). The small **Hotel Eleana** (tel. 0283/22-561) doesn't have harbor views, but the rooms are large and sunny and have balconies. Doubles cost 3325 drs ($25.58). On Leof. Megalocharis near the O.T.E. you'll see the modern **Meltemi Hotel** (tel. 0283/22-881), a pleasant, 43-room hotel favored by groups. The management here seems willing to bargain with individual tourists in the slow season. A high-season double will run you 3850 drs ($29.62).

On several streets behind the port you can find rooms-to-let from 800 drs ($6.15) to 1500 drs ($11.54) for two.

Next to the Hotel Oceanis on Iak. Gkizi we found **rooms-to-let** from a Mr. Giannis, who wasn't home at the time, but whose neighbor let us in to look at the rooms. They were very nice (his home has green shutters outside and a plethora of international flags flying from his balcony), but we couldn't find out the prices. It's worth a look.

RESTAURANTS: Tinos has some particularly good restaurants, probably because their customers are most often other Greeks. Our favorite is **Peristerionas** ("Dovecote"), which is decorated to resemble one of the Venetian towers built as dove perches that are found all over Tinos. The restaurant is found on a small lane uphill from the Lido Hotel, and its outdoor tables and chairs fill the walkway. The Dovecote's special entrées are grilled meats and fish. Their delicious contribution to Greek cuisine is the wonderful dill, onion, and vegetable fritters called *parathoti-ganites;* a plateful is only 120 drs (92¢) and a dinner for two, including the Dovecote's own retsina (from the barrel) will be about 1600 drs ($12.30).

On the harborfront is **Skouva** (tel. 22-741), a cafeteria with good simple food and a metered telephone where you can make late-night international calls after the O.T.E. has closed. A small taverna run by Tannis Krontira that's very popular is **O'Kipos**, almost four lanes inland from the taxi stand (turn left after the Posidonios Hotel). In this quiet, residential section of town you'll see the bright lights of O'Kipos. Behind the kitchen area is a lush garden where you can eat simple taverna fare and consume light white retsina for next to nothing. On this same street, at the harbor, is **Lefteris** (tel. 23-013). The hidden restaurant is identifiable by a blue neon sign over an arched entranceway. Lefteris opens out to a huge garden court decorated with fish plaques on the walls. The grilled sea bass and stuffed zucchini are especially recommended from the varied menu. Dinner for two will cost about 1700 drs ($13.08). A large open area behind the tables invites dancing by enthusiastic tourists and waiters! Nearby is **Xinari** (tel. 23-337), an informal "pizzeria" where a delicious meal can be had by two for less than 1500 drs ($11.54).

At the far end of the harbor, past the Hotel Avra, is the comfortable **Euripidis Coffee Shop**, a great place to watch the sun set or sample some of the famed Tinian pastries long into the quiet night.

WHAT TO SEE: A half day can be spent exploring the **Church of the Evangelistria** and its many museums. About half a block below the church on Leof. Megalocharis is the **archeology museum**, open 10 a.m. to 2 p.m. daily; closed Tuesday. Admission is 150 drs ($1.15). The small collection includes finds from the ancient sanctuary of Thesmophorion (in the Exobourgo region). Of note are some eighth- to seventh-century B.C. red clay vases. In the museum's courtyard are marble sculptures from the second-century A.D. site at Kidomie, the Sanctuary of Poseidon and Amphitrite.

There's a fun **flea market** region behind the port that's easily found if you turn up the street where the Naïas ticket office is. Besides the huge variety of candles and religious paraphernalia, you can find dried herbs and incense, embroidery, weaving, and the wonderful local nougat called *loukoumi,* along with typical Greek souvenirs at lesser prices. Two ceramic shops on the waterfront, **Anna Maria** and **Marina**, also have particularly fine pottery, jewelry, and copperware at moderate prices.

AROUND THE ISLAND: The 800-odd **dovecotes** scattered throughout the island are one of Tinos's most picturesque assets. Many date from the 17th century, when proud Venetians built towers with ornate latticework tiles on top for their doves to sit on. The lazy man's way to see some of these dovecotes is to take about a half-hour walk west from town. Follow the waterfront around the Aigli Hotel and you'll find the west road which takes you by some small break-waters. As you see the dark sand and rock beach come into view, below you on the left will be a charming blue-domed church which has a small ouzeri below it, right at the water's edge. This can be a lovely or perilous spot, depending on the meltemi winds.

From the coast road you can see the large Tinos Beach Hotel, which has two authentic dovecotes (behind the tennis courts) on its property. Along the roadway, just before the hotel (on your right) is the charming **Tsampia Taverna** (tel. 23-142). At the Tsampia you can dine on one of the many-tiered, flowering verandas overlooking the water. Past the Tsampia, on the coast road, you'll find the minimal ruins of the excavated Temple of Poseidon and Amphitrite.

Day Trips

A pleasant day trip from Tinos to Pyrgos will take you through many inland villages to the region of green marble quarries and local sculptors. From Pyrgos you can go to Tinos's best beach (at Panormos), where there are rooms to rent. Buses leave the port at 11 a.m. for the one-hour trip, and return from Pyrgos at 3 p.m., costing 280 drs ($2.15) each way.

For dovecote fans, a short detour would include **Tarampados** or **Koumaros.** These villages are in the Exbourgo region, the old acropolis of Tinos where the ruins of a Venetian castle can be seen. Every two hours a Tinos bus runs the route through the villages of **Steni** and **Mesi,** then up to **Falatados,** a typical hill village (fare is 90 drs 69¢). Ornithologists should purchase the white-covered map which gives the bird types found in each region of Tinos (found at any of the harbor newsstands).

BEACHES: Seekers of isolated beaches should try **Kolymbithra** on the better-protected north coast. Local buses run five times daily to **Komi** from Tinos, a beautiful ride through the hills. From here it's only a three-kilometer walk to the dark sand beach, and there's a campsite nearby. Since there is no public trans-port, only a moped will give you access to the little-known **Lychnaftia** and **Porto** beaches on the southeast coast.

GETTING THERE: Several ferryboat companies service Tinos because of the large number of year-round Greek tourists. There are two or three **ferries** daily from Piraeus; schedules should be confirmed with Tourist Information in Ath-ens (tel. 171 or at 45-11-311). Information on vessels returning from Tinos to Piraeus can be obtained from the **Panagia Tinous Office.** The voyage to or from Rafina cuts about an hour off the normal six-hour time, and fares are about 20% less. The **Chryssi Ammos Company** has an office on Tinos; departure times from Rafina can be checked at 0294/23-300. There are seven sailings daily from nearby Mykonos, and several daily excursions to Mykonos and Delos, at 1400 drs ($10.77). Tinos also has daily connections to Syros and Andros.

9. Andros

Evergreen-covered Andros is the second-largest island in the Cyclades. Its name means "man" and may be derived from Phoenician. Greek families often vacation on Andros because of its verdant hills and valleys.

Today visitors arriving from the mainland port of Rafina will dock at Gavrion. From there, public service will take you to the main port village of Batsi. Most readers (and all Greek tourists) head for the fully equipped kitchen-ette apartments-to-let in many local "villas." The **Chryssi Akti** (tel. 0285/41-

236) is a popular C-class lodging that dominates the town beach. Here there are over 60 comfortable double rooms with private baths each running 3650 drs ($28.08) a night. The older **Krinos Hotel** (tel. 0285/41-232) has 13 beach-view rooms with common bath and shower that rent for 3100 drs ($23.85).

In 1833 there was a major discovery on Andros when archeologists unearthed two statues, one called the Hermes of Andros, the other of a large woman from Iraklion. All of the furor was over the artist, originally thought to be Praxiteles, and later deemed to be a first-century B.C. sculptor from a little-known Parian workshop. Both figures are on display in the National Museum in Athens (Room 21).

If you're bored with total relaxation, you can hop another local bus to the inland capital, **Chora**. The 1½-hour trip along Andros's mountainous roads leads to the many shops selling *loukoumi* candy and *amigdaloto* (almond cookies), both island specialties. After you've stocked up with bus food, continue on for a short way to a small, charming village of traditional Cycladic housing, **Stenies**. Stenies has been well preserved by the merchant seamen who still live here and in Chora. Be warned: their native pride in this very Greek island has made them wary of tourists. Because there's such an annual influx of Greek tourists, foreigners are not as warmly welcomed as at other ports.

10. The Western Cyclades

If any islands within the Cyclades are on the frontiers of tourism, the most likely candidates would have to be Serifos, Sifnos, and Milos. None is nearly as developed for tourism as their more publicized cousins, though they are beginning to receive the overflow from such islands as Mykonos, Paros, Ios, and Santorini. Serifos is the island for those who want to lose the crowd completely. Sifnos is a gorgeous island, with an equally attractive beach, that's just beginning to become popular, while Milos offers the most interesting archeological sites and scenery.

SERIFOS: Among the islands in the Western Cyclades, Serifos is perhaps the least developed, the least wealthy, and the least touristy. Turned around, it's also one of the most untouched, least expensive, and quietest places in all of Greece. Serifos, "the bare," earns its name from the island's rocky landscape, though **Livadi**, the main port town, is filled with trees and carefully tended gardens. **Chora**, the island's main village, is a 45-minute walk from Livadi (wear good walking shoes). Along the meandering roadway are windmills, a few small farms framed by soil erosion walls, and the remains of some Byzantine-era walls. The village is dominated by the ruins of a fortress built by the Venetians. If you look in the cracks of walls and stone you'll find a rare pink flower that's known to grow only on the island. It's indicative of the uniqueness and peacefulness of Serifos.

The boat lands at Livadi (the other port at Megalo Livadi was closed years ago after the island's business of mining iron ore was halted), where there is a beach and the largest concentration of hotels and pensions. There is also a very nice beach at Psiliamos. The bank, post office, and O.T.E. (the area code is 0281) are up in Chora, as are a few restaurants. Don't forget to try the fava beans; they're an island specialty. There's a bus to Chora that is supposed to run hourly, and may actually do so in the high season for a fare of 80 drs (62¢) each way. Otherwise, you may be stuck taking a taxi.

Accommodations

There are two C-class hotels and two pensions in Livadi. The **Serifos Beach** (tel. 0281/51-209) is the larger of the two hotels; all its 33 rooms are equipped with private bath and it's the only inn open all year round. The **Maistrali** (tel. 0281/51-381) is also located on the paralia, about 250 meters from the town. Room rates for the two are about the same; expect to pay about 1850 drs ($14.23) for a single and 3450 drs ($26.54) for a double.

Much cheaper are the pensions Perseus and Areti. The ten-room **Perseus** (tel. 0281/51-273) is right near the beach and Livadi's best restaurant, also called Perseus. Singles cost 3200 drs ($24.62) and doubles run 3750 drs ($28.85). The **Areti Pension** (tel. 0281/51-479) has 12 rooms at prices similar to those at the Perseus. Plenty of people camp on the beach at Serifos but be advised; don't camp under those piney trees near the shore. They are called salt trees, because all day long they absorb the sea air. Every night they sweat it out. If you are under them when you wake up, you and your sleeping bag will be covered with salt!

Getting There

Serifos is a five-hour boat ride away from Piraeus. There are departures four times weekly on the Serifos–Sifnos–Milos route. Serifos is also connected to Kythnos, Ios, and Santorini, although ferries on this route run only once or twice a week. Check with the Port Authority in Athens.

SIFNOS: One of the best kept secrets in the Cyclades, Sifnos is a favorite destination for Greeks who want to escape the hordes of tourists on the more well-known islands. The secret is that Sifnos is a lovely island, the kind that one used to be able to find all over the country: a blend of quiet villages, friendly people, uncrowded beaches, flavorful food, and a totally casual lifestyle. Sifnos is a volcanic island, and its soil is fertile enough to grow grapes and olives as well as support numerous family farms. The villages of Artemonas and Exambela, for example, are set idyllically on rolling hills among white sailcloth masts of windmills which spin in the breeze as they pump water to irrigate the fields. Like Serifos, Sifnos was famed in antiquity for its mines, but in Sifnos's case the ore that was extracted was gold. Sifnos was an exceptionally rich island; each year they sent a solid-gold egg to Delphi as a tribute to Apollo. The Sifnian treasury at Delphi was one of the most elaborately decorated and impressive. One year the islanders' greedier instincts dominated and they made a terrible mistake. Instead of sending their usual golden egg they substituted a gilded egg. Apollo was incensed and in revenge sank the mines deep in the Aegean. Since that time no gold has been found on the island, giving meaning to the island's name—Sifnos, "the empty."

Around the Island

Kamares is the main port, on the western side of the island, with a beach (where you can swim and camp) and a few cafés. The best of the restaurants is **Boulis & Babounis**. The often-crowded bus—costing about 100 drs (77¢), depending on the destination—follows the road to the eastern and more interesting side of Sifnos, to Apollonia and Kastro, the site of the ancient capital, to Chrissopigi and its monastery, and to the beach at **Platy Yalos**.

Apollonia is the main town. It's a loose congregation of one- and two-story Cycladic houses built on a gently terraced hill with the craggy silhouette of the surrounding terrain in the background. The tiered landscape is punctuated by dovecotes and clumps of olive and plane trees. There's a folk-art museum as well as a bank, O.T.E., and post office in the center part of town. Apollonia contains the greatest number of hotels and pensions on the island. The **Hotel Sifnos** (tel. 0284/31-624) is the best of these; its nine rooms have private baths and the hotel's manager, Helen Diaremes, will do her best to make your stay comfortable. Doubles run 3750 drs ($28.85); breakfast is an additional 300 drs ($2.30). The Sifnos is open all year round and is located just off the main square. If you're looking for a cheaper alternative, rest assured that you'll be offered a room to rent when you exit the bus. Expect to pay about 1550 drs ($11.90) for two for a room in a private house. The choice restaurant in Apollonia is **Fasolis**, although **Flora's** (formerly Kalliafe's) is another popular spot.

As you approach the ancient capital of **Kastro** you'll see meandering rock walls that enclose the town's family farms. Farther up the rough-edged hill are sugar-cube-shaped homes that spill down toward the valley floor. Wide zigzagging stone walls, built by the Venetians, mark the medieval line of defense. The Venetians took Sifnos in 1307 and built the fortress on the foundation of the ancient acropolis. Venetian coats-of-arms are still visible above the doorways of the older houses that abut the fort. Kastro is built overlooking the sea, and the view from this lovely hill town is one of those perfect Greek snapshots.

The bus stops at **Panaghia Chrissopigi**, near the village of **Apokofto**, a remarkably sited monastery built on a sacred rocky promontory. The double-vaulted whitewashed church is built on a rock that was split after two women prayed to the Virgin Mary for protection against a band of pirates. The icon inside the church was said to have radiated light when it was discovered. There is good swimming immediately below the monastery and along the coast where secluded bays protect swimmers from rough water. Apokofto has a beach, a couple of tavernas, and a recommendable pension. The **Synodinos Pension** (tel. 0284/31-503) has ten rooms, is a five-minute walk from the beach, and costs 2800 drs ($21.54) for a double. The pension is built in Cycladic style with a whitewashed-village look.

The last stop on the bus line is at the long sandy beach at Sifnos's slowly evolving resort of **Platy Yalos**. The development has been slow enough so that local Sifnians haven't become jaded by the increasing number of tourists. Nevertheless, if any part of this as-yet-unspoiled island is to become victim to the ravages of tourism it's here at Sifnos's best beach. There are coves on either side of the beach where nude sunbathing is the rule rather than the exception. In case you get bored sitting on this great stretch of sand, you can always catch one of the caïques to **Vathi** beach or one of the larger boats to faraway Paros. Also at Vathi, directly on the beach, is a working kiln that produces some of the rough pottery Sifnos is famous for. Many people camp on Platy Yalos beach, but if you want to stay in a covered abode there's an ample supply of rooms. The best bet is the B-class **Platy Yalos** (tel. 0284/31-224), a 22-room hotel right on the beach. You can save money by staying in the rooms without a private bath. Prices for a double without bath are 3600 drs ($27.69); with bath, 3900 drs ($30). Breakfast is additional.

Readers Anna and Eliana Gerotto from faraway Venice, Italy, wrote us to check out the **Panorama Hotel** (tel. 0284/31-334), run by the Benakis family. We received other favorable letters and are happy to report that the hotel is inexpensive—3750 drs ($28.85) for a double with bath—and offers a lovely sea view. The nearby sandy beach is long and, for most of the year, uncrowded.

Loukataria Brothers is our favorite eatery in Platy Yalos. Ask if they have kakavia fish soup, a Sifnian specialty.

Getting There

There are boats leaving from Piraeus every day except Sunday, in addition to connections to the other Western Cyclades, Serifos and Milos. The boat running between Paros and Platy Yalos is an excursion and operates when there is sufficient demand, though they try to go every Wednesday and Sunday.

MILOS: Imagine a gigantic harbor, a harbor so big that it could accommodate an entire fleet of battleships. Surround it with a volcanic land mass and that's Milos. Known primarily for the *Venus de Milo,* the fourth-century B.C. statue of Aphrodite that was found in an island cave and spirited away by the French (it's on display in the Louvre), Milos is the site of one of Greece's oldest civilizations. The Minoan-era excavations at Filakopi II demonstrate the considerable sophistication of this early settlement. During Minoan times, Milos became one of the richest islands in the Aegean as a result of its obsidian trade. A particularly dark moment in the island's history took place after the Peloponnesian War when Athens, angry with the Milians for siding with Sparta, systematically wiped out the Milian male population. Thucydides wrote his *Milian Dialogues,* a passionate attack on the abuses of power. Milos is still a prosperous island and has little inclination to exploit its natural beauty for tourism, though the recently constructed airport promises to increase its flow of tourists.

Around the Island

Most of the interesting destinations on Milos are to be found on the eastern side of the island. **Adamas**, at the base of an active volcano, is the port and island accommodation center. The 16-room (in bungalows) **Chronis** (tel. 0287/41-625) and **Corali** (tel. 0287/41-633) hotels are the island's best C-class establishments; doubles with bath run 4150 drs ($31.92). Cheaper is the ten-room **Adamas Pension** (tel. 0287/41-844), where bathless doubles cost 2850 drs ($21.92). The bus travels to Plaka, the modern capital, to nearby Tripiti, farther up the coast to Kastro, and due east to Filokopi and Apollonia.

Plaka is a quiet town, but it does offer two interesting museums: the archeology museum, with neolithic finds from various sites on the island and a French-made cast of the famous *Venus,* and the folkloric museum. Both are near the bus stop.

Within walking distance, in **Klema**, the Roman-era capital, are fantastic catacombs dug by Christians in the first century A.D. (open 9 a.m. to 1 p.m. and 4 p.m. to 6 p.m.). Ancient inscriptions are etched into the walls—along with modern graffiti—and burial crypts that once held a half dozen bodies are now fully excavated. You'll have to walk through very narrow corridors and low tunnels to see the full extent of the catacombs, so if you're claustrophobic, beware! There are remains of a Roman theater and temple a short walk from the catacombs.

The excavations at **Filakopi**, outside of Apollonia, show the influence of both the Minoans and mainland Greeks on this Middle Cycladic (2000 B.C.) settlement. Many obsidian tools were found here that actually date from pre-Minoan times.

The beach at **Apollonia** is one of the best on Milos and is especially popular with campers. Caïques leave from Apollonia for the trip to the nearby island of **Kimolos**. The whole island is built on a foundation of chalk; absolutely everything is white. There's a great beach and some interesting archeological finds dating from Mycenaean times.

Getting There

Like the other islands in the Western Cyclades, Milos is served by **ferry** from Piraeus six times a week (no ferries operate on Sunday). There are direct connections to Sifnos and Serifos, as well as infrequent connections to Ios and Santorini. **Olympic Airlines** has daily flights from Athens. **Adamas Milou** (tel. 0287/22-380) is the Olympic agent on Milos.

Chapter IX

THE DODECANESE

1. Rhodes
2. Kos
3. Patmos
4. Kalymnos
5. Symi
6. Karpathos
7. A Baker's Dozen

RHODES IS THE HEART of the Dodecanese (Dodekannisos), the largest and perhaps most scenically beautiful of the 12 ("dodeka") original islands. In her history you'll find the history of the region. The proximity of the Dodecanese to Turkey has colored them with a richer ethnicity and a strong sense of the Greeks' Asia Minor heritage. We loved the peoples' style and character—the bold colors and solid villas, fearless seamen and hardy farmers. We're sure you've noticed how Greeks everywhere love to discuss politics; well here, where rebellion against Turkish rule first began, opinionated political talk is the order of the day.

Of all the conquerors who overran the islands, the Italians have left the greatest mark. Although they're recalled as merciless tyrants who occupied the Dodecanese between 1913 and 1943, Italian tourists are warmly welcomed. Many of the older citizens speak the language fluently and hints of Italian taste crop up in the cuisine and culture of the region. Romans, Venetians, Genoese, Crusaders—conquerors all—constructed most of the islands' fantastic temples and fortresses. It was under Mussolini's direction that the greatest ancient and medieval sites on Rhodes and Kos were restored, to remind Italians of the heroism of St. John's Knights and to remind everyone else of the Italians' historical claim to world dominance. Though repeatedly occupied by different nations, the Dodecanese have remained essentially Greek.

The warm people, rugged rocky coastline, secluded beaches, fresh seafood, and strong sunshine that we expect from the Greek islands are here. **Rhodes** (Rodos) is a mecca for sightseers, shoppers, party people, and sportsmen. **Kos** (Cos) offers fascinating archeological sights (the Asclepion), golden beaches, and fun. **Patmos** is as well known for the imposing Monastery of St. John as it's little known for the rich and famous who inhabit its restored medieval villas. **Kalymnos** is still a sponge fisherman's isle. **Symi** is an architectural gem, a picturesque island filled with ex-seafarers and sponge fishermen. **Karpathos**, distanced by rough seas from the others, remains aloof from contemporary Greece; some villagers live as they did in the 17th century. The

"Other Dodecanese"—Kassos (Cassos), Halki (Chalkis), Tilos, Nisiros (Nissyros), Astipalea, Leros, and Kastellorizo (Megisti)—many of which can be visited on day excursions from one of the larger neighboring islands, make up our section at the end, "A Baker's Dozen."

Because they're linked in a chain at the eastern edge of the Mediterranean, the Dodecanese are not visited as often as the closer-to-the-mainland Cyclades islands. We think that's great. There are still a few villages left where life doesn't go topsy-turvy in July and August. If your time's limited, island-hop by plane or boat to include at least one of the Dodecanese on your itinerary.

HYDROFOILS: Since 1981 hydrofoils (high-speed ships that glide over the water's surface on sleek underwater wings), have been operating in the Dodecanese islands. Travelers should be delighted to learn that the often grueling, nauseating nine-hour steamer trip from Rhodes to Patmos can now be made in 3½ hours in first-class comfort at less than twice the cost. Two hydrofoil companies are operating in the Dodecanese on a cruise line license, which enables them to cancel runs if too few passengers purchase tickets (though both cite their 90% record on scheduled runs and claim that only weather causes cancellations). In all other respects these ships operate the same as steamers, including the snackbar and Muzak piped into the lounges.

Both the Dodecanese and Alkyonis Lines use Russian-built Cometas; they're 35.1 meters long, 11 meters wide, and seat 116 passengers in airline-type bucket seats. The 2200-horsepower engines allow a cruising speed of 32 to 34 knots, with a top speed of 36 knots, comparable to the velocity of an American destroyer. (A voyage made by a small ferry in 4½ hours, which could be made by a large steamer in 3 hours, can be made by a hydrofoil in 1½ hours.) When we asked why the Greeks had chosen Cometas over their American counterpart, the Boeing hydrofoil used elsewhere in Europe, the answer was simple. Although the Boeing craft has a better automatic stabilizer system, its two gas turbine engines need to be maintained by a skilled aviation crew. In contrast, the diesel engines of the Cometa can be serviced by the much more readily available steamer crew.

The four "flying boats" in operation, the *Alkyonis I* and *II*, the *Marilena*, and the *Tzina*, were built in 1980 and display the latest in navigation and communication gear. If you ask upon boarding, the ship's captain will usually permit you to inspect the bridge. Studying the aluminum-alloy hull will provide clues to the ship's extraordinary speed and stability. Hydrofoils are affected by the weather and water conditions in much the same way as a water skier. These factors are computed by the internationally accepted Beaufort Scale, a measure of wind speed, duration of blowing, and fetch (the distance from the ship to the nearest land mass in the direction of the wind). The Dead Sea would be rated "0" and a hurricane is rated "12"; a "5" on the Beaufort Scale is the maximum allowed for hydrofoil use. (Actually these ships can operate at slower speeds, like conventional vessels, in much rougher conditions.) We heartily welcome these vessels to the Dodecanese, where island hopping has become a pleasure.

In 1987 schedules and fares included the following:

Rhodes–Kos–Rhodes: runs twice daily (one-way travel time: two hours); round-trip fare: 4350 drs ($33.46)

Rhodes–Patmos–Rhodes: twice a day Tuesday, Thursday, and Saturday (one-way travel time: 3½ hours); round-trip fare: 6000 drs ($46.15).

Rhodes–Samos–Rhodes: runs twice only on Friday (one-way travel time: 3¾ hours); round-trip fare: 6375 drs ($49.03).

Kos–Patmos–Kos: runs Tuesday, Thursday, and Saturday (one-way travel time: 1½ hours); round-trip fare: 3180 drs ($24.46).

The Alkyonis and Dodecanese Lines run additional day trips from Rhodes during the summer season, including: to Nisiros (Tuesday, Thursday, and Saturday), to Kalymnos (daily), and to Tilos (on Sunday only).

Check with local travel agents for the latest schedules and fares.

YACHT CRUISES: In 1986, Viking Tours will begin 7-night, 8-day cruises between Rhodes and Samos, including a stop at Kuşadasi, Turkey, for a day trip to the ancient site of Ephesus (see Chapter XVIII, "Exploring the Aegean Coast"). Viking's luxurious yacht will island-hop through the Dodecanese every week between April and October; twin-berth cabins on the half-board plan will run $945 per person. Contact their Athens office: **Viking Travel Bureau,** 3 Filellinon St., Syntagma Square (tel. 32-29-383), or their U.S. office (800/341-3030) for more information.

1. Rhodes

The stories surrounding the origin and name of Rhodes are among the loveliest in Greek mythology. In the lofty heights of Mount Olympus, Zeus, after his battle against the giants, was dividing the spoils of his victory among the other gods. Helios, the god of the sun, was gone when lots were cast for the division of earth. Upon his return, Helios appealed to Zeus to make some compensation, proposing that a piece of land, rising from the "foaming main," be granted as his sole possession. Zeus complied, and as Pindar wrote in the fifth century B.C., "From the waters of the sea arose an island, which is held by the Father of the piercing beams of light, the ruler of the steed whose breath is fire." The legend continues that Helios wed the nymph of the island, Rhodos, daughter of Poseidon, and was so taken with her beauty that he declared he would make the whole island an equal delight.

A further embellishment holds that a child was born of Helios and Rhodes, who in turn begat three sons: Cameros, Iyalysos, and Lindos. Each son established a great city and thus the wealth and fame of Rhodes spread throughout the world.

Identified with the Colossus, one of the wonders of the ancient world, and the impressive walled monastery of the Knights of St. John, Rhodes is today known by many as the most cosmopolitan resort in the Aegean, if not the world.

ISLAND ORIENTATION: Ever since Julius Caesar vacationed on Rhodes the Italians have coveted the island as a resort. They went a long way when, in the first third of this century, they occupied the island and built new buildings, renovated dilapidated ones, and improved the infrastructure. Today, even with its rampant commercialization and high prices, the beauty of the island shines through.

The best beaches lie on the east coast of the island just above Lindos, on Vlicha Bay, and below Lindos, from Lardos Bay 26 kilometers south to Plimiri. There is little development along this coastline. The greatest concentration of Miami Beach–style monoliths is in the north, around the perimeter of Rhodes town, spreading over an area approximately 15 kilometers long along both east and west coasts. The interior section of Rhodes is mountainous and green, with small villages dotting its rugged terrain.

Rhodes is by far the largest and most varied city on the island, and it makes the best base for sightseeing and beach going. Lindos is a scenic gem, with an ancient acropolis, traditional architecture, and a lovely beach cove. Unfortunately, finding a room in Lindos is quirky at best, so unless you have a reservation, a stay in Rhodes is recommended.

LAYOUT OF RHODES CITY: Rhodes is divided into two sections, the old town, dating from medieval days, and the new town. The **Old Town** is surrounded by the massive walls built by the Knights of St. John and overlooks the commercial harbor. The **New Town** extends into greater Rhodes: it includes resorts farther north and **Mandraki Harbor**, once straddled by the Colossus and now used as a mooring for private yachts and tour boats.

Walking away from Mandraki on Plastira Street, you'll come to **Cyprus Square**, where the **National Bank of Greece** keeps extended hours for exchanging currency (8 a.m. to 2 p.m. and 6 p.m. to 8 p.m. Monday through Friday, to 2 p.m. on Saturday, and 9 a.m. to noon on Sunday). Most of the New Town hotels are clustered around this area. Veer left and continue to the park where the mighty fortress begins. On the left at the intersection of Makarios and Papagou Streets is the **E.O.T.** office (tel. 23-655; open 8 a.m. to 3 p.m. Monday through Friday). You can get advice about the whole island, as well as check on the availability of hotel rooms. There is also a **City of Rhodes Tourist Office,** down the hill at Rimini Square near the taxi stand. Their hours are more substantial—8 a.m. to 8 p.m. Monday through Saturday.

USEFUL INFORMATION: Ferryboat tickets can be purchased from several agencies on Amerikis Street or from the very helpful **Triton Tours** office (tel. 21-690) at 25 Plastira St., near the entrance to the Old Town. **Hydrofoil tickets** for the Alkyonis and Dodecanese Lines operating in the Dodecanese islands can be purchased from most of the travel agencies and hotels in the city. **E.O.T.** publishes a weekly schedule of ferryboat sailings.

The telephone **area code** for the island of Rhodes is 0241. There's a **Market and Price Control Police** (tel. 23-849) in Old Town, open 10 a.m. to midnight to handle any complaints of overcharging, theft, swindles, or other price / goods-related problems. The **Tourist Police** are at (tel. 27-423). . . . The local **American Express** agent is **Rhodos Tours** (tel. 21-010), at 23 Ammohostou St. They're open from 8 a.m. to 1 p.m. and 5 p.m. to 8 p.m. Monday through Saturday.

Olympic Airways tickets are sold at 9 Ierou Lochou St. Phone 25-060 for reservations, or 24-571 for information. There's a duty-free shop at **Rhodes International Airport** (tel. 92-885).

Check with your hotel for the nearest post office and O.T.E. . . . Rhodes has one extremely rare sight: a self-service laundry called the **Lavomatique**, at 28 Oktovriou St., no. 32. It will take four kilos per load at 200 drs ($1.54), the dryer is 100 drs (77¢), and it's open from 7 a.m. to 11 p.m. every day. And there's a **dry cleaners** on Eth. Dodekanission Street. . . . For medical emergencies call **Rhodes General Hospital** (tel. 22-222).

Information on taking **folk dance lessons** can be obtained from the **Old Town Theatre** (tel. 29-085), where Nelly Dimoglu performs, or by writing the **Traditional Dance Center**, 87 Dekelias St., Athens 143, Greece (tel. 25-10-80, in Athens). Classes run from June through the beginning of August, 30 hours per week; each week dances from a different region are studied. There are also shorter classes. Call to check.

For more conservative jocks, try the **Rhodes Tennis Club** (tel. 25-705) in the resort of Elli, or the **Rhodes–Afandau Golf Club** (tel. 51-225), 19 kilometers south from the port. For sailing and yacht info call the **Rodos Yacht Club** (tel. 23-287).

GETTING AROUND: Rhodes is a big enough island to warrant public buses, group shared taxis, a rental car, or an organized bus tour for an around-the-island excursion. Within the city of Rhodes, walking is the best and most pleasurable mode of transport; you'll only need a **taxi** if you're going to splurge at one of the farther-out restaurants or if you're decked out for the Casino and don't want to be seen walking!

There's a tremendous **public bus** system throughout the island; **E.O.T.** publishes a schedule of routes and times. Buses to Lindos and east coast beaches leave from the East Side Bus Station, near the Sound and Light Show Square, several times daily. The fare is 225 drs ($1.73) one way. Buses to Ialyssos, Kamiros, and the airport leave from the West Side Bus Station on Averof Street, behind the market. You can also book city tours by bus from many travel agencies, if you're feeling lazy. There are new one-day boat trips to Lindos, which leave about 9 a.m. from the yacht harbor in Rhodes and return about 6 p.m. (1500 drs or $11.54).

There's a large, well-organized **taxi** stand (tel. 27-666) in front of Old Town, on the harborfront in Rimini Square. There, posted for all to see and agree upon, are the set fares for sightseeing throughout the island. The in-town taxi minimum is 160 drs ($1.23). Since many of the cab drivers speak sightseer English, a few friends can be chauffeured and lectured at a very reasonable cost. Taxis are metered and rather costly on short round-the-city jaunts. You can negotiate cab rentals directly with the drivers.

There are several car-rental companies in each community, and a local travel agent may be able to give you the best price. We had luck with **Suncar Rent A Car** (tel. 27-125), which delivered our mini-Fiat to the hotel from their base in Ixia. There are many rental offices on Octovriou Street, where you can compare prices, but count on spending anywhere from 4900 drs ($37.69) to 5875 drs ($45.19) per day. *Caveat Emptor.* Don't just grab the lowest price; make sure you read the fine print and understand your insurance coverage and deductible!

There are several **tour operators** featuring nature, archeology, shopping, and beach tours of the island. **Triton** (tel. 21-690), at 25 Plastira St., is one of the largest and best agencies; they also offer a wide variety of day and evening cruises.

ACCOMMODATIONS IN RHODES CITY:
Hotels and pensions in the Old Town are cheaper and less sterile than those in modern Rhodes. There's also a special feeling when you walk in the evening hours along the dimly lit medieval streets that is unique to the Old Town. With all of the following recommendations, reservations are suggested and in some cases mandatory. Also, keep in mind that there is no youth hostel in Rhodes, so an often less-than-pristine hostel in the Old Town, or a nearby campsite, will have to serve for the true low-budget traveler in expensive Rhodes.

In the Old Town
By far the most pleasant lodging for the lowest price was the **S. Nikolis Hotel** (tel. 0241/34-561), at 61 Hippodamou St., at the top of the Old Town. This place was our first choice to tell friends about. All rooms are furnished, with private bath and phone and heater (they're open all year); there's a lush garden in the back with an ouzeri, and a marble rooftop terrace that overlooks the Old Town, where you're served breakfast everyday. This kind of comfort comes for 5450 drs ($41.92) for two, a bargain for Rhodes.

The **Hotel Kastro** (tel. 0241/20-446), at 14 Arionos, is the best overall value in the Old Town. Its owner, Vasilis Caragiannos, sculpts benches and friezes in a medieval style and speaks fluent Italian. You'll see his artwork in the garden that adjoins the hotel. Eleven spotless rooms run 4125 drs ($31.73) for two with private bath, 4000 drs ($30.77) without. The taverna next door is occasionally noisy with tourists dancing to electric bouzouki, but it usually closes at 11 p.m.

The 12-room **Pension Steve** (tel. 0241/24-357), named for its multilingual owner and bartender, Steve Kafalas, is another great value for budget-conscious travelers. For 1125 drs ($8.70) per person you get a clean room, Garden of Eden breakfast area, laundry facilities, and a friendly and helpful host. You'll find this vacation package at 60 Omirou St.

One block from the taverna-lined Orfeous Street in a quiet residential neighborhood is the lovely **Hotel La Luna** (tel. 0241/25-856). La Luna has a small, beautiful shaded garden where drinks and breakfast are served, but the highlight is the bathroom: built into this old home is a genuine Turkish bath! All seven double rooms are bathless, yet spacious and bright. Reservations are suggested. La Luna, at 21 Ierokleus, charges 3960 drs ($30.46) for a room for two, Turkish bath, and breakfast.

A stay at the **Nikos Pension** (tel. 0241/23-423), at 45 Atistotelous on the Square of the Jewish Martyrs, will satisfy anyone seeking the warmth and hospitality of staying with a Greek family. Nikos and Eleftheria Dallaris (who hosted Arthur Frommer himself long ago) have created three double rooms and two lovely family rooms (sleeping three to five) from over, around, and under their own quarters in this typical Old Town house. Doubles without bath are 3850 drs ($29.62) and the vaulted-roof family rooms with private bath and separate entrance are 4150 drs ($31.92) for three, plus 500 drs ($3.85) per additional bed. The **Ipapandi** (tel. 0241/22-072), at 15 Pericleous, has nine clean, small rooms for the same price as the Nikos, and is another alternative in the Square of the Jewish Martyrs area.

The **Pension Prekas** (tel. 0241/27-849), opposite Valentino's at 224 Prathitelou St., is a very nice place. Simple, clean, and fresh doubles are 2200 drs ($15.38), and the pension has the plus of being just down the street from Kabo N'Toro, a great inexpensive taverna. Inquire in the store below about the rooms.

Nearby is **Mama's Pension** (tel. 0241/25-359), the addendum to Mike's Taverna next door. Mama's is a young people's pension, with 10 rooms sharing three showers and toilets. However, there are also laundry services, a big plus. A double here, amid Japanese, Italian, German, and Scandinavian (when we were there) sightseers, goes for 2300 drs ($17.69). Mike's Taverna downstairs is a Greek club with a floor show every night from 7 p.m. to midnight, so yes if you keep Greek hours, you'll get some sleep if you stay at Mama's.

At the high end, Mr. Dimitri Paraskevas, who speaks more Italian than English but tries hard in both, runs the comfortable **Hotel Paris,** at 88 Ag. Fanouriou St. (tel. 0241/26-356). Compared with the condition and prices of most Old Town accommodations, the 18-room Paris seems like a bargain. Clean, bright double rooms are 4600 drs ($35.48), including breakfast, with clean, modern toilets and baths downstairs. Eight of the rooms do have private toilets and can be had for 5000 drs ($38.46) per night.

If you arrive at the Paris late at night and there are no vacancies, make a left off Omirou to quiet Ierothotou Street. At no. 42 is the small **Pension Massari** (tel. 0241/22-469). A few of its ten clean rooms overlook a well-lit central courtyard and are the cheeriest ones in the house; doubles are 2250 drs ($17.30).

The **Hotel Sydney** (tel. 0241/25-965), at 41 Apellou St., run by Mr. Savaidis and his wife, remains highly recommended in our Old Town lodgings (so you'd better write or phone ahead for reservations as early as possible). The 18 spacious, wood-paneled doubles are 3875 drs ($29.80), with breakfast an additional

325 drs ($2.50), and are a very good value, with clean, modern bath facilities in each. To find the Hotel Sydney, enter the Old Town through the Mandraki Gate (by the harbor), turn left, and continue past Socratous Street to a large rough lot cleared by bombs dropped in World War II.

The "low end" in the Old Town is certainly colorful. The **Attaleia Hotel** (tel. 0241/23-595) is a wildly decorated 12-bed lodging on the first floor of an old home located on Lachitos Street, the first left past the Auberge de France on the Street of the Knights (there's no more eerily medieval a street than this!). The charming Katerina Koliou speaks not a word of anything but Greek, but she'll try her hardest to spoil you—at 1275 drs ($9.80) a bed that's not bad.

The **Pension Pvekas** (tel. 0241/27-849), at 224 Prathitelou St. (across from Valentino), has nice, clean doubles with private bath for just 2185 drs ($16.80).

In the New Town

Hotels in all categories are more expensive in Rhodes. For the same C-class double that runs 2500 drs ($19.23) to 3000 drs ($23.07) nearly anywhere else in Greece, expect to pay 3500 drs ($26.95) to 5000 drs ($38.50). And watch out for exorbitant breakfasts.

From the usual C-class fare, the **Hotel Astoria** (tel. 0241/27-482), at 39 Vasilis Sofias, in the heart of New Town, is the best. The 38-room, twelve-year-old hotel is so well managed by the lovely Moshis family that it doesn't show any signs of age, and their sincere concern for the welfare of their guests (many of whom are Frommer readers) is truly worth the extra drachmas. The manager-ess, Mary Moshis, is as accommodating a hostess as one could ever hope for. Doubles with a much better-than-usual breakfast (which is buffet all-you-can-eat style, free!) are 8400 drs ($64.61). And the Astoria will give Frommer read-ers 10% off and groups of four or more 25% off! The contemporary **Hotel Irene** (tel. 0241/24-761), no. 9 on tree-lined 25 Martiou Street, has 47 spacious rooms with modern tiled private baths and a cafeteria downstairs. Doubles run about $4.50 less per night (without breakfast) than the Astoria; at least you'll get your money's worth in this expensive neighborhood.

The clean, spacious **Marieta Pension** (tel. 0241/36-396), is a welcome addi-tion to the overpriced New Town hotel pool. Hosts Michael and Marietta Potsos ran the Gold Star Supermarket chain in St. Louis for many years. Now they've returned to Rhodes and run a terrific, home-style eight-room pension in a 50-year-old traditional villa. Huge, high-ceilinged doubles are 3125 drs ($24.03).

Off the street, and quieter than most of the New Town hotels, with lots of homey personality, is the pastel-colored **Hotel Anastasia** (tel. 0241/21-815). George Anghelou and his son Pakys are gracious hosts and will help travelers find a room if none is available at their home. Their 25 bathless rooms are 4160 drs ($32) per night, including a hearty breakfast.

The **Hotel Isabella** (tel. 0241/22-651), at 12 Ammohostou (down the street from Rodos Tours), is a very clean, average hotel where high-season doubles are 5400 drs ($41.50). The pleasant rooms have good-sized balconies that over-look the busy outdoor café underneath. The older **Hotel Moschos** (tel. 0241/24-764) is on Ethel. Dodekannisos Street, about a five-minute walk from Old Town. The 35 double rooms rent for a steep 8500 drs ($65.40); here you're pay-ing for the neighborhood, with its proximity to many shops.

Another choice in this price range is the clean, but aging, C-class **Hotel Tilos** (tel. 0241/24-591), centrally located on Cyprus Square at 46 Makariou.

RESTAURANTS IN RHODES CITY: Maybe it's the sea air or the fragrant flowers everywhere or the Italian heritage, but we found the food in Rhodes to be uniformly well prepared, tasty, and imaginative. Unfortunately, prices vary widely, usually from expensive to outrageous, and restaurateurs continue to swindle tourists by overcharging, underweighing portions, or just not displaying a menu. Unless you're in one of the better restaurants, don't be shy about determining the cost of your meal *before* you consume it. If you have any problems, keep that receipt and head for the Market Police (tel. 23-849).

In the Old Town

The Old Town is crammed with tavernas and restaurants, all hungry for tourist dollars. Hawkers stand in front of eateries and accost passersby by handing out business cards, ushering people in for a look at the kitchen, and finally strong-arming them into sitting down. It's all part of the game. The best way to handle a restaurant bully is to continue walking to one of the restaurants listed below. Lest you think that Old Town restaurants are strictly for tourists, many Rhodians consider this section of town to have some of the best food in the city, particularly for fish.

Our favorite place was found by accident, when we were looking for a pension and got lost. The **Kabo N'Toro Taverna** (tel. 36-181), at the corner of Omilou and Parado Streets, is one of the best restaurants in all of Greece, and one of the smallest too. After starting with the aubergine appetizer, which arrived perfectly prepared and golden, we launched into an individual deep-dish moussaka that completely redefined the term, it was that delicious. We finished with baklava and coffee, but not before Sophie, the chef's wife, had brought us each a liqueur on the house. The tariff was 1500 drs ($11.55), which is amazing for Rhodes. A double thumbs-up for the N'Toro.

The **Plaka Taverna** (tel. 25-812), on the first floor overlooking the lovely fountain at Ippocratous Square, provides one of the Old Town's prettiest settings for a great fish dinner. The friendly maître d', Petros, speaks several languages and thoroughly understands what's what in fresh fish (and he's happy to help you order). The taramosalata is flavorful, a great appe-teaser at 275 drs ($2.10). All the fish is excellently grilled or fried, and Petros' favorite, the red mullet, is truly special. Many customers love to share fish dishes and other special ties that run from 2600 drs ($20) to 5000 drs ($38.50).

Low-cost dining in Old Town is a tricky proposition. Most places are mediocre and expensive. There's a great fast-food—that is, souvlaki stand—at 34 Socrateous St. that has great souvlaki, drinks (soft), and ambience. One of each will cost about 150 drs ($1.15), and Attila Kardiler and his daughter will welcome you to their tiny kingdom.

Nearby, behind Alexis Taverna, is the **Ovelistirio Ouzeri** (tel. 28-916), at 144 Od. Kantarzi. The entire place is outdoors, while a kitchenette-size interior serves as the kitchen and supply closet! The 6 outside tables fill up quickly in the evenings with locals. Only appetizers are served, and they're superb. Each separate appetizer runs about 550 drs ($4.25), and coupled with some beer or ouzo you've got the perfect meal before a night on the town.

Splurge: Alexis Taverna (tel. 29-347), outdoors on Socratous 18, offers some of the best fish and seafood we found in all of Rhodes. Particularly pleasing are the tender mussels steamed in a wine broth and thick grilled swordfish steaks—note that the portions are rather hefty. Although the kitchen side of Alexis is sublime, service is iffy, perhaps because of the constant flow of diners that this small taverna attracts. Before setting out for an evening at Alexis call for reservations. While you're waiting for a table, scan the photos on the walls of Alexis' past guests, including Jackie O., Andreas Popandreou, and Miss Mediterranean of 1985. Expect to pay splurge prices, with a complete dinner for two costing $60.

Casa Castellana (tel. 28-803), located at 35 Aristotelous, is near the Ippocratou Fountain. This wonderfully atmospheric establishment is set in a judge's home built in 1480, during the time of the Knights of St. John. Much of the house was accidentally destroyed during an overly enthusiastic bombing run by the British—they overshot the German boats in the harbor and blew up a section of the Old Town. The house was rebuilt with hand-hewn stone about fourteen years ago, and today it houses an elegant but comfortable garden restaurant. George and Nick Tsimetas are gracious and talented hosts. The food is delicious, featuring a combination of Rhodian specialties and a variety of non-Greek dishes. For a delightful meal, start with *trahanas,* an island village soup, move on to the *stifado,* a fabulous pot au feu–style lamb dish with pearl onions and ripe tomatoes, and finish with a salad. Dinner for two with a bottle of Rhodes's own Ilios wine runs about 6100 drs ($46.93), and it's well worth it. Open for lunch and dinner; reservations suggested.

The **Manolis Dinoris Fish Taverna** (tel. 25-824) is located just inside the front gate to Old Town, at 14A Museum Square. These guys aren't kidding; all they serve is fish, fresh from the owner's boats, and it's the best we found. From mussels, about 1800 drs ($13.85), to sea urchin (1500 drs, or $11.50), everything we had was excellent. Expect dinner for two to be expensive: about 6000 drs ($45), but if you have a craving for a fish splurge, then this is the place.

In the New Town

Near the Hotel Astoria is **Mon Ami** (tel. 21-633), at 23 Dragoumi St., with good food and excellent service, and across from the Hotel Spartalis is the always crowded (or closed) **Hermes Snack Bar**. The latter has some of the lowest prices in the city and is frequented by Greek soldiers (who know the best places for inexpensive meals). Hermes is open from noon to 2:30 p.m. for lunch, and 6:30 p.m. to 10 p.m. for dinner.

Around the corner from the Hotel Astoria at 54 Sof. Venizelou St. is **Donald Burger** (tel. 31-923), ostensibly a fast-food place, but actually much nicer and better. Athanassios Tsironis, the owner, is a character, and he alone is worth a trip to Donald's. If you're looking for an inexpensive salad, burger, fried chicken or schnitzel, come to Donald's. Two can eat here for 500 drs ($3.85) or less. We also found the best omelets on the island here, and it's the perfect place to sit and have coffee.

Splurge: If you're tired of taverna fare, try the more continentally oriented **Roma Restaurant** (tel. 30-044), around the corner from the Astoria Hotel at 62 Sofokli Venizelou St. It runs a bit towards the expensive side, at about 3200 drs ($24.65) for two, but the steak flambé is delicious and hosts Zozo and Nick Iconomopoulos are particularly attentive restaurateurs.

THE CITY'S HISTORY:
When the three ancient Doric cities of Ialissos, Lindos, and Kameros banded together in 408 B.C. to create a new capital, they did so to gain even greater access to the rich trading and shipping routes throughout the Mediterranean and Asia Minor, particularly with Egypt. These cities invested heavily in money and labor to develop the new site. When it was finished, the citizens of each city poured in, populating the new city of Rhodes.

Rhodes rapidly flourished under the Dorians, having inherited and expanded lucrative commercial contacts and cultural traditions. Great temples were erected on the Acropolis and a wide, straight road was built down to the harbor. A remarkably modern code of law was instituted. The Colossus was built, a symbol of Rhodian strength and wealth. Proud, autocratic Rhodians were extremely independent and commercially minded, particularly if it meant preserving relations with a trading partner. Nowhere was this more true than in their steadfast opposition to Athens in every major conflict. During the Persian Wars, Rhodes sided with Persia, and in the prolonged Peloponnesian conflict, Rhodes came to the aid of Sparta.

However, Rhodes's authority declined as Rome, once an ally and trading partner, eventually overran and annexed the island. Cassius, one of the assassins of Caesar, orchestrated the forceful and punishing takeover. Not until the early 14th century was Rhodes to emerge again as a major force. The Order of the Knights of St. John of Jerusalem, retreating from a Crusader battle with the Infidels in the Holy Land, took refuge on Rhodes in 1306 and three years later grabbed control of the island.

For over two centuries Knights from Spain, France, Italy, and England came to join the order, dedicated to returning sacred Jerusalem to the Christian fold. The Knights renovated the huge fortifications over the ancient city and built the inns and castle, the hallmarks of Rhodes. Each "Tongue," or foreign contingent with the monastery, had a headquarters, while the grand master, the life-term leader of the Knights, resided in the palace or castle.

Turkish invaders assaulted the city throughout the residence of the Knights, particularly during the siege by Mehemet II in 1422. By 1522 the Knights' numbers had dwindled to a mere 650, after the furious attacks by Suleyman II's 100,000-man army. The ramparts fell and Suleyman realized his dream of conquering mighty Rhodes.

WHAT TO SEE AND DO IN RHODES CITY: The modern-day city of Rhodes has sights dating from every era of her history that will be of interest to all visitors. (You know, many tourists come to Rhodes just to shop for gold or furs and lap up the sun, and never venture out to sightsee!)

In the Old Town

The best introduction to the walled city is to enter through **Eleftherias (Liberty) Gate,** where you'll come to **Simi Square,** containing ruins of the Temple of Venus. As you cross over the small bridge leading into the square, peek over the right side where a colony of kittens has taken up residence. Some civic-minded Rhodian puts food out, and visitors invariably stop to watch the mini-felines.

The **Temple of Venus,** identified as such by the votive offerings found at the site, is thought to date from the third century B.C. The remains of the temple are next to a parking lot (driving hours are restricted in Old Town), which rather diminishes the impact of the few stones and columns still standing. Nevertheless the ruins are a vivid reminder that a great Hellenistic city once stood within these medieval walls.

Simi Square also is home to a small museum containing finely made Rhodian objects and crafts. It's open Monday, Wednesday, and Friday from 8 a.m. to 1 p.m. Continue through the gate until you reach the Kodak shop (with a precious painted tile of the Madonna above its door), then turn right for the Palace of the Knights.

Street of the Knights: This street (Ippiton, on the maps) is known as the Street of the Knights, and is one of the best preserved and most delightful medieval relics in the world. The 600-meter-long, pebble-paved street was constructed over an ancient pathway which led in a straight line from the Acropolis of Rhodes to the port. In the early 16th century it became the address for most of the inns of each country, which housed Knights who belonged to the Order of St. John. The inns were used as eating clubs and temporary residences for visiting dignitaries, and their façades reflect the different architectural details of their respective countries.

Begin at the lowest point of the hill, at the Spanish house now used by the Commercial Bank of Greece. Next door is the **Inn of the Order of the Tongue of Italy**, built in 1519 (as can be seen in the shield of the order above the door). Then comes the **Palace of the Villiers of the Isle of Adam**, built in 1521, housing the Archeological Service of the Dodecanese. The **Auberge de France** now hosts the French Language Institute. Constructed in 1492, it's one of the most ornate of the inns, with the shield of three lilies (fleur-de-lis), royal crown, and that of the Magister D'Aubusson (the cardinal's hat above four crosses) off-center, over the middle door. Typical of the late Gothic period, the architectural and decorative elements are all somewhat asymmetrical, lending grace to the squat building. Opposite these inns is the side of the **Hospital of the Knights**, now the archeological museum.

The church farther up on the right is **Aghia Triadha** (open 9 a.m. to noon daily), next to the Italian consulate. Above its door are three coats-of-arms: those of France, England, and the pope. Past the arch which spans the street, still on the right, is the **Inn of the Tongue of Provence**, shorter than it once was due to an 1856 explosion. Opposite it on the left is the traditionally Gothic **Inn of the Tongue of Spain**, with vertical columns elongating its façade downhill from the arch.

The Inn of France is open daily till 2 p.m. for a view of the garden and an occasional art show. The other inns are now used as office space or private residences and are closed to the public.

Palace of the Knights: At the crest of the hill, through the grand gates, is the Palace of the Knights (also known as the Palace of the Grand Masters or Magisters), thought to be the original site of the ancient Temple of Helios. The palace was neglected by the Turks (they turned it into a prison), and in 1856 was accidentally blown up, along with the Church of St. John. During the Italian occupation the Fascist government undertook the enormous project of reconstructing the castle. Only the stones on the lower part of the building and walls are original; the rest is the work of 20th-century hands. The palace reflects a happy Gothic style of architecture, with large bright windows flooding the interior with light. Inside, offsetting the dark weighty Renaissance furniture are a collection of pastel-colored Hellenistic, Roman, and early Christian mosaics "borrowed" from Italian excavations on neighboring Kos. The intricately painted urns are Japanese and were presented as gifts from Italy's allies across the Pacific. The palace is open from 8 a.m. to 7 p.m. Monday through Saturday, and 9 a.m. to 6 p.m. on Sunday; closed Tuesday. Admission is 375 drs ($2.90). A photo permit costs an additional 300 drs ($2.30).

The Archeological Museum: Walk back down to the base of the Street of the Knights and then turn to your right. Standing in front of you is the medieval hospital, now housing the **Archeological Museum of Rhodes**, with several exquisite Greek sculptures.

The first floor is lined with tombstones of slain knights from the 15th and 16th centuries, many of which are festooned with extravagant coats-of-arms and wonderfully overblown inscriptions. One of the masterpieces of the collection of ancient works is a funeral stele dating from the fifth century B.C. showing Crito, the grieving daughter of Timarista, embracing her mother for the last time. It's an elegant and expressive example of classic Greek art. Equally stunning is the petite statue of Aphrodite, sculpted 400 years later, but also an extraordinarily beautiful work of the Hellenistic period. The head of Helios, patron diety of the island, was found near the site of the palace in this old city. Metallic rays, representing flashes of brilliant flames from the sun, were attached around the crown.

The museum is open from 8 a.m. to 7 p.m. Monday through Saturday, 9 a.m. to 6 p.m. on Sunday (closed on Tuesday). Admission is 375 drs ($2.90).

Other Sights

The **Mosque of Suleyman** and the public baths are two reminders of the Turkish presence in Old Rhodes. Follow Sokratous Street, away from the harbor; the mosque will be straight ahead near Panetiou Street. You really can't miss it, with its slender minaret and pink-striped Venetian exterior.

The **Municipal Baths** (what the Greeks call the "Turkish baths") are housed in a seventh-century Byzantine structure. They warrant a visit by anyone interested in the vestiges of Turkish culture still found in the Old Town, and are certainly a better deal for hygiene than what most pensions charge for showers. The *hamam* (most locals use the Turkish word for "bath") is located in Arionos Square, between a large old mosque and the Folk Dance Theater. Throughout the day men and women enter their separate entrances and disrobe in the private shuttered cubicles. A walk across the cool marble floors will lead you to the bath area—many domed, round chambers sunlit by tiny glass panes in the roof. Through the steam you'll see people seated around large marble basins, chatting while ladling bowls of water over their heads. The baths cost 100 drs (77¢) except Wednesday and Saturday, when you can wash up for only 50 drs (39¢). The baths are open Monday to Saturday from 5:30 a.m. to 7 p.m., though the ticket sellers warn that Saturday is very crowded with locals. Massages are no longer given; none of the young had trained to carry on this exquisite tradition. Bring your own towel and slippers; shampoo and soap are for sale there.

The old town was also home to the Jewish community, whose origins go back to the days of the ancient Greeks. Much respected as merchants, they lived in the northeast or **Jewish Quarter** of the Old Town. Little survives other than a few homes with Hebrew inscriptions, the Jewish cemetery, and the Square of the Jewish Martyrs (also known as Seahorse Square because of the seahorse fountain). There is a beautiful synagogue, where services are held every Friday night; a small black sign in the square shows the way. This square is dedicated to the thousands of Jews who were rounded up here and sent to their deaths at Auschwitz. If you walk around the residential streets, you'll still see abandoned homes and burnt buildings.

After touring the sites of the old city, a walk around the walls is recommended (the museum operates a twice-weekly tour, on Monday and Saturday at 2:30 p.m., beginning at the palace). The fortification has a series of magnificent gates and towers, and is remarkable as an example of a fully intact medieval structure. Admission is 375 drs ($2.90).

In the New Town

The two major attractions within the confines of the new city are **Mandraki Harbor** and Mount Smith. The harbor is perhaps more famous for the legend of the Colossus than its present use. The **Colossus**, a 90-foot-tall image of Helios, was cast from 304 to 292 B.C., but tumbled down in an earthquake only 66 years after its completion. The shattered giant, one of the seven ancient wonders, lay on the ground for over 800 years before it was hauled away and eventually carried through the Syrian desert by a caravan of 900 camels. It was probably melted down to make weapons. The exact site of the Colossus has never been firmly established. Mythmakers and romantics have placed it on either side of

Mandraki Harbor, where mighty ships from Rhodes and foreign ports could pass under its gigantic legs. Recently a psychic led some divers to the harbor, swearing they'd find big chunks of the Colossus. Large pilings were found, but Cultural Minister, Melina Mercouri angrily denied they were part of the Colossus. Two columns capped by a stag and doe, symbols of Rhodes, mark the supposed location of the Colossus. More serious, and perhaps less imaginative, historians and archeologists place the site farther inland, near the once-standing Church of St. John and Temple of Helios (now the Palace of the Grand Masters). Mandraki has a Venetian-era watchtower and three picture-postcard windmills. Today boats of all varieties dock in Mandraki. Excursion boats to Symi and hydrofoils to Kos, Patmos, and Samos leave from this picturesque port. It's a great area to go for a walk, especially for boat watchers. You'll see everything from tall, regal sailing vessels to super-sleek jet-powered yachts.

Mount Smith sounds like a mighty peak in the Sierras, named after some forgotten, grisly-looking pioneer. This Mount Smith, however, is actually a modest hill named after a proper English admiral. So much for names!

North of the present city is the site of the ancient **Acropolis,** which dates from 408 B.C., which, with Mount Smith, the north shoreline, and the Old Town, once bordered the city. Traces of its north-south main street have been found under the modern New Zealand Street. On top of Mount Smith are remnants of temples dedicated to Athena and Zeus Polieus. Archeologists believe that this very large temple complex was easily visible to ships in the Straits of Marmaris, and therefore all treaties and allegiance documents between Rhodes and her warring neighbors were kept here. Below this are the three tall columns and a pediment which remain from the vast Temple of Apollo.

Below the Acropolis is a long **stadium** built into the side of Sandourli Hill. It was reconstructed by the Italians in the early 1940s, though some of the original tiers from the second century B.C. can be seen. To its left is the totally reconstructed 800-seat theater once used to teach rhetoric (an art for which Rhodes was well known). In the vicinity are the remains of a gymnasium; and above it, near the acropolis, a nymphaeon, where caves and water channels indicate that here river goddesses may have been worshipped.

Modern Rhodes has a number of other diverting attractions. Among them is the **Aquarium**, standing on the northern point of the city, where an amazing variety of Mediterranean marine life is on display. The Aquarium, officially known as the Hydrobiological Institute, is open daily from 9 a.m. to 9 p.m. As you walk along the waterside from the Old Town to the Aquarium, you'll see a complex of Italianate buildings. These massive and forbidding-looking structures, put up by the Italians during the Fascist era, are in the style of a medieval fort. Appropriately, these are government offices. (A post office and theater are also located in this limestone desert.)

Just east of the city, a few kilometers from the center, is **Rodini Park**, a hyacinth-filled garden that's ideal for those who wish to relax from a long day's journey into Knights.

NIGHTLIFE IN RHODES CITY: Outside of Athens, Rhodes has the most active nighttime scene in Greece. From Greek studs cruising the harbor for bombshell Swedish girls on holiday (using such subtle lines as "Hey, where you going?") to the suave and sophisticated rich and near-rich who play high-stakes blackjack in the Casino Grand Hotel, Rhodes by night is brimming with energy.

Discos

Depending on the clientele on any given night, the two hottest dance palaces are **HiWay** (tel. 33-666), at 105 Ialysos Ave., and the **Hippodrome Disco** (tel. 82-537), downtown. Another popular place is **Cosmopolitan** (tel. 26-800), at 6 Kountourioti Square on Paralia Elli. Admission to all three is about 1250 drs, or $9.60 (first drink free); each is more sophisticated than the standard Greek disco, with so many different countries represented. So dress up and get down!

You might want to try some of the music bars in town, which have club-volume music (well, almost) in a more intimate setting. The **White Rock Pub** (tel. 30-639), at Othonos and Amalias Streets, was a local favorite when we were there, as was **5 Stars**, at 6 I. Kazouli.

The party-scene street in the New Town is Iroon Politechniou Street; if you don't want to go home alone, this is the street to stroll through, as is the surrounding neighborhood.

Nightclubs

Rhodes sports a variety of Greek nightclubs, where bouzouki bands strum and pluck and singers croon. The best club is **Copacabana**. The custom here, as in many of the top clubs: when the audience is driven to ecstasy by a heart-wrenching performance, send bunches of flowers and bottles of champagne up to the stage. Finally, when the act accelerates into an absolute orgasmic state, the crowd smashes plates with enthusiasm and spontaneity.

Try **Zorba's Café**, on Iroon Politechniou Street, open from 8 p.m. nightly. Zorba's serves complete prix-fixe dinners from 2000 drs ($15.40) to 4000 drs ($30.75), but you came for the music and show, and that starts at 10 p.m. Live bands and popular Greek singers perform until 2 a.m. **Café Chantant,** at 22 Aristotelous St., is another choice in the Old Town, and though not as rousing as others, its repertoire of pop Greek tunes, bouzouki and rebetika is very popular with locals. Expect to spend 1000 drs ($7.70) each here.

Gambling

Gambling is a popular nighttime activity in Greece. Rumor has it that there's a network of private high-stakes (and illegal) gambling dens scattered throughout the city, much as there is in Iraklion. But for those who want to wager in a less subterranean atmosphere, saunter over to one of Greece's three legal casinos, the **Casino Grand Hotel** (the other ones are in Montparnassus, Athens, and in Corfu), open 8 p.m. to 2 a.m. seven days a week (tel. 24-458 or 25-593). The casino attracts visitors from around the world. If you have visions of Las Vegas or Atlantic City, you'll find this casino on the small side.

Admission is for those 21 years and older only; they'll want to check your passport, so remember to bring it along. Dress nicely (in other words, leave your schleppy jeans behind). Closed shoes and, between November and April, jacket and tie are required. The casino is open all year.

Other Entertainment

For a different type of evening, try one of the many outdoor cafés lining the **harborside**. There's a string of them under the lit arches outside the New Market. You'll have a good time watching the Greeks engage in *kamaki,* the ancient sport of girl chasing ("kamaki," actually, is Poseidon's trident, but you get the idea). At the other end of the harbor is a **cinema**, which often shows American films in English (Greek subtitles).

For entertainment of a strictly adult nature, try walking G. Fanduriou Street in the Old Town. On and around the street you'll find bars, music, and willing company.

The **Sound and Light (Son et Lumière)** presentation in the Old Town (on Alex. Papagou Street) dramatizes the life of a youth admitted into the monastery in 1522, the year before Rhodes's downfall to invading Turks. In contrast to Athens's Acropolis show, the dialogue here is more illuminating, though the lighting is unimaginative. Nevertheless, sitting in the lush formal gardens below the palace on a warm evening can be a pleasant and informative experience, and is heartily recommended to those smitten by the medievalness of Old Town. Nightly performances are scheduled according to season (usually 9 p.m. to 10 p.m.); admission is 225 drs ($1.75).

The **Greek Folk Dance Show,** presented by the **Nelly Dimoglou Dance Company,** is always lively, filled with color, and totally entertaining. Twenty spirited men and women perform dances from many areas of Greece in colorful, often embroidered, flouncy costumes. The five-man band plays an inspired, varied repertoire, certainly more interesting than the amplified bouzouki emanating from the Old Town's new tavernas. The choreography is excellent, the dancers skillful, and even the set (an open square surrounded by two-dimensional Rhodian houses) is effective—a thoroughly recommended evening, even better than Dora Stratou's show in Athens. The Traditional Folk Dance Theater is located off Arionos Square in Old Town. Performances are nightly, except Saturday, at 9 p.m. from April to November. Admission is 1200 drs ($9.25) for adults, 750 drs ($5.77) for students.

LINDOS: Lindos is without question the most beautiful town on the island of Rhodes, an island blessed with a great deal of natural beauty. Unless you've come to spend all your time on the beach or in the Grand Hotel's casino, you'd be foolish to pass up a visit to this special place. Be warned, however, that it is often deluged with tourists; the bus and people jams remind us of L.A. at its worst. Lindos in the afternoon could be your best bet. (Those taking the local bus may have no choice: when we visited, the last bus to Rhodes left at 6 p.m.).

Your first view of Lindos is unforgettable. A dabble of traditional white homes saddles two hills; an incredible acropolis tops the higher hill and sparkling blue water laps at the shores of the sandy half moon beach below. The Archeological Society has control over all development in the village (God bless 'em!), and the homes, shops, and restaurants form the most unified, traditional expression in the Dodecanese. You'll have to leave your transport behind, at the place where the road meets a towering, centuries-old plane tree whose roots are enclosed in a pebble-paved bench. Here, next to an ancient fountain with Arabic script, the old village women in black chatter in the shade, watching the skimpily clad tourists cross back and forth to the beach below. Here also you'll see the tourist information kiosk on your right.

Walk right onto the paved path before you and you'll be swallowed by a village so visually charming that Walt Disney might have created it. Even the peasant blouses, ceramic plates, and disco posters hung along the shopfronts can distract you.

The Acropolis

Continue past the donkey stand and follow the "Acropolis" signs. A visit to the superb remains of the **Castle of the Knights** on a hill above the town will help to orient you. From the east ramparts of the castle you can see the lovely beach at St. Paul's Bay below and more of Rhodes's eastern coastline, where secluded beaches can still be found.

The Acropolis contains the ruins of one of Rhodes's three Dorian towns (settled by Lindos, one of Apollo and Rodon's three grandsons), and within its medieval walls are the impressive remains of the **Sanctuary of Athena**, with its large Doric portico from the fourth century B.C. St. John's Knights refortified the Acropolis with monumental turreted walls and built a small church to St. John inside (though their best deed was to preserve the ancient ruins still standing). Stones and columns are strewn everywhere, and at the base of the stairs leading to their Byzantine church is a wonderful large relief of a sailing ship, whose indented bridge once held a statue of a priest of Poseidon. From the north and east ramparts you'll have the most wonderful views of new Lindos below, where most of the homes date from the 15th century. The Acropolis is open from 8 a.m. to 7 p.m. daily, and 9 a.m. to 6 p.m. on Sunday. Admission is 500 drs ($3.10).

Dug into Mount Krana across the way you can see the caves left by ancient tombs. Then scout out a chaise longue on one of the two beaches encircling the main port to admire the luxury yachts docked at the point. If you want to conserve your energy for picture taking, a 375 drs ($2.90) donkey ride is available at the town's entrance.

Accommodations and Dining

Lindos's only drawback is that it's such an idyllic place to visit that it's almost impossible to live there. In the high season 4,000 resident tourists are joined by 7,000 to 8,000 day-trippers from Rhodes. Since no hotel construction is permitted, almost all of the old homes have been converted into pensions (called "villas" in the brochures) by English charter companies, such as John Morgan Travel and Olympic Holidays. In the peak season, the local **police** have a list of the homes that rent rooms to individuals and will help to place you, though plan to pay $15 to $20 a bed in tiny rooms with shared facilities. If Lindos is booked up, they'll recommend one of the few pensions in other nearby towns. Pefkas, Lardos, or Kalathos are on their own (less picturesque) beaches, and from the inland village of Pilonas you can hike out and down the cliff over lovely Vliha Bay (where you may have noted two awesome, snow white resort complexes).

Tiny Lindos had 58 restaurants and bars in 1987, but if we assume the risks of steering you to some, we'd recommend the **Taverna Antika,** in town. Tables are on a flower-draped patio on the roof, and the large variety of reasonably priced meals is prepared by a Canadian chef with a gift for translating Greek specialties into tasty, familiar fare. On the beach, the huge **Triton Restaurant** would get our nod because it offers free showers and dressing rooms, essential for nonresidents who want to splash in the gorgeous water across the way. It's as overpriced as all the others, but you can eat a decent meal for 845 drs ($6.50) and chalk it off to cabana rental. If you're planning to camp nearby, the Acropolis and Paradise discos are on the beach so head south to Pefkas.

What to See and Do

In Lindos, see and do everything. Shop, stroll through the maze of narrow streets, and look for ancient scripts carved in the wooden door lintels. Hike for miles around the coast, or try painting a watercolor of the vista from the Acropolis. In town there's a beautiful Byzantine Church of the Virgin, **Aghia Panagia,** from 1479. Inside there are intricate frescoes painted by Gregorios of Symi in 1779. The floor is paved *chochlakia,* the Rhodian technique done with pebbles, and here it's a perfect sawtooth pattern of upright black- and-white pebbles, worn smooth over the centuries. An elaborate local wedding took place there during our stay. Such glorious lace and embroidery were brought out for the bride and honored guests that afterward it was impossible to consider any of the comparatively primitive lace things for sale in the shops. Embroidery from Rhodes was coveted even in antiquity; it's said that Alexander the Great wore a grand embroidered robe into battle at Gaugamila. And in Renaissance Europe, the French ladies used to yearn for a bit of Lindos lace.

SIGHTS AROUND THE ISLAND: The island of Rhodes is known for her scenic beauty, and one of the greatest pleasures an around-the-island tour provides is a chance to view some of the varied scenery. The sights described below, with the exception of Kamiros, are not of significant historical or cultural importance. By all means, if you only have a few days on Rhodes, visit the Old Town first and roam through the city (one day), visit Lindos (one day), and if you get bored with relaxing, then try some of these sights.

Ialysos was the staging ground for the four major powers that were to control the island of Rhodes. The ancient ruins and monastery reflect the presence of two of these groups. The Dorians ousted the Phoenicians from Rhodes in the tenth century B.C. (An oracle had predicted that white ravens and fish swimming in wine would be the final signs before the Phoenicians were annihilated. The Dorians, quick to spot opportunity, painted enough birds and threw enough fish into wine jugs so that the Phoenicians left without raising their arms.) Most of the Dorians left Ialysos for other parts of the island; many settled in the new city of Rhodes. During the third to second centuries B.C. the Dorians constructed a **Temple to Athena and Zeus Polius** (similar to those on Mount Smith), whose ruins are still visible, below the monastery. Walking south of the site will lead you to a well-preserved fourth-century B.C. fountain.

When the Knights of St. John invaded the island, they too started from Ialysos, by the Byzantine era a minor town. They built a small, subterranean chapel decorated with frescoes of Jesus and heroic knights. Their little whitewashed church is built right into the hillside above the Doric temple. Over it, the Italians constructed the **Monastery of Filerimos**, which remains a lovely spot to tour. Finally, Suleyman the Magnificent moved into Ialysos (1522) with his army of 100,000 and used it as a base for his eventual takeover of the island.

The site is open from 8:30 a.m. to 4 p.m. weekdays, to 3:30 p.m. on Sunday and holidays. Proper dress is required, and admission is 250 drs ($1.95). Public buses leave from Rhodes frequently for the 20-kilometer ride.

The ruins at **Kamiros** are much more extensive than those at nearby Ialysos, perhaps because this city remained an important outpost after 408 B.C., when the new Rhodes was completed. The site is divided into two segments: the upper porch and the lower valley. The porch served as a place of religious practice and provided the height needed for the city's water supply. Climb up to the top and you'll see two swimming-pool-size aqueducts, their walls still lined with a nonporous coating. The Dorians collected water in these basins, assuring themselves a year-round supply. The small valley contains ruins of Greek homes and streets, as well as the foundations of a large temple. The site is in a good enough state of preservation for you to imagine what life in this ancient Doric city was like over 2,000 years ago. You should think about wearing swimsuits under your clothes: there is a very nice stretch of beach across the street from the site, where the taverna and bus stop are.

The site is open from 8:30 a.m. to 4 p.m. (to 3:30 p.m. on Sunday and holidays.) Admission is 250 drs ($1.95).

Petaloudhes, 36 kilometers from Rhodes, is a popular tourist attraction because of the millions of black-and-white-striped butterflies which have overtaken this verdant valley. When resting quietly on flowering plants or leaves, the butterflies are well camouflaged. Only the screaming of mothers, the wailing of infants, and the Greek disco/rock blaring out of portable radios disturbs them.

Then the sky is filled with a flurry of red, their underbellies exposed as they try to hide from the summer crush. The setting, with its many ponds, bamboo bridges and rock displays, was too precious for us. (Real butterfly hounds should make it a point to stop on Paros, in the Cyclades, to see the only other Petaloudhes in Greece. There you'll find, as the Greeks call it, *psychopiana,* an elevated state of the mind and heart.)

Kalithea is an attractive beach resort 11 kilometers south of Rhodes, on the east coast. Most celebrated for its medicinal hot springs, the government-sponsored bathing facilities are sometimes working, sometimes not. Excursion freaks might enjoy a swim in Kalithea's peaceful bay or a dive in its clear, pure waters.

GETTING THERE: Rhodes may win the prize of being the island with the most transportation options in all of Greece. Do you want to fly? Zip by hydrofoil? Chug by steamer? Lounge on a caïque? Cruise from Turkey? Here are the details.

By Air

Olympic Airways offers several international flights via Athens to Rhodes, from such destinations as Abu Dhabi, Philadelphia, and Stuttgart. Within Greece, there is one flight daily from Iraklion, Crete; five flights daily from Athens; three flights daily from Karpathos; one flight daily from Kos; four flights weekly from Paros; one flight daily from Mykonos; three flights weekly from Santorini. Reservations and ticket information can be obtained from the Olympic Airways Office, 9 Ierou Lohou St. (tel. 24-571 or 24-555). Flights on the small (18-person) island-hopping planes fill quickly, so make reservations as much in advance as possible. The **airport** is 16 kilometers south of Rhodes; buses depart from the Olympic office 90 minutes before flight time for a fare of 150 drs ($1.15). Information can be obtained from Olympic in Athens at 0241/24-571.

By Sea

In 1987 Rhodes was connected to Piraeus by **steamer** (it's a grim 18-hour ride) Tuesday, Wednesday, Thursday, and Saturday and once weekly to Crete. Biweekly **ferries** ply the Dodecanese waters to Symi, Tilos, and Nissiros, while daily ferries service the more popular Kos, Leros, Kalymnos, and Patmos. Once weekly you can take the *Sun Boat* or the *Solphrine* to Limassol, Cyprus, and then on to Beirut and Syria, or the *Odyssea,* which continues from Cyprus to Alexandria, Egypt. Once a week there's a ferry to Santorini, two to Paros in the Cyclades, and one to Samos in the Northeast Aegean group. Twice a week there are boats to Karpathos, Halki, and Kassos, but only once a week to Kastellorizo. Your best bet is to check the E.O.T. office for their printed schedule of weekly departures; they can tell you which travel agents sell which company's tickets.

Both the Alkyonis and Dodecanese **hydrofoil** companies are based in Rhodes and offer the most day trips and scheduled service from this port (see the introduction to this chapter for more information).

There are daily **caïque** excursions to Rhodes from Symi, and several times weekly from Nisiros and Halki. (Yacht hitchhiking is not unheard of for a quick cruise to Turkey. Just stroll along Mandraki Harbor and see what you come up with!)

GETTING TO TURKEY: We're delighted to announce that crossing over to the Turkish port of Marmaris has become a reality on Rhodes. Large, comfortable ferryboats from Turkey return to Marmaris from Rhodes every day except Sunday at about 1 p.m. Tickets (3750 drs, or $28.85, one way) are sold at the ANKA Travel Center (tel. 0241/25-095) at 13 Galias St., about one block from the New Market. Manager Andreas Karayannis works closely with the Albatros Travel Agency in Marmaris, and knows when boats will be early, late, or run twice a day. Passport and fee should be submitted one day in advance of departure; their office is open 8:30 a.m. to 2 p.m. and 5:30 p.m. to 9:30 p.m. daily except Sunday.

2. Kos

Kos is blessed with some of the best beaches in the Dodecanese, and for that reason alone it merits a special visit. Wide stretches of clean, white, fine-sand beaches attract visitors by the droves; fortunately, the island has so many good areas that it's fairly easy to get away from the masses during July and August. Unfortunately, Kos can be a frustrating place if you're not a part of the many low-cost tour groups coming from England, Scandinavia, or Holland. Most of the best hotels, and nearly every hotel on the beach, are locked up from June to early September, with cancellations rare. (Other than a few isolated areas described below, your best bet would be to stay in the main town of Kos and day-trip to sunnier parts.) Groups, a word which changes even the grumpiest Greek into a cheerful soul, are shaping the development of the island in the image of Rhodes. Although Kos isn't yet another Rhodes, the island is gearing up to become a stomping ground for an even-greater number of organized tours.

Since ancient times Kos has been associated with the healing arts and the practice of medicine. Prior to the Dorian settlement of Kos in the 11th century B.C. Koans established a cult dedicated to the worship of Asclepios, the god of healing and medicine. Asclepios was either a son of Apollo (from whom he acquired his knowledge) or a mortal (perhaps the physician of the Argonauts) who was deified because of his great healing power. An Asclepion, a sanctuary dedicated to the god, was built for the sick to make offerings in order to receive a cure. Throughout the centuries Kos produced many notable doctors, but none more renowned than Hippocrates (born 460 B.C.), the so-called Father of Medicine. Hippocrates established the first school of medicine, and a canon of medical ethics that is, to this day, the code of doctors throughout the world.

ORIENTATION: Many first-time visitors prefer to settle in the port town of Kos, explore the rich variety of archeological and historical sights, and sample the capital's lively nightlife. Then, after examining the beaches on bicycle excursions, many move out and find accommodations closer to the golden sand.

GETTING AROUND: Residents of Kos town can easily walk to most sights, and in fact a stroll along the harbor or the busy back streets of the Agora is one of the greatest pleasures offered by the island. Public **bus** service is inexpensive (the highest fare is 200 drs, or $1.55, to far-off Kefalos) but infrequent. Check the posted schedules carefully, especially if you're day-tripping. Buses service all the beach areas, but this is nowhere to get stranded after sunset: a return taxi booked by a local hotel will be very costly. The bus station is around the corner from Olympic Airways, next to Mike & Bill's Restaurant.

A **bicycle** is the preferable mode of transportation for nearby tanning. You can rent them anywhere for 310 drs ($2.38) per day, but remember that the best bikes go early, so get there before 9 a.m. **Mopeds** are great for longer excursions (or for lazier people). For all kinds of wheels try **Moto Kos,** at 8 Kanari St. (tel.

28-458), or the bigger shop at 30 Alexandrou (tel. 23-878). Mopeds rent there for about 1000 drs ($7.70) to 1500 drs ($11.55) per day, depending on size. Vespas rent for about 1850 drs ($14.25) a day, plus insurance. And there's a large supply to choose from. Several companies rent cars and Jeeps—including **Avis** (tel. 24-272) and **Interrent** (tel. 24-070)—but this is a needless extravagance on an island like Kos.

USEFUL INFORMATION: Try to arrive in Kos during the morning, or you might find yourself sleeping in the park or on the beach. Your first stop should be the municipal **Tourism Office** (tel. 24-460) to inquire about available rooms. It is conveniently located right in the middle of Akti Kondourioti, the harbor-side strip, and is open 7:30 a.m. to 9 p.m. Monday through Saturday.

The telephone **area code** for Kos is 0242. . . . **Ferry** tickets can be purchased from any of the portside travel agents. . . . Tickets for the **hydrofoils** are sold through **Ialyssos Tours** (tel. 28-473) at 12 Meg. Alexandrou St., **V. Tours** (tel. 22-340) at 20 Elef. Venizelou St., or next door at **Marilena-Tzina** (tel. 22-251)—both V. Tours and Marilena-Tzina are around the corner from E.O.T. . . . The **Olympic Airways** office (tel. 28-330) is at 12 Vas. Pavlou St. Hours are 7 a.m. to 8 p.m. daily.

There are four **banks** in town, which keep regular banking hours (Monday through Friday from 8 a.m. to 2 p.m.), but in the crowded summer months the **National Bank of Greece** (tel. 22-167, on Riga Ferou, one block from the harbor) will sometimes be open for extended hours: 6 p.m. to 8 p.m. weekday evenings and 9 a.m. to noon on Saturday. Since travel agents will cash traveler's checks for a slightly lower rate, try to cash your checks in town before heading off for a prolonged stay in a (bankless) beachside resort. . . . The **post office** and the **O.T.E.** are located on Elef. Venizelou Street and Vironos Street, respectively, about two blocks from the Agora. . . . For medical assistance contact the **Hippocrates Hospital** (tel. 22-300) on Ippocratou Street, no. 32. . . . At 124 Alikarnassou St. (tel. 28-289) is **Speed-O Cleaning,** open 8 a.m. to 9 p.m. (closed Sunday). It's *the* laundromat in town.

ACCOMMODATIONS: Within the town of Kos there are basically three areas for hotels: Lambi Beach to the west, the central area behind the harbor, and the beach on the east side.

Across the street from popular Lambi Beach is the low-key ten-room **Australia Hotel** (tel. 0242/22-104), at 39 G. Averof. Alex and Xanthipi Hatzimihail, who lived many years in Alice Springs, are its friendly husband-and-wife staff, and the price is right at 3325 drs ($25.60) for two.

Alexis Place (tel. 0242/25-321), at 1 Evripilov St., is a brand-new addition to the Kos scene, and a welcome one. It is located on the left side of town, a five-minute walk from the center. This means that it's quiet at night, no mean feat in Kos. Its 17 rooms are spread over three stories that overlook a marble mezzanine and lounge and an outdoor patio, where breakfast is served. Each room has a bath, balcony, and its own metered telephone, so you can reach out and touch someone. Doubles are 3200 drs ($24.65) and breakfast 325 drs ($2.50).

The 19-room D-class **Dodekanissos** (tel. 0242/22-860) is a spotless and spacious inn that feels like an old house. The rooms have wood-shuttered windows and some have balconies that overlook the harbor (and beyond, to Turkey). Doubles go for 3310 drs ($25.50) with bath. The **Hotel Catherine** (tel. 0242/28-285) has 25 good-sized rooms, all with typical C-class decor (which is to say, hardly any!). Yet its terrific manager is a total Woody Allen addict. Doubles are 4350 drs ($33.45) with shower. For the exact same price but a lot fewer laughs you can get a double at the 70-room **Hotel Maritina** (tel. 0242/23-241). It too is a C-class wonder at 5320 drs ($40.95) for a double, with breakfast an additional 400 drs ($3.10), but it's next door to the best sweetshop in Kos, where breakfast can be a real treat.

The Pension Alexis (tel. 0242/28-798) is an inexpensive 2250 drs ($17.30) dorm-style pension popular with the backpack set.

If all else fails and you need a room, try the **Hotel Anna** (tel. 0242/23-030), a simple, family-run place where doubles are 3500 drs ($26.95) with private facilities.

Near the fortress, on the east side of town at 2 Akti. Miaouli St., a good (though high-priced) selection is the 13-room **Hotel Iviscus** (tel. 0242/22-214). It's an older inn with views of the beach; doubles run 5175 drs ($39.80), including shower. The **Hotel Kamelia** (tel. 0242/28-983), C-class with 22 rooms, is on quiet Artemisias Street, overlooking the park. Doubles go for 4750 drs ($36.55). Just 1½ blocks from the harbor is the **Hotel Costel** (tel. 0242/22-969). It's a newer hotel where double rooms are similarly priced.

In a category all by itself is the huge, splashy, C-class **Hotel Oscar** (tel. 0242/ 28-090). It's so big that it seems like a small village: 192 rooms, three bars, a restaurant, and an enormous swimming pool! It's popular with groups and a number of Frommer readers, so if you're in the mood, the Oscar can be a treat. Miami in Kos . . . why not? Doubles rent for 5560 drs ($42.75) a night.

Kos Camping (tel. 0242/23-275) is 2½ kilometers out of town toward the east, opposite a rocky beach. The sleeping bag charge is 375 drs ($2.88) per night, with tents going for an additional 325 drs ($2.50). Dedicated free-campers, find a secluded beach and put down your sheet or bag, but be warned that it can be damp and cool in the summer and fall evenings, and you may wake up with the infamous Greek chest cold.

DINING AND NIGHTLIFE: The best value restaurant in Kos is the **Olybiada**, commonly known as **Mike & Bill's**. You'll find it by walking to the Olympic Airways office on Pavlou Street and turning right at the corner. The food is fresh, flavorful, sometimes original, and inexpensive. Mike and Bill are both nice guys, and the service is good. You could eat here every night and be happy. Prices run about 900 drs ($6.92) per person for meat dinners—fish is more expensive, of course.

In the long row of harbor eateries, **Limnos** is one of the best and least expensive, an attractive café where a meal for two runs about 2100 drs ($16.15). You'll find it at the end of the harbor, near the minaret and Turkish mosque. Down the block behind the taxi stand is the very pleasant **Romantica**, in about the same price range.

Also good is **Sintrivani Taverna** (tel. 24-073), which features real Greek cooking at reasonable rates, about 2000 drs ($15.40) a couple.

On the east side of town is the **Restaurant Avra** (tel. 24-056), serving high-priced Greek and continental food on a lovely beachside patio. For our money, it's a better place to drink than sup. If it's scampi Taj Mahal, chicken à l'American, or porkchop Mexican that you crave, then head straight to **Restaurant 13** (tel. 22-614), next to the Theoxenia Hotel on Artemisias Street. Although the international entrées are not quite as expensive as Avra, the "13" still has a high tariff.

For those with a sweet tooth, Kos has a great dessert spot. One block from Olympic Airlines (on Vironos Street) is the amazing sweetshop run by **Iannis Svinou**. His desserts are sublime!

Cafés and Bars

For a quick, early-morning coffee before your boat leaves, try the **Coffee Bar,** opposite the daily excursion boat to Kalymnos.

There are two imaginative waterfront cafés worthy of a visit in the afternoon or late night. By the port is **Ka-Iki,** with a polished wood "below-deck" motif and plush-cushioned chairs. The young, single, affluent crowd appears very comfortable in this yachting habitat. A romantic alternative is the pricier, luxurious **Imperial Café.** Here you can lounge under a bougainvillea-draped canopy, hold hands, and sip cocktails to the many moods of live piano accompaniment. A cruise down Fereou Street will put you smack in the middle of "Me-Decade Drive," as the sultry singles' street is known. Here, in the old quarter, is also **The Blue Corner,** *the* gay bar in town.

If you'd like to sample a Greek night out we can recommend the **Aquarius Bouzouki Bar,** the **Kriti Bar,** and **Taverna Sambalas.** They're all reached by walking past the discos on Kanari Street and looking around.

For dancing and late-night revelry, walk over to Lambi Beach to one of Kos's premier discos, **Heaven** (tel. 23-874), at 5 Zouroudi St. Within its muraled walls or under the stars, you can dance the night away. On the same street as Heaven are a number of other choices, including the flashy **Club Kalva.** We suggest you stop at a kiosk and pick up a copy of the magazine *Kos: Where and How* for 300 drs ($2.30), and let your fingers do the walking. Check out the ads and see what appeals, then stroll along the harbor.

WHAT TO SEE AND DO: From the time of the Roman Empire to the Allied victory over the Germans in World War II, Kos was occupied and ruled by foreign forces. Nowhere is the legacy of foreign domination more apparent than in the area of the port and capital city, Kos (also called Hora). The town has a network of Greek and Roman excavations, as well as Byzantine remains, Venetian buildings, a medieval castle, and a Turkish Mosque, all within one or two square kilometers of each other. Only five kilometers northwest of Hora is the Asclepion, the most important archeological site on the island.

Kos's many archeological sites can be seen in one day, but remember: the most interesting places are closed Tuesday, and have very short afternoon hours. You might consider touring the outdoor sites like the Odeon, western excavations, Agora, and plane tree after seeing the Asclepion, Roman villa, castle, and museum.

A Day Tour

The best way to get to all of these sites is by bicycle; if you're hardy (fit for about 12 kilometers of cycling) you can visit everything in a day. Starting from town, take the main road to the intersection of Koritsas, Alexandrou, and Grigoriou Streets, and follow the signs for the Asclepion. You'll pass through the hamlet of **Platani,** also called "Turkish Town," where residents still speak Turkish. It's a great place to stop for an inexpensive snack; you might consider returning for dinner in the quieter evening hours. You'll know you're nearing the Asclepion when you enter an exquisite eucalyptus-lined roadway.

The Asclepion: The Asclepion was excavated in the early part of this century, first by the German archeologist Herzog in 1902, then by a team of Italians. The Italians unearthed the lowest of four levels of the terraced site. The second level is the Propylaia, thought to be where the treatment of the sick actually took place (sulfur springs and a Roman-era bath, on the left, were central to the ancients' idea of exorcising disease). This level of the Asclepion (the largest) was bordered by a Doric portico on three sides, and contained many rooms to house visitors and patients. A number of niches and pedestals were found here, as well as statues and other votive offerings. Don't miss the refreshingly cool drinking fountain next to the stairway; it is Pan who, from his shaded enclave, leaps out at the parched visitor. Continue climbing up the magnificent stairway to the two upper terraces, both containing temples from the Greek and Roman eras.

In the center of the third level is the **Altar of Asclepion** and two temples, the left one dedicated to Apollo and the right to the original Temple of Asclepion. Pilgrims placed their votive offerings (sometimes of enormous value) in the cella of these temples, prior to therapy. The Ionic temple on the left, with the restored columns, dates from the first century B.C., while the Asclepion Temple is from the beginning of the third century B.C.

As you ascend the stairs to the highest level, look back toward Turkey and you'll see Kos's seventh-century B.C. ally, Halikarnassos (present-day Bodrum), part of the Doric Hexapolis uniting Kos, Halikarnassos, and Knidos with the Rhodian cities Lindos, Ialyssos, and Kameros. The fourth story contains the once-monumental second-century B.C. **Temple of Asclepion**. This huge sanctuary, built in the Doric style of contrasting black and white marble, must have been an awe-inspiring sight, visible for miles around.

The Temple of Asclepion is open from 8 a.m. to 7 p.m. daily and 9 a.m. to 6 p.m. on Sunday and holidays. Admission is 300 drs ($2.30), 150 drs ($1.15) for students. If you decide to go by taxi, expect to pay about 200 drs ($1.54) each way.

The Western Excavation: Returning to Kos, veer right on Grigoriou Street and proceed until you reach the site of the Western Excavation, on your left; through the tall trees the Odeon is on your right. The Western Excavation, also known as the ancient Greek and Roman city, connects the site by two third-century B.C. perpendicular roadways. Follow the road leading away from the Odeon until you come to the large reconstructed building on the right; it was originally thought to be a **nymphaeum** (a place where virgins were readied for the fulfillment of their destiny); later research led archeologists to conclude that it was a public toilet! Nevertheless it's a great toilet, with a superb mosaic floor; you'll have to climb up on the right side of the building to peer inside. Across from the toilet is the **Xystro**, a restored colonnade from a gymnasium dating from the Hellenistic era. If you continue walking along the road you'll come to a covered area that houses a lovely second-century A.D. mosaic showing the Judgment of Paris and various Roman deities. The buildings in the center of the site are, like the Xystro, from the third century B.C.; you should climb up to discover the fine marble parquet floor and remarkable mosaics (many of which are covered by a thin layer of sand for protection).

Walk back through the site along the road and make a left to arrive at the second part of the site. The remains here date from the Roman and early Christian eras. The highlight is the splendid mosaic in the **House of Europa** (the first on your left) depicting a lovely, terrified-looking Europa being carted away to Crete by Zeus (in the incarnation of a bull) for his pleasure.

Roman Sites: Cross the modern road and proceed to the **Odeon**, excavated during the Italian occupation of the island in 1929. Many of the sites on the island have exceptional carved marble, and the Roman-era Odeon is no exception. The famous sculpture of Hippocrates (among others) was found in the covered archways at the base of the Odeon.

Continue down the modern road to the restored Roman villa known as **Casa Romana**, adjacent to a Roman bath and a Greek Dionysian temple. Reconstruction of the Roman villa was the work of the Italians who, one can only surmise, were going around the Mediterranean world fixing up ancient edifices to demonstrate the connection between the Great Roman Empire and the newly established Fascist state. It's a fascinating archeological achievement, and presents a unique opportunity to tour a complete Roman villa (open 9 a.m. to 3 p.m.; closed Tuesday). Admission is 300 drs ($2.30).

Hippocrates' Tree: Follow the Odeon road for three blocks and turn left to see the recently relandscaped ruins of the Dionysian temple. Continue down Pavlou Street, and to the right of the nursery on Kazousi Square you'll find the ancient **Agora**, a second-century B.C. market. Walking along the edge of the Agora, toward the harbor, you'll come to Lozia Square. Here you'll find a Turkish mosque and the **plane tree of Hippocrates**, under which he was supposed to have taught his students. The stories about this poor tree have been concocted so as to compare it to the apple tree under which Newton achieved scientific enlightenment. It's extremely unlikely that this tree was alive in the doctor's time, but who knows? Anyway, you can't help feeling for the woefully aged trunk which supports still virile, muscular branches. Fortunately, locals have propped up the meatiest of these with old columns and pedestals.

Castle of the Knights: Walk across the bridge and you'll be at the Castle of the Knights of Rhodes. When entering this impressive fortress, built in the late 14th century and restored by the Grand Masters D'Aubusson and D'Amboise in the 16th, you'll see fragments of statues, columns, pedestals, and other architectural paraphernalia from ancient times. To some it may look like a tag sale of worn-out classical items, but it underscores a ubiquitous phenomenon in Greece: succeeding generations pulled down existing structures to build new edifices that were more appropriate to the time. So it's not surprising that the castle was made in large part from ancient stones. You might spot whole doorways taken from houses located in the ancient city, or a giant slice of pure-white Doric column stuck in the middle of an extension wall.

The design of the castle was considered innovative because of its system of inner and outer walls and the numerous subterranean tunnels and rooms which facilitated covert movement within them. As if that weren't enough, the whole fortress was surrounded by a moat. The views of the harbor and beach from the top of the far wall are unsurpassed (but that's why they built it there in the first place!). Hours are 9 a.m. to 3 p.m. Monday through Saturday, 9:30 a.m. to 2:30 p.m. on Sunday; closed Tuesday. Admission is 250 drs ($1.90) for students.

The Archeological Museum: For those tireless souls who need to see it all in a day, a visit to the archeological museum is the grand finale. The central room contains finely executed second-century A.D. mosaics and sculptures found at the House of Europa. The mosaic (completely intact and in color) depicts the two most famous figures in the Koan pantheon, Asclepios and Hippocrates. The "must see" in this museum's excellent collection of Hellenistic and Roman sculpture is the figure of a man assumed to be Hippocrates. Whatever his identity, the statue is a deeply expressive work, showing the pathos of a man who has taken on the suffering of the world. The museum is open 9 a.m. to 3 p.m. Monday through Saturday, 9:30 a.m. to 2:30 p.m. on Sunday, closed Tuesday. Admission is 250 drs ($1.90).

AROUND THE ISLAND: Although there are many fascinating archeological sites, the reason that most people come to Kos is for its wonderful **beaches**. Here's a quick guide to help you pick the beach that suits you best.

The island lies on a 45° angle; at its tip, the port of Kos faces due northeast to Turkey. The two best **beaches** are between Tigaki and Marmari on the north coast and Norida and Kardamena on the south. Both can be reached by bus; from Kos town the closer northwest coast beaches are a mere hour's bicycle ride away and considerably more convenient.

If you do want to stay on the northwest side of the island, an ideal choice is to go farther south to **Mastihari**, a quiet, isolated village with its own fine beach. Try the 15-room, D-class **Fenareti Hotel** (tel. 0242/51-396), where doubles run 3940 drs ($30.30) per night. As at all the beaches on Kos, camping is illegal at Mastihari. (You really shouldn't let that stop you; people camp all the time—just be discreet.) Mastihari is considered by locals to have the best fish on the island. The unnamed taverna on the far left side of the harbor should prove it.

Although **Tigaki** is typical of the beach towns that deal almost exclusively with groups, you might want to visit anyway, especially from April to May, and in September. The nicest hotel is the C-class **Meni** (tel. 0242/29-217), a modern inn with 28 bright, airy rooms, all with balconies and many with ocean views. Rooms for two are 4900 drs ($37.70) with bath. Near the Meni, but farther from the beach, are five new, clean, reasonable, but very similar, C-class hotels. Try the **Villa Andrius** (tel. 29-282), with its very friendly staff. Rates here are about 3950 drs ($30.40) double. Prices are about the same just down the road at the **Ilios** (tel. 29-411) or the **Sun-Set** (tel. 29-428). Beware: all these hotels are busy with groups in the high season.

On the south side of the island you'll find most of the hotels at Kardamena and in the Kefalos Bay region. The latter is the headquarters for the Dodecanese's own Club Med.

Not to be overlooked are the beaches to the west of the port town, Kos. **Lambi Beach**, a ten-minute walk from town, is usually packed, but that's much better for admiring the wonderfully robust bare-breasted Swedes. You can also take advantage of the many tavernas that line the shore (try the Baltica Restaurant for fresh fish). On the other side of the harbor are the beaches extending all the way down to **Agios Fokas**. These also get crowded, and are lined with the greatest number of beachfront hotels.

GETTING THERE: Kos is served by daily boats to Rhodes, both by ferry and the excursion ship. The four-times-weekly boat to Piraeus calls on Patmos, so you can stay at that lovely isle for a few days before returning to the mainland. Service to Samos takes an exhausting 11 hours going by the once-a-week slow boat. Kos is connected to the other Dodecanese by local excursions, which include day trips to Kalymnos and Leros, as well as frequent service to volcanic Nisiros. As everywhere in Greece, double-check the schedules. Tourist Information in Athens (tel. 171) and the Port Authority (tel. 45-11-311) will confirm Piraeus departures.

There's also regular caïque service to Psarimos, a small island off Tigaki that has excellent swimming and a taverna on the beach.

The best way of getting to Rhodes, Patmos, or Samos for those traveling on a tight schedule (or looking for a thrill) is by **hydrofoil.** These islands are serviced three to five times weekly by the hydrofoil companies. **Olympic Airways** has two to four flights daily to and from Rhodes and Athens and three times weekly to Leros; in the summer they generally add flights according to demand. The airport is in an out-of-the-way village called Andimahia (26 kilometers from town), but Olympic provides bus service leaving their office two hours prior to flight time (fare: 185 drs [$1.45]).

GETTING TO TURKEY: Many visitors to Kos find themselves staring longingly at the Turkish coastline, imagining a journey into exotic Asia Minor. You can turn your dreams into reality via thrice-weekly (Monday, Wednesday, and Friday, at noon) boats to Bodrum, across the sea. Procuring tickets to Turkey will give you a feel for how the two feuding nations manage to tolerate each other. The Greek booking companies offer trips to Turkey; check E.O.T. for the latest in ever-changing information. Boats to Turkey leave from the outer harbor; just arrive at the dock and the locals will point the way. There's a daily boat that arrives from Bodrum at 10 a.m. and leaves Kos at 4 p.m. The one-way fare (including "taxes" and "harbor fees") is 5000 drs ($38.45). You can buy tickets on the boat. Contact the port police regarding any necessary papers, as politically motivated visa regulations and rules change frequently.

3. Patmos

"Dear visitor, the place which you have just entered is sacred."

Thus begins the brochure handed out to all who visit Patmos's Holy Cave of the Apocalypse, the site where St. John the Evangelist wrote the Book of Revelation. Many travel devotees would use the word "sacred" to describe the entire island, for Patmos was the first "holy island" in Greece, thanks to St. John.

From a distance, it's all gray stone: barren rocks, no beaches, ascetic. Patmos appears to be a rough-hewn pedestal for the huge walled fortress of the Monastery of St. John. Rounding Point Hesmeris reveals the hidden port of Skala, cluttered with bars, tavernas, and hotels. There's a Wild West quality about this small fishing port that's heightened by the gregarious locals who will meet your boat. They excitedly wait to collect family, friends, and supplies from every ferry. On isolated Patmos, 12 hours by steamer from Piraeus, four hours by hydrofoil from Rhodes, the stagecoach has arrived.

Thousands of Christians make a pilgrimage to Patmos's religious shrines annually, but the majority arrive on Mediterranean cruise ships and depart the same day. Any traveler seeking peace and quiet, good-hearted, gentle Greek people and a disarmingly sophisticated social scene should stick around. Patmos surprises all who stay long enough for a second look.

HISTORY: Since antiquity the isolated, arid island of Patmos has been considered the "Siberia" of the Mediterranean world. Although many believe that Patmos's inhabited history began with the founding of the Monastery of St. John in 1088, the island was originally colonized by the people of Caria in Asia Minor, who brought with them their cult worship of Artemis. Unexcavated ruins (from the sixth to fourth centuries B.C.) found on Kastelli Hill include the remains of an ancient acropolis, walls, temples to Apollo and Dionysos, and a hippodrome.

Patmos's reputation as a "Siberia" fit only for banishment or exile began in the Hellenistic period. It is said that Orestes, son of Agamemnon and Clytemnestra, took refuge on Patmos after he murdered his mother and her lover to avenge his father's death. Unfortunately, Orestes' lover, Erigone, was the product of his mother's illicit relationship, and the distressed woman brought Orestes to trial when she learned he had murdered her mother. The Erinyes (Three Furies) pursued Orestes throughout the Aegean until he landed on the isolated island of Patmos. Orestes was acquitted by the gods, and after founding a temple dedicated to Artemis, left Patmos to ascend the throne of Argos.

The Romans immortalized the island by sending John the Theologian into exile there in A.D. 96 during the Emperor Domitian's wide-scale persecution of all Christians in the empire.

Archeological evidence suggests that at the time Patmos was an active, if minor, Roman port; many scholars believe that John chose the island as a pleasant retreat for meditation. Saint John (in the Book of Revelations) only makes this reference to his sojourn: "I dwelled in an island which is called Patmos, as to preach the word of God and have faith in the martyrdom suffered by Jesus Christ."

For centuries after Saint John's historic visit, Patmians continued to trade with the mainland port of Miletus (see Chapter XVIII), their link to Asia Minor, and to adhere to the Artemis cult worship practiced in Ephesus. In 313 the Emperor Constantine officially recognized Christianity. Patmos fell into relative obscurity, endured devastating raids through the Islamic period, and was eventually retaken by the Byzantine Empire.

In 1088 a devout monk, Christodoulos, went to Alexius I Comnenus to ask permission to found a monastery dedicated to Saint John on the island. Alexius realized the political favor such a bequest could earn him with the already powerful Christian church. The 1088 Chrysobull (Alexius' imperial decree which is still proudly displayed in the monastery) granted to the monks of Christodoulos "the right to be absolute rulers to all eternity." This Chrysobull (it also exempted Patmos from government taxation or judicial interference and granted the monastery the right to own ships tax free) shaped the future development of the island.

Patmos's autonomous religious community flourished. The centuries of Turkish domination which withered Greek culture elsewhere left Patmos almost untouched. The Monastery of St. John became the finest cultural and theological school in the country, even prospering under the Italian occupation. After World War II Patmos was reunited with the Greek nation.

Today Patmos is one of the few Greek islands that has benefited from tourism without having to sell its soul. The monastery's real estate monopoly ensured slow, careful development of the land. The monks never condoned nude or topless sunbathing; this has kept away the more risqué summer tourists. No military construction was permitted, so there is no commercial airport on the island (many foreign residents use Olympic's private helicopter landing pad in Skala). Ferry service is infrequent, but almost daily Holy Land cruises stop to visit the Cave of the Apocalypse. The revenue produced by day-trip visitors is enough to keep Skala thriving; the less commercial sections of the island are supported by the elite foreign population. The fortuitous combination of historical and social factors has made Patmos a unique, unspoiled island "sacred" to many.

ORIENTATION: Most visitors stay at the port of Skala, where the majority of the island's hotels and rooms are located. From Skala you can walk, cruise, bus, or moped to any of the island's sites and beaches. The hilltop Monastery of St. John dominates the port in much the same way that Mount Olympus dominated the consciousness of those who lived beneath it.

The jumble of whitewashed homes that cling to the fortress-like walls of this medieval monastery comprise Chora (or "City"). Chora has been Patmos's main town since the 11th century, and it's an architectural delight on the order of Lindos, Rhodes. Vacationing Greeks, foreign residents, and self-styled "Friends of Patmos" inhabit Chora's restored medieval dwellings. Their tight hold on any available housing effectively prohibits short-term visitors from staying in Chora, but anyone visiting the island must explore the hilltop village and its monastery, even if only for the day.

SKALA'S LAYOUT: The port of Skala is so small that its development has occurred in a line along the waterfront; rarely are the back lanes two or three deep. To the left (south) of the ferryboat pier is the uphill road running east to Chora, and the coastal road running southwest to Grikou. To the right (north) of the pier are most of the town's restaurants, the town beach, and the coastal route leading to **Kampos.**

If you walk from the ferry north to the well-marked Astoria Hotel, you'll pass the busy heart of town, **Emmanuel Xanthos Square**. In the maddeningly irregular, whitewashed lanes behind the square are some hotels and shops. From the Astoria Hotel north along the waterfront are several small tavernas, hotels, bars, and discos. Behind is the little "neighborhood" of **Nethia**, where the excellent Hotel Australis and some fine rooms to let are located. Ten minutes past Nethia on the path curving up to the right and over the hill is the local beach, **Ormos Meloi.** (The island's other beaches are best reached by caïque from the harbor of Skala.)

GETTING AROUND: The port of Skala is small and compact enough to walk around with pleasure. Outside of Skala, goat paths lead up and over the many untouristed hillsides to wild, unexpected natural beauties. Hiking around the island will also bring you into contact with the lovely Patmian people, whose deep religious beliefs make them even more hospitable than the average welcoming Greek citizen.

Hikers have the advantage of not having to rely on the **public buses**. From the ferryboat pier, the island's bus stop is directly ahead, a little to the left, behind the statue of Emmanuel Zanthos. Buses from Skala to Chora run ten times daily, per the schedule posted next to the stop. We actually enjoyed the 30-minute uphill trek to visit the Monastery of St. John, and proudly rewarded ourselves with a soda as soon as we'd reached level ground. The entire island has only two other bus routes: to the beach at Campos three times daily, and to the beach at Grikou five times daily.

Fortunately for beach bums, local fishermen turn their caïques into **beach shuttles** during the summer season, and offer daily excursions to many of the island's private coves. To check their schedules (posted the night before), walk along the harbor and read the chalkboard signs hanging off the stern of every caïque. Before 9 a.m., if there aren't enough customers to warrant the trip, many sailors will adjust their itinerary to tourist demands. We always rode with the Tri Adelphia ("Three Brothers"), who charged 500 drs ($3.85) each way to Psiliamos or Lampi and 125 drs (95¢) to Kampos each way. If you want to get a group together, some of the fishermen will rent out their smaller powerboats, which hold four people, for 6500 drs ($50) per day.

Many tourists enjoy renting **mopeds** to sightsee because of the greater freedom they afford. Those roads on Patmos which are paved are not properly maintained, and moped riding can be risky. We'd recommend mopeds only for experienced riders who are confident about driving on gravel-filled, winding, hilly roads. Skala's moped dealer is **Apostolidis** (tel. 0247/31-541), located at the south end of the harbor near the fishing boats. He charges 1250 drs ($9.60) per day for single mopeds; 1500 drs ($11.55) for a two-seater.

There are some **taxis** available in Xanthos Square, next to the post office. However, they're usually grabbed up by the repeat visitors or commuting residents who rush off the ferry before you. If you're interested in booking one for nighttime dining in Chora, for example, walk over in the afternoon, negotiate, and confirm your departure time. Fares to Chora run 750 drs ($5.80), depending on the time of day, season, and driver.

USEFUL INFORMATION: There is no official tourist office on Patmos, but

Skala's two travel agents are both helpful. They are the **Astoria Shipping and Tourist Agency** (tel. 0247/31-205), in the harborside Astoria Hotel, and the **Apollon Agency** (tel. 0247/31-356), opposite the ferry pier, which is run by Yiannis Stratas and his sharp English wife, June.

The **Town Police** can be found in Xanthos Square; there is no Tourist Police. . . . The **area code** for Patmos is 0247. . . . **Ferry and hydrofoil tickets** can be purchased at the two travel offices mentioned above. . . . The Apollon Agency handles **Olympic Airways** bookings; though there is no airport on Patmos, many travelers prefer to cut their travel time by flying back to Athens from Rhodes or Kos.

The **National Bank of Greece** (open from 8 a.m. to 2 p.m., and 6 p.m. to 8 p.m. Monday through Friday) is located on Xanthos Square. Opposite it is the **Bahaz General Store,** which cashes checks throughout its working hours (usually until 8 p.m., including Saturday). . . . The **post office** is on Xanthos Square. . . . The **O.T.E.** is on the lane behind the Ariston Café and their hours are 7:30 a.m. to 10 p.m. Monday through Saturday (closed Sunday).

The cheerful Antonio Gazis runs the **White Swan Laundry/Dry Cleaning** shop (tel. 37-779) a block behind the National Bank. . . . Patmosophiles will want to read resident Tom Stone's amusing account, *Patmos,* published by Lycabettus Press. It's available, along with foreign newspapers, at **Patinos** on the square. . . . There's no official **medical assistance** on Patmos, but in an emergency you can call a doctor at tel. 31-577, or check with the proprietor of your hotel or one of the travel offices.

Patmos has an unusually long tourist season, thanks to the moderating sea breezes which sweep across the island year round. If you're lucky enough to be in Greece at Easter (late April or early May), try to book a room so that you can witness the **Nipteras**. It's a reenactment of the Last Supper that's only performed on Patmos, at the Monastery of St. John, and in Jerusalem. The festivities and holy days extend from the Monday before Easter to the following Tuesday, when there's great feasting and dancing in Xanthos Square.

ACCOMMODATIONS: There are not many hotels in Skala, so the best ones require reservations two to three months in advance if you're planning to visit Patmos at Easter or in July or August. Last-minute planners should have no trouble finding a room to let in the surrounding hillside; there also may be vacancies in the larger group-booked hotels. If you're interested in renting a kitchenette apartment or villa on a long-term lease, contact the **Apollon Agency** (tel. 0247/31-356) for more information.

Hotels

Our favorite budget hotel in Skala is the **Australis** (tel. 0247/31-576), in Nethia, just a ten-minute walk north of the ferryboat pier. Fokas Michalis runs a 17-room hotel in a blooming hillside oasis that feels like a high-priced villa. He didn't learn to garden during his many years in Australia, but he's managed to cover every surface of the hotel with bright bougainvilleas, geraniums, carnations, pansies, and roses. This jungle paradise stands out in stark contrast to the barren, rocky land around it. The Australis's pleasant communal porch overlooks the harbor. It's very beautiful; make this your first stop. Michalis charges 3725 drs ($28.65) for a double, 4310 drs ($33.15) for a triple, year round, with breakfast an additional 265 drs ($2).

Excellent in its own way, but slightly more expensive, is the classic **Patmion Hotel** (tel. 0247/31-686). This elegant, Spanish-Mediterranean-style villa on the harbor offers 21 spacious rooms, many with balconies and a priceless harbor view. Doubles with bath are 3120 drs ($23.95), but this classy hotel also has four doubles without bath for only 2075 drs ($16). For many, the old-world elegance, service, and quality will warrant the tariff.

The swank **Hotel Skala** (tel. 0247/31-343), just behind the Patmion on the waterfront, won't be worth the price tag—6085 drs ($46.85), including breakfast, for a double—to anyone seeking a harbor view, but it's new, has wall-to-wall carpeting, piped-in Muzak, and tiger-print bedspreads in its 48 huge rooms. Balconies open out onto a pleasant sun terrace. An illuminated archway on the harborfront leads prospective clients to the hotel. (Both the Patmion and the Skala are open year round.)

Nearby is the **Hotel Chris** (tel. 0247/31-403), which also commands a great view of the harbor. The brown-shuttered, Patmion-style Chris has 26 modern, clean rooms with balconies. Breakfast—at an additional 375 drs ($2.89) per person—is served on a patio in front of the hotel, which provides guests with equally good views of morning activity on land or sea. Double rooms are 3765 drs ($28.98).

The mottled yellow-brick façade of the **Hotel Astoria** (tel. 0247/31-205) makes it a handy landmark on the waterfront. This pleasant, 14-room C-class establishment is run by Minas Kamaratos, who also mans the Astoria Travel Office in the lobby. The Astoria has an elevator, and all the doubles have private, checkerboard-tiled bathrooms. Make sure to request one of the six rooms with a harbor view; high-season rates are 3115 drs ($23.96) per double room.

The older **Hotel Rex** (tel. 0247/31-242) is located near the harbor one street over from Xanthos Square. There are 16 clean, bright rooms for a variety of prices: the Rex offers singles without bath for 1355 drs ($10.42), with bath for 2770 drs ($21.30); doubles with bath for 2750 drs ($21.15) and triples for 3575 drs ($27.50). Upper-floor rooms share a large sun terrace, and guests can enjoy the three very musical parakeets who reside in the lobby.

The family-run **Hotel Castro** (tel. 0247/31-554) is located at 21 Nefetis Petralona, about 3 blocks behind the O.T.E. office and about ten minutes from the center of Skala. The Castro's pretty blonde proprietress, Katy Garoufali, takes bookings from Patmos or through an Athens office (tel. 34-70-390). The C-class rating accorded the Castro enables Katy to charge only 3825 drs ($29.42) for the large double rooms, with lively black-and-white checked floors. Close by is the **Hotel Castelli** (tel. 0247/31-665), much in the same style, where a double runs 3700 drs ($28.45).

Nearby is another D-class choice, the **Hotel Diethnes** (tel. 0247/31-357). The Diethnes has 15 spare rooms with balconies overlooking the town; high-season doubles with bath are 2500 drs ($19.17). The Rex, Castro, and Diethnes are open all year.

Rooms-to-Let

Most private homes are off the beaten track, and residents who rent rooms usually don't have telephones. Therefore women often send their children (or come themselves) to meet the ferryboats in search of clients. Don't be afraid to bargain for room rates if you receive a number of offers. Ironically, the best location in Skala is occupied by one of the cheapest hostels, **Theakaki Rooms**, a small whitewashed, green-shuttered pension next door to the Patmion Hotel. There's nothing but Greek spoken here, and if you call ahead (tel. 0247/31-539) you may be able to get a room in Mrs. Theakaki's casual, super-homey pension. The tall old metal-frame beds in her six-room home go for 1200 drs ($7.69) each. Try to get one in the balconied front rooms with harbor views. Hot showers, when available, cost 275 drs ($2.12).

There are few rooms for rent in the Chora, but if you can get one, you should. The man to check with is **John Apostolidis** (tel. 0247/31-675), who has connections and can usually find you a very nice double room for 2250 drs ($17.30), a bargain.

RESTAURANTS: The presence of many foreign residents and long-term tourists tends to create a small-town, "everyone-knows-everyone" ambience in Skala. Most of the locally run restaurants and tavernas cater daily to repeat customers, and we found the food always moderately priced, well prepared, and graciously served.

Casual Fare

Start your day at either the **Plaza Kaffeterion,** off Xarchos Square across from the post office, or the **Seagull Cafe,** which borders the Astoria Hotel (look for the blue-tick awning). The Plaza is more local in feel, with a cappuccino and "danish" going for just 160 drs ($1.25). The Seagull is bigger, with outdoor seating to boot. Breakfast here (from American to French) will run you 550 drs ($4.25). The Seagull is right on the paralia.

Aristo's Acrogiali, on the town beach, is popular for its wholesome, inexpensive food, especially the excellent fish dishes (from 850 drs [$6.55] to 1400 drs [$10.78] per person). Their location can't be beat; although it's a small family-run operation, Aristo has a few tables outdoors on the beach, a few on the sidewalk in front of their tiny restaurant, and some upstairs on a vine-covered terrace which hangs over the street. A new favorite for seafood, next door to the Patmion Hotel, is the aptly named **Fish Taverna** (tel. 31-539). Begin with their special tsadziki, have grilled barbounia, wine and salad, and it's about 850 drs ($6.55) a head. The Fish Taverna, supplied daily by local fishermen, is a great place for a Saturday night fish fry.

Sweet tooths can be satisfied at the **Edelweiss Pâtisserie,** opposite the booking office for the ferries. The Edelweiss advertises "fresh yogurt with blood orange," which prevented Kyle from entering for quite a while. Duty forced us to inquire about the *kourambiedes* (a half-moon-shaped butter cookie covered with powdered sugar) in the window. They're surprisingly delicate (only 40 drs each), but the real specialty here is *poungi,* made by the handsome young shopkeeper's mother. This ancient family recipe starts with the fragile kourambiedes dough, which is then filled with a mixture of vermicelli, nuts, and honey. Each poungi takes nearly 15 minutes to make and they're a sinfully delicious bargain at 155 drs ($1.20) each.

Just as day café crowds favor the **Café-Bar Nautis,** sunset idlers seem to favor the Arion. The elegant old **Arion Café,** on the port, has high ceilings and exposed brick walls. Large old fans stir up a breeze above the long broad polished-wood bar. Ornate iron medieval-style wall sconces produce the intimate lighting. Drinks, snacks, and coffee are served outdoors by the pier.

If it's a terrific bakery you're looking for, follow the yellow and red signs on Xarchos Square until you find yourself in the back of Patmos standing in front of the **Koumanis Bakery** (tel. 31-625), Patmos's premier bakery.

Up in the Chora we found a café where locals go to have coffee in the morning and an ouzo in the afternoon after work. We loved it because the proprietor is a musician who doubles on violin and *santouri* (a hammered dulcimer, sort of) and who has photos and mementos from turn-of-the-century Ohio, where his father was a shoemaker (his brother is the foremost shoemaker in the Dodecanese today). Vassilis Simantiri is the owner of the **Pantheon Café,** which is perched halfway between the entrance to the Chora and the Monastery of St. John. Stop in and say hello; Vassilis speaks no English, but he loves to meet people and show them his instruments while he cooks up an espresso. His brother, Antonio, is located in the heart of the Chora (ask locals "Where is Antonio

Simantiri?" and they'll point you in the right direction) and is the "sandal-maker to the stars" in Patmos. A pair of hand-made sandals as soft as butter will cost you 1875 drs ($14.50).

More Formal Dining

It shouldn't surprise you that Patmos features one of the best Greek restaurants in the entire country. The **Patmian House** (tel. 31-180), set in a restored 17th-century dwelling on the back lanes of Chora, has been glowingly reviewed in *Vogue,* the *Athenian,* and several German periodicals. This elegant eatery was opened nine years ago by Victor Gouras, a Patmian gourmand who worked during winters at New York's Tavern on the Green. Young Nick Gouras (Victor's son) takes the summer off from his job at New York's Russian Tea Room to return to Patmos and help out in his family's restaurant. From several superb hors d'oeuvres we recommend the creamy taramosalata, gigantes (giant beans) in garlic sauce, or the tasty zucchini fritters. The varied selection of entrées includes three chicken specialties: chicken parmigiana, lemon chicken, and chicken marsala, unusual in a country where chicken is rarely used in cooking. Ask Nick if there are any steaks or meat specialties of the day. The Patmian House is open daily for dinner (7 p.m. to midnight); reservations suggested. A deluxe three-course meal will cost 900 drs ($6.92) to 1500 drs ($11.55) per person, a bargain for such excellent, gourmet Greek fare.

One of Skala's nicer restaurants is **Grigori's Grill** (tel. 31-515), located on the harbor opposite the ferryboat pier. From sunset till the wee hours, Grigori's is the center of Patmian chic. We recommend any of the grilled meat dishes: well-cooked veal cutlets are 600 drs ($4.60); their large, tender lamb chops are 650 drs ($5). Grigori's has an extensive menu with vegetarian Greek specialties as well. The grill is open only for dinner (from 6 p.m. to midnight, daily).

A new combination club/creperie opened recently in Skala called **Rabella** (tel. 31-415), on Main Street just up from the Meltemi Disco. Rabella's will instantly remind you of a chic New York single's bar, with banquette seating, white stucco walls, and blue trim. From 2 p.m. to 7 p.m. they serve very good crepes, from various meats to sweets, ranging from 375 drs ($2.88) to 500 drs ($3.85). At night crepes give way to tapes, and Rabella becomes the hottest singles scope-and-attract scene on the island. Here's where you'll find the jet set.

Another night-on-the-town choice is the **Sea View Barbecue**. This restaurant warrants a mention more for its romantic ambience than for its cuisine. The outdoor café tables are attached to an elegant, traditional home that's set back from the town beach. From Skala's waterfront path, patrons walk through a flowering vegetable garden to reach the dining area. All around, soothing Greek music plays. The Sea View's barbecued chicken is delicious, at 640 drs ($4.92), and when accompanied by a tasty Greek salad makes a very healthful, inexpensive meal. The Sea View Barbecue is open only for dinner, from 6:30 p.m. on, daily.

Another nice place that is inexpensive and tasty is the **Pantelis Restaurant** (tel. 31-230), right behind the Astoria Hotel. Try the calamari: tender, lightly fried, and scrumptious, for 400 drs ($3.10). The Pantelis is also open for lunch, and it has 3 small tables outside, though it's cooler to eat in.

AROUND THE ISLAND: Other than the towns of Skala and Chora, most of Patmos's limited development has centered around the beach areas. Short-term visitors should allow a day to visit Chora and the Monastery of St. John; after that, the island's exquisite beaches can be explored by caïque excursions from Skala.

Chora

Exploring Chora can be an exercise in futility. The narrow, twisted lanes which encircle the monastery are lined with two-meter-tall white stucco walls which surround the private residences of Chora's elite international set. Even during the siesta the ornately carved brown wood doors rarely open to reveal the elegant, stylish homes within. The town is a mini-mecca for the wealthy who scorn the splashier resort islands: actors, writers, publishers, diplomats, tycoons, and their friends. Chora is like Bar Harbor, Newport, Malibu, and Positano; generations may pass, but the houses never change hands. Buyers interested in available villas are carefully (and silently) screened by the current residents. However, Chora's exclusivity rarely affects the day visitor. The town's streets seem refreshingly deserted, even in the high season.

In the square created by several converging twisted lanes are three small restaurants. The **Chora Restaurant** is one lunchtime choice situated just below the monastery entrance. Past the baker on the left is the popular **Vagelis Restaurant** (at no. 390), with a small garden behind it. Also on Theofakosta Square is the **Olympia** (at no. 396), less frequented because of its limited menu. All are adequate for a midday break. The only other commercial establishments in Chora are the shops on the monastery lane, which sell gold, silver, and tin votive ornaments. Make sure to buy one before you enter the monastery if you have a particular ailment.

The wealthy who couldn't get into Chora have begun building villas "down below," near the beaches. Their presence and their anonymity add the spice and mystique that make Patmos such a special island. (A day trip to the beach can be a fascinating social study!)

Beaches

Patmos has some excellent beaches. Die-hard beach bums can always enjoy the sandy patch just 500 meters from the ferryboat pier. However, the **town beach** offers no privacy; it's usually filled with Greek families who don't mind sunbathing in full view of the clothed tourists who stroll along the waterfront promenade.

The nearby **Meloi Beach**, just a 15-minute walk from Skala, is a little more secluded. At Meloi, virile young Greek men who've come with their tourist girlfriends are likely to be playing cassette tapes of the latest European hits. This crescent-shaped stretch of fine brown sand extends into the sea, ensuring a very pleasant dip for sensitive feet. "Nudity Is Forbidden" signs are prominently posted, and the locals often complain when this rule is ignored. Meloi has a large canopied taverna, where windsurfers can be rented (850 drs, or $6.50 per hour) and a smaller one where a young girl does all the home-style cooking herself. Scattered in the nearby fields are some rooms to let and the well-situated, popular **Meloi Camping**. Because accommodations are difficult to obtain in downtown Skala during the busy months, this convenient campground becomes very crowded in the high season.

It takes a moped, car, or willing taxi to reach **Agriolivado Beach**, about three kilometers north of Skala. Along this unspoiled, tranquil sandy cove you'll find one taverna and some prebooked efficiency apartments that are very economical for long-term rental. Before the season, you can try **Petrus Apartments** (tel. 0247/31-133) for short-term availability.

The next beach cove north of Agriolivado is **Ormos Kampos**, popular with families. Its pale sand is shaded by trees and the water is shallow far enough out to make it ideal for children. Kampos village has about 400 residents and is quite lively in the high season. There are very few rooms to let because most overnighters rent homes long term, although a local travel agent can find a room if any of the villas become vacant. (Often a short "sublease" is proportionately more of a bargain than what the leaseholder would pay.) **George's** is a popular restaurant on the beach that's not expensive; there are also two small tavernas on Kampos Square. Two buses ply the Kampos–Skala road daily, but most residents hop the frequent, inexpensive beach shuttles for the 20-minute ride.

Still farther north is **Ormos Lampis.** Daily boat trips can be made to the beach at Lampi, famous for wonderful striped and patterned smooth stones. The deep earth tones of cream, gray, lilac, and coral are particularly striking when wet, and a small bottle filled with Patmian seawater and Lampi stones makes an unforgettable souvenir of your stay. The cruise along Cape Geranos takes about one hour from Skala, and the round-trip fare is 1000 drs ($7.70). There are rooms to let by the beach at Lampi and a few tavernas for light snacks.

Four kilometers south of Skala is the resort village of **Grikou,** where many foreigners have built villas for their summer holidays. As you descend from the coast road toward the shores of Grikou Bay, you'll see the islet of Nea Traonisi, its hills framing the large boulder that sits in the middle of the bay. This is called Kalikatsou, or "cormorant," by the Greeks, because of its appearance at the tip of a narrow, curved spit of land. The natural caves within this rock formation have been enhanced by human hands, leading Patmian author Tom Stone to speculate that monks might have inhabited these caves from the fourth to the seventh centuries, much as they did in Turkey's Cappadocia region.

Grikou is not yet as self-contained as Kampos; you may prefer to make day trips to the beach there and spend evenings in Skala. There's a sand beach right in town, and one in the cove just south at Petras. The **Xenia Hotel** (tel. 0247/31-219) is at the north end of the cove. The 35 spacious B-class doubles, many overlooking the bay, rent for 5650 drs ($43.45). The **Panorama Apartments** (tel. 0247/31-209), two- and three-person units with kitchenettes, are often fully booked in July and August—at 4750 drs ($36.53) for a double, 7580 drs ($58.30) for a triple—but can accommodate guests for short stays in the low season. Try their popular restaurant downstairs.

There's a very nice new addition to the lodging scene in Grikou, the **Hotel Artemis** (tel. 0247/31-555), on Grikou Bay. Built in traditional style, the Artemis is furnished simply with local handcrafts, which lends an air of enchantment to the place. All rooms have balconies facing the water and a phone, and there's a TV room downstairs adjoining a lush garden, where breakfast is served. La dolce vita in Grikou costs 4100 drs ($31.55) for two.

The owners of Chora's chic Patmian House Restaurant maintain eight villas, the **Patmian House Apartments** (tel. 0247/31-180). Rents vary according to season; in the high season it's 4850 drs ($37.30) for two per day. Each efficiency apartment has its own cooking facilities and is furnished in a spartan, easy-to-maintain beachhouse manner.

Bambakos Taverna, a popular local eatery, on the rise as you approach the second cove, rents simple inexpensive rooms; see Flores for bookings. Like Bambakos, the **Stamatis Taverna**, closer to the shore, is known for its authentic, inexpensive cuisine. Grikou can be reached by infrequent buses or by caïque from Skala, although most residents rely on mopeds or personal cars.

On the other side of the island's southern point is what's universally acclaimed as Patmos's best beach—the kilometer stretch of **Psili Amos** (Greek for "fine sand"). This protected cove, tucked in the craggy south coast, provides a special bathing experience. The water at Psili Amos has waves, truly a rarity in the Aegean! Because it's isolated and only accessible by caïque—day trips from Skala are 625 drs ($4.80) round trip—nude bathing is as condoned as it ever will be on this orthodox island.

WHAT TO SEE: The island's two great Christian monuments, the Monastery of St. John and the Holy Cave of the Apocalypse, are of such historical and artistic significance that they should be seen by everyone visiting Patmos.

The Monastery of St. John

The Monastery of St. John was founded in 1088 by the monk Christodoulos. Tall gray stone walls were constructed to protect the hilltop retreat from pirate raids, giving it the appearance of a solid medieval fortress.

Upon crossing the monastery's main threshold, the visitor is transported by the stillness and ethereal calm into a private world. The building materials contribute to the silence; the pebble-paved courtyard is enclosed by broad whitewashed arches. Supported by heavy gray brick columns, the large covered cistern containing holy water in the center of the courtyard (an ideal bench for contemplation) held wine in the days when 200 monks inhabited Chora. Except on major Greek Orthodox holidays, the monastery's religious activities are not as impressive as its museum-quality collection of manuscripts, religious icons, Byzantine art, and frescoes.

The **Outer Narthax**, to the left of the entrances, is richly painted with 17th-century frescoes depicting traditional tales from the life of St. John (a flashlight is needed for a thorough examination of the dark chapel). Tour guides will lead you through the maze of cells, storerooms, chapels, and stairs for 125 drs (96¢) per person in groups of eight or more. Their anecdotes of monastic life and vivid descriptions of the many parts of the monastery which are now off-limits make a tour worthwhile.

For centuries the remarkable collection of more than 13,000 documents in the monastery **library** has drawn scholars to Patmos. The earliest text is a sixth-century fragment from the Gospel of Saint Mark; on Patmos there are 33 leaves of this priceless work, which has been divided among museums in Leningrad, Athens, Britain, the Vatican, and Vienna. The 1088 Chrysobull issued by Alexius I Comnenus granting the monastery sovereignty over Patmos is displayed, as well as an eighth-century text of Job and Codex 33, the tenth-century illustrated manuscript of the discourses of Saint Gregory the Theologian. In the **Treasury** are jewels and icons donated by Catherine II, Peter the Great of Russia, and other dignitaries and the fourth-century B.C. marble tablet describing Orestes' visit to Patmos.

After 200 years of tourist abuse (many valuable texts were taken back to Europe by visiting scholars) the library and original Treasury have been closed to view. For 175 drs ($1.35) one may visit the "Treasury-Library-Museum", where a sampling of the rich vestments, icons, and religious artifacts belonging to the monastery are displayed.

The roof of the monastery is closed now because too many tourists chose to linger and sunbathe there. From its height one could see a spectacular panorama of the Aegean, which included the islands of Ikaria and Samos to the north, Leros, and beyond it, Kalymnos, to the southeast Amorgos, and in the far southwest Santorini.

In printed literature the monastery requests that you "Respect the Holy Places, our traditions and our morals by your dignified attire, serious appearance, and your general behavior." Visiting hours are 8 a.m. to noon and 3 p.m. to 6 p.m. daily, except Wednesday and Thursday when they are only open from 8 a.m. to noon.

The Holy Cave of the Apocalypse

The Monastery of the Apocalypse was built at the site of the grotto where Saint John received his revelation from God. Located a five-minute walk below the hilltop monastery, it can be easily visited on the pleasant, vista-filled descent to Skala.

A rousing brochure written by Archimandrite Koutsanellos, Superior of the cave, provides an excellent description of the religious significance of each niche in the rocks, and the many icons in the cave. The little whitewashed monastery that surrounds the cave was the 18th-century home of the Patmias School, an institute of higher learning unparalleled during the Turkish occupation. A large modern structure built after World War II to accommodate the school and a theological seminary dominates the barren hillside above Skala.

As with the Monastery of St. John, appropriate attire is required at the Cave of the Apocalypse (appropriate means no slacks for women, no shorts for anyone). This dress code applies when visiting any of the island's religious sites, including the several other monasteries and nunneries, which have fine frescoes and religious icons. Those with an interest in Patmos's significance in Christian history will be fascinated by Otto Meinardus' *St. John of Patmos and the Seven Churches of the Apocalypse,* published by Lycabettus Press.

Local Landmarks

If you stay on Patmos long enough, you'll begin to hear about the hundreds of "must see" sites cherished by the locals. We'll only explain two sites that you're likely to encounter.

A little way out in the harbor, opposite the Patmion Hotel, is a large red buoy that marks "**Devil's Rock.**" This submerged plateau is marked not only as a warning to sailors—it keeps sinners on their toes! For here, nearly 2,000 years ago, the Devil used to preach to local citizens by communing with the spirits of their ancestors. The alternate telling of this folktale suggests that the Devil was Kynops, a local magician sent by priests from the Temple of Apollo to challenge Saint John's influence. In either case, one day the Devil/Kynops offered to enlighten Saint John himself, but when he dove underwater to display his powers, Saint John crossed himself and the Devil was halted there, frozen in stone. Even though this is a convenient fishing perch, today the local fishermen avoid it because "the fish caught off this rock smell funny."

Another local landmark you might be curious about is the bright-blue wrought-iron fencing that encloses a nondescript flat rock, located on the waterfront just past the Meltemi Bar. Devoted Patmians have enclosed the stone slab where Saint John is said to have baptized more than 14,000 converts from among the local population.

GETTING THERE: Part of Patmos's special appeal is its isolation—getting there can mean a long, sometimes arduous, trip by **steamer** from Piraeus. There are four midday departures from Piraeus weekly; check with Tourist Information in Athens (tel. 171) or with the Piraeus Port Authority (tel. 45-11-311) for schedules. The F/B *Alcagos, Omiros,* and *Kamiros* provide daily sailings to Leros, Kalymnos, Kos, and Rhodes. Tourists with limited time often catch these ferryboats in order to meet an Olympic Airways flight from Kos or Rhodes back to Athens, thus saving five or six hours of travel time. The Apollon Travel Agency (tel. 0247/31-356) sells Olympic tickets in Skala; for Olympic Airways information in Athens call 92-92-555.

The F/B *Panormitis* makes a once-weekly run to Samos, but during the high season, smaller excursion boats cruise to Samos in three hours, making the round trip for 2100 drs ($16.15). To our minds, the best method of transport is the **hydrofoil** which services Patmos daily from Rhodes (3½ hours), three times a week from Kos (1½ hours), and, depending on demand, sometimes from Samos (1¾ hours).

4. Kalymnos

Kalymnos is best known for the puffy natural sponges that have been her principal industry since the 1700s; but the island also offers some fine beaches, a few resort developments, and peace and quiet rarely found on her better-known neighbors, Rhodes and Kos. The thriving sponge-fishing industry (10% of Greece's total output) used to give Kalymnos an autonomy from the tourist industry that was quite refreshing; now the sponge-fishing industry has fallen on hard times, and tourism is being courted by the island as a source of income.

Historically, Kalymnos has played a role similar to the other Dodecanese; first, as a participant in the Trojan War, then in the wars between the city-states. During Alexander the Great's reign a great sanctuary to Apollo was built (nothing remains today) and the island fell, in succession, to the Romans, Byzantines, and Persians. In 1306 the Knights of St. John based in Rhodes took over. Kalymniots, like most other islanders, claim to have led the insurrection against the Turks during the War of Independence (it *is* true that the first stirrings of rebellion came from the Dodecanese). Soon afterward the island was put under Italian rule (1912–1945). Many of the older locals speak the language fluently, and are proud of the Italian tourists who return each summer.

SPONGES: The sponge-fishing industry dates back to 1700 when divers, weighted by a stone belt, would dive 10 to 15 meters down (holding their breath), collecting up to ten sponges per dive. The sponges, a plant living on rocks at the bottom of the sea, were then cleaned and treated. In 1885 the *Skafandre* (a primitive diving suit) made it possible for the divers to remain underwater at depths of 30 to 40 meters for nearly an hour! In heavy, rubberized canvas suits, with an air tube attached to a fishbowl helmet, these men would walk the sea bottom, cutting sponges with their knives and gathering them with jai-alai racquet-style baskets. On board, other workers would trample the dark sponges to squeeze out the dark membrane and milky juices. This harvest occurred annually. Each May 10, the ships would depart Kalymnos, after much celebration, prayer, and a blessing from the high priest of Aghios Nikolaos. On October 30 another festival was held to thank God for those who returned home safely.

The riskiness of this occupation, in which many died or were crippled by the "bends," has reduced the number of divers from several thousand to about 400. Today the fleets sail to Libya and around the African coast, and the men wear modern scuba gear. The export of sponges has declined due to competition from plastic sponges and from the poorer quality natural sponges processed in the Philippines and Malaysia. Nonetheless, visitors who come to Kalymnos purchase sponges enthusiastically because they are cheaper and of finer quality than those found in Europe, and on a reduced scale, this industry still thrives. Incidentally, many Kalymniots emigrated to Florida after the war, settling in Tampa and Tarpon Springs to continue their trade off the coasts of the Bahamas.

ORIENTATION: If you've come to Kalymnos on a day trip from Kos you'll probably only have time for a visit to one of the sponge treatment centers (plus a splash or wash at the beach). If you orient yourself while you're approaching the harbor at Pothia, it becomes obvious by the spread of the old pastel homes that the waterfront, packed with active boats, still dominates the life here. To the left, silver-domed spires top the cream-colored **Ag. Nikolaos Church**, a treasure trove of icons and frescoes. Indeed, this is one of the most elaborate churches in the Dodecanese, as it was the object of tribute by the well-to-do sponge fishermen and their families. The barren hillside above the town is capped with a 30-foot-tall cross, standing alone as a beacon to the returning fishermen. To the right, built over the water, is the **Ag. Christoss Church**, whose rotund pink basilica is paired with a tall, slim clock tower.

In the middle of the pier is a modern bronze sculpture of a nude sponge diver, arms raised above his head, who, I suppose, should be viewed upside-down for maximum effect. He's the work of local sculptor Michael Kokkinos, whose 28 other sculptures pop up in the oddest, most pleasant places.

Nearby the statue is the **Tourist Information** hut (you'll see the sign), open from 8:30 a.m. to 1 p.m. and 2 p.m. to 7 p.m. daily. It's run by two women who are very helpful and delighted to see you.

USEFUL INFORMATION: Along Eleftherios Street (the harbor road) you'll find the **Police** (tel. 29-301), the **National** and **Ionian Banks**, and two travel agents, **Kalymnos Tours** (tel. 28-329) and **Stelios Tours** (tel. 22-162). A few blocks inland from the harbor is the taxi stand; there you'll find the **O.T.E.** and the **post office**. **Irene's Rent-A-Motor** (tel. 47-155), next to the Crystal Hotel, has the best prices (mopeds for 875 drs, or $6.75; Vespas seating two for 1125 drs, or $8.65), and you'll be helping to put its proprietor, Sakis, through Brock University in Ontario! Sakis also rents dune buggys for 6875 drs ($52.85) a day, plus 625 drs ($4.80) for full insurance. The **area code** is 0243.

ACCOMMODATIONS AND DINING: If you want to make Kalymnos your headquarters in the Dodecanese, stay in Pothia for a night until you find your own retreat.

In the Ag. Nikolaos part of town, around the church, there's the modern all-white **Olympic Hotel** (tel. 0243/28-801), with 42 large, C-class rooms. Balconied doubles overlooking the harbor are 4400 drs ($33.85). Just before the Olympic, on the harbor, are five simple, clean double rooms for 3350 drs ($25.80), with great views as well. Vlaskos manages these rooms above his popular **Faros Taverna** (tel. 0243/29-559). His specialty, grilled chicken, is terrific and very economical at 460 drs ($3.55) a portion.

Turning the corner around the Olympic you'll see the small pastel green D-class **Hotel Crystal** (tel. 0243/28-893), where doubles without bath are 3500 drs ($26.95); ten added-on doubles with private bath are 3850 drs ($29.65). Generally the Ag. Nikolaos section is a little more quiet than other parts of town. Our favorite restaurant, with a terrace overlooking the town beach, was here. The locals called it N.O.K., but it's the **Kalymnos Yacht Club**, an old seafarers' club draped in fishnets with a huge mural of a sponge fisherman (what else?) floating above a background of the city. Two can eat a hearty Greek meal —about 1200 drs ($9.25)—surrounded by crusty old Greek sailors and local youngsters who practice their diving at the beach.

In the Ag. Christoss area, across town, there are several rooms to let and the small **Hotel Alma** (tel. 0243/28-969), run by Michael Kypreous from Kent, England. High-ceilinged doubles without bath are 3150 drs ($24.25). Like those mentioned above, the Alma is open year round. Nearby, behind City Hall, are small ouzeris where you can join the locals enjoying ouzo complemented by small plates of octopus and olives, the only food a Kalymniot would ever eat with ouzo!

Directly behind the Tourist Information hut is the **Pension Patmos** (tel. 0243/24-751) on Odos. Nikolaos, where the eight rooms (all with private bath) each go for 1875 drs ($14.45) nightly and keep you in the heart of the harbor.

When you get hungry head straight over to the **Taverna Sefterios** (tel. 28-642), in the Christoss section of town, just off the harbor and down a street.

This is the best taverna in town. The first thing you'll notice is the Flintstone's-style frescoed walls. Then you'll notice that there's a subtle cool breeze always blowing through the room. Order the stifado with a delicious large salad. The entire menu is delicious, and at 650 drs ($5) a head, a truly great value.

An inexpensive and good harborside restaurant is the **Myrthies Stalas** (tel. 28-916), located on the pier from which the boats for Leros depart. Ask for their *saganaki*, a delicious fried cheese dish made with *kefalotiri*, a very sharp cheese.

The **Kelaris Pub,** just up the hill from the pier, has a large outdoor seating area and red bamboo walls; it's a great place for nightcaps as well as food if smooth jazz and starlight haunt you.

To start your day in Pothia head to the **Cafeteria Gallery** (tel. 28-469), a café that is frequented by the Greek literary crowd. The Gallery's interior is stunning, a slightly tattered reminder of another time. There are oak and glass bookcases, which hold copies of works by local writers, sold by the owner. This is the perfect place to start your day or end your afternoon, when the local fishermen stop by with the days' haul.

WHAT TO SEE: You can't leave Kalymnos without learning something about the islanders' major occupation; the day-trippers from Kos have made a sponge-fishing education easy to obtain.

To get to Pothia's sponge factory, either tag along after a tour guide (who will probably speak a Scandinavian language) or take the stairs at the left of the pier, past the tavernas up into town. About halfway up, a cement path on your right leads to the **Astor Workshop of Sea Sponges** (tel. 29-815), run by Nick Gourlas. Here you can see the sponges at each stage of preparation: their blackish original color, their softening after being beaten with sticks to loosen pebbles and fibers, and the subsequent whitening after a bath in sulfuric acid. Think that's rough? You can watch one of the workers trimming them into a round shape with gardening shears. Sponges here are for sale according to their size and grade. The cheaper unbleached sponges are more durable for cleaning chores; the light ones with big pores are for bathing; the finest quality smooth ones, with tiny pores, are for sensitive skin and cosmetic use. If you get really turned on by this, the Astor Workshop has inexpensive rooms to rent right upstairs.

The sponge-fishing industry has left another cultural legacy as well. A typical Kalymniot mansion, once owned by sponge magnate Mr. Vouvalis, has been donated by him to the city as a museum, and it's filled with archeological finds and personal and business memorabilia. The **museum** is in the Aghia Triada section, a few blocks up from the harbor. You'll notice that almost every taverna or shop displays a barnacle-encrusted amphora or other ancient sea treasure brought back from the depths by the local fishermen.

AROUND THE ISLAND: There's more to see on Kalymnos than Pothia's sponge factory. A **round-the-island tour** may be taken by taxi—at about 8000 drs ($62.50) a day for five people—and if Spyros is available, you'll end up knowing more about Kalymnos than you ever wanted to! **Stelios Tours** (tel. 22-162) has a bus tour around the island once a week for 1250 drs ($9.60). Call for date information and locations.

Beach seekers should head directly to the taxi stand at Stratmos Square to share a cab to **Massouri Beach**. Because there's only one bus that plys this route daily, the island's taxis are required to car-pool and divide the fare among as many passengers as will fit inside. This is accomplished by charging everyone 100 drs (75¢), so as you can see it's well worth it. Because the roads and sites are not very well signposted, we don't recommend mopeds for sightseeing.

Many of Kalymnos's major sites are along the east-west road that bisects the island, and though often charming, they're not exactly on par with Delphi. Just outside of Pothia is the small **Castro Chrissocherias**, where a basilica is hidden underneath a fortress. At **Pera Kastro**, above the old capital of Chorio, you can see small white chapels clinging like barnacles to the rocky hillside around a tenth-century fortress. At the island's proudest shrine, the **Church of St. Christos Ierusalem**, are the ruins of a domed basilica and some columns that were built over what is now thought to be the Sanctuary of Apollo. At Panormos the road forks south to the beach at Kantouni.

BEACHES: **Kantouni** is the first sandy part of the Platis Ialos western coast. Hotels and rooms line this beach and the next cove. The beach is crowded and strong, direct winds make it rough for swimming. Continue north along the oleander-lined road to **Myrties**, a very pretty gray-pebbled beach below a stretch of road that appears somewhat less developed, perhaps because the housing is at a higher level above the shoreline.

Just one kilometer away across the shimmering blue water is the small island of **Telendos**, with its few houses looking square at Myrties. Local boats will take you across for 200 drs ($1.55) if you're not up to swimming to it. To one side is the beach where the locals tell you "people who don't like clothes" go. A favorite Kalymnos folk story tells of a young princess who died so in love with her little island of Telendos that its one hill took her reclined shape; with an active imagination it's possible to see the sway of her hips and the profile of her young face.

At Myrties there's a very popular, inexpensive taverna called **Stallas**, many rooms to rent, and the D-class **Marilena Hotel** (tel. 0243/47-289) and the **Myrties** (tel. 0243/28-912). Bathless double rooms at both hotels run 1265 drs ($9.75) to 1700 drs ($13.07).

Our favorite place to stay is reason enough to visit Myrties: **Le Petite Paris Pension** (tel. 0243/47-239). This pension, situated at a fork in the road 100 feet before the bus stop (look for the Melitsaha Beach Hotel sign), has a mustard-yellow wrought-iron fence around it and is run by a lovely part French, part Greek woman named Kalliopi. She has four doubles and two triples, with each bed going for the bargain price of 750 drs ($5.80)!

The most pleasant of the developed beaches is **Massouri**, just one kilometer north of Myrties. The few hotels and houses are set up on the rocks above a fine-sand beach about one kilometer long. The one coastal road above the beach serves as the town square, a spot to be avoided between 2:45 and 3:15 p.m., when the day-trippers and their group taxis create a traffic gridlock. For those of you who want to stay, there are six clean rooms at the **Massouri Restaurant** (tel. 0243/47-322), run by Nomiki and Theo Pizania. The rooms have private baths, are right off the beach, and are a steal at 1875 drs ($14.42) for a double! Even if you're only in Massouri for the day, walk into the restaurant to study an authentic *skalandre,* the ancient sponge fisherman's diving gear.

Another choice, a bit more on the splurge side, is the **Massouri Beach Hotel** (tel. 0243/47-555), just past the Massouri Restaurant. For 4625 drs ($35.60) a clean modern double with private phone can be yours, complete with air conditioning.

Other areas to explore include the winding mountain road between Vathis and Stimenia, where thousands of mandarin groves fill the valley. Everyone will tell you the best beaches are between **Arginontas** (where the public bus ends) and **Emporios** (along the northwest coast above Massouri). From the small village of Arginonta you can take a moped (or an older cab) up through the 12-family village of Skalia to Emporios, with its 20 resident families. Rooms to rent are available in all three towns and promise a thoroughly "Greek-style" vacation.

Campers can head south to **Ormos Vlichadion** (accessible only by cab) for a beautiful rock-and-sand beach populated only by one part-time taverna.

GETTING THERE: Kalymnos is serviced each morning from Kos by three excursion boats: the *Delfini, Kos Sky,* and *Themis.* Their day-long, round-trip cruises depart Kalymnos for Kos at 4 p.m., and cost 1560 drs ($12). For some mysterious reason, one-way tickets are only 600 drs ($4.62). Kalymnos is also serviced three to five times a week from Piraeus; schedules should be confirmed in Athens at Tourist Information (tel. 171) or at the Port Authority (tel. 45-11-311). There is also irregular service to Kalymnos from the other Dodecanese islands; again, schedules should be checked at the port of departure.

5. Symi

Among the smaller islands of the Dodecanese is Symi, a rugged isle that has made a point of preserving its elegant architecture. Symi's signature is the broad sweep of pastel-yellow neoclassical homes that line its two towns: Symi Town and Yalos, the port. A symbol of Symi's trading and shipbuilding wealth, richly ornamented churches are sprinkled throughout the entire island. Islanders proudly boast that there are so many churches and monasteries that one could worship in a different sanctuary every day of the year.

The absence of modern-designed buildings on the island is due to an archeological decree (as in the case of Lindos and Patmos) that severely proscribes the style and methods of construction for all old and new buildings. Picture-perfect traditional-style Symi is now the star of many Greek postcards, and a magnet for monied Athenians in search of long-term real estate investments. Symi's architectural structures have the potential of making the island seem too precious (one of Lindos's unfortunate side effects), but Symi somehow escaped this—the island feels like a real place.

WHAT TO SEE AND DO: Ferryboats dock at **Symi** or **Yalos** in the barren, rocky northeastern half of the island. Symi's only paved road connects the tiny villages in this region. The southwestern portion is hilly and green; located here is the medieval **Panormitis Monastery**, popular with Greeks as a refuge from modern life. Young Athenian businessmen speak lovingly of the monk cells and small apartments which can be rented (for a few hundred drachmas per day) for R & R. The whitewashed compound is appreciated more for its verdant, shaded setting than for any particular aesthetic value. The town of **Panormitis Mihailis** is most lively and interesting during its annual festival in early November, but can be explored year round via local boats. The hardy can hike there (it's four hours from town) and enjoy a refreshing dip in its sheltered harbor as reward for their labors.

If your boat docks at Yalos, by all means hike the gnarled, chipped stone stairs that ascend to **Symi town**. This picturesque community is filled with images of a Greece in many ways long departed. Heavy-set, wizened old women sweep the whitewashed stone path outside their homes. Occasionally a young girl or boy or a very old man (too old to have left for America or Australia to make his fortune) can be seen retouching the neon blue trim over the doorways and shutters. Nestled between the immaculately kept homes are the abandoned villas, their faded trim and flaking paint lending a wistful air to the village. While young emigrés continue to support their parents who inhabit Symi, entrepreneurs have begun to renovate the classic villas for rent to an increasing number of tourists.

There's a small **museum** in Symi town that seems to be a conglomeration of the one or two items that each islander considered important enough for public exhibition. It has no name other than "museum" (you can't miss the blue arrows that point the way), but it should be called "Folk Museum." It's open from 9 a.m. to 2:30 p.m. Monday through Saturday.

Crowning Symi town is the **Church of the Panaghia**. The church is surrounded by a fortified wall, and therefore called a castle. It is adorned with the most glorious frescoes on the island, which can only be viewed when services are held (7 a.m. to 8 a.m. on weekdays, all morning on Sunday).

Symi is, unfortunately, not blessed with wide, blond sandy beaches. Close to Yalos, the main town, are two beaches. The first is called **Nos**, and it sports a 50-foot-long rocky "beach," with a daytime drink bar that transforms into a nighttime disco called **Gogo**. **Nymborio** is a pebble beach a bit farther than Nos (a 15-minute walk from Yalos); it's a much larger beach but has no snackbar or taverna (bring a picnic). Trying hard to keep everyone happy, Symi offers a nude beach several coves down from Yalos. The only way to get there is to take a half-day boat trip—at about 450 drs ($3.50) per person each way—leaving the port daily.

Two local crafts that continue to be practiced on this island are **shipbuilding** and sponge fishing. Walk along the water toward Nos beach and you'll probably see boats under construction or repair. It's a treat to watch the men fashion planed boards into a beautiful boat, an old tradition on Symi: it was a boatbuilding center in the days of the Peloponnesian War, when spirited seabattles were waged off Symi's shores.

Sponge fishing is a declining industry in Greece, and Symi is no exception. Only a generation ago 2,000 sponge divers worked waters around the island; today only a handful undertake this dangerous work. Working at depths of 50 to 60 meters (often without gear), many divers died or were crippled by the turbulent sea and too-rapid depressurization. The few sponges that are harvested are sold at Konstantinou Lambru's Sponge Shop at the port. These are the real thing and they make fabulous, inexpensive gifts to bring to friends. Sponges run 250 drs ($1.92) to 2500 drs ($19.25), depending on size and quality.

ACCOMMODATIONS AND DINING: There are nine newly built rooms in the traditionally styled **Hotel Dorian** (tel. 0241/71-181), where doubles run 5525 drs ($42.50). Steep narrow stairs lead up to the **Hotel Glafkos** (tel. 0241/71-358), which is really more like a guesthouse or pension. This 1890s villa has small, homey rooms for 2600 drs ($20), including shower.

There's a very beautiful splurge category hotel on Symi, the **Aliki** (tel. 0241/71-665), located one block off the waterfront on a side street. Its 15 rooms are exquisite, old-world-style examples of elegance. The tariff is steep: 8100 drs ($62.30) for a double, but if you can swing it and want to see Symi in style, then we say head straight to the Aliki.

The majority of tourists bypass hotels for private apartments or houses. Like Lindos, the island has opened its many houses (over 120) for visitors. Rooms for two, with shower and kitchen access, go for about 3125 drs ($24.05); for four, 5000 drs ($38.45). The best way of tapping into this alternative is to visit **Symi Tours** (tel. 0241/71-307), which also conducts day trips and cruises to various points around the island. The three partners, Nikos Sikallos, Ewen Clark, and Steven Clark run a very tight agency, and they're the first place to turn to if you need a room, although they told me that the demand for rooms on Symi means you should book a room at least three months in advance of your visit. That sounds like a lot, but it's worth it: many Athenians vacation in Symi, it's so gorgeous. Symi Tours handles over 100 rooms around the island, and they can take care of your other travel needs such as flight bookings, boats, tours, etc. They're located on the left-hand side of the harbor. Expect to pay about 3100 drs ($24) for a room, but it'll be nice.

As for restaurants, the island has 30, but our favorite (and that of other Symians) is **Café-Bar Leftaris**, serving some of the cleanest and freshest food you'll find on the islands. Try the octopus, salads, and stuffed vegetables. Prices at Leftaris can only be called cheap, with a full lunch for two, including beer, running 900 drs ($7.21). You'll find Leftaris at the head of the main road running perpendicular to the harbor. Just ask a local for the fellow with the moustache and the great food! Also very good is the **Stathis** (tel. 71-225), at the middle of the harbor.

Other tourist services include three banking agents, who stay open Monday through Saturday from 9 a.m. to 1 p.m. and 5 p.m. to 8 p.m. There is one bank on the island, and only two taxis. The police, located near the post office and O.T.E., are open 24 hours a day, and encourage tourists who think they may have overpaid for a room or meal to bring a receipt; they'll check the official prices.

GETTING THERE: Finally, a word on getting to Symi. The Symian people operate a boat, the *Symi I,* booked locally in Rhodes through **Triton Tours** (tel. 0241/21-690). Round-trip tickets are 2500 drs ($19.23). The *Symi I* leaves Rhodes at 9 a.m. every day from Mandraki Harbor. The boats leave Symi promptly at 3:50 p.m. (an amused fisherman shuttled us out to the ferry when we missed its departure) and arrive at Rhodes at 6:30 p.m. Even if you consider Symi only as a day trip from chic Rhodes, take a change of clothes in case you decide to stay.

6. Karpathos

When speaking of Karpathos the same adjectives always crop up: "traditional," "wild," "mountainous," "beautiful," "rugged." The second-largest of the Dodecanese group is a stark contrast to the sophisticated international resort of Rhodes. Because of its relative isolation—midway between Crete and Rhodes, but southwest of the island chain paralleling Turkey—Karpathos has remained distinctly its own place. The local dialect (peppered with ancient Doric words) still spoken at the village of Olimbos is so indigenous that even other Karpathians cannot understand it. Although 95% of the islanders have emigrated to America for study or work during their lifetimes, when on Karpathos they shed the title "Greek-Americans" and become simply "Karpathians."

ORIENTATION: Lawrence Durrell calls Karpathos "an ideal hide-away." Tourists who moor at the southern port of Karpathos, or **Pigadia**, will find a sparkling village of chiseled stone houses, whose red terracotta-tiled roofs peek above the treetops. Pastel-colored façades are broken by bas reliefs of Doric columns; many of their ornate wrought-iron balconies depict the double eagle symbol of the Byzantine Empire. The southern half of the island—large, verdant plains, fruit trees, and trellised vineyards—contrasts with the barren, mountainous reaches of the north. **Aperi**, a small village ten kilometers north of Pigadia and once capital of the island, features the island's most important monastery and traditional stone homes built on both sides of a flowing stream. **Arkassa**, on the opposite coast, shows signs of the ancient Arkaseia on the bluffs above fruit orchards.

A newly built highway crossing the once-impassable Mount Kalolimni (3,675 feet) now unites Pigadia with the northern port of **Diafani**. Eight kilometers away, perched on the side of Mount Profitis Ilias, is the famous village of **Olimbos**. Ethnologists have studied the oldest settlement on the island to learn more about the roots of contemporary Greek folk tradition. The villagers are said to live 300 years behind the times, and it's a rare treat to visit this intimate community. Olimbian women wear full cotton skirts and lace-trimmed blouses, covered by a flower print or black apron. Even the faces of the young, swathed in black cotton head scarves, seem timelessly Greek. The old men in their baggy black pants and stiff cotton overshirts continue to farm or herd as always; now many of the young men have gone to Athens or abroad. Olimbos is particularly interesting during one of its many festivals. The post-Easter festivities are very colorful and elaborate, involving all the villagers, who wear traditional holiday costumes. Karpathian music is much faster-paced than the bouzouki played elsewhere, and the lively dances are thought to be unique to the island. A wedding ceremony, often lasting three days, is the ideal festivity to catch for those interested in seeing Greece as it used to be.

ACCOMMODATIONS: Other than in Pigadia, most of the island's villages offer accommodations in rented rooms, an ideal way to share village life. In Pigadia, the C-class **Porfyris Hotel** (tel. 0245/22-294) is one of Karpathos's oldest and best choices. All double rooms have private facilities, and cost 4950 drs ($38); the Porfyris has singles with or without bath at 2680 drs ($20.40) to 3420 drs ($26.30). Their comfortable restaurant serves moderately priced food, but we enjoyed the local portside tavernas at lunch or dinner. The newer **Pension Romantica** (tel. 0245/22-460) is located about one kilometer from the heart of town and has a miniature golf course! The 20 spacious doubles cost the same as the Porfyris. The **Karpathos** (tel. 0245/22-347), a D-class inn, is well run by the Margaritis family. It's located two blocks from the waterfront at 25 Vass. Konstantinou. Doubles with bath are 1500 drs ($11.55); without, 1235 drs ($9.50). The **Anesis** (tel. 0245/22-100) is another D-class choice nearby on Metaxa Street. Both the Karpathos and the **Anesis** are open year round, with a double room going for 1700 drs ($13.10).

USEFUL INFORMATION: The **local police** (tel. 22-226) are housed by the ferryboat pier. . . . Karpathos is serviced by **steamers** from Piraeus via Crete twice weekly, and by steamers from Rhodes three times weekly. . . . . **Olympic Airways** offers three flights daily from Athens via Rhodes, nonstop from Rhodes or twice weekly from Kassos. Tickets can be purchased at the **Prokymaia Travel Office** (tel. 22-291). Buses depart Pigadia for the half-hour ride to the airport 90 minutes before departure time, and the fare is 80 drs (62¢).

Try to car-pool for taxi tours around the island. The local bus is infrequent and unreliable, and solo cab rides are very costly. . . . The main **post office** and **O.T.E.** are in Pigadia. . . . The area code is 0245. . . . There's a small **Health Clinic** (tel. 22-228). . . . Homespun fabrics and local handcrafts are good value gifts from the island.

7. A Baker's Dozen

As we mentioned earlier, the name "Dodecanese" comes from "twelve," the original number of islands counted. Although we're only discussing 13, there are hundreds of other small islands tucked in and around the better-known ones. Most are only occupied by a few fishermen and their families, if at all, and present little interest to the average tourist.

KASSOS: Kassos, just three nautical miles southwest of Karpathos, is separated from her larger neighbor by the treacherous waters of the Karpathian

Straits. Forbidding vertical cliffs which form most of the coastline have caused Kassos's development to be confined to settlements in the northwest. Few inhabitants remain since the first tide emigrated to Egypt to build the Suez Canal; many Kassiots return now only for the holidays. Ironically, every July 7th, Kassos commemorates the massacre of its citizens by the Egyptian troops of Ibrahim Pasha who overran the tiny island in the Ottoman offensive of 1824.

Just one kilometer from the port is the principal town, **Fri**. Peek into any of the fine stone houses and you'll see interiors which have been lavishly decorated with artwork brought home by generations of seafarers. The most popular site on Kassos is the **Sellai Cave**, also called *Hellenokamera*. The cave is known for its beautifully colored stalactites. The Pelasgian walls (masonry consisting of large, hand-hewn stones) which surround the grotto once provided the islanders with a refuge from private invaders.

If you didn't bring your yacht, plan to spend a few days on Kassos; ferries stop here only twice weekly on their way from Piraeus, Crete, and Rhodes. (Piraeus-bound ferries stop only once a week.) Desperadoes can hop on one of Olympic's twice weekly flights to Karpathos, or their thrice-weekly flights direct to Kassos from Rhodes and Crete! Fri boasts two C-class hotels as well as some rooms to let. The **Agennissis** (tel. 0245/41-323) is the better value: in the low season doubles are 1560 drs ($12) without private facilities, 2190 drs ($16.85) with; between July and September they're 2025 drs ($15.60) and 2699 drs ($20.75) respectively. The **Anessis** (tel. 0245/41-201) has seven doubles with private baths at 2200 drs ($16.90); open year round.

HALKI: Halki (Chalkis), one of the smallest of the Dodecanese, is most often visited as a day excursion from her larger, glitzier neighbor, Rhodes. Tired of discos, beach umbrellas, casinos, and honking horns? Sharing the life led by the 300 villagers who've remained on the island may bring welcome relief to those who've been "Rhode-ed out."

Caïques pull into the small port of **Emborio**, where you'll find outdoor ouzeris and tavernas serving inexpensive, fresh seafood. Overnighters can find a room to let in many of the traditional pastel stone houses overlooking the water.

A few kilometers' hike above the port is **Chora**, the island's capital during the 18th and 19th centuries, built around a 15th-century fortress (constructed by the Knights of St. John) to protect villagers from sea-level attack by Turkish pirates. Halki offers some antiquities (including a black mosaic-paved stone path nearly a kilometer long and remains of several temples to Apollo), two Byzantine monasteries, and uncrowded, sandy beaches. The island can be reached by caïque from Kamiros, Rhodes, three times weekly for 385 drs ($2.95) or by steamer from Karpathos, also three times weekly.

TILOS: Tilos, equidistant from the much more intriguing islands of Kos and Rhodes, rarely gets foreign visitors. Local boats from Symi and Nisiros stop regularly at the port of **Megalo Horio**, called **Skala**. If you hop off, head for the southern port of **Livadia**, the island's most interesting village. Here you'll find the ruins of four Genoese fortresses, sandy beaches, and several freshwater streams. It's possible to rent rooms in the attractive arcaded houses, which face east to the Turkish coast. Tilos has its own hilltop capital, **Chora**, where you can visit the Monastery of Ag. Panteleimon.

NISIROS: Nisiros (Nyssiros), a volcanic island south of Kos, is often compared to Santorini by tourists. A volcano is the only thing these islands have in common! The island is shaped like a Circle-in-the-Square; myths tell of an angry god who threw a plump demon to the earth, perhaps creating the huge pit in the island. **Laki**, the four-kilometer-wide volcano, is rimmed by gray stone hills which fall squarely to the sea. Within dormant Laki are two extinct craters, Alexandros and Polyvotis; flowering almond trees sprout from the rich volcanic soil around them. The rest of Nisiros is predominantly barren, and visitors complain of the fierce heat reflected off the black stone landscape. In fact, tourists are urged to wear leather-soled shoes because plastic sandals and sneakers have been known to melt, adhering their wearers to the ground.

Local sights include a Venetian fortress above the port of **Emborios**; monasteries clustered among the half dozen villages that rim the volcano; and Pelasgian walls made of black trachyte, remnants of the ancient acropolis near Mandraki. Most tourists go for the volcano. (By the way, rumor has it that Nisiriots are experimenting with a geothermal plant that would draw steam power from seawater pumped into the volcanic crater!)

Nisiros is serviced by steamers from Astipalea or Rhodes four times weekly and by excursion caïques from Kos.

ASTIPALEA: The butterfly-shaped Astipalea, the westernmost of the Dodecanese, is situated 90 miles from Rhodes. Her architecture has been most greatly influenced by the sensual, whitewashed homes of the neighboring Cyclades islands. The pretty fishing village of **Analipsi** (east of Astipalea's port) has seven Mykonos-style windmills on a hill above the harbor. (The hike uphill to visit these windmills is well worthwhile for the beautiful vista over Maltezana Bay and its many rocky islets.)

The **Chora** of Astipalea is dominated by a 13th-century Venetian fortress and will remind readers of Patmos's Chora (which is dominated by the Monastery of St. John). Within the castle is a well-preserved icon of the Madonna, and above its door is the Quirini family's coat-of-arms. These noble Venetians ruled "Castello," the capital of "Stampalia," from 1207 to 1522. One of their enduring legacies is the odd local dialect which incorporates many Italian words.

Astipalea's beach fills up with Greek families on July and August camping holidays, but three new D-class hotels have been built to accommodate tourists. At the port is the **Aegeon** (tel. 0242/61-236), the **Astynea** (tel. 0242/61-209), open year round, and across Mich. Karageorgi St., at no. 24, the **Paradissos** (tel. 0242/61-224).

LEROS: You run out of the house without your wallet and when you go back to get it you realize you've locked the keys inside. One Greek would say to another: "I'm going to buy you a one-way ticket to Leros."

For years isolated Leros was best known for its mental health hospital. No more. The hospital has closed, and now this quiet yet urbanized island receives day visitors seeking a change from the more touristed Kalymnos and Patmos. Six major bays create tranquil deep-water harbors ideal for boating or swimming. Centuries ago Venetian and Genoese fleets kept these harbors busy refitting their ships for battle.

Today Leros is poised for an expected and welcome rise in tourism, as it accommodates the overflow from various other Dodecanese islands. Though there are still military bases on the island, its lush landscape and natural beauty await the traveler grown weary with the commercialization that has distorted the Greek ideal of sea, sky, rock, and quality of life.

Leros is most easily approached from Patmos, a 1½-hour ferry ride away. You arrive at the harbor of Agia Marina. The first establishment you see as you walk away from the dock is the **Kamaki Cafe** on the waterfront; stop and have some lunch or a drink. Lunch will set you back about 650 drs ($5). If you continue walking down the street you'll come to the **DRM Travel Agency** (tel. 0247/23-568), which provides information on the entire island. Chris Kokkonis, his wife, Christina, and Naomi Smith-Dekker have at hand every piece of information you'll require—from hotel rooms to pension and villa bookings, from the best local eateries to round-the-island tours. These wonderful people made our brief stay on Leros a richly satisfying one, and they can do the same for you. Make this your first stop and let them show you their Leros.

Next door to DRM is a great café, run by Kostas Capaniris and his wife, where you can get breakfast, lunch, and an after-work ouzo. In the evening the place is full of locals, who sip coffee and argue about politics until midnight.

Lining the sloped banks above the port is Leros's main town, **Platanos**, the administrative capital and more picturesque village. Stately old homes are built on tiers below a Venetian fortress. Boxy, whitewashed, flat-roofed houses cluster around a bustling main square. Many visitors enjoy renting bicycles (offered everywhere, at approximately $3 per day) to tour the town. Beach seekers should head directly to the charming fishing village of **Alinda**. On the island's best beach is the C-class **Maleas Beach Hotel** (tel. 0247/23-306), a bright, three-story lodging whose balconies overlook the bay. The Maleas Beach also features a restaurant/roof garden, ideal for early-morning sunbathing. A double room here is 3860 drs ($29.70), and well worth it.

Alinda is the main beach area, and it has cafés, tavernas, and sun-drenched tourists who become party animals once the sun goes down. There's a disco in town, and several hotels to choose from. Again, consult with DRM Travel to find a place that fits your needs.

About 3½ kilometers away is **Lakki**, the other main port, situated on the west side of the island. This is where the big boats come and go; the houses here were built by Italians, as were the road system and public buildings. To this day the islanders feel a special affinity for their northern neighbors.

If you want to stay in Lakki, we recommend the **Hotel Katerina** (tel. 0247/22-460), a clean, "plain jane"–style house where a double goes for 2750 drs ($21.15), with breakfast an additional 375 drs ($2.90). Nearby is the islands' premier moped dealer, Giannakos (tel. 0247/24-027), where for 1000 drs ($7.70) you can rent a Vespa for the day to go exploring around the area.

Also nearby is the village of **Panteli**, where the island's fishermen trade their goods and where the best restaurants are. A local favorite—ours too—is **Zorbas**, where a fresh fish dinner for two runs about 1600 drs ($12.30). After dinner check out the **Savannah Bar** (tel. 23-969) for a nightcap or two and make the scene. This is the place for good music, drinks, and two Polynesian-style outdoor tables that beckon you to bring on the night.

At the other end of the island is **Xerocambos**, where you get the boats to Kalymnos and where campers can roost in a lush and well-designed campground, **Xerocambos Camping** (tel. 0247/23-372). Adults are charged 300 drs ($2.40) a night, which includes a hot shower, dining area with snackbar, and an honest-to-God laundry room!

If you'd like to explore Leros but don't have much time, there's a taxi tour of the island and its charms that DRM can arrange for you with an English-speaking driver/guide. The tour runs about 3 hours and costs 4500 drs ($35), and among its many pleasures are visiting a local beekeeper who will sell you honey, for which Leros is justly famed, straight out of the honeycomb. You'll also see some of the marvelous monasteries that dot the island. If you don't have much time, this is the way to go.

Hopefully in these few paragraphs about Leros we've induced you to visit the goddess Diana's stomping grounds. Leros is still unspoiled; it's the Greece you've been looking for.

KASTELLORIZO: Kastellorizo (Megisti) is more important as a symbol of Greek independence than as a tourist attraction. This tiny droplet of stone is 65 miles southeast of Rhodes and less than two miles from the Turkish port of Kaş. (There's a lively black market tourist-and-goods trade between the two.) The 250 residents (said to remain only to keep the population above the 200 mark at which the land reverts to Turkey) are totally dependent on supplies brought in thrice weekly by ferry or twice weekly by plane from Rhodes.

The name "Kastellorizo" comes from the Venetian occupation of the island, when it was renamed after the red-stone fortress (Castel Rosso) built by the eighth grand master of the Knights of St. John. The Greeks call it Megisti, the "Biggest." Some will tell you it's because Kastellorizo is the largest among a cluster of tiny islands; others claim that the islanders deserve this title for their bravery in overcoming past misfortunes.

The island has been occupied by at least seven nations, including the Egyptians, Italians, Turks, and Venetians. Even the grand fortress built by St. John's Knights was used as a prison for wayward members of the Order. In 1913 local citizens revolted and quickly came under French control. After World War I the Italians regained the island; during World War II they forced the remaining islanders to evacuate. Kastellorizo was occupied by Allied troops, who drew German bomb attacks; most of the town was burned and pillaged. The few citizens who returned after the war (the island was returned to Greece in 1948) had nothing to come home to.

The port town, now partially rebuilt, is tiered amphitheatrically to the water's edge. The pastel-colored, red tile-roofed houses will remind some of Symi, but here the ornate wooden balconies (vestiges of Turkish influence) overhang the oblong harbor. The sea bottom can easily be seen through the crystal-clear waters. As Kastellorizots only occupy themselves with fishing, the few portside tavernas serve the most superb seafood in the Dodecanese.

If sitting over a plate of shrimp or lobster and admiring the Turkish coast gets wearing, stroll over to the harborside mosque. It's been turned into a **museum** of local folklore and handcrafts, and displays some fascinating photographs of the island in her heyday. Otherwise, organize a group to charter a caïque for a trip to the east coast "blue grotto" **Parasta.** Compared to the one at Capri, this fantastic grotto, filled with stalactites and stalagmites, reflects every hue of blue light from its deep waters. Plan a morning trip with your boat captain so you can be in and out of the grotto during low tide, when the overhanging entrance is passable. If you're stuck there you may see why the cave is also called "Fokiali," after the seals which are said to live inside.

There are several rooms to let and one licensed hostel, the **Pension of Dimou Meghistis** (tel. 0241/29-072). With 17 rooms overlooking the water, two can share one, with private bath, for a steep 3850 drs ($29.60). Bathless singles in the high season cost 2750 drs ($21.15), singles with bath 3500 drs ($26.92) year round.

Though the nearby port of Kaş (in Turkey) is close to Kastellorizo, neither place is an official entry port, making a quick hop from one country to another impossible. These laws change often, so check with the local authorities for the latest regulations.

Chapter X

CENTRAL GREECE

1. Boeotia
2. Delphi
3. Evia
4. Thessaly
5. Volos and Mount Pelion
6. Kalambaka: Gateway to Meteora
7. The Mount Olympus Region

JUST READING the list of chapter headings alone should give you that classical tingle all tourists seem to get when sightseeing in Central Greece. Imagine Thebes, Delphi, Mount Parnassus, Thermopylae, the Argonauts, Chyron the Centaur, Zeus and Hera's wedding place, Mount Olympus, Meteora (where James Bond recently dangled off the edge of one of its precariously perched, sky-high monasteries)—all these sights and more in one chapter. As always in Greece, too much to see, not enough time. . . .

Fortunately, Central Greece is blessed with a practical and functional transportation infrastructure. To most major sights you'll have a choice of train or bus, and often a plane. Renting a car is still the most efficient way to cram everything in, but the lack of one here won't prove detrimental to your enjoyment of the natural and man-made beauties.

There are no weather limitations here either, though we prefer spring or fall, when the tourist crush has decreased to a mere press. In late April and May there's still some snow on the slopes of mounts Parnassus and Olympus and a bevy of wildflowers illuminating the Thessalian Plain. In the dry, hot summer you'll probably be tempted to blow off a lot of the classical sightseeing and instead dive off the mainland directly out to the islands. By mid-September things have simmered down, the Greek children are back in school, and Central Greece returns to the relaxed state that makes it so lovable.

1. Boeotia
This province of such immense interest to classicists extends from the Aegean coast to the Pindus Range. Boeotia (pronounced *Bo*-ee-sha) includes such legendary sights as Mount Helicon, haunt of the Muses; the Pass of Thermopylae, where the Spartan Leonidas and his men fell; Aulis, the port used by warships setting sail for Troy; its capital City of Seven Gates, the legendary Thebes; and most important, nestled at the foot of Mount Parnassus, the site of the Oracle of Delphi. If you do nothing else during your visit to Greece, try to pay a call to one of the most remarkable places on the face of our earth.

THEBES: The journey from Athens to Delphi on the Athens-Lamia high-speed motorway will take you through the heart of Thebes, ancient capital of Boeotia. Thebes's prominent position in the classical world has been assured by the vast number of quality literary works that survive from antiquity. Works by Aeschylus *(Seven Against Thebes),* Seneca *(Oedipus),* Statius *(The Thebaid),* and one of the ancient world's great masterpieces, Sophocles' *Oedipus Rex,* were all set in Thebes. These works are mainly tragedies; it's because of what Thebes endured in those times, and the onslaughts, pillages, and wholesale ravaging that it was to experience in later epochs, that modern-day Thebes (Thiva) is nothing more than a slowly developing city and industrial park.

One of the greatest stories of Thebes was the War of the Seven, which began when Polynices, son of Oedipus, decided to reclaim his father's throne. He enlisted the help of Adrastus, king of Argos, who brought seven famous warriors, each a champion in an art of war, to Thebes to join in the battle. Polynices assigned one champion to attack each of Thebes' Seven Gates. His brother Eteocles, current ruler of Thebes, sent seven of his best warriors to defend the gates. At each gate, both champion warriors battled mercilessly. It's said that one champion, Capaneus, boasted that even Zeus couldn't defend himself against the onslaught he'd prepared, but when he approached the gate, Zeus zapped him with a bolt of lightning and he turned into ashes on the spot. Polynices saw that his attack was not succeeding and offered to meet Eteocles in one-on-one combat to decide who would rule Thebes. Eteocles agreed and they fought until both were dead, thereby fulfilling the prophecy Oedipus was told about his two sons. Creon, one of the last surviving Thebans, urged his fellow fighters on and the battle finally went to Thebes's side. In keeping with Theban custom, Creon gave Eteocles a grand funeral but left Polynices' body to rot outside. Antigone, Polynices' sister, swore to herself that she would put her brother's shadow to rest, and was condemned to death for her deed (in the process creating the plot of one of Sophocles' great works, *Antigone).*

A brief ten years later, the seven sons (Epigoni, or After-Borns) of the seven champion warriors returned to attack Thebes, and ironically, the only one killed was Aegialeus, son of the only original champion to survive the War of the Seven. The glory of Thebes was reached in the 450s B.C., when it twice defeated mighty Athens in battle; after that the Fates turned against her and Thebes was crushed by Sparta (382 B.C.). Between 371 and 362 B.C. Thebes enjoyed an unusual decade of prosperity as an ally to Athens. The invincible city-state introduced a new fighting formation called the *phalanx,* the close-knit line of battle we take for granted today. When Alexander the Great arrived in Thebes in 336 B.C., he flattened the entire city, with one exception—the house of the poet Pindar. (Pindar was one of Greece's greatest lyric poets; born near Thebes in 518 B.C., he'd gone to Athens where he befriended Aeschylus and began to write.)

Between the days of Alexander and the liberation from Turkey Thebes was devastated or razed at least eight times, numbering among its conquerors the Bulgars, Normans, Franks, Lombards, and Turks. No wonder that the city lives on only in books!

The Archeological Museum

It's small, but certainly worthwhile if you're in town. Outside in a garden of steles is an "antique" picnic table made up of columns and sculptural fragments, shaded by a grape arbor, that makes a pleasant picnic spot. Large mosaics mounted outside include an early-Christian floor depicting the months of the year as young men bearing gifts. In the first room straight ahead is a collection of Mycenaean *larnakes* (clay coffins) from 1400–1200 B.C. Excavated at a site near

Thebes, this important find revealed a great deal about Mycenaean funeral customs, through both the primitive paintings on the coffins and their content of gifts. This display at Thebes is unique in all of Europe. There is also a unique collection of 40 lapis lazuli cylindrical seals from far-off Mesopotamia, recovered near Thebes. The sculpture room houses votive offerings from the sanctuary of Apollon-Ptoios, one of the most famous sanctuaries in ancient Greece.

The archeological museum is at the foot of Pindarou Street, about a five-minute walk from Epaminandou Square. The museum is open from 9 a.m. to 3 p.m. weekdays and Saturday, to 2 p.m. on Sunday and holidays; closed Tuesday. Admission is 200 drs ($1.54) for adults, half price for students. There's an excellent catalog by Demakopoulou and Konsala for sale at the front desk for 500 drs ($3.85).

Useful Information

The **bus station** is on Epaminandou Street, near the square which represents the main part of town. . . . The **railroad station** is on the west side of town, and train riders will probably want to take a **taxi** to reach the archeological museum. Once you're at Epaminandou Square, though, you'll be within walking distance of several local tavernas, the museum, and the Palace of Cadmus (now only a rock-filled lot at Pindarou and Antigonas Streets). . . . The **Hotel Niobi** (tel. 0262/29-888), at 65 Epaminandou, is a pleasant choice for an overnight lodging; bathless doubles are 2500 drs ($19.20).

For those of you who are doing Greece the leisurely way, we offer the attractive city of . . .

LIVADIA: Livadia's one "must-see" sight can be combined with a café or picnic break in your tour of classical Greece. This is the **Trophonios Oracle**, a well-marked spot just one kilometer off the Athens-Delphi highway. Here you'll find the **Xenia**, a picturesque and costly café overlooking a stream. In ancient times it was called the Fountain of Memory, to refresh those who were to consult the Oracle. The Xenia is a popular hang-out for Livadians, particularly on weekends and holidays.

While awaiting your order, you can contemplate the importance of this classical site as recorded by Pausanius, author of the original "Hellas on 30 Drachmas a Day" (and a talented Roman scribe). Trophonios was an ancient god of the Underworld whose advice was very popular in the sixth century B.C. As you admire the Fountain of Memory, glance to the left at the large square niche in the cliff. This was the Sanctuary of the gods Daimon and Fortune, where pilgrims were fed the flesh of sacrificial victims after a draught of the waters of Lethe, the Fountain of Forgetfulness, which flows beneath it. Having forgotten the past (or more likely, what he was about to eat), the pilgrim would be primed at the Fountain of Memory. Late in the evening he was annointed with oil and led up to the Oracle (thought to be in a gorge of Mount Haghios Ilias, behind you), and with honeycakes in each hand, was slid into a coffin-like pit in the floor of the mantic cave. After his revelation the pilgrim was hoisted out feet first, totally dazed, by the priest who would question him and record his impressions.

Walking through **Trophonios Park** is popular with those seeking good scenery and revelations. The Xenia's an ideal spot on a hot day to recuperate, under the shade of the trees, beside the waterfall, where you can cleanse your mind for the remainder of your touring in Boeotia.

After 37 kilometers of winding, uphill roads the scenery will grow richer, alternating rocks and olive trees and with prospects over the Gulf of Corinth, with an occasional peak at Mount Parnassus. The bleak new highway will bring you right into a charming village called . . .

ARACHOVA: Just ten kilometers north of Delphi is the lovely mountain town of Arachova, perched on the slopes of Mount Parnassus at 950 meters above sea level. Although the main street suffers from the invasion of the tour buses, a descent or ascent by hand-hewn rock stairs leading from it will take you into another world.

The many shops that line the main street feature the village's most celebrated products—their strong, fragrant red wine or *krassi;* the sharp white cheese *fromaella;* and most apparent, the elegant, finely patterned weavings—and carpets—called *chalia.* Just as Americans might flock to Vermont in the fall for maple syrup or cheese, so the Greeks in the cities come on a long winter weekend to tiny Arachova for its specialties and nearby skiing.

There are two holidays that really draw crowds to Arachova. On April 23, San Georgiou Day, the death of the village's patron saint is celebrated with a traditional bacchanalia on the plaza outside the church. At Easter these festivities are extended over several days and encompass all those who are fortunate enough to be in town.

Useful Information

In the height of the tourist season, many readers may prefer to stay overnight in Arachova when visiting the overcrowded village of Delphi. There are several local **buses** running back and forth between Delphi and Arachova; the fare is 90 drs (65¢).

Shopping in Arachova is a treat because so many small tempting stores line the main street. Several markets display local cheese, wine, and honey in the windows, and souvenir stores are draped with weavings. If this specialty is what's drawn you here, go straight to the shop of **Katina Panagakou** (tel. 31-743), on the south side of main street at the east end of the village. Katina herself is a superb weaver and her shop features the work of many local artisans. There you can purchase new or antique *karpiti* (carpets) or *chalia* (weavings). Though her prices are reasonable, quality costs.

Accommodations and Dining

If you're planning to be in Arachova for the San Georgiou festivities, arrive early or telephone ahead for reservations. One alternative is to stay in a private home, although you will have a problem making reservations. The town has formed a housing coop and has set prices for a double at 3210 drs ($24.70). As for hotels, the ten-room **Hotel Apollon** (tel. 0267/31-427) is run by Andreas Louskou, and his family keeps a spotless, homey hillside lodging with wonderful views from most of its rooms. Next door to it is the nine-room **Hotel Parnassos** (tel. 0267/31-307), also run by the Louskous, with similar accommodations but without its own breakfast room downstairs. Both hotels are the town's best choices at 2560 drs ($20) for a double.

For those of you looking for affordable resort luxury, the modern **Hotel Anemolia** (tel. 0267/31-640) commands the best real estate on a hillside about two kilometers west of town. The less pleasant, deteriorating **Xenia Hotel** (tel. 0267/31-230) also offers fine views from the west end of town. The cheaper Xenia has double rooms for 5340 drs ($41), plus compulsory board plans on holiday weekends.

Eating in Arachova is a treat too, whether you order roasted paschal lamb or the usual souvlaki. There are two excellent, inexpensive tavernas on the main street, **O Elatos,** on the north side, where Nikos will charm you with his warmth and hospitality, and **O Karmalis,** across the street, where the outdoor patio makes a sunny luncheon spot.

Because Arachova draws so many Greek tourists, there are several sophisticated restaurants serving Greek haute cuisine, which charge about 3200 drs ($25) for two with wine. Above the main street, in the uppermost lanes of town, is the popular **To Kastro.** Keep climbing and ask the locals how to get there; even if you never find this hideaway restaurant, you'll enjoy the hike up the shallow stairs lined with red-painted olive oil drums, filled with flowers and herbs.

While we're in Arachova, let's go a bit farther north to . . .

MOUNT PARNASSUS: E.O.T. has established a full-service ski resort based at Fterolaka with an altitude of 2,252 meters, a 27-kilometer or 50-minute drive from Arachova. There are 12 ski runs; beginners get the chair lifts while you more experienced skiers will have to make do with the two upper-level T-bars. There's a ski rental shop, snackbar, cafeteria, and clothes and accessories boutique at the **Fterolaka Center.** The ski center is open from December to April; contact their office (tel. 0234/22-689) for more information. Daily lift tickets can be purchased for under $10, they give lessons, and you can rent gear (tel. 0267/31-552) for reservations.

Why would anyone consider skiing here? Because Parnassus, one of the highest mountains in Greece, is where Deucalion and Pyrrha landed in their boat as the last survivors of Zeus' Great Deluge. Because the mountain was sacred to the Muses, to Dionysos, and to Apollo, who requested that his Oracle be set up on its slopes. With those endorsements, at those prices, why not?

In good weather, hikers may want to try the three- to four-hour ascent to the top of Parnassus. The Delphi Youth Hostel has tourist-drawn maps of the route; they suggest hitching a ride to Kelaria and hiking from there. In Athens, contact the Hellenic Federation of Mountaineering (tel. 0132/12-429) for information.

2. Delphi

If there is only one archeological site in Greece that you'll allow yourself to see, it must be the Oracle of Delphi. Nowhere will you find more interesting remains, a more beautiful setting, and a higher quality collection of art gathered in the same place. If any of our readers can write and tell us that they didn't hear the Oracle calling, then we can only assume that they weren't listening. Delphi is simply the most mystical and magical site in the entire country.

THE ORACLE OF DELPHI: According to Plutarch: "There are two sentences inscribed upon the Delphic oracle, hugely accommodated to the usages of man's life: 'Know thyself,' and 'Nothing too much'; and upon these all other precepts depend."

There is some controversy surrounding the question of what one should visit first at Delphi, the archeological site or the museum. Kyle and many near-experts suggest the visitor first tour the museum. They argue that this will orient or enhance your walk through the remains at the site. John believes one should buy a detailed map or guidebook at the museum and head straight for the site. Then when you go to the museum, you'll be much happier and more interested in trying to translate those little signs in French that describe the museum artifacts. Let's examine the . . .

Delphi Museum

One of the first things you'll see upon entering the museum is an **omphalos**, a marble cone sculpted to appear as if covered with braided wool. In antiquity Delphi was held to be the center of the world and the omphalos was the symbol of the "navel of the earth" (umbilicus). To the right in the next room is a **frieze** from the Treasury of the Sifnians (525 B.C.), depicting the war between the Greeks and the Tartans, the gods at Mount Olympus, images of Athena, Aphrodite, and Hermes, and the war between the gods and the giants.

For some reason the next room is often closed, but lean over the guardrail and in the corner you'll see the famous **winged sphynx of the Naxians**. The sphynx, part bird, lion, and woman, stood atop a tall pedestal at the base of the Temple of Apollo.

Enter the room with the two still and imposing archaic *kouroi*, (600 B.C.); to the right are the remains of sacred offerings found in a secret passage under the Temple of Apollo, one of the most exciting exhibits in the museum.

The fifth-century B.C. **offerings**, thought to be from one of the Ionian cities because of their style, are made of chryselephantine (gold and ivory) and of such value even in the ancient world that they were moved from storage in the Treasury of the Corinthians to an underground vault after a fifth-century A.D. fire. In 1939 French archeologists found at least three life-size figures (of Apollo, Artemis, and possibly Leto) and a huge bull. The bull is made of wood, covered with hammered and cast silver and decorated with gold and ivory. The human figures, now charred, are made of solid ivory. Then don't miss the beautiful censer in the corner (450 B.C.).

As you return to the main hall, continue through the rooms displaying metopes from the Athenian Treasury; admire the forceful imagery of the "Labors of Heracles." The exhibit of remnants and restored sections of the Tholos from the Sanctuary of Athena Pronaia is of particular interest if you have already viewed the extraordinarily beautiful circular building standing below the main site of Delphi.

In the remaining rooms there are three highlights that you should search out. The first is a figure of **Agias**, a star athlete of the fifth century B.C. He's the best preserved of a group of six related figures, and is thought to be a copy of a bronze executed by Lysippus. The second sculpture of note is the downcast, **contemplative youth** from Caudiopolis, sculpted by Antinoos in Roman times, and found below the Temple of Apollo. The final sculpture is the trademark of Delphi: the **bronze charioteer**, offered by King Polyzalos in 474 B.C. This lithe young man was part of a larger sculpture that included a chariot, the whole commemorating the victory of the charioteer in the Pythian Games. The eyes of the victor still sparkle.

Before you rush off to the site, examine the marble **Acanthus column** (330 B.C.). Three elegant women in dancing positions pose atop this acanthus-stalk-shaped column and bud, once used as part of a votive tripod.

Sanctuary of Apollo

Along the hillside which hugs the road to Arachova is the Sanctuary of Apollo. If you don't have a site guide, wait a few minutes to join a guided tour in the language of your choice (on any given day you'll have a choice of English, French, German, Italian, or Greek). Up the stairs from the ticket booth is the **Sacred Way**, which was once lined with bronze statues offered to Apollo by Sparta, Arcadia, and several other city-states. On both sides of the walk are the **Treasuries**, housing many of the offerings now preserved in the museum. After the beautiful Treasury of the Athenians (labeled), on the left you'll see the **Rock of Sybil** (grandmother of all soothsayers), where the Pythias (a priestess of

Apollo at least 50 years old) would sit on her tripod and deliver oracles interpreted by the priests. Oracle season lasted only one month a year, and the lines were quite long. Behind this is the long "polygonal wall," covered with inscriptions on each of its beveled faces.

The vast foundations of the **Temple of Apollo** and the few Doric columns that remain invoke images of his beautiful Temple at Vassae. Climbing higher to the theater will reward you with a wonderful view of the temple and the Temple of Athena Pronaia in the valley below. This view of the landscape clearly illustrates why the ancients chose this as "the navel of the world"—it's serene and magnificent. The compact **amphitheater** at this level held 5,000 spectators for dramatic presentations, music, and poetry readings. At the very top of the site is the long **stadium,** (which began hosting theatrical events in 1987), the best preserved in Greece. The stadium is remembered as the venue for chariot races during the quadrennial Pythian Games (begun in 582 B.C., these athletic competitions did for Apollo what the Olympic Games did for Zeus).

There are two more sights that cannot be missed if you're to appreciate Delphi in its entirety.

The Castalia Fountain

At the bend on the road between the Temple of Apollo and that of Athena Pronaia, under the huge maple trees, the pilgrims to Delphi would cleanse themselves with water from sacred Mount Parnassus. Walk up the path and at the old fountain you'll see niches carved in the Yambia rock, which contained offerings brought to the Nymph of Castalia. Stairs lead up to the gorge (now blocked off) formed by the Yambia and Naupflia crags.

The water from the spring was sprinkled over the Temple of Apollo, and you can taste the deliciously pure water yourself—this is your price of admission into the Cult of Apollo. The Castalia Fountain is also a lovely shaded picnic spot, away from the hordes of international shutterbugs.

The Temple of Athena Pronaia

From the roadway, continue past the Castalia Fountain to the Tourist Café. Below it are the uninspiring remains (closed for excavation) of the **Gymnasium,** which had racetracks, boxing and wrestling rings, and baths for the training of local athletes. Keep walking along the roadway, past the laurels, till you see three white Doric columns, topped with one of the few *in situ* pediments in Greece. In the relative isolation of the fourth-century B.C. Temple of Athena you can admire the remains of the mysterious, circular **Tholos.**

Thought to be the work of master architect Theodoros (ca. 380 B.C.), it was originally composed of 20 outer columns which surrounded 10 Corinthian semi-columns, in two tiers. This is the spot from which to admire all the ruins of Delphi, contemplate its role in the ancient world, and listen to the prophecy of the birds.

The Delphi Museum (tel. 0265/82-312) and the Sanctuary of Apollo are open Monday through Saturday from 8 a.m. to 7 p.m., on Sunday and holidays from 8 a.m. to 6 p.m.; the museum is *closed Tuesday.* Admission is 400 drs ($3). The Castalia Fountain is always accessible and the Temple of Athena Pronaia is open 8 a.m. to 7 p.m. daily.

In order to see the remarkable sights at dawn and dusk, the two best moments, when the ominous clouds swoop by mottling the marble façades with prophetic shadows, one must find a place to sleep.

ACCOMMODATIONS: Delphi is a small mountain village built above and below both sides of its main highway, called Frederiki Street. Hotels and pensions are cheek to cheek with bookshops, souvenir stands, and expensive tavernas, but there are some excellent places to stay which make Delphi an ideal base camp for touring this region.

Walk downstairs in the center of town and you'll see two pension signs, for the Maniati and the Odysseus, on a small street lined with red planters. The **Odysseus** (tel. 0265/82-235) is an ideal pension: low priced, fantastic views, clean rooms, quiet, and a spacious terrace. The effusive hostess Toula encourages her guests to buy food at the local markets and bring it back to eat or drink at one of her terrace tables. Her eight bathless rooms are 2000 drs ($16) for two, 1500 drs ($12) for one; showers are 200 drs ($1.55) extra. Across the way, at 2 Isaia St., is the **Pension Maniati** (tel. 0265/82-134). This family-run, clean, and homey lodging was closed at our visit but plans to reopen.

The **Hotel Athina** (tel. 0265/82-239) is a small hotel on Frederiki Street, whose 12 rooms offer superb views from the balconies. Manager Nicholas speaks English and is very helpful. A bathless double costs 1935 drs ($15), and a private-facilities double costs 2435 drs ($19). Just down Frederiki Street is the **Hotel Sibylla** (tel. 0265/82-335), whose ten rooms, all with private bath, share the same scenic views. For 2700 drs ($21) a double, the Sibylla, which has a comfortable coffeehouse off the lobby, is a good value.

The **Hotel Phivos** (tel. 0265/82-319), also on Frederiki Street, is managed by Nicolas Kouroumalis. Its excellent views and comfortable accommodations can be had at 1935 drs ($15) for a double, 2200 drs ($18) for a triple. Check in the gift shop at the peaceful south end of the main street for the host of the clean, modern **Hotel Pan** (tel. 0265/82-294). All 14 rooms have private facilities and share a terrace with that same wonderful valley view. At 3500 drs ($27) for a double with breakfast, the Pan is a good bet.

In a higher price range there's a choice of several newer, C-class hotels that cater to large bus groups as well as individual tourists. The **Hotel Hermes** (tel. 0265/82-318) is built on a hillside on a quiet part of Frederiki Street. The lobby is decorated with local weavings, and the top-floor rooms have the same view one can enjoy in the pleasant breakfast room. All 30 rooms have private bathrooms; rates are 2500 drs ($19) for a bed-and-breakfast single, 3750 drs ($29) for a double. Owners Tony and Nick Droseros happily told us, "Your boss, Arthur Frommer, slept here!"

The **Delphi Youth Hostel** is well known on the budget travelers' circuit for its gracious, helpful, and friendly staff and its better-than-average accommodations. It's located at 31 Apollonas St. (the block above Frederiki Street), and you can call 0265/82-268 or write ahead for reservations. There are three double rooms with private bath for 1875 drs ($13.50), but the 100 beds, at 625 drs ($4.65) each, are what's really in demand. In the high season new arrivals should sign up for a bed between 7:30 a.m. and 10 a.m., before they begin sightseeing. The youth hostel will also put overflow crowds out on the roof for 375 drs ($3) a night.

Apollon Camping is very basic but is the best-situated campground in the vicinity of Delphi. It's located off the main highway two kilometers south of the village, and offers tentsites which overlook the mountains, the valley, and the Gulf of Corinth beyond.

READER'S HOTEL SUGGESTION: "During our last trip to Delphi we stayed at a charming, practically new inexpensive hotel with one of the best views in the world. The **Hotel Acropole** (tel. 0265/82-676) charges $19 for a single and $27 for a double and this includes a continental breakfast" (Nicholas J. Kontras, St. Louis, Mo.).

RESTAURANTS: Even with the huge demand put on lunchtime restaurants, there are some fine, reasonably priced meals to be had day or night in the village of Delphi. For those of you aching to get out and eat some eggs, or at least not have to look at another "breakfast complet," try the **Pâtisserie,** opposite the Hotel Vouzas, at the end of the main street nearest the archeological site. For 550 drs ($4.20) you can have a large glass of fresh-squeezed orange juice, a cheese omelet, a variety of pastries, rolls, breads, and other snack food. It's a plant-filled, elegant little cafeteria that's open daily from morning till night.

If you climb up one block above Frederiki Street to Apollonos Street you'll find the **Taverna Vakzos,** next door to the youth hostel. This was our favorite place, partly because of its gorgeous views. Vakzos has a typical taverna menu, but it's bright and spacious and bargain priced. The youth hostel staff recommended it to us, and they should know about budget eating. Also on Apollonos Street is the **Macedonia Grill** for breakfast, souvlaki, sandwiches, and sodas.

When it comes to dinnertime, there are a few tavernas whose atmosphere and more varied menu make a refreshing change. **Taverna Sunflower** is two doors down from the Hotel Hermes, in the middle of the lower main street. A pleasant atmosphere and spectacular views combine with good beef and lamb dishes, excellently prepared vegetables, and a bottle of wine to make a relaxing evening, at a cost of about 1500 drs ($11.55) to 2000 drs ($16) for two. The little **Taverna Pan** (tel. 82-473) and the small **Omphalos** are up three steps off the alley called Isaia Street (the Hotels Sibylla and Castalia are down on Frederiki Street here; just walk uphill across from them to reach the Pan). Both offer complete soup-to-nuts meals from 800 drs ($6.45) in the "cater to groups" fashion, but the Pan's à la carte menu is varied and all the Greek specialties are reasonably priced. The interior is decorated with locally made weavings and folk art, and the round tables are spaced for views of the stucco fireplace.

A note for those who take our picnicking advice seriously: There's a good **supermarket** on Apollonos Street across from the Hotel Stadion. And another note for those who just get going after dinner: Delphi has three discothèques, listed in order of current "hotness": **Zodiaque, Delphi By Night,** and **Discothèque For You.**

USEFUL INFORMATION: The new Delphi Tourist Office (tel. 82-900), on Frederiki Street, is open 9 a.m. to 7 p.m. daily. Outside the Kafeteria Kastro on the south end of Main Street is the stop for the Athens bus; last year they left four times daily for the three-hour ride, at a cost of 1250 drs ($9.62). Buses to Amfissa, the beaches at Itea or Nafpaktos, or to the Peloponnese leave from the Kafeteria several times daily. Check with the Kafeteria staff or at the youth hostel for schedule information. From this point on Frederiki Street you can catch the local bus to Arachova throughout the day; the fare is 90 drs (60¢). To get to Ossios Loukas (see the next section) you can get a bus to Distomo (or exit the Athens bus at the highway intersection), then you must walk three kilometers to catch the bus directly to the monastery. From Delphi, you can share a taxi with up to four people for about 4000 drs ($30.75), a bargain for the 45-minute scenic drive to Ossios Loukas.

There are two **banks** on Frederiki Street, which are open the standard 8 a.m. to 2 p.m. hours (they reopen from 5 p.m. to 7 p.m. during the summer). The main post office and kiosk at the museum change money also. Skiers can contact the **Fterolakas Ski Center** for more information about skiing at Mount Parnassus (tel. 0234/22-689). Hikers can contact the **Hellenic Federation of Mountaineering** in Athens (tel. 0132/12-429) for information about climbing Mount Parnassus; the Delphi Youth Hostel (many of whose clients have actually done this) has a great deal of information and advice about this climb too. The **area code** for Delphi is 0265.

EXCURSIONS FROM DELPHI: With Delphi as a base, you can visit Arachova or Mount Parnassus (already covered in this chapter), areas of great scenic beauty. Southwest of Delphi is the 11th-century Byzantine Monastery of Ossios Loukas; an exquisite chapel in this lovely compound boasts gold-backed mosaics that rival those at Dafni (when the Dafni Monastery was open) for the affections of Byzantiophiles. Many readers enjoy alternating archeological sites with a refreshing splash in the sea, something easily done at the nearby Gulf of Corinth coastline. We'll cover beaches from just south of Ossios Loukas all the way west to Nafpaktos, near the Antirion crossover point for entry into the Peloponnese.

For those readers who are proceeding up the eastern coast of Greece to Mount Pelion, Volos, or the Sporades Islands, or due north to Meteora and on to Thessalonika, we'll take you up Boeotia on the Lamia highway.

If you are traveling (as do many of the tours from Athens) from Delphi to the Monastery of Ossios Loukas, you'll pass a spot of great importance in Greek literature. Where the road continues straight to Livadia and splits right (south) to Distomo and Ossios Loukas is thought to be the **triple way**, the crossroads where Oedipus killed his father, King Laius. Oedipus (his name meant "swollen foot") was walking from Delphi to Thebes, having received a horrible omen from the Oracle that he would kill his father and marry his mother from whom he had been separated since childbirth. At this very fork in the road a distraught Oedipus met an older man riding in a royal chariot who refused to let him pass. The man whipped Oedipus and, in defense, Oedipus killed his attacker, fulfilling the first part of the Oracle's terrible prophesy.

The Monastery of Ossios Loukas

The Church of Ossios Loukas is one of the most ornately decorated and well-designed Byzantine sanctuaries in Greece. Its brilliant gold-backed mosaics and innovative octagonal structure make Ossios Loukas a must for those interested in Byzantium. Set on the slopes of Mount Helikon, the church is dedicated to the hermit Saint Loukas (not Saint Luke the apostle), and is part of a larger monastery that is run by four bearded monks.

Ossios Loukas Stiriotis established a kind of medieval oracle, a church known for prophecies and the ascetic life. He founded his church in A.D. 942, and lived there until his death in 953. Loukas' original church was replaced during the 11th century by Romanos the First, the new church designed as a local variation of Haghia Sophia in Constantinople. Loukas' relics, recently kept in the Vatican, were moved to the church in 1987, converting the status of the site from a museum to a holy place. Accordingly, both men and women are required to wear suitable clothing, meaning no shorts or halter tops. Monks screen visitors to ensure that they are wearing the proper attire; those not dressed appropriately will be provided with a bright orange pajama-like covering.

As you enter the narthex, where the admission fee—300 drs ($2.65)—is collected and postcards are sold, look up and you'll see some of the best and the brightest of the sparkling mosaics. Proceed into the church and turn left at the second niche. When you step up, Loukas will be above you, sporting a helmet and beard, his intense eyes watching over tourists, arms up in resignation. Many of the mosaics, including the one decorating the main dome, were severely damaged or destroyed by an earthquake in 1659. Paintings and frescoes, which in turn were damaged by Turkish troops in the 19th century, replaced the last mosaics. Notice the lace-like carved marble pillars in front of the altar and the patterns and columns of the marble floors.

We mistakenly entered the monastery from the back and walked down a narrow path (where we were blessed by a monk who was chopping wood) that led to the church and the crypt where old Loukas was originally buried. The crypt contains some interesting and colorful frescoes festooned with graffiti from the ages.

Within the grounds of the monastery is the flagstone "village" of Ossios Loukas, complete with taverna. Don't miss the view of the valley below from the flagstone patio. There isn't a sign of modern life (except the road), so the panorama is strictly medieval. The monastery is open from 8 a.m. to 4 p.m. daily.

The Beaches Near Delphi

Delphi, nestled in a lovely and cool alpine setting, is hardly a place from which to beach-hop. Nevertheless, for those of you who can't wait, we offer the following areas, accessible by frequent local buses.

Antikira, 14 kilometers south of Distomo (the turnoff for Ossios Loukas), provides one of the most scenic swimming holes near Delphi. This tiny port town is built at the center of a natural cove.

It doesn't take long to find out why the hordes haven't ruined this sunny spot. At the north end of the cove is **Aspra Spitia**, a model town straight from the *atelier* of Le Corbusier, which houses the personnel of the well-guarded French Picheney Aluminum factory. In contrast, the sleepy south end of the village is protected by barbed-wire fences surrounding an air force base, which seal off the nicest beaches around. Discreet signs along the shore insist "No Pictures."

If you're dying for a swim, we strongly recommend that you head southwest out of Delphi to **Itea**, a larger port on the Gulf of Corinth just 17 kilometers away. Once blessed with a ferry running to Egio on the Peloponnese, Itea resembles a ghost tourist town. Its broad, once-crowded, echo-filled streets are lined with signs in every language; old hotel marquees dot the horizon.

If you must, stay at the C-class **Akti Hotel** (tel. 0265/32-257) or try the Itea Beach campsite. If a view of supertankers doesn't thrill you, the road north to Delphi is lined with olive groves and provides excellent shaded free camping in leveled plots. The city of Itea, of course, has markets and other services if you need them.

If you drive along the coastline east from Itea you'll soon reach **Nafpaktos**, just 12 kilometers northwest of the ferry crossing at Antirion. In 1407 the Venetians took this sleepy (but strategically located) Greek port and secured the top of Mount Rigani with a fortress, whose walls spread down to protect the harbor. Although ruins can still be seen behind the town, what's so special about Nafpaktos is the beautiful half-moon cove formed by the old walls and guard towers. It's all spread out in front of the main platia. Here, fishing boats unload their wares and the old women and merchants huddle around to bargain for the day's catch. At the east end of town is the pebble beach called **Gribovo**, and at the west, the **Psavi**.

This charming gulfside port is a perfect place to relax near the busy port of Patras. The city is filled with cafés shaded by tall old trees, and if you cannot afford the gulfside **Hotel Lido** (tel. 0634/22-501), where spacious, modern doubles with terraces cost 5000 drs ($38.50), with breakfast, there are several other budget choices. Nearby on Psavi Beach is the **Hotel Amaryllis** (tel. 0634/27-237), a clean, simple lodging with a reading lounge on each floor. Across the street is the **Hotel Diethnes** (tel. 0634/27-342), whose five cozy, older rooms are managed by three charming grandmas. For a bathless double at both, the charge is 2250 drs ($17.30). On the port at 14 Botsari is the **Hotel Nea Hellas** (tel. 0634/27-400). The 12 rooms in this 20-year-old pension have waterfront views upstairs and fortress-wall views downstairs. Bathless doubles are 2250 drs ($17.30) for the upper rooms and 1800 drs ($13.80) for the lower level. We liked both views equally well and found looking in on life in the platia and along the waterfront to be the biggest treat of all.

HEADING NORTH: To work our way back to the north of Boeotia requires returning to the main highway at . . .

Amfissa

Amfissa has little to offer the tourist. Surrounded by mountains and situated on the same plain as Itea, Amfissa serves mostly as a major marketplace for all the local hillside villages. Amfissa's abundant supply of water, hot temperatures, and flat terrain (easier for watering and makes a more tender olive) make it an ideal area for growing olives! One local resident claimed that the area is planted with over five million olive trees; and if you check your at-home supermarket shelves to see where your salad dressing is made, they could be right. The town is like an oven in summer and remarkably cold in winter, so unless you want to watch the olives grow, we suggest that you move on to the highpoint of your northward journey . . .

The Pass of Thermopylae

The mountains (west) will be to your left, the sea (east) to your right, and straight ahead the national highway system has paved its track directly through one of the most famous places of antiquity. Watch for the statue of Leonidas, celebrated Spartan leader, who stands erect, shield and spear in hand, marveling at the amount of vehicular traffic that flows through this strategic pass.

It all dates from 480 B.C., when Xerxes and the Persians reached Thermopylae and knew that to conquer Greece they would have to fight their way through this pass. Leonidas, commander of the Spartan forces and general of all the Greek troops, had 7,300 men stationed in the middle. Weeks of standoff went by, until an Amalian soldier, angry at the confederation, turned traitor and decided to show Xerxes a new back route over the mountains. The traitor, Ephialtes, led the Persian captain to the path over Mount Phrikion, where they found 1,000 Phokidian troops stationed. The Persian, Capt. Hydarnes, returned at night with 2,000 men and slew the Phokidians, emerging the next morning on the east side of the pass. As he'd planned with Xerxes, at the appointed hour the attack against the Greek forces began from both sides. Leonidas realized at once what had happened and dismissed most of the troops. He kept with him 700 Thespians, 300 Spartans, and 300 Theban hostages.

Leonidas and his Spartan troops have long been heralded for their bravery that day. Byron wrote of Greece's 19th-century struggle for independence: "Earth! Render back from out thy breast a remnant of our Spartan dead! Of the three hundred grant but three, to make a new Thermopylae!" (from *Don Juan,* Canto III). One terrible aspect of the story recorded by Herodotus told of the moment when Leonidas himself fell in battle. Savage fighting broke out between the Persians (who hoped to exhibit his body as proof of victory) and the loyal Spartans (who wanted to protect it). Two of Xerxes' own brothers were killed in the struggle, and over many deaths the Greeks retook it four times. Of course, soon all the Greeks had been slaughtered and Xerxes and his men pushed on to Attica.

Herodotus has left us one of the most beautiful epigrams in literature, the quote from the burial mound of the Spartans: "Go tell the Spartans, thou that passeth by, / That here, obedient to their laws, we lie" (translated by W. L. Bowles).

Thermopylae means "Hot Gates" in Greek, and the pass was named for the hot springs that flowed through it in antiquity and are now routed to several spas on the east coast. If you've had enough driving for the day, the **Camping Leonidas** grounds are just off the highway, and to the east (about 30 kilometers from the pass), on the coast, the pretty beach resort of **Kamena Vourla**. The narrow strip of beach is matched across the highway by a row of new white two-story hotels, the architecture of a pleasant middle-class resort overlooking the island of Evia. At nearby Ag. Nikolaos and Ag. Konstandinos regular car ferries shuttle people and their vehicles over to this popular Athenian weekend stomping ground. Drivers can also approach Evia by leaving the old highway at Thebes, bearing right, and crossing the narrow Euripos Channel right into the capital of Chalkis (Halkida).

3. Evia

The island of Evia (Euboea) is the Long Island, Atlantic City, Rehobeth, and Santa Monica of Athens. Its proximity and sand beaches make it the place for weekend homes and mini-vacations. This section is for readers who need a quick break from the Athenian heat. Readers who seek the way to the lesser known pleasures of Skyros should turn to the section on Kymi, the port city nearest to this Sporades isle.

Older Greeks will swear that the island of Evia was actually part of the mainland until Poseidon (angry over some mortal who'd flirted with a mermaid) took his trident and sliced the Evia piece off. Since that long-ago time the Greeks have done everything possible to reconnect it, while simultaneously enjoying the benefit of two additional coastlines. Daily ferry service connects Oropous with Eretria, Grammatikos with Almiropotamos, Ag. Marina with Nea Stira, and Rafina with Marmaris and Karistos. The only land bridge, which connects Ag. Minas in Boeotia to Chalkis (Halkida), extends a mere 210 feet.

CHALKIS: Evia's capital is Chalkis (Greek for "bronze"), and in antiquity this thriving port was well known for the metalwork it contributed to the sanctuaries at Delphi and Olympia and for the weapons produced during continuous wars. Over the centuries Evia, in whole or in part, fell under the rule of the Athenians, Spartans, Thebans, Macedonians, Franks, Venetians, and Turks. Meanwhile its sailors were opening new trade routes for the Hellenic world and founding cities in northern Greece (Chalkidiki), Italy, and Asia Minor.

The **Euripos Channel** is the most interesting thing about present-day Chalkis because of its irregular currents, which change direction between 7 and 14 times a day, or sometimes don't change at all, depending on the moon and the season. The rapid shift and brief lulls in between made it very dangerous for boats to pass through, and it's said that Aristotle drowned himself here in frustration at not being able to explain the currents. Today scientists only guess that the Euripos acts as a sluice between two water levels of the Euboean Channel, but don't let that stop you from attempting an explanation.

Expensive hotels and cafés line the promenade of Chalkis's harbor, with the restaurants on one side of the street and their café tables overlooking the water on the other side. The blue-and-red striped awning of **No. 36 Boudari** (tel. 21-556) is about the least expensive place to hang out and watch the action. Before you settle in, check on the next transportation out.

The **bus station** is on Venizelou Street (tel. 22-640 or 22-436), and the **train station** is nearby (tel. 22-530). . . . If you have some waiting time, the **archeological museum** is at 13 Venizelou St. (about two blocks up from the harbor), where you can see a small collection of finds, particularly from Eretria. There's also an attractive Turkish mosque near the Euripos Channel bridge.

NORTHERN EVIA: Signposted as "B. Evia" or "Boreios Evia," this area features a medicinal hot springs spa at **Loutra Aedipsos**, and many hotels with mineral water bubbling into the rooms have been built for arthritis and rheumatism sufferers. If this interests you, the E.O.T. in Athens can provide you with more information about it and other Grecian spas. **Limni**, 85 kilometers north of Chalkis, was so picturesque a port that Zeus and Hera got married there, but times have changed: as with all good nearby places, hotels and speedboats have followed in the wake of suntanned Athenian weekenders, and idyllic Limni is no more.

SOUTHERN EVIA: Heading south of Chalkis (these road signs confusingly read "N. Evia" or "Notios Evia") you'll notice occasional signs of resort life. Eretria Beach, Holidays in Evia, and the Golden Beach are all huge, full-service resorts packed with locals on summer weekends. Instead, in the sleepy waterfront village of Eretria you'll find the spiffy, large **Delfis Hotel** (tel. 0221/62-380; doubles are $28) and the B-class **Hotel Perigali** (tel. 0221/62-113; doubles with breakfast are $42). Four kilometers south of town is **Evia Camping**. The most comfortable choice to our minds is the spotless, quiet pension run by the **Theodorous** (tel. 0221/62-479), at 6 Apostoli. It's just a block from the beach and offers doubles for 1400 drs ($10.97) a night, but in July and August their 19 rooms with kitchen go by the month only. Eretria's narrow pebble beach makes it a nice day trip or a convenient weekend away from the Athenian *nefos*. A car-ferry runs ten times daily to Oropos on the mainland at a fare of 120 drs (92¢) for adults, 100 drs (77¢) for children, 600 drs ($4.62) for cars. There's also a **Budget Rent-A-Car** office in Eretria (tel. 62-909), but the roads are often unpaved and so hair-raisingly curved through the steep hills of Evia that you're better off avoiding the gray hairs by taking a convenient, usually comfortable local bus.

If you're continuing south, you'll find small mountain villages and tiny fishing villages off the main road. At **Nea Stira** is the most efficient ferry crossing (time and money-wise) if you're driving up to Kimi. A car-ferry (tel. 0294/63-491) runs five times daily to Ag. Marina, near Marathon, on the mainland. Fares are 300 drs ($2.31) for adults, and 1000 drs ($7.70) to 1250 drs ($9.62) per car. If for some inexcusable reason you're stuck here overnight, the **Hotel Plaza** (tel. 0224/41-429)—no relation to New York's—has doubles for 3700 drs ($28.46).

KIMI: Kimi is the only place on Evia worthy of a one-night stand. It's a charming mountaintop fishing village, and the one explanation for this apparent contradiction is that the plateau it's on was more spacious and hospitable than the narrow coast. Tall, narrow stone houses are stacked in among the pine and fir forests, but everyone finds their way into the main square. Here you'll find the **Hotel Krineion** (tel. 0222/22-287), a charming, wood-trimmed 50-year-old lodging that's seen a lot of visitors. Large, clean doubles are 2850 drs ($21.92). The front rooms have great views, but beware: like much of Kimi, the hotel is only open from May to September. Kimi's only other accommodation is the bright, modern **Hotel Kymi** (tel. 0222/22-408), up the hill by the post office. Doubles here are 2010 drs ($15.46).

The best of Kimi's cuisine can be sampled at the **Markos Grill**, one block from the square. This is the time to try out your French, as Mr. Markos transforms himself from an ordinary souvlaki chef into an elegant French headwaiter —a surprising character in this isolated outpost! For breakfast there's a bakery below the platia (they also sell picnic supplies for the boat), or try the small café-pâtisserie on the square which features Kimi's unique all-almond baklava. The charming **Folklore Museum of Kimi** (filled with sailors' memorabilia and brought-home treasures) is set in a traditional house below the platia. It's open daily from 4:30 p.m. to 7:30 p.m., on Saturday from 5:30 p.m. to 7:30 p.m., and on Sunday and holidays from 10 a.m. to 1 p.m. and 4:30 p.m. to 7:30 p.m. Call 22-480 for more information.

Paralia Kimi

The nontown at water's edge, Paralia Kimi is one big pier and the few services needed to maintain it. There's the **Hotel Beis** (tel. 0222/22-870), whose 35 rooms are perfectly okay at 3000 drs ($23.07) a double. A better deal here are the 15 doubles without bath for only 1950 drs ($15). Nick Beis whiles away the hours at his bar with guests, but since the boats to Skyros don't leave till 5 p.m., and there's scheduled public bus service or taxis (from the square up top, 850 drs, or $6.54) down to the paralia, only the truly lazy should spend the night here. Tickets for the C/F *Skyros* or the C/F *Aegeus* can be purchased on the day of departure in Paralia Kimi; call 0222/22-020 for schedule information on car-ferries. There are also passengers-only ferries from Kimi. Besides daily departures for Skyros, there's a Thursday afternoon sailing to Alonissos and Skopelos, and one a week to Skaithos, Limnos, and Kavala (in Thrace). Weather and demand play havoc on sailing schedules from this little port; check in Kimi for information on departures to Samothraki, Alexandropoulis, and Volos (as well as in those respective sections of this book).

4. Thessaly

In his *Histories,* Herodotus describes the Thessaly that Xerxes and his Persian troops crossed in 480 B.C.: "Xerxes could see from Therma the Thessalian Mountains—the towering peaks of Olympus and Ossa, and on being informed that between the two mountains there was a narrow gorge through which the River Pinios ran, and also a good road into Thessaly, he suddenly felt that he would like to go by sea and inspect the mouth of the river. . . . To the eastward is the great barrier of Pelion and Ossa, two mountains whose bases form a continuous chain; then there is the range of Olympus on the north, Pindus on the west, and Othrys on the South. In the center of this ring of mountains lies the low plain of Thessaly. A number of rivers pour their waters into it . . . all unite into a single stream and find their way to the sea through one narrow gorge. . . . Ages ago, before the gorge existed and while there was as yet no outlet for the water, these rivers . . . poured down from the hills as much water as they do today, and so made Thessaly an inland sea. The natives of Thessaly have a tradition that the gorge which forms the outlet for the river was made by Poseidon, and the story is a reasonable one; for if one believes that it is Poseidon who shakes the earth and that chasms caused by earthquakes are attributable to him, then the mere sight of this place would be enough to make one say that it is Poseidon's handiwork. It certainly appeared to me that the cleft in the mountain had been caused by an earthquake. . . ."

Lamia is the gateway to Thessaly for drivers from Athens, and the changing scenery, lowlands, and lofty heights that are immediately visible make clear that one is entering a new region.

Herodotus touched on most of the province's charms. Mount Pelion, towering above the industrial port of Volos, is still the countryside inhabited by frolicking centaurs and wood fairies. The port of Volos is also the gateway to some of Greece's most beautiful Aegean islands, the Sporades.

In the western part of the Thessalian Plain are the startling *meteora* ("rocks in air"), just outside the provincial town of Kalambaka. When the visitor sees these incredible monoliths standing proud and tall in the midst of flat plains, it's easy to understand why the ancients tried so hard to comprehend the geology of this region. (Which is saying nothing about the miracle-built monasteries that crown many of these isolated peaks.)

Mount Ossa must be conquered before we reach what may be the world's most famous mountain, Olympus, home of the gods. Its heights define Thessaly's northern border, but its north face leads us to Chapter XIV, a look at northern Greece.

When you pass through the provincial town of **Lamia**, notice the medieval castle of the Catalan Duchy (built 1319–1393) towering on the heights above you to the northeast. From this prospect it could guard the narrow waterway curling around Evia into the mainland ports. Scholars have found that its walls were largely built over the remains of classical ones, proving once again that once a fortress, always a fortress.

An old local through-road that wends its way around tavernas, beaches, kids on bicycles, and erratic coastline is the slower, more difficult route compared to the modern toll road leading the 110 kilometers to Volos, your springboard for the Mount Pelion region.

5. Volos and Mount Pelion

Two stories from mythology, that of Jason and the Argonauts and of Chyron and the Centaurs, constitute the only appeal the modern-day city of Volos will have for many. Because of the devastation of two earthquakes in 1955, today's rows of concrete housing, functional commercial buildings, and an active but unattractive port are what confront the visitor. Long ago, 79 years before the Trojan War, Jason set sail on the *Argo* from his father's kingdom of Iolkos in search of the Golden Fleece. On board with him were 55 sailors, including such luminaries as Theseus, Orpheus, Heracles, Dr. Asclepios, and Castor and Pollux. Jason returned from Colchis with the Golden Fleece and the woman who'd helped procure it, the enchantress Medea. Medea was only the first in a long line of romantic conquests that included Hypsiple, queen of Lemnos, and Glauce, daughter of the king of Corinth. When Jason finally abandoned Medea, she killed their two sons and fled to Athens. Her tale is eloquently told by Euripides and Seneca, while the Casanova Jason's is the basis of Chaucer's *The Legend of Good Women*.

VOLOS: High up on the slopes of Mount Pelion is Ano Volos, a hill village, undamaged by the quakes, where some 18th-century tower houses (similar to the Mani towers in the Peloponnese) still protect inhabitants from raiding pirates. It's thought that this was the ancient Iolkos, and in the wooded forests above it, the cave where Chyron the Centaur lived. Jason was only one of the remarkable heroes that Chyron (also spelled Cheiron) schooled in the finer arts. Achilles, Heracles, Asclepios, Aeneas, and Peleus all sat at his hooves (according to Homer) and listened to the wisdom of the half-man, half-horse creature. Though most centaurs were renowned for their bawdy behavior and drunkenness, Chyron was an expert at music, shooting, and the medicinal use of herbs and plants for which Mount Pelion is still justly famed. (It was he who cut the spear, or *pelios,* from one of the pine trees on Mount Pelion that saved the life of Achilles.) All the centaurs were known to live in the Pelion region, where they frolicked and wreaked havoc with pretty river nymphs and wood fairies who inhabited the lush, verdant highlands. Their high jinx kept the area from ever becoming overpopulated, and anyone touring one of the most beautiful, scenic regions in Greece will have much to thank them for.

Volos is also, of course, the gateway mainland city to the Sporades islands of Skiathos, Skopelos, and Alonissos (Skyros is more easily reached from Kymi,

Evia). Once touched by the wooded, fairyland beauty of the Pelion you may decide to sample these equally blessed, verdant islands and leave the sunbleached, arid Cyclades to others.

Orientation

Whether you're arriving by train (at Papadiamandi Street) or by bus (the K.T.E.L. station is at 2 Metamorfosseos St. and the O.S.E. station is at 40 Iassonos St.) you'll be within a five-minute walk of Riga Fereou Square, the home of the Thessaly region **E.O.T.** This helpful tourist office is open Monday to Saturday from 7 a.m. to 2:30 p.m. (tel. 23-500 or 36-233), and even when they're closed, much useful information is posted outside on their bulletin board. Ask for George Hadjinicolaou or Eva Koula (who speaks French and English well), who are both very knowledgeable and extremely helpful. A sidelong glance will bring the International Pier into view; walk along the waterfront to reach the **Argonafton**, a catchy name for the main piers where the Sporades ferries leave from, and where you'll find the most attractive hotels and tavernas. If you continue to walk east along the water, past Platia Georgiou (a pleasant park) and past the Ag. Konstantinos Church, you'll come to the **archeological museum**, on Athanasaki Street (open Monday through Saturday from 9 a.m. to 3 p.m., on Sunday from 10 a.m. to 2 p.m.; closed Tuesday), famous for its exhibits of prehistoric finds from throughout Greece, recent local artifacts from an area thought to be Iolkos, as well as Hellenistic-era painted stelae from the village of Dimitris.

Useful Information

Ferry tickets to the Sporades can be purchased from the **Sporades Travel Agency**, 32 Argonafton (tel. 23-400), or from the **Nomikos North Aegean Lines** (tel. 25-688). There are twice-daily sailings to Skiathos, once daily to Skopelos, daily except Monday to Alonissos, and Tuesday and Friday to Skyros (12 hours!). . . . The **Cyprus Shipping Company** has a ferry that leaves from the International Pier every fifth day for the 55-hour trip to Syria. For a double cabin, fares are $310 per person; call 22-501 for more information, and contact the Syrian Embassy in Athens or its consulate in Thessalonika for visa information.

The **Miltos Travel Office**, at 25 Argonafton (tel. 35-910), can provide you with ferryboat schedules, probably the most convenient way for a group to sightsee in the Mount Pelion region. Day rates are about 6000 drs ($46.15) for a compact car, including tax and mileage.

There are several **banks** around Argonafton and Riga Fereou but none keeps extended hours. . . . The **post office** is at 67 Pavlou Mela St. (about four blocks inland from the port), open 7:30 a.m. to 8:30 p.m. weekdays. . . . The **O.T.E.** is nearby at Elef. Venizelou, open 24 hours. . . . Emergency **medical assistance** can be obtained at the Volos Hospital by calling 27-531, 2, 3, or 4. . . . The area code is 0421.

If you're boarding a ferryboat and want to picnic en route, try the **markets** along Iassonos (that's Jason in Greek, by the way) Street; it's one block in from the water. . . . A dining suggestion in the unremarkable cuisine culture of Volos: try Dimitra retsina—it's locally made and widely acknowledged to be the best in Greece. And the **Tsafolias**, **Skratis**, and **Metaftsis tavernas** on Argonafton are all recommended.

Accommodations

The only place to stay when you're in centaur land is up in the hills of Mount Pelion. Since we understand that there's always someone who will prefer a bed nearest to the ferryboat, train, or bus, here are some suggestions for passing the night in downtown Volos.

The best deal around the port is the older **Hotel Iason** (Jason) (tel. 0421/26-075), at 1 Pavlou Mela St. The friendly manager keeps a tidy place whose spacious rooms have balconies with port views. The Iason has the C-class bonus of an elevator, yet only charges 1900 drs ($14.62) for a double with private bath.

The **Hotel Sadi** (tel. 0421/33-341) is an older, C-class place at Iassonos and Topali Streets. It has 40 comfortable doubles with a 1950s kitschy feel; some even have big, old-fashioned bathtubs. Ask the accommodating management for a side-street room so you don't have to listen to the moped-motorcross around your block in the wee hours.

The **Hotel Philippos** (tel. 0421/37-607) is at 9 Solonos and Dimitriados Streets, two blocks from the port back toward Riga Fereou. This recently built addition to the Volos skyline arrived in the era of dark-wood beams, fluffy polyester pile bedspreads, and factory-made "local weavings." The rates at the Sadi and Philippos are the same, 3750 drs ($28.85) for a double.

Getting to Volos

It's not complicated. From Athens there are five O.S.E. buses daily from the Larissis station (tel. 22-222 in Volos for schedule information); and nine K.T.E.L. buses daily from the station at 260 Liossion St. (tel. 83-17-186 in Athens or 25-527 in Volos for information). There are four O.S.E. buses and four K.T.E.L. buses daily north to Thessalonika. For train information, call 24-056 or 23-712 in Volos; O.S.E. runs nine trains daily to Athens (with a daily nonstop train leaving at 3:30 p.m.), six to Thessalonika, 12 to Larissa, and one to Kalambaka (for Meteora). Check with the local E.O.T. for schedule information regarding the ten daily local buses that brave the narrow, twisting roads up to Makrinitsa on Mount Pelion.

THE PELION: The area around Mount Pelion is very popular with Greeks, who rush up on long winter weekends or for the traditional Easter ceremonies. Leaving Volos, the air is immediately cooler and fresher, and within minutes the scent of pines and basil eradicates the fumes of commercial industry. You'll find that the farther you climb, especially when you reach the other side of the 5,305-foot massif, the more beautiful and timeless the scenery becomes.

You'll pass through the pretty village of Anakassia on the way to **Katihori**. Tucked up off the main road are a few traditional, "Pelion-style" 18th-century houses lining narrow cobblestone streets. Local citizens stroll through their village, skinned lambs ready for roasting tossed over their shoulders, impervious to the occasional tourist. Right on the side of road is one of those special places worth coming to for a quiet and peaceful stay in the old Greek style, the **Guest House Matsatgou**. Lily Matsagou's nine rooms are, like the exterior of the mansion, renovated in the traditional Pelion style. High-ceilinged, stucco-walled rooms have wood and flagstone floors, antique handcrafted furnishings, woven rugs, and tall, plush-mattressed beds. Grapevines grow over the trellis-roofed patio, which overlooks the Pelion range and pine forests descending into the sea, a view undisturbed by modern life. Matsagou is open year round, but Lily requires a minimum booking to open in winter. Call 0421/99-380 for reservations; doubles with shared bath are 3900 drs ($30).

Three kilometers from Katihori is **Portaria** (altitude 600 meters), where a 13th-century Chapel of the Virgin stands next to a Pelion-style, mid-18th-century Church of Ag. Nikolaos. A modern Xenia Hotel intrudes on the mansions whose roofs have been restored to their original gray slate (villagers usually opt for the cheaper, red terracotta tiles). Around the picturesque square of this "commercial" center are a small bank, post office, and some rooms to let. A fountain dated 1927 offers delicious spring water; it's located at the bend in the road, under the aging plane tree. Portaria is far enough into the mysterious Pelion world to provide endless hikes and walks leading pleasantly to nowhere.

Then, 17 kilometers from Volos, off the west fork from Portaria, is **Makrinitsa**, the star village of the Pelion. It's the most traditional in style and feel; centered around the charming Erinis Square are three-story mansions, fountains, and spectacular old plane trees (one's so large you can walk into it!). The stone façade of the tiny Ag. Iannis Church is decorated with ornate marble plaques. Next to it is a marble fountain guarded by finely sculpted foo dogs (taste its cold, fresh water). Right on the square, facing the church and fountain on one side and the breathtaking valley view on the other, is the **Pantheon Café** (tel. 0421/99-143). They serve up rich Greek cuisine under the swaying plane trees; two can sample the hearty *spetsofai* (peppers and sausage), moussaka, or *stamnas* for about 1600 drs ($12.31). Tables are set up on the square outside the Pantheon's 1903-era building; the wood-trimmed interior with fireplace shouldn't be missed.

Whether you've come to spend the night or not, Makrinitsa is the perfect place to sample the laudable restoration work being done by the Greek government under the auspices of its Traditional Settlements Program. In Makrinitsa three mansions have already been restored as hotels. The **Arhontiko Sisilianou** (tel. 0421/99-556) is located up the cobblestone steps behind the Ag. Iannis Church. This restored mansion has a simple white stucco interior that's enlivened by traditional, dark earth-tone woven fabrics, gray slatted-wood doors and window shutters. Bed-and-breakfast doubles are 5250 drs ($40.38) at all three arhontikos.

Downhill from Erinis Square is the **Arhontiko Mousli** (tel. 0421/99-228), whose best feature is the immaculate slate-paved patio shaded by plum and plane trees. The tall stone mansion is capped with a second-story façade broken up by old wooden shutters and beautiful stained-glass windowpanes. The E.O.T.'s third Traditional Settlement is the **Arhontiko Xiradaki** (tel. 0421/99-250), on the 17 March 1878 Street (their name, not ours!), which is the entry road into the village if you're coming by car.

Our great find was the **Hotel Diomidis** (tel. 0421/99-114). Just follow the signs to the Sisilianou and you'll walk first into Diomidis' courtyard! The Routsos have decorated the house beautifully in traditional Mount Pelian style, and each floor has a floor-length late-night sitting lounge. Room No. 10 is the double to ask for: it has a balcony overlooking all of Volos, right to the Sporades.

The souvenir to buy from this region is honey, but nuts and homemade fruit preserves are also widely available and delicious. Makrinitsa is also famous for selling fresh herbs gathered on Mount Pelian (2,000 kinds!).

Continuing through nine kilometers of chestnut trees, evergreens, and hairpin turns brings us to **Hania**, at 1,200 meters, the ski center of the region. You can contact the Ski Center in Agriolefkes nearby (tel. 39-136) for ski information, or the Mountaineering Club Lodge (tel. 25-696 in Volos), which sponsors area hikes and climbs. From July 7 to August 15 there's a **youth hostel** operating in Hania; call Mr. Farfitis at 25-565 for information. Orchards of apple trees block out most of the views until you reach those magical twists in the road when the blazing sun, reflected off the glassy face of the Aegean, suddenly bathes you in light.

After several kilometers of hairpin turns a left fork will take you to **Zagora**, the largest town of Pelion where traditional and more recent houses slope gently down the hillside to the tilled fields in the valley below. Taking the right fork leads south, from Makrirahi to **Tsangarada**, a more rural, agricultural area. Trucks of hay tangle up traffic (only one passes at a time); donkeys carrying bundles of wood and old ladies out picking herbs vie for a portion of roadway. **Milopotamos**, eight kilometers from Tsangarda as the road forks east, is considered one of the prettiest, unspoiled beach areas of Pelion.

Vizitsa, about a hair-raising hour of driving away from the Tsangarada region, is one of the more interesting villages. The E.O.T. has opened five Traditional Settlements (tel. 0423/86-373; they all share the same phone number!). Among the few inhabited homes are several decrepit mansions with caved-in roofs (a continual problem with slate), broken windows, and eroded stone siding that contrasts vividly with the lovely, restored ones used as hotels. If you go to Vizitsa, don't drink the water gushing down the main stone street to the bus stop. Instead, let the old Vizitsians, sitting at the café-bar in the square above, usher you to another spring. On the way, you can sample the tunes on their aging Greek jukebox.

Milies is a busy village with a post office that you'll pass through to reach Vizitsa (it's often hard to tell when these villages begin and end). Though many of the houses are new, residents have decked them out in bougainvillea or surrounded them with fruit trees and flowering plants. Coming around the right bend in the main street, you'll see a small sign reading "TYPOΨOMO" (pronounced tee-*ro*-so-mo), or "Cheese Bread." Don't be startled when the woman who takes this thick, heavy feta-cheese pancake out of the cupboard climbs up on top of her old oak baking table. She keeps the cashbox up on the top shelf and can climb back down without stepping on your bread to give you change.

LARISSA: The 60 kilometers between Volos and Larissa on the toll motorway pass quickly. Lots of watermelon, heat, and unpaved roads make Larissa feel like a midwestern cow town on a summer's day—in other words, a place to steer clear of. If your car breaks down, try the **Hotel El Greco** (tel. 041/25-24-11) on Alexandrou (two blocks off the main square). Equally acceptable is the **Atlantic Hotel** (tel. 041/25-02-01), on Cyprus Street; a cheaper alternative is the **Olympion** (tel. 041/22-60-41), on the square, or the **Aris** (tel. 041/22-12-94), next door to the Atlantic. Larissa is a well-connected transportation hub, and yes, there are several recently built hotels, but we think you'd do better to continue on.

TRIKALA: From Larissa, make a sharp left turn and head due west to Trikala. Here's another 60-kilometer drive one could do without; however, any route that shortens the way to Kalambaka and the legendary Monasteries of Meteora is okay with us. Trikala, a totally undistinguished urban center, is thought to be the birthplace of Asclepios, god of healing. In the southwest part of town, Hellenistic-era walls and Roman baths mark the site of the oldest Asclepion in Greece. The ancient Doris became the Homeric city of Trikki; it rose near the acropolis built above the Litheos River. A rather picturesque Venetian fortress sits on St. Nicholas Heights, south of the city, and an old Moslem mosque can be found near the bus station.

All you ever need to know about Trikala is that the train station is on one side of the Litheos River and the bus station is on the other. No matter which means of transportation you choose, if you're stuck overnight in Trikala, you'll want to work your way back to Vass. Georgious Square on the banks of the river. From the bus station, follow the curving riverbed away from the abandoned mosque and up toward the square. If you've chosen the ultra-convenient **Hotel Lithaeon** (tel. 0431/20-690), a large, acceptable C-class hotel built right over the exit ramps (doubles with breakfast are 3810 drs, or $29.30), you'll want to walk over there for some nightlife, tavernas, and classier local color. A budget alternative is the small, older **Hotel Palladion** (tel. 0431/28-091), at 4 Vyronos St. There, 18 simple, clean rooms with shared toilet facilities cost 1530 drs ($11.80) a single, and 2370 drs ($18.20) for a double.

What's there to do at night in Trikala? Well, the locals seem to have flipped over **Paboraea**, a rooftop cafeteria (about the sixth floor) on top of a modern-style office building which overlooks the river.

Transportation Connections

Buses run from Athens to Trikala seven times daily, departing from the terminal at 260 Liossion St. (tel. 83-11-434). The fare for the five-hour trip is 2110 drs ($16.20). Between Trikala and Larissa there's a bus every half hour; to Volos four times daily, to Kalambaka every 20 minutes all day, at 100 drs (80¢), to Ioannina two times daily, at 550 drs ($4.40); to Meteora directly, three times daily, at 60 drs (47¢).

There are five **trains** daily from Athens which pass through Karditsa; the fare is 840 drs ($6.40) for a second-class ticket. Trikala trains depart from the Larissis railroad station (tel. 82-13-882 in Athens, or 041/222-250 in Larissa).

On to Kalambaka

The 29 kilometers of highway left before you reach Kalambaka build up the suspense in a very theatrical fashion. "What could Meteora [which means 'Rocks in Air'] possibly look like?" you're wondering. Then, all of a sudden, a bizarre lone boulder will pop up in a corner of the scrub-brush plains you're speeding by. As fast as it appeared it's gone, but just in time for another one, then a shorter clump of two or three, then again one, huge, towering rock in the air will appear and you'll crane your head out to see if there's a tiny monastery built on top of it. Don't worry—when you're getting near Kalambaka the "Camping Rocks," "Camping Perilous Boulder," "Camping Wonders of the Earth" signs will make it all too obvious.

6. Kalambaka: Gateway to Meteora

In this part of Thessaly the two great mountain ranges of Pindus and Ossa split apart to let the Pinios River flow into the Vale of Tempi, and from there to the sea. Kalambaka, at the foot of the Pindus massif, sits at the point where the Pinios reaches the level valley floor; the unique rock formations of Meteora are thought to be the heavily eroded riverbed of the Pinios dating from a time when it was a much more active and deeper river. It is said that the monks from Meteora believe that during the time of Noah's ark all of Thessaly was under water, which had disappeared as the result of an earthquake. In much the same way that the ark landed on the peak of Mount Ararat when the waters receded, the persecuted monks of the Convent of Stagon built their churches atop inaccessible pinnacles of time-worn stone. In the 12th century these small religious cells began to draw the devout from all over the Byzantine world, and by the 14th century Meteora was a community of such religious learning, art, and wealth that its only rival was Mount Athos. At this point the monks of the Monastery of Meteoron (Grand Meteoron, the largest) had freed themselves from the rule of the abbot of the Convent of Stagon and tried to take over control of the other, less influential monasteries in the area. Such in-fighting caused the number of monasteries to decline from a high of 24 to 14 only 200 years later.

The Turkish occupation of Greece had a favorable effect on Meteora because leader Suleyman the Magnificent put strong bishops in charge of Thessaly's ecclesiastical matters. Varlaam and Roussanou were the monasteries which benefited most from the influx of funds and new recruits; their libraries were enriched with new manuscripts, their churches decorated with brilliant frescoes, and their chapels enlarged and refurbished. Over the next few centuries the fortunes of the Meteora monasteries again declined, and now only four still function.

ORIENTATION: Kalambaka is a small provincial town whose main development has occurred in a line along the north-south highway. The monasteries of Meteora are reached via an access road that veers east at the north end of town. Approaching the town from Trikala, from the south, you'll pass the campgrounds called Theopetra, International, and Kalambaka (this one's uphill and has better views). At the south end of Kalambaka is a roundabout with several outdoor cafés and small shops circling it; this open area is known as **Riga Fereou Square.** Within one kilometer the main highway runs into another, larger, less commercial area, called **Central Square.** From here the road veers right up to Meteora. Between Riga Fereou and Central Square you'll find the railroad station (on the west side of the highway) and the K.T.E.L. bus stop (along the highway). Local buses to Meteora leave from the turnoff for Ioannina and Kastoria (Vass. Pavlou Street). There are tavernas on both squares, some hotels near the railroad station, and several hotels in the little streets around Central Square and the road to Meteora, where they can take advantage of the remarkable views.

USEFUL INFORMATION: The local telephone **area code** is 0432. . . . Kalambaka's **taxi stand** (tel. 22-310) is on the main street; for about 3500 drs ($26.90) you can book a taxi for the 19-kilometer circuit to the five monasteries that are open, including half an hour's waiting time at each one.

The long-distance **bus station** is near the taxi stand; the first morning bus north from here stops at Meteora. The local buses to Meteora stop at Vass. Pavlou Street three times daily (9 a.m., 11:30 a.m., and 1:30 p.m.); but check with your hotel reception for schedule information. . . . The **railroad station** (tel. 22-451) is open daily from 8:30 a.m. to 6 a.m. There are five trains daily to Athens and three from the Larissis station in Athens (fare: 940 drs, or $7.20, for the seven-hour trip); four trains daily to and from Thessalonika (1050 drs, or $8.10, for the five-hour trip); and two trains daily to and from Volos (580 drs, or $4.50, for the 2¾-hour trip). Tickets can be bought at the station.

The **National Bank of Greece** keeps banker's hours (8 a.m. to 2 p.m. weekdays). . . . The **post office** is one block above Central Square. . . . The **O.T.E.** is on top of the hill above Central Square. . . . Call 22-288 for **medical emergencies.**

ACCOMMODATIONS AND DINING: Up the Monastery road at 45 Kastrakiou is the clean, C-class **Hotel Helvetia** (tel. 0432/23-041). Its upper-floor rooms have a view across the street to the pockmarked "cave" rocks where many hermits had hidden homes. The Helvetia's 15 pleasant double rooms with private facilities rent for 3300 drs ($25.40); breakfast is an additional 350 drs ($2.90) per person. Chritos and Vassiliki Gasos are friendly hosts who encourage camaraderie among guests in their café-bar. Their daughter is usually working the reception desk, and she speaks perfect English.

Next we have to mention the **Hotel Aeloic Star** (tel. 0432/22-325), right above the Central Square, even though it doesn't have private baths or a marvelous view of the Rocks in Air. Mr. Papadeli rushed out at 9 p.m. to rescue us when he saw that our car had gotten a flat tire. Our double was clean and comfortable—a bargain at 2310 drs ($17.80)—and sharing clean, modern men's and women's toilets with only two neighbors was no problem.

Just down from the Helvetia is the plain, C-class **Hotel Odission** (tel. 0432/22-320). The 21 simply furnished rooms are divided between private-facility and bathless doubles; rates vary from 2000 drs ($15.40) to 2750 drs ($21.10), depending on which you choose. The elderly owner, Mr. Kommatea, speaks little English but is a warm host just the same.

Directly across from the railroad station, literally a stone's throw from the tracks, is the modern **Hotel Atlantis** (tel. 0432/22-924). The Atlantis, managed by Mr. Papadimitriou, takes advantage of its location with a large lobby whose picture windows overlook Kalambaka's old station. The breakfast room is right here, perfect for those who want to wake up to trains. Large rooms with new, tidy furniture are 2750 drs ($21.10). A smaller and older E-class hotel, just two blocks up from the station at 93 G. Kondili St., is the **Astoria** (tel. 0432/22-213). The ten double rooms offer private facilities for two at 2750 drs ($21.10).

We enjoyed a filling meal of broiled chicken, stuffed tomatoes, and fresh peasant salad at the **Platanos Taverna**, where a large open patio overlooks Central Square. You can't miss the Platanos's flower-covered archway entrance; dinner for two came to less than 1250 drs ($9.60). Another popular favorite at Riga Fereou is the **Nikos Taverna**. Nikos has a limited range of Greek dishes but their food is well prepared. Also around the roundabout are a few small pâtisseries for a light breakfast or snack at midday. There is a very good pizzeria, the **Santa Lucia**, near Central Square. They deliver too! We also liked the **Bufidis Restaurant,** down the road in nearby Kastraki.

THE MONASTERIES OF THE METEORA: If one were to drive the 19-kilometer circular path through the valley of monasteries, they would be approached in this order: Aghias Nikolaos, Metamorphosis, or "Grand Meteoron," Varlaam, Rousanou, Aghias Trias, and Aghios Stephanos.

Monastery Schedules and Other Useful Information

Not all the monasteries are open every day. The following schedule is accurate as we went to press in late 1987:

Aghias Nikolaos (tel. 22-375), open daily from 8 a.m. to 1 p.m. and 3 p.m. to 6:30 p.m.

Metamorphosis (tel. 22-278), open Wednesday to Monday (closed Tuesday) from 9 a.m. to 1 p.m. and 3 p.m. to 6:30 p.m.

Varlaam (tel. 22-277), open Saturday to Thursday (closed Friday) from 9 a.m. to 1:30 p.m. and 3:30 p.m. to 6:30 p.m.

Rousanou—closed to the public.

Aghias Trias (tel. 22-220), open daily from 8 a.m. to 1 p.m. and 3 p.m. to 6:30 p.m.

Aghios Stephanos (tel. 22-279), open Tuesday to Sunday (closed Monday) from 8 a.m. to 1 p.m. and 3 p.m. to 6:30 p.m.

Bus Transportation: From Vass. Pavlou Street (at the turnoff for the Ioannina and Kastoria highway) the local Kalambaka bus stops first at the Ag. Nikolaos Monastery. The next and last stop is in front of Metamorphosis (Grand Meteoron); you can walk 150 meters from here to the Varlaam Monastery. To reach the Ag. Trias and Ag. Stephanos monasteries requires a walk of five kilometers along the paved roadway. Buses make this run four times daily;

the fare is 100 drs (80¢). If you don't have a car we recommend taking a taxi around the 19-kilometer circuit. It shouldn't run more than 3500 drs ($26.90), and the cab will wait half an hour or more at each monastery. The drivers are also very knowledgeable and can point out things not found in guidebooks.

Dress Code: "Men in Shorts and Women in Trousers or Sleeveless Dresses are Not Allowed to Enter." This sign is posted in front of each monastery and convent, and they are quite serious.

For the Disabled: The exquisite configuration of Meteora and its monasteries is best appreciated at a distance, but if you want to enter one, Ag. Stephanos is the most easily accessible, being just 20 meters across a footbridge (wheelchair capable) from the paved road. The easiest climb up is the three-minute hike to Varlaam, which has lovely examples of frescoes and religious objects that are found in the others. If you have only *one solid ten-minute hike* left in you, then you must see the area's largest creation, the Metamorphosis (Grand Meteoron).

Let's examine the individual monasteries in order of importance:

Metamorphosis (Grand Meteoron)

The first monastery of Meteora was founded by Saint Athenassios, a monk from Mount Athos, between 1356 and 1372. The church was built atop Platy Lithos (Broad Stone), one of the largest flat-topped rock formations. Meteoron achieved its autonomy and religious authority after the king of Serbia's son became a monk there. The new monk, Joasaf, ensured royal donations to the monastery's coffers, making the Meteoron the most wealthy and powerful of the existing units. The sanctuary was enlarged in the middle of the 16th century to the size of the present-day church. It's decorated with colorful frescoes, elaborately carved wood, and an inlaid ivory pedestal for the bishop. Notice the particularly gruesome images in the narthex of the saints being tortured.

The museum is housed in the old dining room, part of the 16th-century addition to the original monastery. The museum contains a collection of rare manuscripts, most of which are modest illuminations of the Gospel and the Book of St. John, dating between the 9th and 16th centuries. Next to the ancient dining room cum museum is the old and dusty kitchen that once served up meals for the guests of the Meteoron Hostel. At the base of the stairs exiting from the museum and church, turn left. A small wooden door with a hole large enough for your head contains a bizarre array of skulls from monks who served the monastery long ago.

Varlaam

The Monastery of Varlaam, about 150 meters from Grand Meteoron, is an easier walk up, and well worth a visit. The stone corridors are filled with signs proclaiming "Do Not Make Noise," "No Smoking," "Private Entry," etc., but the lovely flowering garden softens the austerity of the place. The frescoes in the chapel (on the right) were done by Franco Catellano in 1565, 48 years after the monastery's founding by two wealthy brothers from Ioannina. These frescoes were restored in 1870.

Aghios Nikolaos

The first monastery you'll come to on the road north from Kalambaka (and the first bus stop) is Ag. Nikolaos, perched on a lone rock towering above the road. You'll have to climb up there to see it (notice the pulley-and-basket system the monks once used), but the stairs can easily be managed in five to ten minutes. Halfway up, the path forks; a wonderful painted sign, now faded badly, indicates a young man and woman walking up the stairs to the left and an old hobbled couple with canes using the ramp to the right.

Ag. Nikolaos is no longer inhabited and gets few visitors, making it the nicest of the monasteries because of its intimacy. The monastery was built in 1388 and later expanded. Its small chapel is filled with excellent frescoes by the Cretan School painter Theophanes the Monk (done in 1527), which are low enough for close study. The chapel's ornately painted and carved-wood ceiling is in surprisingly good condition. A young boy selling tickets (100 drs, or 80¢) enthusiastically offers *loukoumi* (the popular sweet from Siros) and water to visitors. We heartily recommend Ag. Nikolaos to sightseers with energy to spare after the Meteoron.

Aghios Stephanos

The Convent of Ag. Stephanos, a hermitage founded by Jeremias in 1312, is the most southeasternly one open at Meteora. The fresco-less church has obviously been renovated, but the presence of a nun studying in the back pews by the old wood stove adds a great deal of ambience. Ag. Stephanos was transformed into a monastery in the 1330s by Emperor Andronicus III Paleologos. We guess that this monastery is so popular with tour groups because it's directly accessible from the roadway. A small museum inside displays ecclesiastical items such as robes, painted icons, and documents, but you may have to wait in line to get a peek.

On the road between the Ag. Nikolaos and the Ag. Trias monasteries is the **Rousanou Monastery**, which was built as a hermitage in 1388 and became a monastery, by decree, in 1545. Rousanou is astonishingly intact on its lonely, precarious perch, but has been closed to the public in recent years.

Aghias Trias

The Convent of Ag. Trias, founded by the monk Dometios in 1438, is perhaps the most amazing sight of Meteora. Its solitary placement is bewildering. Ag. Trias is approached by 139 steep steps, though (thank God!) they stop numbering them in the 90s. After you've rested long enough to enter, you can see in the first room the platform attached to guide wires that swings out to the nearby plateau, bringing back materials and people. Inside, the small chapel is filled with frescoes, which are, sadly, blackened by the smoke from votive candles and the modern heater.

Ag. Trias, on its lone, seemingly inaccessible peak, was the star location of *For Your Eyes Only*, a fairly recent James Bond movie. The monastery is a superb construction that's best admired from afar, and for most its interior is just not worth the climb.

The Byzantine Church of the Assumption

This church is worth a visit for anyone spending time in Kalambaka. It's located on the highest street in the village, Koimos Theotokou, and can easily be found by following the signs: "Izantin Church 11th Century." The church, however, was originally built in the seventh century and restored in 1326, and is the only three-aisled basilica of its type other than Aghia Sophia in Istanbul. The worn frescoes inside are the work of the Cretan monk Neophyte, the son of Theophanes who painted the fine frescoes in the Ag. Nikolaos Monastery of Meteora. Inside is an ancient sun throne where the bishop and local priests sat to address the entire congregation. In a corner of the apse closed to the lay public are mosaic fragments of a peacock image (perhaps from the Roman era). A brief history of the church, in several languages, is available at the door. When we visited, a local religious holiday was being celebrated and all the women in their traditional black cotton, apron-covered dresses insisted on giving us cookies and servings of a delicious wheat, walnuts, and cinnamon cereal called *koliva*. It was one of those surprise moments that make Greece so delightful.

7. The Mount Olympus Region

From Kalambaka, the road continues west to the picturesque hill village of **Metsovo**, and 125 kilometers later, to **Ioannina.** This is the province of Epirus, bounded by the Pindus Range to the east and the Ionian Sea to the west, a region of varied and lush scenic beauty.

There's an active "Scenic Attraction" road stop at **Aghia Paraskevi**, where you'll see hundreds of cars parked and Greek men grabbing their children and wives by the hand to pull them across the busy highway to the shaded rocks and gushing waterfall. A narrow footbridge crosses the river: to one side is a modern chapel; on the other, a pleasant café and souvenir shops selling tokens of Paradise.

Continuing north of the vale, one can't help but notice the near-perfect façade of an impressive castle. It crowns the hill above **Platamonas,** from which it guarded the Gulf of Thermae. The castle was built between 1204 and 1222 by the Crusaders, and was spared by the Turks only because they used it to guard against pirates from the east.

About 70 kilometers north of Larissa is the tiny village of **Litohoro,** the jumping-off ꞓ nt for the climb up Greece's legendary Mount Olympus, 2,917 meters high. ⅂ⲏe **Federation of Mountaineering and Skiing** has a regional office at Kentriki Square (tel. 0352/81-944) in Litohoro, or you can call them at 0132/34-555 in Athens. They maintain four refuges on Olympus: one at Spilios Agapitos (altitude: 2,100 meters; 22 kilometers from Litohoro); on the eastern face of Olympus at Vryssopoules (altitude: 1,900 meters); a 15-bed refuge at King Paul (altitude: 2,700 meters; 1½ hours away from Spilios Agapitos); and at Stavros (altitude: 1,000 meters; 1½ hours from Litohoro), which is maintained by the **Thessaloniki Alpine Club** (tel. 0312/78-288). There are some English-speaking guides available in Litohoro.

Mount Olympus, considered the equivalent of Heaven or the Top of the Sky by the ancients, was of course home of the gods. Apollodorus, Homer, and Aeneas all tell of the Gigantomachy, the War between the Giants (sons of Uranus/Sky and Gaia/Earth) and the Olympians. The Giants were the creators of our cosmos, the ordered world created from chaos. Their many sons, the Titans, included the one-eyed monster Cyclops. His brother Cronus eventually led an uprising of Titans to take over leadership of the cosmos. Uranus predicted that someday Cronus too would lose his throne to one of his sons. Each time his wife Rhea (the Earth Mother) bore him a child, Cronus swallowed it whole to forestall the outcome of Uranus's prediction. Finally, when her sixth child was born, Rhea dressed a large stone in baby clothes and fed it to Cronus. Her hidden son Zeus was given to the goat Amalthea, to be raised in Crete. When Zeus reached manhood, his mother helped him to feed a special potion to Cronus, which made him throw up the other five children, all gods, who were ready to do battle. Zeus (with the help of his siblings) took over Cronus's kingdom and established his home on Greece's highest peak, Olympus. Homer describes the attempt made by the Giants to return the attack: "Ossa they strove to set upon Olympus, and upon Ossa leafy Pelion, that so the heavens might be scaled." Zeus had cunningly enlisted the aid of the Cyclops, uncles of Cronus, who forged for him the powerful thunderbolt that became his symbol. Wrote Ovid about the battle's outcome: "Then the omnipotent Father with his thunder made Olympus tremble, and from Ossa hurled Pelion. . . ." Thus was Mount

Olympus secured for the gods, and it wasn't until 1913 that a mortal dared to scale its highest peak.

Just over the crest of Olympus the outer reaches of Macedonia come into view. In Chapter XIII we'll begin our exploration of Alexander the Great's homeland, in Thessaloniki, capital of the province. But first we'll visit the Sporades islands, and then the Ionian coast of western Greece.

Chapter XI

THE SPORADES

1. Skiathos
2. Skopelos
3. Alonissos
4. Skyros

ASK A GREEK ABOUT the islands and this is what you'll hear: "The Cyclades? Filled with tourists, expensive, too dry and rocky. They all look alike. The Ionians? Ah, Corfu! But it's so expensive. The Dodecanese? Rhodes is so built up, so is Kos, and they're as expensive as Corfu. The Northeast Aegean? Who goes there, it's too far. The Saronic Gulf? Too close. What about the Sporades? Of course, the Sporades! That's where we go."

Greeks have been vacationing on the Sporades for years, attracted by fragrant pine trees growing down to the edge of golden sand beaches. Few foreign tourists ventured to any of the Sporades, preferring the well-trod paths leading to the Cyclades. With so few foreign visitors, prices stayed low and hotels and restaurants remained relatively empty. It was only a matter of time before this idyllic state of affairs would come to an end. Groups began to visit Skiathos, and later Skopelos. An airport was built on Skiathos with flights going back and forth from Athens two or three times a day. A convenient hydrofoil service began operating in 1985, transporting even larger numbers of foreign guests. Now those same Greek tourists who pioneered travel to Skiathos and Skopelos party along the shores of Alonissos and Skyros. Still, with all the development and dramatic change in the Sporades, nothing has altered their most basic appeal. The islands are as lush as ever, with plum, fig, olive, grape, and almond orchards planted in the midst of pine and plane forests. The long crescent-shaped beaches—some sandy, others of polished snow-white stones—are superior to nearly any in the Aegean islands. Prices, though on the increase, are still lower than on many Aegean islands.

Skiathos and Skopelos are to the Sporades what Rhodes and Kos or Mykonos and Paros are to their respective groups: the most popular islands, with excellent beaches, chic boutiques, a cosmopolitan following, and great scenic beauty. Alonissos is dramatically less developed for tourism, but with many of the attractions of its more famous neighbors. Skyros, more remote than the other Sporades, is a Cycladic look-alike with whitewashed cube architecture, an arid landscape, and some terrific beaches. It's an ideal destination for those who want to get away from the crowd. *Note:* As we go to press, Viking Tours has announced a schedule of yacht cruises through the Sporades. Contact their office in Connecticut (tel. toll free 800/341-3030) or Athens (tel. 0132/29-383) for prices and departure dates.

1. Skiathos

Long known as queen of the island group most famous for its natural beauties, Skiathos today is just as gorgeous as ever. Her allure comes from the purity of the water and the fine sand beaches; the most famous, Koukounaries, is considered one of the very best in Greece. Elegant shops, flashy nightlife, excellent restaurants, and charming pensions are the glittering amenities created by the booming tourist trade.

Greeks used to frequent Skiathos because it was one of the island gems that tour operators had overlooked. Now charter flights breeze into the airport regularly, and boatloads of budget-tour groups unload three times daily in July and August. The Greeks stay on the ferry until Alonissos, one of the Sporades they can still afford.

If there's any possibility of seeing Skiathos before July 10 or after September 1 (when the tourist crush is at its worst), try to do so. If not, the severe hotel shortage may make your foray into a day trip. But make the effort anyway; we tourists generally know from beautiful islands, and Skiathos is really a charmer.

ORIENTATION: Hydrofoils, excursion boats, and ferries dock at the port town called Skiathos, on the island's southern coast. It lies on the main roadway that links the 35 kilometers of southern resort developments together. Skiathos's north coast is much more rugged and beautiful: steep cliffs, pine forests, and rocky hills are its only inhabitants. Unless you've arrived with reservations at one of the resort communities, we'd recommend setting up a base for exploration in the port town. From here, you can try caïque excursions to the island's magnificent beaches or take public buses to different villages.

Skiathos is a relatively modern town, built in 1830 on two low-lying hills, then reconstructed after heavy German bombardment during World War II. Two-story whitewashed villas with bright red tiled roofs line both sides of the V-shaped harbor, which juts out into the water like a boomerang. At its tip is the lovely little **Bourdzi**, one of many islets that poke up off Skiathos's coastline, but this one has an elegant café and restaurant on its peak. Ferryboats moor at the east side of the harbor, where you'll find more recent construction, slicker, C-class hotels, and the main street (with cars on it) that shoots up through town. This street is named Papadiamantis, after the island's best-known son, an author who made his fame writing about island life and Greek customs. (His villa has been turned into a museum filled with his works and memorabilia, and is open to public view.) About 200 meters from the harbor on Pl. Laskov Street (2nd floor, on your left) you'll find the occasionally English-speaking **Police** (tel. 22-005). Down the street toward the harbor is the **post office** (open 8 a.m. to 4 p.m. daily) and the **O.T.E.** (open 7:30 a.m. to 9 p.m. Monday through Saturday, until 3:15 p.m. on Sunday). **Olympic Airways** (tel. 22-200) is farther up the street, on the right.

On the west flank of the harbor (the left side as you disembark the ferry) are several cheerful outdoor cafés, a few traditionally built small hotels, the excursion caïques that post their beach and island tour schedules on signs over the stern, and in the corner, a staircase leading up to the town's next level. Mounting the stairs above the Oasis Cafe will lead you to **Trion Ierarhon Square**, a charming, stone-paved mall next to a church, with many boutiques, bars, and ornate villas around it.

GETTING AROUND: For most of the places you'll want to visit, Skiathos is well equipped with public transportation. From the bus station at the harbor, **buses** run every half hour between 7:30 a.m. and 10:30 p.m. back and forth to

Koukounaries, the south coast's most popular beach. (Most of the resorts are on this stretch as well.) The north coast beaches and the historic kastro are most easily reached by **caïque**; these sail frequently from the west side of the harbor to all the sights and cost about 750 drs ($5.77) for a five-hour excursion to Calaria Beach and Kastro. If you're on Skiathos for a long period of time and get stir crazy, you might consider renting a **moped.** They're available from **K. Dioletta Rent a Car,** on Papadiamantis Street, for 1100 drs ($8.46) per day. Dioletta and his partner, E. Aivalioti, also rent Pony Jeeps from 4500 drs ($34.62) per day.

USEFUL INFORMATION: The telephone **area code** for Skiathos is 0427. . . . Volos, a 1½-hour ride away on the mainland has the nearest official **E.O.T.** (tel. 0421/23-500). They're very knowledgeable about the Sporades.

    Ferry tickets for the Nomikos Lines can be purchased through several local travel agents (Skiathos information is 22-216 or 22-209). The **Miltos Travel Office** (tel. 22-955 or 6), on the west side of the harbor, is open from 7 a.m. to 10 p.m. daily and sells tickets to many of the around-the-island and beach caïque trips, as well as booking Olympic flights and hotel rooms and exchanging currency. Ask for Anastasia, who is very sharp and speaks excellent English. **Olympic Airways,** with three flights daily to Athens, provides a bus to the airport from their office, 55 minutes before flight time; the fare is 60 drs (50¢). . . . The **National Bank of Greece** is open from 8 a.m. to 2 p.m. Monday through Friday. For **medical emergencies** contact the **Skiathos Hospital** (tel. 22-040) or the **police** (tel. 22-005).

    Directly across the street from the bank, on Georg. Panora Street, is the **Miele Laundromat.** It's open from 8 a.m. to 11 p.m. daily. Two blocks away at the corner of Adriou Sigrou and Antipl. Laskou is **Lido Dry Cleaners,** who also do laundry and have a 24-hour turnaround on cleaning. There is another combination cleaner/laundry right in front of the San Remo Hotel, at the end of the port. The **Flying Dolphin agent** is right on the paralia; they have three boats daily to Skopelos and Alonissos and two boats weekly to Skyros. Call 0427/22-018 for up-to-date departure schedules. This is the easiest and most convenient way to visit the various islands.

    Shopping is as good on Skiathos as on Mykonos; it's not cheap, but there's some excellent merchandise. We loved the **Galerie Varsakis** (tel. 22-255), on Trion Ierarhon Square, for its collection of folk antiques, embroidered bags and linens, and other collectibles. We found very reasonably priced gifts and window-shopped their superb antiques, and better yet, discovered that Harris, the proprietor, speaks English and is quite a character himself. He knows and is known by all the locals, and can help you out a lot.

    There is a gorgeous men's clothing shop (mostly Italian, some Greek, all pricey) on Politohniou Street just up from the Kirki Bar. Perfect for that special gift.

ACCOMMODATIONS: Between July 1 and September 1 it can be literally impossible to find a room in Skiathos. If you're traveling at this time of year, try phoning ahead from Athens to book a room. Many hotels will accept reservations when a deposit equal to one-third of the proposed rent is wired to them through an Athens bank. (For those of you who make plans in advance, most of these hotels request that reservations by mail be made two or three months prior to the summer season.) If you're getting off the ferry cold and arrive between 8 a.m. and 10 p.m. head to **Miltos Travel** (tel. 22-955), right on the port to the right. They'll help you secure a place when all else fails.

    On the east side of the harbor, opposite the many moored yachts, is the modern and comfortable **Hotel Meltemi** (tel. 0427/22-493). The Meltemi's 18 spacious rooms all have private baths and are usually booked by April, but give them a try. Hosts Yorgo and Giuliana Rigas run a very friendly bar out on the waterside. Low-season doubles, bed and breakfast, are 4800 drs ($36.92), high-season rates are 6200 drs ($47.69). The front rooms, which face the harbor, are noisy.

One of the nicest and least expensive lodgings is the **Karafelas Hotel** (tel. 0427/21-235), at the back end of Platia Laskou Street; walk away from the port, past the post office, and where the street forks left, just on the left you'll see the hotel's blue iron door. Ask for a ground floor room in the back garden; what you'll get is your own little villa with two beds, bathroom and shower, a front porch overlooking a garden, and your own clothesline! And the owners are wonderful, fastidious, and obliging. All this for just 2750 drs ($21.15), a real bargain on Skiathos. At the eastern end of the port is the popular **San Remo Hotel** (tel. 0247/22-078), an attractive new hotel that has half-baths in each room and balconies in the front rooms overlooking the port. This slightly noisy and comfortable place goes for 6600 drs ($50.77), with breakfast an additional 500 drs ($3.85)—no great bargain.

Potted hydrangeas greet you at the modern **Hotel Kostis** (tel. 0427/22-909), located at 5 Evangelistrias St., just off Papadiamantis Street. Cozy rooms with balconies overlooking the heart of town rent for 3580 drs ($27.54) to 4300 drs ($33.07).

Around the corner from the fancier Kostis is the 11-room **Australia House** (tel. 0427/22-488), where doubles with private baths are 3860 drs ($29.69) in the high season and 2500 drs ($19.23) in the low, if they're ever available.

A 20-minute walk south of the port will bring you to the suburban beach resort of Ftelia. Just before this, in a verdant setting filled with flowers, is the **Hotel Sophia** (tel. 0427/22-656). The Sophia is one of the very few that hasn't been booked up by group-tour packagers on a summer-long basis. The Sophia's hosts are very charming and maintain their hostel in a familial way. There are eight doubles with bath for 4100 drs ($31.54) and four suite apartments sleeping three for 5200 drs ($40).

Another out-of-town choice nearby is the **Lalaria Apartments** (tel. 0427/22-900 in Skiathos, or 01/52-29-435 in Athens). This stark-white concrete edifice looks like it fell to Greece from southern California! Large balconies overlook Ftelia Beach. Paneled, spacious rooms with flight-lounge decor vary from 4000 drs ($30.77) to 4800 drs ($36.92) for two, including bathroom and kitchenette.

Up above the east side of the harbor, two levels above the Meltemi Hotel, is the **Agnadema Hotel** (tel. 0427/22-356). You'll get a preview of the homey bathless rooms upstairs after entering the flower-print front hallway. Doubles are 4340 drs ($33.40) and singles are 3640 drs ($28), plus 100 drs (77¢) for a shower. Also in this price range is Stephanos Theodoris' **Hotel Meteora** (tel. 0427/22-182), on Glikofilousis Street opposite the unmarked street leading to the Agnadema. All their 12 rooms have private baths and balconies overlooking Skiathos town and the valley behind it.

All over the hillside above the eastern harbor are several unlicensed "hotels," which are newly constructed rooms to rent. Inquire from passersby when you're hotel hunting and you'll be surprised at which buildings turn out to be lodgings.

Down on the waterside, along the western harbor, is the old-fashioned-looking **Hotel Avra** (tel. 0427/22-044). This 14-room D-class hotel has its front door on the street just behind the harbor (there are now so many commercial establishments eager to be on the waterfront that the Avra moved its front door to the back). This clean and quiet hotel has some rooms with superb views over the water and Bourdzi; doubles start at 3200 drs ($24.62) with bath, depending on season.

The alternative to these hotels is to look for private rooms in the quieter western hill above the bay. Wander down the streets and ask merchants about rooms-to-let. If you come via Volos by ferry to Skiathos, stop in to the E.O.T. office there (see pg. 317) and request a copy of their "Accommodations in the Sporades," listing. It's indispensable if you want to lease a villa or apartment for an extended stay.

RESTAURANTS: The western harbor and the lanes around Papadiamantis Street are lined with medium- and overpriced tavernas and cafés. As is the case with most of the overdeveloped tourist resorts, there is a plethora of ice-cream parlors, souvlaki stands, mini-markets . . . you get the picture. This just means that in Skiathos you'll have to walk a little farther for that genuine Greek meal.

Tavernas on the Water

One of the best tavernas on the western harbor, opposite the day-excursion caïques, is **Mandraki**. As you approach the stairs at the eastern most end of the harbor, which lead up to Trion Ierarchon Square, it's the third one from the end (they're so close together here that you have to make sure the chair you sit in matches the color of the taverna's canopy, or you're in the wrong one!) The Mandraki offers a varied menu with several excellent fish selections, all reasonably priced for such a desirable location. The Mandraki is open for lunch and dinner daily; two can eat grilled fish, salad, and wine for 1250 drs ($9.62) to 1500 drs ($11.54).

The **Mezetzidiko Ouzeri**, next to the bank (a little farther down, toward the ferries), is one of the most "Greek" eateries in town. You can have the authentic ouzo and octopus combo at 130 drs ($1) or sample their rich supply of cheese pies, fried feta, olives, and other piquant hors d'oeuvres. Mezetzidiko was John's favorite place to while away the evening—lounging over ouzo, munching on light, tasty tidbits, and admiring the steady parade of suntanned beauties out for a stroll along the waterfront.

The attractive **Bourdzi Café** draws a wholly different crowd. It seems tawny-haired women, silver foxes, or dashing Greek tycoons hop right off their yachts and onto the Bourdzi's willing barstools. The bar action is great fun to meddle with; the Bourdzi's a good value at cocktail hour, when you can admire their priceless sunset view. For breakfast, lunch, and dinner there are two dining areas: an overpriced tourist cafeteria on the south side of the peak and an elegant, expensive restaurant with candlelit tables on the rocky outcroppings at sea level. Entrées from their limited Greek-continental menu run 2100 drs ($16.15) to 2600 drs ($20) each, but we say "Go for it!" and splurge in a truly elegant, pretty, and uniquely Skiathan spot.

There are two other excellent restaurants, which fall between the Bourdzi and a taverna; the first is **Chez Julian,** an intimate, chic French restaurant at 25 Martinou St., about three blocks behind Trion Ierarhon Square. There's a deco-style neon sign on the second story facade in case you get lost. To whet your appetite there's onion soup (375 drs, or $2.88), real bouillabaisse (450 drs, or $3.46), beef Bourgignon (800 drs, or $6.15), and a host of other delectables, prepared and served beautifully in a trés romantique setting! **Ronnie's Miramare,** located at the end of the yacht harbor toward the western tip, has an ideally located exterior dining area overlooking the harbor and features French and Italian food. We had Chicken Fricassee, rice, a calamari appetizer, salad, and retsina for 2800 drs ($21.54) for two. And it was terrific. Ronnie and his "significant other," Lisa, are from the States and they're all go in the kitchen. Fanatic Yankees fans are directed to the Miramare to share Steinbrenner stories with Ronnie.

Tavernas in Town

The **Skiathos Taverna**, on Papadiamantis Street, is right in the heart of town and provides high-quality, moderately priced dining amid boutiques, news stands, the telephone exchange, and other places you find yourself in on a rainy day. Try it for lunch; we loved their individual casseroles of moussaka, at 450 drs ($3.46), and their crispy gigante bean salad with herb dressing, at 250 drs ($1.90). A filling meal will cost 1000 drs ($7.69) to 1200 drs ($9.23) each, with beverage.

Fifty meters off Papadiamantis Street on Evangelistria Street is the very popular **Stavros Taverna**, open for dinner only. The simple, spacious restaurant has a large fireplace in the front room, and behind that a pleasant outdoor garden. The walls surrounding the back garden are frescoed with scenes of Skiathan village life. One of the Stavros's specialties is stuffed calamari, large ringlets of squid stuffed with a tasty vegetable-and-herb mix, deep-fried in batter. The Stavros management is obviously accustomed to dealing with groups; they're friendly, welcoming, and happy to explain the contents and preparation of the Greek specialties displayed in their front room. This restaurant is sure to please even those reluctant to try local cuisine.

By general consent among Greek-cuisine connoisseurs, the best taverna in Skiathos is **Ilias**. It's a five-minute walk beyond Stavros on Evangelistria Street (just follow the painted arrows pointing left which say "Elias Restaurant" on them). Ilias (its name, when you finally arrive) is not very attractive: tables are jammed together outside on the path in apparent disregard for passing goats and herders. However, the Ilias is packed with Greeks and savvy tourists wolfing down large portions of lamb, beef, and vegetable dishes. Dinner for two should cost between 1200 drs ($9.23) and 1500 drs ($11.53). Ilias is open for dinner only, from 6:30 p.m. to 11:30 p.m., daily.

Just before this book went to press, we had an opportunity to visit Skiathos again, taking a casual cruise through the Sporades. Our ship docked in the harbor and was boarded by the harbormaster, presumably for our formalities. As he left, we asked him about his favorite in-town restaurant. "Ilias, that's very good, yes, but I prefer Carnayio." Sure enough, Kyle and I headed straight for it, walking and walking in an easterly direction along the quay, doubting if the taverna actually existed. At last, across from the Alkyon Hotel on the waterfront was **Carnayio Fish Taverna**, totally packed. It's mostly Greek families that dine at Carnayio, more or less an open-air taverna lit by thousands of tiny bulbs strung in the surrounding trees. No need for specific menu suggestions; everything is delicious. A first-rate addition to the Skiathos dining scene, Carnayio is medium priced and quintessentially Greek.

We found two wonderful places to dine for under 500 drs. **Delifrance Croissanterie**, at 6 Riga Fereou St., boasts about 15 different varieties, from fruits to meats, for 250 to 400 drs ($1.92 to $3.07), piping hot and tasty. Across to the left of the Varsakis Gallery is a souvlaki stand with a green awning that ranks as one of the two best in all of Greece! Outside you'll see pine picnic-style tables and a chalkboard menu; for 90 drs (69¢) you can appease even the biggest Big Mac attack. Chase it down with soda, beer, wine, or ouzo, order their peasant salad with feta for 225 drs ($1.73), and you'll be ready to tackle some more sights.

Bars and Cafés

A lot of the Skiathos scene takes place on the streets: along the waterfront, outside of ice-cream parlors on Papadiamantis Street, in the lanes behind Trion Ierarhon Square. The **Scorpio** is the island's hottest disco, and draws a mixed crowd every night. Drinks serve as the cover charge here; expect to pay 400 drs ($3.07) each. The **Albatross** is another popular bar catering to the island's Australian and German clientele. The action centers on the long, intimate bar, but some dancers find room in the back to shake to the steady beat of today.

The hottest and coolest place in town is definitely the **Kentavros Bar,** two blocks in from the port. This place sizzles; here is where you party down, meet the beautiful people from around the world and have a wild, wild time. Behind the bar you'll see the Greek version of Jack Nicholson; that's Kostas, the ringleader. He and his DJ make sure that you have as good a time as they do, from 9:30 p.m. to 4 a.m. every night. Where do you take that person you met at Kentavros to speak softly to each other? To the **Mythos Bar,** right on the harbor next to the Mezetzidiko ouzeri. The decor is white-with-tufted-seats and sleek without the cost. If you like to have videos with your drinks, try the **Oasis Cafe** at the western end of the harbor. Here the beer (draft) is only 150 drs ($1.15) a stein, and if there's a game of any sort being played they'll have it on the tube. They also serve a nice breakfast for 500 drs ($3.84) that you can have sitting outside while watching the fishermen mend their nets.

WHAT TO SEE AND DO: Skiathos's great natural beauty makes it a perfect island for the outdoors lover. From the port to the northern tip, Kastro, is an enjoyable 2½-hour hike over scrubby brush, rolling green hills, and fields of wildflowers. The northeastern coast is lined with secluded sand-and-pebble beaches accessible only to the hiker or boatsman. If there's one thing Skiathos is famous for, it's for having the best beach in all of Greece. Through the years, Europeans and Greeks alike have voted Koukanaries the best beach in the Aegean. We actually bestowed that award on Lalaria, another of Skiathos's magnificent beaches. Our point is, head straight for the beaches!

The Beaches

Examining the island's beaches clockwise from the port, we first reach **Megali Amos**, the sandy strip below the popular group-tour community of Ftelia. Ten minutes farther west by bus is **Vromolimnos**, on the Kalamaki peninsula, a better beach by virtue of being less crowded. There are several small pebble-and-sand patches along the south coast road, but the next big exit for bus takers is **Troulos**. Many afficionados appreciate the picturesque islets that can be seen right off the coast here.

We prefer the beach next door, the world-famous **Koukounaries**. The bus gently edges its way uphill (it's so packed with barefoot bikini-clad tourists that it's a wonder it doesn't tip over) past the spectacular Pallas Hotel luxury resort. As the bus descends, it winds around the inland waterway, Lake Strofilias, then stops at the edge of a fragrant pine forest. Koukounaries means "pine cone" in Greek, and behind this grove of trees is a kilometer-long stretch of fine gold sand in a half-moon-shaped cove. Tucked into the evergreen fold are some changing rooms, a small snackbar, and the concessionaire for windsurfers. The beach is crowded but not objectionable, and the easy mix of topless, families, singles, and discreet nudists are all out to polish their suntans. No doubt, Koukounaries is gorgeous and fits the Greek notion of the perfect beach by having shady trees meet a fine, gold sand beach. On the west side of the cove is the island's **Xenia Hotel** (tel. 0427/22-042), whose 32 rooms run 4800 drs ($36.92) for a double and half-board (two meals) plan.

A short but scenic walk from the Koukounaries bus stop (the end of the line) due west to the tip of the island is to the broad **Ag. Elenis** cove. This beach is popular for windsurfing, because it's a bit rougher than the south coast beaches but not nearly as gusty as those on the north. **Limonaki Xerxes** is a nearby cove named for the spot where Xerxes brought in ten triremes to conquer the Hellenic fleet moored at Skiathos during the Persian Wars. This is also called **Mandraki Beach**, and is a 20-minute walk up the path opposite the Lake Strofilias bus stop. Mandraki is a pristine and relatively secluded beach for those who crave a quiet spot.

A hefty 1½-hour walk from the bus stop at Troulos Beach leads to **Megas Aselinos**, a windy, sandy north coast beach where free camping has taken root. Most of the other north coast beaches are only accessible by boat, the exception being the acceptable **Ormos Xanema**, a windy, unprotected cove that can be reached by car, driving east from the port town.

Lalaria, on the island's northern tip, near Kastro, is to our minds the most beautiful beach in Greece. One of its unique qualities is the Tripia Petra, perforated rock cliffs that jut out into the sea on both sides of the cove. These have been worn through in time by the wind and the waves to form perfect classical archways. From the shore these "portholes" frame an incredibly beautiful landscape: while gulls squawk in the distance, you just lie on the gleaming white pebbles, admiring the neon-blue Aegean and cloudless sky through their rounded openings. If you swim through the arches against the brisk meltemi winds, you can play with the echo created inside them. Out in the water is a perfect vantage point to admire the glowing, silver-white pebble beach and jagged white cliffs above it. The water at Lalaria beach is an especially vivid shade of aquamarine because of the highly reflective white pebbles and marble and limestone slabs which coat the sea bottom. There are many naturally carved caves in the cliff wall that lines the beach, providing privacy or shade for those who've had too much exposure. Lalaria can only be reached by caïque excursions from the port; the fare is 600 drs ($4.61) for the half-day trip. Excursion boats usually stop at one or more of the other sights described below.

The Kastro

In the 16th century, when the Turks overran the island, the inhabitants moved to its northern tip and built a fortress. The village of Kastro remained occupied until 1829. Once joined to firm ground by a swaying drawbridge, this impregnable rock can now be reached by cement stairs. The remains of over 300 houses and 22 churches have mostly fallen to the sea, but two of the churches, with porcelain plates imbedded in their worn stucco façades, still stand. From this prospect there are excellent views to the Kastronisia islet below and the sparkling Aegean. The Kastro can be reached on foot, a 2½-hour hike from the port. Starting out on the uphill path just west of the harbor will take you by the monasteries of Ag. Fanourias, Ag. Dionisios, and Ag. Athenasios to Panaghia Kardasi, where the road officially ends. The lazy can cruise to Kastro or hire mopeds and try Skiathos's latest roadway, which runs to the north coast from just south of Ftelia.

The Caves (Spili)

There are several extraordinary caves carved in Skiathos's rugged coastline, and the caïque drivers seem most proud when they take tourists to see them. Along the coast of Pounta on the island's eastern side, opposite Kamini, is **Spilia Kaminari**, a huge roofless cave at the water's edge. Farther north is **Shotini Spilia**, a fantastic 20-foot-tall sea cave reached through a narrow crevice in the cliff walls. It's just wide enough for caïques to squeeze through for a close look (we took the *Alexandros,* and she just fit!). Seagulls drift above you in the cave's cool darkness, while below, fish swim down in the 30-foot subsurface portion. This odd pattern of erosion has created spectacular scenery and many sandy coves along the east and north coasts, though none are as beautiful or well sheltered from the meltemi as Lalaria beach.

GETTING THERE: Olympic Airways offers six or seven flights daily from Athens; contact Olympic information in Athens (tel. 92-92-444) for reservations.

Skiathos can be reached by either **ferryboat** (three hours) or **hydrofoil** (90 minutes) from Volos or Ag. Konstantinos; there is also ferryboat service from Kimi, on Evia (5½ hours). In the high season, there are three hydrofoils daily from Volos, two from Ag. Konstantinos. If you are in Athens, depart from Ag. Konstantinos, but from the north, Volos is closer and offers the option of a quick side trip to the Mount Pelion region. Kimi makes little sense for going to Skiathos, unless coming from Skyros. For hydrofoil information, contact the **Ceres Company** at Piraeus (45-27-107), Ag. Konstantinos (0235/31-614), or Volos (0421/39-786) for schedules and details about bus service. For ferryboat information, contact the **Nomikos Lines** in Volos (tel. 0421/25-688). Plan your itinerary carefully in order to connect between buses and ferries or hydrofoils.

2. Skopelos

You'll know as soon as your boat pulls into the harbor of Skopelos that you've come to one of Greece's most architecturally pristine islands, on a par with Hydra and Symi. The main town, also called Skopelos, scales the low hills around the harbor and has the same winding, narrow paths that characterize the more famous Cycladic islands to the south. A walk through the back streets and alleyways will delight anyone with an eye for intricately trellised gardens, whitewashed houses with precariously overhanging wooden balconies, and meticulously constructed green and gray slate roofs. Old women sit outside in front of their houses in groups of three and four, knitting and embroidering, the speed of their needles only topped by the velocity of their conversation.

The rest of the island is rich in vegetation, with wind-swept pines growing down to secluded coves, wide beaches, and terraced cliffs of angled rock slabs. The interior is densely planted with fruit and nut orchards. The plums and almonds from Skopelos are legendary, and are integrated into the island's unique cuisine. The coastline, like that of Skiathos, is punctuated by impressive grottos and bays. A camera is a must.

ORIENTATION: Skopelos has two major towns, **Skopelos town**, on the southeast coast, and **Loutraki**, on the northwest coast directly across from Skiathos. The ferries from Alonissos, Skyros, and Kimi, hydrofoils, and most of the boats from Skiathos dock at both Loutraki and Skopelos. Loutraki is connected by a short ferry shuttle from Skiathos. A paved road runs from Skopelos due south to the two beaches at Ormos Stafilos and back up along Skopelos's west coast to the four villages in the north: Loutraki, Klima, Glosa, and Mahalas. If you've never been to Skopelos, it's best to find a room in Skopelos town and begin your exploration there; you'll find all of the necessary tourist services, the starting point for many bus and boat excursions, as well as a large group of hotels. After you've acquainted yourself with the balance of the island, you can move to one of the villages or beaches.

Skopelos is built amphitheatrically around a C-shaped harbor. To the right, as you exit the boat, are only a few of Skopelos's 123 churches (which must be an ecclesiastical record for such a small village). The waterfront is lined with banks, cafés, travel agencies, and the like. Interspersed between these prosaic offerings are some truly regal-looking shade trees. Many of the hotels are on the far left end of the paralia. There are beaches on both sides of the harbor; **Konstantinos** beach, on the north end, is a 15-minute walk away. The bus and taxi stand is under a giant plane tree about 200 meters to the left of the dock. Most of the shops and the O.T.E. (open from 8 a.m. to 10 p.m. daily, until 2 p.m. on Sunday) are up the main street leading off the paralia. The back streets are amazingly convoluted; the best plan is to wander up and get to know a few familiar landmarks.

GETTING AROUND: Skopelos is infrequently served by public transportation. **Buses** run three times a day in high season, twice a day in low season, beginning in Skopelos and making stops at Stafilos, Agnodas, Panormos Bay, Elio, Klima, Glossa, and Loutraki—in other words, nearly anyplace you'd want to go. For more isolated coastal destinations, **excursion boats** call at Sares beach, Ag. Konstantinos beach, and from Agnodas, Limnonari beach. Most of the caïques leave the dock at 10 a.m., but beware—if they fill up before that they'll leave early. There's a 600 drs ($4.61) caïque tour of the island that departs at 7 a.m. and returns at noon. The most convenient way to see the island is to rent a **moped** at one of the two shops on the port. The cost should be about 1250 drs ($9.61) per day. A jeep will run around 6000 drs ($46.15).

USEFUL INFORMATION: The telephone **area code** for Skopelos is 0424. . . . There are **O.T.E.s** in Glossa, Klima, Moni Evangelistrias, Moni Prodromou, Ormos Agnonda, and Ormos Panomous . . . **Ferry tickets** can be purchased at the Nomikos Lines office on the left side of the boat. For information about the ferry lines, contact the **Port Authority** (tel. 21-180). . . . The English-speaking Salpadimos sisters run an excellent travel agency, **Skopelos Tours** (tel. 22-622); they can help you find a room and know the island inside out. . . . The **National Bank of Greece** and the **Commercial Bank** are on the paralia. . . . There's a **police station** in Skopelos town (tel. 21-235) and Glossa (tel. 33-505). They can help you find a room as well as handle emergencies. . . . **Livadia Disco** is the hottest place on Skopelos, in fact the only "place" on Skopelos.

ACCOMMODATIONS: Skopelos is nearly as popular as Skiathos, and because of its increasing flow of tourists several new hotels have cropped up, especially in Skopelos town. If you need advice about one of the in-town hotels or pensions or accommodations available in the outer limits, talk to the Salpadimos sisters at **Skopelos Tours** (tel. 22-622) or the officials at the town hall.

Warning: The hotel classification system, so widely used with consistency on most Greek islands, has been turned topsy-turvy on Skopelos: there are D-class hotels that are more expensive than C-class inns; some D-class rooms are equipped with private showers while a few C-class places have shared facilities. In other words, make sure to look at a room and agree on a price before accepting anything, or you may be unpleasantly surprised.

Two of the best hotels in Skopelos are atop the village overlooking the town and command spectacular views of the harbor and Aegean. (Before hiking up the steep road, call for a pick-up and to check for room availability.) The C-class **Hotel Denise** (tel. 0424/22-678) was built in 1981, but fits in well with Skopelos's architectural style. Each of the Denise's four stories is ringed by a wide balcony and the rooms have hardwood floors and furniture. Doubles cost 6500 drs ($50); singles, 5400 drs ($41.54). Next to the Denise is the D-class **Drosia** (tel. 0424/22-490), of the same vintage as the Denise but with slightly less expensive rooms: doubles with bath are 3800 drs ($29.23).

The other recommended hotels are down at waterside, generally on the side opposite from the ferry dock. The **Hotel Eleni** (tel. 0424/22-179) is a gracious modern hotel, whose 36 rooms all have bath and balcony. Owner Charlie Hatgiorosis returned from the Bronx to build his establishment. A double runs 4100 drs ($31.54); a single, 3900 drs ($30). The **Amalia** (tel. 0424/22-688) is a B-class hotel, just beyond the Eleni, at 5400 drs ($41.54) for a double with bath. Inquire at the **Rania Hotel** (0424/22-486) about their clean simple rooms, or the apartments next door, complete with kitchen.

Rooms are easily found in the town above the waterfront. Especially recommended are the rooms of **George Kaliountzis**, on Magerisias St. (tel. 0424/22-533). George can usually be found meeting the boats, offering his considerable hospitality for around 1600 drs ($12.30).

To get away from the tourist trade and the tour crowds, we can highly recommend the **Hotel Atlantes** (tel. 0424/33-233, 33-489, 33-767) in Glossa. Born in Mississippi, raised here, host Les Chocalas has returned to his native island after a 30-year absence to build a lovely 10-room hotel, on the edge of the hill town, opposite the church. All rooms have baths and balconies looking down on the flower-filled garden or out to the sea. Doubles cost 2500 drs ($19.23); singles, 2250 drs ($17.30).

A special recommendation goes to the **Skopelos Villas** (tel. 0424/22-517), located one kilometer away from the center. The villas are actually duplex apartments equipped with kitchen, private bath, and generally two bedrooms. The 33 villas share a common swimming pool, barbecue, and snackbar where breakfast is served. The buildings are tastefully constructed as "traditional island houses," though we doubt if most island houses share a pool or a barbecue. Each villa can comfortably sleep from two to six people, depending on their feelings about each other. A villa runs approximately 8500 drs ($65.38).

RESTAURANTS: There are several normal tavernas along the waterfront, with **Kymata** standing out in the crowd. It is the last one to the right of the waterfront, just off the ferry dock. The food is excellent, although fish in Skopelos is expensive, just as it is on most of the Sporades. A medium-sized red snapper runs almost 2000 drs ($15.38) alone. (The scarcity of fish in the middle of the Aegean Sea is something of a mystery, though some point to overfishing, others to the fact that fishermen can make much more money taking tourists around.) Anyway, the mullet is a cheaper alternative, and a good dinner for two can be had for 1400 drs ($10.77), unless one goes for snapper. Other good tavernas are **Eklamatoria** and **Yannis**, just down from Kymata.

For breakfast in high season and a late-night drink anytime, try **Platanos**, the jazz pub, beneath the enormous plane tree just to the left off the ferry dock. The morning fruit salad with nuts and yogurt is world renowned in the country of no breakfast. All day long their collection of American jazz records and the view from the outside tables just blows you away, especially if you sip an after-hours ouzo. This is the after-hours place to be on Skopelos.

WHAT TO SEE AND DO: As might be expected, Skopelos is much like Skiathos, with most of the activities and sights taking place outdoors. The whole of Skopelos's 90 square kilometers is prime for hiking, biking, climbing, horseback riding (ask at the Skopelos travel agencies), and most of all, sunning and swimming. There's a kastro in Skopelos town, as well as numerous churches and monasteries. If you're island-hopping, you might want to take advantage of Skopelos's two ports. The northern port at Loutraki is a short jaunt from Skiathos, while Skopelos town is close to Alonissos. Depending on where you've been and where you're going, consider starting at one end of the island, crossing to the other and moving on to the adjoining island.

The following is a run-down of the **beaches** on Skopelos. The one truly sandy beach on the island happens to be in **Skopelos town**, to the south of the paralia. A 15-minute walk to the north will take you to **Ag. Konstantinos**, where there are villas and a few places to eat. **Sares** beach is a short caïque ride away from Skopelastown and is much less crowded than the two town beaches. **Ormos Stafilos** is on the south coast. There is a long and often-packed beach along the sheltered coastal stretch; a 15-minute hike due east will take you to **Velanio**, Skopelos's nude beach. There is a taverna and a ten-room pension at Stafilos. One of the island's best beaches, **Limnonari**, can only be reached by caïque from Agnodas. The longest beach, and one of the nicest and least crowded, is the enormous stretch between **Milia** and **Panormos**, where scruffy pines and shrubs grow down to the sand's edge. There's a taverna in Panormos, but bring a picnic if you plan on staying at Milia all day; there aren't any places to eat. Milia is the better of the two beaches and our favorite on the island. The public bus goes to Milia four times daily and drops you off about half a kilometer above the beach. The best way to go is by car or moped, so you can come and go without waiting for the bus.

The four northern towns—Klima, Mahalas, Glossa, and Loutraki—offer fabulous views. Of these **Glossa,** for the particularly intrepid, offers a native purity rarely found on any island in all of Greece. The ferry docks at **Loutraki** and you can stay at the **Flisvos** (tel. 0424/33-526) or the **Avra** (tel. 0424/33-550).

GETTING THERE: The **ferry** to Skopelos from Skiathos takes 90 minutes if you call at Skopelos, or 45 minutes if stopping at Loutraki. The price for a ticket is the same; about 600 drs ($4.61). The **hydrofoil** takes 15 minutes to Loutraki, 45 minutes to Skopelos. From Skiathos you can take the daily scheduled ferry on the Nomikos Lines or hop on one of the many excursion boats. Similarly, it's possible to catch a normal ferry from Alonissos, or ride on one of the **excursion boats**. Expect to pay a little more on the excursion boats, but if they're not full you can usually negotiate the price. There are infrequent connections to Kimi. Check with the **Port Authority** (tel. 22-180) for current schedules; they change frequently. We felt the extra expense of the hydrofoil was well worth it for hopping from island to island.

3. Alonissos

If recent history is a guide, then the least known and one of the most beautiful of the major Sporades, Alonissos, would have to be considered a star-crossed island. For many centuries Alonissos was a major producer of wine, vineyards covered over one-fourth of the island. Then, in 1950, a blight hit the crop, which killed the vines and contaminated the soil. To this day the island is unable to resume any significant farming. And 1965 was another trying year for Alonissos: a minor earthquake hit the island, damaging the hilltop Byzantine capital. Roofs caved in and many walls were cracked, but ironically the real damage was dealt by a military commission sent in to study the situation. Instead of recommending rebuilding the old town, they suggested moving the entire population of the capital down to a minor port, Patitiri ("wine press"), and making it a model community. If you think this sounds like American urban renewal, you're right; the government appropriated funds to build a slum. As you might imagine, the substandard housing has created yet another blight on the island. A Canadian film crew came to Alonissos a few years ago to make a documentary on how not to build a town.

With all this doom and gloom, it's a pleasure to report that luck seems to be turning for underdog Alonissos. Nine locals, eager to return to their homes, and a band of French, German, and English devotees, have moved up to old

Alonissos to rebuild it, using traditional materials, methods, and designs. They have gone so far as to forego electricity, rejecting modern comforts and conveniences for some greater psychic connection to the past. Tavernas, bars, and a couple of craft shops have opened in the last year, and it looks like the capital may once again regain some of its lost dignity, although locals in Patitari resent the foreign invasion of their old hometown. It's a complicated world, even in far-away Alonissos.

ORIENTATION: The total population of Alonissos is about 1,500; most people live between Patitiri and the old capital, so you can imagine how little development has taken place on the rest of the island. Actually, that's part of the lure for the many Greek visitors who've been displaced by the foreign invasion on Skiathos and Skopelos. They used to flock to Sporades for beautiful beaches, lush vegetation, and uncrowded villages. They still come, but so do boatloads of foreign tourists who have also discovered these special islands. Alonissos is the last frontier for those who long for the good old days of cheap living, deserted beaches, and utterly unsullied scenery (with the obvious exception of the port).

Excursion boats and the Nomikos ferry call at **Patitiri,** on the southern tip of the island. **Alonissos** is connected to Patitiri by the island's only paved road; almost all of the beaches are reached by excursion boats. The vast majority of the island is mountainous and green, with olive trees and pines accounting for much of the foliage.

The harbor in Patitiri, at the bottom of some steeply rising hills, is fairly small. To your right as you disembark from the ferry is a barren hill with the largest number of private rooms to rent, many overlooking the harbor. The waterfront presents the usual mix of cafés, hotels, fish tavernas, and shops. A good place to begin if you're just arriving is the **Ikos Travel Office** (tel. 65-320), right on the paralia. Panos Athanassiou runs the agency and is one of those who has made the move up to the old capital. He knows the island and its politics—not to mention good hotels and beaches—as well as anyone. There's a cluster of hotels on the southern side of the port. The port's two **telephone booths** and **post office** are on the main road leading from the port back up into the less attractive part of Patitiri and on to Alonissos. The post office is about a five-minute walk up the road.

GETTING AROUND: The **bus** from Patitiri to Alonissos runs three times a day and costs 200 drs ($1.54) each way. That's about it for roads, paved ones at least. There's a much larger network of dirt and "unimproved" roads that crisscross the island. **Mopeds** are available in Patitiri for 1200 drs ($9.23) a day, 1800 drs ($13.85) for a double. Be especially careful if you head to the northern, more remote parts of Alonissos; the roads are often curvy and mountainous. Have you considered traveling by mule? Most of the **excursion boats** to the nearby beaches leave the port sometime between 10:30 and 11 a.m. Ask at Ikos Travel about chartering a boat, or at least convincing a fisherman to go to some of the nearby lesser Sporades. We heard a story from a middle-aged guy from Texas who told us that he ended up spending three nights on one of the islands getting totally plastered with the island's only inhabitant, a monk. It could happen to you.

USEFUL INFORMATION: The telephone **area code** for Alonissos is 0424. . . . The **post office** is open from 8 a.m. to 8 p.m. Monday through Friday. There is a doctor, who can handle most **emergencies** (tel. 65-208, or at home 65-470). . . . The local pharmacy is on the right-hand road, just off the harbor. . . . **Ikos Travel** sells ferry tickets and can book Olympic Airways flights. Ask if they'll give you a discount if you have a valid student card. . . . The **police** have an office in Patitiri (tel. 65-205).

ACCOMMODATIONS: One of the best views of the harbor and the azure Aegean is from the **Galaxy Hotel** (tel. 0424/65-251), a multistory C-class inn where doubles with bath run 4900 drs ($37.69). (You can also make overseas calls from their phone booth.) Up and to the right of the Galaxy are the **Artemis Bungalows** (tel. 0424/65-265), our favorite place to stay. There are 13 rooms, each a bungalow, and every other one has a kitchen. They're clean, simple, and nice, with a perfect view of the harbor below. A bungalow for two is 2600 drs ($20) with kitchen, 2200 drs ($16.92) without.

The **Liadromia Hotel** (tel. 0424/65-521) is a very nice C-class hotel near the harbor. Many of its 18 rooms have great views, and a roof garden provides an extra treat. A double with bath and breakfast is 2600 drs ($20).

There are quite a few private homes that rent rooms, and if you're looking to save money they're usually on a par with most of the D- and some of the C-class hotels and pensions. Expect to pay 850 drs ($6.54) per person for a room. Most of the rooms are on the north side of the port. By the time you arrive on Alonissos there may be accommodations available in the old capital. Inquire at Ikos Travel.

If you really want to get away from it all, there's the **Theodorou Hotel** (tel. 0424/65-558), a C-class inn located about halfway up the east coast of the island in Ag. Petros. Rooms are very simply furnished; expect to pay 2800 drs ($21.54) for a double with private bath. There are no roads to Ag. Petros, so you'll have to take a caïque to get there.

RESTAURANTS: As usual, the best tavernas on the waterfront are the last two on the left (look for the Pepsi-Cola signs). Both serve fish which, unlike many islands, is nearly always fresh on Alonissos. Try the red mullet or bass; they're the most commonly caught fish in the area. The best taverna in town is the **Nea Alonissos** (tel. 0424/65-485), above Patitiri near the school. It's a fairly long walk, but the restaurant is really good (it's the only one open in the winter so it has to keep the locals happy), and if you've made it here to Alonissos you probably have lots of time on your hands anyway.

The perfect place for a before or after-dinner drink is **Pub Denis,** right on the harbor two doors down from the tavernas. Here it's sit and schmooze to jazz and blues. It's also a fine place to watch the sunset each evening.

There are a couple of places to eat in old Alonissos. The view up at the **Paraport Taverna,** close to the bus stop, is unbelievable. The food is very good; it seems to be evolving into a blend of Greek taverna and health food. Meals run about 650 drs ($5) a person. The only other eatery is actually an unnamed café at the top of the town. The view there is equally impressive, but instead of looking west, as one does at the Paraport, the café faces east.

WHAT TO SEE AND DO: Most people come to Alonissos to escape the crowds, find a quiet beach, and bliss out. Lofty ambitions all, but the island offers several other interesting diversions that shouldn't be overlooked.

The Beaches

Excursion boats leave in the morning for the resort on **Marpounda,** on the south coast. The beach is a long strip of sand and pebbles, stretching from Vythisma, where there's windsurfing and waterskiing, to the hotel beach at Marpounda. The remainder of the beaches are along the eastern coast. The best beach on the island, **Akr. Kokkinokastro,** is far out on a point in between two other attractive beaches, **Chrisi Milia** and the beach on **Tzortzi Bay**. Part of the wonder of Kokkinokastro is that there are pottery shards, broken stone slabs, huge carved blocks, and pieces of clay with traces of writing all strewn about, said to be the remains from the ancient city of Ikos. Where else in Greece can one find such a perfect blend of Hellenism and hedonism?

Excursion boats also stop on **Peristera**, an islet immediately adjacent to Alonissos. There are fine beaches within easy walking distance of where the boat docks at **Vasilikon**. The coast is pitted with grottos of exceptional beauty. There is a cave in nearby Votsi, actually a short walk outside of Votsi in Platsouka, that is particularly picturesque (it's most accessible on calm days).

Ikos Travel offers a day trip to several deserted islands. On **Yioura**, you can visit the Cyclops Cave, where Ulysses is said to have met the Cyclops. On **Kyratanagia**, you can visit a tranquil, scenic monastery. The price is 3500 drs ($26.92), including lunch, for a day trip.

Old Alonissos

You can either walk or take the bus up to the old capital. Wear good shoes if you choose to walk; depending on your enthusiasm, it will take 45 minutes to an hour. (There is a footpath shortcut just above the post office.) Once in the village, built in Byzantine times, wander through the streets, climbing up to the top. When you see Astrafregia, an ice-cream parlor, on your left you'll have reached the top. There's a curious mix of exquisitely rebuilt homes, with the same sort of slate roofing seen on Skopelos, and dilapidated and abandoned buildings. A growing community of artisans have set up shop in Alonissos, and their wares are exhibited in the little stores along the main path through the village. Old Alonissos is a very quiet corner, isolated from the turmoil of the world; it's a pleasure just to sit on a ledge, look out to the sea, and let your mind wander.

GETTING THERE: Alonissos is on the ferry line with Skiathos and Skopelos, so during the busy summer months there is usually daily service. The hydrofoils come and go three times a day. Excursion boats from Alonissos's neighbors also operate on a daily basis throughout the summer. There's at least one boat a day arriving from either Volos, Ag. Konstantinos, or Kimi. In spring and fall service to the island drops off considerably; check with the local Port Authority for the schedule.

4. Skyros

Skyros is an island of wide, fine-sand beaches, attractive whitewashed pillbox architecture, picturesque surroundings, low prices, and relatively few tourists. How can this be? First, it's difficult to get to Skyros. The ferry leaves either from the isolated port of Paralia Kimi (with a two-hour boatride to Skyros), on the east coast of Evia, or from Volos, which is the starting point for a 12-hour ride to the island. The Flying Dolphin goes twice a week only, on Thursday and Sunday. Second, Greek tourists prefer the other more thickly forested Sporades, especially Skiathos. In this matter we disagree with the Greeks. Skyros's scruffy vegetation and stark contrast between sea, sky, and rugged terrain make it all the more dramatic and revealing.

Perhaps the biggest damper on tourism placed on Skyros has been by the Greek government, ever since it built a NATO base (not much in evidence other than an occasional sonic boom) on the northern end of the island. The government discourages hotel building by withholding low-interest loans from prospective builders. There are only three hotels on the whole island (but many rooms-to-let).

None of these obstacles should deter you. If you're sitting on a crowded beach somewhere south in the Coney Island atmosphere of the Cyclades, or you're planning a trip from your hometown, be assured that Skyros is an ideal place for an extended stay.

ORIENTATION: The ferries from Kimi and Volos dock at **Linaria**, on the opposite side of the island from the town of **Skyros**. The island's only bus—sometimes they bring another over from the mainland—will meet the boat and take you over winding, curvy roads to Skyros town (75 drs, or 58¢, for the ticket). Depending on the mood of the driver, the bus will stop at Magazia Beach, immediately below the town next to the Xenia Hotel. Taxi service between Linaria and Skyros is available but expensive, about 1000 drs ($7.69). The town itself is built on a rocky bluff overlooking the sea.

Skyros looks quite like a typical Cycladic hill town, with whitewashed cube-shaped houses built on top of each other. The streets and paths that are called streets are too narrow for cars and mopeds, so most of the traffic is by foot and hoof. As you alight from the bus at the platia, head north toward the center of town and the main tourist services. There's a **post office** in the bus square, a bank across the street and rooms, drinks, and food farther up the path. To get to **Magazia Beach**, follow the main street all the way to Rupert Brooke's statue of *Immortal Poetry* and take the switchbacks down. If in doubt, just follow the dung and you'll end up on the donkey path. (If your load is heavy, take a taxi to Magazia; it's a hike.) Magazia is several kilometers long, so if you want to be alone just keep walking.

The best beach on the island is **Ag. Fokas**, on the southern coast near Tris Boukes, at the grave of the poet Rupert Brooke. Locals call it paradise, and like all such places it's extremely difficult to reach. Most Skyrians will suggest walking, but it's a long, hilly hike. To get there, take the bus back to Linaria and begin your hike there.

Far more convenient are **Calamitsa**, a five-kilometer walk south of Linaria, and the two beaches near Skyros, **Magazia** and **Ormos Achilli,** south of the town. Roads and an occasional bus, taxi, or private car lead across the Oros Olympos mountains in the center of the island to **Atsitsa**, where there are a few rooms to rent, and **Kirapangia.**

For water sports, there is a sailing center on the beach at Aherounes. Windsurfing and motorboat rentals are available. See Lefteris Trakos at **Skyros Travel** for details.

ACCOMMODATIONS: The whole island has only a few hotels. First is the predictably expensive but nice **Xenia** (tel. 0222/91-209), built right on the beach. There's a carefully tended garden leading up to the entrance and a Skyrian-style coffee room off the lobby. The rooms are austere. A bathless double with breakfast costs 5853 drs ($45.02); with bath, 7240 drs ($55.69). Far more reasonable is the **Elena Hotel** (tel. 0222/91-738), two blocks downhill from the bus stop in Skyros. None of the rooms has private facilities, but the price is right—2700 drs ($20.76) for two. Also near the beach is the small but delightful **Pension Galena** (tel. 0222/91-379). Some of their rooms have baths and run about 2850 drs ($21.93). At the north end of Magazia Beach, in the town of Molos, you'll find the cheery **Paradise Hotel**, whose 40 rooms all have baths. The rooms are small and plain but a short walk from the beach. A double costs 3000 drs ($23.07) and a single, 2400 drs ($18.46). While the area is somewhat removed from the main town, there is a taverna on the premises and another down the street.

Most visitors to Skyros take rooms in private houses. It takes more work, but the rewards are great. Unlike private rooms on other islands, you'll actually stay in a part of the house where a Greek family lives. The best rooms are in the upper part of the town, away from the bus stop, where women in black dresses accost you with cries of "room, room." Walk beyond the platia, up the main street. Women will offer you rooms here, so investigate and make your choice. A more efficient procedure is to stop in at **Skyros Travel Center,** the Olympic Airways representative in Skyros. Lefteris Trakos offers tourist services and can help place you in a room. He may be driving up the prices a bit, but it can save you some effort. Before agreeing to anything check out the rooms to ensure they are what you want. Skyros is somewhat more primitive in its facilities than other islands, but compensates by its authenticity. Rates for in-town rooms during the high season are 1600 drs ($12.30); on the beach 1800 drs ($13.84); and A-class rooms, 2000 drs ($15.38). *Warning:* Very few people in Skyros speak English, so negotiating a room can be tricky. Lefteris speaks very fine English, but can be overburdened. Patience is the trick.

RESTAURANTS: Dining is, like hotels, somewhat of a problem on Skyros—there just aren't a lot of places to eat. People often go to grocery stores and bakeries to buy food for a picnic. In Skyros town, the best fish restaurant is **Kampanera,** located off the main street at the sign marked "The Aquarium." **Volietis** is centrally located but overpriced, especially for its standard taverna fare. The reason to go there is that it seems to attract a cross section of locals and tourists: young moped-riding beer drinkers who try to dance in a stupor to old card-playing men dressed in their baggy pants and wildly complicated sandals. (The sandals on Skyros are among the most convoluted and uncomfortable in Greece; if tempted, you can try them on in the stores on main street.) There's a good taverna on the main path to the statue, about half way up. It's family run, has a green-metal exterior with tables outside, and is inexpensive.

For a good coffee and turnover there is **Omitsos,** right on the main drag. The best **bakery** in the town is hidden away up in the hills on the edge of Skyros. Walk up along the stairs to the weird statue of *Poetry,* bear right up the white-washed stone path, and ask a local. It's tucked away, but your nose will be your guide. A loaf costs 50 drs (39¢).

USEFUL INFORMATION: The only tourist office is **Skyros Travel Center** (tel. 0222/91123 or 91732). Lefteris Trakos can be very helpful on many counts, including rooms, changing money, Olympic Airways flights (he is the local ticket agent), long-distance calls, bus and boat tours. He speaks very fine English and is very helpful. There's only one **bank** (with no extended hours), but the store with the "Food Market" sign on the right-hand side of the path and the newspaper shop opposite, on the main street, will change money at a fairly good rate. The best idea is to bring plenty of drachmas. . . . The island has two discos. **Disco on the Rocks** is reached by foot, midway off the switchback path from town to Magazia. The other danceteria, **Sciropola,** is down the hill from Disco on the Rocks. . . . The **Dorothea Gift Shop,** on the main street, has interesting ceramics, Greek shadow puppets, and a great selection of postcards. For Skyrian plates try the small shop at no. 307, across from Fragoules hardware. Also popular for plates is the studio of **Yiannis Nicholau,** next to the Xenia. He makes all of the plates and also serves as the beer distributor for the island. Good hand-carved wooden chests and chairs made from beech (in the old days it was blackberry wood) can be purchased at **Baboussis,** up in Skyros town. . . . The telephone **area code** on Skyros is 0222.

THE WILD HORSES OF SKYROS: Skyros is the home of a unique breed of wild and very small horses, often compared to the horses depicted on the frieze of the Parthenon. The Meraklides, local Skyrians who care for these rare animals, have moved most of the diminishing breed to the nearby island Skyriopoulou. Ask around and you might be able to find a Meraklide who'll let you ride one.

WHAT TO SEE: The island has the kind of history that inspires tales of adventure and romance. During the Byzantine era, the head clerics from Epirus sent ten families to Skyros to serve as governors. With the exception of St. George's Monastery, they were given every inch of land. For hundreds of years these ten families dominated the affairs of Skyros. The island prospered as a trading center, and consulates opened from countries near and far. The merchant ships were soon followed by pirates, who pillaged and plundered with reckless abandon. Instead of fighting the pirates, the ruling families went into business with them; the families knew what boats were expected and what they were carrying, and the pirates had the ships and bravado to steal the cargo. This unholy combination worked for only a short while, until the pirates turned their plundering on the islanders. The town moved up to the acropolis, high above the port, and by 1830 pirates had ceased to attack the island.

After Greek independence the ruling families were forced to leave. Since they were unable to take all the booty that had accumulated over the centuries they left many of the less valuable objects on the island. Chief among these were sets of dinnerware. **Dinner plates** from China, Italy, Turkey, Egypt, and other exotic locales became a sign of wealth. Skyrian families made elaborate displays of their newly acquired plates. Whole walls were covered, and by the 1920s local Skyrian craftsmen began making their own plates.

If you don't believe this, peek into the doorway of any Skyrian home and nine times out of ten you'll see what looks like a room from a dollhouse: tiny table and chairs and plates, loads of plates, hanging on the wall. This unusual state of affairs is wonderfully celebrated in the island's two museums, the folk art and archeological museums. The **folk art museum** is the private collection of one man, Costas Faltaites, and it's the best island folk art museum in Greece. The museum contains a large and varied collection of plates, as well as examples of embroidery, weaving, woodworking, and clothing. There's a workshop attached to the museum where young artisans make lovely objets d'art using traditional patterns and materials. A stenciled gauze scarf sells for 1500 drs ($11.53), and the proceeds from the sale of workshop items go to the upkeep of the museum. The folk art museum is open daily in the summer from 10 a.m. to 1:30 p.m. and 5:30 p.m. to 8:30 p.m., and in the off-season whenever you can find someone to open it for you. The **archeological museum** has a small collection of Mycenaean and late Helladic funerary objects, and a room dedicated to the very popular arts of Skyros.

The northwest quadrant of the island is covered in dense pine forests, spreading down to the rocky shore and opening into gentle bays and coves. This area provides wonderful hiking for sturdy walkers. Take a **taxi** (1000 drs, or $7.69) to **Atsitsa**. (The cautious will arrange for the taxi to return in five or six hours.) Explore the ruins of the ancient mining operation at Atsitsa, then head south for about four and one half miles to **Ag. Fokas**, a small bay with a tiny taverna perched right on the water. Kali Orfanou, a gracious hostess, will provide you with the meal of your trip—fresh fish caught that morning in the waters before you, vegetables plucked from the garden for your salad, and her own feta cheese and wine. Stay, swim in the bay, and hike back to your taxi. The ambitious will continue south for seven or eight miles to the main road and catch the bus or hail a taxi. This part is mainly uphill, so walker beware. In case you tire or can't pry yourself away from this secluded paradise, Kali offers two extremely primitive rooms with the view of your dreams. There is no electricity or toilets (in the formal sense), but where else can you experience Greece at its most elemental level?

GETTING THERE: Olympic Airways now has one flight a day between Athens and Skyros, landing at the NATO base. The planes are small, so reserve well in advance. The local office is **Skyros Travel** (tel. 0222/91-123 or 91-600).

There is now only one **ferry company** serving Skyros, and it is owned by a company whose stockholders are all citizens of Skyros. The old company provided great service in the busy summer months and lousy service in the off-season. So the citizens of Skyros bought their own boat and only allow it to dock at Skyros. From June 16 to September 15, it runs twice daily from Kimi to Skyros (11 a.m. and 5 p.m.) and twice daily from Skyros to Kimi (8 a.m. and 2 p.m.). Off-season, there is one ferry each way, leaving Skyros at 8 a.m. and Kimi at 5 p.m. The fare is 850 drs ($6.54). For schedules to Kimi, call the **Nomikos Ferry** (tel. 4179-404 or 4178-080) in Kimi. For Skyros ferry schedules, call **Skyros Travel** (tel. 0222/91-123 or 91-600).

The **Flying Dolphin** now goes to Skyros twice a week, on Thursday and Saturday, from Skiathos and Alonissos. The hydrofoil leaves Skiathos at 8:55 a.m., stops in Alonissos, then continues to Skyros. It leaves Skyros at 4:30 p.m. the same day and costs 2300 drs ($17.69). This is easily the most convenient way to go, though pricey compared to the ferry.

The tricky part of getting to Skyros is the connection with the ferry from the other Sporades islands. The off-season ferry from Skiathos, Skopelos, Alonossis, and Volos is scheduled to arrive at Kimi at 5 p.m., but is usually late. It is not uncommon to see the Skyros ferry disappearing on the horizon as your ferry pulls into Kimi. Oh well, make the best of the twenty-four-hour layover and get a room in **Paralia Kimi** (port of Kimi, located up on the hill). The **Hotel Belis,** on the paralia, has doubles with bath for 2750 drs ($21.53). Rooms can be had along the paralia. We recommend the **Taverna To Amanaki,** for a good meal and for rooms in a pinch. The best restaurant in Paralia is **Spanos,** on the water. Walk all the way down past town for a swim on the local beach. Hike the four kilometers up the hill to Kimi and visit the local folk museum.

From Athens, buses run regularly for the 3½-hour trip to Kimi, from which you take a local bus to Paralia Kimi. Just make sure of your connection.

Chapter XII

WESTERN GREECE

1. The Ionian Coast
2. Epirus

THE IONIAN COASTLINE is one of the magnificent, uniquely Greek landscapes in the country. If you've heard about Corfu's legendary beauty (the setting for Shakespeare's *Tempest*) or read about Odysseus' home, Ithaca, in the *Odyssey,* you may well imagine what divine sights greet those who follow the mainland coast and look out to these verdant, rocky clumps of paradise. The Ionian Sea is as well known for its deep emerald color as the Aegean is for its turquoise hue, and from the elevated coastal highway, you can appreciate its fiery depths. If we can't persuade you, wonder about Aristotle Onassis and Paul McCartney, two vacationers with an unlimited range of possibilities, who chose to make their homes-away-from-home here.

Epirus is that mountainous region that begins at the coast and stretches inland, hugging the Pindus range and reaching out to Thessaly on the eastern side. Its fiercely independent mountain people have retained many of their traditional customs, clothing, and building styles in villages such as Metsovo and on Nissi Island in Ioannina.

1. The Ionian Coast

"The mountains look on Marathon, And Marathon looks on the sea; And musing there an hour alone, I dreamed that Greece might still be free"—*Don Juan.* George Noel Gordon, Lord Byron, composer of the above verse, died in Messolonghi, Greece, in 1824. We'll start a tour with one of those places on Greece's beautiful west coast that anyone could do without. (Even Byron fans should not come and get depressed about where he unfortunately died after a happy respite on nearby Kephalonia.)

MESSOLONGHI: Messolonghi was founded 400 years ago after the Evinos River began to silt up, uniting three islets. The shallow lagoons surrounding the town provide excellent fishing and breeding grounds for eel and *avgotarcho* (a local fish roe). Instead of charming, seaside tavernas, which should be serving up these local delicacies, Messolonghi features incomplete tract housing overlooking dirty marshland to the sea. From the local army base, hundreds of uniformed soldiers spew forth to roam the streets or crowd the ouzeris.

This town actually does have an interesting, illustrious history. Its inhabitants held out bravely for four years against the Turkish assault (Byron was part of that) in the 1821 War of Independence, but in 1826 there was a great massacre and the town was razed by fire. Lord Byron died at Messolonghi during the fighting there. For those who've come this far to see it, **Byron's grave** is in the

Garden of the Heroes, signposted "Heroe's Tomb" just before you enter the town.

From Messolonghi north, the road curves inland through verdant fields striped with plastic tents where tobacco is drying. Olives and cypress trees alternate vertically. About 48 kilometers north is the lovely port of **Astakos**, whose houses line the gentle slope of forested hills that surround this cove. Beautiful 19th-century villas line the broad streets, clogged with taverna tables. The simple quay juts out into the placid water, where an infrequent caïque takes passengers to **Kalamos Island**, farther north. There are no formal accommodations in Astakos, but it's worth an admiring glance if you happen to be driving this way.

MITIKAS: Mitikas is another charming port on the Ionian coast, 81 kilometers north of Messolonghi. This one-street village has a few hotels and some excellent tavernas, built during the boom times when the Ionian Lines ferries docked here going to and from Ithaca and Kephalonia. All that's changed. Now if there's enough interest, local cruise companies from Lefkas circle the nearby Prigiponissi (four private islands) so tourists can ogle Skorpios. These boats occasionally stop at Mitikas for lunch.

The friendly inhabitants seem little touched by their brush with tourist fame. They proudly tell Americans of the days when John-John Kennedy and Aristotle Onassis used to waterski off their shores. The calm waters are broken now by fishermen who bring back their mullet and eels to local tavernas. The most satisfying thing to do in Mitikas is watch life go by. Older women, dressed in black, sweep their patios along the waterfront. Crisply dressed young girls promenade along the main street, holding hands. Old men in dusty blue and gray sit at the café bars and watch you watch them. Robust young men clean the eels on the long thin stretch of pebble beach, swapping stories about Australia, where they return each winter to earn money for their families in Mitikas.

The one C-class hotel is the **Simos** (tel. 0646/81-380), a 28-room modern structure that seems to have been dropped in from a Corfu beach resort. Clean, well-furnished doubles are 5000 drs ($38.50) a night during the high season. Across the street is the charming D-class **Akroyali** (tel. 0646/81-206), where our high-ceilinged, pastel-pink double with antique wrought-iron bed and flapping shutters cost us 2250 drs ($17.30). A shower down the chilly hallway was free. The Akroyali is above a popular taverna whose weathered old bartender reads pretty good sign language.

As for tavernas, the **Dionyssos**, its back facing the water (push all the way in to get to the outdoor, seaside tables), is very comfortable and friendly. Its proprietor can really cook up a storm, and for bargain rates too.

The Ionian coast banks sharply here, leaving drivers at a 30° angle to admire the fairyland greenery and small stone fragments that appear to have been tossed randomly into the sea. We'd say how poor the road is, but things change so quickly in Greece (where a flooded spring or a frozen winter can cause terrible destruction to macadam paving) that it may look like U.S. 40 when you attempt it. Crossing over to **Lefkas** on a modern tow raft is a wonderful example of the level of technology. From the town of Ag. Nikolaos a thin ribbon of concrete stretches across the marshland to a buttressed concrete pier with a refreshment truck parked alongside. At water's edge are more ramparts from the well-preserved Venetian fortress at **Santa Maura** (built by Giovanni Orsini in 1300). As they must have done for hundreds of years, men and machine work to pull the vehicle-carrying raft over to the opposite shore, crossing the less-than-60-meter span of water efficiently, and at no charge to the passengers.

Continuing north to Igoumenitsa along this irregular coast still offers some of the best scenery in Greece. The changing light, especially as the day wears on, creates subtle images throughout the drive. As striking as Delphi, the Ionian coast is a region where the magic of that "Greek Light" is illuminated.

At **Aktio** on the mainland there is another break in the road, the entry into the Gulf of Amvrakikos. Here a mini-car-ferry shuttles back and forth across the half-kilometer waterway from the parking lot of Aktio to the busy, crowded harbor at . . .

PREVEZA: For the Aktio-Preveza shuttle, cars are charged 250 drs ($1.95) and people 50 drs (40¢) each. There are several pleasant cafés along Preveza's harbor, all in full view of the steady crawl of vehicles waiting for the next shuttle. The old, narrow back streets of town are much more interesting, and a good place to stock up on picnic supplies for your journey.

If you decide to stop your wanderings here, overlooking the water is the C-class **Hotel Minos** (tel. 0682/28-424), where double rooms cost 3740 drs ($28.80). Nearby are the 16-room **Metropolis** (tel. 0682/22-235) and the 17-room **Hotel Aktaeon** (tel. 0682/22-258); both have bathless doubles for about 2250 drs ($17.30).

For archeology buffs, there's the large, intriguing site of Nikopolis nearby, and veering east, the transportation hub of Arta. **Nikopolis** is eight kilometers north of Preveza, a Roman town built in A.D. 31 by the Emperor Octavius to commemorate his naval victory against the fleets of Anthony and Cleopatra. Several walls have survived with triple gates, and you can climb around to see the remains of the temples of Mars (Ares) and Poseidon, part of an aqueduct, and some baths. In the Byzantine period Nikopolis prospered and the remains of four basilicas with fine mosaic floors can be examined at the site. Shaded by olives and carpeted with grass, Nikopolis is the right place to be on a sticky August day. Travelers without wheels can catch the local bus from Preveza to Igoumenitsa or Arta and get off at the site.

Arta is the second-largest town in Epirus after Ioannina, and is known for the Arta bridge, which spans the Arachthos River (it's the oldest stone bridge in Greece). Legend has it that the bridge's builder, in order to make it stand, bricked his wife into one leg. The Church of Panagia Parigoritissa, in the center of town, has been converted to a museum for local finds from Roman and Byzantine times. The church is an interesting 13th-century work; it, the ruins of a temple along Pyrrou Street, the nearby remains of the ancient theater, and a crumbling fortress above the town are the major sights. In Ag. Vasilios and Ag. Theodora, rare icons and fine frescoes, gifts of the Komnines and Angeloi Imperial families, are exhibited.

Beach lovers should head back out to the Ionian coast road and continue for 57 kilometers, to Parga, a very pretty resort that is perfect for R&R, especially in the low season. You'll find it very built up, to accommodate Corfu's overflow traffic, but the two long beach coves which fan out like outstretched wings from its long central quay provide enough room for everyone to enjoy the clean, calm waters.

PARGA: The town beach is a scenic stretch of white sand (and a few scattered rocks) with a view over the gorgeous bay. The water is emerald and turquoise, with tiny islands tastefully positioned for even the most discerning tourist.

Small paddleboats are ideal for touring the other nearby coves. Caïques advertise their **excursion trips** from small signs on the quay; our favorite is "Day Trip to Hades," which departs at 9 a.m. (does it ever return?). There are several boats running to **Paxi** (600 drs, or $4.60) and to the **Necromantia Cave**, on the River Styx (500 drs, or $3.85).

If you walk up the lane running behind the harbor, the tost, burger, and disco joints disappear. You can explore the walls of the **Venetian fortress** that straddles Parga's two coves, or cross over and reward yourself with a swim at long, sandy **Valtos beach** (the best locally).

Accommodations and Dining

The unpaved, newly leveled "streets" behind the port are filled with new construction; cheap, three-story buildings are stuccoed in between hotels. It seems that everyone is waiting to add a third story to their own home—all signs of a fast-disintegrating village and newly emerging resort.

The **Hotel Calypso** (tel. 0684/31-316) is one of the larger, C-class places that got in first. It's clean and family-run, and the balconied rooms that overlook the water are comfortable and modern. Ask for a high-floor room; the Calypso is one block from the water and you'll appreciate this view. High-season doubles are 4000 drs ($30.80); prices are better in the low season and it's a better time to be in town.

Behind the **Villa Rosa Taverna**, a popular eatery (set in a pink stucco villa) that's moderately priced and luxuriously situated, are the small apartments of **Lisa Lambropoulis** (tel. 0684/31-237). Linens are changed twice weekly for long-term guests; one of her eight double rooms rents for 2875 drs ($22.10) per night in summertime, with use of a fully stocked communal kitchen.

If you walk toward the center of town, a crowded maze of shops and homes in the shadow of the fortress, you'll find the **Hotel Paradissos** (tel. 0684/31-229), uphill near the post office and an excellent bakery. The weathered bit of paradise has spacious, well-kept bathless doubles for 2715 drs ($20.90); with bath they're 3210 drs ($24.70).

There are rooms to rent everywhere, and rest assured, if you're in Parga anytime other than July 15 to August 30 you can bargain down anyone's prices by at least 25%.

Besides the favorite Villa Rosa on the beach, there's an excellent seafood taverna called **Tsimas**, the last one down on the harbor. It's clean and bright, opening onto the quay where you can see the truly fresh fish being hauled in off the boats. For 1400 drs ($10.80) two can drool over fried calamari, fresh salads, and tangy taramosalata with fresh-baked bread.

Walk in off the harbor to the center of "town" and you'll find **To Kantouni**, in a niche off Vasila Street. Under a canvas canopy sit a few tables and chairs; wander into the dark, cool interior of this little storefront to decipher what's bubbling in all of the pots. This is one of those local places where you can eat a filling meat-and-potatoes type of feast for under 400 drs ($3.10) per person—not an easy thing to do in Greece anymore.

Useful Information

If you want to check on the Igoumenitsa sailings for Corfu, there's an **O.T.E.** office uphill of Vasila Street (open 7:30 a.m. to 3:10 p.m. Monday to Friday). . . . There are two **souvenir shops** that act as banker's agents: the **Parga Tourist Shop** (tel. 31-214) and the **Efthimiadis Tourist Shop** (open 8 a.m. to 11 p.m. daily); both are across from each other in the tiny square. . . . The **West Travel Tourist Office**, on the quay, sells ferry and excursion tickets to the local caïques, and can help you with other travel-related problems. . . . Several of the souvenir shops sell snorkels, masks, and fins—snorkeling is the thing to do in this transparent water. . . . The **Big Apple Mini-Market**, along Vasila Street, is run by two young guys who lived in New York. The Big Apple has a large selection of wine, picnic and camping food, and the style and flair these two brought home to Parga is a real treat.

From Parga, the most popular day trip is to . . .

NEKROMANTIO: This site is 25 kilometers south at the village of **Messopotamos**. At the ancient grounds of the "Necromantic Oracle" is the estuary of the Acheron River, where the souls of the dead used to board the ferry to Hades. Today you can explore the subterranean lake of **Acherousia** and visit the famous **Oracle** at the Ephyros of Thesprotia, recommended to Odysseus for its wise counsel. Excavations have revealed a dark, twisting corridor leading into the main sanctuary, a labyrinth created to remind pilgrims of the tortured wanderings of restless souls in Erebos, the last stop before Hades.

IGOUMENITSA: This west coast city is the jumping-off point for maritime excursions to Corfu and Italy. Fortunately, there is frequent service to these points because there's absolutely nothing to do in the town besides waiting for your ship to come in. The restaurants are generally awful, and if you should be unlucky enough to spend the night, you'll find the hotels vastly overpriced. There are no archeological points within proximity, and the beaches are few (the water in this heavily trafficked channel isn't so great either).

Those coming from Italy with EurailPasses should resist all urges to jump ship unless you're going to travel in northern Greece first. Since the trains don't run to Igoumenitsa, you'll have to pay for a bus; continue on to Patras, where you can get a train free to Athens or other parts of Greece.

Useful Information

The **bus** to and from Athens runs three times daily on the K.T.E.L. lines (tel. 01/51-25-954 in Athens); the nine-hour ride costs 1420 drs ($10.95).

The most commonly asked question in Igoumenitsa is "When does the next ferry leave for Corfu?" The informative Balaskas Brothers at **Milano Travel** (tel. 0665/23-565) can answer this (usually every hour during the high season) and much more; they're located on Ag. Apostolon Street, opposite the ferry pier. Passenger fares are 380 drs ($2.90) per person, 2600 drs ($20) for a car and driver, and the ferries depart about twelve times daily. The Milano Travel Office is open 8 a.m. to 10:30 p.m. daily in summer.

The **Stability Lines** (their name, not ours) and **Ventouris Ferries** run steamers to **Bari, Italy,** every two days in July and August from Igoumenitsa; fares range from 3875 drs ($29.80) to 5500 drs ($42.30) in the high season. Contact the Milano Travel Office for information, or call their Piraeus office at 01/41-32-392.

The cheapest place to be stuck overnight is the **Hotel Aktaeon,** at 27 Ag. Apostolon (tel. 0665/22-308); 21 simple rooms, kept clean by a gentle old couple, are 2750 drs ($21.10) for a bathless double. The **Epirus** (tel. 0665/22-504) is behind the Milano Travel Office at 20 Pargas St.; their six rooms with bath run 4000 drs ($30.80) for two. The **Oscar** (tel. 0665/22-675) is on the harbor-side Ag. Apostolon at no. 149. The huge lobby is just dripping with ferns; it's lively, and the managers are good-time, wild 'n' crazy guys. They've got a big café that's across from a big parking lot, with the wide-open Ionian beyond that. We checked their license and found that their spacious, modern doubles should cost 4875 drs ($37.50) with breakfast, per night.

2. Epirus

Turning inland from Igoumenitsa, we travel 100 kilometers east to the capital of Epirus, Ioannina. This city of nearly 45,000 inhabitants boasts a highly regarded local university, a picturesque setting on ancient Lake Panyotis, and several colorful sights associated with its most infamous resident, Ali Pasha. The archeological museum has surprisingly interesting finds from Epirus, including objects related to Zeus' Oracle at Dodoni. The Aslan Tzami Mosque (in the city's special old walled-in section near the lake) houses an intriguing collection of folk art and political memorabilia. Four kilometers outside of town, in the village of Perama, is a spectacular, two-kilometer-long cave filled with galleries of stalactites and stalagmites which are well lit and fun to explore. With so much to see, one could certainly spend a few days in Ioannina. However, in light of the congestion offered by the raging student hordes, motorcycles, bus tours, and general industrial activity in this bustling metropolis, we think one day and night are plenty. Don't leave without visiting Nissi, the islet in Lake Panyotis (now Lake Ioannina) where a small community of homes and monasteries has been built; it's one of northern Greece's most colorful and pleasant excursions. And more important, don't leave the region without a visit to Dodoni, site of an ancient Oracle much revered in antiquity, that still speaks to the modern pilgrim who goes with open ears. From Ioannina you can work your way through dramatic mountain countryside over the Athamanon range to the traditional hill village of Metsovo, where embroiderers and craftsmen thrive in a foundation-funded, creative environment that's totally respectful of their past.

IOANNINA: The "village in the lake," as it's known to many, slopes down an acropolis-topped hillside to the banks of tranquil **Lake Ioannina**. Drivers entering the city will come east along Mavrogiani Street or Venizelou Street until it descends at Averoff Street to the lake. From the west, the road meets Vass. Georgiou Street, then Central Square, which becomes Averoff Street until it bumps into the walled-in fortress that has captured the old city. Along this stretch of Vass. Georgiou (King George) Street, and around Central or Pyrrus Square, there are several hotels, cafés, and tourist services.

From the central Pyrrus Square it's a five-minute walk downhill to explore the walled-in fort, then another five minutes around its perimeter or through an opposite gate out to the shore of Lake Ioannina. The tall brown brick **Litharitsia prison** is on a rise in the green park surrounding the old clock tower; this can be used to orient you to nearby Pyrrus Square. Ioannina's other major artery, **28 Oktovriou Street**, runs perpendicular to Vass. Georgiou St. from their intersection at Pyrrus Square. There are some hotels along this busy street, and several in the triangle formed by Vass. Georgiou Street, Venizelou Street, and 28 Oktovriou Street, the area in which most of the bus terminals are located. Our best suggestion is to find the Palladion Hotel, at 28 Oktovriou Street, no. 26, and ask for their brochure. It's the only printed map of Ioannina around!

Useful Information

There's an **E.O.T.** (tel. 0651/25-086) in Ioannina at King Pyrrus Square at 2 Nap. Sena St. They're open from 7:30 a.m. to 3 p.m. weekdays. . . . The **area code** is 0651. . . . **Taxis** are easy to hail near the square, or call 27-111 to book one; they're 2500 drs ($16.30) round trip to Dodoni.

The **bus station** west to Arta, Preveza, or Patras is on Byzaniou Street (behind the Pyrrus Square crossroads). There are two buses daily to Patras; call 25-014 for schedules. The bus to Igoumenitsa or Athens-Thessaloniki leaves from Zosimadion Street (one block above the intersection of Venizelou and Averoff Streets). Buses leave every two hours for the seven-and-a-half hour trip to Athens; call 26-211 for schedule information.

Olympic Airways (tel. 26-518) is at Ano Kentriki Square; from here a bus departs one hour before flight time for the airport (fare: 60 drs, or 47¢). Olympic flies from Ioannina to Athens once daily, to Thessaloniki twice a week, and to Tirana, Albania, once a week. . . . The **post office** is on 28 Oktovriou Street (open 7:30 a.m. to 8:30 p.m. Monday through Friday). . . . The **O.T.E.** is nearby (open 7 a.m. to midnight, seven days). . . . There's a **foreign-language bookstore** opposite the post office.

There are five **cinemas** in town; of these, the Palladion (near the hotel of the same name) and the Bitta usually only play Greek films. . . . In the **Ioannina Theater**, there are often performances of *Ipirotika,* the older singers who specialize in the popular *thimotika,* or workers' ballads and folk songs. Contact E.O.T. for more information, including the date of the one-day only performance of classic theater at Dodoni. . . . If you're heading out to the natural cave at **Perama,** and can't tear yourself away, there's a hotel there, the **Ziakas** (tel. 0651/28-611).

While we're looking at things to do, there's some interesting **shopping** for folk art, hammered copper and tin dishware, jewelry, and trinkets as well as crafts in the old city. Just across from the main gate to the old city there is an interesting little shop filled with what are probably "new" antiquities, some embroidered vests, skirts, and thick, cozy woven socks.

Accommodations and Dining

All the main avenues through Ioannina are terrifically noisy at night, even though most of the hotels were built here. Therefore although most of the hotels listed below will have odd addresses, they are almost all within a block of a main artery—convenient, but quieter.

Near Pyrrus Square: The **Hotel Alexios** (tel. 0651/24-003) is five blocks up from Pyrrus Square, walking along 28 Oktovriou. You'll see it on the right, at 14 Poukevil St. across from Algos Park. It's one of the quietest hotels here—clean, pleasant, and modern; 88 rooms offer private-facilities doubles for 3875 drs ($29.80). The **Hotel El Greco** (tel. 0651/30-726) is at 8 Tsirigotis, just off 28 Oktovriou Street, near the Alexios. There's parking in back, a cheery breakfast room, and doubles cost the same as the Alexios.

The **Hotel Palladion** (tel. 0651/25-856) at 28 Oktovriou St., no. 26, is about two blocks off Pyrrus Square up past the post office, on the right. It's gigantic (135 rooms), but relatively comfy inside; don't forget its "town map"-sporting brochure. Doubles are 3750 drs ($28.90), but since groups often use this hotel it may be hard to get a room.

It may be risky to recommend the **Hotel Galaxy** (tel. 0651/25-056) because it's right on Pyrrus Square, but their 38 rooms seemed to be somewhat soundproofed. High-season doubles are 3875 drs ($29.80). Ask for the lake view, please.

Near the Fortress (Old City): There are a few small, older hotels located near this most picturesque part of Ioannina. The **Metropolis** (tel. 0651/25-507) is at 2 Averoff St., about three blocks up from the fort's main gate. There are 16 bathless rooms, many of them in the charming baby-pink color scheme of the lobby area. Doubles are 2430 drs ($18.70). The **Hotel Tourist** (tel. 0651/26-443) is at 18 Kolleti, just past the Metropole. The Tourist is aging, but conveniently located, and only 4125 drs ($31.70) for a double with bath, 2875 drs ($22.10) for a double without.

Near the Bus Station: The old car-filled narrow streets of markets and shops in Ioannina's lower triangle are invigorating. Here, in the heart of Ioanninan frenzy but convenient to the bus station are a few hotels and many, many fast-food eateries. The **Hermes** (tel. 0651/25-686) is at 2 Sina St., on a busy intersection. The Hermes's 33 rooms are compact and clean, a good deal at 2490 drs

($19.20). The D-class **Hotel Paris** (tel. 0651/20-541) is in a quiet lane off busy
Tsirigotis St., no. 6. It's near the El Greco, but this part of the commercial street
has a different feel; the courtyard entrance to the Paris is filled with potted plants
and is quite nice. Bathless doubles are simple, but only 2375 drs ($18.30). The
C-class **Hotel Egnatia** (tel. 0651/25-667) is on the small part at Scobourdi
Square. Its 52 rooms are plain, but clean; the Gothic-modern lobby decor is the
strongest theme here. High-season doubles, all with private bath, are 3580 drs
($27.50).

    Special Tavernas: In **Litharitsia**, the old Turkish-era prison where Greek
insurgents were kept, you can dine at an old wooden table and look down into
the grate-covered cells below. The best part of this restaurant (whose menu varies from salads to continental cuisine, meat stews to simple Greek fare) may be
its setting, on a hill in the park (marked by the clock tower) near Pyrrus Square.
Its interior is finely crafted wood, the food's just okay and a bit pricey—about
1000 drs ($7.70) per person—but the drinks are good. On Saturday and Sunday
night a live orchestra plays. It's said in local song that the village women used to
come up to this hill to dance during the Turkish occupation; let's encourage a
worthy tradition!
    The **Tourist Pavilion** is up near the Acropolis, near the Ioannina Theater,
and offers splendid views over the lake and town. Check with E.O.T. for theater
schedules, and then combine a show with drinks or a scenic meal here. Another
popular taverna for those going to the airport is the **Gastra**, one kilometer west
of the airport on the Igoumenitsa road. They have a wide variety of Greek
foods, but so well prepared and presented that it's worth a trip to go. We also
discovered the **Rekatos Taverna,** a fine grill about two kilometers from
Litharitsia.
    There are also three excellent seafood tavernas on **Nissi islet**, serving the
regional specialties of frogs legs, eel, and trout, fresh-caught from Ioannina
Lake. If it's seafood you're after, try a local specialty—*caravida,* a shellfish
that's a cross between lobster and crawfish. It's fabulous but only available certain times of the year.

The Island in the Lake

    Nissi is an islet settled in the 17th century by refugees from the Mani in the
Peloponnese. Its most colorful inhabitant was without a doubt the dissident
Turkish ruler Ali Pasha, who came in 1820 and took refuge here for two years.
After much cajoling, he received his royal pardon from Constantinople, which
was just a trick on the Ottoman sultan's part: troops had been dispatched to
Ioannina to end his command. At their arrival, he shouted, "Stop! What's up?"
and was shot dead.
    The local boat, the *Pambotis,* leaves the lakeside in front of the old fortress
every half hour for the island. The ten-minute trip costs 100 drs (80¢)—just
don't look too closely into the depths of the green water. Disembark at a paved-
stone landing where you'll find three **tavernas** announcing trout and frogs' legs
as their specialty. Check trout prices by the kilo at each place and one will reduce theirs to make sure you eat there. They're all about the same, allowing you
to fish through a tank of trout and eels to choose your own. The fish is excellent
and well prepared.
    The **Ali Pasha Museum** is straight up the blessedly car-free pathway of sou-
venir shops. The holes in its wooden floor are ample evidence of Ali's demise.
The "museum" was actually the pre-1820 home of Vassiliki, who betrayed her
husband Ali's presence in the Pandeleimos Monastery. The 17th-century monastery next door is closed to visitors, but just behind the Ali Museum is the

Prodromou Monastery of St. John the Baptist, built in 1506-1507 and filled with frescoes. Only the museum charges an entrance fee, of 125 drs ($1).

An Island Tour: Continue back up Souvenir Street, and where the other side of the island comes into view is the **Moni Philantropinon**, built in 1292. If you walk through the frescoed church you'll come to the wing used as a "secret school" during the Turkish occupation. It's obvious that the frescoes have been grossly defaced (due to the Moslem taboo against worshiping human images). Next door, the **Moni Stratigopoulou** (11th century) was dedicated to Saint Nicholas, whose portrait is inside the first entry. The frescoes are much darker and eroded here. If the door's closed, an old woman in black will open it up for you; expect a 50-drs (40¢) contribution. Farther along this path is the **Eleousis Monastery**, from the 16th century, which is also closed to the public. Even if you've only got a few hours between buses in Ioannina, a brief visit to the island and a stop for lunch is well worthwhile.

If you've got more time, the island can be circled in a half-hour stroll along a gravel-and-dirt path on the lakefront, a perfect place for jogging too.

Folk Art Museum in Ali Pasha Mosque

Displayed haphazardly in the various prayer areas are some fine local costumes, weapons, old documents, and photos of military men, plus memorabilia from the War of Independence and World War II. The eclectic collection includes some Judaica: three *katubahs* (marriage contracts in Hebrew from 1762) and a gold-embroidered velvet curtain from an old Jewish synagogue in Ioannina. The Mosque museum is located on the lake side of the old city, up some hobbled stone-paved lanes. It's open from 8:30 a.m. to 1:30 p.m. and 5:30 p.m. to 8 p.m. Monday through Saturday; closed Sunday. The admission charge is 125 drs ($1).

The Archeological Museum of Ioannina

A special surprise is the lovely, well-lit, modern museum with many artifacts from Dodona and other archeological digs in the Epirus region. Pieces include pottery, jewelry, coins, and icons primarily from the fifth to third centuries B.C., when Dodona was one of the most important Oracles in Greece. A highlight of the museum is the small bronze statuary from Dodona (its detail intricate and amazing on a boy holding a dove and a lion spout from a funerary sarcophagus). Outdoor alcoves adjoining the galleries have pieces of the marble pillars and friezes from various neighboring archeological sites.

The museum is open from 9 a.m. to 3 p.m. Wednesday through Monday, from 9:30 a.m. to 2:30 p.m. on Sunday and holidays. Admission fee: 125 drs ($1), half price for students.

THE ORACLE OF DODONA: Set in a valley amid tall, rugged, gray-blue mountains 21 kilometers south of Ioannina, Dodona was the most famous Oracle of Zeus, and probably the oldest in Greece—it's said to have been founded by Deucalion after the Deluge. "About the [earliest] oracles," writes Herodotus, "that of Dodona in Greece and that of Ammon in Libya, the Egyptians have the following legend: according to the priests of the Theban Zeus, two women connected with the service of the temple were carried off by the Phoenicians and sold, one in Libya and the other in Greece, and it was these women who founded the oracles in the two countries. . . . However, the priestesses who deliver the oracles have a different story: two black doves, they say, flew away from Thebes in Egypt, and one of them alighted at Dodona, the other in Libya. The former, perched on an oak, and speaking with a human voice, told them that there, on that very spot, there should be an oracle of Zeus. Those who heard her understood the words to be a command from heaven, and at once obeyed. . . ." For centuries, kings and commanders would consult both the oracles at Dodona and Delphi, hoping that at least one would answer their queries with an answer they liked.

At the site today you'll see a mass of temples with eroded columns, tossed upon each other in serendipitous patterns. The theater, one of the very largest in Greece, is still impressive in its bulk. In the Roman era the first five rows were removed and replaced with a retaining wall for use in gladiator events. In the still of the setting sun, the oaks (symbol of Zeus and of Dodona) sway gently, leaves rustling, the wind whips through the mountainsides, whispering through the fir and pine groves. To the east, clouds settle in and blanket the mountain peaks; the birds sing, and when no one else is there, you can listen to the Oracle's words . . .

The Oracle of Dodona is open to the public from 7:30 a.m. to 7:30 p.m. daily, from 10 a.m. to 6 p.m. on Sunday (though you can easily sneak over the fence to be here at dawn or dusk). The admission fee is 300 drs ($2.30). From Ioannina there's a public bus to Dodona twice a day, at the marvelous hours of 6 a.m. and 6 p.m. The bus waits here, after a 45-minute ride, for 15 minutes before turning around (they're obviously trying to build this up as a big tourist attraction). Taxis from Ioannina are the other option. They charge about 2500 drs ($16.30) round trip, including waiting time. A theatrical performance is given in the theater once a year, in August, in honor of the Dodona Festivals of antiquity. Check with the E.O.T. in Ioannina for schedule and ticket information.

From Ioannina to the other highlight of Epirus, Metsovo, it is 58 kilometers (or 93 kilometers west of Trikala in Thessaly).

METSOVO: This is a very charming hill village perched at nearly 1,000 meters above sea level, a delightfully refreshing change, like the hill resorts found throughout India and parts of the tropics. Metsovo's position atop a Pindus range hill lures Greeks all summer and on long, holiday winter weekends.

Metsovo's main street provides wonderful shopping for embroidered wool capes, sweaters, carpets, and souvenirs, but you should stick to items indigenous to the north (we've seen embroidered silk blouses from China, synthetic linen tablecloths from Asian factories, and other overpriced junk). Having warned you, we want to rave about the Pratirio Laikis Technis, the **Metsovo Folk Art Cooperative** supported by the M. Tositsa Foundation, which runs the folk art museum. The cooperative store is located in the cobblestone paths about 50 meters above the Egnatia Hotel and has a large variety of weavings, embroidery, and charming sculpted wooden dolls. The Laikis Technis' gifted women will also tailor some great-looking clothes to order; if you don't want to look like an extra from the Dora Stratou Folk Dance Troupe in Athens, they'll whip up a cape, shawl, or suit in heavy hand-carded wool that'll knock 'em out on Fifth Avenue.

The Tositsa family's mansion has been restored as a **folk art museum**. Its heavy wood, stucco, and roomy interior is very typical of the *arhontikos* seen in the hill country of Mount Pelion, Kastoria, and parts of Crete. Simple rooms are filled with decorative woven fabrics, or warmth-giving rugs, tapestries, and carpets. The displays are a little too "stagey" for Kyle's tastes, but overall, it's an excellent introduction to the best of northern Greek folk craft. The museum is open from 9 a.m. to 1 p.m. and 4 p.m. to 6 p.m. daily; closed Thursday.

You can hike, explore, spend days roaming the hills around here, but don't forget that other Metsovo specialty—cheese. Unfortunately, as charming as the side streets are, the main square, with its two cafés and several cheese shops, is the only turnaround for trucks and buses and gets fume-filled regularly. Zip downhill here to Platia Georgios Averoff to catch your bus, sit and watch the traditionally dressed locals stroll and shop for cheese. **Tiropoleio** is one of many such shops, and they give out samples! Smoked cheese is a regional specialty: try *metsovonay* (which can be stored a long time—good for travelers), *vlachoteri* (made from sheep's milk), or *metsovella* (another lighter, sheep's-milk cheese). In the **Grills Restaurant** (the town's one and only), try roast goat and *kokoretsi,* a Metsovo favorite. If you're here on July 26 for the local religious festival, you'll get treated to dancing in the square, as well as traditional costumes (a more elaborately embroidered version of the daily fare), and roasted lamb on publicly shared skewers.

Have we convinced you to spend the night in this magical village?

Accommodations

Hotels in Metsovo all try very hard to keep in the alpine, *Heidi* mood of the village. Therefore our favorite hotels were those which succeeded without getting too kitschy (and with an excellent view over the mist-shrouded mountains).

First prize goes to the **Hotel Victoria** (tel. 0656/41-771), on a plateau level with the highest roadway into the steeply banked village. The gray stone first story is topped with a typically whitewashed stucco-and-plaster second story, covered with a red tile roof. Inside, the gray slate-paved lobby has big picture windows showing off the exquisite views. Natural-wood beams, furniture, balconies, beds, tables, and chairs give a warm, homey feeling that's only enhanced in winter, when the tall stone fireplaces are ablaze. The dining room and bar are trimmed with locally produced weavings and rugs. Spacious, all-facility doubles are 4500 drs ($34.60) with breakfast, in the high season.

The 36-room **Egnatia Hotel** (tel. 0656/41-485) is on the main street. Carved-wood peacocks bear the number of every wood-paneled room, and the flower-trimmed balconies offer splendid views of the hills. The Egnatia has a snackbar, booze bar, and gift shop; doubles are 3125 drs ($24) in the high season, 375 drs ($2.90) per person for breakfast. The **Flokas** (tel. 0656/41-309) is a six-room pension off the main street whose rooms overlook some red tile rooftops and the valley below. Rooms with private bath, warm, natural-wood floors, and simple decor rent for 3125 drs ($24) double or 2500 drs ($19.20) a single.

The **Hotel Kassaros** (tel. 0656/41-662) is another lodging in the traditional style, on the uphill side of main street. Clean double rooms with TV and telephone are 3330 drs ($25.60) per night. The **Hotel Bitouni** (tel. 0656/41-217) has a marquee which claims to be "old style," but it's a little too new to work. Still, for 3390 drs ($26.10) for two, including breakfast, its rooms overlooking the spectacular view are worthwhile. The Bitouni offers free parking for its guests, a real plus in the summer high season.

Metsovo's only real budget choice is the quiet, clean **Hotel Athinae** (tel. 0656/41-332), eight rooms above a tavern. Bathless doubles are 1570 drs ($12), plus 100 drs (77¢) for the common shower.

Useful Information

The **police** (tel. 41-222) here are just the friendly regular town police. . . . The **post office** is on the main street above the square (open 7:30 a.m. to 2:30 p.m. weekdays). . . . There are two banks—open 8 a.m. to 2 p.m. only—on the square, but several shops accept travelers checks and credit cards. . . . The **area code** is 0656. . . . You can call 41-244 for **medical assistance**. . . . Contact the **Metsovo Alpine Club** for information on trails and the nearby ski center (tel. 41-249).

The Tirokomio is the local **cheese factory**, on the right as you enter

Metsovo from the west. Go visit it and sample away, but don't forget to search out a bottle of **Katogi**, the region's legendary, aged red wine that's only sold in single bottles by those few who collect them. . . . The nearby **Cathedral of Ag. Paraskevi** has a carved wood screen, silver chandeliers, and copies of the Ravenna mosaics that are worth a visit.

Two **buses** from Kalambaka, five buses from Ioannina, and three buses from Thessaloniki pull into Metsovo's tiny Platia Averoff daily, so you shouldn't find it hard getting here. The only problem is leaving.

Now that we've seen the Ionian Coast and Epirus, let's take a look at the Ionian Islands.

Chapter XIII

THE IONIAN ISLANDS

1. Corfu (Kerkyra)
2. Paxos and Antipaxos (Paxi and Antipaxi)
3. Lefkas
4. Ithaca
5. Kefalonia
6. Zakynthos

FOR THE MODERN TRAVELER, the Ionians are often the gateway to Greece. Trains, boats, and planes choose this most direct route to deposit visitors, fresh from Europe, into a new land. The cultural transition is least harsh in the Ionians, for if these islands are the most European part of the country, so in many ways are they the least Greek.

Of all the Greek islands, these are the most fortunate recipients of nature's bounty. All have plentiful rainfall, fertile land, temperate climate, and lush, semitropical scenery, attributes that have made them very desirable acquisitions. The Ionians' strategic position in a line paralleling Albania and the west coast of Greece placed them in the way of every conqueror set on annexing the wealthy mainland of Greece. Having withstood years of musical-chair administrations, the Ionian Islands reflect aspects of the many cultures that occupied them.

Corfu (Kerkyra), one of the great tourist meccas, has always been the belle of the Ionian, her culture and architecture reflecting the elegant styles of her French, Italian, and English conquerors. Tiny **Paxi** and **Antipaxi** are small verdant links in the Ionian chain, mini-retreats that offer a change of pace from the frenzy of the others. **Lefkas** is a large, disjointed island known for its Arts and Letters Festival and embroidery exports. **Ithaca** is the island immortalized by Homer, the birthplace of Odysseus, and the most longed-for home east of Dorothy's Kansas. **Kefalonia** is the largest and most self-sustaining of the Ionians; successful sea trade and agriculture have enabled residents to remain aloof to the recent influx of foreign tourists flocking to see her natural beauties and historic sights. **Zakynthos** is the southernmost island, the proximity to the Peloponnese, good beaches, and moderate climate have made it one of the most popular Greek resorts, the right place for those who want to have a good time, Greek style.

Our ideal version of an introduction to Greece for those coming from Italy: Disembark in Corfu and spend a few days; take the ferry to Igoumenitsa and then a public bus along the gorgeous coast of Epirus to Preveza; cross over to Lefkada; and join an excursion that cruises to the port of Nidri, to Ithaca, and to Fiskardo, on the north tip of Kefalonia. From here you can work your way

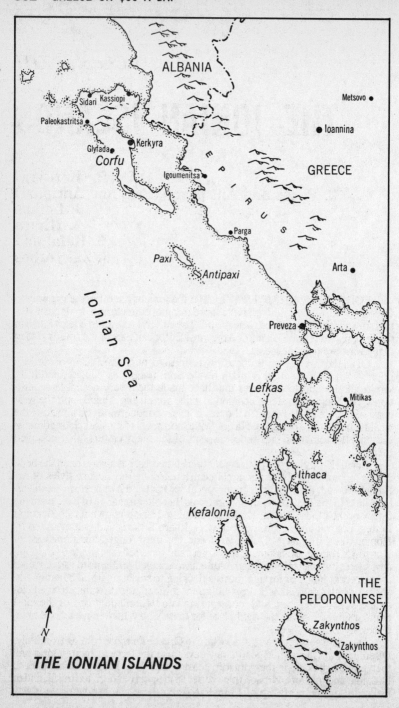

THE IONIAN ISLANDS

around the island to Argostoli or Sami. Then you can fly direct to Athens or take the ferry to Patras, after having experienced the best of the Ionians.

YACHT CRUISES: Viking Tours runs a seven-day Explorer Cruise through the Ionian Islands. What better way to sample these verdant isles? The *Blue Viking* sails from Piraeus through the Corinth Canal to Nafpaktos, then crisscrosses between the Ionians (from Kefalonia to Corfu) and the mainland ports. Viking Travel Bureau has planned cruises in July and August; twin-berth cabins with a half-board plan will cost $795 per person. Contact their U.S. agent, Do As You Like Tours, in Connecticut (tel. 203/259-6030) or their Athens office (tel. 32-29-383) for more information.

1. Corfu (Kerkyra)

It's ironic that Corfu should be the first glimpse of Greece for many travelers; as you'll soon discover, its beauty and culture are unlike anywhere else. Corfu (or Kerkyra as the Greeks call it, after its Dorian name) is a melting pot of its occupiers' cultures: part Italian, French, and British. The Italians have touched her cuisine, art, and language, the French her architecture and education, the British her laws and her lifestyle. Some Greeks say the Corfiots are too refined, too European, too cosmopolitan and artistic to be Greek, yet ever since Homer immortalized the island of the hospitable Phaeacians the Greek people have held Corfu in high regard.

The sumptuous beauty of the island, so unlike the stark-white aridness of the Aegean islands, has drawn visitors for centuries. Most European royalty summered there at one time or another, bringing their native artists and performers with them for entertainment. They left a great cultural legacy which survives in artists such as Dionysos Solomos, the author of the Greek National Anthem and a celebrated modern writer.

Homer tells us how Odysseus was washed ashore on the beautiful island of Scheria, and with Athena's help, came to meet the Princess Nausicaa. Athena urged Nausicaa in her sleep to launder her clothes in preparation for her wedding day. She went to the river (thought to be the stream at Paleokastritsa) with her handmaidens, and when they were done, they began a game of catch ball. Their laughter awoke the bedraggled Odysseus. Although the voyager's appearance frightened off her companions, Nausicaa stayed to hear him out. She encouraged Odysseus to plead with her mother, Queen Arete, for aid in reaching his homeland. Odysseus, still an anonymous traveler, was welcomed into their home and feasted. After supper, when talk turned to the Trojan War, Odysseus' sorrow caused him to reveal his identity. King Alcinoos and the queen were very moved, and listened to his tales all night. A royal ship was outfitted to transport him back to Ithaca the next day. After depositing him on the shore, the Phaeacians set sail for home. Poseidon was furious that they'd assisted Odysseus and turned their vessel into stone. Corfiots claim that the large, free-standing boulder in Paleokastritsa's harbor is the petrified Phaeacian ship, frozen within sight of the port of Alcinoos.

HISTORY: Corfu was first settled by Dorians from Corinth in the eighth century B.C. As Corinth's colony, "Corcyra," prospered, it established its own independent settlements on the mainland. Herodotus notes that: "ever since the original settlement of the island the two people have been on bad terms. . . ." This quarrel between Corcyra and Corinth was a critical factor in the commencement of the Peloponnesian Wars. Since antiquity, because of its strategic position at the head of the Corfu Straights (which separates the island from Albania by less than two kilometers), Corfu has been the center of countless hostilities. Always resilient after defeat, Corcyra remained the prize of the Ionians. Her name was changed to Corfu (Corfou) by European occupiers, who knew it as Koryphos (two summits) or Stous Korfous (breasts) because of the twin peaks its port was built between.

Of her European conquerors, the Venetians, who occupied the island between 1386 and 1797, were perhaps the most influential. They created a titled gentry of Greeks who, with their Venetian overseers, ruled the peasant "serfs" with a heavy hand. The Venetians fortified the entire island; their Old Fort (to the north, separated from the mainland by the celebrated "contra-fossa") and the New Fort (to the right of the domestic harbor) still greet visitors.

Venetian investments in olive cultivation and the extensive trade with Europe made Corfu even wealthier, attracting the attention of many pirates, and eventually the Turks. They attacked the island several times, most notably in 1537, when 30,000 Turkish soldiers under Barbarossa laid siege. The brave Corfiots fought side by side with their Venetian occupiers to defend the island (Corfu remains the only part of modern Greece that was never a Turkish colony). Although they held out, thousands were taken prisoner, brought to Constantinople, and sold into slavery. Such rapid depopulation was potentially disastrous for the Venetians, who recruited Greek settlers from their other possessions. When first Nafplion and then Morea fell to the Turks, the Venetians transported their citizens to Corfu. Soon thousands of Cretans joined them. These immigrants contributed a great deal in learning, customs, and artistic tradition to the already well-educated and cultured Corfiots.

By the 18th century the local islanders were ready for change. Intellectual Corfiots had been stirred by the ideals of the French Revolution, and when Napoleon sent his fleet to "liberate" the island from the Venetian oppressors, they were welcomed with open arms. Within two years the Corfiots were disenchanted by the looting of French soldiers and the rape of their natural resources. In 1799 the Russo-Turkish Alliance wrested Corfu away from the French after many months of siege. The 1800 Treaty of Constantinople declared the creation of the Septinsular Republic (Republic of the Seven Islands), with allegiance to the Ottoman Empire. Corfu sided with Russia in the Russo-Turkish War, and by treaty between Napoleon and Alexander I (the Peace of Tilsit, 1807) was returned to French rule. For the next six years the French behaved much better toward their colony. They contributed to agricultural development and a great deal to education with the founding of the Ionian Academy (the first modern university in Greece). Their most lasting contribution is the charming quarter just west of the Esplanade: on narrow "cantounia" (cobblestone lanes of the Venetian period) they built arcaded homes in imitation of the Rue de Rivoli.

When Napoleon fell from power both Austria and Great Britain wanted control over the Ionians. The 1815 Treaty of Paris created the Ionian Republic, a free and independent state under the protectorship of Great Britain. The United States of the Ionian Islands was to be governed by Lord High Commissioner Sir Thomas Maitland. Islanders thought that liberation might be at hand. Ioannis Kapodistrias (who'd made a name for himself during the Russo-Turkish occupation and was now a Russian delegate) protested Britain's harsh treatment of Corfu; after liberation this outspoken Corfiot became the first president of Greece. The British installed a legal and educational system (Italian was widely spoken on Corfu until 1851), and an infrastructure and network of roads that served the island well, but strictly quelled the local participation in the liberation movements springing up throughout the Greek mainland. On May 21,

1864, in exchange for endorsement of the British candidate Prince William George of Holstein-Glücksburg, Britain returned the island. The Ionians became part of the newly founded Kingdom of Greece, after the accession of the prince as King George I.

Corfu survived World War I as part of Greece, but was rudely awakened in 1923 when the Italians bombed and then briefly occupied the island in retaliation for a political assassination related to negotiations for the Greek-Albanian border. In 1940 full-scale war broke out between Italy and Greece; three years later the Germans reached Corfu, bombing most of the island and destroying much of the port by fire. Many of the elegant Italian and British colonial buildings were burned down. Only in the last half century has Corfu been able to catch her breath and make up her appealing face to welcome the wave of international tourists who flooded in after the war. To our minds, much of Corfu's lustrous beauty has been tarnished by overdevelopment. Whether she can cope with the deluge remains to be seen.

ORIENTATION: The sickle-shaped island of Corfu is approximately 600 square kilometers in area; within this are more than 300 large and small villages. Though it has undergone tremendous development in the recent past, the acknowledged beauty queen of the island is **Paleokastritsa**. Even Lawrence Durrell (blinded by his passion for the islands) wrote: "Paleokastritsa, now half ruined by the tourist-promoters is still a dream-place. . . . About 1930, it rejoined in an enviable solitude and unapproachability. . . . Even now much is left to admire, despite the crowding and the noise. . . ."

If you approach this community from the heavily wooded road running east to Corfu town around the sunset hour, its beauty is still breathtaking. The clear waters, the naked black rocks that break the still surface of the bay, the misty glow of the evergreens in the dying light are an unforgettable picture. We'd heard that only the rich and near-rich attempted to find lodgings in this magical spot; we headed straight there and found lovely bayside rooms in a spacious villa for less than $25 a night! Although tourist development may have lessened the appeal of Paleokastritsa, it's also become a much more democratic resort.

The other unique community on the island, and not a village at all, is the wonderfully picturesque European city of **Corfu**. We found no better place to stay if your interest is in things antique, historical, luxurious, romantic, Oriental, swinging, fashionable, or gastronomic. Ferries arrive at the new port (a five-minute walk from the best budget hotels), the airport is ten minutes away, and the best sightseeing is an arm's length from elegant boutiques, gourmet restaurants, excellent museums, and sophisticated nightlife. If you can afford it, try to rent a car to explore the rest of the island, which is justly famed for its scenic beauties. Otherwise the frequent public buses tour most points of interest at regular, convenient intervals.

The island's eastern coastline, facing Albania and the northern Greek mainland, has been grossly overdeveloped à la Miami Beach. Which isn't to say that Miami's not a lot of fun—it is. It's just that readers who are seeking a full-scale resort package should contact their hometown travel agent, then refer back to our book for sightseeing suggestions when the sun, golf, and tennis gets to be too much. Paleokastritsa and several other known resorts are on the island's west and north coasts, and we'll review many of those in the "Around the Island" section. Enough of our opinions. Now on to Corfu town . . .

LAYOUT OF CORFU TOWN: Try to pick up an E.O.T. brochure about Corfu before your arrival; its map will prove invaluable in guiding you to the local Tourist Office. The most picturesque part of the city is the vicinity behind the **Paleo Frourio** (the Old Fort, on a peninsula just east of the north tip of the island) and the **Spianada** (or **Esplanade**), which lines the coastal route. Ferryboats from Italy dock at the western tip of the breakwater on the town's north coast. From here, at **Stratigou Street**, you have an unhindered view of the dramatically high-walled sanitarium, and to its left, the **New Fort.**

A 15-minute walk east will bring you to the older part of town. On the way you'll pass the harbor for the ferryboats from Igoumenitsa; they moor opposite an attractive park in front of Zavitsianou Street. On the left you'll see the roadway rise up and curl around to meet the Esplanade, built up along the height of one of Corfu's two "breasts." Crossing the park from the Igoumenitsa ferry pier will bring you to the older budget hotels in this quarter; if your luggage isn't too heavy, bear left through the gnarled *cantouni* (cobblestone lanes of the Venetian quarter) and you'll eventually emerge at the Old Fort. The locally organized **Tourist Police** office is located at 35 Arseniou St. (the street rising up to meet the Esplanade); they may help you to find accommodations in the vicinity. If they're busy, they may refer you to the E.O.T. office (which is slated to move next door by 1988). Many tourist services, including ferryboat tickets, travel agencies, and car-rental companies, are in this area of the port.

Buses to several points on the island leave from the terminal at **New Fort Square**, the intersection of Zavitsianou and Solomou Streets by the fortress walls. The other bus station is at **San Rocco Square**, near to the commercial zone in the center of town.

Taxis usually meet all the ferries; you can catch one after you've cleared Customs if you're an international traveler or by the park if you're exiting the mainland ferry.

Tip: Travelers arriving at Corfu from Igoumenitsa should be able to hitch a ride from a tourist who's transporting his/her car on this car-ferry.

GETTING AROUND: Corfu town and most of the island's major resorts are small enough to walk around in, once you're there. The island itself is too large and too heavily trafficked to be fun to walk around; public buses are cheap, fairly efficient, and safer than mopeds.

Around-the-island **buses** leave from two terminals. Buses to Paleokastritsa, Ag. Gordis, Glyfada, Kassiopi, Kavos, and other resorts leave from the New Fort Station, most several times daily. Buses to the major sights such as Achilleion, Ag. Ioannis, and the resorts of Benitses, Kontokali, and Dassia, leave from the San Rocco Square station, also called Theotoki Square, at Avramiou and Theotoki Streets. The no. 2 bus to the well-situated suburb of Kanoni (where the ritzy Hilton and some good C-class hotels are located) leaves from the Esplanade every half hour. Be sure to ask when the last bus returns or you may get stranded.

Taxis are easy to find throughout Corfu town, and if you're having difficulty directing your driver, ask for help from any of the ubiquitous hotel doormen. Expensive, metered taxis should be saved for dining out or discoing at one of the seaside resorts. Taxis are a problem on Corfu. Though the situation is also true of Athens and other highly touristed destinations in Greece, the problem is particularly acute on this island. Nearly every taxi has a meter, though finding a driver willing to use one (and on a legal basis) is as tough as finding inexpensive fresh fish. Below are the legal rates posted for 1987 (expect a 20% increase in 1988–1989):

Minimum	130 drs ($1)
Port, airport, and luggage supplement	30 drs (20¢)
Single tariff	26 drs/kilometer
Out of town, one way, or after 2 a.m.	Double tariff
If taxi waits	240 drs ($1.85)/hour

Although this table is a good guideline, rates can vary by as much as a factor of 10! Of those drivers who use the meter, many actually doctor it to charge a double tariff for a legitimately single-tariff ride. The best advice is to ask a friendly local non-taxi driver for the approximate price of the ride. Armed with that, and insisting that the driver use the meter, you might get there for close to the official rate.

If you think you've been overcharged, such as paying 2500 drs ($19.20) from the airport to the town instead of the more legitimate 375 drs ($2.90), get the driver's identification number and report it immediately to the Tourist Police. It's small consolation, but they are reasonably diligent about prosecuting the reckless. Good luck!

There are several **rental-car companies** around the island: to be exact, 36 in Corfu town and another 17 around the island, according to the printed list the E.O.T. will gladly hand you when you ask for advice. High-season travelers should definitely pay the extra drachmas for a **Hertz** (38 X. Stratigou St.; tel. 38-388), **Avis** (31 Alexandras Ave.; tel. 38-820), **Budget** (82 Stratigou St.; tel. 22-062), or **Hellascar** (2 Dousmani St.; tel. 32-048); their nationwide offices make it easy to reserve one in advance of your arrival. There are several companies on Stratigou Street and along Theotoki Street if you want to shop around; expect to pay from $40 to $50 per day. *Tip:* Check your hotel reception desk first. Every Greek seems to have a cousin or an uncle who can get you a good rate on a rental car!

Mopeds are a fun way to get around if you're just exploring the town (many parts of the old town are pedestrian malls though) or nearby parts of the island. We find them too small to be comfortable for a two- or three-hour ride each way, which is the time it would take you to explore the north or south coasts from Corfu town. But for quick jaunts, try **Corfu Sun Motors**, at 47 Arseniou St. (tel. 36-539). Rates vary from 1000 drs ($7.70) for a one-seater Vespa to 1625 drs ($12.50) for a two-seater mini-motorcycle.

Corfu is so plagued with group tourists that your only problem in finding the right **bus tour** will be sifting through all the catalogues. The helpful E.O.T. will provide their list of the 78 registered travel agencies in town; this doesn't include the 8 domestic agencies selling ferry tickets or the 37 agencies operating throughout the island. **Charitos Travel**, at 35 Arseniou St. (tel. 0661/36-825), has long been helpful to Frommer readers, both for booking tours and arranging hotel rooms, often at a discount. Mr. Charitos and his staff certainly know the island well and provide several bus and boat excursions, for example a Sidari and Paleokastritsa full-day beach tour at 3500 drs ($26.90).

USEFUL INFORMATION: The **National Tourist Office of Greece (E.O.T.)** is located on Arseniou Street (as of 1988), at the port end of the Esplanade. They're open Monday through Friday, from 7 a.m. to 3 p.m. and 6 p.m. to 8 p.m., on Saturday from 9 a.m. to noon (tel. 30-520, 39-730, or 30-360). . . . The **Tourist Police**, at 35 Arseniou St. (tel. 30-265), are open 7 a.m. to 10 p.m. every day. The Tourist Police for the "country" (rest of Corfu island) are at San Rocco Square (tel. 30-669). . . . The telephone **area code** for Corfu town is 0661.

Ferry tickets to the Greek mainland or to Europe can be purchased from travel agents at the respective ports of departure. . . . **Olympic Airways** is at 20 Kapodistrias St. (tel. 38-694). Buses to the airport leave their office 55 minutes prior to departure at a fare of 75 drs (60¢). . . . Several banks have extended hours in Corfu town. The **National Bank** branch at the Customs House is open 7 a.m. to 10 p.m. to meet ferryboats; the **Ionian Bank** and **Commercial Bank** on San Rocco Square have evening hours (6 to 7:30 p.m. Monday through Friday).

Corfu's **American Express** agent (for lost or stolen credit cards, check refunds, and mail) is the **Corfu Tourist Center,** 42 Kapodistrias St. (tel. 31-480). . . . The *Mythos Guide,* an advertiser-supported yet discriminating judge of Corfu, is free and available in most hotels. These are excellent guidebooks. . . . The central **post office** and **O.T.E.** are around the corner from E.O.T. . . . For medical emergencies, contact **St. Irene's Hospital** (tel. 30-033). . . . There's a **luggage storage** opposite the New Port, next door to the Commercial Bank, at 130 Avrami St. (tel. 37-673). There is an excellent book outlet, the **English Bookshop,** at 40 Guildford St., that sells new and used volumes including an excellent assortment of Penguin paperbacks with Greek content. . . . **Pronto Print,** opposite the Credit Bank near San Rocco Square, develops film in one hour; they also sell film.

ACCOMMODATIONS IN CORFU TOWN:

As on Rhodes and Mykonos, hotels tend to be much more expensive on Corfu than on other, less touristed islands. Happily, some of the older lodgings have been maintained and provide clean, if spartan, living for moderate prices. As groups have put pressure on seaside hotels, many C-class inns throughout the older part of town have kept rates at a reasonable level and can often turn up a vacant room at the last minute. Nevertheless, most hoteliers we talked to urged that reservations be made one to two months in advance (particularly at the budget hotels). *Note:* Most hotels operate from April 1st to October 31st unless noted.

One of the better C-class values along the Esplanade is the 55-room **Hotel Arcadion** (tel. 0661/37-671), at 44 Kapodistriou. It offers the virtues of a central location and balcony views over the ancient citadel and Mandraki Harbor without the vices of a noisy, overtrafficked area. Pleasant double rooms are 4960 drs ($38.10) in the summer, with breakfast for two. For those who can't walk very far with their luggage, the **Hotel Ionion** (tel. 0661/30-628), at 46 Stratigou St., opposite the new port (Italy ferry), is very handy. Don't let the faded exterior and worn hallways fool you—the Ionion is friendly, has an elevator and phones, and many of its 89 rooms with bath have balconies overlooking the Ionian Sea. Doubles are 2770 drs ($21.30) in the low season, 4275 drs ($32.90) in the high, including breakfast. If it's full, try the **Hotel Atlantis** (tel. 0661/35-560) next door, where 61 C-class rooms are just a bit higher. Both hotels are open year round.

If the New Port waterside lodgings are too noisy or impersonal for your tastes, the cute, homey **Hotel Europa** (tel. 0661/39-304) may be more to your liking. Though a bit difficult to find, the Europa's isolation from traffic is well worth the minor inconvenience. Rooms run 2500 drs ($19.20) for a double, 1250 drs ($9.60) for a single. There are many signs that will direct you to the Europa, but if you head for the rear of the Argo Restaurant (150 meters beyond the Hotel Atlantis) you're bound to find it.

Our favorite in-town lodging and one of the more original hotels in the C-class price range is the **Hotel Calypso** (tel. 0661/30-723), at 4 Vraila St. The Calypso is off the shore road below the Old Fort, opposite the archeological museum and next door to the town tennis courts. Its 25 rooms have been created from an older, traditional Corfiot home, each spacious, most with private shower or bath. Doubles are 4155 drs ($32) to 5200 drs ($40) with bath, but sign up for their 300-dr ($2.30) breakfast, served in their private back garden. Because the calypso is so small and attractive, it's a very good idea to make reservations well in advance of your stay.

The **Archontico Aparthotel** (tel. 0661/37-222), located in Garitsa along the southern seafront road (farther on than the Calypso), is a retrofitted mansion built in 1903 that still retains some of its original grandeur. Although the floors have been cut up to accommodate a larger number of rooms (20 in all), many of the guest quarters are still large enough to qualify as suites. The first two floors feature cathedral ceilings, some with pastel-colored floral borders. These rooms, like those on the higher floors with lower ceilings, are equipped with telephones, mini bars, radio, and spotlessly clean modern bathrooms. The common spaces are nicely decorated and accented with flowers and ancient urns. Breakfast and snacks are served outside under a vine-covered arbor. Prices are quite reasonable: doubles run 5000 drs ($38.50), singles are 2500 drs ($19.20), including breakfast. What's the catch, you ask? The Archontico is about a 20-minute walk or a short no. 2 bus (from Kanoni) away from the center of Corfu town. That's it. Even the waterside walk is pleasant. Reservations are encouraged.

Budget Bets

The **Hotel Constantinopolis** (tel. 0661/39-826), at 11 Zavitsianou (opposite the mainland Igoumenitsa ferry pier), is an excellently maintained building that's been greeting Corfu visitors for nearly 100 years. The 44 freshly painted, spotless rooms are 1565 drs ($12) single, 2500 drs ($19.20) double and 3125 drs ($24) triple, including showers. The bathrooms are behind the tall ornate wooden doors just down the high-ceilinged hallways. In July and August you'd do well to plan your stay at the Constantinoupolis ahead of time. Go next door, one floor above the traditional kafeneion, and knock on Door 21 to see the old **Hotel Acropole** (tel. 0661/39-569) where well-kept, bathless rooms are the same price.

The High and the Low Ends

At the high end we discovered a special hotel, one that was a favorite of the late William Holden. The **Cavalieri Hotel** (tel. 0661/39-041), at 4 Kapodistriou St. (at the top of the Esplanade), overlooks Corfu town and the water. Originally a 17th-century nobleman's mansion belonging to the family of Count Flamburiari, the building was partly bombed during the Second World War and, by keeping the façade, the Cavalieri Hotel was created. This Venetian-style hotel is decorated with antiques and marble, wallpaper and polish. Though the rooms are fairly standard the common spaces are quite attractive in an Old-European kind of way. The sitting room off the lobby will be your first indication of the glories yet to come, from the back garden where you'll "take" breakfast to the balconies overlooking the water to the elegant fixtures and features that abound. The Cavalieri is almost always booked by European tour groups, so that it's hard to secure a single room without reservations in advance. But don't let that stop you from checking in and checking out the single rooms at 6905 drs ($53.10) or doubles at 9520 drs ($73.20), including breakfast.

Corfu's only youth hostel is the **Kontokali Hostel** (tel. 0661/91-202 or 91-207) in Kontokali village, about eight kilometers northeast of town. Beds here cost 490 drs ($3.80) per night; there are 100 beds available and a small kitchen area. Many low-budget travelers prefer camping to the hostel; the nearest campsite to town is near the hostel, opposite an unfortunately shallow, dirty-water bathing area. To get to Kontokali, take the no. 7 bus from San Rocco Square and ask the driver to let you off at the village.

In Kanoni (Canoni)

Narrow winding roads veer in and out of overhanging plane trees, old oaks, and olive groves, while pungent orange trees scent the air in the lushly over-grown suburb of Kanoni. Years ago Kanoni may have been the idyllic refuge referred to in older guides; now it's a fully developed residential area whose scenic beauty still shines through. There are many luxury and A-class hotels built in the wake of the splashy Corfu Hilton, but there are also two C-class places that warrant a mention. One deserves a rave!

The **Hotel Royal** (tel. 0661/35-343), called the Vassilikon in Greek, is just not to be believed for a C-class hotel. Its 121 rooms tower over three swimming pools, terraced so that each one spills into the one below. The Royal's hydraulic system would make the ancient Romans green with envy. The decor might be described as wildly ornate or simply modern rococo. Bed-and-breakfast doubles are 6200 drs ($47.70) in the summertime. Don't forget to ask for their rate card; its pen-and-ink rendition of the hotel and its pools will provide sure proof to disbelievers back home. Now, what's the catch? Well, the Royal is built on a hillside overlooking the international airport. Was this such a drawback that we couldn't recommend it to you? Luckily, Betty Kaladi wrote us a rave review of her honeymoon stay at the Royal: "It's next to the Olympic runways, but flights stopped in the evening and during the day we were touring the island, so the noise didn't bother us. When we were at the hotel, it was actually interesting to watch the planes take off."

The **Hotel Salvo** (tel. 0661/30-429), at 108 Figareto, Kanoni, is another plush C-class option. Azaleas and wild roses line the Salvo's swimming pool and spacious sundeck, and their rooftop bar and restaurant are very pleasant at sun-set. In the high season the Salvo's 92 doubles run 6200 drs ($47.70), including breakfast. Greek dancing is featured many evenings in their after-supper lounge.

Splurge Accommodations: The **Corfu Hilton** (tel. 0661/36-540), located in Kanoni, is one of the splashiest resorts in all Greece, making it a first-class splurge. This acred 256-room complex includes extremely attractive grounds, with a large outdoor pool (there is an indoor one as well) and a gorgeous garden set above a tranquil, pebbly beach. Guest quarters are spacious and well ap-pointed with balconies, air conditioning, and mini bars. Tennis courts, bowling alleys, and a health club complete the resort facilities, making this an ideal spot for those wanting to relax in active surroundings. The staff, consistent with our experience with Hilton hotels around the world, is extremely well informed and helpful. Our only warning about this comfortable resort is that it is situated atop the hills of Kanoni above the airport. We strongly suggest that you insist on a room overlooking the sea (not the airport side); you'll be rewarded with a better view and a quiet night's sleep. Bed and breakfast for two runs $161 per night, however check for special rates. Currently there is a seven-day price for two at $100 per night (for other promotional rates, contact Charitos Travel at 0661/36-825).

Rooms-to-Rent

The E.O.T. publishes a five-page listing of rooms-to-rent that are govern-ment licensed. This list covers every part of the island and includes rooms in each category (rated according to toilet/shower facilities, privacy, kitchen ac-cess, size, furnishings, etc.). Although you can easily inquire, notice posted signs or follow other clues to available rooms in the smaller villages; in Corfu town we recommend contacting the local police or a local travel agent and letting them make the phone calls. **Charito Travel** (0661/36-825) and **Corfu Sun Club** (tel. 0661/36-539), for example, rent rooms and villas by the week, starting at 1300 drs ($10) per person per day.

RESTAURANTS: Corfu, perhaps because of its Italian heritage, has some excellent restaurants serving Greek and Italian cuisine. Many touristy cafés are under the arcaded portico across from the Esplanade, an area busy all day with people watching cricket matches on the grass, siesta-ing over afternoon ouzo, scribbling away at piles of postcards, or just passing the still of the night. The **Restaurant Aegli** (tel. 31-949), our favorite, is at 23 Kapodistriou, about centerfield from the cricket ground. It's very pleasant to sit on their comfy, leather-cushioned chairs and watch life on the Esplanade drift by, especially if you're waiting for one of the Aegli's Corfiot specialties. They feature *sofrito* (a veal in garlic sauce), *barbounia* (red mullet), a delicious lamb entrée with white beans, spicy salami, and *pastitsada* (a baked veal in tomato and cheese sauce). Dinner for two should cost about 2300 drs ($17.70). The Aegli operates between April 1 and the end of October. The **Rex** (tel. 39-649) is just down the arcade from the Aegli and features many of the same Corfiot specialties, at similar prices.

Two totally casual cafés line the waterside across from the Esplanade. The first, down about 100 meters from the gate to the fort, is **Acteon** (tel. 37-894). Here pizzas, drinks, and a simple menu are outclassed by a first-rate view over Corfu's serene waterway. The best time to visit this inexpensive café is sunset, when the vista is unbeatable. If you continue along the flower-lined walk and take the set of stairs down to the concrete-and-pebble town beach, you'll arrive at the second recommended eatery, **N.A.O.K.** The initials refer to the Nautical Association, presumably connected to the administration of the small marina below. Like the Acteon, the menu is limited and inexpensive, but the panorama is wonderful.

As one can imagine, it's becoming increasingly difficult to find a genuine taverna in Corfu town. One such establishment, on a humble scale, is **Giogias Taverna,** at 16 Guildford St. (a long block behind the Esplanade, near the Calvieri Hotel). Here one can sample such local favorites as *sofrito, kokoretsi,* and numerous other meat specialties for a relative pittance. A filling meal for two should run 1300 drs ($10). Giogias is open daily for lunch and dinner.

We found a great breakfast place, **The Black Cat**, next to the Hotel Constantinople. Bacon and eggs, fresh toast, and more awaits you for about 410 drs ($3.10).

Taverna Ellas (tel. 39-810) is just behind the small park in front of the new port and has pleasant indoor dining as well as shaded outdoor tables. From their varied, well-displayed Greek menu we'd recommend any of the Ellas's veal or lamb specialties. A full dinner for two will run anywhere from 1500 drs ($11.50) to 2100 drs ($16.10) because of the wide range of choices. Another popular taverna, located on a narrow, quiet lane behind the Ellas, is the **Averof**. Many tables are tucked under a flowered canopy outside, and a sampling of the day's dishes is exhibited in their side window. Prices and menu selections are comparable to the Ellas Taverna.

There are a series of lower-priced grills in Mantouki, about 200 meters beyond the Argo Restaurant in the New Port. Among them we prefer **Orestes** (tel. 35-664) and the **Bekios Grill.** A full-course meal with grilled meat and a bottle of wine should run no more than 2000 drs ($15.40).

All the locals agree that the best Italian fare is served up at **Bella Napoli** (tel.

24-958 or 33-338). It's open daily from 6 p.m. to midnight, but many of Corfu's casual restaurants are also open for lunch. Reservations are recommended in summer. Their meat specialty is coeur de filet Provençal at 2000 drs ($15.40) for two, but the Bella Napoli features fresh lasagne, tortellini, and tagliatelle at 625 drs ($4.80) per portion. Try one of their made-to-order pizzas—for about 1000 drs ($7.70) with the tasty house salad for a lighter, weight-watcher's meal. This attractive pizzeria/ristorante is on Skaramanga Square, at 11-13 Voulgareos St., behind the Commercial Bank in town.

For much more casual Italian fare in a scenic, waterside setting, try **Pizza Pete** at 19 Arseniou. Pizza Pete has an outdoor café on the old town promenade, overlooking coveted Vidos Island. It's really one of Corfu's prettiest places and owners Pete and Susie serve some of the freshest food on the island. Pizza Pete opens at 9 a.m., when you can enjoy a full English breakfast for 415 drs ($3.20). Readers from Chicago will be warmed to know that the Pizza Pete in the Windy City is owned and run by the same family! Get there early and watch the sunrise, or come later for the sunset over drinks, pizza, or a late-night café. (We grabbed a take-out pizza for the Corfu-to-Igoumenitsa ride, and boy, did that make the time speed by! We particularly enjoyed their vegetarian pizza, topped with fresh peppers, tomatoes, onions, olives, and mushrooms, for 875 drs ($6.70).

Out-of-Town Dining

The first tip-off that **Iannis Taverna** is a gem of a place is that they have no menu, forcing you to enter that most public of Greek enclaves, the kitchen. Here the amiable staff will take you on a tour of about 20 entrées simmering in sauté pans. The variety, especially in the early evening, is impressive. Even more outstanding is their preparation. At Iannis, if a dish is supposed to be spicy, they'll make it accordingly; there's no holding back. It's difficult to recommend any dish in particular, given that the menu changes frequently; however, we sampled a flavorful stefado with sweet pearl onions, a picante potato *kukya* (a variety of bean), and an octopus stew. All were delicious. Unlike most of the tourist-oriented places, Iannis is open all year and is often frequented by Corfiots. To get to Iannis, either take the no. 2 bus from town and get out in Garitsa (be sure to ask when the last bus runs), walk along the water for about 20 minutes, or take a short cab ride.

Near Iannis Taverna is **Spiros,** a simple pizza restaurant that is about a 15-minute walk from the Archeological Museum. Prices are low, making it an ideal snack stop.

A favorite proverb states that if you have a weakness, make a prop of it. Certainly the noise-weary residents of Kanoni have paid heed by opening a row of pubs, bars, and outdoor cafés, miraculously overlooking the airport at the Kanoni bus cul-de-sac. It was so astonishing to us to see so many people at these popular spots that we joined in one afternoon and discovered that it really is kind of fun to down a frosty beer while jets land and take off. If this gets boring, you can always take the stairs on the other side of the bus stop and plunge into the refreshing water.

A Reader's Selection led us to one of our favorite tavernas in *all Greece:* that's right, *all Greece.* The **Taverna Tripa** (tel. 56-333) in Kinopiastes (a small town 17 kilometers from Corfu town) is quite simply one of the finest meals you will have your entire trip. We'll let Ruth Manton of New York City sell you like she sold us: "It's set in the center of a tiny medieval village south of Corfu. Smoked meats hang from the wooden rafters, wine bottles blurred by cobwebs line every inch of the wall (some of them gifts from Aristotle Onassis), just outside lambs are roasting on a rotating spit. Waiters bring platter upon platter of hors d'oeuvres, salads, cheeses, meatballs, fried vegetables. By the time you feel full plates of succulent lamb and bowls of fresh vegetables come steaming in from the kitchen . . ." What can we possibly add to that? Only that when we went we ate her words, and had a great meal that cost us about $20 each (you can eat for less by ordering from the menu; ask your waiter before the food platters begin). Tripa started as a market with a kitchen in the back and gradually grew into a taverna. Iannis and Spiros Anifadis are the father-son combo that keep the spit spinning, the music playing, and the diners dancing. You'll have to take a taxi to Tripa. Expect to pay 625 drs ($4.80) each way from Corfu town.

Paleokastritsa

Just 26 kilometers due west of Corfu town is the small community of Paleokastritsa, set high on the rocks above a lovely bay. Several rounded coves line the edges, forming rock-and-pebble beaches. The lure of Paleokastritsa is its pure transparent water which have drawn fishermen and divers for years. Bathers seeking less crowded areas should walk down to Ag. Triadha beach (a path descends from the clifftop roadway just past Paleokastritsa Rent a Car) or try some of the less visible pebbley coves around the marina.

What to See: Since the area's renowned for its scenic beauty, leisurely walks are the best way to take in the sights. About an hour's walk uphill behind the Hotel Odysseus (on a beaten donkey path) is the small village where the Corfiot residents of Paleokastritsa live. This harbor and its hilltop acropolis, **Angelokastro**, have long been associated with the Phaeacian kingdom of Alcinoos and Arete immortalized by Homer in *The Odyssey*. A spectacular walk can be made to the monastery above Paleokastritsa. It looks steep, but don't let the path scare you—in actuality it only takes about 15 minutes to the top. This is best done at sunset when the view (and the light) is constantly changing. Beautiful little bays and inlets interrupted by lush greenery endow one with a sense of the vitality of Greek monastic life. The monastery itself is still in use and a walk around the top provides the visitor with peaceful gardens and lots of grape arbors to rest under. Women are reminded that they must wear a skirt, although it's possible you will be given one at the door.

Accommodations: Other than the few super-plush hotels on the cliffs, most housing is in group-booked villas or in rooms to rent. Unfortunately, the recent proliferation of groups has made it extremely difficult to find high-season rooms. The huge, B-class **Oceanis Hotel** (tel. 0663/41-229) is one of the larger resort hotels. Its 71 modern rooms offer spectacular views throughout the region; many overlook the Oceanis's swimming pool and sundeck. Doubles with a compulsory half-board plan (two meals per day) run 9212 drs ($70.90) year round.

At the foot of the road that winds into the village are two other small hotels, both owned by the Ionion Yacht Club. The C-class **Hotel Apollon—Ermis** (tel. 0663/41-211) has 23 double rooms right opposite the town beach for 3750 drs ($28.90). The dark-pink **Zefiros** (tel. 0663/41-244), next door above an ice-cream parlor, offers 16 spotless rooms with showers, but with shared toilets outside. Doubles rent for 4810 drs ($37) with breakfast.

The old waterside **Xenia Café** (tel. 0663/41-208) has eight large, freshly painted, well-maintained rooms upstairs. They're simple enough for sailors, but very charming; bathless doubles run 6240 drs ($48) with bath, 5662 drs ($43.50) including half-board at their café. Write to P.O. Box 81, Corfu, for reservations.

We rented a wonderful room from **George Bakiras** and his wife, who can be written to at: Michalas, Bakiras, Lakones, Corfu. Their "Rooms to Let/Green House/30 m. from Beach/G. Bakiras'" sign on the left of the road past the Odyssey Hotel says "Domatia" (the Greek) also. The Michalas Bakiras family have eight large doubles with private facilities. This apartment complex is a modest bungalow in a comfortable wooded setting; a porch overlooks the marina. Two of the rooms, down toward the beach, have kitchenettes. Rooms are 1920 drs ($14.80) per night, and their hospitality can't be beat.

AROUND THE ISLAND:
Resorts that we'll cover in detail include Paleokastritsa, Ag. Georgious, Sidari, Glyfada, and Kassiopi. All have ample accommodations for a comfortable stay.

There are several rooms-to-let over commercial establishments that line the roadway leading into Paleokastritsa. The clean-kept rooms above the **Belvedere Pizza Parlor** cost 3300 drs ($25.40) for two, with private bath; see the manager for more information. The **Villa Raponas**, tucked up on a wooded hillside beside a roadside souvenir stand, rents ten rooms for the same rate; Vassilias in the souvenir stand can show you what's available. The **supermarket** next door to it has built 16 double rooms with private facilities in a mini-apartment behind the market. Some of the rooms have a balcony and good view.

Camping Paleokastritsa is set in a densely wooded area about a ten-minute walk east of Ag. Triadha Beach. (By the way, some readers may prefer a room farther away from the bay in the height of mosquito season—August.)

Nightlife: For the boogie crowd, there's the **Paleo Disco Club,** at the turnoff for Lakeones, just before the peninsula.

Aghios Georgious

To explore the coastline north of Paleokastritsa you'll have to double back to pick up one of the few through roads. Drivers can take the turnoff for Doukades, a tiny, unspoiled mountain village whose square is still filled with goatherds, women in traditional clothes, and aging farmers playing cards. The **Elisabeth Taverna**, the only one in town, is the place to stop and refuel.

Bear left at Skripero and head straight for **Pagi**, the even more petite village which is the "end of the road" bus stop for those taking the public bus from Corfu town. An hour spent twisting in and out of the shaded, wooded, cool forests and valleys will remind you what all the hoopla was about this island. You must then walk or risk your axle for three kilometers due west, and downhill to **Ormos Ag. Georgious** (not to be confused with the St. George's Beach resort area on the southwest coast). This spectacular two-kilometer stretch of pale gold sand curves gently around a broad bay of the same name. It's an idyllic haven from the white concrete hotel strip lining Corfu's better-known beaches. Ag. Georgious is still so beautiful because it's only accessible by car or by foot from Pagi.

Most of the few accommodations available are thanks to **Sun Med**, that enterprising English budget travel company that stakes out new resort turf with their modest "villas." Comfortable, simple bungalows with private bath are 2200 drs ($17.10) for a double room (rooms can be had if they are not fully booked by charter-flight clients). The friendly **Panorama Taverna**, run by Spyros, has nine rooms which go for 2960 drs ($22.80) or less, when available. There are a few other bungalows and another taverna, the **Nafsika**, which has Greek dancing on Friday nights (we suppose when there are enough people gathered in this tiny outpost to dance). **San George Camping** is a little farther down the beach.

After hiking back up the cliffside to explore the rest of the north country, follow the enchanted fern-filled stretch of road that crosses a stone bridge to the traditional hill village of **Vatonies**. Old women with white cloths shading their heads from the sun and black dresses with colorful aprons carry twigs, herbs, and hay for chickens. The dappled light filtering through the overhead branches makes the lacy black olive nets glow.

The larger road from Kastellani Gyrou leads 12 kilometers north to Sidari. Along its borders are drab, gray-green, ancient gnarled olive trees that convinced us they were of Venetian parentage. In all the crannies and valleys are chartreuse ferns and furry moss patches.

Sidari
Sidari was described to us as "paradise," one of the oldest, best-known beauty spots on the island. Some Scandinavians we met said they heard it was the best beach on Corfu. Folks, it just ain't so. The waters off its fine-sand (but not overly clean) beach are shallow and calm, and better swimming can be had just around the rocky point to the west. This "rocky point" is known to locals as "Canal d'Amour," for it's said that all who sail through the eroded half-cave at the point will be able to marry whoever is on their minds at the time. The Canal d'Amour is ever more picturesque than the bustling, commercialized village.

Accommodations: The best-priced rooms and pensions are monopolized by the travel agencies in the village: walk through the town and you're sure to find an agency that will find you lodgings.

The **Hotel Akti Aphroditi** (tel. 0663/95-247) is centrally located in the village and has 18 doubles—8910 drs ($68.60), including breakfast and dinner—that are usually booked through Manos Holidays in London. If they have vacancies, the Aphroditi's management may rent you one; it depends on the season. The **Three Brothers Hotel** (tel. 0663/95-375) charges 4420 drs ($34) for two, bed and breakfast. They have 52 well-appointed rooms that are nicely decorated and clean. The **Hotel Mimosa** (tel. 0663/95-363) is the most attractive one on the beach; bed-and-breakfast doubles are 4600 drs ($35.40) year round.

Most of these hotels have their own restaurants, and there are several fast-food parlors on the main street of the village. However, **Sophocles Taverna,** on the road out of town toward the Canal d'Amour, is reputed to have the best authentic Greek cuisine on the north coast. The **Lethari Taverna,** in the area, and the **Oasis Taverna,** on the road leading east from Sidari, are both very popular.

Buses run from Corfu town to Sidari four times daily between 7 a.m. and 5 p.m.

The North Coast
From the village of Sidari, the north coast roadway disintegrates into a picturesque, backwoods country lane. If you detour to **Kanalouri** you'll be treated to a lovely little village, where inhabitants wear traditional home spun cotton clothes. Drivers must watch out for the donkeys who like to swing their bottoms out into the road when they hear a car approach! At **Acharavi,** on the coast, there's a good, sandy beach, but from 11 a.m. on it becomes crowded with day trippers from Sidari who are out to find an isolated beach.

The beach at Ag. Ekaterini, known as **Kalamaki Beach,** is just a gray sand-and-pebble stretch by another small village. Just around the bend is **Ag. Spiridon,** named after Corfu's patron saint, where you can rent rooms or lunch in one of the few tavernas. Not until you get to the once totally unspoiled harbor of Kassiopi do you find lots of hotels, restaurants, moped dealers, and pizza parlors.

Kassiopi

In years past travelers have sung the praises of the charming, sleepy fishing village of Kassiopi. Alas, no more—it's now one long, ugly strip of billboards, pizza parlors, souvenir stands, and rooms-to-let, leading to a relatively peaceful, attractive port lined with several tavernas. All the nearby watering holes have narrow rocky banks to sit on, though while bathing you get a distant view of Albania.

If a mediocre summer resort appeals to you, Kassiopi is serviced five times daily by bus from Corfu town. If the charter business from England and Holland is off, there may be rooms available at the ubiquitous "villas" in town. Doubles with bath run 3750 ($28.90) a night. The unfriendly **Kassiopi Tourist Bureau** (tel. 0663/81-388), off Iroon Polytechniou, the main square, will help you find a room as there are no official hotels in the village. For about 4500 drs ($34.60) you can take a day cruise, including lunch, to the sandy beach at Ag. Spyridon, or you can rent a moped (like everyone else zooming through town) for 1200 drs ($9.20) and cruise there yourself. Overnighters may want to sample the **disco** above Jackson's Taverna on Polytechniou Square.

The East Coast

Between Kassiopi and Corfu town is 36 kilometers of cove and beach-lined coastline. Kouloura, Kalami, and Kentroma are small boating ports with pebbly bathing areas. All are densely packed with tourists who've descended from the brush-covered slopes of villa land to partake of the water. Many of these communities have been written of in Lawrence Durrell's *Prospero's Cell*.

The pretty beach community of **Nissaki** has one huge A-class resort, several tavernas, and a hillside coated with newly built whitewashed villas. From Glyfa to Pirgi is the long white sand stretch of **Barbati**, where many water sports are offered. **Ipsos** is a pleasant resort area that reminded us of a New England lake community. Across the roadway from the housing is a narrow pebble shore and very placid water. The town float is packed with kids and sunbathers, and the views of evergreens growing along the waterfront reminded us of New Hampshire.

There are several campsites in this vicinity, until we come to **Dassia**, home of Corfu's own Club Med. At **Kommeno** the coast breaks out into a lush spit of land now occupied by two luxury resort developments. Forget the coast between Gouvia and Corfu. These were hideously exploited villages in the midst of great upheaval and construction when we visited; go at night to any of the many discos and clubs in this area when you won't be able to see what's happening to them.

Perama is the first community south of the inlet below Corfu town. Many villas to let and hotels crowd the coast road, but some hardy olive trees manage to poke their heads through. Just above Gastouri is **Achillio**, the inland retreat of the wealthy where many of the European royal villas (including the Achilleion of Empress Elizabeth of Austria) can be seen. As in so many wealthy enclaves, the lush overgrowth obscures the sightseers' view of many of the finest homes.

Benitses (12½ kilometers south of Corfu town) was one of the most scenic fishing villages along this coast, but has been developed into a friendly, democratic beach town. For two kilometers of coast road there are lots of tavernas, seafood restaurants, discos, and boutiques, but there's a lazy summer feel to the action that's very relaxing.

The enormous 150-room **Potamaki Hotel** (tel. 0661/30-889) is an attractive B-class resort where half board doubles run 8820 drs ($67.90) and bed and breakfast for two is 5640 drs ($43.40). The Potamaki has a good location right across from the beach. The **Corfu Maris Hotel** (tel. 0661/92-181) is a C-class lodging whose balconies overlook the water. Nearby is **Pat's Place Pub**, a popular club at sundown. The 20-room **Eros** (tel. 0661/92-393) and the 15-room **Riviera** (tel. 0661/92-258) are two E-class hotels whose spartan accommodations offer the best budget choice in this high-priced seaside town. Both are located on the main street, in the swing of things, and opposite the beach.

There are a great number of resort hotels all the way down the coast to the once-sleepy beach of **Kavos**, now destroyed by the many boat excursions emanating from Corfu in search of a quiet beach. Along this road is **Moraitika**, home of Valtour, another Club Med-style all-inclusive resort.

The West Coast

Only one major road leads down into the narrow tip of Corfu's "tail." To the west of the road are many less-developed beaches and rooms to let. **Limni Korission**, near Vrakaniotika village and its fortress, is the largest enclosed lagoon. Sand dunes line this fine bathing area, and make comfortable crannies in which to picnic. **Ag. Giordis** is a very popular beach and swimming area, about 40 minutes by public bus from Corfu town.

Most tourists based in Corfu head for **Glyfada** as a day beach trip, for good reason. Glyfada is Corfu's best beach, on all counts. It's long and large, so there's room for everybody, and the sand is remarkably clean. The no. 11 bus from Corfu runs all day to this sandy, active cove (conserve your energy so you can walk back up the banked shoreline to catch the return bus). The hill village above Glyfada beach is justly famed as the place on the island from which to watch the sunset. (Only on Corfu could this attribute create a full-fledged hilltop resort!) The village is overcrowded, overbuilt, and filled with well-dressed hippies and coeds; there are as many moped dealers as rooms to let. Yet the half-hour ascent to the top of **Pelekas Hill** makes your visit here worthwhile. Enjoy a drink at the **Iliovasilema** (Sunset View Café) during the setting sun, but before it goes all the way down, circle the parking area on the hilltop for magnificent views over the entire island and Ionian Sea.

North of Glyfada there's a one-lane roadway that continues along the coast to **Myrtiotissas Monastery**. After a visit to this holy place, you can walk down behind it and arrive at a lovely sand beach. Golf fans can try Corfu's 18-hole course at **Livadi Tou Ropa** (Ropa's Meadow), nestled in a valley near **Vatos**. The agricultural heartland of Corfu is quite remarkable. In the cooler hours of the early evening, the fields fill up with farmers, and you begin to see the true islanders emerge. Old, wind-burnt women in black cotton head scarves just sit out on their stoops, head in hand, contemplating the sky. Wiry old men and young boys and girls comb the countryside, removing olives from the glistening black nets where they've landed. At **Gardelades** you must choose either the left-hand turn to the beautiful Paleokastritsa Bay or the right-hand turn for Corfu town.

WHAT TO SEE AND DO IN CORFU TOWN: Other than touring and sunning, most activity on this hedonistic island can be individually tailored. Museum and old-stone buffs can go wild at Corfu's two excellent collections; shoppers have high-fashion boutiques in the charming old town quarters; sports enthusiasts have a wide range of enterprise; and you hard-core party animals have bars, clubs, and discos where you can move and groove.

The Archeological Museum

The small collection of finds in the archeological museum are well labeled and of surprising interest. The first gallery contains ceramics and a large archaic lion of the seventh century B.C., found near Menekrate's tomb. In the room behind it is the museum's highlight, the **Gorgo Pediment** from the Doric Temple of Artemis. These sculptures (from the early sixth century B.C.) have been installed in a re-creation of their original setting. The broad features of Gorgo are almost Aztec in style; she's surrounded by her children, Pegasus (the winged horse) and Chrysaor (a young man). One look at her face and you can imagine how she turned men to stone; her children are the offspring of the blood shed when Perseus cut off her head. These sculptures are considered the finest extant works of the archaic period, and represent a bold departure in style for the Corinthian artist who sculpted them. Pegasus was the symbol of Corinth, and the two "leopanthers" (half lion, half panther) depicted flanking both sides of the pediment typify the great attention to detail paid by the artist. The temple's remains were discovered two kilometers inland from Mon Repos (the lord high commissioner's palace). All the sculptures have been installed at the museum, leaving the site of little interest.

The archeological museum, located at 1 Vraila St., below the Esplanade, is open Monday through Friday from 8:45 a.m. to 3 p.m., closed Tuesday; Sunday from 9:30 a.m. to 2:30 p.m. The admission fee is 250 drs ($1.90) for adults, 125 drs ($1) for students.

Palace, Library, and Museum of Asiatic Art

The Museum of Asiatic Art is located in the **Palace of St. Michael and St. George**, built as headquarters for this Order of Knights (they recognized English, Ionian, and Maltese subjects for distinguished service). Constructed between 1818 and 1823 after the design of the English architect Sir George Whitmore, the palace is a wonderful example of the neoclassical style seen along the Promenade and throughout the old town. The building is just as much a work of art as the collection it houses.

The collection of Asian art is superb. There are excellent examples of Japanese *netsuke* and wood-block prints, porcelain, sculpture, and watercolors. In the wing adjoining the elaborate throne room is a large collection of Chinese art, so well labeled that it provides novices with a comprehensive introduction to art, culture, and religion from the Shang Dynasty (1500 B.C.) to the Ching (19th century). The museum is comprised principally of the collections of two Greek statesmen, G. Manos and N. Chatzivasileiou, who served many years abroad. Like any collection that's been lovingly assembled, the works at the Asian art museum vary in quality, while always exhibiting their former owner's appreciation of other cultures. This is really a treat for those with any interest in the Orient.

The museum is located at the head of the Esplanade and is open Monday to Saturday from 8:45 a.m. to 3 p.m., on Sunday from 9:30 a.m. to 2:30 p.m.; closed Tuesday. The admission fee is 300 drs ($2.30) for adults, 200 drs ($1.50) for students.

The Old Quarter: Shops and Sights

Anyone with at least a day on Corfu should seize the opportunity to walk around its old quarter. If you're coming from the new port (the Igoumenitsa ferry pier), begin by walking along **Arseniou Street**, the road that leads uphill around the point. This walk provides wonderful views of Vidos Island (the one celebs are always trying to purchase), Epirus, on the Greek mainland beyond it, and the Albanian coast up to the north. You'll pass many elegant neoclassical buildings from the various European occupations: notice the French consulate on the corner of Arseniou and Kapodistriou. From this corner you can gauge the layout of the **Old Fort**, on its own rocky point with the yacht-filled Mandraki Harbor beneath it. On the left of Kapodistrous is the Palace of St. Michael and

St. George, now the Museum of Asian Art, and still a fine building to admire. A statue of Schulenberg (an Austrian mercenary who greatly assisted the defense of the island against the Turks) stands at the entrance to the fort, a footbridge crossing over the **contrafossa**. This moat is 15 meters deep and 23 to 40 meters wide. On the tip of this fortified outcropping is the tiny **Church of St. George**.

Crossing back over the contrafossa brings you to **Dousmani Street**, the road bisecting the Esplanade. These formal gardens are now used for cricket matches. Interested in playing? Call the **Gymnastikos Syllogos** (Gymnastic Association) about temporary memberships (tel. 38-726) or the Byron Club (tel. 39-504). Continue on Dousmani as it crosses Georgious, the busy thoroughfare with sidewalk cafés along its arcaded west wall. We'll return you here at the end of the day to relax over ouzo and watch the cricketeers and playing children.

The streets behind Dousmani—Ouidmandou, Voulgareos, Ag. Panton, and Sevastianou—are full of boutiques, jewelers, souvenir stands, and Greek handcraft stores. The deeper you walk into this old quarter, the more enchanted you'll be. Many little streets never intersect; many alleys are dead-ends, and often a gate or fence will lead nowhere. The magic of old Corfu is in the buildings left from its colonial days, when so many cultures left their mark to create this teeming cosmopolitan town. Old-house buffs (like Kyle) should ask for a copy of the E.O.T. Information Office's listing of **mansions** in Corfu, which gives addresses, dates, and past owners of many of these fine villas.

The Synagogue

Many of the towns in northern Greece once had substantial Jewish populations. One such city is Corfu, where only 70 people survived out of a population of over 3,000. Today the only visible sign of the community is a reasonably well-preserved synagogue built approximately 300 years ago (two others were destroyed during battles on the island). The synagogue is still in use (every Saturday morning beginning at 9 a.m.) and it has much of its original ornamentation. Members of the community claim their ancestors from Puglia, Italy, brought locally made treasures with them. The display of torah crowns is the most interesting aspect of the Sephardic-style interior. To gain access to the synagogue during the week, call the Jewish Community Center (tel. 38-802). The synagogue is located on 4th Pakados Velissariou Street, about two blocks up from the New Fort bus station.

Sports Activities

Sports enthusiasts should continue their walk down along the waterfront. At the end of the Esplanade you'll pass the Maitland Rotunda (commemorating Corfu's first lord high commissioner under the British regime), then the Corfu Palace Hotel. At the next corner, Vraila Street, are the archeological museum and the town tennis courts. For information on booking time, contact the **Tennis Club** (tel. 37-021). Keep strolling on Vass. Konstantinou as it parallels the water. In less than two kilometers you'll reach **Plage Mon Repos** (Beach of Mon Repos). It's not the best beach by any means, but it's close and convenient to the town, and makes a pleasant outing. The beautifully landscaped grounds were part of the overall concept of Sir Frederick Adam, the British lord high commissioner who built this as his summer residence. Begun in 1831, it soon became known as "Sir Frederick's Folly" on account of his own queer reputation. When Greece became independent, Mon Repos was used as the summer palace of the Greek royal family. Since the abolition of the monarchy, Mon Repos Palace has been closed to the public.

Joggers will enjoy the ten-kilometer (six-mile) run to the suburb of Kanoni. From this scenic area you can overlook (or motorboat to) the island of

Pondikonissi (Mouse Island), which has a 12th-century church dedicated to Christ the Pantocrator. The smaller and closer islet just supports the Convent and Church of Vlachernon, reachable from the mainland by a little causeway. The Kanoni peninsula is surrounded by the Ionian Sea on one side and the Chalikiopoulos Lagoon on the other.

The British Cemetery

This beautifully planted cemetery dedicated to the British soldiers and civilians who lost their lives in the Ionian during its term as a British Protectorate may be of interest to some readers. The Commonwealth War Graves Commission maintains these, and the graves of many who died in the World Wars, in a park-like setting lined with tall cypresses and filled with flowers. The cemetery entrance is on Kolokotroni Street, a left turn from the end of Mitropolitou Methodiou Street.

Festivals and Holidays

Corfu's favorite holidays are celebrated in honor of her patron saint, Spyridon, four times a year—on Palm Sunday, Easter Sunday, August 11 (to commemorate the Corfiots' resistance against the Turks in the seige of 1716), and on the first Sunday in November. Saint Spyridon is credited with saving the medieval town from the plague in 1630, from the Turks on several occasions, and again during World War II, when a bomb dropped through the roof of his church but didn't explode. In the **Ag. Spiridon Cathedral**, on Filellinon Street in the old quarter, you can see gold and silver icons and the embalmed body of the saint himself. (It's said that the embalmed body of Spyridon, a fourth-century bishop of Cyprus, was smuggled from Istanbul and put in a silver casket in his Corfiot church.)

Easter, as it is everywhere in Greece, is a major holiday on Corfu. The biggest night is Holy Saturday, when a processional leads to the Esplanade where the bishop will announce at midnight "Christos Anesti" (Christ is Risen). After his proclamation, the hymns, fireworks, bands, bells, and dancing begin, in tune with the turning on of lights everywhere. On Easter Sunday the feasting on roast lambs and wine continues until the afternoon, when everyone goes out again to dance.

The Achilleion

In 1890 the Empress Elizabeth of Austria (always described as melancholy) decided to build herself a retreat away from the intrigues of the Habsburg court. The Achilleion was named after her hero Achilles, and many sculptures of him adorn its outdoor garden. The grounds are well maintained and the interior is extraordinary. Shelf tops, commodes, and mantelpieces are filled with family memorabilia, portraits, and war mementoes. The ground floor has wild murals, frescoes, and a painted ceiling. Wrought-iron handrails sweep up the marble staircase; garish architectural trim, lots of gilt, and a saddle-seated throne of Kaiser Wilhelm II of Germany (who bought the estate for himself after Elizabeth was assassinated by an Italian anarchist) fill the parlor rooms.

The Achilleion Museum is open from 8 a.m. to 6 p.m. Monday through Saturday, from 9 a.m. to 5 p.m. on Sunday. Admission is 200 drs ($1.50). (Public buses from Corfu run directly to the Achilleion, through some old olive groves and refreshing pine forests, four or five times daily.)

NIGHTLIFE: Most of Corfu's swinging nightlife is centered in the resort complexes out of Corfu town, though Corfu town has more than its share of glamour, glitz, and glitter. After you've had dinner and the mandatory walk along the Esplanade you can stop for a drink at the **Black & White Snack Bar** (tel. 0661/43-545) at Platia Vralyoti, just two blocks off the Esplanade. This is where you'll find the Beautiful People; local moneyed beauties, chic Americans, and Greek Apollos all trying hard not to look at each other. The bartenders are elegant and fun and the latest American releases play through the night. Nearby, on the Esplanade, is the **Taonilla Bar,** another very popular spot.

If action is your modus operandi, then two blocks away is a very hot disco called **La Scala**. Over three nights we saw Scandinavian skiers, German, English, and Australians stomping the night away to European and American hits.

Phillipa's Restaurant, in Gouvia, is one hot spot, where gourmet dining can take you into the evening hours when the nearby entertainment halls open up.

In Alikes are three of the most popular nightclubs, those super-energized plugged-in bouzouki joints where plate smashing and Greek crooners dominate the scene. **Esperides** (tel. 38-121), **Akati,** and **Corfu By Night** (tel. 38-123) will provide some of the most unforgettable experiences of your stay.

Another disco we particularly liked was **La Boom** (tel. 31-133), an intimately lit bar and dance floor where up-to-the-minute European and U.S. music is played. La Boom is located on the coastal highway, about one kilometer north of town. Nearby are **Bora-Bora, Hippodrome,** and **Apokalypsos,** all popular danceterias.

We suggest that you talk to the locals to get their advice on nightclubs and discos so you don't drop your drachmas at last-year's hot spot.

There are several bars catering to a gay clientele in and around Corfu town. Perhaps the most popular is **Pompeii,** located along the New Port about 50 meters beyond the Argo Restaurant. As with most bars in Corfu, Pompeii stays open well into the early morning hours.

The **Achilleion** (tel. 30-530) is once again operating as a year-round casino. Gamblers can play French or American roulette, baccarat, or black jack in the luxury of the Austrian palace. The casino also offers a bar (to celebrate your winning, we hope), restaurant, and dance floor. The Casino Achilleion is open daily from 10 p.m. until 2 a.m.

Family Fare

The **Corfu Festival** has been one of the highlights of the September season for the past few years, presenting internationally acclaimed ballet, opera, dance, and music performances. Check with the E.O.T. upon arrival to confirm the season's schedule of events.

The **Sound and Light Show** (Son et Lumière) held nightly at 9:30 p.m. in the ancient citadel can be seen separately from the folk dance performance, but it's not worth seeing alone. The lighting of the trees and some neoclassical buildings along the Esplanade provide very little visual excitement, though the view of the yacht marina and Vidos Island in the waning light is wonderful. Not so the dialogue, and we quote: "Our town has opened like a ripe fig. All around us houses are being built." (This is from two Greeks speaking of the Venetian occupation of Corfu, though it could equally well be the modern tourist invasion.) Since that's the only worthwhile line in the entire evening, you can imagine that the poor performances don't add much. After decimating the lovely Nausicaa legend from *The Odyssey,* the dialogue proceeds to leap from the Venetian to the Turkish to the Napoleonic eras of occupation on the island. When the English take over the dialogue lightens up a little for a few laughs, but not for long. Overheard from an exiting spectator: "Pretty sad."

Access to the Sound and Light Show bleachers is through the citadel in the

Old Fort, which is open 8 a.m. to 7 p.m. for daylight viewing. Admission is 400 drs ($3.10) for this alone, or 450 drs ($3.50) including the folk dance.

Monday through Friday, **folk dance performances** are given before the Sound and Light Show at 9 p.m., in English (Sunday night's show is in French, Saturday's in Greek). If Corfu is your first stop in Greece and you want to brush up on the *sirtaki* before you begin dancing in tavernas, then try this show, held outdoors in the Old Fort. Corfu's folk dance show is not as slick as Dora Stratou's in Athens, or even Nelly Dimoglu's in Rhodes, but it's spirited and joyful. The small troupe gives an unself-conscious display of simple, local dances and festival rituals.

The folk dance ticket is included with purchase of the Sound and Light Show, and cannot be viewed separately. The cost is 450 drs ($3.50) for adults, 200 drs ($1.50) for students.

The **Danilia Village** is the Disneyland of Corfu. Within its confines are a traditional village, fields for goatherds and shepherds, pottery makers, perfume cells, weavers, wine and olive presses, an Orthodox church, a museum displaying traditional Greek objects, fields being tilled—in short, everything you need to see to re-create a day in the life of a 200-year-old Greek village. In the evening the Greek taverna opens, offering a filling meal of local specialties, much free retsina, and loud bouzouki; a troupe of *sirtaki* and *zeimbeikiko* dancers and musicians will entertain you, and ask you to join in with them. The results can be great fun (remember to bring your camera).

Several tour companies offer excursions to Danilia Village, located eight kilometers northeast of Corfu town, off the Paleokastritsa road. The average fee is 5000 drs ($38.50), which includes a tour of the grounds, dinner, wine (as much as you want), entertainment, and transportation to and from your hotel. Reservations can also be made directly with the Danilia Village (tel. 36-833), at 38 Kapodistriou St. It's open Monday through Saturday from 10 a.m. to 1 p.m. and 6 p.m. till the action stops (dinner starts at 8:30 p.m.).

There are two **movie theaters** in Corfu town, the Pallas and the Orpheus.

GETTING THERE: Greece's most popular resort is easily accessible to tourists from all over the world. **Olympic Airways** offers direct and connecting flights from 35 cities around the world—ranging from Dubai, Johannesburg, Cleveland, or Tripoli. From Athens, there are three flights daily, as well as ten other flights midday throughout the week. For reservations and information, contact the Olympic office in Corfu town at 20 Kapodistriou St. (tel. 0661/38-694) or in Athens (tel. 01/92-92-111).

Ferryboats run from Igoumenitsa 12 times daily between 6 a.m. and 10 p.m. (tel. 0661/32-655). There are two ferries daily to and from Brindisi run by two companies (tel. 0661/39-747 and 30-102). Patras has a daily boat at 7 a.m. and a second boat every other day! For information call the above phone numbers; they're in the same lines. Once a week (Tuesdays at 5 p.m.) there is a ferry to and from Yugoslavia, and excursions to the lovely isles of Paxos and Antipaxos run seven days a week (for Yugoslavia info call 0661/32-664; for Paxos 32-655). The local E.O.T. office has a complete schedule listed in their office, and you can stroll down to the piers and check with the various travel agents as to availability.

2. Paxos and Antipaxos (Paxi and Antipaxi)

Paxos (Paxi), about three hours by excursion ferry from Corfu, is a popular outing. It's only ten kilometers long and quite narrow, but its resident fishermen, tiny villages, traditionally dressed women, and lively tavernas provide enough activity to make the trip worthwhile. People go to Paxi looking for peace, quiet, and a much-needed change from the hustle-bustle of Corfu.

Paxos is still authentically Greek enough that the truly affable locals still wish you a passing "Yassos" or "Mera" as you walk along the road. In fact, the whole island has a kind of anachronistic quality to it: the whitewashed stucco houses with green shutters contrast with the neoclassical Ionian style found on the other nearby islands. If anything, Paxos resembles some of the more obscure islands in the Cyclades. Those few buildings that are in the Corfu mold are significantly more modest than their Corfiot cousins.

Even in Gaios, the main town, there is a tranquil feeling. The silence is broken more often by the crowing of a rooster than by the mechanical buzz of a moped.

The island has become something of an antiresort by virtue of rejecting the Corfiot style of development. However, more and more tourists off on a day trip end up spending the night. That way you can soak up the life of the locals, sample the excellent seafood in the portside tavernas, and take long walks around the island.

From the port of **Gaios** there is one main north-south route. A few kilometers south is **Oxias**, known for its mineral springs. North of Gaios there are several villages and beachside communities at **Koutsi** (where you can rent rooms or camp) and at **Lakka**, on the northern tip of the island by a still-water bay. In Gaios itself is a fortress and a monastery, site of festivities that spill over from the islet of Panagia on its holy day, the Day of the Dormition (August 15).

If you've come to Paxos for the beach, head south to **Antipaxos (Antipaxi)**. Most excursion boats stop at the northwest tip of this tiny island (it's about one-fourth the size of Paxi). Yet because of its isolation "chic," a village with some tavernas has sprung up here in Antipaxi. This picturesque port opens out to a broad cove that's almost corked by another verdant islet that just drifted in too close. There are fine, golden sand beaches on Antipaxi that invite topless and nude sunbathing due to their isolation.

Excursion boats from Corfu make round trips four days a week to Paxos for 2500 drs ($19.20) (they will sell one-way tickets as well, and will honor round-trip return coupons on days other than date of purchase). Regularly scheduled boats run daily for 560 drs ($4.30) each way. The mini-cruisers *Petrakis* and *Sotirakis* are two that also sail to Paxi and Antipaxi from the beach resorts of Kassiopi (on Corfu's northern tip) and Kavos (on Corfu's southern tip) once a week. There is frequent boat service between Paxos and Parga (on the mainland).

USEFUL INFORMATION: There is no Tourist Police on the island, but the regular **police** (tel. 31-222) will handle complaints and emergencies. . . . For medical care there is a **clinic** (tel. 31-777) in Gaios. . . . The **area code** for the entire island is 0662. . . . **O.T.E.** is located one block behind the main platia in Gaios. Be sure to check their hours; when we were there last summer they were only open from 7:30 a.m. to 3 p.m. Monday through Friday. . . . Two **banks** for money exchange operate out of general stores and are open Monday through Friday from 8 a.m. to 1:30 p.m. (they have evening hours on an erratic basis). . . . There are a handful of **travel agencies** on the island, mostly concentrated on the waterfront in Gaios; all of these agencies sell boat tickets. In addition, **Paxos Sun Holidays** (tel. 31-201) is an Olympic Airlines representative, located one block in from the waterfront.

GETTING AROUND: The island **bus** runs four times a day from Gaios to Lakka, making a stop in Loggos; the fare is 100 drs (80¢). **Motorbikes** of all sizes are available for hire; contact one of the agencies lining the paralia. The informal **taxi** stand is conveniently located in the main platia of Gaios.

The **boats** to Antipaxos run many times daily during the high season. Captains normally wait for a full boatload of sun worshippers before setting sail for the ten-minute commute. The cost for a return ticket is 625 drs ($4.80).

ACCOMMODATIONS: Though there are only two hotels on Paxos, the latest estimate of beds in private rooms is 4,000; three quarters of these are in Gaios. High season, category A private rooms, with bath, run approximately 3000 drs ($23.10) for a double, 2000 drs ($15.40) for a single. Rooms with common bath run about 600 drs ($4.60) less. Before and after the high season, there is some softness in the market price and negotiating power increases.

As you alight from the boat there will be people in town who will offer you rooms. Make sure to look at the accommodations before making a commitment. If you are unable to find a room, try any of the local travel agencies; they can often make a telephone call or two and find you acceptable lodging.

There is an additional supply of rooms for rent in Lakka, with prices comparable to those in Gaios.

DINING: Though minuscule, Gaios offers a good selection of traditional Greek cuisine. Our two favorites are **Taka-Taka** (tel. 31-323), a grill set two blocks behind the platia, and **Vaganas,** or "Volcano" (tel. 31-251), nestled between two cafés on the platia. The specialty at Taka-Taka is grilled meat and fish. Two can eat a full meal with stuffed tomatoes, shish kebab or fish entrée, and wine for about 1600 drs ($12.30). One of Taka-Taka's main attractions, other than the food and its super-clean kitchen (a rarity), is the vine-covered garden dining area. Vaganas serves one of the better moussakas you'll find in these parts. The restaurant is open from 8 a.m. to 2 a.m.—when do they sleep? Prices are reasonable: two can sup for about 1600 drs ($12.30).

Residents who want to eat fish head for **Restaurant Rex,** just off the platia. They usually list several fixed-price meals, most with locally caught fish. A complete dinner runs about 750 drs ($5.80) per person.

AROUND THE ISLAND: Most people who are curious enough to have ventured to Paxos are keen to hit the beach on Antipaxos. They are well rewarded. Locals (or at least those who are well traveled) call it the "Barbados of Greece" because of its clean white beach. During the high season boats constantly commute between Gaios and Antipaxos.

If Gaios proves to be too busy for your taste, you might want to base yourself in pretty little **Lakka,** on the tip of the island. Planos Holidays (tel. 31-744) can arrange for rooms, excursions, and other travel needs. Among the restaurants, we liked Kapothistrious Taverna and Souris Taverna. Both are inexpensive.

In between Gaios and Lakka is the tiny harbor at **Loggos.** As of this writing there are no rooms to rent, but there is a quiet pebble beach nearby and a few fish tavernas. Nassos, Vassilis, and Iannis were mentioned by local friends as the favorites.

3. Lefkas

The lyric poetess Sappho, born about 600 B.C. on Lesbos, was considered one of the greatest poets of her age, though only fragments now remain of her work. Even Plato wrote of her, in *Phaedras:* "Some say there are nine muses./

So few then?/Sappho of Lesbos makes their number ten."

Although Sappho's name is more often associated with her love for women, it is a legend of love for a man that links her with Lefkas. Myth has it that she was in love with Phaon, a boatman who'd been anointed by Aphrodite to become an exquisitely beautiful man. After sweet romance and several love poems, Phaon grew tired of her. Sappho traveled to Lefkas where for centuries the priests of Apollo had made a devotional leap from cliffs 236 feet high. The Lefkadian Leap (Katapontismos) was thought to cure lovesickness. Sappho threw herself to her death from Kavos tis Kiras, the white cliffs of the Lefkata Cape.

If you've driven over the marshland to Lefkas, it's easy to appreciate the island's non island status. The Corinthians first dug a canal between the semi-peninsula of Lefkas and the outcropping of the mainland. North of their link was the site of the Battle of Actium, a tragic naval loss for Mark Anthony that many believe Cleopatra engineered. In either case Augustus ordered that the canal, now silted up, be redug so that he could appreciate his place of victory more easily. In 1300 Orsini built the Santa Maura fortress to safeguard the narrow canal for Lefkas; in 1807 the Russians (during their brief protectorate of the Ionians) built two fortresses at Acarnania to guard the approach to the canal from the mainland. Today this seems to be much ado about nothing, as locals and tourists blithely load onto a towrope-guided ferry raft for the briefest of floats between the two. There is even a bridge that toally obviates the need for a ferry.

Lefkas (Lefkada) draws many tourists each August to its popular **Festival of Arts and Literature**, two weeks of lectures, folk dances, theater pieces, and exhibitions. (If you're here for the Festival, August 11 is St. Spyridon's Day, when colorful folk dancing, dining, and singing take place in the inland village of Karia.) Although visitors will find accommodations most easily in the main town of Lefkas, we suggest the coastal village of Nidri as a more attractive alternative.

The island's main village, Lefkas, is directly across from the canal, joined through the marshland by a ribbon of paved roadway. Prospects over the silted, marshy lagoon make you turn around and march back into the crowded streets of the market area; these, although recently constructed, are somewhat more interesting. While in the Agora (market), shop for the intricate lacework and embroidery that Lefkadian women are known for. There are no "bargains" among the handmade products, but they are exported to Europe and America, and from the point of view of what you'd pay at home they will seem a bargain.

AROUND THE ISLAND: The east coast of Lefkas faces directly to the mainland and thus offers sheltered coves and inlets ideal for boating and recreational swimming. At **Nikiana**, about eight kilometers south of Lefkas town, there's a mild surf; at Nidri (15 kms) the shore faces the islet of **Madouri**, a perfect spot for sailing. South of Nidri is a very scenic drive along the curving peninsula which forms **Vlicho Bay**. Directly opposite this spit of land is the lush islet of **Skorpios**, famed summer home of the late Aristotle Onassis and his family. **Syvota** is on the island's southeast tip, facing the larger islet of **Meganissi**. This peaceful port is very quiet, and offers three tavernas at the harbor for a relaxing lunch.

The road network winds west to **Vasiliki**; only the daring need hike out to Cape Lefkatas, whose white cliffs invite images of Sappho in her fateful dive. The west coast's beaches open out into the electric-blue Ionian Sea. At **Ag. Nikitas** there's a clean sandy beach and rougher, colder water that's better for windsurfing. The north coast beach at **Tsoukalades** is Lefkas's best windsurfing area. (**Kavos Beach Windsurfers**, at 0645/92-217, rents equipment for 1000 drs, or $8.30, per hour, and provides free instruction.)

Lefkas

The port of Lefkas is definitely the central village on the island. The interior of the village is more appealing than the developed coast; the shore facing the mainland is lined with hotels, tourist offices, parking lots, and a wide roadway. **Dana Travel** (tel. 23-629; Athens tel. 32-30-930), operated by Eva Giannoulatou, is a helpful agency right on the paralia; they're open from 9 a.m. to 10 p.m. daily with information on boat tours, etc. (By the way, these day-long cruises through this part of the Ionian are probably the most enjoyable way to see it.)

If you've arrived by ferryboat, the bus station is at the end of the main road; buses run twice daily in a big circle around the island.

Accommodations: The buff-colored **Hotel Lefkas** (tel. 0645/23-916), at 2 Panagou, is the most visible from the harbor. It's 93 spacious rooms with bathroom, telephone, Muzak, and balcony top a marble-lined restaurant, bar, and disco. The abundant staff and enormous floor space make the Lefkas appear less welcoming than it actually is. Doubles in the high season run 5375 drs ($41.30).

An older but much more budget-conscious choice is the **Byzantio Hotel** (tel. 0645/22-629), at 10 Delpherd St., by the main street leading back into the village. The Byzantio is homey and pleasant (old photos and prints hang in the hallways), and the communal baths and toilets are well kept. Both the older and the new wing have high-ceilinged, well-lit rooms which share a long terrace overlooking the harbor. The Byzantio's nine doubles rent for 2640 drs ($20.30) per night; single travelers pay 1545 drs ($11.90).

The **Hotel Patras** (tel. 0645/22-359), at 1 Meganissiou, is another good choice in this price range. It occupies an older, neoclassical building on the main square, about two blocks in from the harbor. The Patras's 11 small rooms are bright and well cared for. Summertime doubles are about the same rate as the Byzantio.

Any local travel agent can assist you in finding a room to let.

Dining and Nightlife: Near the Hotel Patras is a Lefkiot's favorite restaurant, the **Regantos Taverna**. Its home-style cooking and robust Greek fare are only served up at dinnertime. Also on the main street are two other popular tavernas, open at lunch and dinner. **Orea** (pronounced "O-ray-yah") means beautiful in Greek; their widely varied menu offers local salamis and beef dishes that are the island's specialty. **Kostas Logothetis** runs another good taverna on the main street. Prices at all tavernas should run approximately 1400 drs ($10.80) for two hearty meals. For a quick, inexpensive break, try the **Kanaria** or **Pete's Souvlaki Bar**; both are equally recommended.

Nightlife is limited in the village of Lefkas. If strolling the harbor on a moonlit night doesn't turn you on, maybe one of the few discos that open up every summer will. Otherwise, head straight for the **Phoenix Cinema**, an outdoor affair just around the corner from the yacht marina at the harbor. A Greek B-picture thriller will drain your pockets of 400 drs ($3.10).

Nidri

If the sleepier port of Nidri sounds appealing to you, consider renting a moped when you've disembarked. **Scooter Aravanis** rents mopeds at 1600 drs

($12.10), cars at 5000 drs ($38.50), and bicycles at 500 drs ($3.80), which can be fun and efficient for around-the-island sightseeing.

All of Nidri's tourist eggs are in one basket, the **Nidri Travel Agency** (tel. 0645/92-256). They're right in the center of Nidri's tiny main street and are open from 7 a.m. to 11 p.m. daily. Since Nidri has no hotels, you'll have to count on them to help you find one of the 600 rooms to rent in the village. (Many rooms are actually in "villas" that European budget-tour operators have constructed to house clients.) The office is a wellspring of information on local goings-on, sights, tours, and activities planned for the charterettes who live there.

Vasiliki

Vasiliki offers simple pleasures: a good beach and a windy haven for wind-surfers. If the lure of sand, sun, and sail fail to captivate you consider strolling down the main thoroughfare, where sheep and an odd cow from the town's nearby farms brush against an even more infrequent tourist. Above the town, on the hillside, are a scattering of small pensions and rooms-to-let. Among the best are the **Lefkatas** (tel. 0645/31305) and **Paradise Villas** (tel. 0645/31256). The latter offers 18 rooms, many with small kitchens and refrigerators. Back down in town are a few extremely informal fish tavernas, all serving locally caught denizens of the near blue sea. There is frequent ferry service by local boats between Fiskardo, on nearby Kephalonia, and Vasiliki.

WHAT TO SEE AND DO: As we mentioned earlier, day-long boat cruises are our favorite way to explore this area. The dense green foliage of the Ionians, the ubiquitous islets, the stark black rocks that protrude unexpectedly from the calm waters are all scenic hallmarks of this region that are best appreciated from the water. **Sitia Cruises** (tel. 22-430 or 23-566) sailed last year on Wednesday, Saturday, and Sunday. These small ferryboats would leave the port of Lefkas in the morning (about 9 a.m.) call at Nidri, Fiskardo on the north coast of Kefalonia, Ithaca, the islet of Meganissi (which has an unusually large grotto), circle Skorpios (everyone brings binoculars to snoop around), and then return to Lefkas (about 8 p.m.). Sitia charged 870 drs ($6.80) for the cruise, a great savings on the comparable ferry tariff to all these islands and a pleasant and expedient way to say "I've visited the Ionians!"

GETTING THERE: During the summer, **Olympic Airways** has daily flights to Preveza, a city on the mainland about 25 minutes by bus from Lefkas. In Preveza, tickets and information can be obtained at Spiliadou and Balkou Street (tel. 0682/28-674) for flights back to Athens. (Olympic information in Athens is 01/92-92-111.) Last year, a bridge connecting Lefkas and the mainland was opened, making the overland route that much easier. The trip from Preveza to Lefkas town takes about 30 minutes.

By **boat**, there are many options for reaching Lefkas. Local fishermen offer motorboat connections to the island from Preveza; the ride takes about two hours. The Ionian Lines are the major ferry company plying those waters, but their schedules are very irregular, and the majority of routes only operate between July 15 and August 31. Contact **Dana Travel** (tel. 23-629) for more information. The Ionian Lines connect Lefkas with Nidri, Ithaca, Sami, Poros, and Fiskardo on Kefalonia; and Zakynthos (Zante).

4. Ithaca

Ithaca (Ithaki) is best known as the home of Odysseus, the island that he yearned to return to throughout ten long and lonely years. From its rugged, stony, uninviting coast the modern visitor rightly questions why anyone would be anxious to return; inland, Ithaca boasts wildly beautiful rocky hills and verdant pine-covered valleys. The ferryboat ride into the port of **Vathi** (it means "deep") is almost agonizing; will the barren, forbidding shore ever relent and offer safe mooring? Ithaca is shaped like an irregular bowtie, and the ferry must round its cinched waist before attempting to squeeze into a narrow wrinkle of the southern bow. There, the petal-shaped Vathi opens out; amphitheatrically layered earth-colored houses reconstructed from the rubble left by the 1953 earthquake surround and frame the small harbor. It may be here that the Phaeacians of Scheria (Corfu) left Odysseus to orient himself before returning to his palace.

In 1982 a **Festival of Greek Music** was established on Ithaca, a celebration of national culture (at the beginning of July) on the island of the country's best-loved hero. Visitors to Ithaca invariably choose to camp or rent a room with one of the local inhabitants; communing with brave Odysseus could never be accomplished from the comforts of a resort hotel. Ithaca has most to offer to one who's memorized favorite passages from the *Odyssey* and *Iliad*. Then, guide in hand, you can set off to explore the sights of Homer's world.

Vathi

All of the large boats call at Vathi, Ithaca's main port. Little remains of the old town; most of the buildings date from the last 30 years or so. The town has good white-stone beaches to the south and the greatest concentration of tourist services on the island. Other than that we'd suggest heading up to Kioni or Frikes.

Useful Information: There is a row of travel agencies on the paralia that sell tickets to the other islands, arrange for rooms, and rent cars and mopeds. Among them is **Lazareto Tours** (tel. 0674/32-587); they also organize around-the-island boat excursions. . . . The **National Bank of Greece** has an official-looking branch just off the paralia, before you arrive at the platia; hours are 8 a.m. to 2 p.m. Monday through Friday. . . . The telephone **area code** is 0674. . . . There are **laundry** services in town. . . . The **bus station,** for the very infrequent bus, is in the platia. . . . The **town police** can be reached at 32-205. . . . Information on mooring at any of Ithaca's many harbors can be obtained from the **Port Authority** (tel. 32-909). . . . The **hospital,** near Stavros, can be reached at 32-282.

Accommodations: As with the rest of the island, there are very few hotels. Most people rent private rooms, which are most easily booked through one of the town's many travel agents. Of the hotels, the **Mendor** (tel. 0674/32-433), on the paralia, is the best. This 36-room inn is a B-class establishment that is run by the Papastamos family. Doubles run 6200 drs ($47.60) during the high season.

Dining: We found three fine tavernas. Our favorite is run by a Greek-Australian couple, John Balarurais and his wife (the grill is named after John), and is located across from the bank. The thing to do here is to order the *pikilia* ("little tastes"), a dish that you can customize from the large number of appetizers created in the kitchen—obviously "grazing" has hit remote Ithaca. The grill has a prettily planted and decorated garden in the back, where a fig dropped on Kyle's head and an olive plopped into our salad! Nearby is the **Trohadiri Taverna** and, on the paralia, the pink-painted **Kantouni Taverna;** both serve Greek specialties and are recommended.

AROUND THE ISLAND: A car makes a day tour around the island practical and enjoyable; hilly routes climb up and down through rapidly changing countryside, and in the narrow midriff region the deep blue of the sea is ever-present. The **Cave of the Nymphs** ("Marmarospilia") is a hike up above the port of Vathi; here, it is said, Odysseus hid the gifts and jewels bestowed upon him by the hospitable Phaeacians. **Aeto**, the village at the island's narrowest point, is fondly believed to be the site of Odysseus' own palace; many archeologists differ and offer the port of Polis, on the tip of the island facing west to Fiskardo, Kefalonia, as the better strategic setting. New excavations are certain to inspire new theories and dash old hopes.

South of Vathi two prongs of roadway pierce the mountainous southern half of the island, topped by **Nerovoulo**. Two kilometers from the port is the larger village of **Perahori**; continue on from here to reach the Monastery of Taxiarhon, founded in 1693 and dedicated to the patron saint of the island.

Stavros (17 kilometers from Vathi) has a small archeological museum and is the hub city for the network of spindly roads that crisscross the northern mass of the island. Near here is the Monastery of Katharae, whose belfry provides views over the Bay of Patras and the Greek mainland to the east. Was this prospect what brought Odysseus to build his kingdom in the north? Though only a few kilometers separate Stavros from the pleasant swimming beach at **Frikes**, it can take quite a while to arrive there. To the south is the tiny port of **Kioni**; it's one of the most scenic drives on the entire island.

These twin towns are only five kilometers apart on the northern half of Ithaca and, notwithstanding subtle differences, are almost identical. If you've come to Ithaca to experience life in a remote island port, you'd do well in Kioni and Frikes, which are modest harbors supporting even more humble towns. Boat repair, sailing (mostly in the merchant navy), and some fairly minimal agriculture are the people's trades, lending an uncomplicated and informal air to everyday life.

Cypress, oleander, pine, olive, and an odd palm line the hilly terrain. The harbors in both towns are quiet and clean; the water is so inviting that people swim off the rocks only a few hundred meters from the boats. In both towns there are much better beaches only a short walk away.

Kioni overlooks three abandoned windmills on the hill at the edge of the harbor. From Costa's Taverna, next to the taxi stand in the mini-platia, you can take in the full panorama. Not much happens here so the favorite activity (other than swimming, sailing, or sleeping) is to plant yourself at an outdoor café and soak up the ambience.

There are only a few rental rooms in Kioni, and those that exist are controlled by the Greek Islands Club (an English touring company). When we visited last summer we had to relocate to Frikes, where if you can find a room (or if the Greek Islands Club has an opening) expect to pay between 1500 to 2500 drs ($11.50 to $19.20) per night for a double.

Frikes is about the same size as Kioni, but just a bit busier due to the excursion boats that stop here connecting Lefkas with Kephalonia. Like Kioni, the water is remarkably clean, reflecting a brilliant turquoise color.

The town supports a couple of tavernas and a market (great for picnics). The closest post office is in nearby Stavros (they change money there as well), but if you don't want to make the trip head over to Kiki Travel overlooking the waterfront. Director Angeliki Digaletou sells stamps, changes money, books rooms, rents boats and mopeds, and speaks perfect English. Again, finding a room can be a problem. If possible, write to Angeliki well in advance of your trip or be prepared to improvise. The locals are very hospitable and will go a long way to help you find a rest spot.

There isn't much to do in Frikes at night, but for those in the mood, there is an evening dinner excursion across to lovely Fiskardo, Kefalonia, on the *Romantica* for 1250 drs ($9.60) per person (not including food).

GETTING THERE: Ithaca is served by daily car-ferry connections from Patras on the **Ionian Lines** (tel. 82-36-012); it's a five-hour ride. The *Sitia* sails three times weekly from Lefkas, connecting Ithaca to Fiskardo, on Kefalonia, Lefkas, and Nidri.

5. Kefalonia

Kefalonia (Cephallonia) is one of Greece's best-kept secrets; a large, unspoiled island with spectacular scenery, beautiful beaches, traditional housing, and excellent wine. The Kefalonians have done their best to keep it that way: with an economy long buoyed by the earnings sent home by citizens working abroad, there has been little cause to exploit the island's resources.

Now Kefalonia is undergoing the crisis experienced by many Greek islands. The younger generation which goes abroad to study or work (it's estimated there are 350,000 Kefalonians in the U.S. alone) usually stay, perhaps returning summers to visit or help out in the family business. Their parents remain: too old to farm their land, they sell their fish to tourist-catering tavernas or use their caïques as beach shuttles. The elderly are soon unable to maintain their homes. The fiercely proud Greeks would never sell their property; instead it's left to children who will probably never occupy it, and so, as in many of Kefalonia's villages, the idle houses crumble and the soul of the village withers.

In the last few years the Greek government has taken steps to add tourism to the other revenue-producing industries of agriculture and livestock breeding. The entire island of Kefalonia was leveled by an earthquake in 1953, with the exception of the northernmost village of Fiskardo, where four Traditional Settlements have been established within remodeled 19th-century villas. In the capital city of Argostoli and the newly developed resort of Lixouri, several moderately priced and luxury hotels have been built in emulation of the Ionian's model tourist resort, Corfu.

Full-scale tourism will not come easily to the people of Kefalonia. Since antiquity it's been an island of prosperous sailors and traders. During each period of foreign occupation, local Kefalonians of means took advantage of new ties to Europe to educate their children, import new goods, and learn the ways of new cultures. Today's islanders are very sophisticated; many live abroad and vacation here, or keep in close touch with the world outside their island. It's not enough to say that Kefalonians get around; the Juan de Fuca Strait off Seattle, Washington, was named after a Kefalonian sailor who joined the Spanish navy. (Wealthy shipowners still maintain villas around Argostoli and its sandy beaches; it's not uncommon to see them out there weekends proudly mowing their green lawns.) So many Kefalonians return to the island as tourists that they're not very eager to welcome foreigners. In line with their flush economy, room and board prices are higher than at most comparable islands, and foreigners have little luck bargaining. However, those looking for an island with one of the best beaches in Greece (at Myrtos), the tastiest white wine (Rombola), and superb indigenous architecture (at Fiskardo) should clench their fists and push onward to Kefalonia.

ORIENTATION: The odd-shaped island of Kefalonia looks rather like a high-heeled shoe with a high tongue reaching up to parallel the shores of Ithaca. Under the instep is the main town, **Argostoli**; directly opposite it on the inside of the heel is the newly built resort of **Lixouri**. Behind the heel and up the inside of the tongue (the west coast of the island) are the best beaches, usually at the foot of spectacular, steep powder-white cliffs. On the top of the shoe is the island's other port, **Sami**, a village where most ferries will leave you, to avoid having to round the "sole" of the island to Argostoli. Kefalonia is the largest of the Ionian Islands; the public bus takes 45 minutes from Sami to Argostoli, and a moped ride from Argostoli to the northcoast **Fiskardo** can take over two hours. To our minds, the Traditional Settlements of Fiskardo maintained by the E.O.T. are the best housing alternative on the entire island, and the port of Fiskardo is absolutely charming. Yet many tourists may prefer the busyness of Argostoli.

AROUND THE ISLAND: Argostoli is on the "arch" of the high-heel-shaped island, and the region around the "sole" is called **Livathos**. This area, heavily striped with narrow, scenic, winding roads, has traditionally been one inhabited by wealthy sea captains. Their villas line the roads and climb up the steep embankment for a better view of the water. **Metaxata** (where Lord Byron stayed for four months in 1823) is one village with several modern luxury villas. **Kourkoumelada** is the product of one man's faith in his villagers. After the earthquake of 1953 George Vergotis, a wealthy entrepreneur, rebuilt the entire village and all its former homes by himself. The south coastline of Kefalonia has some other interesting sights. If you sailed past the lovely sand beach at **Ormos Lourda** to Ormos Kateliou, you'd be near **Markopoulos**. As its name implies, the city was founded by ancestors of Marco Polo. During the week before the Feast of the Assumption (early August) local citizens of Markopoulos are said to catch little harmless snakes with black crosses on their heads, which then disappear until the following year.

At the island's "toe" is the village of **Skala**, called Nea Skala by those who've seen the ghost town of half-crumbled houses left over from the earthquake. Getting between these two points is made difficult by **Mount Aenos** (Eagle Mountain), which is also called "Black Mountain" by Kefalonians because of its black color when seen from a distance. Aenos is 1,628 meters tall and is topped by a large antenna that appears to be a NATO installation. The extra-fit can attempt to ascend its northwest face through the dark pine forests and beds of white rock to enjoy the wonderful view from its summit.

For 20 kilometers north of Sami there is good road following the east coast. At the seven-kilometer mark you reach the **Melissani Grotto**, a large, multicolored cave that encloses a huge underground lake. For many years it appeared that water flowed backward into the land at Katavothres, near Argostoli. Now scientists say that in fact this water is flowing due east, through an underwater tunnel into the underground lake at Melissani. This phenomenon, and the large boulder off the shores of Lixouri that rocks back and forth ceaselessly, are some of the reasons Kefalonia is known for "doing everything in a strange and topsy-turvy way" (as the E.O.T. brochures describe it!).

In the small village of **Ag. Efimias** there's an excellent seafood taverna known as "Paradise," located right on the water. From here north the coast rises to tall rocky heights and the roadway moves inland to some charming, small villages. Through the evergreens you can catch glimpses of Ithaca's rocky profile in the distance.

GETTING AROUND: The K.T.E.L. **bus lines** service the entire island on a good network of roads. However, Kefalonia is so big and hilly that it takes forever to get to most places you'll want to go. From Sami, where the ferryboats arrive, to Argostoli, there are two buses daily (last year they were at 7:30 a.m. and 6 p.m.); the fare is 315 drs ($2.40). The northbound Fiskardo bus runs only twice daily, but its route provides the most exquisite scenery in Greece; the fare is 365 drs ($2.80). Information on bus schedules can be obtained from K.T.E.L. (tel. 22-276).

As we mentioned previously, **mopeds** are too slow to cover much ground if you're trying to sightsee in one day. If you're based in a village and want to explore locally, they can be a lot of fun because the roads on wealthy Kefalonia are very good. In high-priced Argostoli, mopeds rent for 1450 drs ($11.15) a day for a two-seater Vespa and 900 drs ($6.90) for a single-seater.

Budget Rent A Car (tel. 28-811) has an office next door to Olympic Airways on Rokkou Vergoti Street. Their rates are approximately $45 per day, and they have the advantage of having offices throughout Greece where you can make advance reservations on a worldwide basis. Mr. Yangos Metaxas is the friendly Budget agent for the island, and can suggest the most practical itineraries for those who band together and rent a car to sightsee. (Most rental cars are taken by visiting ex-islanders.)

The island's main **taxi** station is at Valianou Square in the heart of Argostoli. A four-passenger Mercedes taxi will cost 5000 drs ($38.50) for an around-the-island four- to six-hour tour. On the way the driver may choose to pick up anyone who flags him down, and then charge them whatever fare seems equitable (this in no way reduces your fare!). Most cabbies are used to dealing with Greek-speaking visitors and it helps get your rate down if you can find a friendly local to negotiate on your behalf.

The **ferryboat** to Lixouri (a fun, thirty-minute voyage between two points of land jutting into the Argostolion Gulf) leaves from the western tip of Argostoli. Walk away from the hills toward the harbor and you'll see it in front of the Cephallonia Star Hotel. This large car-ferry runs ten times daily, until 10 p.m., and the fare is 125 drs ($1). For landlubbers, Lixouri can also be reached on a round-about roadway by car or public bus.

ARGOSTOLI: The island's capital is an amusing, lively, modern village totally rebuilt after the devastation of the earthquakes of 1953. Greater Argostoli spreads to the main part of the island and connects to the north-south highway. The village proper is on its own spit of land tied to the rest by the **Trapano Bridge**. This broad causeway was originally built in 1910 by the Britisher C.P. de Bosset in 15 days; two years later it was replaced by masonry. This little bridge so impressed visitors that Henry Holland Fros described it in *Travels in the Ionian Islands* (published in London in 1912–1913) as "of sufficient breadth to admit a carriage to pass . . . and firmly constructed of blocks of solid stones. . . . This was a great undertaking . . . the water in many parts of the channel being six feet in depth . . ." The center portion of the bridge was adorned with a large pyramid dedicated to the "Glory of the British Nation" that was given in gratitude by Kefalonian citizens.

At this point we should talk about one of the island's highlights, the incredible **Corgialenios Historical and Cultural Museum** (open from 8:30 a.m. to 1 p.m., and 6 p.m. to 8 p.m. Monday through Saturday), located a block above Valianou Square (on the ground floor of Corgialenios Library), an absolute must for everyone visiting the island. It includes a large, superb collection of historical memorabilia, folk crafts, European antiquities left by occupiers, and old photographs, maps, and articles about the island's history. One of its most poignant gift items (many excellent lace pieces are for sale) is the collection of black-and-white photos from 1904, now mounted as postcards costing 200 drs ($1.55) each, depicting Argostoli as it was before the earthquakes. An hour spent in this museum is a better introduction to modern Greek history than reading all the history books combined.

Layout

The **Trapano Bridge** is at the south end of the village of Argostoli, off **Iannou Metaxa Street**, the harborside road. In this section of town, running two and three streets in from the water, is the interesting **Agora** section. Some budget hotels, old ouzeris, and disheveled tavernas occupy the quiet lanes. During the day it's a beehive of activity as trucks unload, mules arrive with produce, and fishermen bring their catch into all the shops. This is the area where you'll see behind-the-scenes Greek life; it's also the best place to get Calliga wines (the island's best export and a perfect gift to bring home) and groceries for campers and picnickers.

Walking along the harbor, away from the bridge and toward the Lixouri shuttle ferry, will bring you to the heart of Argostoli. Two blocks in from the water is **Valianou Square**. In the narrow lanes to the south of the square are travel agents, Olympic Airways, car-rental companies, and businesses. To the west of the square the houses are banked on a steeply ascending hillside. If you climb over this and descend the other side (a paved roadway winds down), you'll arrive at the excellent town beaches of **Makri Gialos** and **Plati Gialos**. At the foot of the hill overlooking the square are the village theater, the library, the small archeological museum, and the Corgialenios Historical and Cultural Museum. To the east and north sides of Valianou Square are many tavernas, cafés, and shops. Between the square and the port are several C-class hotels and apartments offering rooms to let.

Although Argostoli is not the most winning village during the day, in the evening, when the square and its cafés are filled with local citizens, the lights are dim, and the scented flowers open on the many nearby trees, it becomes an attractive and enjoyable place to be.

Useful Information

The **E.O.T.** office, open Monday through Friday only, is off Valianou Square (tel. 22-200). . . . The telephone **area code** for Argostoli is 0671; for Sami and Fiskardo it's 0674. . . . The Mouikis Hotel, at Vironos and Kritis Streets, near Valianou Square, gives out the only **map** of Argostoli on the back of their price brochure; pick one up from their desk. . . . **Ferry tickets** to Patras or for excursion boats can be purchased at several travel agents around the square or at the port in Sami (where the ferries depart). **Filoxenos Travel** (tel. 23-055), on the southwest corner of the platia, runs many island excursions and is very helpful. They offer a one-day trip to Assos and Fiskardo for 1875 drs ($14.40).

The **Island Rent a Car** office (tel. 24-154) also serves as the Greek Islands Club representative (an English charter-group company) for Kefalonia and can provide you with information about tours, room availability in villas, and group functions. . . . The **Olympic Airways** office is next to Budget Rent a Car on R. Vergoti Street (tel. 28-808). They have a bus leaving for the airport outside Argostoli about 80 minutes before flight time for a fare of 100 drs (80¢).

Nearby is the **Ionian and Popular Bank**, open 8 a.m. to 2 p.m. Monday through Friday. . . . The **post office** is on Lithostrato Street (open 7:30 a.m. to 2 p.m.). . . . The **O.T.E.** is located behind the E.O.T. and is open daily from 7 a.m. to midnight. . . . **Medical assistance** can be obtained by calling 28-332 or 28-763.

Shopping Tip: The **Calliga Vineyards** is open Monday through Friday for tours. When present shopping, avoid the nicely packaged "Robola" in a burlap sack with French writing and the Calligata wax seal that sells for 850 drs ($6.50). Instead choose the "Calliga Vin de Table Blanc Sec." This is made only from the prize Robola grapes, yet sells for 565 drs ($4.30) a bottle without the pretty wrapping. Also, Kefalonia's "Golden" brand honey is uniquely rich and tasty, a treat for baklava aficionados!

Last summer we discovered what has to be the very best wine in all of Greece. Tucked away in a remote spot in nearby Minies (just above the airport) is the **Gentilini Vineyard.** The superb quality of this modestly scaled winery is testament to one man's determination to produce a Greek export wine. Spiros and Anna Cosmetatos are the very capable vintners, both of whom are also informative, gracious, and fascinating hosts. If you're so inclined, they conduct tours of the vineyard as well as home-style wine tasting; call ahead (tel. 41-618) to make sure someone is home.

Accommodations

The best value in C-class accommodations is the ultra-clean **Mouikis Hotel** (tel. 0671/23-032), on Vironos Street just behind the post office. The spacious marble-floored lobby, swank interior decor, comfortable TV lounge, and friendly clientele impressed us. (Also, the owner's son graduated from the hotel management program at Farleigh Dickinson University—pretty impressive, eh?) Perhaps the best attribute is the Mouikis's rooftop sundeck; it's got a wonderful view over the water to Lixouri and the white cliffs of the coastline. Large, modern double rooms with newly tiled bathrooms are 5500 drs ($42.30), including a hearty breakfast; singles run 3720 drs ($28.60).

The 26-room **Hotel Argostoli** (tel. 0671/28-272) is a few streets up the hill, at 21 Vironos St., in a quiet residential part of the city. Both the lobby and guest rooms are decorated with clean white pine, lending a comfortable, warm feeling to this spotlessly clean C-class inn. High season doubles rent for 5500 drs ($42.30), singles are 4000 drs ($30.80); both prices include breakfast.

Another C-class choice is the **Regina Hotel** (tel. 0671/23-557), one block from the cultural museum at 24 Georgiou Vergoti St. This plush hotel opened in 1982, and the buff-tone marble lobby and gleaming newness of the place are very attractive. If you get bored, you can hang out in the lively café/snackbar, or sit in the lobby and watch the fish swim round their aquarium. The 27 full-amenity doubles run 5500 drs ($42.30) including breakfast.

The **Cephallonia Star** (tel. 0671/23-180) is an older C-class hotel that's an excellent value. It's centrally located on the harbor, opposite the Lixouri shuttle boats at 50 I. Metaxa, and many of its 47 rooms offer fine views over the water. Peter Vassilatos and his warm family are skilled managers; everything is ship-shape and at the same time, homey and comfortable. The Cephallonia Star offers high-season bed-and-breakfast doubles for 5500 drs ($42.30).

The smaller **Castello Hotel** (tel. 0671/23-250) is located at the west side of Valianou Square. The interior decor could be described as go-go moderne: large beige glass globes hang like Christmas tree balls from the lobby ceiling and all the doors are half-moon-shaped Chinese restaurant-style entries. Still, the simple doubles are clean and adequate, and the location is very convenient though it can be noisy next to the square. High-season doubles with breakfast are 5500 drs ($42.30). Opposite it on the square is the **Hotel Aenos** (tel. 0671/28-013). This slightly worn hotel has all the usual amenities, cottage cheese-textured ceilings, dark natural-wood furnishings, and an active outdoor café. The Aenos seems to attract all the returning Greeks, who are really the soul of its lively, active, and social bar. Doubles at the Aenos run 5100 drs ($39.20), including breakfast.

If you want to base yourself outside of Argostoli, consider **Mouikis Village** (same telephone as Mouikis Hotel in town). The so-called village is really a community of 21 apartments, each one sleeping four or five people and equipped with a kitchen and cooking utensils. There is a swimming pool and playground in the complex, making it a good place for families. The only drawback is its proximity to the airport, but with only a few flights a day it shouldn't be too much of a problem. Apartments vary in size but range in price from $40 to $60 per day. Mouiki's Village is located ten minutes away by taxi in Lakithra. If you stay here and feel like going out for a bite, try Kalithea Restaurant, run by Mr. Maravegias.

Budget Bets: We stayed in the rooms-to-rent apartment complex of **Jerry Zervos** (tel. 0671/28-919), a Chicago expatriate who returns to Kefalonia summers to manage his real estate. Spacious, clean doubles with private bath (many with balconies) cost 2730 drs ($21) for a double. Rooms can be booked by telephone or by walking over to the complex, around the corner from the Aegli Hotel, at 3 Metaxa St. The **Aegli** (tel. 0671/22-522) is easy to spot; it's one block east of the square on 21 Maio St. Prices are a little higher, and there's a charge of 100 drs (75¢) for a shower. For bathless rooms these are not as good as the rooms that Jerry Zervos rents (he owns both properties).

As you walk toward the Agora section, there are a few small, older D-class hotels that are of good value. The **Hotel Allegro** (tel. 0671/22-268) is on Anar. Choida Street, two blocks south of the Mouikis Hotel. The good-natured Petros Sklavounakis maintains a clean, comfortable pension where a double with bath goes for 4638 drs ($35.70).

A few blocks farther north, above a taverna in the Agora section, is the **Hotel Paralia** (tel. 0671/22-627), at 144 J. Metaxa. Nearby is the K.T.E.L. bus station for do-it-yourself around-the-island tours. The four rooms at the Paralia are all bathless, but clean and simple. Top-floor rooms have balconies with a good view, and the restaurant/taverna downstairs is open for lunch or dinner. All rooms cost 1000 drs ($7.70) with a common shower.

Dining and Nightlife

Because Kefalonia caters to so many Greek tourists, the restaurants are above average and always busy and lively. Our favorite was the little taverna **Patsoura's** (tel. 22-779), about five blocks from Valianou Square as you walk along Vass. Georgiou Street. Smiling chef Christianthou Patsoura runs this tiny gem (really called "Perivolaki," but no one would know what you were talking about if you got lost). It's opposite the Xenia Hotel in a fenced-in garden setting. Patsoura cooks up a mean *crasato,* pork cooked in wine that's one of the island's specialties. His macaroni pie is also exceptionally tasty. Some stuffed tomatoes and a carafe of crisp Robola wine will bring a satisfying meal for two to about 1950 drs ($15).

Taverna Kaliva (tel. 24-168), also known as the Cottage, is a basic garden dining spot that turns out some very good Greek dishes, including a few Kefalonian specialties. One of the best is *kreatopita,* a meat pie of beef, potatoes, and rice spiced with sabseco, imparting a spicy-sweet fragrance to this well-prepared entrée (surprizingly, it came to our table piping hot!). Other suggestions include a delicious moussaka and the full complement of veal main courses. Dinner for two will run about 1200 drs ($9.20). The Cottage is just off the square, at 2 Vergoti St.

When you eat fish and seafood in Greece there's no getting around it: you're going to pay a lot. To compound matters many seafood restaurants are better at hawking their expensive entrées than in preparing them. Happily, Argostoli is home to the **Port of Cephalos Restaurant** (tel. 23-725), where all things fishy are prepared well and with some style. One can sample shrimp salad in avocado, for example, one of the choices in a large variety of seafood appetizers. We opted for octopus as an entrée and found it tender and fresh. Prices vary wildly with the season and type of fish, so expect this to be a mini-splurge. The Port of Cephalos is opposite the Yacht Harbor near the port offices. The restaurant is open daily, except Monday, for dinner only.

One of the chicest restaurants in Argostoli is **La Gondola**, a fancy outdoor café right on Valianou Square. It's packed with visiting Greeks (who, after all, savor Italian food for a change once in a while) picking at huge, super-combo pizzas. In the front is a large wooden stove and grill used for grilling the various steaks and chops and for roasting the pizzas. From the many different types of pizza, ranging from 550 drs to 1000 drs ($4.20 to $7.70), we thought the seafood pizza, with crispy shrimp and bits of fish, was quite good. Splurge menu items might include some of their juicy steaks, lamb chops, or casserole specialties, priced between 550 drs to 1550 drs ($4.20 to $11.90).

If spending a night at the **Rex Cinema** doesn't excite, there's a popular café/bar at the **Aenos Hotel** off the square. (There are also many cafés right on the square that are fun to hang out in.) If you take the road up behind the square as if you were going out to the beach, you'll see a loud **disco** on the right and the **Katavothres**, an especially popular bouzouki club where all are welcome to dance, a little farther on.

Out of Town: Argostoli has a number of excellent dining establishments nearby, in the "suburban" areas. On the way to the airport and Makris Yalos beach are two of the better ones, **Tratta Seafood** and **Alekos Restaurant.** Two can dine at Tratta for about 3500 drs ($26.90), making it a seafood splurge. Alekos is run by an entertaining mandolin player/cook who serves very good taverna fare. As you head north, along the shore road past the lighthouse, you'll come to what is becoming one of the favorite "in" spots in Argostoli, a tavern called **Memories.** Here one dines in a romantic atmosphere in between Argostoli's best discos, **Midnight Sun** and **Vinarias.**

SAMI: As the principal port, Sami is a village that you need to know something about, especially if you're going to be stuck spending the night there. From the coastline Sami looks like a calm, sheltered harbor in a niche of the white cliffs which score the verdant palisades on the east coast. The ruins of a third-century Roman bath (with its mosaic floor intact) led archeologists to conclude that this was indeed the port of ancient Sami. About an hour's walk from the town to the point is the **Monastery of Agrilia**, where remnants of a Venetian fort and some walls can be seen. Today Sami has lost its prime role to the better-developed (economically speaking) village of Argostoli.

It's possible to rent rooms from some of the many commercial vendors that line the paralia, or hike about 700 meters to **Kamping Karavomilos** (tel. 0674/21-680), where you can rent a moped or sail board. The older, quaint **Hotel Kyma** (tel. 0674/22-064) is on the main street (Platia Kyprou) opposite where the Ionian Lines ferry docks. The 17 spartan bathless rooms at the Kyma rent for 3460 drs ($26.60) for a double with bath, and many have good views over the harbor.

The Ionian Lines cruise company has an office right around the corner from the hotel, on the paralia, and can provide you with information and tickets. The bus to Argostoli leaves from the paralia; in fact, everything you'd need in Sami (including a few unremarkable tavernas) is along the paralia.

FISKARDO: Fiskardo is the one village on Kefalonia that survived the earthquake of 1953 almost totally unharmed. When you arrive at its tiny square (really a roundabout for traffic), you're just within sight of the tranquil harbor at the base of the C-shaped cove. Fiskardo's cove has a lighthouse and tower at one end and the petite village at the other. Flotillas of fabulous yachts moor at its outskirts, in for the day from Corfu or Lefkas. It's no wonder people come to dote on this tiny village; unless you were around before 1953, you've never seen anything like it in Greece. There are cherry and fig trees, peaches and apricots. The Doric-columned schoolhouse still sits proudly amid stucco villas with colonnaded porticos and overgrown grape arbors.

Fiskardo now has a population of 60; you can meet everyone at the port by day, or in the **Thendrinos** or **Herodotus Taverna** by night. The **Captain's Cabin** is popular for pastries and snacks while nostalgic Greeks review the latest news obtained from the nearby post office. The port is made for idlers; sit back in a taverna with ouzo and schmooze with the locals (almost everyone speaks English) while watching youngsters sail toy boats in the water. The Sitia excursion boat from Lefkas stops at this port on its day trips; if you hook up with it, you can visit Ithaca and Lefkas also.

Accommodations: Everyone should try to stay in Fiskardo overnight to sample the essence of Greek life. If you can splurge, you must stay in the Traditional Settlements, renovated 150-year-old villas with modern amenities. Each is named after the family whose home it was, and each has different styles of lodging and facilities. The plushest is the **Artemisia Tseletin House,** where 18 beds have been split into doubles. The other converted buildings are the old **Community House,** the **Anastasios Tseleti House,** and the **Manousaridi House,** all done in the same style of renovation. The ten-year contract covering the Traditional Settlements on Kefalonia expires in 1988. As of this writing the government has not decided what it will do regarding the contract; for further information and reservations (if possible) you can write to: E.O.T./Paradosiakoi Oikismoi, Fiskardo, Kefalonia, or call 0674/51-397 or 51-398. Manager Dennis Messaris is a well of information about the region; he can be found daily in the white building with brown wrought-iron trim at the left of the square. The current price of a double room with bath is 6200 drs ($47.70), doubles without bath run 4820 drs ($37), and singles are 3100 drs ($23.80).

The **Panormos Hotel** (tel. 0674/51-340) is Fiskardo's only other licensed inn (there are rooms to rent in the village), and you can find it by strolling up the road that weaves around the coast. There's good swimming off the rocks below this taverna/hotel, and just dining on their balcony overlooking the scene is a real treat. The Panormos was renovated in the summer of 1987 by the community members of Fiskardo. Doubles with bath are 4200 drs ($32.90).

The E.O.T. estimates that there are 80 private rooms, with 150 beds, for rent throughout the village at rates of 2500 drs ($19.20) for bathless doubles, 3000 drs ($23.10) with bath. Dennis, in the Traditional Settlements office, can point out rental rooms.

Getting to Fiskardo: Fiskardo is 46 kilometers from Argostoli along a mountainous coastal route. By **taxi** the trip is 45 minutes to an hour; by **moped,** 2½ to 3 hours. There are two scheduled public **buses** that leave from the K.T.E.L. station at the port of Argostoli. From the port of Sami to Fiskardo there is one bus that leaves at noon, and from Fiskardo to Sami there is a daily bus at 6:30 a.m. (It's said that sometimes a bus will appear to take afternoon ferry passengers arriving from Patras directly from Sami to Fiskardo.) Fares tend to run about 250 drs ($1.90). The small **excursion boat,** the *Sitia,* cruises thrice weekly between Lefkas, Ithaca, and Fiskardo, and is the fun way to get to this port. Last year it left at 5:30 for Nidri and Lefkas, arriving at 8 p.m. For an additional 700 drs ($5.40) per person you could spend the night on board and cruise back to

Fiskardo at 9 a.m. the next day. Round-trip fare is 970 drs ($7.50). Information can be obtained by calling 0674/51-478, or by asking in the tile-roofed cafeneion under the fig tree. A small **ferryboat** also makes daily runs at 1 p.m. to Vathi, on Ithaca, for 485 drs ($3.75).

The West Coast

The west coast of Kefalonia has the best beaches on the island and some of its most breathtaking scenery. The main road south from Fiskardo winds down through sweet little villages, where one-room schoolhouses can be identified by the crowd of children outside. It's startling to see such traditional life carried on in newly constructed surroundings. At **Assos** (about 13 kilometers south) the tongue of Kefalonia's shoe butts out into another small peninsula. Within its protective arc is the picturesque port of Assos, one of the loveliest in Greece. Topping the peninsula is a Venetian castle from 1595; the buff-colored stones ramble across this acropolis, once used to safeguard Kefalonia's western flank. This round spit of land provides a sheltered cove favored by many small fishing boats. The gray stone shoreline next to the boat launch makes for easy access to the crystal-clear waters. Boxy, pastel-colored houses unified by red tiled roofs are the summer cottages of Greeks who stroll through the portside in bikinis and diaphanous dresses. Everywhere are figs, peaches, flowering oleander, and geraniums.

The village square, bordered by the Platanos Restaurant and a tiny cafeneion, is called Platia Parision, and is dedicated to "Commemoration of the generous contribution of the City of Paris to the reconstruction of Assos after the earthquakes of 1953." Opposite this are the free standing, gutted façades of neoclassical buildings that couldn't be shaken down. During the summer it's difficult, at best, to find a room, but try the following. In the scrub-brush-and-clover-covered hillside behind the town, you'll spot the Pension Geranna and some "Rooms to Rent" signs. The K.T.E.L. bus runs daily from Argostoli to Assos at 2 p.m.

The drive between Assos and **Ormos Myrtos** (about ten kilometers) is one of the prettiest on the island, but unfortunately there's nowhere to stay along the road. Try to sightsee in the early morning or at dusk, when the light is not so harshly reflected from the sparkling Ionian. To reach Myrtos Beach, you either have to walk about two kilometers down from the hilltop village of Divarata (this road is moped-worthy also) or drive if you've rented a car. For your efforts, you're rewarded with a long, wide stretch of fine pearl-colored pebbles and the most Paul Newman-blue waters, with only a scattering of fellow sun worshippers. We voted this one of Greece's top ten beaches.

On the west coast of the Lixouri cape is another beautiful beach, **Ormos Petani**, that can only be reached by taxi or car from Argostoli. South of this, on the green, rugged coast is the **Monastery of Kipoureon,** built in 1744. It's still inhabited by the original sect of monks who zealously guard its fine collection of antique icons. Rounding the cape to Lixouri you'll find many more good beaches, best reached by boat. (Try to get friendly with a boat-owning local so you can take advantage of these.)

The combination of verdant plains, lush, fertile valleys, and pine-covered mountains bordered by a band of fine-sand beaches is what's made Kefalonia such a perfect island from the Greeks' point of view.

GETTING THERE: There are several sea options open to those trying to reach Kefalonia. There are daily departures from Patras via **car-ferries** (call Patras information at 061/277-622 for schedule information). Ferries also depart from Kyllini on the Peloponnese (call 82-36-012 for information) daily for 1000 drs

($7.70). The Ionian Lines (tel. 061/270-948 in Patras) has departures every odd-numbered day from Patras to Kefalonia, Paxi, Corfu, and Brindisi, Italy. Every Thursday and Sunday there are sailings to Ithaca from Sami; for information call 0674/22-359. Those traveling by public **bus** can take the Patras bus from the terminal at 100 Kifissou St., Athens. For information call 51-29-498.

Olympic Airways offers daily flights in summer nonstop to Kefalonia; off-season there are three flights a week, which make stopovers at Zakynthos (Zante); the flight from Zakynthos takes ten minutes! For information, call the Olympic Airways office in Athens (tel. 92-92-111).

6. Zakynthos

Zakynthos, or Zante as it's also known, is the southernmost of the seven Ionian islands. Although it's the third-largest island after Corfu and Kefalonia, its 417-square-kilometer size is just right for a few relaxing days of exploration, allowing enough time to become familiar with the charms and special people of this unspoiled resort.

The island, first noted in history by Homer as Yliessa, was settled by Zakythos, son of Dardanos, king of Troy. In Hellenic times this tiny democracy was wooed by both Athens and Sparta because of its fertile soil and strategic location. In 1204 Zakynthos fell to the Byzantine conquerors and was ruled by a succession of Frankish princes; during this time the kastro, whose ruins reflect the extent of the entire city at that time, was built. In 1484 the Venetians took Zakynthos and ruled it for over 300 years. They began what became one of the nicest legacies of this fertile island: the lucrative cultivation of grapes (made into wine, and, of course, Zante currants). In 1500 the Venetians expanded the city of Zakynthos outside the fortress walls. The narrow streets, open squares, and arcades that form weatherproof promenades along the harbor were designed by these Italians, but date only from 1953. In that year more than 90% of the island's buildings were leveled by a tremendous earthquake that damaged parts of many of the Ionian islands, but which started in Zakynthos. An exception to the rebuilding is the 16th-century Platiafaros, or San Marcos Square, one block up from the harbor. Here you'll find some "fast-food cafés" (the most chic) and the Solomos Museum. Zantiots are fiercely proud of their artistic sons, and this museum houses the memorabilia of Dionysos Solomos, Greece's national poet, and Foskolos and Kalvos, two other celebrated poets of the Ionian School.

ORIENTATION: Zakynthos's southern position in the warm Ionian Sea gives it an especially pleasant climate in the winter; the many sheltered coves on the north end of the island provide cooler water and temperate breezes in the summer. The climate, and its proximity to the mainland, make Zakynthos popular with Greek tourists. The island has yet to be as heavily developed as Corfu and doesn't cater solely to group tourists; however, be warned that prices have climbed dramatically, reaching parity with the other Ionian resorts, and English and Scandinavian holiday makers are in very full force. In contrast to the 90 hotels, there are 3,200 beds to rent privately around the island, and staying with a local is the ideal way to enjoy a vacation inexpensively in a first-class Greece-for-Greeks resort.

To explore the island, you'll want to start in Zakynthos town, the port. From here there are frequent **buses** to every corner and beach, and several shops from which to rent **mopeds**, the preferred mode of transport. **Stamatis** (tel. 23-673), at 9 Filitia St., is one friendly place; **Moto Sakis**, at 3 Leof. Dimokratis, is another; both rent mopeds for 875 drs to 1250 drs ($6.70 to $9.60) per day. Mopeds are fun and as easy to ride as a bicycle (you can rent these too, but the many hills require pretty strong calf muscles!). The faster mopeds allow you to fully explore the cool of the pine forests and the scent of the roses that line every roadway. If you're able to spend a few days on Zakynthos, buy a map (400 drs, or $3.10; available everywhere), enabling you to jog, hike, or just plain wander down all the roadways to appreciate the island's beauty.

LAYOUT OF ZAKYNTHOS TOWN: Zakynthos town is a good base from which to explore if excellent restaurants, elegant (and expensive!) boutiques, and a rousing nightlife make a few kilometers' walk to the beach acceptable. There are several small, reasonably priced Greek-style pensions (spartan accommodations, bathless rooms, impeccably clean) that are tucked away in the back streets, away from the harbor and among the bakeries, markets, and service businesses that the locals use. The harborside lane, **Lombardou Strata Marina**, (or paralia) runs between the two spindly arms of man-made breakwater that form the docking area. You'll disembark facing **Platia Solomou**, where the statue of Solomos dominates the busy port patrol.

The **Tourist Police** office (tel. 22-550) with its blue-and-white flag at 62 Lombardou. Officer Nick Gallifopoulos is the best, most helpful tourist representative we met in Greece; he's terribly knowledgeable and enthusiastic fan of his island. His photographic memory has enabled him to memorize the phone number, number of beds, and other vital numerical information relevant to every hotel or lodging on Zakynthos. Nick will help you find a private room or recommend a hotel. The Tourist Police office is open from 7 a.m. to 2:30 p.m., Monday through Friday.

From their office, you can walk away from the port, up Venizelou Street to the **post office** and **O.T.E.** (open daily from 7 a.m. to midnight). Farther up this street are several **banks**, and opposite them the island's **taxi stand**. If you take the first left off Venizelou Street onto Filita Street, in three long blocks you'll come to the **bus station**. Along this road you'll find several travel agents; **Potamitis Tours** (tel. 23-118) at no. 24 offers an around-the-island tour for 1500 drs ($11.50).

The third right turn off Venizelou is Vass. Konstantinou Street, the town's main drag for shops, restaurants, café-bars, and markets. This street leads into the popular **Ag. Margou Square** (St. Mark's Square), where Greek vacationers crowd the outdoor cafés. On the west side of the square is the Solomos Museum and nearby the **Olympic Airways** office. Several churches crop up in the small alleys and many tree-lined squares, so that a walk through Zakynthos's streets alternates between the screech of mopeds, cars, and hustle-bustle activity and the quiet, shaded relief of monumental churches and plazas.

ACCOMMODATIONS: We've seen many changes on Zakynthos. Among them European tourist groups have established a very strong presence here, locking up many hotels for years in advance. At the same time, many D- and E-class inns have closed, making it tough for the individual budget traveler. Below are the hotels where you have a chance at a room; however, if everything is booked, march over to the Tourist Police and request assistance. They'll likely find you accommodations in a private room. Expect to pay about 3000 drs ($23.10) for a double room with private bath, 1600 drs ($12.30) for shared facilities.

Our favorite C-class hotel is away from the port, across from the E.O.T. beach. You'll recognize the **Hotel Bitzaro** (tel. 0695/23-644) by the thick green vines that have take over the whitewashed facade. Inside the hotel is ultra-clean and extremely well maintained. Though it was built in 1981 it looks brand new. The location, across from the beach and away from the town traffic, is a definite plus. Also, the family that runs the Bitzaro is both amiable and helpful. All rooms have private facilities. High-season doubles run 6230 drs ($47.90), singles are 4545 drs ($35), making this a C-class splurge, but on pricey Zakynthos the Bitzaro represents good value.

Of the many C-class hotels in the port town, there are three that are worth recommending. Two of them (both owned by the same family), the Astoria and the Phoenix, are located on Platia Solomou, with fine views over the waterfront. The **Astoria Hotel** (tel. 0695/22-419) is a small, seven-room home with private facilities in all its singles and doubles. High-season rates are 4568 drs ($35.10) for a double. At the **Hotel Phoenix** (tel. 22-719), Mr. Bonikos manages 38 spacious rooms. Bed-and-breakfast doubles are 5910 drs ($45.50) between July 1 and September 15. The somewhat more basic **Apollon** (tel. 0695/22-838), at 30 Tertseti St., is conveniently located a few blocks up from the harbor. The eight rooms here have rates a little lower than the Astoria; summertime doubles are 4015 drs ($30.90).

Budget Bets

If you're not going to splurge for an all-out resort like the Zante Beach, we think staying in one of the smaller, simpler inns is just fine. The following D-class hotels are noted in order of our preference, based on their location, price, and standards of cleanliness. Few of these have rooms with private facilities.

The **Kentriko** (tel. 0695/22-374), at 25 L. Zoi, is two blocks from the square at Foskolou Street. Seven doubles in this white and green-trimmed hostelry rent for 1125 drs ($8.60) per night. The **Astir** (tel. 0695/22-110) and the **Olympia hotels** (tel. 0695/28-328) are at 5 and 7 Yfantourgiou St. respectively, the road that leads out of town (where there's a turnoff for Lagana Beach or the airport), about a 15-minute walk from the port. Both the Astir and the Olympia charge 1625 drs ($12.50) for high-season singles and 2500 drs ($19.20) for doubles. Nearby is the homey **Omenia Hotel** (tel. 0695/22-113), with similar rates. The eight-room **Pension Iris** (tel. 0695/22-046) offers very basic rooms at a relatively low price. Doubles with private bath run 3125 drs ($24) in the high season. The Iris is centrally located, one block in from the harborside near the main platia and across from Zakynthos Tours.

RESTAURANTS AND NIGHTLIFE: A very acceptable and inexpensive in-town restaurant is **To Roloi**, also known as the Clock Restaurant (tel. 23-587), at 7 21st Maiou St. The cover of the menu says it all: "Mama: The Cook, Papa: The Grill Man." This is a family-run shop. Some breakfast-weary English extolled the virtues of their bacon and eggs, but we like the Clock for lunch and dinner. Their large and varied menu will satisfy meat lovers and vegetarians alike and at prices that will allow you to continue your vacation in style. A full meal for two costs about 1500 drs ($11.50). The chefs deserve special notice for serving hot (not tepid) food.

Zakynthos's greatest concentration of pizza joints, snackbars, and restaurants is in Ag-Margou Square. Of these, we like the pizzas, ranging from 750 to 1000 drs ($5.80 to $7.70), at **Veneziana.** Also worth a look is the **Restaurant San Marco,** serving Greek entrées and Italian-inspired pasta. Both establishments are open quite late at night.

Orea Hellas (tel. 28-622) is a sentimental favorite with Zantiots. It's set at 11 Ioannou Legethetou St., in the heart of what was the restaurant district before the earthquake of 1953. Host Takis Kefalinos is a friendly and excellent chef. The small indoor restaurant is decorated with turn-of-the-century prints of Zante, but the food (well displayed in a glass case) is the true decoration. This indoor section is open for lunch and dinner; across the street is an outdoor lot, lit with Christmas tree lights, that opens at dinner for food, music, and wild dancing. The Hellas has a four-piece band that strums Greek oldies. One of Hellas's best entrées is *saltsa,* an island specialty that's something like a beef goulash. Their lamb with big, rice-flake-like noodles is very tasty, and their loin of pork is one of the best-sellers. Add some side dishes of gigantes (delicious), their cheese-drenched moussaka, and a carafe of krassi, and life can't be beat! Two can dine for 1600 drs ($12.30), including the musical show.

Ximeromata, on Foskolou Street, and Zohio's, on Ignatiou, are two tavernas within a block of the Kentriko Hotel that are inexpensive, frequented by locals, and particularly good. At Ximeromata try the grilled chicken, at Zohio's, the stuffed tomatoes or eggplant. For breakfast, we sleep-walked to Café Olympia at 3 Alex. Roma, opposite the square and the Government House. Cheese pies, yogurt, Greek coffee, butter biscuits, and other treats awaited us each morning—and we always left only 375 drs ($2.90) poorer.

Much farther on, at the E.O.T. beach area, is Alladin, in one of the town's more attractive settings. Our favorite kitsch touch is the illuminated petite concrete mermaid in the center court. Though the menu is fairly exhaustive, we'd suggest ordering the less elaborately prepared dishes, such as salads and grilled chicken. We never could figure out two odd menu items: "Eggplant Shoe" and "Drunks Snack." Like we said, stick to the simple things. Prices are moderate, with the tab for two running 1400 drs ($10.80).

Zakynthos really comes alive at night. Two pub/snackbars that are particularly popular are the Ship Inn, where teenage and early 20s Greek mopeders down beer, and the Castello Cafeteria, a brightly lit shop with crowds eating ice cream to the latest tunes. Both places are on the paralia, down toward the Tourist Police.

The two most popular discos near the town are within close proximity to one another along the road to Argassi. Manhattan is the newest, thereby conferring superior status by local standards. Argassi is just a bit farther on and ranks a close second. If you want to venture to Laganas, you might hit the dance floor at the Cameo Disco. Ela Ka Apsose means "Come Back Tonight." It's also the name of a music bar (tel. 25-192) on 22 Alex. Roma where Greeks eat, drink, and enjoy the night crowd.

Film buffs will appreciate the town's two outdoor, vine-covered cinemas. The Cine Lux is across from the E.O.T. beach near the Plaza Hotel. The other is right in town on the paralia. Film time begins when the sun goes down.

ACTIVITIES: If it's a rainy day in Zakynthos town, head for the Solomos Museum (open from 9 a.m. to 1 p.m. and 5 p.m. to 7 p.m. daily) for a look at the author's lifelong collection of literary memorabilia. The Byzantine Museum offers a small collection of Renaissance and Byzantine-era church paintings from the Ionian School of Art (it's open from 8:45 a.m. to 3 p.m. Monday through Saturday, and from 9:30 a.m. to 2:30 p.m. on Sunday; closed Tuesday). The Cathedral of Ag. Dionissios (St. Denis) is one of the island's finest because of the wrought-silver casket in which relics of Zakynthos's patron saint repose. Twice a year, on August 24 and December 17, there are processions throughout the town for Saint Dionissios, who must pass over streets strewn with myrtle branches.

Outside of Zakynthos, in combination with your other explorations, readers with a scuba license might enjoy a dive into the Ionian. Zante Diving/ Driftwood Club (offices on Lagana Beach, tel. 0695/51-196; or in Athens at 109 Othonos St., Kifissia, tel. 01/80-14-789) offers a range of cruise and dive trips off the west coast, where they claim there are more than 1,000 underwater caves to explore.

There is a Handcrafts Cooperative at 42 Lombardou (on the paralia), where locally made items are sold. We admired tablecloths, place mats, and curtains, as well as hand-knit sweaters and woven rugs. There is also a branch shop in Volimes.

AROUND THE ISLAND: While on Zakynthos, explore. You just may find a beach resort that can lure you away from the gourmet fare in the beachless port town. Our Tourist Police friend, Nick Galifopoulos, recommended his favorite beach (which is, as with all Greeks, in his hometown), but we found that Alikes truly is the prettiest white sand beach on the island.

Alikes is ten kilometers north of Zakynthos town along an inland, partially unpaved road (though it's fine for mopeds) that winds up around the verdant hills through vineyards and olive groves. Along the untouristy beach you'll find three hotels. The best value is the **Ionian Star** (tel. 0695/83-416), where high-season bed-and-breakfast doubles are 4750 drs ($36.50). The Tsoukalas Brothers run the **Montreal Hotel** (guess where they've lived abroad?), where you can rent a canoe for your own exploration for under $2 an hour. All 31 bright, clean rooms are angled to face the sea and overlook the Lefkas trees, which shade the hotel's seaside café. At the Montreal (tel. 0695/83-241) doubles with breakfast run 5150 drs ($39.60).

Across the street from the beach are the better-value **Hotel Alikes** (tel. 0695/83-242) and the **Hotel Calmness,** also known as the Gallini, (tel. 0695/83-264), which both charge 3000 drs ($23.10) for a double room in the summer.

Tsilivi Beach is the resort developed just four kilometers north of the port, in the village of Planos. There are two hotels set back in the sandy, reeded area near the water that have missed the boat: they're the perfectly comfortable **Tsilivi Beach** (tel. 0695/23-109), offering doubles with breakfast at 4500 drs ($34.60), and the **Belle Hélène** (tel. 0695/28-788), where clean, sea view doubles with breakfast are 4250 drs ($32.70). Similarly priced rooms are available at the recently built Tereza (tel. 0695/24-501). They just can't compete with the super-slick **Zante Beach** (tel. 0695/72-230), which has the only swimming pool on the island and overlooks the Ionian to Kefalonia. Doubles with a compulsory half-board plan are 4860 drs ($37.40).

In August, the most preferable location on the island is undoubtedly **Calamaki Beach,** where the Crystal Beach Hotel offers a bird's-eye view of the famous loggerhead turtles which come late each evening during the month to lay their eggs on the shore. The **Crystal Beach** (tel. 0695/22-774) is only one of two that managed to get a license during the years that everyone thought turtle footprints were just tractor marks. The World Wildlife Fund has established a "biogenic reserve" at Calamaki to protect the turtles, which were only discovered nine years ago by locals. This has halted other planned hostelries. Besides attracting curious tourists, the turtles actually serve a secondary purpose: they eat jellyfish, making the waters safer for swimming.

South of Zakynthos town the island becomes heavily wooded with pine and olive forests. At **Cape Gerakas,** civilization can be found at the eight-room **Porto Roma Hotel and Taverna.** (Nearby is the **Mavratsis campground.**) Other than this building there are only turtledoves and hidden coves filled with crafty fishermen who are always alert for the movement of fish. Going back toward the city there are many "Room-to-Let" signs among the olive groves decked out with laundry lines and fields filled with grazing cows. There are all-amenity C-class hotels springing up (or already sprung) in the resort areas of **Vassilikos** and **Argassi.** In Argassi traditionally styled and furnished **Hotel Levante** (tel. 0695/22-833) is the most attractive, but the large **Acti Argasiou** at Argassi Beach (tel. 0695/28-094), on the main street in town, is a better value at 5875 drs ($45.20) for a double room.

Last, and probably least, we should mention the fully developed **Laganas Beach**, where large hotels provide accommodations for foreign tour groups (this resort is its own little world). There are Jeeps on the beach, tavernas, snackbars, and pizzerias as well as a notable lack of charm. Nevertheless, if you find yourself stranded in Laganas Beach as part of a budget package, go out and explore the rest of the island. We're sure you'll soon see why the Venetians dubbed this the "Flower of the Levante."

GETTING THERE: There are several **ferryboats** daily to Zakynthos from Kylini, on the Peloponnese mainland. Once you've arrived in this one-function town, you can inquire from the many English-speaking port patrol guards, or call 0695/22-417 for schedule information. **Olympic Airways** makes a stopover at Zakynthos on their Kefalonia-to-Athens flight three times a week in the low season. During the summertime Olympic often puts on extra planes to service the island directly. For more information, contact the Olympic Airways office on Zakynthos, at 16 Alex. Roma St. (tel. 28-611), or call for information in Athens (tel. 01/92-92-111).

Chapter XIV

NORTHERN GREECE

1. Thessaloniki
2. Chalkidiki and Mount Athos
3. In Alexander the Great's Country
4. Exploring Macedonia
5. Thrace

MACEDONIA'S CAPITAL is Thessaloniki, Greece's second-largest city and the port named in antiquity after Alexander the Great's sister. Yet Macedonia also includes the Chalkidiki peninsula, one of Greece's most scenic resorts and host to Mount Athos, a totally independent religious community over 1,000 years old.

There are great Hellenic-era antiquities at Pella, Vergina, and Veria; Roman ruins at Philippi and Amfipolis; one of the world's great museums in Thessaloniki. New discoveries are being made as you read this, at Dion, Sindos, Vergina, and Philippi; others are about to happen. Macedonia was one of the wealthiest members of the Hellenic Federation more than 2,000 years ago, and still prospers in agriculture, industry, and trade today. The fur industry of Kastoria, the tobacco of Kavala, the shipping of Thessaloniki are the kind of growth industries that will keep Greece alive forever. Unlike so many of the islands or the southern cities which survive on tourism generated by past deeds, much of Macedonia, and Thrace, too, can live on its own. Visiting them becomes an exploration into the heart and soul of modern Greece. Thrace, because of its high Moslem population, smoothly bridges the cultural gap that might exist at the border of two countries with such a volatile past and provides a good introduction to Turkey.

Macedonia, for many, will always be known as the Land of Alexander the Great, the soil from which his father, the great King Philip, was born and raised, the base from which he united the Hellenic world as no man had done before. C. Cavafy wrote in *In the Year 200 B.C.:* "and from this marvelous pan-Hellenic expedition triumphant, brilliant in every way, celebrated on all sides, glorified, incomparable, we emerged: the great new Hellenic world. . . . With our far-flung supremacy, our flexible policy of judicious integration, and our common Greek language which we carried as far as Bactria, as far as the Indians. . . ."

1. Thessaloniki

We dreaded going to Salonica after everything we'd heard about it, but were delighted with the city when we arrived. There's neon, some graffiti, even wildly dressed, gracious, and friendly Greek transvestites. Outdoor cafés, fancy cars, stylishly dressed women, nannies and strollers, art galleries, ice-cream parlors, and motorcycle messengers all reminded us of home.

Everything you've heard about Thessaloniki is probably true, but there's a vitality and life to the city that's never been beat. We like to call it the Big Fig.

A BIT OF HISTORY: Greece's second-largest city and third-largest port is the capital of Alexander's country, a city founded as recently as 316 B.C. by the Macedonian General Kassandros. Just two decades earlier King Philip had staged a decisive victory for his Thessalian allies at the Plain of Crocus; the daughter born to him that year was named Thessaloniki ("Thessalian Victory") to commemorate it. When Alexander's half-sister was wed to General Kassandros, the city given to them as home was renamed after her.

During the Roman occupation the Via Egnatia was paved as a through road between Rome, on the Adriatic coast, and Constantinople, capital of the Byzantine Empire. (Egnatia Odos is still one of Thessaloniki's major arteries, paralleling the sea.) Under the Romans it became the most powerful city of northern Greece. Cicero had been exiled here; Antony and Octavius were welcomed in 42 B.C. after the Battle at Philipi, where Brutus and Cassius, betrayers of Julius Caesar, met their deaths. In gratitude, they made Thessaloniki a free city. Politarchs, or magistrates, were elected from the people to govern this Roman city, now independent like Athens.

Saint Paul arrived in about A.D. 49. From the *Acts of the Apostles* we're told: "They came to Thessalonika, where there was a synagogue of the Jews. . . . And Paul went in, as was his custom, and for three weeks he argued with them from the scriptures . . . and some of them were persuaded, and joined Paul and Silas; as did a great many of the devout Greeks and not a few of the leading women. . . ." After he was forced to leave the city, he wrote his "Letter to the Thessalians" to the newly converted Christians of Thessaloniki.

In 306 the Emperor Galerius had Saint Dimitrios, the city's patron, put to death, a deed which caused many years of bloodshed throughout the Goth's occupation. By the seventh century Thessaloniki was one of the greatest Byzantine cities and enjoyed a rare prosperity. In 1430 the Turkish forces of Murad II laid siege to the city; the Turks continued to rule here until 1912.

The expulsions of Jews from Spain during the reigns of Ferdinand V and Isabella (late 15th to early 16th centuries) caused nearly 20,000 to settle in Thessaloniki alone. By the late 1800s we know the Jewish population was over 35,000, and more than 35 synagogues were in use. (The very few Jews who survived World War II still speak Ladino, the old Sephardic tongue from their Basque homeland.)

Most of the architectural and artistic legacy of the Turkish occupation was eradicated by the Greeks, although two minarets and some hamami (Turkish baths) still stand. In this century alone, Thessaloniki has suffered terrible fires and severe bombings, yet something from each era has survived to sustain the patchwork whole we see today. From the Roman era there is the Arch of Galerius; then the great Byzantine chapels, mosaics, and frescoes; the White Tower on the harbor, a 16th-century Ottoman fortification; a stone on the waterfront which marks where King George I was assassinated by a Greek madman; some exquisite neoclassical office buildings and art deco apartments; the park-like exhibition grounds of the International Trade Fair begun in 1926 (which now draws over a million traders in mid-September); the tiered communications tower which dominates the field opposite the archeological museum. Thessaloniki's Aristotle University complex was built after the war over the old Jewish Cemetery.

Today the city is best known as a Byzantine city, for the wealth of art and architecture that remained from the centuries when Thessaloniki was second only to Constantinople. Recent archeological excavations at Derveni and Vergina (site of King Philip's tomb) have turned up such remarkable artifacts from the Macedonian period that we consider Thessaloniki most notable for its archeological museum and nearby sites.

ORIENTATION: Don't be startled to find that this city of over half a million feels as large and bewildering as Athens. Those arriving by train or bus will be at the west end of the city, near Monastiriou Street, which in a few blocks becomes Egnatia Street. You'll confine most of your sightseeing to the rectangular area (about a 20-minute walk east) bordered by Egnatia Street on the north; Venizelou and Dragoumi Streets, which end at Eleftherias Square, to the west; Nikis Street, the harborside avenue, on the south; and the park, archeological museum, and exhibition grounds to the east.

If you have two days to devote to an exploration of the area, we'd recommend a half-day bus tour to Pella (38 kilometers northwest, the birthplace of Alexander the Great and a fascinating site and museum) and an afternoon in the archeological museum; and then a full-day walking tour of the city itself, its Byzantine and Roman sights, cafés, shops, and waterfront. You can determine your schedule around the weekend-only ferry departures for Lesbos and Chios, or around the Tuesday closing of the archeological sites and museums.

Either way, allow time for a taste of the fine restaurants, pleasant cafés, bustling squares, and sophisticated nightclubs that give Thessaloniki a European charm that the overcongested Athens lost long ago.

LAYOUT: Platia Aristotelous (Aristotle Square) is a central meeting grounds on the waterfront, at Nikis St. Here you'll find the **E.O.T.** at no. 8 (tel. 271-888), open weekdays from 8 a.m. to 8 p.m. Monday through Friday, Saturday until 2 p.m., closed Sunday. At no. 7 Nikis St., across the way, is **Olympic Airways** (tel. 260-121); their airport shuttle service brings you to the square. (Other major international airlines have their offices on Aristotelous Square.)

While you're here, walk over to the waterfront: to the left you'll see Thessaloniki's famous landmark, the **White Tower**, recently converted into a museum of local archeological finds. From there, a five-minute walk inland on N. Germanou Street will bring you to the **archeological museum** and the exhibition grounds behind it. To the right of Platia Aristotelous is **Eleftherias Square** and the large pier for commercial vessels and the North Aegean islands ferry. (In 1987 this ferry left only once a week, Saturday, for a voyage to Lesbos and Chios; call 532-289 for schedule information.) Between the port and the train and bus stations, there are several budget hotels.

If you walk straight up through the square to Aristotelous Street, the next intersection will be Tsimiski Street. The **National Bank of Greece** is at no. 11, to the left. Their extended hours are 8 a.m. to 1 p.m. and 6 p.m. to 8 p.m. Monday through Friday, 8 a.m. to 2 p.m. Saturday, and 9:30 a.m. to 12:30 p.m. on Sunday and holidays. At 19 Tsimiski is the **American Express** bank (tel. 272-791), where you can cash or replace travelers checks and pick up mail. The **central post office** is at Aristotelous and Tsimiski (they also change money until 9 p.m.) the **O.T.E.** is two blocks away at Karolou and Ermou Streets.

The second intersection after Tsimiski is Ermou Street. There are several hotels to the left and the famed eighth-century, domed cruciform-shaped **Aghia Sophia Church**. The next major intersection north is Egnatia Street, for more than 2,000 years a major thoroughfare. Egnatia Street has become so noisy that it's impossible to recommend the older hotels seen everywhere along it; instead, we'll note a few newer ones which have been soundproofed.

To the right, at the intersection of Aristotelous and Egnatia Streets, you can look east to the third-century Arch of Galerius. Straight ahead, across Egnatia, is **Dikastirion Square**. On the left are the arched windows and dusty-brown brick of the 11th century Panagia Halkeon Cathedral; on the right is the Roman Exedra. Dikastirion Square serves as the bus terminal for most of the local Thessaloniki bus lines. There are some excellent moderately priced hotels in this area.

USEFUL INFORMATION: The **Tourist Police** (tel. 522-587) are at 10 Egnatia St. The telephone **area code** for Thessaloniki City is 031. . . . The **American consulate** (tel. 266-121) is at 59 Nikis St. (open 8:30 a.m. to 5 p.m. weekdays) and the **British vice consulate** is at 8 Venizelou (tel. 278-006) . . . You can call 106 for **medical emergencies**; the Thessaloniki hospital is near the port, by the bus station. . . . The most popular of the nearby beaches (the water is polluted at the commercial port) is **Ag. Triada**, where the **E.O.T.** has organized camp-grounds, changing rooms, snackbars, and sports facilities (tel. 0392/51-352). From Dikastirion Square, take bus no. 73. Other, less-crowded beaches include **Epanomi** (bus no. 69) and **Mihaniona** (bus no. 72).

The **Ministry of Northern Greece**, Diikitiriou Square (tel. 270-092), is the place to pick up Mount Athos permits; apply for permits to visit the holy site at the E.O.T. office. Foreign language periodicals can be found at several kiosks near the port or Aristotelous Square, but the best selection can be found at Malliaris Kaisia, at 9 Aristotelous St. This excellent **bookstore** also has a wide selection of regional maps, guidebooks, phrasebooks, tawdry romance novels, cardboard fold-up models of Greek temples, and stationary supplies. They're open 9 a.m. to 9 p.m. daily.

GETTING TO, FROM, AND AROUND THE REGION: Thessaloniki is the major transportation hub for all vehicular, air, train, and water traffic in Macedonia and Thrace. Thousands of Europeans pour through Greece's northern borders every July and August.

By Car

If you've driven into Thessaloniki, good luck trying to find a parking space downtown. Many of the new hotels have parking lots and charge 500 drs ($3.85) to 800 drs ($6.10) a day for parking. To explore Thessaloniki, park your car and walk, or sample the public bus system.

Driving is the easiest way to reach the popular seaside suburb of **Thermae**, just southeast of the city and somewhat comparable to Athens's Glifada. There are some excellent fish restaurants and "hot" outdoor discos in Thermae. **Panorama**, just 12 kilometers from the city center, is another popular suburb, quiet and prettier, with classy hotels, restaurants, cafés, and street life.

Renting a car is the most convenient way (and because of increased bus fares, a good value for two or more people) to explore the Alexander country; such a day tour might include Vergina and the nearby city of Veria, Pella, and Dion, or Kavela and Philipi. There's a **Hertz** office (tel. 224-906) at 4 Venizelou St. and at the airport; an **Avis** office (tel. 227-126) at 3 Nikis St. and at the airport; as well as smaller, local rental companies. A compact car will cost about 4000 drs ($31), including insurance, per day.

By Air

Olympic has several daily flights to most European capitals and major American cities. There are at least six flights daily to Athens, twice weekly to Ioannina, once a day to Limnos and Lesbos, three times a week to Rhodes, and twice weekly to Iraklion, Crete. The Olympic Airways bus departs one hour before flight time for the 16-kilometer ride to the airport; the fare is 150 drs ($1.15). There is a Tourist Police and an E.O.T. office (tel. 425-011, ext. 215 or 221), and a duty-free shop at the airport for international travelers. Call 230-240 in Thessaloniki or 01/92-92-111 in Athens for Olympic schedule information.

By Bus

There are several local and long-distance bus stations in Thessaloniki, depending on where you want to go. The E.O.T. provides the most reliable schedule information, because the telephone numbers listed here are not always answered by English-speaking operators. Buses from Athens leave from the terminal at 100 Kifissou St. (tel. 51-48-856) four times daily for the 7½-hour ride. They arrive at 67 Monastiriou St. (opposite the railroad station); for information call 516-104.

Buses to Pella depart every half hour from Anagenisseos, two blocks south of the train station, for a 45-minute ride northeast of the city; buses to Edessa/Pella and to Volos leave from 22 Anagenisseos St.; call 525-100 for Pella information and 543-087 for Volos information. Around the corner from this station at no. 10, 26 Oktovriou St. is the stop for buses to Veria (tel. 522-160), where you have to change for the Vergina bus (a one-hour trip). Buses to Chalkidiki leave from 68 Karakassi St. (tel. 924-444 for information).

Note: Across the street from the bus station you'll find several companies (with K.T.E.L. signs) selling long-distance bus tickets to all parts of Greece. You may also find it handy to cross over to the railroad station (see below) which has an information desk, city map posted outside, and the nearest taxi stand.

The O.S.E. bus lines has a special Thessaloniki to Istanbul daily bus (the trip is 15 hours long; the fare is $28) and an Athens to Thessaloniki to Paris express stopping in Trieste, Belgrade, Milan, and Lyon. It departs Wednesday and Saturday at 7 p.m., takes 56 hours, and in 1987 cost 14,530 drs ($112). Check with O.S.E. (tel. 238-143) at the train station.

By Train

Trains arrive at the Thessaloniki station on Monastiriou Street (call 517-518 for information).

There is one train daily to Istanbul. You get your money's worth in scenery as you tear through Thrace for the 24-hour ride; the 1987 fare was 3840 drs ($30) in coach class, but EurailPass holders can ride free until Pithion at the Greece/Turkey border, and then catch a Turkish train to Istanbul for about $10.

The Thessaloniki train station is a world unto itself. All day and night trains are pulling in from throughout Greece, all the European cities (lots of EurailPasses go through here!), and from Turkey and east to Asia. The Information Booth is open daily to meet all trains; if they're out of maps, study the mural map of the city outside. There are two banks, and a post office, O.T.E., both open daily, located to the right as you exit. The luggage store is open 24 hours and charges 60 drs (50¢) per piece of luggage until midnight each day.

ACCOMMODATIONS: In Thessaloniki there are more older hotels in the budget-price range and more new ones in the businessman's expense-account range. This probably reflects the surge of visitors who arrive each August and September for the International Trade Fair; during the Trade Fair (when demand is high) many hotels raise their prices by 15% to 20% or make continental breakfast compulsory. Another drawback in the Thessaloniki hotel scene is that many of the city's budget hotels are in neighborhoods that have become intolerably noisy in recent years. So although some of our recommendations mean that you'll have to walk an extra few blocks to sightsee, at least you'll be getting enough sleep to enjoy it.

Around Diikitiriou Square

This prosperous area is a quiet enclave of professional people, fashionable shops, government offices, and a relaxing park three blocks west of Dikastirian Square. The old-fashioned **Hotel Pella** (tel. 031/524-221) is on pleasing Dragoumi Street, at no. 65. Clean, comfortable doubles with private toilets, some with balconies, are a fair price for this ritzy area at 3600 drs ($27.50).

The 56-room **Park Hotel** at Dragoumi 81 (tel. 031/524-121) has a large modern lobby and bar that come as close to a Hilton as you'll find in this price range. The spacious rooms are air-conditioned, have music, telephones, and private bathrooms. Recently the Italians confirmed our enthusiasm by giving the Park their Hotel Oscar! Rates are 4500 drs ($35).

On the other side of the square is the **Hotel Esperia** (tel. 031/269-321), at 58 Olympou St. The rooms are carpeted, each has a large tiled bathtub, and their front balconies overlook the classical Ministry of Northern Greece building. The Esperia offers very high quality, at 4500 drs ($35) for a double. When you exit the Esperia, two blocks to the right you'll find the ruins of the Roman Agora and across the street, the café favored by off-duty policemen and bus drivers.

The top budget choice in this choice neighborhood is the vintage **Mitropolis Hotel** (tel. 031/525-540), located one block north of noisy Egnatia at no. 24 Sygrou St. Plain, but charming and spotless, renovated rooms with high ceilings but without bath run a cheap (for this town) 2100 drs ($16) for two. The management is friendly, the neighborhood pleasant, and our local favorite Taverna Life is just down the street. Another excellent value, with balconies and baths in the large rooms, is the modern **Hotel Bill** (tel. 031/537-666), across the street from the Mitropolis at no. 26. Spotless double rooms that compete with much pricier establishments are kept by the friendly owner, Bill Kitsos; they'll set you back 2800 drs ($21.50). The same room without private bath runs 2400 drs ($18.50).

Around the Port

The port is always Kyle's first choice of where to stay; after all, when in Greece, get a room with a water view! The 39-room **Hotel Continental** (tel. 031/277-553), located at 5 Komninou St., right off the water and a block from the E.O.T. at café-filled Aristotelous Square, is certainly "continental": its elegant, restored façade, glass-doored cage elevator, and wooden moldings all fit the bill. Unfortunately, the high-ceilinged rooms are rather mundane, though perfectly clean and a good value at 3500 drs ($27) for a double with bath, or 2300 drs ($18) for a bathless double. Old-house buffs will prefer the unrenovated bathless rooms for their architectural integrity.

The aging **Hotel Rea** (tel. 031/278-449), down the block at no. 6, is as pretty as the Continental from the outside, but the rooms and the blasé concierge make the interior less appealing. Nonetheless, 29 clean rooms at 2300 drs ($18) for a bathless double or 2800 drs ($21.50) for your own double with a private, modernized facility, cannot be scoffed at.

On quiet Mitropoleos Street is the old-fashioned **Hotel Tourist** (tel. 031/276-335), located at no. 21, one block from the port. A very clean, well-maintained double with shower in the room, toilet in the hall, runs a reasonable 2600 drs ($20). Not far away on not-so-quiet Tsimiski Street you'll find the **Hotel**

Palace (tel. 031/270-885), at no. 21. It's an old-fashioned kind of place with the largest rooms and largest private bathrooms in town. Rooms in the front have balconies and major street noise. We'd head straight to the relative quiet of viewless rear rooms and pay 3750 drs ($29) for a very clean double.

Around the Railroad Station

Though not our favorite neighborhood, the area around the railroad station (leading into Egnatia) may be convenient for late-night bus or train arrivals, even though our other hotel recommendations are all within a five-minute ($2) cab ride or 20-minute walk of the station. The **Hotel Vergina** (tel. 031/527-452) is down the road a bit from the station, at 19 Monastiriou St. This eight-story, white concrete edifice has pleasant, spacious rooms with all the amenities, balconies, and an underground parking lot (for a small fee). Doubles are a pricey 6000 drs ($46).

The closest hotel to the railroad station is across the street and one block to the left—the older C-class **Hotel Rex** (tel. 031/517-051). The Rex is at 39 Monastiriou, and its third-floor sun roof has an urban sort of charm. Clean, bright doubles with bath are 3750 ($29); without bath, 2400 ($18.50).

Egnatia Street Hotels

As befits any inn astride a through-road in operation for thousands of years, the hotels on busy Egnatia Street are, if nothing else, very convenient, but above all, noisy. The **Hotel Delta** (tel. 031/516-321), at 13 Egnatia St., gets top billing here for its small, kidney-shaped rooftop swimming pool. Many of the rooms have air conditioning, they're all clean and furnished in that nondescript style that's so C class, high season, the 113 rooms rent for 4200 drs ($32.30) a double.

The older **Hotel Ariston** (tel. 031/519-630) is at 5 Diikitiriou St., about 50 meters off the corner of Egnatia Street. The Ariston has double rooms with private baths for 2600 drs ($20), but the bathless rooms have strange, amusing "Murphy"-style pull-out showerstalls, with just the toilet outside in the hall. It's quite an adventure staying at the Ariston.

The Low End

In Thessaloniki this consists of two youth hostels, the **YWCA** (or **XEN** in Greek), at the superbly located 11 Ag. Sophias St., and the coed Youth Hostel (tel. 031/225-946) at 44 Svolou St., near the Arch of Galerius. The women-only **XEN** (tel. 0321/276-144) is in a well-kept neoclassical structure just one block from the waterfront. The high-ceilinged rooms, lounge, and TV parlor are cozy and comfortable; there's an inexpensive cafeteria as well. Single rooms are 850 drs ($6.50); beds in a double or triple dorm are 680 drs ($5.25) each. Dorm beds at the Youth Hostel are the same price.

RESTAURANTS: There's a certain joie de vivre about the Salonicans that makes dining out in this cosmopolitan city something of an unexpected pleasure. There are many tried-and-true restaurants that the International Trade Fair has kept alive, as well as many inexpensive, simple taverns and grills, and westernized fast-food chains that a traveler in any budget range can afford.

Along the Waterfront

Here is where you'll find most of the traditional gourmet eateries. **Stratis**, at 19 Nikis, is a very attractive, low-key restaurant across from the harbor with a varied, traditional Greek menu: lots of meats, excellent imported wines, seafood specialties, and a range of excellently prepared and displayed *mezes* (the traditional array of appetizer-size portions of piquant foods, had with ouzo or wine). The regionally-produced Corona white wine is particularly good. In the evening, call ahead for reservations (tel. 279-353), and dress up for Stratis (you'll enjoy it more that way). An excellently cooked, flavorful meal that is impeccably presented should run about 1000 drs ($7.70) per person, with wine.

Just down the harbor road is the more traditional continental cuisine of **Olympos-Naoussa**. Another elegant, older restaurant catering to the suit, tie, and grandmother crowd, it's a bit more expensive than the Stratis, but serves up *midia tiganita*, a local specialty of fried mussels. The service is good, even when busy; call for reservations (tel. 275-715). Both are open for lunch and dinner daily and have less formal, outdoor seating.

For light snacks, heavy ice-cream sundaes, and tart fresh lemonade try the **Gardenia Café Pâtisserie,** on Aristotelous Square. It's open day and night and its comfy, leather-plush chairs are often filled with postcard writers, children, weary parents, and youngsters in love. It's not cheap, but it's alive and lots of fun.

Tavernas

Rogotis, at 8 Venizelou St. (tel. 277-694), known by its former street address but actually named Soutzoukakia, has an interesting menu with varied appetizers, meat dishes, grilled and skewered fish, and a tasty, ground meat *soutzoukakia* that's made there daily. Rogotis is just off Eleftherias Square. This old-fashioned, dark-wood taverna is open daily for lunch and Tuesday, Thursday, and Friday for dinner; closed Sunday.

Another café that's centrally located for day-tour walkers is called **Koumparakia**, (tel. 271-905) and it's across from the Arch of Galerius, behind the Sunken Church. Koumparakia is always filled with Greeks licking their lips over the excellent grilled calamari and broiled whole fish. It's open lunch and dinner; at both tavernas you can feast for about 800 drs ($6.25) per person.

Ta Spata is a large, brightly lit outdoor grill under the arcade at 28 Aristotelous Street and Egnatia Street, at the foot of Dikastirion Square. They're open till midnight. Souvlaki, scrumptious grilled chicken, and gyros are the things to order; lunch or dinner costs 500 drs ($3.85) to 750 drs ($5.75) per person.

Another choice is the popular **Tiffany's** (tel. 274-022), an elegant outdoor and indoor taverna on a shaded, quiet pedestrian mall. It's at 3 Iktinou St., just a five-minute walk from the archeological museum, in the midst of the upscale shopping district. Tiffany's well-heeled Salonican crowd goes for the grilled meats and potatoes along with their *melitzanosalata* and *choriatiki* (about 900 drs/$7 per person). Tiffany's is busy day and night but its tranquil surroundings always seem a respite from the chaotic city.

One of the best of the neighborhood tavernas is **Pizza Grill Life** (tel. 545-337). We were a little confused by the name, but Life has brought small tables and bushy asparagus ferns to the peaceful corner of Philippou and Sygrou Streets, just a two blocks north of Egnatia. The remarkably courteous (for Thessaloniki) waiters suggest the grilled lamb and veal or any of the varied hot and cold vegetable and salad hors d' oeuvres. With retsina or a Henninger and fresh, individual loaves of bread to dunk in taramosalata and olive oil, two can while away several pleasant hours for about 1300 drs ($10).

NIGHTLIFE: Nightlife and dining go well together in Thessaloniki, where many discos have restaurants and many restaurants are pleasant enough to while away the evening in. **Remvi** (tel. 411-233), in the suburb of Nea Krini, is known for its romantic garden setting and excellent seafood. After a dinner of several *mezedes* and some Corona wine, you'll feel light enough to get up and dance on their outdoor patio. The roof-garden of the **Macedonia Palace Hotel,** on Kennedy Boulevard, is another stiff-priced choice, but the beautiful views over Thessaloniki Bay justify one late-night or sunset drink.

The disco and bar scene changes seasonally, so this year's picks may be next year's duds. In 1987 the hot bars were **Belair** and **Enplo**, both near the waterfront east of Aristotoleus Square. The summer disco crowd moves outdoors and out of town, on the road just past the airport, where presumably the decibel level will not disturb sleeping planes. The contenders in this high-stakes play-off are **Amnisia**, with its tropical environs and swimming pool; **Acropol**, for the new wave crowd: and **Swing** ($6 cover charge at each). It's about a 12-kilometer ($4) cab ride to get there, but don't bother going before 11 p.m. because the crowds are still at the bars.

If you're up for a nightime *volta,* that leisurely Greek saunter, there's no better place to do it than along the harbor in front of Aristotelous Square. Between there and the White Tower you'll be entertained and romanced by the moon and the waves. If you wander west to the waterfront around the commercial and ferryboat pier, and particularly up to the region of Polytechniou and 26 Oktovriou Streets, you'll find some colorful ladies of the night, along with clubs, bars, and neon signs.

To escape reality, sample the modern, new **cinemas** along Nikis Street, opposite the White Tower. In a row you'll find one playing the latest Italian fare, the latest Greek fare, and six-month-old American fare. Both the **White Tower** on N. Germanou Street and the **Dimotiko Teatro Kipou** have outdoor performances (check with E.O.T. for the schedule).

WHAT TO SEE AND DO IN THE CITY: If you're only in Thessaloniki for one hour, and it costs you $50 to get there and back, we still say the **archeological museum** and its contents are an unforgettable, not-to-be-missed, once-in-a-lifetime experience. Recent finds at Vergina (site of Philip of Macedon's Royal Tomb) have added such lustrous displays to this newly renovated, well-laid-out, lit, and maintained museum that anyone should be able to enjoy it.

The Archeological Museum

The museum is organized in two circles: the inner galleries are dedicated to recent finds from Sindos; the outer circle is most of the older portion of the museum. A new wing houses the magnificent finds at Derveni and Vergina.

The Sindos wing, opened in 1982, displays sixth- to fifth-century B.C. examples of gold hair ornaments, jewelry, filigree pendants, dollhouse-size tables and chairs, and some delicate miniature glass amphoras. Most of these tombs were found underwater, so all metal other than gold was badly damaged. The buried warrior's golden face mask and helmet from 520 B.C. rival anything connected with Philip's tomb. One case has gold-filigree pomegranates the size of a baby's fingernail, but carved in such detail that you can't imagine anyone's fingers being small enough to create it.

In the next galleries there are grave steles from Veria and fine marble statues from the ancient Agora of Thessaloniki, from around the first to second centuries A.D. In the central gallery you'll find a fascinating display devoted to 2,300 years of Thessaloniki daily life, including a striking third-century mosaic from a local house.

In the fourth gallery there's a bold, strong sculpture of Emperor Augustus, still obviously very much in control even if frozen in stone. The color photographs in the hallway at the end of this gallery announce the new Macedonian Wing.

At Derveni, gold and bronze from the last half of the fourth century B.C., as well as ornate silverwork burial gifts, were found. In the beginning of the gallery there are finds from a royal tomb at Katerini and from Thermi and Stavroupolis. But the real prizes are from Vergina, the first great capital of Macedonia, birthplace of King Philip II. Excavations in the late 1970s unearthed one of the most important archeological finds since the Tut tombs, the royal tomb of Philip himself, untouched in 2,100 years. The riches of the find are staggering, none more so than the exquisite crown of the great king. The solid gold funerary box is another example of the fine level of craftmanship of the Macedonians; even the bones of Philip are displayed, providing an eerie experience for the viewer. Imagine the man that was Philip—a great leader, warrior, king—now a set of surprisingly small bones which today are far overshadowed by the splendor of the objects found with him in the royal tomb. This is a gallery not to be missed.

The archeological museum, two blocks up from the White Tower at the intersection of Angelaki and Tsimiski Streets, is open daily from 8 a.m. to 7 p.m., closed Tuesday. Admission is 350 drs ($2.65). Professor Andronicos' museum guide at 600 drs ($4.60) is great and a must for the quality of the reproductions!

Other Museums

There are some new and interesting additions to the museum scene in Thessaloniki.

The **White Tower**, also called the Bloody Tower (Levkos Pirgos) because it was the site of a Turkish massacre of Christian soldiers, was built in the early 16th century after designs by the renowned Ottoman architect, Sinan. The interior has been recently renovated to house archeological finds from sites within the modern-day city. Broad stone stairs circumnavigate the cool cylinder and lead to five small display floors. Marble architectural ornaments, column fragments, mosaics, fourth to fifth century tombs with wall paintings, and Byzantine-era finds fill the vaulted coves and wonderful low-ceilinged galleries. Don't miss the two enameled, carved gold Byzantine bracelets on the third floor. The fifth floor is used for temporary exhibitions. The White Tower is open daily from 8:45 a.m. to 9 p.m., closed Tuesday; admission 350 drs ($2.70).

The **Ethnological and Popular Art Museum** (tel. 830-591), located at 68 Vassilissis Olgas St., exhibits items connected with the last 250 years of northern Greek history (ornaments, weapons, household items, costumes). It is open daily 9:30 a.m. to 5:30 p.m., closed Tuesday. The **Hellenic Museum of Photography** is located in a small gallery on the second floor of no. 23 Mitropoleos St., between Eleftherias and Aristotolous squares. It has a fine and growing collection of Greek photographs, both current and historical, and revolving exhibits of foreigners' work.

A Walking Tour of Thessaloniki

Our walking tour begins with a quick coffee on Thessaloniki's most attractive square, **Platia Aristotelous**. The platia opens up to Nikis Street, the waterfront drive along the city's busy port. Make a left on the portside avenue and proceed until you come to the **White Tower**, a symbol of medieval Thessaloniki and now, a museum. Continue up Vassileos Georgiou; to your left, two blocks beyond the White Tower, is the **archeological museum**. At this point you might want to stop for a look at what is fast becoming Greece's premier collection.

To continue with the walking tour, turn left on Angelaki, and after five blocks, turn left on Egnatia until reaching the massive **Arch of Galerius**. The arch was constructed in A.D. 303 to commemorate the Roman victories of Emperor Galerius over forces in Persia, Armenia, and Asia Minor. The reliefs, which portray the battle with the Persians, have been badly eroded, though the arch is still impressive. Walk through it, continuing to the domed **Rotunda**. Built only a few years after the arch, the Rotunda served as a mausoleum for the emperor. Later it was converted to a Christian sanctuary and decorated with masterful mosaics. In 1590 it was converted into a mosque and remained in use under the Ottomans until 1912.

The Rotunda has been shrouded in scaffolding for years and will open to the public in the 1990s. It will be worth the wait for the finely executed mosaics within.

The next stop will be of particular interest for those coming from or headed to Turkey. Walk north from the Rotunda, away from Egnatia, until you reach the next main avenue, Ag. Dimitriou. Continue to the right along Dimitriou a couple of blocks up to the Turkish consulate (it's the "compound" on the corner of Ag. Pavlou Street), and next door, the **birthplace of Mustafa Kemal Atatürk**. Born in 1881, Atatürk is revered in Turkey as the father of the modern nation. All political parties in Turkey, from anarchist to totalitarian, rally behind the teachings and ideals of Atatürk. The house (open from 9 a.m. to noon, Monday through Friday) contains historical photos, Turkish-style furniture, and other paraphernalia. Apply to the Turkish consulate for entry to this fascinating site. Don't be alarmed if they request your passport as a "deposit"; it's the price you'll pay for "security" precautions.

Return to Egnatia and cross the street, to the subterranean **Church of the Metamorphosi** (in between the two parallel streets that run perpendicular to Germanou). This one isn't on the normal tour route, but we liked it for its sunken, listing foundation and the perfectly preserved Byzantine brick-and-tile exterior. (If you've stopped at the church and are looking for a bite to eat, try the Koumparakia Restaurant, which overlooks this tiny sanctuary.)

Two blocks down, on diagonally running Patriorhou Ioakim, is one of Thessaloniki's most important Byzantine churches, **Aghia Sophia**. Constructed in the eighth century, Aghia Sophia marked an important turning point in Western architecture by incorporating the Oriental cupola and a cruciform style over the older basilica form. When the Ottomans' ruled Thessaloniki, the church was converted to a mosque. The interior mosaics, including a figure of Christ enthroned on a rainbow and surrounded by the Apostles and olive trees, date from the 11th century.

Return to Egnatia, turn left, and make a right on Ag. Sophia St. to the **Panagia Ahiropiitos**. The name means "Our Lady Not Painted by Human Hands," referring to the icon that is said to have miraculously appeared at this, one of the oldest Byzantine churches in Thessaloniki (fifth century). The mosaics on the upper walls and finely filtered light from the arched windows are reason enough to take a quick look inside (open 8 a.m. to 1 p.m. and 5 p.m. to 7 p.m. daily).

Continue up Egnatia, turning right at the bus station and following the road two blocks to the **Roman Agora and theater**. Thessaloniki was the Roman capital of the Macedonian province, and one of the most significant cities in the empire. The large square contains the few remains of what was once a center of Roman activity; a theater, vestiges of the water system, and a solitary column are all that survive. Above the northern perimeter of the market is a small shaded park that's ideal for a rest, picnic, or cool drink.

For those who may be disappointed that so many of the famous churches are closed or under scaffolding, consider taking an out-of-the-way interlude in this otherwise geographically concentrated walking tour. The eventual destination is **Aghia David**, a fifth-century church with mosaics of the Vision of Ezekiel.

The location is Epimenidou (the "old town," much like the Plaka in Athens), and instead of giving you detailed directions on how to get there (difficult), we'll give some general guidelines. Walk away from the direction of Egnatia, crossing Ag. Dimitriou and past the huge reconstructed church of Ag. Dimitrios (stop in if you're touring on Sunday; they have baptismal ceremonies all morning long and it's quite a sight!). Continue in the same direction up Ag. Nikolaou Street and veer right onto Epimenidou. Somewhere in that neighborhood is tiny Aghia David. Ask any passerby for exact directions.

Return to the Platia Dikastirion on Egnatia and the 11th-century **Panagia Halkeon**. According to an inscription the church was built in A.D. 1028. If such a thing is possible, the Panagia Halkeon could be characterized as a "seductive" sanctuary, with soft Byzantine curves and domes and highly articulated doorways. Alternating brick, mortar, and stone add a subtle pattern to the church's classical design.

Walk down Venizelou back toward the platia and you'll pass the **Bedestan**, or Ottoman bazaar, still filled with jewelers. You'll see the main shopping streets, where shoes and clothes are often a bargain. Our recommendation is to complete the tour by returning to Aristotelous platia, ordering a fresh, delicious Greek lemonade—and congratulating yourself on seeing the best of Thessaloniki.

2. Chalkidiki and Mount Athos

Chalkidiki (Halkidiki), the three-fingered peninsula settled centuries ago by sailors from Chalkis in Evia, is revered by the Greeks for its lush pine forests and gold sand beaches. Now, however, most of the forests have been cut back to make way for the condos and the narrow beach strips are so overcrowded that it's hard to tell the sand from the flesh.

Kassandra, the westernmost (left, on a map) finger of the peninsula was the first to be developed. The roads throughout are packed with condominiums and vacation villas for Thessalonikans, and there are hotels or mega-resort complexes for European group tourists around each sandy strip.

Sithonia, the middle finger, has a more densely forested interior and a very rugged and beautiful coastline, whose few sand beaches have been much less developed. Campers will find ample opportunities along the west coast, especially at Nikitas, Tripotamos, and Porto Koufo. Along the east coast there are campsites at the beaches of Sarti, Ag. Sikias, and Kalamitsion, and as always, rooms to let along the coast road and in the larger inland villages such as Sikea. Sithonia's biggest resort complex is at Neas Marmaras, now renamed Porto Carras after its developer. He planted one million grape vines, almond trees, orange and grapefruit trees, and flowering bushes after filling in a mosquito-breeding lake at this picturesque site. Besides its three hotels—the Meliton, the Sithonia Beach, and the slightly more modest Village Inn—Mr. Carras built a marina, several swimming pools, tennis courts, and an 18-hole golf course. We wouldn't dare quote the prices, but if you have a wild urge to cavort in this playground for the wealthy (or conference center for expense-account types) you can get more information at their offices in Athens (tel. 01/36-46-241), Thessaloniki (tel. 031/268-626), or Neas Marmaras, Chalkidiki (tel. 0375/71-381).

The eastern (or right) finger of Chalkidiki is **Mount Athos** (Agion Oros, the Holy Mountain), the independent Greek Orthodox state revered by the Greeks. The 20 monasteries that inhabit this most scenically beautiful of the fingers are closed to women visitors, and will only allow ten men ashore each day to visit (see the Mount Athos section below on information regarding permits). You can visit Ouranopoli (the closest "open" city) by bus, but this small village gets inundated with day-trippers who join the Round-Athos Cruises and will not exactly provide the spiritual experience that women readers might seek. Instead, you'd do well to join a Mount Athos day trip or quietly explore Ierissos (the ancient Acanthos), Gomati, or Megali Panagia on your own. Also of interest in the eastern sector is Arnea, a mountain town whose women are known for their hand-weaving, making shopping for fabrics and flokati rugs a real treat. Aristotle, the great philosopher, was born in nearby Stagira, where he lived for several years until heading north to tutor King Philip of Macedon's son, Alexander.

A POPULAR DAY TRIP: You can take the public bus to Poligiros, the capital of Chalkidiki, just 69 kilometers from Thessaloniki, but unfortunately the drive doesn't take you through any of the beautiful scenery for which the peninsula is justly famed. **Poligiros** has become a good-sized modern town of little interest to most tourists, save for the **archeological museum** near its north end. Museum and archeology fans will find the collection of primitive clay figurines from the fifth century B.C., and the Picasso esque style of painting on the black figure vases particularly pleasing. For the cognoscenti, there are fragments from the Sanctuary of Zeus Ammon near Kallithea on the Kassandra finger and finds from the ancient city of Acanthos (at Ierissos), where Aristotle taught. The museum is open Monday through Saturday from 9 a.m. to 4 p.m., on Sunday from 10 a.m. to 3:30 p.m. Admission is 250 drs ($2).

If this is as far as you'll get in Chalkidiki, and you have the energy, a hike up **Profitias Elias hill** provides a wonderful prospect. West of Poligiros is the village of **Petralona**, famous for its natural cave, where a skull and some remains were found indicating habitation by a primeval man over 700,000 years old (the first tourist?). The cave is filled with colorful stalagmites and stalactites, and the paleontological museum at the site is quite interesting; open daily from 9 a.m. to 6 p.m. Petralona can be reached by bus via Nea Kallikatia and is also the object of many local day tours.

For those with only a day, we'd recommend one of the **Mount Athos cruise** excursions that originate in Thessaloniki. As offered by **Doucas Tours** (tel. 031/224-100) and others on alternate days, this day trip costs 4500 drs ($35) for a coach tour across Chalkidiki to Ormos Panagia on the central finger of Sithonia, then a cruise along the west coast of Athos to Ouranopolis.

If you'll have an opportunity to visit other parts of Greece (such as the Ionian islands, the western coast south of Ioannina, and much of the Peloponnese), which offer the same lovely combination of green forests and sand beaches, we'd suggest you avoid the crowded Chalkidiki resorts. For those who'd like a break from the urban sprawl of Salonica and need a few day's away, we offer a brief look at—

KASSANDRA: The west coast of Kassandra is less built up and presents possibilities for enjoying the peninsula's evergreen-clothed mountains with some sandy and pebble beaches. From **Nea Fokea**, the small, sandy beach marked by a lone Venetian watchtower guarding rowboats and sunbathers, there are rooms to let until you come to Kallithea, an overbuilt stretch of road with the large, group-oriented Zeus Ammos Resort.

Kriopigi, five kilometers south, is the site of the official **E.O.T. campground** (tel. 0374/51037), which you should call before even considering during the months of June to September. It's on a long, narrow length of sandy beach, and grassy plots are shaded by oleanders and pines. Fees are 500 drs ($4) per person plus 575 drs ($4.50) per tent site. There are rooms to let above the main-road tavernas. Buses to Kriopigi from Thessaloniki run five times daily and cost

780 drs ($6). (There's another E.O.T. Campground at the Xenia Hotel in Paliouri on the south tip.)

Haniotis is ten kilometers south of Kriopigi and is developed enough to satisfy anyone looking for action. Cafés, pizzerias, fish tavernas, and the *Space Odyssey* video-games parlor will occupy those not lying on the long, fine-sand beach. In the modern resort village, the **Sirtaki Taverna** is popular with bused-in tour groups who join the dancing waiters in retsina-inspired revelry. Nice, seaview accommodations are available at the 45-room, C-class **Hotel Strand** (tel. 0374/51-261), where compulsory halfboard is the rule all year. High-season doubles are 9200 drs ($70). In the village there's the small C-class **Hotel Ermis** (tel. 0374/51-245) and the **Hotel Haniotis** (tel. 0374/51-323). For a total Dionysian revel, try the **Hotel Pella** (tel. 0374/51-679, or 031/283-344 in Thessaloniki), a resort with German/Greek comanagement that's got European glitz mixed with bouzouki and a Greek cuisine half-board plan. There are 179 carpeted rooms overlooking the two pools, green lawns, flower gardens, and a long, clean sandy beach. Besides the restaurants, bars, disco, and kids' playground, the Pella has an all-weather tennis court, plus watersports facilities and nearby horseback riding. It's open from April 1 to October 10; doubles with half board range from 8200 drs ($63) to 11,100 drs ($116), depending on the season.

In **Pefkohori** you can rent rooms in the touristy village; better to reap the benefits of so much company at a full-scale resort like Kallithea or head for a hermit's pleasure a little farther away at the village of **Ag. Paraskevi**. Here, on a hilltop with wonderful views over the pine forests to the bright blue Aegean is the **Hotel Aphroditi** (tel. 0374/71-228). Signs lead to Loutra, which draws tourists looking for a cure in the hot, sulfurous waters of the nearby thermal springs. Doubles at the B-class Aphroditi are spacious, with wonderful views, though some of these are blocked by a private home under construction right in front. Aphrodite, the charming German-speaking hostess and good chef, offers double rooms including half board for $63. (There are a couple of rooms to let in some of the private homes on the hill and in the less-well-situated Villa Hotel on this road.)

And now for a look at—

MOUNT ATHOS: The monastic community inhabiting 20 monasteries and 700 related houses perched on the Holy Mountain has remained untouched by time since Saint Anathasios founded the Lavra Monastery in A.D. 963. At its peak, Athos had 40,000 monks; the Crusaders sold 39,000 of them into slavery. Today, Mount Athos is an independent religious state that's not even part of Greece: the monks follow their own Orthodox calendar (whose year begins 17 days after ours); their time zone is four hours later than at Ouranopolis, the nearest lay community. In the 1981 census, Athos had 1,500 residents; only 20 or 25 monks still live at each of the open monasteries.

Many of the customs practiced at Mount Athos are unique, but the basic precepts of the Orthodox religion are the same as those studied at Tinos, Patmos, and Meteora (Greece's other religious enclaves). The Orthodox service you'll hear on Athos is the same you'd hear in Moscow, Bucharest, or Bulgaria. Visitors with some knowledge of the Orthodox faith will gain tremendously from their conversations with the monks, all of whom are well educated and speak several languages. The Bibles, icons, frescoes, and religious art displayed in the monasteries comprise one of the best collections of its kind in the world.

Laymen are able to get permission to stay for up to four days on the Holy Mountain. Days are spent hiking between the monasteries and exploring the lush, forested, and flowering countryside. By sunset you must reach the monastery where you'll spend the night because they lock their doors. The monks work at farming (they grow their own food), study and pray in the early morning, and sleep in the afternoon. Nights are spent dining, and talking with the few guests they receive. Meals consist of locally grown eggplant, onions, olives, and bread, with the occasional tomato, cucumber, or fresh fish (if one is caught). The monks will offer you wine and their homemade ouzo to soften the sudden austerity the lay visitor meets.

Of the 20 monasteries that are open, **Lavra**, the oldest and one of the few that hasn't been rebuilt, is the most architecturally pure. Fortress walls surround this stone, wood-trimmed Byzantine compound. The **Monastery of Simonos Petras** is perched on top of a 6,700-foot-high cliff, where Simon built it in the mid-14th century. It was rebuilt by the Serbians, and after a 1581 fire, was restored by funds from the Orthodox of Bucharest. Between 1821 and 1891 it was closed by the Turks (Mount Athos as a whole remained fairly autonomous under the Turkish occupation), and in 1891 suffered another fire which destroyed the library. Typical of many monasteries, Simonos Petras boasts such treasures as the left hand of Saint Magdalene and the hand of Saint Dionysios of Zakynthos.

The 13th-century **Monastery of St. Gregory** was deserted in 1500, rebuilt by the governor of Moldovlahia, and burned down in 1761. It was restored and its church dedicated to Saint Nicholas. At St. Gregory are the two legs and right palm of Saint Anastasia Romaia, as well as beautiful icons and frescoes in the church. The **Monastery of Zographou** is famous for its library, which contains early ecclesiastical codes and 66 codes on parchment of 16th- to 19th-century Byzantine music. Fortunately, a 1976 fire that destroyed one wing left the library unharmed.

The 12th-century **Monastery of Panteleimon** has been called the Russian monastery since the 14th century, when it was rebuilt with Serbian and Byzantine funds after a fire. After Greek monks abandoned it for one near the coast, a Russian abbot was elected, and for 100 years the main mass has been given in Russian and Greek. The 19th-century influx of Russian Orthodoxy has left its mark visually on all the monasteries that have been partially rebuilt or restored since that time. (New interest expressed by the patriarch of Moscow is said to have the Greek government somewhat concerned.) In 1963 the Holy Mountain celebrated its first millennium of religious occupation, an event which brought the unique Mount Athos to the attention of the world.

Getting to Athos

Only ten foreign male lay visitors are granted permission to remain overnight on Mount Athos each day. It is suggested that interested parties make application three to four months in advance of their planned arrival; a dated entry permit will then be issued. To obtain the permit, you must send a letter including details of your passport (or a photocopy), personal or professional information including why you want to visit Mount Athos, a declaration of your "intention to be a pilgrim," and a letter of recommendation from your consulate to: National Tourist Organisation of Greece, 8 Aristotelous Square, 54623 Thessaloniki; they will pre-apply for you, requesting your dates. Applicants in Athens may contact E.O.T. or the Ministry of Foreign Affairs, who will then forward your request to the Thessaloniki office. Interested readers in the religious profession should apply to the Ecumenical Patriarchate, Istanbul, Turkey, in a letter noting their religious background.

Once you've been notified in writing that your request has been granted and your date is issued, you'll have to pick up your permit personally from the Ministry of Northern Greece on Ag. Dimitriou Street, which is open only Monday through Friday. To reach Mount Athos, you'll have to take a bus from 68

Karakassi St., Thessaloniki, to Ouranopolis on Chalkidiki. There are two boats a day to Daphni (2 hours), the harbor of Mount Athos. You must show your letter of permission to board the boat. From Daphni, you can take the bus 12 kilometers uphill to Karyes, the administrative capital of Athos. There, you'll present your letter for a Diamonitirion, a pass enabling you to visit other monasteries. There is no charge for room or board at any of them, but the boat trip and pass will cost about $50.

Note: Women should not even try to win this battle; **Doucas Tours** (tel. 031/224-100 or 269-984 in Thessaloniki) and others have organized well-guided day cruises around the Holy Mountain for 4500 drs ($35).

3. In Alexander the Great's Country

Hesiod traces the settlement of Macedonia to the descendants of Makednos and Magnes, sons of Zeus who populated the region after about 2000 B.C. These Makedniam tribes spread southward to the Pieria Mountains in the Pindus range, eventually moving over the next thousand years into the Peloponnese as Dorian peoples. Herodotus called the Makednia a "wide-wandering" Greek race, accurately foreshadowing the goals and eventual triumph of Macedonia's most celebrated son, Alexander.

Historians believe that King Perdikkas first founded the Macedonian capital at Vergina in the seventh century B.C. It was known as Aigaes in antiquity. East of the present-day city of Vergina, on both sides of the national highway, small mounds that have contributed a great deal of information about dress, burial customs, and the weaponry and tools manufactured by these families. Archeologists found that some mounds had been opened and reused later during the Hellenistic era by Macedonian settlers. Frenchman Léon Heuzey began excavating at Vergina in 1861, thinking that it was probably the small Macedonian village of Balla. Over the years archeologists uncovered a Macedonian tomb (found in 1937) and a royal palace, both thought to date from the early third century B.C. In 1959 Professors Bakalakis and Andronicos joined the team of Greek archeologists and historians at the site. In the early 1970s they began to feel that this excavation at Vergina might not be Balla at all, but rather the first great Macedonian capital, Aigaes, birthplace of King Philip II. In 1977 Professor Andronicos made the most envied find of the century—he discovered what has come to be considered the Royal Tomb of Philip II. And most astonishing of all, the tomb had never been plundered! The wealth of gold funerary objects discovered at Vergina needs no explanation, for this spectacular discovery took the world by surprise and has received a huge amount of publicity. What may be less well known is that finally, in 1982, Professor Andronicos discovered the first row of seats of an ancient theater. "This is the sort of thing we archeologists and historians dream about. The theater established a direct link with King Philip and his death," said Professor Andronicos, who for many years fought the doubts others had about the importance of the Vergina site. "We know that King Philip II was killed by one of his seven bodyguards while attending the wedding of daughter Cleopatra in the theater of Aigaes."

VERGINA: The **royal tomb** which has yielded such wealth is in the midst of excavation and study, and may not be opened to the general public for several years. One can visit the Macedonian tomb and royal palace near the modern-day village of Vergina, and see from above the early stages of excavation at the theater.

The **Macedonian tomb** has been partially cleared from under the mound of soil that was piled over it in antiquity to thwart vandals. Unfortunately, it didn't work. When the huge white marble doors were pushed aside, the tomb was empty. The façade of the classic tomb is almost perfectly intact; four Ionic semi-columns in relief grace the entry. Through the grated modern, iron protective gate you can see the halves of the marble sealing doors, carved in relief to resemble wood joined by metal studs. If you bring a flashlight, you can see to the right the damaged remains of the marble throne.

The **royal palace** is thought to have been built for King Antigonas Gonatas, who preceded Philip by almost half a century. Although the knee-high remains are difficult to appreciate, what immediately strikes the visitor is the palace's size: it's 144.5 by 94.5 meters. The central courtyard, whose walls of buff-colored Poros stone can be discerned, once had 60 Doric columns. If you explore carefully, you can find the excellent black, white, and tan stone mosaic floral pattern on a raised floor near the grand, oval fluted columns. Archeologists have found traces of several badly damaged mosaics, and have come to the conclusion that early Christian squatters at the site may have been offended by the nudity or religious frolicking portrayed in some; the only intact mosaics are of floral patterns and geometric designs. Along with the obviously high level of artistry, scholars have determined that there was great architectural and engineering sophistication in Macedonia at the time. Even in the largest palace rooms, no trace of internal support columns has been found, indicating a technical expertise capable of designing walls to hold the weight of the heavy, tiled roofs.

The partially uncovered **theater** can be seen in the plains below the hillside palace.

The site of the royal palace is open Monday through Saturday from 9 a.m. to 7 p.m., on Sunday to 3 p.m.; closed Tuesday. Admission is 300 drs ($2.30).

VERIA: Fifteen kilometers northwest of Vergina, and the largest nearby town to make bus connections to the site, Veria is better known for its Byzantine-era churches than for remains of the Roman era. Some are housed in its **museum** (open 9 a.m. to 5 p.m. daily), with exquisite painted stelae, pottery, and figurines from Vergina and exceptionally high-quality finds from the Macedonian tomb at Lefkadia. Veria was later one of two Macedonian capitals during the reform period of Emperor Diocletian (third century A.D.). The **Cathedral of St. John Theologos** and the **Church of Christ** display some fine frescoes from the later Byzantine period.

There are three C-class hotels in Veria for those who miss their returning tour bus: the **Villa Elia** (tel. 0331/26-800), the **Vassilissa Vergina** (tel. 0331/24-886), and the **Polytimi** (tel. 0331/64-902).

Before we head east to the second Macedonian capital, Pella, we'll note some other sites south of Thessaloniki. There is very little of interest at Pidna, but recent finds at the site of Dion may one day prove to be as exciting as those at Vergina.

DION: About 80 kilometers south of Thessaloniki, at the foot of the magnificent Mount Olympus, is the village of Dion. Recent excavations have revealed that this was an important religious center for worship of the gods of the sacred mount. King Philip II celebrated his victories here, and his son, Alexander the Great, came to sacrifice to Zeus to bless his famous expedition. The selection of this site for such important worship is no mystery, for the landscape is very blessed. Springs pour out of the hills and run down to the nearby sea. The thunderstorms that were thought to be the god's battles roll off the mountain and across the oak groves of Dion, lending credence to the legends that grew around it.

Much progress has been made in the excavations in recent years, filling the new museum with some very fine works. As you reach the town of Dion, turn down a small road toward the sea to the east, and you'll pass a small, badly preserved theatre on the right. About half a kilometer farther is the main part of the site, to the left. There are ancient paved roads running by stores, workshops, an odeon, and the well-preserved foundations of public baths. The short, standing pillars supported the floor under which heated air would flow. Across the modern road is the Temple of Demeter, where finds dating to 500 B.C. were found. Farther down the public road on your right, is the most interesting part of the area. Under six feet of water, archeologists found an intact sanctuary of Isis, the Egyptian goddess. Water and mud heaved into place by an earthquake had protected it from vandals for centuries. Rich finds of sculpture were uncovered still standing in place, including the wonderful cult statue of Aphrodite that stands in the museum. A copy sits in the reeds and water that have partially reclaimed the temple, although the foundations are still clearly visible.

The Dion Museum is on the same road as the archeological site, but back in the quiet village. The brand new building (with scholarly teams cataloging new finds out back) contains tasteful displays of very exciting finds from the site. The sculptural works, votive offerings from throughout the ancient world, are especially impressive, particularly the cult statue of Aphrodite found underwater in the Temple of Isis. Upstairs is a collection of household items, including surgical tools, dentist's instruments, and rusted iron nails used in house construction.

The archeological museum and site of Dion are open daily from 9 a.m. to 7 p.m., 10 a.m. to 6 p.m. on Sunday; admission is 400 drs ($3.75) for both.

PELLA: At the end of the fifth century B.C. the Macedonian capital had moved from Aigaes to Pella. It was traditional in the Macedonian culture to bury royalty in the ancient capital (a tradition which was not to be fulfilled with Alexander, who died in Babylon and was buried in Alexandria). This probably explains why Philip's tomb was found at Aigaes. King Philip II ruled his kingdom from Pella, and from here launched more successful military missions than the Greek world had ever seen. The city-states south of the Thermopylae Pass would soon come to know the high degree of civilization achieved in Macedonia. King Philip was an early exponent of Panhellenism, a concept of Greek unity for mutual protection and prosperity that had been proclaimed by Gorgias, Lysias, and then directly to Philip himself in the famous *Philippos* (as well as to the kings of Sparta and Syracuse), by Isokrates. When Philip, after defeating the combined southern Greek forces at the Battle of Chaironeia (338 B.C.), called for peace and unity against the common Persian foe, he was on the verge of realizing this goal. On the eve of his death (two short years later) Philip was proclaimed head of the Hellenic Federation; he'd achieved an alliance with the Corinthian League, which represented all the southern city-states and most of the Aegean islands. The Molossian Kingdom in west-central Greece and Thessaly were his subject allies. In his own right he'd taken control of the entire northern Balkan region. The stage was set for Alexander.

Alexander the Great

From Plutarch's *Lives* we've learned a great deal about Philip and Alexander. Even as a young boy, Philip's favored son, a pupil of the wisest tutor of the day, Aristotle, was aware of his strengths. Plutarch writes: "Being nimble and light-footed, his father encouraged him to run in the Olympic Race. 'Yes' said he, 'if there were any kings there to run with me.'" As a young man Alexander was trained in the sophisticated military tactics and weaponry that the great minds of Philip's court had invented. "Whenever Alexander heard Philip had taken any town of importance, or won any signal victory, instead of rejoicing at it altogether, he would tell his companions that his father would anticipate everything, and leave him and them no opportunities of performing great and illustrious actions." His impatience to lead is legendary; the case of the Gordion Knot tied by Gordius, father of the king of Phrygia, is only one example. Alexander, knowing the legend that whosoever untied the complicated knot would rule over all of Asia, cut it in two with his sword. Plutarch tells us: "Alexander wept when he heard from Anaxarchus that there was an infinite number of worlds; and his friends asking him if any accident had befallen him, he returns this answer: 'Do you not think it a matter worthy of lamentation that when there is such a vast multitude of them, we have not yet conquered one?'"

Alexander (who lived from 356 to 323 B.C.) gathered together the troops his father had readied for him. Allied with a newly unified Greece, he marched east across Persia all the way to the banks of the Indus River in India, conquering all and spreading the arts, ideals, traditions, and language of the Greeks. To his everlasting credit, he admired the peoples he subjugated, and remained to live among them the rest of his life. Just as Ionic columns have turned up in Pakistan and Iraq, Far Eastern religious cults found expression in some areas of southern Greece. It's said that 10,000 of his officers married Eastern women; the young man who'd been schooled by Aristotle to keep an open mind to all thoughts and all men was greatly taken by the beauties and wisdom of the East. After his death the Macedonians could only hold onto their own kingdom until 168 B.C., when the Romans defeated them at the Battle of Pidna, but Alexander's legacy will never be forgotten.

The Archeological Site of Pella

The small site and its few remains have led scholars to speculate on the great wealth and high standard of living achieved by its inhabitants. Graceful fluted Ionic columns still stand within the large areas of beautiful crafted mosaics. The site is only part of the Macedonian capital that Alexander had enlarged according to a master urban plan. In the museum there's a small display of statuary, pottery, and jewelry excavated at the site. The late 4th century mosaics not *in situ* have been carefully reconstructed and placed here. The museum is open Monday through Saturday from 8:45 a.m. to 3 p.m., on Sunday 9:30 a.m. to 2:30 p.m.; *closed Tuesday*. Admission to both site and museum is 200 drs ($1.55) each.

Modern Pella and Environs

In the modern mini-city of Pella there are several moderately priced tavernas and shops. The 65-room **Hotel Avra** (tel. 0384/21-300) is a modern, comfortable, C-class lodging favored by tour groups for its proximity to the site. Many tourists working their way west to Epirus prefer to move onward through the picturesque metropolis of **Edessa**, known for its cascading waterfalls and its Byzantine-era bridge that was one link in the Romans' Egnatia Way.

The two archeological sites that have offered us the richest artifacts displayed in the Thessaloniki Museum are Sindos and Derveni. There is little to see at **Derveni** (ten kilometers east of Thessaloniki on the Kavala highway) or at **Sindos** (23 kilometers west), where a treasure-filled cemetery spanning centuries was found when excavating a site for a new factory in the industrial zone. In both areas, archeological work continues.

GETTING TO THE SITES: Although each of the sites can be reached by public **bus** from Thessaloniki's west side K.T.E.L. stations, we found the schedules too limited to permit viewing more than one or two on any given day. Bus fares to the many connecting points between Pella, Veria, Vergina, and Dion cost $3 to $6 each and add up quickly. Two or more travelers can see more, in less time, by **renting a car** from one of the many companies in Thessaloniki. Rates run about $40 a day, including insurance.

Many travelers prefer the ease and expert narration that comes with a guided bus tour. **Doucas Tours** (tel. 269-984), at 8 Venizelou St., is one of the largest operators in this area. In 1987 they offered an Alexander the Great Tour, including visits to Pella, Edessa, Veria, and Vergina every Friday at a cost of 3000 drs ($23). Their day trip to the newly excavated site and museum at Dion left every Thursday and cost 2850 drs ($22). Doucas also offered a day trip to Philippi, Kavala, and Amphipolis (see section IV: Exploring Macedonia), which cost 3300 drs ($25).

4. Exploring Macedonia

Readers continuing west (hopefully not in the bitter cold winter) will reach first the prefecture of Florina, then that of Kastoria. **Florina**, once home to rebel Greek forces, borders on the Albanian and Yugoslav borders, giving it a somewhat more ethnic feel than is evidenced in the hill country farther south. It's a beautiful verdant region dotted by small cold-water lakes; ice skating is a popular winter activity. In the northwest area tranquil **Lake Prespa** is actually the larger Megali Prespa and tiny Mikri Prespa, two bodies of water separated by a very narrow land bridge at the village of Lemos. Both are partially Greek and partly Albanian; Megali Prespa also has the (possibly unique) distinction of being part Yugoslavian as well. In any case this region of shallow, marshy wetlands has for centuries been an active breeding ground for wildlife and birds. Since 1977 the region around Mikri Prespa has been a National Wildlife Preserve, most noted for its over 185 different species of birds. Mikri Prespa numbers among its happy inhabitants two types of endangered pelicans and some of Europe's rare cormorants.

KASTORIA: This name has cropped up in this book several other times. That's because it's the fur region of Greece, the one place where furs are rock-bottom cheap—cheaper than anywhere else. The city of Kastoria is worth writing home about for its picturesque locale on a promontory jutting into the still gray-blue waters of Lake Orestias (or Kastoria). Because of its influential position as a successful trading center, it is graced with an extraordinarily large number of Byzantine churches. More than 70 churches from the Byzantine and later eras are tucked in between typical Macedonian *arhontiko* (mansions). Many of these mansions have large, open fireplaces and their own exceptional frescoes. The **Kastoria Folklore Museum**, housed in a traditional-style house on Kapetan Lazarou Street, has interesting displays of locally produced embroideries and, of course, a history of the fur trade.

Kastoria's fur trade is based on its skilled craftsmen ("trimmers"), who can take small pieces of furs, or ends, and stitch them together to form a whole cloth, from which lower priced coats are sewn. In several factories you can watch as left overs imported from European and Scandinavian furriers are melded together to form blankets and carpets. "Stop and shop" is what we say for Kastoria. If you find yourself shopping till the wee hours, the **Xenia du Lac** (tel. 0467/22-565), overlooking the lake, is by far the prettiest, though not the cheapest, hotel. The **Kastoria** (tel. 0467/29-453), the **Keletron** (tel. 0467/22-676), and the **Orestion** (tel. 0467/22-257) are smaller, good-quality C-class hotels. For other accommodations, check with the Tourist Police (tel. 0467/22-696), at 25 Grammou St.

Olympic Airways (tel. 22-275), on 15 Meg. Alexandrou Street, has daily flights returning to Athens. Their airport bus leaves the office 40 minutes before flight time for the ten-kilometer ride to the airport. The nearest major **railroad station** is in Florina; there are two trains daily from Athens (tel. 82-13-882 for information.) **Buses** depart Athens from the 100 Kifissou Street terminal once daily for the 11-hour ride to Kastoria; phone 51-29-308 for schedule information in Athens or 0467/24-455 in Kastoria.

While you're waiting for your plane, train, or bus, walk over to **Van Flit Square**, where the timeless outdoor tavernas and idling backgammon players show no evidence of living with a fur trade that's a $100-million-a-year industry. (By the way, the square is named after the U.S. general, Van Fleet, who spoke there when U.S. troops were helping push back the Communist forces from this region into Albania in 1949.)

HEADING EAST: Let's turn eastward from Thessaloniki and look at the Macedonia of Philippi and Kavala, a Macedonia that becomes more Oriental in flavor every kilometer east we go. The scenic way to Drama is along the Kavala highway that hugs northern Chalkidiki; passing **Lake Koronia** and **Lake Volvi** will demonstrate how easily an island could have been made of Chalkidiki had the two lakes been joined! North of Lake Koronia is the famous village of **Langadas**, where each May 21 the Festival of the Anastenarides is held. Local firewalkers will come out and dance on blazing embers in honor of Saints Konstantinos and Eleni. (There's not much here on other days of the year.) On the north side of Lake Volvi is the hamlet of **Filadelfia**, one of many Greek cities called "Brotherly Love."

Amfipolis, a new village on the site of an ancient, prosperous mineral-mining town, is noted for its Byzantine church and for the remarkable marble Lion Statue found in the riverbed of the flowing Strimon River. The Strimon, which contributed to the rich mineral deposits sought after by Thracian, Roman, and Athenian alike, also preserved for us the remnants of a large wooden bridge from the fifth century, which has recently been brought up from its bottom.

The roads leading to **Drama**, called the "Plain of Gold" for its late afternoon amber light, are often lined with shade-giving poplar and elm trees. The plain was the battleground for a fifth-century B.C. defeat of Athens by the more powerful Macedonian forces, yet very little of interest remains from antiquity. Consider a lunch break in one of Drama's pretty public gardens. If you're not prepared to picnic, there's a small taverna, on its own little island in the middle of the healthy Ag. Varvara springs that bubble up in downtown Drama.

PHILIPPI: Depending on whether you're a Roma-phile or a Christiano-phile you'll say Philippi is best known for (a) the Battle of Philippi or (b) the site where Saint Paul preached his first sermon on Christianity. In 42 B.C., Mark Antony and Octavius met Caesar's assassins on the Plain of Philippi (Brutus' fleet had arrived at Kavala) and defeated them soundly, causing Brutus and Cassius to commit suicide. After their victory, Mark Antony and Octavius committed great sums of money to renewing Philippi, and most of its fascinating archeological site dates from this period of largesse. They granted Philippi the status of a Roman colony and a garrison guarding the Via Egnatia and its language, laws, and coinage followed the Roman model.

In the *Acts of the Apostles,* we read about Saint Paul's visit to Philippi, probably about A.D. 49: "We went to Philippi, which is the leading city of the district of Macedonia, and a Roman colony. . . . On the sabbath day we went outside the gate to the riverside, where we supposed there was a place of prayer;

and we sat down and spoke to the women who had come together. . . ." Paul and Silas set up a church in the house of Lydia, one of the women laundering who'd accepted Paul's words and been baptized. Their troubles were caused by a young prophetess who was trying to disclaim the preacher. Impatiently, Paul exorcised the spirit which enabled her to prophesy, a radical disability for one gainfully employed as a seer. In any case it is said that her supporters and "agents" demanded that Paul be jailed for interfering with their livelihood. A small crypt in the Roman forum is supposed to be the cell where Saint Paul and Silas were imprisoned.

The Archeological Site

As you enter Philippi, the site's entrance and museum are on the left of the main road. The **Propylon** has been restored and welcomes visitors. The largest part of the site is the **forum** or agora (on the south side), where there are remains of the arcade that once spanned three sides. There are remnants of a Roman bath, but a much more impressive plumbing feat are the 50 marble seats still in place in the **public toilets** at the southeastern end of the agora. At the north end, finely preserved stairs lead up to a terrace and portico. A bold, hewn-brick arch on top of rectangular columns is the striking remains of a sixth-century basilica. The tawny-colored stone and acanthus leaf-trimmed columns were made up from the Roman-era palaestra and forum, destroyed in clearing the land for the chapel. The smaller basilica A, as it's called, is near the ruins of the theater.

The **theater** dates from the fourth century B.C. and was actively used in Philip's time for the presentation of dramatic works. In the third century A.D. it was converted to a gladiator's arena; wild animal exits and entrances and a guardrail for the spectator seating were added at that time. The theater has been somewhat restored, and during the summer a Historic Drama Festival is held there (you can check with the E.O.T. for schedule information).

The small **archeological museum** at the site exhibits finds from the Neolithic period (Dikili-Tach and Sitagri regions) and from the Hellenic and Roman eras, when Philippi was at its prime. The Museum of Philippi (also spelled Filippi) is open from 8:45 a.m. to 3 p.m. Monday through Saturday, 9:30 a.m. to 2:30 p.m.; *closed Tuesday*. The site is open seven days: 9 a.m. to 5 p.m. Monday through Saturday, 10 a.m. to 5 p.m. on Sunday. The admission fee for the museum is 150 drs ($1.15) and for the site, 250 drs ($2). To get to Philippi from Kavala, take the Drama bus from the K.T.E.L. station, which leaves every 20 minutes. Ask the driver to let you off at "Archaia Philipi"; the half hour ride costs 125 drs ($1).

Our tour of Macedonia comes to a close in the big city of . . .

KAVALA: Located on the slopes of Mount Simvolon over an area occupied at least as long as 3,000 years ago, the modern port of Kavala rests on the remains of the ancient port of Neapolis. Modern concrete-block housing descends from the west, fascinating wood and stucco, traditional Turkish-blend villas descend from the east; the new meets a modern pier for the Thassos ferries and the old meets the original crescent-shaped port and breakwater installed for the Piracus ferries. From the impressive hilltop remains of the Byzantine fortress, one can appreciate the amphitheatrical design of the city. The 16th-century Kamares Aqueduct commissioned by Suleyman the Magnificent still dominates the central part of town. If you confine your stay in Kavala to the old Panaghia quarter, colored by its residents' Turkish heritage, and to the scenic port lined with cafés and shops, you'll have the best possible time in this otherwise industrial and commercialized city.

Besides its successful fishing industry, Kavala is the central market town for the area and Thrace's large tobacco industry. The scented leaves used in "Oriental" tobaccos have been farmed by Anatolian peoples in the Kavala area for centuries, and their integration into the community is one of the more intriguing aspects of this cross-over region.

Orientation

The town you will want to know is all within a quarter mile of the port. The long-distance **ferries** arrive at the east end of the harbor, beneath the old Panaghia quarter on the hill. **Buses** arrive one block up from the west end of the harbor. **Erithrou Stavrou Street** is the main thoroughfare, running east-west next to the fishing-boat docks and intersecting Koudouriotou Street, which runs up the hill next to the Panaghia quarter. **Eftherias Square** is one block above the middle of the port. The higher-priced hotels are on Erithrou Stavrou Street and Venizelou Street which runs parallel one block north; the budget hotels are on either side of Eftherias Square.

There are two museums worthy of mention in Kavala. The **archeological museum,** on the west side of the waterfront, has some excellently displayed finds from Amfipolis (a prosperous mining town near Thessaloniki), Avdira, Neapolis (the ancient Kavala), and Philippi. The museum is open Monday through Saturday from 8:45 a.m. to 3 p.m., on Sunday from 9:30 a.m. to 2:30 p.m. Admission is 250 drs ($2). On the east side of the harbor, up on Panaghia Hill, is the **home of Muhammed Ali** (the ancient one). This traditional-style Turkish house was where Ali, founder of the Egyptian dynasty that ended with King Farouk, was born in 1769. It's maintained courtesy of the Egyptian government, who also own and are partially restoring the Imaret down the hill, also built by Muhammed Ali. This was a priest's school combined with a poorhouse, which at times housed and fed up to 300 people. It is a wonderful, sprawling piece of Islamic architecture, sadly in need of repair.

Muhammed Ali should inspire you (especially those of you continuing east into Turkey) to explore the narrow, cobblestone lanes of the Turkish Panaghia district.

Useful Information

There is an **E.O.T.** office (tel. 051/228-762) in Kavala at 2 Filellinon St., at Eletherias Square. They're open Monday through Thursday 7 a.m. to 2:30 p.m., Friday 9 a.m. to 1:30 p.m., and Saturday 8 a.m. to 2 p.m. . . . The **Tourist Police** (tel. 222-905) are on Omonias Street, near the post office. . . . Besides the many **banks** on the square, the Macedonia Thrace Bank on Omonias and P. Mela Streets is open extra hours, from 6 a.m. to 7:45 p.m. daily and from 10 a.m. to 12:45 p.m. on Saturday. . . . the **bus station** to Philippi (Drama), Thessaloniki, Athens, and other eastern destinations is on Mitopolous Street, about a block up from the harbor. . . . The telephone **area code** for the Kavala region is 051.

The E.O.T. sells tickets to the annual summer-long **Drama Festivals** held on the island of Thassos and in the ancient theater at Philippi; check with them for schedules and show times . . . The **Olympic Airlines** office is at 8 Paraliaki (tel. 225-577). They have an airport bus, costing 200 drs ($1.55), leaving their office 1½ hours before flight time.

Accommodations and Dining

The 150-room **Hotel Galaxy** (tel. 051/224-521) has balconies which face directly over the brightly painted caïques to the hills of Thassos south. The Galaxy is at 51 Venizelou St. and offers a roof garden (great view!), restaurant, bar, and air-conditioned rooms. It's popular with the "Saint Paul in Greece" tour groups

(Saint Paul landed at the ancient port of Neapolis on his way to Philippi), but it's so big you can almost always find a room; doubles with all the frills (no breakfast) are 5900 drs ($45).

If you didn't come to Kavala to live like this, at no. 50 Erythrou Stavrou, one block in from the port, is the more tranquil, 100-room **Hotel Nefeli** (tel. 051/ 227-441). It's near the archeological museum and the rooms are simple and spacious. Doubles here are 3500 drs ($27), and their Acropolis view roof garden competes favorably with pricier neighbors. The **Panorama** (tel. 051/224-205) is at 26C Venizelou, just down from the Galaxy. Prices here are 10% more for similar rooms, and 10% less for shared bath rooms; it's pretty dull, but the views are better from the front-facing rooms.

Budget watchers should consider Kavala's quartet of old-fashioned, typically Greek D-class hotels. The **Parthenon** (tel. 051/223-205), at 14 Spetson St., one block east of Eleftherias Square, has the most charm. Flowered coverlets, wallpaper, and couches create a symphony of Oriental decor in this balconied, high-ceilinged, creaky floors abode. Shared baths are big, old but clean. The blue-trimmed **Hotel Rex** (tel. 051/223-393), at 4 Kriezi St., is diagonally across the street. Similar simple and spotless rooms are just as comfortable, if not as ornate, and Iannis, the manager, is a gracious host. At both, two can have beds and hot showers for 2100 drs ($16). The **Acropolis Hotel** (tel. 051/223-543), at 33 Venizelou, is tucked in next to the posh Galaxy Hotel on the port (the entrance is one street inland). The aquarium and black-and-white photos of guess-where add some style, and back rooms do have a great water view. However, the ambivalent management style leaves a great deal to be desired. The **Attikon** (tel. 051/222-257), just off the square at 8 Megalou Alexandrou, is run by graduates of the same hospitality school but it, too, has fairly clean, old-fashioned rooms and shared baths. Both charge 2500 drs ($19) for two.

Check with the E.O.T. about the availability of the few rooms to rent in the city's most picturesque quarter, the Panaghia District. The E.O.T. **Batis Campgrounds** (tel. 051/227-151) is at Kavala Beach. It's really a luxurious watersports/resort-style camping area.

You should only eat seafood in Kavala, so the best thing to do is head down to Venizelou Street and stroll the harbor. Of the three tavernas at the old port, **Panos Zafira** is very popular, but all are known for grilled calamari and small local fish which are cheaper than most other seafood. Near the stadium at 14 Perigali St. is the **Kiriakos Taverna** (tel. 222-494), which overlooks the beach. Here's the place for *xifias* (swordfish) and *midia* (oysters)—try them fried. Have the day's catch fried or broiled and served with a wedge of lime at **O'Pharos,** at 27 Poulidou, the main street of Panaghia, another popular seafood and mezes taverna. You can watch the neighbors stroll and savor exceptionally well-prepared Greek fare over some of the hearty, regional Limnos white wine. At all these restaurants, a fish dinner for two will average 1800 drs ($14) to 2600 drs ($20) with wine, a meat dinner about 30% less than that. In the newer part of town you'll have a wide variety of stylish, portside cafés and fast-food and souvlaki places. Don't miss the *artopoleo* (bakery) on Poulidou St. as you asend to Panaghia. Their *tiropita, spanakopita,* and *milopita* (apple pie) and whole wheat or sesame breads are wonderful for breakfast.

Getting There

Kavala is the midway point between Thessaloniki and Istanbul (there's a huge "Constantinople 460 KMS" sign on the harbor) and, as such, is easily accessible. **Buses** to eastern Macedonia leave from the Athens terminal at 260 Liossion St. (tel. 01/51-29-363) twice daily for Drama or Kavala (11 hours). Buses run along the Via Egnatia (built in the mid-second century from Rome to

Constantinople) from Thessaloniki every hour. The Kavala Port Authority (tel. 224-472) or E.O.T. has **ferry** schedule information about boats to Limnos (four times a week), Lesbos and Chios (twice weekly), Kymi, Evia (infrequently), and Thassos (eight times daily). **Olympic Airways** has two flights daily to Athens.

From Kavala, continue eastward until you cross the Nestos River. Now, you've arrived in . . .

5. Thrace

The coastal road swings inland as you cross the Nestos and heads north to the fascinating village of **Xanthi,** 63 kilometers from Kavala. This is a tobacco town, but here it's grown, not just traded and shipped, and the fragrance is everywhere. Many of the villagers are traditionally dressed in Turkish peasant clothes of baggy black trousers, full skirts, and headdresses. The women who wear white bandannas indicate they're Pomaki, descendants of the Bulgarian hill people who were converted to Islam from Christianity. Some 70 kilometers farther east, in **Komotini**, the locals are dressed in traditional garb too, but here the head-clothes are black and the faces are pure Turkish. Komotinis are Musulmani, Moslems of direct Turkish descent. In Komotini worship is carried out five times daily in the 450-year-old New Mosque.

Nearly one-fourth of Thrace's population is Moslem, in a country where more than 90% of the population shares the Orthodox faith. This story goes back to the years after World War I when the Greeks developed their *megali idea* of uniting all the areas with an Orthodox population once again under the Greek flag, perhaps reestablishing a great capital at Constantinople. They invaded the weakened Ottoman Empire and got nearly as far as Ankara before they were repulsed by the furious Turks. Since anyone of Orthodox faith in Anatolia now feared for their lives, they fled (more than a million) into neighboring Greece, increasing its population by more than 20%. Under the Treaty of Lausanne the western part of Thrace was given to the Greek nation in 1923. In the last decade the government has made a big push to industrialize this region. The borders shared with Bulgaria and Turkey ensure that it will always be heavily fortified and counted on as a strategic military outpost. Villages such as Xanthi and Komotini are of the past; Alexandroupolis is of the future.

There isn't much to see in **Alexandroupolis,** except for the nearby cave at Makri that tour operators push as the famed cave where Odysseus met the Cyclops and defeated him. Every August there's a Wine Festival; in February a Hunter's Week (the thing to do in this rugged region) is celebrated near the city. At nearby Pithion the O.S.E. train will be rerouted for its trip to the Turkish border. Drivers and hitchhikers will head for the land border at Kastanee to cross into Edirne, Turkey. Frommer readers will anxiously turn to Chapter XVI. But first, some . . .

USEFUL INFORMATION: The **Municipal Tourist Office** (tel. 0551/24-998) is three blocks behind the 1880-era lighthouse, on Dimokratia Street. The ticket agent for the **Samothraki ferry** (which runs four times a week) is one short block from the harbor esplanade, on Kypou Street; call 26-721 for schedule information. . . . There are four **trains** daily from Athens which make the 16- to 17-hour ride up to Alexandroupolis, with stops at Drama and Komotini, leaving from the Larissis station (tel. 0551/26-212). . . . **Buses** from Athens to Thrace depart from the terminal at 100 Liossiou St.; call 01/51-32-084 for information. . . . **Olympic Airways** has two flights daily to Athens. They provide an airport bus one hour before flight time from their office at 6 Ellis St., at the corner of Koleti Street. Call 0551/26-207 or 28-653 for information.

Local buses go to several nearby **beaches**, making for an easy day excursion. Another day trip through pretty, unspoiled scenery is through the **Evros Valley** region, paralleling the Turkish border north from Alexandroupolis. In **Didymotichon**, the double row of walls, ten towers, three gates, a reservoir, and food storage cells of an imposing Byzantine castle can still be seen. It was one of the most important Byzantine cities, home to both the Emperor Iannis Paleologos and to Sultan Beyazit.

ACCOMMODATIONS AND DINING: If you're here waiting for the Samothraki ferry (and it's hard not to be if that's where you're going or coming from) you'll probably want a place to stay. Our first choice is the **E.O.T. Campground** (tel. 0551/26-055), just one kilometer outside town, overlooking the water. It can accommodate up to 900 persons, but call ahead to find out how crowded it will be.

If you want to stay in the heart of things, Dimokratias Street is for you. First choice along hotel row is the **Hotel Alex** (tel. 0551/26-302), at 294 Vass. Georgiou. The Alex has 28 comfortable rooms, and doubles in the high season are 2900 drs ($23). At no. 150 is the **Hotel Galaxias** (tel. 0551/28-112) bathless, whose range of budget-priced rooms includes bathless singles for 1800 drs ($14.60) and doubles for 3125 drs ($24). The rooms are all simple and clean.

The **Park Hotel** (tel. 0551/28-607) is another C-class choice on central Vass. Georgiou St., at no. 458. All 24 rooms have private baths and rent for 3100 drs ($24) a double. The **Metropolis** (tel. 0551/26-443) and the **Tourist** (tel. 0551/26-403) are smaller, family-run D-class places very near each other on Kyprou Street, another major cross street. Both have doubles with and without baths for about 1770 drs ($13.70), plus 400 drs for the private bath.

When in Alexandroupolis, try *lagos* (hare) and the locally produced *telemes* cheese. The **Klimateria**, at 14 Kyprou St., is a popular taverna on a small square where you can sample a spicier-than-usual moussaka with a delicious hunk of Greek bread. The Turkish influence can be tasted in the cuisine here. (Just wait till you get to Istanbul!) Their lamb and beef dishes are also flavorful; try the *katsikaki* (baked goat).

From Alexandroupolis, after a run through the northeast Aegean islands, in Chapter XV, we say good-bye to Greece, and in Chapter XVI, hello to Turkey!

THE NORTHEAST AEGEAN ISLANDS

1. Samos
2. Chios
3. Lesbos
4. Limnos
5. Samothraki
6. Thassos

THE ISLANDS that comprise the Northeast Aegean group, the least visited of any of the Aegean islands, can really be further divided into the eastern islands, Samos, Chios, and Lesbos, and the northern islands, including Limnos, Samothraki, and Thassos. The division reflects both physical and cultural differences. The eastern islands are more autonomous; when you're on our favorite island, Chios, you know you're in a place that exists on its own. It has a history and personality that flourish without reliance on tourism. One can't help thinking that the smaller northern islands are extensions or weekend resorts for the populace of larger mainland cities. Finally, the three eastern islands all share a connection with Turkey, reflecting that country's exotic, Asian heritage.

1. Samos

During the sixth century B.C., in the glory days of the Ionian civilization, Samos was heralded for its rich contribution to art, architecture, and science. The island's favorite son, Pythagoras, is the most notable in a long list of luminaries (including the philosopher Epicouros, Aesop of fable fame, and the mathematician Aristarchos) who brought Samos honor and fame. Herodotus, in his *Histories,* devoted a large portion of his historical writing to Samos: "I have dwelt longer upon the history of the Samians than I should otherwise have done, because they are responsible for three of the greatest building and engineering feats in the Greek world: the first is a tunnel nearly a mile long, eight feet wide and eight feet high, driven clean through the base of a hill nine hundred feet in height. . . . Secondly, there is the artificial harbor enclosed by a breakwater, which runs out into twenty fathoms of water and has a total length of over a quarter of a mile; and, last, the island has the biggest of all known Greek temples."

Samos is mountainous and green; its peaks are the highest in the Aegean islands and sections of the interior are as thickly forested as one finds in the region. Samos's beaches are considered among the best in the region, and because it's the closest Greek island to Turkey, it is a particularly convenient crossover point for those who want to visit Ephesus—one of the most important archeological sites in Asia Minor.

Samos's popularity with group tours makes it difficult to recommend an extended stay on the island. Samos town (sometimes called Vathi) is an old port which has undergone extensive development and Pythagorian, the ancient capital and a lovely south coast village, is excessively crowded with tour groups. For years Kokkari, the island's most unspoiled resort village, was a favorite of the individual traveler. Now it's overrun with tourists who prefer less-touristy villages. The other north coast beaches are plagued by strong winds that make it difficult to sun, but are also undergoing intense development. If you're willing to travel off the beaten track to explore some of the remote sections of the island, particularly in May, June, September, or October, a trip to Samos can be enjoyable.

ORIENTATION: Samos has three ports. Depending on which boat you take you'll either land at Samos town on the northeast, Karlovassi on the northwest, or Pythagorian on the southern coast. The ferries from Chios, Piraeus, and Ikaria normally stop at both Samos and Karlovassi. **Samos** is the largest town on the island and offers the most complete tourist services. **Karlovassi** is little more than a beachless shipping dock with hotels and tourist services lining its harbor. The ferries from Patmos land at **Pythagorian**, a picturesque and friendly village that was the ancient capital of the island. The tunnel and Heraion are located outside of Pythagorian. The airport is to the west of Pythagorian.

Midway on the north coast road between Kokkari and Karlovassi are a cluster of inland mountain villages that one Samian friend describes as paradise. Included in this group are **Ithonia** ("nightingales"), **Margarites**, and **Manolates**. All three villages are set on steeply terraced hills and valleys where Samos's famous muscadine grapes grow—from which muscat wine is made. The South Coast villages outside of **Marathokambos** have some of the best beaches and are slated for the next wave of development. **Platanos** and **Pirgos**, two high mountain villages in the center of Samos, are both known for their production of olive oil and honey and are virtually untouched by tourism.

Excursion boats to Turkey leave daily from Samos town and Pythagorian.

USEFUL INFORMATION: There are three helpful local tourist offices on the island. The **Samos City Tourist Office** (tel. 0273/28-258) is a half block in from the port on the lane behind the portside Alex's Cafe. They're open daily from 8 a.m. to 9 p.m., till 10:30 p.m. in the high season. The **Pythagorian Community Tourist Office** (tel. 0273/61-022) is on Lykourgos, one block up from the harbor. Their kiosk is open daily from 8 a.m. to 10 p.m. The **Kokkari Tourist Office** (tel. 0273/92-333) is in the middle of the village; it's open daily from 8 a.m. to 11 p.m. All are manned by local people who are very helpful and informative; none will make room reservations by phone but will help you find accommodation once you're at their office.

The telephone **area code** for Samos is 0273. . . . The **O.T.E.** in Samos is on Iroon Platia, across from the municipal garden (open seven days a week); in Pythagorian it's on the port (open daily from 8 a.m. to 1 p.m. and 5 to 9 p.m.) . . . The **police station** (tel. 27-980) is on the central platia along the port. In Pythagorian for emergencies, call the local police office at 61-100, all hours of the day.

Both Samos and Pythagorian have branches of the **National Bank of Greece**: in Samos, on the port (open from 8 a.m. to 2 p.m. Monday through

Friday); in Pythagorian, one block up Lykourgos (Main) Street from the port (open from 8:30 a.m. to 12:30 p.m. Monday through Friday). Several travel agents change money at a lesser rate but stay open daily from 8 a.m. to 10 p.m. . . . The **hospital** (tel. 27-407) is in Samos town. . . . The **post office** in Samos is across from the O.T.E.; in Pythagorian, it's four blocks up from the harbor on Lykourgos. . . . **Samian Travel** (tel. 27-146), in Samos town at the port, is extremely helpful and can assist you in booking a rental car and plane tickets. Samian has offices in Pythagorian (tel. 61-116) and in Kokkari (tel. 22-579). . . . Themos Seirlis at **Nova Tours** on Lykourgos in Pythagorian (tel. 61-008) is also very knowledgeable and helpful. . . . **Olympic Airways** (tel. 27-237) is at the corner of Kanari and Smyrnis Streets in Samos town, two blocks behind the Xenia Hotel, or at 90 Lykourgos (tel. 61-213) in Pythagorian. . . . **Pythagoras Tours** (tel. 27-240), on the port in Samos, sells ferryboat tickets to Piraeus, Ikaria, and Lesvos. . . . **Mirsiadis Tours** (tel. 28-571) in Kokkari, near the bus stop, is this village's post office and money changer. They and the Tourist Office have metered phones for long distance calls. Alex Stavrides runs a **laundromat** in Pythagorion on the church street; it's open 9 a.m. to 9 p.m. daily, till 11 p.m. in summer. A load of laundry (up to five kilograms) costs 700 drs ($5) for both machines.

GETTING AROUND: If you're arriving by Olympic Airways, their special airport bus will transport you 17 kilometers to their office in Samos town, or you can take a taxi (which costs about $3.50) to Pythagorian. From there you can catch a public bus to other parts of the island.

There's good public transportation on Samos, and **buses** serve most destinations several times a day. The buses get so crowded that they sometimes leave early. The bus terminal (tel. 27-262) is on Kanari Street, down the block from the Olympic Office. The bus travels five times a day between Samos town and Pythagorian 150 drs ($1.15). If you miss the bus a taxi will cost 725 drs ($6). Buses from Samos go to the inland village of Mitilini four times a day; to Kokkari, Ag. Constantinos, and Karlovassi five times daily; and the south coast beach, Psili Ammos, once a day. There's one bus from Pythagorian to Ireo (near the Heraion); it costs 225 drs ($1.75) and you'd better check the schedule (tel. 27-262).

You can book an all-day **taxi** for an around-the-island tour. Count on paying about $13 per hour or 12,000 drs ($75) for a full day (tel. 28-404 in Samos or 61-450 in Pythagorion). Both Samos and Pythagorian have many **rental-car agencies.** The cheapest car will cost about $40 per day without fuel. **Budget** (tel. 27-146) has an office on the paralia in Samos, in Pythagorian (tel. 61-116), and in Kokkari (tel. 22-579). Also try Samos Car Rent (tel. 27-750); they advertise that they have the cheapest rates on Samos. **John's** in Pythagorian (tel. 61-405) rents mopeds and Vespas for 1300 drs ($10) a day but bargain.

You can also rent a **bicycle** in Samos from Mr. Notaros near the Bank of Greece, or in Pythagorian from a lovely man across from John's, next to the Pythagoras Tourist Shop. Bicycles rent for 400 drs ($3) a day.

Excursion boats from the Pythagorian harbor go to Psili Ammos and to the sandy beach on Samiopoula ("small island"), where there is a taverna and pension.

ACCOMMODATIONS: Vacancies are often tough to come by during the summer. If you don't have reservations, consult the travel agents or the local Tourist Information Office in Samos town. If you land in Pythagorian, head for the Community Tourist office, one block off the paralia on Lykourgou. There are many private rooms for rent in both Pythagorian and Samos town.

In Pythagorian

The **Dolphin Hotel** (tel. 0273/61-205) is located right on the paralia, and if they have a vacant room take it—it's one of the best values on the island. Front rooms have balconies, many with views of the port, beach, and sea. The Dolphin is small and simple but well maintained, and your host, Costas Tsalparas, is very friendly. His 12 bathless doubles run 2500 drs ($20).

The C-class **Pythagoras** (tel. 0273/61-373) is farther along on the paralia from the Dolphin. The rooms all have private showers and balconies, many with views overlooking the beach. The breakfast room faces the water. The price for two, including breakfast, is 3750 drs ($29); for one, 2500 drs ($19).

The six-room **Pension Anna** (tel. 0273/61-298), one block behind the paralia near the town church, is a two-story inn with some rooms with balconies and private baths. The hotel looks like a large villa and its guests often lounge on the terrace overlooking the garden. A room for two, costs 2900 drs ($22).

The **Hotel Fyllis** (tel. 0273/61-296), on the main street, Lykourgos, is an excellent 15-room pension. Clean, bright white rooms with private bath and breakfast cost 3250 drs ($25) for two.

Also on Lykourgou Street, across from the Olympic Airways office, is the nine-room **Efpalinion Hotel** (tel. 0273/61-466). Its older rooms are spacious and the bathrooms have checkerboard-tile bathtubs. The balconies look out to honeysuckle bushes. Double rooms cost 4000 drs ($31), including breakfast.

In Samos Town

The full-amenity lodging closest to the ferry dock is **Hotel Samos** (tel. 0273/28-377), at 11 Th. Sofoulis St. The façade has been restored to resemble that of a classic Samian-style mansion, and the interior is super-clean with first-rate service. The rooms in the back of the hotel are quieter and have larger balconies. Rooms for two are a hefty 4800 drs ($37), 3700 drs ($29) for a single.

The 17-room **Hotel Artemis** (tel. 0273/27-792), at 4 Kontaxi, a little further on the port, is a family-run establishment with simple, clean furnishings and a low price: 2600 drs ($20) for a double room with private bath and balcony. The Artemis has bathless rooms for 2200 drs ($17).

The pretty new **Sibylla Hotel** (tel. 0273/22-396), on St. Nicholas Square, one block in from the middle of the port, is popular with tour groups but a good choice if you can get a room. All are sparkling clean, designed in the old villa style of the local mansions, and rent for 4000 drs ($30) for two. Our favorite pension on the island is the **Pension Avli** (tel. 0273/22-939), at Kalomiri and Areos Streets, two blocks uphill from the port behind the Aeolis Hotel. The Avli is a lovely, restored Samian mansion with a grand marble courtyard filled with plants and breakfast tables. Spyros tends his home well; the 12 bathless rooms are as large as you'd expect, simple but spotless, and have their own water closet. The common showers are down the hall. This grandeur comes with twin beds for 1900 drs ($15); his modernized rooms with private bath are reserved for groups, but you can inquire about their availability. Another pleasant pension, run by the caring Emmanuel Tzivanakis, is the **Pension Cactus** (tel. 0273/28-754), at 5 Zisimou Sideri St., two blocks up from the port behind the Samos Hotel. The largest cactus our Texan friend had ever seen grows right in the front patio of his restored old home. Simple, large bathless rooms with water views are 1750 drs ($13.50) for two.

In Kokkari

Kokkari, off-season, is a tiny fishing village built up around a scalloped shore that boasts many waterside cafés, small, pebble beaches, and pedestrian bridges and walkways. Its small-scale commercialism is very appealing, and draws hordes competing for its few rooms and hotels in the summer months. The Tourist Office (tel. 92-333) will do their best to place you; expect to pay 2500 drs ($19) for a room with bath, 2000 drs ($16) without. Most hotels cost at least 3800 drs ($30) for two.

READER'S HOTEL SELECTION: "I've spent the winter in Kokkari. Mrs. Triantafilio Kypreou runs a new, clean pension with excellent kitchen facilities and a charming courtyard full of citrus trees. It's on a road back toward Samos and has a sign that reads "Chambres à Louer." Lily Moros runs the **Blue Sky Pension** in town and she speaks good English. A restaurant run by George and Kiki Hatzimahalis serves the most consistently good food in town. Most of the restaurateurs in Kokkari have lived in Canada or Australia at some point and English is spoken everywhere. The best bakery in town is off the beaten track, down by the water near Nick's Souvenir Shop. They make BROWN bread in the summer." (Carroll Klein, Vancouver, British Columbia, Can.).

RESTAURANTS: The real specialty on Samos isn't the food (it's tourist-quality, mediocre, and expensive), it's the wine: as Byron exclaimed, "Fill high the bowl with Samian wine!" The wine that most people (those used to California and French wines) prefer is a dry white called *Samaina*. There's also a relatively dry delicious rosé called *Fokianos*. The Greeks go wild over the sweet wines, and when we say sweet. . . . These wines have names like *Nectar, Dux,* and *Anthemis*. Almost any restaurant on the island will serve one or all of these wines, and you really ought to try a bottle.

Dining in Pythagorian

The three best cafés are all on the harborside. **Samaina** (tel. 61-516) serves particularly flavorful vegetable dishes, and a typical meal for two will run about 1700 drs ($13). They also have a good wine list and one of the better views of the port. **Trovas** (tel. 61-373) is especially well regarded by the locals, which accounts for its crowded and festive atmosphere. The food is fairly standard taverna fare—and the prices are a tad higher than the Samaina. **Polycratis,** on the paralia, is another popular choice.

Dining in Samos

It would be hard to top the **Samian Restaurant** (tel. 27-285) for atmosphere, an outdoor garden café enclosed behind thick walls and shaded by a giant palm tree (although we hear it may be renovated!). Their specialties include octopus and onion in red wine sauce and a Samian platter of assorted meats. Two can dine for 1950 drs ($15). The Samian is located next door to the Xenia Hotel. **Tassos** and the **Akriyali** are near the bus station and are filled with Samians who work in that part of the port. If you're looking for a cheap meal try **Gregoris Taverna** near the Olympic office, which specializes in roasted meats and chicken. It's no frills; the food is good and the service friendly.

WHAT TO SEE AND DO: Samos has a lot to offer, but you will have to travel out of the way to discover the truly special spots. Before you make plans for your island hop, inquire whether the Eupalinus Tunnel is open. If it is, and you have any interest in archeology, it alone will justify a special visit to Samos.

In and Around Pythagorian

This ancient village and harbor is named after the most notable of all Samians, Pythagoras, who is still studied ("Reason is immortal, all else mortal") by students for his theories about geometry and mathematics and their relation to the other disciplines. Aesop was one of Pythagoras' contemporaries, and it is he who penned such expressions as "appearances often are deceiving," "the lamb

. . . began to follow the wolf in sheep's clothing," "do not count your chickens before they are hatched," "slow and steady wins the race," "familiarity breeds contempt," and "any excuse will serve a tyrant" (the last being particularly applicable to his times). Samos was ruled by the autocrat Polycrates, under whose administration the island made its greatest strides. The first is the **harbor** at Pythagorian and the three-mile wall built around it; columns from the fortifications and the unexcavated theater are visible on the far left side north of the port.

The second is the **Eupalinus** (or Eupalinian) **Tunnel**, a 1,050-meter-long waterway located just to the northwest of the town and one of the most splendid engineering feats of the ancient world. The purpose of the tunnel was to transport water from mountain streams to ancient Samos. Eupalinus designed the tunnel on two levels. The lower level was the actual waterway, while the upper level permitted workers to gain access to the aqueduct for maintenance. There are air holes dug from the surface down into the upper level of the tunnel to provide both light and fresh oxygen. The tunnel caved in during the 17th century when Samos was abandoned because of a series of devastating earthquakes. It wasn't until a few years ago, when a German engineering team completed eight years of work, that the Eupalinus Tunnel was entirely cleared of debris and rock. It's an astounding human achievement. Some of the spaces are tight, and you'll have to descend a stairway so narrow that you might have to do it sideways, but the experience of walking the length of the tunnel, from one end of the mountain to the other, is fabulous—remember your flashlight! Recently we were informed that the site, often closed for repairs, will reopen by 1988. Call one of the island's tourist offices to learn the most current schedule. If it's open, it's a "must see" site.

It's a pity that all that survives of the **Heraion**, the greatest of all Greek temples, is its massive foundation and a lone reconstructed column. The temple was surrounded by a forest of columns, which was one of its most distinctive and original features. In fact, rival Ionian cities were so impressed that they rebuilt many of their ancient temples in the style of the Heraion. The Temple of Artemis in nearby Ephesus (which was one of the seven wonders of the world) is a direct imitation of the great Samian structure. The Heraion was rebuilt and greatly expanded under Polycrates; it was damaged during numerous invasions and finally destroyed by a series of earthquakes. An ideal way to visit the Heraion is by bicycle (the road from Pythagorian is flat). Alternatively you can walk, but it will take an hour or so. The one bus a day usually leaves Samos or Pythagorian in the afternoon. The site is open from 9 a.m. to 3 p.m. Monday through Saturday. Admission is 200 drs ($1.55).

In Samos

There isn't much to see in Samos town, other than the archeology museum and the old quarter known as Vathi. The **archeology museum** has displays in two buildings; particularly impressive are the sculptural pieces: a giant kouros (five to six meters tall), a group of six archaic statues dedicated to Hera, the sixth-century B.C. cast-bronze griffin heads, and a charming frieze of dimpled cupids, wings uplifted, bringing gifts to Hera. Samos was the sculpture center of Greece; being much in demand, many of the island's best sculptors traveled all over the Hellenistic world to create their art. The Samian artists were especially adept in the craft of casting, which is apparent from the exhibits in the museum. It's open from 8:30 a.m. to 2:45 p.m. Monday through Saturday, from 9 a.m. to 2 p.m. on Sunday; closed Tuesday. Admission is 250 drs ($2).

If Samos town is built amphitheatrically, then the section of town called **Vathi** is in the cheap seats. The homes are neoclassical and the streets narrow and twisting. Vathi is in direct contrast to the town below; up in this quiet village there are few cars, motorcycles, tourist buses, or hotels. It's a residential area that retains a lot of its original character—a nice place to wander about and grab a bite to eat.

Around the Island

Samos has the best-known paleontological remains in Greece, mostly from Stephanidis Valley, near **Mitillini**. Many of the finds excavated in this area are on display in the **paleontological museum** (tel. 51-205), open Monday through Saturday from 9 a.m. to 1:30 p.m. and 6 p.m. to 8 p.m.; admission 150 drs ($1.10). There is bus service to Mitillini four times a day (65¢) from Samos town.

Kokkari is a short bus ride away from Samos town on the north coast. Up until a few years ago it was a traditional Greek fishing village with small cobbled back streets, a few tavernas, and off in the distance, bare grayish hills. Today, small hotels, pensions, and rooms to rent occupy many of the town's older homes. People come to Kokkari for the line of **beaches** that extend westward to Avlakia; they're made of large pebbles and are fairly wide. Be forewarned that the winds on this side of the island are notorious; you may have to move on to sunbathe comfortably.

Samians have dubbed one corner of their island "**Paradise**," an area off the north coast road where densely wooded valleys give way to terraced hills and mountain hamlets. Take the Samos road to Ag. Konstantinos. At about the 18-kilometer point from Samos town there is a left turn to Aidonia (meaning nightingale—they will serenade you all the way up to the highest village).

For oenophiles Paradise features the **Paradisos Restaurant** (tel. 94-208), which is a large garden café located just after the turn from the coast highway. Your host, Mr. Folas, who worked in the vineyards many years, makes his own wine from the excellent Samian grapes. Mrs. Folas' *tiropita* is made from local goat's milk and butter and wrapped in a flaky pastry.

There are two tavernas about 15 minutes up a lonely country road, totally wooded with evergreens and lulled by the sound of a running stream. Near Aidonia is a clear mountain spring that attracts scores of songbirds and is a delightful watering and washing spot.

If you have the stamina (for a half-hour hike uphill) you'll be rewarded by sky-high views of the steeply tiered grapevines growing over the foothills of Mount Abelos (1,140 meters tall) down to the deep-blue sea. Above it all is the small and picturesque hamlet of **Manolates.** It's a typical Samian village, with stucco homes and red-tiled roofs. The narrow cobblestone streets are so steep that you'll find yourself bending forward to avoid falling backward. Manolates has a taverna.

BEACHES: There are beaches near Samos town, the closest and best being **Plaz Gagou**, and on the east side of the port, the beach at **Kalami**. There's an excellent beach at **Potami**, on the far western end of the island, near Karlovassi.

Our favorite part of the coast is on **Marathokombos Bay**, along the extreme southwestern shore. A several sandy beach, several tavernas, and a growing number of hotels and pensions fill the once-tiny village of **Ormos Marathokombos**; it used to be the kind of fishing village that you imagine when you dream about Greece—but the harbor under construction now will soon change that.

Closer to the more populated areas of the island are the resort beaches extending from **Ireo** all of the way to **Pythagorian**. There are lots of luxury hotels, restaurants, beach cabanas, and watersports facilities.

A better grade of beach is at **Psili Ammos**, about five kilometers from

Pythagorian (by excursion boat) on the south coast and ten kilometers from Samos. There's occasional bus service to Psili Ammos from Samos town.

A popular beach excursion is a visit to **Samiopoula**, a boat ride away to an excellent and usually uncrowded island beach. Samiopoula is a small island that has some pensions.

NIGHTLIFE: The best discos in Samos town are **Babylon** and **Flash**. There are several singles bars in the lanes just off the port and a bouzouki club in Samos called the **Green Hill**.

In Mitillini, the **Panorama** is the top bouzouki club. Nightlife in Pythagorian is much more restrained (the **Three Brothers** baizouki club is near the airport.) The new **San Lorenzo,** above the town on the Samos road, is considered the island's best.

There are **cinemas** in Samos, Pythagorian, and Kokkari, all of the outdoor variety and mostly showing kung-fu films.

GETTING TO TURKEY: There are usually boats leaving every day from the docks of Samos or Pythagorian for Kuşadasi, a comfortable resort 20 minutes from Ephesus. During the height of summer there are two boats making the short jaunt. Several travel agents sell boat tickets (it's a $50 day trip, so negotiate a one-way fare); if you submit your passport a day in advance, it won't be a problem to get a seat. You'll have to pay Greece's new 1500-dr ($12) port tax also. (Refer to the section on Kuşadasi in Chapter XVIII for more information.)

GETTING THERE: There are **boats** from Piraeus twice a day. The journey takes 12 hours. Thrice weekly a steamer connects Samos and Chios, taking five hours from port to port. There's one steamer a week to the Dodecanese. Three times a week there are ferries to the Cyclades from Karlovassi and **excursion boats** leaving Pythagorion for Patmos. **Olympic Airways** offers three flights daily from Athens and new service from Mykonos, Chios, Lesbos, and Thessaloniki in the summer.

2. Chios

Compared to the more familiar and heavily trampled Greek islands, Chios (Hios) is on the frontiers of tourism. Few Europeans, and even fewer Americans, have discovered this remote spot, but for the adventurous it offers an almost unlimited variety of beaches, intact medieval villages—where you can rent a room in a 700-year-old house—excellent fishing, and a unique identity. The elite families that control Greece's private shipping empires tend to congregate behind high stone fences on secluded, and usually exquisite, islands, a point of pride for locals.

Chios is the genuine article, a shipowner's island of immense wealth and exceptional scenic and cultural beauty. The names Onassis (who came to the island from Smyrna during the massive population exchange between Greece and Turkey), Livanos, Karas, Pateros, and Chandris are only part of Chios's modern-day pantheon. For the visitor, Chios is one island where tourism is a relative sidelight; the merchant navy employs about 80% of the work force. The home-grown mastic industry produces millions in revenue from Chiclets and other gum products. The island is an ideal destination for those who want to escape the hordes, even in the height of summer, and is also one of the best places from which to cross over to Turkey. From Chios, boats connect to Çeşme, near Izmir, and the journey takes a scant 40 minutes.

ORIENTATION: Boats dock at **Chios town**, the largest town on the island and a thriving, refreshingly Greek port filled with Greeks. Late-19th-century mansions (and some dating as far back as the 14th-century), in various states of repair, line the highways on the outskirts of town. Most are enclosed by tall stone walls, shielding their occupants from inquiring tourists. From Chios, buses and roads lead to the island's many beaches, inland villages, and historical sites. There are beaches on nearly every coast of Chios. The black-stone beach at **Emborios**, on the southern tip of the island, is magnificent. Chios isn't as green as the Sporades, but wide sections of the island are covered with lemon, orange, almond, olive, and pine trees.

The most interesting villages, dating from medieval times, are **Pirgi** and **Mesta**. Both are in the mastic region, in the southern half of Chios, so named because of the gum trees that still grow in the countryside—mastic in the Phoenician language was *chio*, which may account for the island's name. Pirgi is known throughout Greece for the distinctive gray-and-white geometric designs that decorate the façades of most of the village buildings. Mesta, and many of the hamlets surrounding it (including **Olympi** and **Vessa**), are architectural gems; these villages' two-story stone-and-mortar houses are linked by narrow vaulted streets and quiet platias. **Nea Moni**, atop a jagged hill in the mountainous interior north of Chios town, is an 11th-century monastery containing some of the most superb mosaics in Greece.

Although no one knows for sure where Homer was born, most historians believe that he was from Chios. The "Stone of Homer," where the blind poet was supposed to have sat when he composed his legendary works, is outside of Vrodados in a grove of olive trees, at the ancient site of the Temple of Cybele and Rhea.

USEFUL INFORMATION: The **Tourist Police** (tel. 26-555) are headquartered on the far right side of the harbor as you hop off the boat. There is a new Chios **Tourist Information Office** (tel. 0271/20-488), located at 11 Kanari St., one block off the port opposite the O.T.E. They are very helpful and will assist you in finding a reasonably priced room. Open 7 a.m. to 2:30 p.m. and 6:30 p.m. to 9 p.m. Monday through Friday, 7 a.m. to 1 p.m. on Saturday.

There is another mine of information on the harbor, to the far left near the chunky Chandris Hotel, at **Chios Tours** (tel. 29-444). They will assist you with your room search and may even get you a discount. Chios Tours organizes excursions around the island, to Çeşme, Turkey, and to Samos. They rent very serviceable mopeds for 1800 drs ($11) and can make or confirm international air reservations—all in all, a top-notch shop.

There's a **Commercial Bank of Greece** on the port and a **National Bank** in town, a couple of blocks behind the waterfront. Chios Tours or the Tourist Office will change money after the banks' normal hours. . . . The **post office** and **O.T.E.** are a block off the harbor on the right side. The telephone **area code** of Chios is 0271. . . . All of the ferry companies keep offices on the port. The **Olympic Airways** office is in the middle of the port road, (tel. 22-414).

GETTING AROUND: If you arrive by plane, count on taking a cab into town. **Taxis** to and from the airport are about 300 drs ($2.30) for the seven-kilometer ride. All **buses** leave from Chios town; the blue buses serve local destinations, green buses the more remote locales. There are three buses a day to Mesta ($1.25 or $14 by taxi), seven a day to Pirgi ($1 or $10 by taxi), five to Kardamilla, and only one bus a day to Volissos. Chios is a great place for **moped** riding. The roads are generally in good condition and the scenery is some of the best in Greece. There are moped-rental shops on the left side of the port. If you wish to rent a car, try **Budget** (tel. 23-505). They have an office in town, at 6 Petrokkinou, and a desk at the airport to meet incoming passengers. Compact cars rent for about $40 per day, but make sure to inquire about the specific terms of insurance. Also check the prices at **George Sotirakis Rent-A-Car** (tel. 29-754), located next to the Chandris Hotel.

ACCOMMODATIONS: If you're just arriving on Chios, it might make sense to find accommodations in the town before setting off for the rest of the island. This will give you time to wander about and to make arrangements. For budgetary and aesthetic reasons, try to find a room in one of the island's many special villages, although you'll need your own transportation to sightsee.

In the Town of Chios

At the south end of the port behind the modern, styleless but expensive Hotel Chandris is the much older **Hotel Kyma** (tel. 0271/25-551), built in 1917 as a private villa for John Livanos—you can't help seeing a portrait of Mrs. Livanos on the ceiling in the lobby. Though the hotel is of historical interest (the treaty with the Turks was signed in the Kyma in 1922), few of the original architectural details survive; all the rooms have been renovated (to their detriment). On the positive side, many rooms have views of the sea and the breakfast includes fresh mandarin oranges (actually, they're delicious Chios oranges). A room for two with—surprise—a double bed costs 6000 drs ($46). Their breakfast costs an additional 500 drs ($3.80).

The **Hotel Diana** (tel. 0271/25-993) is a 51-room C-class inn located at 92 Venizelou, one block in from the port. The rooms are comfortable and clean, similar to most newly built C-class hotels. Doubles with shower run 5200 drs ($40); singles, 4000 drs ($31).

One of the best values in town can be found at the small but cozy **Hotel Rhodon** (tel. 0271/24-335), located just off the port near the Customs House, at 17 Zachariou St. (Keep going straight in from the port road where it curves). A simple, clean bathless double will cost 2700 drs ($21). A "Rooms to Let" section upstairs in the same establishment runs 1000 drs ($7.50) less. Breakfast is an additional 200 drs ($1.50).

The **Hotel Filoxenia** (tel. 0271/22-813) is an old-fashioned hotel with brass railings, a lobby with a skylight, and a staircase lined with plants. Located at Vupalu 6, about two blocks inland, halfway between the port and the public gardens, it offers very basic rooms, clean but worn, for up to 4000 drs ($31).

It's half past midnight, you just got off the ferry from Piraeus or Samos, don't have a room, and the town is dead. What do you do? Walk straight ahead, away from the port, and into the pleasant **Pension Giannis** (tel. 0271/27-433). You'll pay more than elsewhere, but the rooms are fine, all have private bath, and the garden behind it is a treat. The tariff for two is 3000 drs ($23).

The town has a large number of private rooms; you can expect to pay 1800 drs ($14) for two. Contact the Tourist Office for a reference.

Outside of Town

Six kilometers to the south of town, in the village of **Kampos**, is the **Pension Perivoli** (tel. 0271/31-513). Maria Xeria has renovated the building, making it a very special hostel, much in the style of the old homes in Mesta. The Perivoli offers rooms with and without showers: prices for either are 5000 drs ($38.50) for two. *Note:* The Pervioli is often sold out to groups.

There are also private rooms and houses in **Karfas**, a small village one kilometer farther south.

Marcos Place (tel. 0271/31-990) is an old converted monastery run by Marcos Kostalos. The 15 rooms have been fixed up but are still very simple. Charming monk's cells for two rent for 1900 drs ($15). However, you must call ahead for availability. Marcos and his lovely girlfriend, Erica, book German yoga groups throughout the summer, leaving only a few rooms open.

Just 3 kilometers north of Chios town, in Vrondatos, is the **Xenios Hotel** (tel. 0271/26-758), a new, very tasteful C-class hotel with rooms facing the sea or mountains, for 4550 drs ($35), including breakfast.

Traditional Villages

There are a few villages in Greece that still seem timeless; built in centuries past, life appears to have changed little in the intervening years. Many of these villages are outdoor architectural museums, studied and appreciated for their unique styles of construction. Unfortunately, these isolated villages have been deserted by the younger members of the community who prefer life in Athens or America. **Mesta** is just such a village, and fortunately, the Greek government acquired 33 old abandoned homes to protect them from further deterioration. Four of these homes, originally built 300 to 400 years ago, have been restored and opened by the National Tourist Office of Greece as part of their Traditional Settlements program. The wonderful Dimitri Pipidis (tel. 0271/72-319) manages the houses and each comes equipped with a kitchen, bathroom, and enough sleeping space for two to six people. The price is determined by the number of beds: for one bed, 3300 drs ($25); two beds, 3900 drs ($30); and three beds, 4900 drs ($38).

If there is no answer at the Mesta number, just drive to the village and ask for Dimitri. If his houses are booked, Dimitri will assist you in finding one of the many private rooms in Mesta. Even though it's pricey, don't pass up the opportunity to stay in one of these homes. It's a real treat. In the high season, contact the main office on Lesbos (tel. 0251/27-908) for reservations, a must in the busy summer months.

In the other mastic villages the only accommodation may be a room in the home of a local family. The **Women's Agricultural-Tourist Cooperative of Chios**, like their counterparts on Lesbos, offers a program enabling tourists to share the life of local farm families. In the towns of Mesta, Pirgi, Armolia, or Olimpi, you can enjoy this experience for 2200 drs ($17) for two, plus an additional 250 drs ($2) for breakfast. Though not required, you can weave, cook, or work in the fields with your host. In any of the villages, except Mesta, we think it's the best choice. For reservations, write to the cooperative at Pyrgi 82100, Chios, Greece, or call 0271/72-496.

For the traveler with latent hermetic tendencies, visit Psara, a small island off the west coast of Chios, where rooms are offered in a restored monastery under the same price scale as the Mesta houses. Call the main Lesbos office (tel. 0251/27-908) for information. Ferry service runs to Psara from Chios three times a week.

RESTAURANTS: The paucity of tourists on Chios, usually such a blessing, means that there are few tavernas, pizzarias, bouzouki clubs, and tost shops outside of the port. In Chios town, try **Giannis Taverna** (tel. 28-663), located next to the Hotel Diana at 90 Venizelou St. Large portions of *gigantes,* dolmades, *yuvetsi,* and other taverna standards are ladled out day and night to the Chiotis who work in the area. For a more formal meal (where the locals go to celebrate), try the **Chios Marine Club** (tel. 23-184), or Naftikos Omilos Xios (NOX). The club is a startlingly modern edifice on the shore (behind the Chandris Hotel), where tables with cloths, fresh flowers, and glassware create a luxurious setting.

As befits a wealthy clientele, excellent service and fancy trappings don't try to outdo the food; it's simple Greek fare at its best, with a large variety of vegetable dishes, fresh bread, several wines, and excellently prepared lamb. Its owner, Tassos, has an outdoor summer place where the same standards apply in an informal garden setting across the road from the water, at 6 Livanou St. **Tassos Restaurant** (tel. 27-542) is packed on a nice evening with kids and their families —a great place to watch the island's older generations pay tribute to the young. If you're looking for romance and moonlight, NOX's seaside tables are a better alternative. A feast with wine, at either, should cost about 500 drs ($3.50) a person. Of the many cafés in the port, our nod goes to **Iviskos**, in the mid-stretch. Not only do they serve wonderful bread with their 7 a.m. breakfast, but they also serve a dynamite black forest cake until 2 a.m. Shoppers should head two blocks in from the port to the main platia, where you'll find bakers, butchers, produce vendors, etc. Cheaper are the tavernas clustered on the right side of the port, nothing to write home about but certainly passable.

If you're in **Emborio** or **Pasalimani** make sure to try the fish and squid. Both villages are known for their seafood, and you can watch the fishermen bring in their catch right in front of your table. The same is true just north of **Vrondados** at the **Ormos Lo Restaurant**, near the public beach.

WHAT TO SEE AND DO: Greeks come to Chios for weeks at a time to take advantage of its many secluded beaches. Chios also has some of the most scenic countryside and villages in the country, as well as a monastery that contains some of the best mosaics in Byzantium.

Beaches

Imagine being able to go to a Greek island at the end of June and finding only six or seven other people on a spectacular beach. That dream is a reality on Chios. Beginning with the best, **Emborios** is a small fishing village built around a volcanically formed cove. The water appears black from the dark smooth stones on the ocean floor. Men wade knee-deep to catch squid and pry off crustaceans while snorkelers explore the colorful seabed. Two fish tavernas overlook this cozy little harbor. Walk about 250 meters up the road to the right of the town over to a small man-made black-pebble beach that's filled with families. Don't be disappointed, because just over those rocks to your right is a beach that will knock your socks off. Walking on the black rocks feels and sounds like marching through a room filled with marbles, the sound reverberating against the rough volcanic cliff behind. The panorama of the beach, slightly curving coastline, and distant sea is heaven on earth. Yes, we are fond of this beach! There is a bus from Chios town or from Pirgi (eight kilometers away) to Emborios, or you can try hitching along the main highway from Chios.

Up the coast, about two kilometers, is a white-stone beach at **Komi**. If the best is on the far southern point of the island, it follows that second best should be on the extreme northern coast. **Nagos** is another seaside village that offers some great black-sand beaches. Most people go to the beach right near the town, but it can sometimes become crowded. The secret is to hike to the two small beaches a little to the east—take the small road behind the white house near the windmill and you'll get there. To get to Nagos you'll have to take the Kardamilla bus and hope that it'll continue the five kilometers to the beach. If not, you can usually get a ride by waving down a private car.

If you're looking for a totally isolated beach where you can camp, try the ten-kilometer stretch on the west side of the island around **Limia** (outside of Volissos). There's rarely anyone there, perhaps because the bus only runs once a day, waits two hours and returns.

There are quite a few beaches near Chios town. To the south is **Bella Vista**, a sandy beach that's often crowded. There's a sandy beach at **Karfas**, and a shallow bay. To the north, at **Vrondados**, are two pebble beaches, one public, the other private, but open for a 100 drs (75¢) fee.

Around the Island

The two most interesting excursions are to the mastic villages, including Vessa, Armolia, Pirgi, Olimpi, and Mesta, and to Nea Moni, the 11th-century monastery in the center of the island. If you don't mind a moped, take the road south—remember your map—and follow it inland over the rustic hills and plains to **Pirgi**. Pirgi is the only village in Greece decorated with such a distinctive white-and-gray motif. From the main platia the view is like some strange Op Art dream with the geometric patterns taking on a life of their own. The men who sit at the outdoor cafés don't seem to be fazed at all. The irony is that of all villages in Greece, Pirgi is where the majority of coffeeshop owners in New York City come from. Just off the main square in Pirgi is the 12th-century Byzantine chapel, the Saint Apostle Church, built in the style of the earlier Nea Moni. It's a tiny jewel, with 17th-century frescoes still in good condition.

Mesta is very different from Pirgi. This remarkable 14th-century village was built inside a system of walls, with corner towers and iron gates to fend off invaders. The meter-thick, attached walls of the houses create a labyrinthian maze of streets that will charm, delight, and disorient you. Though many young people have moved away, life is thriving in Mesta thanks to the many renovation projects inspired by the Traditional Settlement Program. The arch-roofed houses that have withstood centuries of earthquakes reveal interiors having a grace rarely seen by Western eyes. Life is slow and quiet here, and the moped has yet to violate the sanctuary that is Mesta. There are two beautiful churches; the newer one (it's 120 years old) is the fourth-largest and one of the wealthiest churches in Greece. Its ornate frescoes, massive chandeliers and lovely icons make it worth a stop on your trip through the main square. The older church, Paleos Taxiarhis, is buried deep in the village; the gatekeeper lives across the street. Its Byzantine frescoes have been revealed beneath the plaster that covered them during its use as a Turkish mosque. Both churches are dedicated to the patron saints of the village, Michael and Gabriel.

Chios is ringed by several private islets that are served by charter boats, if you want to finance a special day trip. The most famous of these is **Oinousai**, an 18-square-kilometer island that is home to 30 multimillionaire families who are said to control 25% of Greece's 2,700 registered-vessel merchant fleet. Constantine Lemos, who supposedly grosses a million dollars a day, is only one among many who form the tightly knit society on Oinousai. The social life on this private isle is rumored to be as wild as anything in Greece.

Five nuns live a much quieter life at **Nea Moni**, a medieval church built by craftsmen brought over from Turkey. It's one of Greece's prettiest monasteries, with an octagonal chapel that is highlighted by exquisite mosaics: marble white, azure blue, and ruby red dominate the glittering field of gold tiles. If you've arrived from Turkey and visited the Kariye Camii in Istanbul, the high quality and style of these mosaics should be familiar (though the work in Istanbul is more recent). These at Nea Moni are the best of their kind, on par with those at Ossios Loukas and Dafni. Be sure to look into the cistern, a cavernous vaulted room with columns, just to your right as you come through the main gate. The small chapel at the entrance to the monastery is dedicated to the martyrs of the 1822 massacre by the Turks. The skulls and bones are the victims themselves.

There are only a few buses each week (check the schedule at the station) to Nea Moni; you may have to take a moped, car, or taxi. The road traverses valleys, ridges, and hills with nary a straight stretch of highway. It's a challenging ride. Nea Moni is closed daily from 1 p.m. to 4 p.m. (the nuns' nap) and after 8 p.m.; otherwise it's open.

GETTING TO TURKEY: During the summer there are daily departures to Turkey from the port of Chios. The price is 3000 drs ($23). In the other months boats run less frequently; check with the portside travel agents such as Chios Tours. All boats going to Turkey call at Çeşme, described in Chapter XVIII. Çeşme is a 45-minute bus ride from Izmir, the Aegean coast transportation hub of Asia Minor. From Izmir, buses run frequently to Istanbul and all the coastal cities.

GETTING THERE: Olympic Airways has three flights daily from Athens to Chios; the flight takes a scant 30 minutes compared to the 10- to 12-hour ferry ride from Piraeus. There are two flights each week to Mykonos, Samos, and Lesbos. There are **ferry** connections to Piraeus or Lesbos (daily except Sunday), and Thessaloniki, Kavala, and the Dodecanese, (once a week). Check with the **Chios Port Authority** (tel. 22-837) or the Tourist Information Office for current schedules.

3. Lesbos

It's impossible to think about Lesbos (also called Lesvos or Mytillini) without the island's two most obvious, and related, associations: the love of women by women and the great classical poet Sappho, whom Plato dubbed the Tenth Muse. Legends abound about the origin of the former, some suggesting that it developed as a cult or college devoted to Aphrodite (possibly founded by Sappho), others theorizing that the island became "lesbian" when the Athenians wreaked vengeance on its inhabitants, after a failed rebellion, by murdering all of its men. As for Sappho, she is an equal mystery because so little of her writing has survived. What is known is that she lived in the seventh century B.C. and was born in the village of Eressos on the western part of the island. She wrote openly about love and desire, of men and women: "Desire shakes me once again/here is that melting of my limbs./It is a creeping thing, and bittersweet./I can do nothing to resist." Sappho's tragic legend of love began with her unrequited passion for Phaon, an attractive younger man, whom Sappho followed across the sea to the mainland. When he finally rejected her in Lefkas, Sappho flung herself over the white cliffs and plunged to her death.

That Lesbos was an artistic center is without dispute (there is still a festival each May called "The Week of Prose and Arts"), but it was most famous in ancient times for its academics and symposia. Theophrastus, director of the Athens Academy, was from Lesbos—both Aristotle and Plato went to Lesbos to teach and study. The maxims "Know thyself" and "Nothing in excess," inscribed on the Temple at Delphi, were taken from the writings of Pitticus, one of the Seven Sages of Greece and a tyrant of Lesbos. The philosopher Epicurus came to Lesbos from Samos to study and write: "Accustom thyself to believe that death is nothing to us, for good and evil imply sentience, and death is the privation of all sentience, therefore a right understanding that death is nothing to us makes the mortality of life enjoyable, not by adding to life an illimitable time, but by taking away the yearning after immortality." He also wrote, "Pleasure is our first and kindred good," which is something that one who has lived on the lovely island of Lesbos has the privilege to say.

ORIENTATION: Lesbos, Greece's third-largest island, is shaped something like a rounded triangle with two inland bays fed by the Aegean through a pair of south coastal channels.

Mytillini (and the airport) are on the southeastern corner of the triangle, just across from Ayvalik, on the Turkish coast. The east coast road, leading up to **Mandamados**, is the most scenic on the island; olive and fruit trees grow down to the water's edge and thermal springs form warm pools that attract bathers. **Mithymna** (now called Molyvos), at the northern tip of the triangle, is a castle-crowned village with stone and pink-pastel stucco mansions capped by red-tile roofs. The town overlooks the sea, its modest harbor, and flanking pebble beaches overflowing with sunners and swimmers. Seven kilometers south of Mithymna is the enterprising village of **Petra**, where the Women's Agricultural-Tourist Cooperative program welcomes visitors to live in local homes.

The paved road to Mithymna meets the west-bound road at **Kaloni**, a sardine center four kilometers north of Lesbos's largest inland body of water. The western half of the island is the least visited; uncrowded sandy beaches run the length of the coast from Sigri to Skala Eressou. The villages on this part of Lesbos are as serene as one finds on the island.

Plomari is 40 kilometers southwest of Mytillini. It's a village very much like Mithymna, but with a significant twist: Plomari is one of Greece's major ouzo centers. If you're there when the potent drink is being distilled your nose will catch the fennel scent wafting in the breeze.

USEFUL INFORMATION: The **Tourist Police** (tel. 22-776) are headquartered on the port in Mytillini. They're open daily from 8 a.m. to 3 p.m. and 5 p.m. to 9 p.m. and have a complete listing of hotels, pensions, and rooms throughout the island, and are willing to make calls for you. . . . There's a cluster of **banks** near the portside hotels (the Sappho and Lesvion) on Pavlou Koudouriotou. They're all open from 8 a.m. to 2 p.m., although the post office and nearby travel agents also change money.

The telephone **area code** for Mytillini is 0251, for Mithymna it's 0253, and for Plomari it's 0252. . . . The **O.T.E.** is a long block up from the harbor on Vournazon near the park. . . . The **post office** is next door.

Olympic Airways (tel. 28-659) has an office at 44 Kavetsou, about seven blocks south of the port (walk up from the harbor and turn left); their airport bus leaves 75 minutes before flight time. . . . The **Cooperative Tourism and Travel Agency** (tel. 21-329) at 5 Constantinoupolis St., next to the bus station, will help you find rooms in any of the island's rural areas. . . . **Theodore** at Olympia Express (tel. 27-082), on the port, can book tickets and make other travel arrangements. **Aeolic Cruises** (tel. 23-960), and other portside agents sell ferryboat tickets.

The **Vostanio Hospital** (tel. 28-457) on E. Votsani St. will take care of emergencies. . . . The **Port Police** (tel. 28-647) is located on the paralia, as is the **Maritime Company** of Lesbos (tel. 23-720), for ferry information.

GETTING AROUND: Lesbos has an expensive and infrequent **bus** system with daily service to Kaloni, Mithymna (two hours, three times), Mandamados (three times), Plomari (one hour, five times), and Eressos and Sigri (once). The **city bus station** and **taxi stand** are on the port near the Sappho Hotel. The round-the-island K.T.E.L. buses can be caught at the south end of the port behind the Argo Hotel. Lesbos is a big island (a taxi to Mithymna cost $20 one way), better suited to cars and buses than mopeds. There are many **car-rental offices** on the port in Mytillini; **Lesbos Cars** (tel. 28-242) has offices in Mytillini and

Mithymna, as well as a desk at the airport. Expect to pay 6000 drs ($45) a day without gas for a Fiat-127. **Aeolic Cruises** (tel. 23-960) offers daily **boat excursions** around the island (costing 1800 drs, or $15).

MYTILLINI: If you approach the capital by sea you'll see the giant tan stone Genoese fortress on the pine-covered mound to the north of the port. The modern city, with little style of its own, is built on the remains of ancient Mytillini; the only vestige of that city is the Hellenistic theater to the west of town. Mytillini is built amphitheatrically around the port and the ornate, peaked dome Church of St. Therapon. The port street, or Prokymaia, is **P. Koundourioti Street**, the most important area of the city for tourists, with nearly all services, shops, and hotels. Behind the new dock is the **archeological museum** (open 3 p.m. to 6 p.m. Wednesday and Thursday and 9 a.m. to 6 p.m. Saturday and Sunday; with a fine sculpture collection. In a small white house in the center of the port is the fine **Folk Art Museum**, open Monday through Friday from 9 a.m. to 1 p.m. and 7 to 9 p.m. Its current curator and guide, Ioanna, will give you a wonderful tour of its fine embroideries, eccentric pottery (much of which came from Çannakale, Turkey), costumes, and historical documents. Three kilometers south, in Varia, is the former house—now a museum—of **folk artist Hadjimichael Theophilos** (1868–1934). Theophilos emigrated from the Mount Pelion region to paint in Mytillini. His watercolors of ordinary people, daily life, and local landscapes are widely celebrated, and they are also exhibited at the excellent Museum of Folk Art in the Plaka, in Athens. The **Teriad Library and Museum of Modern Art** is nearby in the home of the noted art critic Stratis Eleftheriadis-Teriad. Copies of his published works, including the *Minotaure* and *Verve* magazines, as well as his personal collection of works by Picasso, Matisse, and other modern artists are displayed. Both museums are open daily except Monday. There is also a **Traditional House of Mytillini** (tel. 28-550), in front of the cathedral in the center of town, whose interior has been restored and furnished in a 19th-century style. Admission is by appointment only, with Mrs. Vlahou Marika.

After you've seen these, head to the bus station to explore other, more interesting parts of the island.

Accommodations and Dining

Almost all the hotels in Mytillini are located on or very near the port. There aren't many hotel rooms available so if you're stuck in the high season, try the Tourist Police or a portside travel agent for help. The best bet, along the paralia, in between the row of banks, are the C-class hotels **Sappho** (tel. 0251/28-888) and **Lesvion** (tel. 0251/22-038). Doubles run about 3200 drs ($25) in the Sappho for rooms with private facilities, although shared-bath doubles at 2600 drs ($20) can be found in both inns. The Lesvion's rates run about 10% higher but it's a bit better kept. Mid-port is the one hundred-year-old **Megali Vretannia** (tel. 0251/28-449). Kyle has a weakness for these charming white elephants; this is no exception. The Megali Vretannia's rooms are small but neat, with simple furnishings, and although each floor has common toilets, only the middle floor has three showers to share. The exterior really does have more style than the interior, but portside rooms have great views (you'll go moped-crazy at night) and the rates are good: 2250 drs ($17) for two. One of the more convenient pensions is a block behind the portside ferryboat offices on Komninaki Street. Here the tiny **Pansion Afea** (tel. 0251/25-977) has two cots in each brightly painted room, and a nice second-floor sundeck on which to breakfast. We stayed nearby, on Kilkis Street (tel. 0251/21-559), in another townhouse, and can also recommend the bathless, well-kept rooms at **Pansion Sofi** (tel. 0251/25-729) at 22

Giannarelli, about two blocks inland from the O.T.E. All of these rooms (often full till late June, when students at Mytillini's Teachers College vacate them for the summer) cost about $8 a person.

Mytillini, with its youthful, somewhat avant-garde population, has even more portside cafés and tavernas than your average bustling harbor town. **Arapis Grill,** mid-port near the Sappho Hotel, is one of the better grills around, with particularly good beef dishes. At the southern end of the port (opposite the new docks) are several small **ouzeris,** specializing in grilled octopus, squid, shrimp, and local fish. Small portions of tsadziki, patates, and olives accompany wine or one of the many types of ouzo from Plomari. The cluster of chairs around the small lighthouse at the point is the most scenic (as well as the windiest) of these places. For après-ouzo there are several cafés, but on soccer night it's almost impossible to get a seat.

AROUND THE ISLAND: Many visitors to Lesbos prefer to stay in Mithymna, up on the north coast, and take excursions from there. Alternatively one could do the same thing from the south coast village of Plomari, but both locations have been somewhat taken over by groups. If you want to disappear into Lesbos's seductive landscape, head to the west, where few visitors tread.

Mithymna (Molyvos) and the North

The legend told most often about Mithymna concerns Arion, a seventh-century B.C. contemporary of Sappho and poet-musician. Apollo told Arion in a dream that the sailors who were returning him to Lesbos were going to kill him for the prize he won in a music contest. The events unfolded as Apollo had prophesied, and when Arion was granted one last wish, he asked the sailors if he could play his lyre. They consented and Arion, at the very last moment, played and jumped into the sea. He was picked up by a school of appreciative dolphins, who carried him on their backs to the shores at Mithymna. Historians believe that part of the story is based on fact.

The village is a wonderful place to soak up a lot of Greek atmosphere: the men who live in cafés, studying their ouzo, the bright, colorful geraniums and roses that decorate balconies and sills, the unfathomable layout of streets, alleyways, and passages, and the women, always working, who have a special place on Lesbos. The genuine atmosphere draws a European arts crowd that resides there summers. In Molyvos, you can wander up to the Genoese fortress, stroll along the port, or swim at the local pebble beaches.

Two of the more interesting excursions from Mithymna are visits to **Petra,** a fishing village just a few kilometers south, and **Mandamados,** a village known for the manufacture of *koumaria,* ceramic vases that magically keep water cool even in scorching heat. In Petra, the **Committee for the Equal Rights of the Two Sexes** started a housing program to place visitors in local homes, where they can help in the fields, in the kitchens, or in the local women's handicraft cooperative. The **Women's Agricultural–Tourist Cooperative of Petra** (tel. 0253/41-238) has a reception area in the village; stop in to find a double room (2600 drs, or $20 with breakfast), or try their restaurant. The back roads that connect Mithymna with Mandamados are rarely paved; you're more likely to come across a toothless farmer dragging his reluctant donkey than a slick-looking tour bus. Ask the staff at the tourist office, next to the bus stop in Mithymna, for specifics on these short bus trips. The same office will help you find a room in one of Mithymna's traditional gray-stone homes. There are many good pensions as you walk down away from the port, but almost all are presold to group tours. The restaurants at the modest-looking port are the best and least expensive.

Plomari and the South

Located on the south coast, Plomari is another sleepy, tiered fishing village that has been able to accept a little tourist development without selling its soul. The village has the same appeal as Mithymna: winding streets, mysterious passageways, outdoor cafés, a scenic harbor, and a relaxed pace that will make you wonder how you could have lived any other way. Plomari is especially known for its potent ouzo. The in-town beaches are fine for swimming, but travel a few kilometers east to **Ag. Isodoros** for better water, a long pebble beach, and a growing number of pensions and condos. The **Oceanis** (tel. 0252/32-469), a 42-room C-class inn, rents doubles for 3200 drs ($25). Plomari has a large number of private rooms for rent. Maria Tsaramirsis (tel. 0252/32-120) rents them in her lush citrus garden. Due west on Lesbos's south coast is the popular sand beach at **Vatera**, that's 8 km long, 30 m wide, and often jammed.

A really enjoyable day trip is to the rural hamlet of **Agiassos** (as seen in Mytillini's Folk Art Museum, 23 kilometers north), where local craftsmen still turn out their ceramicware by hand. The town, built up on the foothills of Mt. Olympus, consists of traditional greystone houses whose wooden "Turkish" balconies are covered in flowering vines, narrow cobblestone lanes and modest churches.

Skala Eressos and the West

The best beach on Lesbos is far to the west at Skala Eressos. A long stretch of sandy beaches and coves extends north from there to Sigri. The few who stay in this area prefer the village of **Eressos**, Sappho's birthplace, four kilometers north of Skala. When you return from the beach you can visit the archeology museum, behind the Church of St. Andrew, the Byzantine-era fortress (closed Monday), or the fifth-century basilica, Ag. Andreas. The new **Hotel Alkeos** (tel. 0253/53-311), run by Dimitreos Psaradellis and his wife, now has 30 doubles with bath for 2400 drs ($18.50). The Alkeos is a five-minute walk from the beach. If you choose to stay at the beach there's a lot of summer-home construction and some rooms to let.

Sigri, with its Turkish fortress from 1757, is an even more isolated destination. You may have the whole beach to yourself. There's a petrified forest on the way to Sigri that's a victim of the ravages of tourism.

GETTING TO TURKEY: Although few Americans heading to Lesbos realize there's a direct connection to Turkey via the port of Ayvalik, about 30,000 tourists make the crossing annually. During the high season, ships to Turkey sail daily except Sunday. Tickets for the Turkish boats are sold by **Aeolic Cruises Travel Agency** (tel. 23-960) on the port in Mytillini for about $24; submit your passport one day in advance of departure. Ayvalik, a densely wooded fishing village, makes a refreshing base camp from which to tour Pergamum or ancient Troy. For more information, consult Chapter XVIII.

GETTING THERE: The 188-nautical-mile voyage from Piraeus to Lesbos takes 14 hours, just about the longest trip to any Greek island. There are **boats** daily calling at Mytillini from Piraeus. The boat from Chios stops at Lesbos daily except Sunday. There are also steamship connections to Thessaloniki (in the high season only), Kavala, Limnos (both thrice weekly), and Samothraki, Alexandroupolis, and the Dodecanese, on an infrequent basis. Call the **Maritime Co.** (0251/23-720) or the **Port Police** (tel. 0251/28-647) for current schedules. **Olympic Airways** has up to five flights daily to Athens, one daily from Thessaloniki, four flights weekly from Limnos, three from Rhodes, and two flights weekly from Samos and Chios.

4. Limnos

The rough jagged rocks which enclose Limnos's port, Mirina, suggest a volcanic antecedent, perhaps related to the Olympian god of iron and fire, Hephaestus. Born ugly and lame, Hephaestus was cast out by his father Zeus, and as Milton wrote, was "Dropt from the zenith like a falling star, on Lemnos, the Aegean isle." Here he fashioned shields and spears for the Olympians and created a race of cast-gold robotic maidens. They stoked the fiery furnace which caused the volcanic disturbances that mark Limnos. Limnos was, for a short time, dominated by women. Aphrodite made the island's women repulsive to their husbands, because the men had favored Hephaestus over her during the couple's tempestuous marriage. The ignored women turned their mounting sexual tension back onto their men and ultimately slaughtered them—they poisoned their wine, slit their throats, and tossed them into the sea. For a while the island was inhabited only by women, until the *Argo* and its manly crew pulled into Limnos's snug harbor to repopulate the island.

The Venetians controlled the island during the Middle Ages. The vast castle and fortifications on the left hill above the harbor are today balanced by a lovely white chapel on the right hill. Few tourists visit windswept Limnos and even fewer head off to the island's arid interior. During antiquity soil from Limnos was thought to have healing power, and exports were strictly regulated. Today the most sought-after but rarely exported product of Limnos is its delicious wine.

MIRINA: The best activity on Limnos, and in the sleepy town of Mirina particularly, is to go to the beach. There are two excellent **beaches** within a few kilometers south of the port: **Plati** is the closer of the two; **Thanos** is less crowded. The port is lined with a clean sand beach, but why not make the extra effort (you already have if you've made it to Limnos) and day-trip to the above destinations. You can rent a bicycle in town, or a car if you decide to explore further. One kilometer west of town, around the fortified hill, is the complex of luxury, exorbitantly priced bungalows, **Akti Mirina** (tel. 0254/22-681), which dominate the scene with their restaurant, a private beach, and good climbing rocks.

More affordable is the blue-and-white Hotel **Lemnos** (tel. 0254/22-153), on the platia 28 Octovriou. Expect to pay 3000 drs ($24) for private bath doubles with large balconies overlooking the harbor. The **Aktaeon** (tel. 0254/22-258), on the paralia is a smaller, well-maintained hotel with some charm. Double rooms run 3300 drs ($25) with shared facilities, and 3700 drs ($28) with private bath. The **Thraki** (tel. 0254/22-617), is another choice nearby with similar prices. All are open year round. Private rooms are available, but you'll have to bargain, because the Limniots will often double the "expected" rate for the few tourists they meet. The best seaside taverna is behind the sheltered fishing boat mooring.

There is a **Tourist Police** (tel. 22-200), an **O.T.E.**, and **post office** in Mirina. The telephone **area code** for the island is 0254. **Olympic Airways** (tel. 22-214) is on Garofalidi St., in Mirina. Their airport bus departs 90 minutes before flight time and costs 200 drs ($1.60).

GETTING THERE: Getting to Limnos isn't much of a problem because it's connected by boat to Kavala four times weekly, to Lesbos twice weekly, and to Chios, Samothraki, Alexandroupoli, the Dodecanese (departing from Kos), and the Evian port of Kymi infrequently. The schedule changes frequently, so you'll have to contact the **Limnos Port Authority** (tel. 22-225) or the **Port Authority** (or travel agency) from your point of origin. **Olympic Airways** has two flights daily to Limnos from Athens, one flight daily from Thessaloniki, and four flights weekly from Lesbos.

5. Samothraki

Samothraki is a forbidding place. Not only is it a very windy, rocky, mountainous island with a port that's nearly impossible to navigate (there really is no natural harbor), but in ancient times the ultra-secretive Mysteries were practiced here—with a vague suggestion of human sacrifice. Even Samothraki's Mount Moon (Fengari), one of the highest in the region, has a name that resonates with darkness and the unknown. Other than for religious pilgrimages, few people ever visited the island; it successfully avoided the invasions and disasters that befell the other Aegean islands. The situation remains much the same today: Samothraki has staved off yet another army, the legions of tourism.

Like Milos, the island is closely associated with a particular piece of sculpture, the forthright *Winged Victory (Nike) of Samothrace,* on display in the Louvre. The fourth-century B.C. statue was commissioned by Demetrius Polyocretes—who was the patron of the Colossus of Rhodes—for his victory over Ptolemy in Egypt. It was found 2,100 years later, in the middle of the 19th century, by the French consul who somehow spirited the masterpiece off the island and back to Paris. Excavations at the site of the Mysteries, the Temple of the Great Gods near Palaeopolis, began in 1938 when an archeological team from American uncovered the foundations of a complex of temples and initiation sanctuaries. The **Arisinoe Rotunda** (dedicated by one of the Ptolemies' wives) is a circular building on the order of the tholos at Delphi and the largest structure of its kind in Greece. The Mysteries date prior to the Greek settlement of the islands, and may have originated as a Phoenician rite celebrating the cult of the Cabeiri. Herodotus claimed that the Cabeiri were a race of dwarfs who protected the fields, though modern writers believe "The Mighty Ones" (as "Cabeiri" is translated) were a group of fertility gods. The initiation rites of the Cabeiric Mysteries were reinterpreted by the Greeks, and such notables as Philip of Macedon and his wife-to-be, Olympias, journeyed to Samothraki to take part in the ritual. For a more detailed account of the Mysteries, refer to Chapter IV on Eleusis. Samothraki, although a Northeast Aegean island, is now part of the district of Thrace.

AROUND THE ISLAND: **Boats** arrive at the port of **Kamariotissa**, where you may be met by a dinghy that will take you ashore. There's a C-class hotel on the harbor, the **Niki Beach** (tel. 0551/41-561), but you'd be advised to move on up to Chora in the central mountains of the island. The bus (which stops at the major villages in the summer) will stop at the base of the Mountain of the Moon, where **Chora**, the capital, was built to discourage pirates from attacking—how could they! Above the village is a Byzantine fort that seems superfluous in this remote outpost. There's a **bank**, **O.T.E.** (the telephone **area code** is 0551), and **post office** in the village, plus a modest offering of private rooms.

The bus from Chora (it's a pleasant four-kilometer walk downhill) stops in **Paleopolis**, the site of the Mysteries, an excavation, and a museum. Like the museum on Milos, there's a French-made cast of the *Winged Victory,* as well as objects found at the site.

It's possible to climb the 1,600 meter Mount Fengari, but consult the local police about the conditions on the slopes; the mountain is covered with snow for much of the year. From the peak of the mountain there's a fine view of Turkey, and it's said that Poseidon sat atop the crest to watch the battle at Troy.

GETTING THERE: Samothraki is served daily except Sunday by a **steamer** from

Alexandroupolis (tel. 0551/26-721 for information). If you're in Kymi, Evia (tel. 0222/22-606), there's a weekly boat to the island, but be prepared for a 17-hour voyage. In 1987 there was a Wednesday ferry to Kavala. Contact the local Port Authority for the current schedule. **Olympic Airways** offers daily flights between Athens and Alexandroupolis or Kavala, a handy way to save ferry time!

6. Thassos

Thassos is the northernmost island in the Aegean, lying 14 nautical miles off the Macedonian coast near Kavala (now incorporated in the district of Macedonia). Unlike Limnos and Samothraki, Thassos is a wooded, green island with broad sandy beaches and a few Greek- and Roman-era archeological sites. The island's name derives from one of two sources. Most commonly explained, Thassos was Poseidon's grandson, but we recently heard a historian explain that Thassos was the name of a Phoenician explorer who stopped at the island on his way to Europe.

The island has always had a wealth of natural reserves. Marble quarries were exploited by the Parians when they ruled Thassos—marble and other minerals are still being quarried. Herodotus claimed that there were active gold mines on the island when he visited in the fifth century B.C. Apparently the gold was completely mined (there is none today), but oil was recently discovered off the coast, proving once again that the rich get richer.

Most visitors come to Thassos on weekends from nearby Kavala or as the first island encountered on the drive from Europe or Turkey.

ORIENTATION: Thassos is a small circular-shaped island with hilly coastal plains and a mountainous interior. The island abounds with trees: plane, chestnut, fir, almond, olive, and pine account for most of the foliage. Ferries from Kavala dock at the northwest town of Skala Prinos, and from Keramoti at the northeast coast town and capital, **Thassos** (also called **Limenas**). The remnants of an ancient acropolis, harbor, fortifications, and theater are centered around Limenas. A coastal road, with olive trees and tobacco plants on one side and the turquoise sea on the other, completely encircles the island, passing the excellent east coast beaches from **Chrissi Ammoudia** to **Chrissi Akti**. Megalos Prinos and Mikros Prinos, about four kilometers inland from the Kavala ferry pier, are traditional mountain villages. Many of the centuries-old houses display intricately carved wood panels. The west coast road continues down to the extreme south coast to the resort town of **Limenaria**. Tacky shops, cafés, new rooms to let, and pastel-colored houses line the waterfront.

USEFUL INFORMATION: The local police, bus station, and the **Commercial Bank of Greece** are all on the port in Thassos town. The tourist police (tel. 22-500) are open daily during the summer months. Check with the portside **Katha Travel** (tel. 0593/22-546), open 8 a.m. to 8 p.m. daily, for general information. Both have lists of available private rooms as well as current bus and ferry schedules. . . . The **O.T.E.** and **post office**, both in town, are on the street behind the port. . . . The Skala Prinos to Thassos (Limenas) and the Limenas to Limenaria **bus** runs hourly in the high season; the K.T.E.L. bus station is next to the Commercial Bank. Thassos' telephone **area code** is 0593.

The Katha Travel office (tel. 71-202) in Skala Prinos handles all tourist needs in town, including rental cars. In Limenas, there's a **Thassos Rent A Car** office (tel. 22-535), but we easily toured the island by **moped** and they're widely available for 2400 drs ($18.50) a day.

AROUND THE ISLAND: The main reason to go to Limenas is for the archeological ruins. Of greatest interest is the poorly rebuilt ancient theater, where Greek plays are performed each July and August. The agora, acropolis, and other ancient ruins are situated within walking distance; signs mark the way to most of these sites. Finds from Thassos's rich past are on display at the **museum**, two blocks southeast of the port (across from the church). The highlight of the collection is a giant kouros carrying a ram, dating from the sixth century B.C., when Thassos was something of a sculpture center. The museum is open 8:45 a.m. to 3 p.m. Monday through Saturday, to 2:30 p.m. on Sunday; closed Tuesday.

Limenas (also called Thassos) is the most developed town on Thassos, and unless you're thirsting for discos and souvenir shops, you're better off setting up base at the tranquil port of Skala Prinos or near one of the fine east coast beaches (there are rooms everywhere). If you do stay in Limenas you'll have a large offering of rooms from which to choose. Harbor-view rooms can be found at the recently upgraded **Astir** (tel. 0593/22-160), and **Akti** (tel. 0593/22-326), and **Angelika** (tel. 0593/22-387), all charge 3900 drs ($30) for two including private bath, on the paralia. The Astir and the Angelika are open year round.

The nearest **beach**, aside from the private beach at Makryammos, is four kilometers to the west at **Glyfada**. There are better, less crowded beaches at **Chrissi Ammoundia** and **Chrissi Akti**, ten kilometers from Limenas and a short but winding bus ride from the inland villages of **Potamia** and **Panagia**.

As an alternative to staying in Limenas, consider the private rooms and hotels in the beach community at **Skala Potamias**, such as the **Hotel Kamelia** (tel. 0593/61-463). We prefer staying in Skala Prinos, a ferryboat pier like Limenas but with significantly less commercial development. The half-kilometer long town is lined with beaches, both to the east and west. First choice on the Prinos beach is the **Hotel Prinos** (tel. 0593/71-327), where spotless, balconied doubles with modern showers overlook the ferry activity and sunrise (2500 drs, or $20). Next door is our favorite taverna in northern Greece, the superb **Delphini**, where fresh fish and a huge variety of local vegetables are cooked to perfection. A few doors east are comfortable, modern rooms to let from **Malimis Thomas** (tel. 0593/71-451); shared bath doubles cost the same as the Prinos's. The new **Hotel Elektra** (tel. 0593/71-374), on the west side of the beach (where the fishing boats are built), is a bit classier; rates run $9 more per night, including breakfast.

GETTING THERE: Steamers from Kavala (tel. 224-472) make the 70-minute trip to Skala Prinos (the northwest port) up to eight times a day in summer, between 7:40 a.m. and 8 p.m. From Keramoti (tel. 223-716), only 35 minutes from Limenas, there are eight departures a day and two boats daily continue from Limenas to Skala Prinos before returning to Kavala. (Limenas Port Police: tel. 22-106). If you're pressed for time, consider the twice-daily flights between Kavala and Athens. There is an **Olympic Airways** office (tel. 22-546) in Limenas.

Chapter XVI

INTRODUCING TURKEY

1. Highlights and Suggested Itineraries
2. Getting There
3. The ABCs of Turkey

CONSIDER THE FOLLOWING LIST: Troy, Pergamum, and Ephesus; Herodotus, the world's first historian; the eminent physician, Galen; Homer's *The Iliad;* the goddess Artemis; Alexander the Great cutting the Gordian Knot on his way to conquering Asia; King Midas; the graceful lines of Ionian architecture; the capital of the Greek Orthodox church—all are parts of Greece's enormous legacy to the world. Yet none of these personalities, cities, or developments actually belongs to Greece today! Instead they are all from the European and Asiatic shores of the Aegean and Mediterranean, along the coast of western Anatolia in modern Turkey.

Each year greater numbers of tourists visit Turkey and are surprised at the wealth of things to see and do. Many travelers to the Aegean are aware of the extraordinary archeological sites at Ephesus and Pergamum, but few realize, for example, that the stadium at little-mentioned Aphrodisias is the best preserved in the world, or that the Temple of Didyma, with 124 columns, far outshines its counterparts in any area of Greece.

Aside from the country's historical landmarks, the Turkish coast is lined with fishing villages, beaches, and resorts. Bodrum, a coastal town opposite Kos, is one of the prettiest villages on any part of the Aegean, while the endless beaches at Fethiye are the envy of many a Greek isle. Ask people who have been to Turkey what their most lasting impression is and they'll undoubtedly mention Istanbul, the most exotic city of Europe. The Topkapi Palace, Blue Mosque, Covered Bazaar, and Bosporus strait are but few of this remarkable city's highlights. Finally, a visit to Turkey is a journey to Asia, with a vastly different culture, history, language, and of course, cuisine than our own. In our age, when people hopscotch around the world and so many countries are becoming imitative, bland, and homogeneous, it's rare to find a culture that has retained so much of its original identity.

1. Highlights and Suggested Itineraries

The primary purpose of including Turkey in a book that is ostensibly about Greece is to let travelers know the ease with which they can travel between the countries, as well as describing what they can see without having to travel a great distance from any of the ports of entry. We hope that some people will use this section of the guide to help them plan a more thorough trip along the Turkish coast. The following are sample itineraries for those who plan on visiting the country for more than a day or two.

ARCHEOLOGICAL ITINERARY: If you only have a few days, we suggest crossing over from Rhodes or Kos and heading north, along the coast road, to Didyma, Ephesus, and Pergamum. The same program can be done in reverse order by crossing from Lesbos to Ayvalik. If you have more time, by all means visit the continuing excavation at Aphrodisias. The second-tier sites include Miletos and Priene (both near Didyma), Troy, Assos, and the necropolis at Pamukkale. All of these sites can be seen in a week.

THE SEVEN CHURCHES OF ASIA MINOR: One of the most popular special tours of Turkey is a trip to the so-called Seven Churches, where Saint Paul came to preach. The churches are, in the order in which Paul traveled: Ephesus, Smyrna (Izmir), Pergamum (Bergama), Thyatira (Akhisar), Sardis, Philadelphia (Alasehir), and Laodicea. Nearly all travel agents offer a package tour (with charter flights from North America), including bus transportation, meals, hotels, and a guide.

TURKISH RESORTS AND BEACHES: All the best beaches and resort towns are on the southern part of the coast. Among the many seaside villages, we prefer Marmaris for its combination of scenery, beaches, sophistication, and relative lack of development although stylish Bodrum is certainly popular. Kuşadasi is another comfortable but touristy resort and an ideal base for visiting the nearby site at Ephesus. Fethiye has an excellent beach, where sun worshippers can tan and swim in a gorgeous and undeveloped setting.

ISTANBUL: We would include this magical city on all itineraries. Even if you stop over for a day or two, you're certain to fall in love with Istanbul's exotic minarets, mosques, and sumptuous food. If you have the time, be sure to visit the Topkapi Palace, the Blue Mosque, Suleymaniye, Hagia Sophia, the Covered Bazaar, the many Bosporus fishing villages, and Istanbul's fine museums.

2. Getting There

Once upon a time journeying to Turkey was strictly for the rich or adventurous traveler. Today thousands arrive daily by plane, bus, boat, and train, often crossing over from Greece on a convenient ferry.

BY AIR: If you're coming from North America the most direct way to get to Turkey is on **Lufthansa German Airlines**. Lufthansa (toll free tel. 800/645-3880) has daily connecting flights from New York to Istanbul, via Frankfurt (with a change of planes). The super-APEX fare weekdays in 1987 ranged from $889 to $1,049, depending on the day of the week and season of the year. Both **TK** (Turkish Airlines) and **Olympic** have daily service between Istanbul and Athens. The 1987 fare was $121. You can connect to Istanbul from every major city in Europe and the Middle East, either on TK or a national carrier, such as KLM, Alitalia, Air France, Pan Am, British Airways, etc.

Occasionally large travel companies offer special charter flights from New York to Istanbul. **Pacha Tours** in New York will help you find the lowest cost flights; contact Kamil Muren (tel. 212/355-5141 or toll free 800/PACHA88 outside New York state) for excellent guidance, all inclusive tours and land arrangements.

BY FERRY FROM GREECE: There are five crossover points from the Greek islands to the Turkish mainland: Lesbos to Ayvalik, Chios to Çesme, Samos to Kuşadasi, Kos to Bodrum, and Rhodes to Marmaris. Generally there is daily service during the high season. The typical fare is $20 one way. (Specific information regarding ferry service between these points is listed at the end of each section.) There is also regular ferry service from Piraeus (originating in Ancona, Italy) to Izmir and Istanbul offered by the Turkish Maritime Lines. Information on the TML schedule is available in Piraeus at **S.M. Oliver and Co.**, 17–19 Akti Miaouli, Tanpy Building, Piraeus 9 (tel. 41-78-457), in Istanbul at **Denizyollari Ac.**, Rihtim Caddesi, Karaköy (tel. 1440207), and in Izmir at **Denizyollari Ac.**, Yeniliman, Alsançak (tel. 210094).

BY TRAIN OR BUS FROM EUROPE: The *Orient Express,* recently revived, will transport you in ultimate luxury from Paris to Istanbul for $6,000 (contact **Society Expeditions**; tel. 206/324-9400). Of course there are cheaper ways to do it. The *Marmara Express* leaves from London and Paris and makes stops in Lausanne, Milano, Venice, Trieste, Belgrade, and Sofia before arriving in Istanbul. The *Balkan Express* leaves from Vienna and terminates in Istanbul after stops in Graz, Zagreb, Belgrade, and Sofia.

Perhaps the cheapest and most efficient way to get to Turkey from Europe is by **bus**. Both **Bosfor** (tel. 143-2525) at Taksim Mete Caddesi, 14 and **Varan Turizm** offer bus connections between Athens and Istanbul, at 28,800 TL ($36). Also contact **Ast Turizm** in Istanbul (tel. 442006) and **Rika Tours**, 44 Marni, Platia Vathis (tel. 52-32-458) or the O.S.E. network (tel. 513-5768) in Athens for their Athens-Thessaloniki-Istanbul bus connection. The contact in Thessaloniki is Simeonidis Tours, 26 October St., no. 14 (tel. 540-971).

Bosfor has buses beginning in Paris, costing 127,000 TL ($158), making stops in Lyon, Geneva, Milan, and Venice before arriving in Istanbul. Bosfor also runs express service from Munich, at 115,000 TL ($146), and from Vienna. Press and student discounts are offered. Bosfor has offices or representatives in the following cities:

Paris: Gare Routière Internationale, 7/15 Avenue de la Porte de la Vilette, 75019 Paris (tel. 42-05-12-10).

Lyon: Aire Internationale, rue Gustave Nadaud, 69007 Lyon (tel. 858-04-38).

Milan: Autostradale, 1 Piazza Castello, Milan (tel. 893025).

Munich: Seidlstrasse 2, 8000 Munich 2 (tel. 594002).

Geneva: Gare Routière Internationale, Place Dorcière, 1201 Geneva (tel. 320230).

Venice: Stazione Santa Lucia, Piazzale Roma, Venice (tel. 27544).

Vienna: 1040 Wien, Südbahnhof, Argentiner Strasse 67 (tel. 650-644).

Also contact the **Magic Bus** offices (there is one in Athens) for student and discount tickets.

3. The ABCs of Turkey

ACCIDENTS: You are required to notify the police in case of an accident so they can write an official report. If a car is left for repairs or is totaled and you wish to exit the country, check first with the Customs office about removing the automobile endorsement on your passport. Similarly, if the car is stolen you must obtain a certificate from the governor of the province.

AUTOMOBILE CLUB: The main office of the **Turkish Touring and Automobile Club** is in Istanbul (tel. 131-4631) at Halaskargazi Caddesi, 364. There's an office near the Greek border in Edirne (tel. 03 Kapikule/34). The touring club is also involved in many historic preservation projects, primarily in the Istanbul area: Yildiz and Emirgan Parks (they operate a lovely café), Hidiv Kasri (an art nouveau castle-turned-hotel on the Asian side of the Bosporus), and a few 19th-century houses near Sultan Ahmet Square, the Yesil Ev and the Ayasofya Pansiyonlari, that have recently opened as hotels.

CLIMATE: Turkey is a country whose climate varies radically from the east to the west. Fortunately all of the good weather is concentrated in the west coast region, that is, from Istanbul down to the Mediterranean. The warmest clothing ing you'll need, unless you plan to visit in the winter, is a sweater and rain shell.

	Average Temperatures (°F)			
	January	*April*	*July*	*October*
Istanbul	41	54	75	59
Izmir	45	57	79	63
Antalya	52	61	82	68

CLOTHING: Turkish men are born wearing suits and the women dresses, even in the countryside, but for Westerners it's quite all right to don your casual traveling clothes. Remember that 99% of the Turks are Moslem and, especially for women, it's a good idea to dress modestly. Women may, in rare situations, be required to cover their heads and arms when entering a mosque. When mosque-hopping, wear slip-on shoes; you're required to remove them before entering and it's a drag to lace up every hour.

CUISINE: Turkish food may be one of the world's greatest underrated cuisines. It offers a wide variety of taste delights from the *mezes* (hors d'oeuvres) that begin the meal to the pastries and strong Turkish coffee that complete it. The mezes come in hot and cold varieties, ranging from *etli börek* (ground meat filling in between buttered pastry leaves), cheese böreks, *midye dolmasi* (fried mussels stuffed with spiced rice), *menemen* (red-and-green chile-flavored eggs scrambled with melted cheese) to the more common dishes of *imam bayildi* (roasted eggplant with cheese on top, translated literally ". . . and the priest fainted"), *fasulye* (beans in olive oil and tomato), and others too numerous to mention. There is always a salad of the freshest cucumber, and tastiest tomatoes you'll ever see. In spring mezes are eaten with Romaine lettuce leaves; other seasons their sauces are soaked up with fresh-baked bread. Your main course might include one of 20 different kinds of kebab dishes—our favorite is *döner* or *iskender* kebab—very thin slices of charcoal-broiled lamb served on a bed of coarsely chopped pita and yogurt topped with a chile-flavored tomato sauce— or freshly caught fish including *lüfer* (a delicious variety of bluefish), *kiliç* (swordfish), smoked sturgeon from the Black Sea, or *trança,* a thick meaty fish found off the south coast. Fish will be the most expensive choice and meat the most prevalent one, but vegetarians can thrive happily on the meze courses. The desserts will satisfy your sweet tooth, though not complement your waistline, for they are varied and delicious, from the baklava variations of honey, pastry, and nuts to the true and eternal Turkish delight, the *lokum,* a cube of candy dipped in powdered sugar and filled with various delectable nuts.

Warning: Make sure that uncooked vegetables and salads are cleaned in boiled or bottled water, and only drink the bottled water (su) available everywhere. You can easily thrive on a Turkish diet!

CUSTOMS: In most cases the Customs officer will wave you on with little more than an indecipherable chalk mark. When entering the country you are required to declare any valuables, including jewelry, antiques, or any expensive electronics. The Customs officer will record these in your passport to ensure that they leave Turkey when you do. You're allowed to bring in the following articles duty free: personal photographic equipment (one camera and ten rolls of film), camping and sporting equipment, a typewriter, tape recorder, radio, two cartons of cigarettes, 50 cigars, five liters of spirits, and 1,000 grams of coffee.

The U.S. consulate reports that the Turkish authorities are cracking down on people trying to take antiquities out of the country. You can buy them, but you can't export them. This policy also applies to rugs, although enforcement of the law on carpets is less stringent than on old relics. To avoid the problem altogether, make sure you get a receipt and documentation that the item you bought is not an antiquity.

Autos, vans, motorcycles, towed boats, and bicycles are allowed without a *carnet de passage* for up to three months. The registration and engine numbers will be recorded on your passport. Make sure you have a valid driver's license (an international license isn't required) and adequate insurance—a Green Card International Insurance Certificate, endorsed for Turkey, or Turkish or third-party insurance, which can be purchased at frontier posts.

CURRENCY: The **Turkish lira (TL)** is the standard monetary unit. It's divided into 100 **kurus**. As inflation soars the 2-, 5-, 10-, 25-, and 50-TL coins are increasingly irrelevant and rare. More common are banknotes in denominations of 20, 50, 100, 500, 1000, 5000, 10,000, and 50,000 TL. The government continues to pat itself on the back for bringing inflation down from triple-digit levels. As of mid-1987 it was a more manageable 45%, and $1 U.S. was worth approximately 800 TL. Save your exchange receipts; you'll need them to convert TL to dollars when exiting the country.

DOCUMENTS FOR ENTRY: U.S., Canadian, and British citizens need only a valid passport for a stay of up to three months. Beyond that, permission for an extension is by application at the local Tourist Police. No special visas or inoculations are required. If you bring a pet, also remember to bring the animal's current health record, including a valid certificate of vaccination against rabies, issued within 48 hours of departure and translated into Turkish by a consulate or embassy. Check with the Turkish consulate in your country for details.

DRUGS: Narcotics, hashish, and marijuana are illegal in Turkey, and they aren't kidding! Possession of a gram of hash will get you a year in a Turkish prison, and two grams gets you two years. Get the picture? Once caught, there's nothing the American authorities can do for you.

ELECTRICAL APPLIANCES: Bring an adapter: 220-volt, 50-cycle current is the standard.

EMBASSIES AND CONSULATES: The capital is in Ankara, in the center of the country, where the embassies are located. The American Embassy is at 110 Ataturk Blvd. (tel. 4/265-470); the British Embassy at 46A Şehit Ersen Caddesi, Cankaya (tel. 4/274-310); the Canadian Embassy at 75 Nenehatun Caddesi, Gaziomanpasa (tel. 4/275-003); and the Australian Embassy is at 83 Nenehatun

Caddesi, Gaziomanpasa (tel. 4/286-715). However, there are American, Canadian, and British consulates in Istanbul and Izmir. Australian interests outside of Ankara are represented by the British Consulate.

FILM: It's expensive in Turkey and even at the best shops you won't find nearly the variety available at your corner photo dealer. Bring it with you. When going through the security check at airports, it's best to remove film from the luggage to be X-rayed. Turkish security uses a fairly high dosage of radiation to examine bags and it could possibly damage your film, especially fast or high-ASA stock.

GETTING AROUND: As in Greece, getting around Turkey is easy, cheap, and usually pleasant. Language problems arise, but can always be solved with the friendly assistance of the many English-speaking Turks.

Airplanes are probably the least appealing choice, but if you're in a rush, **Turkish Havayollari Airlines** (THY) offers daily service between Istanbul and Izmir for access to the northern and central coasts. The southern coast is served by Dalaman Airport, (about halfway between Marmaris and Fethiye), with at least one daily THY flight to and from Istanbul. THY offers **bus service** between Dalaman and their offices in Fethiye and Marmaris. To get to other cities, you must take a taksi (taxi) or dolmush to the Dalaman bus terminal, then connect to the frequent intercity buses to your destination.

For most Turks and tourists, **long-distance buses** are the best means of transportation. They are modern, comfortable, efficient, and cheap. Varan is the best company for trips between the big cities of Istanbul, Izmir, Ankara, and Antalya. There are several companies serving the smaller cities and coastal resorts; Pamukkale Bus Company has the best reputation. Tickets can be bought either from their office or on the bus. Seats are reserved, so if you want a choice or want to insure getting a seat in the high season, book ahead. You can also flag these buses down on the road. If you have baggage problems, go straight to the local tourist office and ask their assistance.

Rental cars are not expensive and enable you to visit smaller sites which are not near a major city. Driving in Turkey (with the exception of Istanbul) can be a remarkably pleasant experience. The roads are often excellent, road signs are clear and frequent, traffic is light, and Turkish drivers are generally sane. Several international car rental companies serve the Turkish market, permitting advance reservations, a move well-advised to the summer traveler.

Avis has offices in Istanbul and every city on the coast, charges no drop fee, and issues an excellent personalized itinerary free of charge. Other companies have offices in some cities, with comparable rates. A Murat (a Turkish-built Fiat 131) will run about $350 per week, without gasoline. Gas for the trip from Istanbul to Marmaris, a distance of 1,500 kilometers is about $50 in 1987, costing 300 TL (45¢) per liter.

Taksis (taxis) are everywhere, and generally are a cheap transport within a town. Most city cabs have meters, although some have fixed fees. For trips between cities or to out-of-town sites, taxis can get expensive. If there is no meter, determine the price in advance.

Dolmush (meaning "full" in Turkish) is a term used to describe a group taxi. In Istanbul, these are wonderful vintage American cars, many with a bench seat squeezed in the back. In other cities, dolmushes take the shape of small vans holding from 10 to 12 people. Destination signs are in the window or on top and they leave only when dolmush. The fares are a fraction of the taxi price, but you can wait up to a half hour for a crowd to gather.

HITCHHIKING: People do it, and it appears to be pretty safe. Hitchhiking in the countryside is usually more interesting than on the major highways; don't be surprised if you end up sitting on the back of a horse-drawn wagon. Women traveling alone should exercise caution, as some Turkish men may misinterpret your motives. You don't "thumb" a ride in Turkey. The preferred technique is to wave your arm up and down, indicating that you want the driver to stop.

HOLIDAYS AND FESTIVALS: Turkey celebrates the following festivals and national and Islamic holidays:

January 1—New Year's Day.

April—Regaip Kandili (religious festival with mosque illumination); Istanbul Tulip Festival.

April 23—National Sovereignty and Children's Day (national holiday).

May 1—May Day.

Early May—International Ephesus Festival.

May 19—Youth and Sports Day (national holiday).

Late May—Bergama Festival; Berat Kandili (religious festival with mosque illumination).

Early June—Kirkpinar Oiled Wrestling Festival in Edirne (Turkish National Sports Festival).

Mid-June—Marmaris Festival; (May or June—beginning of Moslem holy month of Ramadan); Istanbul Festival of Culture and Arts (until late July).

Early July—Kadir Gecesi (religious festival with mosque illumination).

Mid-July—Bursa Festival; Seker Bayrami (end of Ramadan).

August 15—Mass of the Virgin Mary in Ephesus.

Mid-August—"Trojan Horse" Festival in Cannakale; beginning of month-long Izmir International Trade Fair; Kuşadasi Festival.

August 30—Victory Day (rout of invading forces in 1923; national holiday).

Early September—Bodrum Art and Culture Festival.

Mid-September—Kurban Bayrama (year's most important Moselm festival).

October 29—Republic Day (anniversary of the declaration of the Turkish Republic; national holiday).

The specific dates of festivals and religious holidays are determined each year by local authorities and the Moslem calendar. Consult the Ministry of Tourism for exact dates.

LANGUAGES: One of Atatürk's reforms was to convert the written Turkish language from an Arabic to a Latin alphabet. It's easy to read, but difficult to speak. Turkish Ural-Altaic etymological roots are connected with three unlikely linguistic partners: Hungarian, Finnish, and Mongolian. In the major tourist centers you'll do pretty well with English, though most older Turks speak French and middle-aged "guest workers" and their kids speak German. *Turkish for Travellers,* a pocket guide by Berlitz Publications, is a useful manual for getting by in hotels, restaurants, shops, and the usual tourist haunts (see also the Appendices in this book).

LITERATURE: Poetry was the literary form preferred by most Turkish writers prior to the 19th century. Penguin Books publishes an excellent anthology of classical Turkish verse. Nasreddin Hoca is lionized in Turkish literature as the country's supreme teller of wise and often humorous tales. There are numerous translations of this 13th-century writer's works available in Istanbul's English-language bookstores. Yasar Kemal is Turkey's best recognized modern novelist. His *Memed, My Hawk* (Pantheon Books) has now been translated into 15 lan-

DISTANCE BETWEEN TURKEY'S MAJOR CITIES
Distance in Kilometers

	Istanbul	Bursa	Çannakale	Ayvalik	Izmir	Kuşadasi	Bodrum	Marmaris	Fethiye	Kaş
Istanbul		247	549	725	568	663	810	950	1072	1170
Bursa	247		302	478	321	416	563	703	825	923
Çannakale	549	302		176	409	504	651	791	913	1011
Ayvalik	725	478	176		233	328	475	615	737	835
Izmir	568	321	409	233		95	242	382	504	602
Kuşadasi	663	416	504	328	95		147	287	409	507
Bodrum	810	563	651	475	242	147		140	262	360
Marmaris	950	703	791	615	382	287	140		122	220
Fethiye	1072	825	913	737	504	409	262	122		98
Kaş	1170	923	1011	835	602	507	360	220	98	

guages. The best single volume covering Turkey's great archeological sites is Professor Ekrem Akurgal's *Ancient Civilizations and Ruins of Turkey*. Why not read Agatha Christie's *Murder on the Orient Express?*

MEDICAL MATTERS: If you need medical attention, contact the Tourist Information Office or Tourist Police. The American consulates in Istanbul and Izmir maintain up-to-date lists of doctors.

METRIC MEASURES: The metric system is the standard in Turkey. (See this topic in Chapter III).

NEWSPAPERS: The *International Herald Tribune* and *Wall Street Journal* are distributed in major tourist centers, usually a day or two after publication. The English-language *Daily News* is published in Ankara and carries Turkish and international stories.

OFFICES AND WORKING HOURS: Most shops and offices are open Monday through Saturday from 9 a.m. to 1 p.m. and 2 p.m. to 7 p.m. Banks are open from 8:30 a.m. to noon and 1:30 p.m. to 5 p.m. Monday through Friday (some banks also keep limited hours on Saturday). Government offices keep bank hours, but stay open till 5:30 p.m. Nearly everything is closed on Sunday. During summer in the Aegean and Mediterranean region many private shops and government offices close during the hot afternoon hours.

POLITICS: Turkey is a democratic republic. Mustafa Kemal Pasa, otherwise known as Atatürk, led the Turkish Nationalism Movement, was the first president in 1923, and is considered the father of modern Turkey. His image and writing are displayed throughout the country, and he is the rallying point for almost all Turkish parties, no matter what their persuasion. Atatürk died in the late 1930s. During the last 25 years the military has intervened three times in civilian government. At present, the republic is governed by the president, prime minister and his cabinet, and an elected national assembly.

RADIO: There is a five-minute news broadcast in English at 9 a.m., noon, 5 p.m., and 7 p.m. on the national station, **TRT-3** and on FM.

REST ROOMS: Istanbul's motto "where Europe and Asia meet" can be equally well applied to Turkish toilets. Most hotels and restaurants catering to tourists have Western-style toilets; rural restaurants and lower-priced establishments use Asian toilets, or as Kyle calls them, "starting pads." Most are equipped with a pull-chain flush and running water to maintain better hygiene. In either case, you should bring your own toilet paper and remember to put it into the nearest wastepaper basket (don't try to flush it down Turkey's old, narrow sewage pipes!). Toilets are usually labeled "W.C.," or Bey (Men) and Beyan (Women). Sometimes a tip is required; 50 TL (6¢) is appropriate.

TELEPHONE AND TELEGRAPH: The **PTT** (post office/telephone/telegraph) is easy to spot; look for the bright-yellow sign. Most PTTs are open until midnight for booking telephone calls. *Jetonu,* 50 or 250 TL tokens, can be used to make domestic and international calls in phone booths. These booths are normally located both inside and outside the PTT. For calls to North America it's often better to book it through an operator; you'll get a better connection. Plan on waiting at least an hour for the call to come through. You can also dial direct from the PTT. Cost: 4400 TL ($5.50) per minute. *Note:* It's always cheaper to call collect. Telegrams can also be sent from the PTT. Avoid making calls and sending cables from hotels; they often add a surcharge to all outgoing messages.

TIME: Turkey is ahead of Greenwich Mean Time by two hours in the summer and three hours in the winter, making it seven and or eight hours ahead of Eastern Standard Time. The entire country has only one time zone.

TIPPING AND TAXES: It is not necessary to tip taxi drivers. Most hotels and restaurants add a service charge of 10% to 15%, in addition to the 12% VAT tax. It's customary to leave an additional 5% to 10% for the maid or busboy.

TOURIST INFORMATION: The Ministry of Culture and Tourism has information offices in the U.S. and Great Britain. The North American address is 821 United Nations Plaza, New York, NY 10017 (tel. 212/687-2194); the address in England is 170-173 Piccadily, 1st floor, London W/V9DD (tel. 01/734-8681).

Chapter XVII

ISTANBUL

1. Orientation
2. Accommodations
3. Restaurants
4. What to See and Do
5. Nightlife
6. Istanbul ABC's

ISTANBUL—the name alone summons up images of magnificent jewels, palaces, mosques and minarets, fragrant spices, intricately knotted carpets, ornately painted tiles, and of course, the Grand Bazaar. Few places on earth are as richly endowed, and even fewer live up to their reputation.

Much of Istanbul's wealth is directly related to its extraordinary location. The only city to bridge two continents, Asia and Europe, Istanbul is also the guardian of the Bosporus, the strategic link between the Black, Marmara, Aegean, and Mediterranean seas. Three of the West's most powerful civilizations have made Istanbul their capital, and in each case the new invader rebuilt and embellished the city to his taste. The Romans moved the center of their empire to Byzantium (as Istanbul was called in ancient days) to consolidate control over their Asian conquests. Emperor Constantine constructed elaborate fortifications and dedicated the new capital in A.D. 331; in short order Byzantium became known as Constantinople. The Roman Empire's transition to a Christian-controlled polity was played out within two centuries. By A.D. 530 Emperor Justinian ruled jointly with a bishop, Christianity was the official state religion, and pagan temples and schools were closed forever; the fall of Rome was complete as Constantinople became home to the new Byzantine Empire. Shrines were built, including early Christianity's most innovative and stunning church, Hagia Sophia. After 900 years of Byzantine rule, in the middle of the 15th century Constantinople suffered repeated attacks by marauding Turkish forces as well as an almost constant assault by incoming and outgoing Crusaders. The Turkish Ottoman army, led by Mehmet II, took Constantinople in 1453. Again the new rulers rebuilt the city, adding new structures that far outshone those of the more ascetic Byzantines. Under Suleyman the Magnificent, and with the help of his chief architect, Sinan, the skyline of Constantinople changed dramatically. This time slender minarets, exquisitely domed mosques, and grand palaces heralded an era of Islamic influence.

After the fall of the Ottoman Empire in the second decade of this century, the modern republic took up the banner of successor, constructing new skyscrapers, large municipal halls, and banal concrete apartment blocks.

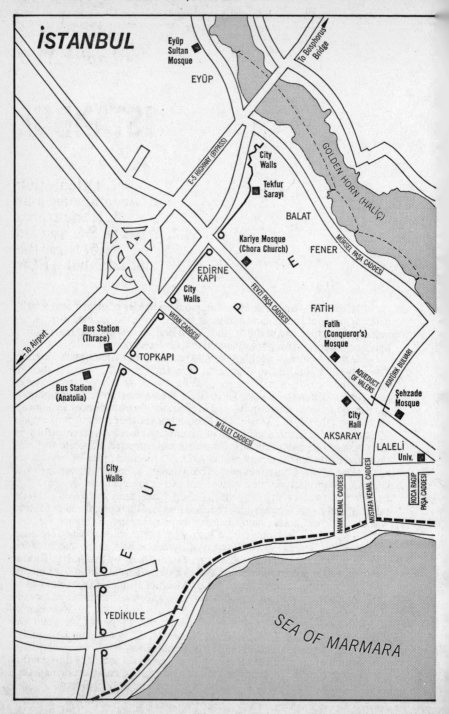

İSTANBUL

Eyüp Sultan Mosque

EYÜP

To Bosphorus Bridge

E-5 HIGHWAY (BYPASS)

City Walls

Tekfur Sarayı

GOLDEN HORN (HALİÇ)

BALAT

Kariye Mosque (Chora Church)

FENER

MÜRSEL PAŞA CADDESİ

EDİRNE KAPI

City Walls

FEVZİ PAŞA CADDESİ

FATİH

Fatih (Conqueror's) Mosque

To Airport

Bus Station (Thrace)

VATAN CADDESİ

TOPKAPI

Bus Station (Anatolia)

ATATÜRK BULVARI

AQUEDUCT OF VALENS

Şehzade Mosque

MİLLET CADDESİ

City Hall

AKSARAY

LALELİ Univ.

E Y U P

E U R O P

City Walls

YEDİKULE

NAMIK KEMAL CADDESİ

MUSTAFA KEMAL CADDESİ

KOCA RAGIP PAŞA CADDESİ

SEA OF MARMARA

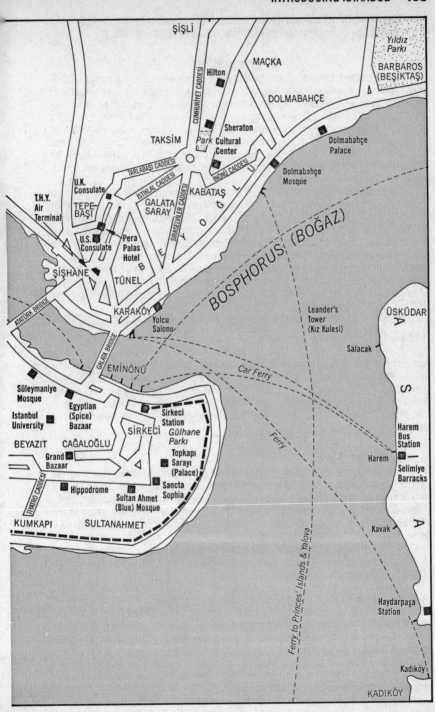

ŞİŞLİ

Yıldız
Parkı

MAÇKA

BARBAROS
(BEŞİKTAŞ)

Hilton

DOLMABAHÇE

CUMHURİYET CADDESİ

Sheraton
Cultural
Center

TAKSİM

Park

Dolmabahçe
Palace

İNÖNÜ CADDESİ

TARLABAŞI CADDESİ

U.K.
Consulate

Dolmabahçe
Mosque

İSTİKLAL CADDESİ

TEPE-
BAŞI

GALATA
SARAY

KABATAŞ

SIRASELVİLER CADDESİ

T.H.Y.
Air
Terminal

BOSPHORUS (BOĞAZ)

U.S.
Consulate

Pera
Palas
Hotel

ÜSKÜDAR

SİŞHANE

TÜNEL

KARAKÖY

Leander's
Tower
(Kız Kulesi)

ATATÜRK BRIDGE

Yolcu
Salonu

Salacak

GALATA BRIDGE

EMİNÖNÜ

Car Ferry

Süleymaniye
Mosque

Egyptian
(Spice)
Bazaar

Sirkeci
Station

Harem
Bus
Station

İstanbul
University

SİRKECİ

Gülhane
Parkı

Ferry

Harem

BEYAZIT

CAĞALOĞLU

Topkapı
Sarayı
(Palace)

Selimiye
Barracks

Grand
Bazaar

TİYATRO CADDESİ

Hippodrome

Sancta
Sophia

Kavak

Sultan Ahmet
(Blue) Mosque

KUMKAPI

SULTANAHMET

Haydarpaşa
Station

Ferry to Princes' Islands & Yalova

Kadıköy

KADIKÖY

The modern city reflects the presence of all of these cultures, making it the most exotic city in Europe and an absolute treasure chest for visitors.

1. Orientation

The narrow Bosporus strait divides the European and Asian continents. It also bisects metropolitan Istanbul. **Üsküdar**, the Asian side, is a combination of recent industrial and suburban development and of lesser interest to most visitors than the European sections, Stromboul and Galata. The European section itself is divided, again by a body of water. The **Golden Horn**, a shallow offshoot flowing into the Bosporus, separates the old city to the south, **Stromboul**, from the new city, **Galata**, to the north. Within the confines of Stromboul (Greek for "to the city") are nearly all of Istanbul's greatest monuments, mosques, museums, and markets.

Legend has it that the Golden Horn earned its romantic name from an enormous treasure of jewels and gold that sank centuries ago in the deep mud of the inlet during Mehmet the Conqueror's reign. Numerous requests were made to dredge the waterway, but the ruling sultan denied them all. Perhaps the most accurate derivation of the name comes from the ancient Greeks, who called it Chrysokeras (literally, "Golden Horn"), so called after the golden sunsets over the scimitar-shaped inlet. Whatever its origin, at the confluence of the Golden Horn, Bosporus, and Sea of Marmara is the tip of old Stromboul, called Sultan Ahmet Square, and here one finds the Blue Mosque, Hagia Sophia, Topkapi Palace, and the Hippodrome.

LAYOUT: There are three major sections of the city of interest to tourists: **Sultan Ahmet Square**, the old quarter around Galata Bridge, and the modern urban center at Taksim Square. Sultan Ahmet Square is the heart of the ancient city and therefore has the greatest concentration of historical sights. The narrow, sloped, winding streets have fired the imagination of every mystery writer since Wilkie Collins and still provide plenty of intrigue. **Taksim Square** is the heart of the new city; most of the tourist services you'll need are located here.

Sultan Ahmet Square

Sultan Ahmet Camii is the Turkish name of the **Blue Mosque**. It also refers to the area of greatest interest to visitors, containing nearly every major tourist attraction in Istanbul. Most of the city's bus lines intersect Sultan Ahmet, making it one of the best transportation hubs in Istanbul—the bus stand is next to the Tourist Information Booth in the square (extremely helpful; open 9 a.m. to 6 p.m. Monday through Friday, until 5 p.m. on Saturday and Sunday; tel. 1/522-4903). Now that new hotels and clean hostels exist in Sultan Ahmet, travelers have a choice of staying here, farther west in Aksaray, or across the Galata Bridge in Şişhane, or Taksim Square.

Aside from the obvious stops at Hagia Sophia, the Blue Mosque, Topkapi, and Kapali Çarşi, the Grand Covered Bazaar, the most interesting section of Sultan Ahmet is within walking distance southeast of the Blue Mosque, toward the Byzantine walls and the Marmara Sea. Here you'll find narrow streets lined with 19th-century two- and three-story wooden homes that once were the dominant style throughout Istanbul. The neighborhood is changing rapidly—many of these homes have been pulled down and some are collapsing on their own—but you can still watch children playing ball in untouched side streets and alleyways that evoke a feeling of Istanbul past.

Around Galata Bridge

Since Istanbul is built along so much water, it's not surprising that one of its bridges, **Galata Bridge**, should also be the city's busiest spot. An enormous number of cars, buses, and pedestrians cross it every day, and the lower level supports a lively fish trade: markets, restaurants, and supplies. What catches many first-time bridge walkers off guard, though, is a strange bobbing sensation, as if the whole package is floating. It is, on a series of pontoons.

Directly to the left as you reach solid ground on the Stromboul side are the piers for **Princes Islands** and Bosporus-bound boats. In front, facing the water, is Yeni Camii, an attractive though undistinguished mosque that seems to attract more pigeons than people. Somewhat behind the mosque is Misir Çarşisi, the old **Egyptian Spice Market**, where you can wander through stalls that sell herbs, from mundane to exotic, and dine in high style upstairs at Pandeli's. This waterfront region is known as Eminönü and was occupied by the Venetians and Amalfians during their brief occupation in the Byzantine era.

All trains from Europe arrive in Istanbul at **Sirkeci Station**, two blocks east of Galata Bridge on Ankara Caddesi in Eminönü. The Victorian-period station is a landmark for romantics, crime-novel enthusiasts, and train buffs, because it was the terminus for the *Orient Express,* operating from Paris to Istanbul and because it has a modest display of antique rail cars and the restored Gar Restaurant, dating from 1890.

The other side of Galata Bridge embraces three neighborhoods: **Karaköy**, Şişhane, and Beyoglu. **Galata Tower**, built by the Genoese, dominates the hill overlooking the bridge and the Golden Horn. There is an underground funicular railway, one of the first of its kind (constructed by the French in the 1870s), simply called **Tünel** (150 TL or 19¢ one way). Tünel runs from Karaköy Caddesi, near the bridge, to Istiklâl Caddesi, on the hill behind Galata Tower. The area around the exit, above the tower, typifies what makes Istanbul such a wonderful city. Called **Pera**, in the Şişhane precinct, it encompasses the old Embassy Row, with shabby-but-elegant limestone palaces that once housed representatives of the great powers of Europe. The stone façades are pockmarked, desecrated by decades of pollution and graffiti, but the grandeur of the buildings and the mystery of the area's dimly lit alleyways and back streets add to Istanbul's exotic character.

Istiklâl Caddesi runs through the Pera district and Beyoglu, straight to Taksim Square; it's lined with boutiques, doner kebab fast-food joints, shoeshine stands, dessert palaces, and a continuous torrent of shoppers. At night Istiklâl's side streets become Istanbul's most sophisticated entertainment center. The sounds of movies, plays, Turkish dancing, and barroom music, the neon haze, and the broad range of nighttime Istanbulus, from beggar to plutocrat, make it the city's liveliest late-night zone.

Taksim Square

If Sultan Ahmet's attractions make it the historical hub of Istanbul, then Taksim Square's broad streets and towering concrete buildings make it Istanbul's modern business center. Located on the Galata side of European Istanbul —meaning that you must cross either the Galata Bridge or Atatürk Bridge from Stromboul—walking in Taksim feels like being in the midst of an efficient 20th-century European city, on the order of Milan. Luxury hotels, sidewalk cafés, chic shops, and wild drivers and traffic jams all seem out of place in most parts of Istanbul (with the exception of the wild drivers and traffic jams), but in Taksim they all fit together.

Like Sultan Ahmet, Taksim is another of Istanbul's transportation centers, both for buses and dolmushes. North of Taksim, up Cumhuriyet Caddesi toward the Hilton, is Istanbul's greatest concentration of tourist and airline offices, as well as discos and nightclubs.

ARRIVING IN ISTANBUL: As a transportation center, Istanbul is reminiscent of New York City. All paths lead there, but where you arrive is not necessarily where you want to be.

From the Bus Station

Most buses from Europe that arrive in Istanbul, other than the Varan Turizm and Bosfor Turizm luxury coaches (which drop you in Taksim Square), will stop at the **Topkapi Otobus Terminali** (tel. 1/582-1010); located at the entrance to the city immediately adjacent to Topkapi Gate. Topkapi Gate and the palace of the same name are quite far apart, so don't make the mistake of trying to walk it unless you don't mind schlepping your heavy bags for seven kilometers. The depot is four kilometers from Aksaray on Millet Caddesi. Unfortunately, there is no Tourist Information Booth at the station; the nearest office is at the Covered Bazaar. If you need any help, telephone the office at Sultan Ahmet (tel. 1/522-4903); they're extremely helpful and speak excellent English. There are buses and taxis aplenty at the station. If you take a taxi, make sure the cabbie uses his meter.

From the Airport

Atatürk Airport (tel. 1/573-3500) is about 30 minutes southwest of the city on the European side. At present all flights via Turkish Airlines (THY) arrive at the old terminal, with the new building serving international flights. There's a free shuttle between the buildings. There's a Tourist Information Office (tel. 1/573-7399) at the new terminal (open 8:30 a.m. to 9 p.m. daily) which will help you with hotel reservations, bus information, and the usual panoply of brochures, maps, guides, and schedules. Next to the kiosk is a bank that will change money.

The Airport Bus leaves from the domestic terminal and stops at the THY terminal (tel. 440296) on Mesrutiyet Caddesi in Şişhane. The bus runs every half hour, from 5:30 a.m. to 11 p.m. and takes 40 minutes. Tickets are 600 TL (75¢) each way. Public bus No. 96 runs between Atatürk Airport and Yeni Kapi Station near Aksaray between 8:25 a.m. and 6:30 p.m. If you don't want to take the bus, there are many taxis willing to shuttle you into town. A ride to Taksim Square will set you back about 5000 TL ($6.25). Before you get into a cab, ask the Tourist Information Office what the rate should be for your destination just to avoid any possible confusion.

From the Pier

Karaköy Maritime Station (tel. 1/149-9222) is on the Galata side of the Galata Bridge; it's the pier for all but day excursion ships. There's a Tourist Information Office (tel. 1/149-5776) at the maritime station.

GETTING AROUND: Unless you plan on staying in Istanbul for a week or more, most of the sights that you'll want to see are within walking distance of each other, and there's really no better way of experiencing the city than on foot. It's almost impossible not to be seduced into walking down a small lane with an open-air market, sampling the delicious street food, discovering an overlooked mosque or *hamami* (Turkish bath), or browsing in a shop filled with dusty, tarnished antiques. Istanbul is that kind of a place—if you only visit the "normal" attractions, you'll miss much of the wonder. If you have only a couple of days in the city or you somehow become bored with walking up and down the seven hills (just like Rome), you'll be glad to know that Istanbul has a terrific transportation system.

By Dolmush

A dolmush (Turkish for "full") is a private car that has predetermined pick-up and drop-off points. There are many dolmush depots, the principal ones are at Taksim Square, Istiklâl Caddesi, the Sirkeci Railway Station, and Aksaray. You only pay for your seat, and prices are usually posted at the stand. One of the delights of traveling by dolmush is that they are almost always refitted American classics (a center bench seat has been installed). The cars are a buff's dream: 1956 Bel Aires, 1961 Impalas, round black Chryslers, long-forgotten DeSotos, and the king of classics, 1957 Chevies. As tourism flourishes, metered taxis multiply, and spare parts become more scarce, dolmushes, too, are fading from the Istanbul scene.

By Taxi

There are lots of them, and, as in most cities, you have to be a little wary of possible price gouging. To avoid problems, take a car with a meter (and make sure the driver uses it). Taxis are marked with checkered stripes or "Taksi" signs and are still a bargain; it's hard to spend more than $3 in town.

By Bus

Travel by local bus is cheap but slow. Tickets, which are on sale near the stop (and at some post offices), and which must be bought before riding, cost a mere 180 TL (23¢). The most convenient ticket booth is in front of the Tourist Information Office in Sultan Ahmet Square. The routes are posted on signs. The most popular route for tourists begins at Taksim Square, crosses the Atatürk Bridge, runs down Atatürk Boulevard in Aksaray, passes the university and Grand Bazaar, stops at Sultan Ahmet Square, and crosses the Galata Bridge on its return to Taksim. Check the Tourist Office for current route numbers, check at the ticket booth, and ask the driver if he's going to your appointed stop; they're used to bewildered tourists. By the way, Istanbul's buses are usually full so you may have to politely push your way on and off.

2. Accommodations

As more and better accommodations are being built in Istanbul, the price of a clean, comfortable room is getting higher. No longer can the two of you find a charming pension for under $10 a night. However, there are more charming pensions than ever before, many of them restored Turkish houses in the fascinating old quarter around Sultan Ahmet Square. The Sultan Ahmet district is our first choice for lodging because it's the heart of old Istanbul and the area you'll be spending most of your sightseeing time in.

The adjoining neighborhoods, known as Lalelei and Aksaray, rise above the Marmara Sea southwest of the Sulemaniye Mosque and the Grand Bazaar. This middle-class section, a mix of the new and old Istanbul in every nook and cranny, is for the traveler who likes to explore the back streets of contemporary cities. The recent influx of European tour groups has spawned a large number of modern, efficient, though not charming, hotels that are well within our budget.

The district marked by the grande dame of Istanbul's hotels, the *Orient Express's* Pera Palas, is known as Şişhane, or the Pera district. If you're not springing for the Pera Palas herself, the nearby smaller, less distinguished inns are only worthwhile for their location and sometimes wonderful Golden Horn views. This neighborhood of embassies, boutiques, and risqué nightclubs is up-hill from the Galata Bridge (a short walk from the Tünel metro exit) and thus relatively convenient to the Sultan Ahmet and Galata areas. Istanbul's business center is around busy Taksim Square, and if business is what brings you here, be prepared to spend more than in any other quarter for a night's rest.

SULTAN AHMET: The area around Sultan Ahmet Square has the greatest con-centration of important sights in all of Istanbul, but like the Plaka in Athens, it had declined into a sleazy neighborhood of second-rate hotels and hippy hang-outs catering to a dope-smoking crowd. We're happy to report that all this has changed. The flophouses are gone, replaced by superbly restored Turkish homes and small renovated pensions. As Istanbul's popularity grows among smart middle-income travelers, the hotel scene in Sultan Ahmet Square (the city's premier location) has grown to accommodate them.

The best of these new pensions is the **Hotel Nomade** (tel. 1/511-1296), at Divanyolu Ticarethane Sokak 7–9, two blocks from the Blue Mosque. The Nomade has 12 small, stylish rooms whose stucco walls are decorated with woven bags, carpets, and camel packs. We met Esra, a helpful hostess who keeps the rooms very tidy and helps serve breakfast (1200 TL, or $1.50) in the cozy, carpet-lined rooftop bar or, in nice weather, on the roof terrace with its wonderful views over the square. The Nomade's rooms should be reserved one to two weeks in advance during the summer; bathless doubles run 21,600 TL ($27), rooms with private shower are 25,000 TL ($31). Reader Josephine Rob-erts of Adelaide, Australia, stayed there last year and wrote: "It's run by English-speaking twins, Hamra and Esra Teker. I found it clean, friendly, and ideally situated, close to all the sights."

Downhill from the Blue Mosque on quiet Ishakpaşa Caddesi at no. 8 is **Barut's Guesthouse** (tel. 1/520-1227). The Barut family runs a clean, modern place with 22 simple rooms. Each has a private bathroom with shower, little decor but on the 3rd floor and above, marvelous views over the back walls of Topkapi Palace out to the Marmara Sea. Across the street is Arap Camii, Istan-bul's oldest mosque. The charming manager Naçiye and the rooftop breakfast room, lounge, and sundeck make the tariff worthwhile. Barut's Guesthouse charges $23 for a single, $33 for a double, and $42 for a triple, all including breakfast.

The **Elit Hotel** (tel. 1/519-0466) is one of the best of the budget places in town. Elit is tucked away above the "Elit Collection" shop at Salkim Söğüt Sokak, no. 14, off Yerebatan Caddesi, three blocks from the Tourist Informa-tion office. This newly renovated pension has good-sized rooms (with private showers) that are newly tiled and wallpapered. Single travelers or a couple will pay 12,000 TL ($15) per room. As you exit the Elit, be sure to check out Istan-bul's sixth-century underground cistern, the Yerebatan Saray, recently repaired and open to the public.

We have high hopes for the newly opened **Optimist Guesthouse** (tel. 1/519-2091), across the street from the Hippodrome and Obelisk at 68 Atmeydani. This tiny European villa has six small, well-kept rooms with a timeless view over the square. Owner Halit Özüdoğru turned the family home, which had been rented to the Social Democrat Party, into a warm, friendly guesthouse with polka-dot sheets and bedspreads! Only two of the rooms have private bathrooms with shower and toilet ($32); four rooms sharing common facilities rent out at $25 each, including breakfast.

There is some good news for the low-budget traveler—the Yücelt Youth Hostel (tel. 1/522-4790), now associated with the International Youth Hostel Federation, has been totally refurbished. Long a favorite stop with travelers, and conveniently located at Caferiey Sokak 6/1 behind the Hagia Sophia church, the clean, carpeted rooms with fresh sheets, newly tiled common bathrooms, and a pleasant garden café all make the Yücelt's rates a bargain. The informative and friendly management ask for payment on a daily basis, but at 6500 TL ($8.15) for two, who's arguing?

Across the street from the classy Elit is the long-standing **Sultan Tourist Hostel** (tel. 1/520-7676), at 35 Yerebatan Caddesi. The Sultan's bathless rooms are too tiny and worn to be fit for one, but they're kept very clean and your friendly hosts make you feel at home. If the Yücelt and the Sultan are fully booked, try the **Hotel Mola** (tel. 1/526-7604), around the corner from the Sultan at 15 Alayköşkü Caddesi. It's worn but pretty clean, and there's hot water each morning and evening. All three charge the same daily rate, although all will bargain in the low season.

If you're stuck for a room, there are two other choices on Divanyolu Caddesi, opposite the Tourist Information office. The trim gray façade of the **Hotel Güngör** (tel. 1/526-2319), next to the bright-orange Pudding Shop, marks another student haunt. The small, clean rooms are well kept, though very simple. Twin-bedded rooms without showers cost 8000 TL ($10); 40% less from November to March. The **Hotel Holiday** (tel. 1/522-4281), distinguished by its illuminated yellow sign at 52 Divanyolu Caddesi, has an unobstructed view (from the terrace) of the Blue Mosque, Hippodrome, and Marmara Sea. World travelers will appreciate the Holiday's bulletin board, where correspondence between lost friends is posted. Most of the rooms are fairly clean, although like the Güngör's they tend to be quite noisy. A double with private shower costs 12,000 TL ($15); without shower, 10,000 TL ($12.50), including breakfast.

Two Splurge Hotels

Set between the Blue Mosque and Hagia Sophia, below Sultan Ahmet Square, is the **Yeşil Ev,** formerly the Konak, (tel. 1/528-6764) a rebuilt Turkish mansion that has been fashioned into a 20-room luxury hotel. The rooms are immaculate and elegantly furnished with Ottoman antiques (even the room phones are old), fine Turkish rugs, calligraphic drawings, and brass beds. Although its four-poster antique bed might not be able to handle the activity, honeymooners should consider the Pasha's Suite, with even more sumptuous decor and its own marble Turkish bath. In addition to its other attributes, service is outstanding at the Yeşil Ev, which is another in a growing list of Turkish Touring and Automobile Association restoration projects. Once a great 19th-century Ottoman mansion, the Yeşil Ev is now on a par with the Pera Palas as one of the finest traditional hotels in all Istanbul. Of course, it's a splurge at 93,000 TL ($116) for a double and 71,000 TL ($88) for a single ($170 for the Pasha Suite), but where else can one live like an Ottoman noble, in a grand residence with views of the magnificent Blue Mosque? Reservations, one month prior to arrival, are necessary. It's worth it.

Nearby, behind the Hagia Sophia church, are nine newly restored 18th-century homes known as the **Ayasofya Pansiyonlari** (tel. 1/512-5732). Located on Sogukçeşme, a cobblestone path which is closed to cars and runs downhill from the Bab-i Humayun gate of Topkapi, each restored pension backs up against the palace's fortified walls. The individual homes, which once belonged to Istanbul's elite, are now divided into five to ten rooms, with a parlor and a dining room on the ground floor. All are furnished in pastel-colored tulle and velvet, embroidered cushions, lace curtains, and silk tassels; guest rooms are small, cozy, with antique beds. Each has a private bathroom with shower, and the only concession to modern telecommunications is an international direct-dial phone. Viewless single and double rooms run $42 and $66, rooms overlooking Haghia Sophia and her minarets cost $77 and $108; all rates include breakfast, tax, and service. If Yeşil Ev is fully booked, the **Ayasofya Pansiyonlari** will provide an equally charming and historical, if not as sumptuous, sleeping experience.

AKSARAY AND LALELI: The adjacent neighborhoods of Aksaray and Laleli offer the greatest variety of low- and middle-priced hotels of any district in Istanbul. Although the main street, Ordu Caddesi, is noisy, the little side streets that surround it are pleasant, tree-lined, and filled with Turks going about their daily business. It's a neighborhood that's convenient to the Grand Bazaar and a $1.50 taxi ride from Sultan Ahmet Square. It's also a ten-minute walk from the wonderful fish restaurants of Kumkapi. If you're stuck without accommodations in the busy summer season, although many places host tour groups, here your chances are the best in the city.

Situated one block south of Ordu Caddesi is the **Hotel Astor** (tel. 1/522-4423), at 12 Laleli Caddesi. The rooms are small, but quiet, and the entire hotel is spanking clean. Doubles are a budget-conscious 26,400 TL ($33); singles cost 19,200 TL ($24). North of Ordu Caddesi is another modern, but older hotel, the **Eyfel Hotel** (tel. 1/520-9788), at 19 Kurultay Sokak. Here a small and somewhat drab double rents for 30,720 TL ($38). The lobby, however, is bright and cheerful and there is an inviting restaurant on the premises.

A block west of the Eyfel you'll find a trio of reasonably priced establishments that offer comfortable rooms with private shower and phone, elevator service, furnished lobbies to gather in, and their own breakfast rooms or coffeeshops. None are fancy but all are clean, quality hotels of good value. The **Hotel Barin** (tel. 1/522-8426), located on a quiet side street north of Ordu Caddesi, at 7 Şehzadebaşi Fevzize Caddesi, sports marble flooring throughout. Trim, well-kept doubles run 26,400 TL ($33), singles are 8000 TL ($10) less. Next door, at 2 Yokuşu Caddesi, at the corner of Fethi Bey, is the **Hotel Diana** (tel. 1/526-9621). Recently built but cheaply constructed rooms run 21,000 TL ($26.25) for two; try the Diana's attractive guest rooms while they're still new. Across the street at Yokuşu Sokak, nos. 1–3, is the older **Hotel Burak** (tel. 1/522-7904). Small, slightly drab rooms cost $1 less, but their corner rooms shaded by a four-story tree outside are quite pleasant. All rates quoted above include breakfast. One of the newest in the area and our current favorite is the **Hotel Piza** (tel. 1/512-5940), a real gem at Fethi Bey Caddesi and Kurultay Sokak 3/1. It's a small, elegantly designed hotel with a European feel (no, it doesn't lean). Single travelers are charged 24,000 TL ($30), two travelers 33,600 TL ($42), bed and breakfast. Families should consider the bargain corner suite, where four can sleep luxuriously and enjoy the added TV and mini-bar for just 44,400 TL ($55.50) a night, including four breakfasts.

Hotels seem to be sprouting up like poppies in this neighborhood, so a stroll down Fethi Bey or Yokuşu Caddesis, between Ordu and Şehzadebaşi Caddesis, should turn up other choices if all of the above are booked.

ŞISHANE AND THE PERA DISTRICT: The grand Pera Palas (see our Splurge section), the Beaux Arts American Embassy, a host of fading examples of Europe's best architectural styles, embassies, and once exclusive town houses make this area very appealing to walk through during the day but of little interest in the evening. Yet Şişhane has some fine restaurants, the lively Çiçek Pasaji (a flower market by day that becomes one big seafood café at night), inexpensive stylish clothing boutiques along Istiklâl Caddesi, and several scenic vistas over the Golden Horn. If you can't find a room near Sultan Ahmet, or its youthful ambience doesn't appeal, if Lalelei and Aksaray are too sterile or group tours are anathema, strongly consider a room in this district. These hotels are fairly priced and conveniently located halfway between the Tünel metro and Taksim Square (it's a 15-minute walk either way).

Uphill from the Pera Palas is the **Otel Alibaba** (tel. 1/144-0781), at 119 Meşrutiyet Caddesi. The Alibaba has freshly painted, spacious twin-bedded rooms which cost 13,300 TL ($17) with private shower, 10,600 TL ($13) without. The shared facilities are kept very clean; although there's no private bathroom the views over the Golden Horn from the street-facing rooms make it worthwhile. The Alibaba lacks the old-world charm of its neighbor, the **Grand Hotel de Londres** (now $36 to $60 a double), but the management is very friendly and it's a great price for this location.

We're not sure if the American embassy or the grand Pera Palas has lured other hoteliers to set up shop in this fashionable part of the city, but we welcome three other budget choices. The **Hotel Kavak** (tel. 1/144-5844), at 201 Mesrutiyet Caddesi, would merit mention, regardless of price, for its amusing, fluffy-stucco and whipped-concrete construction. The lobby looks like the interior of a sand castle. Bedrooms are clean, simply furnished, and above the third floor, have scenic views of the Golden Horn. Doubles rent for 200 TL ($24) nightly. Breakfast ($2 or 1500 TL per person) is served in the amusing restaurant/bar.

Across from the American Embassy, at no. 225, is the renovated **Hotel Inka** (tel. 1/143-1728). Here, natural wood, modern furnishings, and subdued colors contribute to an almost high-tech simple decor. The Inka's new seventh-floor restaurant serves inexpensive drinks and a variety of local hors d'oeuvres until midnight. Bright, spacious rooms have dressing tables, bureaus, and their own private toilets. Doubles are 29,000 TL ($36) and singles are 21,100 TL ($26.40).

In the same price range, but with simpler decor, is the **Yenişehir Palas** (tel. 1/149-8810). The official address is 57 Mesrutiyet Caddesi; tell your taxi driver it's next door to the super-deluxe Etap Istanbul. The Yenişehir Palas is a good bet when other recommendations are fully booked.

A Splurge Hotel

Every once in a great while we run into a hotel that captures the soul of a city, but that's a bit above our budget. The **Hotel Pera Palas** (tel. 1/151-4560), at 98-100 Meşrutiyet Caddesi, is just such a place. The hotel was built in 1892 to accommodate the passengers of the *Orient Express.* Among the hotel's most famous guests are the kings of England, Albania, Serbia, and Rumania, Mata Hari, Greta Garbo, Agatha Christie (who preferred Room 411), Sarah Bernhardt, and Seyyid Ali Bin Hamud, sultan of Zengibar! "Atatürk slept here" can be said of Room 101, now a permanent museum open daily from 9 a.m. to 5 p.m. (closed Sunday). The Pera Palas is magnificently decorated with colorful mosaics and tiles, hand-carved dark-wood doorways and molding, marble floors, crystal chandeliers, and antique rugs. The famed middle hall has a dazzling high ceiling; its skylight domes illuminate the enormous space. The residential rooms are as spacious as you'd expect from such a grand hotel (though many of the single rooms are compact and the beds tend to be a bit lumpy and soft for our taste). The staff is genuinely helpful and not the least stuffy. Double rooms cost $130 and singles are $100, including tax, service, and breakfast, but as stated, this is a truly special place. Reader John Fels of Phoenix, Arizona, agrees: "If we had to miss the Pera Palas, the Golden Horn, or the Topkapi Palace, I think it'd be the last to go. . . ." Even if you can't stay at the Pera Palas, make a point to drop in for a look. With a 98% occupancy rate, the highest in Istanbul, reservations are a must.

AROUND TAKSIM SQUARE: If you want to stay in the posh, modern Hilton quarter of town, be prepared for some steeper prices. Luckily, there are two new choices just a kebab's throw from the international, deluxe Hotel Etap Marmara, which dominates the bustling traffic circle at Taksim Square. Just behind it, making the first right onto Inönü Caddesi and looking up, is the **Hotel Star** (tel. 1/145-0050). The Star is actually on quiet Sağlik Sokak, and many of its 26 rooms offer views of the Bosporus. Simple, tasteful doubles run 30,600 TL ($38), including breakfast.

A few minutes' walk towards the Dolmabahçe Palace, down Inönü at No. 38, is the **Hotel Opera** (tel. 1/143-5528). The Opera's spacious 58 rooms are divided in price by those with and without that priceless Bosporus view; doubles-cum-view and a balcony to enjoy it are 40,900 TL ($51), without a view and overlooking a sometimes-noisy street are 31,800 TL ($40). At both these popular hotels, reservations two weeks in advance of the high season are recommended.

Around the other side of the Etap Marmara, on very busy Siraselviler Caddesi nestled between the fresh juice bars, are two other not-so-budget choices. The **Hotel Dilson** at No. 49 (tel. 1/143-2032) has a bright, modern lobby decorated with framed collages of pressed flowers. Their less-distinctive double rooms cost 40,000 TL ($50); these prices may be warranted by the seventh-floor terrace restaurant, where you can enjoy the breakfast included in the room rates. The older **Keban Hotel** (tel. 1/143-3310) is located at 51 Siraselviler Caddesi. It's one of Istanbul's more popular, aging businessmen's lodgings. Functional double rooms cost 36,800 TL ($46) without breakfast. At both, ask for quieter rooms off the main street.

READER'S HOTEL SELECTION: "The Hotel Konak (telex 27345 otot tr.) was quite comfortable and can be recommended to those who, like ourselves, are traveling on a somewhat limited budget. We had a double room (US $51) and a single room (US $38), each room had a bathroom with shower and tub and a bar-type fridge stocked with beer, wine, and mineral waters: the latter were particularly useful after a hot day of sightseeing. The location is within a few blocks of the Hilton and Sheraton, just off the Cumhuriyet Caddesi. . . .The staff were all friendly and helpful and the little map they gave to guests turned out to be very useful, when returning to the hotel in taxis that were not familiar with the area" (Richard J. Joy, Ottawa, Can.). (Authors' Note: The Joys ended up at this hotel while searching for the first-class Konak Hotel, which recently changed its name to the Yeşil Ev; see the Sultan Ahmet section for details.)

A Splurge Hotel

The **Hilton International Istanbul** (tel. 1/131-4646), which recently celebrated its 30th birthday, still ranks first among the city's five star hotels. Impeccable service and all the modern amenities; spacious, well-furnished rooms with balconies offering views of the Bosporus; a huge pool and sundeck are some of the Hilton's luxury features. Their Roof Rotisserie restaurant is one of the city's most elegant continental dining rooms, serving caviar, champagne, a buffet of Turkish mezes and several French entrées. The Hilton's groomed park setting provides a tranquil respite from Istanbul's usual bustle, but life on the European side (Galata) brings European prices: two will pay $172 to $210, including tax and service, for the privilege.

3. Restaurants

For those who are unacquainted with Turkish cuisine, Istanbul's many excellent restaurants (*lokanta*) may be a bit of a surprise; however, the culinary cognoscenti have known for years that Istanbul rates among the best cities in the world for food. Imagine sitting down to a meal beginning with plates of hot hors d'oeuvres (*siçak mezes*) followed by one of 20 different kinds of kebab dishes. After your entrée, continue on to a *pastahnesi*. Istanbul has dessert palaces offering an amazing selection of sugary treats.

Our restaurant section is organized by neighborhood, and listed in the order of those neighborhoods in which you'll be spending most of your time. Sultan Ahmet Square, a sightseer's paradise, will make few gourmands happy. Both the nearby Galata Bridge area and the Pera District, across the bridge, which runs up along Istiklâl Caddesi to Taksim Square, have some good restaurants, none better than the wonderfully atmospheric Pandeli Lokantasi, at the Stromboul end of the Galata Bridge. Taksim Square has the greatest number of continental eateries and fast-food snackbars, in keeping with its commercial, cosmopolitan air. Aksaray and Lalelei's Kebab salonu keep their package-tour guests well fed, but you should only be lured there by a seafood feast in Kumkapi, a fish-lover's haven that's a ten-minute walk away. For more fish and more scenery, fresh air and a taste of the good life, continue north along the coast and up the Bosporus. Atmospheric dining has its price, and it seems most of Istanbul's super-deluxe, gourmet establishments in our Splurge Section have moved out to the suburbs into larger, more dramatic, and elegant settings. Since these can be 30 to 40 minutes away from town by taxi, we'd suggest saving that splurge urge for evening. The harborside Liman Lokantasi (open for lunch only) is the one exception to this rule.

SULTAN AHMET SQUARE: The Turkish Touring and Automobile Association, which has done so much, through its restoration projects, to provide the Sultan Ahmet area with fine hotels, has also given the traveler some fine new restaurants. **Sarnic** (tel. 512-5732), at Soğükçeşme Sokaği, is just beyond the charming restored houses of the Ayasofya Pansiyonlari, under street level in a Byzantine-era cistern. The cavernous, cool brick walls are arched 21 feet above wrought-iron candelabra, dark-wood tables set with olive-green pottery, and a formidable fireplace. Sarniç was designed as a Roman taverna, serving continental cuisine. Daily specials include Viennese schnitzel, chicken with mushrooms, and tender roast lamb. The türk pilavlari (three kinds of rice) and seasonal vegetables stuffed with onions and raisins are typical Turkish dishes, which are well prepared and elegantly presented. Sarniç has a much larger uniformed staff than we're used to at tavernas, but it's a pleasant place for lunch or supper and reasonably priced at 20,000 TL ($25) for two with wine. Open daily.

Around the corner from the Blue Mosque, in the lovely garden of the Yeşil Ev Hotel, is the **Konak Restaurant** (tel. 528-6764), another continental/Turkish eatery with style. The Konak's tables are set outdoors around a porphyry marble fountain; in cold weather, they are placed inside a greenhouse. Classical music accompanies the fine selection of mezes, Konak Steak with mushroom sauce, lamb şiş kepap, and kadayif pastry. Two can dine well, far removed from the bustle of today's Istanbul, for about 10,000 TL ($12.50) each. The Konak is open daily for lunch and dinner.

For casual snacking or a pick-me-up with style, try any of the **Ayasofya Paniyonlari's dining rooms.** Four of the nine restored houses have ground-floor parlors dressed in velvet, silk embroidery, golden tassles, and turn-of-the-century pastels. Most are open 7 a.m. to 7 p.m. daily, serving tea, coffee, and simple sandwiches or pastry. The parlor of the brown-painted middle building, known as No. 4, serves a daily table d'hôte lunch or dinner of continental fare (6700 TL, or $8.50). This hotel (next to the last house) also runs a tea garden right behind the Hagia Sophia church.

Except for the hotel restaurants, the Sultan Ahmet-area establishments are rather ordinary. However, one of the most essentially Turkish eateries around is the **Çinar Lokantasi** (tel. 527-4757), located at Divanyolu 68, up the hill from the Ayasofya Pansiyonlari. The old-style second-floor dining room, which is popular with locals and has white tablecloths and views of the Blue Mosque and Hagia Sophia, is very pleasant indeed. The most expensive item on the menu is about 1400 TL ($1.75), a bargain.

One of the least touristy and offering the best values of the Sultan Ahmet restaurants is **Meshur Halk Köfeçisi**, at 12A Divanyolu Caddesi, 1½ blocks up from Hagia Sophia. As the name suggests, this kitchen specializes in making *köfte,* fragrantly spiced and grilled Oriental meatballs, at 600 TL (75¢). The salads and meze run 300 TL (35¢) and an order of şiş kepap costs 1000 TL ($1.25).

A little farther uphill on Divanyolu Caddesi is the **Vitamin Restaurant** (tel. 526-5086). It's reasonably priced and the kitchen, right in the front of the restaurant, passes close examination with flying colors. The Vitamin serves mezes, but their Iskender kebab is delicious and the eggplant and meatballs draw raves from the mixed Turkish and tourist clientele. Entrées range from 750 TL to 1400 TL (95¢ to $1.80).

Down the block at No. 6 is an institution in Sultan Ahmet, the **Pudding Shop Restaurant** (tel. 522-2970). We'd be remiss if we didn't mention it, since the Pudding Shop has been the traditional stomping grounds for many a youthful nomad. The food is uninspired and bears only a distant relation to recognized Turkish recipes, but go there to meet travelers on their way to India, to hook up with people heading to Greece, or to exchange ideas about the future of Europe.

The **Sultan Pub Restaurant** (tel. 526-6347), is on the second floor above the bar of the same name at 2 Divanyolu Caddesi. A large selection of mezes (1000 TL, or $1.25 each), followed by any of their quasi-Turkish meat entrées (including chicken Maryland), should run 10,000 TL ($12.50) for two.

For a quick break in your sightseeing, stop at one of the many sidewalk snackbars or tea parlors in the area between the Hagia Sophia and the Blue Mosque. Most serve only sandwiches or pastries, but you can't beat the location.

Finally, if you're touring the Topkapi Palace and experience deep hunger pangs, take heart—there's a restaurant tucked away in a pavilion in the fourth court. The **Konyali Restaurant** (tel. 526-2927) used to be one of Istanbul's best. Unfortunately the food is now merely mediocre, though the view overlooking the Bosporus and Asiatic Istanbul is fit for a sultan. Prices are a bit steep, with the best entrées, konya kebab or *shashlik,* costing 3600 TL ($4.50). The best bet is to sample their meze plate at 3250 TL ($4), which features ten different appetizers. It's a great snack that comes with one of the tastiest red-pepper sauces *(biber)* we've ever tried. In season, the Konyali offers lesser-price cafeteria-style food immediately below the restaurant. The view is every bit as wonderful though service is not a hallmark of this eatery. Expect to pay 2400 TL ($3) for a sandwich and beer. The Konyali Lezzet is open only for lunch.

GALATA BRIDGE AND THE PERA PRECINCT: One of the more comprehensive introductions (though on the splurge side) to the joys of Turkish cuisine is **Pandeli Lokantasi** (tel. 522-5534), an 83-year old restaurant located on the second floor of the Egyptian Spice Market (at the Stromboul end of the Galata Bridge, behind the mosque). As you enter the market, make a left just before the first jewelry store and climb the blue-tiled stairway up to the entrance. The rooms are tiled in bright blue, *kilims* drape over the benches in the booths, and simple chandeliers hang from the painted domed ceilings. Pandeli offers a wide assortment of mezes, including fresh shrimp salad, black caviar, *tarama,* Russian salad, stuffed grape leaves, and the *börek* of the day. The two special entrées are sea bass cooked in parchment at and doner kebab. Vegetarians, or anyone else for that matter, will enjoy Pandeli's many nonmeat dishes and appetizers. Finish the meal with a dessert platter. The bill for two should be about 18,000 TL ($23). Pandeli is open only for lunch, 11:30 a.m. to 3:30 p.m., Monday through Saturday. If you visit Pandeli early at lunch, you'll be more likely to receive service that matches the quality of the food.

The greatest concentration of fish restaurants in Istanbul is on the lower level of the Galata Bridge. Fishermen tether their small boats to the bridge and hawk that day's catch to discerning Istanbulus. Primitive-looking restaurants line the other side of the walkway. Among the more popular and cleaner places are the two **Olimpyats** (one on each side of the bridge). The prices are relatively low—approximately 3600 TL ($4.50) for a portion of the exalted *lüfer*—and the fish is fresh. Readers Dr. and Mrs. King of Brentwood Bay, Canada, wrote to us about their favorite snack. "In the pier area on the Sultan Ahmet side (we believe it was between Piers 3 and 4) a small boat docks and serves freshly caught fish (small), fried and in a piece of bread. It is delicious and very inexpensive . . ."

Stuffed mussels are another thriving bridgeside specialty. Boys and whiskered old men stroll with plates of the scrumptious black-shelled seafood accented with lemon juice—150 TL (18¢) per mussel. Turks pry off the top shell and use it like a spoon. Delicious! For a true Turkish experience, walk back to the middle of the bridge for a smoke on a *nargile,* a rented waterpipe. Even if you don't smoke you shouldn't miss this haze-filled salon with its throng of pipe-puffing Turks.

The main restaurant street between the bridge and Taksim Square is Istiklâl Caddesi. There are several dining treasures hidden on Istiklâl's side streets.

The **Four Seasons Restaurant** (tel. 145-8941), at 509 Istiklâl, like Istanbul itself, reflects both Asian and European styles, thanks to its husband and wife owners, Musa and Gay Hiçdonmez. The same menu that lists "sis kebab" *kademuta köfte* ("lady's thigh"), and *palamut* fish among its specialties also includes steak Diana, with mushrooms and red wine, and various other sauced steaks. For dessert you can choose between English trifle and a selection of seasonal Turkish fruit dishes including a distinctly winter specialty, an Anatolian mousse made with cooked bananas, brandy, and roasted pignolia nuts. The staff makes an elaborate show of making Turkish coffee (not unlike the chefs at the Benihana steakhouses from Japan). The comfortable decor combines old-world elegance with family-style dining. At the Four Seasons; dinner for two, including wine (try the Doluça Riesling), runs 20,000 TL ($25). Open daily except Sunday from noon to 3 p.m. and 6 p.m. to midnight.

Continue up Istiklâl to Sahne Sokak (on your left), which leads to **Çiçek Pasaji (Flower Passage)**, where flowers, as well as fruits, vegetables, and fish are artfully displayed for passageway shoppers. A few unnamed quick-eat fish-and-mezes tavernas are interspersed between stalls. Fried mussels, grilled shrimp, and a glass of beer makes a delicious, inexpensive, and atmospheric meal, especially in a market where fishmongers shout out prices, butchers shave off fat from freshly cut meat, and vegetable-stand owners create their carefully arranged produce sculpture. The market is at its best by midday, tapering off by 7 or 8 p.m., although the tavernas stay open past 10 p.m.

One particular restaurant we like for its authentic local ambience is the **Hasir-2** (tel. 144-3942), on the second lane to the right off of Istiklâl. Pastel-painted, basket-weave cane walls comprise the simple decor. Friendly waiters will bring a huge tray laden with the day's mezes to your table. Choose from dandelion greens, yogurt spreads, eggplant, shellfish, and other tasty offerings, which can be spread on their delicious sourdough bread or scooped up with the pyramid of fresh Romaine lettuce leaves heaped in the center of the table. Add beer, wine, or raki and you can dine until the wee hours for under $5 per person. The piped-in Turkish Muzak comes free of charge.

Across Istiklâl from Çiçek Pasaji on Turnacibasi Sokak (look for the signs leading to Galatasaray Hammam) is Istanbul's best hamburger and pizza joint, **Kral ve Ben** (also known as King and I). Kral ve Ben (tel. 144-9688) is such an astonishingly accurate imitation of an American fast-food outlet, down to the onion rings, fried chicken, and orange plastic trays, that for truly homesick travelers it's the next best thing to being back in the U.S. If you go at lunch (open 11:30 a.m. to 10 p.m. Monday through Saturday) you'll more likely run into a crowd of young Turks than tourists. The pizza, which they claim is 18 inches in diameter and weighs three pounds, costs 5000 TL to 7200 TL ($6 to $9). A burger with everything costs 1200 TL ($1.50). Tasty onion rings cost 600 TL (75¢).

There are two special dessert shops back on Istiklâl. **Inci** (open till 6 p.m.) is a classic pastry and sweetshop with high ceilings, dark wood, and glass display cases. Among their specialties are *profiterolle* at 600 TL (75¢), an unbelievably delicious pastry puff filled with custard and drenched in bittersweet chocolate, and *lokum* (Turkish delight). The opulent **Konak**, at 259 Istiklâl (open 7 a.m. till midnight), serves various pastries and kebabs in a chandelier-lit, old-world setting. Farther up toward Taksim Square, at No. 127/6, is the sweet shop of **Ali Muhiddin Haci-Bekir**, where halvahphiles will find excellent plain, pistachio, or marble *helva* from 2160 TL to 3240 TL ($2.75 to $4) per kilo.

AROUND TAKSIM SQUARE: The eateries around Taksim generally serve more continental than Turkish cuisine, owing in large part to the many luxury hotels and heavy tourist traffic. However, there are a few restaurants that offer excellent Turkish fare at reasonable prices. One of our favorites and a true Istanbul classic is **Hacibaba** (tel. 144-1886), one block off Taksim Square at 49 Istiklâl Caddesi. Don't let the drab doorway and narrow staircase dissuade you —Hacibaba has a delightful, ivy-covered terrace out back that overlooks a classic Orthodox church. The mustachioed staff is genuinely pleased to display their selection of mezes and make suggestions. Three large indoor dining rooms can be boisterous when full, but their *küzu kizartma* (roast lamb), *imam bayildi* (an onion-filled baked eggplant dish), and *Islim kebab* (lamb with pureed eggplant, tomato, and peppers topped with cheese) make this a night to remember. Hacibaba's classic Turkish cuisine and ambience will set a couple back about 20,000 TL ($25); it's well worthwhile.

A cozy neighborhood place that's perfect for a casual Turkish meal is **Yekta** (tel. 148-1183), at 39/1 Vali Konaği Caddesi, a five-minute walk north of the Divan Hotel, bearing right where Cumhuriyet Caddesi forks. Yekta's suited young waiters will whip the mezes tray past you as soon as you sit down. Their huge *enginar* (artichoke heart vinaigrette), *plakiler* (white beans), and *dolmalar* are particularly good. Yekta's crowd of young couples and families mix pasta dishes with şiş kepap and *köfte;* expect to pay about 7,500 TL ($9.25) per person. Another local favorite is a block from Yekta's. **Flora** (tel. 148-9476), at No. 9, is a popular Italian café and pizzeria. On any evening you'll see young Turks huddled over beers, munching on a delicious, thick sourdough-type of crust covered in thick *kayseri*. At lunch, suited businessmen and elegant ladies out shopping can be seen doing the same thing. Pizzas average about 5000 TL ($6.25) each.

Just north of Taksim Square, in Nişantaşi at Mim Kemal Öke Caddesi 21, is a fashionable restaurant called **Ziya** (tel. 147-1708). Ziya offers a standard Turkish menu, including a wide assortment of kebabs and fish, but we particularly enjoy its elegant crowd, courteous service, and delicious mezes. Because Ziya is more often frequented by Istanbulus than tourists, dining here is a more dressy but leisurely experience. Ziya is open daily for lunch and dinner; a complete meal for two should run about $35 to $40. (Equally good but a bit stuffy is the old-world **Samdan** (tel. 140-8368), located across from Ziya at No. 18.

More reminiscent of a Swensen's Ice Cream Parlor than a McDonald's is the new fast-food outlet at Taksim Square. **Taksim Sütis** (Kyle calls it Taksim Sweeties), at 9A Siraselviler Caddesi, is a few doors down from the Etap Marmara. It's filled with busy Turks from 6 a.m. to 1 a.m. seven days a week. Kilos of cheeseburgers, cheese böreks, and omelets (all under $1) are devoured daily. Taksim Sütis is especially recommended for breakfast eaters, who can have a double Turkish coffee, eggs, and fresh rolls for 1200 TL ($1.50).

Speaking of McDonald's, we can report that the Golden Arches have invaded Istanbul and sprung up on the southwest side of Taksim Square, among other fast-food snackbars. The prices are western—1140 TL ($1.40) for a Big Mac—as is the familiar decor. McD's is open daily from 11 a.m. to midnight.

Nearby, behind the main bus stop, are two tea and coffeehouses, both with limited snackbar menus, **Café Pandarosa** and **Café Boulevard,** and the lively **Fiesta Café**, a tourist-oriented but authentically Turkish restaurant, open from 8 a.m. to midnight daily, with prices from 1400 TL to 3600 TL (or $1.75 to $4.50). Just north of the square on Cumhuriyet is the **Divan Otel Pastahanesi**, a tea parlor run by the hotel of the same name. Higher priced, superb pastries, chocolates, Turkish sweets, and ice cream are served in an elegant, contemporary setting.

Up to your ears in eggplant? Try the **Restorante Italiano** (tel. 148-3444), almost next door at no. 6, where pasta and an excellent marinara sauce is served daily for lunch or dinner.

READERS' RESTAURANT SELECTION: "We found a good meze and lamb restaurant near Taksim Square. It is the Antep Restaurant, Istiklal Cad., 3 (across from the French Consulate). Their lamb dishes were as good or better than any we had in Istanbul" (Dr. and Mrs. David King, Brentwood Bay, British Columbia, Can.).

AKSARAY, LALELI, AND KUMKAPI:

A well-traveled friend of ours refers to Kumkapi, the neighborhood immediately south of Aksaray and Laleli (a 15-minute walk for those staying in this area) as the Left Bank of Istanbul. Here a bustling street scene comes to life every night because of the concentration of excellent fish restaurants. If you come to Kumkapi by the Marmara Sea road (Kennedy Caddesi), you'll see fishmongers working their trade at all hours of the day and night. Turn up Çapariz Sokak and you'll discover what all the excitement is about. It's difficult to choose a favorite eatery when so many abound, but among ours are **Cemal Balik, Akvaryum, Beyaz Balina, Sandal,** and **Evren.** As an example, Cemal Balik (tel. 527-2288), at 27 Çapariz Sokak, serves *pavurya* (fresh crab), *karadisğuveş* (an exquisite shrimp-and-peppers casserole topped with cheese), grilled *lüfer* (bluefish), *tonuk* (tuna steak) or fried *barbunya* (red mullet) in a lively, casual bistro setting. The staff is gracious though busy and the flavors and scents that waft past your table provide a true culinary adventure. Fish is billed by the filet or kilo and a portion averages 4200 TL ($5); two can gorge themselves on fresh seafood for under 18,000 TL ($22.50).

Moving up into Laleli and Aksaray, the pickings are rather slim. There are many Iskender kebab joints lining the streets, but don't expect anything great. Better than most is **Hacibozanoglu Restaurant** (tel. 528-4492), at 214 Ordu Caddesi. Hacibozanoglu offers a very good Kerisik kebab or mixed grill for 2200 TL ($2.75), and for dessert an excellent baklava loaded with nuts. It's no surprise that **Haci Bozan Ogullari** (tel. 522-8268), at 279 Ordu Caddesi (across the street and one block away), is the name of the new sweetshop opened by these successful restaurateurs. This lively gilt *salonu* serves up the honey daily between 7 a.m. and 1 a.m. A small, casual, more intimate Turkish eatery is **Özlale Restaurant** (tel. 511-4775), at 64 Zeynep Kamil Sokak, off Fethi Bey Caddesi. Özlale is wood-panelled, a bit more dressy than the neon-lit kebaberies in this quarter. The friendly, laid-back staff serves diners on the main level and on the small balcony which overlooks it; two can have a solid şiş kepap and mezes for 10,000 TL ($10.50). Özlale is open daily for lunch and dinner. Directly under Hacibozanglu, below street level, is a meat-and-potatoes restaurant called **Murat** (tel. 528-1928). Among our recommended dishes are *turlu guvel* (beef and vegetable stew), *karni yarik* (eggplant stuffed with tomato, peppers, and meat), and *icli pilau* (brown rice spiced with pine nuts, raisins, and liver). Expect to pay about 1800 TL ($2.25) for most dishes.

DINING ALONG THE BOSPORUS:

DINING ALONG THE BOSPORUS: On the far side of the Bosporus Kuruçesme Bridge, from Kuruçesme to Bebek, are several excellent restaurants and bars open daily for lunch and dinner. **Merih Sarap Mahzeni** (tel. 163-5977) is an intriguing wine bar built in a Byzantine-era cellar (the owners bottle their own wine). The bar is located on the coast highway, along the bus or dolmush route, at 24 Kuruçesme Caddesi. (Call to make sure that they're open.) After a glass of wine in Kuruçesme, many people proceed one kilometer north to the **Kuyu Restaurant** (tel. 163-6750) in Arnavutköy on the coast, for excellent fish and seafood mezes at moderate prices.

Yeni Bebek (tel. 163-3447), next to the Bebek Hotel, at 123 Cevdet Paşa Caddesi, is among our favorite fish restaurants in all of Istanbul. Set above a small marina overlooking the Bosporus, Yeni Bebek, with its well-dressed and hip-looking crowd reminded us of an oceanside café in Malibu. We sat outside, sampling the expertly prepared mezes and fish and watching the ships ply the water under a bright, full moon. All of this romance runs about $40 for two, including wine.

Far up the Bosporus, in and around Tarabya, are two more excellent restaurants, Palet II and Façyo. On the south side of Tarabya's yacht-filled harbor lies **Palet II** (tel. 162-0020), a luxurious catery with 20-foot-high wooden ceilings and a large central fireplace. This octagonally shaped restaurant offers a 180° view of Asia and the bay. Try the grain-and-walnut salad as well as the *palamut* (fish) with parsley and lemon. Expect to pay about 8000 TL ($10) per person.

Façyo (tel. 162-0024) is at 13 Kireçburnu Caddesi, but is actually to the north of the town. Again, the specialty is fish and seafood mezes. Prices are lower than at Palet II and the view over the Black Sea is fantastic.

The last stop on the Bosporus cruise is the much smaller fishery village of Rumeli Kavagi, whose lanes are filled with cheap and casual seafood cafés. Try the fried mussels *(midye)* on a stick; they're delicious at 500 TL (65¢) a portion.

SPLURGE DINING:

SPLURGE DINING: **Liman Lokantasi** (tel. 144-1033) is for that one very special meal in Istanbul. Set on the harbor at 44 Yolcu Salonu Üstü, near the Maritime Terminal Tourist Office, Liman is popular with businessmen at lunch who want to dine in a formal environment. The service is always good, the seafood is the best in the city, and the view of the harbor is superb. Much less expensive and totally informal is the **Liman Cafeteria** in the downstairs section. Both the restaurant and cafeteria are open only for lunch. Closed Sunday.

Among Istanbul splurge restaurants there is one that stands out because of its reputation for serving the city's finest meat dishes. In fact, this restaurant, called **Beyti** (tel. 573-9373), at 33 Oman Sokak, in the suburb of Florya, is often referred to as a "Meat Palace." This ultramodern cast concrete and wood structure with 11 separate dining rooms is quite unusual in these parts. Their helipad makes lunch convenient for the royalty and dignitaries who dine here. The interior decor, in contrast, follows traditional Turkish lines with tiled panels, stained glass, hand-woven rugs and bright chandeliers. One dines at Beyti, however, not for the ambience but for its extraordinary kebabs. Beyti is open for lunch and dinner. (Florya is about 40 minutes away from the city, toward the airport and is best reached by taxi; the fare is about $8 each way.) Dinner for two should run $40 to $50.

If you're overtaken with the urge to splurge after the sun goes down, the famous Abdullah, founded in 1888, fills the bill. **Abdullah Lokantasi** (tel. 163-6406) is now housed in a modern, semicircular glass observatory atop a hill in Emirgan, overlooking the Bosporus. The large reception area is decorated with flower-filled antique vases and ornately stamped copper serving pieces; from there a bevy of waiters will lead you into a formal, gracious dining environment. The cuisine, like the aesthetic, is Turkish continental. The celebrated sturgeon Abdullah is baked on a bed of spinach and topped with a béchamel and cheese sauce ($13.50). The mezes range from black Black Sea caviar ($33 for 100 grams) to meat-filled ravioli with a yogurt dressing, or superb grilled squash and eggplant. The Abdullah's drawback is its location at Emirgan Koru Caddesi 11, which is about a half-hour ($7) taxi ride from Taksim Square. Brunch lovers should contemplate the journey for its daytime Bosporus view; Abdullah is open from noon to 3 p.m. and 8 p.m. to midnight.

4. What to See and Do

If you're interest was whetted by the spectacular "Suleyman the Magnificent" art show that toured Amenza last year, your first stop should be the Topkapi Palace. The sultans' collections and the Harem offer the best glimpse of life in the royal Ottoman court to be found anywhere in Anatolia. The exquisite Blue Mosque and its neighbor, Hagia Sophia (the Church of St. Sofia), are just down the street from Topkapi and are two more "must sees."

Beyond these few points, the rest depends wholly on individual interest. Shoppers should march directly to the Grand Bazaar—actually it's recommended to anyone who wants to see one of the world's best markets. Museum fans should visit the **Ibrahim Paşa Museum of Art** and wander down the hill from Topkapi to take in Istanbul's marvelous triad: the archeological museum, Çinili Köşk (the tile museum), and the Museum of the Ancient Orient. All are excellent. Those who wish to see Turkey's most architecturally perfect mosque will be fascinated by Suleymaniye, the mosque of Suleyman the Magnificent; this particular mosque is all the more interesting because it still functions as a place of worship and gathering point for a large community of devout Moslems. The best display of classical Turkish tiles is found in the Rüstem Pasa mosque. Kariye Camii is a sacred Christian church that contains the most extraordinary mosaics created in the Byzantine world. A day or evening cruise up the Bosporus is the highlight for many first-time visitors to Istanbul. Also highly recommended is a stop at Dolmabahçe Palace, a fabulously ostentatious abode built for the sultan on the banks of the lower Bosporus. We were fascinated by a visit to Yerebatan Sarayi, the newly opened underground cistern sure to delight those who are interested in engineering marvels. Finally, no visit to Turkey is complete without experiencing the pleasures of a Turkish bath. Now it's time to go out and explore one of the most exciting cities on the planet!

THE BLUE MOSQUE (SULTAN AHMET CAMII): From the Marmara Sea, among the most stunning silhouettes in Istanbul is that of the Blue Mosque, perhaps comparable only to the Taj Mahal in India. Piercing the skyline are six minarets on the corners of a multidomed exterior. Sultan Ahmet I, in the early 17th century, ordered its construction, placing it only 200 yards from Hagia Sophia. The architect, Mehmet Aga, designed the mosque under the sultan's orders to challenge both the size and shape of its neighbor. The Blue Mosque's middle dome swells to 23½ meters in diameter and 43 meters in height; four five-meter-wide ribbed-stone columns create the support. As a result of its grandeur (now undergoing a grand restoration), the Blue Mosque became the reigning sultan's place of prayer.

Prior to entering you are required to take off your shoes, respecting the Moslem custom. Half of the interior is cordoned off to separate the tourists from the Moslems in prayer. Foreigners should make an effort to observe certain customs: don't wear shorts, miniskirts, or sleeveless tops, but it's not necessary to wash your hands and feet before entering.

Over 250 stained-glass windows light up the cavernous interior. Although earthquakes and disrepair destroyed the originals, the existing windows are harmonious with the rest of the mosque. Over 21,000 exquisite blue Turkish tiles line the walls, the majority of the designs of the four-flower variety, with tulips (they were originally grown in Turkey and sent to Holland), roses, carnations, and lilies. Many of the best designs begin around the walk ledge running along the perimeter of the mosque approximately seven meters above rug level, an area, restricted to women in prayer. As is typical in the Moslem faith, separate areas of prayer are maintained for men and women.

The internal dimensions, the plethora of designs and colors on the tiles, the rugs, and the stained-glass windows make a visit to Istanbul's most famous mosque an overwhelming experience. The Blue Mosque is open daily. A donation is requested at the door when you leave your shoes; 500 TL (60¢) is appropriate.

Carpet and Kilim Museums

Tucked away to the left of the main entrance to the Blue Mosque are two small but fascinating museums for anyone interested in antique Oriental rugs. For some reason the museum has been divided into two parts and charges two separate admission fees: 500 TL (65¢) for adults, half price for students. No matter, walk down into the cool barrel-vaulted galleries under the Blue Mosque for a look at some of the oldest and richest rugs on display in a public museum. Both museums have examples of prayer rugs, folk rugs, and rugs made for the sultans and their palaces. The Carpet Museum, with rugs that date from the 13th century (making them some of the oldest in existence) and range from worn fragments to perfectly preserved samples is closed for renovation. The Kilim Museum also contains many colorful wall rugs, prominent in their use of Caucasian blue and Turkish red. Open Tuesday through Sunday from 9 a.m. to 5 p.m.; closed Monday.

Hippodrome

On the long landscaped mall that borders the Blue Mosque stood a 100,000-seat Hippodrome (the civic center of Roman Constantinople). Chariots raced around the narrow spine of the giant stadium, today distinguished by three lone columns and obelisks (in order, going from north to south: the Egyptian Obelisk, the Serpentine Column, and the Colossus). Constantine the Great, after rebuilding the Hippodrome, chose it as the site of the ceremony dedicating Byzantium as the new capital of the Roman Empire. The Hippodrome was also a notorious meeting ground for the four major rival political parties. Its reputation was based on a revolt in A.D. 531 that ended only after 30,000 deaths and the near collapse of Emperor Justinian's regime.

Museum of Turkish and Islamic Arts

Along with the Topkapi Palace Treasury, the Museum of Turkish and Islamic Arts, or Ibrahim Paşa Muze, (located along the Hippodrome Mall, across from the Blue Mosque) is the most impressive collection of Turkish crafts in the world. Housed in the recently renovated 16th-century palace of Ibrahim Paşa, a fabulously wealthy Grand Vizier to Suleyman the Magnificent, this collection features a selection of classic 16th- and 17th-century Uşak court carpets (the finest examples we've ever seen), miniature paintings, illustrated manuscripts and calligraphic drawings, and fine ceramic, wood, stone and metalwork from the Selçuk and Ottoman periods. One of the highlights of the museum is the ethnographic display (downstairs from the gallery of huge Uşak carpets). This section illustrates the customs, styles, and modes of housing for diverse ethnic groups living in 19th- and 20th-century Turkey. Especially interesting is their exhibit on yurts, tents, and nomadic life.

After wandering through the museum, be sure to stop in the highly atmospheric coffeehouse, set in an arched and vaulted Ottoman kitchen (located across from the Ethnographic section). The museum is open daily, except Monday, from 10 a.m. to 5 p.m. Admission is 800 TL ($1), half price weekends.

The Tomb of Sultan Ahmet I

To the right of the entrance to the Blue Mosque is the tomb of Sultan Ahmet I, built in 1620 by Osman II for his father. The impressive, square-plan tomb is filled with the small and large coffins of many generations of sultans. The wrapped white turbans on top of the coffins indicate the deceased's status. Architect Sedekfar Mehmed Ağa (who designed the Blue Mosque) here uses a band of gilt calligraphy, yeşil Iznik tiles, and stained-glass florettes in the arched niches above the windows. Although a lesser sight in comparison to many of the Sultan Ahmet Square wonders, the devotion of the Turkish people who come to pay homage to the pantheon of former sultans is very moving.

Medresseh (Market of Istanbul Arts and Crafts)

The Touring Club has just restored the Medresseh, a classic Islamic school across from the Blue Mosque. The vaulted study rooms and simple courtyard have been renovated for use by local craftsmen, who demonstrate the traditional techniques of calligraphy, bookbinding, miniature painting, the making of ceramics and copperware, and mother-of-pearl inlay to visitors. Handcrafts and artworks are for sale at reasonable prices; the quality is high, but there's no bargaining here. The craftsmen and their work can be seen daily between 9 a.m. and 7 p.m.

HAGIA SOPHIA: Hagia Sophia (Ayasofya) is testimony to the religious diversity of this Eurasian city. In the fourth century A.D. Christians constructed a basilica at this site, laying down the ultimate foundation of the current building. Christened Hagia Sophia and dedicated to divine wisdom, this church-turned-mosque-turned-museum has undergone tremendous religious and structural transformation. A fire in the fifth century and one in the sixth century destroyed the original basilica, leaving only the foundation. In A.D. 532 the Byzantine Emperor Justinian commenced the five-year project of constructing the basic inner form as it appears today. Given the materials used and the ambitious design of the massive dome, the architectural work required the best architects and engineers of the time. It was little wonder, though, that when earthquakes occurred in the ninth and tenth centuries the dome shattered (it was rebuilt several times). So stunning was this architectural achievement of the Byzantine era that Hagia Sophia became a model for Christian churches in Greece and Italy. For example, the great Monastery of Ossios Loukas, south of Delphi, was patterned after this sixth-century design.

Although pillaged and ransacked by waves of thieves, Hagia Sophia remained an essentially Christian building until May 1453, when Turkish forces, led by Sultan Mehmet II, invaded and took Constantinople. Within a week Moslem services were being held in a Christian building whose tradition had extended more than a millennium. Throughout the ensuing Ottoman reign Hagia Sophia underwent significant structural and decorative alterations to accommodate the new religion. Minarets were added, external buttresses were built to reinforce the interior columns, and Islamic calligraphy was painted on the domes. Because of the Islamic law against re-creating human imagery, all of the ninth-century Christian mosaics were covered up with plaster. Having been given a facelift, Hagia Sophia remained a center of Islamic worship for centuries.

Hagia Sophia evolved to its current level of incongruous Christian and Islamic design after the reforming Sultan Abdul Mecit I ordered the restoration of the building. The mosaics were exposed and protected from any further damage. In 1935, under the guidance of the Byzantine Institute, venerable Hagia Sophia was declared a museum.

What a museum! There are exquisite mosaics of the Virgin Mary up in the galleries above the ground floor; wonderful tenth-century portraits of the Emperor Alexander and Empress Zoe as well as Christ and Constantine Monomachos adorn the walls up in the rafters. Not far away, eight huge black disks with Islamic calligraphy hug the corners of the central dome. Clever observers will notice that the Moslem prayer platform (mihrab) near the apse looks off-center relative to the rest of the building. In fact, the mihrab faces exactly 10° away from the front of the apse in order to properly align it in the direction of Mecca, a consideration Justinian certainly never contemplated when he originally set about building the church. Some of the best mosaics are in the narthex (the entry hall); both Justinian and Constantine are depicted on a gold-leaf background.

One of the main attractions in the left aisle of the main sanctuary is the weeping column of Saint Gregory, the miracle worker. It is said that water oozes out of the column from some miraculous source. Medieval fable has it that the moisture was a general panacea and that worshippers would be cured of any ailment by the water. Fertility and clear eyesight are supposed specialties of this sacred water. The source of the moisture remains a mystery. Centuries ago it was said that the column drew water from a cistern below, but nobody ever found the cistern. Others explain that moisture results from the reaction of the marble with the metal girder around the column. Whatever the explanation, a lot of people must have believed in its power, because there's a three-inch hole in the marble where the curious have poked their fingers for centuries.

Unlike most of the mosques in the area, you don't have to remove your shoes before entering, for after all, Hagia Sophia has been converted again, this time from religious to secular status. The entrance fee is 600 TL (65¢), and hours are 9:30 a.m. to 4:30 p.m. Tuesday through Sunday; closed Monday.

If you have an extra moment, look at the tombs of the Ottoman emperors, Selim II and Murad III (both are in the garden to the south).

THE TOPKAPI PALACE: If the city of Istanbul is a gigantic treasure trove, then the Topkapi Palace ("Topkapi Saray" in Turkish) is literally its vault. Within the palace's sprawling grounds are the most precious objets d'art of the sultans: an array of mind-boggling jewels, including the emerald-studded Topkapi Dagger; one of the world's finest collections of Chinese ceramics; a display of Ottoman arms and armor; and an unparalleled gallery of miniatures.

The buildings that house these remarkable objects are themselves outstanding. Organized in four courts, the third court contains another of the sultans' grand treasures, the harem.

Immediately below the palace, to the west, is a complex of three museums. These form a continuity of Anatolian wealth with the collections at the Topkapi Palace. The largest building, the archeology museum, is devoted to finds principally of the Greek (the Turks call them "Western Anatolians") and ancient Roman era. The second is devoted to ancient objects from the Near Eastern world, while the third, the Çinili Köşk, is an Ottoman-era kiosk converted into a tile museum.

Today, the **first court** is little more than a tree-lined parking lot, with taxis, buses, and souvenir hawkers. Tour groups and guides waiting to enter the palace clog up the area. The original function of this court was as a staging ground for the Janissaries, the sultans' most elite regiment, so its current use seems to fit nicely with the original design. This court was also used for public executions which, according to historical accounts, occurred frequently. Notice the fountain (called Cellad Cesmesi) and low pillars to the right of the gate. This quiet corner was where the executioner cleaned his sword (on display in the arms collection). After his work was completed, the executioner mounted the recently detached heads on the short pillars; thus they were called Example Stones, for obvious reasons.

The majority of the palace was built between 1459 and 1465, during Mehmet the Conqueror's reign. The gate leading into the second court, called the **Middle Gate** or **Gate of Salvation**, is reminiscent of the military architecture in the old city of Rhodes; the fortress-style walls were comfortable for a band of newly settled nomads, yet they kept the interior of the palace light and exposed to the open air. Topkapi, instead of being a huge medieval stone monolith, feels like an open park, full of life and fresh air.

The **second court** is by far the largest of the four, and served five distinct purposes. Each function had its own building and a corresponding path radiating from the Middle Gate. As you enter the second court, the path on your extreme left leads to the **stables**, which are now used to display quaint sedan chairs used by harem ladies. The second path from the left connects to one of the entrances to the harem.

The **Harem** was built nearly 100 years after Mehmet laid the original plan of Topkapi. Until the late 16th century the sultan's female entourage was housed in an older palace (far away on the third hill of Constantinople.) Murat III, undoubtedly a man of great prowess (let's face it, the man probably had over 300 wives), built a new harem attached to the Topkapi Palace. Actually, Murat may also have been lacking in judgment. By placing a bevy of attractive, influential, ambitious, and intelligent women that much closer to the sultanate, he threatened his own power and that of his heirs and successors. Within a short span of time numerous plots would be hatched from the harem involving African eunuchs, jealous ministers, assassinations, fratricide, and political intrigue. Its power grew to such an extent that by the 18th century many contended that the Ottoman Empire was ruled from the harem. As an architectural monument, the harem is a marvel, both for its complex and convoluted design (there are over 400 rooms on six levels), as well as its supreme elegance. Many of the rooms that have been restored are the most impressive in all of Topkapi. The 500 TL (65¢) tour of the harem is a must; it's conducted in English and offered approximately every half hour from 10 a.m. to 4 p.m.

Returning to the Middle Gate, the third path leads to the meeting hall of the **Divan**, or **Imperial Court**. The Divan was an administrative and judicial body that advised the sultan and carried out the main functions of government. Just to make sure his ministers' advice was to his benefit, the sultan hid in a small room next to the Divan's chamber and listened through a screen. A prominent activity of the Imperial Court was imposing and collecting taxes. The treasury, a storehouse of records and collected funds, was conveniently located next door to the Divan—a rare expression of political candor. The Divan members took their expenses off the top and left the rest to the treasury. The treasury now functions as a gallery for the collection of arms and armor. This is a particularly fine collection, showing off two prominent Ottoman characteristics: rare craftsmanship and an eagerness to enter (or start) a good fight. Don't miss the intricately inlaid battle helmets and, of course, our favorite, the execution sword.

The fourth path, lined on both sides by cypress trees, leads to the **Arz Odasi**, or **Throne Room**. This structure is situated in the third court, but is functionally connected to the second. The throne room was as far as anyone outside the royal family was allowed to go. Grand viziers, Divan leaders, foreign dignitaries, and honored citizens met with the sultan here only on rare occasions, often to request his final approval of a law or treaty.

The fifth path, on the extreme right, reaches out to a bank of low buildings capped by a row of chimneys that look like nuclear reactor cooling towers. This is the **kitchen**. Consistent with Ottoman organization, each of these ten separate cooking chambers served a separate segment of the palace: one for the sultan, one for the harem, etc. When the cooks were operating at peak efficiency, they could feed 5,000 people a day. The kitchen houses the porcelain collection, one of the world's finest displays of Chinese Sung and Yuan period ceramics. The 10th- to 14th-century pieces were produced during the zenith of Chinese ceramic artistry; their celadon-colored glazes and clean flowing lines, created over 600 years ago, are remarkably modern. Most of this collection (only a fraction is displayed out of the 10,000 items acquired by the sultans) was undoubtedly hauled off to Constantinople during centuries of pillaging and plundering.

Walking through the **Gate of Felicity**, past the Throne Room, you'll enter a part of the palace no outside visitor entered until the early years of the 20th century. This, the **third court**, was the private domain of the sultan, the royal family, the harem, and the highest officials of the inner palace. Apart from the many buildings that served the Sultan, the third court was also used as the palace **school**.

The highlight of Topkapi Palace, and for many the premier attraction in all of Istanbul, is the **Treasury**, situated on the right side of the third court. Head straight for the second room. There, illuminated behind a pane of thick glass, is the glittering Topkapi Dagger. Festooned with three of the largest emeralds we've ever seen, the dagger looks otherworldly, as if it landed on earth as a gift from a neighboring galaxy. The overgrown emerald on the top is hinged, covering a watch that's hidden inside. If the Topkapi Dagger whets your appetite for all things glittering, proceed to Room 4 to examine the brilliant 86-karat Spoonmaker's Diamond, fifth largest in the world. The other objects in the Treasury of particular note are the four thrones (one in each display room), each more ornate and ostentatious than the next.

The third court also contains the sultan's collection of Ottoman and Turkish miniatures, the Shrine of the Holy Mantle (relics of Mohammed), and a small display of costumes. All are recommended. One of our favorites in the palace is the library of Amhet III, the compact pavilion situated behind the throne room, which has recently been closed for renovation. It's an altogether elegant interior that combines the warmth of Moslem hospitality with the exotic and luxurious tastes of the Ottoman Turks.

The **fourth court** is most renowned for its terraced gardens, small pavilions, and fountains (around which Crazy Ibrahim had harem dancers stage water ballets). Here was the sultan's famous tulip garden (tulips were originally taken to Holland from Turkey). Nowadays the gardens are little cared for and the rest of the court functions as a restaurant run by the Konyali family (they also operate a snackbar in the garden below the dining rooms). The food is only fair and expensive, but the view overlooking the Golden Horn is wonderful. Topkapi Saray is open daily from 9:30 a.m. to 5 p.m., closed Tuesday during the winter. The admission is 1500 TL ($2). There is a Charge Bureau and long-distance telephones at the Konyali Restaurant.

Hagia Eirene

Hagia Eirene (Church of Divine Peace) stands as the oldest, and until the rebuilding of Hagia Sophia, the most important church of Byzantine Constantinople. Contrary to its name, Hagia Eirene's history is anything but peaceful. Thousands died in A.D. 346 during riots incited by Orthodox believers who supported the Nicaean Creed against Arian reformists. Hagia Eirene was destroyed by fire in the sixth century, and like Hagia Sophia was rebuilt by Justinian. Under the Ottomans the church was enclosed within the first court of Topkapi; the Janissaries used the church as an arsenal. This shrine of peace was later converted into a storehouse of Ottoman foreign military gear. Today the church is remarkably empty, little used except for presentations during the Istanbul Festival.

The church is constructed along the simple lines of a basilica. The interior is unadorned; only the chalky brick and mortar remain. Its most striking feature is the semicircular rows of seats at the bema, looking much like a small odeon. Other than that, Hagia Eirene has finally become what its name stands for: a divinely peaceful and contemplative resting place.

Hagia Eirene is temporarily closed for renovations, although open during the Istanbul festival and to Turkish TV as a backdrop for epic dramas.

Historical Museums

Three relatively small but excellent collections are clustered together 200 meters down the hill from the Topkapi Palace as part of the Istanbul Archeological Museums. The classical section of the **archeological museum** features a superb collection of Greek- and Roman-era sarcophagi, including the lavishly carved Alexander Sarcophagus. The collection, begun in 1881 for the Ottoman's Imperial Museum, numbers more than 85,000 objects. Some of the best Greek sculpture unearthed in Turkey is on display throughout the many rooms of the museum, though the Ephebos Room contains the most sublime works. The museum is open daily (closed Monday in winter) from 9:30 a.m. to 4:30 p.m.; admission is 500 TL (65¢), half price weekends.

The Çinili Köşk (Tiles Pavilion), situated directly across from the classical section, was built by Mehmet II in 1472 as a retreat from Topkapi. Today it functions as a tile museum, highlighting one of the Ottoman's greatest art forms. The art of Turkish tile making reached its zenith during the 16th century, with the most distinguished designs coming from the ceramic studios south of Istanbul in Iznik (then called Nicaea). The superb mihrab in the center room from the central Anatolian Isa Bey Mosque is decorated with these colorful tiles from the Iznik period. The exterior of the Çinili Köşk was once covered with many more tiles; those that have survived have recently been cleaned or repaired.

The third museum in this extraordinary complex is devoted to objects of the ancient Orient. Besides its rich collection of Hittite art (including the two lions welcoming you at the door), the **Museum of the Ancient Orient** features a fabulous set of turquoise-colored tiles from Nebuchadnezzar's (sixth-century B.C.) grand procession way in Babylon (the rest of the tiles and enormous sections of the famous tiled gate are on display in the Pergamon Museum in East Berlin). The museum also contains three "firsts": Hammurabi's Code, the first canon of laws set in writing; tiles from 2200 B.C. that are presumed to be the first example of printed (stamped) writing; and the Treaty of Kadesh (1269 B.C.), the first written peace treaty. The Museum of the Ancient Orient was closed in 1982 for renovation.

THE SULEYMANIYE MOSQUE: While it rivals the grandeur of the Blue Mosque, its purity of religious purpose remains untouched by generations of admiring foreigners. The Suleymaniye was built in 1557 as part of an overall urban plan, which situated it in the midst of hospitals, schools, and housing. The functional design called for a landscaped complex of great simplicity overlooking the Golden Horn. The stone enclosure walls of Sulemaniye are decorated with Iznik tiles but lack the opulent design of better-known mosques; the bare marble walls within are broken by panes of sombre-hued stained glass which cast an austere light over the vast interior. The main dome reaches 60 meters high and has a diameter of nearly 30 meters; this immensity, and the classic simplicity of its almost minimalist decor, make the Suleymaniye a masterpiece of Ottoman architectural design. The architect Sinan (who also contributed to the Topkapi Palace, Hagia Sophia, and Selimiye Mosque of Edirne, among others) used his ingenuity to maintain an interior uncluttered by all save the structural necessities. There are surprisingly few galleries and no aisles; the vast rotunda is supported by only four massive columns. The Suleymaniye's four minarets indicate that it was commissioned by the fourth sultan of Istanbul, and its ten serifes (balconies on minarets) symbolize the sultan's position as tenth Ottoman ruler.

The Suleymaniye continues to fulfill the religious mission for which it was built. There are few tourists, but outside, at the 20-odd sculpted faucets, local devotees scrub their hands and feet before entering to pray. Worshippers are dressed like Anatolian peasants: baggy black workpants for the men and thick black veils enveloping all but the women's faces. Do as the locals do: take off your shoes and carry them with you inside. When the prayers begin, the imam may ask all non-Moslems to leave the mosque. However, a few minutes spent outside on the steps listening to the rhythmic chanting of his words and the worshippers' response will help you to feel the pulse of this nation. Although there is no formal admission fee, we think a contribution of 500 TL (65¢) would be appropriate.

Before you hurry off to another sight, walk around back to visit the several türbes (mausoleums). Sultan Suleyman himself is buried here; his türbe of 1566, decorated with exquisite Iznik tiles, is only open sporadically, but peer inside for a look if it's closed. The eight-sided design of the sultan's türbe will help you locate it.

Also behind the mosque, in its personally chosen locale, is the hand-hewn türbe of Sinan, the architect. Not only did he live at the mosque during construction, but Sinan also prepared for his burial there (in 1588) by designing his personal türbe. It's noteworthy that Sinan was neither Moslem nor Turk; he was instead Christian and Greek (a biographical note which troubles the proud Turks). He did not arrive in Istanbul till 1511 (at the young age of 21 years), yet this infidel's style represents the height of Ottoman mosque design.

Also in the back are the türbes of Suleyman's wife, Roxelana, and that of his daughter Princess Mihrimah.

YEREBATAN SARAYI (BASILICA CISTERN): Istanbul has so many wonderful sites from every era that it's difficult to choose which should be included on our list of "must see" list. However, the newly opened Yerebatan Sarayi, or Underground Palace, one of the largest water cisterns in the city, is such a marvel of engineering and grace that it shouldn't be missed.

It was built under Justinian in 532, probably as part of an enlargement of an earlier waterwork. This structure, of vaulted brick ceilings held up by eight-meter-tall columns at four-meter intervals, covers an area that is one and a half times the size of a football field (140 meters long by 70 meters wide). Its 336 columns, some fluted, have a variety of simple Doric or ornate Byzantine-era Corinthian capitals. When the municipality of Istanbul drained one meter of water for its restoration project, two huge carved Medusa heads (similar to those found at the Apollo Temple of Didyma but thought to have come from Rome) were uncovered. These beautiful sculpted reliefs, turned upside down and reused as column bases, are only a few of the architectural fragments from antiquity that were scavenged for use in the cistern's construction. The city's fine restoration includes a long walkway that enables visitors to fully explore and a new lighting system that reveals the cistern's beauty. The Basilica Cistern, which originally brought water from 12 miles away, now only collects rain water, but a visit to its interior, so much cooler than the streets of Sultan Ahmet, is as refreshing as a cool drink. The Yerebatan Sarayi is open daily from 9 a.m. to 5 p.m. The entrance is on Alemdar Caddesi, just off Divanyolu by the Hagia Sophia; admission is 1200 TL ($1.50).

THE GRAND BAZAAR: The covered market (Kapalicarşi) that lent its name to a high-fashion magazine (Harper's Bazaar) and is the setting for countless spy novels can't be missed by anyone visiting Istanbul. Tourists and Turks make pilgrimages to this consumers' paradise, but often more for its intriguing ambience and life than to actually buy anything. Nevertheless, merchants don't live on soul alone: there are over 4,000 shops selling everything from junk to jewelry, leather gear, rugs, knits, antique guns, copper, tiles, and other bric-a-brac. The Grand Bazaar is open daily (closed Sunday), and you'll find that shops carrying the same type of merchandise cluster together. Since the multitude of narrow, winding, amber-lit lanes don't wind in any logical pattern, the best thing to do is wander around.

One hint: There's an inverse relationship between the quality of the goods and the amount of barking the store owner emits. At modern uninspiring gold jewelers, the owner and his relatives will accost you in several languages, saying their goods are without equal; more often than not it's just not true.

Our strategy for conquering the bazaar is simple: first find the best quality (often, most expensive) goods and see what you like; then hunt out equally high-quality, lower-priced bargains. To do this, your first stop should be the **Bedesten** (the Old Bazaar at the heart of the Grand Bazaar) to see the finest objects and steepest prices. When you find something you like, ask the price, and then comparison shop in the rest of the bazaar. If the Bedesten has the only goods you covet, at least you can comfort yourself by knowing you're an educated consumer.

In addition to housing the finest antiques, the Bedesten is the oldest and most picturesque section of the Bazaar. Tall, vaulted ceilings enclose the small shops; the ablution fountains outside are frequently used by Moslem shoppers. Even the pace in the Old Bazaar is different; store owners don't shout at you to buy this or that. Nor will there be much bargaining, in fact in some stores none at all.

Where to Shop

We found four particular stores in the Bedesten which offer top-quality goods at fair value. For antique metalware, such as samovars, scales, lanterns, copper pots, etc., try the shop of **Murat Bilir** (tel. 520-7046) at Şerifag. Sokak 2223. At the age of 15, Murat claims he developed his passion for Oriental metalwork; after an education at Istanbul University, he has for 15 years continued to refine his knowledge of this subject. He speaks excellent English and knows the detailed history of each piece he sells as well as its virtues and flaws. The majority of them are 100 to 250 years old, and of fine quality; although Murat may come down from the posted sticker price, he generally does not bargain. (The staffers from the American consulate are regulars here, so you can rest assured that Murat is no fly-by-night operator!)

For kilim carpets, **Adnan and Hasan** (tel. 527-9887), located on the periphery of the Bedesten at 92 Halicilar Çarsisi, offers a fine selection. Adnan and Hasan, both former schoolteachers, now sell only the best Anatolian tapestries. As opposed to the knotted carpet (the floor covering of royalty) the kilim is the flat-woven carpet of the poor. Both men find folk aspects of the kilim interesting and are very skilled at explaining the meaning of patterns, or farming utensil, bird, or poppy-flower designs. Their carpets cost between $80 and $120 for the newer kilims (made within the last 40 years). Older kilims can become very expensive and are considered collectors' items; when we were there a neighboring merchant sold one for $22,000 (although not to us!).

For exquisite old and new embroideries and traditional clothing, try the **Çevre Antique Shop**, at 18 Şerifaga Sokak, near the copper stalls. Half-century-old dowry linens start at $50 and unique, gold-embroidered satin kaftans run $500 and up. If you bypass their museum-quality goods there are many inexpensive gift items to consider!

The traditional skills of fine gold and silver workmanship demanded by the sultans have been passed down to the silversmiths of Mahmutpaşa. **Cap Gümüş** (tel. 527-1447), at 13 Kalcilar Han, stands out among shops crowding the lanes next to the bazaar for their fine repoussé and filigree tea services, candlesticks, vases, and other decorative items. Their merchandise is priced according to weight, and because the cost of fine labor is so much less than in our country, heirloom quality pieces and reproductions of classic English patterns are excellent value. For low-cost, easy-to-carry gift items, why not buy some traditional Turkish tiles? Yaglihciler Caddesi (which also features clothing) in the new bazaar has two small shops, at nos. 56 to 58, which sell the largest variety of small and large newly made ceramic tiles and plates. Floral patterns or animal designs decorate six-inch-square tiles, which cost about 5000 TL ($7.25) each.

A Rest and a Snack

In addition to shops, the bazaar houses a bank, a PTT, and some restaurants. The restaurants are all quite adequate; however, they tend to share, perhaps by osmosis, the hustle-and-bustle ambience of the rest of the bazaar. One

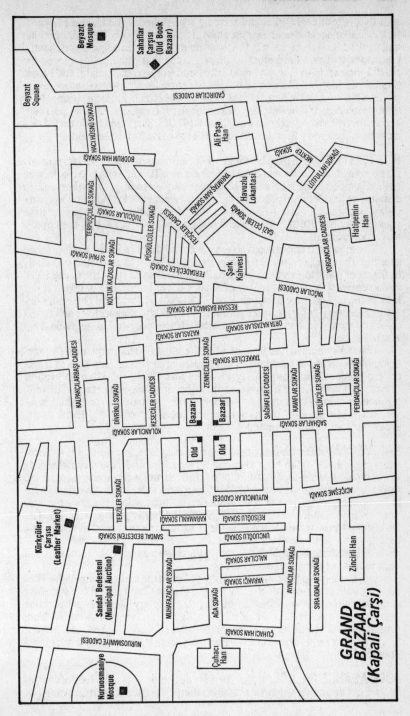

Beyazit Mosque

Sahaflar Çarşısı (Old Book Bazaar)

Beyazit Square

ÇADIRCILAR CADDESİ

HACI HÜSNÜ SOKAĞI

BODRUM HAN SOKAĞI

Ali Paşa Han

MEKTEP SOKAĞI

TERPUŞÇULAR SOKAĞI

TUĞCULAR SOKAĞI

PÜSKÜLCÜLER SOKAĞI

YARIM HAN SOKAĞI

FESÇİLER CADDESİ

LÜTFULLAH SOKAĞI

Havuzlu Lokantası

GAZİ ÇELEBİ SOKAĞI

Hatipemin Han

Sİ PAHİ SOKAĞI

FERDACİLER SOKAĞI

Şark Kahvesi

YORGANCILAR CADDESİ

KOLTUK KALAASLAR SOKAĞI

RESSAM BASMACILAR SOKAĞI

YAĞCILAR CADDESİ

KAZASLAR SOKAĞI

ORTA KAZASLAR SOKAĞI

KALPAKÇILARBAŞI CADDESİ

ZENNECİLER SOKAĞI

TAKKECİLER SOKAĞI

KAVAFLAR SOKAĞI

TERLİKÇİLER SOKAĞI

PERDAHÇILAR SOKAĞI

DİVRİKLİ SOKAĞI

KESECİLER CADDESİ

Bazaar

SAĞHAFLAR CADDESİ

Bazaar

Old

Old

SAĞHAFLAR SOKAĞI

KOLANCILAR SOKAĞI

TERZİLER SOKAĞI

KIYUMCULAR CADDESİ

ACIÇEŞME SOKAĞI

KARAMANLI SOKAĞI

REİSOĞLU SOKAĞI

Kürkçüler Çarşısı (Leather Market)

SANDAL BEDESTENİ SOKAĞI

UNCUOĞLU SOKAĞI

Zincirli Han

Sandal Bedesteni (Municipal Auction)

MUHAFAZACILAR SOKAĞI

KALCILAR SOKAĞI

AYNACILAR SOKAĞI

VARAKCILAR SOKAĞI

SIRA ODALAR SOKAĞI

AĞA SOKAĞI

ÇUHACI HAN SOKAĞI

NURUOSMANİYE CADDESİ

Çuhacı Han

GRAND BAZAAR (Kapali Çarşi)

Nuruosmaniye Mosque

spot that is soothingly quiet and recently refurbished is the **Havuzlu Lokanta** (tel. 273-346), located near the post office at Sokak no. 3 ve 6. The ceiling is high and vaulted, and there are windows way up top that let in a few rays of light; a place to rest after a hard morning of bargaining and walking. John loved the *pideli kebaplar donerli,* a pita bread full of stuffed eggplant, tomato, and onion. Stuffed zucchini, bonfile, and other kebaberie staples are available at moderate prices. (No bargaining here, please.) If your appetite is for local cuisine more than ambience, try **Sevim**, the bazaar dealer's hangout. A delicious soup, kebab, and salad lunch costs about 2200 TL ($2.75). Their *irmik helvasti* (75¢), a cinnamon-flavored wheat dessert, is one of the bazaar's best bargains.

RÜSTEM PAŞA CAMII: This is one of our favorite mosques, and fortunately it's rarely included on the major tourist itineraries. Tucked away two blocks west of the Egyptian Spice Market (on Kutucular Caddesi) and easily within walking distance of the Galata Bridge, the mosque was named after Rüstem Paşa, son-in-law and grand vizier to Suleyman the Magnificent. As you might have guessed by now, Rüstem Paşa was designed and built in 1561 by the equally magnificent Sinan.

The mosque is constructed above a series of shops (rents from these shops subsidize the charitable activities of the mosque). You'll have to climb two dimly lit flights of stairs to reach the portico. From the outside this little masterpiece looks remarkably similar to many of Sinan's larger buildings, but take a closer look at the façade. Like the Çinili Kiosk, it's decorated with the Ottoman's finest 16th-century Iznik tiles. Let your fingers trace the sinuous lines and raised colors of these ceramic polygons, particularly the deep-red glaze made from Anatolian bole.

Like Suleymaniye, the mosque of Rüstem Paşa is still frequented by practicing Moslems; it has a soul that's less evident in such inanimate halls as Hagia Sophia or the Blue Mosque. Try to arrive just before the afternoon call to prayers, when you'll see a cross section of the area's shopowners, taxi drivers, businessmen, and street cleaners wandering in to prepare for the midday service. You'll also see how the mosque functions, as it has for 400 years, as the area's most important community center.

KARIYE CAMII: For those brought up on Renaissance, impressionist, and classical Greek and Roman art it's especially difficult to understand or appreciate works created during the Byzantine era. Of all the major Byzantine works in the world, among the most "accessible" (and certainly more impressive than Istanbul's mosaic museum) is the extraordinary cycle of mosaics decorating the interior of Kariye Camii, the Church of St. Savior in Chora ("in the country"). The mosaics and frescoes inside the Funerary Chapel are works created at the peak of Byzantine aesthetic development (early 14th century) and foreshadow aspects of Renaissance art. It's advisable to purchase a guide to the mosaics if you want to follow the progression of the cycle.

Not literally "in the country" (though prior to the construction of the Theodosian walls it was outside the city limits), Kariye Camii is near the sixth hill, and a fair distance away from any of the other primary sites in Istanbul. Your best bet is to take bus no. 34 or 87 from Toksim Square or bus no. 86 from Emunönü. Ask the driver to let you off at Nestor Sokok; Kariye Camii is three blocks to your right. The church is open daily from 9 a.m. to 5:30 p.m.; closed Tuesday.

DOLMABAHÇE PALACE: If the open-air design of Topkapi's four courts reflects the Ottoman's nomadic tradition, then the opulent marble "vault" at

Dolmabahçe, built on the banks of the Bosporus, represents an attempt to enter the mainstream of 19th-century Europe. The palace was built by Sultan Abdul Mecit I in 1853 as a symbolic break with a then-declining Ottoman Empire.

The style of the building can only be called Turkish baroque. The reception/throne room, lit by a 4½-ton crystal chandelier and bordered by a crystal staircase, is of gigantic proportion. The sultan's alabaster bathroom must have provided the world with a new definition of the word "ostentation."

After the founding of the Turkish Republic, Atatürk took up residence in Dolmabahçe during his visits to Istanbul, and he died there in 1938. Since that time the palace has hosted numerous dignitaries and is the primary venue for official state functions. Because of its present use, visiting hours often change; however, the normal schedule is 9:30 a.m. to noon and 1:30 p.m. to 4:30 p.m. daily, closed Monday and Thursday. Admission is 800 TL ($1), half price weekends.

VISITING A TURKISH BATH: Going to a *hamami,* or public bath, is as much a daily ritual in the fabric of contemporary Turkish life as it was in Ottoman times. The tradition of public baths actually extends back to the Romans. Remains of giant bathing complexes have been found at nearly every Roman archeological site in Anatolia. For the Turks the hamami was traditionally run at a profit to subsidize the social welfare programs of the mosques. The Cağaloğlu Hamami, for example, one of the oldest and most ornate baths in Istanbul, was built by Mahmut I in 1741 to underwrite a library that he supported near Hagia Sophia.

An excellent introduction to the world of the Turkish bath is the same **Cağaloğlu Hamami** (tel. 522-2424), off Sultan Ahmet Square, 200 meters up the hill from Hagia Sophia, at 34 Prof. Kazim Ismail Gürkan Caddesi. Taking a bath at Cağaloğlu is an absolutely perfect way to end a tiring day of touring. The bath is divided into two sections, one for men and another for women (the women's entrance is around the corner). As with all traditional Turkish baths—directly modeled after Roman designs—one enters a large room, called the *camekan,* where bathers change clothes, sip tea, and generally lounge about.

After deciding what sort of bath you want—self-service, at 2800 TL ($3.50); with massage, at 5600 TL ($6.75); with massage and scrub, at 8000 TL ($10)—proceed to a changing room where you are expected to don a thin cotton wrap that feels something like a dish towel. You'll have to remove your shoes and negotiate the wooden-clog slippers that are provided by the hamami. Passing through the *sogukluk,* a chamber that functions as a passageway or anteroom (also called a tepidarium by the Romans), you'll come to the *haraet,* or as the Romans appropriately named it, the calidarium. This 300-year-old white marble hall is crowned by a dome pierced by six pointed stars and circles. Each design is covered with stained glass that allows colored shafts of light to permeate the steamy haze. Self-service bathers sit by large scalloped sinks and ladle warm water over themselves. Cağaloğlu Hamami is open every day from 7 a.m. to 8 p.m. for ladies; to 10 p.m. for men. The Galatasaray Hamami, on Istiklâl Caddesi, is a less touristy, cheaper alternative.

CRUISING THE BOSPORUS: Traveling by boat up the Bosporus, past old Istanbul, Dolmabahçe Palace, and the coastline leading up to the Black Sea, is a glorious way to view some of Turkey's exceptional scenery. The Bosporus's shores, lined with cypress and pines, are punctuated by rocky coves and centuries-old mansions and castles. The shoreline abounds in attractive fishing villages: Bebek, Rumeli Hisari, Tarabya, Sariyer, and the somewhat distant hamlet at Rumeli Kavagi are the most interesting, both for their settings and food. (Gourmands take note: prices for locally caught fish are significantly lower than in most Istanbul restaurants, and the fish is always fresh—see our restaurant recommendations.)

The ancient waterway is associated with two stories from mythology. The name "Bosporus" literally means "Ford of the Cow" and derived its inspiration from Zeus' amorous affair with the Princess Io (whence the name Ionian). Zeus transformed the beautiful Io into a white heifer to disguise and shield her from the jealous reprisal of his wife, Hera. Of course Hera knew that the odd-looking cow was in fact Io; she sent a gadfly to hound the tormented princess, driving her into the water. Io crossed the strait and thus "Ford of the Cow," or Bosporus.

The second legend relates to the actual creation of the waterway and centers on Jason and his search for the Golden Fleece. Writing in the *Argonautica,* Apollonius Rhodius relates that Jason consulted a prophet who warned the Argonauts that they must follow a dove through a treacherous section called the Symplegades ("clashing rocks"), so named because the rocks would close on any but the most skillful navigator. Following these instructions, Jason and crew vigorously rowed through the rocks, led by a white dove. Just as Jason's boat was approaching safe water the rocks closed, and only through Athena's divine power was the boat permitted to pass. The watchful protectress forced the rocks to separate to the position they're in today.

Cruising the Bosporus presents significantly fewer problems today than in Jason's time. Your only concerns are the cost of a ticket and the schedule: 1200 TL ($1.50) buys a round-trip ticket to any destination (you could, if desired, stay on the boat for the entire time). Normally, a minimum of two boats operates each day, leaving from Pier 4 adjacent to the Galata Bridge on the Stromboul side of the Golden Horn. Times vary according to season, but there are usually boats at 10:30 a.m. and 1:30 p.m. You can also return from most ferry stops by bus. As always, check with the Tourist Information Office.

Tarabya

From a corrupt form of the Greek *therapeia* (therapy), Tarabya is a small fishing village on the Bosporus known for its relaxing and tranquil ambience. The summer villas of wealthy Istanbulus and the French, German, and British embassies hug this golden coastline. In Tarabya's harbor you'll see sleek yachts pulling in from Bodrum, Izmir, Marmaris, and other southern ports.

The older community of mansions—clapboard homes rising to three stories above the roadway—overhang the harbor. The villas of the nouveau-comers, in deference to the acknowledged water pollution of this beautiful resort, are built up on the hills overlooking the inviting Bosporus.

Sariyer

Sariyer, a quaint fishing town just north of Tarabya, is known for the **Sadberk Hanim Museum**. Their collection is a precious sampling from upper-middle-class life of the 18th to 20th centuries set in an enormous three-story mansion on the water that is well suited to the display within. China, ceramics, and ornate woven shawls from central Anatolia can be seen on the ground floor. Upstairs are the *uc-etek* (literally, "made-in-three-pieces") dress work by Anatolian women. The uc-etek are long dresses with two vents which were typically worn with a *gumus* (heavy, sculpted belt) around the waist.

Your only opportunity to see the traditional five-day wedding ceremony of last century's upper middle classes is on the third floor. Mannequins people a set re-creating the ritual. Handcrafted cigarette and moneybags are strapped to the wedding bed to bring luck and prosperity. Elaborate ritual cloth is draped over the floor for the bride to walk on. This aspect of the collection is very special, but on the whole this small museum cannot compare with the folk treasures of the Topkapi Palace. The Sadberk family, who put together this collection, is considered the Turkish equivalent of the Rockefellers.

A maintenance fee of 500 TL (65¢) is charged. The Sadberk Hanim Museum (tel. 142-3813), 27 at Piyasa Caddesi, is, unlike most other museums, closed on Wednesday. Museum buffs should try to plan their Bosporous tour on either a Monday or Tuesday, when most of Istanbul's historic sights are closed anyway. Summer hours are 10:30 a.m. to 6 p.m.; 10 a..m. to 5 p.m. in winter.

THE PRINCES ISLANDS (BÜYÜKADA): The Büyükada (the Big Island) of the Princes Islands group is located just 20 kilometers south of Istanbul.

Dr. Ariel Teitel of Washington, D.C. wrote us: "I very much enjoyed a day trip to Büyükada." It's the largest of five islands, and available round-the-island tours enhance the excursion. It's such a fascinating place because it's been frozen in time, in the 19th century. With the exception of police and service vehicles, there are no automobiles or trucks on Büyükada; like Spetsai in Greece, horse-drawn carriages provide the local and tourist transportation.

In the good old days Büyükada was a place of exile for dethroned royalty. The most notorious period on this paradisical Alcatraz was during the eighth and ninth centuries, during the reign of Queen Irene. After the death of her husband, the reigning king, Irene realized that her ten-year-old son Constantine V would be heir apparent. Thinking quickly, she poked out her son's eyes and set about planning the demise of her daughter, the other heir. Queen Irene enrolled her daughter, Orfozin, in a convent on Büyükada to prevent her from becoming a threat. As the Fates had it, Irene had succeeded in preventing her own family from taking her throne, but lost her kingdom to a stranger named Nikeferos, who easily dethroned the mad queen. Where was she exiled? To Büyükada, of course, where she soon died.

In the 20th century Büyükada is a self-imposed retreat for wealthy Turks. The absence of cars, very strict zoning laws, and 19th-century Victorian architecture make it easy to lose all sense of time and place on the island. The vegetation is as lush as you'll find anywhere: aged pine trees, willows, palms, and cypress give shade to this wind-swept island. Many of the houses are three-story wooden mansions designed a century ago under the combined influences of Ottoman and Victorian taste, resulting in stunning clapboard homes with extremely ornate façades, large second-floor wrap-around porches, widow's walks, and finely painted grillwork for the windows. Now many of the exteriors are badly in need of a fresh coat of paint, but they're delightful to see anyway.

Touring the Island

Walking around the inhabited core of Büyükada allows you to examine the homes at your own pace, but an eight- or ten-kilometer hike may be too much to accomplish in one day. Walkers should continue straight forward from the pier and then bear right at the Clock Tower to Cankaya Caddesi. From this main street you'll weave in and out of side streets where dense, jungle-like gardens alternate with these architectural dinosaurs.

One of the more popular sightseeing options is the **horse-drawn carriage tour.** You'll have a choice of the Büyük Tur (Grand Tour) or the Kuçuk Tur (Short Tour). The Grand Tour takes about an hour and a half, running the entire perimeter of Büyükada. Because so much of the coast is densely forested, a great deal of time is spent admiring the scenic beauties of land and sea—very relaxing but not for the architectural maniac. The Short Tour detours inland to view only the homes that are included on the Grand Tour, leaving you the opportunity to explore the coast on your own. Standard rates seem to be 6400 TL ($8) for the Short Tour and 8000 TL ($10) for the Grand Tour. *Caveat emptor:* make sure your route (note "büyük" or "kuçuk") and the price are set down in writing before you gallop off!

Accommodations and Dining

There's only one hotel on Büyükada that warrants one night of your limited holiday, but it's so special (and expensive) that you may want to save it for a honeymoon, anniversary, or other super-splurge. We're singing the praises of the suitably 19th-century **Splendid Oteli** (tel. 1/331-5167). It's a splendid, aging Victorian colossus set up on the cliffs to maximize an extraordinary ocean view. The wooden clapboards and shutters are in need of a paint job, and the proud Splendid may look run-down to some, but in its heyday it was obviously the *only* place for the well-to-do who summered here. The large iron gates are flanked by two fine Greek statues. After ascending the marble steps, you'll confront 14 tall wooden doors and a myriad of oversize windows. The Splendid's cavernous lobby has cool, worn marble floors and a ceiling that's a good seven meters high. Overhead, two floors embellished with interior-facing balconies defy gravity. The Splendid has 72 rooms, all with grandiose bathrooms whose aging fixtures are definitely of yesteryear (would you want it any other way?). When you open the shuttered French doors of the balconies, the strong sea breeze knocks you backward into your room, into another era. . . . The Splendid is open during the summer season (June to late September) and charges 60,000 TL ($75) for two, 35,000 TL ($33) for one, including their obligatory full board. Definitely a place to work on your Gothic novel.

Dining options are limited on Büyükada, where the seaside cafés, such as Milto or Kapri (to the left of the ferry pier as you disembark), are just overpriced, tourist-supported eateries. We found and liked the **Orman** restaurant, farther inland on the left, as you walk toward the Clock Tower. The Orman's food is not gourmet, and they have simple decor and unbreakable plastic plates (for Greeks?), but it's certainly the better value compared to what's up along the waterfront. A tasty *köfte, bonfile,* or grilled *barbunya* (red mullet) depending on the season, are all recommended. The Orman's fish and tomato soups are local favorites, and worth sampling.

Getting to Büyükada

You'll find the docks of the Sirkeci Commuting Ferry Lines about 500 meters from the foot of the Galata Bridge on Pier 5. For an overall view of the Princes Islands, travelers with time may prefer the "milk-run" boat that calls on each port, taking an hour and a half to reach Büyükada. The boats depart Istanbul at 7:15 a.m. and seven more times till 11 p.m. Slow boats leave Büyükada for Istanbul between 7 a.m. and 9 p.m. The fare is 1000 TL ($1.25). Candy, snacks, tea, and freshly squeezed orange juice are sold on board, but a breakfast picnic (stop at a *pastanesi* for some fresh-baked bread or butter biscuits) is always satisfying.

The Tourist Information Office or the Sirkeci Ferry company has current schedules.

5. Nightlife

Turkish nightlife for hundreds of years has been synonymous with belly dancing, that age-old form of art and titillation. Nowadays few treat it as an art, and those who excel at its trade often wind up shaking their coin-encrusted G-string in a higher-paying American or European nightclub. What's left in Istanbul, for the most part, is a watered-down version, though a resurgence of the real thing is taking place on the Asian coast. Even in bourgeois surroundings it's still an interesting way of spending an evening.

BELLY DANCING AND NIGHTCLUBS: The major hotels in Taksim Square all have nightly floor shows, as does the **Kervansaray** (tel. 147-1630), at 30 Cumhuriyet Caddesi. The price of a show plus dinner is 31,000 TL ($39); the show only with one drink cover is a steep 19,200 TL ($24). Most shows include not only belly dancing but different types of folk dances from around Anatolia. Some programs resemble an evening of vaudeville instead of traditional belly dancing. Don't be surprised if a crooner, juggler, or magician is thrown into the evening's activities. Although the management tends to be obnoxious and rude, the **Galata Tower** has a restaurant with decent food, an entertaining floor show, and an unbelievable view of nighttime Stromboul, all for 12,000 TL ($15).

CASINOS AND GASINOS: Both the **Hilton** and the **Etap Marmaris hotels** have casinos for gambling. Foreigners must have their passports and foreign currency and are allowed to play the full range of games. Turks can only play the one-armed bandits. You will find other casinos down the coast, in the major resorts. Turkey also has many "gasinos," which are more like nightclubs with no gambling.

The **Maksim Gasino** (tel. 144-3134) is well known for both classical and popular Turkish entertainment. Dinner and show will run 10,000 TL ($13) per person.

THE ISTANBUL FESTIVAL: The festival takes place over a four-week period, from mid-June to late July, and features a wide range of music, dance, and theater. Performances are given all over the city by world-renowned artists. Tickets and schedule information are available at the Atatürk Cultural Palace in Taksim Square, or by calling tel. 160-4533. Tickets cost from $2 to $18.

TURKISH NATIONAL FOLK DANCE GROUP: Like the performances in Athens and Rhodes, this energetic and talented troupe presents a wide range of folk dances from across the country. The dancers wear colorful native costumes and performances are given outdoors, either at the open-air theater near the Hilton Hotel or the fortress at Rumeli Hisari on the Bosporus. Inquire at the Tourist Information Office for the current schedule.

SOUND AND LIGHTS: No stay in Istanbul is complete without experiencing the Blue Mosque Sound and Light Show. From May 1 to September 30, at 8:30 or 9 p.m. according to season, the sweet young voice of the Blue Mosque begins to recite her impressions of ancient Istanbul. The gruff voice of Sultan Ahmet I demands of his shy, young architect that this new mosque surpass the Hagia Sophia across the way. In one of the show's more dramatic moments, the blue and gold lights dim on the Blue Mosque and yellow lights come up on the Hagia Sophia. A Turkish guide yells to the audience to direct their attention to the illuminated monument behind them! This show is free, entertaining, and utterly captivating under the midnight-blue Istanbul sky. Contact the nearby Tourist Office for schedule information, or call 522-1516; the show is in English every fourth night.

DISCOS: The best disco is **Hydromel** (tel. 140-5893), at 12 Cumhuriyet Caddesi. Drinks and cover are 6000 TL ($7.50) and they present a live show after midnight. Among the better nearby nightspots are **Regines** (tel. 146-7449), at 16 Cumhumiyet Caddesi, and the club atop the **Sheraton Hotel** in Taksim

Square which draws an older, more upscale crowd. Although neither place has a minimum, both charge 3200 TL ($4) per drink. The music is international; they don't play any Turkish tunes. Hydromel and Regines opens at 10 p.m. and closes at 5 a.m.

6. Istanbul ABCs

AIRLINE OFFICES: The main office of **Turkish Airlines (THY)** is at 131 Cumhuriyet Caddesi, at the entrance to the Hilton (tel. 147-0121). The **Lufthansa** office (tel. 146-5130) is at 179-185 Cumhuriyet Caddesi, between the Hilton and Taksim Square. Office hours are 9 a.m. to 5:45 p.m., Monday through Friday, closed for lunch 12:30 p.m. to 1:30 p.m. Most of the other air-lines offices are on Cumhuriyet Caddesi in the same area.

AMERICAN EXPRESS: Turk Ekspres is the local representative for American Express. The head office (tel. 130-1515) is at 91/1 Cumhuriyet Caddesi, across from the Divan Hotel, near Taksim Square, it's open 9 a.m. to 6 p.m. Monday through Friday. There is also a branch office in the Hilton Hotel (tel. 141-0248), open daily from 8:30 a.m. to 8 p.m. Lost traveler's checks or credit cards should be reported to the Turk Ekspres head office on weekdays and to the Hilton of-fice on weekends. Both offices cash traveler's checks and offer travel services, though only the Hilton office has a postal service.

BANKS: Banks are open from 9 a.m. to 1 p.m. and 2 p.m. to 5 p.m. Monday through Friday. The bank at the airport is open when there are scheduled flights. The bank at Sirkeci Railway Station is also open Saturday and Sunday from 9 a.m. to 5 p.m.

BEACHES: Are there beaches in Istanbul? Yes. Are they good? Sort of. Actu-ally there are beaches all around Istanbul, though as you can imagine they're none too clean and much too crowded. Best to take a boat up the Bosporus to the far-away sands at **Kilyos** (on the European side) and **Sile** (on the Asian side).

BOOKSTORES: There are two English-language bookstores on Istiklâl, near the entrance to the Tünel. **Hachette Bookstore**, at 469 Istiklâl, is by far the larg-er; they also sell periodicals. Hachette also has a small bookstore next to the THY office near the Hilton.

BUS COMPANIES: The bus to Athens from **Bosfor Turizm** (tel. 143-2525) or **Varan** (tel. 143-2187) leaves from the Topkapi Terminali in the morning and ar-rives in Athens the next morning (the trip takes approximately 22 hours). A one-way ticket to Athens costs 29,000 TL ($36). Bosfor operates the most comfortable buses to Europe, while Varan handles the long-haul domestic routes to major cities, such as Izmir, Antalya, Ankara, etc. **Pamukkale Bus Company** (tel. 582-2935) is the best of the short-haul intercity lines and operates out of the Topkapi Bus Terminal. Service to most cities is frequent and good.

BUS TERMINALS: Most buses leave from **Topkapi**, which is on the western edge of the city, but some of the luxury coaches also have earlier pickups at Taksim Square. The special bus to the airport leaves every half hour from the THY in-town terminal (tel. 144-8457) at 30 Mesrutiyet Caddesi; the fare is 800 TL ($1) each way.

CAMPING: The Ministry of Tourism has graciously set up a cluster of campgrounds along the Edirne-bound E-5 highway on the European side of the Sea of Marmara. **Camping Yesilyurt** (tel. 573-8408), and camping **Ataköy** (tel. 572-4961) are the two best, but be prepared for a long bus ride back into town. Campsites are closed during the off-season, from November to March.

CAR RENTAL: Budget (tel. 145-0766) and Avis (tel. 148-7752) have offices in Istanbul as well as the other major cities in Turkey; Avis has an office in the Hilton and at the Divan Hotel. Budget has an office at Inönü Caddesi Kunt Apt. 33/1, near Taksim Square, and at Bağdat Caddessi 177/7, in the Kadiköy area. Weekly rentals with insurance and unlimited mileage for a Renault 12 or Murat 131 (Turkish-assembled Fiat) are about $400, excluding gasoline.

CONSULATES: The **American Consulate General** (tel. 151-3602) maintains offices at 104 Mesrutiyet Caddesi, next door to the Pera Palas. Office hours are 8:30 a.m. to noon and 2 p.m. to 4 p.m. The Canadian consulate (tel. 172-5174) is at Büyükdere Caddesi Bengün Han 107/3 in Mecidiyeköy, about 30 minutes from Istanbul. The British consulate (tel. 144-7540) is located one block down from the American headquarters, at 34 Mesrutiyet Caddesi, and also handles Australian affairs.

COPPER AND BRASS: Depressed by the high cost of old pounded-out tea kettles? Looking for a bargain? Try **Bakircilar Caddesi**, running from the Grand Bazaar out to the university, where copper and brass dealers will sell, clean, or repair many unusual and often lower-priced heirlooms.

CRIME: There is no problem whatsoever walking around late at night and no need to do anything special other than take the precautions one would normally take in any large city.

DOCTORS AND DENTISTS: The American consulate publishes a list of recommended doctors and dentists, including specialists.

EMERGENCY: The main number for the **Tourist Police** is 527-4503; they can refer you to the appropriate agency.

FERRIES: Ferries run continuously, some crossing over to Asia, others cruising the Golden Horn, Bosporus, and the Prince Islands. Longer-range steamers head south, through the Sea of Marmara, down through the Dardanelles and out to the Aegean. Generally, the short-range ferries leave from the many piers next to the Eminönü side of the Galata Bridge; the long-range boats leave from the maritime Station on the Kanaköy side. It takes about 15 minutes to make the ferry crossing to the Asian coast.

HAIRDRESSING: If you don't want to gamble, go to one of the big international hotels. They all have hair salons, and they're used to foreign visitors' requests. The best cut is at the **Divan Hotel**.

HOSPITAL: The **Admiral Bristol Hospital** (tel. 131-4050) on Güzelbahçe Sokak in Nişantaşi, is an American-founded and registered hospital. Dr. Warren Winkler is the medical director. For your information, Dr. Winkler recommends drinking only bottled water and avoiding uncooked fruit and vegetables.

INFORMATION OFFICES: The Ministry of Culture and Tourism has set up **Tourist Information Offices** all over the city: Sultan Ahmet Square (tel. 522-4903), Karaköy Maritime Station (tel. 149-5776), Atatürk Airport (tel.

573-7399), Hilton Hotel entrance (tel. 133-0592), and the Regional Directorate of Istanbul at 57 Mesrutiyet Caddesi (tel. 143-3472) in Galatasaray. These offices are particularly helpful for suggesting hotels and providing current schedules, maps, and brochures and are open daily from 9 a.m. to 5 p.m.; the Atatürk Airport office is open 8:30 a.m. to 9 p.m.

MAPS: The best Istanbul city map is called "Buses of Istanbul," published by Aypa; the card shop of **Aykut Uysal**, at 80 Divanyolu Caddesi, at Sultan Ahmet Square, sells it, along with other maps and a great variety of postcards, giftcards and local books.

POST OFFICE: The main post office, called the Sirkeci **PTT** (Post/Telegraph/Telephone), is open 24 hours a day and is located at 25 Yeni Postahane, two blocks from the Galata Bridge on the Stromboul side, in Eminönü. This is the only branch that accepts *Poste Restante* mail; *Poste Restante* service is available from 9 a.m. to 5 p.m. Monday through Friday. Remember to bring your passport for identification. There are smaller regional post offices around the city. Most post offices remain open until midnight for booking telephone calls and selling stamps. The most convenient post offices are the branch next to Çiçek Pasaji on Istiklâl, near the Pera Palas and the branch in the Grand Bazaar. The Parcel Post Office (Tophane) is the only place from which to send copper and carpets with correct customs forms.

RAILROAD INFORMATION: There are two rail stations: **Sirkeci** (tel. 527-0051) on the European side, and **Haydarpasa** (tel. 336-0475) on the Asian side. The TCDD (Turkish State Railway) is an inefficient means of transportation. An exception to that rule is the Istanbul-to-Ankara connection; there is express service to both Ankara and Izmir. Since the days of the *Orient Express,* trains coming from Europe have had an element of romance associated with them. Unfortunately today's trains are slow and fairly dreary.

RELIGIOUS SERVICES: **Roman Catholic** services are held at St. Anthony of Padova, 325 Istiklâl Caddesi (tel. 144-0935), and St. Esprit at 250 Cumhuriyet Caddesi (tel. 148-0910) near the Hilton; English-language **Protestant** services are held at the German Protestant Church at Emin Cami S. Aynaliçeşme (tel. 150-3040); **Jewish** services are held at Neve Shalom (tel. 144-7566), near the Galata Tower at 61 Büyük Hendek Sokak, and at Beth Israel on Şişli Square.

SUBWAY: While not exactly a subway, the Tünel does operate underground, transporting weary tourists from the base of the Galata Bridge up to the beginning of Istiklâl Caddesi, all for 200 TL (25¢).

TRAVEL AGENCIES: Cumhuriyet Caddesi is lined with travel agencies, some helpful and informative, others not. You might want to try **Act Tours** (tel. 146-7157), at 12/c Cumhuriyet Caddesi (turn the corner and go up the stairs to the second floor). Halil and his staff will help you book hotels, especially in the Taksim area, often at a modest discount. They also organize their own tours of other parts of Turkey. If you're interested in booking a cruise, try **Bodrumtour** (tel. 141-6518), at 22 Cumhuriyet Caddesi. Bodrumtour also books ferry tickets between Turkish ports to Kos, Samos, and Rhodes.

TURKISH DELIGHT: Some call it by its Turkish name, *lokum;* others call it heaven. How bad can anything be that's sticky, chewy, and made primarily of sugar? The undisputed capital of Turkish delight is **Haci Bekir**, a shop whose name has been associated with the candy for over 300 years. The original Haci Bekir store is at 72 Hamidiye Caddesi, two blocks east of the Egyptian Spice Market. For 1400 TL to 3000 TL ($1.80 to $3.80) you can bring back a kilo of plain or nut lokum that will last for months—a great present. Haci Bekir has a second store at 127/6 Istiklâl. If you want lokum that's every bit as good, but wrapped in fancier foils and cardboard, go to the **Divan Pastry Shop**, next to the hotel of the same name. In the interests of science, we invite readers of the book who've sampled the Greek *loukoumi* from Tinos to write us with their preference.

Chapter XVIII

EXPLORING THE AEGEAN COAST

1. Bursa
2. Troy (Truva)
3. Assos (Behramkale)
4. Ayvalik
5. Bergama (Pergamum)
6. Izmir
7. Çesme and the Chios Connection
8. Ephesus (Selçuk)
9. Kuşadasi
10. Bodrum
11. Marmaris
12. Fethiye
13. Kaş

TURKEY'S WESTERN COASTLINE extends 800 miles along the blue-gem water of the Sea of Marmara, the Aegean, and south to the Mediterranean. At five separate points along the coast, ferries transport visitors to and from the Greek islands. The coast includes four of the ancient world's most glorious cities: Troy, Ephesus, Pergamum, and Aphrodisias. Farther south are the beaches, resorts, and yacht harbors at Fethiye, Bodrum, Kuşadasi, Kaş, and Marmaris—among the Aegean's best. Bursa presents a deeper look into traditional Moslem culture, as well as a vast network of healing thermal springs.

1. Bursa

Bursa is a contrast of the old and new Turkey. The same city that now makes Mercedes-Benz buses and Turkish Fiats is also the city of the first Ottoman capital, established by Osman Bey in the 14th century. Although the budding empire moved to Edirne and then Istanbul, the sense of early Ottoman aesthetics is unmistakably preserved in Bursa's museums and mosques. The city's mosques and *türbes* (mausoleums) are decorated in *yeşil*, or green, considered to be the favorite color of the prophet Mohammed, and therefore holy. The tiles came from the kilns at nearby Iznik, the most renowned of all Turkish tile centers. Bursa is in a region that still adheres to fundamentalist Moslem

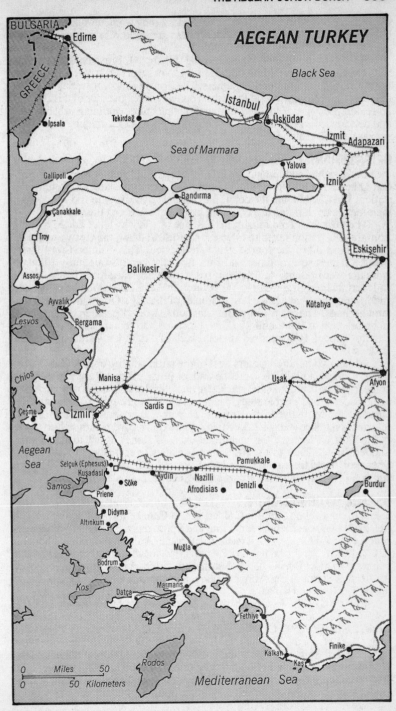

AEGEAN TURKEY

BULGARIA

GREECE

İpsala

Edirne

Tekirdağ

Black Sea

İstanbul

Üsküdar

İzmit

Adapazari

Sea of Marmara

Yalova

İznik

Gallipoli

Bandırma

Eskişehir

Çanakkale

Troy

Balıkesir

Kütahya

Assos

Ayvalık

Lesvos

Bergama

Chios

Manisa

Uşak

Afyon

Çeşme

Sardis

İzmir

Selçuk (Ephesus)

Kuşadasi

Pamukkale

Aegean
Sea

Söke

Aydın

Nazilli

Afrodisias

Denizli

Burdur

Samos

Priene

Didyma

Altınkum

Muğla

Bodrum

Kos

Datça

Marmaris

Fethiye

Finike

Kalkan

Kaş

Rodos

Mediterranean Sea

Miles 50

50 Kilometers

ways, despite Westernization under Atatürk. Young women walk through the bazaar covered in the outlawed black Moslem dress and veil, then stop to enjoy the city's new plazas and outdoor cafés.

Nestled at the base of Mount Uludağ (Olympus), Bursa boasts a thriving sulfur hot springs and Turkish bath industry. Not surprisingly, a towel business has developed to accommodate bathers. The Roman Emperor Justinian used to frequent the spas here, as did Pliny the Younger, once governor of this Bithyni-an region. Because of its early Ottoman architecture, charming urban parks, and delicious local specialty, Bursa kebab, Bursa makes a unique, worthwhile stop as you travel along the Turkish coast.

ORIENTATION: Most people arrive in Bursa at the bus station, an area south of the hotels, sights, and restaurants in the main part of town. A **Tourist Informa-tion Office** is open there during the summer. Across the street in front of the station, **Ulu Caddesi**, are the dolmushes and taksis. Make sure taxi drivers turn their meters on, if riding in a dolmush, inquire ahead about the fare.

The town is laid out roughly in the shape of a T, with Ulu Caddesi running from the bus station north to intersect **Atatürk Caddesi**, the east-west axis on which almost all of the tourist sights are located. This main east-west street changes names several times and runs from the central Cumhuriyet Square (with the ever-present Atatürk statue) west to Çekirge, an area of hotels, parks, and thermal springs, and east to Yeşil Camii and Yeşil Türbe, the Green Mosque and Mausoleum that are the best examples of the city's Ottoman-era architec-tural heritage. The main Tourist Information Office is located in the new park and plaza next to **Ulu Camii**, the largest mosque and centerpiece of downtown activity, (about two hundred meters west of Atatürk's statue of Atatürk Caddesi).

About two hundred meters west of the park, where Atatürk Caddesi be-comes Cemal Nadir Caddesi, are the walls of Bursa's Byzantine-era castle, now home to several outdoor cafés stacked up the hillside. This area's new landscap-ing includes broad marble steps leading up the hill to Kaplica Caddesi and the Ottoman-era Muradiye tomb complex. This area, **Tophane**, has its own Tourist Information Office (tel. 24/213368), in a white trellis-covered house next to the cafés. West of Tophane the main road changes names again, to Altiparmak Caddesi, which leads to the pleasant and extensive recreational **Kültürpark**, where you'll find the Archeological Museum and Yeni Kaplica, a Suleyman-era *hamami* (Turkish bath) that is part of the Çekirge thermal springs area.

USEFUL INFORMATION: The Turkish **Tourist Information Office** is located below street level on Atutürk Caddesi in Ulu Camii Park, No. 7. You can call (tel. 24/212359) or visit between 8 a.m. and 6 p.m. daily. . . . For a **police** emer-gency, call 148300. . . . For a **medical emergency**, call the government hospital (tel. 214071). . . . Local **bus** nos. 2A and 2B will take you any and everywhere you want to go in Bursa. . . . **Dolmushes** stop in front of the theater, opposite the Atatürk Statue at Cumhuriyet Square, and opposite Ulu Camii can be found the PTT and several **banks**.

Buses make the four-hour trip to Istanbul every half hour for 2400 TL ($4.50). There are approximately 50 buses a day (we didn't count them) to Izmir; the fare is 3250 TL ($3). There are many buses daily to Çanakkale, a 5½ hour (3600 TL, or $4.50) trip. . . . There are two flights weekdays, one flight Saturday, but none on Sunday, from Istanbul to Bursa. The **THY office** (tel. 212838) is on Cemal Nadir Caddesi. The fare is 18,000 TL ($18) one way. . . . Passenger **boats** leave Istanbul from Kabataş (near Dolmabahçe Palas), and car ferries leave from Kartal (about a half hour south), but both go only as far as

Yalova about 50 kilometers north of Bursa; from here a $5 dolmush will bring you into Bursa's main square. The Istanbul–Yalova boats depart five times daily in summer, three times daily in winter, and cost $2 from Kabataş. The car ferry from Kartal leaves hourly and costs 7000 TL ($9) per car, plus 650 TL (80¢) per passenger. Check the Tourist Office for pier and schedule information. Overland sightseers will head west from Bursa to the city of Çanakkale, past the infamous World War I battleground of Gallipoli and south to another infamous battleground, Troy.

ACCOMMODATIONS: The most convenient location in Bursa is near the no. 2A or 2B bus route, which runs east to west along the base of the mountainside.

Directly across from the Ulu Camii at Atatürk Caddesi is the **Artiç Hotel** (tel. 24/19500), a convenient, modern hotel that's one of Bursa's best choices. The 63 rooms are very well kept though basically modest; the Artiç is a no-frills kind of place. All rooms have private baths; doubles are 12,000 TL ($15), singles 8700 TL ($11). The Artiç faces the Ulu Camii and traffic, so request a room facing the rear if you prefer quiet to the view. Up behind the Artiç, at Ulu Cami Karşisi Inebey Caddesi, is the blue-mosaic façade of the small **Otel Çağlayan** (tel. 24/211458). Everything in this spartan hostel is spotless. Simple, small doubles with showers are 9,300 TL ($12).

Continuing farther west, we reach the city's most luxurious, only five-star hotel, the **Çelik Palas** (tel. 24/19600). The Çelik Palas, known for its private Turkish bath, is across from the Kültür Park and at the entrance to Çekirge, the thermal quarter of Bursa. After checking in, one can change into a bathing suit and put on the bulky bathrobe provided in each room. Once you've showered in the Turkish bath wing, you can enter the steamy, all-marble coed pool. The water is very pure, hot, and ennervating; graduates should head over to the plush leather couches to recuperate after their cleansing. If this isn't your idea of bathing, all of the Çelik Palas's 173 rooms have private bath facilities. Elegant doubles in their traditional or new wing range from a steep 72,000 TL to 96,000 TL ($90 to $120).

If the Çelik Palas is not your style, nearby the Kültür Park, at 47 Çekirge Caddesi, is the **Hotel Diyar** (tel. 24/365130), an excellent budget choice. Although it doesn't boast a private Turkish spa, the Diyar's modern, spacious doubles, with park views and private baths (24,000 TL, or $30), or with views back to the tranquil side streets (20,000 TL, or $25), are well worthwhile. Breakfast, served in the Diyar's pleasant restaurant, is included in their rates. An older, more modest but adequate choice next door is the **Otel Ilman** (tel. 24/367706) at Fuar Karşisi. Singles start at 8500 TL ($10.50) with shower; doubles at 12,000 ($15) with shower, $2 more with bath.

DINING: With aching feet and a well-scrubbed body, you should be in the mood to sample Bursa's gift to the wonderful art of Turkish cuisine—the **Bursa kebab**, the local version of Iskender or Döner kebab. Sliced lamb is laid on top of diced pita cubes with a ladleful of rich tomato sauce and a dollop of yogurt seasoned with fresh parsley. Delicate slivers of fresh tomatoes and green peppers garnish the platter. In Bursa, kebabs can best be consumed with a large glass of freshly pressed grape juice. Here are some notables among the myriad kebaberies. The first is off Sirin Square, across from the bus station and about half a block up. It's called **Uludağ Kebabçiş**, or **Cemal and Cemil**, and the unmistakable interior, where old fans whip up the smoke created by crowds of local bus drivers, laborers, lawyers, and the famished from all walks of life, cannot be missed. A Bursa kebab runs 1300 TL ($1.60). The most historically interesting, as well as gastronomically satisfying, is **Işkender Kebab**, one block south of Cumhuriyet Adani and down the first right lane. Işkender Kebab was closed for renovation at our last visit but we hope they retain the trio of old black-and-white photos that feature the family that claims to have invented the Işkender or Bursa kebab. The **Hünkar Kebap Salonu** (tel. 18091) combines an excellent *iskender* (Bursa Döner) kebab with a panoramic vista of the sprawling city. Conveniently situated for tourists, across the street from the Yeşil Mosque, the Hünkar provides a clean, well-decorated venue or terrace café to experience the local cuisine. A casual lunch for two should run a painless 5600 TL ($7). For a quick, cheap no-frills lunch or dinner, try **Saray Restaurant** (tel. 211067), located about two blocks south of the Atatürk statue at 22 Yeniyol Caddesi. Saray has a wide variety of entrées.

For a Turkish taste delight after touring the Ulu Camii or prowling the bazaar, stop in at **Ulu Pastry Shop**, two doors west of the mosque at 92 Atatürk Caddesi. A box of candied chestnuts (the local sweet-tooth specialty), a bag of honey-soaked figs, or a handful of candied orange rinds filled with cream should provide enough sugar to keep the sightseeing muscles going. The sweets run about 3000 TL ($3.75) per kilo.

A *çay* or *kahve* is necessary to cap off the Bursa kebab experience. Just west of Ulu Camii are several cafés which are built on a terraced hillside overlooking a busy traffic circle. Traffic and Turkish ambience make this a fun place to stop.

Bursa's delightful Kültür Park is the city's focal point for many day and evening diversions. It combines a zoo, museum, swimming pool, amusement park with rides, disco, a garden and many fine open-air restaurants. One eatery is the **Dörtler Restaurant** (tel. 367656), where meals are served on a brightly lit patio with a multicolored fountain. The Dörtler, the **Yusuf** and many of the park's restaurants have a large and varied selection of mezes. Dinner for two runs about 12,000 TL ($15). Entrance to the park (there are four entrances) is 100 TL (1.24), plus 360 TL (30¢) for cars.

WHAT TO SEE AND DO: The visitor's activities in Bursa and include exploring some early Ottoman architecture and Uludağ Mountain and eating a Bursa kebab. To work up your appetite, walk over to the **Yeşil Camii** and the **Yeşil Türbe** (the Green Mosque and Mausoleum). The decorative carved marble over the entry and around the windows, large hexagonally shaped interior tiles, and finely crafted woodwork distinguish this 15th-century mosque, built for Mehmet I. Some of the mosque's finest deep-green Iznik tiles are preserved in the niches, which were custom-made for the sultan's harem, governors, and members of his entourage. The Yeşil Camii mosque has endured several earthquakes; its excellent state of preservation is due to the restoration work carried out by native architect Asim Bey.

Across the street is the **Yeşil Türbe** of Sultan Mehmet I (1387–1421). Sultan Mehmet died in Edirne but his body was brought to Bursa for burial 40 days after his death. The türbe, completed during the reign of Murat II, also holds the sarcophagi of his nurse and children. Ewaz, the mosque's architect, designed the hexagonally shaped türbe, which is filled with splendid Iznik tiles and gold calligraphy of the sayings of the prophet, Mohammed. Next to the Yeşil Camii is Bursa's newest museum, the **Turkish Arts Museum**, set in a restored *medressah* (Islamic holy school). All of Bursa's museums are open daily except Monday from 8:30 a.m. to 12:30 p.m. and 1:30 p.m. to 5:30 p.m. in summer; 8 a.m. to noon and 1 p.m. to 5 p.m. in winter; admission is 600 TL (75¢).

On Atatürk Caddesi you'll find the 14th-century, and quite special, **Ulu Camii** (Great Mosque). Begun under Mehmet I in 1379, it took 42 years to complete the elaborate interior: 20 squat domes and 12 broad, heavily sculpted square supports dominate the prayer area. Take a moment to admire the extensive Arabic calligraphy that decorates the columns. Ulu Camii's numerous domes and stocky minarets give the exterior a clumsy appearance, so unique in Moslem architecture (especially compared to later designs) that we found it somehow charming and worth a visit.

The city of Bursa unveiled Ulu Camii Parki in 1987, a marvelous plaza and park just outside the mosque. An ornate marble ablution fountain overlooks a small garden of roses, and beyond, an elegant outdoor café and restaurant. Behind a central fountain are several shops, and the two-story Silk Bazaar (Koza Han Carşişi) in a restored *kervansaray* (caravan palace). Several smart shops and restaurants line the east side of the plaza (where the Tourist Office is located) and the tunnel leading to the other side of busy Atatürk Caddesi.

Just below Ulu Camii is Bursa's major bazaar. The covered **Bedesten** offers a variety of goods found in other markets, and is the local version of an urban shopping mall. However, there is an older market (Eski Carşi), whose intriguing 500-year-old ornate arched architecture and huge supply of towels is bound to remind you that you're in the middle of Turkish bath country. There are great deals on bold, often garishly patterned terry-cloth squares, or $20 terry-cloth and velour robes.

From here, you can take a dolmush or no. 2A or 2B bus along Altiparmak Caddesi to the **Muradiye Kulliyesi**. Along the cobblestone streets of this old hillside quarter you'll find one of the most exquisite cemeteries in the Ottoman world. The interiors of beautifully crafted *türbes* for the likes of Sultan Mehmet II, or Cem Sultan, can be seen with the cooperation of the likely-to-disappear grounds keeper.

Nearby, within view, is an 18th-century Ottoman house preserved as a **cultural museum**.

The **Eski Kaplica** is the most historic and grandest of Bursa's Turkish baths. Eski Kaplica is located in the western section of town, Çekirge, which draws Turks from all over the country to bathe in its famous sulfurous springs. This ancient bath, built by the Roman emperor Justinian, has fresh and mineral spring waters to bathe in; only the daring should contemplate a dip in the untempered, steaming spring waters. Even if you're staying in the Çelik Palas or Kükürtlü hotels, which have their own Turkish bath, a wash-up in the ever-more-picturesque Eski Kaplica provides a timeless communion with classic Turkish customs. Eski Kaplica is about 15 minutes by dolmush from Ulu Camii (150 TL or 15¢). If making an effort to get there isn't your idea of a relaxing time, you can walk through Kültürpark to Yeni Kaplica (New Spring), a newer, hamami (14th-century) dating from the reign of Suleyman the Magnificent. I've heard the men's section, with its huge marble pool and ornate carving, is still worthy of sultans; the women's quarters are more modest. In Bursa, the hamami is still the root of the grapevine, the source of all local socializing and gossip. Both baths are open 8 a.m. to 11 p.m. daily; admission is 600 TL (75¢), plus 600 TL for a three-towel package and 2000 TL ($2.50) for a scrub-a-dub massage.

Lesser-known Ottoman sites to the east of the Yeşil Camii are the **Emir Sultan Mosque** and one of Bursa's earliest, the **Yildirim Beyazit Mosque**. If you walk to the Muradiye tombs by ascending the stairs by the Tophane cafés, you'll reach the small restored türbe of Pasha Okçubaba. Continuing right along Kaplica Caddesi, you'll pass narrow, cobblestoned streets reminiscent of 19th-century Istanbul. On the right, offering beautiful vistas of the city from its café, is **Yildiz Park**. Here are two historically important türbe from the Ottoman period. The 14th-century **Tomb of Sultan Orhan** (1281–1360) was built on the foundations of a Byzantine church, whose mosaic floors can still be seen. Orhangazi was the second Ottoman ruler, and it was during his reign that Bursa was taken from the Byzantines. Across the way is the **Tomb of Osman Gazi** (1257–1326), founder and namesake of the Ottoman Empire. The interior is painted in traditional Islamic floral patterns and his sarcophagus, draped in silver-embroidered velvet, is enclosed by a mother-of-pearl inlaid gate. If you walk back to the clock tower, you can catch the gleam of the tomb's lead-covered dome. Both tombs and the park were restored in 1863 after a bad earthquake. West of Çekirge on the road to Uludağ are the **mosque and mausoleum of Sultan Murat I.** Bursa's small **Archeological Museum** (in Kültürpark), and a lovely Victorian house known as the **Atatürk Museum** (on Çekirge Caddesi next to the Celik Palas Hotel), are two more sights to keep you busy for a two- or three-day stay.

In winter, Bursa's popularity is due to Mount Uludağ and the village at its base, Teleferik. Swiss cable cars take you up the mountains in three stages. You pass through the cloud level in the last stage, and everything about Uludağ Mountain (including the air) is breathtaking! Skiers from all over Turkey crowd the slopes all winter, but it's a good excursion year round. There's a dolmush stand in Teleferik, right at the cable-car station.

2. Troy (Truva)

When we mentioned to a Turkish friend that we were to visit Troy, he said, "Troy—big name, little stones." This heralded and ancient city overlooking the wide plains of Troas seems to have gotten a bad rap of late. Although it doesn't begin to compare with the enormous finds at either Pergamum or Ephesus, there really *is* something to see at Troy.

Before visiting the site, consider reading Homer's account of the Trojan War, one of the most legendary tales in the *Iliad.* In brief, the war began when Paris, a Trojan prince, was given Helen ("the face that launched 10,000 ships") as a reward for selecting the alluring goddess Aphrodite in a beauty contest. Unfortunately, lovely Helen was married at the time to none other than King Menelaus of Sparta. Paris incurred the wrath of what one would have to consider an all-star team of Greeks; the Spartan king Menelaus and his warriors; King Agamemnon (Menelaus' brother); plus Nestor, Odysseus, Achilles, and Ajax. Among Troy's warriors were Paris, King Priam (Paris' father, although Paris didn't know who his father was), Hector (Paris' brother), and Astyanax. Troy also had a mighty fortress. The Greeks sailed to the Anatolian coast, hauled their gear across the plain, and fought tirelessly for ten years. The most famous battle story occurred when Achilles, who was arguably the most courageous warrior of them all, met his death outside the Trojan walls. Thetis, Achilles' mother, had immersed the newborn into the magical river Styx, making his skin inpenetrable. But Paris, never one to be outwitted, shot a poison-dipped arrow straight into mighty Achilles' heel, the only area which Thetis had failed to dip into the charmed river.

The war raged on, with the Trojans repeatedly repelling the Greeks. One night the Trojans discovered that the Greeks had departed. Their camps were disbanded and their ships had set sail. All that was left was a huge wooden horse, an offering to the gods, outside the city walls. The Trojans were jubilant. The soldiers wheeled the immense horse through the gates—the statue was so big that they had to remove the giant stone lintel above the gate just to get it in. They rolled their booty up a long ramp so that it stood triumphantly atop the city's acropolis and then plunged into a night of orgiastic drinking and dancing, until they began passing out wherever they happened to be. A few hours later, a little door cut into the belly of the great wooden beast was flung open. Greek soldiers quietly scampered out, some to usher in additional troops outside the walls, others to take their position for the final attack. At once the Greeks thrust every spear and sword, arrow and bludgeon into the heart of the groggy Trojan army. Not a man was left after the massacre; the city was torn apart.

This is the legend ("Beware of Greeks bearing gifts"), and like all legends the truth can only be discovered after stripping away centuries of embellishment. Archeologists and historians believe that a long battle did occur, sometime around 1250 B.C., between Troy and a large Achean force from the mainland. The Acheans were only able to take the fortified citadel after it was destroyed by an earthquake. As for the Trojan horse, the Acheans made an offering to Poseidon, the earth-shaker, in the form of a large wooden animal in gratitude to the gods' divine intervention. The rest belongs to Homer.

EXPLORING ANCIENT TROY: The site is situated a short distance (17 miles) out of Çanakkale (there's a three-mile turnoff to Troy from the Çanakkale-Izmir highway). In the tiny town are numerous schlock shops and Schliemann's House (the 19th-century German "amateur" archeologist and dreamer who discovered, among other things, a rich deposit of gold in California and the ruins in Knossos and Troy).

As you approach the site, you'll notice a 40-foot-tall, frighteningly angular and kitschy representation of the Trojan horse, looking like a combination of a Japanese movie monster and Atlantic City's own Lucy the Elephant. Needless to say, we loved it.

When Schliemann opened up Troy in 1870 to a shocked Europe (they considered old Heinrich to be a rich crackpot), he brought out a treasure of gold and jewels. He gave these to his wife to wear. Schliemann thought he'd discovered the Troy and treasure of King Priam. In fact he had unearthed a much older Troy, dating back to between 2500 and 2300 B.C. As later excavations showed, there were nine different Troys, one built over another. An American team in the 1930s further delineated 30 distinct habitation levels.

The site now has examples from all nine major periods of Trojan history, from the thick inner walls of Troy I (3000–2500 B.C.) to the enlarged Temple of Athena and twin theaters from Troy IX (Roman era).

Troy Late VI (1425–1250 B.C.) is the Troy of Homer and the *Iliad*. The walls of this city are the first set of walls you see, and are in a good state of preservation. In the northwest corner are the remains of a watchtower, and an unusual set of parallel walls that formed the city gate. These walls formed a concentric circle around the acropolis and were the main line of defense against the Acheans. The houses on top of the acropolis are also of "Homeric" Troy.

The site is open every day from 8:30 a.m. to noon and 2 p.m. to 8:30 p.m. Admission is 600 TL (75¢) Monday through Friday, 300 TL (38¢) on Saturday and Sunday.

GETTING TO TROY (VIA ÇANNAKALE): Whether you're driving or busing it from Bursa to Troy, there are two stops of note, one for the site and one for an overnight stop. If Mel Gibson and Peter Weir have stimulated your interest in the World War I battlefield, *Gallipoli*, with their film, you'll never be closer than on the coast road just 30 kilometers east of Çanakkale. In the tiny fishing village of Lapseki you can catch the ferry to Gelibolu, which leaves at roughly two-hour intervals from 7:30 a.m. The battle site is now a military cemetery, where thousands of fallen Australians and Allied forces lie buried. Continuing on to **Çanakkale**, you may find it convenient to stop overnight on the journey south. There is little of interest except a small archeological museum with some finds from Troy, though it is a charming village, with quiet back streets and a port that centers on the ferryboats that cross to Eçeabat. The best accommodations in town can be found at the **Hotel Anafartalar** (tel. 1961/4454), a no-frills hotel with balconied rooms overlooking the ferry port. Double rooms with shower run 19,200 TL ($24), singles $5 less. A slightly drab alternative, the **Hotel Barik** (tel. 1961/4090) located on the waterfront at Rihtim Caddessi 12, costs a few dollars less. The best meal in town is at Liman's Yalova Restaurant, at the south end of the waterfront. Delicious fresh fish, mezes, and vegetables make a satisfying meal for two for only 9000 TL ($11). (Seafood gets cheaper after you leave Istanbul.) After dinner, stroll along the harbor and stop at the Dondurmasi (ice-cream shop), at the corner of the Anafartalar hotel. A cone of fresh, homemade vanilla will set you back 200 TL (25¢), a Turkish ice-cream sandwich 300 TL (38¢). Bet you can't eat one.

From Çannakale your best bet is to take a dolmush or taxi to the site of Troy, which is 27 kilometers south of town and 5 kilometers off the main road. There are travel agents on the main street in Çannakale who offer day trips. Return to Çannakale to continue your journey or flag down a southbound bus on the main road.

3. Assos (Behramkale)

If you visit Troy, it is difficult to imagine that this low mound in the middle of a wide, open plain was once a thriving port city. At Assos, the location is still miraculous, with the acropolis perched high above the coastline, looking out toward the Bay of Edremit, and in the far distance, Lesbos. The agora and theater are built several levels down, and a wonderful little harbor lines the shore.

Assos was something of a philosophy center. During the middle of the fourth century B.C. it was ruled by a student of Plato, Hermias (a eunuch). Aristotle studied and wrote here (348–345 B.C.). Kleanthes, one of the founders of the Stoic School, also came from Assos.

Most of the structures that have been unearthed are a combination of Doric and Ionic styles, much like Assos' bigger cousin at Pergamum. The walls surrounding the city, the major highlight other than the view, are the most complete fortifications in the Greek world. The Turkish government is funding a long-term dig and restoration, under the direction of one of Turkey's leading archeologists, Professor Umit Serdar-Oglu. The restored Temple of Athena (530 B.C.) is situated like the Temple of Poseidon at Sounion, its columns and architrave are visible from the water below.

There are two motels along the harbor, the **Behram** and the **Eden Beach**, as well as a couple of cafés.

To get to Assos you must catch a minibus, at 750 TL (95¢), at Ayvacik (not Ayvalik) for the 17-kilometer ride. Ayvacik is a thriving little trading town that has a colorful weekly bazaar. Unlike the markets in Istanbul or Bursa, Ayvacik's bazaar covers most of the town. Old men carry newly tanned sheepskins over their shoulders, yelling out prices. A man from a carpet cooperative clutches his three knotted rugs hoping to snare a big-city buyer. Thousands of secondhand suits and discarded army uniforms hang on sagging racks, and in the midst of it all, a particularly brusque shepherd will herd his flock right through the stream of buyers.

Assos is a short steep walk above the stone houses of Behramkale. Don't miss the 14th-century Ottoman bridge with the pointed arches as you approach the town.

4. Ayvalik

A typewritten note on the inside of one of the town's international phone booths reads: "On your first visit you will be a guest. On your second visit you will be a member of the family. Tourism Office, Ayvalik."

Welcome to one of the friendliest towns in the Aegean. Most people come to Ayvalik as a way station to or from Lesbos, some two hours away, but the helpful Tourist Office always convinces some to stay longer. Need a bicycle to find that out-of-the-way hotel? Just ask; they keep one out front for tourists. If you're feeling a bit overcome by the sun, stop by and recover in their quiet first-aid station in the back.

If you do stay, you'll discover the 23 gorgeous pine-tree-covered islands that punctuate Ayvalik's rocky, wildly irregular coastline. (In the summer there are thrice-weekly cruises of Ayvalik's islet group.) Ayvalik is known for its 12-kilometer-long beach, some of Turkey's best fish restaurants, and endless groves of olive trees—not a bad package for a little-known port town.

ORIENTATION: The **Tourist Information Office** (tel. 6631/2122)—open 8:30 a.m. to 5:30 p.m. (till 8 p.m. in summer) Monday through Friday, 9:30 a.m. to 1:30 p.m. on Saturday—is located about one kilometer south of the center of town, to your right as you alight from the boat. The **bus terminal** is three kilometers north of town. Either way, it's a short dolmush, bus, or taxi drive.

The center is an energetic port town, whose new shops, harbor cafés, and promenades make it attractive to growing numbers of tourists. Most hotels, camping spots (the site of Çamlik has a lovely view of the islands), and restaurants are situated in a three-kilometer stretch between the tourist office and the 12-kilometer-long **Sarmisakli Beach**. All of the town's **banks** are clustered around Atatürk Square in the center of town. Banking hours are normal, though the ferry arrives after 5 p.m., after the banks have closed. Hotels and restaurants will change money.

ACCOMMODATIONS AND DINING: The first hotel you'll see as you disembark from the Lesbos ferry is the eight-room **Motel Kiyi** (tel. 6631/1448), next to the main pier at 18 Gumrück Meydani. Velvet couches and silk lampshades lend an elegant, homey atmosphere to this simple hostel. Nearby at the **Ipek Otel** (tel. 6631/1201) small, spotless twin-bedded rooms rent for 8400 TL ($11) a night; the showers in the newly tiled common bathroom down the hall are free. The Kiyi's front rooms overlook the multicolored fishing boats moored at the pier, but the town-view Ipek has a wonderful manageress. There is a similar, less homey lodging 1½ blocks up from the pier at 20 Gumrück Caddesi, the small **Otel Canli Balik** (tel. 6631/2292). Clean, spartan rooms on the top floors, with a minaret's-eye view of the town and only a hint of street noise, range from 5000 TL ($6) for a single to 14000 TL ($18) for four beds. The Canli Balik's sunny breakfast terrace is a perfect picnic spot.

If you're after the sunny sands of Ayvalik's Sarimsakli Beach (a $3 cab ride or 25¢ bus ride from the pier) there are two fine hotels, the Ankara and the Buyük Berg, among the many new ones. **Hotel Ankara** (tel. 6631/1195) is named after the hometown of its gracious owner/manager, Murat Özek, whose Austrian wife has helped to build the business. The lobby and common space are decorated with Turkish batiks, carved dark-wood molding, colored glass panels, and a collection of woven-cane models of houses in which Atatürk lived. Both hotels share the pool behind the Buyük Berg, rent small boats and windsurfers, and are set side by side on the sandy beach. Spacious, simple doubles with bath and breakfast cost 17,600 TL ($22). At the **Buyük Berg** (tel. 6631/2311) the rooms and facilities are decorated in a more modern style. The restaurant becomes a disco in the evening, although the ground floor outdoor café always resembles a thatched-roof *posada*. Compulsory half board in July and August brings a double room rate to 26,400 TL ($37) a night. In the low season, prices range from $20 to $28 for a double with breakfast; both solar-heated hotels are open year round. For beachside quality at in-town prices, try the new pensions on Alibey Island.

Situated in a tranquil cove of Ayvalik Bay, between the port and Sarimsakli Beach, is the **Murat Reis Hotel** (tel. 6634/1456), an isolated resort worthy of mention. The manicured gardens, cool sand beach, and large swimming pool set up on Angel's Rock (a small plateau with views over Ayvalik's 23 islets) may warrant the $70 full-board tariff for two in the high season. A nearby eatery, the **Seytan Sofrasi**, is farther up the Murat Reis's private road at Devil's Rock (a much larger scenic lookout). Cafeteria food is available at this picturesque site; it's best at sunset.

Ayvalik's best cuisine is the focal point of its economy: seafood. At nearby Alibey Island, a ten-minute ride by frequent ferries from Ayvalik's port, one can find fresh fish cooked so exquisitely that to eat here warrants a detour through Ayvalik. Of the many establishments near Alibey's pier, the **Saray Gazinosu** is particularly good. One moonlit night, as guests of Mr. Bariş, whose fishing fleet supplies the local market, we feasted on shrimp, *midye dolmasi* (stuffed mussels), *tarama* (red caviar spread), *istakos* (octopus), and a variety of mezes, followed by a delicious *kirlangiç* (a tender, local flying fish) poached with dill and tomatoes. You can share our bliss for under $10 per person. In the town of Ayvalik, **Öz Canli Balik Restaurant**, to the left end of the harbor from the Lesbos ferry pier, is one local favorite. Other good, in-town meat restaurants (of course, all serve fish, too) are **Sahil** and **Elifa**. As Kyle reminds me, there are *pastanesis* galore.

GETTING TO LESBOS: The Ayvalik-Lesbos connection is one of the least-used crossover points between Turkey and Greece. One-way tickets are $15; round trip, $25. The 1987 summer schedule had boats running on Monday, Wednesday, and Friday but only Wednesday during the off-season, though this schedule is subject to change. Check with their agent near Atatürk Square, the **Barish Office** (tel. 1756) or **Ayvalik Tur** (tel. 2740) for the current schedule, or ask at the Tourist Information Office. Generally, reservations should be made one day prior to sailing and can be called in over the telephone.

GETTING TO AYVALIK: There is regular bus service to Izmir, nearly every hour, for 1500 TL ($2). Buses to Bergama, costing 750 TL ($1), run hourly, while Istanbul-bound coaches, at 6000 TL ($7.50), depart several times daily.

5. Bergama (Pergamum)

After the conquest of Asia Minor by Alexander, the kingdom of Pergamum became one of the great centers of Hellenistic culture. It still is. Ranking among the best preserved and largest sites within the ancient Greek and Roman world, Pergamum is an absolute must for anyone visiting the Aegean coast.

ORIENTATION: The site is divided into three areas: the Acropolis, the town, and the Asklepion—all within walking distance of one another. But wear your best-soled shoes—it's a hike. Don't despair; any part of the tour can be serviced by a taxi. The bus will let you off near the base of main street. (*Note:* Make sure your bus stops *in* Bergama, rather than at the intersection of the main highway. The town is actually four miles from that spot.) Walk up toward the town where you'll find the **Tourist Information Office** (tel. 5411/1862) as well as the archeological and ethnographic museums (open daily from 8:30 a.m. to 5:30 p.m., till 7 p.m. in summer, 600 TL, or 80¢). Neither museum is outstanding, largely because the best relics are on display in Istanbul or were hauled off years ago to Berlin, London, or Rome.

ACCOMMODATIONS AND DINING: The town has several acceptable hotels, nothing fancy, with the **Tusan Hotel** (tel. 5411/1173), on the outskirts, being the best at 9600 TL ($12) for two. In town, about 300 meters up the main street from the archeological museum is the **Pergamon Pansiyon** (tel. 5411/2395). This small pension has set up shop in a charming, vividly painted turn-of-the century town house. High-ceilinged, simply furnished rooms look out over the city's red roofs or over the small courtyard and café. Beds are billed at 3000 TL ($3.75) per person including breakfast. Another choice for hostel-like simplicity is the **Park Hotel** (tel. 5411/1246), at Sokak 6 off the main street, one block from the Bergama Restaurant. The pink-and-blue shades of "Miami Vice" that make the exterior so remarkable are not in evidence inside. However, rooms are spacious and clean (especially room 25, with its balcony) and the shared toilet, bath, and shower are neat. If you want a private bathroom in Bergama, you'll have to head out to the Tusan Hotel.

The best restaurant in Bergama is the **Kardeşler**, near the PTT. Across the street from the archeological museum is the glitzy **Bergama Restaurant**, a popular group stop and a pretty good place to grab lunch. Nearby is a good Kebab parlor and an excellent *pastanesi*.

ANCIENT PERGAMUM: The absolute best way to see the site is to share a taxi (about $8, but definitely worth it) to the top of the Acropolis and walk the rest of the way down (there are always people at the Tourist Information Office looking to share a cab, and the office will keep you posted on the latest official rates). If it's a hot day—and it's almost always hot up on the big rock—remember to carry a canteen of water. You'll be the envy of every parched tourist.

The Acropolis

The cab will let you off at the foot of the main ramp leading to the upper city. The Acropolis really incorporates three separate cities, built on three levels in concentric semicircular terraces. The **upper city** was for the nobility, high-ranking soldiers, dignitaries, and scholars. Several of the buildings on this level were directly modeled after those on the Acropolis in Athens, but with one important difference: the Acropolis at Pergamum was devoted almost exclusively to the secular life. Pergamum was a center of medicine, art, learning, business, theater, and a bit off to the side, religion. For example, at the head of the ramp you'll come to a terrace that houses one of Pergamum's most notable institutions, the **library** (the foundation is on the far northern side). During the height of Pergamum's wealth (283–133 B.C.) the city built a library second only to that of Alexandria, containing over 200,000 volumes. Although Egypt had a clear hold on number one, they were concerned that Pergamum's library might one day surpass their own. As a countermeasure to Pergamum's growing reputation the Egyptians stopped exporting papyrus. Faced with a dearth of writing material, one of Pergamum's own, Hirodicus, invented Charta Pergamena, or parchment. After Julius Caesar's Egyptian campaign, which included the burning of the Alexandrian Library, Mark Antony seized 200,000 volumes at Pergamum to present to Cleopatra (all were destroyed in a later fire).

Continue to the **theater**, a few steps to the west of the library. Nowhere else is a stage for the ideas of man—drama, comedy, philosophy, and poetry—so elevated by its site and construction. The theater literally hugs the mountains, built on a grade that rises 108 feet from the orchestra to the upper entrance. Its 80 rows overlook the surrounding plain and city in the manner of an ideal fortification. At Pergamum the idea, largely Dionysian, was to connect the audience with nature. To underscore it, they built a Dionysian temple at the base of the theater (at the far right of the processional road), so that the god of the vine—and of the force of life in all growing things—would always be honored. Imagine being one of 10,000 spectators at a Greek drama with the mountains, river, and plains serving as the backdrop.

Return to the upper level and walk north to the Roman-era **Trajaneum**, a Corinthian temple built in later years to honor the emperor. The German Architectural Institute has been restoring the temple since 1981. The surrounding buildings on this upper level are various palaces, temples, stoas, and military buildings.

The Acropolis's major religious building is the renowned **Altar of Zeus**, located on a slightly lower level below the first terrace you encountered (below the site of the Parthenon-inspired Temple of Athena). Nothing remains except for the base of the altar, but the temple was Pergamum's largest and most important. (If you want to see the rest of this horseshoe-shaped altar, you'll have to visit the Pergamum Museum, inconveniently centered in East Berlin.) In 1871 a German engineer, Carl Humann, discovered fragments of remarkably sculpted high reliefs used as supports for the Byzantine-era city wall. He assembled the surviving sections of the frieze, depicting combat between gods and giants, and sent it off to Berlin. The entire altar was subsequently reassembled, with the metopes and frieze put in place. Humann's discovery led to the eventual excavation and restoration of the Pergamum Acropolis.

Follow the path down to the **middle city**. This level contained the three gymnasia as well as cult temples supported by the less sophisticated and more superstitious classes. Some of these shrines, especially the Temple of Demeter, were scenes of blood rituals and animal (and perhaps human) sacrifice.

After exploring the middle city, walk through the middle gymnasium and at the far east end you'll find a vault-covered stairway. Descend to the lower city through the finely crafted tunnel, one of the oldest and best constructed Greek-era vaulted archways on the site. Walk through the lower gymnasium, built for the children, to the main road, paved with gigantic blocks of andesite (notice the chariot ruts!). Along this road are remains of old shops and houses, some of which have been restored by a team of German archeologists. The road leads down past the city walls, through the lower agora (it now houses visiting scholars) and eventually back into town. The Acropolis is open daily from 8:30 a.m. to 5:30 p.m. and later in summer. Admission is 600 TL (75¢).

In the Town of Bergama

The second major area to visit is the modern town. Make a stop at the city's largest building, the **Temple of Serapis**, or as it's now known, the **Red Courtyard**. In the second century A.D. the Roman world was racked by an interest in cults and foreign religions. Among the most popular were the Eyptian deities Isis and the god of both medicine and the Underworld, Serapis. This temple was dedicated to Serapis and was, unlike its crumbling-brick Alamo-like appearance of today, a multicolumned marble-faced edifice of great distinction. Some of the marble facing is still intact on the upper parts of the temple. The temple still has a river running under its main courtyard.

For museum hounds, continue down Bergama's main street for the two collections, one archeological, the other ethnographic.

The Asklepion

The third attraction in Pergamum is the city's Asklepion (open 8:30 a.m. to 5:30 p.m. (later in summer) daily; 75¢ entrance fee), located in the southwest area of modern Bergama. Ranking in importance with those at Kos and Epidaurus, it was built in the fourth century B.C. An Asklepion was a center of healing and study. Diagnosis was largely made through analysis of dreams, suggesting that patients' maladies were often brought on by psychological disorders and revealed in a subconscious state. Various treatments were prescribed, usually involving music, massage, different kinds of baths, dietary restrictions, ointments, herbs, and a strange form of psychiatric treatment. Patients went to special rooms where they were to sleep and dream. After waking, patients discussed the dreams with doctors. Once this process was completed, the patient ran down a long tunnel from the sacred pools and fountains and the house of treatment toward the Temple of Telesphorus. Doctors and priests yelled encouraging comments, bolstering the patients' strength and morale. These "incubation cells" and tunnels formed the psychological part of the cure. The rest was either religious or physical therapy.

Many doctors studied and practiced at the Asklepion, but none more famous than Galen. His work in Pergamum augmented his anatomical studies afforded by the rulers of the Roman Empire (who allowed him to dissect live humans, using dying gladiators as experimental subjects).

6. Izmir

Driving south along the coast from Istanbul to Izmir one begins to see advertising billboards, a relatively uncommon sight in Turkey. The billboards are the first warning about this overindustrialized port which mars an otherwise attractive shoreline. *Oy vey*-Izmir!

On September 9, 1922, Turkish locals under the leadership of Mustafa Kemal won back the Greek-occupied town, then Smyrna. Under siege, this beautiful port caught fire and in one brief day was razed. Virtually no significant architecture built prior to 1922 survives. (The destruction of Smyrna/Izmir is well chronicled in a moving photographic display at the Byzantine Museum in Athens.) Izmir is the Landsoutheast headquarters for NATO in Europe. That and its lucrative Trade Fair give the city an international flavor on a par with Thessaloniki. Although Izmir is a valuable transportation hub, there is little left of historic merit, and an overnight stay, unless mandated by a bus or boat schedule, is not particularly recommended.

ORIENTATION: Izmir's two main arteries run parallel to the Aegean. The **Birinci Kordon** is the First Cordon, and parallel to it, one street inland, is the **Ikinci Kordon**, the Second Cordon. They are actually named **Atatürk Caddesi** and **Cumhuriyet Bulvari**, respectively, but since there are few Izmiris who use the official names, we can only suggest that you memorize them both!

At the center of the waterfront is the large, open **Cumhuriyet Meydani**, or Democracy Square. A shining statue of Atatürk on horseback dominates the square and is a handy landmark. Cumhuriyet Square is the site of many political and official ceremonies and at night becomes a teenage roller-skating disco. It's not unusual to see a five-star general or Arab oil sheik strolling the tree-lined avenues. The waterfront is lined with Izmir's best and most expensive shops.

Several blocks inland from Cumhuriyet Square lies **Kültür Parki**, a park occupying a large portion of urban real estate. During most months industrial trade expositions are held here. (Many foreign countries are represented in the summer trade show, whose great success leaves the sightseeing tourist extremely hard pressed to find decent accommodations during these two chaotic months.)

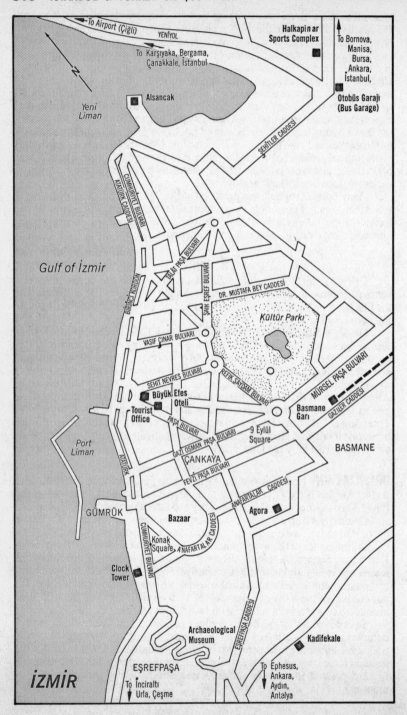

To Airport (Çiğli)
YENİYOL
Halkapinar
Sports Complex

To Bornova,
Manisa,
Bursa,
Ankara,
İstanbul,

To Karşıyaka, Bergama,
Çanakkale, İstanbul

Otobüs Garajı
(Bus Garage)

Alsancak

Yeni
Liman

ŞEHİTLER CADDESİ

Gulf of İzmir

CUMHURİYET CADDESİ

ATATÜRK CADDESİ

TALAT PAŞA BULVARI

ŞAİK EŞREF BULVARI

BİRİNCİ KORDON

DR. MUSTAFA BEY CADDESİ

Kültür Parkı

VASIF ÇINAR BULVARI

ŞEHİT NEVRES BULVARI

REFİK ŞAYDAM BULVARI

MÜRSEL PAŞA BULVARI

GAZİLER CADDESİ

Büyük Efes
Oteli

Tourist
Office

Basmane
Garı

BASMANE

Port
Liman

PAŞA BULVARI

GAZİ OSMAN PAŞA BULVARI

ATATÜRK

9 Eylül
Square

ÇANKAYA

FEVZİ PAŞA BULVARI

GÜMRÜK

Bazaar

ANAFARTALAR CADDESİ

Agora

Konak
Square

CUMHURİYET BULVARI

ANAFARTALAR CADDESİ

Clock
Tower

ESREFPAŞA CADDESİ

Archaeological
Museum

Kadifekale

İZMİR

EŞREFPAŞA

To İnciraltı
Urla, Çeşme

To Ephesus,
Ankara,
Aydın,
Antalya

There's one more focal point to mention. About two kilometers (20 minutes) south along the waterfront from Cumhuriyet Square is **Konak Square**. This is the terminus for most of the local city buses and the home of the utilitarian Izmir Bazaar.

USEFUL INFORMATION: The **Tourist Information Office** (tel. 51/142147) is located next to the Büyük Efes Oteli in Cumhuriyet Square. The staff is very helpful and speaks very good English. It's open daily from 8:30 a.m. to 5:30 p.m. (later in summer) and on weekends from 9 a.m. to 5 p.m. . . . The **American Consulate** (tel. 51/131369) is at 92 Atatürk Caddesi. The **British Consulate** (tel. 51/211795) is located at 49 Mahmot sat Bozkurt. . . . There is the "**American**" **Hospital** (tel. 211101), which is so American the operator speaks no Turkish. It's located on 1375 Sokak, quite near the Büyük Efes Oteli.

Banks are open from 9 a.m. to 12:30 p.m. and 1:30 p.m. to 5 p.m. Monday through Friday, but are closed on Saturday and Sunday. If you're stuck on a weekend, try your hotel, a travel agent, or the local **American Express** branch, located in the **Egetur Travel and Tourism Agency** (tel. 217925), at 2 Talatpasa Bulvari near the NATO complex.

Foreigners starved for reading material should visit **Haşet Kitapevi** (tel. 214264), at 143 Cumhuriyet Bulvari very close to the Büyük Efes Oteli. Although a small shop, it carries all major international newspapers. The selection of magazines is even more impressive (there are even movie-buff magazines) and their hardcover books range from spy novels to Dickens. Haşet also has a Xerox machine. Next door is the **Izmir Sinemasi**, where we saw the handsome Robert Bedfort (sic) star in *Brubaker*. There is a small but fine archeological museum.

Directly facing Cumhuriyet Square lies the **PTT**, for making international calls or purchasing stamps. . . . Below the Büyük Efes Oteli is the **THY office** (tel. 141226) and a THY affiliate, **Agency Doktoroglu** (tel. 145020). Go see them for ticket purchasing or advice about major travel plans by ship, train, bus, or plane. Several **rental car companies,** including **Avis** (tel. 211226), located near the Büyük Efes Otel, have local offices. . . . There are many travel agencies in town, but one, **Cemtur** (tel. 144609), at 122B Sehit Fethi Bey Caddesi, is run by an experienced guide named Engin Deniz and his American wife, both quite helpful. Romantic horsedrawn carriages will transport you along the waterfront in style for $4 per half hour.

GETTING TO AND FROM IZMIR: Since we're hoping that most of you are in Izmir because it's a transportation hub, especially for those arriving by boat or plane, we'll examine your travel options carefully. Most visitors will want to visit either Bergama, to the north, or Ephesus, to the south. If you're considering basing yourself in Izmir to visit these sites as day trips, we'd recommend moving on (during the trade festival days, you may not have an option).

Ephesus

Ephesus can be reached by either **bus** or train. Because the ruins are spread over several kilometers, the public bus to Selçuk will leave you in a convenient place to sightsee, about three kilometers from the site. Selçuk is on the main highway running south along the Aegean coast, and many buses to and from Marmaris, Bodrum, and other points pass through. The earliest bus from Izmir leaves the Otobus Garaji about 6 a.m.; others run every 15 minutes thereafter until 9 p.m. The fare is 720 TL ($1). Travel at night to beat the heat and reserve seats mid-bus for a tranquil ride. From Selçuk, the last public bus leaves about 9 p.m. for the 1½-hour trip to Izmir.

Trains to Ephesus (Selçuk) leave from Basmane station daily at 8 a.m., 3:30 p.m., and 6 p.m. The trains cost 900 TL ($1.10) and make the trip in two hours. In the past two years travel times have fluctuated as wildly as bus fares; phone Basmane information (tel. 135087) for current schedules. We enjoyed taking the train; you'll find that it's a good way to see the country, and a pleasant change from the highway. If this is a day trip we would definitely advise taking the bus back to be safe, since these run regularly to Izmir (and the same may not be said about the trains). Several travel agents offer day tours to Ephesus for $25.

Kuşadasi

Those wanting to visit the seaside before hitting Ephesus may want to go to this nearby port. Buses leave the Octobus Garaji from the **Elbirlic** company (tel. 163127). The first bus is at 7 a.m., and they depart approximately every hour thereafter. The last bus leaves Kuşadasi for Izmir at 7:30 p.m. The price is 960 TL ($1.20).

Istanbul

Istanbul is accessible by plane, bus, boat, or train. **THY** (tel. 141226) flies between Istanbul and Izmir four or five times daily ($42 for the 40-minute flight).

The **Varan Bus Lines** (tel. 191919), a classy outfit that will take you on a nine-hour journey to Istanbul in comfort and style, is located at Gazi Osman Paşa Bulvari across from the Büyük Efes Hotel. From here they'll shuttle you free of charge to the Otobus Garaji to catch their seven daily buses. You should consider taking the night bus; it's a much cooler ride in the summer when the days are really hot! The one-way fare (no student discounts) is 9000 TL ($11.25). Varan's offices are open daily between 7 a.m. and 11 p.m.

The **Turkish Maritime Lines** (tel. 210077) runs several ships up the Aegean coast to Istanbul and on to Venice leaving from Yeni Liman. Contact the Turkish Tourist Office (tel. 142147) for schedule and fare information.

Trains depart two times daily for the express trip (12 hours, $5) to Istanbul. For information about departures (from the Alsançak station), contact the Tourist Office or call the station at 210014.

Çeşme

Çeşme, with its beautiful beaches and scheduled boat departures for the Greek island of Chios, may be some travelers' destination. Buses leave for Çeşme from Izmir's Konak Square (1½ kilometers south of Cumhuriyet Square) every hour, between 6:30 a.m. and 8 p.m. The **Çeşme Pirlik Bus Company** (tel. 141783) controls this route and charges 840 TL ($1) for the 1½-hour trip.

GETTING AROUND IZMIR: The **bus terminal** is **Otobus Garaji**, the main terminus for public bus transport between Izmir and other cities. The no. 50 local bus departs from Cumhuriyet Meydani, goes to Konak Square (where you would catch the Ephesus minibus or the Çeşme bus), and then brings you to the Otobus Garaji. Fares are 125 TL (15¢) for adults, 55 TL (8¢) for students. You can, of course, take a dolmush or taxi to the terminus instead.

Getting to the **airport** is made fast and convenient by the private bus run by THY for its passengers. Buses depart from THY's offices (tel. 141226) below the Büyük Efes Oteli and return new arrivals directly to the hotel. THY allows 75 minutes before flight time for the 20-kilometer ride.

Izmir has two **train stations**. To reach **Basmane Gari** (the station for regional destinations or southern towns), take the no. 4 bus; you can catch it from Cumhuriyet Meydani or Konak Square. To reach the **Alsançak Gari** (used for Istanbul- or Ankara-bound trains), take the no. 2 bus from Cumhuriyet Square. Please double-check with your local travel office or the Tourist Information Office to make sure you're heading to the correct train station (we don't want to receive any nasty letters).

Getting to the **port** is difficult at best, and really warrants a dolmush or taxi for anyone with luggage to carry. It's a short, inexpensive ride, but budget watchers can take a bus: no. 120 cruises the coast and stops at both squares.

ACCOMMODATIONS: Izmir is a large, busy city where low-price, good-value hotels are difficult to come by. A steady flow of tourists and the popular trade fair each summer and fall keep the hotel market strong enough so that hoteliers don't have to bargain to keep beds filled. The two best areas for hotels are the vicinity of Cumhuriyet Square and by the Basmane Railroad Station, about five blocks in from the port. We recommend trying the Cumhuriyet Square hotels first and settling for the Basmane area for lower-cost accommodations.

Around Cumhuriyet Square

Cumhuriyet Meydani (Square) is the focal point of Western luxury in Izmir, and if money is no object or you're in search of a treat, stay at Izmir's finest, the **Büyük Efes Hotel** (tel. 51/144300). It's located right on the square and features a disco, terraced garden for snacks or breakfast, two-story reception area and lounge, and a news stand that carries the *Wall Street Journal, International Herald Tribune,* and several of the English Fleet Street papers. The Büyük Efes's swimming pool may be the best-known feature locally; one of its walls is glass and fronts onto a cocktail lounge, whose customers are treated to a subterranean view of swimsuits in action. It's got the glitter quality of a James Bond set, is lots of fun, and is a great place to meet the world's military leaders. By the side of the pool is a brand-new Turkish bath decorated in tastefully modern tiles.

This luxury hotel's 450 rooms do not come cheap. The good news first: they're fully air-conditioned with the largest, most opulent bathrooms in Turkey; several rooms overlook the lovely inner garden court. Now the bad news; doubles range from $77 to $86 according to season, and garden-view rooms cost $110.

A luxury lodging made more affordable by the strong dollar is the **Izmir Palace** (tel. 51/215583), at Atatürk Bulvari, about two blocks north along the waterfront. Here 150 rooms, air-conditioned with private baths and luxurious appointments, rent for $54 a night for two, $44 for one.

An excellent mid price choice is the **Otel Karaca** (tel. 51/144445), at 1379 Sokak, 55, a block in from the square. The Karaca's lobby is well decorated and quiet, and all 68 spacious rooms have private facilities, air conditioning, TV, mini-bar, and comfortable furnishings. Balconied front rooms overlook the Büyük Efes's pool and gardens. Bed-and-breakfast doubles cost 41,000 TL ($50), singles cost 31,000 TL ($40), and street-facing rooms cost $5 less.

A terrific new entry in the mid price range is the **Otel Kismet** (tel. 51/217050), at 1377 Sokak, No. 9, one block inland from the square. Quiet, soothing beige-painted rooms range from 19,200 TL ($24) for a single to 27,000 TL ($34) for a double with bath to 32,000 TL ($40) for a suite to accommodate three. Since groups favor the Kismet, try to make high-season reservations two weeks ahead.

The **Otel Kilim** (tel. 51/145340), a good choice that's popular with business people, has gotten more costly. The Kilim is at 1 Atatürk Bulvari, two blocks south of Cumhuriyet Meydani in the direction of Konak Square. The Otel Kilim is an older but well-maintained hotel whose 89 simple rooms are enlivened with brightly patterned, often pretty Turkish carpets. Doubles with bath now cost 39,000 TL ($49), singles are 31,000 TL ($40).

Around Basmane Railroad Station

There are few hotels or lodgings in this area that could be called luxurious, and even fewer whose simplicity might be called quaint. Yet there are several budget choices in this working-class neighborhood, and since tourists rarely choose to stay here, you'll often be able to find a room when all others in the Cumhuriyet Meydani area are sold out.

The best value is the **Atlas Oteli** (tel. 51/144265), located between the Meydani and Basmane circle, about three blocks inland at the intersection of Sair Esref Bulvari and Gazi Osman Pasa Bulvari. The rooms are plain but relatively clean, and the price is right: 10,000 TL ($13) for a double with bath, or 5000 TL ($6.20) for a single with bath. To assure yourself a room at the Atlas, call in the early morning to talk to one of their English-speaking receptionists. If no rooms are available they can make other recommendations, but at least you'll have made your play before the morning buses from the provinces arrive and all rooms are taken.

The **Billur Hotel** (tel. 51/136250) is located right on the Basmane traffic circle, at 783 Garkarşisi, and its rooms are somewhat noisy. Inspect your room before making a commitment, accommodations are clean and surprisingly pleasant; each of the Billur's 70 rooms has a mini-tub, sink, and toilet within the room, and many overlook the entrance to the railroad station. A twin-bedded double room runs 26,400 TL ($33) a night, but a "French-bedded" (the Turks' name for a double bed) room only costs 19,200 TL ($24), including breakfast in their scenic open-air rooftop restaurant.

RESTAURANTS: Finding a cheap meal in this bustling city isn't always easy. Dining in Izmir is principally geared to Turkish businessmen and Trade Fair visitors. For the low-budget-minded, far and away the best area to eat is near the Basmane Railway Station. It's cheap and off the path beaten by international tourists.

Zeybek (tel. 135231), at 1368 Sokak no.6/A, is a small eatery located just off the Basmane circle. Good-quality food is well prepared and inexpensive. For a hearty dish of Bursa kebab with lamb, yogurt, tomato sauce, onions, and pita bread, the cost is a mere 1500 TL ($2).

Two doors down is another of our bargain favorites. **Guzel Izmir** (tel. 140501), at 1368 Sokak no. 8/B, offers cooked dishes simmering in steam pans, which are equivalent to cafeteria-style presentation.

While you're in the Basmane area, walk a few feet back toward Kyle's favorite discovery, the **Aligalip Pastanesi**, on the corner of Basmane circle and 1368 Sokak.

Back toward the center, next to Cumhuriyet Square, is the **Reis Cafeteria**, a low-price döner kebab and burger joint; it's around the corner from the Etap Hotel. Near the Kilim Hotel, a few meters from the water, is **Kordelya**, specializing in traditional Turkish cuisine.

There are several restaurants featuring continental/Turkish cuisine along the harbor in front of Cumhuriyet Square. One of the most pleasant is the **Bergama Restaurant** (tel. 135709), but expect to pay international prices. The Bergama is located on the Birinci Kordon with a panoramic view of the Izmir harbor. We loved their spinach soufflé at 5000 TL ($6), but it's only available in the fall harvest season. Another tasty choice was the *kalamar tava*, or fried squid, for 10,000 TL ($13).

Actually, caution should be exercised when ordering any fish in Izmir restaurants. Because the fish is usually imported from the southern fishing villages, it's often expensive—26,000 TL ($33) per kilo is not unheard of here.

If you're set on fish, try either of the elegant **Deniz Restaurants** (tel. 220601) along the waterfront (one in the Izmir Palas Hotel and the other a ten-minute stroll north). Both serve varied mezes and a large selection of seafood; two can dine well for 12,000 TL ($15).

The splashiest dining establishment in Izmir, and a definite splurge, is the **Palet Café Restaurant Kordon,** (tel. 118436), set on its own micro-pier in the harbor off of Atatürk Caddesi, 503. Fish is the featured food, but expect to pay about $30 per person for a complete meal. The scene, the entertainment, and view are among the best in Izmir.

WHAT TO DO: There is a **bazaar** of sorts in Izmir, located across the street from Konak Square. If you've experienced either the bazaar in Istanbul or Bursa, Izmir's pales by comparsion; it's closer to being the main shopping area for daily needs such as clothing, shoes, and children's toys.

Shoppers needn't despair. There is an authentic and interesting **poorman's market** in another location on Saturday and Sunday. On 1369 Sokak you'll find a motley collection of local junk. Odds are that there'll be nothing here you want to buy, but to see bargaining at its best, check this place out. Secondhand clothing, 15-year-old hi-fidelity equipment, bicycle spikes, used watches, and vintage Turkish comic books and sex magazines are being hawked at any price the seller can get.

To get to this area from Cumhuriyet Square, walk down Gazi Osman Paşa Bulvari to Çankaya Square, where the Atlas Hotel is, and walk one block down Gazi Bulvari to 1369 Sokak. Here there is a small, but excellent, archeological museum.

7. Çeşme and the Chios Connection

The port of Çeşme ("Fountain") is set on a hilly peninsula that's become a popular retreat for locals from nearby Izmir, 80 kilometers to the east. Çeşme itself is the jumping-off point for Chios, one of Greece's most fascinating islands (and best kept secrets). Other than the 14th-century fortress (expanded in 1508 during the reign of Sultan Beyazit II); and many hot springs there's little to see or do in Çeşme. If you're coming from Chios move on to Izmir for other travel connections.

ACCOMMODATIONS AND RESTAURANTS: Çeşme's growing tourist industry and the new Turkish-built holiday villages seem to attract more tourists each season. A splurge hotel choice but one with great charm and fascination is the newly restored kervansaray, the **Kanuni Kervansaray Oteli** (tel. 5492/6490), in the center of town. The Kanuni Kervansaray now has 32 rooms for travelers rather than camels. Double rooms decorated in traditional Turkish style are 35,000 TL ($44), including breakfast; it's open year round. The **Ertan Hotel** (tel. 5492/6795) overlooks the harbor near the Chios ferry dock. Here clean but comparably drab rooms cost 24,000 TL ($30) for two, 18,000 TL ($22) for singles, including breakfast. Street-facing rooms are a few dollars less, but the harbor views are priceless at sunset. The **Cesurlar Pansiyon** (tel. 5492/6022), at Inkilap Caddesi, is one of the many which have recently opened near the port. Simple rooms with private bath and breakfast cost 15,000 TL ($19).

Much cheaper is the 20-room **Captain's Pension** (no telephone), just three or four blocks down from the harbor off Çeşme's main street. Although the rooms and baths (in the hall) are very basic, the price is right: 8000 TL ($10) for two, including breakfast.

As for restaurants, be warned that Çeşme has some of the highest prices we've seen anywhere in Turkey, especially for fish. The popular **Korfez Restaurant**, for example, charges 26,000 TL ($33) per kilo for *çipura* or *barbouni!* Much cheaper and definitely less touristy is the **Sahil Restaurant**, next to the Ertan Hotel on Cumhumiyet Square.

USEFUL INFORMATION: The **Tourist Information Office** (tel. 5492/6653), at Iskele Meydani 6, is open seven days a week (9 a.m. to 6 p.m.) and is 100 meters from the ferry dock. . . . **Banks** are also open from 9 a.m. to 6 p.m., but foreign currency can usually be exchanged at the Erturk Ferry Boat Agency, shops, or restaurants during off-hours—important if your boat arrives late from Chios. . . . The **PTT** is 200 meters from the ferry and open until midnight, seven days a week, for telephone service.

There is dolmush and bus service to the nearby resort, hot springs, and beach at **Ilica** for 200 TL (40¢); a taxi costs 3000 TL ($3.80). A more secluded beach is two kilometers north at **Agia Yorgi**, near Dalyan, a small fishing village and yacht harbor. The fish tavernas in Dalyan are considerably cheaper than those in Çeşme. A taxi to Dalyan costs 3000 TL ($3.80).

During the summer, **buses** to and from Izmir operate hourly, though the last bus from Çeşme usually leaves at 9 p.m.

GETTING TO CHIOS: The Erturk Ferry to Chios operates from May through October on a regular schedule, with daily sailings except Monday from mid-July through August. During the other months the ferry usually goes twice or thrice weekly. The ten-kilometer, 1½-hour excursion costs $18 (1987 price) one way, $30 round trip. The ferry has space for motorcycles and cars as well. A Greek-based company also runs a ferry between Çeşme and Chios. The **Erturk Agency**, half a block from the harbor at 11 Cumhuriyet Meydani (tel. 5492/6768), sells tickets for both ferry companies and can advise you on the current schedule.

Those not returning to Greece via Çeşme will leave the bustle and pollution of Izmir's port behind, and follow the road veering inland toward the town of Bergama. The recently built two-lane highway is already being expanded to accommodate the guest workers' BMW's and Mercedes, which now strain impatiently to pass lumbering vegetable trucks and long-distance buses. Overhead phone lines skew the symmetry of neatly ploughed peanut and wheat fields. Occasionally, a flock of Turkish women dressed in brightly colored kaftans and flower-print harem pants, bowed heads covered by black or white scarves, are seen working in the fields. As you head south, crimson poppies and sunny buttercups poke through the less hospitable, scrub-brush terrain. The bonanza of tourists visiting ancient Ephesus has left its mark on the no-longer sleepy village of Selçuk. Large storks which have nested in the chimneys of local farmhouses for centuries now roost above cheap pensions and pizza parlors. Readers can choose between the touristic frenzy of the nearby, scenic port of Kuşadasi and the more Turkish small-town life of Selçuk, but none should pass up one of the country's historic wonders—Ephesus.

8. Ephesus (Selçuk)

Among the many extraordinary archeological ruins within Turkey, Ephesus (Efes) stands as the country's banner site. Throughout antiquity the city was the commercial and population center of western Anatolia, and it boasted one of the seven wonders of the world, the Temple of Artemis, within its boundaries. The wealth of Greek- and Roman-era remains are only part of Ephesus' appeal, for since medieval times Christians marked a visit to Ephesus (one of the seven churches mentioned by St. John) among the holiest of pilgrimages. St. John and the Virgin Mary were reputed to have lived in Ephesus (after living on Patmos), and St. Paul came to the city to preach the gospel. The modern town of Selçuk remains relatively oblivious to the tourist trade (although the 7 pensions that existed two years ago have grown to 33), with old men puffing on *nargiles* (hookahs) and women, dressed in flower-patterned harem pants and tunics, carrying goods to the local market.

ORIENTATION: For beach lovers, the most convenient way to reach the site is to stay in Kuşadasi. It's only a 20-minute minibus ride away, costing 425 TL (55¢); in the high season the minibus runs every 15 minutes.

The minibus stops on the road near the Ephesus site, then in Selçuk, a modern agricultural town that adjoins the ancient site. As Selçuk is on the main road, buses run approximately every half hour from Izmir, 76 kilometers away. The Kuşadasi minibus and Izmir stops are in the center of Selçuk, around the corner from the Tourist Information Office (tel. 5451/1328), whose summer hours are 8:30 a.m. to 6:30 p.m. weekdays, 5:30 p.m. on weekends.

ACCOMMODATIONS AND DINING: The archeological site of Ephesus receives about 3,000 guests each summer day, and more are opting for the quiet, still typically Turkish life of Selçuk than for the glitzier, almost overdeveloped beach resort of Kuşadasi. Since most of the fine new pensions have been built under contract with European tour operators, you may have to walk a few blocks before you find an available room. If none of our suggestions pan out, ask Cihaan at the friendly **Tourist Information Office** (tel. 1328 or 1945) for help.

One of the best of the newer hotels is the **Ak Otel** (tel. 5451/2161), at 14 Kuşadasi Caddesi, just 20 meters down from the wonderful archeological museum. All simply furnished, clean double rooms have private tiled showers and small balconies overlooking a garden patio and café. Stylish decor, carpets, copperware, and etchings justify the 21,600 TL ($27) tariff, which includes breakfast. Typical of the many new pensions is **Tomurcuk** (tel. 5451/2401), off Selcuk's main street near the old square that's dominated by brick columns, all that remains of a Roman-era aqueduct. The Tomurcuk's young proprietor is justifiably proud of six spotless double rooms with attached baths; each rents for 12,000 TL ($15). A spacious four-bedded room with common shower but a tiny balcony rents for 24,000 TL ($30). Breakfast, included in this price, is served in a natural wood-and-batik-decorated lobby. Around the corner is the bigger **Artemis Hotel,** and nearby, the **Aksoy.**

Another choice is the 24-room **Otel Aksoy** (tel. 5451/1040), where clean, spartan rooms (decked out in Turkish carpets and flowered curtains) cost 11,400 TL ($15) for two, with private shower and breakfast; singles run 7800 TL ($10). The Aksoy is located in the middle of town, at 17 Atatürk Caddesi.

The **Artemis Hotel** (tel. 5451/1191), has 20 rooms and a gracious English-speaking host, Muskadder Basterzi. All rooms have built-in showers, doubles are 14,400 TL ($18). Breakfast, at 1500 TL ($2), is served on their pleasant roof terrace. The Artemis is 2½ blocks off the main road, on Atatürk Caddesi at Çarşi ici, 15.

The town's old luxury motel is the **Tusan** (tel. 5451/1060), located on the tree-lined road between the temple and the entrance to Ancient Ephesus, and it has the only convenient campground.

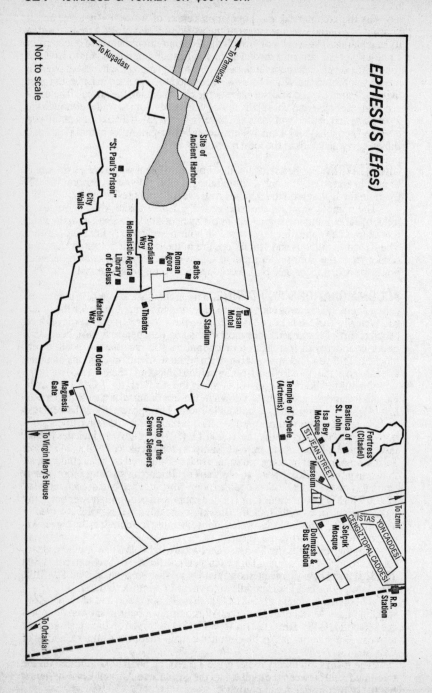

EPHESUS (Efes)

Not to scale

To Kuşadası
To Pamucak

Site of
Ancient Harbor

"St. Paul's Prison"

City
Walls

Hellenistic Agora
Arcadian Way
Library of Celsus
Roman Agora
Baths

Tusan Motel

Marble Way
Theater
Stadium

Odeon

Magnesia Gate

Grotto of the
Seven Sleepers

To Virgin Mary's House

Temple of Cybele
(Artemis)

Basilica of
St. John
Isa Bey
Mosque

ST. JEAN STREET

Fortress
(Citadel)

St. John Museum

To İzmir

İSTAS
CENGİZ TOPAL CADDESİ
YON CADDESİ

Selçuk
Mosque
Dolmuş &
Bus Station

R.R.
Station

To Ortaklar

Those constantly on the prowl for new and different regional food, take note. Selçuk is the place for *çop şiş*. Simply, çop şiş is made with tiny pieces of grilled beef skewered on a toothpick-thin bamboo stick and dipped in cumin powder. Usually five to ten sticks constitute one portion—delightful. The best place in town for çop şiş is the **Hitit Restaurant** (tel. 1960) on the main street, at 1200 TL ($1.50) for nine skewers. With beer, salad, and a healthy number of çop şiş skewers, lunch or dinner should cost no more than 2400 TL ($3). Next door is a *pastanesi* and, about 200 meters up, towards the museum, is the Hitit Restaurant's affiliate, **Yeni Hitit** (tel. 1920).

One of the better eateries among the many new ones is the **Girne Restaurant,** an outdoor café just below the fortified walls of the St. John Church, on Atatürk Caddesi. Girne specializes in meat dishes and serves excellent çop şiş, kebabs, and salads.

THE ARCHEOLOGICAL SITE: There are three areas of interest for sightseeing: Ayasoluk Hill, ancient Ephesus, and the House of the Virgin Mary. Ayasoluk Hill overlooks modern Selçuk and is an easy walk from the bus stop. On the hill stands St. John's Church and the Mosque of Isa Bey. Off the main street, back toward the Tourist Information Office, is the small but excellent archeological museum. **Ancient Ephesus** is three kilometers from the Tourist Information Office. You can walk, cab it at 1800 TL ($2.25)—a taxi carries up to five people—or ride the Kuşadasi-bound minibus for 250 TL (31¢). Either way, you'll pass the Artemision (the Temple of Artemis) on your right, halfway between Selçuk and ancient Ephesus. A visit to the **Home of the Virgin Mary**, nestled in the foothills opposite the ancient city, is seven kilometers from Selçuk, and because of the rough terrain, requires a car (taxis go there for 6600 TL, or $8.50 round trip). Check with the Tourist Information Office before hiring a car; they know the official rates and perhaps can match you with other people who want to go.

Ayasoluk Hill

As you pass through the gate of the fortifications, built mostly of stones taken from the ancient city, you'll come to the sixth-century A.D. **Church of St. John**. This sacred Christian shrine was built around the grave of Saint John, and has been totally reconstructed according to the plan of Justinian.

Below the church is the **Mosque of Isa Bey** (A.D. 1375), a Selçuk-era structure that is distinguished by its intricate carving and decoration. Admission to Ayasoluk Hill is 800 TL ($1).

Next to the Tourist Information Office is Selçuk's fine **Archeological museum,** open every day from 8:30 a.m. to 7 p.m.; admission is 800 TL ($1) weekdays and half price weekends. The museum contains a collection of mosaics, statues, reliefs, and frescoes removed during the recent excavations of Ephesus and the surrounding sites. Of particular note are a small bronze Roman era cupid riding a dolphin (second century A.D.), a series of Roman stone masks made eerily modern by their eroding features, and two statues of Diana of Ephesus represented in the Artemesian style of Anatolia—with 20 breasts to suckle all living things.

Ancient Ephesus

Not much is left of the **Temple of Artemis** other than the foundation, and like its counterpart on Kos, a single, crudely restored column, but during the period of the Greeks the **Artemision** was the largest edifice in the Hellenic world and the first important structure to be built completely of marble. It was surrounded by a staggering array of columns and created such a monumental impression that it was counted among the wonders of the ancient world. Strangely, the temple was built on a swamp (as was its model, the Heraion, on Samos), and is, as it was over 2,000 years ago, deluged by water. Ironically, it was fire that ultimately ravaged the original Artemision when an arsonist set the ceiling and architrave ablaze in 356 B.C. The temple was rebuilt in the more elegant Ionian design with columns that measured over 60 feet in height, but was torn apart in later years to provide building materials for roads and Christian and Moslem shrines. (Admission is 350 TL, or 45¢).

After a walk of two kilometers you'll come to the entrance of the ancient city of Ephesus, open every day from 8 a.m. to 5:30 p.m., and 6:30 p.m. in summer; admission is 1200 TL ($1.50). To your right, after passing the stadium, is the **Church of the Virgin Mary**, the site of one of the most important ecumenical councils in the history of Christianity and the first church to be named in honor of the Virgin. It was here, in A.D. 431, that the church officially declared that Jesus was the Son of God as well as the son of the Virgin Mary. Controversy continues as to whether Mary actually lived in Ephesus (her "house" can be visited near this site), though passages in the New Testament have been interpreted by church historians to support the claim that she came to Ephesus in the middle of the first century A.D., under the care of Saint John. The wide marble road that runs parallel to the church led to the old harbor. It's a little mystifying to think that the end of this stretch (no more than a few hundred meters), once reached the sea, now several kilometers away. Over the centuries, silting eventually made Ephesus a land-locked city.

Head back to the marble road that once connected the Artemision with Ephesus and walk south to the **theater**, another of the city's important Christian sites. Though the 24,000-seat theater was built during the Greek era, its true glory came later in Roman times, during Trajan's reign. When Saint Paul came to Ephesus, he delivered his oration in the theater, but the Ephesians were a devotedly pagan lot and not particularly sympathetic. Their attachment to the goddess Artemis led to a near riot when Paul suggested abandoning cult worship of the deity for Jesus' teachings—perhaps giving meaning to his plea "Put on the whole armor of God." There is an apocryphal story that local merchants, engaged in the flourishing Ephesian trade of Artemis statues, organized a demonstration against Paul, fearing that if he was successful their business would vanish.

Perhaps Ephesus' most distinctive relic is the recently reassembled façade of the **Celsus Library** (the work was undertaken by a team of Austrian archeologists). If you want to appreciate the enormous wealth of ancient Ephesus, take a detailed look at the intricately carved cornices, architraves, niches, and inscriptions on the façade. Although the library was much less important than that at Pergamum, it was still endowed with richly decorated and well-crafted features.

If the theater and library are too refined for your tastes, walk across the street from the Celsus façade to the Roman-era **brothel**. This ancient cat house originally had two stories: the guests were downstairs and the girls were on top. In case you can't find the brothel, look very carefully at the marble road; you'll occasionally see carved footprints with Greek writing crudely pointing the way.

As you turn the corner and head up the marble road, you'll pass two more of Ephesus' most notable highlights. On your left is **Hadrian's Temple** (second century A.D.), a Corinthian-style edifice with an elegantly designed arch and local goddess crowning the remains of its façade. Directly across the street from the temple are the houses and shops built on the gentle foothills of Mount Koressos. This area is currently being excavated; its many exquisite frescoes and mosaics dating from the first through fifth centuries A.D. are on display in the covered buildings.

The marble road continues, passing many fountains (built by wealthy citizens in honor of themselves), shops, homes, and ultimately the Municipal Building, adjacent to the Upper Agora. The **Odeon** is particularly well preserved and worth a visit.

The House of the Virgin Mary

The little stone house containing an array of offerings from around the world is actually a late Byzantine chapel. Pilgrims of all faiths as well as tourists frequent this cool, wooded spot and its sacred spring, located about 7 kilometers uphill from Ephesus as you exit by the Magnesia Gate. The House of the Virgin is currently attended by three nuns and two monks who welcome visitors; there's a small restaurant at the site as well (admission 600 TL, or 75¢).

9. Kuşadasi

Kuşadasi may well be your introduction to the fascinating country of Turkey if you, as 270,000 others did last year, arrive by boat from Samos to see the incredible ruins of Ephesus. Kuşadasi, meaning "Island of Birds," is the port of ancient Ephesus, which spread in earlier times from its acropolis to the Aegean shores.

The modern-day city is known for its sparkling, sandy-bottom bays and the centrally located 17th-century Kervansaray, which has been converted into a hotel. Huge ocean liners moor at Kuşadasi's picturesque harbor so day-tripping passengers can visit Ephesus and shop in the many local leather, jewelry, and carpet stores. The new Turban Marina moors nearly 400 visiting yachts from the north coast and abroad, whose crews have come to enjoy the city's restaurants, sights, and shops. Among the high-rise hotels you can still see white minarets poking up between the palm trees, and flowering cactus are planted in the broad traffic islands. For those intending to stay in Turkey to visit sights in Pamukkale, Miletus, Didyma, Aphrodisias, and Priene, Kuşadasi is now a touristy but efficient and pleasant base of operations. It's a widespread, growing town where walking is the best transport, and it's lively and easier to cope with than the bustling city of Izmir to the north.

ORIENTATION: The harbor road is **Atatürk Bulvari** and runs approximately north–south. About 200 meters south of the yacht harbor, Akincilar Caddesi splits off and runs into town by the Otobus Garaji **(bus terminal).** At the north end of town is the new Turban **yacht harbor and marina;** at the south end, the **ferryboat** docks at Immigration and Customs and the **Tourist Information Office,** followed by the Ada Restaurant on Bird Island at the end. The main tourist shopping street, **Kahramanlar Caddesi,** runs off the harbor road next to the **Kervansaray Hotel,** a major landmark. Kahramanlar eventually intersects Akincilar Caddesi to create a triangle with the sea that defines the area of interest for tourists. However, the unstoppable march of development is spreading hotels beyond this area and up the hills above the town. The closest **beach,** Woman's Beach, is south and west of the town, about two kilometers beyond the Ada Restaurant.

USEFUL INFORMATION: The **Tourism and Information Office** (tel. 6361/1103) is located on Liman Caddesi, the shop-filled plaza at the main pier. The staff is well informed, courteous, and friendly. If you wish to call or write in advance, the Tourist Office will make hotel reservations in any of the local inns, a necessity in June, July, and August. The office is open from 7 a.m. to 9:30 p.m.

daily in summer, to 5:30 p.m. daily in the off-season. **Banks** are open from 8:30 a.m. to 8 p.m. every day, including the weekends to cash travelers' checks. . . . The local **police station** (tel. 1382) is on Kahramanlar Caddesi one block from the port. . . . The **hospital** (tel. 1026) is on Atatürk Caddesi. . . . Any yachting families among our readers will be sure to appreciate the many facilities offered by the huge new **Turban Marina** (tel. 1752). . . . The **Central Post Office** (PTT) is up on Kahramanlar Caddesi, near several smart shops, and is open 24 hours a day. . . . For foreign newspapers, books, and magazines try the new branch of **Haşet Kitapevi A.S.** (tel. 1828) at 10A Kibris Caddesi . . . There is a local **Avis** office (tel. 1475) on the harborside Atatürk Caddesi. . . . For nighttime strollers, mosquito repellent is recommended. . . . The **area code** is 6361.

ACCOMMODATIONS: The hotels of Kuşadasi tend to be less expensive than in Izmir but are often presold to European tour groups. One of the best values is a super-centrally located hotel, the **Akdeniz** (tel. 6361/1120), on Arslanlar Caddesi. If you walk up Kahramanlar Caddesi and take the first right turn, you'll find the Akdeniz by the heavy ivy and grape-leaf blanket overhanging the street from its terrace restaurant. There are 42 simple rooms, most with private facilities; a bed-and-breakfast double runs 17000 TL ($21) and a single is 9600 TL ($12). The Akdeniz is now open year round and offers a 35% winter discount. Farther uphill on the right is the small, very Turkish-style **Otel Ada** (tel. 6361/4282), where kilims, copperware, and carpets predominate. You'll feel more Turkish than tourist but at 1100 TL ($14) for a tidy, ethnic double with bath this place is a find. The lefthand lane below the Akdeniz, Eski Pazayeri Sokat, offers very simple but plain accommodations for the same price at No. 15, the modest **Hotel Kuşadasi** (tel. 6361/1315).

Kuşadasi has several fine pensions clustered on the side streets between the town center and south to the old marina. The **Yunus Pansiyon** (tel. 6361/2268) is at 7 Istiklâl, off the harborside Atatürk Bulvari. It's an 11-room pension where guests can throw open their windows without the din of tourists nightspots. Doubles cost 16,000 TL ($20) with breakfast; all have private baths.

Next door at no. 9 is the **Ci Dem Pansiyon** (tel. 6361/1895). The 20 rooms are clean, well maintained, and functional. Doubles with private bath cost 16,000 TL ($20), and bathless doubles with private shower and toilet down the hall cost 12,800 TL ($16); all rates include breakfast, served on their pleasant flower-filled terrace.

On the same street, at 3 Istiklâl Caddesi, is the **Gurup Pansiyon** (tel. 6361/1230), a family-run place with 21 rooms with private facilities. Couples will pay 20,000 TL ($25), single travelers 14,400 TL ($18) for a room, use of the second-floor sundeck and breakfast on their vine-covered front porch. Up the block at No. 13 is the new **Akman Hotel** (tel. 6361/1501). Forty-seven balconied rooms offer views of the town and harbor; the Akman has a small bar, roof sundeck with chaises longues, and Ping-Pong table to accommodate guests. Double bed and board runs 30,000 TL ($37). One block farther from the town on the lane parallel to Istiklal is the small, often overlooked **Posaci Turistik Pansiyon** (tel. 6361/1151). Some of the Posaci's spartan rooms have private bathrooms; all cost the same—10,000 TL ($13) for a single, 16,000 TL ($20) for a double, including breakfast.

As Kuşadasi's sea-level real estate is consumed by gold, carpet, and leather salesmen, hoteliers have begun moving south two kilometers to the crowded Kadinlar Denizi beach, north among the condos above the Turban Marina, and straight up above the heart of town itself. A steep stairway (for the hardy only) leads to several pensions and a few hotels which hug the hillside overlooking the ferry pier. The **Hotel Stella** (tel. 6361/1632) is one of the best of these. Five stories of front-facing balconied rooms offer wonderful views over the harbor and tiny Küçük Ada (the islet with the medieval castle on it). All have private baths, terra-cotta tile floors, and carpets (for sale of course) galore. It all makes for a cozy Turkish sense of hospitality. Double rooms with breakfast cost 29,000 TL ($36). Up behind the Stella, at 4 Kaya Aldoğan Caddesi, is the **Aran Turistik Otel** (tel. 6361/1076). The Aran was discovered by Frommer reader Mary Mabie, of Montana, and even though the rates have gone up since her stay, it's still a good deal for the area. Most of its 22 rooms have balconies offering city and harbor views; they're well kept and comfortably furnished, have private facilities, and include breakfast in their rate of 14,400 TL ($18) for two. Nearby, the **Hotel Neptune** (tel. 6361/1540) has comparable facilities in the same price range.

Back in town, there's another choice among the many crowding the side streets off busy Kahramanlar Caddesi. The **Bahar Pansiyon** (tel. 6361/1191) is at 12 Cephane Sokak, the first lane to the left as you walk away from the harbor. The Bahar has very neat, newly tiled rooms with natural-wood furnishings and tiled private showers. The friendly management rents doubles (when not booked by groups) for 21,000 TL ($26), including breakfast. If all else fails (and in high season, it will), contact the Tourist Information Office (tel. 6361/1103) for assistance, since so many hotels are currently under construction.

Campers should have better luck; try the **Mehtap Kamping** (tel. 6361/3012) at Kadinlar Denizi. They and **Olmez Kamping** have the best beachside facilities.

Two Splurge Hotels

The most interesting but now touristy hotel in Kuşadasi is the **Kervansaray Hotel** (tel. 6361/4115), originally built in 1618 by Öküz Mehmet Paşa as a way station for his caravan of camels, servants, and subjects. It's an intriguing place to stay, with low, arched stone doorways leading into narrow passages. Graceful vaulted ceilings, heavy wooden doors, large fireplaces, and brightly colored kilims add to the ethnic ambience. No matter which of the 40 rooms (all with private bath) you book, you'll be able to enjoy the Kervansaray's stunning two-story courtyard, centered around a beautifully sculpted stone fountain. Unfortunately, it now becomes a boisterous nightclub after dark. If you can't get a room here (group-tour alert) or can't afford it, come in for a drink and look around. Bed-and-breakfast doubles cost $54 and singles cost $38 (compulsory half-board in the high season adds $7 per person).

Our favorite splurge, one noteworthy for its beautiful views over land and sea, is the **Otel Kismet** (tel. 6361/2005). The Kismet is perched high up on the cliffs overlooking the old-yacht marina (the one-kilometer walk into the heart of Kuşadasi keeps the touristic frenzy at a safe distance). The Kismet is favored by visiting dignitaries and a chic foreign crowd; however, the tennis courts, pool, scenic outdoor café, and elegant restaurant may sway some of you. Its 65 luxurious rooms cost $57 for two and $42 for one, including breakfast.

RESTAURANTS: Kuşadasi caters to the hordes of day-tripping tourists from cruise ships, English tour groups, and Greek excursions. Most restaurants get in on this action, serving prepackaged groups. Fortunately there are still some good, moderately priced restaurants throughout the town.

Along the main shopping street, Kahramanlar Caddesi, three lanes up from the harbor just before the police station, on the left, is a little side street called Bozkurt Sokak. Make a right and a sharp left to find **Kral'in Yeri**; a pleasant walled-in garden where Turkish musicians serenade you through the night. Kral'in Yeri is popular with tourists more for its authentic ambience than for its typical food.

Farther down this gourmand's alley, at no. 8, is a unique pizza parlor named **Meshur Dede** (tel. 3403). You'll find the proprietor; grandson of the deceased founder, poking his head into an antique oven, which he stokes with wood. His pizza looks more like a pastry or meat pie than the goopy-cheesey thing we're used to, but the *wiande pizza* of diced lamb, tomatoes, onions, parsley, sweet peppers, and basil was out of this world, and only $1 a portion.

For a heavier, more filling meal, sample one of the hearty stews offered at the **Konya Restaurant** (tel. 1484), at 3 Kahramanlar Caddesi. Kuşadasi's fishermen, who sell off the fish they catch for the high prices it will fetch on the market, enjoy eating meat dishes here. Our favorite is the *haslamalar*, a local peasant concoction of stewed ground meat, served with rice and white beans in tomato sauce, for 1000 TL ($1.25). Back down Kahramanlar, opposite the police station on the second floor is another good choice for simple, typical cuisine, called **Haci Dede.** On a sheltered terrace you can sip "aged" Turkish red wine and admire the view over the turrets of the Kervansaray Hotel. This dry, tasty wine from the barrel goes superbly with the warm pita and walnut spice spread that's served as an appetizer. Haci Dede does a big tourist trade, but the staff is accommodating and two can dine on *paklican* (eggplant) kebabs, good mezes, and a variety of lamb dishes for 8000 TL ($10). Another restaurant that's popular for its ambience and authentic cooking is **Sultan Han** (tel. 3849), which occupies two floors of a restored house at 8 Bahar Sokak, the second lane off Kahramanlar. Diners are seated in small parlors and larger common rooms, then surrounded by carpets, kilims, copperware, and carved wood. Reservations are recommended here; prices are about the same as Haci Dede.

Our favorite choice for seafood—always a luxury item on the Aegean coast—is **Ferah** (tel. 1281), a longtime local favorite that's moved out to the port to compete with the more expensive Kazim Usta and Toros cafés. Ferah is on a quiet stretch of the harbor (Liman Caddesi) just past the Tourist Information Office and the cruise ship, férry Samos pier. We dined outdoors, away from the din, with our good friend Zaki, who ordered *yaprak sarmak* (rolled grape leaves stuffed with rice and spices), *imam bayildi* (stuffed eggplant), crisp fava beans, and an excellent Russian potato salad to accompany our raki. For an entrée we had freshly grilled şiş kepap of *trança*, a local fish served in large, fleshy cubes with peppers and tomatoes. Our three hours of feasting under the stars only cost 9600 TL ($12) each.

READERS' RESTAURANT SELECTIONS: "The best restaurant we ate in at Kusadasi is the **Öz Urfa,** Doner ve Kebab Salonu, Kazim Zorlu. The food was excellent, the clientele almost entirely German or Turkish and very little English was spoken" (Dr. and Mrs. King, Brentwood Bay, British Columbia, Can.) . . . "Downhill from the Akdeniz Hotel is a baklava shop . . . it's a great place to eat and they have the best and freshest baklava in town. They don't even want to let you have it if it isn't fresh" (Ms. J. Maureen Bangston, San Clemente, Calif.).

NIGHTLIFE: There are alternatives (though not many that are better) to whiling away an evening under the stars. Kuşadasi's sudden thrust into the tourism mainstream has brought a nightlife scene with it.

Every Wednesday evening at **Ada** (tel. 1725), the seafood café that hugs the shore of the tiny Kücük Ada (the pigeon-covered Bird Island that gave its name to the town), there is a special Turkish Night. Belly dancers, folk musicians, and classical Turkish music replaces the usual disco scene. On Wednesday, their set menu of regional specialties and entertainment cost 7200 TL to 9000 TL ($9 to $11.25) per person. If you want to dine elsewhere, the cover charge for the show only is 4500 TL ($6). The **Kervansaray Hotel** (tel. 4115) has nightly entertainment in its beautiful stone courtyard. From Monday to Thursday they offer a Turkish special evening that includes dinner and a floor show-cum-belly dancer for 25,000 TL ($31). Reservations recommended; performances during summer months only.

Another turn-on of a more personal nature is a traditional Turkish bath and massage. Two old hamami have recently been restored, thanks to tourism demands. The **Belediye Hamami** (tel. 1219) is in the center of the old town (off Kahramanlar Caddesi), behind the post office. The **Kale İçi Hamami** (tel. 1292) is on Yildirim Caddesi, up behind the Akdeniz Hotel. Both are open Monday to Saturday from 7 a.m. to 10 p.m., unless a coed tour group commandeers the main domed chamber for themselves. Reservations are recommended for their bath and massage session; this costs 6000 TL ($7.50), self-bathing only 1200 TL ($1.50).

WHAT TO SEE AND DO: In Kuşadasi activity revolves around shopping and taking day trips elsewhere to sightsee.

Shopping

As mentioned, the main shopping street, other than the harborside plazas, is **Kahramanlar Caddesi**, the unmistakable call of the multilingual merchant will be heard everywhere. Fortunately for the comparison shopper, all the carpet, jewelry, and leather shops are within close proximity and can be carefully examined in a few hours. We found prices about the same as those in Istanbul (no more than 20% higher if you avoid the harbor shops), and all the shops sold similar merchandise.

Our most pleasant souvenir of Kuşadasi is the evening spent in the shop of antique merchant Zaki Bilge. **Zaki Baba** (tel. 2967), at 32 Kahramanlar, is a fascinating shop filled with Anatolian crafts, jewelry, and folk art. After receiving his law degree in Paris, Zaki returned to practice in Turkey. Claiming "Lawyers, by definition, must lie, and I cannot," Zaki decided to open a shop of personally chosen antiques and crafts. What's so appealing about Zaki in comparison with other Turkish merchants is his obvious preference for socializing with customers in French, English, or Turkish, rather than actually selling them something. He's really worth dropping in on.

Day Trips

Kuşadasi is a good base for boat and bus day trips.

To Samos: Regularly scheduled car-ferries line up at the main pier daily, from June through December, for the 2½-hour trip to Samos. Boats depart at 8:30 a.m. and 5 p.m. both to and from the port of Samos town. Tickets can be purchased at the pier before departure, or from the several nearby travel agents, such as **Diana** (tel. 1399), **Skalanova** (tel. 3268), **Azim** (tel. 1553). The 1987 fare was $25 one way, $30 same-day return, $45 round trip.

To Ephesus: Since this is the site most people come for, minibuses shuttle back and forth from the Otobus Garaji all day; the fare is 425 TL (50¢). Allow a full day for your Ephesus excursion to appreciate the many wonders of this ancient city. Several travel agencies offer guided bus tours of Ephesus for $18.

To Aphrodisias and Pamukkale: The archeological dig at Aphrodisias, where a New York University team has uncovered a Hellenistic city with a well-preserved stadium, has one of the best museums of sculpture in the region. An intellectual's visit here, and a hedonist's visit to the bubbling, calcium-filled mineral springs of Pamukkale (intellectuals can go the necropolis) are often combined in a one-day excursion offered by several local travel agents. Both places can actually be visited more cheaply by public transportation, but we can't endorse wasting ten hours of your vacation getting lost or missing buses just to save $30.) One of the many travel agencies offering this full-day package is **Turquoise Tours** (tel. 1392), at 10 Yali Caddesi; they charged about $30 in 1987. You can also check with your hotel or the Tourist Information Office about current local tours and about taxi fares, currently $80 for a cab seating four.

To Didyma, Priene, and Miletos: Didyma is best known for the Didymaion, a sixth-century B.C. Temple to Apollo. The priests, called branchids, served as Oracles in one of the most important Ionian sanctuaries. When Alexander the Great rebuilt it in the third century B.C., it stood as the third-largest temple in the ancient world. Nearby was the once-prosperous city (built according to an urban plan instituted by Hippodamos at Philippi) of **Priene**, excavated to reveal a large theater, Bouleuterion (Senate meeting hall), and the Temple to Athena designed by Pytheos, the father of Ionian architecture. This site is vastly more impressive than what can be seen at **Miletos**, but archeologists have uncovered Minoan and Mycenaean remains at lower levels of Miletos which prove its importance in archaic times. These sites constitute another popular package sold by tour and excursion operators for about $21. Because they are located so close to one another, you might prefer to make a group of four and book a taxi for the day. For $50 your group can have the freedom of movement that tour buses just don't allow.

GETTING TO AND FROM KUŞADASI: From Kuşadasi, there are hourly buses daily to Izmir, departing from the Otobus Garaji. The nearest train north to Izmir or Istanbul can be caught in Selçuk, the way station of ancient Ephesus (Selçek is about 20 minutes away). The Central Garage has minibuses running to Selçuk every half hour from 7 a.m. to 8:30 p.m. for a fare of 425 TL (55¢).

Note that Selçuk is the through point for buses south from Kuşadasi to Bodrum or Marmaris (they cannot be caught in town). Every half hour one should be pulling into the Selçuk bus stop. If Bodrum is your destination, three buses depart Kuşadasi's Central Garage each morning for Bodrum direct. The 2400-TL ($3) fare may be worthwhile for the increased speed and comfort of the ride. Turkish Maritime Lines has thrice weekly cruises from nearby Mersin to Cyprus ($39 one way). Check the Tourist Office for information.

BETWEEN KUŞADASI AND BODRUM OR MARMARIS: Here is the town of **Milas**, where two of the region's newest and oldest businesses coexist: a statewide industry of electric power generation and a local cottage industry of the manufacture of hand-woven carpets. Many of the most beautiful Turkish carpets and kilims sold in cities and tourist centers come from the nimble fingers of the women of Milas. Even today most of these women card their own wool and dye it with the powdered roots of indigenous plants. Most carpets larger than five by seven feet are woven by two people; when husbands are not ploughing their fields or working at the electric plant, they lend a hand. The ten or twelve carpets woven annually by each of these families are sent to the **Milas Bazaar**, where dealers and distributors shop for retail stores and foreign markets. Readers who are seriously interested in purchasing a rug can stop in Milas; it's on every bus route to or from Kuşadasi, Bodrum, or Marmaris.

Small shops along **Hacilyas Meydani Kadiaga Caddesi**, in the bazaar, and the large showroom of **Ahmet Gürdağ** (tel. 1844), at Güveşde de Caddesi, offer a wide selection of rugs at 30% to 50% less than what you'd pay at a retail shop. Mr. Gürdağ can often supply the name of the woman who wove the rug.

Those touring the coast will travel overland from Kuşadasi to Bodrum, along dusty inland roads where traffic competes with sheep and stray cows. The verdant pine forests that cover the peninsula crowned by Bodrum provide welcome relief to those who trampled through the gravel and buckthorn of Priene, Miletos, and Didyma on the way.

10. Bodrum

A town blessed by nature and man, Bodrum is the finest Aegean resort in Turkey. The clean beauty of its natural harbor and the abundance of pine trees are a refreshing change from the arid north. Bodrum was noteworthy in antiquity—when it was called Halikarnassos—both as part of the Dorian confederation as well as for the Mausoleum, another of the ancient world's seven wonders. Halikarnassos was the birthplace of Herodotus, considered the father of history, whose writing about the ancient world is both poetic and amusing. The Castle of St. Peter, a magnificent 15th-century fortress built by the crusading Knights of Rhodes, juts out into the bay at the midpoint of the waterfront, creating two distinct harbors.

Today, tarred pine-wood and white stucco construction give the town a sparkling antique aura. Bodrum has maintained its historical appearance due to stringent zoning laws that prohibit building higher than two stories. To further reduce the effects of commercialization (and cars), roads running through the center of town and by the eastern bay are closed to traffic; the whole town becomes a lovely pedestrian thoroughfare in the busy summer season.

Like its Greek model Mykonos, Bodrum has the most fun-loving and active party scene on the Turkish coast. Bohemian nightspots abound, with revelers often reveling until four in the morning. Bodrum is alluring despite the recent influx of group tours. Although it has survived years of tourism, however, its intensive development indicates it may succumb to the "quick buck" syndrome of other Turkish resort areas.

ORIENTATION: You're approaching Bodrum when you begin to see newly constructed white stucco houses adorned with miniature turrets. This design, a peculiar architectural habit, clearly echoes the crennellations of Bodrum's centerpiece, **Saint Peter's Castle**. Centuries ago this fortification was an island in the center of the bay. The link between island and mainland was made after subsequent additions to the original fort. Bodrum now consists of two small bays running east to west and divided by the castle. The eastern bay, around which are the majority of nightspots and accommodations, is referred to as **Deniz** ("sea"). **Cumhuriyet Caddesi**, the road around Deniz, is the summertime boardwalk (cars are routed to the back of town). **Yat Limani** (Yacht Harbor) is the western bay, and it's lined with Bodrum's more expensive and expansive open-air restaurants. The Tourist Information Office and the main pier are at the base of the castle, in the center of town. The Central Garage, where all the buses and dolmushes operate from, is on the western side of town near the market, about 250 meters inland from the castle.

USEFUL INFORMATION: The **Tourist Information Office** (tel. 6141/1091), at the base of the castle, is open Monday through Saturday from 8:30 a.m. to 5:30 p.m. (closed from noon to 1 p.m. for lunch) and until 8:30 p.m. in peak season. Mr. Baki Pala, the office director, and his staff are very helpful. . . . The **post office,** across from the bus garage, is open until midnight for making phone calls, their branch next to the castle is open till 5:30 p.m. . . . . **Banks** are open Monday through Friday from 8:30 a.m. to noon and 1:30 p.m. to 5:30 p.m., but several money changers near the Tourist Office are open until 8 p.m. every day. . . . The **hospital** (tel. 1068) and **police** (tel. 1004) are both located by the castle base. . . . **Yeşil Marmaris** (tel. 6141/2375), the travel agency that began the Blue Coast cruises out of Marmaris, now has a Bodrum office at Atatürk Caddesi. Contact them about budget yacht cruises along the Aegean and Mediterannean coasts. . . . The **area code** is 6141.

GETTING AROUND: The town itself is ideal for **walking**; all of the restaurants, hotels, and historical sites are within an easy stroll of each other. Beachgoers can rent a **bicycle**, at 4200 TL ($5) per day, the dreaded **moped**, at 8000 TL ($10) per day, and a **Jeep** (try **Avis** at tel. 2333) or take a **minibus**. A fun way is by boat; **caïques** visit various destinations starting out at the dock next to the Tourist Information Office. Normally caïques depart when there are enough people to fill a boat.

Among the ports along the Turkish coast, Bodrum is known for **yacht rentals**. It's certainly romantic, but such romance comes at a steep price. A 15- to 20-meter skippered boat that can hold 10 to 12 people costs $200 to $350 per day (assuming you make arrangements through the captain). Several travel agencies specialize in booking yachts, such as **Gündüz Travel and Yachting** (tel. 1551), **Aegean Yacht Services** (tel. 1734), at 202 Neyzen Tevfik Caddesi—they also have offices in Istanbul, London, and Paris—and **Bodrumtour** (tel. 1786), at 218 Yar Limani Caddesi, or in Istanbul. Many people come to Bodrum in the height of the summer expecting to find a boat for rent and are disappointed that nothing is available. Other agencies that arrange boat trips are: **Anba Travel and Yachting** (tel. 1587) and **Durukos Travel** (tel. 1868), located near the Tourist Information Office.

ACCOMMODATIONS: There are now hundreds of hotels and pensions in Bodrum, but finding a room in summer, especially because Bodrum attracts European group tours, may require persistence. At the low end are places that call themselves pensions but are really homes which have a spare room or two. Most hotels are of fairly recent vintage and moderately priced for such a popular resort.

Deniz

Most of the best-value lodgings are concentrated in a compact half-kilometer stretch between the center of town and Otel Halikarnas. However, a special place to stay is a recently built five-room complex called the **Villa Bergamut** (tel. 6141/1716), 500 meters farther east, around the corner and over the hill, from the Halikarnas. Mehmet Aran, a young and well-educated architect, built and owns these exquisite villas. Each room has a full kitchen, fireplace, double and single bed, and bathroom. The kilims on the floor are of first quality and design, and all rooms are spacious enough to comfortably accommodate two to four. At 32,000 TL ($40) for a room, the luxurious Bergamut is a great value.

Bodrum's landmark *Love Boat*–style **Otel Halikarnas** (tel. 6141/1073) crowns the Deniz (or Kumbahçe area) hotel and café strip. Readers who don't want to sleep above the town's biggest disco should look elsewhere for accommodations. One uphill block above the Otel Halikarnas is the small **Otel Merve** (tel. 6141/1278), at 103 Atatürk Caddesi. Its less attractive location is compensated for by a peaceful night's rest. The Merve's homey details (Oriental throw rugs, soft pink guest towels, and a host who croons Turkish ballads from the flower-covered terrace) make their comfortable new rooms a good deal: rooms with private facilities and phones run 16,000 TL ($20) for a single, 17,600 TL ($22) for a double, and 22,000 TL ($28) for a triple.

Downhill from the Merve is the **Artemis Pension** (tel. 6141/2530), on the waterfront, at 117 Cumhuriyet, and closer to the center of town. The Artemis has 23 rooms, all carpeted and with showers. A double costs 27,000 TL ($34), including breakfast.

Another choice is the **Karya Otel** (tel. 6141/1523). The Karya is nearby on the waterfront; its whitewashed exterior and pine-trimmed rooms are similar to those of the Artemis. Next door is the **Dinç Pension** (tel. 6141/1141), another of Bodrum's wood, wrought-iron, and whitewashed waterside inns. Though the name is pronounced "Dinge," the pension is anything but, with 20 spic-and-span, fully carpeted rooms. Doubles are 28,000 TL ($35); singles run 19,200 TL ($24), including breakfast.

Down the street from the Dinç is the **Hotel Gozegir** (tel. 6141/2541), where there are 48 rooms, all with showers, and all clean and comfortable. Downstairs is an open-air restaurant with a perfect view of the castle—a nice place to dine, watch the sun set, and let the world go by. Bed and breakfast for two costs 28,220 TL ($35.25); for one, 20,700 TL ($25).

There are pensions closer to the heart of Bodrum, but since this is a late-night town, expect late-night noise. Walking westward toward town, you'll come to a right fork off the boardwalk called Üç Kuyular Sokak. About 200 meters up this street is the eight-room **Çem** (tel. 6141/1757), a pension with a warm and cozy ambience. Two can stay for 24,000 TL ($30); this price includes breakfast.

Directly next door, at 17 Üç Kuyular Sokak, is the **Murat Villa** (tel. 6141/1710), with a new pool and marble-tiled sundeck next to the blue-and-white umbrellas of an outdoor café. Small, simple rooms with private facilities run 24,000 TL ($30), including breakfast.

Adjacent to the Çem and the Murat Villa, at 11 Üç Kuyular Caddesi, is the **Otel Alize** (tel. 6141/1401), a whitewashed 30-room lodging set back from the road. This new hotel's stark courtyard surrounds a good-sized pool; comfortable rooms with private facilities and breakfast cost 26,400 TL ($34) for two. A bit farther down, toward the port, is a small bougainvillea-covered pension called the **Evin Pansyon** (tel. 6141/1312). The Evin, at 7 Ortanca Sokak, has very simple rooms with bath and a pretty rooftop terrace. Double rooms, when not group-booked, rent for 16,200 TL ($20). The 14-room **Mylasa Hotel** (tel. 6141/1846) is a new addition to this end of the waterfront, at 34 Cumhuriyet Caddesi. A tasteful lobby and rooftop sundeck add some class to an otherwise ordinary place; rooms are 10,400 TL ($13) for one, 16,800 TL ($21) for two, and 28,000 TL ($34) for three, with breakfast. Farther down, at 217 Cumhuriyet Caddesi, is the small, clean **Villa Bakiş Pansyon** (tel. 6141/2225). Some of their bathless rooms have a good view of the Aegean and cost only 13,000 TL ($16) for two, with breakfast. The Villa Bakiş, though not fancy, is at least quieter.

One of the better in-town inns, at 88 Cumhuriyet Caddesi, is the **Mercan Pansiyon** (tel. 6141/1111). The new lobby restaurant appears to be below sea level; when breakfast is served you could swear the water's lapping at your toes! Refurbished rooms with tiled bathrooms and spectacular harbor views run 17,600 TL ($22) for two, including breakfast.

Yat Limani

The area on the bay is preferred by some because of its proximity to the Kos ferry pier, the yacht harbor, and quieter accommodations. The most inviting pension is the **Herodot** (tel. 6141/1093), at 116 Neyzen Tevfik Caddesi. This 15-

room lodging is simple but clean, drenched with sunlight, and has small balconies overlooking the yachts. A double room with cold running water and bathing facilities in the hallway costs 10,400 TL ($13); a bathless single runs 8800 TL ($11). There's an additional 3000 TL ($3.75) charge for private showers in the room.

Most of the other accommodations near the ferry pier are small, spartan pensions with only cold water, a clean sheet, and a cheap price to recommend them. The **Tepe Pansiyon** is at 24 Nevzen Tevfik, opposite the mosque. A friendly family here keeps five neat rooms with cots that rent for 3600 TL ($4.50) each. The **Şehirioğlu,** next door, is another option (also without phone) that could be tried in a pinch.

A Splurge Hotel

There was a day on Turkey's Aegean coast when only a five-star hotel could be called a splurge, but those days are long gone. Bodrum's newest three-star hotel, the **Hotel Manastir** (tel. 6141/2858), has just been added to the hillside above Deniz in the Kumbahçe Mahallesi, and it's special enough to warrant a splurge. Its 43 rooms each have their own patio with aerial views over the harbor, castle, and bay. Built on the grounds of a former monastery, Manastir offers tennis, a large attractive pool and sundeck, and an elegant bar and outdoor café. Furnishings are in the de Stijl vein; geometric wood forms in shades of blue complement the whitewashed stucco basics. Evil eyes hover over the doorways, adding an amusingly Turkish touch to such an internationally chic place. Their compulsory half-board plan brings a double room rate in season to 53,000 TL ($66).

READERS' HOTEL SELECTION: "In Bodrum we found all accommodations booked and went to Gümbet, about 3 kilometers north. It is situated on a cove, nice beaches, and is undergoing a lot of building. . . . Our hotel, the **Bavaria** (tel. 6141/1944), was about two to three minutes' uphill from the beach. There is a reasonably good restaurant on the beach in a campground and trailer park; it's a very scenic setting. The proprietors Gülten and Cekti Göksu were extremely nice and accommodating. Their hotel (actually called a pension) has 18 rooms, lots of hot water, new furniture, and superb hosts. They do not speak English but we conversed readily in French and German. Their rates for a double including breakfast were $18 to $22" (Dr. and Mrs. David King, Brentwood Bay, British Columbia, Can.).

RESTAURANTS AND NIGHTLIFE: Everything is so compact and integrated in Bodrum that eating, drinking, and listening to live music are events that all tend to fall together naturally.

One of our favorite spots is **Amphora** (tel. 2368), at the far end of Liman (164 Neyzen Tevfik Caddesi) on the waterfront. The restaurant, with wooden tables under a grape-leaf canopy, has a fine view of the harbor. During the off-season Amphora's cozy interior with carpets and a fireplace makes it a popular café for locals. Specialties include *antepezme* (tomato, hot ground pepper, onions, parsley, olive oil, all finely chopped) and *tatar meze* (made with eggplant, yogurt, green pepper, chile, and garlic). At No. 36 is **Meryem Ana** (tel. 2239). Even though Meryem Ana is a fish restaurant, we'd recommend the şiş kepap—it's cheaper than their fish şiş and very flavorful. A complete meal for two shouldn't cost more than 8000 TL ($10) at either.

A few doors down is the **Korfez Restaurant** (tel. 1105). There are actually two Korfezes in Bodrum; both are attractive but this is a quieter, more out-of-the-way café (the other one is in the center of town with a beachside patio). Tables are set under trellis-trained vines and hanging plants. Gentle breezes from the harbor filter through the dense foliage. The two specialties are fish soup, *balik corbasi,* and the local favorite, *Adana köfte,* grilled chopped meat that's probably hotter and spicier than any köfte you may have eaten before. Fish is fresh and well prepared, but as usual, check prices before ordering or you might find yourself writing an unexpected traveler's check to cover the charge.

If you want to eat in a more lively area, head to a café- and bar-lined street —it's actually more of an alleyway—called **Eski Banka**, just off the main shopping avenue in the center of Bodrum. A large trellis stretches across some of the buildings, and vines crisscross this cobblestone lane overhead. Casual strolling is almost impossible because tables from the various establishments spill out onto the street and are jammed together; it's a cozy atmosphere.

On Eski Banka Sokak dining and nightlife become one; two especially good restaurants—the **Ibo** and the **Ilyada**—are across from a couple of bars and music clubs. All serve the same variety of food and all are low to moderately priced. One of the things that makes dining in these cafés so interesting is that they serve a huge variety of mezes. You could literally spend the evening grazing, sampling delicious plates of Turkish appetizers. We even found *manti,* a meat-filled ravioli in a yogurt and spice sauce. Another local specialty is *kiymali pide,* a ground meat, onion, and spice-filled bread "canoe" sold with spinach böreks; you'll find the pide shop down the main street opposite the Cinaj Hotel on the Deniz waterfront.

Actually, some of the best low-budget dining spots are the outdoor cafés on the east side of Bodrum, along the picturesque harborfront. Again, these restaurants (including the other Körfez) are near some of Bodrum's best bars and clubs. On the harbor street, Cumhuriyet, directly overlooking the water, is one of Bodrum's favorite hangouts, the **Big Ben.** It's a pretty splashy place, including live bouzouki music, dancing, and an "American bar" (a bar where you stand while the bartender mixes drinks).

The next 300-meter stretch along the concrete, trafficless boardwalk is lined with great Turkish fast-food joints, mostly operating out of family kitchens. The **Bursa Inegöl Köftecisi** serves a regional specialty—a cheese-filled meatball.

The best bars are on the far side of either shore. The friendly **Jazz Café,** on the Yat Limani near the Kos-bound ferry, is one of Bodrum's best. Print cotton cushions on low banquettes, antelope skins, African masks over a fireplace, and the frisky black-and-white dog, Melissa, make up the decor. Good-looking, English-speaking Gengiz and Mete serve their guests to the tune of modern jazz till 3 a.m. nightly.

Another favorite café, the **Mavi,** is at the far end of Deniz. Be careful entering, because nearly everyone trips over a raised floorboard near the door. Once inside, look around and admire the works of local artists, white stucco walls, and pine beams. The plethora of comfortable cushions, couches, and lamps makes it feel anything but outdoors, but it is. Live jazz, folk, and blues bands provide entertainment, and it's possible to sit indefinitely sipping liqueurs and watching the stars.

Just up the hill from the Mavi is the previously mentioned Halikarnas Hotel, the mecca of upscale disco-goers and Bodrum's all-night party.

READER'S RESTAURANT SELECTION: "I found *monte* (a delicious homemade pasta) on my first night in town. It is available at the **Lugano Restaurant,** located on the little square in the heart of Bodrum. Monte is not available until about 3 p.m. because it takes a long time to make and that's when the lady in the house next door has it ready. The Lugano is an all-around great place to eat" (Ms. Maureen Bangston, San Clemente, Calif.).

WHAT TO SEE AND DO: Although Halikarnassos was an important port in antiquity, Bodrum offers aesthetic and hedonistic pleasures more than ancient ruins. However, the portside Crusader **Castle of St. Peter** is a lot of fun to walk around and contains an excellent and unique **Museum of Underwater Archeology.** The castle is an eclectic edifice, partially constructed with stones, pillars, and friezes from the Mausoleum (see below), much in the way the fortifications on Rhodes were constructed from the ruins of the ancient acropolis. Rhodian knights, including the French, Italians, English, and Germans, laid the basic foundation for the fort in 1402, and then constructed a tower. Many of the halls and towers display superb collections of objects found underwater, some dating as far back as 1300 B.C. The majority of objects are utilitarian pottery and tools of great archeological worth. By far the more interesting part of the collection is the Mycenean and Islamic blown glass. It's open daily 8:30 a.m. to noon, 1 p.m. to 5:30 p.m. but in summer reopens at 3 p.m. till 7 p.m., closed Monday. Admission is 800 TL ($1), free for students.

The tomb of King Mausolus, otherwise known as the **Mausoleum** (thus the term), was built by the king's wife in 350 B.C. A 24-step pyramid, set on a high base, was crowned by a four-horsed chariot at a height of 40 meters! The impression of this ancient tomb, as reconstructed in the display area, is spectacular, and, according to Pliny, it was one of the seven wonders of the ancient world. Unfortunately, generations of pirates, Turks, and medieval knights totally ransacked the monument. Even the few statues that were found (one of the king, another of his wife) have been carted off to the British Museum. Walk two blocks in from the Liman side of the harbor and you'll find the site. The Mausoleum keeps the same hours as the Castle; admission is 300 TL (35¢).

BEACHES: Beaches are somewhat of a problem in Bodrum. The best beaches are at **Turgutreis and Akyalar Villages,** where there's camping. There are several beach boat trips. Fishing-style boats leave the pier next to the Tourist Office at about 11 a.m. and return at 6 p.m. The 3600 TL ($4.50) trip is a relaxing, inexpensive, and fun way to get a feel for the Turkish Aegean, although the beaches (some are just rocks you jump off) sometimes leave cleanliness to be desired. From the numerous competing boats, look for the funky *Yasmin,* captained by Unal Sencicek (his last name means "Happy Flower"—very apt). Unal may burst into spectacular Turkish songs if he's in the right mood. . . .

You can also rent private boats at a daily rate of $30 to $60, depending on size. These can take you to farther-away beaches, some of which are accessible by minibus. Check with the Tourist Office for this year's most popular beaches, and information on public transportation to them.

Bodrum's fame as a center for underwater archeology has spawned a scuba diving mini-industry. Contact the local **Data** (tel. 1443), **Turquoise Diving** (tel. 1244), **Triton** (tel. 1174) or **Sea Tour** (tel. 2454) agents for information about day trips.

SHOPPING: True to its Mykonos-like appeal, Bodrum offers some of the most sophisticated shopping in this part of Turkey. The ubiquitous **Mudo**, the Benetton of Turkey (and now Benetton itself) has a large shop diagonally across from the Tourist Information Office. There you'll find a bright and happy selection of the latest international fashions, from casual to almost naked, and at near-budget prices (most bathing suits run $15 to $20). Along Yat Limani and on Deniz's main street are some of the chicest **leather shops** we've discovered in Turkey. Italian-inspired designs made with the country's best skins at reasonable prices distinguish these shops. Wander down the main street along the Deniz side and you'll find numerous high fashion shoe- and sandal-makers, all waiting to fit you into the latest in intricate, multistrap foot fashions. For less than the price of an inexpensive hotel room you can pick up a custom-made pair.

GETTING TO KOS: Two boats depart every day (leaving at 9:30 a.m. or 10:30 a.m. and returning at 5 p.m. or 6 p.m.) for the Greek island of Kos (the nine-mile voyage takes 1½ hours). Tickets are $15 one way and $20 return. Tickets are sold at **Karya Tours** (tel. 1759) and other travel agencies. Boats run infrequently during the off-season; contact the portside Tourist Information Office for the current schedule.

GETTING TO AND FROM BODRUM: Two bus companies—**Pamukkale Otobus** (tel. 1369) and **Karadeveci Otobus** (tel. 2560)—serve Bodrum and depart from the Central Garage. Buses to Izmir leave almost hourly from 5 a.m. to 7 p.m., costing 3000 TL ($4); to Istanbul twice a day—it's a 14-hour journey—costing 9600 TL ($12); to Marmaris five times daily, costing 2100 TL ($3); and to Fethiye (Antalya) twice daily, costing 3400 TL ($4.25). The two ways of getting to and from Dalaman Airport are to take the Fethiye bus, which goes directly, or to go to Muğla on the Marmaris bus and transfer to Dalaman. Check with the THY office, which may also offer bus service.

11. Marmaris

It's impossible to describe the scenery around the port city of Marmaris as anything less than breathtaking. Whether you approach from land or sea, the pine-covered craggy peaks, turquoise bay, eucalyptus groves, and fjord-like geography make this the most dramatically scenic spot along the Turkish Aegean coast.

Marmaris has long been home to Turkey's yachting set. During the past decade European sailors have steadily migrated south, making Marmaris today a cosmopolitan seaman's haven. A stroll down the town's attractive waterfront tells the story: a vista of deep-blue bays, scores of bright-white hotels, bars and restaurants, and bobbing boats hailing from as far away as Southampton, England, and Fort Worth, Texas. For those who've forgotten their vessels at home, be assured that this sailor's delight offers a varied program of day trips, bareboat and crewed yacht rentals, and weekly yacht cruises. Even if you don't like sailing, Marmaris has some fine beaches and over 50 carpet shops. There really is something for everyone.

Marmaris is one of Turkey's major jumping-off points for Greek island-hoppers, with ferries making the 2½-hour trip to Rhodes. If you're coming or going, Marmaris is a lovely destination.

ORIENTATION: Marmaris is a small, but bustling town; the best hotels are to the left of the ferry pier and the large resorts are as much as a 15-minute taxi ride away. The dock for the Rhodes boat bisects the two halves of the marina.

The portside road west (left) of the ferry dock is Atatürk Bulvari, or Kordon (Seaside) Caddesi; to the east and around the town's closed fortress is Barbaros Caddesi, or Yat Limani (Yacht Harbor). Shops fill the lanes inland from the **Tourist Information Office** (tel. 6121/1035), open every day except Sunday from 8:30 a.m. to 5:30 p.m., (closed between noon and 1 p.m.), and until 6:30 p.m. in summer. You'll find their warm, helpful staff opposite the Rhodes pier at 39 Iskele Meydani, along with a selection of brochures and town maps. . . . To **change money**, the Halkbankasi, at the passport control booth on the Rhodes ferry pier, stays open daily in summer from 9 a.m. to 8 p.m., as do some of the money changers on the Yat Limani. . . . There is a **THY office** (tel. 3751) and an **Avis** (tel. 2771) rental-car office on the Kordon. . . . The local **police** (tel. 1494) are in the center part of town. . . . . The **hospital** (tel. 1029) is nearby. . . . . The **PTT** is a block off the Kordon. . . . . The **area code** is 6121.

ACCOMMODATIONS:

They're pricey and often fully booked in summer. The best deal at the port for a clean, simple bathless room, with a balcony with town and harbor views, breakfast on a sundeck, and a friendly desk clerk is the little **Otel Pina** (tel. 6121/1053), at Iskele Meydani. It's above a shop on the first right-turning lane after you leave the Tourist Information Office. Double rooms with toilet cost only 11,000 TL ($13), $2 less without a toilet. (Since Marmaris has always catered to a well-heeled crowd, its accommodations are relatively expensive for this coast.) Another choice as you leave the boat is the small **Otel Kaptan** (tel. 6121/1251), on the right. The older, well-maintained Kaptan faces the water and is situated pluck in the middle of a row of sidewalk cafés. Simple, bathless doubles cost 19,200 TL ($24), including breakfast, but room 302, a sloped-roof loft with a small balcony and exposed wood beams, is a treat. This triple room 24,000 TL ($30) has twin beds up on the sleeping loft and a single bed in the spacious living area; it's a great place to hang out. The Kaptan has only 25 rooms and fills up early.

Our "choice" hotels are a 10-minute walk from the ferry, close to one another at the far western end (to your left) of the town. Before you start cursing that you have to cab it or schlep your heavy luggage a long way, note that these places are quiet and offer a fairly clean beach—not a bad tradeoff.

The 50-room **Hotel Karadeniz** ("Black Sea") (tel. 6121/1064) is so-called by its owner who moved from the Black Sea region in 1983. The rooms are carpeted and have balconies; many overlook the palm trees by the sea. The interior of the Karadeniz is distinguished by an unusual three-story skylight/atrium, throwing light on the upper stairway. Prices are 29,000 TL ($36) for two people, 22,000 TL ($27) for one, including breakfast. The Karadeniz is across from the beach on Atatürk Bulvari.

If you like Turkish kilims, you'll love the **Halici** (tel. 6121/1683), literally the "Carpet Motel." It's behind the Hotel Marmaris; about 100 yards off Atatürk Caddesi. Before entering the lobby, you'll cross over a small footbridge and follow a stone-lined walk past their swimming pool and colorful flower garden. The real treat for carpet lovers is the traditionally inspired coffee room, entirely covered in layers and layers of kilims. The 128-room hotel is rather drably modern, so all the carpets do a wonderful job of breathing life into the place. The Halici's owner, Ahmet Urkay, runs a thriving carpet store on the waterfront in town, and everything on the floors and walls in the hotel is for sale. The only problem here is that it's popular with groups, particularly Finns, so finding a vacant room may be difficult. Bed-and-breakfast prices are 22,400 TL ($28) for a double, 17,600 TL ($22) for a single.

If the Karadeniz and Halici are full, walk over to the **Otel Marmaris** (tel. 6121/1308); it's right on the main drag, across from the beach. The 70 clean, balconied rooms run 30,000 TL ($37) for a double, $2 less for a back view, including breakfast.

A splashy alternate choice is the **Otel Yavuz** (tel. 6121/2937), a recent addition to the harbor, on Atatürk Caddesi. The Yavuz's rooftop pool, cabañas, sundeck, and bar make the 39,000 TL ($48) double-bed-and-breakfast tariff worthwhile for pool-lovers.

The **Otel Karaca** (tel. 6121/1992), at 48 Atatürk Caddesi, is another comfortable, portside hotel whose rooms have small balconies and bright vistas. Bed-and-breakfast doubles cost 29,000 TL ($36). In the shadow of the high-rise hotels on Atatürk Caddesi is an area of pleasant, low-cost pensions, most of which can be found on 9th Sokak Street, the second lane back, between the side street next to the Maksim 5 disco and the street next to the Karaca Hotel. Most will cost between 4000 TL and 6000 TL ($5–8) per person, with breakfast. None have private baths; all are in private homes with vine-covered patios on the quiet lane. Though farthest from town, our favorite is the **Gülnür Pansiyon** (tel. 6121/2237), located on the second driveway to the left behind the Karaca Hotel. Mr. Dursur and his family will welcome you to their clean, comfortable home to share breakfast on their shaded porch. Stroll on down Ninth Street, just opposite the Gulnur's drive, and you will pass the **Gardenia Pansiyon** (tel. 6121/4131), the **Güven** (tel. 6121/3421), the **Yilmaz** (tel. 6121/3754), and the **Onay** (tel. 6121/1330). None of these qualify as luxury housing, but even in the busy months, you should be able to find a room.

READER'S HOTEL SUGGESTION: "A good clean place to stay in Marmaris is above a small store called Korton Market. This is about 75 meters to the left of the Customs Office on the waterfront road. Enquire in Korton market for rooms, which are up 2 or 3 flights of stairs. The rooms are a good size, have their own bathrooms and a lovely view of the waterfront and in December 1986 cost about $2" Mrs. Leone Marsden, Bucklands Beach, Auckland, New Zealand. (*Authors' Note:* Times have changed!)

DINING: Our favorite breakfast spot in Marmaris is the small **Taşlik café** on the waterfront, opposite the day-excursion boats. At tranquil outdoor tables ringing this bustling restaurant you can enjoy yogurt and toast, fresh-squeezed orange-juice, and thick Turkish coffee or freshly brewed tea for under 1600 TL ($2) per person. Midday, walk down the center of the three parallel bazaar lanes till you reach the bakery. Spinach and cheese pies, sweets, donuts, and whole-wheat bread are displayed on large baking trays out on the sidewalk, and the smell is heavenly.

You can pick up some picnic food to eat on the waterfront, and then finish your meal with a *dondurma* (ice cream). There are several ornately carved wood and copper stalls along the harbor promenade, which are manned by Turks in wild glitter and fur Anatolian folk costumes, who chant out invitations to sample varied flavors of ice cream. More casual lunch food can be had at the **Deva Pide Salonu,** opposite the day-trip boats along Kordon.

To hobnob with the yacht set or just savor a meal with a view, head over to Yat Limani. **Birtat, Kontes Restaurant,** and **Düses** are new outdoor cafés with excellent (not cheap) food. The smaller **Café Sail** is another popular choice. We enjoyed the new **Zühal** (tel. 4792), around the corner past most of the cafes and distinguished by its purple-wood trim and color scheme (including lilac ruffled tablecloths). Zühal's Australian and Turkish chefs whip up some gourmet Turkinental cuisine. Their rice has currants and nuts, vegetables are crisply al dente, böreks are airy and light, and their fish and meat dishes are prepared with a variety of rich sauces. Such fine fare runs about 20,000 TL ($25) for two, with wine. The harborfront's **Marmaris Pastanesi** is next door for some sweets.

For a lighter lunch or dinner, try any of the other appealing restaurants on the yacht harbor. **Dede, Kumkapi** (remember that district of yummy seafood places in Istanbul?), **Fanya, Gök,** and **Divan** hug the sidewalk opposite the elegant yachts. Mezes run 1000 TL ($1.20) to 1800 TL ($2.25) and fresh-caught fish ($6 to $12 a portion according to season) is always an excellent entrée. **Liman** and the **Hotel Karadeniz** restaurant, near the day-excursion boats, are other good seafood eateries a bit away from the general crush on the Kordon.

Terrific meals without a view can be had at **Öz Yalçin,** Marmaris's famous meat eatery. Öz Yalçin (tel. 2934) is located about four blocks inland from the port, up the PTT street and to the right. Here, in the lane crowded with yachting- supply and black-pine-honey stores by day are dozens of tables and chairs filled with customers by night. Along the bustling Gözpinar Sokak are several storefronts with only a wood-fired oven or barbecue inside, turning out döner, şiş, and iskender kebabs. You'll see young boys delivering lamb, veal, and beef from the local butcher all evening to satisfy demand. Barrels of tomatoes and cucumbers are hastily chopped and the round puffed *ekmek* is toasted before serving. A kebab, salata, and a bottle of rosé can be had for 6000 TL ($7.50) a person. After you've sampled their baklava, ask for directions to the nearest butcher, **Pinar Et.** Next door is the tiny new shop, **Turkish Delight House,** at 9 Talatpaşa Sokak. This gift shop packages its own excellent lokum. A good-looking young architect and ship's captain moonlight selling Turkey's favorite treat ($2.25 for 500 grams) to passersby, all lured in by the free samples displayed outside. The Turkish Delight House is open until 10 p.m. every night in season.

CRUISING THE BLUE COAST: Marmaris is the Newport of Turkey; it's impossible to stroll along the water and not feel the glamour, elegance, and luxurious ease of the yachting set. Boating is the town's preoccupation: the bazaar sells buoys, anchors, and life jackets. Like Homer's Sirens, discreet notices requesting crew ("Inexperienced Okay!") for private yachts call out from the lampposts. John and I nearly abandoned this update to jump aboard a 65-foot schooner on its way to Cyprus. **Yeşil Marmaris** (tel. 6121/2290), at 11 Barbaros Caddesi, offers group yacht tours so that everyone can be swept away by the turquoise seas. Their eight-day voyages sail round trip between Marmaris and Fethiye, Marmaris and Bodrum, or Bodrum and the tiny villages along the Gokova Gulf. Full board on their sleek, 12- to 16-person yachts cost $300 per person in 1987.

If you're pressed for time, you must, at least, take a day-excursion boat. They typically cruise around Marmaris's uneven coastline to small pebble beaches and isolated fishing coves. Pack a picnic, bring a beach towel, and luxuriate under the sun to the serenade of Turkish crooners over the P.A. system. Boats leave when full, from about 9 a.m. to 11:30 a.m. for the six- to eight-hour trip; the fare is 4800 TL ($6).

Another popular day trip generated by an increased number of tourists with an archeological bent is to the ancient city of Caunos. Caunos is 90 kilometers (2½ hours by boat) east of Marmaris, along the Kögez Canal near the modern-day city of Dalyan. Ruins include Roman baths, various temples, and a Roman-era theatre. Caunos's well-preserved rock-cut tombs date from the fifth century B.C. to the Roman era. Day-long excursions leave from the Kordon side piers three times a week about 8 a.m.; cost is 16,000 TL ($20).

GETTING TO RHODES: Last year over 29,000 people crossed over from Rhodes to Marmaris, continuing an increasing trend since the tense days of the Cyprus War. During the summer boats ply the waters between Marmaris and Rhodes every day except Sunday. At least one boat makes the 2½-hour trip; another ferry is added if there's greater demand. On most days the boats leave Marmaris harbor at 8:30 a.m. The price for a one-way ticket to Rhodes is $20, the round-trip fare is $36. Unlike some of the Turkish-Greek ferries, the boats leaving Marmaris can accommodate up to seven automobiles (and 270 passengers). Tickets for the ferry trip are sold in nearly every travel agency in Marmaris, all at the same rate. The most convenient agency we found is **Yeşil Marmaris Travel Agency** (tel. 2290), under the Otel Kaptan (open 7:30 a.m. to 9 p.m. every day).

GETTING TO MARMARIS: If you're not approaching Marmaris by sea from

Rhodes, you have the option of flying or busing from Istanbul and points north or busing from points east and south. **THY** currently offers five flights per week from Istanbul to Dalaman Airport—the 1987 fare was 33,000 TL ($41) one way. The **THY** airport bus departs from their office about 2½ hours before flight time; the fare to or from the airport is 2400 TL ($3).

Twelve **buses** depart daily from the center of Marmaris heading north to Istanbul (10,000 TL, or $12.25—15 hours) and Izmir (4000 TL, or $5—6 hours). Several buses run daily to Bodrum (3 hours to this attractive seaside resort) or to Kuşadasi (the town nearest to the ruins of Ephesus); take the Izmir bus to Selçuk. The Pamukkale and Varan Bus Companies also service the eastbound Antalya route, and run south to Fethiye (3000 TL, or $4—3 hours). You can check with their Atatürk Bulvari ticket office or with the Tourist Information Office for current schedules and fares.

12. Fethiye

Fethiye, 120 kilometers south of Marmaris, is not a crossover point from Greece, but it's included in our book because its nearby beaches are utterly exquisite. The small port town, once only an outpost of veteran overland travelers and local fishermen, now offers several hotels, pensions, and harborside cafés. The magnificent beach at **Ölü Deniz** (14 kilometers away) has retained much of its startling purity despite increasing development. The Ölü Deniz community that only five years ago had nine telephones, all hand-cranked, now boasts several hotels (some with international direct dialing), myriad pensions, campgrounds, and windsurfing lessons. Thanks to the Turkish government, the best beaches at Ölü Deniz and **Kidirak** (3 kilometers away) have been preserved as national parks, so development has been contained.

The tranquil cove of Ölü Deniz (literally "Dead Sea"), a still-water bay enclosed by pine forests, is sought after by visiting yachts and remains a natural wonder. The sandy spit of land (a national park) separating Ölü Deniz from the kilometer-long white pebble-and-sand beach, called Belcegiz, absorbs sunbathers and picnickers without relinquishing its unspoiled beauty. **Belcegiz,** bisected by the paved road leading back to Fethiye town, is lined with pensions and cafés built back far enough from its smooth, broad beach to fade into oblivion when compared with the dazzlingly clear turquoise sea. Around the next cove, 2 kilometers south, is **Kidirak.** Still totally undeveloped, this park boasts a long sand stretch bordered by evergreens, which shelter its campsite from view. Only a 15-minute walk beyond Belcegiz, Kidirak is still remote and uncrowded enough to have retained that "Me Tarzan, you Jane" way of life that was Fethiye's claim to fame. Even at Ölü Deniz or Belcegiz we'd recommend renting a tent (many with cots) or a primitive wood bungalow with outdoor showers to best appreciate a lifestyle in tune with nature.

Fethiye, no longer an undiscovered tropical paradise, is still a marvelous, secluded destination where the elemental beauties of nature dominate the inventions of man.

USEFUL INFORMATION: The Fethiye **Tourist Information Office** (tel. 6151/ 1527), on the east side of the harbor at 1 Iskele Meydani, is open daily from 8 a.m. to 10 p.m. and 8:30 a.m. to noon in summer, and 1 p.m. to 5 p.m. Monday through Saturday in the off-season. They are all extremely helpful, especially about the often-impossible-to-find spare room. There is no information office at Ölü Deniz. . . . The **police station** (tel. 1040) is in town. . . . The local **hospital** is at tel. 1045. . . . Fethiye town **banks,** located around the harbor, are open

Monday through Friday from 8:30 a.m. to noon and 1:30 to 4 p.m. In Ölü Deniz most hotels will change foreign currency (particularly Deutsche marks or dollars) but not traveler's checks. . . . The **PTT** is on Atatürk Caddesi, about a five-minute walk east of the Tourist Office; it's open daily till midnight. The Ölü Deniz PTT is near the entrance to the national park; it's open from 8 a.m. to noon and 2 to 6 p.m. . . . The **area code** is 6151.

The **Central Otobus Garaji** is 1½ kilometers east of Fethiye town. **Pamukkale** (tel. 2437) has eight buses daily to Marmaris (2½ hours—$2) and one bus daily to Bodrum (6 hours—$2). **Köseoğlu Bus Lines** (tel. 1973) has buses daily to Selçuk (for Ephesus or Kuşadasi), which take 6 hours and cost $2. To get to Kaş, take any of the several daily buses to Antalya; it's a 2½-hour ride ($1.50). To get to Ölü Deniz, take a dolmush from the bus station or from the stand behind the PTT. They leave every 20 minutes, cost 400 TL (50¢) and stop at the Cetin Motel in the center of Belcegiz beach. A **taxi** from town (they wait at the harbor, bus station, and PTT) will cost 5000 TL ($6). To reach **Dalaman Airport,** take a Köseoğlu bus to Dalaman town, then a taxi the last 8 kilometers from there. Their bus leaves every half hour throughout the day and takes one hour (the cost is $1). Fetur Travel (tel. 2034), the local THY agent and a helpful bunch, at 2 Atatürk Caddesi, has an airport bus for 50¢.

If the beach makes you stir-crazy, Fethiye, the ancient Telmessos, has a small archeological museum behind the PTT and some fine Lycian rock-cut tombs in the hills behind the port. Their carved facades imitated important buildings of the era; the Tomb of Amyntas (fourth century B.C.) is particularly impressive. If the sea calls, there are daily boat tours from the Fethiye port or, less often, from Belcegiz, to visit 12 neighboring islands. They leave about 9:30 a.m. and cost 4500 TL ($5.50).

ACCOMMODATIONS AND DINING: Fethiye is a bustling little fishing village that will represent civilization if you, as we did, become enchanted with the primitive life out at the beach and remain for some days. Then a trip to downtown Fethiye will mean stopping for ouzo or fried calamari along the pier, savoring rosé and hummus (a chickpea dip) at a harborside café, watching the flying fish leap in and out of the still water, browsing through its back streets, lined with small boutiques, checking on the bus schedules. We recommend trying to find accommodations along the beach, but they're *very* simple, as close to *Robinson Crusoe* beach huts as any of you thought you would ever come. We loved the simplicity of a life led almost totally outdoors: showering under the rustling leaves in a roofless cabaña and dining under a thatched roof on the beach or on a patio exposed to the light of the stars. (This coast, by the way, because of its isolation, is a mecca for star-gazers.)

In Fethiye Town

The reason to go to Fethiye is for the beach, so it's best to stay there if you can find a room. If you can't or prefer the town ambience, try the hotels and pensions that lie beyond the Tourist Office toward the Yat Limani. The splurge among these is the **Hotel Likya** (tel. 6151/1169), a six-story stucco building right above the harbor. Newly built, its large simple rooms with modern baths have splendid views of the harbor, with a not-so-splendid 36,000 TL ($45) price tag. The **Hotel Prenses** (tel. 6151/1305) and **Hotel Dedeoğlu** (tel. 6151/4010), both almost next door to the Tourist Office, are similar in style, but with lesser views and a lesser tab—26,000 TL ($32) for a double, with breakfast. The two neighborhoods uphill from and beyond these hotels are thick with pensions, most built into modified private homes in middle-class areas. The **Inci Pansiyon** (tel. 6151/3325) is up the first left above the Likya, at Karagözler Mah. Gençlik Yolu no. 9, and it's the fanciest and best around. Private baths with hot water, phones, a bar, a lovely breakfast terrace, and splendid sea views can be yours for 18,000 TL ($23) for two. Much more simple, but clean, with common baths and the same views is the **Panorama Pansiyon** (tel. 6151/2096), next door at no. 7. Beds are 3600 TL ($4.50) each. Another 500 meters beyond the harborside Likya Hotel is another pension neighborhood. The **Konuckçu Family Pension** (tel. 6151/2903) and the **Sonnen & Panorama** (tel. 6151/3055) are both good choices, the former with common baths and the latter with private facilities but less personal warmth; the cost is 5000 TL ($6) per person, plus 1000 TL ($1.25) for breakfast.

There are a lot of dining possibilities in Fethiye. **Rafet** is probably the best of the harborside cafés. On the two narrow shopping streets which parallel the harbor road are many tiny kebab, mezes, and grill restaurants.

READERS' RESTAURANT SELECTION: "We found a good restaurant in Fethiye, the **Sun, Sol, Soleil.** Leaving the Tourist Information Office, follow the main street toward the restaurant area (turning slightly right beyond the pizza place). Turning right at the third cross street brings you to the Sun" (Dr. and Mrs. David King, Brentwood Bay, British Columbia, Can.).

The **Motel Meri** (tel. 6151/1482) is the only "hotel" on the tranquil Ölü Deniz cove, and its prices reflect this monopoly. White bungalows and attached motel-style rooms are well kept but the composite concrete floors, hard, narrow twin beds, and stall showers hardly warrant their tariff of $69 for two or $47 for one, including their compulsory half-board in-season meal plan. If you have to sleep at Ölü Deniz (rather isolated at night), head downhill to the **Osman Kamping** ground on the bayshore. It's a great location but caters to a party crowd.

The **Çetin Motel** (tel. 6151/1430), in the center of Belcegiz beach by the road to Fethiye, has almost identical rooms to the Meri's. Their private-bath "chalet" rooms cost 24,000 TL ($30), their bathless, small bungalows cost 15,500 TL ($20), both including breakfast in their beachside café. Tent sites rent for 2400 TL ($3), plus $1 per person. The **Belcegiz Motel** (tel. 6151/1430) is about 100 meters towards Kidirak and is newer, so a bit spiffier. Their private-bath "motel" rooms cost 34,000 TL ($33), their bathless bungalows 30,000 TL ($27), again with breakfast. The most luxurious accommodations on Belcegiz beach are at the far end on the rise to Kidirak—the newly opened **Hotel Ölü Deniz** (tel. 6151/3993). Their 64 white-stucco rooms are large, have all-tiled bathrooms with showers, small patios, and surrounding landscaping. Meals are served in their two-story sea-view restaurant. Two of you can wrest a room from the claws of the European travel agents who have latched onto the Ölü Deniz for about 38,000 TL ($35), including breakfast.

The "You Tarzan, me Jane" set is best served at Kyle's old stomping grounds, the **Deniz Camping Motel** (tel. 6151/1430), now a veritable miniresort. Simple A-frame bungalows for two run 9600 TL ($12) to 19,200 TL ($24), depending on season; the higher price includes their compulsory half-board full-season meal plan. There's outdoor camping, a laundry area, and clean, common toilets and baths. You can rent a car, bicycle, motorcycle, boat, or beach umbrella. Deniz Camping's restaurant is one of the most popular nightspots on this part of Belcegiz, and becomes a disco after 9 p.m. If you want a larger portion of peace and quiet, walk up the road from the Çetin Motel to several lanes filled with family-run pensions. The **Ölü Deniz Pansiyon** (tel. 6151/1516) and good **Kardeşler Restaurant** have bungalows for 17,000 TL ($21) for two with breakfast, and rent tents with cots for 7200 TL ($9) for two. A little farther up, down a lane on the right, are the **Yildiray** (tel. 6151/1430, line 28) and **Ceyhan** (tel. 6151/1430, line 27) **pansiyons.** (Note that these smaller places have old-fashioned phone service connected through the PTT switchboard.) The Unsäl family runs the Yildiray and tends a host of nearby chickens and tomato greenhouses. Each of their five large clean rooms have private showers and cost 7200 TL ($9) for two, with breakfast. The Ceyhan is a more modern place with bathless rooms at 6000 TL ($7.50) and private facility rooms at 8500 TL ($11), including breakfast. Reservations at all the Fethiye town and beach hotels are recommended and, if you're coming in July or August, they should be made two months ahead.

There are several nearby campsites with tent rentals. At the gorgeous Kidirak beach, there is only camping. You must check with the park's gatekeeper in person for availability. Kidirak's only facilities are toilets, showers, and a water faucet.

Dining in Ölü Deniz is a matter of where you can find an available table. The roadside **Kardeşler** is good for kebabs, while the **Deniz Camp** has some fine Turkish food and a rowdier crowd. The **Cetin Hotel** has long stood out for its local specialties. For more formal service and tablecloths, walk down the beach to the **Hotel Ölü Deniz.**

13. Kaş

The tiny fishing village of Kaş has been added to this year's edition because the tourist boom that swept Turkey in 1986 so altered the Aegean resorts that we had to stretch our boundary to the edge of the Mediterranean to find a harbor with the charm once commonly found along the Aegean.

Individual travelers and Turkish tourists have long favored Kaş, but the port's relative isolation kept the group tours at bay. The main street, which hugs the harbor along a half mile cove, is filled with women in flowered harem pants and crusty old fishermen who stroll, oblivious to the occasional traffic. Pastel-painted fishing boats, large wooden day-trip cruisers, and sexy yachts from Istanbul and Antalya bob up and down in front of lively cafés and the imposing Atatürk statue. Evening is heralded by the sudden illumination of several Lycian rock-cut tombs scattered in the brush-covered hills above the village. Lights behind the shuttered windows of small hotels and bougainvillea-draped pensions sparkle in the cobblestone back lanes.

Despite the carpet shops, boutiques, and travel agents that have sprung up among the yachting supply and grocery stores, Kaş has retained an immense amount of charm. The indolent life of a Mediterranean resort, flavored by its proximity to the Greek island of Kastelorizo (only two miles away but closed to tourists in 1987 for political reasons), has blessed this village with the ability to absorb tourism and be little affected by its commercialism.

USEFUL INFORMATION: The **Tourist Information Office** (tel. 3226/12308) is in the center of the port, at 5 Cumhuriyet Meydani. They're open daily from 8 a.m. to 7:30 p.m. in the summer, 8 a.m. to 5:30 p.m. Monday through Friday in the off-season. . . . The **local police** are next door (tel. 1024). . . . The **hospital** (tel. 1014) is 400 meters west. . . . The **PTT** is one block up from the port; it's open till 11 p.m. . . . The **area code** is 3226. . . . There is only one bank in Kaş, and it doesn't change money. Instead, a **portable bank** in a trailer has been towed to the port's center, where money is changed daily from 8 a.m. to 8:30 p.m., with a noon-to-1 p.m. lunch break.

The **Otobus Garaji** is about 300 meters up the main street, Elmasi Caddesi, where the town ends at the coastal highway. Most buses between Fethiye and Antalya stop at Kaş; if you're going to Dalaman Airport you'll have to change buses at Fethiye. Contact **Antalya** (tel. 1045) or **Pamukkale** (tel. 1168) for their schedules.

The **Andifli** (tel. 1315) and **Simena** (tel. 1416) travel agencies will have the latest information about reaching the Greek island of Kastellorizo (see our chapter IX, The Dodecanese). Up until May 1987, they had thrice weekly day trips ($15) from the port. Since Kastellorizo is not a legal port of entry, you couldn't spend the night or fly to other parts of Greece from there. As of this writing, unfortunately, you can't even go there. Console yourself with a day cruise to the sunken, ancient city of Kekova ($6), more of a Mediterranean sun-and-fun excursion than an archeological expedition.

Kaş, once a central city in the Lycian league, boasts an **amphitheater** (opposite the hospital) and several hillside Lycian rock-cut tombs. It's said that Apollo was born at nearby Pataras (though others would say at Delos in the Cyclades) and that Saint Nicholas, founder of the Christmas tradition of giving, was born at nearby Myra. All we can say without question is that this is, indeed, a charming and special place.

ACCOMMODATIONS AND DINING: Kaş's 2,000 beds fill up quickly every summer, when an estimated 20,000 tourists arrive on holiday. Book a hotel room early or ask the helpful Tourist Information Office for assistance in locating one of many pensions. The town's most luxurious hotel is the boldly wood-trimmed **Mimosa** (tel. 3226/1272). A double room with a private bathroom, phone, and a small balcony overlooking Elmasi Caddesi (the main street) cost 36,000 TL ($45), with breakfast. Our favorite is the little **Hotel Turquoise** (tel. 3226/3226), on a tiny shop-filled lane between the port and the PTT. Turquoise railings on the balconies, geranium-filled flower boxes, stairs, and a rooftop sundeck lend a happy air. Simple doubles with bath and breakfast cost 15,000 TL ($19) year round. East of the port, a few hundred meters toward the tiny, pebble-filled town beach, are a cluster of pensions, surrounding the good **Likya Hotel** (tel. 3226/1070). The best of these is the popular **Nur Pansiyon** (tel. 3226/1203). Modern, natural wood-trimmed double rooms with small balconies and private facilities cost 12,000 TL ($15) each. There are several other pensions in this area, located along the main street above the shops and west along the port toward the amphitheater and Kaş campgrounds.

Perhaps because it's farther east and on the more ethnically Turkish Mediterranean coast, Kaş has a different and delicious local cuisine. Several restaurants serve a larger variety of mezes (including hummus, taramasalata, sesame-covered pita, and a moist spinach börek) than we've come across, outside of Istanbul's top restaurants. Mezes are displayed in trays (in some cafés there are up to 20 choices), and guests are invited to fill up their own plates with these for a 2,000-TL ($2.50) per plate fee. Thick cuts of beef for kebabs, lamb for *köfte,* and many types of fish, like the locally-caught *lagos* for balik kebab (or fish şiş), are cooked with lots of garlic, paprika, and oregano and served at an extra charge. A small lane running away from the port, near the harborside **Noel Baba Pastanesi** (another local delight), contains three such restaurants. At night, their tables and the crush of hungry diners surveying their displays of mezes make them difficult to miss. There are several harborside cafés, some frisky bars, and the aforementioned Noel Baba Pastanesi and dondurma (ice cream) parlor, with café tables along the port. Across from the Turquoise Hotel is a traditional bakery where fresh loaves, *pide,* or a sweet muffin can be bought daily.

CAPSULE VOCABULARY

1. Greek Words and Expressions
2. Turkish Words and Expressions

WHILE YOU MIGHT NOT have the right inflection, the right accent, or the right pronunciation, almost anyone will warm to you almost immediately if you try to speak to them in their own language. It can't hurt to give it a try—and in some areas, your English (or other northern European language) will do you no good at all. While the following will hardly make you sound like a native, at least it'll get you going.

1. Greek Words and Expressions

To aid your pronunciation, in this section we have written the *accented syllable in capital letters* and the rest of the word in lowercase. (Note that since Greek does not use the "Western," or Latin" alphabet, we have not included the written Greek here.) As a general rule in modern Greek the *accent* of the word is *on the middle or last syllable,* unlike English where you usually find the accent on the first syllable of a word. This simple difference in pronunciation often determines whether or not you will be understood. Don't worry about it too much—so many people in Greece have learned English in school that unless you're well off the tourist path you may find this vocabulary handy only for courtesy or for fun.

Good morning	kah-lee-MEH-ra
Good evening	kah-lee-SPEH-ra
Good night	kah-lee-NEEK-ta
Hello or Good-bye (informal)	YAH-sahs!
Hello or Good-bye (formal)	HEH-re-te
What is your name?	POSS-ssas LEH-neh?
Glad to meet you	HAH-ree-kah po-LEE
Yes	neh
No	O-hee
Excuse me	sig-NO-mee
Does anyone speak English?	mi-LYE-kan-EES on-glee-KAH?

Thank you (very much)	**ef-kah-ree-STOH (PAH-rah-po-lee)**
Please	**pah-rah-kah-LO**
You're welcome	**pah-rah-kah-LO**
Where is . . .	**poo-EE-neh . . .**
the bus station	**stas-EE-mos lee-oh-for-EE-oh**
the train station	**stas-EE-mos TREN-oh**
the airport	**ar-ro-THRO-me-oh**
the hotel	**ksen-oh-tho-HEE-oh**
Hot, Cold	**Zesto, KREE-oh**
Here, There	**eh-THO, eh-KEE**
Near, Far	**kon-DAH, ma-kree-AH**
Breakfast	**pro-ee-NOH**
Lunch	**messee-maree-A-noh**
Dinner	**vrah-three-NOH**
The bill	**lo-gar-ee-YAZ-mos**
Left, Right	**a-rees-ter-AH, thexi-AH**
Cheap, Expensive	**stee-NOH, a-kree-VOH**
Today, Tomorrow	**SEEM-er-ah, AH-vree-oh**
Good, Bad	**kah-LO, kah-KOH**
Open, Closed	**ahn-EEK-toh, KLEES-toh**
Old, New	**pahl-eh-OH, keh-NUR-io**
Pretty (Nice)	**po-LEE-oh-RAY-oh**
Good Health! (Cheers!)	**stee-nee-YAH-sou (singular)**
	stee-ne-YAH-sass (plural)
	stee-nee-YAH-mas (us)
I don't understand.	**THEN-kah-tah-lah-VEH-no**
Please repeat it.	**PEH-steh-toh PAH-lee,**
	pah-rah-kah-LO
What time is it?	**TEE O-rah EE-neh?**
How much is it?	**PO-so KAH-nee?**
It's all right.	**en-DAX-ee**
It's not all right.	**THEN EE-nai en-DAX-ee**
Men's room	**an-THRON**
Ladies' room	**pe-nai-KON**
What?	**TEE?**
Why?	**yah-TEE?**
When?	**POH-teh?**
How?	**POHSS?**
How far?	**POH-soh mah-kree-AH?**
How long?	**POH-soh ke-ROH?**
Can you tell me?	**boh-REE-teh nah-moo-PEE-tah?**
I am lost.	**EH-khan-sah ton-THROH-moh**
I am sorry.	**lee-POO-mee**

I want to go to the airport.	THEH-loh na PAH-oh stoh ah-eh-roh-THROH-mee-oh
Please call a taxi for me.	sahss pah-rah-kah-LO fo-NAX-teh EH-na ahf-toh-KEE-nee taxi
Show me on the map.	THEEK-steh-moo stoh KHAR-tee

0	Mee-den	20	Ee-kohsee	400	Tetra-Kosya
1	E-nas	30	Tree-an-dah	500	Penda-Kosya
2	Dee-oh	40	Sar-an-dah	600	Eksa-Kosya
3	Tree-ah	50	Pe-neen-dah	700	Efta-Kosya
4	Tes-era	60	Ek-seen-dah	800	Octa-Kosya
5	Pend-ah	70	Evdoh-meen-dah	900	Enaya-Kosya
6	Ek-see	80	Oct-don-dah	1000	Hi-lia
7	Ef-tah	90	Ene-neen-dah	2000	Dee-oh Hi-li-A-dess
8	Oct-to	100	Eka-toh	3000	Trees Hi-li-A-dess
9	Enaya	200	Dee-ah-Kosya		
10	Deka	300	Tra-Kosya		

Day	Mia	Month	E-nas
Monday	Def-Tera	January	Ye-Na-ris
Tuesday	Tree-tee	February	Fi-voo-Arios
Wednesday	Te-Tar-tee	March	Mar-tios
Thursday	Pemp-tee	April	A-Pree-lios
Friday	Para-skevee	May	Ma-yos
Saturday	Sah-vato	June	Yoo-nios
Sunday	Kiria-Kee	July	Yoo-lios
		August	Av-Goos-tos
		September	Sep-Tem-vrios
		October	Ok-To-vrios
		November	No-Em-vrios
		December	De-Kem-vrios

THE ALPHABET

Aα	álfa	Nν	ní
Bβ	víta	$\Xi\xi$	xí
$\Gamma\gamma$	gáma	Oo	ómikron
$\Delta\delta$	thèlta	$\Pi\pi$	pí
Eϵ	èpsilón	Pρ	ró
Zζ	zíta	$\Sigma\sigma$	sigma
Hη	íta	Tτ	táf
$\Theta\theta$	thíta	$\Upsilon\upsilon$	ipsilón
Iι	yóta	$\Phi\phi$	fí
Kκ	kápa	Xχ	hí
$\Lambda\lambda$	lámtha	$\Psi\psi$	psí
Mμ	mí	$\Omega\omega$	oméga

2. Turkish Words and Expressions

Turkish is written phonetically. If you give each letter its sound—never combine two or more into diphthongs as in English—you should have little trouble with pronunciation. The main snags for foreigners are the six letters that do not appear in English and the two that are pronounced differently. A letter with a cedilla under it is pronounced like its English equivalent with an "h" after it. Turkish "ç" therefore, is like our "ch," and "ş" like "sh," as in "church," "should." Turkish has two "i's," one with a dot, one without. The dotted one is pronounced like our "e," the undotted one pronounced "uh." The "ö" and "ü" are like the same sounds in German, made with pursed lips. The Turkish "c" is exactly the same as English "j," while Turkish "j" is like the French "j"—softer, more like an English "zh." Finally, the funny-looking "soft 'g'"—with a curved line over it—is usually not pronounced at all. Your best bet is to ignore it altogether.

German, English, and French are spoken by many Turks, and workers who have been in Europe may know Dutch or a Scandinavian language as well. No one will expect you to know Turkish, but will be delighted if you have learned a few words and phrases. In price bargaining, we have found that prices arrived at completely in Turkish tend to be lower, so practice your numbers. Here is a useful glossary of common words and phrases. If you have the chance, and if you're going to do much traveling in Turkey, you should consider buying *Turkish for Travellers,* by Berlitz. This handy phrase book covers virtually every common situation you're liable to get into, and is available in most good bookstores.

Hello	Merhaba	MEHR-ah-bah
How are you?	Nasilsiniz?	NAH-suhl-sin-iz
Very well	Çok iyiyim	"choke" EE-yum
Goodbye	Allahaismarladik	ah-LAHS-mahr-lah-duhk
Good morning	Günaydin	gu-NYE-dun
Good evening	Iyi akşamlar	ee-yee OCK-shum-lar
Good night	Iyi geceler	ee-yee geh-SHELL-er
What time is it?	Saat kaç?	sah-AHT KOTCH?
At what time?	Saat kaçta?	sah-AHT KOTCH-ta?
Bon voyage	Güle güle	gew-LAY gew-LAY
Yes, No	Evet, Hayir	EH-veht, "higher"
Please	Lüften	LEWT-fehn
Thank you	Tesekkür ederim	tesh-eh-KEWR eh-dehr-im
Excuse me	Affedersiniz	AHF-feh-DEHR-si-niz
You're welcome	Bir sey degil	beer shey day-EE
Please have some (one) . . .	Buyrunuz . . .	BOOY-roo-nooz
What's this?	Bu ne?	BOO nay?
Where is . . . ?	. . . Nerede?	NEH-reh-deh
the station	Istasyon	ees-tahs-YOHN
a hotel	Bir otel	beer oh-TEHL
a restaurant	Bir lokanta	beer loh-KAHN-tah
the toilet	Tuvalet	too-vah-LEHT
someone who speaks English	Ingilizce bilen bir kimse	een-geel-EEZ-jeh beel-ehn-beer keem-seh
Left, Right	Sol, Sağ	sohl, saah
To the right	Sağa	sah-AH
To the left	Sola	sohl-AH
Straight ahead	Doğru	doh-ROO
Here, There	Burada	BOO-rah-dah
Over here	Surada	SHOO-rah-dah

Over there	Orada	OHR-ah-dah
Near, Far	Yakin, Uzak	yah-kuhn, oo-ZAHK
Give me . . .	. . . bana veriniz	bah-NAH vehr-rin-eez
I would like . . .	. . . istiyorum	ees-tee-YOHR-oom
a menu	bir yemek listesi	beer yeh-MEHK lees-teh-see
a meal	bir yemek	beer yeh-MEHK
breakfast	kahvalti	kah-vahl-TUH
lunch	ögle yemegi	ewy-LEH yem-meh-yee
dinner	aksam yemegi	ahk-SHAHM yem-meh-yee
the check	hesap	heh-SAHP
the price list	fiat listesi	fee-YAHT lees-teh-see
a room	bir oda	beer oh-DAH
for one, two	bir, iki kisilik	BEER, ee-KEE kee-shee-leek
with . . . beds	. . . yatakli	yah-tahk-LUH
twin beds	çift yatak	CHEEFT yah-tahk
a double bed	genis yatak	geh-NEESH yah-tahk
a shower	bir dus	beer DOOSH
a bathtub	bir gömme banyo	beer gewm-MEH bahn-yoh
without bath	banyosuz	bahn-yoh-SOOZ
for one night	bir gece için	BEER geh-jeh ee-chin
It's very noisy	Çok gürültülü	"choke" gew-rewl-tew-lew
What does it cost?	Kaç para?	KAHCH pah-rah
Something cheaper	Bir sey daha ucuz	beer shay dah-HAH oo-jooz
Something more expensive	Bir sey daha pahali	beer shay dah-HAH pah-hah-luh
Service charge	Service ücreti	sehr-VEES ewj-reh-tee
Tax	Vergi	VEHR-gee
Very expensive	Çok pahali	"choke" pah-hah-luh
How?	Nasil?	NAH-suhl
How long?	Ne kadar zaman?	NEH kah-dahr zah-mahn
When, Which?	Ne zaman, Hangi?	NAY zah-mahn, HAHN-gee
When does it leave?	Ne zaman kalkar?	NAY zah-mahn kal-kahr
When does it arrive?	Ne zaman geliyor?	NAY zah-mahn gehl-ee-yohr
. . . hours . . . minutes	. . . saat . . . dakika	saa-AHT, dah-kee-KAH
Eight o'clock	Saat sekiz	saa-AHT seh-KEEZ

Now, Later	Simdi, Sonra	SHIM-dee, SOHN-rah
Before, After	Once, Sonra	EWN-jeh, SOHN-rah
Yesterday	Dün	dewn
Today	Bugün	BOO-gewn
Tomorrow	Yarin	YAHR-uhn
Ticket	Bilet	bee-LEHT
Reserved seat	Numarali yer	noo-mahr-ah-LUH yehr
First, second class	Birinci, ikinci mevki	beer-EEN-jee, ee-KIN-jee mehv-kee
Train	Tren	trehn
Railroad	Demiryolu	deh-MEER-yohl-oo
Railroad station	Gar, Istasyon	gahr, ees-tahs-YOHN
sleeping car	Yataki vagon	vah-tahk-LUH vahg-ohn
Dining car	Yemekli vagon	yeh-mehk-LEE vahg-ohn
Bus, Bus station	Otobüs, Otogar	oh-toh-BEWS, OH-toh-gahr
Airport, Airplane	Havaalani, Uçak	hah-VAH-ahl-ahn-uh, oo-CHAHK
Baggage checkroom	Emanetçi	eh-mahn-EHT-chee
Timetable	Tarife	tah-ree-FEH
Cheap, Expensive	Ucuz, pahali	oo-JOOZ, pah-hah-LUH
Hot, Cold	Sicak, soğuk	suh-JAHK, soh-OOK
Good, Bad	Iyi, Fena	ee-EE, feh-NAH
Big, Small	Büyük, Küçük	bew-YEWK, kew-CHEWK
Old, New	Eski, Yeni	ehs-KEE, yeh-NEE
Open, Closed	Açik, kapali	ah-CHUHK, kah-pah-LUH
Money	Para	PAH-rah
Small change	Bozuk para	boh-ZOOK pah-rah
Do you have?	Var mi?	VAHR muh
There is none.	Yok	"yoke"
Cigarettes, Matches	Sigara, Kibrit	see-GAHR-ah, kee-BREET
With a filter	Filtreli	FEEL-tray-LEE
Map	Harita	hahr-ee-TAH
Laundry	Çamasir	chah-mah-SHUHR
Dry cleaning	Kuru temizleme	koo-ROO teh-meez-leh-meh
Turkish bath	Hamam	hah-MAHM
Shower	Dus	doosh
Soap	Sabun	sah-BOON
Towel	Havlu	hahv-LOO
Not	Değil	day-EEL
And	Ve	veh

Or	**Veya**	ve-yah
Pretty	**Güzel**	gew-ZEHL
Gorgeous	**Şahane**	shah-ha-NEH

Note: When speaking of money, mention lira and kurush, as in saying 3.50 TL: "üç lira, elli kurush." It is also common to give prices under ten liras only in kurush, as "üç yüz elli kurush" (350 kurush).

1	**Bir** beer	9	**Dokuz** doh-KOOZ	60	**Altmis** ahlt-MUSH
2	**Iki** ee-KEE	10	**On** ohn	70	**Yetmis** yeht-MISH
3	**Uc** ewtch	11	**On bir** ohn BEER	80	**Seksen** sehk-SEHN
4	**Dört** "dirt"	12	**On iki** ohn ee-KEE	90	**Doksan** dohk-SAN
5	**Bes** besh	20	**Yirmi** yeer-MEE	100	**Yüz** yewz
6	**Alti** ahl-TUH	30	**Otuz** oh-TOOZ	1000	**Bin** been
7	**Yedi** yeh-DEE	40	**Kirk** "Kirk"	Half	**Yarim** YAHR-um
8	**Sekiz** seh-KEEZ	50	**Elli** ehl-LEE	Half	**Buçuk** boo-CHOOK

Note: "Buçuk" is never used alone, but always with a number, as "Dört buçuk," 4½; "yarim" is used in all other situations, as "yarim porsiyon," a half-portion, or "yarim veriniz," Give me half (of that).

Gün	Day	**Ocak**	January
Pazartesi	Monday	**Şubat**	February
Sali	Tuesday	**Mart**	March
Çarşamba	Wednesday	**Nisan**	April
Perşembe	Thursday	**Mayis**	May
Cuma	Friday	**Haziran**	June
Cumartesi	Saturday	**Temmuz**	July
Pazar	Sunday	**Ağustos**	August
Hafta	Week	**Eylül**	September
Ay	Month	**Ekim**	October
Yil, sene	Year	**Kasim**	November
		Aralik	December

MENU TRANSLATIONS AND RESTAURANT TIPS

1. Greek Menu Terms
2. Turkish Menu Terms

THE FOLLOWING MENU TERMS are not meant to be all-inclusive. Far from it, for the cuisines available in both Greece and Turkey are wide-ranging, and would each require at least a chapter—but we don't have the room. These lists of menu items are just to get you started. The more adventurous among you will have fun trying out new foods and taste sensations as you go along.

1. Greek Menu Terms

HORS D'OEUVRES—ORETIKA

Taramosalata	Fish roe with mayonnaise	**Midia fassolia salata**	Dandelion salad
Tiropita	Cheese pie	**Piperies yemistes**	Stuffed green peppers
Spanokopita	Spinach pie		
Melitzanosalata	Eggplant salad	**Tsatziki**	Cucumber with yogurt
Tomates yemistes me risi	Tomatoes stuffed with rice		

FISH—PSARI

Astakos (Ladolemono)	Lobster (with oil and lemon sauce)	**Glossa (Tiganiti)**	Sole (fried)
		Kalamarakia (Tiganita)	Squid (fried)
Bakaliaro (Skordalia)	Cod (with garlic)	**Kalamarakia (Yemista)**	Squid (stuffed)
Barbounia (Skara)	Red mullet (grilled)	**Oktapodi**	Octopus
		Soupies yemistes	Stuffed cuttlefish
Caravides	Crayfish		
Garides	Shrimp	**Tsipoura**	Dorado

MEATS—KREAS

Arni souvla	Spit-roasted lamb	**Kotopoulo yemisto**	Stuffed chicken
Arni yiouvetsi	Lamb in tomato sauce	**Loukanika**	Spiced sausages
Arni avgolemono	Lamb with lemon sauce	**Moussaka**	Meat and eggplant (or potato)
Brizola moscharisi	Beef or veal steak	**Paidakia**	Lamb chops
		Pilafi, risi	Rice pilaf
Brizola hirini	Pork steak or chop	**Souvlaki**	Lamb (sometimes veal) on the skewer
Dolmadakia	Stuffed vine leaves		
Keftedes	Fried meatballs	**Youvarlakia**	Boiled meat balls with rice
Kotopoulo souvla	Spit-roasted chicken		
		Yuvetsi	Lamb with noodles

2. Turkish Menu Terms

SOUPS—ÇORBALAR

Balik çorbasi	Fish soup	**Mercimek çorbasi**	Lentil (pea) soup
Domates çorbasi	Tomato soup		
Dügün çorbasi	Mincemeat, egg, and lemon soup	**Paça**	Lamb shank soup
		Sebze çorbasi	Vegetable soup
Et suyu (yumurtali)	Broth (with egg)	**Sehriye çorbasi**	Vermicelli (noodle) soup
Haslama	Boiled meat in broth	**Yayla çorbasi**	Yogurt and barley soup
Iskembe çorbasi	Tripe (stomach) soup		

MEATS—ETLER

Böbrek	Kidney	**Köfte**	Spiced grilled meat patties
Bonfile	Small filet steak	**Kuzu**	Lamb, mutton
Çerkez tavugu	Chicken with crushed walnut sauce	**Macar gulyas**	Hungarian goulash
		Pastirma	Turkish pastrami
Ciger	Liver	**Pirzola**	Chop, usually lamb
Dana	Veal	**Şigir**	Beef
Domuz, jambon	Pork, ham	**Şatobriyan**	Châteaubriand
Karisik et izgara	Mixed grill (lamb)	**Şinitzel**	Wienerschnitzel (breaded veal)
Koç yumurtasi	Ram's "eggs" (testicles)	**Tavuk, piliç**	Chicken

KEBABS—KEBAPLAR

Adana kebabi	Spicy grilled rissole	**Kagit kebabi**	Lamb and vegetables cooked in paper

Bursa kebabi	Sliced grilled lamb, tomato sauce, butter, and yogurt	**Orman kebabi**	Roast lamb with onions
Çöp kebabi	Diced skewered lamb	**Patlican kebabi**	Stewed meat and eggplant
Döner kebab	Lamb grilled on vertical spit	**Şiş kepap (kusbasi)**	Skewered lamb
Güveç	Meat and vegetables cooked in crock	**Tandir kebabi**	Roast lamb
Halep isi kebap	Grilled rissoles, onions, and spices	**Urfa kebabi**	Lamb stew with onions
Iskender kebabi	Mixed lamb kebab plate	**Tas kebabi**	Grilled meat rissole

Note: Kebabs are served three ways: as chunks of meat, as ground meat patties, or as sliced meat. The meat is almost always lamb, and in the ground meat dishes savory spices are added. Ingredients are usually the same—it's the preparation that's different. Adana kebabi is heavily spiced, though they let you put the red pepper on by yourself. Yogurt can be ordered with kebabs. Many kebabs are served with pide bread, under the meat or separately.

FISH—BALIKLAR

Alabalik	Trout	**Lüfer**	Bosporus bluefish
Barbunya	Red mullet	**Mercan**	Red coral fish
Dil baligi	Sole	**Midye**	Mussels
Hamsi	Anchovy (fresh)	**Palamut**	Tuay, bonito
Istakoz	Lobster	**Pisi**	Plaice
Kalkan	Turbot	**Sardalya**	Sardines
Karagöz	Black bream	**Tarama**	Roe, red caviar
Karides	Shrimp	**Trança**	Aegean fish
Kefal	Gray mullet	**Uskumru**	Mackerel
Kiliç	Swordfish	**Yengeç**	Crab
Levrek	Sea bass		

Note: Prices for fish are sometimes marked in profit percentages of wholesale price. Make sure you know what you're paying. Often you can bargain for a good price. Fish are very seasonal, and very expensive out of season.

SALADS—SALATALAR

Amerikan salatasi	Russian(!) salad	**Domates salatalik salatasi**	Tomato and cucumber salad
Beyin salatasi	Sheep's brain salad	**Karisik salata**	Mixed salad
Çoban salatasi	Chopped mixed salad	**Marul**	A sweet delicious romaine lettuce

Patlican salatasi	Eggplant salad (puree)	Söğüs	Plain sliced vegetables
Rus salatasi	Russian salad	Tursu	Pickled vegetables
		Yeşil salata	Green salad

Note: Salads are ordered "sirkeli" (with vinegar) or "limonlu" (with lemon juice), and if you don't like hot peppers, "bibersiz."

VEGETABLES—SEBZELER

Ayse kadin fasulye	French beans with meat	Karnabahar	Cauliflower
Bamya	Okra	Kuru fasulye	White beans
Barbunye	Red beans	Lahana	Cabbage
Bezelye	Peas	Patates	Potatoes
Biber	Peppers	Pilav	Rice
Domates	Tomatoes	Salata	Lettuce
Havuç	Carrots	Salatalik, hiyar	Cucumber
İç pilav	Rice with pine nuts and currants	Sogan	Onions
		Taze fasulye	String beans
Ispanak	Spinach	Turp	Radish
Kabak	Squash	Türlü firin sebze	Assorted baked vegetables

FRUITS—MEYVE

Armut	Pear	Kiraz	Cherries
Ayva	Quince	Mandalin	Tangerine
Çilek	Strawberries	Muz	Banana
Elma	Apple	Nar	Pomegranate
Greyfurut	Grapefruit	Portakal	Orange
Incir	Figs	Seftali	Peach
Karpuz	Watermelon	Uzüm	Grapes
Kavun	Melon	Visne	Morello (sour) cherries
Kayisi	Apricots		

SIDE DISHES

Biber dolmasi	Stuffed green peppers	Kabak dolmasi	Stuffed squash
Çaçik	Yogurt with cucumber and garlic	Kadin budu köfte	Batter-fried meat and rice rissoles
İç pilav	Rice cooked in broth with currants, liver, and pine nuts	Karniyarik	Stuffed eggplant served hot
		Kiymali börek	Pastry with ground meat
Imam Bayildi	Stuffed eggplant served cold	Lahana dolmasi	Stuffed cabbage

TURKISH MENU TERMS **559**

Makarna, spaket	Macaroni, spaghetti	**Sigara böregi**	Fried pastry stuffed with sheep's cheese
Menemen	Spicy tomato slices with eggs	**Su böregi**	Pastry (hot or cold) filled with cheese or mincemeat
Musakka	Ground meat and vegetable pie	**Yaprak dolmasi**	Stuffed vine leaves
Peynirli börek	Pastry with goat's cheese		
Pilaki, piyaz	White beans and onions in olive oil (cold)		

Note: Dolmas (or sarmas) are served either hot with meat stuffing or cold with rice stuffing and olive oil. Specify which you want by saying "etli" (hot) or "zeytinyagli" (cold). Börek is a general term for flaky pastry stuffed with meat, sausage, cheese, etc., usually served hot.

DESSERTS—TATLILAR

Asure	Sweet pudding with walnuts, raisins, and peas	**Keskü**	Milk, almond, and pistachio pudding
Baklava	Sweet many-layered pie, with nut stuffing	**Komposto**	Stewed fruit
Bülbül yuvasi	Shredded wheat with pistachios and syrup	**Krem karamel**	Caramel custard
Burma kadayif	Shredded wheat bun stuffed with pistachios, in syrup	**Krem sokolade**	Chocolate pudding
		Muhallebi	Mild, rice flour, and rosewater pudding
Dondurma	Ice cream	**Peynir tatlisi**	Cheesecake
Ekmek kadayifi	Crumpet in syrup	**Samsa tatlisi**	Pastry in syrup
Güllaç	Flaky pastry with pistachios and milk	**Sütlaç firin**	Baked rice pudding (cold)
Helva	Halvah	**Sütlac**	Rice pudding
Hurma tatlisi	Semolina cake in syrup	**Tavuk gögsü**	Milk, rice flour, and chicken pudding
Kabak tatlisi	Candied squash	**Tel kadayif**	Shredded wheat in syrup
Kadin göegi	Doughnut in syrup	**Yogurt tatlisi**	Yogurt and egg pudding
Kazandibi	Baked "Tavuk gögsü"	**Zerde**	Sweet of saffron and rice

Note: Baklava is made with different things: pistachios, walnuts, or clotted cream (kaymak). Most Turkish desserts are smothered in syrup; best to look before you order.

BEVERAGES—ICKILER

Ayran	Buttermilk-like yogurt drink	**Boza**	Fermented wheat (millet) drink
Bira, beyaz/siyah	Beer, light/dark	**Çay**	Tea
		Kahve	Coffee

Türk kahvesi	Turkish coffee	**Sarap**	Wine
Amerikan kahvesi	American coffee	**Beyaz**	White
		Kirmizi	Red
Fransiz kahvesi	Coffee and milk	**Rose**	Rosé
Kanyak	Brandy	**Köpüklü**	Sparkling wine
Limonata	Lemonade	**Su**	Water
Maden sodasi	Mineral soda	**Süt**	Milk
Maden suyu	Mineral water (naturally carbonated)	**Vermut**	Vermouth
		Viski	Whiskey
Raki	Arrack, anisette	**Votka**	Vodka
Sahlep	Hot milk and tapioca root drink		

CONDIMENTS AND OTHERS

Bal	Honey	**Pasta**	Pastry
Beyaz peynir	White sheep's milk cheese	**Peynir**	Cheese
		Pide	Flat bread; pizza
Bisküvi	Biscuit	**Reçel**	Jam preserves
Buz	Ice	**Sarmisak**	Garlic
Ekmek	Bread	**Seker**	Sugar; candy
Hardal	Mustard	**Sirke**	Vinegar
Kara biber	Black pepper	**Siyah biber**	Black pepper
Kasar peynir	Yellow milk cheese	**Tereyagi**	Butter
Ketçap	Ketchup	**Tuz**	Salt
Limon	Lemon	**Yogurt**	Yogurt
Lokum	Turkish Delight		

COOKING TERMS

Buglama	Steamed	**Piskin**	Well done (same as iyi pismis)
Etli	With meat		
Ezme, pure	Puree	**Rosto**	Roasted
Firin	Baked	**Salçali**	With savory tomato sauce
Haslama	Boiled		
Iyi pismis	Well done (said of grilled meats)	**Sicak**	Hot
		Soguk	Cold
Izgara	Charcoal grilled	**Terbiyeli, soslu**	With sauce
Kiymali	With ground meat	**Yogurtlu**	With yogurt
Kizartma	Broiled	**Yumurtali**	With eggs
Peynirli	With cheese		

Note: The suffix -li (or -lu, -lü) means "with," so "pilavli" is "with rice." The -siz (or -suz, -süz) suffix indicates "without," so "bibersiz" means "without peppers."

NOW, SAVE MONEY ON ALL YOUR TRAVELS!
Join Arthur Frommer's $35-A-Day Travel Club™

Saving money while traveling is never a simple matter, which is why, over 26 years ago, the **$35-A-Day Travel Club** was formed. Actually, the idea came from readers of the Arthur Frommer Publications who felt that such an organization could bring financial benefits, continuing travel information, and a sense of community to economy-minded travelers all over the world.

In keeping with the money-saving concept, the annual membership fee is low—$18 (U.S. residents) or $20 U.S. (Canadian, Mexican, and foreign residents)—and is immediately exceeded by the value of your benefits which include:

(1) The latest edition of any TWO of the books listed on the following pages.

(2) An annual subscription to an 8-page quarterly newspaper *The Wonderful World of Budget Travel* which keeps you up-to-date on fastbreaking developments in low-cost travel in all parts of the world—bringing you the kind of information you'd have to pay over $35 a year to obtain elsewhere. This consumer-conscious publication also includes the following columns:

Hospitality Exchange—members all over the world who are willing to provide hospitality to other members as they pass through their home cities.

Share-a-Trip—requests from members for travel companions who can share costs and help avoid the burdensome single supplement.

Readers Ask . . . Readers Reply—travel questions from members to which other members reply with authentic firsthand information.

(3) A copy of *Arthur Frommer's Guide to New York*.

(4) Your personal membership card which entitles you to purchase through the Club all Arthur Frommer Publications for a third to a half off their regular retail prices during the term of your membership.

So why not join this hardy band of international budgeteers NOW and participate in its exchange of information and hospitality? Simply send $18 (U.S. residents) or $20 U.S. (Canadian, Mexican, and other foreign residents) along with your name and address to: $35-A-Day Travel Club, Inc., Gulf + Western Building, One Gulf + Western Plaza, New York, NY 10023. Remember to specify which *two* of the books in section (1) above you wish to receive in your initial package of member's benefits. Or tear out the next page, check off any two of the books listed on either side, and send it to us with your membership fee.

Date_____

FROMMER BOOKS
PRENTICE HALL PRESS
ONE GULF + WESTERN PLAZA
NEW YORK, NY 10023

Friends:

Please send me the books checked below:

FROMMER'S $-A-DAY GUIDES™

(In-depth guides to sightseeing and low-cost tourist accommodations and facilities.)

☐ Europe on $30 a Day $13.95	☐ New Zealand on $40 a Day $10.95
☐ Australia on $25 a Day $10.95	☐ New York on $50 a Day............. $10.95
☐ Eastern Europe on $25 a Day $10.95	☐ Scandinavia on $50 a Day........... $10.95
☐ England on $40 a Day.............. $11.95	☐ Scotland and Wales on $40 a Day..... $11.95
☐ Greece on $30 a Day............... $11.95	☐ South America on $30 a Day $10.95
☐ Hawaii on $50 a Day............... $11.95	☐ Spain and Morocco (plus the Canary
☐ India on $25 a Day $10.95	Is.) on $40 a Day $10.95
☐ Ireland on $30 a Day............... $10.95	☐ Turkey on $25 a Day............... $10.95
☐ Israel on $30 & $35 a Day $11.95	☐ Washington, D.C., & Historic Va. on
☐ Mexico on $20 a Day $10.95	$40 a Day $11.95

FROMMER'S DOLLARWISE GUIDES™

(Guides to sightseeing and tourist accommodations and facilities from budget to deluxe, with emphasis on the medium-priced.)

☐ Alaska............................ $12.95	☐ Cruises (incl. Alaska, Carib, Mex,
☐ Austria & Hungary $11.95	Hawaii, Panama, Canada, & US) $12.95
☐ Belgium, Holland, Luxembourg $11.95	☐ California & Las Vegas $11.95
☐ Egypt............................ $11.95	☐ Florida........................... $11.95
☐ England & Scotland $11.95	☐ Mid-Atlantic States $12.95
☐ France........................... $11.95	☐ New England..................... $12.95
☐ Germany......................... $12.95	☐ New York State $12.95
☐ Italy............................. $11.95	☐ Northwest........................ $11.95
☐ Japan & Hong Kong $12.95	☐ Skiing in Europe $12.95
☐ Portugal (incl. Madeira & the Azores) . $12.95	☐ Skiing USA—East $11.95
☐ South Pacific...................... $12.95	☐ Skiing USA—West $11.95
☐ Switzerland & Liechtenstein $12.95	☐ Southeast & New Orleans............ $11.95
☐ Bermuda & The Bahamas........... $11.95	☐ Southwest........................ $11.95
☐ Canada $12.95	☐ Texas............................ $11.95
☐ Caribbean $13.95	

TURN PAGE FOR ADDITIONAL BOOKS AND ORDER FORM.

THE ARTHUR FROMMER GUIDES™

(Pocket-size guides to sightseeing and tourist accommodations and facilities in all price ranges.)

☐ Amsterdam/Holland	$5.95	☐ Mexico City/Acapulco	$5.95
☐ Athens	$5.95	☐ Minneapolis/St. Paul	$5.95
☐ Atlantic City/Cape May	$5.95	☐ Montreal/Quebec City	$5.95
☐ Boston	$5.95	☐ New Orleans	$5.95
☐ Cancún/Cozumel/Yucatán	$5.95	☐ New York	$5.95
☐ Dublin/Ireland	$5.95	☐ Orlando/Disney World/EPCOT	$5.95
☐ Hawaii	$5.95	☐ Paris	$5.95
☐ Las Vegas	$5.95	☐ Philadelphia	$5.95
☐ Lisbon/Madrid/Costa del Sol	$5.95	☐ Rome	$5.95
☐ London	$5.95	☐ San Francisco	$5.95
☐ Los Angeles	$5.95	☐ Washington, D.C.	$5.95

FROMMER'S TOURING GUIDES™

(Color illustrated guides that include walking tours, cultural & historic sites, and other vital travel information.)

☐ Egypt	$8.95	☐ Paris	$8.95
☐ Florence	$8.95	☐ Venice	$8.95
☐ London	$8.95		

SPECIAL EDITIONS

☐ A Shopper's Guide to the Caribbean	$12.95	☐ Motorist's Phrase Book (Fr/Ger/Sp)	$4.95
☐ Bed & Breakfast—N. America	$8.95	☐ Swap and Go (Home Exchanging)	$10.95
☐ Guide to Honeymoons (US, Canada, Mexico, & Carib)	$12.95	☐ The Candy Apple (NY for Kids)	$11.95
☐ How to Beat the High Cost of Travel	$4.95	☐ Travel Diary and Record Book	$5.95
☐ Marilyn Wood's Wonderful Weekends (NY, Conn, Mass, RI, Vt, NH, NJ, Del, Pa)	$11.95	☐ Where to Stay USA (Lodging from $3 to $30 a night)	$9.95

☐ Arthur Frommer's New World of Travel (Annual sourcebook previewing: new travel trends, new modes of travel, and the latest cost-cutting strategies for savvy travelers) $12.95

ORDER NOW!

In U.S. include $1.50 shipping UPS for 1st book; 50¢ ea. add'l book. Outside U.S. $2 and 50¢, respectively.

Enclosed is my check or money order for $_____

NAME _____

ADDRESS _____

CITY _____ STATE _____ ZIP _____

It's 2 am.
It's far from home.
It's more than
a tummyache.

**American Express Cardmembers can get
emergency medical and legal referrals, worldwide.
Simply by calling Global Assist.**℠

What if it really is more than a tummyache?
What if your back goes out? What if you get into a
legal fix?

Call Global Assist – a new emergency referral
service for the exclusive use of American Express
Cardmembers. Just call. Toll-free. 24 hours a day.
Every day. Virtually anywhere in the world.

Your call helps find a doctor, lawyer, dentist,
optician, chiropractor, nurse, pharmacist, or an
interpreter.

All this costs nothing, except for the medical
and legal bills you would normally expect to pay.

Global Assist. One more reason to have the American Express®
Card. Or, to get one.

 TRAVEL RELATED SERVICES For an application,
call 1-800-THE-CARD.

Don't leave home without it.®

If you lose cash on vacation, don't count on a Boy Scout finding it.

Honestly.

How many people can you trust to give back hundreds of dollars in cash? Not too many.

That's why it's so important to help protect your vacation with American Express® Travelers Cheques.

If they're lost, you can get them back

from over 100,000 refund locations throug out the world. Or you can hope a Boy Scou finds it.

Protect your vacation.